SCIENCE FICTION
TELEVISION SERIES

SCIENCE FICTION TELEVISION SERIES

*Episode Guides, Histories,
and Casts and Credits
for 62 Prime Time Shows,
1959 through 1989*

by MARK PHILLIPS *and*
FRANK GARCIA

with a foreword by KENNETH JOHNSON

McFarland & Company, Inc., Publishers
Jefferson, North Carolina, and London

Dedicated to my family;
my parents Frank, Sr., and Angelita
and my sisters Rosamar and Beatriz
—FG

Dedicated to my Mom and Dad,
Elizabeth Lundell and Gary Phillips,
and to my sister Angie
—MP

British Library Cataloguing-in-Publication data are available

Library of Congress Cataloguing-in-Publication Data

Phillips, Mark, 1959 July 22–
    Science fiction television series : episode guides, histories,
and casts and credits for 62 prime time shows, 1959 through
1989 / by Mark Phillips and Frank Garcia ; with a foreword by
Kenneth Johnson.
      p. cm.
    Includes bibliographical references and index. ∞
    ISBN 0-7864-0041-2 (lib. bdg. : 50# alk. paper)
    1. Science fiction television programs—Encyclopedias.
I. Garcia, Frank, 1961–   . II. Title.
PN1992.8.S35P48   1996
791.45'656—dc20   95-47667
                                        CIP

Manufactured in the United States of America

McFarland & Company, Inc., Publishers
  Box 611, Jefferson, North Carolina 28640

ACKNOWLEDGMENTS

The following people graciously agreed to be interviewed for thirty years of television science fiction, or offered us help in other ways. This book would not have been possible without their continued friendship, support and assistance.

Frank Garcia Interviewees: Philip Akin, Ralph Alderman, Desi Arnaz, Jr., Ray Austin, Scott Bakula, Steven Barnes, Peter Barton, Hagan Beggs, Donald Bellisario, Peter Benison, Stan Berkowitz, Paul Bernbaum, Ben Bova, Chuck Bowman, Rob Bowman, Ray Bradbury, Randy Bradshaw, Ellen Bry, Robert Butler, Michael Cavanaugh, Richard Chaves, Maury Chaykin, Arthur C. Clarke, John Colicos, Nick Corea, Joe Cortese, Wes Craven, Brad Creasser, Steven de Souza, Philip DeGuere, Neill Fearnley, Richard Flower, D.C. Fontana, Jonathan Frakes, Jeff Freilich, Matt Frewer, Mick Garris, Gary Goddard, Daniel Goodman, Jonathan Goodwill, Jeff Gourson, Lynda Mason Green, Kenneth Griffin, Stacy Haiduk, Nicholas Hammond, Gregory Harrison, Richard Hatch, Robert Hays, Peter Howell, Peter Hyams, Michael Ironside, Kenneth Johnson, William Jordan, Gerald Kelsey, Bruce Kessler, Winrich Kolbe, Martin Kove, Martin Landau, Glen Larson, Stan Lee, Hal Linden, Harold Livingston, Jack Lowin, Paul Lynch, Peter MacNeil, Stuart Margolin, Jared Martin, Kent McCord, Jim McMullan, Cameron Mitchell, Donald Moffatt, Sheila Moore, John Haymes Newton, Kerry Noonan, David Nutter, Gordon Pinsent, Andreas Poulsson, Deborah Pratt, Stanley Ralph Ross, Sarah Rush, Ronald Satlof, Andrew Schneider, Michael Shannon, Lionel E. Siegel, Robert Silverberg, Parker Stevenson, Dean Stockwell, Greg Strangis, Malcolm Stuart, Jo Swerling, Jr., Attila Szalay, Kristoffer Tabori, David Tomblin, Gus Trikonis, Glynn Turman, Brad Turner, Ilse Von Glatz, Lyle Waggonner, Fred Waugh, James Whitmore, Jr., Thomas Wright, and Peter Wyngarde.

For generously providing permission for the use of material they owned: Steven Ricks for the quotations from David Tomblin, Jack Lowin, Peter Howell and Kenneth Griffin in his documentary *The Prisoner Investigated*; Elyse Dickenson, at *The Blackwood Project*, for the Richard Chaves interview and help on the *War of the Worlds* chapter and episode guide; Ken MacIntyre for the Jared Martin and Matt Frewer quoted material; Sally Smith for Scott Bakula, Dean Stockwell, Deborah Pratt and certain Donald P. Bellisario quotations; Sally Smith, Jason Dzembo, Kitty Woldow, Debbie Brown and Anita Kilgour, for the template serving as the *Quantum Leap* episode guide.

The following clubs have also been helpful. (If you would like to contact a club for information, please include a self addressed stamped envelope.) Vicki Werkley, Todd Andrews, Jill Wells, Lil Sibley, Gayle Highpine and Jean Laidig at Spotlight Starman, 784 Holmdel Rd., Holmdel NJ 07733-1635 (to whom thanks go for help with the *Starman* chapter, fine-tuning the episode guide and connecting me precisely when I needed it with Michael Cavanaugh); Pete Chambers, Esther Nash and Connie Colvin at the Alien Nation Appreciation Society, 110 Richmond St., Coventry, CV2 4HY England.

Thanks also to all those with unique talents who helped: Eileen Kernaghan for assistance with contract matters; Hardip Randhawa and Canada Wide Magazines, Ltd., for their generous assistance with photos; Valorie Hoye for the amazing editing workshop; the Academy of Television Arts and Sciences Library; Roger Brown and Nan Santarpia for transcripts and Galactic advice; William K. Atkinson, Betsy Garcia, Debbie Holberton and Al Betz for access to important videotapes; Bob and Julie Abraham, Dave Dundas, Herbert Fung, Steve Griffiths, Kyle R. Kirkwood, John Larocque, Mike Levenston, Asif Quadri and Lorne Walton (Canada); Mimi Braverman, Michael L. Brown, *Phoenix* producer Mark Carliner, Scott Clark, Nancy Durgin, Jeff Elbel, George Fergus and Alan Morton, Barbara Fullerton, Raelyn Harris, Loren Heisey, Linda Knights, R. Maximilian Mendoza, Charles Pappas, Sci-Fi Channel's Sean Redlitz, Rod Rehn, Kate Shaklee and Jeffrey Zahnen (U.S.A.); Marina Bailey (South Africa); Andrew Burford, Ailsa Jenkins, Art Mulder and D.W. Rowlands (drhi@reading.sgi.com) (England) for invaluable videotape and assorted researches via the Internet; Mary May and Wiebe DeJong for *Quantum* and *Heroic* Research; Bob Furnell at TASC, Jason Katayama, and Stan Woo for valuable research and materials; Andy Mangels for generously opening his research files to me at the last minute; Darren Ryall, Tracy Robin Somerville, Lynne Henderson for data entry assists; and Linda Currie, Tim and Gloria Dalmatov, Michael Dean, Leonard "Swifty" Wong, Stuart Royan, Lois Balzer, Cathy Mayo, Jim Hay, Vicki Holden, Cynthia and Gerry Baron, Rhea Rose and Jim Rondeau at Quantum Quarterly, Gary Ewing, Michael and Rachel Levenston, Elan Park, Mary Jane Reid, Linda Richards, Garth Spencer, and at White Dwarf Books, Jill Sanagan and Walter Sinclair.

Mark Phillips Interviewees: Frank Aletter, Larry Alexander, William Alland, Corey Allen, Howard Alston, John Anderson, Sylvia Anderson, Margaret Armen, Alan Armer, John Badham, Bob Barbash, Allen Baron, Orson Bean, Terry Becker, Harve Bennett, Alan Bergmann, Ed Bishop, Jerome Bixby, Earl Booth, Arthur Browne, Jr., Martin Caidin, George Chan, Linden Chiles, Thom Christopher, Calvin Clements, Jr., Robert Collins, Booth Colman, Michael Constantine, Elisha Cook, Jr., Randy Crawford, Patrick Culliton, Henry Darrow, Bill Davidson, Bill Derwin, Walter Doniger, Rudi Dorn, Donna Douglas, Robert Douglas, Cindy and Cathy Downes, Hal Dresner, Robert Easton, Don Eitner, Melinda Fee, Terence Feeley, Al Francis, Fred Freiberger, J. Bret Garwood, Harold Gast, Larry Gates, John Gaynor, Prof. James Gunn, Kevin Hagen, Susan Hampshire, Ron Harper, Nancy Hayes, Robert Hecker, David Hedison, Karl Held, Buck Houghton, Allan Hunt, Lou Huston, Jill Jaress, Kenneth Johnson, Russell Johnson, Jay Jones, Robert Justman, Stephen Kandel, DeForest Kelley, Gerald Kelsey, Paul King, George Kirgo, Norman Klenman, Don Knight, Richard Landau, Otto Lang, Charles Larson, Darrell Larson, Anthony and Nancy Lawrence, Ted Lehmann, Seeleg Lester, George Lindsey, Vic Lundin, Jean Marsh, Don Marshall, William Marshall, Leslie Martinson, Don Matheson, Gerald Mayer, Tom McDonough, Nigel McKeand, Allan Melvin, Lee Meriwether, Jan Merlin, Michael Michaelian, Herman Miller, Richard Milton, Robert Mintz, Lawrence Montaigne, Thomas W. Moore, Sean Morgan, David Moses, Bill Neff, Erik Nelson, William O'Connell, Tim O'Connor, Robert O'Neill, James Parriott, Michael Pate, Gregg Peters, Philip Pine, Suzanne Pleshette, Gene Polito, Katharyn Powers, Pat Priest, David Rayfiel, Robert Redford, Ed Richardson, Peter Mark Richman, David W. Rintels, George Robotham, Elizabeth Rogers, Sutton Roley, Gerald Sanford, Ralph Sariego, John Saxon, Howard Schwartz, Ralph Senensky, Richard Shapiro, Jill Sherman-Donner, Mark Slade, Jerry Sohl, Herbert F. Solow, Alvin Sapinsley, Robert Specht, Aaron Spelling, Ellis St. Joseph, Joseph Stefano, Leslie Stevens, Larry Stewart, Herbert L. Strock, Liam Sullivan, Jeannot Szwarc, Joey Tata, Bruce Taylor, Roderick Taylor, Roy Thinnes, Donald Todd, Art Wallace, Robin Ward, Nick Webster, Dawn Wells, Stan Whitmore, John Williams, Shimon Wincelberg,

William Windom, Robert Vincent Wright, Peter Wyngarde, Amanda Wyss, Dean Zanetos, and Paul Zastupnevich.

Thanks also to Robert Coyle for the Roderick Taylor and Bruce Taylor interviews, videotapes of series and assistance in the *Otherworld* episode guide; Karen Myatt for the Jean Marsh interview and providing videotapes of series; Candy Krause for the quoted matter from Robert Redford and Donna Douglas; Sherry Krause for the Allan Melvin, Ted Lehmann, Larry Gates, Russell Johnson and Robert Easton material; Merle Mason for the Gerald Kelsey, Terence Feely and Peter Wyngarde interviews; Alain Bourassa for his invaluable help with the *Men into Space, World of Giants, Science Fiction Theater* and *Champions* episode guides and providing the Otto Lang and Walter Doniger interviews; Cheryl Horton of the Writer's Guild of America for her good humor and help in contacting writers; my uncle, Brian Lundell, who provided me with the invaluable assistance and *Starlog*'s Dave McDonnell for his encouragement and advice over the years and for providing some of the photos in this book.

The following clubs have also been helpful. (If you contact a club for information, please include a self addressed stamped envelope.) Kathy Lewis of the Mark Slade Club, 38 Joppa Road, Worcester, MA 01602; Helen Weber of the UFO Fan Club, 514 Delaware Ave., Lansdale PA 19446; Diane Albert at the TV Collector, P.O. Box 1088, Easton MA 02334; Betty Cole of the David Hedison Fan Club, 928 North Patrick Henry Place, Alexandria VA 22205; Friends of Deanna Lund, 545 Howard Dr., Salem VA 24153.

People who helped with advice and information: Howard A. Anderson, Lee Bacchus at the Vancouver Province, Gwen Bagni-Dubov, Dan Borgman, Ben Brewster (assistant director for Film and Theater Research, University of Wisconsin), Steve Clayton (University of Missouri–Columbia), Laurie Close, Robert Colbert, Evelyn Daniels, Doug Diamond, Charles Dubin, Marj Dusay, Fred Eichelman, J. Bret Garwood at Aaron Spelling Productions, Vicki E. James, Paul J. Jeffers, Leonard Katzman, James Killian, George Kirgo, Al Lewis, Brian Lundell, John Lundell, Quinn Martin, Lynda Mendoza, Tim E. Peck, Doug Powell at *Unique Magazine*, Revelstoke, B.C., Vincent Price, Mary Ann Sell, Carol Serling, Loraine Starr, Mary Anne Stone, John Waldsmith, Bill Winckler, Paul Zastupnevich, the Director's Guild of America, and the Screen Actors Guild.

Portions of the following interviews, reprinted with permission from, and conducted by the authors for, *Starlog* magazine (1986–1993) were used in the book. Our thanks to Starlog Press, editor Dave McDonnell, publisher Norman Jacobs and Kerry O'Quinn. We thank the following writers, directors, and actors for material that we have quoted from them:

Arthur Batanides, Lee Bergere, Barbara Bouchet, Paul Comi, Robert Duncan, Michael Forest, Robert Hamner, Craig Huxley, Don Knight, Robert Lees, Don Matheson, Esther Mitchell, Lou Morheim, Stewart Moss, Susan Oliver, Vic Perrin, Roger Perry, Mann Rubin, Joseph Ruskin, Richard Shapiro, Ron Soble Robert Specht, Leonard Stadd, Sheldon Stark, Liam Sullivan, Jack Turley, William Read Woodfield, Morgan Woodward, Celeste Yarnall.

Finally, thanks to Kenneth Johnson for writing the foreword to this book.

TABLE OF CONTENTS

FOREWORD

From the time we humans first gathered around our stone-age campfires and watched the flickering firelight, we have amazed each other with fantastic tales. We created extraordinary myths and legends to explain the unknown and to give ourselves hope in the face of the great mysteries. We created heroic archetypes to which we could aspire, and mystical demons to tempt and teach us darker lessons. And by these fables we also sought to lighten our load with humor and the enjoyment of a gripping story.

We have passed the tales down, reinventing them with each new generation—even as Shakespeare's magically splendid Ariel from *The Tempest* evolved into the intriguing Robby the Robot of *Forbidden Planet*.

When we view it with this historical perspective we see that "science fiction," though considered a relatively modern literary form, truly has its roots in our earliest mythology. Much in folklore and legend easily qualifies as science fiction. Certainly the worldwide wealth of fairy tales is a prime example.

The people chronicled in this book must take their places alongside the earliest practitioners of the art. They stand beside Homer, Virgil, and the greatest of historic myth-makers (who was probably a woman)—Anonymous. They continue the work of Jonathan Swift, Aldous Huxley, H.G. Wells, Arthur Conan Doyle, Robert Louis Stevenson, Mary Shelley and George Orwell.

Another grand master, Jules Verne, writing about the work of Edgar Allan Poe, once said, "In the midst of these impossibilities, there sometimes exists an appearance of reality which takes possession of the reader's beliefs."

Indeed, that was the pursuit to which Verne himself was most committed: making the unreal, prophetic, outrageous new idea seem not only wildly entertaining, but plausible. He filled the background with details so believable that the foreground action was merely a logical extension—even as H.G. Wells later convinced us that invisibility might just be possible (setting aside the trouble the Invisible Man would experience in dealing with his transparent eyelids). Verne's imagined submarine *Nautilus*, with its design, electric propulsion, diving planes, etc., proved a stunningly accurate prototype for the first real submarine. Writers like Verne and Wells are always ahead of their time.

In congenial interviews, this volume brings front and center the women and men who are carrying into the present the traditions of fanciful creation. Herein are those who fight the daily battles to have some measure of wit and intelligence triumph over pure commercialism; who struggle against the numbing, mundane, leveling influences of network television's lowest-common-denominator mentality.

Included here are those journeypersons who openly admit they only did the work because it was a job and they had to eat (although like Mozart, who also toiled under those conditions, many of them have managed to leave behind some rather exceptional work). Also here are those who have continually been courageous enough to consciously stretch themselves—and us—by making their work aspire to true artistry.

Fantasy and science fiction have always sought to look at the world through a prism, skewing the images of reality, and freeing us, inspiring us—even forcing us—to be imaginative. Within those inspired realms, the best work asks us to find more similarities than differences between ourselves. Thus even at the farthest reaches of space and time, behind even the most grotesque and off-putting facade, we discover there exists a worthy soul to be appreciated, learned from and welcomed as a blood sister or brother: a member of the universal race and consciousness, who has something profound to teach us about ourselves.

KENNETH JOHNSON
Encino, California

(Kenneth Johnson is a writer, producer and director whose credits include The Six Million Dollar Man, The Bionic Woman, Cliffhangers, The Incredible Hulk, "V," *and* Alien Nation.*)*

INTRODUCTION

Welcome to the fantastic, exhilarating and sometimes thought-provoking world of television science fiction.

Whether traveling to other worlds, or galloping through time in this one, the characters portrayed in this genre provide a more provocative level of entertainment than the living room histrionics of situation comedy denizens or the catching-the-robber premise of many a crime show.

Most of the television series covered in this volume, whether good, bad or unflinchingly awful, did accomplish one important thing despite their often meager budgets: they created another world, another reality, and made you believe that these people of other worlds or other dimensions were really out there.

The broad appeal of the genre allowed youngsters to enjoy the fantastic premises and far-out stories of *Lost in Space* and *Land of the Giants*, while sublime series such as *Outer Limits* and *Star Trek* often put the human experience in dramatic perspective. That's more than most television fare offers.

Even at their most primitive, many series have projected bold heroes who embodied the most admirable attributes of humanity: nobility and strength, curiosity and a sense of adventure in the face of the strange and bizarre.

Science fiction series have generally had mediocre ratings during their original runs, but many have proved durable over time, inspiring conventions, fan clubs, video releases, reruns on cable networks and magazine retrospectives. With the debut of America's Sci-Fi Channel in 1991, many of the shorter-lived science fiction shows are enjoying a rebirth in popularity. By contrast, many of the crime and medical series that ranked high in the ratings during their network runs fluttered into obscurity after cancellation.

With one exception, this book covers shows that began their runs between 1959 and 1989. We examine their genesis, their network and syndicated histories and where they stand today in the world of television. All this is conveyed via extensive research as well as interviews with over 250 writers, directors, actors, stuntmen and craftsmen plus the shows' creators. Many are telling their stories here for the first time. Uncovered are a myrid of production stories, some trivial, some groundbreaking. Why was a *Spiderman* episode in danger of sparking a disastrous international incident? How did a dying actor on *Night Gallery* use his impending demise to create a vivid performance? What was the unusual secret of a Detroit auto worker who guest starred on *The Immortal*?

The exception to the time frame is *Science Fiction Theater*, which aired from 1955 to 1957. Had it been possible to cover the 1950s as completely as the later years, we might have set an earlier starting date for the book, enabling us to include other imaginative early programming (such as *Captain Video* and *Tom Corbett*). Unfortunately, the tapes of many 1950s programs have been lost over the years. Thus 1959—which happens to coincide with the launching of the most durable science fiction/fantasy show ever, Rod Serling's *Twilight*

Zone—is a logical starting point for complete coverage. Nevertheless, so significant was *Science Fiction Theater*, which used science as a serious source storytelling and influenced later anthology series, that it seemed impossible to discuss the later shows without describing this important predecessor. Thus we felt compelled to include it despite the unavoidable absence of its contemporaries.

Since this book includes only series that began their runs by 1989, you won't find such 1990s shows as *The Flash*, *seaQuest DSV*, *Babylon 5* or *Star Trek Deep Space Nine*. However, we have included complete episode guide coverage of *Quantum Leap*, *Star Trek: The Next Generation* and *The Adventures of Superboy* beyond 1989 because they all began before 1989.

The 62 series included were chosen as representatives of science fiction as a genre. Television series classified as horror, including *Thriller* and *Way Out*, are covered briefly in Appendix A, as are shows that only skimmed the science fiction genre such as *Wild, Wild West* and *The Man from U.N.C.L.E.*

Situation comedies with a science fiction twist such as *Mork and Mindy*, *It's About Time* and *Quark* are excluded. Saturday morning live-action shows such as *Land of the Lost* and *Space Academy* and animated series are also not included. Since we are covering primarily American series, many foreign shows, including Japan's *Ultraman* and Britain's *Dr. Who* and *Blakes' 7* are not covered. However, the British productions *UFO*, *The Prisoner*, and *The Champions* are chronicled here. One criterion we used for their inclusion was that they all enjoyed national exposure when they were carried by the major American networks. A fourth British series, *Space 1999*, while not network-based, was in full American syndication during its 1975–1977 run, featured American actors and was aimed specifically at American audiences.

We have tried to provide complete and accurate historical records of these series without introducing our opinions into the writing.

In this one book, you will also find the most comprehensive episode listings ever. We have made every effort to have the episode guides be as complete and accurate as possible. In some cases, however, character names for guest stars just were not available.

In fact, we are open to information from readers who would like to offer additional data on any aspect of this book for any future editions that may appear.

The bibliography will provide readers with additional source material on series of interest.

It has been a fascinating and gratifying journey for us. To the people who helped us put this book together, and to the individuals who granted us interviews, we offer our thanks.

Whether you grew up with these shows as we did or are just discovering them in reruns, we hope you will have an entertaining and interesting journey.

FRANK GARCIA
Vancouver, British Columbia

MARK PHILLIPS
Victoria, British Columbia

SCIENCE FICTION
TELEVISION SERIES

Alien Nation
September 1989–September 1990

Aliens from the planet Tencton, who are dubbed "The Newcomers," arrive on Earth and become acclimated into modern society. A young human cop, Matt Sikes, is paired with a Newcomer partner, George Francisco, who's married with a family. In the course of the series, we watch their personal and professional lives unfold, and we see how society deals with the world's newest minority.

Cast: The Humans: Detective Matt Sikes (Gary Graham); Capt. Brian Grazer (Ron Fassler); Jill, Emily's friend (Molly Morgan); Burns, the photographer (Jeff Doucette); Sgt. Dobbs (Lawrence Hilton-Jacobs); Dr. Lois Allen (Michele Lamar Richards); Detective Beatrice Zepeda (Jenny Gago). *The Newcomers:* Detective George Francisco (Eric Pierpoint); Susan Francisco (Michelle Scarabelli); Buck Francisco (Sean Six); Emily Francisco (Lauren Woodland); Cathy Frankel (Terri Treas); Albert Einstein, the janitor (Jeff Marcus); Uncle Moodri (James Greene).

Based on the characters created by: Rockne O'Bannon; *Executive Producer:* Kenneth Johnson; *Supervising Producer:* Andrew Schneider; *Producers:* Tom Chehak, Arthur Seidel; *Co-Producer:* Diane Frolov; FOX/Twentieth Century–Fox; 60 minutes.

Cops and Coneheads. That's what writer-producer-director Kenneth Johnson thought *Alien Nation* was all about when he saw the 1988 feature film starring James Caan and Mandy Patinkin.

"When Fox first came to me and asked if I could turn *Alien Nation* into a series, I didn't want to do science fiction and was anxious to do something else," recalls Johnson. "I agreed to look at the film, which I enjoyed half of. I thought it was a lovely premise they had created, the world's newest minority. I found halfway through the movie it turned into *Miami Vice* with coneheads. It was a cop show I've seen a thousand times. The most interesting part of the piece was the little moment when the family waved to Mandy Patinkin. I said, 'Wait a minute! Those people! They're the ones I want to know! I don't need another damn cop show!' When I took over the chore for Fox, it was the absolute understanding I was to do a social drama. Not another cop show, nor a science fiction show. What I wanted to do was a story to examine what it's like to be a minority."

To pull the show off with a sense of style,

Johnson reassembled a few key colleagues from *Incredible Hulk* days. He brought onboard the husband-wife team of Andrew Schneider and Diane Frolov; cinematographer promoted to director John McPherson; and veteran director Chuck Bowman.

Although the show lasted for only one season, in those 22 episodes, *Alien Nation* was a broad exploration in the sociology of how human society would feel about and interact with new-found alien neighbors in their everyday lives. Episodes dealt with human-alien relationships via a collection of characters. Forefront was an often stormy relationship between human cop Matt Sikes and his alien partner George Francisco, as they walked the beat in Slagtown Los Angeles. Secondary explorations dealt with Sikes' growing interest in his apartment neighbor, Newcomer Cathy. There was also the running story of the Newcomer kids trying to fit into human society. Daring for television was direct exposition of discrimination and racial issues, plus stories about the unusual sexual practices of the Newcomers.

In preparing Graham and Pierpoint for their roles, all Johnson had to do was plant a seed in their minds. "I said to [them], 'Eric is the first black police officer in Jackson, Mississippi, in 1962.' And, bingo, you immediately get the picture. That's what it was all about. What *Alien Nation* was about was discrimination. Prejudice. Intolerance. Within that framework, Andy and Diane and I would sit down and say, 'Well, what's this week's show going to be about? Let's take greed for an example. How does greed manifest itself in the alien culture versus the human culture?' Then we'd get into all of that."

From those discussions, other ideas took shape, and the most unusual of those was Johnson's suggestion that for Newcomers, it was the male of the species that gave birth. "Also, I came up with the notion that it took more than two to have sex!" laughs Johnson. "It gave us an opportunity to, again, examine stereotypes and intolerance towards religious beliefs. In a subsequent episode when I suggested that George give birth [for the episode "Real Men"], Andy and Diane immediately hit on the opportunity that I suggested to create a show about male stereotypes. When I said, 'George has to have the baby, let's do a show about what makes a man.' Setting that show about a pregnant man in a police milieu, where they were investigating a crime that took place in a body building arena where all these guys all pumped up, gave us an opportunity to explore masculinity. As George said, most people of his species don't feel like they've really fulfilled themselves as a man until they've given birth!"

The sexual mores and practices of the Newcomers were explored early on the show in an episode titled "Fifteen with Wanda." It was directed by *Star Trek: The Next Generation* veteran, Rob Bowman, who remembers that, "Fifteen with Wanda" was a funny show because it was basically about the sexual desires of these aliens. Once you get this husband and wife who are about to mate, and they take this certain pill that heightens their sexual desires, it makes them almost sexually crazy! As soon as the guy takes the drug, he gets kidnapped. He witnesses a murder and needs police protection. And he's got this drug that's making him sexually in demand! His wife is home and is dying to be with him. And all he wants is 15 minutes with his wife, 'Just give me 15 with Wanda and I'll be fine.' There was some action and suspense in it, but basically, it was about the heightened sexual activities of the aliens and it was very funny."

Bowman's memory of his one directing stint on the show was that he had to film it *fast*. "The show wasn't quite [fine-tuned] yet. I think I could have helped in several areas to bring those characters to the screen. It was an *extremely* difficult show to shoot because of the schedule. My memory of that was we shot fast as we could move the camera to the next location. I didn't have a lot of rehearsal, it didn't have a lot of polish, but we did our best. It's not one of my favorite all-time shows. I just barely had time to get it together."

So effectively did Johnson and his team spin their Newcomer tales in this show that various ethnic groups in Los Angeles bestowed upon them commendations and awards. "The New York Board of Jewish Education, an organization in New York City that services 400 schools in the New York area, asked us to send them every episode of *Alien Nation* so they could use it in their schools as a teaching tool about discrimination," says Johnson. "The Hispanic community here in Los Angeles, a multicultural organization including Hispanics and Asian-Americans and black Americans, gave us several awards, and we were acknowledged by several multicultural groups as being a very moving force in the community for making people step back and taking a look at how they view minorities. When you can do this through a science fiction framework, through allegory, you can do it *without* offending anybody! That's the *beauty* of it."

As an example of this, Johnson cited a scene written for the pilot of the show. "The people of all races and colors are trying to keep the [Newcomer] kid out of their school, because that kind doesn't belong there. The whole idea of the purists reflects a lot of the American fundamentalists, the right wing minorities, that don't want to admit that anyone else might be as good as they are. They're trying to keep all the doors closed."

Of his cast, Johnson points to Eric Pierpoint as "a consummate actor and someone I had worked with on a short-lived series previously called *Hot Pursuit* for NBC. I realized what a good guy Eric was, and when *Alien Nation* came along, I went to Fox and said, 'This is the guy I want for George'. I knew that not only did Eric have a wonderful range, but that he would have the *patience* required for getting in and out of that makeup everyday. It was a two-hour job getting in and 25 minutes getting out."

Director Chuck Bowman, who worked on the episode called "The Red Room," also has some good words for the cast of the show. "They are consummate, conscientious actors in that they are there, well-prepared, hardworking and flexible. Eric's father is Robert Pierpoint, an NBC news correspondent for 37 years, so Eric is a quite well-traveled young man and brings a lot of experiences to his role, and you can see that in his portrayal," says Bowman. "Terri Treas is an absolutely wonderful actress. She was also a consummate, well-prepared actress with a good attitude and a work ethic."

Bowman knows Kenneth Johnson very well, having worked with him previously in *The Incredible Hulk* and *V*. "Kenny Johnson has a wonderful way of getting a community of actors in these projects to really bond together," notes Bowman. "He's a good leader. First, he's a fabulous director and a wonderful writer. His strongest attribute is in his directing. He's very creative. He

Kenneth Johnson (right) directs Gary Graham (middle) and Eric Pierpoint (left) in a scene from *Alien Nation*. Photo courtesy of Kenneth Johnson.

pushes the envelope in that he's bold and risky in his direction. His actors get into that. They know that with Kenny they're going to get the best product they can possibly get for the time and money that they have. Kenny's a good team leader, he has a good attitude, he doesn't bark at people, he's intelligent. He respects his actors as human beings. When he reads actors for his directing episodes, he reads with them in casting. Generally, a casting director—someone who works in casting—will read and the producers and directors will watch. But Kenny wants to make sure that they have everything going for them. He reads the other parts of the scene, and he's wonderful. I'm a huge fan of the quality of human being and creator that Kenny is."

Bowman recalls the days of the show as being "really an experience for everyone to pull together with a deep desire to do a good job. Everyone contributed like that."

Johnson says that the makeup design—which won an Emmy award for the artists Michelle Burke and Rick Stratton, posed problems for the actors. Not only did it become very hot after several hours of shooting; it also made it very difficult for the actors to hear. "To get a

sense what it was like, if you put your hands over your ears and you talk, and listen to people talking around you, that's what it sounds like," says Johnson. For one episode, his daughter, Katie, appeared as an orphaned child at a funeral and got a taste first-hand of the makeup experience. Piercing earholes into the makeup helped alleviate the problems somewhat.

One other problem with makeup became evident in shooting scenes that called for crowds of Newcomers: "When you need extras, you call casting, but when you need a bunch of *alien* extras, we had days when we had 20 makeup people working as opposed to the usual two."

To this day, Johnson receives mail regarding the show. "We got a huge amount of mail. And virtually all of it was positive. It was astonishing the amount we got. We *still* get mail! There are *Alien Nation* societies all over the world. I just got a newsletter from England yesterday." This newsletter, *The Tencton Planet,* produced by the Alien Nation Appreciation Society, is a fan effort by a man named Pete Chambers. To demonstrate the enthusiasm fans have for this show, Chambers has somehow managed, via the International Star Registry, to give a star the name of Tencton.

The show was canceled because of poor ratings in a Monday night time slot opposite the CBS smash sit-com *Murphy Brown*. Johnson remembers the fateful phone call announcing that the ax had fallen on the show. "When Peter Chernin [then president of Fox Entertainment, now head of 20th Century–Fox] called me to say they were not picking up the show for another season, I said, 'Peter, this is a *huge* mistake you're making!' [It was] foolish of Fox to cancel the show when it had another four or five years, easily, to it. Now, fade out and fade in a year later, Peter stands up in front of the television critics association and says, 'Last year, we made a *huge* mistake! We canceled *Alien Nation!*' He apologized for canceling the show," laughs Johnson. "Again, it was an example of the network community *not* understanding what a show was *about* or not giving it time to grow and to find its audience. It's very frustrating when that happens."

Post-cancelation, several efforts were made to continue the show. Syndication was one possibility, but the roadblock for a continued effort was the show's expensive budget, composed largely by makeup for aliens. "We could not get the costs of the show down far enough to do it as a viable syndication show. We couldn't get the kind of budget that *Star Trek: The Next Generation* was doing," informs Johnson. "They were saying, 'Well, if you can do it for $600,000...' Well, the show cost a million and two. There was no way to do any kind of quality. We would have a show called *Alien Nation*, but it wouldn't have the quality. We tried getting Fox to doing a couple of TV movies. Andy and Diane wrote a couple of wonderful scripts which carried the relationship of Cathy and Sikes to a full-blown sexual relationship, which was very funny and topical with all this talk of safe sex in this world today. Fox, in their infinite wisdom just decided not to."

Fox Television's rationale in canceling the show was that since *Alien Nation* had a 10 share rating, something else in the time slot would garner a 15 rating. But when something new did air, ratings took a further dive, destroying Fox's hopes. Everyone connected with the show had been confident of its renewal, largely because Fox had commissioned six scripts for a second season. A cliffhanger episode, "Green Eyes," was created and aired to entice viewers to tune in again next season. But the show's resolution never came to be. "We thought we were going on!" exclaims Johnson. "Andy and Diane already wrote the follow-up, and

we got a very clear idea where the show was going, and we wanted to leave the audience wondering what was going to happen and wanting more so they would tune in again next season."

Johnson recalls that while *Alien Nation* was often a nightmare to create, "The good side is I made a lot of friends. I'm very close to virtually everybody we worked with in the show. We didn't shoot on the Fox lot. We shot on old warehouses on East L.A. You needed visas to get into the neighborhood. We were all there working together. It was the best kind of family operation by all of us. The loss of *Alien Nation* is always going to be painful for all of us. It was one of those rare situations where everything came together, the theme of the show, good people working together on a good product. I've come to realize the journey is sometimes more important than the destination," explains Johnson. "In *Alien Nation* the journey could not have been more positive. When I was casting *Alien Nation* and I had the sense that it could go on for a while, I was careful in the selection of the cast, writers, and the crew. I've always told my crew there's two things I'm always concerned about. The first is, 'Let's do the highest quality show we can possibly do and I will not take second best,' and they all loved that. And the second thing is, 'We gotta have fun.' Life's too short to not have fun. That's how I operate. I have a very happy crew and a very happy set. It starts at the top. I always feel the executive producer sets the tone, and the stars pick it up and pass it along, and the crew picks it up, and everybody feels good. It was wonderful for people to come on our show and do just a one-day part or something and say, 'My god! I've never been on a set like this! Everybody's happy!' It was a real loss."

But Johnson's perseverance has paid off. *Alien Nation* returned to television in October, 1994 as a Fox TV movie titled *Dark Horizon*. The entire cast reassembled after a four-year hiatus to resolve the cliffhanger story that began in "Green Eyes," the final series episode. "After *Dark Horizon* aired, it got the highest ratings Fox had in that time period in two and a half years," says Kenneth Johnson in a followup interview. "Ratings are always inspiring to them, so they bought two more movies."

The broadcast of this two-hour Halloween special was so successful, both creatively and in the ratings, that Fox TV commissioned three additional scripts for a series of made-for-TV movies. The second story to be filmed was *Body and Soul.* In this story, George and Matt make a startling discovery about the slave ship that brought the Newcomers to Earth, and of the vicious Overseers who ran the ship. "*Body and Soul* is from an original script by Andrew Schneider and Diane Frolov, and was rewritten by Renee and Harry Longstreet," informs Johnson. "It turns out that the love relationship between Matt Sikes and Cathy, his alien girlfriend across the hall, has progressed to the point where they have to take sex classes together. It deals with interspecies sex."

The third script *Millenium* (formerly titled *Dangerous Portals*), was a sequel to the episode "Generation to Generation," set in the last week of the millenium. During December, 1999, people think it's the end of the world and a cult leader misuses the sacred box introduced in "Generation." The box is a virtual reality device Overseers use for religious purposes. "The network is very excited about the films. *Millenium* particularly, has quite a staggering look to it," says Johnson. "We have more special effects in *Millenium* than there are in *Forrest Gump*. Our editing team is the same team that worked on that film and when they added it up, realized there were more shots of special visual effects than there were in that feature."

Pleased with the successful return of *Alien Nation*, the Fox network commissioned three additional television movies. In the spring of 1996, two of them, *The Udara Legacy* (previously titled *Time Bombs*) and *The Enemy Within*, were filmed back to back. A sixth script, titled *City of Angels*, was also planned.

Responding to a query whether the series would ever have an opportunity to return to a weekly schedule, Johnson revealed that the studio is interested in that but the Fox network is more reticent. Both the studio and the network is 20th Century–Fox. This is a case where separate divisions of the same corporate entity have differing ideas of how to treat their child. It's the left hand fighting with the right.

"I love the concept and I love the characters that we've created here, and I'd love to see them carry on regardless of whether it's [long form or as a series]," says Johnson. "I think, frankly, there should be one hour episodes playing, they allow for more personal stories. The studios and the network always want the TV movies a little bigger with a more 'save the world' quality to them. That works against us sometimes when we're trying to do more personal stories. "From the standpoint of the series and the characters, I would prefer to go back to one-hour but if two hours is the only life for them, that's what we'll do."

Alien Nation is a rare example, *Star Trek* notwithstanding, of a television show that refused to die. It is a tribute to the continued and unflagging interest by the entire cast and of key production personnel that the show returns to the airwaves after an extended break to pick up where they left off.

CAST NOTES

Gary Graham (Det. Matt Sikes): "Sikes is a cop because, number one, he loves it, and number two, he just can't see himself doing anything else." says Graham. "He's a rule breaker but he gets the job done. Instinctual, compulsive, the type of guy I'd want to go in battle with."

To prepare for the role, Graham spent time with the Los Angeles policemen. "I must have been doing something right, they took me in as one of their own," he says.

Graham's motion picture debut was in Paul Schrader's *Hardcore* (1979) and followed by *Hollywood Knights* (1980), *All the Right Moves* (1983), and Stuart Gordon's SF film *Robojox* (1990). Since the show, Graham has appeared in the short-lived 1994 series *M.A.N.T.I.S.* and *Star Trek: Voyager* (1995).

Eric Pierpoint (George Francisco): "George carries himself with an inner confidence while adapting to his new surroundings. Even though he approaches his new lifestyle with curiosity, George is comfortable with who he is and can tolerate virtually all obstacles directed toward him. It's his self-confidence that's the key to George's strength," says Eric.

Pierpoint's credits include *In the Heat of the Night* (1967), the TV series *Beauty and the Beast*, and *Hill Street Blues* and a starring role in *Hot Pursuit*, a 1979 TV movie directed by Kenneth Johnson. He also appeared in *Windy City* (1984) and the remake of *Invaders from Mars* (1986). Since the series, Pierpoint has appeared in *Time Trax* and *Star Trek: The Next Generation*.

Michele Scarabelli (Susan Francisco): "My hope was to develop and explore basic assumptions we have about gender roles by seeing Earthlings through the eyes of someone completely different," says Scarabelli.

Scarabelli hails from Montreal, Canada, and

The cast of *Alien Nation*, left to right: Gary Graham, Terri Treas, Eric Pierpoint, Lauren Woodland, Michele Scarabelli and Sean Six. Copyright 1989 ABC/Twentieth Century–Fox Television.

has starred in *The Hotel New Hampshire* (1984) and *Cover Girl* (1984). On television, she has appeared in *Night Heat*, *Air Wolf II* on USA Network, and *Dallas*. Since the series, Scarabelli went to South Africa to work on a television series there and guested on *Star Trek: The Next Generation*.

Lawrence Hilton-Jacobs (Sgt. Dobbs): Born in 1953, Jacobs began his career at the age of 14. His acting assignments have been many and varied. Best known as student "Boom Boom" Washington in the 1970s hit *Welcome Back Kotter*, Jacobs has also guested in *Simon and Simon*, *Hill Street Blues*, *Fame*, and the mini-series *Roots*. Jacobs is a skilled commercial cartoonist and keyboardist, and likes sports ranging from basketball to ice skating.

Terri Treas (Cathy Frankel): "She's had very few romantic experiences. When she encounters Matt

Sikes across the hall of her apartment building, she has no perception of what it really means to have a relationship. She is someone who is very bright, yet so naive," says Treas of her character, Cathy.

Born in 1959, this Kansas-born actress got her big break on TV's *Seven Brides for Seven Brothers* (1982–1983). Feature credits include *The Nest* (1988), and *The Fabulous Baker Boys* (1989), and television appearances include *Murphy Brown*, *Matlock* and *The A-Team*. When *Alien Nation* folded, Treas concentrated on film acting and in holding women's defense workshops.

Lauren Woodland (Emily Francisco): "I think Emily wants the best of both worlds. She wants to be accepted by her classmates, but she also wants to preserve her alien heritage," says Woodland. Her acting appearances include the CBS Special presentation of *An Enemy Among Us*, as well as *Our House, L.A. Law, St. Elsewhere, Superior Court* and *The Judge*. Woodland is also a veteran of 40 national commercials.

Sean Six (Buck Francisco): "Buck Francisco is a teenager who is trying to connect with something, but the truth he connects with isn't the right one," says Sean Six. "The whole teenage thing is about finding out about who you are. Buck is doing just that, trying to relate with something, his parents, friends, anything. He can't connect with his father since he considers his father to be a sellout. He takes a liking to a gang because he needs to identify with a figure of strength."

A native of New York, Six's first professional job was *Fiddler on the Roof* in San Francisco. "I want to do everything and try everything…. How many actors get to say they portrayed an alien? Not too many."

When *Alien Nation* closed its doors, Six returned to his hometown in Portland, Oregon, and joined the forestry service. To film *Dark Horizon*, Six had to take a leave of absence, but with the advent of a continuing film series, Six relocated to Los Angeles.

EPISODE GUIDE

Alien Nation (2 hours)
On their first case together, Matt and George investigate the death of a transient. They also attempt to solve a series of murders that may belong to an insect creature but the Purist movement could be involved.

Meanwhile, Matt is given his former partner's materials and learns that the Overseers might have an involvement in his partner's death. Wr: Kenneth Johnson. Dir: Kenneth Johnson.

Lyddie L. (Scott Caldwell); Jill's mother (Diane Civita); Purist leader (William Frankfather); Teacher (Ketty Lester); Puente (Loyda Ramos); Ketnes (Tim Russ); Priest (Brian Smiar); Dr. Lee (Evan Kim); Jill (Molly Morgan); Marcos (Tony Acierto); Randall (Jeff Austin); Newcomer cop (Terry Beaver); Miranda (Lisa Donaldson Bowman); Mark (Jade Calgory); Rowdy #2 (George Cheung); Linen manager (Gus Corrado); Blentu (Trevor Edmond); Salvage manager (Robert Allan Curtis); Vagrant (John William Evans); Receptionist (Brooke Anne Hayes); Tito (Marco Hernandez); Person #2 (Kevin Hurley); Supporter (John Kirby); Amos N. Andy (Aaron Lustic); Female Purist (Melora Marshall); Informant (Joe Mays); Dr. Hurwitz (Richard Mehuna); Street person (Martha Melinda); Diane (Catherine Paolone); Ramna (John Patrick Reger);

Bernardo (Bert Rosario); Homeowner (Andrea Stein); Black kid (Tiere Turner); Rowdy #1 (Steve Vandeman); Newcomer (Ed Williams); Man (Biff Yeager).

Fountain of Youth
When George's friend is shot, George visits him at the Newcomer clinic. But when he dies of respiratory failure, George becomes suspicious and quietly investigates to discover others have died in the clinic before. Wr: Diane Frolov. Dir: John McPherson.

Trenner (Jason Beghe); Windsor (Joel Polis); Harriet Beecher (Susan Gibney); Lisa (Gretchen Graham); Celinite priest (Robert V. Barron); Celeste (Crystal Carson); Man (Randy Harrington); Beth Meadows (Wendy Kaplan); Henry James (Steve Rankin); Executive (Barry Sherman); Pathologist (Liz Torres); Mrs. James (Bonnie Urseth).

Little Lost Lamb
George and Matt try to save the life of a Newcomer prostitute, but she's killed by Dorian Grey, the pimps' henchman. Their only lead is a talent agency. Meanwhile, the devotion George's Uncle Moodri shows to the Tenctonese religion compels Buck to confess to an accidental murder. Wr: Diane Frolov. Dir: Kevin Hooks.

Mary Shelley (Heather McAdam); Dallas (Kimberly Kates); Charlotte Bronte (Shannon Wilcox); Dorian Gray (Will Bledsoe); Blentu (Trevor Edmond); Receptionist (Catherine Lansing); Harry Marcus (Robert Maniardi); Svabo (Noon Orsatti); Rudy (William Wellman, Jr.).

Fifteen with Wanda
Matt is having problems with his daughter just as George copes with a rebellious Buck. But they're both too busy protecting a witness from a mobster. Wr: Steven Long Mitchell and Craig Van Sickle. Dir: Rob Bowman.

Buster Keaton (Dave Bowe); Victoria Fletcher (Joan McMurtry); Kirby Sikes (Cheryl Pollak); Sal (Lori Petty); Wanda (Sachi Parker); Thor (Wayne Pere); Principal (Haskell V. Anderson III); Blentu (Trevor Edmond); Granny (Jean Sincere); Maitre'd (Michael Wilson); Officer (Thomas J. Hoageboeck); Prep #1 (Mike Worth); Salesgirl (Nikki Tyler); Svabo (Noon Orsatti); Wayne Joshua (Ron Howard George).

The Takeover
Matt and George are stuck at the station with office work during a city-wide riot. But some thieves think the Police Station is easy prey for contraband and drugs. Wr: Tom Chehak. Dir: Steve Dubin.

Diane Elrea (Gwynyth Walsh); Andrew Craig (Ji-Tu Cumbuka); Kenny Dunstan (Charley Lang); Tom Mulden (Tracey Walter); McKnight (Michael Fairman); Harry Dundee (Will Egan); Letitia Rosario (Camila Griggs).

The First Cigar
Needing cash to pay the IRS, George gets a loan from Newcomer businesswoman Betsy Ross. Betsy also gives George tips about deals involving a highly addictive and illegal narcotic, "Jack." Wr: Diane Frolov and Andrew Schneider. Dir: John McPherson.

Betsy Ross (Diana Bellamy); Yamato (Cary-Hiroyuki

Tagawa); Ruth Steelman (Carolyn Mignini); Ramna (John Patrick Reber); Vahan (Steve Susskind); Nina (Jennifer Banko); Cliff (Mike DeLuna); Blentu (Trevor Edmond); Alverez (Carlos Lacamara); Bouncer (Faith Minton); Newcomer junkie (James Nixon); Svabo (Noon Orsatti); Delivery man (Jeff Skier); Korean drug dealer (Joon B. Kim); Newcomer drug dealer (Salvator Xuereb); Also with: Doug McKeon.

Night of the Screams
A series of murders seems related to the Tenctonese legend "Tagdot" the equivalent of the "boogeyman". George and Matt are assigned to solve the murders. Wr: Tom Chehak. Dir: Gwen Arner.

Paul Revere (David Opatoshu); Macy (Brad English); Richard (James Polk); Jean Paul Sartre (Mitch Pileggi); Officer #1 (Michael Miladan); Car Buyer (Harry Caeser); Car Buyer (Gwen E. Davis); Newcomer usher (Suzanne Levelle); Tagdot (adult) (Steven Majewicz); Tagdot (child) (Jessica Pesscas); Lost child (Gabe Witcher); Car dealer (Wayne Powers).

Contact
An astronomer is murdered before he can announce a discovery of a radio source at the galaxy's edge. George and Matt target an Overseer who wants to send a signal to a probe telling them Earth has four billion more slaves. Meanwhile, Matt receives a trunk from an uncle containing personal belongings. And, George and Susan agree to have another child. Wr: Joe Menosky. Dir: John McPherson.

Carl Peterson (Joel Polis); Marissa Meyers (Annabelle Gurwitch); Sergius (Jeffrey Josephson); Bob (Stuart Fratkin); Concierge (Curt Lowens); Jerry Bielack (John Apicella); Mr. Kim (Michael Paul Chan); Professor Tower (Donald Hotton); John Barrymore (Alexis Arouette); Dr. Morales (Vincent Leahr).

Three to Tango
George asks Albert to serve as the "Binnaum," in a ritual where two Tenctonese males impregnate a female. Meanwhile, a number of Binnaums have been found dead lately, and George and Matt investigate. Wr: Diane Frolov and Andrew Schneider. Dir: Stan Lathan.

Drevni (Alan Scarfe); May O'Naise (Dana Anderson); Coroner (Meagan Fay); Bjorn (Ivan G'vera); Goran (Charles Hayward); Isaac Newton (Patrick Johnson); Mrs. Sartre (Anva Liffey); Guest (Fiama Fricano); Female Newcomer (Laura Herring); Male Newcomer (James Polk); Craig Keller (Charlie Skeen).

The Game
On the anniversary of "The Day of Descent" (the arrival of the Newcomers on Earth), George is disturbed when reports of "The Game" on Earth crops up. "The Game" is a deadly Russian roulette–like sport where jet sprays of salt water burn away the victims' chest. Wr: Steven Long Mitchell and Craig Van Sickle. Dir: David Carson.

Coolock (Andreas Katsulas); Tom Edison (Sam Anderson); Dr. Roscoe Brennan (Teddy Wilson); Deon Flack (Billy Ray Sharkey); Joe Comet (Joel Swetow); Mrs. Comet (Maggie Egan); Ruhtra (Bill Allen); Attorney (Craig

Richard Nelson); Challenger (Henry Stolow); Alva Edison (Isabel Wolfe); Cop (Martin Valinsky).

Chains of Love
George and Matt believe that Newcomer Clara Bow is a 'Black Widow' killer, mating with and killing sexual partners via a dating service. Unable to pin her down, George sets up a date with her and becomes infatuated. Wr: Andrew Schneider and Diane Frolov. Dir: Harry Longstreet.

Jenny Hoffat/Clara Bow (Caitlin O'Heaney); Marvin Gardens (S.A. Griffin); Emma Bovary (Diana Barton); Dr. Roscoe Brennan (Teddy Wilson); Ted Healy (Jeffrey Nordling); Leonard (Darren Dalton); Johnny Appleseed (Theodore Raimi); Ralph Emerson (Bennett Liss); Daniel (Thom Zimerele); Roland (Kurt Verbaarschot); Lance Lot (John Hese).

The Red Room
George and Matt are annoyed when they're taken off a murder case by the FBI. Wr: Steven Long Mitchell and Craig Van Sickle. Dir: Chuck Bowman.

Dr. Marcie Wright (Katherine Justice); Jeffries (John P. Connelly); Silas Marner (Tom Dugan); Amanda Russle (Patricia Heaton); Dr. Chris Pettit (Ray Reinhardt); Marcus Byer (Chuck Bennett).

Memory Flash—Director Chuck Bowman: "I thought it was a very exciting episode. The series was set up as an eight day production. When I arrived they informed me I had to do it in seven days. And then a day and a half before I was about to do it, they informed me that I had to do it in six days. I saw that the potential for production values was going to be limited.

"So, I worked on how best I could utilize that and see how I could give that episode some life without costing more money or more time from our schedule. I think we were successful in doing that.

"It became one of the best episodes."

The Spirit of '95
Susan and Buck become involved in politics when an amendment is considered to allow Newcomer voting. Matt and George investigate a series of violent attacks against the campaign that are being blamed on the Purists. Wr: Tom Chehak. Dir: Harry Longstreet.

Wyatt Earp (Mark Thomas Miller); Max Klay (Mark Joy); Jack Pearlman (Clarence Felder); Mr. Hopper (Harvey Jason); Jesse Parker (Henry Brown); Mrs. Giller (Frances Bay); Mike Wilmington (Mark L. Taylor); Carol Wilmington (Marla Fries); Cop (Michael Milhoan); Reporter (Ron S. Herbes); Desk sergeant (Arthur Seidel); Officer (Martin Valinsky).

Generation to Generation
In another series of murders, victims are being burned to death, and it has something to do with a Tenctonese box that's passed along from person to person. Meanwhile, Matt becomes a "Big Brother." Wr: Andrew Schneider and Diane Frolov. Dir: John McPherson.

Lowell Bratigan (Timothy Scott); Henry Glass (Scott Jaeck); Sydney Foley (Michael Faustino); Howard Thayer (Francis Guinan); Auctioneer (Aubrey Morris); Lucille (Peggy Doyle); Krasava (Ernestine Mercer); Philip Dunaway (Ryan Cutrona); Girl (Stephanie Baldwin); Boy (Damon Gourdine); Ruiz (Tony Muvor).

Eyewitness News

A local TV station follows George around for a week alienating his family and friends. Meanwhile the detectives investigate an assault on a video sex-line operator. Wr: Charles S. Kaufman, Larry B. Williams. Dir: Lyndon Chubbuck.

Renee Longstreet (Angela Bassett); Virginia Hamm (Deborah Goodrich); Arvin Kaufman (Gene Butler); Ernie Denton (Hugh McGuire); Mrs. Denton (Kelly Jean Peters); Mr. Denton (Rob King); Roger Rose (John Mese); Female executive (Evelina Fernandez); John (Ian Patrick Williams); Joe (David Hoskins); Male executive (Terry Nunn); Cameraman (Kerrigan Mahan); Tilly (Jennifer Roach); Bailey (Joseph Graham).

Partners

George sees a mobster kill another man and becomes the state's strongest evidence against him. Plus, after a drug bust, George is accused of lifting seven grams from the $1 million worth of Jack. Wr: David Garber and Bruce Kalish. Dir: Stan Lathan.

Theo Miles (Gilbert Lewis); Bud Anderson (Tom Byrd); Sgt. Dustin Baxley (Terry Beaver); Ken Jester (Bill Kalmensc); Allison Wolfe (Maria Rangel); Chester Charles (Crofton Hardester); Con (Wilson Raiser); Haney (Branscombe Richmond); Rankin (Arthur Seidel); Garrison (Gary Morgan); Rickman (Brad Orrison); Pretty Boy Whalen (Robert Romanus); Also with: Tony Rizzoli.

Real Men

Newcomer hormones are being sold as steroids for humans, while George is fully pregnant and undergoes mood swings. They trace the hormone thief to a gym, where a struggle causes George to enter premature labor. Wr: Diane Frolov and Andrew Schneider. Dir: John McPherson.

Nick Coletta (William Shockley); Victor Wendkos (A.D. Muyich); Dan Zimmer (Robert Neary); Marty Penn (Hank Garrett); Karina (Debbie Barker); Doctor (M.E. Loree); Sol Birnbaum (Martin Garner); Guest (Jeff Skier); Andrew (Neil Nash); Nurse (Patty Toy); Carl (Oscar Dillon); Rankin (Arthur Seidel); Cop (Joe Hoke).

Crossing the Line

Vacation time is ruined for Matt when a serial killer turns up. His M.O. is similar to a case Matt covered a decade ago. Wr: Steven Mitchell and Craig Van Sickle. Dir: Gwen Arner.

Doctor Death (Tobin Bell); Tool and die foreman (Robert Alan Browne); Dutchman (Ivory Ocean); Wounded officer (Robert Balderson); Cyndy (Heather McComb); Nurse Adele (Eva Von Widman).

Rebirth

George and Matt chase after a robber, Peter Rabbit. But during a struggle, Matt is electrified, and Tenctonese technology must be used to save him. Wr: Tom Chehak. Dir: Tom Chehak.

Peter Rabbit (Brian Thompson); Okno (Ellen Wheeler); Dr. Milt Kogan (Milt Kogan); Billy (Raffi DiBlasio); Sike's dad (John Sudol); Young Sikes (Ryan Cash); Officer (Rif Hutton); Nurse (Terri Semper).

Gimme, Gimme

Matt invests $10,000 into a Tenctonese fabric company. When the owner dies mysteriously in a salt water swimming pool, Matt and George investigate. Wr: Andrew Schneider and Diane Frolov. Dir: David Carson.

Sleepy Phil (Alan Fudge); EPA Official (Beege Barkette); Marilyn Houston (Kim Braden); Cyril Roman (Armin Shimerman); Edgar Allen Poe (David Selburg); Rita Allen Poe (Beverly Leech); Mr. Elias (Michael Zand); Cop (Bob Minor); Delivery man (Lance E. Nichols); Thug (Stephen Hart); Lee Smith (Joseph Cali).

The Touch

Cathy rediscovers a youth she befriended on the slave ship, but he's cold and distant now. Worried, she enlists Matt and George's help in finding out what happened to him. Wr: Steven Mitchell and Craig Van Sickle. Dir: Harry Longstreet.

Rigac (Mike Preston); Lorraine (Barbara Bush); Andy (Jonathan Brandis); Ella Day (Dorothy Fielding); Mr. Eugene (Doug Ballard); Troy (Martin La Platney); Andron's mother (Margaret Howell); Helen (Yvette Freeman); Andron (Mitchell Allen); Desk clerk (Vlado Benden); Newcomer boy (Dustin Berkovitz); Female Overseer (Eli Guralnick); Newcomer girl (Marin May); Newcomer sacrifice (Tom Pabst); Male Overseer (Van Quatro).

Green Eyes

After sharing his first kiss with Cathy, Matt is frightened and seeks the help of a counselor. Cathy declares Matt must accept her as she is or there can be no future between them. Meanwhile, in an effort to rid Earth of the Newcomers, the Purists have developed a bacteria that's deadly to the Tenctonese. Matt's shocked to learn that Susan and Emily are infected. Wr: Diane Frolov and Andrew Schneider. Dir: Tom Chehak.

Marilyn Houston (Kim Braden); Lorraine (Barbara Bush); Rick Parris (John Calvin); Darlene Bryant (Lee Bryant); Michael Bukowski (Geoffrey Bryant); Marc Guerin (David Purdham); Principal Fisher (Haskell V. Anderson III); Martha (Edith Fields); Noah Ramsey (Andras Jones); Dr. Bogg (Geoff Pierson); Judge Kaiser (Thomas Knickerbocker); Joshua Tree (Thom Zimerele); Newcomer cop (Joe Hoke); Delivery man (Michael Najjar).

Alien Nation: Dark Horizon (1994 TV Movie)

As radical humans plot to spread a deadly virus that has hit George's family, Overseers in deep space pick up a signal from Earth. They send an agent to see if the 250,000 missing slaves are still alive and ripe for the picking. This agent, Ahpossno, helps develop a cure for George's family while quietly working on his hidden agenda. Wr: Diane Frolov and Andrew Schneider. Dir: Kenneth Johnson.

Ahpossno (Scott Patterson); May O'Naise (Dana Andersen); Marc Guerin (David Purdham); Priestess (Susan Appling); Penny (Diane Cary); Ordnance officer (Mary Komatar); Supervisor (Michael Zand); Avid Fan (Michael Durrell); Detective Zepeda (Jenny Gago); Store owner florist (Lew Palter); Dr. Lois Allen (Michele Lamar Richards); Darlene Bryant (Lee Bryant); Sherriff (Robert Donner); Tom (John Meyers); Mitch (cop) (Don James); Communications officer (Daine Markoff); Cashier (Patience Cleveland); Teri Cloth (Sondra Currie); Slave mother (Elizabeth Storm); Jill (Risa Schiffman); Moe Goodluck (Rick Zumwalt); Elliot Riley (Jim Fyfe); Lorraine (Susanna Thompson); Transient (James Cooper); Rancher (Terrence Evans); Sam (Kevin Greviuox); Reporter (Khin-Kyaw Maung); Dr. Quinn (Haunani Minn); Kenny Bunkport (Blumen Young).

Alien Nation: Body and Soul (1995 TV Movie)
George and Matt uncover a devastating secret about the slave ship that brought the Newcomers to Earth, and about the fate of the vicious Overseers. Meanwhile, the romantic relationship between Matt and Cathy finally reaches a sexual consummation. Wr: Andrew Schneider, Diane Frolov and Harry and Renee Longstreet. Dir: Kenneth Johnson.

Dr. Lois Allen (Josie Kim); Tivoli (Pamela Gordon); Benson (Leon Russom); Giant (Tiny Ron); Child (Danielle and Aimee Warren); Balboa (Marva Hicks); Felker (Monte Russell); Elinor (Judith McConnell); Karina Tivoli (Kristin

Davis); Weapons commander (Ruth Cordell); Tech #1 (Robert Prentiss); Tech #2 (Ned Van Zandt); BNA guard (Daniel Chodos); Female Cop (Zilah); Pilot (Peter McKernan); Man #1 (Rick Davis); Phil Dirt (Ben Martin); Penn (Glenn Morshower); Jones (Jeff Austin); Costell (Miguel Perez); Smithford (Paul Tuerpe); Attendant/Assassin (Richard Snell); Registrar (Susan Appling); Bud the Guard (Brent Scarpo); Trash #1 (Greg Longstreet); Trash #2 (Darion Basco); Off-duty cop #1 (Harry Longstreet); Turner (Harry Johnson); Cop (Catherine Bell); Boy in hospital (Zane Graham).

Alien Nation: Millennium (1996 TV Movie)
On the eve of the end of the millennium, December, 1999, emotions are running high and people are expecting the end of the world. Some see the Newcomers as the second coming of Christ, while others view them as the incarnation of Satan. Events are complicated when a Newcomer cult leader misuses the sacred box first glimpsed in "Generation to Generation." Wr: Kenneth Johnson. Dir: Kenneth Johnson.

Jennifer (Kerrie Keane); Calaban (Steven Flynn); Jill (Risa Schiffman); Vivien (Freda Foh Shen); Jason (Brian Markinson); Alana (Herta Ware); Norton (Ellis Williams); Marina Del Rey (Susan Diol); Bigelow (Rick Snyder); Shivan (Pamela D'Pella); Polly Wannakraker (Susan Graham Lavelle); Landlady (Harriet Leider); Lawyer (John Towey); Whacko Human (Irene Forrest); Cop (David Correla); Randy (Jason Behr); Felix (David Faustino).

Amazing Stories
September 1985–May 1987

A weekly half-hour series of "amazing" tales of fantasy and adventure. This show brought a wide variety of stories, ranging from serious drama to pulse-pounding suspense and broad comedy.

Developed by: Steven Spielberg, John Falsey, Joshua Brand; *Executive Producer:* Steven Spielberg; *Production Executives:* Kathleen Kennedy, Frank Marshall; *Producer:* David E. Vogel; *Supervising Producers:* John Falsey, Joshua Brand; *Associate Producers:* Skip Lusk, Stephen Semel, Steve Starkey, Cheryl Bloch, Cleve Reinhard; *Theme:* John Williams; NBC/Universal, 30 minutes.

Steven Spielberg may have become a feature film superstar director since the journeyman days when he was directing *Columbo*, *Night Gallery* and *The Psychiatrist*, but years after his feature successes with *E.T.* and the *Indiana Jones* films, his continued fascination with television led him to *Amazing Stories*. The vision of the show came up because Steven had ideas and stories flowing out of his head like a water spigot. An opportunity to return to television seemed to be an ideal way of sharing all of those exciting stories with the millions of television viewers.

In 1985, Spielberg was introduced to NBC chairman Grant Tinker and NBC president Brandon Tartikoff by pal Gary David Goldberg, producer of *Family Ties*. In an unprecedented agreement, Spielberg convinced Tinker and NBC to give him a solid two years and 44 episodes to run his show. Grabbing the title from the science fiction digest magazine that has been running since 1926, Spielberg asked for and got a budget of $750,000 to $1 million per episode. He also was given more lead time to prepare the show and control publicity and marketing. All 22 episodes of the first season were completed by the week the first episode aired, an accomplishment unheard of in television. So jealously did Spielberg guard the show, that NBC did not see their first film print until six weeks before the premiere of the series. Additionally, Spielberg made sure the network had "hands off" in the making of the series so he could work in peace and quiet and not have undue pressures.

Going from features to television is often seen as a step backwards. But not for Spielberg, who saw his return to the small screen as a celebration of the medium. Returning to NBC was a sentimental journey for Spielberg, since his first professional directing job was for a segment of the *Night Gallery* pilot in 1969. It was also an opportunity for him and his fellow directors to go back and shoot *fast* again. Many filmmakers say they lose interest in their work if a particular project takes too long to complete.

So unique was the deal that Spielberg was able to attract many of his feature director buddies into doing a half-hour of fantasy television. Industry shakers such as Martin Scorsese, Clint Eastwood, Burt Reynolds, and Peter Hyams signed aboard to direct. "Name" actors such as Kevin Costner, Rhea Perlman, Helen Shaver, Charlie Sheen, Keifer Sutherland, Patrick Swayze and Sam Waterston picked up the scripts. "Steven asked me to do one of the first episodes of the show," says director Peter Hyams, who helmed the episode "The Amazing Falsworth," starring Gregory Hines. "It had a sense of humor, it was not the kind of thing you see on everyday television. Steve Spielberg is simply somebody I personally liked so much and admire so much that I jumped at the chance because he is somebody I like to be with, to work with. It seemed to be such an ambitious thing at the time for television. You take a bunch of disparate filmmakers and try to bring the feature film technique and quality on a television schedule. I think a lot of people in drama think that's too difficult."

Hyams felt that the idea of the show was "a wonderful idea to create something that tried to push the limits of television, to attract actors, directors and writers that we don't normally attract to form a showcase. I felt it was extraordinary."

Hyams felt the two-year experiment by Spielberg and company succeeded admirably. "He succeeded because he got Clint Eastwood, Martin

Scorsese, Paul Bartel, Phil Joanou, and he had Kevin Costner, Gregory Hines. We had first-time directors, we had veteran directors," says Hyams.

The only person who turned down an invitation was *Lawrence of Arabia*'s David Lean, who said he just couldn't shoot that fast. He wanted six months to do a half-hour. Reminded of this, Hyams says that filmmaking brings certain demands to directors. "It's an exercise in fighting against one's limitations. If you're used to shooting something in sixty days and you only have six days, well, you have to make compromises. You cannot expect the same level of complexity and finish in six days as in sixty days. The question is, what kind of compromises are you willing to make? And what can you do to make the six days better than anybody else? Part of it is fun, part of it is dealing with the craft of filmmaking. And the craft of filmmaking can be hard and not always go your way. And that brings in your innovative thinking."

For Hyams, the only feedback that mattered was Steven Spielberg's. "I think Steven was pleased. That says a lot. That meant the world to me," says Hyams. "I didn't want to disappoint him. The fact that he seemed pleased made me happy. Anytime you get the chance to spend time with somebody that bright and gifted is an exciting time. And I think he's as gifted and intelligent a guy as I've ever worked with in my life."

But *Amazing Stories* wasn't merely a celebrity fest; it was also a professional training ground for people who had never before worked on television. The series was Spielberg's attempt at a professional film school clique. He wanted a revolving door of talent, experienced and inexperienced.

Mick Garris was a young man who paid his dues by doing film publicity, operating R2-D2 for Lucasfilm, and directing documentaries before Spielberg tapped him as a story editor for the series. After writing nine episodes and making his directorial debut with the episode "Life on Death Row," Garris today reflects on his experiences with the show. "I'm proud of many episodes; some of them I don't think of too well for a number of reasons," says Garris. "Probably I'm happiest with the one I directed, 'Life on Death Row,' just because it was very different from a lot of them. It was very serious and dramatic, and I think I've grown a lot as a director by the experience. It came out really well. It had wonderful performances in there, it's very dramatic, it takes its time and had some genuine suspense. 'Amazing Falsworth' I like a whole lot, too," notes Garris. "Steven and I won an Edgar Mystery Writers of America award for that. That was one of the few suspenseful and scary things made for episodic television, and I'm very proud of that. They did a real good job on that one. Some of them I think came out much less. 'Such Interesting Neighbors' is probably my least favorite of any of them."

On other episodes, Garris points to "both of Steven's shows—I thought 'Ghost Train' was wonderful. I thought 'The Mission' was wonderful. I liked the period pieces; I thought 'Thanksgiving' by Todd Holland was good. Both of Tom Holland's episodes were really interesting. The first Joe Dante ['Boo!'], was a really good one. I thought that Richard Matheson's script, 'The Doll,' that Phil Joanou did with John Lithgow was absolutely wonderful. 'The Doll' was unique in that it was written for *The Twilight Zone* in 1959 by Richard Matheson. We managed to get that script

In the episode "Secret Cinema" (directed by Paul Bartel), an idea to make a film without the leading lady's knowledge sparks a hit called *The Adventures of Jane*. The unsuspecting star of the show (Penny Peyser) begins to think she's going insane. Copyright 1985 NBC/Amblin Entertainment.

for the show. I thought it worked great. There was very little rewriting to bring it up to date. It was very faithful to the original script. 'Dorothy and Ben' was a terrific episode—it had a lot of heart and soul to it. A lot of them worked really well."

In his job as a story editor it was Garris's responsibility to sift through the many different ideas and scripts that were generated for the show. Scripts were written largely in-house or from stories suggested by Spielberg. Garris mainly rewrote scripts to conform to the parameters Steven wanted. "It was an unusual series because most of the story ideas were generated by Steven himself," points out Garris. "The whole

time I was on the show, a year as a story editor and another year as a freelancer, I never once spoke to anyone at NBC or Universal about the content of the show. That was dealt with by much higher echelons than me. I never really accepted any scripts. I was involved in either writing or rewriting and doing whatever changes needed to be done to fit the schedule and meet the requirements of the show. Whatever the producers or directors felt was problematic. Basically, I was a script doctor. Scripts were basically in-house and were also handed out to freelance writers. People who wanted to work on the show were excited by the idea of an anthology series."

A couple of unusual folks take a bus ride in Beverly Hills in "Fine Tuning."
Copyright 1985 NBC/Amblin Entertainment.

more fun than that. It really started from scratch on the rewrite. I pretty much completely rewrote that episode, not because Joe Minion's script wasn't good, we just felt it needed to be more appropriate for the series."

Not so well known is that *Amazing Stories* was responsible for not one, but two spinoffs. *batteries not included** (1987), a film directed by Matthew Robbins and starring Hume Cronyn and Jessica Tandy, was an outgrowth of an *Amazing Stories* script. *batteries not included** was a tale of young and old tenants in a decrepit apartment building in New York who are visited by a bunch of friendly little blinky-winky flying saucers.

"*batteries not included** was indeed an *Amazing Stories* script that Steven had written, and he offered me the opportunity to adapt it as a screenplay, and he worked with me on it," says Garris. "He very generously gave me the full credit on the original script, although it was going to be written by the two of us. There were so many people involved in the arbitration of that script that he allowed my draft to be submitted with just my name. Again, a generous man."

Garris says that regular brainstorming sessions provided catalysts to many of the stories produced for the show. "In the second season, we did a weekly round table where people would talk about the scripts and critique the ideas. Bob Zemeckis, Bob Gale, Steven, myself, Michael McGill, Richard Matheson, a whole bunch of people, and it was really exciting! Really intimidating at first to a newcomer like myself."

Providing an example of what happens on his job on the show, Garris offers the episode "Mirror, Mirror," directed by Martin Scorsese. [It] was a really good script for *Amazing Stories*, but it was relentlessly dreary and very, very dark. My job as story editor was to do whatever rewriting needed to be done. They wanted a show that was

The second spinoff took a little bit longer. "Family Dog" first appeared as an animated episode of the show. Spielberg liked the idea of the show so much he tried developing it, with director Tim Burton, as a series in the same mode as *The Simpsons*. As early as 1991, CBS announced the show as a prime-time series. The adventures of an unnamed pooch who lives with the Bickfords and is picked on by their kids, the show was hooked on the dog's wry observations of life in suburbia. Reaction was not so hot, so it took another two years for retooling. And it wasn't until in 1993 that "Family Dog" premiered and ran for 10 episodes.

Although *Amazing Stories* lasted for two years, it was not renewed, and audiences and critics gave it mixed reviews. On why the show did not receive a better reception, Garris says, "I think the main reason *Amazing Stories* didn't work for the audience was they never knew what to expect each week. One week would be an animated show, another week would be kid-oriented fantasy show, another week a dark thriller. It really was scattered in its approach, and there was no Alfred Hitchcock or Rod Serling, or any identifiable core to the series other than a trip into the fantastic."

With the suggestion that the show advertised "amazing stories" but did not deliver for the most part, Garris disagrees hotly. "I don't know if that's really fair, because you want to keep it within the realm of possibility and believability and [you don't want to] take them to the point of being way too amazing. I think a third of the shows were terrific, and a third of them were OK, and a third of them were not very good. It was so up-and-down, it was very difficult for an audience to link onto. Series television these days relies on an audience getting to know a family of characters on a week-to-week basis. You get to know them, get to like them and feel comfortable with them."

Of his tenure working under the Spielberg banner and of working with Steven himself, Garris has nothing but glowing comments, revealing that he is a fan himself. "Steven's stories, which were all on paper, were very well brought out, with a beginning, middle and end, were well written," notes Garris. "He's really, really terrific in putting his thoughts on paper and presenting them to you verbally. I think my experience with Spielberg was the best. I mean, how can anyone complain about him? The guy's incredibly, creatively generous. He's wonderful to work with. Ideas flow out of him just like hair out of a balding man. He's just so fun and enthusiastic about what he does and sharing that with the people that do it with him. Can you imagine going from [working] food stands to writing for Steven Spielberg and having scripts produced? To have my scripts directed by Joe Dante, Robert Zemeckis, Peter Hyams is really unbelievably exciting," laughs Garris. "I worked with Steven off and on for about two years and would do any-

thing he wanted me to do. I will always be grateful to him. I learned a lot. It was my film school."

Garris goes as far as to say that Spielberg is someone "who has suffered the slings and arrows of the prejudices and jealousies [of his peers], but I think he deserves all the success he's had and I would love to work with him again at any time. He's a brilliant guy. Probably the most intuitive filmmaker on the planet."

The experience allowed Garris to move further up the hierarchy of the filmmaking business. "It established me as someone who's quite cheap to write, which was certainly new. It opened a lot of doors and aside from the open doors, it provided an incredible learning experience." Garris recently completed a horror feature, *Sleepwalkers*, and brought to television an ABC mini-series of Stephen King's massive tome *The Stand*.

Garris feels that the show's unique contrast in using famous, established names alongside no-name casts and production people was an ideal combination. "You had reliable filmmakers who, most of them, haven't really worked in television, even to this day, taking feature-quality production values and making television," points out Garris. "Some of them weren't used to the restrictions in time and money, but there weren't as many restrictions on this as there were on many other TV shows. You've got a lot of people with something to prove, trying to do some of their best work on this show. Some of the best shows on *Amazing Stories* were from the newcomers. If not exactly first-timers, then at least first-time studio people. There was some really good talent discovered on the show. Steven used it as an opportunity to try people out, like Mickey Moore, who did second unit directing on all the *Indiana Jones* movies. He directed an episode. There were those kinds of relationships on this show."

Actor Timothy Hutton was another one of those first-timers, writing and directing an episode. Previous to that, he had directed rock videos. Other discoveries were directors Lesli Linka Glatter and 23-year-old Phil Joanou. The first season alone had eight first-time directors.

Amazing Stories belongs to a very exclusive club of anthology TV shows. Fantasy and science fiction anthology dramas had last been produced in the 1960s, the decade that gave us *The Outer Limits* and *The Twilight Zone*. Oddly, *Amazing Stories* appeared on the tube in 1985 with revivals of *Alfred Hitchcock Presents* and *The Twilight Zone* as well as *Tales of the Darkside*.

On this, Garris muses, "I don't think the *Twilight Zone* or *Alfred Hitchcock* revivals, or *Tales of the Darkside*, had much to do with *Amazing Stories*. The original *Twilight Zone* did, though; it's hard to grow up in the 1960s and not feel the influence of the original *Twilight Zone*, *Outer Limits* or *Alfred Hitchcock*. Spielberg was one of those growing up in that era. I certainly was a child of that era as well. No doubt, all of us were influenced. But I don't think it had much to do with the later anthologies. I know I didn't see many of the new *Twilight Zone*s, or the other shows. Everybody had a different approach to the shows that were produced. We were trying to do something in one field, and *Twilight Zone* was trying to recapture what had been done before. And the *Alfred Hitchcock*s were mostly remakes of the original stories brought up to date. So, I don't know if any one of them fed on the other."

Why are the anthology shows like *Amazing Stories* such a rarity on network TV? Garris believes that "TV has changed over the years. People turn to TV for news, for information, and when they want series television they like to see familiar faces and get to know them and treat them like the members of the family. An anthology, good, bad or indifferent, doesn't handle it that way.... In syndication, the requirements for the size of an audience are much, much lower. So, things like 'The Hitchhiker' can ... find their audience. It doesn't need to be a huge audience. By and large, network viewing audience has to be massive. Generally, it's character shows, whether it's drama, comedies or whatever, that are the people you spend time with every week. The nature of television viewing has changed since the 1950s when anthologies peaked."

If the show had continued further, says Garris, "I would have loved to have seen more suspense and more serious shows, but we did a number of those, so I think it delivered on a lot of its promise."

EPISODE GUIDE

Season 1: 1985-86

Ghost Train
Trains of ages past are about to crash into the present world of a young boy. Wr: Frank Deese, story by Steven Spielberg. Dir: Steven Spielberg.
Old Pa (Roberts Blossom); Fenton (Scott Paulin); Joleen (Gail Edwards); Brian Globe (Lukas Haas); Dr. Steele (Renny Roker); Conductor (Hugh Gillin); Engineer (Sandy Ward); Brakeman (Iggie Wolfington); Train passenger (Drew Barrymore); Train passenger (Amy Irving); Train passenger (Priscilla Pointer).

The Main Attraction
A high school football jock gets magnetized and pays for his arrogance. Wr: Brad Bird and Mick Garris, story by Steven Spielberg. Dir: Matthew Robbins.
Brad Bender (John Scott Clough); Shirley (Lisa Jane Persky); Mr. Hiller (Richard Bull); Mrs. Bender (Barbara Sharma); Wylie (Tom Napier); Cliff Ratte (Bill Allen); Scientist #1 (Nicholas Mele); Scientist #3 (Joan Foley); Scientist #2 (Brad Bird); Billy Johnson (Dominick Brascia); Francine (Isabelle Walker); Stan (Eric Briskotter); Kid (Michael Joshua Cramer); Girl #1 (Megan Wyss); Darcy Cook (Piper Cochrane); Geek (Larry Spinak).

Alamo Jobe
A young messenger during the fight at the Alamo is transported to twentieth century San Antonio. Wr: Joshua Brand and John Falsey, story by Steven Spielberg. Dir: Michael Moore.
Alamo Jobe (Kelly Reno); Col. Travis (William Boyett); Harriet Wendse (Lurene Tuttle); Davy Crockett (Richard Young); Curator (Robert V. Barron); Lefferts (Michael Cavanaugh); Sam (Benjie Gregory); VCR/man #2 (Dick Yarmy); Tour guide (Pattie Pierce); Dad (Chip Lucia); Jim Bowie (Jon Van Ness).

Mummy, Daddy
Starring in a mummy film, an actor finds himself caught in a nightmarish world when he leaves the set to reach his pregnant wife. Wr: Earl Pomerantz, story by Steven Spielberg. Dir: William Dear.
Harold (Tom Harrison); Director (Bronson Pinchot); Willie Joe (Brion James); Ezra (Tracey Walter); Jubal (Larry Hankin); Librarian (Lucy Lee Flippin); Mayor (William Frankfather); Town Sage (Arnold Johnson); Ra Amin Ka (Michael Zand); Old grave robber (Len Lesser); Old blind man (Billy Beck); Actor (Brian Bradley); Ruta Mae (Joann Willette); Asst. director (Pamela Seamon); Freckled-faced kid (Eldon Ratliff); Doctor (Dalton Cathey); Young grave robber (Oliver Dear); Harold's wife (Susan Dear); Guard (Bill Martin).

The Mission (1 hour)
During World War II, men in a bomber are caught with a no-win scenario when their belly gunner gets trapped inside his seat and the plane has no wheels for landing. Wr: Menno Meyjes, story by Steven Spielberg. Dir: Steven Spielberg.
The Captain (Kevin Costner); Jonathon (Casey Siemaszko); Static (Kiefer Sutherland); Jake (Jeffrey Jay Cohen); Bullseye (John Philbin); Sam (Gary Mauro); Dave (Glen Mauro); Officer (Terry Beaver); Mechanic #1 (David Grant Hayward); Commander (Peter Jason); Liz (Karen Kopins); Mechanic #2 (Anthony La Paglia); Tail gunner (Gary Riley); Lamar (Ken Stovitz); Father McKay (Nelson Welch).

The Amazing Falsworth
A psychic showman realizes while performing that there's someone in the audience who wants to commit murder. Frightened, he calls the police, and a detective shows up to investigate. Wr: Mick Garris, story by Steven Spielberg Dir: Peter Hyams.

Falsworth (Gregory Hines); Trent Tinker (Richard Masur); Messenger (Don Calfa); Gail (Suzanne Bateman); Young man (Robert Lesser); Jimmy (Joseph G. Medalis); Older woman (Sally Stark); Showgirl (Nori Morgan).

Fine Tuning
Aliens from space arrive on Earth and imitate characters from 1950s television. Wr: Earl Pomerantz, story by Steven Spielberg. Dir: Bob Balaban.

Andy (Matthew Laborteaux); Jimmy (Gary Riley); George (Jimmy Gatherum); Milton Berle (Himself); Alien (Debbie Cunningham); Alien (Daniel Frishman); Alien (Patty Maloney); Alien (Ricky) (Kevin Thompson); Vaudevillian #1 (Vance Colvig); Vaudevillian #2 (Moasie Gardner); Vaudevillian #3 (Don Davis); Vaudevillian #4 (Happy Hall); Vaudevillian #5 (Jack Spoons); Vaudevillian #6 (Whitey Roberts); Vaudevillian #7 (Angelo Rossito); Tour guide (Tom Amundsen); Tourist (Charlie Cirillo); Father (Bryan Gordon); Waitress (Starr Hester); Weatherman (Peter Kwong); Used car salesman (Titus Napoleon).

Mr. Magic
A fading illusionist has a last shot at the spotlight, thanks to a deck of very special old cards. Wr: Joshua Brand and John Falsey. Dir: Donald Petrie.

Mr. Magic (Sid Caesar); Murray (Leo Rossi); Harry (Larry Gelman); Joe (Julius Harris); Jack (Tim Herbert); Dora (Eda Reiss Merin); Danny (Larry Cedar); Young magician (Nick Lewin); Johnny (Hugh Warden).

Guilt Trip
The emotion Guilt, feeling overworked, takes a vacation cruise and becomes taken with Love. Wr: Gail Parent and Kevin Parent. Dir: Burt Reynolds.

Guilt (Dom DeLuise); Love (Loni Anderson); Assistant to the Boss (Charles Durning); Mother (Carol Arthur); Father (Gordon Jump); Enchantress (Abbe Lane); Father McClintley (Charles Nelson Reilly); Larry (Rick Ducommun); Maitre'd (Fritz Feld); Man on boat (John Fiedler); Female newscaster (Nancy Nelson); Susan (Beverly Sanders); Large man (John D'Aquino); Bald man (Ben Kronen); Sweet woman (Jeanne Jensen); Robert, the waiter (C.J. Hunt); Waiter #2 (Louis Silvers); Boyfriend (Michael R. DeLuise); Daughter (Kristi Blackburn).

Remote Control Man
A henpecked man finds solace in a unique TV set that brings lifelike images to him. Wr: Douglas Lloyd McIntosh, story by Steven Spielberg. Dir: Bob Clark.

Walter Poindexter (Sydney Lassick); Grendel (Nancy Parsons); Salesman (Charlie Dell); Thug (Sid Haig); Underling #1 (Steve Liebman); Thug #1 (Jocko Marcellino); M.C. (Rod McCary); Old woman (Eve Smith); Underling #2 (Bill Wiley); Also with Philip Bruns, David Stone. *Cameo Appearances by*: Kristian Alfonso, Lyle Alzado, Dirk Benedict, Barbara Billingsley, Gary Coleman, Leann Hunley, Jim Lange, Ed McMahon, LaWanda Page, Clara Peller, Richard Simmons, Jake Steinfeld, Shawn Weatherly.

Santa '85
A little boy helps Santa when the legendary man gets thrown into the slammer while delivering presents. Wr: Joshua Brand and John Falsey, story by Steven Spielberg. Dir: Phil Joanou.

Santa (Douglas Seale); Sheriff Horace Smivey (Pat Hingle); Bobby Mynes (Gabriel Damon); Deputy (Marvin J. McIntyre); Mrs. Santa Claus (Frances Bay); Dad (Stephen Lee); Mom (Joan Welles); Drunk #1 (Dick Balduzzi); Drunk #2 (Gerry Gibson); Drunk #3 (William McDonald).

Vanessa in the Garden
When an artist becomes devastated by the death of his wife, he finds a way for her to live on in his paintings. Wr: Steven Spielberg. Dir: Clint Eastwood.

Byron Sullivan (Harvey Keitel); Vanessa (Sondra Locke); Teddy (Beau Bridges); Eve (Margaret Howell); Dr. Northrup (Thomas Randall Oglesby); Mrs. Northrup (Jamie Rose); Waiter (Milton Murrill).

The Sitter
Two boys get the best of every babysitter in the town, until they meet Jennifer Mowbray, who employs voodoo to settle them down. Wr: Mick Garris, story by Joshua Brand and John Falsey. Dir: Joan Darling.

Jennifer Mowbray (Mabel King); Lance (Seth Green); Dennis (Joshua Rudoy); Mother (Wendy Phillips); Mrs. Abbott (Fran Ryan); Patti (Suzanne Snyder); Indian (Michael Horse).

No Day at the Beach
A GI tries to be a hero during an amphibious assault during World War II in Italy. Filmed in black and white. Wr: Mick Garris, story by Steven Spielberg. Dir: Lesli Linka Glatter.

Casey (Charlie Sheen); Arnold Skamp (Larry Spinak); Ira (Ralph Seymour); Stick (Philip McKeon); Evergreen (Leo Geter); Tiny (Tom Hodges); Irish (Ray "Boom Boom" Mancini); Granville (Luca Josef Bercovici); Sergeant (Jed Mills); 1st sergeant (Keith Joe Dick).

One for the Road
Depression-era bar regulars trick a patron into signing an insurance policy, hoping he will drink himself to death so they can collect. Wr: James D. Bissell. Dir: Thomas Carter.

Francis (James Cromwell); Dan (Geoffrey Lewis); Joe (Joe Pantoliano); Tony Maroni (Al Ruscio); Mike Malloy (Douglas Seale); Salvation Army officer (Royal Dano); O'Farrow (Mark Tymchyshyn); Customer (Mike Finneran); News kid (Matt Amott).

Gather Ye Acorns
An 18-year-old dreamer who collects rare comic books takes the advice of a tree troll and follows his heart to gain wealth and happiness. Wr: Stu Krieger, story by Steven Spielberg. Dir: Norman Reynolds.

Jonathon (Mark Hamill); Troll (David Rappaport); Alma (Louis de Banzie); Elmer (Royal Dano); Young Jonathon (David Friedman); Mariel/wealthy lady (Joanna Merlin); Treadwell (Frank Schuller); David (William Dear); Jerry (Forest Whitaker); Auctioneer (John Carlyle); Gas station attendant (Conrad Dunn); Sister (Kelly Henson); Brother (Brian Parker); Also with Mary Jo Deschanel.

Boo!
Ghosts in an attic try to get rid of a couple who

moved into their house. Wr: Lowell Ganz and Babaloo Mandel. Dir: Joe Dante.

Ghost-husband (Eddie Bracken); Ghost-wife (Evelyn Keyes); Richard (Bruce Davison); Barbara (Andrea Marcovicci); Tony (Robert Picardo); Sheena (Wendy Schaal); Scott (Taliesin Jaffe); Deena (Heidi Zeigler).

Dorothy and Ben

After 40 years in a coma, Ben Dumpfy awakens and discovers he can communicate with a seven-year-old girl, who is unconscious after a bike accident. Wr: Michael de Guzman, story by Steven Spielberg. Dir: Thomas Carter.

Ben Dumfy (Joe Seneca); Dr. Caruso (Lane Smith); Dr. Templeton (Louis Giambalvo); Samantha (Kathleen Lloyd); Merle (Joe Regalbuto); Dorothy (Natalie Gregory); Dr. Haller (Rick Andosca); Dr. Fredericks (Alice H. Sachs); Doctor (Judith Durand); Nurse #2 (Lynn Kuratomi); Nurse (Kaye Bess).

Mirror, Mirror

A popular horror novelist is terrorized by a strange figure in his bathroom mirror. Wr: Joseph Minion, story by Steven Spielberg. Dir: Martin Scorsese.

Jordan Manmoth (Sam Waterston); Karen (Helen Shaver); Dick Cavett (Himself); Jordan's phantom (Tim Robbins); Producer (Dana Gladstone); Host (Valorie Grear); Jail attendant (Michael C. Gwynne); Chauffeur (Peter Iacangelo); Cameraman (Jonathon Luria); Guard (Harry Northup); Jeffrey Gelb (Glenn Scarpelli); Tough guy (Jack Thibeau).

Secret Cinema

A young woman believes her mother, her fiance and a psychiatrist are secretly filming her life. Wr: Paul Bartel. Dir: Paul Bartel.

Jane's mother (Eve Arden); Dr. Schreck (Paul Bartel); Dick (Griffin Dunne); Jane (Penny Peyser); Nurse (Mary Woronov); Mr. Krupp (Richard Paul); News dealer (Barry Dennen); Boy (Justin Darby); Lady customer (Alex Elias); Doorman (Gary Goodrow).

Hell Toupee

A new hairpiece causes a peaceful man to feel the urge to kill the first lawyer he sees. Wr: Gail Parent and Kevin Parent. Dir: Irvin Kershner.

Harry (Tony Kienitz); Beth (Cindy Morgan); Mitchell (Stanley Brock); Mr. Simon (Gary Allen); Chief Hansen (James Avery); Floyd King (Mitch Kreindel); Clifford Monroe (Ken Olfson); Murray Bernstein (E. Hampton Beagle); Officer Schmidt (Fredric Cook); Guard (Cal Gibson); Officer Montgomery (Jonathan Luria); Guard (Thomas F. Maguire); M.C. (John McCook); Woodsman (Robert Tessier); Mr. Zahl (Jack Wells).

The Doll

A lonely bachelor is fascinated by a doll he bought for his niece. Wr: Richard Matheson. Dir: Phil Joanou.

John Walters (John Lithgow); Mary Dickenson (Anne Helm); Sally (Sharon Spelman); Vin (John Christopher Jones); Doris (Rainbow Phoenix); Liebemacher (Albert Hague).

Trivia Alert: This script was originally written for Rod Serling's *Twilight Zone*.

One for the Books

An elderly custodian suddenly gains incredible knowledge. Wr: Richard Matheson, based on his short story. Dir: Lesli Linka Glatter.

Fred (Leo Penn); Eva (Joyce Van Patten); Dr. Fetlock (Nicholas Pryor); Professor Rand (John Alvin); Professor Gilbert (Gary Bergher); Dr. Barth (Rodney Kageyama); Professor Smith (Ben Kronen); Ms. Harris (Pamela Seamon); Mr. Wilson (Jack Slater).

Grandpa's Ghost

A man tries to reconcile his grandmother with the death of his grandpa. But the ghost of the old man keeps reappearing only in the presence of his wife. Wr: Michael de Guzman, based on a short story by Timothy Hutton. Dir: Timothy Hutton.

Edwin (Andrew McCarthy); Grandma Helen (Herta Ware); Grandpa Charlie (Ian Wolfe).

Season 2: 1986-87

The Wedding Ring

A wax museum dresser takes a ring from a statue, transforming his overworked wife into a femme fatale. Wr: Stu Krieger, story by Steven Spielberg. Dir: Danny DeVito.

Lois (Rhea Perlman); Herbert (Danny DeVito); Haggerty (Louis Giambalvo); Tina (Bernadette Birkett); Blaze (Tracey Walter); Woman (Jacqueline Cassel); Loner (Fred Scialla); Mr. Rhine (David Byrd).

Welcome to My Nightmare

A horror film buff's attraction to the girl next door lands him in a terrifying scene from *Psycho*. Wr: Todd Holland. Dir: Todd Holland.

Harry (David Hollander); Bud (Steve Antin); Mom (Sharon Spelman); Kate (Robyn Lively); Holly (Christina Applegate); Larry (Parker Jacobs); Dad (Robert L. Gibson); Attendant (Sharon Powers); Kate's mom (Cheryl McWilliams).

You Gotta Believe Me

Awakened by a dream of a light plane crashing outside of his home, a man tries to convince people of his premonition. Wr: Stu Krieger, story by Steven Spielberg. Dir: Kevin Reynolds.

Earl (Charles Durning); Nancy (Mary Betten); Female airline rep #1 (Jennie Sadler); Guard #2 (Lance Nichols); Controller #1 (Richard Burns); Man #1 (Gregory Wagrowski); Pilot (Joel Lawrence); Old woman (Eve Smith); Security Guard #1 (Tim Russ); Airline rep #2 (Wade Meyer); Fashionable woman (Rosemarie Castellano); Child (Erinn Canavan); Red bag lady (Cassandra Gava). Also with Ebbe Roe Smith, Wil Shriner, John Roselius.

Go to Head of the Class (1 Hour)

A teacher's bizarre discipline causes two students to seek revenge with a spell culled from a rock song played backwards. So intense was this episode, NBC announced it may not be suitable for all family members. Wr: Mick Garris, Tom McLoughlin and

Bob Gale, story by Mick Garris. Dir: Robert Zemeckis.

Professor B.O. Beanes (Christopher Lloyd); Peter Brand (Scott Coffey); Cynthia Simpson (Mary Stuart Masterson); Cusimano (Tom Brezhnahan); Caretaker (Billy Beck).

The Greibble
A housewife has a very real nightmare, encountering a large creature that has a taste for inanimate objects. Wr: Mick Garris, story by Steven Spielberg. Dir: Joe Dante.

Mrs. Simmons (Hayley Mills); Fred, the mailman (Dick Miller); Bobby (Justin Mooney); Greibble (Don McLeod); Greibble's voice (Frank Welker); Man in commercial (Jim Jansen).

Life on Death Row
An inmate is struck by lightning, giving him miraculous healing powers and sparking a last-minute attempt to save him from the electric chair. Wr: Rockne S. O'Bannon, based on a story by Mick Garris. Dir: Mick Garris.

Eric David Peterson (Patrick Swayze); Erhardt (James Callahan); Meadows (Hector Elizondo); Bradshaw (Nicholas Love); Fowler (Hawthorne James); Johnny (Arnold Johnson); Doctor (Paul Eiding); Marshall (Jed Mills); Warden's guard (George Jenesky); Priest (John Hamelin); Inmate (Alan Fine); Trustee (Roberto Contreras); Casey (T.J. Worzalla). Also with Kevin Hagen.

Thanksgiving
A farming couple digs a hole and discovers an underground community. Wr: Pierre R. Debs and Robert C. Fox. Dir: Todd Holland.

Calvin (David Carradine); Dora Johnson (Kyra Sedgwick).

The Pumpkin Competition
An old spinster, tired of losing a pumpkin competition, receives some special advice from an agricultural professor. Wr: Peter Z. Orton. Dir: Norman Reynolds.

Elma Dinnock (Polly Holliday); Mildred (June Lockhart); Prof. Bertram Carver (J.A. Preston); Mayor Chestor A. Barnsworth (Ritch Brinkley); Ernie (Britt Leach); Ma (Ann Walker); Billy (Joshua Rudoy).

What If...
A boy ponders what would happen if his parents didn't return from one of their many social gatherings. Wr: Anne Spielberg. Dir: Joan Darling.

Jonah Kelly (Jake Hart); Pam Kelly (Clare Kirkconnell); Raymond Kelly (Tom McConnell); Crosswalk man (Ric Cane); Marsha (Susan Swift); Woman in car (Sherry Landrum); Man in car (Dennis Haskins); Pregnant woman (Ann Bell); Male friend (Michael Horse); Female friend (Diane Lewis); Woman #2 (Laurel Green).

Eternal Mind
A dying scientist volunteers to be the first human being to merge with a computer. Wr: Julie Moskowitz and Gary Stevens. Dir: Michael Riva.

John Baldwin (Jeffrey Jones); Katherine Baldwin (Kathryn Borowitz); Ben Oltman (Gregory Wagrowski); Frank (Robert Axelrod); Tech #1 (Paul Tauger); Tech #2 (Aaron Seville).

Lane Change
Traveling a deserted highway, a woman facing a divorce sees her past through the windshield after she picks up a stranded woman. Wr: Ali Marie Matheson. Dir: Ken Kwapis.

Charlene "Charlie" Benton (Kathy Baker); Older Charlie (Priscilla Pointer); Father (Cletus Young); Little girl (Misty Forrest).

The 21-Inch Sun
A desperate television writer is handed an opportunity to write a comedy sit-com in one night. The unusual source of inspiration comes to the man from his plants. Wr: Bruce Kirschbaum. Dir: Nick Castle.

Billy Burliss (Robert Townsend); Mr. Marvin (Michael Lerner); Dick Castel (Craig Richard Nelson); Woman actor (Bridget Sienna); Actor (Alan Solomon); Castel's assistant (Richard Chudnow); Italian man (Jeremy Iacone); 2nd man (Alec Murdock); Woman (Caroline Parton); Production assistant (Charlene Nelson); 2nd assistant (Jim Nelson); Personal secretary (Jean Pflieger); Secretary #1 (Lisa London). Also with Robert Starr.

The Family Dog
An animated episode. The antics of a family are seen from the point of view of the family dog. Wr: Brad Bird. Dir: Brad Bird.

Father-Skip Binford (Stan Freberg); Mother (Annie Potts); Miss Lestrange (Mercedes McCambridge); Burglar (Marshall Efron); Burglar (Stanley Ralph Ross). Also with Jack Angel, Scott Menville, Brooke Ashley, Brad Bird.

Blue Man Down
Two patrol cops attend to a supermarket robbery, but when the younger partner is killed, a new female partner helps him avenge his friend. Later, he discovers she's the ghost of an officer who died 12 years earlier. Wr: Jacob Epstein and Daniel Lindley, story by Steven Spielberg. Dir: Paul Michael Glaser.

Duncan Moore (Max Gail); Patti O'Neal (Kate McNeil); DeSoto (Chris Nash); Capt. Redmond (Sal Viscuso); Maurici (Eddie Zammit); Dr. Levin (Michael Villella); Beckloff (Frank Doubleday); Market owner (Tad Horino); Lieutenant (Jay Ingram); Atwood (Mark Erickson); Herrington (Charlie Hawke); TV reporter #1 (Lynn Kuratomi); TV reporter #2 (Richard Epcar); TV reporter #3 (Robert Benedict); Cop (Robert Louis Cameron); Hostage (Debby Lynn Ross).

Gershwin's Trunk
A Broadway lyricist seeks inspiration by contacting the spirit of Gershwin through a psychic. Wr: John Meyer and Paul Bartel. Dir: Paul Bartel.

Jo-Jo Gillespie (Bob Balaban); Sister Teresa (Lainie Kazan); Jerry Lane (John McCook); George Gershwin (Dana Gladstone); Logan Webb (Hurd Hatfield); Det. Watts (Paul Bartel); Carmen (Irene Olga Lopez); Pepi (Danny Ponce); Trish Charlton (Pamela Galloway); Girl #1 (Barbara Turvett); Boy #1 (Alan Bardsley); Girl #2 (Pattie Brooks); Boy #2 (Christopher Blande). Uncredited: Laurie McNamara (Carrie Fisher).

Miscalculation

A high school student searching for a date accidentally spills some chemicals and conjures up a dog. He tries desperately to create a beautiful woman, but a few things go wrong... Wr: Michael McDowell. Dir: Tom Holland.

Phil (Jon Cryer); Angela (Joann Willette); Bert (Jeffrey Jay Cohen); Ms. Allure (Lana Clarkson); Ms. Eyeful (Galyn Gorg); Ms. Awesome (Catherine Gilmour); Ms. Laura (Elizabeth de Turenne); Miss Crowning Shield (Rebecca Schaeffer); Cashier (Wynonna Smith); Mousy girl (Penelope Sudrow); Dr. Blitz (Harry Woolf); Cop #1 (Al Lampkin); Cop #2 (Alden Millikan).

Such Interesting Neighbors

The Lewises think the Hellenbecks are causing some strange repeats in time. Wr: Mick Garris and Tom McLoughlin, based on the story by Jack Finney. Dir: Graham Baker.

Al Lewise (Frederick Coffin); Nell Lewise (Marcia Strassman); Randy Lewise (Ian Fried); Ann Hellenbeck (Victoria Catlin); Ted Hellenbeck (Adam Ant); Brad Hellenbeck (Ryan McWhorter).

Without Diana

A father meets his long-lost daughter, who appears to him exactly as she appeared forty years ago. Wr: Mick Garris. Dir: Lesli Linka Glatter.

George Willoughby (Billy Green Bush); Kathryn Willoughby (Dianne Hull); Diana Willoughby (Gennie James); Dr. Wittenberg (Fredric Cook); Policeman (Rick Andosca).

Moving Day

A teen learns his family is bound for a new home—a planet 85 billion miles away. Wr: Frank Kerr. Dir: Robert Stevens.

Alexander Webster (Steven Jeffreys); Mr. Webster (Dennis Lipscomb); Mara Webster (Mary Ellen Trainor); Karen (Kristen Vigard); Big Boy (Bill Wesley).

Miss Stardust

An alien threatens to destroy Earth unless a beauty pageant promoter allows entrants from other planets to participate. Wr: Thomas Szollosi and Richard Christian Matheson, based on the short story by Richard Matheson. Dir: Tobe Hooper.

Joe Willoughby (Dick Shawn); Miss Schroedinger, Joe's secretary (Laraine Newman); Mike (Rick Overton); Emcee (Jack Carter); Judge (James Karen); The Cabbage Man ("Weird Al" Yankovic); Mendelheim (Gabe Cohen); Businessman #1 (Anthony James); Businessman #2 (Robert Kim); Stage manager (Wade Mayer); Ms. Colorado (Wendy Sherwood); Beauty #2 (Victoria Ellen Powells); Beauty #1 (Lisabeth Aubrey); Man (Norman Friedman). Also with Jim Siedow, Angel Tompkins.

Magic Saturday

A man temporarily exchanges bodies with his grandson so he can recapture his youth on the baseball field. But while the man is enjoying his new life, the boy discovers his grandfather's old body is dying. Wr: Richard Christian Matheson. Dir: Robert Markowitz.

Grandpa (M. Emmet Walsh); Mark (Taliesin Jaffe); Dorothy (Caren Kaye); Eddie (Jeff B. Cohen); Umpire (David Arnott); Boy #2 (David Donnelly); Boy #1 (Jeff A. Kinder). Also with David Crowley.

Automan

September 1983–April 1984

A police computer jockey, Walter Nebicher, invents a crime-fighting three-dimensional computer hologram he dubs "Automan." As Automan and Walter jump into the field solving difficult cases, Walter's colleague, Lieutenant Jack Curtis, becomes constantly amazed and befuddled at his successes. Assisted by Cursor, another holographic creation of Walter's, Automan employs a car, a helicopter, a motorcycle and a plane to fight crime.

Cast: Walter Nebicher (Desi Arnaz, Jr.); Automan (Chuck Wagner); Roxanne Caldwell (Heather McNair); Lieutenant Jack Curtis (Robert Lansing); Captain Boyd (Gerald O'Loughlin).

Created by: Glen Larson; *Executive Producer:* Glen Larson; *Co-Executive Producer:* Larry Brody; *Associate Producer:* Gil Bettman, Randall Torno; *Supervising Producer:* Sam Egan. *Produced by:* Donald Kushner, Peter Locke; *Co-Producer:* Harker Wade; ABC/Universal; 60 minutes.

Holograms. High technology. Knight Rider: The Next Generation. Predicament humor. With these key elements combined and orchestrated into a one-hour dramatic television series, you arrive at *Automan*. When creator-producer-writer Glen Larson stirred these ideas into a television series in 1983, he invented what has been described by several of those involved as a television series that was "a little bit ahead of its time."

"I'm just a nut about this subject matter,"

confesses Larson. "The whole idea was doing a 3-D [computer generated] figure and doing it with lifelike quality. I guess we were definitely ahead of *Quantum Leap* in using a computer with a cursor to weave and spin the tale. It's always been something of interest to me. I created *Knight Rider*, and I was looking for something that had the fun and cars and high-tech but the next generation, going one step beyond what we were doing on *Knight Rider*."

Finding the series difficult to describe, Larson labels *Automan* as a "drama that had humor. It wasn't meant to be pure comedy. As opposed to situation comedy, I call it predicament humor. You put your hero in a predicament and make the audience smile. It's not that he's foolish or doing pratfalls, [Walter Nebicher] creates a personage that's virtually from another dimension. How do you explain this to anybody? Nobody is going to believe you."

Desi Arnaz, Jr., was star of the show as the mousey, somewhat nerdish police computer jockey, Walter Nebicher. Arnaz recalls his experiences on *Automan* with great fondness: "I thought it was a great idea! The thing that was so interesting was that it was a superhero [show], and it was also a comedy, which was different, and the people that produced *Tron* (1982) [Donald Kushner and Peter Locke] were also the producers of *Automan*. The idea of a superhero coming out of a computer was very interesting because *Tron* was the opposite—about a fellow who goes *into* a computer. Also, the characters were very unique because the superhero Automan was like [Walter's] alter-ego. It was everything that he wanted to be. He programmed the superhero to be everything he dreamed of. It was a great idea for a show because [together, Walter and Automan] were fighting the forces of evil, and at the same time there was a lot of humor."

Arnaz's co-star, Chuck Wagner, was cast as the hologram crime-buster Automan. "Chuck was great," says Arnaz. "He and I got along really well. The thing that was good about Chuck was he was an actor who was trained in musical comedy so he could dance and sing. He was also a good comedian. So he combined all of that in order to create his character. He also had a very proper kind of persona in real life.

"Walter had programmed Automan to be every great detective throughout the ages, [like] James Bond and Sherlock Holmes, which was interesting. Automan had kind of an English persona. He almost had kind of an English accent.

Chuck Wagner sparkles in his role as the computer-generated hologram *Automan*. Here, he's with Cursor, who transforms into a car, a helicopter and a plane. Copyright 1983 ABC/Universal.

And Chuck was able to do that very well. He was very talented, and he incorporated [his skills] into the character."

Glen Larson says that looking for a man to fill Automan's suit was difficult. "We looked for all kinds of people, from bodybuilders to not quite Hulk Hogan, to see what we could find, but ironically, Chuck came in and had a wonderful quality when he read. It was quite a surprise. He hadn't done much. We were having trouble casting that role. He just came in and did it. He was quite good. I thought he did a nice job, and I just liked his quality. I thought he was a good contrast. He was big. They were great together."

Of working with creator and producer Larson, Arnaz says happily, "He was a great support.

He told me how much he loved the show and how unhappy [he was] that the show didn't do better. He felt it was one of the best shows he'd ever done. Curiously, I came in the last day of casting. I was thought of originally, but for some reason they didn't see me until right before they had to decide. They brought me in on the last day, and I had to read for the network the next day, and I got the part the following day. We had a nice time together. I really enjoyed working for him."

The show was one of the most expensive to produce at that time because of the extensive special effects needed to bring Automan alive. Arnaz believes the show's short, one-season life span was probably the longest it could have run. "It was something like over one million dollars an episode. In those days that was very unusual."

Director Winrich Kolbe agrees that the show was well executed but says, "I think it was overly ambitious. We had a lot of technical problems. At that time video and blue screens were not that well developed. We began to go to video."

Arnaz says that "one of the special effects men, David Gerber, did things with live effects and computer graphics and in-camera effects that were never done before." When the audience saw Automan's glowing, blue-white starfield suit, it was done by projecting a light through a camera lens device called a beam splitter. "They had never used that before, so it was very unusual. They were getting this traveling matte on his suit. Computer graphics would then put in this animated starfield. It also added to the various vehicles—the car, the helicopter, the plane and the motorcycle," says Arnaz.

What also added to the special effects budget was not just Automan and the collection of vehicles used in the show, but Cursor. Cursor was a computer hologram that created and literally transformed itself into Automan's many unique vehicles. Using the name "Cursor" was one of Glen Larson's many pokes at computer slang. The cursor is the icon in a computer screen that directs users to create graphics or prompts them in word processing.

Working with Cursor proved to be a challenge for actors, who never saw anything until a computer effect was added later. "Cursor was never really there," says Arnaz with a grin. "You'd have to come up with the pantomime as to what … the director thought, where the Cursor would be. People didn't quite understand the 'computerese' language we were using a lot of the time!" he adds. "Nowadays everyone has a computer.

But back then, ten years ago, it was ahead of its time."

What was Automan, exactly? Arnaz says, "The whole concept of Automan was, he was a three-dimensional electromagnetic entity that was a hologram, but he also had his own electronic power source." Automan also had the ability to draw on electrical sources around him to power himself, creating scenes where he would inadvertently create blackouts in his immediate surroundings. Larson calls that "just great fun. When the lights go out because of something you've done. It does great humor. I mean, it's funny, but hopefully it's also sort of real."

A high point for the show, says Larson, was the first segment after the pilot, "Staying Alive While Running a High Flashdance Fever." Chuck Wagner threw on a white suit and launched his way into a disco. "In a Las Vegas hotel, Automan gets carried away [on a dance floor full of people] and takes his suit off and reveals his electronic substance underneath. A girl starts getting into the dance and starts getting carried away. Wally comes in and sees this, and it's 'Oh my god!' because he's given himself away." Automan watched television and imitated what he saw, generating many take-offs and spoofs galvanized by studies in soap operas and Dirty Harry characters.

Larson describes Arnaz's character as " 'nebbishy.' We called him Nebicher—nerdy—except that he could also be a young hero because he is a good-looking guy, having been a bit of a teenage idol." Arnaz says that Nebicher "was frustrated as a policeman in fighting crime. And being the computer expert allowed him to fight crime on a much more phenomenal level. It was really fun to play. The character was kind of insecure, and he had a good sense of humor, but underneath his insecurity, he was incredibly smart. That's what was interesting about him. He created this superhero that came out of the computer [so] there was something about him that was remarkable. At the same time he didn't understand about getting along with women, and the people of the police department viewed him as being nerdy. [Because he couldn't] … solve crime the way they did, they would always make fun of him, putting him down. He didn't have the experience in the real world."

In Arnaz's eyes, this was not an ordinary show by any means. "*Automan* was a very moral show with values in it. I just loved doing it and playing Walter," he says. "The whole idea, in my mind, of the superhero, was symbolic of a spiritual battle. For some, you need something higher, more supernatural to fight evil. In any science fiction show in my mind there's elements of the unknown and the supernatural that are able to come into a person's life and overcome whatever dark forces.... In fact, [in] the opening of the show, the statement was [that] Automan was a force for good."

Most fascinating for Arnaz, in playing Walter, was having to keep Automan's existence a secret. "All superheroes have to have a secret identity!" laughs Arnaz. "And the other part of the show that was interesting was Walter and Automan would combine to be one entity. He would merge with Automan. It was actually a very funny part of the show." What a twist. Instead of leaping into someone else's *body*, Arnaz got to leap into a *hologram*. Oh boy.

"I would [dub dialogue over] Automan's voice and so Automan would have Walter's voice because Walter was inside of Automan's energy field. It was kind of funny, so a lot of strange things happened. Walter could actually experience being a superhero. He would merge with Automan to protect himself during crime-fighting adventures."

In describing the relationship between Walter and Automan, Arnaz says, "Automan was everything Walter wanted to be, and in a way, Walter was everything that Automan wanted to be because [Automan] wasn't human—kind of like Data in *Star Trek: The Next Generation.*" That would make Automan a "pre-Cursor" to Data. "An early Cursor," quips Arnaz. "One of the first Cursors...."

Challenging for the technical staff of the show and the lead actors was dealing with Automan's glowing blue suit. It didn't photograph well during daylight, so Automan made the bulk of his appearances at night—suggesting that crime happens only at night! "In the pilot," says director Kolbe, "I understand they had to shut down all the lights around a downtown street because they wouldn't have been able to properly film Automan's sparkling special effects suit. It's a tremendous amount of work. A lot of the show was shot at night. It's not a very life-enhancing way to make a living!"

"We tried during the day, but it didn't come out as good," Arnaz remembers. "It was very difficult because of the hours. We were trying to get him to appear in the daytime undercover in regular clothes. What would happen is he could then 'rez up' (electronically create) any outfit he wanted, then he could go out during the daytime.

The only thing that glowed was his collar.... That made it a lot easier for us to shoot the show because we didn't have to shoot nights anymore! So we tried to get him into other clothes whenever he would change persona." As a result of technical difficulties, Automan evolved into a more versatile character. Donning such guises as an FBI agent or a special intelligence officer for the government dubbed "Ottoman," he became an undercover superhero.

Director Kolbe reinforces Arnaz's and Larson's assessment of the show's predicament humor. "It's the reactions of the character that made it funny." Kolbe says it was he who invented a whimsical ride with Automan in his Autocar. "I'm not tooting my own horn here, but I think I believe I was the one who introduced that whenever a crime was made, a 90 degree left or right turn would make Desi, inside the AutoCar, slam into the left or right side. For the car, there's no gravity to consider. But Desi would obviously be the one to slam into the side windows. We all thought it was very funny."

Of the two leads, Kolbe remarks, "I thought the two of them were perfect. I liked Desi. He was so frenetic, and that really worked for his character. But he was his character off the set as well! The guy was like live wire all the time! He was a lot of fun. I liked working with him." Commenting on Chuck Wagner's portrayal of Automan, "the only thing that struck me funny was he was very serious all the time," says Kolbe. "Now, keep in mind that at the time I was not exposed to *Star Trek* and people actually taking science fiction that serious. So, when Chuck began talking about 'No, I wouldn't do this or that,' I said, 'Wait a minute. The guy's supposed to be a computer image!'

"I think *Automan* was his first big chance at series television. Sometimes that can be a handicap, to get involved in science fiction shows.... Producers sometimes look at science fiction as something for kids." As Kolbe explains, "the moment you say, 'I've done this science fiction show,' it's possible to get typecast or lose credibility as a serious actor."

D. C. Fontana, best known for her work on *Star Trek* and *Star Trek: The Next Generation,* co-wrote with her brother Richard two unproduced *Automan* scripts. "Fly by Night" was an original script, and "If Looks Could Kill" was a rewrite of someone else's idea.

"'Fly by Night' was a story we originated about a theft of highly classified information from a top-security computer company which

Desi Arnaz, Jr., played Walter Nebischer in *Automan*.

was involved in providing equipment for an Air Force stealth plane," says Fontana. "This was before it was verified that the U.S. actually had stealth planes! We had it that the information stolen was in regard to the device that would provide protection for the plane against any type of radar or other detection equipment. It was a sort of a cloaking device. Because the information was useless without the actual equipment, it was decided Automan and his friends would be disguised as Air Force personnel transferred to the base where the stealth plane was being tested in order to protect the plane from being tampered with or stolen by the people behind the information theft. Naturally, in the course of the adventure Automan winds up flying the stealth plane."

Fontana recalls the script as "a pretty good story with humor and a number of plot twists. It helped a lot that my brother is an Air Force veteran and a private pilot and was able to supply a lot of technical information himself." The second script involved race car drivers, professional models and murder, and culminated in Automan driving in a race.

Overall, Arnaz feels that *Automan* was well received. "We had quite a faithful following during the year it was on," he says. "A lot of people enjoyed the show. But I think a lot were watching *Magnum P.I.* We were opposite the number one show on television. Unless ... [a show] had become the number one show, ... [the network] didn't think it was financially affordable. Science fiction shows hadn't really taken off. [The network heads] weren't interested in it at that point— I was! I've always been a science fiction buff."

Summarizing his feelings towards *Automan*, Larson says, "I'm a big fan of that show. It's obviously not on my list of my biggest hits. But I tell you, it's one of my favorite accomplishments in terms of having pulled off what I wanted. I remember the young lady at ABC in charge of development, when she saw the pilot, she actually came out...and I remember her just saying, 'It was just stunning!' It was like a jewel. The way these effects came on, it just knocked her hat off.... If it hadn't got buried in that time slot, it would have gone on to be a major hit. They're just too impatient. I stayed very involved with that show, and I was very happy with it."

If the show had continued further, Larson says his only change would have been to restrain the use of gadgets and Automan's appearances. "One thing in execution that one of my associates at Universal accused me of—and I agree with him—I think we frontloaded it a little bit too much," says Larson. "By frontloaded, I [mean] we revved up that wonderful car, a Lamborghini. We also did a helicopter for the same show. I think we should have saved some of those devices and used them more sparingly when we were getting started. It's like if you saw the Hulk too often. I think we could have used some of that a little more sparingly. Desi has to do a little more on his own and not give Automan quite as many power tools in the beginning. At least let the audience get up to speed and discover you a little more. We gave them too many sweeps at once.

"If I could do it over, I would go a little more slowly. Help the audience to believe in a new concept. Holograms are kind of a new concept. Computers weren't as big then, and graphics on computers were almost unheard of then."

Cast Notes

Desi Arnaz, Jr. (Walter Nebischer): Born 1953. The son of Lucille Ball and Desi Arnaz, this actor appeared with his parents and his sister Lucie on *Here's Lucy* from 1968 to 1971. Today, Arnaz is very involved with the New Life Foundation, a non-profit organization for studies in spiritual psychology. He has continued to be active with such features as *Mambo Kings* (1992), theater productions of *Is There Life After High School?* and *Alone Together*, and talk show appearances on *Larry King Live*, *Oprah Winfrey*, *Regis and Kathie Lee*, and the *Maury Povich Show*.

Robert Lansing (Lieutenant Jack Curtis): Born 1928. After *Automan*, Lansing had a supporting role in Edward Woodward's *Equalizer* series.

"He was a lot of fun to work with," says Desi Arnaz, Jr. "He was really one of the first people who did science fiction in the early fifties. There's a certain quality that Robert Lansing has, always mysterious and magnetic. I always thought Robert Lansing was a very, very good actor. He also had a good sense of comedy. He plays it very straight, but he could also be very funny as well." Lansing died in 1994 shortly after co-starring in television's *Kung Fu—The Legend Continues*.

Chuck Wagner (Automan): Chuck Wagner remains busy in musical theater, appearing in *Beauty and the Beast* and *Les Misérables*.

Gerald S. O'Loughlin (Capt. Boyd): Born 1921. This New York actor is best known as Lt. Ryker on the 1970s crime drama *The Rookies*. He co-starred in the gentle family series *Our House* in the late 1980s and starred with Peter Barton on the *Powers of Matthew Star* original pilot in 1982.

EPISODE GUIDE

Automan (90 minutes)
Walter becomes entangled in a missing persons case when Lt. Jack Curtis disappears. With Automan's help, he learns a top security agency may be involved. This leads Walter and Automan to Switzerland, where they locate abducted engineers and technicians. Wr: Glen Larson. Dir: Lee Katzin.

Det. Ted Smithers (Doug McClure); P.J. Hawkins (Steve Franken); Lydell Hamilton (Patrick MacNee); Marty Peterson (Robert Hogan); Collins (Steven Keats); Cramer (James Antonio, Jr.); Chuck Wilson (Robert Dunlap); Martin Wills (Don Galloway); Tanya Dubois (Camilla Sparv); 1st gang (Sid Haig); 2nd gang (Mickey Jones); Landlady (Gloria Le Roy); Swiss guard (Herman Poppe); Joanne Wills (Carol Vogel); Taxi driver (Dennis Fimple); Stewardess (Kristina Hayden); Parking valet (Ed Hooks); Wills girl #1 (Angela Lee); Wills girl #2 (Tricia Tomicic).

Staying Alive While Running a High Flashdance Fever
A kidnapped girl leads Walter and Automan to the discovery of a judge who has been accepting payoffs with overseas bank accounts. Wr: Glen A. Larson. Dir: Winrich Kolbe.

Judge Alexander Farnsworth (William Windom); Ellen Fowler/Miss Simmons (Mary Crosby); Leonard Martin (Don Gordon); Bartender (Angela Aames); Jason (Robert F. Lyons); Jackson (Jorge Cervera, Jr.); Drunk (Jack Perkins).

The Great Pretender
With Automan's help, Walter is able to shut down a crime czar's diversified operations. When Jack gets caught by them, it complicates matters. Wr: Sam Egan. Dir: Kim Manners.

Rudolph Brock (Clu Gulager); Kevin Mayhew (Michael Callan); Robinson (Richard Derr); Seymouor Laird (Ed Griffith); Russo (William Long,, Jr.); Gritch (Todd Martin); Solt (Fil Formicola); Lauren Robinson (Andrea Howard); Parsons (James Andronica); Nelson Trotter (Rick Jason) Minister (Ken Sansom); Blond (K.C. Winkler); Carty (Marc Vahanian); Uncredited: Pool player (Michael Pataki); Also with Cliff Emmich, Paul Lambert.

Ships in the Night
When six men disappear at a remote island while trying to purchase illegal drugs, Jack and Roxanne are sent to investigate. Little do they know that Walter and Automan are following them to provide back-up support. Wr: Park Perine. Dir: Bob Claver.

Robert Sawyer (Scott Marlowe); Liang Lew (France Nuyen); James Dowling (Frank Aletter); Captain Romano (Cesare Danova); Woody (Steve Hanks); Police sergeant (Abraham Alvarez); Johnson (Branscombe Richmond); Bank guard (Rick Garcia); Desk clerk (Javier Grajeda); Beautiful girl (Melanie Vincz); Croupier (Bridget Sienna).

Unreasonable Facsimile
When a co-owner of a helicopter company realizes that defective parts are the cause of many accidents, his partner kills him. Walter is put on the job to find his killer. Wr: Sam Egan. Dir: Winrich Kolbe.

Henry Innes (Robert Sampson); Jarrett Powers (Glenn Corbett); Rachel Innes (Delta Burke); Christine (Lina Raymond); Bartender (Conroy Gedeon); Francine (Toni Nero); Hortense Behrens (Ruth Warshawsky); Theodore Behrens (Walter Brooke); Edward M. Scanlin (Gerald Gordon); Norman (David Sheiner); Herself (Tawny Schneider); Reedy (Dennis Scott); Lisa (Tammy Alverson).

Flashes and Ashes
When a fellow police officer is killed, Walter sets to find out who's responsible, but a crooked lieutenant sets him up. Walter loses his badge in the processs. Wr: Doug Heyes, Jr. Dir: Kim Manners.

Malcolm Whittaker (Jeff Pomerantz); Tennis Pro (Roscoe Tanner); Madame Russo (Anita Dangler); Dean Springer (James Emery); Rollie Dumont (Hari Rhodes); Jeff Coe (Michael Horsley); Street guy (Africanus Roscius); Frank Cooney (Ron Harvey); Laurie (Tami Barber); Tisha (Tammy Brewer); Also with Dan Thorpe.

Biggest Game in Town
A computer genius blackmails the entire city for $10 million, threatening to throw the city into chaos via electronics. But when he's captured, he sets a bomb to go off inside the police station. Wr: Larry Brody, story by Larry Brody and Shel Williams. Dir: Winrich Kolbe.

Ronald Tilson (Rick Lenz); Ellie Harmon (Kristen Meadows); Bart Johnson (Felton Perry); Sam Maroni (Timothy Blake); Man (Stefan Zema); 2nd air controller (Michael Holden); Chief air controller (Bill Ewing); Bomb squad #1 (Robert Gribbin); Flood control engr. (Paul Savior); Doctor (Lee Burlington); Bomb squad #2 (Richard Milholland).

Renegade Run
Friends contact Walter because a corrupt sheriff is forcing them to sign over the deed of their parents' home. But Walter is thrown into jail and it's up to Automan and Jack to save the day. Wr: Larry Brody and Doug Heyes, Jr. Dir: Allen Burns.

Sheriff Clay Horton (Richard Lynch); Chico Fuentes (Billy Drago); Teresa Fuentes (Gina Gallego); Gretchen Lewis (Greta Blackburn); Carl Donovan (Richard Anderson); Stone (Terry Kiser); Miss Lucy (Carol Webster); J.P. Crazy (Michael McRae); Travis (Bobby E. Green).

Murder MTV
Walter is assigned to protect a rock star when her life is threatened. But her father and manager are in deep with extortionists. Wr: Doug Heyes, Jr., story by Guerdon Trueblood. Dir: Bruce Seth Green.

Monica Cole (Laura Branigan); Sid Cole (Michael McGuire); Frank Ladrone (Albert Paulsen); Sam Clementine (Sander Johnson); Josie (Christie Claridge); Leo Shane (Gerald Berns); Delivery boy (Paul Haber); Tony Lupus (Michael Gregory); Joanne (Ola Ray); Carlo Crane (Zitto Kazann); Parking valet (Miguel A. Nunez, Jr.).

Murder Take One
When a leading Hollywood gossip columnist is killed after arguing with an actress, Walter and Automan enter the film soundstages to investigate. Wr: Sam Egan. Dir: Kim Manners.

Michael Hagedorn (Ed Lauter); Veronica Everly (Michelle Phillips); Sheila Dunham (Hilary Thompson); Kitty Hopkins (Winnie Gardner); Oscar Selby (Tim Rossovitch); Frank Loren (Bart Braverman); Seymour Grodkin (Floyd Levine); Roland Green (Mark Wheeler);

Philip Eames (Greg Mullavey); Keith Gillette (Peter Marshall); Guard (Jonathan Gochberg).

Zippers
A microchip lists members of the federal witness program, and criminals are desperate to retrieve it. Wr: David Garber and Bruce E. Kalish. Dir: Alan Crosland.

Carlos (John Vernon); Gary Baxley (James Morrison); Victor (Erik Stern); Buck (Billy Ray Sharkey); Dennis Stanton (James Callahan); Stanley (Tom Everett); Freddie (Reginald T. Dorsey); Robin Hood (Don Mirault); Woman (Gertrude Marx); Karl (Cliff Carnell); Guard #1 (Eric Lawson); Guard #2 (Charles Walker); Kevie Wright (Mindi Iden); Policeman (John Mahon); Mrs. Stanton (Nancy Jeris).

Death by Design
After Jack's former partner is killed by the mob, he's pulled off the case. To help, Automan takes on the persona of "Mad-Dog," a Dirty Harry type, and manages to infiltrate the mobsters. Wr: Sam Egan. Dir: Gil Bettman.

Woodrow "Woody" Oster (John Ericson); Eric LeBlanc (Luke Askew); Nate Hester (Edward Mallory); Noah Jeffries (J.D. Hall); Tracy Morgan (Anne Lockhart); Model (K.C. Winkler); Gill (Eric Server); Simon Rafferty (Lance LeGault); Tom Sholes (David Spielberg); Joseph Sylvana (Johnny Crear); Bookie (Danny Dayton). Also with Michael Gazzo.

Club Ten
Roxanne bumps into the trendy and very private Club 10 and discovers that it is a central clearinghouse for smuggled diamonds. Wr: Michael S. Baser and Kim Weiskopf. Dir: Kim Manners.

Crandall (Dennis Cole); Geri (Barbara Horan); Felipe (Brett Halsey); Randy (Bruce Bauer); Ted (Marshall Teague); Laura Ferguson (Robin Eisenman); Waiter (Edward Crotty); Inspector Mercer (Don Knight); Rummy (John Alderson); Valet (Abraham Gordon); Girl #2 (Mae LaBlanc); Girl #1 (Cis Rundle); Bikini girl (Dona Speir).

Battlestar Galactica
September 1978–August 1979

On the eve of a peace conference between the 12 colonies and the evil, hated Cylons, warriors Apollo and Starbuck find out that the conference is a cover for an attack. When virtually all civilization is destroyed by the Cylon attack, Commander Adama orders the last battlestar warship Galactica *and every available ship to join together in search of the legendary planet Earth.*

Cast: Captain Apollo (Richard Hatch); Lt. Starbuck (Dirk Benedict); Commander Adama (Lorne Greene); Baltar (John Colicos); Lt. Boomer (Herb Jefferson, Jr.); Athena (Maren Jensen); Cassiopea (Laurette Spang); Sheba (Ann Lockhart); Jolly (Tony Swartz); Boxey (Noah Hathaway); Col. Tigh (Terry Carter).

Executive Producer and Creator: Glen Larson; *Supervising Producers:* Leslie Stevens and Michael Sloan; *Producers:* John Dykstra, Donald Bellisario, Paul Playdon and David O'Connell; *Associate Producers:* Winrich Kolbe (Pilot), David Phinney; *Theme:* Glen A. Larson and Stu Phillips; *Music Score:* Stu Phillips and The Los Angeles

Philharmonic Orchestra; ABC/Universal; 60 minutes.

Newsweek called it "Son of Star Wars," and at the time of its premiere in September of 1978, nearly everyone assumed that *Battlestar Galactica* was created to capitalize on the success of that famous film. But Glen Larson, creator and producer of the show, said he dreamed the idea for the show in the late 1960s.

"It really started as a concept I had as a novice when I first started to sell something for," remembers Larson.

His fascination with Howard Hughes, the billionaire, led him to create a billionaire-type character named Adam who invites "all the people who had ever been on *Time* magazine, at a meeting ... [in] the giant, brand new superstructure at the outskirts of Las Vegas, where he had bought property and land. They would all be gathered together in a main auditorium. They would feel a

The cast poses, left to right: Maren Jensen, Lorne Greene and Richard Hatch. Copyright 1978 ABC/Universal.

strange rumbling, and someone would leave the room and go up the stairs and around to a flight deck and realized they had taken off from the Earth. I called it *Adam's Ark*. Adam's computers had projected the end of the world. He was taking—as opposed to every animal—representatives of all of our highest forms of achievement on this planet to seek out destiny somewhere in the stars, if only against their will."

At the time he wrote this scenario, science fiction was not saleable. On the shelf it went. But in 1977 when *Star Wars* hit it big, "everyone was looking for science fiction. So I turned it around, and instead of leaving Earth looking outward, people were leaving outward looking for Earth," says Larson. "That's what happens in this day and age. When you go and sell a show … the networks will take what you have and say, 'You know, so-and-so is successful, why don't we take advantage of that,' and that, in effect, is why so many cars look alike. Imitation is the sincerest form of flattery. That's why you can say *Buck Rogers* sold at the same time! Someone's got to come along and make something commercial, and then you can sell your idea."

When *Battlestar Galactica* premiered in the fall of 1978, with Patrick MacNee's rich melodic voice opening the titles, it came with high audience expectations, driven by a thundering fanfare in the media. It was heralded as the pinnacle of science fiction shows. With so much promise, so much money invested, and such stellar talent on screen—the best Hollywood had to offer—it just couldn't fail. But *Battlestar Galactica* ended after 21 episodes. What happened?

Richard Hatch, star of *Battlestar Galactica* as Captain Apollo, says, "I think a lot of mistakes were made on *Galactica*. A golden opportunity was finished. It generated a great deal of money for everybody. It had the potential to be an exciting show and a good money maker at the same time, but I think there were too many egos. and too many people had different opinions. Not enough people understood the show, and once again, science fiction gets cut short before it gets a chance....

"It was a very exciting and interesting story. As a science fiction reader and believer, I thought it held a lot of similarities to a lot of things I felt inside my own heart. I liked the premise very much. The graphics of the artwork for the initial three-hour script were spectacular! The visuals were very powerful on that script. So when I was reading it, I had a chance to look at these wonderful art pictures … describing the places and events that were really quite stunning. That was

one of the things that persuaded me to take a chance at this project."

Remembering the early days of production, Hatch muses, "The trouble was, it was supposed to be a seven-hour mini-series that was already scripted out and planned. And then, it got turned into a series halfway through the first three-hour movie. They never quite got caught up, they were so far behind the gun, so far behind schedule. Everything was rush, rush, eighteen-hour days, six days a week. This first year, it was hard to tell whether you were coming or going. It was frustrating, in a sense, because you didn't get a chance to put in the planning and caring that would make the show much more effective in the first year. We were always getting pages and lines in the last second, a rough-and-tumble first year for everybody. [But] any first year series goes through that kind of stuff. No matter how much you plan, it always seems there are a million problems that come up. We were trying to find a format. [Actors] were trying to find their characters. The show was trying to find its own unique [identity]. They didn't quite know what to do with the show."

While Larson believes the show was "by and large, what I wanted to do," he also concedes that "when we went to a one-hour form, we were really rushed. We should not have gone on the air as fast as we did. We really should have taken from six months to a year. If you are dealing with a sitcom, you can rewrite a script overnight. But in space, everything you write, every piece of imagination, has to trigger a whole series of developments with sets, costumes. It's so difficult to do things so they're not hokey and they don't look thin and transparent."

Richard Hatch agrees, noting that the typical progression for developing a project is "delay, delay" followed suddenly by "'We want it for this season. We want production for next month!' and so they have to hurry and there's no time for proper planning. It's very difficult to find people who are gifted in planning things well. We do the best we can in this business. It's always a very traumatic, helter-skelter, roller coaster ride whenever you make a project.... Everybody hangs on for dear life to survive. *Galactica* … had more problems than most because we had a huge cast, sets, special effects, and it took ten days per episode to film. We were all doing something unique for television."

Hatch also recalls *Battlestar Galactica* as a frustrating experience for an actor. "When I read for the show I was hoping I would get a lot more material that would be challenging as an actor. I was told, before I did the show, there would be a lot of interesting storylines that would be very challenging dramatically. Unfortunately, with all the pyrotechnics and battles and running around, there wasn't much time to do human stories about people. I wanted to have more people-oriented stories. There's nothing wrong with playing a hero, but at the same time I like playing a human being. [I wanted to get] sensitive and get involved in human interest stories. And I just felt my talents were never used and never made the best of me as an actor. It was wonderful to be *in* the show. It was wonderful to be doing science fiction, but I wanted more kinds of stories that would give me a chance to use my special sensitivities and talents more effectively. It was very difficult under the conditions to do your best work sometimes. Because of the hours that we shot ... we were all tired, the conditions were not easy. They never are in television series, but it was harder for us. Captain Apollo was a very underdeveloped character."

Having said all that, Hatch does cite the father and son relationships as highlights of the show. "I wanted scenes between me, my father and my son. That gave me a chance to deal with the kind of material I like to do. [Jane Seymour as the reporter Serina] was asked to stay on by Glen Larson. But she opted not to."

Hatch was also very critical of the stories chosen for the show, since as a science fiction fan he wanted the genre's potential realized. "I wanted to have good science fiction shows. I thought that *Galactica* had a lot of potential to explore a lot of different, exciting probabilities. *Star Trek*, the wondrous thing about that—and I watched it for years—they explored a lot of different, unique concepts, and it's such a wonderful genre for us. And I felt *Galactica*, during that first year, never got its footing, never got a chance really to do the kind of wonderful science fiction shows that science fiction is so famous for.

"There were *so many* stories to be explored! We had so many problems from so many different people, and so many different egos involved, and so many people wanting it this way or that way. There's a lot of battling going on. Networks, producers, actors, directors, syndication, p.r., distributors; there's a lot of competition going on. ABC was not receiving the revenues from the movie and the merchandising. I think that Universal was. They weren't sharing the money that *Galactica* was generating." Hatch adds that "Glen Larson ... tends to take a lot of old stories

that were well done, and he updates them and puts them into a different genre.... Now, I don't have absolute proof of this, but this is what I was told: A lot of old storylines and stories from other shows were used and updated [for *Galactica*]."

Larson declares that he didn't necessarily enjoy this sort of borrowing "That came from network, who said, 'Let's do movies. Let's do Westerns. Let's do *Shane*. Let's do *Towering Inferno*.' It's tough to fight those guys. They're the buyer, and when we went to sell this, they weren't sure what we were going to do with it. And one of the things they bought was this epic kind of stories. Again, had we [had] a second season, we would have had a chance to avoid that particular stigma, if there was one."

Indeed, in hope of that second season, Larson had already planned for better stories by flying to New York and sitting down with a grandmaster of science fiction: author Isaac Asimov. "We did a projection for year two," says Larson. "We sat down and worked out how it would all go, and he would be involved and help us with concepts and things. We were so busy getting things up and running. Mr. Asimov agreed to come aboard as our science fiction writer—as our expert. That would have brought a whole level of credibility. ... We came up with a lot of directions, a lot of stories, and a lot of concepts."

Of Glen Larson's creative visions as the builder of the *Galactica*, Hatch declares, "Anybody who has the courage to put science fiction on the air, number one, is a pretty courageous person. Number two, Glen Larson is talented in many, many areas, as a writer, singer, musician, you know, so he brings a lot of his talents to play to put this together. This is his baby. He put a lot of hard work into it, and it was a monumental effort. Unfortunately the network just didn't want to go to a second year for this show that was so promising! Networks don't understand the genre of science fiction. They tend to be very conservative and play it safe. I don't blame them; there's a lot of money at stake and a lot of pressure. But I do know one thing about this business: Those who have the wherewithal and courage to take chances, are usually the ones who succeed."

Was Hatch ever reluctant to speak his mind during filming? "I had meetings just about every day with Glen Larson. He always bent over backwards to lend ears whenever I wanted to speak to him, and he always made himself accessible. He would come over, pick you up and go to lunch, and you would talk. I had meetings every day

The fleet's best warriors: Starbuck (Dirk Benedict) and Apollo (Richard Hatch). Copyright 1978 ABC/Universal.

with writers and producers, discussing my ideas, thoughts, feelings, and everybody was very amenable. I must say, with all the pressure and all the craziness of that show, that amongst ourselves, the actors, producers and directors, we all got along very well. There was a great deal of harmony and supportiveness. The problem was with Universal and the networks. Sometimes when there's great potential, everybody's ego gets involved, and everybody sees it differently, and there's a lot of infighting about how it should be done and what should not be done. Too many cooks in the kitchen. By the time they brought it back for *Galactica 1980*, it was too late. We were offered to do the second show, but most of us were busy at the time." But not all memories were bad ones. Hatch made many friends during the show and recalls them with fondness today.

As Adama, the commander of the *Galactica* and leader of the rag-tag fleet of humans, Lorne Greene "had this wonderful, booming, Shakespearean voice," laughs Hatch. "And truly he was a very simple, down-to-earth, loving, caring gentleman. He was very amenable and open to people. He came to my Christmas party, and you would find him in a corner talking with anybody who would want to sit down and talk with him. He had no ego, [no] attitude ... [nor was he] con-

descending in any way. He was just ... very ordinary folk. People who got to know him got very warm and comfortable in his presence."

Dirk Benedict, who was Apollo's sidekick and fellow warrior, Starbuck, "tended to be very warm on the set. But it's funny, he could be very volatile. I mean, he could at one moment be friendly, and the next moment, he would be withdrawn and want to be alone or off to himself. Dirk was very much an introverted-extroverted kind of person. You don't always know what's going on with Dirk. He tends to be a little bit disguised in that sense. There are a lot of hidden feelings inside Dirk, and you don't always know what they are. But he's a good guy, we never had a problem on the set. But I think that he's a complicated person. ... He's very warm and outgoing, and yet he's aloof at the same time.

Another important warrior was Boomer, played by Herb Jefferson, Jr. "I haven't seen Herb in a long time. I think his marriage broke up, I think he had a child. He was ... very crushed by the marriage breakup. It kind of put him on a tumble. He went through a very difficult time ... trying to find himself after that. Last time I saw him I was walking in Venice and he was walking down the street. He seemed like he was moving around a lot, busy with different things and different places. He left the business for a while. I think he's struggling to find his bearings. To me he was one of the most eloquent, intelligent, sensitive men I've ever met. I'm just amazed his career isn't going for him. I think he's a very good actor and he's a classy gentlemen. I think he'll bounce back."

Maren Jensen as Athena, Adama's daughter and communications specialist aboard the *Galactica*, "was very beautiful, but she was never uppity. She was always very approachable, very friendly and very down to earth. A very sensitive girl, but I have seen *nothing* of her since the show.

Laurette Spang as medical technician Cassiopea, Starbuck's girlfriend, "was always a sweetheart. She's one of those girls that if you didn't want her as a lover or a girlfriend you'd definitely want her as a good friend. She is such a neat person that you just enjoyed being around her. I think she was just very cute, spunky, and ... I think she had a very maternal quality about her. Even though she played a little sexpot on the show."

Anne Lockhart, as Sheba, a warrior from the Battlestar *Pegasus* introduced in the two-parter "The Living Legend," was "like everybody's best friend. She's one of those girls that you could trust with all your money. Someone who's just a good, down-to-earth, old-fashioned lady who's counted upon in a pinch. She's one of those people you thought of as a good friend."

Then there was Sarah Rush, who played Corporal Rigel, another communications specialist aboard the *Galactica* bridge. "I don't know about Sarah Rush," says Hatch candidly. "I know that she's a classically trained actress, who's done a lot of theatre who's wondrous on stage and wondrous in classical theatre. I'm sure she's ... married with children or working in the classical theatre somewhere. I'm surprised that lady hasn't done something more. I've never seen someone with so little screen time make such a huge impression. I had a mini-crush on her, to tell the truth. I don't think I ever told her that."

On hearing this very interesting comment, Sarah Rush laughs and replies, "Oh! I had a big crush on him! But I never told him. I was too shy. Isn't that funny? Richard gave the greatest back and neck rubs. [He] was very sensitive and gentle. Dirk was great. I thought both Richard and Dirk were just gorgeous."

Sarah Rush entered the world of the Battlestars as a contract player at Universal Studios. "*Battlestar Galactica* was the very first thing I'd ever done film-wise," remembers Rush. "I studied theatre in drama school and was in New York, and I got brought into contract with Universal, which was what brought me to Los Angeles. I had a very small role. I just kind of came in and out, now and then. I had my twenty-second birthday on that show. We had a birthday lunch with Lorne Greene, Richard and Dirk, and we're all in our little space suits. You have to remember I was a very small-town girl. For me it was great fun. I was thankful for the job. There were so many nice people involved. I did not have a very challenging role, but I was grateful for it because it literally paid my rent for years."

As Rigel, Rush was the show's voice of doom as she calmly counted down the 'microns' of when Cylons would attack. We saw Rigel primarily on the *Galactica* bridge set.

"It was an incredible set," says Rush. "I was very much a method actress and tried to make it my system, as though this was a part of my daily life and I knew what I was doing. I didn't know anything about computers. I just made up my own system there."

Another participant in this gigantic saga for television was Canadian actor John Colicos. He remembers *Battlestar Galactica* quite fondly. As the treacherous Baltar, Colicos got to play a role many actors say they prefer: the bad guy. "I wish we had gone on to a second year with that. We were just beginning to settle down to a marvelous format," says Colicos. "I love the part of Baltar, who's this galactic Judas. We were exploring all kinds of possibilities. He was sort of a flawed Lucifer and might have turned out eventually to have been a bastard son of Adama, which would have been a very interesting twist between the good and the evil and all that kind of thing. But there just wasn't time to do that." Beheaded in the feature version of the premiere episode to give the film finality, Baltar lived on in subsequent episodes to give Adama headaches.

"Glen himself reshot the final scene where Baltar was to be beheaded and stopped it before the beheading," recalls Colicos. "And [he] had the great lizard make a deal with me.... Being human, I would become a fine aide-de-camp, as it were, for the aliens, and I would live. So Baltar, being Baltar, decided to betray the entire human race and work for the aliens. But then he was going to take over himself the powers-that-were and become the supreme dictator of the galaxy. That was sort of the long-term plan that we had. Thank goodness we reshot it and had him not be killed and we continued the character."

But what was Baltar's motivation, when it was clear that if he did succeed in destroying the last of the human race, he too would be killed by Cylons?

"My opinion of Baltar's motivation was that it was just ... a cowardly self-preservation. That he was just not prepared to die for any sort of cause whatsoever. He was very selfish. We had one episode where he was trying to explain that his entire family had been destroyed and he was left alone and in a sense was wreaking vengeance on the world. And unfortunately his conscience was burned along with the rest of his family. It's where he explains to Adama that he's not the bastard that Adama thinks he is. His plan was eventually—and we wanted to develop this—to become a ruler of the Cylons."

Of Glen Larson, Colicos says, "He was highly overworked. But he was a very extraordinary, intelligent, imaginative, energetic individual. He had tremendous creative energy. He's never happy unless he's doing things, working 24 hours a day. I think he's a man who can't be idle at any point in time. He's a very dynamic and very creative person."

Working with Lorne Greene was a special

treat for Colicos because "Lorne and I had known each other for years and years and years. We had worked on radio back in the 1950s when he ran a radio training school in Toronto. I knew Lorne when he played the ghost to my Hamlet on radio. We had done a number of shows together. I think we knew each other for 40 years ... just like meeting an old friend again."

Overall, in speaking with *Galactica*'s cast and crew, one gets the impression of great collegiality and mutual admiration on the set, to say nothing of talent and drive. But according to some critics, the obstacles presented by *Galactica*'s premise were more than even the most energetic and harmonious efforts could overcome. In the book *The Best of Science Fiction TV* by John Javna (Harmony Books, 1987), screenwriter and novelist David Gerrold says, "I know they tried to do their best ... but as the season went on it got worse and worse. The problem was that these people did not have a heroic mission. They were running away from Cylons. They weren't running to something. They weren't searching out something ... Galactica was 'Run like hell—we're being chased.' And that's cowardice. You can't make cowardice noble, no matter how hard you try."

In response, Larson says, "That's taking a very narrow perspective of what this was about. There's such a thing as tactical retreat. But in this case these people were going out to warn their brothers in space [Earthlings] of this menace [Cylons]. And regrouping to fight another day. ... I don't think they show themselves to be cowards at all, but very often you have to pull back in order to win. A military strategist doesn't fight to the last man. He regroups. And I would say to find the planet Earth *is* a noble move, warning their brothers of this menace." Larson adds that perhaps Gerrold's criticism "should have generated an episode where they say, 'We have to fight another day.'"

And fight they did. The "Living Legend" two-parter with Lloyd Bridges, and the last episode, "The Hand of God," were segments that dealt with our intrepid heroes fighting back against the Cylons and the dreaded Basestars.

Of the show's much-heralded budget, Hatch remembers, "There was a tremendous amount of money spent on that show. One or two million per episode, a huge expense."

Glen Larson, however, looks at the show's budget slightly differently. "It didn't have a big budget. Relatively speaking you could say a big

budget, but to compare it with motion picture vehicles, it had a very low budget. We had to do the best we could. We were constantly compromising. Because of John Dykstra's genius, we were able to execute a lot of the things. It was costing more than a million dollars an episode in a time where that was pretty unheard of. If we were able to amortize that show over more than one season, the price of the show would have come down! You have to take the costs of all those costumes, all of those special effects, and if you amortize them against one season, it's expensive, but if you can lay it over over two, three, four or five seasons, it's not so expensive anymore!" What's more, Larson points out, "When they recut them into three movies which played overseas, they made a lot of money."

Six months prior to the premiere of *Battlestar* on television, Universal released the three-hour premiere in Canada as a feature, garnering good box-office receipts that helped bring the show's expenses closer to black.

"We didn't set out to make it as a feature," says Larson. "They took away the budget, and a lot of the things we would have needed to make it different. In *Buck Rogers* (which Larson co-created) we were allowed, by the network, to pull it off and reshoot it and add things that we thought would help it in the theater."

Of course the notion of a feature to be released in Canada and outside of the United States came from Universal marketing. Larson says, "There was some anger from Canada, from people who thought it was a totally different picture. And of course, it wasn't. It was a different version [of] essentially the same body of film."

With the release of that feature, media and audience attention snowballed, as Larson recalls. "The hype came about naturally because of the comparison to *Star Wars* and the fact that when you have people like Dykstra, the 20th Century–Fox lawsuit, and all of those things coming together, it created a feeding frenzy. *Time* magazine was there, *Newsweek*, *People*, all these magazines descended upon us. It wasn't that we were out there looking for the hype. In a way, it creates an unfair comparison, because we didn't have the same tools to work with as motion pictures had. That was difficult.

"I don't look upon it with any regrets, because we were able to do a great deal, and we had a pretty huge following for that show.... If *Battlestar* was able to continue financially, beyond the first year, I think the network's success would have been far beyond *Star Trek*'s. *Star Trek* never attained enormous popularity in its network run, and it was not until syndication that it found and consolidated its audience. We had the opportunity to do a lot more. Finances really crippled us, and ABC at the time was so strong that they were enjoying 50 shares in everything they had. They really threw us away, and they regretted it ... later, that's why they were willing to bring us back. But really, it was almost impossible to try and remount it because it lost a lot of its key people, and a lot of its potential. But at the time it wasn't a failed experiment. Our numbers for the year were very, very strong. Far greater than any of *Star Trek*'s ever were. If you look at the actual numbers for the year it was on, it was like nineteenth place in the whole year. The trouble was with the network. They had all top ten shows, and they got very greedy."

In effect, ABC's expectations for *Battlestar*'s performance were higher than those of the audience.

The lawsuit that Larson mentions was when 20th Century–Fox, who owned *Star Wars,* slapped Universal with a suit claiming that *Battlestar Galactica* infringed on the copyright to their blockbuster. There was also a countersuit in which Universal charged that *Star Wars* infringed on their feature *Silent Running.* In the end, the case was settled out of court.

"The original complaint encompassed *Buck Rogers* too," says Larson. "They had a tough time making that case. One's pride soars with that kind of success, and one begins to think he has a proprietory interest in all space vehicles, otherwise they wouldn't have mentioned *Buck Rogers.* We actually sat down and worked out a lot of things with [the *Star Wars* producers]. We agreed not to use laser streaks. We agreed to do a number of things they asked us to do. They actually leased us Industrial Light and Magic [Lucas's special effects facility] at the time. So we couldn't have made the show without positive help. But George wanted the lawsuit, and I think it was very much a personal decision on his part. It was an intrusion on his domain.

"The truth of the matter is, all these things are derivative. Many things in *Star Wars,* John Dykstra will tell you, are derivative. [Lucas] put his concept together brilliantly. I think it's a masterpiece. One has to expect that when you do something that original and that unique, it's going to throw into a lot of other things. And in fact, it did. It influenced a lot of shows, includ-

John Colicos played bad guy Baltar on *Battlestar Galactica.*

ing our own. If the number one car in the world is a Mercedes, you're going to find that car influencing other things. They're not supposed to be direct ripoffs, but ... it happens all the time. I don't think there has been a successful show that hasn't generated a lawsuit. There are very few shows that don't generate some kind of litigation from somebody."

Many viewers complained that *Battlestar Galactica* became too enamored with Cylons as the recurring villains. They wanted to see other types of life in the universe, and stories more closely centered on characterization.

"It's an interesting perspective," says Larson. "You don't know until you step back and get a perspective. I haven't talked to a lot of people to see what they thought. It could be that there was an awful lot of emphasis on ... [the Cylons]. You think of a story like *The Fugitive*, you didn't see the one-armed man very much and you didn't see Lt. Gerard very much. Perhaps we could have used [the Cylons] less."

Donald P. Bellisario, supervising producer of the show, also believes the show suffered from Cylons and space battles. "It became too hung up on the technology and not enough on the stories," says Bellisario, *Quantum Leap*'s creator. "The special effects I thought were terrific for the time. I thought the acting was just fine on the show. I thought the cast basically worked." When talking about the show's shortcomings, however, he notes that "in order to create a show where someone's being pursued by an enemy, a villain, an antagonist, you have to have a realistic enemy. Even in a science fiction show. There was no reality to the antagonist there, to the Cylons."

Bellisario says that if you repeatedly blow the enemies away, the viewers will see them as no longer a threat. "A hero—a protagonist—is only as strong as his enemy can be," he explains. "The network, the standards people, could not allow the humans to be killed. They only had one person die, the Jane Seymour character in the pilot; other than that, you couldn't do it! That was probably the biggest single thing that didn't work. Had it been realistic (for a series), having battles going on and people dying and a real conflict trying to escape from being pursued, I think it would have worked. I would have liked to ... [make viewers feel] something was at stake here. You don't always win. Why tune in every week if you don't feel any danger here? The unexpected is what always gets people."

On an optimistic note, in October 1993, a *Battlestar Galactica* 15-year reunion convention reassembled the cast of the show at Universal City. As he prepared for that event, Hatch said, "I want to bring together all the people that were associated with *Battlestar Galactica* to 'reignite' the dream of the show, to bring back an awareness to the industry and everybody who followed the show of how special that show was, and the great potential it had. I want to rekindle that enthusiasm because of the advent of the Sci-Fi Channel. Science fiction is becoming huge, and I always felt that *Battlestar Galactica* has a definite place in the science fiction community. As you know, it has taken off in syndication more than ever in network. It shows you the huge audience out there."

But Hatch has a bigger agenda. He wants to launch the *Galactica* back into space in a theatrical trilogy, a TV-movie series or even in regular episodic form.

"*Battlestar Galactica* deserves a second chance. I've sent letters to Universal and the Sci-Fi Channel about doing a trilogy of *Battlestar Galactica*. Let's see what happens with that."

To that end, Hatch has written a story treatment of a trilogy resolving the premise of the show. It is his hope that with the proper personnel, space battles will once again come alive.

"We've never been off the air in 15 years," Hatch explains. "No other science fiction show with 21 episodes has ever had the longevity all over the world like *Battlestar Galactica*. It was the highest rated network science fiction show of all time." Refusing to describe his story in detail, Hatch does give a few hints. For starters, the story ignores the events of *Galactica 1980* and acknowl-

edges the death of Commander Adama, Lorne Greene. "It will address all the unresolved issues and deal with some 20 to 30 yarns [years] since we last saw the *Galactica*. The commander ... died, and [there will be] a fight to establish who's going to be the leadership of the *Galactica* ... and [it] deals with what happens to Captain Apollo and Lt. Starbuck, and basically, puts the ship on course to really find its true home. The odyssey really was about re-establishing contact with the true race, where humans had begun and trying to trace its steps back to its evolutionary heritage."

Reactivating the Cylons, who surely are waiting in vaults inside Universal Studios, is not in Hatch's plans. "Cylons will no longer be. They will be the future evolutionary strain of the Cylons—far more dangerous, more scary, than anything that has ever been seen in the galaxy. They will have evolved into a far more lethal race."

Hatch hopes the few small steps he takes will snowball into a new series. The first step, however, is to find someone to finance the venture. "I'd like to do it as a feature," says Hatch. "Science fiction is huge now. I think you can have an incredibly dynamic show. And the nice thing about it is it's not a new premise, it's a show that has deep roots in the science fiction community. It's well known and has strong name value. It has a built-in marketing value. With old elements and new elements you can create a real exciting show."

Essentially, Hatch is hoping to give *Battlestar Galactica* what the networks never did: a chance to realize its potential. "The network should have given us a second year in order to really do the show the way everybody really knew and hoped it could be. I think everybody knew the first year was a shakedown cruise, and had we been given a second year, *Battlestar Galactica* could have been one of the most exciting TV shows ever on the air. I think we had the capability of being an extraordinarily exciting show, with some ability to go out there and compete with *Star Trek*. With its popularity, I really thought that we never got a second year that we deserved."

Larson wishes he had been better equipped to fight for that year. "I'll say this, if I knew then what I know now, I would have worked a lot differently in terms of how I position myself with the network; I would have worked more politically to platform ourselves with the network. We would know how to survive a little bit better. Our failure was not being able to sustain that great expectation," Larson says, musing that things might have been different "if we had put it in a different perspective—if we had been on either of the two other networks!"

CAST NOTES

Richard Hatch (Apollo): Born 1947. This popular soap opera actor broke into prime time as Karl Malden's new police partner during the last season of *Streets of San Francisco* (1976-77).

"I have been doing a lot of movies all over the world," says Hatch. "I just did a series of short stories called *The Hitchhiker*. I did a play called *Pepper Street*. I'm also working on a couple of movie projects. I'm teaching seminars around the country, inspiring and empowering people to stand up and be counted and learn to speak, training them how to get involved in what's happening in this world and not sit back and let others speak for them. I'm teaching them how to find their own voice in the world. And I use acting as a means of communicating more effectively. It's teaching people how to listen to their own inner voice and … how to trust, have faith and, with courage, make that inner voice come out. I do these lectures at colleges and I … help develop original material from the everyday citizen who has never, ever created anything. And help them write their feelings, thoughts and ideas down. I break them into scenes … and I put them up on a stage and present them as a production."

Dirk Benedict (Starbuck): Born 1944. Prior to *Galactica*, Benedict starred in *Chopper One* (1974). Features include *SSSSS* (1973) with Heather Menzies, and *Scavenger Hunt* (1979). His career remained healthy with four years on *The A-Team*. He has written two books, the autobiography *Confessions of a Kamikaze Cowboy* (1991) and *And Then We Went Fishing* (1993), both available from Avery Publishing Group. Benedict is interested in writing and directing his own films.

Lorne Greene (Commander Adama): Born 1915. This Canadian-born actor found fame as Ben Cartwright for 14 years on TV's *Bonanza* (1959–1973). He also starred in *Griff* (1973). Greene died of pneumonia in 1987.

Terry Carter (Col. Tigh): Born 1929. For seven years he played Sgt. Broadhurst on Dennis Weaver's 1970s series, *McCloud*. Carter is an award-winning producer/director with more than 30 years in broadcasting and film. He's embraced the fields of broadcasting, documentaries, education and episodic television. Presently, Carter has many television programs in distribution around the world. He's president of Meta-4 Productions, Inc., a production company, and also is involved in a non-profit organization called Council for Positive Images, Inc., a company that produces film and video to promote intercultural and inter-ethnic understanding.

Noah Hathaway (Boxey): This young actor returned to theater screens as the teenage hero in the film fantasy *The Neverending Story* (1984). He's also appeared in the sit-com *Family Ties*. He's had parts in *The Last Convertible* (1979), *High Midnight* (1982), and the premiere of *Call to Glory* (1985). He also attended the Director's School of UCLA.

John Colicos (Baltar): Born 1928. Colicos, a native of Canada, has made himself a name playing wonderfully wicked villains and working as a character actor in many TV shows. Colicos also is known for guesting in science fiction shows such as *Starlost*, *Star Trek*, and *War of the Worlds*. He also appeared as a regular in *General Hospital* (1981). More recently, Colicos performed as King Lear for the Canadian Broadcasting Corporation (CBC) radio in Canada. He also had an opportunity to reprise his famous Klingon role, Kor, in *Star Trek's Deep Space Nine* with William Campbell and Michael Ansara, in the episodes "Blood Oath" and "The Sword of Kahless."

Maren Jensen (Athena): Born 1957. This actress first came to attention on television with a guest shot in *The Hardy Boys*, which led to her regular role in *Galactica*. Later, she starred in *Deadly Blessing* (1981) with Sharon Stone and Lisa Hartman, and put in an appearance in *Fantasy Island*. She retired to Hawaii in the early 1980s and now lives in Beverly Hills.

Laurette Spang (Cassiopea): In addition to *Galactica*, Spang had a recurring role in *B.J. and the Bear*. She has also appeared in several TV movies: *Short Walk to Daylight* (1972), *Maneater* (1973), *Runaway!* (1973), *The Rangers* (1974), *Sarah T: Portrait of a Teenage Alcoholic* (1975), *The Love Boat* (1976), *Tourist* (1980), and *The Day* *the Bubble Burst* (1982). Spang is married to actor John McCook.

Herb Jefferson, Jr. (Boomer): Born 1946. Jefferson appeared in *Rich Man, Poor Man* (1976). After *Galactica* he was a regular in *The Devlin Connection* (1982). He has also been involved with the United States Marine Corps Reserves' Toys for Tots program, the USO, and California Special Olympics. He continues to work today with voice-overs in commercials.

EPISODE GUIDE

Saga of a Star World
In the midst of an intergalactic peace conference, inhabitants of the 12 Colonies come under attack from their 1000-year-old enemies, the Cylons. With their civilization reduced to rubble, Commander Adama, leader of the last battleship *Galactica*, gathers all the remaining citizens of the colonies together in a quest for the lost colony—Earth. Wr: Glen A. Larson. Dir: Richard A. Colla.

President Adar (Lew Ayres); Anton (Wilfred Hyde White); Dr. Payne (John Fink); Serina (Jane Seymour); Sire Uri (Ray Milland); Ensign Greenbean (Ed Begley, Jr.); Zac (Rick Springfield); Statesman (Norman Stuart); Omega (David Greenan); Rigel (Sarah Rush); Operative (David Matthau); 1st warrior (Chip Johnson); 2nd warrior (Geoffrey Binney); Pilot (Paul Coufos); Deckhand (Bruce Wright); Little Supreme (Myrna Matthews); Other Supreme (Stephanie Spruill); Big Supreme (Pattie Brooks); Seetol (Sandy Gimpel); Dealer (John Zenda); Gemon (Rene Assa); Commentator (Jim Peck); Wounded man (Don Maxwell); Man #1 (David Byrd); Man #2 (Richard Bronda); Woman #1 (Lois Adams); Woman #2 (June Whitley Taylor); Woman #3 (Carol Baxter); Sandell (David Tress); Lobe (Lee McLaughlin); Old woman (Louise Lorimer); Crewman (Stoney Bower); Pit Boss (Ben Frommer); Guard (Michael J. London); Imperious leader (Dick Durock); Lotay (Diannel Burgdorf); Centurion #1 (Ted White); Young woman (Randi Oakes).

Lost Planet of the Gods, Part 1
When two Viper pilots bring back a contagious disease from a patrol, almost all of the pilots succumb. Shuttle pilots must be recruited for defense against the pursuing Cylons. Wr: Glen A. Larson and Donald Bellisario. Dir: Christian Nyby II.

Serina (Jane Seymour); Dr. Salik (George Murdock); Ens. Greenbean (Ed Begley, Jr.); Deidra (Sheila De Windt); Brie (Janet Louise Johnson); Rigel (Sarah Rush); Omega (David Greenan); 1st guard (Bruce Wright); 2nd guard (Paul Coufos); 2nd girl warrior (Jennifer Joseph); Sorell (Janet Lynn Curtis); 1st girl warrior (Leann Hunley); 3rd girl warrior (Gay Thomas).

Lost Planet of the Gods, Part 2
The *Galactica* comes upon a planet called Kobol.

Finding ancient pyramids, Adama seeks more clues to locate Earth. Meanwhile, Baltar launches an attack. Wr: Glen A. Larson and Donald Bellisario. Dir: Christian Nyby II.

Serina (Jane Seymour); Dr. Salik (George Murdock); Ens. Greenbean (Ed Begley, Jr.); Deidra (Sheila De Windt); Brie (Janet Louise Johnson); Rigel (Sarah Rush); Omega (David Greenan); 2nd girl warrior (Jennifer Joseph); Sorell (Janet Lynn Curtis); Giles (Larry Manetti); 3rd girl warrior (Millicent Crisp).

The Lost Warrior
Apollo is marooned on a wild west–like planet where he meets a woman and her son. In town, "Red-Eye," the local enforcer, turns out to be a Cylon centurion whom Apollo challenges to a shootout. Wr: Donald Bellisario, story by Donald Bellisario and Herman Groves. Dir: Rod Holcomb.

Bella (Katherine Cannon); Bootes (Lance LeGault); Puppis (Johnny Timko); Red-Eye (Rex Cutter); Marco (Red West); La Certa (Claude Earl Jones); Giles (Larry Manetti); Jason (Jay Donohue); Macy (Carol Baxter); Vi (Mary Kay Mars).

The Long Patrol
Assigned to test-pilot a long-range Viper with no laser equipment, Starbuck loses the ship to a robber. He winds up in prison by those believing him to be the robber. There, he discovers the prisoners are the descendants of the original captives. Wr: Donald Bellisario. Dir: Christian Nyby II.

Robber (James Whitmore, Jr.); Croad (Ted Gehring); Assault (Sean McClory); Adultress (Tasha Martel); Forger (Ian Abercrombie); Rigel (Sarah Rush); Omega (David Greenan); Enforcer (Robert Hathaway); Slayer (Nancy DeCarl); Waiter (John Holland); Voice of Cora (Cathey Paine).

Memory Flash—Actor James Whitmore, Jr. "I remember the food at the end of that movie. We had a big banquet. They had the strangest looking food you ever saw in your life. Green turkey, orange cabbage, all kinds of strange stuff on the table there.

"There's also a true story about the scene we shot where Starbuck knocked me out. In the story, my character and his wife and daughter escape from prison. The problem was we filmed it at night and kids can't work [due to child labor laws]. It was shot about one a.m. So I'm yelling after my wife and daughter, who's being taken away. And in the scene, my 'daughter' runs up to me and jumps into my arms and she has a moustache. The problem was they couldn't use the little girl at night so they brought a dwarf in to play my daughter. And my 'daughter' smells of whiskey and cigars…!" laughs Whitmore. "They couldn't use the kid, so they used the dwarf…!"

Gun on Ice Planet Zero, Part I
Galacticans realize they're headed straight for a pulse gun on an ice planet that's capable of destroying the

fleet. Apollo and Starbuck and a team of skilled criminals are sent down to destroy the gun. Wr: Michael Sloan, Donald Bellisario and Glen A. Larson, story by John Ireland, Jr. Dir: Alan J. Levi.

Croft (Roy Thinnes); Ser Five Nine (Denny Miller); Tenna (Britt Ekland); Thane (James Olson); Leda (Christine Belford); Wolfe (Richard Lynch); Giles (Larry Manetti); Cadet Cres (Alan Stock); Haals (Curtis Credel); Komma (Jeff McKay); Rigel (Sarah Rush); Omega (David Greenan); Cadet Shields (Larry Cedar); Cadet (Alex Hyde White); Killian (Richard Muholland); Vickers (Walt Davis).

Gun on Ice Planet Zero, Part 2

On the planet, Apollo's commando team encounters a small colony of clones created by Dr. Ravashol, who lives in the caves of the gun planet. Together, they join forces to destroy the gun fortress. Wr: Michael Sloan, Donald Bellisario and Glen A. Larson, story by John Ireland, Jr. Dir: Alan J. Levi.

Croft (Roy Thinnes); Tenna (Britt Ekland); Thane (James Olson); Leda (Christine Belford); Ser Five Nine (Denny Miller); Wolfe (Richard Lynch); Dr. Ravashol (Daniel O'Herlihy); Giles (Larry Manetti); Cadet Cres (Alan Stock); Haals (Curtis Credel); Rigel (Sarah Rush); Omega (David Greenan); Vickers (Walt Davis); Uncredited clone (Liam Sullivan).

The Magnificent Warriors

When a food crisis erupts, Commander Adama must deal with an old flame to obtain equipment needed to engineer a food trade. Meanwhile, Starbuck unwillingly becomes sheriff to protect the local farming community from pig-like creatures. Wr: Glen A. Larson. Dir: Christian Nyby II.

Belloby (Brett Somers); Carmichael (Olan Soule); Bogan (Barry Nelson); Digger (Eric Server); Ens. Greenbean (Ed Begley, Jr.); Duggy (Dennis Fimple); Farnes (Rance Howard); Rigel (Sarah Rush); Omega (David Greenan); Nogow (Ben Frommer).

The Young Lords

After crashlanding on a planet, Starbuck is rescued by a group of children whose father is being held hostage by Cylons in a castle. Wr: Donald P. Bellisario, Frank Lupo and Paul Playdon. Dir: Donald Bellisario.

Kyle (Charles Bloom); Megan (Bruce Glover); Miri (Audrey Landers); Ariadne (Bridgette Mueller); Robus (Jonathan B. Woodward); Nilz (Adam Mann).

The Living Legend, Part 1

While on patrol, Apollo and Starbuck encounter the Battlestar *Pegasus*, commanded by the legendary Commander Cain. Wr: Glen A. Larson, story by Ken Pettus and Glen A. Larson. Dir: Vince Edwards.

Commander Cain (Lloyd Bridges); Bojay (Jack Stauffer); Tolan (Rod Haase); Omega (David Greenan); Launch officer *Pegasus* (Junero Jennings).

The Living Legend, Part 2

Together, the *Galactica* and *Pegasus* plot to strike at a Cylon base, but Adama has reservations. Wr: Glen A. Larson, story by Ken Pettus and Glen A. Larson. Dir: Vince Edwards.

Commander Cain (Lloyd Bridges); Bojay (Jack Stauffer); Tolan (Rod Haase); Helmsman (Ted Hamaguchi); Omega (David Greenan).

Fire in Space

A Cylon attack leaves Adama injured and most of the *Galactica* in flames. Wr: Jim Carlson and Terrence McDonnell, story by Michael Sloan. Dir: Christian Nyby II.

Sheba (Anne Lockhart); Dr. Salik (George Murdock); Fire leader (William Bryant); Giles (Larry Manetti); Komma (Jeff McKay); Omega (David Greenan).

War of the Gods, Part 1

Hounded by strange, mysterious lights, the *Galactica* encounters an alien man, Count Iblis. His charisma and powers win the trust of many in the fleet. Wr: Glen A. Larson. Dir: Daniel Haller.

Count Iblis (Patrick MacNee); Statesman (John Williams); Dr. Salik (George Murdock); Brie (Janet Louise Johnson); Bojay (John Stauffer); Ens. Greenbean (Ed Begley, Jr.); Dr. Wilker (John Dullaghan); Old man (Kirk Alyn); Old woman (Paula Victor); Rigel (Sarah Rush); 1st pilot (Paul Coufos); 3rd pilot (Chip Johnson); Guard (Bruce Wright); Girl warrior (Leann Hunley); Omega (David Greenan); Carmichael (Olan Soule); 2nd statesman (Norman Stewart).

War of the Gods, Part 2

Count Iblis delivers Baltar to the Council, but Adama's suspicious. He sends Apollo and Starbuck down to a planet to learn the real identity of the count. Wr: Glen A. Larson. Dir: Daniel Haller.

Count Iblis (Patrick MacNee); Statesman (John Williams); Dr. Salik (George Murdock); Brie (Janet Louise Johnson); Bojay (John Stauffer); Ens. Greenbean (Ed Begley, Jr.); Dr. Wilker (John Dullaghan); Old man (Kirk Alyn); Old woman (Paula Victor); Rigel (Sarah Rush); 1st pilot (Paul Coufos); 3rd pilot (Chip Johnson); Guard (Bruce Wright); Girl warrior (Leann Hunley); Omega (David Greenan); Carmichael (Olan Soule); 2nd statesman (Norman Stewart).

The Man with Nine Lives

An aging con man tries to escape from Borellians who want his life, so he convinces Starbuck that he is Starbuck's father. Wr: Donald Bellisario. Dir: Rod Holcomb.

Chameleon (Fred Astaire); Siress Blassie (Anne Jeffreys); Maga (Lance LeGault); Taba (Anthony DeLongis); Bora (Robert Feero); Cpl. Lomas (Bruce Wright); Crewman (Dan Barton); Zara (Patricia Stitch); Zed (Frank Parker); Female pilot (Leann Hunley); Male pilot (Alex Hyde White); Omega (David Greenan); Maitre D' (John Holland); Dealer (Lynn Halpern).

Murder on the Rising Star

When a game of Triad ends in murder, Starbuck is tried for the crime. It's up to Apollo and Boomer to clear him. Wr: Donald Bellisario, Jim Carlson and Terrence McDonnell, story by Michael Sloan. Dir: Rod Holcomb.

Solon (Brock Peters); Barton (W. K. Stratton); Chella (Ben Frank); Pallon (Lyman Ward); Ortega (Frank Ashmore); Dr. Wilker (John Dullaghan); Komma (Jeff McKay); Elias (Newell Alexander); Zed (Frank Parker); Zara (Patricia Stitch); Official (Ted Noose); 1st Guardian (Paul LeClair).

Greetings from Earth (2 hours)

Intercepting a primitive spaceship, Apollo and Starbuck believe the cyrogenically preserved humans may be from Earth. After helping them reach the planet Paradeen, the Galacticans learn that the planet is in combat with its neighboring enemies, the Eastern Alliance. Wr: Glen A. Larson. Dir: Rod Holcomb.

Michael (Randolph Mantooth); Commandant Leiter (Lloyd Bochner); Hector (Bobby Van); Vector (Ray Bolger); Doyle (Gary Vinson); Sarah (Kelly Harmon); Geller (Murray Matheson); Dr. Salik (George Murdock); Dr. Wilker (John Dullaghan); Aggie (Lesley Woods); Sec. officer Reece (Frank Marth); Josh Moreland (Curt Lowens); Security officer (Ron Kelly); Lanceman (Alex Rodine); Denner (Lester Fletcher); Omega (David Greenan); Charity (Michelle Carol Larson); Melanie (Gillian Greene); Todd (G. Eric Larson); Loma (Kimberly Woodward); Baby Walker (David G. Larson); Med. Technician (Donald Mantooth).

Baltar Escapes

Baltar tries to escape from prison with the help of the Eastern Alliance captives. Held in blackmail, Adama must deliver himself to save the fleet. Wr: Donald Bellisario Dir: Winrich Kolbe.

Siress Tinia (Ina Balin); Leiter (Lloyd Bochner); Domra (John Hoyt); Maga (Lance LeGault); Bora (Robert Feero); Taba (Anthony Delongis); 4th guard (Bruce Wright); Dr. Wilker (John Dullaghan); 1st guard (Ron Kelly); Rigel (Sarah Rush); Omega (David Greenan); Control operator (Mitchell Ret); 2nd guard (Paul Tinder); 5th guard (Paul LeClair).

Experiment in Terra

Apollo and Starbuck catch up with an Eastern Alliance craft back to its planet, Terra. But before they can land, the mysterious lights that saved them from Count Iblis ("War of the Gods") intercept. Wr: Glen A. Larson. Dir: Rod Holcomb.

Brenda (Melody Anderson); President (Peter D. McLean); John (Edward Mulhare); Supreme commandant (Nehemiah Persoff); Mr. Moore (Logan Swanson); Max-Well (Ken Swofford); Stone (Sidney Clute); Dr. Horning (Kenneth Lynch); Brace (Jordan Rhodes); Officer (John de Lancie); Alliance member (Russ Marin); Omega (David Greenan); Alliance leader (Milt Jamin).

Take the Celestra

Just as Starbuck rediscovers a lost love, a power struggle erupts onboard one of the rag-tag ships, the *Celestra*. The mutineers try to flee from the fleet. Wr: Jim Carlson and Terrance McDonnell, story by David G. Arthur, David G. Phinney, Jim Carlson, and Terrance McDonnell. Dir: Daniel Haller.

Kronus (Paul Fix); Charka (Nick Holt); Aurora (Ana Alicia); Ramon (Randy Stumph); Hermes (Richard Styles); 1st mutineer (James B. Parkes); 2nd mutineer (Michael Horsley); Omega (David Greenan); 2rd crewman (Ted Hamaguchi); Duty officer (Robert Murvin).

The Hand of God

Tired of running away from Cylons, Adama prepares a bold plan in which Apollo and Starbuck infiltrate a basestar and blind the scanners so that the *Galactica* can attack. Wr: Donald Bellisario. Dir: Donald Bellisario.

Omega (David Greenan).

Beyond Westworld

March 1980

John Moore is security chief of the Delos Corporation, a futuristic amusement park using androids as the centerpiece of its attractions. Moore is confronted with the task of hunting down the renegade scientist Simon Quaid, who has absconded with a collection of androids and plots dastardly deeds against humanity.

Cast: John Moore (Jim McMullan); Pamela Williams (Connie Sellecca); Joseph Oppenheimer (William Jordan); Simon Quaid (James Wainwright); Laura Garvey (Pilot) (Judith Chapman); Foley (Pilot) (Stewart Moss); Foley (Series) (Severn Darden).

Based on the film Westworld *by* Michael Crichton; *Developed for television by:* Lou Shaw; *Executive Producer:* Lou Shaw; *Producer:* Fred Freiberger; *Supervising Producer:* Leonard B. Kaufman; CBS/MGM TV; 60 minutes.

Beyond Westworld is easy to describe: James Bond hunting robots. The series is based on Michael Crichton's 1973 feature film *Westworld*, where robots provided visitors their every pleasure in a futuristic amusement park, until the electronic servants suddenly ran amok. Although a 1976 sequel, *Futureworld*, was filmed, the television series was a setup for an ongoing struggle between man and machines (controlled by an evil leader with world conquest ambitions) and shares no relationship with the sequel. To counter the evil one's intentions, John Moore, security chief, joins forces with assistant Pamela Williams and the true genius behind the robots, Professor Joseph Oppenheimer. They are pitted against the villainous Simon Quaid, their version of the James Bond villain, "Blofeld."

"I loved the idea," says star McMullan. "Michael Crichton and I worked on his first movie for television that he directed, *Pursuit*, and a film he wrote right after that called *Extreme Closeup*. Now, Michael had nothing to do with *Beyond Westworld*. He just gave them the rights to do it and then stepped away.

"The pilot was a well-written script, and in this genre you need good scripts that are well thought out and will intrigue the audience and are tricky and will go in different directions. The pilot had that. They waited and finally got an OK from the network to go ahead with it. Then, on short notice, they had to come up with all these scripts, and they were not very good. They got worse as they went along because they were in a real hurry to deliver them. It's such a shame, and that's why the series fell."

Co-star Jordan recalls the fall of the show similarly. "The idea was confined to the limitations of television," he says. "There's a matter of production qualities. I think that to some extent we achieved quality work in the first two or three shows. But I think the production costs were too much for the network. There were lots of special effects in terms of robotics and in terms of people's chests having to be opened and circuitry being shown. I didn't think it was a major problem, it was just costly." For Jordan, this show was something of a small blip in his career, and he did not find it satisfying. "Doing television isn't very fulfilling unless you're doing a movie of the week, that has to do with history or some kind of innovative piece of material," he notes. "Pilots start out as ambitious, but ... [episodes] peter out. Exposition takes over for any hollowing in the dialogue. There's lots of efforts to cut costs,

Jim McMullan, who starred in *Beyond Westworld* as John Moore, security chief of the Delos Corporation.

and sometimes there's an attempt to tell a story through exposition rather than visually."

Five episodes is an embarrassingly small number to have filmed, but airing only *three* on prime-time television is the action of a network who pulled the plug very fast.

"They would have loved this to go on much longer, but it was like asking someone to deliver a weekly show like *Mission: Impossible* and not give much time to write these intricate scripts," acknowledges McMullan. "They could have been wonderful. We were very disappointed because each time we would get a new script, we were rushing to get it finished. So, we ended up with all this junk, and you could feel each show was a little worse than the last one. We tried hard."

McMullan believes that had the show been given the time it needed to be properly put together, viewers would have seen deeper characterization, more interesting relationships and of course, more action. McMullan says, "As it was, *Beyond Westworld* degenerated into a chase show, and not even the villains were interesting. James Wainwright's character became something of a caricature. We had a couple of scenes, mostly him watching me in a television monitor. I actually saw him as more of a Burgess Meredith character when I first read the script. They felt it was important to make him my age. I didn't feel comfortable with that. At that time that's how they saw it; they figured the audience just wanted action. Today, if you did the same show, you would start to see much more relationships. Even in *Baywatch*, I did a recurring part as the father of one of the boys—they're bringing in intimate relationships with families."

Executive producer, Fred Freiberger, when contacted for comments on the show, responded with just two words: "Impossible concept!" McMullan concedes, "From a writer's viewpoint, that may be true." And McMullan also admits that in the right hands, *Beyond Westworld* could very easily have been a comedy, a *Get Smart*–style show.

Despite the disappointments, working on the set was pleasant enough for the actors.

"Connie was wonderful and so was Bill," remembers McMullan. "We got along very nicely, and we had fun working together. This show was a big boost for Connie. It was a good opportunity for her to get started. ... As a matter of fact, Connie and I did a movie of the week called *She's Dressed to Kill* (1979) just after the show."

Sellecca was not present for the pilot. For reasons McMullan doesn't understand, her role was played as a different character by actress Judith Chapman. The casting was also adjusted for Foley, a sidekick legman who would implement Quaid's plans, played in the pilot by Stewart Moss and later by Severn Darden.

"Connie was just getting started," says William Jordan. "I think it was her first series. She was a very sweet, bright, able actress. She was a real delight. She still is a very pleasant person. Jim, I still see regularly. We're still good friends. I run into him every month or so. We've worked together on other projects, so it's not like it was the only one. It was kind of like a family here sometimes. And not just because of the series. It's like when you go out for different interviews and projects and you are similar in age, qualities, naturally you run into that person reading the same part."

However disappointing and unsuccessful the show was, McMullan remains fascinated by its concept and viability, so much that he declares it can be done again.

"I would love to see them do this again properly," says McMullan. "If I had the opportunity, I'd like to try to bring this back again. It was very exciting to me. You never knew *who* the robot was. The concept was simple. A villain who's disgruntled with what they were doing with his androids, pitting them back at society, doing

dastardly deeds, that's wonderful. And you have a James Bond character that I played; running around with all his expertise, being a troubleshooter, checking them out.... You never knew who the android was. That was the mystery each week. I thought the pilot was *great*, and it got fabulous reviews, and that's why they put it on opposite the toughest show on television, *Eight Is Enough*. They refused to move it. The ratings started to drop because they were fighting a show that was well ensconced."

Cast Notes

Jim McMullan (John Moore): Born 1938. McMullan has had a long career in Hollywood, with over 200 TV episodes and feature films to his credit. He's appeared in the features *Assassination* (1987), *Incredible Shrinking Woman* (1981) and *Downhill Racer* (1969); in the TV movies *Scruples* (1981) and *Francis Gary Powers Story* (1976); and in such diverse TV series as *Dallas*, *The Young and the Restless*, and *Chopper One*. Most recently, he has had a recurring role in *Baywatch*.

Connie Sellecca (Pamela Williams): See *Greatest American Hero*.

William Jordan (Professor Oppenheimer): See *Project UFO*.

Episode Guide

Westworld Destroyed
After the events of Westworld, John Moore is assigned to hunt down Simon Quaid, who has made off with a collection of androids for his own deadly purposes.

In the opener, Moore must find the renegade android aboard a U.S. nuclear submarine. Wr: Lou Shaw. Dir: Ted Post.

Capt. Farrell (Dennis Holahan); Parker (Morgan Paull); Dudley (John Kirby); Horton (Paul Henry Itkin); Sailor (Nicholas Guest); Jan (Mo Lauren); Gunfighter (Alex Kubik); Roberta (Ann McCurry).

My Brother's Keeper
Quaid blackmails an owner of the Stoner Oil company for the company's profits. John and Pamela must find the android in the company's ranks before Quaid can win. Wr: Lou Shaw and Howard Dimsdale. Dir: Rod Holcomb.

Nick Stoner (Christopher Connelly); Dean Stoner (Jeff Cooper); Earl Case (Denny Miller); Jason (John Shearin);

Danny (Bobby Van); Police officer (William Elliott); Charles Vincent (Jack Carter); Stickman (Greg Lewis); Woman (Inga Nielsen); Reporter (Frank White).

Sound of Terror

When Quaid steals uranium from a nuclear power plant, John and Pamela's mission is to find the robot in a rock band before it can be used to build a bomb. Wr: Martin Roth. Dir: Paul Stanley.

Power (Rene Auberjonois); Ruth Avery (Ronee Blakely); Lingo (Dwayne Jessie); Bobby Lee (Louis Welch); Spooner (Robert Ayers); Ryder (Lawrence Casey); Mace (Dirk Blocker); Nuclear plant guard (John Lafayette); Hakim Fader (Sirri Murad); Pilot (Hank Chorra); Doctor (Ed Bernard); Roberta (Ann McCurry); Head nurse (Mary Carver).

Takeover

A top police captain is Quaid's target when he's in charge of the state governor's visit. John and Pamela must thwart Quaid's efforts and locate the robot among the many police officers protecting the gov-

ernor. Wr: Gregory S. Dinallo, Steven Greenberg and Aubrey Solomon, story by Gregory S. Dinallo. Dir: Don Weis.

Capt. Mike Nicholson (Monte Markham); Liz Nicholson (Julie Sommars); Commander Riley (Hari Rhodes); Sgt. Al Benedek (Chip Lucia); Vickie Greene (Judy Pace); Jack Edwards (Martin Kove); Governor Eric Harper (Robert Alda); Patrick (Russell Johnson); TV reporter #1 (Robert Clarke); TV commentator (Scott Ellsworth); Jim Roberts (Arthur Roberts); Doctor (George Takei).

The Lion

When an experimental car explodes and Westworld circuitry is discovered in the wreckage, John and the Delos team must figure out Quaid's latest scheme. Wr: Martin Roth and David Bennett Carren. Dir: Jack Starrett.

Diana Lionstar (Christine Belford); Corey Burns (Michael Cole); Eric Lionstar (William Bryant); Carlos Menotti (Paul Liapis); Aldo Ortiz (Michael Pataki); Bill Johnson (Ron Trocatty); Narrator (Larry Carroll); Commentator (Robert Clarke); Roberta (Ann McCurry); Nurse (Mary Ayres); Nurse (Trish Guzey).

The Bionic Woman
January 1976–September 1978

Jaime Sommers, former tennis pro, is fitted with super-powered bionic limbs and a bionic ear after a skydiving accident. While working as a schoolteacher at an Air Force base, she goes on undercover missions for the government's intelligence division.

Starring: Jaime Sommers (Lindsay Wagner); Oscar Goldman, her boss (Richard Anderson); Dr. Rudy Wells (Martin E. Brooks); *Created by:* Kenneth Johnson; *Producers included:* Kenneth Johnson and Arthur Rowe; *Executive Producer:* Harve Bennett; ABC (1976-77); NBC (1977-78)/Universal; 60 minutes.

When it looked like *The Six Million Dollar Man* was headed for the scrap heap in early 1975, bionic man Steve Austin (Lee Majors) was given a mate to attract more viewers. As Steve's doomed high school sweetheart, Jaime accepted Steve's proposal of marriage. The storyline was born when Universal executive Frank Price wanted to grab older viewers for *The Six Million Dollar Man*. Kenneth Johnson came up with the character, naming Jaime Sommers "after a water-skier I had once met." However, Jaime Sommers lasted for only one story. Her body rejected her bionic limbs, and she died. That was supposed to be the end of the bionic woman.

"When she died, Universal was inundated with a tidal wave of telegrams and phone calls," recalls novelist Martin Caidin. "People were bitching, 'You can't kill her off.' Picketers outside the studio were raising all kinds of hell." ABC-TV received 200,000 letters, and a psychologist warned the producers that children had been deeply shaken by Jaime's death. It was clear to Universal and ABC that the bionic woman had to be brought back from the dead.

"My phone rang at 2 a.m.," recalls Caidin. "[The producers] said, 'We're starting production in a few hours on "The Return of the Bionic Woman." We have 12 people listening to you on loudspeakers and this call is being taped. How do we bring her back to life? We need an absolutely justifiable, acceptable, scientific-medical method.' I suggested cryogenics—putting her on ice. That's what they did. I had been the technical consultant on *Six Million Dollar Man* for two years and they never called me. But this one phone call was worth it to them. *The Bionic*

Lindsay Wagner, producer Kenneth Johnson and guest star Ted Cassidy (as Bigfoot) on the set of *The Bionic Woman*. Courtesy of Kenneth Johnson.

Woman turned out to be a fine series. Lindsay Wagner was fabulous."

The Six Million Dollar Man opened its third season with "The Return of the Bionic Woman." Still mourning Jaime's death, Steve Austin begins to doubt his sanity when he sees visions of her. It turns out that what he's seeing is real. Jaime Sommers has been revived from suspended animation, and new drugs have eliminated her bionic rejection. Her recovery results in partial amnesia, and she no longer knows or loves Steve Austin. The return of Jaime was a ratings smash, and ABC decided to give Jaime Sommers her own show. However, actress Lindsay Wagner, who had only guest-starred on *The Six Million Dollar Man* because it was her fourteen-year-old sister's favorite show, wasn't thrilled to be tied to a series. "Lindsay had a movie career going when she did her first guest appearance on *The Six Million Dollar Man*," recalls writer James Parriott. "She played the love interest in the film *The Paper Chase* (1973) and got fabulous reviews. She felt she was on her way to a movie career." As a Universal contract player, her contract was dropped in 1975. Ironically, her option expired during filming of her first *Six Million Dollar Man*

appearance. Executive producer Harve Bennett had to get her contract extended on a day-to-day basis to finish the shoot.

"Then the ratings for her appearance went through the roof," says Parriott. "ABC wanted to bring her back. But Lindsay's contract at Universal had lapsed by that time." Sally Field and Stephanie Powers were seriously considered as replacements, but ABC was adamant that it had to be Lindsay Wagner. This allowed Wagner, a relative newcomer to acting, to dictate terms to one of the most powerful studios in Hollywood.

"ABC and Universal kept throwing more and more money at Lindsay, trying to get her to come back," says Parriott. "At one point, Wagner's agent said, 'You've got to take it.'" Wagner, who had begun as a $162-a-week contract player, ended up being paid a substantial sum for her second appearance on *The Six Million Dollar Man* and even more for her resulting series. "But I think she regretted it," says Parriott. "She had to give up a movie career. Subsequently, her attitude was not stellar that first year and a half. She liked us, and was a hard worker and did a good job, but she had an underlying resentment about having to do *The Bionic Woman*."

"Lindsay reminded me of a young Judy Garland," says producer Harve Bennett. "She had that image of everybody's girl next door. She was also extremely bright, competitive and physical. She has a naturalness about her acting. She could also carry the action quotient believably. Another woman might have looked silly doing those stunts."

Writer Lionel Siegel agrees: "The series benefitted from Lindsay's warmth, charm, intelligence and sincerity." When *The Bionic Woman* began in January 1976, Wagner was the highest paid dramatic actress on television. However, Lee Majors was upset with having a *Bionic Woman* series spun off from his show. The actor felt Wagner's series could diminish the interest in his own series. "Lee's concern was eventually tempered by the fact that Majors was given—or more likely, he forced Universal to give him—a [financial] piece of Wagner's series," says producer Lionel Siegel.

The Bionic Woman was softer than her high-tech counterpart. Jaime taught at an Air Force base near her hometown of Ojai, California. Since her parents had been killed years ago in a car crash, she stayed with Steve Austin's parents (played by Martha Scott and Ford Rainey). Jaime's school scenes provided a comedy lilt as she occasionally disciplined her unruly class. "I believe in the gentle approach," she says as she tears a phone book in half with her bionic hands in the first episode. However, Jaime's main thrust was as a reluctant agent for the O. S. I. (Office of Strategic Intelligence), headed by her sympathetic boss, Oscar Goldman.

"We picked up tremendous things with Lindsay that we didn't have with Lee Majors," says Harve Bennett. "Lee's character was quiet and reserved. But here we had a bionic person—a woman—who could cry and tell us how she feels. So we were able to develop much more feelings in the show. In fact, Lindsay even sang the song 'Feelings' in one episode. She played an undercover nightclub singer, and Lindsay sang beautifully. Those were the things we could do with Lindsay that we were not able to do on *The Six Million Dollar Man*."

"*The Bionic Woman* had greater depth because of Lindsay," agrees unit production manager and producer Ralph Sariego. "She was a fine actress and a sensitive, lovely person. She wanted more of a dramatic show than action-adventure. On *Six Million Dollar Man*, Lee Majors didn't care. He just grunted, moved his eyebrow and

took the money. Lindsay fought for better stories and character relationships. The producers were reluctant to do that. They were more interested in a formula show, which did seem to work better in the ratings."

"Lindsay worked hard and had a great sense of humor," recalls director Larry Stewart, "but she didn't enjoy being a 9,000-pound gorilla. She wanted to play it more feminine. In one show I directed, she had to chase the bad guys into a mine shaft and throw gold carts at them. Lindsay hated that kind of stuff. There was another episode where she had to chase bad guys at a rodeo. Lindsay got pissed off with the story and walked out. The producer, Arthur Rowe, said to me, 'Boy, she really hates this script.' I said, 'Let me kick it around,' because I'm also a writer. I rewrote it as a love story set in a rodeo."

Writer Philip DeGuere recalls that the series was caught between being a superhero show and a drama. "Talk about network interference," he says. "Freddie Silverman [head of ABC programming] used to call Universal five days a week with directives on how we were supposed to do the show. Problem was, he would flip-flop between two major directives. He wanted to make Jaime into a superhero like Wonder Woman or Superwoman. His other directive was exactly the opposite: to hide her super powers and play it more natural. So I would meet with writers and tell them, 'OK, we want this to be an action-adventure show and Jaime's a superhero!' The writers would come up with a bunch of storylines. At the end of the day, Silverman had decided to go the other way. So I put away all of the superhero storylines and told the writers, 'OK, she's not a superhero anymore. We've got to do everyday stories.' So we came up with everyday-type stories. The next day, Silverman decided that he wanted her to be a superhero again. I developed a severe case of schizophrenia." DeGuere, who left the series during its first year, says, "We finally decided that the non-superhero approach was the way to go. That's how the series eventually worked. She was ladylike and operated her bionics discreetly. The conventional wisdom at the time was that an audience wouldn't buy a real strong, aggressive female character. Lindsay did very well in the role. She was fun, and I liked her as a person."

"We tended to do stories that got more into issues and character studies," says creator Kenneth Johnson. "That made the show more unique. We also had more comedy than *The Six*

Jaime (Lindsay Wagner) takes off. Copyright 1976 ABC/Universal.

Million Dollar Man. Lindsay has a wonderful sense of humor, and I used that. That's part of the reason *The Bionic Woman* took off. It wasn't just an action show. I spent a lot of time with Lindsay, developing scripts that would play into her strong suits. She was very glib and natural. After a script would be written, I'd sit in her trailer during lunch and we'd read the script out loud. She read Jaime and I read the other parts. She could embrace the dialog and make it play very comfortably."

"Lindsay was a terrific person and actress," says James Parriott. "She was best when she had a good character conflict. I liked putting her in more emotional situations, but the network still wanted an action show. In most episodes, it was the guest stars who were in conflict. Jaime was there to console and rescue them. In the best shows, it was Jaime who had the emotional and moral dilemmas." Parriott's script, "Mirror Image," won Lindsay Wagner an Emmy as best actress. In the segment, Jaime is kidnapped and replaced with an evil southern belle who, through plastic surgery, is made to look like Jaime. "That was, for me, my most rewarding work for the series," he says. However, Parriott admits that the actress never thanked him for the teleplay. "Everyone was deeply offended," he says, "not just for me but because she didn't thank anyone from the show. Everybody was going, 'Huh?' But again, Lindsay wasn't thrilled to be doing *The Bionic Woman.* That was the state of her mind at the time. Even later, when she did the two bionic film reunions (in 1987 and 1989), she did them mainly as a favor to Richard Anderson, who was the producer."

Larry Stewart has a warmer memory of Wagner's Emmy win. "At the time, I was president of the Academy of Arts and Sciences. Lindsay won the Emmy as best actress in 1976. My job as Academy president was to be backstage as the winners came off the stage. I'd take their Emmy to have it engraved for them. Lindsay and I hadn't met before, and she didn't know that the next day I was scheduled to direct a *Bionic Woman.* So when she came off the stage with her Emmy, I congratulated her and took the Emmy, promising it would be back to her in a few days. She said okay and started walking away. I yelled, 'Oh, and I'll see you tomorrow at five a.m.!' She turned around with a bewildered look of, 'What does that mean?' So the next morning, as she came out of her dressing room, the producer introduced us. 'Lindsay, meet your director.' She looked at me and said, 'Oh my God. It's you.' We got a good laugh out of that. Two days later, we were filming on the lawn of a local college in front of all of these college students. Lindsay's doing a scene where she's picking up some books. I had her engraved Emmy, and with the cameras rolling, I snuck up to her and said, 'Lindsay?' She turned around. I said, 'I thought I'd give this to you in person.' I handed her the Emmy in front of 1500 students. It was captured on film. She was extremely pleased. It was a very satisfying moment."

Important to Kenneth Johnson was keeping *The Bionic Woman* believable. "We had bionic rules that we lived by. Writers would come in and say, 'I've got an idea where Lindsay picks up a truck.' I said, 'No. Lindsay can't pick up a truck.' The writer would look at me puzzled and say, 'What do you mean? She's bionic!' I'd say, 'But she can't pick up a truck. She can turn over a car, but

Jaime (Lindsay Wagner) swings into action. Copyright 1977 ABC/Universal.

trucks are too heavy for her. She can jump up to the second floor of a building but not to the third floor.' You had to keep the credibility. Otherwise, the audience will throw up their hands and say, 'This is stupid.' That's happened to too many science fiction series. Once you decide on your rules, you've got to play by them. After I left *Bionic Woman* [in late 1977], the rules got lax. The show kind of went off the deep end. It got too far out to understand or care about."

Time and budget were constant challenges for Johnson during his *Bionic Woman* tenure. "When I worked on the *Mike Douglas* talk show back East, we did it on a dollar-and-a-quarter budget," he says. "So when I started producing *Six Million Dollar Man*, with a $500,000-per-episode budget, I said, 'Wow!'" But Johnson found the money didn't last long in the high-cost world of TV. "In many ways, doing the bionic shows was like doing the old movie serials. We had very little time. *Six Million Dollar Man* was shot in six days. After working with all of the special effects and stunts, the crew would be beat. When we did *The Bionic Woman*, it was the first Universal series to get seven days per episode.

There was a lot of to-do from the *Six Million Dollar Man* guys about that: 'Hey, how come *The Bionic Woman* gets seven days?' I said, 'Because Lindsay's makeup takes longer than Lee's, for starters.'"

Johnson's fiscal ingenuity kept *The Bionic Woman* under budget. "We did an episode with Max, the bionic dog (who wasn't my favorite premise, but the network loved him). The story had Jaime and Max trapped in a forest fire. So I went to the stock footage library and raided an old Irwin Allen movie called *Fire*. It was about a town caught in the middle of a horrific fire. There was a great sequence of a train moving through the fire. I said, 'This is great. We'll write our story so that Jaime travels on a train.' But the only train Universal had was the one on the Universal Tour. It only had about 30 feet of track. So we put Lindsay on the train, and shot 12 different angles of this train going its 30 feet. At one point, we had the train stand still and we gave it the illusion of movement by having a half-dozen extras run beside it, holding up burning trees. With the smoke blowing past the train, it made it look like it was really moving past a burning forest."

Then there was the time Johnson faked an

audience for the Miss America pageant in the episode "The Bionic Beauty." "I thought, 'How am I going to show a beauty pageant on a TV budget?' You can't do a Miss America story without Jaime walking out on stage in front of a thousand people. So we hired 100 extras, put them at the front and made the rest of the theater dark. My propman, Rick DuNarry, had his special effects guys rig up 30 flashbulbs all over the theater. When Lindsay came out on stage, the flashbulbs went off, the spotlights were flashing, and we had our crowd of 100 people. It was an illusion that worked."

As a substitute for an expensive set, Johnson once used a location inspired by a newspaper. "In "Doomsday Is Tomorrow" we needed to show Jaime running through a giant complex. My eye caught a photo in the L.A. *Times* of a great-looking tunnel that was 12 feet in diameter. It turned out to be a power station under construction outside of L.A. That gave me the idea to scout the area for other locations that nobody had used. I found some remarkable and offbeat places owned by the Department of Water and Power. In the finished episode, it looks like Jaime has traveled through this huge underground complex when actually, it was the unconstructed power station. There's also a scene where this computer tries to suffocate Jaime by filling up a tunnel with foam. We got a big foam machine that the fire department used, and it was great. We sort of pieced together the episode with nickels and dimes, but the overall look of the episode—especially when we added Joe Harnell's music—was terrific."

Ever loyal to his crews, Johnson adds, "Joe Harnell had worked with me on *The Mike Douglas Show* as musical director. I brought him out here, and I kept saying to Harve Bennett, 'We gotta use Joe—he's really good!' Harve kept putting me off. Finally, I used Joe on the Miss America episode ["The Bionic Beauty"]. Harve said, 'Geez, why haven't we used Joe before. He's great!' I punched Harve in the arm and said, 'You bozo!' Harve and I had a good relationship. I look at him as a mentor who really helped me get cooking in this town." When Johnson left *The Bionic Woman* to produce the *Incredible Hulk* pilot, he used many of the *Bionic Woman* crew. "I still work with many of the same people today," he explains. "Fortunately, they like working with me, mostly because I believe in listening to other people. So many people in this town are megalomaniacal. I don't work that way. If a grip or a makeup man has a good idea, I'll listen. You never know when they'll have a good idea. If you give them credit for that idea, you've made a friend for life."

The most famous special effect involved Jaime Sommers making her bionic leaps. "The stunt woman would jump backwards off ledges and land on an airbag," Johnson says. "Then we'd reverse the film so it looked like Jaime was leaping up on the ledge." As Ralph Sariego notes, this process required some practical costuming decisions: "We tried to keep Lindsay and her stuntgirl in pants. When they wore skirts, we had a problem keeping their skirts from jumping up during bionic leaps"—which would not only expose too much skin for a family show, but also look mighty silly when the film was shown in reverse.

However, there were more serious considerations, as Kenneth Johnson states flatly: "It was dangerous. It's not easy to jump backward, blind and straight. Rita Eggleston was Lindsay's double, and Vince Deadrick, Sr., doubled for Lee Majors. They got incredibly adept at making these things look real.

"We had one script that called for Lindsay Wagner to jump up to a second-floor of a balcony. Normally, Rita would stand on the balcony railing and jump backward. This time she said to me, 'I've got an idea. Watch this.' She stood up on the balcony railing and jumped forward, onto the balcony, which didn't make any sense to me. Then I realized that she had put a mini-trampoline on the balcony. When she landed on the balcony's mini-trampoline, that propelled her backward, over the railing and into the airbag on the ground. When you reverse that film, you got a woman flying up toward the building and gliding right over the railing and into the balcony. We cut the film just before Rita hit the mini trampoline. So it was a very subtle but smooth effect. Rita was constantly developing ways to enhance the jumps and make them better. She worked her ass off for *The Bionic Woman*. She was also a dead ringer of Lindsay from ten feet away. People couldn't tell them apart. Rita also did most of the running for Lindsay. Lindsay, bless her heart, *can* walk, act and chew gum, but when it comes to being physical, oy! We really had to labor to make her look like a tennis pro on the show. She wasn't a sportswoman, but she was always game and was the first one to say, 'Let me try that!' So she'd try it. We'd say, 'Ok, Rita, come on in!'"

Even so, says writer Lionel Siegel, "the physical feats Lindsay had to do were taxing. Physically, it was a tough show to do."

When *The Bionic Woman* finished its second year in 1977, ABC made a stunning announcement: They were cancelling the show, despite its number 14 finish in the ratings. Universal pitched the series to NBC, who purchased the show for 1977-78. "We were pulling a 30 share when ABC canceled us," says James Parriott. "ABC felt that *Bionic Woman* was slipping, and their researcher told them, 'Drop the show while it's still hot and get something else in there because *Bionic Woman* is gonna fail next season.' They may have been right, because we went over to NBC and only lasted a season."

"It got a reprieve by moving to NBC," continues Harve Bennett. "But in moving to NBC, we lost the crossover appearances of Steve Austin on *Bionic Woman* and Jaime on *Six Million Dollar Man*. We could only do this while both shows were on ABC. So we couldn't perk up the shows that way. We also lost the potential that Steve and Jaime might restart their love affair."

The show's move to NBC gave Ralph Sariego the chance to produce an episode. "Universal promised Fred Silverman [now head of NBC programming] a show where Jaime would fight sharks. After a few episodes, Silverman called them and said, 'Where's my shark story?' So I was allowed to produce the shark show. I spent two months reading books on sharks and looking at shark footage from all over the world. I'd always been a sun-and-surf guy, but to this day, based on what I saw in those films, I'm afraid to go into the water. We shot the episode off the coast of California. We used real sharks—a 12-foot and 9-foot nurse shark—and had a double for Lindsay. Every morning we put ropes on the tail of the sharks and filmed their run-bys. On the last day of filming, the sharks were so tired that we took the ropes off them. It was a great adventure for one episode."

When it looked clear that *The Bionic Woman* wouldn't be picked up for a fourth year, Lindsay Wagner asked writer Steven de Souza to write a finale. "She told me over lunch, 'I feel Jaime Sommers has never been comfortable as a tool of the government. She's basically a peace-loving person, and she's only doing it because she's grateful the O.S.I. saved her life. What would happen if they called her one evening and told her she had to be airborne to Russia that night...and she doesn't want to do it anymore?' So I wrote a story that really brought that to the fore."

De Souza found the script proved a perfect mirror for Wagner's real-life situation: "Lindsay,

who was tired of doing a network show, played Jaime Sommers, who was tired of being a spy. Jaime quits her job, and suddenly she's confronted by a government man who she's never seen before. He tells her she can't quit. She tries to run, and these people, who are like the evil C.I.A., are chasing her. It was a great opportunity to turn the series upside down. In the end, because *Bionic Woman* was going into syndication, we had to put a little coda where she says, 'OK, one more mission.' Even though these government guys framed her for a murder, tried to shoot hypodermics into her, tried to kidnap her, drugged her dog, and fired Oscar Goldman from the O.S.I., she says, 'Okay, I'll keep working for the government.' On that level it was phoney. In general, though, the episode was a great switch."

Had the series continued, there were plans to capitalize on the popularity of the film *Close Encounters of the Third Kind*, and reunite all of the alien characters who had appeared on *The Bionic Woman* for an intergalactic get-together. When the series ended, Harve Bennett was philosophical. "The series had gotten more expensive every year because it took longer to shoot," he says. "For that reason, Universal was less anxious to continue it than *The Six Million Dollar Man*. But I'd say we squeezed out as many years as we could from what the industry calls 'high concept' shows."

Director Larry Stewart sums up the feelings of many of the *Bionic Woman* team by saying, "It was a fine series. It was action-adventure-myth, and it humanized its premise to a great degree. It worked out well. Nobody has anything to be ashamed of with that show."

CAST NOTES

Lindsay Wagner (Jaime): Born 1949, a former rock singer and model, Wagner got her first big movie break in *The Paper Chase* (1973). She has starred in many TV movies in the 1980s and 1990s.

Richard Anderson (Oscar): See *The Six Million Dollar Man* listing.

EPISODE GUIDE

Season 1: 1976

Welcome Home, Jaime
An industrialist is determined to film Jaime in

bionic action so that he can sell her to a foreign country. Wr: Kenneth Johnson. Dir: Alan Crosland, Jr.

Carlton Harris (Dennis Patrick); Helen Elgin (Martha Scott); Jim Elgin (Ford Rainey); Don Harris (Kip Niven); Charles Butler (Gordon Jump); Sayers (Robert Bralver); Bailey (Nick Pellegrino); Teddy (Christian Juttner); Gwen (Alycia Gardner); Joey (Kraig Metzinger).

Angel of Mercy
Jaime and an American pilot get caught behind enemy lines while trying to rescue an American couple from a collapsed building. Wr: James D. Parriott. Dir: Alan Levi.

Jack Starkey (Andy Griffith); George Morehouse (James Karen); Julio (Claudio Martinez); Judith Morehouse (Jean Allison); Andrew (Robbie Rist); Guerilla (Bert Santos); Soldier (Paul Berrones).

A Thing of the Past
Bus driver Harry Anderson gets publicity for a heroic deed, but it could cost him his life: he went into hiding after witnessing a murder. Wr: Philip DeGuere, Jr., story by Terrence McDonnell, Jim Carlson. Dir: Alan Crosland, Jr.

Harry Anderson (Donald O' Connor); Glen Morgan (Don Gordon); Stone (Roger Perry); Steve Austin (Lee Majors); Raines (W. T. Zacha); Teddy (Christian Juttner); Gwen (Alycia Gardner); Mark (Robbie Walcott); Mills (Brian Cutler); Caroline (Lori Busk).

Claws
A peaceful African lion is blamed for livestock killings. Jaime has to protect the animal from angry ranchers. Wr: Sue Milburn. Dir: Phil Bondelli.

Susan Victor (Tippi Hedren); Uncle Bill (William Schallert); Charles Keys (Jack Kelly); Katie (Alicia Fleer); Rancher (George Wallace); Sheriff (Mills Watson); Andrew (Robbie Rist).

The Deadly Missiles
A tycoon is wrongly accused of using his ranch as a missile site. Jaime tries to nail the real culprits. Wr: Wilton Denmark. Dir: Alan J. Levi.

J. T. Connors (Forrest Tucker); Steve (Lee Majors); Warren Riker (Ben Piazza); Katie (Alicia Fleer); Teddy (Christian Juttner); Guard (Gary McLarty).

The Bionic Beauty
Jaime enters a rigged beauty pageant and learns Miss Florida will be delivering top secret microchips to enemy agents. Wr: James D. Parriott. Dir: Alan Crosland, Jr.

Sally Bartell (Cassie Yates); Ray Raymond (Bert Parks); Helen (Martha Scott); Brady (Gary Crosby); Mrs. Belding (Helen Craig); Reporter (Charlotte Moore); Man (Henry Pollick); Miss Tennessee (Lisa Parks); Miss Oklahoma (Katie Hopkins Zerby).

Jaime's Mother
Oscar investigates a woman claiming to be Jaime's mother, who was reportedly killed some years before. Wr: Arthur Rowe and Worley Thorne. Dir: Leo Penn.

Ann Sommers (Barbara Rush); Mrs. Noah (Norma Connolly); Mark Russell (Sam Chew, Jr.); Vic Boylin (Joseph George); Henderson (Dan Barton); Jaime as child (Carlene Gower).

Winning Is Everything
Jaime competes in a motor race to find a vital cassette tape before enemy agents do. Wr: James D. Parriott. Dir: Phil Bondelli.

Carlo Scappini (Alejandro Rey); Tim Sanders (John Elerick); Russian woman (Nancy Jeris); Bartender (Frank Cala); Attendant (Rene Assa); Man (Stephen Coit).

Canyon of Death
An Indian student can't get anyone to believe that he saw thieves stealing flying suits that could undermine American security. Wr: Stephen Kandel. Dir: Jerry London.

Mallory (Gary Collins); Karen (Dee Timberlake); Paco (Guillermo San Juan); Henderson (Paul Covonis); Andrew (Robbie Rist); Briggs (Don McGovern); Elora (Annette Cardona); Phillips (Jack Stauffer); Radioman (Jim Ingersoll); Gen. Fuller (Bill Conklin); Stan (Todd London); Felicity (Nina Weintraub).

Fly Jaime
Stranded on a remote island, Jaime tries to protect Rudy from assassins. Wr: Arthur Rowe, Mann Rubin, story by Mann Rubin. Dir: Barry Crane.

Marlow (Christopher Stone); Connors (Jerry Douglas); Reed (Spencer Milligan); Romero (Vito Scotti); Mrs. Griffith (Arline Anderson); Pilot (Dick Valentine); Co-pilot (Jim Raymond).

The Jailing of Jaime
Jaime grasps at straws to clear her name after being jailed for betraying her country. Wr: Bruce Shelly. Dir: Alan Crosland, Jr.

Dr. Ellis Hatch (Barry Sullivan); John Naud (Philip Abbott); Cindy Wilson (Anne Schedeen); Gregory (Skip Homeier); Carlson (Ron Hayes); Gen Partridge (Ross Elliot); Ted Ryan (Tom Bower); Mark Russell (Sam Chew, Jr.).

Mirror Image
A plastic surgeon creates a sinister duplicate of Jaime. Wr: James D. Parriott. Dir: Alan J. Levi.

Dr. Jim Courtney (Don Porter); Boxley (Herb Jefferson, Jr.); Matthews (Terry Kiser); Mark Russell (Sam Chew); Perkins (John Fink); Tipsey (Harry Wiere); Bartender (Fuddle Bagley); Intern (Chris Barrett).

The Ghost Hunter
Jaime poses as a governess in a mansion plagued by ghostly events that tie in with a scientist's work. Wr: Kenneth Johnson, Justin Edgerton. Dir: Kenneth Johnson.

Amanda Cory (Kristy McNichol); Alan Cory (Paul

Shenar); Emil Laslo (Bo Brundin); Nurse (Merry Lomis); Lisa (Susan Fleming).

Memory Flash—Kenneth Johnson: "I cast a 14-year-old Kristy McNichol. I think it was like her second gig in the industry. She was great. In fact, I read her and Valerie Bertinelli for the part. I didn't hire Valerie because even at 14 she was too sexy."

Season 2: 1976-77

The Return of Bigfoot
The Bigfoot android, programmed for destruction by a renegade alien, delays Jaime's efforts to retrieve serum to save Steve's life. Continued from an episode of *The Six Million Dollar Man*. Wr: Kenneth Johnson. Dir: Barry Crane.
Shalon (Stefanie Powers); Nedlik (John Saxon); Bigfoot (Ted Cassidy); Gillian (Sandy Duncan); Dallett (Stephen Young); Apploy (Severn Darden); Steve (Lee Majors); Faler (Charles Cyphers); Pilot (Jim Gavin).

In This Corner, Jaime Sommers
Jaime poses as a wrestler to investigate an agent's disappearance. Wr: Robert L. McCullough, Kenneth Johnson, story by Robert L. McCullough. Dir: Alan Crosland, Jr.
Dr. Brandes (Marj Dusay); Bigelow (Norman Fell); April Armitage (Marcia Lewis); Mary Maddox (Marsha Shapiro); Esther (Margaret Shocklee); Referee (Gene Le Belle); Jimmy Lynon (Lew Palter); Wayne Haley (Brett Dunham); Epstein (Bill Keene); Man (Bill Conklin); Battling Betty (Sandy Parker).

Assault on the Princess
Unstable energy cells hidden aboard a casino ship will explode unless Jaime can locate the double agent who stole them. Wr: Wilton Denmark. Dir: Alan Crosland, Jr.
Lucky Harrison (Ed Nelson); Romero (Vito Scotti); Grover (John Durren); Tanner (Steve Kanaly); Ice man (Dick Dinman); Creighton (Tony Giorgio); Joe (Ron Wilson); Lt. (Abraham Alvarez); Crewman (Don Maxwell).

The Road to Nashville
Jaime suspects friendly country singer Buck Buckley is being used to carry top secret codes to enemy agents. Wr: James Parriott. Dir: Alan J. Levi.
Big Buck Buckley (Hoyt Axton); Penn Mathers (Bert Kramer); Muffin Calhoun (Doc Severinson); Tammy Dalton (Fionnula Flanagan); Bill Womullun (Scott Arthur Allen); Announcer (Dick Haynes); Pam (Robin Harlan); Harold (Roy Daniels, Jr.).

Kill Oscar, Part 1
Oscar is taken prisoner by an army of android women. They're controlled by a scientist who wants to steal a weather machine. Wr: Arthur Rowe, story by Arthur Rowe, Oliver Crawford. Dir: Alan Crosland, Jr.

Dr. Franklin (John Houseman); Steve (Lee Majors); Lynda Wilson (Corinne Michaels); Katy (Janice Whitby); Baron Constantine (Jack Colvin); Callahan (Jennifer Darling); Hanson (Jack Ging); Rawlins (John Dewey-Carter); Gen. Williams (Eugene Peterson).

Kill Oscar, Part 3 (Part 2 of this story was aired on *The Six Million Dollar Man*)
Steve and Jaime endure a hurricane and Fembot androids to break Dr. Franklin's stronghold. Wr: Arthur Rowe, story by Arthur Rowe, Oliver Crawford, Wilton Schiller. Dir: Alan Crosland, Jr.
Dr. Franklin (John Houseman); Steve (Lee Majors); Hanson (Jack Ging); Gordon (Jim McMullan); Callahan (Jennifer Darling); Lynda Wilson (Corinne Michaels); Katy (Janice Whitby); Rawlins (John Dewey Carter); Admiral Wilkins (Byron Morrow); Adm. Ricter (Sam Jaffe).

Black Magic
Jaime stays at a spooky mansion to find out which family member is planning to sell a special alloy. Wr: Arthur Rowe. Dir: Barry Crane.
Manfred/Cyrus Carstairs (Vincent Price); Warfield (William Windom); Claudette (Julie Newmar); Tess (Hermoine Baddely); Barlow (Abe Vigoda); Barry (Alvah Stanley); Maitre'd (Roger Til); Boatman (George N. Margo).

Sister Jaime
Posing as a nun, Jaime tries to find missing diamonds, whose theft was blamed on a priest. Wr: Kenneth Johnson. Dir: Alan J. Levi.
Mother Superior (Kathleen Nolan); Sister Barbara (Ellen Geer); Sister Beverly (Catherine Burns); Father Thomas (Ron Hayes); Sister Margo (Dran Hamilton); Marlene Stoler (Cynthia Whitham); Trucker (Al Hansen).

The Vega Influence
An alien life form, awakened from the permafrost, takes over people's minds. Wr: Arthur Rowe. Dir: Mel Damski.
Laurie Boylin (Jamie Smith Jackson); Mike Marchetti (Rick Lenz); Andrews (Philip Carey); Capt. Colter (Don Marshall); Dr. Boylin (Roy Poole); Sgt. Roberts (John Lawrence).

Jaime's Shield, Part 1
Jaime, posing as a police cadet, befriends a troubled fellow cadet as she tries to ferret out an enemy agent. Wr: James Parriott. Dir: Alan Crosland, Jr.
Bob Welton (George Maharis); Herb Partnow (Linden Chiles); Arlene Hart (Diane Civita); Parker (Rebecca Balding); Commissioner Hart (Arch Johnson); Capt. Godfrey (James McEachin); Jetton (William Bryant); Rosignano (Amy Joyce); Baxter (Mike Santiago).

Jaime's Shield, Part 2
Jaime and her friend are to escort Premier Gabrin's motorcade, but enemy agents plan to kill the two cadets and replace them with assassins. Wr: James D. Parriott. Dir: Barry Crane.

Bob Welton (George Maharis); Arlene Hart (Diane Civita); Herb Partnow (Linden Chiles); Comm. Hart (Arch Johnson); Parker (Rebecca Balding); Jetton (William Bryant); Gabrin (Amapola Del Vando).

Biofeedback

Jaime's efforts to recover a top secret code analyzer from East Germany is complicated by the relationship between two brothers. Wr: Dan Kibbie, story by Kenneth Johnson. Dir: Alan J. Levi.

Payton Jones (Peter Haskell); Ivan Karp (Lloyd Bochner); Darwin Jone (Granville Van Dusen); Narek (Jan Aaris); Terry (Inge Lindgreen).

Doomsday Is Tomorrow, Parts 1 and 2

A peace-loving scientist puts his doomsday device in the control of a super computer in hopes it will scare the world into peaceful co-existence. In Part 2, Jaime tries to disarm the computer, but first she must get through its defenses. Wr and Dir: Kenneth Johnson.

Dr. Elija Cooper (Lew Ayres); Satari (David Opatoshu); Victor Dimitri (Kenneth O'Brien); Mark Russell (Sam Chew); Kurosawa (James Hong); Alex (Guerin Barry); Technician (Ed Vasgersian); Navigator (Stack Pierce); Pilot (Ned Wilson).

Memory Flash—Kenneth Johnson: "I did some work on *The Bionic Woman* that I was very proud of. This episode was one of my favorites. Jaime had to take on a computer to stop a doomsday machine from trashing the world. It was a sort of philosophical piece too. Working with Lew Ayres was terrific. He's not only a great pacifist, as I am, but a wonderful actor."

Deadly Ringer, Parts 1 and 2

Jaime is kidnapped, and her villainous duplicate, Lisa Galloway, replaces her in the O.S.I. In Part 2, Lisa uses a drug to give herself super-powers. Jaime escapes from prison and is hunted by authorities. Wr: James D. Parriott. Dir: Alan J. Levi.

Dr. James Courtney (Don Porter); Dr. Harkens (Katherine Helmond); Warden Cooper (Warren Kemmerling); Woody (Donald "Red" Barry); Weber (John Zenda); O'Hanian (Don Fenwick).

Jaime and the King

To protect a shah, Jaime poses as a tutor for his son. Her life is jeopardized when an evil prince discovers her true identity. Wr: Robert L. McCullough, C. Robert Brooks, Arthur Rowe. Dir: Alan Crosland, Jr.

Ali Ben Gazim (Robert Loggia); Prince Ishmail (Lance Kerwin); Hassan (Joseph Ruskin); Ezelda (Brioni Farrell); Marahna (Tanya L. George); Emerlad (Annette Cardona).

Beyond the Call

Jaime must locate a runaway girl and stop the girl's father from stealing a missile guidance system. Wr:

Dan Kibbie, Arthur Rowe, story by Dan Kibbie. Dir: Alan J. Levi.

John Cross (Sam Groom); Kim (Mariel Aragon); Col. Banning (Sandy Ward); Willet (Madison Arnold); Luddick (Ron McCabe).

The Dijon Caper

Jaime and an art forger join forces in Paris to nail a thief but her cover is blown when she's arrested. Wr: Arthur Rowe. Dir: Barry Crane.

Pierre Lambert (Rene Auberjonois); Moreau (Sydney Chaplin); Alain (Erik Holland); Rochette (Roger Til); Fournier (Ben Wright); Beaumont (Bernard Behrens); 1st gendarme (Maurice Marsac).

Night Demon

A shady rancher is using a man-made demon to scare people. Wr: Justin Edgerton. Dir: Alan J. Levi.

Lyle Cannon (Gary Lockwood); Thomas Bearclaw (Jeff Corey); Capt. Anders (Jay J. Saunders); Don Woods (Howard McGillin); Hawkins (John Quade).

Iron Ships and Dead Men

The skeleton of Oscar's brother Sam is found in a sunken ship at Pearl Harbor. Jaime investigates when rumors surface that Sam was a traitor during the 1941 Japanese attack. Wr: James D. Parriott. Dir: Mel Damski.

Bob Richards (Ray Young); Duke (Stephen Elliot); Zanetos (Edward Walsh); Warner Williams (Ted Wilson).

Once a Thief

Jamie infiltrates a group of bank robbers, but finds herself an outlaw when she's forced to rob a bank. Wr: Kenneth Johnson. Dir: Alan J. Levi.

Inky (Elisha Cook); Saul (Ed Barth); Capt. Blank (William Boyett); Rogers (Dick Balduzzi); Talvin (Dick Bakalyan); Reggie (Fuddle Bagley); Marchese (Sonny Klein); Steinhauer (Frank Cala).

Season 3: 1977-78

The Bionic Dog, Part 1

The O.S.I. may kill Max, the bionic dog, because of his erratic behavior. Jaime and Max run away into the mountains, and Jaime learns Max's condition is caused by a fear of fire. Wr: James D. Parriott, story by Harve Bennett, James Parriott. Dir: Barry Crane.

Judy McHugh (Carlene Watkins); Crosby (Taylor Lacher); Harley (Will Hare).

The Bionic Dog, Part 2

When a forest fire erupts in the woods, Max goes berserk, leaving Jaime and a forest ranger trapped in the inferno. Wr: James D. Parriott, story by Harve Bennett, James Parriott. Dir: Barry Crane.

Roger Grette (Dale Robinette); Harley (Will Hare); Bill Tyler (Lee Jones De Broux); Sheriff (Jack Garner); Old man (Jason Johnson); Trucker (Al Hansen).

Fembots in Las Vegas, Part 1

Jaime tries to rescue a scientist from the army of killer fembots, who are out to snatch his energy weapon. Wr: Arthur Rowe. Dir: Michael Preece.

Rod Kyler (James Olson); Tami (Melinda Fee); Carl Franklin (Michael Burns); Callahan (Jennifer Darling); Nancy (Jeannie Wilson); Gina (Nancy Bleir); Billie (Lorna Sands); Ellen (Lisa Moore); Dan Mayers (Alexander Courtney).

Fembots in Las Vegas, Part 2

Dr. Franklin launches the energy weapon into space and orders his army of robots to kill Jaime and Oscar. Wr: Arthur Rowe. Dir: Michael Preece.

Carl Franklin (Michael Burns); Rod Kyler (James Olson); Tami (Melinda Fee); Callahan (Jennifer Darling); Nancy (Jeannie Wilson); Gina (Nancy Bleir); Billie (Lorna Sands); Ellen (Lisa Moore); Lt. Rogers (Ted Schliesman).

Rodeo

Enemy agents want to plunder a rodeo rider's mind for a vital secret code. Wr: Herman Groves, story by Kenneth Johnson. Dir: Larry Stewart.

Billy Cole (Andrew Prine); Crowley (John Crawford); Radnick (Jason Evers); Janos (Thomas Bellin); Teak (Don Gentry).

The African Connection

Freedom fighters capture Jaime and an English agent, mistaking them for allies of a dictator in Africa. Wr: William Schwartz. Dir: Alan J. Levi.

Harry Walker (Dan O' Herlihy); Azzar (Raymond St. Jacques); Leona Mumbassa (Joan Pringle); Hopper (Marc Alaimo); Duma (Don Pedro Colley); Serrano (Kipp Whitman).

The Motorcycle Boogie

Daredevil rider Evel Kneivel helps Jaime retrieve a computer reel in West Germany. He must jump his bike over the Berlin wall. Wr: James D. Parriott, Kenneth Johnson. Dir: Ken Gilbert.

Evel Kneivel (as Himself); Petrov (Bernard Behrens); Schmidt (Spencer Milligan); Guard #1 (Chris Anders); Guard #2 (Erik Holland).

Memory Flash—creator Kenneth Johnson: "This was done around the time Evel Kneivel was working on a stunt to bail out of a plane without a parachute and land in a bale of hay in the middle of a stadium. Evel was amazing, but he was a banana! He invited [the *Bionic Woman* producers] to dinner, but we ended up paying! He would say to the waiter, 'Bring me a bottle of Rothschilds!' So they brought him this 100-dollar bottle of wine. He autographed it and gave it to me. 'Here you go, Kenny! It's from me to you, pal. My pal, Kenny!' Who do you think ended up paying for the wine?"

Brain Wash

Callahan is revealing top secrets, leading Jaime to an enemy hairdresser who uses a shampoo to brainwash O.S.I. personnel. Wr: James D. Parriott. Dir: Michael Preece.

John Bernard (Michael Callan); Benny (David Watson); Callahan (Jennifer Darling); Mark Russell (Sam Chew); Pineda (Pepe Hern).

Escape to Love

Jaime tries to rescue the son of a scientist from behind the Iron Curtain. Wr: Ellen Wittman, Lionel Siegel. Dir: Alan J. Levi.

Arlo Kelso (Philip Abbott); Dubnov (Peter Mark Richman); Sandor Kelso (Mitch Laurence); Hober (John Reilly); Pruska (Michael Richardson); Rodi (Ed Sancho-Bonet).

Memory Flash—Lionel Siegel: "When it was decided that I would do the *Bionic Woman* series, I had dinner with Lindsay Wagner [and her boyfriend, Michael Brandon]. I drank too much and accepted their invitation to follow them home. I ended up on their bathroom floor, practically unable to move, and I slept there. I left them a note early in the morning before I left. That was my first day on the job with Lindsay."

Max

Max, the bionic canine, and a female scientist are kidnapped by agents who want to study Max's bionics. Wr: William Schwartz, story by William Schwartz, Lionel E. Siegel. Dir: Don McDougall.

Valerie Breuer (Neile Adams-McQueen); Bobby (Christopher Knight); Jack Carson (Rudy Solari); Yvon Sanders (Sandy Kenyon); Mark Russell (Sam Chew); Hobbs (Bill Fletcher).

The Over the Hill Spy

A bitter ex-agent returns to duty to battle his nemesis, a master of disguises. Wr: Joe Viola. Dir: Ken Gilbert.

Terence Quinn (Richard Erdman); Boris Slotsky (Michael Thoma); Vilmos Vanovic (Jeff David); Juan Robles (Felice Orlandi); Wolfe (Whit Bissell); Carol (Alana Collins); Manning (Rick Buckner).

All for One

Jaime locates a computer hacker and learns that criminals are going to use his skills. Wr: James D. Parriott. Dir: Larry Stewart.

Tom Tharp (Roger Perry); Benny (Franklyn Ajaye); Mrs. Simpson (Viola Kates Stimpson); Raul (Garret Pearson); Stubbs (Gary Barton); Mango (Henry Kingi); Mr. A. A (Joe Al Nicassio).

The Pyramid

Trapped in a pyramid, Jaime discovers an alien sentinel, who must contact his spaceship before it reaches the atmosphere and unwittingly causes Earth's destruction. Wr: Margaret Armen, Alf Harris. Dir: Barry Crane.

Ky (Eduard Franz); Chris Williams (Christopher Stone); Jim Burns (Gavan O'Herlihy); Laura Kane (June Barrett); Inca warrior (Henri Kingi).

Memory Flash—Margaret Armen: "The interesting thing in writing for a female lead was that you could use her feminine reactions. In this episode, we could show a growing attraction between Jaime and the alien. At first, I was not impressed by the *Bionic Woman* series and I didn't care for Lindsay Wagner's acting, but I got to like her work."

The Antidote
An enemy nurse plans to kill a poisoned Jaime. Meanwhile Chris searches for Dr. Wells, who has the antidote. Wr: Arthur Rowe, Tom and Helen August, story by Dan Ullman. Dir: Don McDougall.
    Chris Williams (Christopher Stone); Henderson (John Milford); Nurse (Suzanne Charny); Dr. Hamilton (Brett Halsey); Carson (James Blendick); Callahan (Jennifer Darling); Sarah (Linda Wiser); Dmitiri Zhukov (John Myhers).

The Martians Are Coming, the Martians Are Coming
Jaime suspects a terrestrial explanation when Oscar sees Rudy beamed up by a hovering U.F.O. Wr: Robert A. Urso, Tom and Helen August, story by Robert Urso. Dir: Larry Stewart.
    Ray Fisk (Jack Kelly); Spencer (Frank Aletter); Bill Robbins (Frank Marth); Casey (Jim McMullan); Norma Fisk (Lynn Carlin); Nena (Amanda Davies).

Sanctuary: Earth
Jaime befriends Aura, a young alien princess on the run from killer aliens. Wr: Rudolph Borchert, story by Craig Schiller, Tom and Helen August. Dir: Ernest Pintoff.
    Aura (Helen Hunt); Chris (Christopher Stone); Verm (Jim Hager); Dier (Jon Hager); Belden (David Matthew).

Trivia Alert: On the NBC show *Later* with Bob Costas, Helen Hunt admitted that if she could burn one piece of film, this episode of *The Bionic Woman* would be it.

Deadly Music
Scuba diving to investigate submarine detection sabotage, Jaime is unaware that enemy agents plan to kill her with sharks. Wr: Conner Everts, Lionel Siegel. Dir: Thomas Connors.
    Jed Kimball (Frank Converse); Anton Dasovic (Henry Darrow); Henry Klempt (Robert Ellenstein); Frank Dade (Roger Cruz); Ritter (Chip Lucia); Steve (Greg Barnett); Reese (Igus Darrow); Marsden (James Crittenden).

Which One Is Jaime?
Callahan is captured and used as bait to lure the bionic woman into a trap. Wr: Jim Carlson, Terrence McDonnell, story by Martha Humphreys, Ted Pederson. Dir: Jack Arnold.
    Jack Stratton (Brock Peters); Callahan (Jennifer Darling); Mark Russell (Sam Chew); Roger Fowler (Regis J. Cordic); Ray Burns (James B. Sikking); Eddie Dwyer (Robert Feero); Julie (Adrien Royce); Colin Lee (Marcus Mukai).

Out of Body
Captured and tied to a bomb, Jaime's only hope of rescue is from the spirit of Tommy Littlehorse, who lies in a coma but is having an out-of-body experience. Wr: Steven de Souza, story by Steven de Souza, Deborah Blum. Dir: Ernest Pintoff.
    Philip Jennings (Nehemiah Persoff); Tommy Littlehorse (Charlie Hill); Denton (Richard Lynch); Mauro (Antony Ponzini); Jacoby (Allan Magicovski).

Long Live the King
Assassins target Jaime so that they can assassinate a Middle Eastern king. Wr: Mel Goldberg, David Ketchum, Tony De Marco, Tom and Helen August. Dir: Gwen Arner.
    Sam Sloan (John Reilly); King Kusari (Carmen Argenziano); Byron (Brian Burgess); Kia (Rene Assa); Sharokah (Dov Gottsfeld); Beth (Elise Cattlin); Lynette (Rachel Bard).

Rancho Outcast
Jaime goes undercover to a Central American compound to recover currency plates. Wr: Arthur Rowe. Dir: Ivan Dixon.
    Gustave (Keenan Wynn); Petrie "The Weasel" Regan (Donald Calfa); Madeline (Diane Civita); Colonel (Robert Easton); Janos (Dave Cass); Agent (George Cheung); One Eyed One (Henry Kingi).

On the Run
Jaime finds herself on the run from her own government when she learns her resignation from the O.S.I. means confinement to a retirement compound. Wr: Steven de Souza. Dir: Tom Blank.
    Chris Williams (Christopher Stone); Parr (Andrew Duggan); Renshaw (Skip Homeier); Sarah (Linda Wiser); Salesman (Kenneth O'Brien); Harding (Juno Dawson); Reiko (Mariel Aragon); Tommy (Johnny Timko); Balloon man (Bob Benedetti); Black woman (Hannah Dean).

Buck Rogers in the Twenty-Fifth Century

September 1979–April 1981

Space Probe III, *piloted by Capt. William "Buck" Rogers, is thrown off course by meteors in the year 1987. Frozen in suspended animation when his life-support systems fail, Buck awakens in the year 2491.*

Befriended by Dr. Elias Huer and Col. Wilma Deering in New Chicago, Buck joins the Earth Federation as a pilot to ensure the safety of Earth from alien forces.

In the second year, Buck and Wilma command the spaceship Searcher *with their new alien ally, Hawk. They explore the galaxy and search for humans who fled Earth during the nuclear holocaust hundreds of years ago.*

Cast: Captain William "Buck" Rogers (Gil Gerard); Col. Wilma Deering (Erin Gray); Dr. Elias Huer (year 1) (Tim O' Connor); Hawk (year 2) (Thom Christopher); Twiki (Felix Silla); Twiki's voice (Mel Blanc, Bob Elyea); Dr. Goodfellow (year 2) (Wilfred Hyde-White); Admiral Asimov (year 2) (Jay Garner); Dr. Theopolis's voice (Eric Server); Crichton's voice (year 2) (Jeff David); Narrator (year 1) (William Conrad); Narrator (year 2) (Hank Sims).

Based on the character created by: Philip F. Nowlan; *Developed for television by:* Glen A. Larson, Leslie Stevens; *Producers:* (year 1) David O'Connell, John Gaynor; (year 2) John Stephens, Calvin Clements, Sr.; *Executive Producer:* (year 1): Bruce Lansbury; *Executive Producer:* (year 2): John Mantley; NBC/Universal; 60 minutes.

Buck Rogers' rockets fizzled the first time he tried to blast off in a TV series. In 1950, a live, videotaped New York production starred Kem Dibbs as Buck, Lou Prentiss as Wilma and Harry Sothern as Dr. Huer. After a few episodes, Robert Pastene stepped in as Buck. The series, done on an extremely low budget, was creaky even by primitive TV standards and exhausted its welcome within a year. Buck had been a lot more successful as a comic strip in the newspapers (1931-1956), and in 1939 Buster Crabbe played him in the movie. (Crabbe was better known as another comic hero, Flash Gordon). In 1967, ABC-TV got serious and agreed to mount an expensive Buck Rogers series using state-of-the-art special effects. Buck was going to be portrayed as a witty superhero in this MGM production. The project burned out during the storyboard stage.

With the success of the film *Star Wars* in 1977, and the popularity of *Battlestar Galactica* a year later, Universal studios decided to launch a Buck Rogers series for the 1979-80 season. According to writer Dorothy C. Fontana, it took awhile for the studio and network to decide what kind of series they wanted.

"Originally, Buck Rogers was planned as a series of two-hour movies," she says. "My brother, Richard, and I wrote a two-hour script for producer Leslie Stevens. Unfortunately, Universal decided to go ahead with an hour format instead. The next producer, Andrew Fenady, had a different take on the series. This would have been a true adventure series. Fenady had a good sense of character and the action-adventure genre. David Gerrold was on that version as story editor."

This version was also aborted during the script stage, and the next metamorphosis took Buck into the orbit of campy adventure. "There was too much emphasis on Buck being just a happy-go-lucky kinda guy, with too many jokes and cute characters, including the beede-beede-be robot [Twiki]," says Fontana. "The versions that would have worked best would have been the Leslie Stevens two-hour movies."

Stevens and writer Glen A. Larson, who had just finished *Battlestar Galactica*, joined forces to create the light-hearted version of *Buck Rogers.* "I wrote a two-hour script with Leslie Stevens and that's what sold the series to Universal," claims Larson. Larson and Stevens had a good working relationship that dated back almost a decade. "I had been a protege of Leslie's many years earlier on *McCloud*, and we worked together on *Battlestar Galactica.* He had great style and wit. We flew to Hawaii to discuss the *Buck Rogers* script, and Leslie lay on the beach at night and stared up at the constellations. He knew them

Left to right: Guest star Buster Crabbe (the original Buck Rogers in the 1939 serial) poses with Erin Gray (Wilma) and Gil Gerard (Buck Rogers). Copyright 1979 NBC/Universal.

completed, Larson's involvement with the weekly series was minimal. "I only supervised or hired people who produced the episodes. One thing I didn't want either *Battlestar Galactica* or *Buck Rogers* to become was a monster-of-the-week show. That represents the poorest level of writing. I wanted them to represent good drama with some intellectually challenging concepts. That viewpoint was not necessarily shared by the people who produced the weekly *Buck Rogers* series. They did their own thing, and I'm not going to knock them. I had been paid handsomely by the studio [to do the pilot], and I had other things to work on."

It's a wonder actor Tim O' Connor ended up playing Dr. Elias Huer on the series. As a small child, he had had trouble pulling off his Buck Rogers space helmet. "The darn bubble on top of the helmet would catch my hair every time I tried to pull it off," the actor laughs. Darting around the neighborhood with his ray gun primed O'Connor's interest for the series 40 years later. As Dr. Elias Huer, O'Connor envisioned the scientist as "a genius who is very capable but also a bit of a fuddy-duddy. He uses this fuddy-duddiness to escape the day-to-day goings-on in this large organization. Most people leave him alone because they think he's a crazy guy. Buck and Wilma discover that he's a great friend, and Huer is taken with them as well. That's the kind of character I was working towards. But that slipped away as the series progressed. Huer ended up behind his desk all of the time, and Buck and Wilma would come to him for their briefings about their next mission. That was a mistake.

forwards and backwards! We discussed the fanciful approach to the character and developed the pilot as a Trojan Horse story. Princess Ardala's flagship is brought through Earth's defenses under the guise of peace. I took one section, Leslie took another and we worked out a script. I then brought in Gil Gerard as Buck without so much as a reading and without any discretion from the network. It was a foregone conclusion in my mind that Gerard was going to play Buck. That's a rarity. That was the only time in my career where the leading man was cast without any network input at all."

Although filmed for TV, the pilot was released in theaters to capitalize on the post–*Star Wars* success of space operas. Once the pilot was

"There was an early episode where Huer is given a plant. For the next three episodes, the plant keeps growing, and Dr. Huer becomes leery of it. He feels the damn thing is spying on him. Huer gives it double-takes, and the scenes are very funny and cute. But the producers decided to cut that back. Instead, Huer ended up sending Buck off on missions. Originally, Buck was supposed to get his orders from a main office somewhere. That's when he and Wilma would come to Dr. Huer's lab. Huer would offer them some kind of weapon or tool for their mission, and his lab would be loaded with far-out, special-effects experiments. It was an opportunity to show, technically, how the world of the future worked. Funny things would happen in the lab, and we'd see Huer's reaction to them. The first episode had me staring into this bubbling tank of chemicals, and some weird object is inside it. The camera filmed me from the other side, and my eyes looked like saucers three feet wide. In another episode, I'm fascinated by some of Buck's old toys. I blow up a balloon, and it flies out of my mouth and shoots around the room making a funny noise. Those were the kinds of things I wish had been kept as the series progressed."

While O'Connor became straight man, he also noted that Gil Gerard and Erin Gray had some reservations about their character relationship as well. "Gil and Erin worked very well together, but the writers never developed their relationship. Buck and Wilma had a kind of adversarial relationship as well as one that bordered on being sexy and sensual. They also cared for each other. Some of the directors understood this, others didn't. The characters' relationship was often reduced to an adolescent level. Gil and Erin complained about that. Gil in particular was very forceful whenever he felt the series drifted away from its original premise."

In terms of the stories, O'Connor appreciated the camp quality of *Buck Rogers*. "It was part of the show's allure," he says. "Originally, *Buck Rogers* was designed to shoot for the kid audience. They planned to market all of these little dolls of Buck, Wilma and Dr. Huer. It turned out the age of our audience went up to 45! Men in particular enjoyed seeing it after a hard day's work. It was undemanding, it had lots of special effects, lots of good-looking people, some tits and ass, and lots of action. The humor and camp were also part of the appeal. That's what *Buck Rogers* was, a tongue-in-cheek show. But while it was camp, it couldn't be treated as such. If you perform it that way, you're going to fail."

Captain Buck Rogers found the twenty-fifth century filled with larger-than-life space villains. There were also space casinos, galactic space pageants and futuristic rock 'n' roll bands. One running joke throughout the series (devised by story editor Alan Brennert) was Earth's landing bay reception room. Attentive viewers listening closely to the background loudspeaker voice would hear names such as Isaac Asimov and Christopher Pike (*Star Trek*'s first captain), announced as arriving guests.

Occasionally, the writers were inspired by dramatic themes, but their episodes were retitled with names that conjured up pulp fiction. "I wrote one episode where Buck was forced to land on a hostile planet," says Dorothy Fontana. "Once there, he discovers that the entire defense of the planet is in the hands of women. Unfortunately, the war hasn't gone their way, and the enemy is coming for them. Buck helps them defend their planet the best they can, and the women make it through. The story was based on the way women rallied to replace men on the homefront during World War II and the way Israeli women served in their armed forces. But the title they gave my script, 'Planet of the Amazon Women,' makes me shudder!"

Despite its equally silly title, one exciting episode that stands out in Tim O'Connor's mind is "Planet of the Slave Girls." "Buster Crabbe made a guest appearance, and he had some dialogue that played off the fact that he had been the original Buck Rogers," he recalls. Crabbe fit right into the high tech world of *Buck Rogers*. "He had been out of the business for a while, but he was no dummy," says O'Connor. "He wasn't standing there scratching his head and wondering what was going on. He was impressed by the changes in film technology. He was a very knowledgeable guy, and he shared a lot of wonderful old stories. I think his mother had been a Hawaiian princess."

O'Connor remembers other episodes for less pleasant reasons. "I had the hell scared out of me once. Gil, Erin and I were walking down the hall of a corridor, and the doorway was supposed to blow out. It exploded a couple of seconds too late. It just missed us. The door roared past us and slammed against the far wall. We could have been seriously hurt. It took the special effects guys 45 minutes to reset the explosion. So we did it again, and believe me, you're seeing three

The second season of *Buck Rogers in the Twenty-Fifth Century* included Hawk (Thom Christopher, right) as an ally of Buck Rogers (Gil Gerard). Copyright 1980 NBC/Universal.

cracking mechanical partner. The actor inside the suit was Felix Silla, a short-stature actor who had played Cousin Itt on TV's *The Addams Family.* "Felix had the toughest job of anybody on that show," says Stewart. "He had to stay in that bloody robot suit all day. During the summer he would cook inside that thing. We couldn't take him out of the suit because it took too long. We could at least take his mechanical head off, and we'd put cold rags over his face and neck. He never lost his sense of humor and he was never nasty. He was a wonderful guy."

"Felix was a sweet, family man," recalls O'Connor. "Once he and I had to fly to New York to do a 15-minute show for PBS. We stayed three or four days. I called Felix at his hotel and asked him to meet me in the city for lunch. Felix had an excuse that sounded reasonable. I said, 'Well, then, maybe we can meet for dinner this evening?' He politely balked at the suggestion. The conversation now struck me as being rather odd. I said 'Felix, what's wrong? You've been cooped up in that hotel all day. Don't you want to get out?'

"Felix replied, 'Actually, Tim, I can't go out unless I have somebody with me. I'm so small that somebody could just pick me up and run away with me. That happens frequently with dwarves.' I was absolutely stunned. I realized that was a valid concern."

O'Connor also enjoyed working with Gil Gerard and Erin Gray. "This was one of the first shows Erin ever did," says O'Connor. "She was a very successful model, and she picked *Buck Rogers* as her first dramatic series. She was a very

extremely nervous actors as we go down that hall, carrying on dialogue as if we were nonchalant. We got past the door, it exploded on cue and we got sprayed with bits of junk. All part of the job!"

Director Larry Stewart recalls, "We had constant problems with those sliding doors. We kept slicing actors in half. The propman who operated the doors off-camera would have to guess when to open and shut them. At one point I had a button that I pressed in my hand. A lightbulb would go off next to the propman, telling him when to open and close the doors. But every now and then, the propman got antsy and he'd close the door too soon. He'd cut an actor in half!"

One robotic effect was Twiki, Buck's wise-

serious actress, but also fun-loving, very smart, and she had a wonderful time on the show."

"The network wanted to replace Erin at the very beginning," recalls producer John Gaynor, "so we had to test dozens of girls as a replacement. None of them worked out, and the network had to go back to Erin and eat a little crow. She was a lovely girl and very cooperative to work with. One thing she didn't like was to dye her hair blonde. Over the season, we let her gradually return to her normal hair color, which was light brown."

As the star of the series, Gil Gerard felt the responsibility that was on his shoulders. The week the series premiered, he told the *Denver Post*, "If the audience likes me, *Buck Rogers* will be a success. If they don't, it will fail."

"Gil worked very hard to make the show a success," says Gaynor. Larry Stewart agrees. "Gil was very dedicated and a hoot to work with. Gil had an interesting problem. He had very fine and delicate hair. Whenever he took his helmet off, he had to go through a whole hairdressing process to make it look right again. You'll notice as the series went on, Buck kept his helmet on. He'd be in these dumb positions with his helmet on and you got to wonder, 'Why the hell doesn't he take his helmet off?'"

The production of *Buck Rogers* involved huge sets, expensive miniatures and big casts. "It was a tough show to produce," notes Gaynor. "It was the most expensive hour-long show being made at the time. Pressure from the studio and the network to keep costs down was constant. The network was also concerned with violence. Every act of violence was counted, and you were allowed only so many. The skimpy costumes on the girls, which we liked, were also an issue. The network always wanted to approve the costumes beforehand. They didn't like surprises! David O'Connell [producer] and I were proud of receiving an award for having the most chauvinistic show on TV because of the way we presented women. It was our intention to use beautiful girls in brief, futuristic costumes. N.O.W. and other women's groups objected strongly to that. That gave us quite a few laughs!"

"The special effects on *Buck Rogers* were very good," recalls director Larry Stewart. "One of the reasons I was hired was because of my early training on the Sam Katzman serials. I knew about using the optical printer, which was the basis of most special effects at the time. If someone on *Buck Rogers* held a gun and went *zap*, the actor had to hold that gun in position for a beat before he could move his hand again. That gave the optical guys time to animate the zap beam shooting from the gun.

"The special effects ran smoothly, but every now and then, the effects house at Universal would come up with a problem that really wasn't a problem. In 'The Flight of the War Witch,' Buck Rogers warped into a new universe, so we needed a new starfield. The optical house guys suddenly said, 'Geez, we've got the spaceship and we've got the new starfield but we haven't had a chance to put them together. We're not gonna make the production deadline!' I went over to them and said, 'You've got the spaceship, right? And you've got the starfield…put the two damn things in the optical printer and press the button that says *Forward*.' They looked at me and said, 'Oh, we'll try that.' They did, and it worked. So sometimes the effects problems were makework problems that would be shifted down to us on the set to solve."

As for the acting, Stewart, a former casting director, recalls, "We were able to get some pretty fair actors to guest-star on *Buck Rogers*. There was nothing cheap about the series. The episodes were well done and actors were having fun on them."

"The only way you can do episodic TV is to pretend that it's the greatest damn thing that you've ever done in your life," says Tim O'Connor. "*Buck Rogers* wasn't the greatest thing I had ever done, but I did want it to succeed. I worked on it as if it was the best material I had ever read." O'Connor admits that the futuristic trappings were a critical part of the show. "They put a lot of money into the show's original production and sets. The wonderful effects, elaborate sets and the beautiful girls were an important part of the first season's success."

Although *Buck Rogers* was usually in the top 40, NBC felt that the series could be improved upon. "Fred Silverman was the head of NBC, and although the series had reasonably good ratings, he decided he was either going to kill the show or make some drastic changes," says O'Connor.

"It was a particularly annoying situation," recalls Larry Stewart. "Silverman decided to fix something that wasn't broken. *Buck Rogers* had been doing well with a comedy lilt to it and Silverman decided he wanted *Gunsmoke* in space. [Executive producer] Bruce Lansbury and the other producers were let go, and John Mantley, who had produced *Gunsmoke*, was brought in."

"We had a steady following and good

ratings," says Gaynor. "It was a children's show that also had tongue-in-cheek for the adults. The network wanted to change the formula. They ruined it by trying to turn it into an adult show with messages."

One character who wouldn't be returning for the show's second season was Dr. Huer. "I really found out by accident," says O'Connor. "Everyone else on the show knew that I wasn't going to be back, but I didn't find out until much later. They even had a big party at NBC, introducing the next season's shows. They introduced me even though Fred Silverman knew I would no longer be in the show. Gil and Erin also knew, and I suspected from their tone that there was something afoot. After the party, I said to myself, 'Hmmm … I think I've been dropped from the show!' I called the producer, and he told me. I was disappointed. I was also saddened that they were going to change the show. I almost called Silverman, not to complain, but to tell him that he was taking a big risk with the series by changing it."

O'Connor did watch some of the second season out of curiosity, recalling, "It began to look a lot like that old fantasy show of the 1960s that got goofy, *Lost in Space,* with the funny old character and the talking robot. For me, it wasn't *Buck Rogers* anymore. It seemed very talky and pretentious."

"They lost the humor," says Larry Stewart, "and the uncomfortableness Buck had being out of his own time. We used to have shows where Buck would try to teach ping-pong to people, or introduce slang from his century. I felt the second year got rid of Buck's humanity. It became a much more serious, 'We gotta get the bad guys!' The writing was pedantic. Interestingly, none of the directors from the first season were called back. John Mantley was interested in purging the lightness and comedy from the show. It wasn't that the direction they took was bad. It was that the audience said, 'Hey, what happened to the show we liked?' Another factor was that Gil Gerard had made the show work with his sense of humor. However, Gil was not a Charles Bronson or Clint Eastwood type. The 'new' Buck didn't fit the actor."

"The series probably got changed because Fred Silverman said, 'We're looking for an excuse to renew a show that probably needs a boost,'" notes Glen Larson. "Science fiction has always suffered from low ratings. Mantley may have been brought in because of his success with

Gunsmoke. NBC felt he would tell 'people' stories in a space environment. Therefore, they might attract people who might otherwise not watch science fiction."

The second season's momentum was hurt by an actors' strike in Hollywood. The new *Buck Rogers* premiered in January 1981. Buck and Wilma were now aboard the starship *Searcher* with Admiral Asimov (Jay Garner) and kindly old scientist Goodfellow (played by veteran english actor Wilfred Hyde-White). In their search for other humans, the *Searcher's* crew took on a *Star Trek*–like exploration of the universe, encountering alien life forms and helping to maintain intergalactic peace.

The most intriguing cast addition was the character of Hawk (Thom Christopher). When his people are killed by humans, Hawk seeks revenge and becomes Buck's mortal enemy in the season's debut segment, "Time of the Hawk." Hawk gradually strikes a truce with Buck, and they become friends. Thom Christopher infused the alien Hawk (part hawk, part humanoid) with a quiet strength and loyalty.

"NBC's casting director, Joel Thurm, called my agent and told him, '*Buck Rogers* is writing in a new character—a bird man. Would Thom come out to the West Coast and read for it?" recalls Christopher. "I was in New York. The fortunes of the fates were generous, and the role became mine." Christopher had a definite point of view as he portrayed the character, who was the last of his species. "Inherent in the role from the first reading was the sense of Hawk being an outsider—the outcast—the lone pilgrim in space," says Christopher, "and ultimately, the noble savage in the romantic sense. These were the elements I used to make such an exotic character believable. I enjoyed exploring the valley of hurt that Hawk seemed to exist in. The loss of his people, his family and the loss of his wife, Koori, by Hawk's own accidental hand. He was the 'stranger in a strange land.'"

Christopher's favorite episode was "Time of the Hawk." "It was as all launchings should be," he marvels. "Perfect. Director Vincent McEveety was incredible to work with. He 'presented' Hawk, not just introduced him. The actors and crew treated the moment [of Hawk's presentation] as something special. I knew working with all of these unique people that my life from that moment on would never be the same."

As the new season progressed, vocal fans of the series made two things clear. First, they didn't like the new voice for Twiki (Bob Elyea). Voice master Mel Blanc (best known as the voice of Bugs Bunny and many other cartoon characters) returned to the part. Secondly, mail reflected an enthusiastic acceptance of Christopher and his alien character. Unfortunately, the intriguing dimensions Hawk could have provided the series didn't materialize, though Christopher remembers that "John Mantley, our executive producer, said to me during production that if the series continued, there would be more opportunities for Hawk to generate some strong storylines of his own as opposed to just responding to them."

Christopher recalls Mantley "as a writer, an actor and a man of strong professional taste. He gave science fiction an added dimension on TV. His very sharp intelligence combined with a true sense of drama and theatrical compassion made all of the elements work." Overall, the actor says the second year was represented by "some wonderful work done by everyone involved. Gil Gerard and Erin Gray were wonderfully generous in sharing the work with me. Never once did they, as the stars of the show, attempt to have this exotic character of Hawk—feathers, spandex and breast plate—moved into the shadows. Gil is one of the nicest actors I've ever worked with."

Christopher, who later won an Emmy award for his role as Carlo Hesser on the daytime soap opera *One Life to Live* in 1992, recalls a moment on the *Buck Rogers* set where he was the recipient of an unexpected, very personal award. "We had been doing the show for two months prior to airing," he says. "It was Christmas, and NBC had prepared a large party on the set of the *Searcher*. As John Mantley was thanking everyone for their hard work, he started talking about a character that he himself had no idea would become what it had. I was sitting there with Gil and Erin, wondering who he was talking about. Suddenly, he called out to me. The entire set erupted in loving applause. My wife, Judith, suddenly appeared from behind a group of crew members. She had flown in from New York a day earlier without me knowing! Erin Gray had been the generous soul behind everyone giving me this magnificent Lalique crystal Hawk's head. I'll always cherish it for the flood of love and respect I felt from that incredible cast and crew!"

Buck Rogers was canceled after its second year and went into syndication. In retrospect, Glen Larson suspects that the hour format of the series in general diluted the premise. "It would have been better as a series of two-hour movies,

the way they did the Perry Mason films," he says. "*Buck Rogers* had a wide-open concept. It should have been a show that took advantage of location filming and larger special effects. It would have lent itself better to a longer form."

Cast Notes

Gil Gerard (Buck): Born 1940. Gerard was a New York cabbie when he got the job of an extra in the film *Love Story* (1970). A few years later he was one of the stars of daytime's *The Doctors*. He occasionally turns up in TV movies.

Erin Gray (Wilma): Born 1952 in Honolulu. Gray moved with her family to California when she was eight years old. She became a New York fashion model at the age of 16. She co-starred in TV's *Silver Spoons* (1982–86).

Tim O'Connor (Dr. Huer): Born 1926. O'Connor played Elliot Carson on TV's *Peyton Place* (1965–68). A more recent role was in an episode of *Star Trek—The Next Generation*.

Thom Christopher (Hawk): He devoted time to daytime TV and theater (including a production of *The Sound of Music* in upstate New York in 1993).

Wilfred Hyde-White (Dr. Goodfellow): Born 1903 in Gloucester, England. His childhood dream was to become a magician, but that ambition gave way to acting. His stage debut was in the 1922 production of *Tons of Money*. He died in 1991.

EPISODE GUIDE

The Awakening (1979 TV movie)
Buck, awakened from suspended animation, finds himself the prisoner of Princess Ardala. She plans to use a peace conference as a way of launching a devastating attack on Earth. Wr: Glen A. Larson, Leslie Stevens. Dir: Daniel Haller.

Princess Ardala (Pamela Hensley); Kane (Henry Silva); King Draco (Joseph Wiseman); Young woman (Caroline Smith); Supervisor (John Dewey-Carter); Tigermen (H. B. Haggerty, Duke Butler); Pilot (Kevin Coates); Comtel Off (David Cadiente); Technician (Gil Serna); Guards (Larry Duran, Kenny Endoso); Officer (Eric Lawrence); Wrather (Colleen Kelly); Pilot #2 (Steve Jones); Pilot #3 (David Buchanan); Wingman (Burt Marshall).

Trivia Alert: Shown in theaters before being telecast. Joseph Wiseman's character was edited from the TV version.

Season 1: 1979-80

Planet of the Slave Girls (2 hours)

Buck must rescue Wilma from a would-be conqueror who has immobilized Earth's fighter fleet. His forces are about to attack the planet. Wr: Steve Greenberg, Aubrey Solomon, Cory Applebaum, story by Steve Greenberg, Aubrey Solomon. Dir: Michael Caffey.

Kaleel (Jack Palance); Gov. Saroyan (Roddy McDowall); Brig. Gordon (Buster Crabbe); Dr. Mallory (MacDonald Carey); Duke Danton (David Groh); Galen (Robert Dowdell); Stella (Karen Carlson); Ryma (Brianne Leary); Julio (Don Marshall); Regis Saroyan (Mike Mullins); Maj. Fields (Sheila DeWindt); Pilot (Diane Markoff); Woman (June Whitley-Taylor); Husbans (Borah Silver); Technician (Nathaniel Brian Wise); Worker (Mike Masters); Guard (Don Maxwell).

Vegas in Space

Buck infiltrates a space casino to rescue a woman from the city's leader. Wr: Anne Collins. Dir: Sigmund Neufeld, Jr.

Armat (Cesar Romero); Morphus (Joseph Wiseman); Falina (Ana Alicia); Tangie (Pamela Susan Shoop); Velosi (Richard Lynch); Marla Landers (Juanine Clay).

The Plot to Kill a City, Parts 1 and 2

Buck poses as a killer to infiltrate the Legion of Death assassins, who are planning to wipe out Chicago. In Part 2, Buck has to act fast when his cover is blown. Wr: Alan Brennert. Dir: Dick Lowry.

Kellogg (Frank Gorshin); Joella Cameron (Markie Post); Sherese (Nancy DeCarl); Quince (John Quade); Richard Selvan (James McEachin); Varek (Anthony James); Markos (Robert Tessier); Barney (James Sloyan); Argus (Victor Argo); Technician (Mitch Reta); Cop (John Furlong); Rowdy (Richard Reed); Pirate (Seamon Glass); Woman (Sena Black); Hartsteen (Whitney Rydbeck); Clerk (Gwen Mitchell); Katrina (Nonice Williams).

The Return of the Fighting 69th

A group of retired space fighters returns to the skies to help Buck battle gun runners who are going to attack Earth with nerve gas. Wr: David Bennett Carren. Dir: Philip Leacock.

Noah Cooper (Peter Graves); Roxanne Trent (Elizabeth Allen); Corliss (Robert Quarry); Big Red Murphy (Woody Strode); Harriet Twain (K.T. Stevens); Clayton (Robert Hardy); M. K. Schultz (Eddie Firestone); Eli Twain (Dan Sturkie); Alicia (Katherine Wiberg); Westlake (Duncan McKenzie); Technician (Cliff Turknett).

Unchained Woman

Buck springs an innocent woman from an intergalactic prison, but their escape is shadowed by an indestructible android. Wr: Bill Taylor. Dir: Dick Lowry.

Jen Burton (Jamie Lee Curtis); Malary Pantera (Mike

Delano); Sergio Sanwiler (Bert Rosario); Ted Warwick (Robert Cornthwaite); Majel (Tara Buckman); Hugo (Walter Hunter); Gymon (Danny Ades); Captain (Jim B. Smith); Zimmerman (Charles Walker).

Planet of the Amazon Women

Buck is sold as a slave to a powerful leader on a planet ruled by women. Wr: Dorothy and Richard Fontana. Dir: Philip Leacock.

Ariela (Ann Dusenberry); Prime minister (Anne Jeffreys); Cassius Thorne (Jay Robinson); Nyree (Liberty Godshall); Linea (Teddi Siddell); Flight controller (Sean Garrison).

The Cosmic Whiz Kid

A child genius from the twentieth century is kidnapped by a criminal. Wr: Alan Brennert, Anne Collins. Dir: Leslie H. Martinson.

Hieronymus Fox (Gary Coleman); Roderick Zale (Ray Walston); Lt. Dia Cryton (Melody Rogers); Koren (Albert Popwell); Toman (Lester Fletcher); Selmar (Earl Boen).

Memory Flash—Leslie Martinson: "Gary Coleman was about 11 at the time. He was a real space buff. He had a simulated space capsule in his garage. Even though he was a superstar on *Diff'rent Strokes*, he told his agent, 'I'd do anything to appear on *Buck Rogers*.' During filming, Gary kept asking me if he could keep the *Buck Rogers* spacesuit that he wore. On the last day of filming, I walked into his dressing room and gave him his spacesuit. He was very appreciative. He's an exceptionally talented young man."

Escape from Wedded Bliss

Princess Ardala threatens to destroy Chicago unless Buck is turned over to her for marriage. Wr: Cory Applebaum, Patrick Hoby, Jr., Michael Bryant (Alan Brennert). Dir: David Moessinger.

Princess Ardala (Pamela Hensley); Kane (Michael Ansara); Tigerman (H. B. Haggerty).

Cruise Ship to the Stars

Buck tries to protect Miss Cosmos from a mysterious woman. Wr: Michael Bryant (Alan Brennert), Cory Applebaum, story by Michael Bryant. (Alan Brennert). Dir: Sigmund Neufeld, Jr.

Alison Michaels (Kimberly Beck); Sabrina (Trisha Noble); Miss Cosmos (Dorothy Stratten); Jalor (Leigh McCloskey); Captain (Brett Halsey); Tina (Patty Maloney); Man (Timothy O' Hagan).

Space Vampire

Mysterious deaths on a space station are linked to a space vampire who is now stalking Wilma. Wr: Kathleen Barnes, David Wise. Dir: Larry Stewart.

The Vorvon (Nicholas Hormann); Royko (Christopher Stone); Dr. Ecbar (Lincoln Kilpatrick); Bill Nelson (Phil Hoover); Twiki (Patty Maloney); Captain (Jeannie Fitzgibbons); Technician (David Moses).

Happy Birthday, Buck

Plans to cheer Buck up during his birthday are spoiled by an assassin who turns people into marble, and is now after Dr. Huer. Wr: Martin Pasko. Dir: Sigmund Neufeld, Jr.

Raylyn (Morgan Brittany); Dr. Delora Batliss (Tamara Dobson); Traeger (Peter McLean); Carew (Chip Johnson); Roruik (Bruce Wright); Niles (Tom Gagen); Garth (Eric Mason); Alien leader (Harry Gold); Woman (Gina Gallego); Guard (Abe Alvarez); Technician (Victoria Woodbeck); Marsden (Clay Alexander).

A Blast for Buck
To discover who's threatening Earth, Buck agrees to a mind probe that propels him through his past adventures. Wr: Richard Nelson, story by John Gaynor, Alan Brennert. Dir: David G. Phinney.
Hieronymus Fox (Gary Coleman); Twiki (Patty Maloney); Kaleel (flashback) (Jack Palance); Noah Cooper (flashback) (Peter Graves); Ardala (flashback) (Pamela Hensley); Zale (flashback) (Ray Walston); Brig. Gordon (flashback) (Buster Crabbe); Ryma (flashback) (Brianne Leary); Tangie (flashback) (Pamela Susan Shoop); Jen Burton (flashback) (Jamie Lee Curtis).

Ardala Returns
Four duplicates of Buck are created by Princess Ardala to destroy Earth. Wr: Chris Bunch, Allan Cole. Dir: Larry Stewart.
Ardala (Pamela Hensley); Kane (Michael Ansara); Tigerman (H.B. Haggerty); Pilot (James Emery); Technician (Betty Bridges); Guard (Bob Minor).

Twiki Is Missing
Evil superwomen kidnap Twiki and threaten to ignite Earth's atmosphere. Wr: Jaron Summers. Dir: Sigmund Neufeld, Jr.
Clare (Janet Bebe Louie); Kerk Belzak (John P. Ryan); Stella (Eddie Benton); Dawn (Eugenia Wright); Pinchas (David Darlow); Oto Anad (Ken Letner).

Olympiad
A defecting athlete during the twenty-fifth century's Olympic games finds his escape plans complicated by an explosive booby-trap on his body. Wr: Craig Buck. Dir: Larry Stewart.
Lara (Judith Chapman); Karl (Paul Mantee); Alaric (Nicholas Coster); Jorex Leet (Barney McFadden); Quarod (Jerry Quarry); Rand Sorgon (Bob Seagren); Zogan (Paul Coufos); Satrap (John Zee); Olympians (Thomas Henderson, Elgin Baylor, Anthony Davis, Carlos Palomino).

A Dream of Jennifer
While searching for a woman who looks like his old girlfriend, Buck finds a plot to start an intergalactic civil war. Wr: Michael Bryant (Alan Brennert). Dir: Harvey Laidman, David G. Phinney.
Jennifer/Leila (Anne Lockhart); Reev (Paul Koslo); Nola (Mary Woronov); Merlin (Gino Conforti); Rekoff (Jessie Lawrence Ferguson); Toby Kaplin (Cameron Young); Supervisor (Shawn Michaels); Guard (Dennis Haysbert); Mime (Mitchell Young-Evans); Clerk (Marsha Mercant).

Space Rockers
The rock group Andromeda tries to control millions of teens with music and incite them to riot in major cities. Wr: Chris Bunch, Allan Cole. Dir: Guy Magar.
Kyrana (Nancy Frangione); Lars Mangros (Jerry Orbach); Joanna (Judy Landers); Cirus (Leonard Lightfoot); Yara (Richard Moll); Rambeau (Jesse Goins); Tarkas

(Paul LeClair); Elaine (Cynthia Leake); Mark (Jeff Harlan); Technician (Mitch Reta); Guard (Joseph Taggart).

Buck's Duel to the Death
Buck tries to free a peaceful planet by battling the dictator Trebor. Wr: Robert W. Gilmer. Dir: Bob Bender.
Trebor (William Smith); Darius (Keith Andes); Kelan (Fred Sadoff); Vionne (Elizabeth Stack); Neil (Edward Power); Albert (Robert Lussier); Maya (Heidi Bohay); Greta (Stephanie Blackmore); Officer (Douglas R. Bruce); Karem (Francisco Lagueruela).

Flight of the War Witch, Part 1
Buck travels to an alternate universe where he and Princess Ardala join forces against a female dictator. Wr: Robert W. Gilmer, William Mageean, story by David Chomsky. Dir: Larry Stewart.
Zarina (Julie Newmar); Tora (Vera Miles); Ardala (Pamela Hensley); Keeper (Sam Jaffe); Chandar (Kelly Miles); Kane (Michael Ansara); Kodus (Donald Petrie); Spirot (Sid Haig); Councilman (Larry Ward); Pantherman (Tony Carroll); General (Brent Davis); Guard (Gary Adler).

Flight of the War Witch, Part 2
The evil ruler Zarina plans to destroy a peaceful planet and Buck and Ardala work against time to stop her. Wr: Robert W. Gilmer, William Mageean, story by David Chomsky. Dir: Larry Stewart.
Zarina (Julie Newmar); Tora (Vera Miles); Kane (Michael Ansara); Ardala (Pamela Hensley); Chandar (Kelly Miles); Keeper (Sam Jaffe); Kodus (Donald Petrie); Spirot (Sid Haig); Councilman (Larry Ward); Pantherman (Tony Carroll); Soldier (Don Maxwell).

Season 2: 1980-81

Time of the Hawk, Parts 1 and 2
While eluding two assassins, Buck forges an uneasy alliance with the alien Hawk. Buck tries to save Hawk's injured wife by getting her to a powerful alien. Wr: Norman Hudis. Dir: Vincent McEveety.
Koori (Barbara Luna); Llamajuna (David Opatoshu); Flagg (Lance Le Gault); Simmons (Susan McIver); Thordis (Andre Harvey); Pratt (Sid Haig); Officer (Dennis Haysbert); Judge (Michael Fox); Lt. (J. Chris O'Connor); Bailiff (Tim O'Keefe); Clerk (Ken Chandler); Also with Ken O'Brien.

Journey to Oasis (Part 1) and Journey to Where (Part 2)
Crash landing on a savage desert, Buck and Wilma accompany an ambassador to a city to reach a vital peace conference. Wr: Robert and Esther Mitchell. Dir: Daniel Haller.
Duvoe (Mark Lenard); Devlin (Paul Carr); Odee-X (Felix Silla); Zite (Len Birman); Rolla (Mike Stoka); Zykarian (Donn White); Technician (Alex Hyde-White).

The Guardians
A dying alien gives Buck a glowing box that conjures

up childhood memories for Buck. Meanwhile, the spaceship *Searcher* is locked on an unknown course. Wr: Paul and Margaret Schneider. Dir: Jack Arnold.

Koori (Barbara Luna); Buck's mom (Rosemary DeCamp); Janovus (Harry Townes); Guardian (Vic Perrin); Devlin (Paul Carr); Boy (Shawn Stevens); Mailman (Howard Culver); Helmsman (Dennis Haysbert).

Mark of the Saurian

Buck realizes that a visiting ambassador is actually an evil lizard-creature, but no one believes him. Wr: Francis Moss. Dir: Barry Crane.

Sorens (Linden Chiles); Nurse Paulton (Kim Hamilton); Elif (Barry Cahill); Dr. Moray (Vernon Weddle); Devlin (Paul Carr); Crewwoman (Andrea Pike); Willie (Allan Hunt); Officer (Stacy Keach, Sr.); Martin (Alex Hyde-White); Captain (Frank Parker).

The Golden Man

Stranded on an asteroid, the *Searcher* crew encounters a golden boy. He's being pursued by criminals who want to exploit his powers of transformation. Wr: Calvin Clements, Sr., Stephen McPherson. Dir: Vincent McEveety.

Relcos (Russell Wiggins); Velis (David Hollander); Devlin (Paul Carr); Alphie (Bob Elyea); Graf (Anthony James); Hag (Diana Chesney); Loran (Bruce M. Fisher); Marcos (Roger Rose); Jailer (Mike Masters); Onlooker (Richard Wright); Also with Arthur Eisner.

The Crystals

Buck, Wilma and Hawk befriend a young woman who has amnesia. She can't recall her past, but the mummy stalking her is the key to her future. Wr: Robert and Esther Mitchell. Dir: John Patterson.

Laura (Amanda Wyss); Hall (Sandy Champion); Kovick (James R. Parkes); Martin (Alex Hyde-White); Johnson (Gary Bolen); Petrie (Leigh C. Kim); Mummy (Hubie Kerns, Jr.).

The Satyr

After befriending a woman and her son on a desert planet, Buck begins exhibiting signs that he's turn-

ing into the dreaded creature called the Satyr. Wr: Paul and Margaret Schneider. Dir: Victor French.

Syra (Anne E. Curry); Delph (Bobby Lane); Pangor (Dave Cass); Midshipman (Dennie Freeman).

SHGORATCHX!

The *Searcher* takes aboard seven tiny men who are fascinated by Wilma—they've never seen a woman before. Wr: William Keys. Dir: Vincent McEveety.

Yoomak (Billy Curtis); Xces (Tommy Madden); Zoman (John Edward Allen); Sothoz (Harry Monty); Moore (Alex Hyde-White); Zedht (Tony Cox); Towtuk (Spencer Russell); Kuzan (Charles Secor).

The Hand of Goral

Buck and a landing party return to the *Searcher* and find that the crew has undergone strange personality changes. Wr: Francis Moss. Dir: David G. Phinney.

Reardon (Peter Kastner); Goral (John Fujioka); Cowan (William Bryant); Parsons (Dennis Haysbert); James (Michael Horsley).

Testimony of a Traitor

A recovered video from 1987 shows that Buck was a traitor who started the nuclear holocaust that ended his world. Buck's efforts to clear himself only confirm the damning evidence. Wr: Stephen McPherson. Dir: Bernard McEveety.

Bergstrom (Ramon Bieri); President (Walter Brooke); Myers (William Sylvestor); Official (John Milford); Sergeant (Carl Reindel); Peterson (John O'Connell); Turner (Bill Andes); Arnheim (David Hooks); Crawford (Thomas Bellin); Biles (Buck Young); Marine (Eric Lawrence); Pilot (James Emery); Marine Sgt. (Dean Brooks).

The Dorian Secret

Buck is mystified by his female passenger, who is being pursued for a murder charge by aliens. Wr: Stephen McPherson. Dir: Jack Arnold.

Asteria Eleefa (Devon Ericson); Koldar (Walker Edmiston); Saurus (Denny Miller); Demeter (William Kirby Cullen); Chronos (Eldon Quick); Falgor (Thomas Bellin).

Captain Power and the Soldiers of the Future

1987–1988

In Earth's far-flung future in the year 2147, after the long and violent "Metal Wars," humanity is on the brink of total destruction. Captain Jonathan Power and his band of soldiers, hiding in their Power Base, are Earth's last hope of salvation against the insidious New Order, a vision of the planet's evil leader, Lord Dread. Half-machine and half-human, Dread's evil dreams are to create a machine empire. Ruling from Volcania, a massive iron fortress, he plans the implementation of the Bio Dread Empire.

Cast: The Heroes: Captain Jonathan Power (Tim Dunigan); Major Matthew "Hawk" Masterson (Peter MacNeill); Lt. Michael "Tank" Ellis (Sven Thorsen); Sgt. Robert "Scout" Baker (Maurice Dean Wint); Corporal Jennifer "Pilot" Chase (Jessica Steen); Dr. Stuart Power/Mentor (Bruce Gray). *The Villains:* Lord Dread (David Hemblen); Soaron (voice) (Deryck Hazel); Blastarr (voice) (John Davies); Overmind (voice) (Tedd Dillon); Overunit Wilson (Kelly Bricher); Laccki (voice) (Don Francks).

Created by: Gary Goddard and Tony Christopher; *Executive Producers:* Gary Goddard, Tony Christopher, Douglas Netter and John Copeland; *Producer:* Ian McDougall; Syndicated/Landmark Entertainment Group; 30 minutes.

Captain Power and the Soldiers of the Future was created to sell toys. Yet even with 42 million dollars worth of merchandise sold, the show ended production after 21 episodes because Mattel Toys oversold their stock, leaving a 22 million dollar problem sitting on warehouse shelves across America.

It was a show that married a dramatic, action-adventure, science fiction premise with the technology of interactivity—sending broadcasting signals from the program into toys that would activate guns, lights, and ejecting action figures. Plus, *Captain Power* was a platform where computer-generated images (CGIs) would be used to create, for the first time on film, shining robot characters that spouted dialogue and actually participated in plots.

Gary Goddard, director of the feature film *Masters of the Universe* and owner of the Landmark Entertainment Group, first invented the concept of *Captain Power* when he knew that Mattel was looking for a new toy aimed at young boys. "I always liked science fiction, and there was a lot of animation on television at that time," recalls Goddard. "My idea was to create a new live-action series, kind of like the ones I grew up with. I took a character named Captain Jonathan Power, the concept and story to Mattel and said, 'This should be your next toy line.' It was the idea they would be fighting in the future against robotic armies. We went to Mattel about a concept of a live-action television series with computer-generated animation images to be developed as robot creatures."

Mattel liked the ideas and, in fact, had been working on the interactivity technology in-house but didn't know how to apply it. They asked Goddard if he could create the CGIs he was proposing on a decent budget and if interactivity could be applied to it. "To do that every week was a big challenge. And the technology was nowhere near where it is today. We were a little bit ahead of our time, I tell you!" laughs Goddard. After some research, Goddard returned and said, "Yes." From there, *Captain Power* was born and ready to fly.

"Not only was the show groundbreaking in terms of being the very first show to use CGIs on a weekly series interacting with live-action characters, but it was also the first interactive television show!" says Goddard proudly.

Although the practice of sponsoring animated shows was common, for the first time, a toy company was financing a live-action television show. So blatant was the tie-in with Mattel as the toy developer and financier of the project that the Captain Power toys didn't need to be advertised with the show.

The five toys produced in conjunction with the show included two jets, the PowerJet XT-7 and the Phantom Striker, which interacted with the onscreen targets from as far as ten feet away and scored points each time a target was hit. The TV enemies could return fire and take away points, resulting in each vehicle's cockpit being ejected when the score reached 0. Other jet features included a light-emitting diode (LED) that indicated a "target lock" and a power check button indicating scores.

The Power On Energizer transfer unit illuminated, emitted sounds and sent light beams through the Captain Power action figure when the live-action Captain Power on television gave his "Power On" battle cry. The accessory also caused other vehicles within range to gain or lose points.

Interlocker was an anti-aircraft throne of Lord Dread. It could exchange fire with the television screen and featured an LED "target lock." A digital score readout, ejectable throne, and a "battle scope" for viewing the action from the figure's eye level were also supplied.

The miniature Power Base featured a fold out mega-weapon with the same interactive and scorekeeping capabilities as the jets. The mega-weapon also had sensors that triggered "explosions" or caused action figures to be ejected.

Each toy could be played with independently of the TV show.

As accessories to the show, Battle Training Tapes (animation, not live-action) were supplied in VHS format. Each tape featured 15 minutes of interactive battle and chase footage at a different skill level. Locked into the concept of interactivity to support the toys, filmmakers were required to imbed three to five minutes of interactive signals into each episode. The writers and producers sometimes complained.

"We like action," says Goddard, "but the fact we *had* to work in action in every single show led to a bit of a headache. Not just minor action, but at least two to three minutes of battle distributed throughout the show." Goddard thinks the interactivity interfered with storytelling at least "a little bit." Nevertheless, Goddard claims that the production crews and cast went into the project solely with the goal of creating dramatic television. "We did not produce the show with children in mind although we were sure children would like the show," he says. "We took more of a Disney philosophy. Walt Disney always said he never made shows for kids. He always made them for adults but put things for kids in them. We were always aiming for the same audiences who watch *Star Trek* and *Star Wars,* and we were making the show for ourselves, feeling confident that kids would like the gadget aspects, the CGI characters and things. Kids liked the show, but overall we had very good reaction from adults. You'll see that in the reviews. People like the stories, people like the fact there is characterization, they can see the production values of the show. Our sole goal was to have a quality science fiction television show within the limitations and parameters that were set up by ... doing a show with a very direct toy tie-in. It required some creative thinking. But I think we did some good, creative problem solving. The majority of those shows stand up on their own merits. You could show any one of those shows today without the interactivity."

The show was originally titled *The Metal Wars*, and Goddard laughs when reminded that story editor J. Michael Straczynski accused him of creating a childish title in *Captain Power and the Soldiers of the Future*. "He thought it was a dumb title. Because it was being done by Mattel, because they were selling toys, the name of the show had to be the same as the toys," explains Goddard. "I know Straczynski holds me responsible for that, but it was a given. If we didn't call it that, we couldn't have made the show. I like the title. Each season would have been another year in the Metal Wars."

The storylines for *Captain Power* were surprisingly adult in nature if the viewer looked beyond the battle scenes in every episode. For example, one episode, "The Abyss," featured an insane commander in an uncharted sector who believed the Metal Wars were still raging and had marked Jonathan Power and Hawk for execution.

"Generally speaking, the storylines were aimed at a much more older audience," Goddard agrees. "We tried very hard to make sure there wasn't [just] one dimension and just good and evil. We tried to make sure the characters had their own backgrounds and stories, including the bad guy. On the surface it *is* basically a good vs. evil kind of thing. I think you'll see that over the course of the shows, everything gets much more dimensional. We used World War II as a model of what we were doing. If you look underneath ... you'll see a lot of the same things at work."

As a result of the production staff's conscious decision to further the World War II allegory, "the entire setup, the entire mission of the first series is to keep the battle in terms of the favor of the Allies," says Goddard. "In this case, Captain Power. As the story unfolds, we find an underground resistance that is trying to help the battle to end the domination of the machines. If you look at the costume design for the bad guys you'll see some very similar designs on the Nazi uniform. There's a lot in there. Again, Joe Straczynski was responsible for that."

Cinematographer Peter Benison, who photographed every episode, agrees with Goddard that in *Captain Power* "we were doing drama television. Technically, we had to support the toy, but no, we were telling stories to a wide age and interest. I think the toy overshadowed, from an adult point of view. I think the times the show was on, and the publicity the show had in connection with the toy, made adults not want to see it, [or] bother trying to see it. It was just parents of kids who were watching it, they would say, 'It wasn't as much of a kids' show as I thought.'"

On whether the interactivity gimmick was a good element of the show, Benison candidly says, "I never really talked to many people or kids who had the toys and who were using them. It was certainly novel, an extra aspect of the show. But at no time was the show dependent on the toys. It stood on its own."

"What was unique about the use of the interactivity," says Benison, "was that it was built into the characters. Initially, that was going to be the only interactive part of the show. They were very concerned with the violence, so you could only shoot a robot or these computer characters.

Ready for action! The Power Team were: (from left to right) Sven-Ole Thorsen as Michael Ellis (Tank), Jessica Steen as Jennifer Chase (Pilot), Tim Dunigan as Captain Jonathan Power, Peter MacNeil as Major Matthew Masterson (Hawk) and Maurice Dean Wint as Sergeant Robert Baker (Scout).

For humans on the show there was no signal.... So, you wouldn't have a child directing his gun and shooting at a human. There was no interactive signal. Interactive signals were only on inanimate objects; robots or vehicles or computer-generated characters. Computer characters took a long time to do and were expensive. At one point the worry was there wasn't going to be enough interactive signal on the computer-generated characters to support the toys through the show. So we had to introduce the interactive signal onto other objects in the show like vehicles and robots."

That's where the technical prowess came in. Benison designed a light bulb that was strung on the chests of all of Dread's robot troopers to give the animators a frame of reference when animating the glowing red light onto their chests. Interactive signals were then added to that.

Benison recalls his experience on the show as a time when "every department went crazy with their specialties and was able to experiment and allow for their imaginations to grow wild, and do things without having their hands tied."

Like many science fiction shows throughout television history, *Captain Power* was a show that

could only be done if everything was created from scratch. Filming the entire season took five months, from June to November of 1987, at a budget averaging $1.2 million per half-hour with a total of about $26 million for the entire season.

The show was filmed in Canada.

"We took over a bus maintenance depot in Toronto," recalls Benison. "This huge building was abandoned for years, it was filthy. We had to turn the power back on, the pipes were bursting, rusted. Even though we got the building from the city for free, it cost us a fortune to clean it up and bring it up to proper safety standards. After that was done, we had a filmmaking studio. Once we set it up, it became cheaper and cheaper for each show."

But the place had no air conditioning and when Toronto had heat waves, everyone felt it. Cold weather was equally uncomfortable in the cavernous building. While an effort was made to soundproof the stages for filming, sounds from the outside world often filtered into the building, ruining many a take. Scenes had to be redone when, for example, cars would drive by or honk their horns.

Camera operator Attila Szalay remembers that the bus depot was so big that almost everyone needed two-wheel scooters with baskets to carry equipment around and get from set to set. To create the interior of the Power jumpship, the shell of a plane was carted through the streets of Toronto, installed at the studio, and redesigned for the show.

Today, according to Brad Creasser, second assistant cameraman, who worked under Benison and with Szalay, the former Captain Power studio has been converted to townhouses and condominiums.

Benison marvels at the diversity of people gathered as cast and crew for *Captain Power*. "It was put together from quite a few different walks of life. We had both American and Canadian [actors]. We had those fresh from acting school, we had people with no experience. It was a real collection, so it was interesting to see their different personalities fit into this rather unusual concept. Everyone got on pretty well. I think the whole crew on the set was unique. We were shooting a fantasy. That put everybody in a different frame of mind."

Szalay remembers it as a difficult show, with "massive amounts of special effects and explosions and fires that went on all day long." Creasser, whose job was to slate the takes before every shot, load the cameras and keep track of the film inventory, agrees wholeheartedly. He also remembers dealing with explosions every day.

"Once, we were waiting to do a shot, and squibs from Dread's soldiers went off and flew between Attila and me, just missing us. There were always technical mishaps," he says. Szalay confirms this, saying he lost many a shirt from flying sparks and squib misfires. Eventually they had to give him a fire blanket for protection. To prevent any serious accidents, during any special effects or explosions, all crewmembers wore plastic goggles, and plexiglass shields were strategically placed to protect them and the cameras.

Creasser goes so far as to say, "I became a guinea pig towards the end. So rarely you get to work in dangerous situations with explosions, and it's exciting. Your adrenalin gets going when you're filming things that are blowing up. Several occasions, we were working inside the sets and I would slate and *run* and get out of the way before they would set off an explosion or squibs. And they have me on camera trying to clear the frame. And I'm yelling, 'Don't blow me! Don't blow me!'"

At the time of *Captain Power*, says Creasser, slate boards or clapper boards, which are used so editors can identify scenes and synchronize sound and video during post-production, had to be wired to the soundman's tape recorder. (Wireless models were available, but the company opted not to use them because the bulk of shooting took place indoors.) Occasionally, the cable of Creasser's clapper board would get tangled amid the rubble, and he would frantically try to collect the wiring and hurriedly get out of frame.

"I have one image in my head that I'll never forget," says Creasser. "We were shooting outside at night, at the back of the warehouse. We were filming a building, and the script girl, Susan, has to be there with me to read the numbers on the slate, just as I close the sticks. Everyone is way back. There were two or three cameras in safety boxes closer to the buildings. We're there, I have to slate two cameras and then get out of the way before they cue this explosion. I just have this image of Susan and me running back towards everyone else 50 feet away"—with a $2,000 slate board in one hand and cable flying behind.

"We were halfway back before they cued the explosion. I would have loved to have a picture of the two of us running away. From their perspective it must have looked great to see these two people running away, silhouetted by the fireball behind us. Towards the end we were blowing up every set. 'Oh, what are we blowing up today?' I was more than happy to go in there! It became an everyday occurrence."

Of the cast, according to Szalay, Sven Thorsen as "Tank" had it the hardest because, wearing the unbending battle armor, he couldn't even sit down. A special wooden platform had to be built so he could rest.

"I remember him lifting his visor, wearing a Tank outfit, he'd sit there, smoke big cigars and crack jokes, watching people do their work. It was hilarious. That was quite fun. ... And we always made fun of Jessica's breastplates, of course!" says Szalay.

Peter MacNeill, as Major Matthew "Hawk" Masterson, says, "I don't think anyone was able to estimate the enormous expense of developing the technical wizardry needed to make the show interactive. I believe ground was broken in many disciplines, including sound recording, set design, animation and computer graphics. In this regard, *Captain Power* was a success for many people."

Asked if he ever felt overshadowed as an actor by all the special effects that were thrown into the show, MacNeill replies that the show was always a battleground for two schools of thought. "Constantly warring was, should the show be a vehicle to sell toys and to that end must be highly interactive and plot be damned? Or a solid action drama aimed at a science fiction buffs sort of audience, much like *Star Trek*? When the interactive school, who in fact held the purse strings, won out, in my mind the storyline, the actors and common sense were overshadowed. But then, I'm just an actor."

Hardly bitter, MacNeill fondly recalls his fellow cast members on the show. He remembers many moments on the set that included "laughter and puzzlement dealing with the costumes and sets that were at times being invented for us on the spot," says MacNeill. "My friends and cast members—who, in spite of not being able to move in a cumbersome outfit, were still asked to get out on that limb and act—were for me heroes of the first order. When you're breaking new ground with new ideas and materials, always inventing, always innovating, not everything works first time out. As a result there were long stretches of overtime and many delays while a new prop or effect was put together. The power suits were awkward and hot to wear, the props sometimes cumbersome, however much magic was worked!"

Benison's thoughts about the costumes echo MacNeill's memories. "In the summer, the studio got very hot, and there was smoke and dust flying around," says Benison. "It got very, very uncomfortable in the suits. That was a major problem, for them to be constricted by that. I was surprised it didn't get worse than it did. It was as good as it could be under the circumstances. But we had a lot of fun with it. We were doing something new and different, and that reflected in everybody's attitude."

Of the scripts, MacNeill says, "I felt they had great potential. I mean, the drama of people fighting for life and dignity in a collapsing world run by machines—how could one lose? However, editors were told to insert battle scenes one after the other in order to sell the interactive toy. This destroyed, at times, wonderful scripts, and I wondered if instead of being an actor I was in the toy industry. ... I was pleased with the insight and sensitivity with which writers developed the characters, including mine. However, once the 'action editors' got started, not much was left."

So proficient was the crew in creating the special effects, says Benison, that "sometimes we'd get to a sequence where everything is heavily storyboarded and the directors had no say whatso-ever. We'd just send the director off somewhere for a couple of hours. 'Go read a newspaper, go make a couple of calls, there's nothing you can do here. We all know this sequence, we know exactly what happens. There's nothing you can direct or supervise.' So directors would get very frustrated too. They'd get overcome by the technical requirements."

Szalay remembers that the signature scene for the show, the "Power On!" sequence in which all the soldiers would electronically don their battle suits by standing under a machine, was very difficult and tedious to film. "We'd have to lock off the camera and have them stand in the machine without the suits, then leave and change into the armor and come back, and we had a still frame of how they were standing on the previous shot on video, and we had to match everything. It had to be within a centimeter of the same place! It had to be exact, otherwise it would look like a jump cut between the segments. One of the first times we did it was quite difficult. It's critical that the camera is locked off. The actors had done the first sequence and were putting on their power suits, and just before they came back, the camera got bumped by the boom man. He was backing up his sound equipment. We wasted a good hour and a half. We had to go back and take off the suits and start from scratch."

Jessica Steen's character, Pilot, would play a pivotal role in the series' final two-part episode, "Retribution." In this episode, Lord Dread finally discovered the Power Base location and sent his soldiers to destroy it. It was Pilot who made the base self-destruct so that Captain Power and the rest of the team could survive. Steen's character was always destined to die. Jessica did not want to do a five-year series.

After a season of shows, and millions of toys sold through Christmas, *Captain Power* fizzled to a stop for three reasons. First, Mattel had oversold the toys to retailers, projecting the idea that it wasn't a $40 million best seller, but a product that had a $22 million shortfall in sales. Second, parents were crying out against the show's violent battle scenes, even though Captain Power was a fantasy show set in the far-flung future. And third, Writers Guild and Screen Actors Guild residuals were expensive for the toy company.

Goddard believes the marketing mismanagement was the primary missile that defeated Captain Power. "[Overselling toys] was something toy companies were doing back then. They were overshipping to run the numbers up. That practice doesn't happen as much anymore, but unfortunately, we were a victim of that."

Benison agrees and adds, "Mattel was also quite a bit in trouble. They lost a fair bit of money, not just because of the show but because of toy sales in general. I think executives got changed, and new people came in and didn't want anything to do with it. So the show never had a chance to get rolling."

But Szalay offers a different perspective on *Captain Power*'s abrupt demise. "Ultimately," he says, "the downfall of the show was because [kids] really got into watching the show for the stories, the plots, and the characters. If I watch that show now, and I try playing the video game, it turns *into* a video game and I don't follow the plot or the story. All I care about is the flashing light on the screen and scores gained. However, kids found that they got into the story too much and then the game became [trivial]. That's why they didn't sell! Everyone I talk to tells me they liked the stories and the drama and you can't play with the toys! It's a different mindset to play video games than it is to watch a science fiction drama."

Peter MacNeill recognizes that had the show continued further, there were many directions scripts and characters could have taken. He wishes the show had caught a broader audience by starting with a decent time slot.

"Many of us, crew and actors, hoped for an afternoon or early evening spot," says MacNeill. "When I realized that the focus was the interactive toy, it became impossible to call it anything else. I had hoped it would have a broader appeal when we started. Kids, yes, but the 'kid' in all of us!"

Best ratings were garnered either before or after *Star Trek—The Next Generation*, although TV station operators would also program the show at 5:30 or 6:30 on Saturday mornings.

Characterizing the feedback he received from being in the show, MacNeill laughs that "actor friends were not over the moon, but tech freaks were in love!"

Illustrating how popular the show was, Benison remembers that once, while sailing in the Virgin Islands, he walked into a grocery store and bumped into *Captain Power* cereal on the shelves.

Goddard believes that had the deal included "a television company, a production company doing it with us, or a distributor or network, the show would have kept going for another season at least, if not more. But, because it was toy related, Mattel basically just abandoned it."

In retrospect, Goddard believes that the interactivity was not good for the show. "Everyone related to the [show] as a toy thing," he sighs. "But that was what I had to agree to in order to get the series made. But I don't think [story editors] Joe Straczynski or Larry DiTillio or myself or any of us involved in the production ever let that affect us. We set out to make a quality television show within the guidelines of having at least three minutes of the show to be interactive programming for the kids who had toys at home. But we made a show that plays just like a normal show. The only way you know it's interactive is if you bought one of the toys. The toys tell you what to look for. The show plays on its own merits. There's nothing on the show that says, 'OK, kids, hold up your guns now.' We got excellent reviews. Even Siskel and Ebert, on their Christmas review show, where they covered videos and gifts, gave us a good review."

Confident that the show would continue, Goddard and company commissioned 22 scripts for a projected second season. Today those scripts are gathering dust on shelves, waiting for a resurrection.

Discussing the further adventures of *Captain Power and His Soldiers of the Future*, Goddard envisions that "we'd introduce newer characters. Our guys would be on the run. The first show of the season would be a five-part episode called "The Archers." They wind up in the last forest on Earth. They're saved by a band of archers, a Robin Hood type of group. Captain Power and his men are ready to help them as they're able to help him. We hoped to release that five-parter as a feature in Europe. But again, we only got as far as the script."

Using the world as a landscape, the second season would have the team being hunted down and on the run from Lord Dread's forces.

"They have to use their wits, they have to encounter new people, visit different areas, and essentially rebuild their defenses against Lord Dread and the robotic empire."

Cast Notes

Tim Dunigan (Capt. Jonathan Power): Born in St. Louis, Missouri, this actor had a recurring role in 1983's fantasy series *Wizards and Warriors*. Later, he went on to do a short-lived TV series, *Davy Crockett*.

Jessica Steen (Jessica "Pilot" Chase): Steen became a regular on the 1990s series *Homefront* (1992-93). She also guested on the Fox sit-com *Herman's Head* (1993). In the fall of 1994 she joined the cast of *Earth 2*.

Peter MacNeill (Matthew "Hawk" Masterson): MacNeill has appeared on television and in films. On USA Cable, he's acted in *Beyond Reality* and *Matrix*, and for CBC in *Road to Avonlea*. He has made movies of the week such as *Law of the Jungle*, and guest appearances on *ENG, Top Cop, Street Legal, My Secret Identity* and *War of the Worlds*. Features include *Body Parts, Renegades*, and *Physical Evidence*.

David Hemblen (Lord Dread) is a well-known Canadian actor who has appeared in *Family Viewing* (1987), *Short Circuit II* (1987), and most recently in William Shatner's TV movie adaptation of his novel *TekWar* (1994).

Sven Thorsen (Michael "Tank" Ellis): This muscled man has appeared in *Dragon: The Bruce Lee Story* (1993).

Maurice Dean Witt (Sgt. Robert "Scout" Baker): Like Hemblen, Witt is a well-known Canadian actor who also appeared in William Shatner's TV movie *TekWar* (1994).

EPISODE GUIDE

Shattered
Scout penetrates an Energy sub-station and, while narrowly escaping capture, manages to destroy it. Lord Dread, angry of Power's efforts to set back his New Order, uses an old girlfriend as bait to lure him. Power receives a message from Athena, but he doesn't realize that she's been digitized by Dread and that he is heading into a trap. Wr: Larry DiTillio. Dir: Mario Azzopardi.
  Athena Samuels (Ann-Marie MacDonald).

Wardogs
An unknown group has been raiding Dread's forces. Power and the team investigate with the possibility of recruiting support against Dread. Elsewhere, Tank and Scout find another Dread station. Wr: Larry DiTillio. Dir: George Mendeluk.
  Col. Vi (Kate Trotter); Cherokee (Graham Greene); Keiko (Jane Luk); Overunit Webber (Michael Woods).

The Abyss
An old military code is picked up by both Capt. Power and Dread. Investigating, Power and Hawk

are captured by military soldiers under General Briggs. After interrogating Power and Hawk, he orders his second in command to execute them. Wr: J. Michael Straczynski. Dir: Mario Azzopardi.
  Maj. General Briggs (Michael J. Reynolds); Col. Masters (Hardee T. Lineham); Interrogator (Victor Ertmanis); Hamilton Price (Ray Paisley); Soldier (Tim Koetting).

Final Stand
To learn Dread's next operation, a Bio Dread transmitter is planted on soldiers, who lead Power and his crew to a genetically engineered super-human who holds humans hostage. Hasko challenges Tank to a one-on-one fight to the death to settle an old score. Wr: J. Michael Straczynski. Dir: Doug Williams.
  Kasko (Charles Sexias); Woman (Susan Conway).

Pariah
A teenager escapes from Dread troopers. Hawk finds and saves the boy and learns that Dread had been experimenting with him at a lab. But the boy is a prototype of a new biological weapon against the humans. Wr: Marc Scott Zicree. Dir: Otta Hanus.
  Mitch (Gordon Woolvett); Commander Lorek (Wayne Best).

A Fire in the Dark
Pursued by Dread, who wants her help in perfecting his mechanical warriors, Jessica Morgan seeks safekeeping with Power, but Dread warns he will kill Jessica's friends every hour she's away. Wr: Marv Wolfman. Dir: Doug Williams.
  Jessica Morgan (Patricia Collins); Arthur (Gerry Pearson); Henry the Elder (J.R. Zimmerman); Adam (Robert O'Ree).

Mirror in Darkness
A fake Capt. Power is luring humans into being digitized. Power hears of people mysteriously disappearing, and he must investigate. Wr: Marc Scott Zicree and J. Michael Straczynski. Dir: Otta Hanus.
  Jason (David Elliot); Zig (John Dee); Mother (Anne Anglin); Man (Tom Diamond); Second man (Dwayne McLean); Fal (Colin O'Mera).

The Ferryman
Power plans a dangerous but important mission against Epsilon Station. The plan is successful, and Lord Dread is furious as more details of the New Order become revealed. But as Power begins to analyze the information obtained, a self-destruct signal is sent, destroying the data. Wr: J. Michael Straczynski. Dir: Otta Hanus.
  Rivvik (Ric Sarabia); Commander (Peter Snider).

And Study War No More
When Power and his team arrive at a sector they are investigating, they're surrounded by Dread Troopers. Retreating into a cave, they discover a self-contained community called Haven and its inhabitants. Wr: Michael Reaves. Dir: Jorge Montesi.
  Miles Williamson (Graeme Campbell); Chelsea Chandler (Tonya Williams).

The Intruder

In the course of delivering medical supplies, a man stows away inside Power's shuttle. Entering the base, he triggers an alarm. But Dread has them under surveillance and sends out Blastarr and units in the hopes of locating Power's base. Wr: J. Michael Straczynski, story by Marc Scott Zicree and J. Michael Straczynski. Dir: Jorge Montesi.

Andy Jackson (Barry Flatman); Jim Mitchell (Ted Simonett); Scavenger #1 (Steve Whistance Smith).

Flame Street

Disguised while on an intelligence mission to a city seeking information on Project New Order, Power is recognized by someone who immediately contacts Dread. Meanwhile, Power discovers the Web, a highly dangerous computer network that links directly to the human brain. To battle Power, Dread and Overmind meet him inside the Web. Wr: Michael Reaves, story by J. Michael Straczynski. Dir: Otta Hanus.

Mindsinger (Laurie Paton); Zone boy (Brock Johnson); Dr. Stuart Power (Bruce Gray).

Gemini and Counting

A powerful virus strain is sweeping the land. Power and his team must send a vaccine to the afflicted humans. But there isn't enough for everyone. Pilot suggests infiltrating Dread's Chem Labs to get more, having worked there before during the Metal Wars. Wr: Christy Marx, story by J. Michael Straczynski. Dir: Otta Hanus.

Erin (Laurie Holden); Doctor (Ana Ferguson).

And Madness Shall Reign

Encountering a group of raving, insane people, Power must discover how they became this way. Dread monitors them and orders their capture. Just as the Troopers get there, Power takes the leader and returns to base. Mentor learns that chemicals in the water supply have drugged the group. But Tank drank some of that water and is turning on the team. Wr: Larry DiTillio. Dir: Jorge Montesi.

Colonel Cypher (Lorne Cossette).

Judgment

Learning new data about Project New Order, Power and Pilot are shot down by Soaron. Stranded in the desert and incommunicado from the team, Power's got a broken leg, so he sends Pilot to a nearby community for help. But as Pilot gets there, she's recognized as someone who's helped Dread in the past. Wr: Larry DiTillio. Dir: Jorge Montesi.

Randall (Hans Jason Engel); Arvin (William B. Davis); Clegg (Jan Filips); Gaelan (David Gardner); Martin (Rich Parker); Jack (Kerry Rossall).

A Summoning of Thunder, Part 1

Returning to his father's gravesite on an anniversary, Power remembers working for his father as a teenager during the Metal Wars. He remembers when Dr. Power was upset at the creation of Overmind and a younger Dread's devotion to it. Meanwhile, Soaron is created. Wr: J. Michael Straczynski. Dir: Otta Hanus.

Young Jonathan Power (Dylan Neal); Landry (Anthony Dean Rubes); Commander (Vincent Orle); Soldier Jack (Jonathan Wilson); Dr. Stuart Power (Bruce Gray).

A Summoning of Thunder, Part 2

Dr. Power invents the Power suits, but Jonathan is captured by the future Lord Dread and Dr. Power is ordered to deliver himself or his son will be killed. Masterson discovers the doctor's gone but finds a hologram of him called Mentor. He must use the experimental and untried Power suits to rescue the doctor and his son. Wr: J. Michael Straczynski. Dir: Otta Hanus.

Young Jonathan Power (Dylan Neal); Dr. Stuart Power/Mentor (Bruce Gray).

The Eden Road

Is Eden 2 a myth? A resistance fighter arrives at the base and tries to convince Capt. Power and his team that it exists and is a location safe from Dread's forces. But Dread manages to intercept a shuttling mission. As proof, Vi's Wardog uniform is presented to Power, who must decide if all said is true. Wr: J. Michael Straczynski. Dir: Ken Girotti.

Overunit (Rafe MacPherson); Col. Six (Cypher) (Lorne Cossette); John (Brent Stait); Vi (Kate Trotter).

Freedom One

Freedom One is an eastern resistance radio broadcast that declares victories over Dread forces. When the station is located by Dread Troopers, a secret message is directed at Capt. Power, and the team goes to the rescue. Meeting Christine, Power discovers her plans of assembling all resistance leaders together. Wr: Christy Marx, story by J. Michael Straczynski. Dir: Aihen Scherberger.

Elzer Polarski (Raymond O'Neil); Christine Larrabee (Gwynth Walsh); Col. Cypher (Lorne Cossette); Gundar (Nick Nichols); Overunit (Laing Maybee).

New Order, Part 1: The Sky Shall Swallow Them

Power and Scout meet an informant named Locke who's got data on Project New Order, but the arrival of Blastarr and Soaron interferes. Returning to the Base, Power learns that Dread has an orbiting satellite that will mass-digitize the human population. Power's only got a few hours before the entire human race will be destroyed! Wr: Larry DiTillio. Dir: Otta Hanus.

Locke (Paul Humphrey); Overunit Gerber (Todd Waite).

New Order, Part 2: The Land Shall Burn

The Space digitizer is destroyed and plummeting towards Earth right at Volcania! Although Soaron collides with the machine, Volcania is destroyed. But Dread and Overmind survive. Wr: Larry DiTillio. Dir: Otta Hanus.

Locke (Paul Humphrey); Overunit Gerber (Todd Waite).

Retribution, Part 1
Celebrating the defeat of Volcania, Power and his team are nevertheless worried where Dread will strike next. Wr: J. Michael Straczynski. Dir: Jorge Montesi.
Overunit (Tom Quinn).

Retribution, Part 2
Using a device to track Power's shuttle, Dread locates Power's Base. But the team hears Colonel Cypher has been captured and the Soldiers must rescue him. It's a trap. They're ambushed. Meanwhile Pilot is alone at the Base when Dread's troops arrive, bent on destruction. Wr: J. Michael Straczynski. Dir: Jorge Montesi.
Locke (Paul Humphrey); Overunit (Tom Quinn).

The Champions
June 1968–September 1968

Three international agents are killed when Chinese soldiers shoot down their plane in the mountains of Tibet. The agents are revived and given special powers by strange beings from an ancient civilization. The two men and one woman now have improved senses, strength and telepathic abilities.

The trio keep the source of their powers a secret and go to work for Nemesis, a Geneva-based, top secret international agency dedicated to law, order and justice.

Cast: Craig Stirling (Stuart Damon); Sharon Macready (Alexandra Bastedo); Richard Barrett (William Gaunt); Lawrence Tremayne (Anthony Nicholls).

Created by: Monty Berman, Dennis Spooner; *Producer:* Monty Berman; *Script Supervisor:* Dennis Spooner; *Creative Consultant:* Cyril Frankel; NBC/ITC Productions; 60 minutes.

With TV's spy craze coming to an end, *The Champions* tried to enliven the genre by combining science fiction with espionage. Writer Dennis Spooner, who had written for many of Gerry Anderson's supermarionation shows in the 1960s, proposed a realistic superhero show. Producer Monty Berman, whose prior credits included *The Saint*, had the more metaphysical idea of people who had returned from the mountains of Tibet with strange powers.

The compromise was to crash-land three secret agents (Craig, a pilot; Richard, a cryptographer; and Sharon, a biologist) in Tibet and have inhabitants of a forgotten civilization bestow ancient superpowers on the trio.

The powers of the three were underplayed throughout the series. They exchanged looks of concentrated energy while trying to locate a missing person, and on rare occasions they bent a jail bar or knocked out a small section of a wall. In many episodes, their superpowers were so subtle that they had a negligible effect on their missions.

The comic-strip plots pitted the champions against would-be world conquerors, traitorous scientists and revived Nazis. Although filmed in England by ITC, *The Champions* was purchased by the NBC network for the summer of 1968. ITC wanted an American lead for the show to appeal to an international market. Stuart Damon, an American actor who had moved to England, was cast as the lead hero, Craig Stirling.

Several actresses were considered for the role of Sharon, including Illona Rogers and Australian actress Annette Andre. Because model Alexandra Bastedo had the exotic look the producers were looking for, she won the role despite her lack of acting experience. English actor William Gaunt was cast as the third agent, Richard. Shakespearean actor Anthony Nicholls played their boss, Tremayne.

"*The Champions* was more of a run-of-the-mill idea for TV than *The Prisoner*," says writer Gerald Kelsey, who wrote for both series. "The supersensory element was not particularly original." Kelsey was invited as a freelance writer to script two segments for the series. "I mostly dealt with Dennis Spooner as far as details of stories and scripts were concerned. I was given a very free hand. Dennis would ask me to think of an idea. I would then tell him the show's teaser. If it hooked him, I'd go away and write it."

Kelsey recalls that *The Champions* was set on a very strict budget. Despite globe-trotting stories,

The Champions, left to right: William Gaunt, Stuart Damon, Alexandra Bastedo. Copyright 1968 ITC.

the filming of the series was mostly confined to a soundstage. "It was emphasized in story briefings that they wanted to use stock footage of interesting and spectacular backgrounds. We talked about story settings in jungles, deserts and volcanoes."

Kelsey's first script, "Operation Deep Freeze," took place in the Antarctic. Since filming there was out of the question, Kelsey came up with an idea. "I had seen travelogues of the Antarctic, and I called Dennis. I asked if he could organize some of these travelogues for me to see again. I sat in the studio theater and watched five of the films. I made notes of all of the impressive and dramatic shots, including a large transport aircraft landing at Scott Base, ice breakers and icebergs, and penguins scattering into the sea. When I finished viewing the films, I had 150 shots. I then devised and constructed a story that featured the most spectacular cuts. I linked them together with the studio exteriors, which were polystyrene snow spread across the studio floor with a background

of white backcloth. My final script specified almost 100 stock shots of Antarctica."

Kelsey felt the result was sensational. "'Operation Deep Freeze' effectively showed the 'wide ice wastes.' The episode received complimentary notices in the national press for its feature film quality! There was actually no location filming in the Arctic at all. I was very impressed and delighted with the way the shots I had selected looked in the final film."

The economical series was obsessed with getting a return on its investments. When the producers bought a mock-up of a submarine, they used it in four episodes to make the most of their purchase. On another occasion, while filming inside a studio, the producers heard that a building was on fire nearby. A film unit raced to the inferno, and as firefighters battled the blaze, the film crew got spectacular footage of the fire. It was later written into the episode "The Happening."

The Champions unpack for a jungle safari. Left to right: Stuart Damon, Alexandra Bastedo and William Gaunt. Copyright 1968 ITC.

Guest star Peter Wyngarde feels the show was better than it was given credit for. "*The Champions* had three protagonists, and this limited the budget for the series considerably. The budget was the series' biggest problem. This may explain why the producers have not had the recognition [for the show] which they so richly deserve." Wyngarde, who starred in the segment "The Invisible Man," had worked with *Champions* director Cyril Frankel before in such series as *Jason King*. He recalls him as a man who "brought an artistic quality, which helped the visual presentation. He was sensitive, and technically, an immensely proficient director."

The Champions aired in America during the summer of 1968, but it contained many of the qualities American TV was getting rid of, including violence and action-adventure formats. A dozen of the episodes were screened, but the response was tepid from viewers and hostile from critics. It was not picked up for NBC's January 1969 schedule.

Without a network slot, it was financially impractical to continue with a second season. *The Champions* was retired after 30 episodes. The series has been seen only in sporadic syndication since. The pilot and the episode "The Interrogation" were spliced together in the early 1980s to form the TV movie *Legend of the Champions*.

CAST NOTES

Stuart Damon (Craig): Born 1937. The American-born actor was 11 years old when he played his first role, as the Cowardly Lion in a summer camp production of *The Wizard of Oz*. His big break was playing the Prince in the 1966 TV special *Cinderella* (with Lesley Anne Warren). He's been one of the stars of daytime's *General Hospital* since the 1970s.

William Gaunt (Richard): Born 1937. An English actor who turned to situation comedy in the 1980s. Gaunt's most recent success was in the London play *Travels with My Aunt* (1993).

Alexandra Bastedo (Sharon): Born 1946. The former model continues acting, with occasional TV appearances in England, including game shows and theater. She was one of the stars of the English stage comedy *Pickwick* in 1993.

Anthony Nicholls (Tremayne): Born 1902. Nicholls began his film career in 1937 and served with the Royal Artillery during World War II. He died in 1977.

EPISODE GUIDE

The Beginning
After crashing in the mountains of Tibet and receiving their special powers, the trio are pursued by Chinese agents. Wr: Dennis Spooner. Dir: Cyril Frankel.
Old man (Felix Aylmer); Whittaker (Kenneth J. Warren); Chislenkan (Joseph Furst); Ho Ling (Eric Young); Chinese major (Burt Kwouk); Chinese commander (Anthony Chinn).

To Trap a Rat
Sharon poses as a drug addict in the streets of London to expose a dealer who is selling an exotic powder that makes people crack. Wr: Ralph Smart. Dir: Sam Wanamaker.
Walter Pelham (Guy Rolfe); Sandra (Edina Ronay); Jane Purcell (Kate O'Mara); Edwards (Michael Standing); Peanut Vendor (Toke Townley); Ambassador (Michael Mellinger); Doctor (John Lee); Ambulance man (Michael Guest).

The Experiment
Sharon is one of the guinea pigs used by a mad scientist intent on creating a race of super-humans. Wr: Tony Williamson. Dir: Cyril Franken.
Dr. Glind (David Bauer); Dr. Margaret Daniels (Madalena Nicol); Cranmore (Allan Cuthbertson); Marion Grant (Caroline Blakiston); Susan Francis (Nita Lorraine); Jean Giraud (Jonathan Burn); Paul Lang (Peter J. Elliot); Officer (Philip Bond); Barman (Russell Waters); Farley (Nicholas Courtney).

The Invisible Man
Under the control of a scientist, Craig finds himself involved in a plot to rob a bank. Wr: Donald James. Dir: Cyril Frankel.
John Hallam (Peter Wyngarde); Charles Sumner (James Culliford); Frederick Howard (Basil Dignam); Van

Velden (Aubrey Morris); Boursin (Steve Plytas); Weightlifter (Dave Prowse).

The Search
Modern-day Nazis take over a British nuclear sub and threaten to destroy London unless a ransom is paid. Craig and Sharon manage to get aboard the sub. Wr: Dennis Spooner. Dir: Leslie Norman.
Kruger Haller (John Woodvine); Conrad Schultz (Reginald Marsh); Rudolf Mueller (Joseph Furst); Suzanne Taylor (Patricia English); Allbrecht (Ernst Walder); Innkeeper (Gabor Baraker).

The Dark Island
Missing agents lead the trio to an uncharted atoll where they discover a missile installation and a plot to start World War III. Wr: Tony Williamson. Dir: Cyril Frankel.
Max Kellor (Vladek Sheybal); Admiral (Alan Gifford); Controller (Bill Nagy); Perango (Benito Carruthers); Kai Min (Andy Ho); Radarman (Richard Bond); Withers (Brandon Brady); Tsi Chong (Robert Lee); Sailor (Nick Tate).

Shadow of the Panther
While investigating a scientist's disappearance in Haiti, Sharon is put under a voodoo trance. Wr: Tony Williamson. Dir: Freddie Francis.
Prengo (Zia Mohyeddin); David Crayley (Donald Sutherland); Riley (Tony Wall); Ralph Charters (Hedger Wallace); Doctor (Christopher Carlos); Waiter (Kenneth Gardiner); Girl (Tania).

The Iron Man
The Champions work as domestic servants for a former dictator whose life has been targeted by assassins. Wr: Philip Broadley. Dir: John Llewellyn Moxey.
El Caudillo (George Murcell); Pedraza (Patrick Magee); Callezon (Robert Crewdson); Gen. Tornes (Michael Mellinger); Carlos (Stephen Berkoff); Cabello (Norman Florence); Maid (Lisa Thomas).

Twelve Hours
An assassin's bomb sends a submarine to the sea floor, where Sharon must operate on a critically injured foreign leader. Wr: Donald James. Dir: Paul Dickson.
Raven (Mike Pratt); Admiral Cox (Peter Howell); Street (John Turner); Captain (John Stone); Madame Drobnic (Viola Keats); President Drobnic (Henry Gilbert); Jackson (Laurie Asprey); Telegraphist (Rio Fanning).

Operation Deep Freeze
A Central American dictator locks Craig and Richard in a deep freeze and prepares to launch his atomic weapons. Wr: Gerald Kelsey. Dir: Paul Dickson.
Gen. Gomez (Patrick Wymark); Hemmings (Robert Urquhart); Capt. Jost (Walter Gotell); Margoli (Peter Arne); Captain (Dallas Cavell); Santos (George Pastell); Mendoza (Michael Godfrey); Gregson (Martin Boddey); Zerilli (Derek Sydney); Hoffner (Alan White).

The Fanatics

Agents are killing world leaders. Richard infiltrates the assassin's outfit, learning that the next target is Tremayne. Wr: Terry Nation. Dir: John Gilling.

Croft (Gerald Harper); Col. Banks (Donald Pickering); Anderson (Julian Glover); Roger Carson (David Burke); Krasner (David Morrell); Faber (Barry Stanton); Collings (John Robinson).

Get Me Out of Here!

A woman scientist is held captive at police headquarters in the Caribbean. Wr: Ralph Smart. Dir: Cyril Frankel.

Anna Maria Martes (Frances Cuka); Commandante (Ronald Radd); Angel Martes (Philip Madoc); Minister (Eric Pohlmann); Enrique Cuevos (Anthony Newlands); Josef (Godfrey Quigley); Captain (Norman Florence); Detective (Richard Montez).

The Ghost Plane

Sharon gets put in cold storage when she investigates a scientist who has sold his super-plane to the Chinese. Wr: Donald James. Dir: John Gilling.

John Newman (Andrew Keir); Vanessa Bailey (Hilary Tindall); Coates (Michael Wynn); Bridges (Dennis Chinnery); Hardwick (Tony Steedman); Admiral (Derek Murcott); Pilot (Paul Gist); Crolic (John Bryans); Captain (Michael Miller).

Reply Box No. 666

Sharon and Richard race to the rescue when Craig, searching for a secret plane, is dumped into the sea after his cover is blown. Wr: Philip Broadley. Dir: Cyril Frankel.

Jules (Anton Rogers); Nikko (George Murcell); Bourges (Brian Worth); Corinne (Nike Arrighi); Clive (Linbert Spencer); Semenkin (George Roubicek); Cleo (Imogen Hassall).

The Gun Runners

While searching the Burmese jungle for missing weapons, the Champions are captured by a ruthless arms dealer. Wr: Dennis Spooner. Dir: Robert Asher.

Hartington (William Franklyn); Guido Selvameni (Paul Stassino); Filmer (David Lodge); Schroeder (Guy Deghy); Police captain (Eric Young); Nadkarni (Wolfe Morris); Clerk (Nicolas Chagrin); Sergeant (Anthony Chinn).

The Mission

A plastic surgeon furnishes escaped convicts with a new identity. Craig and Sharon pose as Mafia people to infiltrate the organization. Wr: Donald James. Dir: Robert Asher.

Hogan (Dermot Kelly); Pederson (Anthony Bate); Sophia (Patricia Haines); George (Harry Towb); Maltman (Robert Russell); Emil Boder (Paul Hansard).

Project Zero

Richard summons the help of Craig and Sharon when his undercover mission to investigate a giant fusion gun is imperiled. Wr: Tony Williamson. Dir: Don Sharp.

Dr. Voss (Rupert Davies); Antrobus (Peter Copley); Forster (Geoffrey Chater); Grayson (Reginald Jessup); Miss Davies (Jan Holden); Postmaster (Nicholas Smith); Sloane (Donald Morley); Travis (John Moore); Wittering (Maurice Browning); Chairman (John Horslay); Hedges (Eric Lander); Stewardess (Jill Curzon); Pilot (Bruce Beeby).

The Interrogation

Flashbacks of previous adventures are included when Craig is fiercely interrogated. Evidence suggests that Craig may be a double agent for the enemy. Wr: Dennis Spooner. Dir: Cyril Frankel.

Interrogator (Colin Blakely).

The Night People

Sharon's disappearance is linked with a man's uranium mine and his efforts to increase nuclear testing for his own profit. Wr: Donald James. Dir: Robert Asher.

Douglas Trennick (Terence Alexander); Mrs. Trennick (Adrienne Corri); Porth (David Lodge); Jane Soames (Anne Sharp); Dan Hedgely (Michael Bilton); George Whetlor (Walter Sparrow); Hoad (Jerold Wells); Clerk (Frank Thornton).

Full Circle

Craig poses as a prisoner to gain the trust of a fellow convict who can reveal top secret information. Their escape is sabotaged, and Craig is captured by enemy agents. Wr: Donald James. Dir: John Gilling.

Paul Westerman (Patrick Allen); Garcian (Martin Benson); Sarah (Gabrielle Drake); Alfred Booker (John Nettleton); Carrington (Jack Gwillim); Pickering (James Donnelly); Fairfax (Lawrence James); Collins (Victor Brooks); Boulton (Harvey Hall).

The Gilded Cage

Kidnapped, Richard is forced to reveal a top secret formula or an innocent young woman will be killed. Wr: Philip Broadley. Dir: Cyril Frankel.

Samantha (Jennie Linden); Symons (John Carson); Lovegrove (Clinton Greyn); Orley (Charles Houston); Brandon (Tony Caunter); Haswell (Sebastian Breaks); Manager (Vernon Dobtcheff).

The Silent Enemy

The Champions duplicate the submarine voyage taken by an ill-fated crew, and become stranded on an island where a scientist has developed a deadly nerve gas. Wr: Donald James. Dir: Robert Asher.

Sam Baxter (Paul Maxwell); Parker (Warren Stanhope); Stanton (James Maxwell); Minoes (Marne Maitland); Minister (Esmond Knight); Lighthouse men (David Blake Kelly, Rio Fanning).

A Case of Lemmings

A Mafia leader has made several Interpol agents take their own lives. When Craig tries to bring the mafioso down, he finds himself caught in the same self-destructive grip. Wr: Philip Broadley. Dir: Paul Dickson.

Del Marco (Edward Brayshaw); Claudine Merval (Jeanne Roland); Umberto (John Bailey); Jacquet (Michael

Graham); Pillet (Michael Slater); Madame Carnot (Olive McFarland); French couple (Jacques Cey, Madge Brindley); Woman (Ann de Vigier).

The Body Snatchers
Investigating the deaths of two newsmen, Richard and a dying American general are captured and cryogenically frozen for a foreign government. Wr: Terry Nation. Dir: Paul Dickson.

Squires (Bernard Lee); Inge Kalmutt (Ann Lynn); Yeats (Philip Locke); Frank Nichols (J. G. Devlin); David Fenton (Gregory Phillips); Lee Rogers (Christina Taylor); White (Fredric Abbott).

The Survivors
Investigating the murders of three students in the Austrian Alps, the Champions find a horde of underground Nazis. Wr: Donald James. Dir: Cyril Frankel.

Frank Reitz/Col. Hans Reitz (Clifford Evans); Richtter (Donald Houston); Schmeltz (John Tate); Emil (Bernard Kay); Mine attendant (Frederick Schiller); Hans (John Porter Davison); Pieter (Stephen Yardley); Heinz (Hugo Panczak).

The Nutcracker
A top government official is caught stealing top secret documents, forcing the Champions to test the security of a sophisticated vault that is programmed to kill intruders. Wr: Philip Broadley. Dir: Roy Ward Baker.

Duncan (William Squire); Lord Mauncey (David Langton); Manager (Michael Barrington); John Warre (John Franklyn-Robbins); Walcott (John Bown); Travers (David Kelsey); Guard (Dervis Ward); Assistant (Robert Mill).

Happening
A super-bomb is set to destroy most of Australia.

The only hope of stopping the explosion rests with Richard, who has lost his memory and is stranded in the desert. Wr: Brian Clemens. Dir: Cyril Frankel.

Banner (Jack MacGowran); Gen. Winters (Grant Taylor); Joss (Michael Gough); Aston (Bill Cummings).

Desert Journey
The Champions must transport the son of a deposed regime to an Arab state to prevent war, but assassins are everywhere. Wr: Stuart Black. Dir: Paul Dickson.

The Bey (Jeremy Brett); Yussef (Roger Delgado); Said (Nik Zaran); Curtis (Reg Lye); Branco (Henry Soskin); Sheikh (Peter Madden); Tuat (Tony Cyrus); Sonia (Yole Marinelli); Man (Dave Prowse).

The Final Countdown
A group of Nazis locate a missing A-bomb that was to have destroyed London during World War II. They now plan to use the bomb to launch the Fourth Reich. Wr: Gerald Kelsey. Dir: John Gilling.

Von Splitz (Alan MacNaughton); Dr. Neimann (Wolf Frees); Kruger (Derek Newark); Wolf Eisen (Basil Henson); Anna Eisen (Hannah Gordon); Gerhard Schultz (Morris Perry); Heiden (Norman Jones); Tom Brooks (Michael Lees).

Autokill
Nemesis agents are killing each other after being given a deadly drug. Richard is given the drug and ordered to kill Craig. Wr: Brian Clemens. Dir: Roy Ward Baker.

Barka (Eric Pohlmann); Klein (Paul Eddington); Dr. Amis (Harold Innocent); George Brading (Richard Owens); Loretta Brading (Rachel Herbert); Mechanic (Conrad Monk); U. S. Colonel (Bruce Boa).

Cliffhangers: The Secret Empire
February 1979–May 1979

Jim Donner, a U. S. marshal in Cheyenne, Wyoming, in 1880, is on the trail of gold robbers when he discovers an underground city named Chimera. The futuristic metropolis is inhabited by aliens who escaped from their planet long ago. Donner joins up with the friendly Princess Maya, who helps him battle Thorval, the evil dictator intent on conquering the surface world.

Cast: Marshal Jim Donner (Geoffrey Scott); Millie Thomas (Carlene Watkins); Thorval (Mark Lenard); Princess Tara (Diane Markoff, Stepfanie Kramer); Princess Maya (Pamela Brull); Jess Keller (Peter Breck); Billy (Tiger Williams); *Cliffhangers* Title Narrator (Brad Crandall); *Recurring Characters:* Hator (David Opatoshu); Yannuck (Sean Garrison); Kalek (S. Newton Anderson); Roe (Peter Tomarken); The Taz (Tommy Madden); Demeter (Jay Robinson).

Created by: Kenneth Johnson; *Producers:* Richard Milton, B. W. Sandefur, Paul Samuelson; *Executive Producer:* Kenneth Johnson; *Writers for the three segments under the* Cliffhangers *title included:* Jeri Taylor, Sam Egan, Richard Christian Matheson, Craig Buck, Peggy Goldman, Andrew Schneider, Harry and Renee Longstreet; *Directors included:* Joe Pevney, Alan Crosland, Jr., Kenneth Johnson; NBC/Universal; 60 minutes (17 minutes per segment).

"It was the most expensive TV series at the time," says *Cliffhangers* creator Kenneth Johnson. Raised on the matinee serials of the 1940s, Johnson wanted to recreate the thrills for audiences of the 1970s. He came up with an unusual format for television. Under the title *Cliffhangers*, three continuing series were presented. They consisted of *Stop Susan Williams*, a spy spoof with Susan Anton as an adventuress; *The Secret Empire*, an adventure that mixed science fiction and the Old West (and because of its science fiction flavor, the only one of the series included in this book's episode guide), and *The Curse of Dracula*, starring Michael Nouri as an anguished vampire who poses as a California college professor. Each of the three segments ran 17 minutes each, and each ended with a cliffhanger. Susan Williams might be trapped on a river raft, surrounded by hungry piranha; Dracula would usually be about to bite a trapped heroine; and Marshal Jim Donner would be in his own fix, perhaps thrashing about in the web of a giant spider. Audiences had to wait until the next week to find out what happened. Just like the old movie cliffhangers, however, the heroes always found a last-minute reprieve from death.

The *Cliffhangers* concept thrilled Johnson. "Freddie Silverman [NBC's programming chief] asked me to create a show that would be reminiscent of the old Republic movie serials. I had watched all of that great stuff as a kid: *Don Winslow of the Navy, Robinson Crusoe on Clipper Island,* and *Radar Men from the Moon.*

"Over Labor Day weekend, 1978, I wrote a premise for five different serials. I went to NBC and said, 'Okay, here's five. These are the three I think we should go with.' One was a contemporary *Perils of Pauline,* which was *Stop Susan Williams.* The second was *The Secret Empire,* my science-fiction western, and the third was a contemporary, sexy retelling of the *Dracula* story. NBC said, 'Great! Let's do it.' I proceeded to write the one-hour pilot, which was three separate shows in one, in ten days."

Once the series was geared for production, Johnson realized just how complicated the show was going to be. "Casting three separate shows simultaneously was something of a nightmare," he says. "We also had three different film units shooting, and three sets of writers. The whole series cost over a million dollars per episode because of the multiple requirements. While it was a lot of fun to write for, it was a monster to produce. When I realized I needed three writing

Producer Kenneth Johnson (right) poses with Tommy Madden, who played one of the Taz in *Cliffhangers: The Secret Empire.* Courtesy of Kenneth Johnson.

staffs, I put out a cattle call for writers. I think 17 writers showed up and I hired them all." Johnson's next step was to get the series rolling. He admits that he was forced to make some compromises. "Geoffrey Scott was cast the day before we started shooting," he says of the actor who played Marshal Donner in *The Secret Empire.* "I'm not sure if he was my best choice. Everyone looks for that magical, 35-year-old leading man that nobody's seen. Geoff had sort of a western feel about him, and he turned out to be adequate."

The Secret Empire also needed a futuristic city. Although Universal studios made a lot of stock footage available, Johnson was determined to make *Cliffhangers* as fresh as possible. "I didn't give any thought to how much it would cost to build these things. The cost didn't seem to matter to Freddie Silverman, either. Part of the alien city was created by matte painting. Another part was actually beautiful downtown Long Beach, California. We put a sky of rock over it with a matte painting. We had about six matte paintings

Geoffrey Scott as lawman Jim Donner in *Cliff-hangers: The Secret Empire.* Copyright 1979 NBC/Universal.

... and they cost around $12,000 each. They were very expensive, and they would only be on screen for six seconds." One interesting twist in *The Secret Empire* was the novel use of color. Scenes that took place above ground were filmed in black and white, while all of the underground city scenes were filmed in color. "They [NBC] gave me all kinds of shit over the black-and-white western idea. They said, 'You can't do that!' But it turned out well. We ended up using very little stock footage."

One of the *Cliffhangers* producers, Richard Milton, recalls, "All of the staff writers brainstormed every day. I produced the *Dracula* segments; Bill Sandefur, a former dentist, produced *The Secret Empire;* and Paul Samuelson produced *Stop Susan Williams.*" Milton, however, feels that the combination of three series under one title ultimately doomed the show. "Having each segment as 17 minutes long wasn't time enough to develop them properly," he says. "It was like squeezing three series into one. There should have been only two segments per show at a half hour each. The three 17-minuters didn't work, and people found them hard to follow. The storylines were fairly complicated, whereas the original movie cliffhangers were simpler to understand. The first episode started out pretty well in the ratings with a 25 share. Within a few weeks it had gone down to a six share. The production was also rushed, and no one expected the costs of the series to be so high. Fred Silverman wanted *Cliffhangers* as a mid-season show. We pleaded with the network to put us on in the fall so that we could develop it properly. When *Cliffhangers* failed, Silverman blamed himself for it."

"Good ol' Freddie put us on opposite *Happy Days* and *Laverne and Shirley,*" notes Kenneth Johnson. "*Happy Days* was getting a 45 share in reruns. I said, 'Fred, what are you doing? This is crazy!' He said, 'Don't worry. If it doesn't work, I'll move it right away.' He didn't, and we never picked up an audience. NBC didn't even air the final episode. That infuriated the enormously loyal following that we did have."

Had the series continued, Richard Milton thinks *The Secret Empire* would have been dropped. "It was the least successful. *The Curse of Dracula* was the most successful. *Stop Susan Williams* probably would have been dropped as well. Susan Anton was its star because Fred Silverman demanded that she be there. She was great as a variety singer. She has a damn good voice, and she's terrific on live stage in Las Vegas and terrific to work with. She wasn't, however, much of an actress. After the first day of seeing dailies for *Stop Susan Williams,* Silverman was ready to replace her with somebody else."

"Susan was a very nice lady, but she didn't have much experience as an actress," agrees Kenneth Johnson. "Freddie had a thing for her at the time."

Milton and Johnson both give high marks to the *Curse of Dracula* segment. "We got a lot of fan mail about Dracula," says Milton. "Even today, it's the only *Cliffhangers* segment shown in syndication [glued together as a TV movie, *The World of Dracula*]. There's something about the Dracula stuff that holds up. However, even with Dracula, we never really decided what we wanted to do. Did we want a serious show or tongue-in-cheek? But Michael Nouri was well cast. He had a great sense of humor and went on to be a fairly big-name star."

"Michael Nouri was a dazzling Dracula," says Johnson. "He walked into my office talking like Bela Lugosi. The out-takes of *Curse of Dracula* are some of the funniest stuff you'll ever see. Michael is a hysterically funny fellow. Dramatically, the Dracula segments were the best. They had a lot of soul, and we focused on character more. Dracula was sexy, dangerous and vulnerable. At the time, I wrote a one-hour pilot to spin off a separate series. It was similar to *The Incredible Hulk*. It was Dracula's desire to try to get off the blood, i.e. the bottle. You couldn't totally trust him because he couldn't trust himself. Had *Cliffhangers* gone on, that spin-off might have happened. It would have been a very interesting show."

Johnson still has a soft spot for *The Secret Empire*, however, and thinks it may have been just slightly ahead of its time. "It was the most imaginative of the three. We were on just before Indiana Jones reared his head. What intrigued me in seeing the Indy films was that there were the snakes and the hero who used a bullwhip—all of the things we had done in *The Secret Empire*.

"*Cliffhangers* was an enormously challenging series," he concludes. "It was great fun to write for. We had a good stable of writers, many of whom went on to successful careers. It was just very frustrating that we didn't last longer."

Cast Notes

Geoffrey Scott (Jim Donner): Scott spent time on TV's *Dynasty* (1982–84).

Carlene Watkins (Millie:) Born 1952. Watkins appeared later in several situation comedies, including *Bob* in the mid 1990s.

Pamela Brull (Maya): This California-born actress currently appears in TV guest roles.

Peter Breck (Keller): Born 1929. Breck played one of the sons on TV's *The Big Valley* (1965–69). Currently, he runs an acting school in Vancouver, Canada.

Diane Markoff (Tata): After *Cliffhangers*, Markoff had a recurring role on the Jack Klugman series, *Quincy* (1980–83).

Stepfanie Kramer (Tara): Born 1956. Kramer costarred in the 1980s crime series *Hunter*.

Mark Lenard (Thorval): See *Planet of the Apes*.

Episode Guide

Plunge into Mystery
Marshal Jim Donner learns that gold robbers are from an underground city. The city's evil alien dictator intends to keep control over his subjects and invade the surface world as well.

Prisoner of the Empire
Donner races to save Billy, who has been sentenced to death by Thorval and placed in a compression tube.

The Mind Twisters
Marshal Donner has only one hope in escaping a freezing death: pledge his allegiance to Princess Tara and become her slave.

Seeds of Revolt
Using the stolen gold to power his mind control device, Thorval tries to take over Donner's mind and make him a slave.

Attack of the Phantom Riders
Donner desperately struggles to escape from the city as Thorval prepares to make his first assault on the surface.

Sizzling Threat
Jim's plans to undermine the Phantom Riders' next raid is stalled when they capture Billy.

Mandibles of Death
Donner infiltrates the Phantom Riders to thwart a gold mine robbery, but lawmen mistake him for a raider and he's thrown into jail.

The Last Gasp
Thorval makes a deal with gold smuggler Jess Keller. If Keller helps Thorval attack the surface of Earth, Thorval will give him the power he craves.

Return to Chimera
Maya is left to perish in the surface atmosphere, but her long-missing father, Demeter, appears and rescues her. He pledges to help Donner in his battle against Thorval.

Powerhouse
Jim needs to free the Partisans (the aliens who are opposed to Thorval) from the compliatron mind-control effect. He enters Chimera's nuclear reactor room and faces its explosive dangers.

The Fantastic Journey
February 1977–June 1977

Shipwrecked on an island in the Bermuda Triangle, a group of travelers finds that the island is subdivided into different time zones. The travelers make their way through the zones, which represent the past and future, to reach a land known as Evoland, which can return them home.

Cast: Varian (man from the 23rd century) (Jared Martin); Jonathan Willoway (from the 1960s) (Roddy McDowall); Dr. Fred Walters (Carl Franklin); Scott Jordan (Ike Eisenmann); Liana (half earthling, half extra-terrestrial) (Katie Saylor); Main Title Narrator (Mike Road).

Created by: Merwin Gerard; *Producer:* Leonard Katzman; *Executive Producer:* Bruce Lansbury; NBC/Columbia; 60 minutes.

"Science fiction series generally weren't successful in the past because the audience wasn't ready," said producer Bruce Lansbury just before *The Fantastic Journey* began on NBC. "We now have a generation who love science fiction movies like *Futureworld, Rollerball* and *Logan's Run.* They are loyal fans and their numbers are multiplying." Unfortunately, they didn't multiply enough for *The Fantastic Journey.* A fresh, unique TV series, it debuted on television during a spate of situation comedies and dramas. The reaction proved that American audiences still preferred the hijinks of *Welcome Back Kotter* to the troubles of travelers crossing through fantastic lands to reach their home.

The fanciful premise marooned a group of survivors on an island in the Bermuda Triangle. Their goal: to reach a shore named Evoland where they could be returned to their rightful time. What proved difficult was deciding which characters should be on the journey. In the original unaired pilot, Desi Arnaz, Jr., played a World War II pilot who crash-lands on the island and meets fellow travelers Scott Jordan and Dr. Fred Walters (both from 1977). "My role was based on a real-life lieutenant who disappeared in the Bermuda Triangle," says Arnaz. "My character encounters all of these pirates from the sixteenth century, and I had a big swordfight scene with actor Ian McShane." Shortly after the filming, Arnaz was cut from the pilot. "My part just disappeared," he says. "My footage is probably floating around Columbia studios somewhere. Call it the Columbia Triangle."

Writers Katharyn Powers and her then-husband Michael Michaelian were asked to rewrite Merwin Gerard and Ken Pettus's original script. "One of the problems was that the original pilot had too many characters," she says. "Our main contribution was adding Varian [the man from the year 2230]. In fact, one of the studio executives had reservations about giving the go-ahead to *Fantastic Journey* until she read the version with Varian. She fell in love with the character, and the pilot was accepted. This isn't to vitiate the work done by the original script workers. It was simply the total contribution of all the creative talents involved that made it work."

Varian was a peace-loving, articulate man whose futuristic spaceship crash-landed on the island. He befriends Scott and Fred, and the three join forces to find Evoland. "Michael and I had written an unusually long speech for Varian in the pilot where he describes who he is and what his world is like," recalls Powers. "We felt the speech established the thrust of the character. We were met with instant objection from everyone! We were told to cut the speech way down. In the meantime, our speech was what they used to audition Jared Martin with. When Jared read the speech, everyone was deeply moved. The speech stayed. I was privileged to meet Jared on the set. He was absolutely perfect in the role. 'A role like this doesn't come along very often,' he told me. We also had a chuckle over the infamous long speech by Varian. I thanked him for making it work. He thanked me for writing it."

It still took some juggling to come up with the right character combination. In the second episode, "Atlantium," Liana joins the travelers. Her father was a descendant of the lost people of Atlantis; her mother was an extra-terrestrial. Katharyn Powers made the contribution of Sil-L, Liana's telepathic cat.

In the third episode, another important character was added: Jonathan Willoway. "In the original script," says story editor Dorothy Fontana, "Willoway had been totally evil. He was

Cast of *The Fantastic Journey*, left to right: Katie Saylor, Roddy McDowall, Ike Eisenmann, Carl Franklin and Jared Martin. Copyright 1977 NBC/Columbia.

destroyed in the climax of the story. I rewrote the script and made him into someone who was merely manipulative and not entirely trustworthy. As played by Roddy McDowall, he was very compelling. He became the fifth and last character added to the group. It took us until the third episode to establish all of the regular characters. From then on, we had to start working out their relationships to each other. The growing relationships and humor between the characters were partially effective."

"The addition of Roddy McDowall was a real coup," adds Powers. "He's a superb actor, and he added a dimension of importance to the show."

Now the five could begin their journey. "Bruce Lansbury envisioned the island as a honeycomb of different time zones," recalls Powers. "Past, future and present existed simultaneously. It allowed the writers to concoct the widest possible variety of scenarios." Every week, a blue glow would transport the travelers to a new time zone. The characters never knew what lay ahead.

Powers' strongest memory of the series relates to rewriting the pilot. "We were all under a tremendous amount of pressure to get the script completed. There was a scene on the beach, just after the scientists are shipwrecked, where one of the young women becomes hysterical. For some reason, the scene was a bitch to write. Around 3 a.m., Michael and I were exhausted. We had reached our breaking point with this scene. We couldn't make this woman's transition [to accept her predicament] believable. No matter what we changed, we hated it. We had a technique to break through such creative quagmires. We talked the scene through in an X-rated version. The absurdity of the technique really worked for us. We made the necessary changes that morning. However, we slipped the X-rated page into Bruce Lansbury's script (and only his!) as if it were a part of the final rewrite. Well, Bruce is one of the most able, creative producers I've ever worked with. He has a great sense of humor. He let us know that we had given him a good laugh. He kept that page after all these years."

"I remember one of the network people

Guest star Lew Ayres (left) as a peaceful leader in "The Innocent Prey." Also with (left to right) Roddy McDowall, Jared Martin, guest star Cheryl Ladd, Ike Eisenmann and guest star Jim Payner. Copyright 1977 NBC/Columbia.

wanted to shoot that page," says Michael Michaelian. "Unfortunately, they didn't. But it was discussed appreciably ever after!"

As a mid-season replacement, *The Fantastic Journey* was, in Dorothy Fontana's words, "rushed into production without enough lead time. I started with the show in early December 1976. At that point, only the pilot was in the can, and it was being re-cut. We had a few scripts on hand, but they had to be rewritten to fit the revised format, i.e., take out Scott's father, add Liana and Willoway. The show went on about a month after the staff was assembled and production began. As a result, we were constantly close to the edge. We were pushed to get scripts done, principal photography completed, film edited, scored and dubbed. We had to have answer prints ready to go on the air on schedule. It's not possible for people to do their best work under such hectic and pressured circumstances."

Story consultant Calvin Clements, Jr., says, "*Fantastic Journey* went by like a blur. Every day was like a sprint. Good science fiction is very hard to write. Most of what passes for science fiction is updated westerns or simplistic human allegories with people who have Martian sounding names like Og. When science fiction isn't good, it's frankly very bad. Most of the time they're not successful. *Battlestar Galactica* and *Buck Rogers* were both financial disasters. In *Fantastic Journey*, it became somewhat formalized. In terms of production, it was very ambitious. Any show that is visiting new worlds every week has to build that world. You can't just go out in the street and film it, unless it's one of those plots where they go, 'Hey, look! It's a mirror image of Earth!' That meant building the sets, dressing the people, and using optical effects. The budget went for making that razzle-dazzle effect each week. Every time they skipped over to another time zone, you needed the optical blip, and that costs money. It was like building the land of Oz every week!"

Clements enjoyed his stint, but *The Fantastic Journey* doesn't stand out as a particular memorable series. "As a young writer, I was just happy to get a job offer. It was an intriguing premise, and the creative people were nice. Bruce Lansbury is a terrific producer. The cast was fairly decent. Roddy McDowall's character was an interesting, spunky fellow. He was a kind of a pixieish villain. Katie Saylor's character was fun. She had that eerie sensitivity for animals. Ike Eisenmann was a good young actor. He had done a lot of work at Disney. But audiences just didn't bite. There were never any Ike Eisenmann fan clubs. I don't say that with derision. The show may have had a look that people didn't like. We rushed to get those shows on the air. Some of the episodes shouldn't be held up as examples of our best work."

While *The Fantastic Journey* languished in the ratings, it did pick up a loyal core of viewers, as well as encouraging reviews from the critics. *TV Guide* urged viewers to give the series a chance before it was too late. *Seattle Post-Intelligencer* TV columnist Susan Paynter said a tear could be shed for *The Fantastic Journey*'s impending cancellation because "at least it tried to be different."

"Every new series takes time to 'shake out' and find itself," notes Powers. "*Fantastic Journey* was doing that. If it had been given a chance, I think it would have run for a very long time."

"It had an awful time slot [Thursdays at 8 p.m.]," says Michaelian. "And the network was unwilling to give it a chance. The series' strength was that it had a pretty good cast. Roddy and Jared worked particularly well together. Roddy was excellent in an episode I wrote for him, 'Funhouse' [where Willoway is possessed by a sorceror]."

"The series did not draw satisfactory ratings at any point in its life," reveals Fontana. "However, it began to rise in the ratings around the sixth episode. Publicity had begun to pay off, and audiences were discovering it. It took us until the fifth episode to find the full tone of the characters' relationships and strengths. The scripts began to improve steadily, and the characters became increasingly more interesting. Unfortunately, NBC began preempting the episodes with specials. This contributed to the low ratings. Under the circumstances, many episodes turned out quite well."

The character of Liana had to be written out of the last two episodes when actress Katie Saylor became seriously ill and had to leave the show. "Had we continued, another character, preferably another woman, would have been added to fill the niche vacated when Katie left," says Fontana.

Many series don't resolve their premise when cancellation strikes, but Fontana recalls that producer Lansbury was interested in having a concluding episode. "He planned to have the characters reach the end of the island and find Evoland. Evoland was Bruce's creation. Drop the 'and' and it's love spelled backwards."

The quick cancellation dashed hopes of a final episode, although the second-to-last episode, "Riddles," provides the travelers with a stone that will guide them safely to their destination.

For Jared Martin, who would later star in the 1987–89 series *War of the Worlds*, the character of Varian was a pleasant departure from the killers and drug fiends he had been playing up until that time. "I've been really boxed in by playing bad guy roles in series like *Switch* and *The Rookies*," he said at the time. "And when I'm not playing a heavy, I'm playing a reformed junkie like on *Columbo*." Today, the actor notes, "I see pictures of Varian and I'll say, 'Wow, he's like my son.' He was a dear character and it was a dear series. It died because of the furious and merciless economics of television. It was between *Welcome Back, Kotter,* the year John Travolta hit it big, and *The Waltons*. No show is going to last stuck in that atmosphere. We ran for only ten episodes."

Although there was a strong letter-writing campaign to save the show, NBC's decision was final. "I don't think we were given enough time," concludes Martin. "NBC at that time was a very weak network [in terms of programming] and they didn't want to pour money into a show that might or might not be successful."

CAST NOTES

Jared Martin (Varian): Born 1941 in New York. Martin played Dusty Farlow in *Dallas* (1979–82) and starred in the syndicated *War of the Worlds* (1987–89).

Roddy McDowall (Willoway): See *Planet of the Apes*.

Katie Saylor (Liana): Born 1951. Growing up in Connecticut, Katie dreamed of being an actress from the age of four. Her movies included *The Godfather* (1972). "Katie became seriously ill during the filming of *The Fantastic Journey*," recalls writer Dorothy Fontana. "She had to leave the series. To the best of my knowledge, she has not worked as an actress since."

Carl Franklin (Fred): This young black actor turned to directing in the 1980s. His film *One False Move* (1992) received critical acclaim.

Ike Eisenmann (Scott): Born 1962. As a child actor, he starred in the Walt Disney film *Escape to Witch Mountain* (1975). He was also Scotty's ill-fated nephew in *Star Trek: The Wrath of Khan* (1982).

Episode Guide

Vortex
Marooned on the island, shipwrecked survivors encounter sixteenth century pirates and a man from the far future. Wr: Michael Michaelian, Katharyn Michaelian-Powers and Merwin Gerard, story by Merwin Gerard. Dir: Andrew V. McLaglen.

Dr. Paul Jordan (Scott Thomas); Eve (Susan Howard); Ben Wallace (Leif Erickson); Carl Johanson (Scott Brady); Sir James Camden (Ian McShane); Paget (Don Knight); Jill (Karen Somerville); Enid Jordan (Lynn Borden); Dar-L (Gary Collins); Rhea (Mary Ann Mobley); Atar (Jason Evers); Source voice (Mike Road); George (Bryon Chung); Andy (Jack Stauffer); Star (Tom McCorry).

Atlantium
The travelers come across a futuristic city ruled by a giant brain-creature that intends to drain the earthlings of their energy. Wr: Katharyn Michaelian-Powers, story by Michael Michaelian and Katharyn M. Powers. Dir: Barry Crane.

Dar-L (Gary Collins); Rhea (Mary Ann Mobley); Atar (Jason Evers); Source (Mike Road); Iltar (Albert Stratton); Under (Ian Jon Tanza); Maron (Lawrence Bame).

Beyond the Mountain
Green-skinned creatures ask Fred and Varian to save their dying leader. Meanwhile, Liana is forced into a marriage by Dr. Willoway, who commands a fleet of androids. Wr: Harold Livingston. Dir: Irving J. Moore.

Rachel (Marj Dusay); Cyrus (John David Carson); Aren (Joseph Della Sorte); Chef (Lester Fletcher); Toren (Frank Corsentino); Robert (Ron Burke); Daniel (Brian Patrick Clarke); Veteran (Bud Kenneally); Michael (Crofton Hardester).

Children of the Gods
The travelers are captured by a group of children who hate adults. They sentence Willoway to die when he blunders into a sacred temple. Wr: Leonard Katzman. Dir: Alf Kjellin.

Alpha (Mark Lambert); Sigma (Bobby Eilbacher); Delta (Cosie Costa); Beta (Stanley Clay); Gamma (Richard Natoli); Omega (Al A. Eisenmann); Rho (Michael Baldwin).

A Dream of Conquest
Willoway pretends to befriend a ruthless military leader who plans to invade and conquer the other time zones. Wr: Michael Michaelian, story by Bruce Lansbury. Dir: Vincent McEveety.

Tarant (John Saxon); Lara (Lenore Stevens); Argon (Morgan Paull); Nikki (Johnny Doran); Neffring (Bobby Porter); Luther (Robert Patten).

An Act of Love
Varian decides to marry a young woman, but the couple are unaware that he's been consigned for volcanic sacrifice. Wr: Richard Fielder. Dir: Virgil W. Vogel.

Gwenith (Christina Hart); Maera (Ellen Weston); Zaros (Jonathon Goldsmith); Baras (Vic Mohica); Arla (Belinda Balaski); Guard (Jerry Daniels); Heras (Jeffrey Byron).

Memory Flash—story editor Dorothy C. Fontana: "I thought it was the best episode we did. It wasn't entirely satisfactory as a story, but the emotional relationships in it were excellent."

Funhouse
The travelers face terrifying rides and illusions at a carnival, where a sorceror intends to take over Willoway's body. Wr: Michael Michaelian. Dir: Art Fisher.

Apollonius (Mel Ferrer); Roxanne (Mary Frann); Barker (Richard Lawson); Gwenith (Christina Hart).

Turnabout
Women banish their men to a limbo world, and Liana pretends to join the women in an effort to free her fellow travelers. Wr: Dorothy C. Fontana, Ken Kolb. Dir: Victor French.

Halyana (Joan Collins); Morgan (Paul Mantee); Adrea (Julie Cobb); Connell (Beverly Todd); Obril (Charles Walker, III); Masel (Amy Joyce).

Riddles
The travelers stay at a mountain cottage where they're subjected to frightening illusions. The images are designed to scare them away from a stone that could point them to Evoland. Wr: Katharyn M. Powers. Dir: David Moessinger.

Kedryn (Dale Robinette); Krysta (Carole Demas); Simkin (William O' Connell); Enid Jordan (Lynn Borden); Rider (Dax Xenos).

Memory Flash—story editor Dorothy C. Fontana: "In a youth- and beauty-oriented society, this episode had a nice message. It was a story about a couple who would do anything to fight the aging process. They were desperate to remain young forever."

The Innocent Prey
The travelers must stop the evil plans of a twenty-first century convict who is about to exploit the

riches of a friendly civilization. Wr: Robert Hamilton. Dir: Vincent McEveety.

York (Richard Jaeckel); Rayat (Lew Ayres); Tye (Nicholas Hammond); Natica (Cheryl Ladd); Raddison (Burt Douglas); Thomas (Gerald McRaney); Roland (Jim Payner).

Future Cop
May 1976–September 1978

The Los Angeles Police have just gained a new partner in the fight against crime. His name is Haven, he's a robo,t and he's been assigned to Officer Joe Cleaver, who will show him how things work on the streets. Cleaver's old partner, Bill Bundy, and all Los Angeles criminals had better watch out. Using the unique abilities and talents at his command, Haven shows Cleaver a stricter interpretation of the law.

Cast: Officer Joe Cleaver (Ernest Borgnine); Officer Bill Bundy (John Amos); Officer John Haven (Michael Shannon); Captain Skaggs (Herbert Nelson); Dr. Tingley (Irene Tsu); Peggy, the Waitress at the Cafe (Angela May).

Executive Producer: Anthony Wilson, Gary Damsker; *Producer:* Everett Chambers; ABC/Paramount; 60 minutes.

The future of law enforcement, contrary to what other sources are claiming, really began in 1976. To fully understand the development of *Future Cop* as a television series, one has to start with two well-known and award-winning science fiction novelists, Harlan Ellison and Ben Bova. Trying to develop a short story for *Analog* magazine in the late 1960s (during the reign of its celebrated editor John Campbell), Ellison and Bova collaborated on a tale of futuristic law enforcement titled *Brillo*. It's the story of how police officer Mike Polchik got assigned to a robot named *Brillo* and was instructed, for one night, to take the non-humanoid metal robot on a trial by fire through the streets of upper Manhattan. Polchik had the street smarts, but Brillo had the textbook interpretation of the law. And therein lay the conflict.

Brillo was published in *Analog* in 1970 (and is still available in Ben Bova's paperback short story collection, *Future Crime*, from Tor Books). Soon thereafter, the ABC television network and Paramount Television expressed interest in developing the story for television and commissioned an on-spec teleplay from the two authors. However, the corporates requested some changes: make the robot human-looking (an android), and make the place of the story in present-day Los Angeles. No way, said Ellison and Bova, who wanted to preserve the ideas and characters already laid out in their tale.

Ben Bova picks up the story: "They dropped the show. They said they weren't going to do it. And then we heard about a year later that a show called *Future Cop* was coming out starring Ernest Borgnine, whom we had suggested as the lead for the *Brillo* teleplay, dealing with a pair of policemen, one human and one machine. The only difference we could discern in seeing the show, was that instead of a robot that looks like a machine, they had decided to use an actor and have him pretend to be a robot. This was a point of argument between Paramount and ourselves as we were developing *Brillo*. We wanted to be faithful to the original story and wanted the machine to *look* like a machine. Sort of like R2-D2, although this was before *Star Wars*. We wanted it to be a robot that looked like an animated fireplug. And ABC and Paramount said, 'It doesn't cost too much to get an actor and just have him play it as if he had arthritis, you know, very stiffly, and pretend he's a machine.' We argued about that. I always thought that was the major reason why they dropped the show."

Bova was first made aware of *Future Cop*'s existence when he received "some 17 calls from people around the country who saw it, and felt it looked so much like the story *Brillo* that they felt it was probably something that Harlan and I had done, and yet they didn't see our names in the credits."

That was the problem. "It *was* our script. I saw a videotape of what ABC had aired, and Harlan did too, of course. I realized they had used the script we had written virtually word for word. There were only minor changes. It was the most blatant case of plagiarism I have ever seen,"

Academy award winner Ernest Borgnine (right) stars as Cleaver, a veteran cop; John Amos (left) stars as Bundy; and Michael Shannon (inset) joins the team as Haven, the android rookie, in *Future Cop*. Copyright 1977 ABC/Paramount.

remembers an amazed Bova. So, Ellison and Bova took the only course clear to them: They sued Paramount and ABC for stealing their ideas and failing to acknowledge their work. Paramount and ABC had just taken the *Brillo* script and made the changes they wanted—an android cop and a modern-day Los Angeles setting—without acknowledging or consulting the two authors.

"It took four years to get to court," Bova continues, "and their defense was, essentially, 'Yes, we stole it, so what? Everybody steals everything in this business.' And then they said *Brillo* was essentially stolen from Isaac Asimov's *The Caves of Steel* [also about a detective and a

robot/android partner, Elijah Baley and R. Daneel Olivaw, set in the far future in an underground city]. Well, we had depositions from Isaac and everybody else in the science fiction field, pointing out the major differences between *Brillo* and anything else that had been done before. So, their case fell apart very quickly. They thought they could get away with it because up until that time, no writer had successfully sued a major Hollywood studio for plagiarism. Thousands of such suits have been pursued in Hollywood for many years, and the studios always won. In this case, they were so incredibly guilty that I just told Harlan and our lawyer, 'Just get this case in front

Known only to Cleaver (Ernest Borgnine, right), Haven (Michael Shannon, left) is a computerized biosynthetic android in ABC's *Future Cop*. Copyright 1977 ABC/Paramount.

of a jury. Let them see the videotape of *Future Cop*, let them read our script for *Brillo*, and then they'll find the defendants guilty.' Which is exactly what happened."

Four years after the premiere of *Future Cop* on TV, after a five-week trial, culminating in a court decision on April 25, 1980, Ellison and Bova were awarded $337,000 in damages in the copyright infringement of *Brillo*.

Harlan Ellison said in a news brief from *Starlog* #37, in August 1980, "We won. And we didn't just win with some piddling amount where they could say, 'Well, you know, the jury was in doubt.' It's a big, big judgment and it's rocking the entire town."

"We were very relieved it was over," sighs Bova. "It had been a big drain, especially on Harlan, since he carried most of the financial and emotional burden, being out there on the West Coast dealing with our lawyer, Henry Holmes. And of course, ABC and Paramount simply played a delaying game for as long as they could, hoping that sooner or later we would run out of money or patience. But they picked the wrong customer in Harlan—he would have sold his house to get them." Asked if he'd seen any of the other seven hours of the *Future Cop* series, Bova

was surprised, as he was not aware the other episodes existed. If there have been any changes in Hollywood, specifically towards writers, as a result of this suit, Bova isn't aware of it. "I'm not close to Hollywood," says Bova. "But from everything I hear from people who are there, writers are still not held in the highest esteem. There's even a joke about the stupid starlet who's so dumb that she went to bed with the writer. Writers are at the bottom of the totem pole. So, for the starlet to go to bed with a writer would do her career no good at all."

Of their *Brillo* teleplay, Bova reveals that "Harlan did most of the writing. We worked on it together. He's the expert in screenwriting. We had developed the short story together, and Harlan did most of the work in turning it into a television form. I have several friends in the industry, but it's such a different art form, aimed at such a different audience from the kind of things I write, that I even doubt I would ever try to write a screenplay. There are several novels of mine that Hollywood has asked about to produce as films, but I've never really closed the deals on any of them."

In 1992, ABC aired a television series titled *Mann and Machine*, starring David Andrews and

Yancy Butler, which bore a great resemblance to the human detective/robot partner theme except that this time, the robot was female.

"Not every show that has a human cop and a robot partner is a ripoff of *Brillo*," cautions Bova. "What we were trying to do with the story that we wrote, was to contrast what people *say* they want from the law with what they *really* want. Everybody says they want absolutely impartial and utterly certain enforcement of the law. If somebody is parked overtime, they want that car to get a ticket. But if it's their car, then they want the law to bend. So people want strong law enforcement for everyone except themselves. And that's what *Brillo* was all about. The human cop understood the system and could bend when it was necessary. But the robot only knew the law and infractions thereof. That was the point of *Brillo*. And that's something that television is not deep enough to understand or even attempt to do.

"[This was] social commentary. Using science fiction to make a social point. Most science fiction is a very good vehicle for commenting on society by changing the society we live in and exaggerating the change to show a particular aspect of society that we all take for granted.

"Take a policeman who is absolutely honest and cannot bend no matter what the situation— can do nothing except make strict enforcement of the law—and then you see that's not really what you want at all! You want compassion, understanding, you want a wink and a nod and a look the other way while I'm doing something that I shouldn't be. But if somebody else is doing something wrong, you want that sucker in jail!"

If there's anyone who's happy that *Future Cop* came to be a series, it's Michael Shannon. He was tapped to play Haven, Ernest Borgnine's robot partner on the beat. Shannon had been in Los Angeles for only a month prior to being cast. *Future Cop* was his first time in front of the cameras, and it was his goal to provide some solid characterization to this robot cop opposite the veteran actor Borgnine. "It happened very quickly," remembers Shannon. "I read for the director and producer, read for the network, tested on film, and started the very next day. It was all very fast, as most things are on television."

Filmed in February and March of 1976, the pilot aired on May 1. Shannon recalls, "[It was] one of the most difficult things I ever did. It was a very narrow scope emotionally to play with. The comedy came from the character's confusion in trying to understand human beings. The irony

was that the android was in some ways a better example of humanity. It required a lot of technical skill, concentration, and a relentless exploration of ways to make the character interesting and versatile."

And he had to do all that within a grueling schedule. "Locations were difficult, but the days were very long. [Often we'd work] 16-hour days.

Of his relationship with Ernest Borgnine and John Amos on the set of the show, Shannon says, "I recall it as a real whirlwind. Borgnine was very committed to the show, and he certainly was involved in the final casting decision. I tested with him as did several others. Ernie was totally professional, loved the crew, full of beans, and a lot of fun. He created a good atmosphere on the set. Amos was friendly, but I didn't have many scenes with him."

A staple of the triad relationship between these cops was that Cleaver's former partner, Bundy, did not know that Haven was a robot. Thus Bundy was ever amazed by Haven's knowledge and abilities, and compatriot Cleaver always had to cover for the robot. Yet Bundy never really got suspicious of Haven.

"This is what's called dramatic license," says Shannon wryly. "If Bundy had been in on the gimmick, it would have detracted somewhat from the relationship that was developing between Haven and Cleaver." Not until the final two hours of *Future Cop*, in the 1978 TV movie *Cops and Robin*, was Bundy clued in on Haven's secret— and then only because he was promoted to sergeant and became Cleaver's boss.

Comedy was often the object of the robot's behavior. Writers would use Haven as a mirror to humanity. For example, in "Fighting O'Haven," as a boxing contender, Haven could not understand the meaning of the phrase "Take a dive!"

"This was for the sake of comedy," says Shannon. "It gave Cleaver a chance to be worried, do a double take, have to explain the facts of life, etc. In a way, it gave Cleaver an opportunity to parent the android, educate him to some extent, and consequently provided an opportunity for the relationship to develop."

As the show began to develop, was there ever confusion over whether *Future Cop* was a science fiction series or a police drama? "The show started to develop more and more towards being a science fiction show," muses Shannon. "Originally, it leaned more towards a cop show with a science fiction element. However, as it developed and as the writers began to discover they had virtual carte blanche with this android, it must have been tempting to push the science fiction elements. Of course, this left Cleaver as more of a straight man to the robot, which was a problem."

Shannon's strongest memory of his experience was "enjoying the challenge of the show. It was an interesting exercise from an acting point of view. Like a child, I had to make discoveries all the time. It seemed to me this was the most interesting aspect of the character. And of course, Borgnine was my mentor. Ernie enjoyed that. It allowed him to show a fatherly side of himself as well as be the tough cop. Later on, they opened up the Haven character, allowing him more skills, and this seemed to be the direction in which the series was headed. Certainly, the writers were pushing for that. Borgnine felt, however, the relationship would take a backseat and was concerned." Other memories include working with Joan Collins on "The Kansas City Kid," an episode that took place at a racetrack. "Joan was very sleek and a lot of fun. Great costumes, atmosphere, drinks I couldn't drink as the android, good stuff." Shannon also remembers "getting punched by my stuntman" in "The Fighting O'Haven." "I got a black eye. There was no time to rehearse. I was put into the ring with my opponent (a stuntman) and he simply called out right or left, depending on which punch he was going to throw, and I was supposed to dodge one way or the other. This worked for a while, but then as the pace picked up, he caught me with a punch and I had a real shiner." The stuntmen had their own problems; Shannon recalls his stuntman getting a concussion doing a fall into an inflated mattress from 50 feet.

Of the short-lived series *Mann and Machine* (1992) that featured a *female* robot, Shannon confesses, "I haven't seen it. It's difficult to comment. It must satisfy every male fantasy! A beautiful robot who needs to be taught the facts of life. It should run and run..." Sorry, Michael.

Shannon also admits that he wasn't very aware of the litigation surrounding *Future Cop.* "I heard about it," he says, "but only vaguely, and I have no idea if it affected the longevity of the show. Personally, I'm glad they got their [money]. I write as well and am certainly aware these things go on. Sometimes the problem can be subliminal. A writer may not even remember where he got the idea."

Of John Haven's ultimate fate in the series' universe, Shannon speculates that "Haven could have been continuously updated and so could have continued to express new technology, newer insights, especially with genetic engineering moving closer and closer to creating life itself.

"The silicon chip has enabled science to reduce the mechanics. In terms of the show, however, a world full of robots did seem to be on the cards. What I thought was interesting about the concept is that it forced human beings to examine their beliefs and attitudes, particularly in a social way. The robot raised some intriguing questions so you had a kind of reversal of roles. The robot student became the teacher." And exactly this theme is expressed in the *Brillo* short story.

In summary, Michael Shannon looks back at *Future Cop* as a good introduction to Los Angeles and to series work. "The role was a bit confining, but they had started to open it up. I did the gambler with a Damon Runyon accent, I did the boxer, I did a Bogart-type lover with Sheree North. The series had to move in this direction. As it did, it became more of a gimmick show. But the original idea had some mystery and subtle humor. I felt I brought something original to it. However, it was difficult to sustain as a series, especially for the writers."

Harold Livingston, executive story editor for *Future Cop,* remembers being on the job and always seeking "stories of interest, humor, *humanity* and suspense. The humanity aspect, I think, was vital. [Haven] was more human at times than the humans." Best known to science fiction fans as the screenwriter of *Star Trek: The Motion Picture* (1979), Livingston recalls *Future Cop* as "one of the few shows that I ever truly *enjoyed* working and writing on. It was also a challenge. I was very adamant about retaining credibility, so you really couldn't get too broad or you would have tipped over into farce. We had to be very careful about that. In that regard, I know we succeeded."

Livingston also believes that the science fiction element on the show—Haven and his abilities—was well maintained. "The audience accepted Haven. And so did I!"

If the show had continued further, Livingston would have liked to have the robot "take on increasingly human traits and foibles. It would eventually have posed big problems for Cleaver. As I recall, I wrote several lines for Cleaver to say, 'He's like a son to me.' I'm very grateful to know that someone appreciated the show. I truly believed we got a raw deal by ABC not continuing us."

CAST NOTES

Ernest Borgnine (Officer Joe Cleaver): Born 1915. Winner of an Academy Award for his starring role in *Marty* (1955), Borgnine also starred in the 1960s comedy series *McHale's Navy* and in the 1980s action series *Airwolf.*

Michael Shannon (Haven): Born 1943. This American actor has been working and living in London in recent years. Features he's acted in include *Little Shop of Horrors* (1986), *Sheena* (1984), *Death of an Angel* (1985), *Making Love* (1982), and *That Lucky Touch.* Television movie appearances include *Poor Little Rich Girl* (1987), *The Two Mrs. Grenvilles* (1987), and *The Teddy Kennedy Jr. Story* (1986). TV guest appearances include *The A-Team, Partners in Crime, Scarecrow and Mrs. King, Remington Steele* and *Simon and Simon.*

"I just did an American play in London, called *Violent Peace*," says Shannon. "I also did a series called *The Big Battalion* filmed in Ethiopia and Israel. And, I'm doing some writing. Plays and screenplays."

John Amos (Officer Bill Bundy): Born 1941. Amos played the husband on the 1970s sitcom *Good Times* and gained critical acclaim as the adult Kunta Kinte in the 1977 mini-series *Roots.*

EPISODE GUIDE

Future Cop (1976 TV movie, 90 minutes)
John Haven, a human-looking robot, joins Los Angeles Police Department beat officers Cleaver and Bundy in the field to test his worthiness as an officer. Wr: Anthony Wilson. Dir: Jud Taylor.
    Klausmeier (Herbert Nelson); Avery (Ronnie Claire Edwards); Paterno (James Luisi); Dorfman (Stephen Pearlman); Young rookie (James Daughton); 1st terrorist (Lorry Goldman); 2nd terrorist (Tony Burton); Cocktail waitress (Nancy Belle Fuller); Della (Ruth Manning); Hippie (Eddy C. Dyer); Grandmother (Shirley O'Hara); Fowler (Sandy Ward); Evans (Sandy Sprung); Teenager (Michael Francis Blake); Fugitive (Bill Dearth); 1st kid (Michael Goodrow); 2nd kid (Eric Suter).

Season Episodes (1977)

Fighting O'Haven
Cleaver's charge, the android, infiltrates a corrupt boxing syndicate, posing as Irish Paddy O'Haven, a rising contender. Wr: Mann Rubin. Dir: Robert Douglas.

Charlie Willis (Michael V. Gazzo); Jack Cassey (Rod McCary); Kurtz (Steve Gravers); Gang leader #1 (Mwako Cumbuka); Ollie Dawson (Stan Shaw); Man (Jesse Emmett); Airport aecurity (Morris Buchanan); Referee #1 (Wally Rose); Referee #2 (Gene Le Bell); Bartender (Jimmy Joyce); Reporter #1 (Glen Douglas); Reporter #2 (Dorothy Dells); Reporter #3 (Darren Dublin); Woman in plane (Victoria Carroll); TV commentator (Jim Healy).

The Mad, Mad Bomber, Part 1
Police receive threats from a deranged bomber who wants them to free a revolutionary. Cleaver, Bundy and Haven think they know who's behind the terrorism. Wr: Ken Kolb and Harold Livingston, story by Ken Kolb. Dir: Ted Post.
    Brad Bannock (Harry Guardino); Chief Ross Wheeler (Albert Salmi); Cliff Yancy (Gerrit Graham); Red (Dennis Bowen); Lt. Fisk (Bill Zuckert); Roberts (Bob Hanley); Zack (Rick Sawaya); Warehouse clerk (Mike Lally Sr.); Sports arena policeman (Bob Golden); Desk sergeant (Paul Schumacher); Bramlett (John Andersonjo); Young patrolman (John Kirby); Cindy (Mary Moon); Shore patrol guard #1 (Guy Remsen); Shore patrol guard #2 (Michael Payne); Spectator (George Sawaya); Lt. Commander (Fred Draper); Wave (Sharon MacGee).

The Mad, Mad Bomber, Part 2
Yancy has planted a bomb inside Haven and continues his revolutionary rampage throughout Los Angeles. Wr: Ken Kolb and Harold Livingston, story by Ken Kolb. Dir: Ted Post.
    Brad Bannock (Harry Guardino); Chief Ross Wheeler (Albert Salmi); Cliff Yancy (Gerrit Graham); Red (Dennis Bowen); Deputy mayor (Jack Bannon); Lt. Fisk (Bill Zuckert); Roberts (Bob Hanley); Zack (Rick Sawaya); Warehouse clerk (Mike Lally Sr.); Sports arena policeman (Bob Golden); Bramlett (John Andersonjo); Young patrolman (John Kirby); Cindy (Mary Moon); Shore patrol guard #1 (Guy Remsen); Shore patrol guard #2 (Michael Payne); Spectator (George Sawaya); Lt. Commander (Fred Draper); Wave (Sharon MacGee).

Girl on the Ledge
A young woman threatens to jump off a 10-story building unless her estranged father pays a visit. Wr: Mann Rubin. Dir: Earl Bellamy.
    Girl (Katherine Cannon); Natalie Bundy (Tracy Reed); Darlene Montoya (Gloria Manon); Asst. Chief Joseph (Robert Symonds); Nick Redmont (H.M. Wynant); Sal (Francine York); Lt. Fisk (Bill Zuckert); Carl Jadwin (Steven Marlo); Hotel clerk (Raymond Singer); Marge (Sarah Kennedy); Pedestrian (Bob Hoy); Bradley (John O'Connell); Cummings (Craig Ludwin); Ford (Richard Doyle); Fire chief (Dan Priest); Dr. Wallace (Joe Bratcher).

The Carlisle Girl
A businessman uses his cosmetics concern as a front for a drug ring. Wr: Harold Livingston. Dir: Vincent McEveety.
    Claire Hammond (Sheree North); Herb Conroy (Peter Donat); Natalie Bundy (Tracy Reed); June Bundy (Kim Hamilton); Officer Fitzgerald (Edward Bach); Bruce (Louie Elias); Gardener (Fred M. Porter); Policeman (Michael Edward Lally); Atkinson (Morris Buchanan); Carlilse girl (Cynthia Wood).

The Kansas City Kid
Haven poses as a Runyonesque cardsharp to win back the Police Benevolent Fund that was gambled away by the irresponsible investment counselor. Wr: Harold Livingston. Dir: Robert Douglas.

Geary (Don Reid); Eve Di Falco (Joan Collins); Andrew (Joshua Bryant); Fisk (Bill Zuckert); Bank teller (Sharon McGee); Dugan (Regis J. Cordic); Phillips (Victor Izay); Sgt. Monroe (Zachary A. Charles); Doctor (Alvah Stanley); Nolan (Michael MacRae).

The Cops and Robin (1978 TV movie, 2 hours)
When the wife of Cleaver's first partner, who's been hiding for years, agrees to testify against a rich and wealthy businessman for the murder of her husband, Cleaver and Haven protect her five-year-old daughter, Robin, so she can testify. Wr: Brad Radnitz and John Anthony Mulhall, story by John Anthony Mulhall. Dir: Allen Reisner.

Robin Loren (Natasha Ryan); Dr. Alice Alcott (Carol Lynley); Wayne Dutton (Terry Kiser); George Garfield (Philip Abbott); Lt. Dan Morgan (Richard Bright); Walter Costello (Jeff David); Det. Furie (J. Kenneth Campbell); Richard (James York); Tyler (Gene Rutherford); Judge Wheeler (Ivan Bonar); Marge Loren (Elizabeth Farley); Housekeeper (Peggy Converse); Laura (Linda Scott); Supermarket checker (Linda Gillin); Secretary (Ketty Lester); Policewoman (Gail Cutchlow).

Galactica 1980

January 1980–August 1980

Half a generation has passed since the adventures of Battlestar Galactica, *and Adama and his fleet have finally found Earth, sending down teams of warriors to be assimilated into the society and make contact. Warriors Troy and Dillon meet up with a television reporter, Jaime Hamilton, who helps them in their adventures on Earth.*

Cast: Troy (Kent McCord); Dillon (Barry Van Dyke); Jaime Hamilton (Robyn Douglass); Commander Adama (Lorne Greene); Dr. Zee (Robbie Rist) (pilot); Dr. Zee (Patrick Stuart) (series).

Executive Producer and Creator: Glen A. Larson; *Producers:* David O'Connell, Frank Lupo, Jeff Freilich; ABC/Universal; 60 minutes.

In 1980, the men and women of *Battlestar Galactica* finally landed on Earth. But the mission aborted when the saga landed a 7:00 Sunday night time slot. "It changed the nature of what the show was intended to be," says star Kent McCord.

Galactica 1980's time slot actually dictated the content of this TV show. "There was an FCC [ruling] where the 7:00 time slot was given back to the networks if the programming were public affairs, news-related or children's programming," explains McCord. "So, by dictate from the FCC, any program going in there had to meet one of those three criteria. And if you're programmed in that slot, and you're trying to do an action-adventure show, what follows is that action-adventure show had better be a children's show."

Because of this, Glen Larson was faced with the dilemma of how to do an action-adventure science fiction show that fit within the boundaries of children's programming. Jeff Freilich, a

Galactica 1980 producer who apprenticed in science fiction with *The Incredible Hulk*, explains how Larson accomplished this feat. "There had to be at least one educational message every act. That means four times an hour," says Freilich. In "The Super Scouts," "when the kids go off with Kent and Barry, they go to the RCA building in New York, and one of the Galactica kids takes apart and puts back together a television camera. Glen decided that's going to be educational, but it's also a wonderful character moment for a futuristic child, raised from another planet, to demonstrate to people how a television camera works. That was Glen's idea of how to be educational without being preachy.

"We had to come up with a premise that could be exploited from an educational standpoint, which is why we did one about toxic waste in waters, why we did one about migrant farm workers. There were several shows that had messages, which for television is very difficult to get away with, because generally [series] television shows things that people won't see on the news, and they want to escape a little bit of the reality of the world. We were really forced to deal with it as much as we could. Because we had to mix the intention of the show, I think we got a little bit lost on how the show was supposed to run."

Why ABC decided to slot *Galactica 1980* in this position on Sunday night escapes McCord. "I guess ABC felt it would meet one of those areas," he muses. "It would be counter-programming to *60 Minutes* or whatever it was on NBC at the time."

"They just hammered us," says Larson of ABC's time-slot decision. "That's where they wanted us. That was the whole point of putting us on the air, so they could fill it as a 7:00 show. They were more powerful then than they are now. They said it virtually has to be this way. By getting on the air, we figured we could steer people in the right direction. We would do it their way until we could eventually move on and into what we wanted."

The first three hours of the show featured Troy and Dillon acclimating to Earth, and dealing with a renegade council member who traveled back in time to World War II. The villain, Xavier, planned to upgrade Earth's technology to help it meet any Cylon attacks that might come to be during the present. It was Larson's initial intention to do a Galactica time-travel show before it became mired in the FCC's programming straitjacket. Scripts were written that dealt with Cleopatra and Helen of Troy.

"We did some of those," admits Larson. "I'm not sure if that was a good idea or not. In retrospect, maybe we shouldn't have toyed with it too much to begin with. We should have stayed right where we were instead of going back and doing [time travel stories]. I have mixed emotions. It may have been a mistake.

"Essentially what Glen Larson and I talked about when we sat down together, when he was coming back with *Galactica*, was 'I want to try to do something akin to *The Day the Earth Stood Still*,'" recalls McCord. "Something along the lines that these two beings from outer space with all this great knowledge … were coming as peacemakers and trying to bring peace to Earth. But then, all of a sudden we got set with the 7:00 time slot and we got strapped down with a bunch of kids, doing baseball shows as Scouts. We kind of lost the direction, I thought. And also, the fact it was programmed so quickly, I don't think Glen wanted to delay the premiere of the show. We had done the pilot in December [of 1979] and had worked for three or four weeks on the pilot. We started work on it, and then all of a sudden they wanted a show right away! I know that Glen had asked that we be delayed for a September [1980] premiere so we could prepare scripts and not be put under the gun.

"I felt that … had the show gone on in the time slot that everybody thought was going to be, an 8:00 or 9:00, we could have developed the show the way Glen originally envisioned it—a *Day the Earth Stood Still* type of series, where these two characters with vast knowledge from the stars would come to Earth and bring peace. …The pilot we did went into all the things we could have done with the show. With the characters meeting scientists and all that area. That was very interesting, and I thought it played very good. And then we got off on a tangent and got into a 7:00 time slot and the kid thing and all of that. When you ask how would I have taken the show, I would have done exactly what Glen tried to do. Go get a copy of *The Day the Earth Stood Still*, put it on your VCR and watch it. It is an absolutely wonderful film."

McCord is philosophical about the show's low order of ten episodes, and he explains the modern realities of Hollywood filmmaking and network rationale, giving audiences less and less of a show they watch.

"That's life. It's a different world here. In the old days … you'd get an order for 13, a back 13 and the following season you'd get an order of 26. That's the old days. In the new days, you get an order for four or five or six and a producer hopes lightning strikes. If it doesn't, hell, I've seen shows pulled off the air—gone forever—after a couple of episodes. *Galactica 1980* was opposite *60 Minutes*. I think we came in second in the time slot, but I don't know if it was enough to counter the high cost of doing the show."

Although Larson's original intention in doing *Galactica 1980* was to create a show that would be more economical than *Battlestar*, that quickly disintegrated when the network declared they wanted a product immediately for speedy airing.

"The purpose of finding Earth," says McCord, "was supposed to have been so we could bring down the costs. [But what happened was] in trying to get scripts ready and shooting, sometimes we had three first units shooting at the same time, in different episodes. I don't know if the show was economically feasible or viable to continue without being an all-out hit. *Battlestar Galactica* was the most expensive hour here at the time. This happens when you go into production and you don't have enough lead time. Mistakes are made and things become costly. So Glen was writing to try to get the show for September 1980 instead of that January or February that we debuted, which was very, very short lead time."

"What made it expensive was they gave that show just a few weeks to get started to get it on the air," agrees Larson. "I'll tell you a true story. I was dubbing the show on the lot on a Sunday afternoon. You don't dub on Saturday and Sunday, that's how expensive it was. I saw a guy walking around in one of the Galactica warrior uniforms. (I have one in my closet, by the way.) I saw this guy walk by and I was furious! I was so mad because the [Universal Studios *Battlestar Galactica*] tour was using so many of our props and they weren't paying for them, and I thought we were getting victimized. I was ready to call it. 'This is exactly what I'm talking about. They're taking our money and they're spending it on the tour, and I'm not getting it on the screen.' I made a phone call. A very impatient voice on the other end of the phone said, 'That's not the tour.' I said, 'What are you talking about?' 'You better check your schedules. I know you're on the dubbing stages but we're shooting today.' We were actually shooting the show on weekends in order to get it on the air. That's how ridiculous it got. There were guys driving out that gate every weekend in campers ... and they were buying their overtime. The show was costing a fortune because the network rushed it. How fast can you get on the air? I was terrible that way. They ring the fire bell and I answer it, figuring I could do almost anything.

"There was a super-rush because it took eight or nine days to make [each episode] ... and we couldn't make airdates unless we shot around the clock. One of the things that hurt the show was that I wouldn't allow them to just throw it together.... I insisted that we make it look good and try to hold the quality. To do that we had to shoot a lot of overtime, a lot of weekends. The cost ran up there so ... that cost our pickups [extra footage to increase coverage for editors]. We virtually couldn't afford to keep shooting them. The network was probably willing to keep it going, but it was costing them so much money."

So hectic was the filming schedule, it made for a memorable moment for the two lead stars of the show.

"This probably points up the chaos that we had to deal with. [It] was the day we were shooting the scene on the Universal 747 stage," recounts McCord. The episode was "The Night Cylons Landed," and "we had probably 30 or 40 or 50 extras plus a crew. About noon, on this day with all this very difficult stuff, one of the associ-ate producers came down and handed Barry and me eight pages of dialogue and said, 'At 4:00, you have to go to stage 25 and you have to shoot these eight pages. And no matter where you are here, you have to be over there to do this because we need this stuff to finish cutting a show that's being done.' So at 4:00 Barry and I had to go over to a different stage and leave all these extras and the whole crew ... on this 747 soundstage and shoot eight pages of dialogue in a Viper. That dialogue had no reference to anything. It was Galactican language written for us. It's not easy stuff to learn. We had eight pages, and we didn't have time to learn it because we were shooting another show in another stage! That pointed out a couple of things. We had that unit shooting on a 747 stage and we had another unit shooting with us on stage 25, and I even think there was another unit out shooting with the kids or something," laughs McCord. "That was the way that show was done—to make airdates. It's very unusual."

Kent McCord, surprisingly, was originally slated to appear in *Battlestar Galactica* as one of the lead characters. "Glen wanted me in it, the studio wanted me in it. But it was a person on the network who had some conflict of interest," says McCord. "I've known Glen now for over 30 years, and when he called me and said, 'I got this great concept and I want you to meet with me,' I went over and met him. We had lunch together, and we drove out to the special effects studio where they were doing all the miniatures, and they had shot some tests of some things, and we went to a screening and looked at them. Yeah. I was *very* excited by that project. I thought it was going to be *terrific*! I think the original was plagued by airdates and a difficult time. It was a very, very difficult show to do. One of the most expensive hours that was being shot for television at that time! It was tough for everybody who worked on that show. Yeah. I was looking forward to having done that show. Unfortunately, I didn't get the opportunity to do it."

As to the change in premise from the earlier show to *Galactica 1980*, McCord says, "I think that if you're going to follow a show that has had some success, with some following, I think you have to keep you lineage alive. Glen chose to do a time some 25 or 30 years later of which I was supposed to be the grown Boxey. So there was a whole other generation. Lorne Greene was the tie between the old show and the new show. That kept the fans they had accumulated from the original show interested."

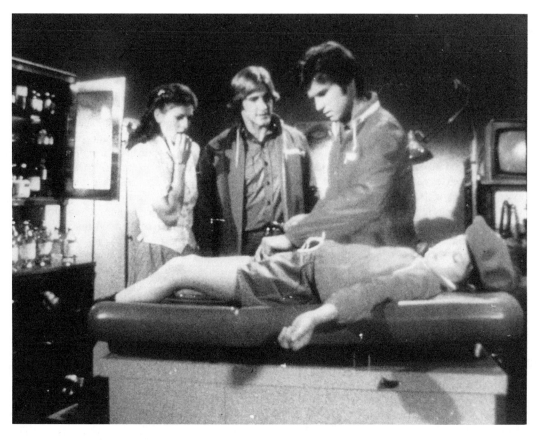

From an episode of *Galactica 1980*, Robyn Douglass (left), Barry Van Dyke (middle) and Kent McCord (right) gather together to help an injured Galactican child while on their adventures on Earth.

Working with Lorne Greene was an opportunity for McCord to see a television veteran at work. "He was a very nice man. Very professional and very dedicated. Lorne had a very limited time. He would come in and do his scenes. Everything was set up for him. I enjoyed working with him. He was an interesting man."

And of McCord's co-star, Barry Van Dyke? "Barry is a wonderful, wonderful man. I had a great time with him and we had a lot of fun together. I still see Barry from time to time."

Oddly, at the end of every episode of *Galactica 1980* was a paragraph on Project Blue Book that said, "The United States Air Force stopped investigating UFOs in 1969. After 22 years they found no evidence of extra-terrestrial visits and no threat to national security."

"The network put that for 7:00 kids. That's standards and practices," says Larson.

McCord doesn't recall this paragraph at the end of the show; however, he notes, "I would imagine that if you're going to deal with outer space and things like that, that little paragraph at the end of the show, about Project Blue Book, is a nudge for people to think about what's out there in outer space."

McCord and co-stars Barry Van Dyke and Robyn Douglass appeared in only nine of the ten episodes shot for the series. Number ten was "The Return of Starbuck," with guest star Dirk Benedict returning as the sly, wisecracking warrior. In this episode, kid genius Dr. Zee recounts a dream to Commander Adama. In the dream, Boomer and Starbuck are on a mission, and Starbuck's Viper is hit during a Cylon attack, forcing him to crash-land on a rocky, deserted planet. The only other presence to keep him company is a deactivated Cylon robot, which Starbuck rebuilds. With his newfound Cylon robot friend, "Cy," Starbuck faces up to the reality that he could probably spend the rest of his life on this ruddy rock—especially since a woman about to give birth has appeared. But a homing beacon from Cy's ship brings more Centurions, and in order to save

Starbuck's life, Cy sacrifices himself against his compatriots.

The director of that episode, Ronald Satlof, recalls, "I didn't care about the final fate of Starbuck. I liked it because of the anthropomorphization of the machine, the robot that Starbuck fixes who turns into a friend and sacrifices himself for Starbuck. I thought there was a lot of human interest in a theme like that. I thought that was a wonderful theme from science fiction because it is a mirror to ourselves. This was an irrationally programmed robot who ultimately became rational and saw the folly of its ways. People need each other, even if one of the people is a robot."

When asked why this episode was such a departure from the regular series, Satlof responds flatly: "They were trying to save the show. They were shooting two other episodes with Kent McCord, and it was written as a way of putting an entirely different unit [to work while] the regular shooting company of the series [was filming elsewhere]. Getting Dr. Zee and Adama in for one little scene to tell the story—that's about all that unified the two shooting companies."

Satlof recalls filming at Red Rock Canyon, "a horrible location." When they were scouting the location, it was nice and warm, and they thought it would be a perfect place to do the story. "But when we got there to shoot, there was a hailstorm and [the temperature] was in the 30s," he says. "The actress Judith Chapman had a little thing to wear, it was see-through, and she was out there with her knees shaking, trying to act. It was unbelievable. We'd wrap blankets around her. We'd roll the camera, snap the camera slate, and she'd [get] ready to go, pull off the blanket and step forth [to] the cameras and say her lines and try to act before the shakes started. It was just horrible. It's what we do for television."

Of Benedict's performance in the episode, Satlof says, "He had a kind of lovely egotism tempered by a flare of humanism ... so I thought he was terrific. I liked him a lot."

At the end of the story, it's hinted that we've seen the very last of Starbuck, but with the appearance of the team of Centurions, who ultimately will destroy Cy, Larson also hints that there's a Cylon vessel elsewhere on the planet in perfect working order for Starbuck to use.

"That's right. If the series had survived—and Starbuck certainly had a chance to survive—he'd rejoin the series," notes Satlof. "He'd somehow get to that Cylon ship and somehow get back to the star fleet."

"I'm not absolutely sure about this, but I really suspect that Glen ... left a door open ... to have him somehow get back into it in a new age, a new Galactic mission and all the rest of it, without having to age because you can explain it away with time differences in space."

Potential for resurrection aside, with this episode Glen Larson was also able to close the series with a measure of personal satisfaction. Larson cites the episode as probably his all-time favorite *Galactica* segment, next to the premiere episode and the two-hour films like *War of the Gods* and *The Living Legend*.

"We were virtually going back to the original premise," he says. "That was really the series brought to a whole different level, even though it didn't need a lot of pyrotechnics."

Viewers liked this show so much that Larson got a request to do the show in London as a play. "We were approached on the subject and they never got around to doing it," he sighs. "It was a big hit in England. If you think about it, it was very much a play."

McCord recently bumped into a videotape of *Galactica 1980*. Curious to relive some of his work on the show, he rented it, only to find a badly edited film culled from three different episodes. "It's terrible! It's awful! I couldn't even watch it. It was just the worst. I remember they came to me and asked, 'Can you do some voiceovers?' It was probably one of the most dreadful things I've ever seen in my life. They should have just released *The Night the Cylons Landed*, a two-parter episode. That was just a mish-mash. It didn't cut together. It didn't make sense."

Like others involved with the show, Jeff Freilich says the *Galactica 1980* failed, "not because the show was doing so badly, but because it was in a time slot that was a death time slot [with] CBS's *60 Minutes*. At the time NBC and ABC deluded themselves into believing they could make inroads into the *60 Minutes* audience with adults on one channel and under-25's on another.

"The other prerequisite [of the time slot] was there couldn't be more than ten incidents of violence in an episode, and that meant if ten Cylons got shot out of the sky, that was all we could do. You couldn't have anything else, which included hitting somebody on the head with a stick, or punching somebody in the mouth or a car into a wall."

The competing show on NBC, *The Wonderful*

World of Disney, got away with more violence because it fell under the category of previously released theatrical motion pictures. Censors did not have to cut those films—but they kept their scissors sharpened for *Galactica 1980*.

"I remember one very particular night," says Freilich, "when Frank Lupo and I were sitting there on a Sunday and we got phone calls from ABC standards and practices, Susan Fetterman. She declared, 'You cannot air this show tonight!' She had just looked at it that day and we could not understand why. She had counted 11 Cylons being shot out of the sky, and she would not allow the show on the air with 11 incidents of violence. We had to go back to my office that afternoon with her, Peter Roth (a vice president of ABC at the time; now executive vice-president of Fox Broadcasting), and we had to sit there and watch the show and count, yes, 11 of them.

"Our argument was these were not people, they were robots, Cylons were animatrons and it wasn't hurting anybody. She put on such a stink, and we reminded her that it would probably cost upwards of $50,000 to cut one of the shots, recut and redub the film and be ready for satellite that night. We got away with it that time, but these are things you never have to deal with anywhere else."

One night while writing the episode "Spaceball," Freilich received a very unusual phone call from Texas. "Every show that I've ever worked on has its own group of really obsessive fans. Regardless of the show you work on, there is a group of people who watch the show religiously and know the show better than you do, even if you are the creator of that show. They will read things into your shows that you as the creator or writer would never think about. They see people on your show as being in the real world, whereas you know they're fantasy. I got this call from a man who is very upset because he's been watching the show and he swears that's not how Galacticans talk, because he's met them. Because they've actually landed in his yard and he put them up for a few days in his barn. They don't talk like that. He's calling to tell me that in the future there are several expressions Galacticans use that we don't use on the show, that we oughta use if we're going to be accurate about them. I couldn't believe I was hearing this. I took him seriously because I didn't want to make fun of him. But I could not believe that somebody truly believed what he was telling me. And yet, this was a middle-aged man, he must have been at least in his late forties if not early fifties. He was a devotee of the show."

Taking him seriously could have been a good idea. Freilich accepted the man's advice and incorporated the expressions into the show. Sadly, Freilich can't recall the specifics of what he added.

Working with Glen Larson was an enriching experience for Freilich. "Glen always had his finger on the pulse of the American television audience," he says, "and he was very good at creating shows that critics might pan, but the audiences tuned into in droves. He never paid much attention to anybody but the audience. What Glen taught me more than anybody else, was to exploit whatever your own ideas were and don't pay attention to networks and studios. Your own success or failure should be measured by your ideas without having them polluted or changed [by other people].

"He was really very much of an individualist. He had, more than any other producer I've ever worked for, a high respect and reverence for the writer. Glen started as a writer, a pure writer, and that's all he was. He wasn't a producer, and he built an incredible reputation as one of the faster writers in television. Speed in television is really important because things are done so quickly. I learned to go with your instinct when you are writing; to close yourself off from phone calls, make sure to have other people to handle the nuts and bolts of making a television show, to lock yourself behind a door. Glen would disappear to his home in Hawaii or Malibu and not answer the phone until he was finished with what he was doing. He also had an amazing ability to make incredibly expensive television shows despite the protestations of the networks and studios and then take those television shows, and in the case of *Galactica*, which is a prime example, make it into a theatrical film, release it overseas, and make back any deficit he might have incurred by making a TV show. It was very, very rare to do that.

"Glen was one of the first people to market toys and games and cards and all sort of ancillary things that could come from a television show.

"I had heard a tremendous amount of negative things about Glen Larson before [working with him]. In retrospect, most of the stuff I heard about that was not positive came from jealous people.... My experience with him was a very pleasant one, and it paid off particularly well about a year and a half ago. I was in Paris on vacation from Spain, where I was doing an episode of *Dark Justice*, a show I created. Glen called me in Paris to tell me that CBS had just shown him the pilot I had written and directed for *Dark Justice* because he was interested in writing a late night show, and how he thought it was really wonderful and how proud he was and stuff. I said, 'In a lot of ways you taught me all I know.' He took no credit for that at all, kind of laughed it off. Truthfully, the other person that he really helped was Frank Lupo, who created the *A-Team*." (Lupo also worked on *Greatest American Hero* and invented, with John Ashley, *Something Is Out There*.)

If the show had continued further, Larson says, "We would have just expanded on our basic premise but refined our storytelling. There are an infinite number of stories you could tell in outer space. It had a lot more scale and potential than, I think, *Star Trek* did in many ways.... We had better hardware to work with and a lot less limiting. We could have done a great deal, but we needed more time."

The last word on *Galactica 1980* comes from Glen Larson, musing on a revival of the adventures of the Battlestar *Galactica*. "There was a point where Universal was talking about doing it the same way as *Star Trek*—that we might have done it as a prime access sold to stations [i.e., syndication]. But with the sale of Universal to Japan, and some of the other things, I don't know if the people [who are there now] have the imagination to do that. Right now it's a little less likely, but nothing's impossible. With the success of *Star Trek* and its spin-off, it's possible that this will come up again."

And would Larson be interested in doing it? "Yeah, I would, because I really think having been there once, I have a better idea of what we could do. But who knows?" he shrugs. "We'll have to see."

CAST NOTES

Barry Van Dyke (Dillon): Born 1951, the son of comedian Dick Van Dyke. In the late 1980s he starred with his father in a short-lived sitcom called *Van Dyke and Company*. He also joined his father in a pair of TV movies, first *Diagnosis of Murder* (1992) and then *The House on Sycamore Street* (1993), which successfully spun off into a series titled *Diagnosis: Murder* beginning in late 1993.

Kent McCord (Troy): Born 1942. McCord was Officer Jim Reed on *Adam-12* (1968–75). He also appeared in *Airplane II* (1982) as the co-pilot with Peter Graves and played a cop in *Predator 2* (1990). He also guested on *seaQuest* (1994).

Lorne Greene (Adama): see *Battlestar Galactica*.

Patrick Stuart (Dr. Zee): Born 1966. A child actor in *Galactica 1980*, he made a successful move to *All My Children* as rapist Will Cortlandt. Stuart is the son of Chad Stuart, of the singing duo Chad and Jeremy. He continues to act on the stage in New York.

Robyn Douglass (Jaime): Born in 1953 in Japan. Douglass has also starred in a TV movie with Marc Singer, *Her Life as a Man* (1984) and with Steve Martin in *The Lonely Guy* (1984).

EPISODE GUIDE

Galactica Discovers Earth, Part 1

The Battlestar *Galactica* and her rag-tag fleet finally find Earth. But before they announce themselves, Adama and Dr. Zee review the ramifications of their arrival. Troy and Dillon are sent on a covert mission to Earth and try to contact scientists. Wr: Glen A. Larson. Dir: Sidney Hayers.

Professor Mortinson (Robert Reed); Secretary (Sharon Acker); Carlyle (Pamela Susan Shoop); Brooks (Fred Holliday); General Cushing (Richard Eastham); 1st cop (Vernon Weddle); 2nd cop (David Moses); Willy (Brion James); Donzo (Mickey Jones); 1st pilot (Duncan Mackenzie); 2nd pilot (Douglas Bruce); Derelict (Eddie Firestone); 1st guard (Frank Downing); 2nd guard (Don Maxwell); Willie (Adam Starr).

Galactica Discovers Earth, Part 2

Troy and Dillon are summoned back to the *Galactica* for an emergency mission. A council member, Xavier, has traveled back in time to speed up Earth's technology by altering the course of World War II. Wr: Glen A. Larson. Dir: Sidney Hayers.

Xavier (Richard Lynch); Sheriff (Ted Gehring); German commander (Curt Lowens); Father (James R. Parkes); Aide (Bruce Wright); Willie (Adam Starr); Little girl (Missy Francis); 3rd German (Todd Martin); 3rd cop (John Zenda); 2nd German officer (Erik Holland); 1st German officer (Eric Forst).

Galactica Discovers Earth, Part 3

Meeting up with an American WW II agent, the Galacticans and Jaime try to find Xavier and stop his mad plan of changing Earth's history. Wr: Glen A. Larson. Dir: Sidney Hayers.

Xavier (Richard Lynch); Professor Mortinson (Robert Reed); Stockwell (Christopher Stone); Brooks (Fred

Holliday); Boomer (Herbert Jefferson, Jr.); Colonel (Hank Brandt); 3rd guard (Duncan MacKenzie); 2nd guard (Jonathan Williams); 4th guard (Paul Brown); Newspaper boy (Ray Duke); Air Force major (Doug Hale); Tucker (Billy Jacoby); Little girl (Missy Francis); German officer (Louis Turenne); "The Old Man" Resistance leader (Michael Strong); Also with Albert Paulsen.

Superscouts, Part 1

The Cylons have caught up with the *Galactica*. Troy and Dillon have been assigned to bring a group of children to Earth, and they disguise themselves as Scouts. But in making the purchase for the clothes, Dillion accidentally robs a bank. Wr: Glen A. Larson. Dir: Vince Edwards.

    Stockton (Mike Kellin); Col. Sydell (Allan Miller); Dr. Spencer (George Deloy); Brooks (Fred Holliday); Nurse Valerie (Carlene Watkins); Bank teller (Caroline Smith); Collins (Jack Ging); Boomer (Herbert Jefferson, Jr.); Captain (Simon Scott); Saleslady (Helen Page Camp); Co-Pilot (Ken Scott); Moonstone (Eric Larson); Starla (Michelle Larson); Jason (Eric Tablitz); Superscouts (Mike Brick, Jeff Cotler, Nicholas Davies, Mark Everett, George Irene, Tracy Justrich, Lindsay Kennedy, David Larson, Jerry Supiran).

Superscouts, Part 2

When one of the children becomes ill because of polluted water, Troy and Dillon try to do something to stop the waste from being released into the environment. Wr: Glen A. Larson. Dir: Sigmund Neufeld, Jr.

    Stockton (Mike Kellin); Col. Sydell (Allan Miller); Sheriff Ellsworth (John Quade); Denver (Mikeal Swan); Spencer (George Deloy); Brooks (Fred Holliday); Nurse Valerie (Carlene Watkins); Bank Teller (Caroline Smith); Collins (Jack Ging); Boomer (Herbert Jefferson, Jr.); Captain (Simon Scott); Saleslady (Helen Page Camp); Co-Pilot (Ken Scott); Moonstone (Eric Larson); Starla (Michelle Larson); Jason (Eric Tablitz); Superscouts (Mike Brick, Jeff Cotler, Nicholas Davies, Mark Everett, George Irene, Tracy Justrich, Lindsay Kennedy, David Larson, Jerry Supiran).

Spaceball

While playing baseball with the children, Xavier tricks Troy and Dillon and traps them on a Viper in space. Meanwhile, he holds the children hostage. Wr: Frank Lupo, Jeff Freilich and Glen A. Larson. Dir: Barry Crane.

    Col. Sydell (Allan Miller); Billy (Paul Kolso); Hal (Bert Rosario); Brooks (Fred Holliday); Xavier (Jeremy Brett); Tommy (Wayne Morton); Stratton (Trent Dolan); Red (Bill Molloy).

The Night Cylons Landed, Part 1

When a Cylon ship crash-lands on Earth, Troy and Dillon must find it before it can transmit a message to Cylon basestars telling them about Earth. Wr: Glen A. Larson. Dir: Sigmund Neufeld, Jr.

    Shirley (Lara Parker); Norman (William Daniels); Col. Briggs (Peter Mark Richman); Andromus (Roger Davis); Wolfman Jack (Himself); Col. Sydell (Allan Miller); Stewardess (Sheila DeWindt); 1st Officer (Rene Lavant); 2nd Officer (Ed Griffith); Cabbie (Jed Mills); Kanon (Timothy O'Hagan); Briton (Robert Lunny); Moonstone (Eric Larson); Starla (Michelle Larson); Jason (Eric Tablitz); Superscout: (Mike Brick, Jeff Cotler, Nicholas Davies, Mark Everett, George Irene, Tracy Justrich, Lindsay Kennedy, David Larson, Jerry Supiran).

The Night Cylons Landed, Part 2

Picked up by a group on the way to a Halloween party, two Cylons go along for the ride while looking for a radio transmitter. Meanwhile, Troy and Dillon close in, but they must save the life of a child trapped in a penthouse fire set by the Cylons. Wr: Glen A. Larson. Dir: Barry Crane.

    Mildred (Marj Dusay); Arnie (Val Bisoglio); Singer (Heather Young); Andromus (Roger Davis); Cop (Bernie Hamilton); Grover (Ken Lynch); Cabbie (Arthur Batanides); Officer Trauma Room (John Finnegan); Pop (Herb Vigran); Chuck (John Wildlock); Police sergeant (Dan Ferrone); 1st tough (Alexander Petala); 2nd tough (Cosie Costa); 3rd tough (Tony Miratta); 4th tough (Louis Sardo); Fireman (Paul Tuerpe); M.C. (Chip Lucia).

Space Croppers

When Cylons destroy the agricultural dome, the fleet's food supply is in grave danger. Troy and Dillon join some farmers to grow food for the fleet. But a land baron wants to put the farmers out of business. Wr: Robert L. McCullough. Dir: Daniel Haller.

    Steadman (Dana Elcar); Gloria (Ana Alicia); Louise (Anna Navarro); Trent (Bill Cort); Garrett (Bill McKinney); Boomer (Herb Jefferson, Jr.); Hector (Ned Romero); Rogers (Booth Colman); Chris (Joaquin Garay III); Maze (Andy Jarrell); Dante (Phil Lavien); Creature (Dennis Haysbert); Foley (John Dantona); Deacon (Gordon Haight); Channon (Stefan Haves); Pilot (Lance Mugleston).

Return of Starbuck

Dr. Zee's strange dream reveals the fate of the long-lost Starbuck: After being stranded on a barren planet after a Cylon attack, Starbuck reactivates a Cylon robot for companionship. Wr: Glen A. Larson. Dir: Ron Satlof.

    Starbuck (Dirk Benedict); Boomer (Herbert Jefferson, Jr.); Angela (Judith Chapman); Centurion (Rex Cutter); Girl (Ellen Gerken).

The Gemini Man
September 1976–October 1976

An underwater explosion turns diver Sam Casey into an invisible man. By wearing a watch that stabilizes his DNA, he's able to control his invisible condition. Casey reluctantly agrees to work as a secret agent for the government agency Intersect. However, Sam can disappear only for 15-minute intervals—any longer and his molecular structure will disintegrate.

Cast: Sam Casey (Ben Murphy); Dr. Abby Lawrence (Katherine Crawford); Dr. Leonard Driscoll (William Sylvester).

Based on the novel by H.G. Wells; *Created by:* Leslie Stevens, Harve Bennett, Steven Bochco; *Producers:* Leslie Stevens, Robert F. O'Neill, Frank Telford; *Executive Producer:* Harve Bennett; NBC/Universal; 60 minutes.

The Gemini Man sprang to life from the wreckage of the previous season's *The Invisible Man*. When the latter proved a ratings dud in 1975, NBC was convinced that it was the treatment, not the concept, that failed. They quickly commissioned the same producers to try again. *The Gemini Man's* story editor, Steven de Souza, was surprised by the whole affair. "It was the first time I had seen a network cancel a show and then want it back immediately! On *The Gemini Man*, they took the unfilmed *Invisible Man* scripts and filmed them. As story editor, I knew the scripts were recycled. They had crossed out the names on the *Invisible Man* script and put the *Gemini Man* names in the margins."

"When *The Invisible Man* was not renewed, Universal ordered *The Gemini Man* in its place," says executive producer Harve Bennett. "It was the conversion of one format into another. Something similar had happened a few years earlier at Universal. A show named *Toma* had been converted into the series *Baretta*. It was a kind of common experiment at the time."

Producer Robert O'Neill helped to reincarnate *The Invisible Man*. "Since *The Invisible Man* wasn't working, there was an attempt to save the show in a different form. Universal was anxious to save the premise. The head of TV at Universal, Frank Price, had a meeting with me and Leslie Stevens, and we were brainstorming ideas. We were desperate to come up with another format that would work. We came up with the idea of an agent who had limited invisibility. Leslie Stevens came up with the idea of putting a wristwatch on

Sam Casey. This gave him 15 minutes worth of invisibility at a time." This technique gave Casey far more flexibility and vulnerability than Dr. Daniel Westin in *The Invisible Man*, who had to wear a human mask and clothes to hide his invisible form.

With NBC and Universal anxious to give the concept another go-around, casting was crucial. The network and studio wanted a more athletic lead. "Since *The Gemini Man* was a more conventional action-adventure show, we wanted a handsome, American action hero," says Harve Bennett. Ben Murphy was cast as the playboy agent, Sam Casey.

"Ben was a more physical kind of guy than David McCallum," notes Robert O'Neill. "It was felt he had the sex appeal required, and he was certainly capable. The network and studio liked him, and Murphy was interested in finding another series [Murphy had previously co-starred in *Alias Smith and Jones*]. We wanted to seduce the audience into thinking *The Gemini Man* was a whole new show."

Leslie Stevens, however, didn't see any future for the invisible men. "Universal assigned me to help Harve Bennett bail out a sinking ship, *The Invisible Man*," he recalls. "When it failed, the studio had felt David McCallum wasn't appealing enough to carry a series. They wanted the more dashing, brainless Ben Murphy. I came up with a new approach called *The Gemini Man*, which put the hero in a little more jeopardy. I came up with the wrist gizmo and other futile stop-gaps, but I knew from the outset that "invisibility" was a creaky franchise. I argued that the disappearing act hands the hero a cowardly solution to his problems. It was like a squid hiding under a cloud of ink. The original H.G. Wells classic was great, but from *Topper* on, invisibility sucks."

Harve Bennett felt that Murphy added a new dimension to the invisible theme. "Ben brings an energy level and a sense of humor David McCallum didn't have in the role," he told *TV Guide*

Ben Murphy as Sam Casey, *The Gemini Man.* Copyright 1976 NBC/Universal.

during the series' run. "David's character was serious about the whole invisibility business. Ben realizes that it might be fun to use it to get into the girls' dormitory. Ben is the best action hero since Errol Flynn."

"I loved working with Ben. He was a real trooper," says Bennett today. "He enjoyed doing the show." Associate producer Richard Milton was less enthusiastic. "Ben Murphy was a contract player at Universal, and he was impossible. He certainly wasn't the actor McCallum was. *The Gemini Man* was a more action-oriented show, but it didn't go anywhere either."

"There was one problem common to *The Gemini Man* and *The Invisible Man*," notes Bennett. "You're asking the audience to love somebody who isn't there most of the time. There is only so much you can do with audio. The joke wears a little thin when a bad guy walks into a room and suddenly, *whap*, he reacts to an invisible blow. He falls down, and you laugh. But you don't laugh every week. It became very difficult to find inventive ways of using invisibility. The other problem was that being an invisible man has a certain prurient quality. On *The Gemini Man*, we had Kim Basinger in a train in an upper berth. Ben Murphy, invisible, is trying to escape the police, and he ends up in the berth with her. It's a funny

scene, but you can't play it for more than, 'Oops! Pardon me. I'm outa here!' At least, not on TV."

The Gemini Man was mainly a crime series with a unique gimmick. "The espionage plots were easier to write," says Robert O'Neill. "The only time we moved into science fiction was with one I wrote, "Minotaur," about a robot. We weren't sure what kind of stories would be successful."

Steven de Souza believes a dull episode was used to kick off the series' premiere. "There were two episodes that had a lot of adult themes," he says. "They were more sophisticated, more intriguing and had some romance and production values. But the episodes couldn't be edited in time to make the airdate. What went on was an episode with a much more familiar storyline.

"That happens a lot with science fiction shows. They're given very little love by studio executives. Science fiction shows are generally regarded as juvenile. The attitude is, 'Well, it's just for kids.' You get executives who have a certain scorn or who are indifferent to the material. Because it's science fiction they don't think the story has to make any sense."

De Souza recalls one *Gemini Man* episode that enraged not only TV critics but viewers as well. "It was a very chaotic situation between the transition of *The Invisible Man* and *The Gemini Man*," he says. "*The Gemini Man* didn't have any scripts. One of the studio execs said, 'Wait a minute. Remember we did a show last season on *The Bionic Woman*, where the bad guys did plastic surgery on someone and made them identical to Jaime Sommers? Let's do that for *The Gemini Man*.' So they took *The Bionic Woman* script, over the misgivings of its writer [James Parriott], and used on it *The Gemini Man*. They just changed the names. Well, around this time, Lindsay Wagner was involved in a car accident. *The Bionic Woman* went into reruns for awhile, and they just happened to run her "identical twin" episode. This was on a Tuesday night. The next night, *The Gemini Man* aired *his* "identical twin" episode ["Sam Casey, Sam Casey"]. Well, the same audience watches both shows. You would not believe the amount of letters that came into NBC and Universal. 'Do you think we're idiots out here? Just because we watch science fiction, do you think we're morons? We won't watch *The Gemini Man* again because you're ripping off *The Bionic Woman*.' Newspaper columnists wrote about how creatively bankrupt Hollywood minds are."

"I was on the staff of *The Bionic Woman*, and

I was asked to redo a version of my "twin" script for *The Gemini Man*," James Parriott says, in a tone that suggests he'd rather have gotten his teeth pulled. "Well, after it aired, I was lambasted by the press. A reporter caught me and said, 'It's the same story as *The Bionic Woman!*' I said, 'I did what they told me to do!'"

The Gemini Man also faced the old story of budgetary constraints. "We just didn't have the budget to do the effects the way we wanted," says Robert O'Neill. "Today, with computer-generated opticals, we could have done a much better job."

"We had a lot of special effects," recalls Richard Milton. "We had tons of blue screen, tons of second unit stuff, we floated things around on thin wire and nylon. It was very complicated and time consuming. It really screwed up the production schedule. But the effects on TV looked pretty good."

The Gemini Man vanished after two months on the air. It was up to Harve Bennett to break the news to his star. "I had the task of going down to the stage and telling Ben it was over. I found him dozing off in a chair—actors in TV series work horrendous hours. I said, 'Ben?' He looked at me and I said, 'Ben, I gotta give it to you straight. We weren't picked up.' He said, 'Oh, that's okay. Now I can do what I've always wanted to do. I'm gonna become a senior tennis champion of the world.' Well, I'm a tennis player, and I had played with Ben. He was better than I was, but he wasn't … well, you know. And Ben continued, 'My age is right. I just turned 36, and if I work real hard, I can go knock their socks off.'" Bennett tried to explain to the actor that he would have formidable competition, but Murphy was determined. "I finally said, 'Well, follow your dream, Ben.' And he did become a superb tennis player. But after five years, he went back to acting!"

Cast Notes

Ben Murphy (Sam): Born 1941. Murphy's first big break was as Kid Curry on TV's *Alias Smith and Jones* (1971–73). He continues to appear in guest shots in TV series such as *Dr. Quinn, Medicine Woman* (1993).

Katherine Crawford (Abby): Born 1944. The daughter of TV writer Roy Huggins and wife of Universal TV executive Frank Price, Katherine Crawford distinguished herself with several strong performances in the 1960s and 1970s. She is currently retired from acting.

William Sylvester (Driscoll): Born 1922. This character actor had a major role in *2001: A Space Odyssey* (1968).

Episode Guide

Code Name: Minus One (1976 TV movie)
Saboteurs of a space capsule try to frame Sam for the capsule's destruction. Facing conviction from the authorities, Sam uses his newfound power of invisibility to get to the truth. Wr: Leslie Stevens. Dir: Alan J. Levi.
Leonard Driscoll (Richard Dysart); Harold Schuyler (Dana Elcar); Charles Edward Royce (Paul Shenar); Vince Rogers (Quinn Redeker); Ballard (H. M. Wynant); Whelan (Len Wayland); Receptionist (Cheryl Miller); Officer (Gregory Walcott); Dietz (Jim Raymond); Guard (Mike Lane); Dive officer (Austin Stoker); CHP officer (Richard Kennedy); Mechanic (Dave Shelley); Controller (Robert Forward).

Season Episodes

Smithereens
Sam transports fuel canisters cross-country for testing, but hijackers threaten his mission. Wr: Frank Telford. Dir: Alan J. Levi.
Stark (Andrew Prine); Arthur Hale (Alan Oppenheimer); Buffalo Bill (Jim Stafford); Hank (Gil Serna); Girl guard (Jeannie Wilson); Worker (Lawrence Bame).

Minotaur
A super robot will be turned loose on the city unless a scientist is paid half a billion dollars. Wr: Robert F. O'Neill, Frank Telford, story by Robert F. O'Neill, Robert Bloch. Dir: Alan J. Levi.
Carl Victor (Ross Martin); Nancy Victor (Deborah Winters); Officer #1 (William Boyett); Date (Cheryl Miller); Minotaur (Loren Janes); Clerk (Robert Hackman); Secretary (Dale Johnson); Guard (Michael Jay London).

Sam Casey, Sam Casey
Plastic surgery turns an assassin into a duplicate of Sam. Driscoll's life is the target. Wr: James D. Parriott. Dir: Michael Caffey.
Armistead (Nancy Malone); Susi (Jo Ann Pflug); Robbins (Leonard Stone); Alf (Mickey Morton); Tanner (Tony Young); Barby (Pamela Susan Shoop); Dora (Joan Crosby); Guard (Leslie Moonves).

Night Train to Dallas
Sam stows away on a train to protect the rebellious daughter of a dead scientist from enemy agents. Wr: Steven de Souza. Dir: Alan J. Levi.

Amy Nichols (Lane Bradbury); Mrs. Price (Ann Shoemaker); Conductor (Michael Fox); Sheila (Kim Basinger); Leslie (Dawn Jeffory); Steward (Bob Delegall); Moose (Michael L. McManus); Agents (Ryan McDonald, Carl Reindel).

Run, Sam, Run!

Awakening with amnesia, Sam is startled to find Driscoll accusing him of murder. Now a fugitive, Sam tries to reconstruct his last 24 hours. Wr: Frank Telford. Dir: Charles Rondeau.

Ted Benton (Terry Kiser); Harris (Warren Berlinger); Bruce (Michael Richardson); Willie (Ron Pinkard); Dan (Jack Bannon); Maggie (Laurette Spang); Frank DeBlazio (Ted Hartley); Proprietor (Rai Bartonious).

Targets

Sam tries to help a defecting woman's daughter escape from a Middle Eastern country, but his cover is compromised. Wr: James Carlson, Terrence McDonnell. Dir: Michael Caffey.

Valerie Dawson (Katherine Woodville); Nina Dawson (Cindy Eilbacher); Victor (Cesare Danova); Guards (Paul Lukather, W. T. Zacha, George Ball); Carlyle (Cort Brackett); Driver (David Mauro); Also with Paul Mantee.

Buffalo Bill Rides Again

Driscoll is a man obsessed: He knows Robert Denby is sabotaging America's defenses but cannot nail him. Sam is sent in as a race driver to get the goods on the traitor. Wr: Frank Telford. Dir: Don McDougall.

Buffalo Bill (Jim Stafford); Robert Denby (Ed Nelson); John Hillier (Don Galloway); Tina (Smith Evans); Elmo (Mickey Gilbert); Mort (Ben Bates); Hoods (Fred Waugh, Alan Oliney); Also with John Milford.

Escape Hatch

Sam sneaks aboard a cruise ship to rescue a businesswoman from the ship's captain. The captain is forcing her to help a hostile foreign country. Wr: Leslie Stevens. Dir: Paul Stanley.

Miss Carisle (Jane Wyatt); Daphne (Pamela Franklin); Capt. Brenner (Bert Kramer); Hammond (Walter Brooke); Stanton (Morgan Jones); Pat Sloane (Polly Middleton); Miss Evans (Florence Halop); Stoller (Larry Delaney); Admiral (Lane Allan); Steward (Barry Van Dyke).

8, 9 , 10 ... You're Dead

Sam poses as a boxer after a prizewinning fighter is blackmailed to throw a fight. Wr: Frank Telford, Richard Fielder, story by Richard Fielder. Dir: Andy Sidaris, Alan Crosland, Jr.

Arch Kingston (Herb Jefferson, Jr.); Trent (Henry Darrow); Pop Kingston (Charles Lampkin); Del Reese (James "Skip" Ward); Referee (Gene Le Belle); Caster (James York); Moore (Tony Burton); Sportscaster (Thomas J. Kelley); Boy (Derek Welles).

Return of the Lion

When their helicopter is shot down, Sam and a dictator travel across African terrain to elude ruthless mercenaries. Wr: Steven de Souza. Dir: Alan J. Levi.

Jamada (Raymond St. Jacques); Brighton (Quinn Redeker); Hauser (Mills Watson); Wife (Adrian Ricard); Daughter (Merriana Henrio); Headman (Joel Fluellen); Soldier (Don Maxwell); Radioman (George Ranito Jordan).

Suspect Your Local Police

Sam goes undercover as a cop and finds that policeman Nik Radinski is being forced to participate in the planned killing of a fellow officer. Wr: Steven de Souza, story by Steven de Souza, Rick Mittleman. Dir: Paul Krasny.

Nik Radinski (Richard Jaeckel); Josef (Joby Baker); Alex Kadescho (Ben Hammer); Mrs. Stapoli (Naomi Stevens); Captain (Bill Zuckert); Oscar (Scott Arthur Allen); Lisa Korlavitch (Barbara George); Kristina (Peggy Walton).

Memory Flash—story editor Steven de Souza: "There was another episode, never aired, that was written by Steven Bochco. When the series was cancelled, they stopped shooting the episode after three days."

Greatest American Hero

March 1981–February 1983

A high school teacher, a frenetic FBI agent and a female lawyer all have a close encounter in the desert with aliens in a flying saucer. Given a super suit that will give him unusual powers, Ralph the teacher (with Bill Maxwell and the FBI in his pocket), fight crime. But wait—Ralph dropped his instruction book in the desert. Flying, and discovering just what powers he has, is not an easy task.

Cast: Ralph Hinkley/Hanley (William Katt); FBI agent Bill Maxwell (Robert Culp); Pam Davidson (Connie Sellecca); *The High School Kids:* Tony Villicana (Michael Pare); Rhonda Blake (Faye Grant); Cyler (Jesse D. Goins); Paco Rodriquez (Don Cervantes).

Created by: Stephen J. Cannell; *Executive Producer:* Stephen J. Cannell; *Co-Executive Producer:* Juanita Bartlett, Jo Swerling, Jr. (years 2 and 3); *Producer:* Alex Beaton, Christopher Nelson, Babs Greyhosky; *Supervising Producer:* Frank Lupo; *Theme:* "Believe It or Not" by Mike Post and Stephen Geyer, sung by Joey Scarbury; ABC/Universal; 60 minutes.

Stephen J. Cannell is quite probably the most unlikely person for a network to approach about a fantasy superhero show. He is well known for creating, producing and writing some of television's most enduring crime drama shows such as *The Rockford Files, Baretta, 21 Jump Street*, and most recently, *The Commish* and *Cobra*. When ABC asked for a superhero show from Cannell's company, it took him awhile to develop the premise. "He didn't want to just come up with a show about a guy with superhuman strength or with X-ray eyes," says co–executive producer Jo Swerling, Jr. "That was too straight—it had been done before. And he thought, 'How can I make a superhero who's a little different?' That led to the development of a character who had super powers but didn't like to use them. And then he came up with the specific details of the aliens who selected him to be there to save the world. They were always referred to as 'the little green guys.' And they gave him this suit with magic powers and an instruction book on how to use it, and he loses the instruction book. So now he has the suit and doesn't quite know how to use it, and he crashes into walls and so on. That was a way of putting humor into the concept, and making it distinctive from Superman."

Director Bruce Kessler, who directed many segments of the show (other credits include *Alias Smith and Jones, B.J. and the Bear, Barnaby Jones, Baretta*, and *I Dream of Jeannie*), describes the show as "a fun concept. It appealed to me—a guy with a suit who had lost the instructions. Yeah—I thought it was terrific."

According to Swerling, it's amazing that *Greatest American Hero* lasted for three seasons. "Traditionally," he says, "fantasies have a rough time in one-hour formats. But many fantasies have been very successful in half-hour sitcoms. *Bewitched, Ghost and Mrs. Muir, I Dream of Jeannie*. With an hour show, it's an uphill battle to get it to succeed. *Greatest American Hero*, which is a fantasy, stayed on the air for three years, which is a credit to everybody involved.... *Quantum Leap* is one of the few fantasies that has stayed on for as long as it has, but it never had very good ratings."

When Ralph Hinkley receives his super suit, he realizes he can fly (although very badly; he has a nasty habit of slamming into brick walls or landing into bushes). He's able to lift cars with his super strength and can deflect bullets (though cowering and covering his face with his arms for protection), and can run at speeds that would make the Six Million Dollar Man blush. Later, with a burst of concentration, he is able to make himself invisible, an ability that spooks FBI agent Maxwell. The super suit also gives Ralph an ability to see events telepathically and to locate someone while holding an object belonging to that person. This "holograph" connects Ralph to the owner or whoever was last in contact with the object. For instance, when it is believed that Bill Maxwell has died, Ralph and Pam learn he is still alive when Ralph accidentally puts on Bill's fishing cap. And much later, when he recovers the instruction book from the "green guys," Ralph even learns to shrink himself. But any time Ralph launches himself into the world with his suit, he has to let FBI agent Maxwell take the credit and disappear (often literally) before anyone can see him. Keeping a secret identity is a problem common to all superheroes, a problem writers frequently exploit for comedy.

Both Kessler and Swerling describe the show as an action-adventure type with a thread of wry, character and situation-based humor running through it. Swerling concedes that, in "broad strokes," *Hero* was a formula show. "Stories had to contain an amount of action, the flying and so on, and action elements and a line of attitude humor running through it. I don't recall anyone sitting down and saying, 'We've had a bunch of these kinds of stories, now we should look for something issues-oriented.' Or very serious drama or Three Stooges comedy. The effort to create stories was focused on being true to the show. We wanted to do stories that were interesting from one [to] another. So you weren't doing the same story every week."

William Katt, who played the idealistic, energetic high school teacher, was introduced to the show via Stephen Cannell, who had seen him in the feature *First Love* with Susan Dey. Katt bought the show's concept on the strength of Cannell's enthusiasm—but for one element of his role, Katt could never muster any enthusiasm of his own. According to Swerling, William Katt hated "the magic red jammies" (as character Bill Maxwell dubbed them) so much that he refused to do publicity wearing the suit.

William Katt stars as a reluctant hero, Ralph Hinkley, chosen by extraterrestrial aliens to wear the magic suit that gives him super-powers. Copyright 1981 ABC/Stephen J. Cannell Productions.

want.' Bill signed on to do the character in the show, but he felt he had associated with a comic strip character. But he didn't want to be associated with the character in any other way. That included publicity. He would wear it during filming, but it still embarrassed him. But he wouldn't wear it on a talk show or publicity session, and *TV Guide* wasn't interested in that. So, we lost a *TV Guide* cover as a result of that." Katt could not be swayed, even by prodding from his boss, Stephen Cannell. When he did talk to *TV Guide* in 1982, he talked about the suit. "I know it's part of the job," he said, "but to this day, after a year and a half of the show, I still don't like it. Every time I have to put it on, I'm uncomfortable."

"Ultimately," says Swerling, "we got the *TV Guide* cover and they had an artist draw him. So, that made sense and that's what they ended up doing. I always felt the best anecdote about the show was that the star was embarrassed by the wardrobe. He wanted to forget about the suit every chance he got."

"He hated the suit and wore it with some reluctance," recalls Swerling. "He didn't hold up production, or say, 'I won't wear it,' he knew it was part of the show.

"*TV Guide* wanted to do a cover of the show, and a *TV Guide* cover is important to any series. It's not just something they do for every show. The editors decide that they want to give you a cover.

"At the time, the title song had been a top 40 hit, and *TV Guide* wanted to set up a photo session with him, and Bill said, 'That's fine—but I won't wear the suit.' They said, 'But that's what we

Notwithstanding this impasse, Swerling and Kessler remember Katt as excellent in his work on the show. They also concur in their high praise of Katt's co-stars, Robert Culp and Connie Sellecca.

Robert Culp played FBI agent Bill Maxwell in a very straight-arrow, dogmatic style. "I don't know how much he was enjoying himself because I didn't get that close to him personally," comments Swerling. "My observation is, he was a very dedicated professional who worked very hard to do his role. I think he very much liked the role.

There was no embarrassment, of course. He didn't have to wear funny wardrobe. He really got into that character, and his particular style of acting worked extremely well in the character of Maxwell. He was delightful to watch. He always came in prepared."

Kessler agrees with Swerling, "Bob was a true professional. I don't think he came in looking at it as a 'fun day.' He looked at it as being a professional actor doing the best job he could. Not that he disliked the part, but work is work. Bob was not the kind of guy who had a lot of fun on the set and socializing and goofing around—he came in to do the job and did it very, very well."

Swerling goes on to say that "Bob was multi-talented. Bob was not difficult, but he was not as malleable for me as Bill [Katt] was, to work with. I could do more with Billy than I could with Bob. Bob was not a difficult actor to work with, but we never developed a real close relationship. We were just people working together and did what we had to do. He had a very definite ideas about the character, and because he also writes and directs, he would have ideas on how things should be done. So he wasn't just a guy who would come in and say, 'Where do you want me to stand? What do you want me to do?' As Bruce said, he wouldn't fool around [on] the set." So involved was Culp with the show and his role that he told Associated Press he'd worked out Bill Maxwell's character all the way back to his childhood.

Culp had a longstanding declaration that he was not interested in doing another series after burning out on *I, Spy*. But a friend cajoled him into reading the pilot's script. Thirty pages into it, he picked up the phone and called Cannell for a meeting. (Years earlier, buddy Robert "Baretta" Blake had told him that he should never miss a chance to work with Cannell.)

To avoid creating a show that was dependent on just two lead characters who often disagreed vehemently about values and priorities in life, Cannell invented Pam Davidson. Played by Connie Sellecca (fresh from the 1980 series *Beyond Westworld*), Pam helped the duo on their cases and eventually married Ralph Hinkley. Swerling and Kessler remember Sellecca fondly.

"Connie was great to work with. Bill and Bob had certain aspects of their personalities that made them a little difficult," says Swerling. "With Bob I would say that it would be his very strong, rigid opinions on how things should be done. With Bill, it was a tendency to be moody. His atti-

tude about the suit was a separate issue. Bill could be the most delightful, charming guy around. Other days, he was kind of down, and that would have its contagiousness. It's not fun to be around somebody down in the dumps, it kind of brings you down too, and that was an effect Bill would have on the crew from time to time. Connie, on the other hand, was the consummate professional and nice person. I always felt she was kind of the glue that kept it together. Her demeanor was so friendly to everybody. It certainly helped the morale of the set at times when the morale might have been affected by other stresses and strains, which might have had to do with the actors, or bad weather, or whatever pressures there are. Everyone loved her, and I would work with her anytime, anyplace, and anywhere."

After listening to Swerling's comments, director Kessler succinctly agrees: "Connie was everything Jo said. She was a stabilizing force on the set."

However, filming *Greatest American Hero* with Sellecca at one point took some creative filmmaking. Just prior to the start of the show, Sellecca became pregnant by then-husband Gil Gerard, so directors had to discreetly film around her increasingly apparent condition. In fact, scenes degenerated to shots of Pam carrying objects that hid her body and finally to phone conversations between Pam and Ralph.

Early in production, Sellecca asked if Pam could try out the supersuit but producers balked. "I would have loved to do that. I think it would have been hilarious, but they didn't have my sense of humor, I guess," Sellecca told *TV Guide* in 1984.

One of the problems on *Greatest American Hero* was that while Ralph, Bill and Pam dashed off to their adventures saving the world, it became obvious that the high school kids from Ralph's special education class were shoved into the background, their appearances eventually dwindling.

Asked if including the kids in the various plots of the stories became difficult, Swerling reports that "it *was* cumbersome to involve all the school kids. They were around during the year I worked on the show—I remember they kind of faded out. They were not as important to the stories." But Swerling also says, "I don't remember any conscious effort to put them into the episodes. I never heard anything like, 'The audience misses the kids.' The stories were the stories as the writers wrote them."

Comparing *Greatest American Hero* to the many shows he has directed over the years, Kessler says the series "was always a challenge in making it new and keeping it alive, like in any series. Part of directing is figuring out how to figure out how to do it, and so forth. The actual directing is very satisfying, but you have no time—you're on a dead run all of the time. That's the nature of the business."

As an example of the kinds of problems he had to deal with, Kessler remembers he was directing an episode called "The Hand Painted Thai," a script that he loved very much, when a message arrived from the network. "Before we shot it, the network decided they wanted to take out the biggest joke in it, which was every time Billy said a certain word, it put Bob to sleep. The word was 'scenario.' They'd be in the middle of a crisis and Billy would say, 'Well, if we follow this scenario,' and Bob would go to sleep."

This joke related to a scene earlier in the plot in which Maxwell, despite his skepticism, was placed under a trance in a visit to a hypnotist. "Word came down just before we shot it to take that joke out of the show," says Kessler. "I remember saying, 'What? They want to take that out?' and Jo talked to someone to take care of it. They did. Because if you took that joke out of the show, you wouldn't have an episode." The episode was filmed with the joke intact.

Like Ralph himself, the show couldn't seem to fly straight and true. It slammed right into a lawsuit even before it aired. Warner Brothers and D.C. Comics, the owners of Superman, had sued Universal because they felt Hinkley was too close to Superman. Warners and D.C. Comics said that *Greatest American Hero* was copyright infringement, unfair competition, and misappropriation of Superman. An injunction preventing the air of the pilot was requested—and denied. A federal judge later viewed the *Superman* movie and the pilot and found that there was no "substantial similarity between the two characters." He thought Superman was "a broad shouldered, big-muscled, calm and confident square" while Hinkley was a "model American young man of the 70's and the 80's. Trim, hungry looking, non-macho, concerned with family and the every day problems of life but [has gained powers] which he accepts with reluctance and internal confusion." The judge granted ABC's request for dismissal of the suit.

During the show's run, a man named John Hinckley took a shot at fame by attempting an assassination of President Reagan. Although the would-be assassin's name was spelled differently, the producers of *Greatest American Hero* decided to change Ralph's name immediately. Ralph Hinkley suddenly became Ralph Hanley, sometimes just "Mr. H" to the school kids. Later, when the change was deemed inconsequential, the name went back to Hinkley.

After 41 episodes and three seasons, *Greatest American Hero* was canceled by ABC even before five episodes "in the can" got aired. Later, these last five were included in syndication, along with one more item that rose from the ashes. *The Greatest American Heroine*, guest-starring Mary Ellen Stuart, was intended to be a 30-minute presentation film to the network as a spin-off of the show. In this film, Ralph Hinkley's secret identity is blown wide open and the world learns who their mysterious flying benefactor is. Bill Maxwell, however, hides in the shadows and remains the silent partner. The green guys frown on Ralph's sudden celebrity and decree that the suit be transferred to someone else. After a search, Ralph chooses a girl named Holly Hathaway to carry on his deeds in the suit. When the news is delivered to Bill Maxwell, he responds with amazement: "A skirt! You gave the suit to a skirt!" Offended, Pam Davidson replies, "It's a girl, Bill!"

Of *Greatest American Heroine*, Swerling says, "It wasn't the final episode per se. The series had been off the air quite a while. *Greatest American Heroine* was … an effort to sell a new show. Somebody came up with the *Greatest American Heroine*. [Mary Ellen Stuart, who played the replacement character] would be the secondary character. The network financed it, looked at it and went, 'Ugh!' They passed. It did go into syndication as part of the package because we expanded it to an hour by taking footage from other [episodes]. We didn't shoot any new footage for *Greatest American Heroine* aside from the original 30-minute presentation."

Cast Notes

William Katt (Ralph Hinkley/Hanley:) Born 1955. Son of actor Bill Williams and actress Barbara Hale, Katt played gung-ho investigator Paul Drake, Jr., in several of the *Perry Mason* movies in the 1980s, performing with his mother. Later, he acted again for Stephen J. Cannell, in the short-lived series *Top of the Hill.*

Robert Culp (Bill Maxwell): Born 1930. Actor-writer Culp starred with Bill Cosby in *I, Spy* (1965–68) and reprised the role with Cosby on the *I, Spy* reunion (1994). Culp also narrates books-on-cassettes.

Connie Sellecca (Pam Davidson): Born 1955. This New York–born actress started out as a stewardess in the short-lived *Flying High* TV series and later spent several seasons on the 1980s series *Hotel*. She is married to *Entertainment Tonight* host John Tesh.

Episode Guide

Greatest American Hero (2-hour pilot)
En route through the desert with a busload of high school children for a field trip, Ralph meets Bill Maxwell at a diner. Later, when his bus breaks down, Maxwell gives him a lift, and together they get a visit from a flying saucer. Bill's partner hands the super suit to Ralph and decrees they work together. But when Ralph gets home, he realizes he's lost the instruction book.

When a holograph tells Ralph that Bill has been kidnapped by religious fanatics, he and Pam Davidson join forces against the fanatics, who plot a takeover of the U.S. government with the help of the vice-president. Wr: Stephen J. Cannell. Dir: Rod Holcomb.

Adam Taft (Richard Herd); Nelson Corey (G.D. Spradlin); Col. Shackelford (Ned Wilson); John Backe (Bob Minor); David Knight (Edward Bell); Brother Michael (Hank Salas); Officer (Robert Dunlap); Officer Cowan (Jeff MacKay); Debbie the babysitter (Carol Jones); Also with Jason Corbet, Robert Jean Williams, Jody Lee O'Hara, Robbie Kiger, Ed Deemer, James King, Corkey Ford, John Caliri, Lydia Fernandez, Cheryl Francis.

Season 1: 1981

The Hit Car
After 20 years of cat-and-mouse with a drug dealer, Bill and Ralph protect the ex-girlfriend who's willing to testify, from an armored hit car. Wr: Stephen J. Cannell. Dir: Rod Holcomb.

Starlet Wild (Gwen Humble); Johnny Damanti (Gianni Russo); Arnold Turner (Kene Holliday); Mike (Arnold Charnota); Larry Miller (W.T. Zacha); Agent Billings (Arnold Turner); Bob Aaron (Ernie Orsatti); Man (Melvin F. Allen); Hatcheck girl (Quin Hessler); Maitre d' (Bob Goldstein); Woman (Virgina Palmer); Waiter (James Arone).

Here's Looking at You Kid
A top-secret jet fighter disappears from the air, so Bill tries to convince Ralph to help out, but he's too busy with Pam's visiting parents. Later, Ralph discovers new powers of invisibility. Wr: Juanita Bartlett. Dir: Bob Thompson.

Alice Davidson (June Lockhart); Gordon McCready (James Whitmore, Jr.); Harry Davidson (Bob Hastings); Cliff (Red West); Consul general (Zitto Kazann); Van Kamp (F.J. O'Neil); General Morehead (Laurence Haddon); Captain (Roger Etienne); Carrie (Denise Halma); Colvin (Thomas W. Babson); Aide (Daniel Chodos); Bus driver (Bert Hinchman); Mechanic (Al Dunlap); Consul person (Nick Cinardo); African representative (Will Gill, Jr.); European representative (Eric Forst); Asian representative (Gerald Jann); Policeman (Blake Clark).

Saturday on Sunset Boulevard
Bill fails a lie detector test about recent strange happenings. With his job on the line, Bill recruits Ralph to help rescue a missing Italian heiress from Russians, and the stakes are raised when Pam gets kidnapped. Wr: Stephen J. Cannell. Dir: Rod Holcomb.

Serge Valenkov (Kai Wulff); Theresa Chimerosa (Alexa Hamilton); Mikhail (David Tress); Sherman (Mel Stewart); Dept. Bureau Chief Harlan Kane (Joseph Warren); Russian official (Ian Teodorescu); Frederic (Lev Mailer); Kerner (Will MacMillan); Craig (Christopher Thomas); Hollinger (Lawrence Benedict); Kavolstock/Stunt (Glenn Wilder); Pilot (Richard R. Holley).

Reseda Rose
Ralph's having a busy day: Rhonda's mother has vanished, Pam wants a romantic drive, ex-wife Anita wants him to look after their son Kevin, and Bill wants help in speeding up FBI work. Wr: Juanita Bartlett. Dir: Gabrielle Beaumont.

Rose Harris (E.J. Peaker); Alicia Hinkley (Simone Griffith); Yuri Semenenko/Simpson (Peter White); Manny (Dave Shelley); Leonard (Nicholas Worth); Merv (Stephen Kahan); Station attendant (Al White); Vladimir Zorin (Kurt Grayson); Submarine seaman (Jens Nowak); Technitron guard (Don Dolan); Submarine captain (George Ganchev).

My Heroes Have Always Been Cowboys
When a near-accident occurs during a flying chase, Ralph wants to hang up the suit. But Bill's LAPD mentor is turning bad and wants to heist a diamond for himself. An encounter with the Lone Ranger plants some seeds in Ralph's mind. Wr: Stephen J. Cannell. Dir: Arnold Laven.

Tracy Winslow (Jack Ging); Lone Ranger (John Hart); Abe Figueroa (Ferdy Mayne); Edward Castelli (Frank McCarthy); Tim Carson (Joseph Chapman); Norm Woods (Robert Gooden); Sam Watson (Bruce Tuthill); Pete King (Glenn Wilder); Announcer (William Woodson); Man (Charles Walker); Policeman (David Clover).

Fire Man
When Tony is accidentally pegged for a series of arson fires, it takes everything Ralph and Pam have to convince Bill of his innocence. Wr: Lee Sheldon. Dir: Gabrielle Beaumont.

Shaffer (Mark Withers); Kaufman (Raymond Singer); Lane (Steven Hirsch); Robert Moody (Woody Eney);

Cameron (Timothy Carey); Lt. Rafferty (Sandy Ward); Thompson (Paul Cavonis); Joyner (Danny Glover); Policeman (Henry G. Sanders); Fireman (Duane Tucker); Young boy (Scott Thomson); Bag lady (Gayle Vance); Woman (Mercedes McCloskey).

The Best Desk Scenario
Bill's down when his branch has been taken over by someone else, Ralph's temporarily appointed vice-principal, and Pam has been offered a junior partnership at a firm. But when the firm's partner gets threatened, the trio investigates. Wr: Juanita Bartlett and Stephen J. Cannell. Dir: Arnold Laven.

    Clarence Carter II (Eugene Peterson); Palmer Bradshaw (Duncan Regehr); Kyle Morgan (Eric Server); Theodore Sevenson (Rod Colbin); Principal David Kane (Michael Ensign); Chet Kanaby (William Frankfather); Agent Genesta (Tom Pletts).

Season 2: 1981-82

The 200 Mile an Hour Fastball
When an important baseball player gets beat up, Bill convinces Ralph to join the team to make sure they win. That way, hoods who are trying to fix the game won't succeed with an arms deal. Wr: Stephen J. Cannell. Dir: Georg Stanford Brown.

    Debbie Dante (Markie Post); Shorty Robinson (Bruce Kirby); Nick Castle (Carmen Argenziano); Henrique Diaz (Hector Elias); Raymond Sloane (Michael J. London); Mike Douglas (Himself); Don Drysdale (Himself); Big Al (Stanley Brock); Manny Garcia (William Marquez); Tommy the Greek (Charles McDaniels); Russ Decker (Richard Gjonola); Man (Ralph Mauro); Umpire #1 (Hank Robinson); Manuel Cortez (Porfirio Guzman Berrones).

Operation Spoilsport
Missiles are malfunctioning. Someone has tapped into the computer system and programmed a stack of missiles to launch towards Russia. The aliens contact Ralph and want him to avert World War III. Wr: Frank Lupo. Dir: Rod Holcomb.

    General Gerald Stocker (John Anderson); Nancy Ratner (Robin Riker); Agent Carlisle (William Bogert); Capt. Reilly (Al White); Sergeant Jenson (John Difusco); Charles Ratner (Dudley Knight); Mayor Dyle (James Burr Johnson); Admiral Bailey (John Brandon); Secretary of defense (Russ Marin); Smitty (Ronald Spivey); Guy under bridge (John Bristol); Motorcycle cop (Don Maxwell); Sgt. at computer (Dein Wein); Man near phone booth (Rex G. Yon).

Don't Mess Around with Jim
Though a billionaire is declared dead, he's actually alive and has kidnapped Ralph and Bill and knows about the super suit. It turns out he and his partner used the suit a generation before them, but the powers corrupted him. Wr: Stephen J. Cannell. Dir: Robert C. Thompson.

    James J. Beck (Joseph Wiseman); Jordan Heath (Stan Lachow); Jilly Mitchell (Luke Andreas); Marshall Dunn

(Byron Morrow); Vern (Michael Alldredge); Dr. Springfield (Bernard Behrens); Greg Mathews (W.T. Zacha); Mike (Fred Lerner); Jerry Dunphy (Himself); Keith Asherman (Chuck Bowman); Cab driver (Barry Cutler); Croupier (Barry Davis); Girl #1 (Phyllis Hall); Girl #2 (Zan Daes); Gil (Don Pulford); Phil (Dave Ziletti); Diggs (Sonny Shields); Pilot (Carl Wichman).

Hog Wild
Members of a motorcycle gang beat up Ralph and Bill. Later they manage to nab the suit for themselves and take over a small Midwest town. Wr: Stephen J. Cannell. Dir: Ivan Dixon.

    Preacher (Dennis Burkley); Bad B. (Paul Koslo); Sheriff Mark Vargas (Gregory Sierra); Curley (Tony Burton); Deputy Kyle (Dennis Fimple); Stella (Marianne Muellerleile); Sandra (Carol Jones); Sam Watson (Al Dunlap); Dr. Worley (Hoke Howell); Ted (Gary Lee Davis); Coleen Watson (Anne Bellamy); Flo (Kerrie Cullen); Basil (Marland Proctor); County sheriff (Terrance Beasor).

Classical Gas
When Ralph and Pam help the kids with their rock band, they don't realize the rock promoter is a terrorist planning to poison 10,000 people with nerve gas. Wr: Frank Lupo. Dir: Bruce Kessler.

    Charley Wilde (Ed Winter); Hydra (George Loros); Sgt. Crane (Blake Clark); Col. Hansen (Garnett Smith); Man (Christopher Thomas); Doug (Joe Horvath); Huey (Steve Liebman); Biker (Dennis Madalone).

The Beast in the Black
When a benefactor donates the contents of a house to the school, Ralph and the kids go to remove belongings. But when Bill is possessed by a dead woman's spirit, Ralph enters another dimension, where the suit doesn't work to save him. Wr: Juanita Bartlett. Dir: Arnold Laven.

    Sheila Redman (Christine Belford); Edith Morabito (Rae Allen); Betty (Jane Merrow); Dr. Weinstein (Jeff MacKay); Workman (Vince Howard); Arnold (John Macchia).

The Lost Diablo
Bill tricks Ralph and the kids into prospecting in the hills, because he wants Ralph to help find a gold mine. Wr: Juanita Bartlett. Dir: Lawrence Doheny.

    Fletcher Casco (John Miranda); Doyle Casco (Gary Grubbs); Pop Casco (Fred Downs); Harlan Blackford (Bill Quinn); Sheriff (Joseph Whipp); Student #1 (Michael O'Leary); Student #2 (Patti Mariano); Student #3 (Wayne Scherzer).

The Plague
When a mercenary dies from a plague, Ralph and Bill ask around for a known fanatic. Bill is kidnapped, and it's up to Ralph to stop a group from releasing deadly germs. Wr: Rudolph Borchert. Dir: Arnold Laven.

    Harlow Bunker (Ed Grover); Reo Crocker (Jeff Cooper); Dr. Kelly (Arthur Rosenberg); Jeff Sharp (Chip Johnson); Agent Spiegel (J.P. Bumstead); Cadre man (Hank Salas); Arnold Diggs (Melvin F. Allen); Dr. Keene (Richard Brand); Radar operator (Blake Marion); Medic (James

Dyers); Truck driver (Robert Curtis); Harvey Locke (Glenn Wilder).

Train of Thought
Stopping a train, Ralph gets amnesia and has no memory of Bill or the suit. Meanwhile, terrorists are planning to use radioactive waste against a small town. Wr: Frank Lupo. Dir: Lawrence Doheny.

Azziz (Jean Le Clerc); Dr. Gardner (David Tress); Atkins (Dave Shelley); Marshall (Frank McCarthy); Richards (F. William Parker); Sonja (Sonja Petrovna); Mohammed (Judd Omen); Deacon (Robert Alan Browne); McGivers (James Lydon); Fenster (Dabbs Greer); Shaeffer (Arnie Moore); Brakeman (Nick Shields); Josef (Ari Barak); Doctor (Milt Kogan); Engineer (Warren Munson); Sylvester (Nick Cinardo); Carter (Perry Cook).

Now You See It
While practicing with some fins to help him fly, Ralph discovers a new power: foretelling events. The plane that crashes in his vision is the same one that Pam will be taking later in the day. Wr: Patrick Hasburgh. Dir: Robert C. Thompson.

Richard Beller (Jon Cypher); Sen. Henderson (Chris Lofton); Phillipe (Richard Beauchamp); Oliver (Matthew Faison); Burke (Laurence Haddon); Col. Cullen (Charles Bateman); Guard (David Clover); De Jesus (Robert Covarrubias); Juan (Joe Mantegna); Smitty (Patrick Cameron); Trigg (Dennis Haskins); Capt. Fredericks (Glenn Wilder); Capt. Williams (Gary Jensen).

The Hand Painted Thai
Hypnotized years ago in Vietnam by enemy military, reactivated U.S. soldiers plot to destroy a dam, ravaging prime farm land and an important scientific meeting. It's up to Ralph and Bill to change the scenario. Wr: Frank Lupo, Stephen J. Cannell and Patrick Hasburgh. Dir: Bruce Kessler.

Col. Shawn Liang (James Shigeta); Gen. Vin Chow (John Fujioka); Tim Lider (Kurt Grayson); Marty Boxx (Terrance O'Hara); Erika Van Damm (Hilary Labow); Watchman (Terrance Evans); Eugene Zale (Michael Cornelison); Stevens (J.P. Bumstead); Marv Keegan (Chris Hendrie); Kelly Kim (James Saito); Nurse (Odessa Cleveland); Shirley (Lori Michaels).

Just Another Three Ring Circus
Upset with Bill's performance, the FBI assigns him to find a missing circus clown. Ralph enters the circus as the Human Cannonball. Wr: Stephen J. Cannell. Dir: Chuck Bowman.

Erica (Catherine Campbell); Klaus Vorman (Alex Rodine); Peter (Kai Wulff); Keith (Terrence McNally); Biff #1 (Richard Doyle); Biff #2 (Jim McKrell); John (David Winn); Alicia (Lisa Donaldson); Julian (Joe Anthony Cox); Chuck (Patrick Stack); Sharp (Chip Johnson); Lisa (Jourdan Fremin); Spielman (Derek L. Thompson); Yuri Yovanovich (Gene Lebell).

The Shock Will Kill You
The space shuttle has malfunctioned, and Ralph has to maneuver it safely to a landing. As a result, Ralph becomes a super-magnet, and an electrically charged creature that came with the shuttle has run amok.

Wr: Stephen J. Cannell and Frank Lupo, from a story by Patrick Hasburgh. Dir: Rod Holcomb.

Gen. Enright (Rod Colbin); Crocker (Don Starr); Lieutenant (Leonard Lightfoot); Col. Nelson (Ray Girardin); Newscaster (Doug Hale); R.J. (Ned Bellamy); Rider (Randy Patrick); Guard (Bert Hinchman).

A Chicken in Every Plot
Arriving in the Caribbean on the invitation of Bill's friend, Ralph and Bill discover he's been killed by a voodoo cult. After many voodoo-related incidents, the team learns the cult is out to take over the government. Wr: Danny Lee Cole and Jeff Ray. Dir: Rod Holcomb.

Phillipe Augereau (Ron O'Neal); Louis Davout (John Hancock); Victor Suchet (Thalmus Rasulala); Orin Le Masters (Lincoln Kilpatrick); Ted McSherry (Todd Armstrong).

The Devil in the Deep Blue Sea
Vacationing in Bermuda, Ralph thinks he's discovered the Triangle's secret. He thinks a dinosaur has been prowling and sinking ships. Wr: Frank Lupo. Dir: Sidney Hayers.

Le Clerc (Glynn Turman); Devereaux (Jeremy Kemp); Collins (Michael Halsey); Linda Harrison (Anne Bloom); Drunk (Will Hare).

It's All Downhill from Here
Vacationing in a ski resort, Ralph and Pam discover that a U.S. skier has died of foul play. A Czechoslovakian skier wants to defect, and there is a plot by foreign agents to stop him. Wr: Patrick Hasburgh. Dir: Sidney Hayers.

Samantha Brice (Sandra Kearns); Robert Allen Klein (William Lucking); Karpov (Stefan Gierash); Fred Blandin (Red West); Anna Kurienna (Sarah Torgov); Yuri Petchernec (Norbert Weisser); Talenikov (Michael Billington); Weber (Bill Cross); Zhilov (Curt Lowens); Sports announcer (Robert Hastings); Scotty Templeton (Dan Sherwin); Boy in lift line (Craig Schaeffer); Lift attendant (Stan Howard).

Dreams
A man imprisoned by Ralph and Bill gets paroled and plots to kill them. Frightened, Bill hangs onto Ralph and his super suit for dear life. Wr: Stephen J. Cannell. Dir: Bruce Kessler.

Johnny Sanova (Michael Baseleon); Evan Thompson (Fred Stuthman); Red (Nick Pellagrino); Norm (Nicholas Worth); Principal Knight (Edward Bell); Margaret Ditweiler (Elizabeth Hoffman); Dr. Moran (Milt Kogan); Duffy Magellan (James Costy); Matty (Johnny Crear); Irma Keever (Jean Le Bouvier); Ted Keever (Charles Hutchinson); Seminar guest speaker (Peter Trencher).

There's Just No Accounting
Successfully foiling a kidnapping plot, Ralph arrives home with the ransom money and finds an IRS agent waiting for him. Meanwhile, Bill's bosses read him the riot act because he guaranteed the return of the money. Wr: Frank Lupo. Dir: Ivan Dixon.

Byron Bigsby (James Whitmore, Jr.); Jack Martel (Jerry Douglas); Donnie Armus (Marc Alaimo); Harve Sherwin

(Ryan MacDonald); Julie (Carole Mallory); Michael Fattah (Eugene Peterson); Counterman (Ted Gehring); Debbie Sherwin (Emily Moultrie); Penny Sherwin (Cloyce Morrow).

The Good Samaritan
Tired of chasing after crime and crooks, Ralph wants to use the suit for something "nice," like saving the life of an old man who's having everything he owns taken from him by the government. Wr: Rudolph Borchert. Dir: Bruce Kessler.

Ira Haggert (Keenan Wynn); Dave Tanner (Dennis Lipscomb); Murph (Carmen Argenziano); Harlan Blackford (Bill Quinn); Nino (Harry Grant); Guard (Ron Thompson); Commander (Will MacMillan); Judy (Sandra McCulley); Alison McKay, the reporter (Wendy Wessburg); Woman (Pat Wilson); Jonathan (Joshua Miller).

Captain Bellybuster and the Speed Factory
A superhero icon for a hamburger fast food chain realizes his company is engaging in illegal drug trafficking, and he immediately calls Bill. Ralph is needed when a reporter dies and Capt. Bellybuster knows who's behind it. Wr: Stephen J. Cannell and Frank Lupo. Dir: Arnold Laven.

Mickey "Bellybuster" Michaelson (Chuck McCann); Donato Federico (Anthony Charnota); Cal Freeman (Stanley Grover); Bruce Warfel (Danny Wells); Herb Teil (Colin Hamilton); Cabbie (Jim Greenleaf); Cop (Rex Ryon); Passenger (John Roselius); Receptionist (Janet Winter); Kid (Bob Jacoby).

Who's Woo in America
Ralph's mother arrives in town announcing she's getting married to Philip Kaballa, a man Ralph's age. And when Ralph is mistaken for him, it turns out that a lot of thugs are interested in Kaballa. Wr: Patrick Hasburgh. Dir: Bob Bender.

Paula Hinkley (Barbara Hale); Philip Kaballa (Tom Hallick); C.C. Smith (Hugh Gillin); Heller (Jon Ceder); Prentice Hall (Michael Prince); Goodwin (Dave Cass); Nasher (Daniel Chodos); Brackman (Don Maxwell); Haffa (Daniel Dayan); Dr. Woo (Gerald Jahn); Computer clerk (Milt Tarver); Jill (Terri Hanauer); Waiter (Ted Richards); Racquetball clerk (Brian Sheehan); Woman in C.C.'s office (Dinah Lindsey Smith).

Lilacs, Mr. Maxwell
Breaking into the FBI archives to solve unsolved cases, Ralph helps Bill become a hero. But the KGB has hired a lovely assassin to kill Bill. Wr: Robert Culp. Dir: Robert Culp.

Samantha O'Neill (Dixie Carter); Carlisle (William Bogert); David (Ted Flicker); Insurance guy (Arnold Turner); Newscaster (Gay Rowan); Mailboy (Michael Cornelison); Yuri (Adam Gregor); Jane (Stephanie Faulkner); Mr. Bunker (Ralph Clift); Mr. Rogers (Gary Pagett); Mr. Newton (Craig Shreeve); Annie (Trisha Hilka).

Season 3: 1982-83

Divorce Venusian Style
While neo–Nazis are plotting to kill Ralph and Bill, the duo have been arguing. Ralph gives up the suit in disgust, putting them in more jeopardy. Wr: Patrick Hasburgh. Dir: Ivan Dixon.

Jackson (Dean Santoro); Franz Zedlocker (Jeremy Kemp); Billy Boy Floyd (James MacIntyre); Hertzog (Kurt Grayson); Morgan (Jason Bernard); Phillips (Robert Gray); Steve (Al W. Coss); Patrolman (Joe Clarke); Lutz (Frank Doubleday); Police officer (Wayne Storm); Ranch guard (Shane Dixon); Also with (Eugene Brezany).

The Price Is Right
When Ralph is invited to a high school reunion by a famous pro football player, he realizes the man's wife is being held hostage because thugs want him to throw the game. Wr: Stephen J. Cannell. Dir: Ivan Dixon.

Price Cobb (Steven Shortridge); Coach Andrews (Dick Butkus); Coach Farley (Claude Jones); Gertmanian (Patrick Collins); Wendy Cobb (Heather Lowe); Stan Hawn (Martin Speer); Florenzia (Jack Andreozzi); Sports announcer (Bob Hastings); Caprice (Doug France); Gloria (Cathryn Habit); Roberta (Louise Hoven); Miller (Don Pulford); Angie (Susan Duvall); Maid (Edith Fields); Also with Chip Johnson, Anthony Davis, Ben Powers, Tom Harmon, Ted Dawson.

This Is the One the Suit Was Meant For
When Ralph continues to be late for Pam's appointments because of 'suit business,' the three agree a vacation is best. But when they arrive at a remote Bermuda island, Bill shows up with the suit and wants Ralph to help him find a missing jet. Wr: Babs Greyhosky. Dir: Ivan Dixon.

Stanislov (Bo Brundin); Cortez (Pepe Serna); Bunny (Loyita Chapel); Fernandez (Jay Varela); Alejandro (Randall Nazarian); Mitchell (Dein Wein); Sandy (Maurie Lauren); Employee (Bobby Don McGaughey); Also with Bob Basso.

The Newlywed Game
During wedding preparations for Ralph and Pam, the team meets up with a former U.S. secretary of state who wants Ralph to take on a mission for him. Wr: Babs Greyhosky. Dir: Chuck Bowman.

Martin (Woody Eney); Harry Davidson (Norman Alden); Matthew Powers (Hansford Rowe); Alice Davidson (June Lockhart); Mrs. Pilburn (Alice Backes); Campbell (Terrence McNally); Videoman (Frank K. Wheaton); Boom Boom (Pamela Bowman); Stripper (Dan Peterson); Party guest (Cynthia Steele); Minister (Tom Pletts).

Heaven Is in Your Genes
It is believed that Bill has died, but Ralph discovers it's not true when he holographs that Bill has been kidnapped and taken by crooked scientists conducting genetic experiments. Wr: Patrick Hasburgh. Dir: Christian Nyby II.

Dr. Striegel (William Prince); Rutter (George McDaniel); Gardner (Dennis Lipscomb); Kris Peterson (Carolyn Seymour); Bradley (Rick Barker); Plummer (Gene Ross); Marge Lutz (Patricia Wilson); Gas station attendant (Ruben Moreno); Receptionist (Gina Alvarado); Monster (Andre the Giant); George (William Marquez); Also with Ted Gehring, Paul Barselou, Santos Morales.

Live at Eleven

While at a retirement party for a TV anchor, Ralph bumps into someone's briefcase and via a holograph learns that mercenaries are trying to steal radioactive material from a nuclear plant. Somehow, the TV anchor is connected. Wr: Babs Greyhosky. Dir: Arnold Laven.

Henry Williams (William Windom); Chuck Cole (Alan Fudge); Sherwood Dawes (Eugene Peterson); Fields (Will MacMillan); Canton (Miguel Fernades); Security guard #1 (Melvin F. Allen); Shelton (Charles Walker); Coursey (Woody Skaggs); Vicki (Victoria Boyd); Policeman (Mark York); Nurse (Eileen Saki); Gladine (Amanda Harley); Foreman (Dudley Knight); Schneider (Terence Bensor).

Space Ranger

A CIA radio informant known as "Space Ranger" is a student of Ralph's. He's invented a way to tap into spy satellites, and everyone from the CIA to the KGB wants this kid. Wr: Rudolph Borchert. Dir: Ivan Dixon.

Allen Longstreth (Douglas Warhit); Agt. Henry Fetchner (Joe Santos); Agt. Ballantine (Kene Holliday); Principal Knight (Edward Bell); Oscar (James Beach); Proslov (Alex Rodine); Zatkoff (Jan-Ivan Dorin); Clarence Mortner, Jr. (Billy Zabka); Zelda (Evonne Kezios); Milton (Steve Altermann); Mortner (Jay Gerber).

Thirty Seconds Over Little Tokyo

While dining at a Japanese restaurant, the team witnesses a kidnapping. Ralph rescues the man and discovers they are up against Japanese criminals. Meanwhile, Ralph's tenure as a teacher is under review. Wr: Danny Lee Cole and J. Duncan Ray. Dir: Arnold Laven.

Ernie Shikinami (Soon-Teck Oh); Dotty Parker (Christine Belford); Isoroku Shikinami (Lloyd Kino); Maitre d' (Dana Lee); Principal Knight (Edward Bell); Master of Flowers (Mako); William Frankfather (Robert Alan Browne); Tanaka (Peter Kwong); Benning (John Wyler); Landlady (George Paul); Security guard (Bert Hinchman).

The Resurrection of Carlini

When the anniversary of a famous magician's mysterious death comes up, Bill is named in the will. Three competing magicians show up for the reading. But the house goes on fire and later, the other magicians are nearly killed. Wr: Frank Lupo. Dir: Arnold Laven.

Chris Stoppard (Andrew Robinson); Toby Roberts (Jack MacGee); Blatchard (Timothy Carey); Marco the Magnificant (Ferdiand Mayne); Reporter (Tawny Little); Beverly (Randi Brooks); Woman (Sandy Martin); Little boy (Troy Slaten); Magician (Robert Aberdeen); Magician's Assistant (Melanie Vincz); Pool cleaner (Ken Lerner); Also with Wiley Harker.

Wizards and Warlocks

When a Middle Eastern prince plays a fantasy role-playing game on a college campus, he's marked for assassination. Bill meets with the king, who wants him to find his son. Wr: Shel Willens. Dir: Bruce Kessler.

Norman Fackler (James Whitmore Jr.); Margolis (Steve Peterman); King Abou Al Fahaad (Nico Minardos); Prince Aha Mohammed Ali Fahaad (Shunil Borpujari); Omar Stambouli (Harvey Solin); Gamer (Michael Huddleston); Gamer (David Paymer); Student (Toni Hudson); Rook (Bob Saget).

Desperado

Spending a weekend in horse country, Ralph and Pam find that a rustler is obsessed with recovering a previously owned stallion. Wr: Stephen J. Cannell and Frank Lupo. Dir: Christopher Nelson.

Justin King (John Vernon); Sheriff (James Hampton); Charley (Red West); Matt (Luke Askew); Martha Wells (Linda Hoy); Judge (Beach Dickerson); Veterinarian (Rick Lenz); Hunter (Conlan Carter).

It's Only Rock 'n' Roll

While a rock band is in the air, a bomb on board is announced, and Ralph flies to disarm it before the plane lands. Later, a motorcycle gang harasses the band leader because he was once one of them. Wr: Babs Greyhosky. Dir: Christian I. Nyby II.

Dack Hampton/Harmony (Judson Scott); Christopher Bunch (Anthony Charnota); Brick (Robert Dryer); Station house MC (Rick Dees); Official (David Sage); Mr. Norton (George Dickerson); Lenny (Andy Wood); Training officer (Sheila E. Frazier); Also with Lesley Woods, Dennis Stewart, Michael Mancini.

Vanity, Says the Preacher

When a foreign country pays tribute to Bill Maxwell for past deeds, Bill's kidnapped because they need him once again—their government is collapsing. Ralph and Pam fly to the rescue and find matters are not as easy to resolve here. Wr: Robert Culp. Dir: Robert Culp.

Senora Estelita Del Vera (Isela Vega); Dr. Francisco (Julio Medina); Marco (Dehl Berti); Marco (Luis Moreno); Bartender (Frankie Pesce); Sons (Joseph Culp, Jason Culp).

Greatest American Heroine

When Ralph's identity is finally revealed to the world, the "green guys" instruct Ralph to find a replacement hero who will work with Bill. Ralph finds a woman, Holly Hathaway, to take on the adventures. Wr: Babs Greyhosky. Dir: Tony Mordente.

Holly Hathaway (Mary Ellen Stuart); Sara Hathaway (Mya Akerling); Alien (John Zee); Timothy (Jeffrey Markel); Also with Jerry Potter, Wayne Grace.

Hard Time on Planet Earth

March 1989–July 1989

A revolutionary from another world is cast out for causing trouble on his planet and is sentenced to serve time on Earth, where his human form has great strength and speed. The length of Jesse's sentence is determined by Control, a floating computer observer who guides and advises Jesse in his mission to do good on Earth.

Cast: Jesse (Martin Kove); Voice of Control (Series) (Danny Mann); Voice of Control (Pilot) (Charles Fleischer).

Created by: Jim and John Thomas; *Executive Producers:* Richard Chapman, E. Jack Kaplan, Jim and John Thomas; *Supervising Producers:* Ric Rondell, Michael Piller; *Co-Producer:* Janice Cooke-Leonard; CBS/Touchstone Television; 60 minutes.

One of the best ways to use science fiction is to create a character totally unfamiliar with our world, then watch him grow and be educated as he interacts with us in our everyday lives. In the process, we can learn about ourselves as well as be entertained. *Hard Time on Planet Earth* presented such a character in Jesse, an intergalactic warrior from the planet Andarius who had long ago abandoned the confines of a physical body.

The show was created when CBS asked brothers Jim and John Thomas for a series in the mold of *The Incredible Hulk.* In reply, the Thomases suggested a more "alien" idea. Fresh from their work on *Predator* (1987), they conjured up an alien who arrives on Earth against his will and is constantly frustrated in everyday life.

"It was a chance to live out of our own alter-egos. The frustrations we feel with day-to-day life sometimes lead us to want to wreak havoc on our surroundings and our fellow human beings, so we gave our alien superhuman strength and a backstory that made him an exiled warrior. He could convincingly say, 'I've had enough and I'm not gonna take it anymore!'" says Jim Thomas.

The hidden backstory of this character is that Jesse had triumphed in a cosmic battlefield of unimaginable scale and returned home a hero. But his victory was short. His services were no longer needed. Trouble followed him, and promises were not kept. The ruling classes grew intolerant of him. Rather than terminate Jesse and make a martyr of him, the rulers banish him to the backwater planet called Earth. Parole for Jesse comes in the form of good deeds on Earth; if he did enough of these, he will be freed.

Acting as warden while Jesse does his time on Earth is a cybernetic, slightly misprogrammed, pestering motor-mouth of a sidekick named Control, who supervises his stay. "The idea of Control," John says, "came about because we realized Jesse needed an alter-ego, another aspect of his own personality with whom he could develop an uneasy partnership."

Control's backstory is this: Flawed programming gave him a mind of his own at times, with a tendency to become too involved in assignments rather than standing by as an unbiased observer. When Jesse was exiled, Control was tapped as the perfect agent. Of course, Control advises Jesse *badly*, creating many predicaments and confounding his learning and adjustment. Control has a nasty habit of wandering off on his own and enjoying the sights on Earth. Bright things, computers and neon signs fascinate Control, and sometimes he might be off studying chimneys or a ventilation shaft.

Jesse was played by Martin Kove, a familiar face from the long-running *Cagney and Lacey* as well as other TV series. Jim Thomas says, "Every other actor who read for the part was overly dramatic with it. Marty made us laugh, and we knew he could handle the humor in the material, the tongue-in-cheek scenes we wrote depicting a frustrated alien in a human body trying to make sense of it all. And thanks to Marty, as we developed the show, we realized we could explore more of the innocence and the comedy in the characterization and less of the warrior. Instead of playing anger and toughness all the time, we focused on the alien's complete naivete in the face of the complexities of modern life as we know it."

Martin Kove admits that when he was first approached with the idea of the show, he was not so hot for the script, although he liked the concept. "I met with the producers and everyone," he says. "I liked them and felt very comfortable with them. They were very excited about the script. I loved Jim and John Thomas—they were terrific—and the people at Disney."

No agreements were made at first, and as the months passed, Kove moved on to other projects. One day, he asked his agent if anyone had been cast for the show. When he learned that the role was still open, and that the Thomas brothers wanted to see him again, Kove became excited. "Ultimately, we made a deal and scheduled me around a movie of the week I had to do. All these schedules were moved around so that Disney and the network could use my services to shoot the pilot."

The character appealed to Kove, who wanted an opportunity to stretch himself as an actor, since he had become so well known for *Cagney and Lacey* and various action films. "I'm always playing wise guys and heavies in movies," Kove says ruefully. "What was interesting [about Jesse] was he's vulnerable and quite sensitive to some of the situations around him. It's a stranger in a strange land. His vulnerability [comes about] ... because he's so naive." Kove believes the charm of the character Jesse was that he received everything at face value. Of course, humans are sometimes very confusing, even deadly under certain circumstances. Kove points out that Jesse "takes things at face value because that's the way they function at his planet."

Viewing humans through alien eyes has long been a favorite theme in science fiction, with the help of such classic characters as Mr. Spock, Starman, the Phoenix, Gene Roddenberry's Questor from *The Questor Tapes*, and of course, our old pal Mork from Ork. Kove wanted a similar theme to come through in *Hard Time on Planet Earth*. "That's what we wanted to do. I find a lot of our shows didn't touch upon that. Some of our shows did a great deal about that," says Kove. He points to an episode called "Battle of the Sexes" in which Sandahl Bergman plays a female terminator from his planet, sent to kill him—but not before both of them fall in love.

Hard Time on Planet Earth demanded a great deal from Kove, since he was the only regular character from week to week other than Danny Mann's off-screen voice as Control. "Sometimes you're up against handling too much," says Kove. "I learned a lesson there where you can't do everything. Often, you would do a scene for the day, and then there's second unit stuff for the previous show, and then a director comes up and wants to talk to you about a show coming up in the future. So there's three shows you're chatting about. It's very hard to function. It's not impossible—you really need to be pre-

Martin Kove stars as the alien revolutionary sentenced to Earth in a human body. He's guided by a biosynthetic electronic observer called Control. Copyright 1989 Disney/NBC, photo courtesy of Martin Kove.

pared. If I had to do it again, I [would] focus my energy in certain areas [only]."

Although Kove enjoyed the work and what the show had to offer, he says very candidly that he felt it needed a harder edge and a stronger gearing for an adult audience. "I had everybody screen the *Highlander* movie before we started shooting," he says. The character is loosely based on the Highlander." Kove says he had worked with the Highlander's creator, Gregory Widen, on a *Tales of the Crypt* episode, and they had entered into a discussion on why Jesse couldn't have been "more with an edge, like Christopher Lambert played. In television you can't do that. You have to work with the format as the series changes ... [from] conception of the pilot to the regular episodes. What I think happened was, people weren't sure about the viability [of the character]. I think it changed."

Kove believes that Jesse came off as an 11-year-old whereas Kove envisioned him as 18—wiser and less childlike. "I read the original treatment for this show and it was much harder-edged than what you saw. It got soft and more of an 8:00 show," he says.

To ensure proper character development as the show progressed, Kove kept a notebook in which he wrote down all the different things that Jesse learned. "I kept a bible, a diary. In the first episode, he learned about money. The second episode is about love. He learned about a kiss and about love. I kept a diary for every episode so when it came up in the next episode, he knew what it was. You have to remember we're dealing with a character that's like a newfound baby who knew nothing about our customs and had to play everything by ear. He would learn by television, by talking to other people."

Kove feels very strongly that had the show continued further, Jesse's character growth would have continued. "The audience deserves it," he emphasizes. "Audiences are so sophisticated now. They fly in with their remote control, and you have to ... [engage] their imagination. If you contribute enough, they'll stay with the show, but if you don't, they won't. Their emotional involvement will dissipate in a 48-minute episode."

With no regular sets for the show, the company filmed in and around Southern California, creating unique hardships (and rewards) for Kove. For "Battle of the Sexes," Kove says his love and dedication for the show came through when a scene had to be filmed very late night at a planetarium. "We had to stop at 12 a.m. I was off the clock because I needed 12 hours to turn around again," explains Kove. "At 2 a.m. my double was going to shoot a huge chase scene with Sandahl Bergman. I didn't want them using my double. I wanted *me* so we could get close to the camera. I said, 'Don't use the double! Use me!' Technically, you're not paid for that because you're off the clock! But I wanted the camera work to be close. So I volunteered to do it. The stuff we got was brilliant. I had to be on the set again at 6 a.m. So, it was like a 20-hour day and I only got 3 hours of sleep."

In terms of storytelling, Kove says he preferred deeper science fiction plots and less Earthbound melodrama. "['Battle of the Sexes'] was the kind of episode I wanted for intergalactic reference; more information from above. We didn't do too many episodes that way, but if the show had stayed on the air, we would have done more intergalactic, more science fiction–oriented episodes," says Kove. The opportunities for science fiction were there, he says, but not enough of the desired elements were played up. Surprisingly, Kove would have liked Jesse to experience time travel, deepening the "stranger in a strange land" theme and broadening the landscape of his encounters with humans.

"The audience would have gotten a bigger kick out of it.... I truly wanted the audience of the show to use as much of their imagination as possible. I wanted more galactic stories. We had a few stories like that. [In one episode, "The All-

American"], a boy came down from my planet 20 years ago, and I met him and he wants to take over the world. The best episodes were the ones that involved sophisticated storytelling. Mostly science fiction audiences like scenes of ... the terminator coming down to get me."

Ultimately, says Kove, the character Jesse would have undergone major changes in his life. "What would have happened is he would have lost Control, the warden. If the show had gone past 13 episodes, I would have lost that ball that was following me around. I felt the show didn't need that. It would have been better to lose that and have him by himself."

Control was an electronically created animation character that was added into the episode during post-production. This meant Kove never saw Control until the final product was assembled. For any scene with Control, Kove just acted to empty space and the character would be added in. Not an easy task. This style of acting is not unlike the task of Desi Arnaz, Jr., in *Automan* when he had to act to Cursor, another character electronically created in post-production.

Kove wanted a show that was less juvenile. "I think it had elements that eliminated an older audience. The concept became more juvenile than necessary. It didn't need that talking, animated element of the show." Addressing Jesse's final fate, Kove says, "He would have succeeded in going back, but ultimately, they couldn't afford to let this popular, political revolutionary figure come back. That's where the [main title] credits came from. It was done very well. It was like a tribunal. They found him guilty on the political front. More so than a socialist. It's like, you don't have any need for a gunfighter any more on the planet. I envisioned him as a gunfighter up in the stars."

For a show with only 13 episodes, *Hard Time on Planet Earth* has achieved a worldwide recognition that's surprising. Kove says he had been in the Philippines shooting a film and found the show airing there. "It's playing all over Asia. Asia loves it!"

Cast Notes

Martin Kove (Jesse): Born 1947. Kove has a long career in television, films and stage. Features include *Lightning in a Bottle* (1993), *Shootfighter* (1993), *White Line Fever* (1975), and *Death Race 2000* (1975). Television regular roles included six

years on the 1980s series *Cagney and Lacey, Code R*, and *We've Got Each Other*. Kove also had supporting roles in the *Karate Kid* feature films. Most recently he did guest roles in *Burke's Law* (1993) and *Kung Fu—The Legend Lives* (1993 and 1994).

EPISODE GUIDE

Hard Time on Planet Earth (Pilot)
Banished from his planet, Jesse arrives on Earth at an abandoned gas station, and the first thing he discovers is television. When the police open fire on Jesse, he steals a truck and saves a woman from sliding off a cliff. Later, she helps him when he arrives in Los Angeles and is pursued by the police. Wr: Jim and John Thomas. Dir: Robert Mandel.

Karen (Marita Geraghty); Capt. Ralston (Roscoe Orman); DeSalvo (Robert Schenkkan); Deputy #2 (Michael G. Hagerty); Deputy #1 (James Lashly); Woman thief (Laura Malone); Clerk (Jeanne Bates); Van Dyke (Brian Brophy); Jewelry store manager (Don Draper); Detective Smits (David Dunard); Guard (Terrence Evans); Beautiful woman (Ann Gillespie); Fast food junkie (Stephen Lee); Sheriff Sarandon (Brendon McKane); Chicken boy man (Dean R. Miller); Cop #1 (Howard Mungo); News commentator (Minerva Perez); News person (Juney Smith).

Something to Bank On
Hungry, Jesse takes some food without paying and learns he needs money. But Jesse lands in jail when trying to return the bucks spit out by an automatic teller. Wr: Richard Chapman and E. Jack Kaplan. Dir: Roger Duchowny.

Dr. Laura Rowlands (Jamie Rose); Felix (Terry Kiser); Kohler (Rod Arrants); Lt. Dan Lawry (Gerry Gibson); Phil Marker (Raymond O'Connor); Reinhardt (William Lanteau); Anchorwoman (Marcia Brandwynne); Vendor (Anthony de Fonte); Pickett (Hector Mercado); Bellman (Kent Stoddard); Hotel clerk (Barry Dennen); Mrs. Rosetti (Catherine Paolone); Ms. Yardley (Timothy Blake); Young man (Brad Kepnick); Exerciser (Perry Anzilotti); Salesman (Ed Levey); Model (Karen Todd).

The Way Home
Jesse befriends a young delinquent and helps to reunite the troubled teen with her estranged family. Wr: Michael Piller. Dir: Timothy Bond.

Erin Parker (Darcy Marta); Mrs. Parker (Karen Landry); Mr. Parker (James Handy); Offcr. Rollman (Bill Sadler); Offcr. Stoff (Roger Aaron Brown); Tim (Marcus Chong); Taxi driver (Charles Gruber); Bellman (Kent Stoddard); Hotel clerk (Barry Dennen); Mrs. Rosetti (Catherine Paolone); Mr. Yardley (Timothy Blake); Cook (Barry Doe); Kid #2 (David Katz); Punk #1 (Tony Mangano); Gardener (Julio Medina); Kid #1 (Danny Oberbeck); Larry (Stephen Quadros); Freak (Shane Tyler Ralston); Jogger (Joe Nesnow); Punk #2 (Keith Tellez).

Losing Control
Jesse and Control visit Disneyland to see how humans rejuvenate themselves. But Jesse ages a few years when he loses Control. Wr: Daniel Freudenberger. Dir: James A. Contner.

Sullivan (Robin Riker-Hasley); Harry Newcomb (Adam Arkin); Ruth Newcomb (Anne Wyndham); Herb Leavitt (Christian Clemenson); Sgt. Burdick (Ken Jenkins); Jonathan Newcomb (Tim Eyster); Mark (Michael Faustino); Alvarez (Rick Garcia); Man (Jeremy Roberts); Archie (Marc Silver); Patrolman (Franz Turner); Boy (Ryan McWhorter); Son (Malachi Pearson); Railroad leader (Trith Doolan); Car salesman (Chuck Sloan).

Battle of the Sexes
Jesse faces the ultimate battle when he's confronted by a female assassin from his planet. Wr: Bruce Cervi. Dir: Michael Lange.

Danielle (Sandahl Bergman); Connie Russo (Lycia Naff); Frank Russo (Paul Comi); Mike Russo (Mark Thomas Miller); Tom Caretti (Stephen Liska); Vic Caretti (Tom Silardi); Salesperson (Rhonda Aldrich); Young man (Darren E. Burroughs); Cop (David Glover); Lana (Julie Hayek); Man (Rod Fitzgerald); Janitor (Jonathon Hugger); Bartender (Paunita Nichols); Businessman (Jim Raymond).

All That You Can Be
Jesse joins the U.S. Army and saves a young corporal from the influence of his old street gang. Wr: Bruce Cervi and Nicholas Corea. Dir: Roger Duchowny.

Corp. Curtis Tillman (Larry B. Scott); Master Sgt. Stryker (Marshall Bell); Lt. Arlene Michaels (Jayne Modean); Capt. Vance Butler (Tim Ryan); Deacon Powell (Real Andrews); Toots (Chico Brooks); Mrs. Tillman (Judyann Elder); Vanessa Tillman (Shana Washington); Hudson (Jon Stafford); Franco (Tony Colitti); Wright (V.C. Dupree); Master Sgt. Hurley (John Disanto); Jewelryman (B'Nard Lewis); Woman (Linda Lutz); Nun (Patricia Wilson); Tommy (James Brown, III); Strider #2 (Eric Chambers); M.P. #1 (Brent Dehart); Driver (Jake Jacobs); Reporter (Julie Moran).

Death Do Us Part
Jesse becomes a winning contestant in "The Dating Game" and saves his attractive bachelorette from making a big mistake. Wr: Michael Piller and Ed Zuckerman. Dir: Charles Corell.

Jeff MacGregor (Himself); Jane (Lise Hilboldt); Michael (Tim Dunigan); Bobby (Scott Lincoln); Bruno (Vance Colvig); Lt. Taylor (Scott Jaeck); Date #1 (Sussannah Woodside); Date #2 (Kelly Andrus); Date #3 (Kelly Miller); Chauffeur (John Batis); Waiter (Jerome Front); Truck driver (Bill Dunham); Bachelor #1 (Michael Scoggins); Bachelor #2 (James Casey); Also with Jack Riley.

The Hot Dog Man
As a professional wrestler, Jesse saves a family business from the grip of an unscrupulous real estate developer. Wr: Rob Ulin. Dir: James A. Contner.

Annie (Conchata Ferrell); Billy (Jacob Vargas); Sandra (Pamela Cumming); John Henry ("Tiny" Lister, Jr.); Tao (Tao Logo); Mongo ("Pistol" Pete Marquez); Bullwhip (Magic Schwarz); Announcer (Ronnie Schell); Concession girl (Paige Price); Burns (Michael Canavan); Morrow (Malcolm Groome); Mt. Fiji (Emily Dole); Babe, farmer's daughter (Ursula Hayden); Vicky Victory (Peach Janae); Sally, farmer's daughter (Becky Mullen); Jake (Richard Epcar); Promoter (Fran Montano); Fan (Bert Rosario); Receptionist (Christine Cattell); Fan #2 (Vince Colvig); Ted (Raymond Davis); Coach (Dick Durock); Referee (Mando Guerrero).

Jesse's Fifteen Minutes

Jesse becomes a top fashion model and learns that stardom can win friends and foes. Wr: Michael Eric Stein. Dir: Bill Corcoran.

Donna (Rebecca Staab); Perry (Gregory Wagrowski); Zack (Brad Lockerman); Fred Waterman (Sandy Simpson); Romy (Stan Ivar); Agent (Gregory Procaccino); Kiosk operator (Bill Stevenson); Gladys (Julia Sweeney); Male model (Tom Alexander); Second punk (Dylan Coleridge); Makeup woman (Martha Hackett); Bouncer (George Kyle); First punk (Claudio Martin); Magazine vendor (Greg Rusin); Reporter #1 (George Siegal).

Rodeo

Jesse joins a rodeo and convinces an old cowboy star that he can be a great person again. Wr: Van Gordon Sauter and David Percelay. Dir: Michael Lange.

Travis Brady (Grainger Hines); Mark Brady (Christian Jacobs); Shelby (Greg Kean); Buck McGrew (Michael Alldredge); Joe Pierce (Michael J. Cutt); Rodeo announcer (Art Bradford); Fan #1 (Charles Dierkop); Director (Shelly Lipkin); Cop (David Starwalt); Fan #2 (Robert Devlin); Serviceman (Jim James); Kid (Josh MacDonald); Customer (R. Leo Schreiber).

Not in Our Stars

Jesse attempts to communicate with his home planet but fails when a scientist tries to stop him for his own gains. Wr: Rob Swigart. Dir: Al Waxman.

Dr. Cyrus Jordan (Sam McMurray); Carrie Robbins (Lezlie Deane); Coldstream (Paul Tuerpe); Chancellor Payton (Richard Roat); Nurse (Cathy McAuley); Bookstore clerk (Lisa Mende); Co-Ed (Elizabeth Cox); Military VIP (Bill Dearth); Jerry (Mitch Ford); Cashier (Terri Hoyos); Bus passenger (Danny Mann); Freshman (Mark Swussman).

The All American

Jesse recognizes a young boy as a fellow alien from his planet and tries to stop him from entering a political life that will take over Earth. Wr: Michael Piller. Dir: Roger Duchowny.

Bill Mitchner (Doug Johnson); Janet Gleason (Caryn Richman); Mr. Roberts (Dave Shelley); Frances (Patricia Tallman); Mr. Boothby (Charles Bouvier); Ginger (Kristine Blackburn); Vendor (Vinny Argiro); Matt (Daniel Jordan); Jojo (Michael Stoyanov); Teacher #1 (Alice Borden); Rebecca (Kathy Christopherson); Chris (Tyrone Jackson); Mrs. Tucci (Laura James); Detective (Raymond Lynch).

Wally's Gang

Joining a kid's show as a regular, Jesse learns that the father of one of the kids is in trouble. It's up to Jesse to save the father's life. Wr: Richard Chapman and E. Jack Kaplan. Dir: Ric Rondell.

Wally Banks (Gordon Jump); Timmy Hogan (Brandon Bluhm); Bill Webber (Brad Kepnick); Merrick (Leon Russom); Mr. Hogan (Rick Lieberman); Mrs. Hogan (Katherine Cannon); Kevin (Greg Mortensen); Karen (Patricia Sill); Harry (Eric Server); Galloway (Clayton Landey); Executive (Jeffrey Lampert); Reed (Chuck Picerni, Jr.).

The Immortal

September 1970–September 1971

Ben Richards, a test driver, discovers that a genetic fluke has given him blood that contains immunities against all diseases. His blood also enables him to fight off the ravages of age for several centuries.

Transfusions of Richards' blood can give others temporary youth, a fact that keeps him on the run from a frail old tycoon named Maitland, who wants to use Ben as his own private blood bank.

Maitland uses the resources of his National Research Institute to hunt Richards down. The immortal keeps one step ahead of Maitland's men and searches the country for his long-lost brother, Jason, who may have the same kind of blood.

Cast: Ben Richards (Christopher George); Fletcher, Maitland's henchman (Don Knight); Main Title Narrator (Paul Frees).

Based on the novel The Immortals *by James E. Gunn; Series concept created by:* Robert Specht; *Producer:* Richard Caffey (two segments); Howie

Horwitz; *Executive Producer:* Anthony Wilson; *Music:* Dominic Frontiere; ABC/Paramount; 60 minutes.

"You know, that ABC is crazy!" giggled Judy Carne on *Laugh-In.* "They gave us a show called *The Immortal.* Thirteen weeks later, it died!"

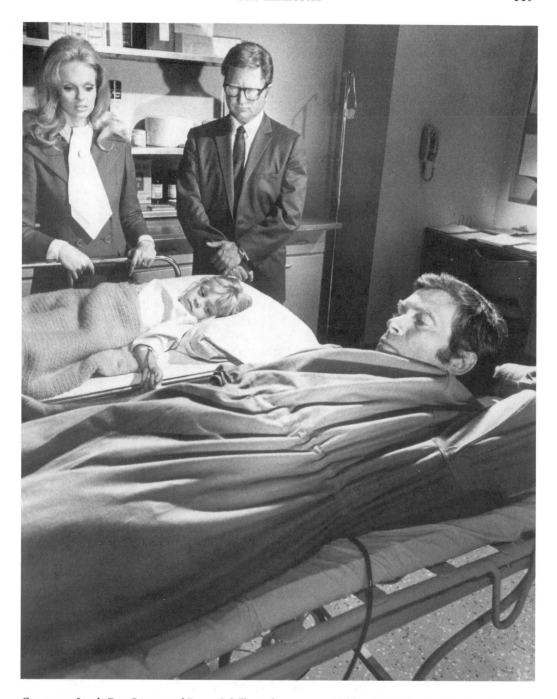

Guest stars Lynda Day George and Barry Cahill watch as a young girl (Lori Busk) is given a life-saving blood transfusion from the immortal (Christopher George). Copyright 1970 ABC/Paramount.

According to writer Robert Specht, *The Immortal* could have been one of TV's biggest hits. The 1962 novel on which the series was based was a success. The 1969 TV movie called *The Immortal* was also a hit. But as a weekly series, *The Immortal* grew anemic and died. "It was a disaster," Specht laments.

The novel, written by James E. Gunn, was titled *The Immortals*. In it, a drifter sells his blood to a hospital to make some money to buy wine.

The doctors learn that his blood carries immunities to all diseases and that a transfusion brings temporary health and restored youth. *The Immortals* examined how this rejuvenating blood, later synthesized, could change society. Gunn, now a professor of English at the University of Kansas and still a science fiction novelist (his books include *The Joy Makers* and *The Listeners*), was approached by writer Robert Specht in 1966. Specht thought the novel would make a terrific movie and was interested in securing the rights. Because of the novel's complexities, Gunn felt a movie adaption would be nearly impossible.

In scripting the ABC Movie of the Week version, Specht took only the germ of the novel. He changed the book's drifter to a test car driver named Ben Richards. "I was fascinated by the way James Gunn's novel got into the hunger of older people for immortality," says Specht. "What would a man's life be like if he were the lone sparrow and there were ten cats waiting to devour him? He's got this blood that no one else has. People would go to any lengths to take advantage of that." Specht's script had Richards innocently donating a pint of blood that is used to save a dying tycoon named Braddock (played by Barry Sullivan). When Braddock is rejuvenated by the transfer, it's discovered that Richards has "special blood." The bad news is that Braddock, now lapsing back into old age, wants Richards imprisoned in his mansion so that he can continue getting transfusions. Ben escapes and begins a quest to find his missing brother, Jason, and to ponder what to do with his blood.

Ben Richards was played by Christopher George. "Chris was a very conscientious actor," says the film's producer, Lou Morheim. "I was familiar with his work on the *Rat Patrol* series. It was his aggressive energy that got him the role."

The film was a success, and ABC and Paramount studios immediately signed up *The Immortal* as a series for 1970-71. "I was surprised by that decision," says Morheim. "The danger in making it a TV series was that it would regress into a one-joke idea."

Chris George continued his role as the immortal, but a new tycoon, Arthur Maitland (played by David Brian), replaced Braddock as the bloodthirsty old man. Each week, Ben had to stay ahead of Maitland's men.

Although James Gunn's novel had given birth to the immortal, the novelist's influence on the TV film and series was minimal. The producers were too busy gearing the immortal up for his chase to delve too deeply into the moral and political consequences of Richards' blood. "In March of 1970, I met with Robert Specht," recalls Gunn. "I suggested we recruit science fiction writers such as Ted Sturgeon, Harlan Ellison and David Gerrold. In fact, Gerrold had written me a letter, asking to write for *The Immortal*." However, Paramount studios wanted a new regime for the series and brought in Anthony Wilson as executive producer and Dan Ullman as story editor. Specht and Gunn were reduced to making suggestions from afar. While Wilson in particular was interested in Gunn's analysis of the upcoming series, the edict handed down from the network was that *The Immortal* would not be a quote-unquote "science fiction show." It was to be, first and foremost, an action-adventure series (in fact, the first of several TV series in the budget-conscious 1970s to use science fiction as a sidecar gimmick to enliven ordinary crime or adventure plots). Ben's blood was going to ignite countless chases by car, bike and dune buggy. The series was not going to deal with how an immortal's blood could change a society's social and political structure.

When a writers' strike loomed in the spring of 1970, Anthony Wilson was forced to solicit scripts with haste. These scripts were rushed to him before the strike could immobilize the industry. "[Wilson] knew the scripts would be scratched out by harried writers trying to beat a deadline," recalls writer Stephen Kandel. "To his dismay, the strike was settled, and he and the studio were left with 17 scripts of dubious perfection."

Writer Jack Turley illustrates an example: He was asked to dust off one of his old scripts for *The Fugitive* and turn it into an *Immortal* story. "When one of the guys at ABC read my script, he got his shorts in a knot," recalls Turley. "He called Tony Wilson and told him that I had plagiarized my own *Fugitive* script. Tony laughed and told the guy to forget it. All he wanted was a shootable script. The guy who blew the whistle crawled back into his hole, and we shot the thing."

The rushed, derivative nature of the scripts hurt the show early on. Two months before the series even aired, the network was stunned by the poor reception test audiences gave two of the completed episodes. While reaction to the TV film a year earlier had been excellent, reaction to the series product was dismal. Some ABC insiders knew they had a doomed show on their hands. At the same time, there were changes in *The*

Cast of *The Immortal*, left to right: Christopher George, Don Knight and David Brian. Copyright 1970 ABC/Paramount.

Immortal's creative staff. Producer Richard Caffey was out, Howie Horwitz was in. Associate producer William Hole, Jr., was out, Gregg Peters was in. Story editor Dan Ullman was out, Stephen Kandel was in.

"You can almost predict whether a show is going to be a dog or not," says Robert Specht. "I saw a sampling of the scripts, and it was clear that they were going to turn this immortal into a social worker every week. They also had him running every week. I told Tony Wilson, 'The pace is too frantic. It'll only make people nervous. The stories are all hyped up. People don't want that kind of nervous energy in their living room every week.'"

Gunn's offer to be a consultant on the series fell on deaf ears. "I watched the series with white knuckles," he admits. "I was hoping they would get into stories that would deal with the problems of an immortal in a mortal world. Instead, they never got beyond the chase."

The TV movie was rerun a week before the series premiered. It clocked strong ratings. The series, however, debuted to poor ratings in its Thursday night time slot. Stephen Kandel was brought in to untangle the show's choppy direction. "Howie Horwitz and I had worked together on a schnitzel called *The Reporter* [in 1964]. We had been brought in at the last minute for major emergency surgery. We saw *The Immortal* as another victim of an accident. There wasn't much time for tender loving care."

Kandel describes the experience as "making love to an alien inside a rotating barrel filled with smoke and alternate strips of grease and sand paper. All first-season shows are frantic. This was more frantic than most. There was little time to write and to prepare. Most of all, there was a lack of time to evaluate. We found unexpected strengths in the premise but no time to re-do the earlier scripts to emphasize the newly discovered values. We literally wrote it on the run."

Ben Richards was also on the run every week, usually being pursued in a car chase. "The network had a religious faith in the efficacy of car chases," Kandel says. "They were an unfortunate function of the chase theme. There was a feeling that those viewers who were intellectually incapable of following a plot could follow a chase." The guy doing all of the chasing was Fletcher, played by English actor Don Knight. He categorizes his nasty character as "a man on a personal vendetta. It infuriated him that Richards kept out of his reach. Fletcher was obsessed with the hunt. I saw him as going to bed, waking up, taking a shower and going to the bathroom while thinking of nothing else but capturing Ben Richards." Little was learned about Fletcher during the series' run. Knight says, "I liked the idea he was mysterious. You began to wonder where he came from. Was he even human? Originally, the idea was that he would be an android." Fletcher grew to respect his quarry. In the episode "To The Gods Alone," when Fletcher and Richards are trapped in a snowbound lodge, Fletcher says, "You're the kind of man I wish I could be, Ben. I can't allow myself the luxury."

Knight preferred the series when the late Anthony Wilson was in charge. "Tony felt *The Immortal* was too slow, and he wanted to tighten it up and make it faster. If he had [retained control] of the series, I think it would have lasted longer." Knight wasn't impressed when Howie Horwitz took over as producer. "Howie and I didn't get along," he says. "We had one fight in particular. I was ready to walk off the show because he had changed some of Fletcher's lines. He wanted Fletcher to say how scared and frightened he was. I could never see Fletcher saying that. I told Howie he had a choice: Let me say the line as it was originally written, or he could hire another Fletcher. Everything came to a grinding halt for ten hours. We got it reconciled."

Chris George also had his problems with some scripts. As the show's star, he had script approval and made his displeasure known to the producers. "Some of the scripts are rotten," he told *TV Guide* at the time. "In one show, they've got me playing an introspective character who practically sucks his thumb. In the next show, I'm a finger-snapping, gum chewing wise guy."

"Chris had difficulty with the character at the beginning," admits Stephen Kandel, "but he got into it as time went on. Toward the end of the series he was a lot happier."

Director Leslie Martinson notes, "I had done *Run for Your Life* with Ben Gazzara. He played a man who had a year or two to live. That premise had great margins in which to work. Gazzara had a motivation to live life to its fullest. But Chris George's character seemed much more unrealistic. He's an immortal. Instead of helping mankind with his blood, he spends his time being chased by cars. Had he devoted his life to experimentation, he would have become a powerful force in advancing modern science and medicine. Ben Richards never seemed to have a purpose."

The Immortal was unique in being the first science fiction series that didn't show off science fiction hardware. Optical effects were never used to dramatize Ben's remarkable healing from vicious beatings or accidents. Occasionally, viewers got a hint of Ben's subtle powers. He was resistant to cold temperatures, he didn't get sick and he had a slightly stronger stamina than the average human. He was not, however, a superman. His strength was comparable to that of any mortal, and he was susceptible to the tranquilizer darts used by Fletcher's men. Aside from the chase, Ben's adventures mainly consisted of meeting everyday people who needed his help or were in a position to help him. The stories rarely focused on Ben's unique blood and never explored other science fiction themes.

Al Francis was the director of photography for *The Immortal*. Francis, who had previously filmed *Star Trek*, is astonished when he learns of the writing headaches that occurred during production. "I didn't know about any of those problems," he says. "For me the series was a wonderful working experience. It was a tough show to do because we moved from location to location. Very little of the series was filmed on a soundstage. From the producer to the crafts service man, everyone was cooperative. We had one of the most effective crews in television and always brought the show under budget. Sam Strangis, head of the production department, couldn't get over the amount of work we'd get done in a day." According to Francis, episodes for *The Immortal* were shot in five days. The clean, crisp photography, a trademark of the cinematographer, has stood well the test of time. "Every night after we finished filming, we had a meeting in Sam Strangis's office. Tony Wilson, Ted Leonard [executive production manager] and Howie Horwitz were there. We spent a half-hour discussing what we could do to keep the show's momentum up and talking out any problems."

One important member of *The Immortal* team was stuntman Hal Needham, who doubled for Chris George. "Hal and I used to race motorcycles together," says Francis. "I suggested him to Howie. From 20 feet away, Hal and Chris looked identical. That's why Hal got the job. Chris George also did a lot of the action stuff that he didn't have to do. He was a hard-working guy. We never had to wait for Chris, and he was never temperamental. He was a regular guy. He was very generous and thoughtful. He was the kind of guy who would give you the shirt off his back. I admired him tremendously."

Francis recalls that the hard-working crew sometimes cooled off with fun and games. "On location, the minute you had a chance to rest, you would get splashed with water from someone. One day, Howie Horwitz came down to the set to check on things. Unlike Tony Wilson, who was an easygoing fellow, Howie was intense and no-nonsense. He was always dressed in immaculate, fancy clothes. Well, Howie got doused with a bucket of water. I got a phone call from Sam Strangis shortly afterward. He wanted a meeting that night. I went to his office and found Howie Horwitz, Ted Leonard and some other guys looking at me. Sam said, 'I've got a complaint.' I was stunned. We never had complaints. Sam said, 'Howie says that there's too much horsing around going down on the set.' I said, 'He does? Is it because he got doused with a bucket of water today?' Sam said, 'Howie says the playing around has got to stop.' I said, 'Look—we've done eight shows so far. Have we ever fallen behind schedule? Have we ever cost the company money for re-takes? Haven't we, in fact, saved money by bringing the shows under budget?' Sam admitted we had. 'Then what are you talking about?' I said. 'We're doing our work. If the boys are having a good time, it shows everyone is getting along.' So Sam finally said, 'Okay, but just make the guys slow down a bit.' The next morning, I called the guys together and said, 'I got called into the office last night. They're upset because we're having too much fun out here. We're going to have to cut it down.' I made my way back to the truck to get some stuff and the prop man was ahead of me. Just for fun, I goosed him. I turned around and there was Howie Horwitz staring at me. I said, 'Well, Howie, that's the way it goes. There's nothing you can do about it.'"

Associate producer Gregg Peters recalls a time when an entire town rebelled against *The Immortal*'s production team. "We filmed several episodes up at Lake Piru, California," he recalls. "It was a quaint, old-fashioned little town. One day I got a call from the production people.

'Gregg, you had better come down here. We can't shoot the episode.' The townspeople had gotten fed up with having a camera crew in their midst. They protested by yelling and turning up their music full blast. This totally disrupted filming. I went up there and gave the townspeople some money and beer. They quieted down. Actually, it was kind of funny. I think they 'held up' every production company from then on!"

The fun and games came to an end with the show's cancellation. "There were rumors of it ending," recalls Francis, "but we thought, 'They can't cancel it. We're making it on schedule and saving Paramount money.'"

"We were told we were going to be picked up for the remainder of the season," recalls Don Knight. "[Doug Cramer, executive in charge of Paramount's production] gave us a big party. The cast and crew were there. It must have been 300 people. Then I looked around and I said to Chris George, 'That's odd. None of the producers have shown up.' Suddenly we were both handed a telegram. It said, 'Sorry. You've been canceled. Best regards, Doug.' We were fit to be tied. When *The Immortal* went into reruns, it became the highest rated show of the summer. Because of the tremendous ratings we were told that the network was considering bringing us back. Chris even went on the road and tried to get a letter campaign started to save the show."

"The network had considerable ambivalence about canceling the show," says Kandel, "and given some prodding from Paramount, they did consider a revival. There were also endless discussions about continuing the series for syndication."

In February 1971, James Gunn was invited by *TV Guide* to write an article about *The Immortal*'s history. In that article, "An Author Watches His Brainchild Die," Gunn expressed his feelings that a good concept had been homogenized by the Hollywood industry to "look and sound and feel and smell like everything else." Gunn received over 125 letters from readers in response to the article. One asked Gunn, "You said that you wanted *The Immortal* to evolve as a series. Where could it have gone after the Movie of the Week?" Another expressed a preference for *The Immortal*'s leanings toward drama rather than science fiction. "It seemed to deal more with relationships than with the possibilities of immortality, but that wasn't entirely bad." Opinion in the letters varied widely. One couple wrote, "The pilot film was excellent. We looked forward to the series but it was a disappointment. We watched it only because we liked Chris George." Meanwhile, another viewer totally disagreed with Gunn's assertion that the series didn't come up to standards. "I didn't stay up until 11 o'clock every week to watch a show with no variety. All that garbage about 'nobody knowing what to do with *The Immortal*' is just that—garbage!"

"Most of the letters were thoughtful and understanding," notes Gunn. "It showed that a good science fiction series *could* get an audience."

While Stephen Kandel was interested in placing more emphasis on the immortal's superblood, he says, "There was never any hint of jazzing up the series with science fiction melodrama. It was what it was. It would either survive or it wouldn't. It had begun to find its audience, but the network, driven by the normal network fear of science fiction, canceled it. We tried for human stories and as a distinct advantage, we were able to set them in a wide range of American vistas. In the best sense we were a road show.

"I haven't thought of *The Immortal* in years," he says quietly. "It ignites some regrets. But series TV is not a business that encourages too much vain sentiment."

CAST NOTES

Christopher George (Ben Richards): Born 1929. Best known as Sam Troy on TV's *Rat Patrol* series (1966–68). George starred in several films in the 1970s including *Grizzly* (1976) and *Day of the Animals* (1977). He was married to actress Lynda Day. Christopher George died of a heart attack in 1983.

Don Knight (Fletcher): Born 1934. An English actor who moved to Los Angeles in 1965, Knight was a frequent guest star on *Hawaii 5-0*, usually as a bad guy. Knight is also a minister.

David Brian (Maitland): Born 1914. Brian, a leading man in the 1940s, made only two appearances in *The Immortal*, but his presence as the withering tycoon was always felt. He died in 1993.

EPISODE GUIDE

The Immortal (1969 TV movie)
Ben Richards is imprisoned in a mansion, where his blood is to be used as a fountain of youth for an aging businessman. Wr: Robert Specht, based on the novel by James E. Gunn. Dir: Joseph Sargent.

Sylvia Cartwright (Carol Lynley); Jordan Braddock (Barry Sullivan); Janet Braddock (Jessica Walter); Dr. Matt Pearce (Ralph Bellamy); Locke (Vincent Beck); Pilot (William Sargent); Detective (Garry Walberg); Doctor (Martin Silberscher); Nurses (Claudia Bryar, Lillian Adams, Mimi Dillard); Mechanic (Joseph Bernard).

Season Episodes

Sylvia
Ben reunites with his ex-fiancée, Sylvia, and finds that she still wants him. Meanwhile, Fletcher sets up a trap for the immortal. Wr: Robert Malcolm Young. Dir: Don McDougall.

Sylvia Cartwright (Carol Lynley); David Hiller (Glenn Corbett); Sherry Hiller (Sherry Jackson); Maitland (David Brian); Moniton (Joey Tata); Walter Hiller (Paul Langton); Mrs. Hiller (Angela Greene); Thugs (Bob Orrisson, Frank Orsatti, Bill Burton, Alan Oliney).

White Elephants Don't Grow on Trees
Ben hitches a ride with truck driver Eddie Yeoman. Eddie is transporting unstable explosives to make money to gain custody of his teenage son. Wr: Shimon Wincelberg. Dir: Michael Caffey.

Eddie Yeoman (Ross Martin); Jud Yeoman (Mitch Vogel); Tucker (Read Morgan); Manager (William Wintersole); Aunt Marge (Elizabeth Harrower); Waitress (Victoria Carroll); Attendant (Ed Begley, Jr.); Superintendent (Karl Lucas); Auctioneer (Larry J. Black).

Reflections on a Lost Tomorrow
Dr. Koster is experimenting on Ben's blood when Maitland makes a deal with Koster: Turn over Ben and the tycoon will fund research to synthesize the blood. Wr: Robert Hamner. Dir: Leslie H. Martinson.

Dr. Walter Koster (Jack Albertson); Anne Koster (Rosemary Forsythe); Arthur Maitland (David Brian); Paul Hubner (Philip Bourneuf); Moderator (Gene O'Donnell); Waitress (Alice Borden); Arnie (Walt Davis); Mother (Treva Frazee).

The Legacy
Imprisoned by miners who are digging for illegal ore, Ben tries to summon help for several workers who are dying from typhoid. Wr: Robert and Wanda Duncan, Dan B. Ullman. Dir: Robert Douglas.

Annie Williams (Susan Howard); Ramos (Mario Alcalde); Luis (Manuel Padilla, Jr.); Martinez (Armand Alzamora); Rodriguez (Felipe Turich); Jensen (Michael Vandever); Smith (Chuck Taylor).

The Rainbow Butcher
Ben is forced to work in a town park by a sadistic sheriff. His only chance for freedom lies with Clarice Evans, who needs Ben to recover an incriminating file from the sheriff's office. Wr: Jack Bradford Turley. Dir: Nick Webster.

Sheriff Dan W. Wheeler (Vic Morrow); Clarice Evans (Collin Wilcox); Charley (Jerry Ayres); Deputy Collis (Byron Mabe); Martha (Tani Phelps); Donny Evans (Jimmy Bracken).

Memory Flash—Nick Webster: "It wasn't a very exciting project but I remember on the Paramount lot they had parking places for the directors. They were designated by the names of the directors' shows. When I directed *Mannix*, I parked in the space marked *Mannix* Director. When I directed *Immortal*, I parked in the space marked *Immortal* Director. Unfortunately, it won't prove to be true!"

Man on a Punched Card

Ben is being tracked by a super-computer across the state. Programmer Terry Kerwin will help him only if he'll donate his super-blood to save her ill daughter. Wr: Shimon Wincelberg, Stephen Kandel. Dir: Don Weis.

Terry Kerwin (Lynda Day George); Duane Hollenbeck (Lee Patterson); Dr. Joe Lacey (Barry Cahill); Bonita Kerwin (Lori Busk); Betty (Karen Arthur); Morton (Hal Riddle); Brockaw (Dave Willock); Deputy (Ford Lile); Attendant (Jim Wagerman).

White Horse, Steel Horse

Fletcher has to help Ben escape from land baron George Allison. Allison is planning to kill Ben and a biker for the accidental death of his friend. Wr: Gene L. Coon, Stephen Kandel, Dan B. Ullman, story by Gene L. Coon. Dir: Leslie H. Martinson.

George Allison (John Dehner); Nat King (Stephen Oliver); Judge Atkins (Warner Anderson); Robert Allison (Robbie Porter); Katcher (John Pickard); Mort (Frederic Gavlin); Ray (Bill Burton).

Queen's Gambit

Taken to a jungle mansion, Ben is offered a century's partnership with a playboy. The man wants to use his fortune to cure the world's ills, but he must remain young to do so. Wr: Stephen Kandel. Dir: Robert Douglas.

Sigrid Bergen (Lee Meriwether); Simon Brent (Nico Minardos); Dom DiLorenzo (Karl Swenson); Casey (Dom Tattoli); Benson (James O'Hara); Girl (Jayne Brechenridge); Man (Joe Thomas).

Trivia Alert: Joe Thomas was a Detroit auto worker hired to play a villain on *The Immortal*. Thomas earned $12,000 a year by selling his rare blood to a pharmaceutical house. Paramount dubbed him "a true-life Ben Richards."

By Gift of Chance

Ben encounters injustice and murder on a tomato plantation ruled by a sadistic foreman. Wr: Ken Trevey, Stephen Kandel. Dir: Irving J. Moore.

Alpha Henderson (Jacqueline Scott); Monte Loomis (Michael Conrad); Garland Colley (Herb Jefferson, Jr.); Portland Bill (Arthur Lewis); Peters (Paul Nickles); Danson (Don Haggerty).

Dead Man, Dead Man

Ben has to contend with hostile townspeople when he assumes the identity of a dead detective. However, Ben does trick Fletcher into believing he died in a car accident. Wr: William Wood. Dir: Allen Baron.

Helen Stoner (Joan Hotchkis); Dr. Kinneson (Henry Beckman); Dave Holley (Byron Keith); Tom McWade (John Garwood); Frye (Lal Baum); Deputy Barry (Lee Stanley); Bryer (Kem Dibbs).

Memory Flash—Allen Baron: "We sent a car down a steep cliff and it didn't turn over. So we had to haul it back up and do it again."

Paradise Bay

Ben's efforts to investigate the death of a man who might have been his brother are complicated by a greedy industrialist. Wr: Ben Masselink, Stephen Kandel, story by Ben Masselink, Dan B. Ullman. Dir: Don Weis.

Julie/Nancy Dudley (Tisha Sterling); Arthur Cameron (Howard Duff); Frank Brady (Scott Brady); Pete Cameron (Aron Kincaid); Warren Harron (Don Diamond); Ralph (Ronnie Rondell); Eddie (Joe Hooker).

To the Gods Alone

Trapped in a snowbound cabin, Ben and Fletcher recount the time when tycoon Jordan Braddock and Ben had to work together to fight their way out of the Florida jungle after a car crash. Wr: Ken Trevey. Dir: Leslie H. Martinson.

Jordan Braddock (Barry Sullivan); Grace Lee Canby (Lynn Loring); Luther Seacombe (Bruce Dern); Check Hutchins (Robert Sampson); Wesley Beacombe (Bucklind Noah Beery); Mrs. Strom (Peggy Rea).

Sanctuary

Fletcher tries to bribe an Indian tribe into handing Ben over. Instead, the Indians map out an escape plan for the immortal. Wr: William Eastlake. Dir: Michael Caffey.

Tsinnajinni (Sal Mineo); Klabo (Paul Picerni); Djanni (Iron Eyes Cody); Reese (Don "Red" Barry); Delgado (Fred Lerner); Espargo (Allan Gibbs).

Brother's Keeper

Ben and Jason Richards, who may be the immortal's brother, escape from Maitland's men by hiding in the mountains. Fletcher retaliates by kidnapping Jason's wife. Wr: Robert and Wanda Duncan, Stephen Kandel, story by Robert and Wanda Duncan. Dir: Charles Rondeau.

Jason Richards (Michael Strong); Allison Richards (Marj Dusay); Administrator (James B. Sikking); Dalby (Michael Masters); Assistant (Tom Stewart); Heavy (Frank Orsatti).

Return

Ben's reunion with his adoptive father, Joe Carver, a black man, is marred when Carver critically injures the white fiance of his daughter. Wr: Robert Specht. Dir: Michael Caffey.

Joe Carver (Richard Ward); Roy Adkins (Harry Townes); Mrs. Adkins (Martine Bartlett); Carol Carver (Marlene Clark); Dr. Arliss (Ted Knight); Sheriff Billy (Ford Rainey); Player (William Benedict); Ralph (John Gallaudet); Nurse (Patience Cleaveland).

The Incredible Hulk
March 1978–June 1982

A scientist, Dr. David Banner, in search of hidden human strengths, accidentally overdoses himself with gamma radiation. As a result, whenever he gets angry or outraged, he involuntarily transforms into a giant green creature. He's pursued by Jack MacGee, an investigative reporter who's convinced the creature killed Dr. Banner and a female scientist. On the run across the country, Banner seeks to cure his affliction while trying to escape the dogged hunt by MacGee.

Cast: Dr. David Banner (Bill Bixby); The Creature (Lou Ferrigno); Jack MacGee (Jack Colvin).

Incredible Hulk created by: Stan Lee; *Developed for television by* Kenneth Johnson; *Executive Producer:* Kenneth Johnson; *Supervising Producer:* Nicholas Corea; *Producers:* Nicholas Corea, James D. Parriott, Chuck Bowman (year 1-2) Jeff Freilich (year 3), Robert Bennett Steinhauer, Karen Harris and Jill Sherman; *Associate Producers:* Alan Cassidy, Craig Schiller; *Theme:* Joseph Harnell; CBS/Universal; 60 minutes.

In the comic books, the Incredible Hulk is a not-so-jolly, muscle-endowed green giant perpetually garbed in purple pants. Bounding up and down, covering miles at a time, he spouts fantastic dialogue such as, "Hulk smash!" or, "Puny humans! Hulk kill all!" Transforming such a campy, wildly comic premise into a believable, dramatic one-hour television show was a task that very few in Hollywood wanted to take on. But writer-director-producer Kenneth Johnson ingeniously found a way to do it, and the Incredible Hulk smashed his fists from the comic pages into our television screens in the winter of 1977.

Frank Price, the head of Universal Television at the time, had acquired the rights of several Marvel Comics characters for translation to television, and he thought of Kenneth Johnson as a potential producer-writer to take on the challenge. But Johnson's initial reaction was very negative: "I'm *not* interested in doing any more superhero, comic book–type shows." He was in the heat of working on *The Bionic Woman* at the time and didn't want to be typecast as someone doing superhero shows. "I was afraid that was all

people would look after for me in the future, you know? I was really trying to duck it." Some of the other characters snapped up for an over-the-air-waves makeover were the Human Torch, Captain America, Thor, Doctor Strange and Daredevil. "I was literally standing at home trying to figure out how to say, 'No!' because I just didn't *want* to do any of them." But after a conversation with pal Steven Bocho (creator of *Hill Street Blues*), Johnson realized that if he did *Incredible Hulk* for Universal, he could get another pet project, a mini-series adaptation of Walter Scott's *Ivanhoe*, off the ground as a favor.

The concept that would turn the Incredible Hulk into a television character came from the unlikely inspiration of *Les Miserables*. "I was thinking of *The Fugitive* and Inspector Javert," says Johnson, "and I thought, 'Well, wait a minute, maybe there's a way to take a little bit of Victor Hugo, Robert Louis Stevenson, and this ludicrous premise called Incredible Hulk and meld all of these together,'" said Johnson. "So I went to Frank Price and said, 'I think I can make the Incredible Hulk work, but I want to do it this particular way, a sort of *Fugitive* manner, and … make it totally different, classy and classical."

The deal was struck. Johnson would later do *Ivanhoe* if he'd bring the Hulk to life. (*Ivanhoe* was produced by CBS in 1982, but it was not Johnson's script or project.)

He researched his subject, but Johnson confesses that the actual Hulk comic books didn't give him much to go on, "except the basic premise of a man exposed to gamma radiation, and that somehow altered his body chemistry. I just sort of took that as a red-liner and went from there. Over Easter weekend of 1977, I guess, I wrote … the pilot for *The Incredible Hulk*." The possibilities of what he could do with the character became so intriguing that on Easter Sunday, in a white-hot fever over the course of a 12-hour period, Johnson wrote in longhand 43 pages of script.

"That's sort of a record, I've never gone faster than that. This was before computers. The more I got into it, the more I realized there was a delicious character here that I could give some psychological depth; raise it above the levels of its comic book origins. George Burns said, 'If you're going to tell a lie, put as much truth as you can in it.' So I did a tremendous amount of research into cellular structure, various kinds of metamorphoses and possible ways something like this could happen."

In the end, the Hulk of the comics bore little resemblance to the Hulk of television. Several alterations were necessary—the television Hulk would not have Tarzan-speak and would not be as powerful as the comic book character (read: the television budget just wouldn't allow that!). Plus, there was an entire layer of emotional and physical consequences that had to be addressed, making the adventures of David Banner more dramatic and three-dimensional than in comics. Finally, no super-villains. Grim reality, not camp, was the order on the plate.

The drama and dimensions came first in casting a respected comedy and dramatic actor, Bill Bixby, as Dr. David Banner. (Johnson never thought of anyone else—even though when his agent first showed him the script, Bixby reportedly moaned, "Oh pleeuuzz! I don't want to get involved in anything called *The Incredible Hulk!*") Further depth came through in the types of stories the writers and producers chose to tell, many of which tackled weighty social problems.

Nevertheless, nearly everyone required some time to warm up to the project. "I was so embarrassed that the title of my original script was 'The Hulk,' not 'The *Incredible* Hulk,'" laughs Johnson. "I couldn't deal with writing 'Incredible.' It's a comic book title, you know? It had been around for a couple of years, and they insisted on keeping the title. I did manage to change the name of the lead character. I couldn't deal with Bruce, so I changed it to David Banner. And eventually compromised and gave him the middle name of Bruce."

A little-known fact is that Lou Ferrigno was not the original choice to play the creature. Richard Kiel, best known for a pair of appearances as the character 'Jaws' in the James Bond films *The Spy Who Loved Me* and *Moonraker*, was the original choice.

"I met Lou, but he had absolutely no acting experience," remembers Johnson. "I saw that it would be very difficult to make an actor out of him. Richard Kiel, on the other hand, *was* an actor and happened to be seven and a half feet tall. We shot a whole week, and then I think it was Frank Price's son who came in to a screening and said, 'It's a neat show but the guy doesn't look like the Hulk!' We had four weeks scheduled. I had shot a whole sequence at the lake. So, I had to go back to Lou, and he's not as big as Richard, he's a whole foot shorter. But I had a little movie magic and a lot of patience [to make the illusion believable]."

Asked why he originally chose Kiel, who, though tall, is not muscled, Johnson explains, "I wanted an actor. You have to understand I wasn't out to do a comic book. I was out to do something solid, like *Frankenstein* by Mary Shelley. I wanted somebody who could act, play the emotions I wanted the creature to have. I didn't want him to just crash through the wall, you know? I wasn't sure I could get that from Louie. But it turned out that Lou was quite good and a real natural, and once we got to working together and got comfortable with what he had to do and how to do it, it worked out fine."

The first Hulk telefilm, written and produced by Ken Johnson, made about $7 million when it was released in Europe as a theatrical, running for about two months.

Nicholas Corea, supervising producer, screenwriter and sometime director for *The Incredible Hulk*, recalls his experiences on the show as "the best time of my life. Universal studios was at the height of its TV power—12 to 14 series on each year—and Reagan's tax laws weren't on the books. You could put a lot of time, energy and money into a production—even go over budget without any flack from the 'big boys' [at the studio]. All that ended about the time *The Hulk* ended. Suddenly it was about *money* and how much was spent that determined the quality of a show. Those four or five years were also an incredible learning time for me, brand new in the biz and *learning* something each new day. Working my rear off, and never realizing it. I was enjoying myself so much. There were no fat writer-producers in '78 to '82."

Moving up the ladder quickly from story

The Hulk (Lou Ferrigno) runs through Times Square in New York. Copyright 1978 CBS/Universal, photo courtesy of Kenneth Johnson.

of action and special effects. But also—especially after the show was a hit—we wanted tales that had something universal in them (like all good stories) that would really strike a chord in the audience." That is to say, we *all* have the green monster inside of us trying to break out, and the show would provide a catharsis by manifesting that monster in a safe, nonviolent way. "This element was very important in all the shows, all the way through. *What makes you angry?* Figure that out, then write a show about it."

This approach inspired episodes dealing with such issues as child abuse, mental health, terminal illness, mental retardation, teenage alcoholism, drugs, teenage runaways, family estrangements, paraplegism, and yellow journalism. Occasionally, various government institutions got the stab, as when Banner got stuck in a phone booth and the Hulk had to smash his way out.

editor to writer-producer, Corea was eventually tapped as supervising producer, which "scared the hell out of me" until Ken Johnson explained that "common sense was the only talent needed for the position. The technical aspects would come with time. He was right, of course. Common sense and, I would add, cinematic taste—an introverted history of *living* at movie houses and/or in front of a TV—is all one needs to produce."

To generate stories for the series, producers and writers would gather together and throw ideas back and forth. As Corea explains, the thrust for Banner's life in the world was to find stories that were more than just run-of-the mill adventures. They wanted stories that would touch viewers' emotions. "We wanted a show that 'did numbers' and was successful, so we laid in a mess

"Another criteria was, if you show an episode in Botswanaland, Africa, will the viewer *get it?*" says Corea. "That's why, I believe, the show has a kind of natural universality."

Says Andrew Schneider, story editor for *Hulk*'s third season, "I tried to find stories that were emotionally powerful and socially relevant, that would put David Banner in crisis and conform to our 'two Hulk-outs per episode' format. It *was* difficult to keep from digressing into formula, but we tried very hard to make each episode fresh in its own way. I haven't seen any *Hulk* episodes recently, but I'm satisfied with the show in that we were able to raise it above the level of a comic book. We tried to tell meaningful stories, and by and large, I think we were successful."

Corea agrees. "I think the show was more

Bill Bixby directs Lou Ferrigno in *The Trial of the Incredible Hulk* (1989), the second *Hulk* reunion TV movie. Photo by David Cooper/NBC 1989.

than its comic book origins. I know, for a fact, that it had a lot more meat on its bones than, say, *Wonder Woman*, being produced at Warner Brothers at the same time."

For Johnson, his goal for the series was simply to create "a show that adults could watch. What happened to *The Hulk* was that kids would watch to see the big green man smash through the wall, but very quickly adults would watch and realize there's more going on here in terms of story. This was really a psychological drama about a man with a major problem he's trying to solve in a realistic way, and he was a very sympathetic character. In each of the episodes we wanted it to be *about* something. Writers would come in with an idea and start talking about *plot*. And I'd say, 'No, I don't want to hear about plot. I want to know what's it *about*.' They'd say, 'What do you mean?' I'd reply, 'Well, is it about anger?'

"The show comes in different forms. For some people David Banner/Hulk is anger, drugs,

for some it's alcohol, and others yet it's obsession or vengeance. They get upset, and their Hulk comes out. People 'Hulk out.' We've developed a phrase in the English language, a 'Hulk-out,' the same way that 'bionics' did. We wanted each episode to somehow reflect that thematic material. And that's what sets *The Hulk* apart from other shows." Johnson also claims that David Banner's line, "Don't make me angry, you wouldn't like me when I'm angry!" became "a catch phrase not only in the series and in the industry but around the world."

The Incredible Hulk was one of the most expensive shows filming at the time, and near the end of its run, the studio asked those running the show to cut the Hulk's appearances to one per episode.

"This attempt to emasculate the show—in its third year, for God's sake—led to Kenny Johnson and myself saying, 'No!' and being let go," remembers Corea. "However, this state of affairs lasted only about 48 hours, and everything was brought back to normal by our star, Bill Bixby, making it clear that he *needed* our services to carry on."

Johnson adds his detailed recollection: "There's a guy named Peter Thompson who took over the production department at Universal. He called me one day and said, 'Kenny, the studio doesn't want to deficit finance any more. You gotta take $100,000 out of every episode. And that's the rule.' I said, 'No problem, Peter. Now, are you going to call them and say we can only afford one 'Hulk-out' instead of two?' 'No, no, no! It has to be the same show!' and I said, 'Let me explain something to you, Peter. I can do a show called *Incredible Hulk* for $7 or $700, $700,000 or $7 million. The only thing they have in common is the title! Now, if you want me to do the same show, it has to be the same money!' He said, 'Are you refusing to cut?' 'It can't be done, Peter!' so he said, 'You're suspended!' I said, 'Ok, Peter, let's call Nick.' So he called Nick and said, 'You're in charge!' Then Nick said, 'F--- you, Peter!' Peter Thompson went to the whole staff and managed to suspend everybody. All of a sudden, there's no staff anymore. This lasted for 24 hours, and then everything went on as normal afterwards, except that Peter Thompson was thrown out of his job about a month later!"

What was life like on the *Hulk* set? Corea offers this anecdote: When Lou Ferrigno first started the show, his hearing aids were not of the best quality, and it was necessary to get someone to signal him at the start and end of a scene. "Usually, a trainee from the Directors' Guild or a second assistant director would lie on the ground below [the camera] frame line. [It was his job] when the director yelled 'Action!' to tap Lou on the leg once to start, and when the director yelled 'Cut!' to smack him twice so he'd stop wrecking the set. [I'm not sure precisely] how the code worked, but the actual event was a daily occurrence until Lou was able to invest in a much better quality hearing device that made this no longer necessary."

As for working with Kenneth Johnson, Corea says, "[He] took a basic comic book idea and turned it into a classic investigation into the soul of man à la *Portrait of Dorian Grey* and Jekyll and Hyde. Instead of a character who could make himself Hulk out, Kenny created a tortured individual who'd overdosed and was now cursed with a side of himself he could not control. David Banner thus became Everyman and not 'special

man,' searching for an answer to a very universal and human dilemma.

"Kenny's writing was always superior, and his directing was terrific. He taught me a hell of a lot, and I've always looked on him as mentor and guru. Our backgrounds—he was from the 'aristocracy' and me from 'ethnic roots'—always kept us from being best friends, but we were definitely good pals and co-workers from 12 to 18 hours a day."

Asked if he was satisfied with his work on this show of many years ago, Corea replies, almost insulted, "I pity the TV writer, producer [or] director who is ever 'satisfied' with the work accomplished. To me, that's death! Walking out of a screening room, winking at the men and women who work with you and chortling: 'Perfect! Terrific stuff!' God, it makes me gag to think about it. There were quite a few executive producers in those days who said just that—who believed they'd found the key to infallibility. Most of those jerks are looking for work right now. Sure, there were many, many things we didn't get to accomplish with the show, mainly because CBS canceled us without much warning. At the time I remember that our biggest problem with the cancelation was the fact they never gave us the chance to wrap up the show. To do a final, blockbuster, two-hour episode that put Bix in the wringer and saved him from the monster inside— a kind of addiction story where David Banner had to finally turn himself inside out and explore the dark zones of his soul, etcetera. Also, we wanted a trial to be part of this two-hour—an inquisition of our hero that would cause him to *Hulk out on the stand*."

Over the course of the series, reporter Jack MacGee never really understood that the Hulk was David Banner. Only late in the second season, in the two-parter "Mystery Man," did he learn that the Hulk was a man who transformed into the creature and back. Would it have been a better idea, dramatically, for MacGee to *know* the Hulk's identity? Corea considers the question.

"My answer is that Kenny, Bill Bixby, [and] CBS thought it *more* exciting that MacGee didn't. [But] I agree with you. It was strictly a consensus that a MacGee who was in the dark, so to speak, would be a much better protagonist than a MacGee who understood Banner's plight. A MacGee who suddenly was no longer a threat and possibly even a partner or friend. Of course, if we'd been able to do that last wrap-up show, you can be certain MacGee would've had that shock."

For the show's cancelation, Ken Johnson lays the blame on Harvey Shepherd, then head of the CBS television network. "Harvey felt there wasn't a season left in it," growls Johnson. "It was a particularly foolish choice because at the time we had been canceled we had seven episodes in the can that hadn't aired yet! I said, 'Harvey, buy five or six more episodes, and you'll have a whole half-season right there! Then you'll see! The show's got another year in it.' He decided in his infinite wisdom not to, and I razzed him a good deal about it since then."

As the series developed, producers and the studio went looking for another producer to bring some freshness to the show. They snagged Jeff Freilich. He came aboard *The Incredible Hulk* as a producer and writer during the third season to see what ideas he could contribute. "When I was producing the show, Bill Bixby's concern was that the Hulk was becoming too repetitive," says Freilich. "It was fairly predictable that if David Banner got confronted by, you know, violent or threatening people, he would turn into the Hulk. That was always based on anger. He was afraid the series wouldn't last much longer because it was the same note over and over again. And what I came up with was an idea that I thought would keep us going for a little bit. I [wrote] a story that … involved Banner as a logger in Oregon, working near a river. He gets stung by a bee and turns into the Hulk. He stubs his toe and turns into the Hulk. David Banner is not only confused, but terrified that now it seems to be the slightest trauma that does it. What we discover [in the course of the story] is that a B-29 plane bound from Los Angeles to Japan at the end of the war, carrying a nuclear device on it, went down and was underwater near where he is logging and has been underwater for 40 years. Because of added radiation, it was accelerating the Hulk-outs. It became, then, a key. Any scientist who discovers that a change in a phenomenon can be instigated by some outside substances—in this case, radiation—would immediately start to work on a cure or reverse of that. It gave Banner a new kind of quest."

The ideas were interesting, but we never saw this story on the air. "I got into a fight, basically, with the people on the show," sighs Freilich. "Part of it was because I was more involved with the star than some people wanted me to be."

Freilich left the show and went down the block to Glen Larson, who was also at Universal, to produce *Galactica 1980*. Meanwhile, Freilich says, "Ken Johnson proceeded to basically borrow the idea and do the big two-parter which opened next season, which was David Banner at NORAD, where there is an overexposure [fourth season's premiere, *Prometheus*]. To me, it was the most obvious departure of the series. To accelerate the Hulk-outs, to make them so frightening and confusing that instead of traveling from city to city aimlessly, which is what Bixby's character did, that he should now kind of rechannel his energies to finding a cure for his problem, which was the original premise of the show. The problem was, he was very rarely looking for the premise. It was basically *The Fugitive*."

Freilich believes that the show enjoyed continued success because "it had heart to it, basically. The show always involved some everyday person. It was what makes any comic book work. The best *Superman* stories involve people who are in impossible situations that can only be rescued by a superhero from another planet. In the case of the Hulk, it was people up against very tough odds who are saved by a seemingly everyday man, who has this incredible power that torments him. So, he was a wonderful anti-hero. Bixby played it as a man tormented and obsessive, and at the same time, because he was a doctor, it was in his character to help people. He couldn't turn his back on helpless victims, knowing full well that in the process [of helping] he'd probably be subjected to this horrible transformation into this large, green, angry monster, which was something he didn't want to put himself through. [He] subjected himself to it as a sacrificial donation to other people's betterment. It is an interesting, compelling, human thing.

"The other reason the show is successful is there still is a dearth of quality children's programming. What I found fascinating about the Hulk … and made me feel valuable as a writer, was that I got involved with a large number of child psychiatrists who all thought that *The Hulk* was an outstanding children's program. The reason why was that it demonstrated to children, when Bill Bixby turned into Lou Ferrigno … that David Banner was acting out his anger, and that it was okay to become angry. Many children have a tremendous difficulty … expressing anger appropriately. I was told by a therapist that a lot of children, in a very healthy way, would become the Hulk when they became angry. Parents were complaining that the Hulk provoked violence in their children. Not that they broke walls or stuff like that, but they'd growl and they'd throw

Writer-producer Kenneth Johnson poses with "white eyes" Bill Bixby on the set of *The Incredible Hulk*. Photo courtesy of Kenneth Johnson.

pillows around. They would act out as if they were the Hulk. So I got concerned about that. I have two children of my own now. I'm a little sensitive to what they watch. At the time, I was particularly sensitive because I didn't want to be creating stories that would have really serious negative repercussions, particularly among children. So, I talked to a few people I knew. I had gone to medical school at the University of Southern California and knew a lot of psychiatrists who would have been graduates with me, and they all did research. I started to get calls back from Children's Hospital in Los Angeles, a place in New York and a couple of other places, and they all said, 'When children act out anger, it's because they can't express it otherwise, and if they can't find a way to act out it will become repressed, and if it does become repressed, they will grow into violent adults.' It was a wonderful outlet for children. It was a way to validate and express anger when they might otherwise repress it or internalize it and cause problems in themselves or their future. To me, all of a sudden, gee, I'm working on a show that actually has some value!"

Freilich remembers feedback for *The Incredible Hulk* as "very positive. I think that Ken Johnson really tried to make each individual episode have some meaningful, accessible human story. Each of these stories could be told without the Hulk."

For Freilich, *The Incredible Hulk* was a pivotal assignment because it was his first production. "I was hired as the producer of *The Hulk* for no particular reason," he says, "except for the fact that I was a very good writer and both Ken Johnson and Nick Corea wanted to branch out and try other shows, other things, and wanted me to become heir apparent to the show. The fact that Ken Johnson and I had a personality clash precluded me from taking that show over, which I'm glad I didn't do in retrospect. Nick Corea, whom I have a lot of admiration and respect for as a creative person, should really have been writing something closer to his heart. Nick's a former police officer, and a marine in Vietnam. He's got a wonderful background for writing gritty politics. If he could have been born again, he'd like to be either Ernest Hemingway or Raymond Chandler. Nick was the best *Hulk* writer I think there was. He was also the best director of the ones who directed episodes."

Asked to describe Ken Johnson, the show's television creator, Freilich first emphasizes that Johnson "took the Hulk seriously. I mean, he took everything seriously and, in fact, wanted the show to be as reality-based as possible. Which, when you're doing a show about a man who, when he gets run over by a steam roller, has his eyes go white and comes out a green person, is very difficult to accept."

Freilich then supplies an extended anecdote that reveals Johnson's commitment to his craft and, in particular, to the Hulk. During the second season of the show, for an episode titled "Killer Instinct," Freilich, Johnson and episode director Ray Danton were all sitting in the editing room, viewing dailies. "There's a scene that takes place in the Los Angeles Coliseum during a football game where stock footage is used, but there is a young boy who is sitting in this 100,000-seat coliseum, way up high, watching, and he has a relationship to David Banner. He sees David Banner running across the field, and Banner runs right through a play, and [with] the combination of the two teams ramming over him, he winds up with 2300 pounds of bodies over him, and he becomes the Hulk.

"Instead of tearing apart Los Angeles Coliseum, Lou is supposed to look around and spot this boy sitting up in the coliseum, and a tear appears under his eye and drips down his cheek," said Freilich, relishing the tale. "This is a Hulk moment. Ken Johnson reached over to the controls on the console and paused the film and turned to Ray Danton and said, 'Ray, I don't understand this! This isn't real!' He says, 'How could the Hulk come out of the scrimmage, look up and spot this boy out of a hundred thousand people? This is crazy, nobody's going to believe this. Why did you do this?' There was a long pause, and Ray leaned over and said, 'Kenny, why is he green?' Ok? It was like Ken bought this myth to the point where if everything else isn't real, then it would become a cartoon, is what he would think. We kept reminding him it *was* a cartoon and that nobody would ask how Superman or Batman can leap or fly out of the sky and arrive just in the right time to stop a mugger from roughing up a family. ... Nobody would ask that question because it goes with the mythology and fantasy involved. In this instance, why would anyone wonder how the Hulk could spot this boy? But Ken really thought it was very important and couldn't answer why he was green at all. It was a funny kind of situation, but it made all of us fall over because it made us think, jeez, what are we doing here? Were we making a comic book or a television show?"

The story is recounted to Johnson, who says, "Jeff is certainly correct in my dedication to keep the show as real as possible. The Hulk was green because I had it forced on me. In the original comics he was grey, then Stan Lee wanted a color. The printer said they could do a nice consistent green. Stan said okay. I wanted him *red*, the color of rage, anger, danger—and my favorite word, logic."

Freilich believes that *The Incredible Hulk* was one of the best children's television shows ever made. "I think, for me, it opened up my career [just] because someone anointed me and said, 'Now you're a producer," recalls Freilich. "I didn't know what I was doing. It took me a few months to figure it out, and after that I was able to work quite well on *Galactica 1980* and after that, creating my own shows and becoming executive producer and running things."

The *Incredible Hulk*'s creator from the comics, Stan Lee, wasn't too far away during the show's production. He was labeled as creative consultant. Lee remembers that although Ken Johnson had changed the Hulk in a number of ways (with his approval), the result was "an intelligent job."

"I felt the changes he wanted actually would make it a better television show," says Lee. "Apparently, we were right, because it was quite successful." Lee cited the first *Hulk* telefilm as a favorite of all the *Hulk*s. "I felt it was so beautifully done. I thought it just proves how brilliant Ken Johnson was. It was an adult show that happened to have a monster in it. But you only saw the monster for about five minutes for each hour. A couple of minutes in the beginning and a few minutes at the end, and for the most part, the show was the story of this fellow, David Banner, and the things that happened to him and the romances he would get into, and personal problems. So it was a show that any intelligent adult could watch and could enjoy. I thought it was very well done."

As to whether he met with the production staff or contributed ideas to the show, Lee just says, "It was basically Ken Johnson's show. He made all the major decisions. Anything that changed the Hulk from the way we had him in the books, he would discuss with me and we would work it out. Mostly, I agreed with virtually everything he wanted to do."

In 1988, New World Television acquired the rights to several Marvel Comics characters and, in an effort to generate television series pilots, released a TV Movie titled *The Incredible Hulk Returns*, written and directed by Nicholas Corea. This film guest-starred actor Eric Kramer as the comic book character the Mighty Thor. Later, in 1989, New World also released another movie, *The Trial of the Incredible Hulk*, written by Gerald DiPego and directed by Bill Bixby. This time around, the guest super hero was Daredevil, essayed by soap opera veteran Rex Smith. When neither film was successful in launching a TV series for the new characters, Bixby (still at the helm as director) and company decided to go back to the roots of the series and complete the long journey of David Banner by killing him. *The Death of the Incredible Hulk*, released in 1990, did just that.

Stan Lee, asked his opinion of the three post-series *Hulk* TV movies, says, "The one with Thor, I thought, they meant well. They had the best of intentions, but ... maybe ... the only way they felt they could do it, because they felt Thor was such an unbelievable character, was to do it humorously. But it didn't seem to work. I don't know why. It was just a bad idea. They changed

Thor tremendously from the way he is in the comic books. They split him into two characters; him and Donald Blake, so it was a different character, a different mood. I felt there was no reason to have changed it that much."

To explain why some of those changes were necessary, Nick Corea describes his work on that production: "I was given this assignment, I wanted to do it, but then when I saw I had to put in the Marvel Comic character, I looked through them all, and Thor was the one I felt that I could do something about—make it a little humorous, and have him be basically a big old Viking that comes back into our time now and bumps into events in our world. I like the idea of somebody out of time and out of place in our world that can show us and tell us about ourselves from a different perspective. We had very little money to do it, and even though I had brought him way down from the original Thor, I wasn't going to have him in Valhalla, talking to his father in the clouds. In the comic book he takes out his hammer and just flies with it. I basically brought it down to the places where we could film him for the amount of money we had. My memories were very good of everybody below the line, the crew and all the stunt people."

Regarding the second movie, *The Trial of the Incredible Hulk* with Daredevil, Stan Lee was more generous. "I thought that worked a little bit better. But again, I don't know why they changed Daredevil the way they did. He's always had a red costume, and they had him in a black costume. They made the mask a bit different, and I think what that did was alienate a lot of the comic book fans who watched the show. It would be like doing Superman in a green polka dot cape! It might not affect the story, but it would get the fans a little upset. But I thought the acting was rather good, and it was well-written and it was a good show."

For the *Trial of the Incredible Hulk* (filmed in Vancouver), Lee wanted to participate in the filming, so Bixby invited him up from Los Angeles and inserted him into the film as the foreman in the court sequence. "I was in the jury box, and there was a scene where the Hulk lifts the jury box up and all the people are scared out of their trees," laughs Lee. "And I wasn't allowed to be in that scene because all the people had to be stuntmen. And I said, 'Well, there's nothing difficult about sitting in a scene and jumping out of it when the Hulk starts shifting it.' But they said, 'No, no, we can't take a chance. According

to union rules, it has to be a stunt person.' When the Hulk started lifting the box, I was not there. And it was somebody else, and I thought, 'This is great! Here I am, and I've got my own stuntman!'"

Regarding the *Death of the Incredible Hulk*, the one that ended it all, Lee says, "I thought it was very well done. For some reason, the network said there was supposed to be another show following that in which he comes back to life, but they never produced it. I don't know why. But I thought the death was okay."

David Banner dies when a plane is trying to take off and the Hulk hangs on to the doorway. Attempting to get rid of him, the pilot takes the plane through some air gymnastics and shakes the creature off, and he falls through the night sky, lands on the airport runway and dies.

"Again, it wasn't in keeping with the way the Hulk has been portrayed in the comics, because he could've survived that fall," explains Lee. "But from the point of view of the television show, it seemed if they wanted to kill him, it was as good a way as any. That was a clever story."

Today, Stan Lee works at Marvel Productions, a company currently involved with an animated *X-Men* television series and with generating other projects to bring Marvel characters to film and television.

Rumors were rampant for a brief period that the Hulk would come back in a *Revenge of the Incredible Hulk*–type of story bringing the character back to life. Brigette Nielsen, who would go on to action films such as *Rocky IV* and *Cobra*, tried out for a *She-Hulk* feature, but financing couldn't be found.

Jill Sherman-Donner, a story editor for the original series, claims, however, that *She-Hulk* did get off the ground, although it was reeled back to earth after only five days. "We went to the Caribbean. I just don't think the casting made it for them," says Sherman-Donner. "I think when you take a woman it's a very sensitive thing. But it was an ABC–New World TV and it was a pretty good script. It could have worked, and I was very disappointed it didn't go. It would have been hugely expensive."

Sherman-Donner says it was a wonderful reunion for her and Bixby. "He's a wonderful man, very complicated, and I'm thrilled that I got to know and work with him. *The Incredible Hulk* (series) would never have happened if it hadn't been for Bill Bixby, and *She-Hulk* would never have been launched if he hadn't agreed to help launch it, so he was pivotal in that whole area."

CAST NOTES

Bill Bixby (Dr. David Banner): Born in San Francisco in 1934. Bixby started acting in television's *Dobie Gillis* and *Lonely Are the Brave* (1962). He's best known as the lead in several popular TV series: the fantasy sit-com *My Favorite Martian* (1963–66), *The Courtship of Eddie's Father* (1969–72) and *The Magician* (1973). After a short stint hosting *The Wonderful World of Magic*, he landed *Rich Man, Poor Man Book II,* for which he received a directing Emmy nomination. The second and third Emmy nominations bestowed on Bixby as an actor were for *The Courtship of Eddie's Father* and a *Streets of San Francisco* segment. After *The Incredible Hulk,* Bixby starred with Mariette Hartley in *Goodnight Beantown* (1984).

TV-movie acting appearances include *Congratulations! It's a Boy!* (1971); *The Couple Takes a Wife* (1972); *Shirts/Skins* (1973); *Invasion of Johnson County* (1976); *The Great Houdinis* (1976); *Fantasy Island* (1977); *Black Market Babies* (1977); Agatha Christie's *Murder Is Easy* (1982); and *Sin of Innocence* (1986).

Bixby's directing credits include the series *Barbary Coast, Bert D'Angelo, Mannix, Kate McShane, Oregon Trail, The Magician, Spencer's Pilots,* and *Sledge Hammer!*; the TV-movie *Three on a Date* (1978); and the series *Murphy's Law* (1988). And of course, *The Trial of the Incredible Hulk* (1989) and *The Death of the Incredible Hulk* (1990).

Bixby was a director on the NBC sitcom *Blossom* when he died in November 1993 of cancer.

Lou Ferrigno (Hulk): Born 1952. His first exposure to film cameras came when *Pumping Iron* (1975) documented the Mr. Olympia bodybuilding competition, in which Ferrigno landed third place. In 1976 he played briefly with the Toronto Argos as a defensive tackle, but because he didn't have "the killer instinct," he quit. A leg injury sent him back to Los Angeles. Ferrigno was with the Weider Company promoting bodybuilding products when he was approached with the role of *The Incredible Hulk.* Life has never been the same.

When four seasons of destroying sets ended in 1982, he segued into another show called *Trauma Center,* playing an ambulance driver. Ferrigno moved to starring roles in Italian epics produced by Cannon Films: *Hercules* (1983), *The Adventures of Hercules* (1985), and *Sinbad* (1987). Then, he went on the road across the country in the classic comedy play *Arsenic and Old Lace.*

His most recent lead roles as an actor were a comedy with George Segal and Sally Kellerman, *All's Fair* (1988), and *Cage* (1989) with Reb Brown. Ferrigno also completed a pilot with Sid Caeser called *No Place Like Rome* and made an appearance on the TV series *Wolf.*

Between films, Ferrigno likes to train people one-on-one in the gym, "to keep my sanity" he says. Lou Ferrigno is married to his wife, Carla. They have a daughter and a son. Ferrigno has returned to bodybuilding full-time.

Jack Colvin (Jack MacGee): This Kansas-born actor later became a director. He's performed roles in *Amelia Earhart* (1976), *Benny and Barney: Las Vegas Undercover* (1977), *Exo-Man* (1977), *Footsteps* (1972), *Hurricane* (1974), and *The Spell* (1974).

EPISODE GUIDE

The Incredible Hulk (1977 TV movie, 2 hours)
David Banner, a research scientist, searches for ways of tapping—and possibly controlling—hidden strengths all humans have. A gamma ray experiment changes his body chemistry, and he becomes a giant green creature. With fellow scientist Dr. Marks, Banner explores his affliction but they are hampered by a reporter who noses around. Wr: Kenneth Johnson. Dir: Kenneth Johnson.

Dr. Elaina Marks (Susan Sullivan); Laura, David's wife (Lara Parker); Mrs. Jessie Marie (Susan Batson); B.J. Marie (Eric Deon); Mrs. Epstein (June Whitley Taylor); Martin Bran (Mario Gallo); Girl at lake (Olivia Barash); Man at lake (George Brenlin); Ben (Charles Siebert).

Death in the Family (aka **Return of the Incredible Hulk**) (2-hour 1977 TV Movie)
David discovers his new employer secretly administering a drug to her crippled stepdaughter, a young heiress he has befriended. The girl is hunted by killers, a helicopter and other dangers created by her family. Wr: Kenneth Johnson. Dir: Kenneth Johnson.

Julie (Laurie Prange); Margaret (Dorothy Tristan); Denny (Gerald McRaney); Dr. Bonifant (William Daniels); Michael (John McLiam); Sheriff (Mills Watson); Rafe (Victor Mohica); Phil (Robert Phillips); 1st nurse (Ann Weldon); 2nd nurse (Linda Wiser); Lab technician (Robert

Aaron Brown); 3rd nurse (Janet Adams); Receptionist (Swan Socorro); Maid (Rita Gomez); Cuban (Rick Garcia).

Season 1: 1978

The Final Round
Mugged by hoods in an alley, a prizefighter saves David and hires him as his physician. Soon, David finds out that the boxer is involved in drug operations. Wr: Ken Johnson. Dir: Ken Gilbert.

Rocky (Martin Kove); Sariego (Al Ruscio); Mary (Fran Meyers); Tom (John Witherspoon); Also with Paul Henry Itkin, Tony Brubaker, Tony Miratti, Ron Trice.

Memory Flash—Martin Kove: "I enjoyed it very much. It was the biggest guest star role I ever had. I met my wife while shooting that show. I thoroughly enjoyed it. It was broad. I haven't done an episodic show for so long. But *The Hulk* was a terrific experience."

The Beast Within
At a zoo, David meets another research scientist carrying on work similar to his before the tragic accident. A criminal smuggling operation gets in the way. The Hulk fights with an ape. Wr: Karen Harris and Jill Sherman. Dir: Kenneth Gilbert.

Claudia (Caroline McWilliams); Dr. Malone (Dabbs Greer); Carl (Richard Kelton); Jagger (Jean Duran); Joe (Charles Lampkin); 1st zoo security guard (Norman Rice); 2nd zoo security guard (Joe DeNicola); Rita (Billie Beach).

Of Guilt, Models and Murder
Disoriented after coming out of another Hulk blackout, David realizes his alter-ego may have killed a young model. He returns to the scene of the crime to investigate. Wr: James D. Parriott. Dir: Larry Stewart.

Sheila (Loni Anderson); Joslin (Jeremy Brett); Terri Ann (Deanna Lund); Sanderson (Ben Gerard); TV reporter (Doug Hale); Elkin (Rick Goldman); Ellen (Nancy Steen); Jackson (Bill Baldwin); Security guard (Vince Howard); 1st policeman (Art Kimbro); Collins (Ross Durfee); Dr. Elaina Marks (flashback) (Susan Sullivan); Also with Jane Alice Brandon.

Memory Flash—Larry Stewart: "On [this episode] the actress said, 'I have an audition for a series job coming up, can I take a slightly long lunch?' I said, 'Sure.' We gave her a two-hour lunch. She came back and didn't know if she had gotten the job. She tells this story now all the time but never mentions my name: 'This wonderful director let me go on this two-hour lunch and I got the job.' It was Loni Anderson of *WKRP*.

"Seymour Klate was *Hulk*'s art director. In this episode, Hulk goes into a mansion, breaks down the front door and goes crackers. ... Well, I walked on the set and the walls are painted green. I sent for Seymour and said, 'Seymour, what color are the walls? and he said, 'Green.' 'What color is our Hulk?' and he said, 'Oh!' At that moment, Loni Anderson walked into the room wearing a green dress. Everything was green! Well, the cameraman, John McPherson, was terrific. 'We'll handle it with lighting.' He lit it in such a way that the background was darker and the Hulk was lighter, so it didn't look like green against green."

Terror in Times Square
Employed in a New York arcade, David encounters murder, testing a friendship with his employers. The Hulk runs through Times Square in this episode. Wr: William Schwartz. Dir: Alan J. Levi.

Norman (Jack Kruschen); Carol (Pamela Susan Shoop); Leo (Amy Freeman); Jason (Robert Alda); Jonathan (Karl Held).

747
David's on an airplane hijacked by the pilot and his girlfriend, who are after some jewels. With the help of a young passenger, he tries landing the plane without transforming into the Hulk. Stock footage from *Airport 1975* in this episode. Wr: Tom Szollosi and Richard Christian Matheson. Dir: Sigmund Neufield, Jr.

Kevin (Brandon Cruz); Phil (Edward Power); Stephanie (Sondra Currie); Stewardess (Denise Galik); Jack Howard (Kevin Honig); Cynthia Davis (Susan Cotten); Mr. MacIntire (Don Keefer); Mrs. MacIntire (Shirley O'Hara); Controller (J. Jay Saunders); Pilot (Del Hinkley); Captain Brandes (Ed Peck).

Trivia Alert: Brandon Cruz was Bill Bixby's costar in the series *The Courtship of Eddie's Father*.

The Hulk Breaks Las Vegas
Working in a Las Vegas casino, David assists a reporter on a story about a gambling scandal. In the course of the story, the Hulk saves Jack MacGee's life. Wr: Justin Edgerton. Dir: Larry Stewart.

Wanda (Julie Gregg); Tom Elder (John Crawford); Lee (Don Marshall); Campion (Dean Santoro); Charlie (Paul Picerni); Kathy (Simone Griffith); First patrolman (Phil Hoover); Also with William Molley, Paul Koufas, Tony Miller, Wally K. Berns, David Zelliti.

Memory Flash—Larry Stewart: "The Hulk comes out of a sand quarry, and we thought, 'Boy, how do we manage this one? If we put him under the sand, and he gets sand under his contact lenses, Lou could be in real trouble.' So we set Lou under the sand without the lenses and had him come up, turning, so you couldn't see his eyes. Then I cut, we put in his lenses and overlapped the turn, and it worked well. It took extra time to do, but our first concern was to protect the actor and not to destroy his life doing *The Incredible Hulk*."

Never Give a Trucker an Even Break
David helps a female trucker retrieve her father's tanker truck from hijackers. Stock footage from

Steven Spielberg's *Duel* is used in this episode. Wr: Kenneth Johnson. Dir: Kenneth Gilbert.

Ted (Frank R. Christi); Mike (Grand Bush); Gas station man (Charles Alvin Bell); The Irishman (John Calvin); Also with Jennifer Darling, Peggie Doyle, Don Starr.

Life and Death
Volunteering to a hospital for a DNA experiment, David meets up with a pregnant young woman whose life will intertwine with his. Wr: James D. Parriott. Dir: Jeffrey Hayden.

Ellen Harding (Julie Adams); Young woman (Sarah Rush); Dr. Rhodes (Andrew Robinson); Crosby (Carl Franklin); Carrie (Diane Civita); Chief nurse (Mitzi Hoag); Dan (John Warner Williams); 1st detective (Gil Garcia); 2nd detective (Judd Laurance); Young nurse (Takayo); Tina (Lillah McCarthy); Trucker (Al Berry); Man in elevator (Ben Freedman).

Earthquakes Happen
Posing as a scientist at a nuclear research facility to gain access to gamma radiation equipment, David is caught in the middle of an earthquake. Footage from the film *Earthquake* is used in this story. Wr: Jim Tisdale. Dir: Harvey Laidman.

Hammond (Peter Brandon); Diane Joseph (Sherry Jackson); Paul (Kene Holliday); Marsha (Pamela Nelson); Nancy (Lynne Topping); Also with John Alvin.

The Waterfront Story
Working in a bar in Texas, David becomes involved in a war for the control of dock workers' unions. The Hulk intervenes and assists in solving the problems. Wr: Paul M. Belous and Robert Wolterstoff. Dir: Reza Badiyi.

Josie (Sheila Larken); Tony (Jack Kelley); McConnell (James Sikking); Sarah (Candice Azzara); Vic (William Benedict); First mate (Joe Perry); Night watchman (Robert Hackman); Dock worker (John Zenda); Trucker (Tonyo Melendez); 1st policeman (Anthony Davis); 3rd policeman (Brian Baker); 2nd policeman (Blake Marion); Customer (John Colton); Marty (Ted Markland).

Season 2: 1978-79

Married (2 hours)
In Hawaii, David teams up with a psychiatrist (who has a terminal illness) to find ways to rid himself of his affliction. They marry, not realizing what consequences lie ahead. Actress Mariette Hartley won an Emmy for her performance. Wr: Kenneth Johnson. Dir: Kenneth Johnson.

Dr. Caroline Fields (Mariette Hartley); Brad (Brian Cutler); The girl (Diane Markoff); Mark (Duncan Gamble); Boy (Meeno Peluce); Receptionist (Rosalind Chao); Conservative man (Russ Grieve); 1st messenger (Nat Jones); 2nd messenger (Russell Takaki); Justice of the peace (Joseph Kim).

Memory Flash—Kenneth Johnson: "When I showed Mariette Hartley the script, I said, 'Here's your Emmy, Mariette.' And her reaction was the same as everyone: 'Oh, please! Come on! *The Incredible Hulk*! Give me a break!'

"When I set out to do that episode, it was to talk about what it's like to be close to death and how one faces death. A psychologist friend of mine had been doing research on hypnotherapeutic treatment of disease, and it was really the cutting edge of medical treatment. I thought it was a great idea. It gave me an opportunity, for the first time, to put Bixby and Ferrigno together in the same scene. My Federico Fellini sequence, you know?" Johnson went to a desert location in Barley, California, just north of the Mexican border. There was a heatwave. "The temperature of the sand was 160 degrees. It was so hot, Lou's makeup kept [running]. Instead of being green, he'd be blue and yellow! The special green makeup came from Germany, but the heat kept separating the primary colors off him. ... It was an amazingly difficult sequence to shoot. We were there for two days."

The Antowuk Horror
In a dying town where the Hulk makes an appearance, townsfolk try to revive their homeland by creating a werewolf creature to generate publicity. Wr: Nicholas Corea. Dir: Sigmund Neufeld.

Harlan (Bill Lucking); Samantha (Debbie Lytton); Brad (Lance Le Gault); Mayor (Claire Murphy); TV reporter (Bill Deiz); Also with Gwen Van Dam.

Ricky
In New Mexico at a racing track, David meets a racing driver's retarded brother. Wr: Jaron Summers. Dir: Frank Orsatti.

Irene (Robin Mattson); Ricky Detter (Mickey Jones); Buzz Detter (James Daughton); Ted Roberts (Eric Server); Sam Roberts (Gerald McRaney); Mac (Gordon Jump).

Rainbow's End
A vitamin used to calm down a troublesome racehorse may be the key to curing David. But first he must prevent the horse from being killed. Wr: Karen Harris and Jill Sherman. Dir: Kenneth Gilbert.

Thomas Logan (Ned Romero); L.H. Carroll III (Craig Stevens); Jim Kelley (Gene Evans); Kim Kelley (Michele Nichols); Andy Cardone (Larry Volk); Man on bus (John Myers); Security guard (Warren W. Smith).

A Child in Need
Taking a job as a school gardener, David meets a child who has wounds on his body. He learns they are created by habitual abuse from his father. Wr: Frank Dandridge. Dir: James D. Parriott.

Mark Hollinger (Dennis Dimster); Jack Hollinger (Sandy McPeak); Margaret Hollinger (Sally Kirkland); Mary Walker (Rebecca York); Reporter (Marguerite De Lain); Middle aged man (Thomas H. Middleton); School kid (Nyles Harris).

Another Path
David meets up with a wise old Chinese man, Li Sung, who teaches methods of controlling the

autonomic nervous system. It may provide an off-beat solution for David in curing himself of the Hulk's curse. In return, the Hulk helps in resolving some problems for Li Sung. Wr: Nick Corea. Dir: Joseph Pevney.

Li Sung (Mako); Frank Silva (Tom Lee Holland); Mr. Fong (Joseph Kim); Simon Ming (Richard Lee Sung); Gramma Loo (Jane Chung); Jim Fong (Sam Tampoya); Receptionist (Helene T. Nelson); Driver (Eric Stern); May Chuang (Irene Yah-Ling Sun).

Alice in Disco Land

Working in a disco, David realizes a young dancer is an alcoholic. He helps her quit the habit and resolve problems with the owner of the palace. The Hulk tears apart the disco in this episode. Wr: Karen Harris and Jill Sherman. Dir: Sigmund Neufeld.

Alice (Donna Wilkes); Louie (Jason Kincaid); Rosalyn Morrow (Mo Malone); Ernie (Marc Alaimo); Molly (Julie Hill); D.J. (Freeman King); Alice as a child (Lisa Lambert); Art Philbin (Dennis Holahan); Al (Brian James); Joan Roberts (Betty Ann Rees); Bernard (Miles McNamara); Sarah (Denise Kumagi).

Killer Instinct

As an assistant trainer on a football team, David meets a player who is overly aggressive. The Hulk intervenes and teaches him that winning is not everything. Wr: Joel Don Humphreys and William Whitehead. Dir: Ray Danton.

Tobey (Denny Miller); June Tobey (Barbara Leigh); Dr. Stewart (Rudy Solari); Bowers (Wyatt Johnson); J.P. Tobey (Herman Poppe); J.P. Tobey as child (Tiger Williams); Coach Haggerty (Pepper Martin); Kurt Donahue (Frank Orsatti); Mitch Adams (Tom Kelley).

Stop the Presses

Working at a restaurant that's a target of the National Register, David's photo is accidentally taken. To protect his identity, David must break into their offices to retrieve the print before MacGee finds him out. Wr: Karen Harris, Jill Sherman and Susan Woolen, story by Susan Woolen. Dir: Jeff Hayden.

Jill (Julie Cobb); Karen (Mary Frann); Charlie Watts (Art Metrano); Fred (Pat Morita); Joe Arnold (Sam Chew Jr.); Samuelson (Judson Pratt); Lenette Logan (Janet Brandt); Geller (Mike Griswold); Game warden (Tain Bodkin); Printer (Sandy Champion); Copyboy (Donald Petrie).

Escape from Los Santos

Hitchhiking to Phoenix, David is jailed by a policeman. There he meets a young woman who is framed for the murder of her husband. Wr: Bruce Kalish and Philip Taylor. Dir: Chuck Bowman.

Holly Cooper (Shelley Fabares); Deputy Evans (Lee deBroux); Sheriff Harris (Dana Elcar); Deputy Munro (W.K. Stratton); Forrest (Kerry Mahan); Jill (Desiree Kerns); Mexican man (Ben Frommer); Mr. Mallard (Al Valletta); Mrs. Mallard (Toni Handcock); Chase (Vernon Weddle).

Wildfire

At an oil rig, sabotage breaks out and David finds himself face to face with the man responsible. Wr: Brian Rehak. Dir: Frank Orsatti.

Mike Callahan (John Anderson); Linda Callahan (Christine Belford); Ray Thomas (Billy Green Bush); Frank Adler (Dean Brooks); Haze (Ernie Orsatti); Tim Wade (John Petlock).

A Solitary Place

Desiring isolation, David seeks out a remote area, but his solitude is quickly quashed by a young woman who joins him at his camp. The only problem is, Jack MacGee is chasing her, too. Wr: Jim Tisdale and Migdia Varela. Dir: Jeff Hayden.

Gail Collins (Kathryn Leigh Scott); Frank Sloan (Jerry Douglas); Raul (Hector Elias); Richard Sloan (Bruce Wright); Pablo (Tony Melendez); Ramon (Jay Varela).

Like a Brother

David's car wash job turns into a conflict involving a co-worker, a preacher and drugs. Wr: Richard Christian Matheson and Thomas E. Szollasi. Dir: Reza Badiyi.

Rev. Williams (Austin Stoker); Fantine (Rana Ford); Jimmy (Jesse Dizon); Bobby (Dale Pullum); Mother (Elizabeth Chauvet); Mike (Stuart K. Robinson); Taylor George (Tony Burton); Lee (Ernie Hudson); Oscar (Carl Anderson); D.J. (Michael D. Roberts).

The Haunted

As a driver, David helps a young woman move to a new city but quickly becomes involved in a mystery involving the death of the woman's twin sister many years ago. Wr: Karen Harris and Jill Sherman. Dir: John McPherson.

Renee (Carol Baxter); Bernard (John O'Connell); Fred Lewitt (Johnny Haymer); Dr. Rawlins (Jon Lormer); Renee as a child (Randi Kiger); Woman (Iris Korn).

Mystery Man, Part 1

As a result of a plane crash, a masked and amnesiac David is stranded in a forest with MacGee. To survive, they must help each other before a forest fire wipes them out. Wr: Nicholas Corea. Dir: Frank Orsatti.

Rose (Victoria Carroll); Doctor (Don Marshall); Pilot (Skip Riley); 3rd nurse (Barbara Tarbuck); 1st man (John C. Colton); Nurse Phalen (Aileen Towne); 1st nurse (Nadeja Klein); 2nd man (Norman Merrill); Hospital guard (John McKee).

Mystery Man, Part 2

Still stranded near a raging forest fire with Jack MacGee, Banner finds his memory slowly returning—and along with it, the Hulk. Wr: Nicholas Corea. Dir: Frank Orsatti.

Bob Cory (Howard Witt); Hal Pollock (Michael Payne); Helen Cory (Bonnie Johns); Cory Child (Cari Anne Warder); 3rd nurse (Barbara Tarbuck); Betty (Laura Lizer).

The Disciple

A sequel to *Another Path*. Li Sung meets David

again, but this time a disciple of Li Sung, a policeman, must regain confidence in himself when an incident shakes him up. Wr: Nick Corea and James G. Hirsch. Dir: Reza Badiyi.

Li Sung (Mako); Michael (Rick Springfield); Colin (Gerald McRaney); Tim Roark (Stacy Keach Sr.); Newscaster (Bill Deiz); Lynch's henchman (Fred Ward); Michael's mother (Anne Bellamy); 1st cop (Rene Levant); Lynch's doctor (Frederic Franklyn); Thayer (Brian Baker); Al (Doug McGrath); Lynch (George Loros); Jolee (Lina Raymond).

No Escape

Picked up for vagrancy, David is placed in a police van. Inside he finds a man who feels betrayed by his wife and doctor. The Hulk breaks them out of the van, and as a result, David frees his mad companion. Wr: Ben Masselink. Dir: Jeff Hayden.

Tom Wallace (James Wainwright); Kay (Mariclare Costello); Robert (Sherman Hemsley); 1st officer (Howard Bruner); 1st reporter (Lynne Randall); 2nd reporter (George J. Cooper); 2nd officer (Jerry Fitzpatrick); Steve (Chris Petersen); Jimmy (Andy Enberg); Matthews (Tom Lowell); Simon (Thalumus Rasulala); Dr. Stanley (Skip Homeier).

Kindred Spirits

Archaeological digs uncover a Hulk-like creature. This gives David some hope relating to his condition. But MacGee is nearby, a girl recognizes Banner, and the Indians disapprove of the expedition. Wr: Karen Harris and Jill Sherman. Dir: Joseph Pevney.

Dr. Gabrielle White (Kim Cattrall); Professor Williams (Whit Bissell); Rick Youngblood (A. Martinez); Lone Wolf (Chief Dan George); Security guard (Melvin F. Allen); Reporter (Brian Pevney); Michael (George Gonzales); Frank (Eloy P. Casados); Little Jim (Don Shanks).

The Confession

Jack MacGee gets an assistant in his never-ending quest for the Hulk while a young man arrives at the offices claiming to be the Hulk. Wr: Deborah Davis. Dir: Barry Crane.

Harold (Barry Gordon); Pamela (Markie Post); Mark Roberts (Richard Herd); Ernie (John Armstrong Marshall); Alan O'Neil (Angus Duncan); Newman (Michael Laurence); Gladys (Fritzi Burr); Night guard (Clint Young); Mrs. Goldsmith (Holly Irving); Woman at desk (Gloria Delaney); Girl (Yusy Flanigan); Crewman (Kenny Davis); Man (Ron Taft); Harry (Earl Corbert); Carl (Walter Janowitz); Sandy (Elaine Joyce).

The Quiet Room

David discovers research scientists using mind-controlling drugs on patients. As a result he is labeled a lunatic and strapped into a straitjacket. Wr: Karen Harris and Jill Sherman. Dir: Reza Badiyi.

Dr. Joyce Hill (Joanna Miles); Dr. Murrow (Philip Abbott); Kathy (Sian Barbara Allen); Sam (Robert F. Lyons); Dr. Caldwell (John Petlock); Mark (Vince Howard); Houdini (Kopi Sotiropulos); Tom Vincent (Lawrence Howard); Frankie (Gino Ardito); Laundry man (Dick Winslow); Bully (Drew Michaels); Counting man (Behrouz); Gene (Robert Feero).

Vendetta Road

David becomes involved with a gangster couple who blow up gas stations in revenge for the corporation's killing of their son. David's attempts to reach the press are hindered when MacGee shows up. Wr: Justin R. Edgarton. Dir: John McPherson.

Ray Floyd (Ron Lombard); Cassie Floyd (Christina Hart); Madrid (Morgan Woodward); Greg Bantam (Chip Johnson); Sheriff (Robert Ackerman); Spaulding (Michael Potter); Jed (Justin Smith); Hank (Larry French); Earl (Tobias Anderson); Sam Butler (Don Furneaux); Waylon (Tom Kindle); Del (Michael Champion); Guard (Jesse Doran); Damian Fielding (Howard Morton).

Season 3: 1979-80

Metamorphosis

Hired as a sound technician for a New Wave rock band, David soon discovers one of the band members attempting suicide on stage. The Hulk appears in the midst of a packed house. Wr: Craig Buck, story by Frank Dandridge. Dir: Alan Levi.

Lisa Swan (Mackenzie Phillips); Jackie Swan (Katherine Cannon); Greg (Gary Graham); Diane Markon (Jennifer Holmes); Ken (James Reynolds).

Blind Rage

At a chemical warfare research station, David and a friend get blinded, but company officials obstruct their efforts at finding an antidote. Wr: Dan Ullman. Dir: Jeffrey Hayden.

Colonel Drake (Nicolas Coster); Major Anderson (Jack Rader); Carrie Banks (Lee Bryant); Lt. Jerry Banks (Tom Stechschulte); Sgt. Murkland (Don Dubbins); Sgt. Sam Stanley (Michael Alldredge); Patty Banks (Michelle Stacy); Ambulance driver (Michael Horsley); M.P. (Meshach Taylor); Brubeck (Leonard Lightfoot); Mahalovich (Mitch Reta); Sentry (Gary Devaney).

Brain Child

Driving across the country, Banner meets up with a young, super intelligent runaway from an institution who is in search of her mother. Banner must help her in her quest before they are caught. Wr: Nicholas Corea. Dir: Reza Badiyi

Joleen (Robin Dearden); Dr. Kate Lowell (June Allyson); Elizabeth Collins (Lynn Carlin); Dr. Saltz (Henry Rowland); La Bruja (Madeleine Taylor-Holmes); Cop (Stack Pierce); Mr. Sweeney (Fred Carney); Boy (Tony Ramirez); Federal agent (Jonathan Williams); Mr. Arnold (Joseph Mascolo); Ramon Alvarez (Tonyo Melendez).

The Slam

Arrested for vagrancy again, David is sent to a work camp where prisoners want their grievances aired to the press—but it's MacGee who appears. It takes the Hulk to work out the problems. Wr: Nick Corea. Dir: Nick Corea

Blake (Charles Napier); Doc (Julius Harris); Holt (Marc Alaimo); Harris (Charles Picerni); Old convict (John Steadman); Reporter (Linda Lawrence); Guard (David Zellitti); Driver (Cecil Reddick); Farmer (Hank

Underwood); Rader (Robert Davi); Roth (Skip Riley); Sheriff (Brad Dexter).

My Favorite Magician

David becomes a magician's assistant and gets involved in a benefit performance. Wr: Sam Egan. Dir: Reza Badiyi.

Jasper Dowd (Ray Walston); Lily (Joan Leslie); Giancarlo Corleone (Robert Alda); Kimberly (Anne Schedeen); Edgar McGee (Scatman Crothers); Earl (Bob Hastings); Rose Brown (Fritzi Burr); Justice of the peace (Archi Lang); Maurie Brown (Franklin Brown); Ben (Bill Capizzi).

Trivia Alert: Ray Walston starred with Bill Bixby on the series *My Favorite Martian*.

Jake

At a rodeo, David discovers a cowboy performing with an illness that could kill him. Cattle thieves also figure in this story. Highlight: the Hulk wrestles with a charging bull. Wr: Chuck Bowman. Dir: Frank Orsatti.

Jake White (L.Q. Jones); Maggie (Sandra Kerns); Leon White (James Crittenden); Terry (Jesse Vint); Buford (Richard Fullerton); Bob Long (Buck Young); Marvin (Fred Ward).

Behind the Wheel

Hired by a cab company, David helps combat dope smuggling operations that are taking over the company. Wr: Rick Rosenthal, Todd Susman, Andrew Schneider, story by Rick Rosenthal. Dir: Frank Orsatti.

Coleen (Esther Rolle); Michael Swift (Michael Baseleon); Sam Egan (Jon Ceder); Jean (Margie Impert); Eric (John Chandler); Owner (Raymond O'Keefe); Dealer (Jim Staskel); Driver (Ed Reynolds); Calvin (Albert Popwell).

Homecoming

David gets homesick and drifts towards the family home. Although he has no plans to stay, David accidentally bumps into his sister and takes up old antagonisms with his father, whose farm has hit hard times. Wr: Andrew Schneider. Dir: John McPherson.

Helen Banner (Diana Muldaur); D.W. Banner (John Marley); Young David (Reed Diamond); Steve Howston (Guy Boyd); Croft (Drew Snyder); Newscaster (Barbara Lynn Block); Entomologist (Richard Armstrong); Young Helen (Julianna Tutak); Dean Eckart (Regis J. Cordic); Elizabeth Banner (Claire Malis); Teenage David (Steve Burns).

The Snare

A friendly game of chess with a weird millionaire sends David on a hunting trip that traps him in a one-on-one game of survival. Wr: Richard Christian Matheson and Tom Szollosi. Dir: Frank Orsatti.

Michael Sutton (Bradford Dillman); Pilot (Bob Boyd).

Babalao

In New Orleans David helps a doctor get her patients out of the ages of voodoo and superstition. Wr: Craig Buck. Dir: Richard Milton.

Dr. Renee Dubois (Louise Sorel); Luc (Michael Swan);

Celine (Paulene Myers); Louie (Jarrod Johnson); Antonio Moray/Babalao (Bill Henderson); Girl (Morgan Hart); Local (John D. Gowans); Denise (Christine Avila); Ballerina (Patti Jerome).

Captive Night (aka Hostage Night)

David is under the gun when working in a department store because of inventory discrepancies. When thieves break in one night, they hold him and two co-workers hostage. Wr: Sam Egan. Dir: Frank Orsatti.

Karen (Anne Lockhart); Mr. Slater (Mark Lenard); Jim (Paul Picerni); Gary (Stanley Kamel); Raymond (Parley Baer); Cliff Edwards (Dennis Holahan).

Broken Image

David meets his lookalike mobster and finds it an amusing advantage to have a double to thwart the police, a rival gang and newspaper reporter MacGee. Wr: Karen Harris and Jill Sherman. Dir: John McPherson.

Lorraine (Karen Carlson); Teddy (Jed Mills); Steve (John Reilly); Danny (Chris Wallace); Woman with dog (Erica John); Pete (George Caldwell); Larry (Enrique Castillo); Police lieutenant (Donald W. Carter); Police sergeant (Al White); Miriam (Sally Sommer).

Proof Positive (aka Nightmare)

In an episode that's mostly from Jack MacGee's point of view, MacGee's obsession with finding the Hulk costs him his job when a new publisher forbids him to continue the search. He quits and gets back on the trail. Wr: Karen Harris and Jill Sherman. Dir: Dick Harwood.

Muriel (Isabel Cooley); Chuck Schlosser (Wayne Storm); Also with Caroline Smith, Walter Brooke, Charles Thomas Murphy.

Sideshow

A brief romance between David and a woman figures in this tale of terror in a carnival filled with characters, including a pretty mind reader and an avenging madman. Wr: Len Jenkin. Dir: Nicholas Corea.

Nancy (Judith Chapman); Belle Star (Marie Windsor); Benedict (Robert Donner); Luther Mason (Allan Rich); Jimmy (Bruce Wright); Candy (Tam Eliot); Cox (Essex Smith); Cecil (Terence Evans); Beth (Louisa Moritz).

Long Run Home

Hanging out with a motorcycle gang is bad for David, who experiences prejudice and alienation in the middle of a gang war. Wr: Allan Cole and Chris Bunch. Dir: Frank Orsatti.

Carl Rivers (Paul Koslo); Johnny (Robert Tessier); Doc (Mickey Jones); Fitzgerald (Stephen Keep); Bob (Edward Edwards); Ann (Pamela Bryant); Doctor (Albert Popwell); Foreman (Galen Thompson).

Falling Angels

When working with orphans, David discovers they're under the command of a man who teaches them the tricks of the crime trade. His efforts to help the children are hampered by the appearance of Jack

MacGee. Wr: Eric Kaldor, D.K. Krzemien and James Sanford Parker, story by Eric Kaldor and D.K. Krzemien. Dir: Barry Crane.

Rita Montoya (Annette Charles); Don Sipes (Anthony Herrera); Jodie (Deborah Morgan-Weldon); Peter Grant (Timothy O'Hagan); Jeff (William Bronder); Lee (Earl Billings); George (George Dickerson); Mrs. Taylor (Arline Anderson); Tom (Vincent Lucchesi); Society woman (Joan Benedict); Mickey (Cindy Fisher).

The Lottery

One-in-a-million strikes David when he wins a lottery, but he can't pick up his winnings. He sends a friend to do it for him, but that only sets up an elaborate scam. Wr: Allan Cole, Chris Bunch, story by Dan Ullman. Dir: John McPherson.

Harry (Robert Hogan); Hull (Peter Breck); Clark (David McKnight); Announcer (Russell Arms); Steve (Adam Thomas); Guard (Jimmy Hayes); Clark (David McKnight); Man (Jack Denbo); Lover (Peter Bruni); Mugger (Christi Corso); Official (Luis Avalos).

The Psychic

Meeting a psychic endangers David when the psychic talks to MacGee. With her powers she foresees a murder—something the Hulk must prevent. Wr: Karen Harris and Jill Sherman, based on a story by Karen Harris, Jill Sherman and George Bloom. Dir: Barry Crane.

Annie Caplan (Brenda Benet); Manager (Nick Pellegrino); Switchboard girl (Sue Ann Gilfillan); Johnny Wolff (Stephen Fenning); Mrs. Donner (Judy Jean Berns); Robbie Donner (David Anthony); Joe "the Green" grocer (Bert Hinchman); Beat cop (Jason Ross); Doctor (Thomas Hilliard); Woman (Marilyn Allen); Young girl (Andrea Pike).

A Rock and a Hard Place

David is caught between the FBI and a gang planning a big robbery. Both sides are aware of his identity, so he must cooperate with each side to save his life. Wr: Andrew Schneider. Dir: Chuck Bowman

Lucy Cash (Jeanette Nolan); Preston Dekalb (John McIntire); Randolph (Eric Server); Granett Simms (J.J. Saunders); Russky (Robert Gray).

Deathmask

Brutal murders of young women are attributed to David after a victim mutters his name. The true culprit is a demented cop. Wr: Nicholas Corea. Dir: John McPherson.

Frank Rhodes (Gerald McRaney); Joan Singer (Melendy Britt); Mayor (Frank Marth); Miriam Charl (Marla Pennington); J.J. Hendren (Lonny Chapman); Young blond woman (Desiree Kerns); Young man (Kieran Mullaney); Sid Fox (Michael Bond); Man (Don Marshall); Dale Jenks (Dennis Bowen); Newsman (Robert Lunny).

Equinox (aka Masquerade)

During a masquerade party, David comes face to face with MacGee, who continues to try to capture the creature. Wr: Andrew Schneider. Dir: Patrick Boyriven.

Diane (Christine DeLisle); Allan Grable (Paul Carr); Donald (Henry Polic III); Pierce (Louis Turenne); Inquisitor (Kathie Spencer-Neff); Also with Danny Dayton.

Nine Hours

To save the lives of a kidnapped child and a reformed crime figure, David helps an alcoholic police officer. Wr: Nicholas Corea. Dir: Nicholas Corea.

Joe Franco (Marc Alaimo); Rhonda (Sheila Larken); Nurse Grasso (Doris Dowling); Timmy (David Comfort); Sam Monte (Frank De Kova); Fats (Phil Rubinstein); Slick Monte (Sam Ingraffia); Timmy Wilkes (David Comfort); Capt. Deeter (Hal Bokar); Guard (Dennis Haysbert); Danny (John Medici).

On the Line

Assisting in putting out a forest fire is doubly dangerous for David when MacGee shows up. Trapped with a female firefighter, the Hulk emerges to save her and his alter-ego. Wr: Karen Harris and Jill Sherman. Dir: L.Q. Jones.

Weaver (Bruce Fairbairn); Randy (Kathleen Lloyd); Wilson (Don Reid); Bennett (Peter Jason); Mackie (Joseph di Reda); Reporter (Tony Duke).

Season 4: 1980-81

Prometheus, Part 1

A mysterious meteor's radiation stops David's transformations halfway. The military believes he is an alien and captures him. They take him to a underground complex known as Prometheus. Wr: Ken Johnson. Dir: Ken Johnson.

Katie Maxwell (Laurie Prange); ; Captain Welsh (Roger Robinson); Col. Harry Appling (John O'Connell); Sergeant (Stack Pierce); Lieutenant (Jill Choder); Pilot (Chip Johnson); Storekeeper (Lew Palter); Also with Ric Dresin.

Prometheus, Part 2

David tries to find a way to escape from military brass who believe that he's an alien creature. Wr: Ken Johnson. Dir: Ken Johnson.

Katie Maxwell (Laurie Prange); Charlena McGowan (Carol Baxter); Colonel (Monte Markham); Dr. John Zeiterman (Whit Bissell); Jason Spath (Arthur Rosenberg); Corporal (John Papais); Young man (Steve Bond).

Freefall

David gets in between a skydiver and the son of a corrupt politician. Wr: Chris Bunch and Allan Cole. Dir: Reza Badiyi.

Jean Combs (Kelly Harmon); Hank Lynch (Sam Groom); Jack Stewart (Jared Martin); Woody Turner (Michael Swan); Max Stewart (Sandy Ward); Ike (Ted Markland); Mead (Erik Holland); Fowler (John Zenda); Hughes (George Brenlin).

Dark Side

Using drugs to further alter his body chemistry creates more negative effects for David. His "evil" nature grows and extends to the Hulk, who is now more than ever capable of murder. Wr: Nick Corea. Dir: John McPherson.

Mike Schulte (Bill Lucking); Lori Schulte (Philece Sampler); Ellen Schulte (Rosemary Forsyth); Jimmy Ellison (Jonathon Perpich); Butcher (Nick Cinardo); Huntress (Marilia); Judy (Lisa Carole); Cynthia Farber (Taafe O'Connell).

Deep Shock
An electrical shock gives David the ability to see future disasters created by the Hulk, events he must prevent from happening. Wr: Ruel Fischmann. Dir: Reza Badiyi

Edgar Tucker (Tom Clancy); Dr. Louise Olsen (Sharon Acker); Frank (Ed Power, Stefan Gierasch); Walt (Bob Hackman); 1st security officer (M.P. Murphy); Nurse (Helen Boll); Receptionist (Harriet Matthey); Reporter (Saundra Sharp); 2nd security officer (Charles Hoyes); Foreman (Robert Alan Browne).

Bring Me the Head of the Hulk
A mercenary finds a way of bringing the Hulk out from hiding to destroy him. Wr: Alan Cole and Chris Bunch. Dir: Bill Bixby.

Alex (Sandy McPeak); La Fronte (Jed Mills); Dr. June Cabot (Jane Merrow); Mark Roberts (Walter Brooke); Pauline (Barbara Lynn Block); Neil Hines (Laurence Haddon); Ludin (Murray MacLeod).

Fast Lane
David doesn't know it, but the car he's driving contains a suitcase filled with money. Gangsters and fortune seekers are all after it. Wr: Reuben Leder. Dir: Frank Orsatti.

Joe (Robert F. Lyons); Callahan (Dick O'Neil); Nancy (Victoria Carroll); Leo (Lee deBroux); Danny (Frank Doubleday); Clyde (Alex Rebar); Mechanic (John Finn); Clint (Ben Jeffrey).

Goodbye, Eddie Cain
David meets forties-style, hard-boiled detective Eddie Cain. It's a story that involves murder, passion and profit. Wr: Nick Corea. Dir: Jack Colvin.

Eddie Cain (Cameron Mitchell); Victoria Lang (Jennifer Holmes); Dante Romero (Anthony Caruso); Mac (Gordon Connell); Sheehan (Thomas MacGreevy); Sheldon (Roscoe Born); Norma Crespi Lang (Donna Marshall); Jack Lewis (Ray Laska); Mrs. Stauros (Virgina Hahn).

Memory Flash—Cameron Mitchell: "A good script. It was well written. Scripts aren't [always] that good. It was more outside of the show itself. It was that kind of script, you know? That script would have stood up even without the green monster."

Mitchell enjoyed "the way we did the narration. The narration really made it. It was my voice about [Eddie Cain's] life."

King of the Beach
Lou Ferrigno plays Carl, a bodybuilder-restaurateur in this offbeat story. David makes sure his friend Carl isn't manipulated by a girlfriend into a bodybuilding competition just to get money he needs. But competition managers quickly come in with

blackmail so he won't win. Wr: Karen Harris. Dir: Barry Crane.

Carl Molino (Lou Ferrigno); Mandy (Leslie Ackerman); Sol Diamond (Charlie Brill); Rudy (George Caldwell); Annette (Carol Swarbrick); Trainer (Leo DeLyon); Steve (James Emery); The Lady (Nora Boland); Little girl (Angela Lee); King (Ken Waller); King's girlfriend (Kimberly Johnson).

Wax Museum
The owner of the wax museum where David is working is slowly going insane—since her father died in a fire she believes she caused. Wr: Carol Baxter. Dir: Dick Harwood.

Leigh Bamble (Christine Belford); Walter Gamble (Max Showalter); Kelleher (Ben Hammer); Andy (Kiki Castillo); Woman (Natalie Master); News vendor (Michael Horsley).

East Winds
Policemen and gangsters converge on David's apartment because his bathtub is made of solid gold. Wr: Jill Sherman. Dir: Jack Colvin.

Sgt. Jack Keeler (William Windom); Kam Chong (Richard Loo); Tam (Irene Yah Ling Sun); The lieutenant (Del Monroe); Officer Bill Menning (Tony Mumolo); Landlady (Beulah Quo).

The First Part, Parts 1 and 2
David investigates a small, quiet town where rumors abound of another Hulk-like creature that once terrorized the countryside. In Part 2 he must confront Frye's creature and search for an antidote for his affliction. Wr: Andrew Schneider. Dir: Frank Orsatti.

Dell Frye (Harry Townes); Sheriff Carl Decker (Billy Green Bush); Elizabeth Collins (Lola Albright); Willie (Jack Magee); Case (Bill Beyers); Frye's Creature (Dick Durock); Linda (Kari Michaelson); Cheryl (Julie Marine); Janitor (Hank Rolike).

The Harder They Fall
David, crippled after an accident, meets a bitter young paraplegic who can't cope with his disability. At the same time, David considers reviving the Hulk in order to regain the use of his legs. Wr: Nancy Faulkner. Dir: Mike Vejar.

Paul (Denny Miller); Dr. Hart (Peter Hobbs); Judy (Diane Shalet); Al (Joe Dorsey); Bartender (Ralph Strait).

Interview with the Hulk
A colleague of MacGee manages to get an interview with David Banner. Wr: Alan Cassidy. Dir: Patrick Boyriven.

Emerson Fletcher (Michael Conrad); Stella Verdugo (Jan Sterling); Mark Roberts (Walter Brooke).

Half Nelson
A midget wrestler has trouble adjusting to the world of normal-sized people around him. Wr: Andrew Schneider. Dir: Barry Crane.

Buster Caldwell (Tommy Madden); Marsha (Sandy Dryfoos); Gregor Potemkin (H.B. Haggerty); Mitzi (Elaine Joyce); Channing (Paul Henry Itkin); Kelly (David Himes).

Danny
Farm machinery thieves give David a hard time. Wr:
Diane Frolov. Dir: Mark A. Burley.
　　Nat (Don Stroud); Rachel (Robin Dearden); Ben
(Bruce Wright); Red (Taylor Lacher); Hugh (Art LaFleur).

Patterns
Loan sharks are after David when his boss at a cloth-
ing manufacturing plant makes him a partner. Wr:
Reuben Leder. Dir: Nick Hazinga.
　　Sam (Eddie Barth); Liz (Laurie Heineman); Malamud
(Paul Marin); Sonny (Robert O'Reilly); Solly (Joshua
Shelley); Marvin (Larry Marko); Gladys (Thelma Pelish).

Season 5: 1981-82

The Phenom
David and the Hulk help out a baseball pitcher. Wr:
Reuben Leder. Dir: Bernard McEveety.
　　Cyrus (Dick O'Neil); Audrey (Anne Lockhart); Devlin
(Robert Donnor); Joe Dunning (Brett Cullin); Charley
Sepikis (Ken Swofford).

Two Godmothers
Three escaped women prisoners, one of whom is
pregnant, hold David prisoner. Wr: Reuben Leder.
Dir: Mike Vejar.
　　Freida Hackett (Kathleen Nolan); Barbara (Suzanne
Charny); Sondra (Sandra Kerns); Mary Grubb (Gloria
Gifford); Lannie (Penny Peyser); Phil Giles (John Stead-
man); Matron (Gay Hagen).

Veteran
David tries to stop the murder of a Vietnam war
hero. Wr: Nick Corea and Reuben Leder. Dir: Mike
Vejar.
　　Doug Hewitt (Paul Koslo); Harrison Cole (Bruce
Gray); Lisa Morgan (Wendy Gerard); R. Harnell (William
Boyett); Frank Rivera (Richard Yniguez); Arthur Hewitt
(David White); Howard Miller (Alexander Zale); Jr. cham-
ber of commerce emcee (Michael Boyle); Jimmy the Kid
(Barrett Oliver); Viet interpreter (James Saito); Vietnamese
(Jerry Loo); Cosgrove (Wayne Grace).

Sanctuary
As a clergyman, David befriends an immigrant. Wr:
Deborah Davis. Dir: Chuck Bowman.
　　Patrero (Henry Darrow); Sister Anita (Diana
Muldaur); Rudy (Fausto Barajas); Roberto (Guillermo San
Juan); Sister Mary Catherine (Edie McClurg); Father Costa
(Michael Santiago); Father Young (Paul Tuerpe); Franco
(Bert Santos); Sister Rebecca (Barbara Beaman); Truck
driver (Rick Garcia); Sheriff (Jerry Hardin).

Triangle
A love triangle develops between David, a woman
and a ruthless land baron. Wr: Andrew Schneider.
Dir: Mike Vejar.
　　Ellis Gale Weber (Andrea Marcovicci); Jordan (Peter
Mark Richman); George Rothman (Mickey Jones); Bert
(Charles Napier); Lyle (Jerry Sloan); Foreman (Bill Cross);
Detective (John H. Fields); Guard (Don Maxwell); Land-

lady (Eve McVeagh); Librarian (Georgia Schmidt); Servant
(Christine A. Hayden); Les Creaseman (Lewis Arquette).

Slaves
David Banner meets a hostile black man who is
determined to make him his slave. Wr: Jeri Taylor.
Dir: John Liberti.
　　Isaac Whittier Ross (John Hancock); Christy (Faye
Grant); Roy Darnell (Charles Tyner).

　　Memory Flash—director and producer Chuck
Bowman: "Jeri Taylor [now one of the producers of
Star Trek—The Next Generation] showed some real
wonderful talent for writing. She gave me a spec
script she had written, a prison story. I was somewhat reluctant to get started.... I anticipated it to be
just an awful thing because it was coming from a
woman who I knew to be a gentle human being.
But, my goodness, it had bite! It had drama! It had
a wonderful structure. I went to Kenny and said,
'Here's someone to look at. She's going to be a
terrific writer.' He called her in and gave her what I
believe was her first writing assignment."

A Minor Problem
A bacterial germ endangers David in a deserted
town. Wr: Diane Frolov. Dir: Mike Preece.
　　Cunningham (Linden Chiles); Patty (Nancy Grahn);
Rita (Lisa Jane Persky); Tom (Xander Berkeley); Mark
(John Walter Davis); Jordan (Brad Harris); Sperling (Gary
Vinson).

Reunion TV-movies

The Incredible Hulk Returns (1988)
When Banner infiltrates a research laboratory to
gain access to a gamma ray machine, an old stu-
dent, Donald Blake, approaches him with the dis-
covery of an ages-old hammer that conjures the
Mighty Thor. Pilot for an unsold series. Wr:
Nicholas Corea. Dir: Nicholas Corea.
　　Dr. Maggie Shaw (Lee Purcell); Mike (Charles Napier);
Josh Lambert (John Gabriel); Zachery Lambert (Jay Baker);
Jack LeBeau (Tim Thomerson); Thor (Eric Kramer);
Donald Blake (Steve Levitt); Jack MacGee (Jack Colvin);
Police sergeant (William Riley); Police lieutenant (Tom
Finnegan); Mr. Elwood (Donald Willis); Bonner (Carl
Nick Ciafalio); Security guard (Bobby Travis McLaughlin);
Reporter #1 (Nick Costa); Reporter #2 (Peisha McPhee);
Also with William Malone, Joanie Allen, Burke Denis.

Trial of the Incredible Hulk (1989)
Banner is jailed for kidnapping a woman. He meets
up with Matt Murdock, who is secretly a crime-
fighter named Daredevil. His obsession is to bring
down the kingpin of crime, Wilson Fisk. Pilot for an
unsold series. Wr: Gerald DiPego. Dir: Bill Bixby.
　　Matt Murdock/Daredevil (Rex Smith); Wilson Fisk
(John Rhys-Davies); Ellie Mendez (Marta DuBois);
Tendelli (Joseph Mascolo); Christi Klein (Nancy Everhard);
Al Pettiman (Richard Cummings, Jr.); Edgar (Nicholas

Hormann); Danny (John Novak); Nurse (Linda Darlow); John (Dwight Koss); Farmwoman (Meredith Woodward); Turk (Mark Acheson); Landlord (Richard Newman); Judge (Don MacKay); Prosecutor (Doug Abrahams); Jay (Mitchell Kosterman); Loma (Beatrice Zeilinger); Guest #1 (Ken Camroux); Orderly (Charles Andre); Large farmhand (John Bear Curtis).

Death of the Incredible Hulk (1990)

Posing as a janitor, Banner secretly assists a colleague in research similar to the experiments that led to his gamma ray nightmare. But when David is caught, Dr. Pratt helps him explore solutions to exorcise the Hulk forever. Meanwhile, Jasmin, an agent for a terrorist group, wants Pratt's research to assemble the perfect soldier. Wr: Gerald DiPego. Dir: Bill Bixby.

Jasmin (Elizabeth Gracen); Dr. Ronald Pratt (Philip Sterling); Amy Pratt (Barbara Tarbuck); Kasha (Andreas Katsulas); Bella (Anna Katerina); Zed (John Novak); Betty (Chilton Crane); Bank Teller (Carla Ferrigno); Tom (Duncan Fraser); Brenn (Dwight McFee); Crane (Lindsay Bourne); Pauley (Mina E. Mina); Luanna Cole (Marlane O'Brien); Shoup (Garwin Sanford); Dodger (Justin DiPego); Aaron Colmer (Fred Henderson); Carsino (Judith Maxie); George Tilmer (French Tickner).

The Invaders

January 1967–September 1968

Architect David Vincent witnesses the landing of a craft from another galaxy. He learns that alien beings from a dying planet have taken human form to take over the Earth. Vincent wages a one-man battle against the aliens and tries to alert the authorities to their presence before their invasion is complete. In the second year, Vincent is joined by industrialist Edgar Scoville, who helps David in his battle.

Cast: David Vincent (Roy Thinnes); Edgar Scoville (last 13 episodes) (Kent Smith); Narrator (William Woodson); Main Title Announcer (Hank Sims)

Created by: Larry Cohen; *Producer:* Alan A. Armer; *Associate Producers:* Anthony Spinner (year 1), David W. Rintels (year 2); *Executive Producer:* Quinn Martin; *Music Theme:* Dominic Frontiere; ABC/A Quinn Martin Production; 60 minutes.

The invaders were extremely treacherous because they could look like anyone—a bus driver, a paper boy, a secretary or a little old lady. They could smile, they dressed well and they were polite. They were also here to rob Earth of its future. Their mission was one of desperation: With their planet dying, they needed a new world. Architect David Vincent knew they were here and devoted his life to exposing the invaders. He was tireless in his efforts to try to convince "a disbelieving world that the nightmare has already begun."

The Invaders was first conceived by creator Larry Cohen as a half-hour, twice-weekly serial. (*Peyton Place* had worked for ABC in this format.) Ultimately, however, the network went with the more conventional one-hour format.

Originally, the aliens were supposed to get their orders from an eyeball that opened and closed in the palms of their hands. The network rejected the idea as too scary. The aliens ended up with a variety of other idiosyncrasies. They didn't have blood or heartbeats; some aliens had pointed little fingers; they didn't display emotion because they had none; and since their "human" disguises required periodic regeneration, they occasionally glowed before losing their earthly forms. Three episodes, "Genesis," "The Enemy" and "The Prophet," gave viewers a hint of what the aliens looked like in their native forms. When killed, the aliens glowed and vanished, which proved frustrating for David Vincent since the only evidence left was an outline of ash. The aliens were also experts at covering their tracks. Whenever Vincent found an alien outpost housed in an abandoned warehouse or town, the evidence was gone by the time the authorities got there. The aliens also had an impressive technology: They all carried glowing discs that, if applied to a human being's neck, caused instant death. Some aliens also carried disintegration guns that could melt cars like butter.

Although the special effects in the series were often excellent, the producers limited the visual tricks to add to the show's realism. "This is a strange series," admitted producer Alan Armer to the *New York Times* in 1967. "We combine science fiction with reality. People like to be scared out of their wits but they're no longer frightened by three-headed monsters. So we've made the invaders look like the folks next

Technicians construct a flying saucer for a scene in *The Invaders*.

door. ... We're after fear, not brutality and violence."

Today Armer says, "It was an intriguing, workable concept that should have been better than it was. We began with an exciting pilot and it was marvelous. The pilot was originally 75 minutes long, and we had to cut it by 20 minutes. It had believability, color, genuine fear and enormous excitement. My William Morris agent called and declared it to be the finest pilot he had ever seen."

Armer was forced to cut it down. "We eliminated footage slowly, trying to preserve the pilot's strengths. But cutting those 20 minutes forced us to mutilate our baby. We ended up with all of the peaks and none of the valleys. We lost a lot of richness and reality. [It had] excitement, but not the texture that makes the excitement believable. Although we produced a dozen solid shows for *The Invaders,* we never captured the suspense and believability of the first, overlong pilot film."

The Invaders was a hit for ABC, and the series held its top 20 status for its first few months. Caught off guard by the show's popularity, executives at CBS and NBC tried to hide their dismay by plastering bumper stickers on their cars that read, "*The Invaders* Are Coming." The show also became a hip topic at Hollywood dinner parties. Even critic Rex Reed, who had groused over the show's violence, admitted, "This show threatens to over-throw the *Batman* craze."

The series was immediately renewed for a second year, but the producers realized that the tricky format was beginning to have a corrosive effect on its viewers. Audiences found David's struggle to expose the aliens frustrating. In the last episode of the first season, "The Condemned," the producers tried to remedy this by giving David a major triumph: exposing all of the important alien leaders on Earth. Associate producer Anthony Spinner recalls that they also tried to keep David Vincent alive week after week. "The question all of the writers used to ask was, 'Why don't the aliens just kill the son of a bitch?' Getting around that question was always a challenge. We came up with a nebulous theory that, 'Oh, if they kill Vincent, it'll bring too much attention.' Often, when a writer asked, 'Why don't the aliens kill him?' we'd say, 'Because, they don't!' That was not a great answer."

Spinner tried to deal with the question in

one of his own scripts, "The Experiment." "Rather than kill him, I had the aliens try to brainwash him. This way he was valuable to them. But you couldn't do that every week. Actually, a lot of the episodes did work dramatically, but you put them all together, you go, 'Oh, yeah—more of the same.'" Spinner left the series at the end of its first year, cordially telling Quinn Martin that the highly rated series was doomed.

"*The Invaders* was an ambitious undertaking with little time or money," says art director George Chan, who was called in during the series' frenetic first year. "When I arrived, the production unit was in total disarray." Chan adds, "I was not prepared for this kind of operation. There was little time for research, and it took many weeks for me to become comfortable with *The Invaders*. The network was only thinking of rushing production and financial gains. Storylines and sets were of minor importance to them.

"There were also numerous artistic and creative differences that were never solved. I kept questioning why David Vincent, who had no means of income, always wore expensive clothing. Quinn Martin placated me by adding the Edgar Scoville character in the second year to show some financial responsibility."

Series production settled down as Chan and art director James Vance took turns working on every other episode. Even so, "It was, because of the special effects and gadgets, the most challenging work of my career up to that time," says Chan.

Some viewers were downright hostile to the show because aliens were being portrayed as evil. Armer tried to present the aliens as realistically as possible. "The aliens' motives were inconsistent," he admits. "Occasionally, the aliens were shown with understandable motives. They were fleeing from a dying world and striving to take over ours. One script by David Rintels even portrayed them as the good guys and us as the bad guys ["The Peacemaker"]. We had to make the aliens both frightening and powerful since we were selling paranoia. But inevitably, the aliens degenerated into despicable, comic strip monsters. I suspect our problem lay not in the alien characterizations, but in our revealing too much of them. Things unseen are far scarier than the things we can examine. Suggest rather than show."

One hint of the aliens' nature was, according to Armer, in the closing moments of the pilot. "The final shot of Diane Baker [as an alien] implied that beneath the alien mask might lie the face of an emotional, dimensional being."

The series propelled Armer and star Roy Thinnes into the real-life world of UFO buffs. Thinnes and his wife, actress Lynn Loring, claimed to have seen a UFO a week before *The Invaders* premiered. Thinnes played down the incident, saying, "I didn't want to look like a self-serving actor out for publicity." The actor was intrigued by the show's premise. "I liked the simple dramatic structure of one man's paranoia," he says. "I think we all share that kind of paranoia. Is the government telling us the truth? Does the government want to hear the truth? That thread carried through all of the shows. Larry Cohen had a good idea, and the series was masterfully produced by Quinn Martin. He hired a lot of good writers, like Alan Armer, Anthony Spinner and David Rintels."

The Quinn Martin production offices often received phone calls from people claiming to have seen aliens from other worlds. "I was astonished at the number of credible witnesses to UFO sightings," says Armer. "These were not little old ladies in tennis shoes. These were responsible, intelligent individuals whose stories were generally believable. At the time, I was invited to do an interview with a Colorado radio station. There had been a burned circle in a hayfield and a dead, skinned horse nearby. UFOs had been sighted in the area. Personally, I was skeptical, but there is evidence that can't be shrugged away."

Production manager Howard Alston's job was to keep *The Invaders* on budget and handle many aspects of production. "Our biggest challenge was to manufacture this alien culture, but everything we dreamed up—a gun, a costume, a spaceship—always looked like something we had seen before."

One of the most eye-catching effects, the "flaming out" of dying aliens, was a painstaking process. "The immolation effect was a new technique at the time, and it drove the directors nuts," says Alston. "Setting up the incineration effects took valuable time out of their shooting schedules. It required an advisor from the Howard Anderson optical company to be on location and to ensure all of the elements were present to add in the optical effect later." Another time-consuming effect was the aliens' flying saucers. Although the saucer looked like a full scale mock-up, the effect was a bit of technical trickery. "There was never a mock-up," recalls actor and extra Randy Crawford. "The saucer only consisted of landing pads and a drop-stairway. The middle and top half of the saucer were always superimposed."

Alston recalls that transporting the spaceship's lower half proved challenging. "Moving the spaceship around to desert locations was an involved and costly process. The location had to be scouted and the saucer had to be set up in advance. We tried to figure out ways to avoid having the saucer land on location!"

Crawford, who had served as a double for Roy Thinnes in his previous series, *The Long Hot Summer* (1965-66), was invited by Thinnes to work on *The Invaders.* "Roy was a warm and friendly person," says Crawford. "I was in almost every episode as either an alien or a double for Roy. I was also one of the aliens in the spaceship [in the main title sequence], and I'm the guy driving Roy Thinnes' car in the opening credits."

Crawford has scattered memories of the series. "In the pilot, the aliens were portrayed as having special powers in their eyes. Contact lenses were used on actor Skip Ward in his fight with Roy Thinnes. The contacts were never used again because they were too complicated to fit every actor. Although the series had regular sets at Goldwyn studios, we filmed a lot of episodes on location in Los Angeles, Santa Monica and the Mojave Desert. Dumping water on each other was a favorite pastime in the heat of the desert. We averaged a 12-hour day but we occasionally extended to 16. My fondest memory is going into stores and having kids recognize me as an alien. They would point their finger at me and go ZAP! They remembered me as the alien who didn't bleed ["The Ivy Curtain"]."

For Roy Thinnes, *The Invaders* was a big break early in his career. His 1963-65 stint on daytime's *General Hospital* led to his popular co-starring role in NBC's *The Long Hot Summer.* On *The Invaders,* Thinnes projected David Vincent with a quiet, dignified strength. The character was obsessed with saving his disbelieving world from the invaders. Vincent knew it would take enormous determination and strength for one man to make a difference against such overwhelming odds.

"Roy Thinnes was well cast," says director Robert Butler. "He was a concentrated and riveted guy. That made for a good, strong, heroic characterization."

"Roy Thinnes was a fine actor, but not the vulnerable, compassionate figure that, for instance, David Janssen was in *The Fugitive,*" says Alan Armer. "Roy sometimes played the role with a sullen quality, as if resentful of the world. That was an attitude unlikely to win the hearts of view-

A friendly alien (Barry Morse, left) needs the help of David Vincent (Roy Thinnes) to help stop the invasion in "The Life Seekers." Copyright 1968 ABC/Worldvision.

ers. To his credit, Roy accepted the protagonist's beliefs as his own. He attended UFO meetings and listened attentively to stories from witnesses."

"Roy may have been enthusiastic about the series, but he wasn't close to the production crew," recalls Howard Alston. "We had very little personal relationship with him even though he was on the set every day. In other Quinn Martin productions, the lead performers—Efrem Zimbalist, Jr., William Conrad, Karl Malden, David Janssen, Buddy Ebsen—were all wonderful team players. Roy was not."

"Quinn Martin had a good sense of casting," says writer Robert Collins, "and Roy Thinnes was very good in the role. He had a subtle sense of humor. He was a terrific series lead."

As *The Invaders* headed into its second year, there were efforts to steer the show in a different direction. The series had faded from a top 20 hit to a top 40 contender. Research showed that the first season had done something no one had counted on: It had literally scared older viewers away. "The show was popular with audiences under the age of 21," says Armer. "It did fairly well with audiences between 21 and 35. It died with audiences over 50. Older audiences didn't have enough acceptance of science fiction."

In the series' first year, the aliens often

hatched a sinister plot-of-the-week that bordered on the fantastic: carnivorous insects, alien moon-bases, killer hurricanes and oxygen-depleting crystals. The second year grounded the alien threat in more realistic terms. Drama was often emphasized over science fiction. The aliens tried manipulating humanity through religion, racial strife and the threat of a nuclear war. In addition, the series used current political and social issues as background material. During the second year, stories touched upon the Vietnam War, drug abuse and the Cold War. In one episode, "The Trial," the sexual relationship between a human woman and her alien husband is revealed. Many episodes benefited from this mature approach. Other segments, robbed of their imaginative science fiction value, slipped into a dreary routine that made even the most dedicated fan restless.

"David Rintels [the associate producer for the second year] had a lot of input," recalls Robert Collins. "He's a very socially responsible person with great cares and concerns. He's one of the most socially and politically aware writers in town. You can credit Rintels for examining some of those issues on *The Invaders*."

Rintels, an Emmy award–winning writer who wrote such TV films as *Fear on Trial* (1975) and *Washington: Behind Closed Doors* (1977), recalls, "I had never written or even read science fiction before *The Invaders*. The series gave me a chance to work on something that related to contemporary themes. It was something television didn't do enough of at the time. Using the series format, I could write about things I cared about.

"*The Invaders* script I was happiest with was called "The Peacemaker" [in which Vincent convinces a U.S. general that the invasion is taking place]. I wrote it as a deliberate allusion to our Vietnam involvement. The theme examined to what lengths the military should go in dealing with a threat, and indeed, whether there were any limitations."

For Robert Collins, *The Invaders* proved to be an important beachhead in his career. "I sold my first script to them," he says. "I was a film editor on the *Tarzan* series. We were working seven days a week, 16 hours a day for months to meet airdates. One morning at three a.m., I was sitting at the Moviola watching Tarzan swing from tree to tree, and I turned it off. I called a producer friend of mine and said, 'I'm really tired of watching this guy swing from tree to tree. I know I can write, certainly better than the people writing for *Tarzan*. How can I get into writing?'

"He said, 'Pick your favorite TV show and write the best script you possibly can. Submit it to them on spec.' I chose *The Invaders* because I watched it every week. It had tension, mystery and it was intriguing and unpredictable. It was a terrific show. I had always been a fan of *Twilight Zone* and particularly *The Outer Limits*. *The Invaders* had that same kind of mystery and suspense, and a fair attention to character development. It had all of the qualities of a good television series."

Collins submitted his script to the series. "They didn't buy it because of the subject matter. At the time, Ronald Reagan was governor of California. In my script, he turned out to be one of the invaders. I didn't use his name, of course. It was about a state governor and while he's making his inaugural address, his little finger is sticking out. The producers liked my work, and I was invited by David Rintels to write a treatment for "The Ransom" [in which Vincent holds an alien leader captive]. David said, 'I'm going to go to bat for you. If they're afraid of a first-time writer, I'll rewrite it for you.' So David really was my mentor, and we later became good friends."

Collins turned in "The Ransom," recalling, "Since this was my entry into television, I worked as hard as I could to make it the best script possible. After they accepted it, I quit my job at *Tarzan*. I became a full-time writer and never looked back."

The writer feels the aliens on *The Invaders* were excellently conceived. "The fact that they looked just like us attracted me to the show. I never liked monsters. That's one of the reasons I didn't like *Star Trek*. The monsters were silly to me. But on *The Invaders*, the idea of a monster looking like everybody else was frightening. At that time, the aliens were a metaphor. Beings from other worlds would either save the world or destroy it. The threat of the Cold War was dramatically unsatisfying. As a people, we had become more sophisticated by the late 1960s. The Russians weren't enemies. You couldn't say they were terrible people who were gonna destroy us all. Aliens, on the other hand, were an acceptable enemy."

The Invaders went into its second season with mediocre ratings. To help elevate audiences' frustration with Vincent's lonely crusade, electronics expert Edgar Scoville (played by Kent Smith) was brought in as Vincent's ally. With Scoville's contacts and electronics empire, David made impressive gains against the invaders. In

"Counterattack," David videotapes the incinerations of two aliens; "The Miracle" ends with Vincent driving off to Washington, D.C., with an alien crystal as proof; in "The Pursued," six members of Congress see an invader incinerate in a hallway.

Yet the creative thorns in the side of the series weren't easily extracted. Edgar Scoville turned out to be a dull paternal figure for Vincent. Although well portrayed by Kent Smith, his underdeveloped character remained murky.

Vincent himself underwent changes. In the first year he was brash and independent, but also vulnerable as he criss-crossed the country in search of aliens. Toward the end of year two, Vincent was transformed into something of a space-age urban guerilla. His battles no longer took place in rural American towns. He spent most of his investigations in major cities, and with his suit and tie, he looked like a dour businessman.

ABC moved the series from its struggling 8:30 p.m. Tuesday slot and put it in a Tuesday 10 p.m. slot in January. *TV Guide* was inundated with letters from younger fans protesting the late time slot. Shortly afterward, the series was canceled.

Despite the changes, Howard Alston feels *The Invaders* was not set for a long run. "The series generated a great deal of interest at first, but it lost its honesty when so many people, week after week, didn't believe David's invasion story. The ratings were marginal when it was canceled. I suppose it was destined to be a short-lived series based on one fact alone: The aliens had the ability to kill David every week, but they were too dumb to do so."

Alston felt the addition of the believers was a good idea, but notes, "The idea wasn't conceived in time. It could have prolonged the show, but the network didn't give it enough of a chance to develop."

"There was always a sense of frustration at the end of many episodes," says David Rintels. "Roy Thinnes and company achieved at best a stalemate or a short-term victory against the bad guys. You knew the aliens were certain to be back in force next week. That may have been a factor in the show's cancelation. TV ordinarily ends with definitive resolutions and, almost invariably, happy endings. The format of *The Invaders* may not have allowed that."

"What could have been a quality series ended up, alas, getting a little silly," says Alan Armer. "The network panicked and badgered us to take some other directions when the audience didn't respond positively. Another factor was that Quinn Martin and his assistant, Adrian Samish, really didn't understand the concept. Quinn was totally honest about it. He stated from the beginning that this type of series wasn't his bag. He was far more comfortable in the police genre."

"The show simply didn't attract audiences over 35," continues Armer. "Older folk demanded, I guess, more traditional fare. We told ourselves that the series was ahead of its time. That may or may not be true."

The Invaders went into syndication in 1969. Its 75-minute pilot was aired at the Museum of Modern Art that same year. There have also been flickers of a revival. In Quinn Martin's 1977 suspense series *Tales of the Unexpected, The Invaders'* pilot film was loosely remade as "The Nomads." David Birney played a man who tries to convince authorities that aliens have landed.

In 1980, Quinn Martin made the telefilm *The Aliens Are Coming*. It was an unsuccessful pilot starring Tom Mason and Melinda Fee.

In 1985, in response to popular demand, episodes of *The Invaders* began airing in England. The same year, Roy Thinnes sold an *Invaders* project to ABC. "We had a commitment for a three-hour pilot and six one-hour episodes," says Thinnes, who would have produced the series. The deal fell through, but he's still interested in seeing a resolution to the series. Thinnes reprised his role in Fox TV's *Invaders* movie (1995), but it ended with the aliens still among us.

The actor didn't fully approve of the aliens' hostile nature in the original series. He remarked to *Science Fantasy Film Classics* magazine in the 1970s, "The producers abandoned any concept which depicted planetary integration in favor of an old SF formula depicting aliens as plunderers and conquerors."

Today the actor says, "It wasn't so much that I disliked the aliens being hostile, [but] if human nature is so violent and our nature is to conquer, why should that also be the aliens' nature? Certainly if the aliens had the technology to reach our planet, they had the technology to conquer it."

The actor proposes that David Vincent could have been more of a mediator between his race and alien visitors. "That sort of storyline could have been sustained just as easily as the format we went with," says Thinnes. "One idea would be to do a satire on mankind. The aliens who arrive here are on a quest for benevolence. The humans' resistance to superior, benevolent beings would provide the real drama. For example, say the aliens brought a cure for cancer. Before the cure could be defined, the military complex would probably blast them out of the skies."

According to Thinnes, *The Invaders* is regarded as a cult show in France. "It's a huge smash there," he says. "They celebrated the show's twenty-fifth anniversary with screenings of the episodes in the oldest movie house in Paris." The actor found himself literally mobbed by the fans. "The turnout was as if the Beatles had arrived. It was incredible. The first time I went to Paris [1989], I was being driven from the airport in a limousine, and two reporters in the limo kept asking me all of these questions about the show. They wanted to know about the love story with Suzanne Pleshette [in the "Mutation" episode] and if I believed in extra-terrestrials. I said, 'Please—can we wait until we get to Paris? I'm trying to see the Eiffel Tower!' I go to Paris about twice a year as their guest, and I'm treated like royalty. It's as if *The Invaders* is happening all over again. It has an incredible following."

"Perhaps we should do a two-hour movie, *Return of the Invaders*," muses Howard Alston. "It would be kind of fun. The aliens finally killed David, and this could be about his son."

"I would like to see the series revived," says Armer, who still receives mail from *Invaders* fans. "It's heartening to know that people still remember the series. Audiences weren't turned on by such a far-out concept then, but they might well watch such a series today."

CAST NOTES

Roy Thinnes (David Vincent): Born 1938. Thinnes played the co-pilot blown out of the 747 in *Airport 1975*. He also starred in several TV movies including *The Norliss Tapes* (1973). In 1990, he played Rev. Trask in the new *Dark Shadows* series. Two years later he joined the daytime series *One Life to Live*.

Kent Smith (Edgar Scoville): Born 1907. As a leading man during the 1940s, Smith starred in the cult film *The Cat People* (1942). By the 1960s, he was working consistently as a durable supporting actor. He died in 1985.

EPISODE GUIDE

Season 1: 1967

Beach Head
Marked for death by the aliens after seeing a landing saucer, David Vincent seeks help from a young widow. He discovers an alien outpost in a hydroelectric plant and tries to alert the authorities. Wr: Anthony Wilson. Dir: Joseph Sargent.

Kathy Adams (Diane Baker); Sheriff Ben Holman (J. D. Cannon); Alan Landers (James Daly); Lou Carver (John Milford); Aunt Sarah (Ellen Corby); John Brandon (James "Skip" Ward); Mrs. Brandon (Bonnie Beecher); Kemper (Vaughn Taylor); Nurse (Mary Jackson); Dennis (Dennis Cross); Secretary (Shirley Falls); Intern (Charles MacDaniels); Fire chief (E. A. Nicholson).

The Experiment
A passenger plane is blasted out of the sky. It's another failed attempt by the aliens to kill a scientist who has conclusive evidence of the invasion. His life is soon threatened by his son, who is being controlled by the aliens. Wr: Anthony Spinner. Dir: Joseph Sargent.

Lloyd Lindstrom (Roddy McDowall); Dr. Curtis Lindstrom (Laurence Naismith); Dr. Paul Mueller (Harold Gould); Alien (Lawrence Montaigne); Minister (Dabbs Greer); Lt. James (Willard Sage); Houseboy (Soon Teck-Oh); Proprietress (Jackie Kendall); Superintendent (Stuart Lancaster); Cabbie (Roy Sickner); Male nurse (Mel Gallagher); Trooper (John Ward); Alien (Randy Crawford).

The Mutation
David discovers a crippled flying saucer in the Mexican desert. He and a friendly alien woman must flee from the saucer's crew. Wr: George Eckstein, David Chandler. Dir: Paul Wendkos.

Vicki (Suzanne Pleshette); Mark Evans (Edward Andrews); Fellows (Lin McCarthy); Alien (Roy Jenson); Miguel (Rodolfo Hoyos); Manager (Val Avery); Cobbs (William Stevens); Cabbie (Ted Gehring); Mama (Tina Menard); Boy (Tony Davis); Guides (Roberto Contreras, Pepe Callahan); Beggar (Pedro Regas).

Memory Flash—Suzanne Pleshette: "I barely remember doing *The Invaders* except I did one hell of a strip! I would love to share astute insights into the character and have scintillating stories about the show. The absolute truth is, I only remember that there was a great caterer on 'The Mutation.' I ate Osso Bucco for the first time out on the desert location. With almost 1,000 TV appearances under my belt, a good lamb shank is easier to remember than a long-ago performance. I'll be searching the channels for a rerun. My interest is piqued!"

The Leeches
David and a cynical helicopter pilot explore an abandoned mine shaft to reach several top scientists whose knowledge is being drained away by alien machines. Wr: Daniel B. Ullman. Dir: Paul Wendkos.

Warren Doneghan (Arthur Hill); Tom Wiley (Peter Mark Richman); Eve Doneghan (Diana Van Der Vlis); Hastings (Robert H. Harris); Noel Markham (Theodore Marcuse); Millington (Peter Brocco); Pyschiatrist (Noah Keen); Alien (William Wintersole); Man (Hank Brandt); Cabbie (Tom Signorelli); Guard (Ray Kellogg).

Memory Flash—Peter Mark Richman: "I almost lost my head in this episode. I stepped out of a helicopter and the wind was gusting. I didn't duck enough. The blades came swooping down and just missed me! It was scary. The aliens on the show all had crooked little fingers that stuck out. My finger was already crooked because of an old football injury. Since I played a human on the show, I had to hide my finger from the camera!"

Genesis

A dying policeman's last words about a giant slug-like creature in the back of a car lead David to an undersea lab. He finds experiments are being conducted to create life. Wr: John W. Bloch. Dir: Richard Benedict.

Dr. Selene Lowell (Carol Rossen); Greg Lucather (John Larch); Grayson (Frank Overton); Hal Corman (Phillip Pine); Ken Harrison (William Sargent); Steve Gibbs (Tim McIntire); Joan Corman (Louise Latham); Andy (Dallas Mitchell); Jimmy (James Devine); Kevin Ryan (Jonathon Lippe); Manager (Bill Erwin).

Memory Flash—Phillip Pine: "I had to keep a frozen look of horror on my face during the episode [after his character sees an alien in its true form]. When I read the script, I recalled the stunned, stony, blank look of one of the soldiers in a documentary about the first troops to enter the Nazi death camp at Buchenwald. That was my motivation in playing the role here."

Vikor

A dying lineman's last words about a glowing skeleton lead David to an industrial complex. He meets George Vikor, a man whose bitterness has caused him to sell out to the invaders. Wr: Michael Adams (Meyer Dolinsky), Don Brinkley. Dir: Paul Wendkos.

George Vikor (Jack Lord); Sherri Vikor (Diana Hyland); Nexus (Alfred Ryder); Sergeant (Richard O'Brien); Hank (Sam Edwards); Phil (Joe di Reda); Houseboy (Larry Duran); Guards (Hal Baylor, Max Kleven); Edward McKendry (Hank Sims).

Nightmare

A young schoolteacher is nearly eaten alive by a swarm of flesh-eating insects. This puts David on the trail of experiments that have turned insects into carnivorous killers. Wr: John Kneubuhl. Dir: Paul Wendkos.

Ellen Woods (Kathleen Widdoes); Ed Gidney (James Callahan); Miss Havergill (Jeanette Nolan); Ames (Robert Emhardt); Gabbard (William Bramley); Deputy (Wayne Heffley); Lena Lapham (Nellie Burt); Clara Lapham (Irene Tedrow); Fred Danielson (Jim Halferty); Danielson (William Challee); Carl Gidney (Logan Field); Cook (John Harmon); Hank Braden (Carey Loftin).

Doomsday Minus One

An idealistic general covers up the crash of a saucer so that he can trick the aliens into helping him stage a nuclear incident. He's hoping this will bring about nuclear disarmament on Earth as well as expose the invasion. Wr: Louis Vittes. Dir: Paul Wendkos.

Rick Graves (William Windom); Gen. Ted Beaumont (Andrew Duggan); Carl Wyeth (Robert Osterloh); Tomkins (Wesley Addy); Spencer (Tom Palmer); Agent (Lee Farr); Nom Com (Lew Brown); Attendant (Rick Murray); M. P. (Dave Armstrong); Guards (K.L. Smith, Don Kennedy).

Quantity: Unknown

A dying guard's last words about glowing, vanishing assailants put David in the possession of an alien cylinder. The device is used to guide flying saucers into Earth's atmosphere. Wr: Don Brinkley, story by Clyde Ware. Dir: Sutton Roley.

Harry Swain (James Whitmore); Diane Oberly (Susan Strasberg); A.J. Richards (Milton Selzer); Frank Griffith (William Talman); Farley (Doug Henderson); Walt Anson (Barney Phillips); Investigator (Byron Keith); Leo Rinaldi (Ernest Sarracino); Driver (Mike Harris); Minister (Melville Ruick); Guard (Raymond Guth); Rescuer (Ron Doyle); Security man (Randy Crawford).

The Innocent

Dodging laser beams, a fisherman makes off with an alien disc. Meanwhile, a young army officer needs David to testify at a congressional hearing to expose the invaders; David, however, is whisked away to a beautiful paradise as proof of the aliens' benevolent intentions. Wr: John W. Bloch, story by John W. Bloch, Norman Klenman, Bernard Rothman. Dir: Sutton Roley.

Magnus (Michael Rennie); Nat Greeley (William Smithers); Helen (Katherine Justice); Edna Greeley (Patricia Smith); Mitchell Ross (Dabney Coleman); Billy Stears (Paul Carr); Ruddell (Robert Doyle); Alien (Frank Marth); M. P. (Erik Holland); Nat, Jr. (Johnny Jenson); Alien #2 (Harry Lauter).

The Ivy Curtain

Newly arrived aliens are being taught how to act like human beings in an Ivy League school. David joins up with a pilot to expose the indoctrination center. Wr: Don Brinkley. Dir: Joseph Sargent.

Barney Cahill (Jack Warden); Stacy (Susan Oliver); Burns (David Sheiner); Reynard (Murray Matheson); Alvarado (Barry Russo); Gilbery (Byron Morrow); Dispatcher (Paul Pepper); Nova (Clark Gordon); Sobbing woman (Jacqueline Mayo); Alien (John Napier); Aliens (Ted Markland, Laurie Mock); Intern (Garth Pillsbury); Bartender (Bud Perkins); Injured alien (Randy Crawford).

The Betrayed

David's efforts to alert the FBI to a series of saucer landings in a Texas oil field are complicated by his love for Susan Carver. Wr: John W. Bloch, story by Theodore Sturgeon. Dir: John Meredyth Lucas.

Simon Carver (Ed Begley); Susan Carver (Laura Devon); Neal Taft (Norman Fell); Evelyn Bowers (Nancy Wickwire); Alien #1 (Bill Fletcher); Butler (Joel Fluellen); Joey Taft (Victor Brandt); Older alien (Ivan Bonar); Waiter (Gil Stuart); Doctor (Garrison True); Alien technician (Ron Stokes).

The Storm
Hurricanes are tearing the East Coast apart, but a small fishing village is spared. This leads David to an alien weather machine. Wr: John Kneubuhl. Dir: Paul Wendkos.

Father Joe (Joseph Campanella); Lisa (Barbara Luna); Malcolm Gantley (Simon Scott); Danny (Paul Comi); Clerk (John McLiam); Luis Perez (Carlos Romero); MacLeuen (Dean Harens); Weatherman (John Mayo); Organist (Allan Emerson); Alien (Edward Faulkner).

Panic
The frozen body of a truck driver is the third victim of alien Nick Baxter, whose touch brings on a freezing death. David chases Baxter as the panicked alien hitchhikes across West Virginia to rendezvous with a saucer. Wr: Robert Sherman. Dir: Robert Butler.

Nick Baxter (Robert Walker); Madeline Flagg (Lynn Loring); Gus Flagg (R.G. Armstrong); George Grundy (Ford Rainey); Wallace (Len Wayland); Jorden (Ross Hagen); Molly (Helen Kleeb); Attendant (Robert Sorrells); Deputy (Rayford Barnes); Joe Bagely (Joseph Perry); Woman (Merecedes Shirley); Deputy in charge (Ralph Thomas); Ed Larson (Don Ross); Webster (Don Eitner).

Moonshot
A glowing red mist kills two astronauts. It's the first clue that aliens are sabotaging a spaceflight to protect the existence of an alien moonbase. Wr: Rita Lakin, John W. Bloch, Alan A. Armer, story by Rita Lakin. Dir: Paul Wendkos.

Gavin Lewis (Peter Graves); Hardy Smith (John Ericson); Angela Smith (Joanne Linville); Stan Arthur (Kent Smith); Tony LaCava (Anthony Eisley); Banks (John Lupton); Charlie Coogan (Strother Martin); Riley (Richard X. Slattery); McNally (Ross Elliot); Owens (John Carter); Correll (Paul Lukather); Col. Howell (Robert Knapp); Roberts (Charles A. MacDaniels); Reporters (Morgan Jones, Lee Millar, Robert Duggan, Ollie O'Toole); Attendant (Steve Cory); Technician (Steven Ferry).

Wall of Crystal
The tragic death of a young newlywed couple leads David to a crystal that dissolves oxygen. David convinces talk show host Ted Booth to show the crystal on nationwide television. Wr: Don Brinkley, Daniel B. Ullman, story by Daniel B. Ullman. Dir: Joseph Sargent.

Theo Booth (Burgess Meredith); Robert Vincent (Linden Chiles); Taugus (Edward Asner); Grace Vincent (Julie Sommars); Joe McMullen (Lloyd Gough); Miss Johnson (Karen Norris); Groom (Jerry Ayres); Bride (Peggy Lipton); Harding (Russ Conway); Mrs. Endicott (Mary Lou Taylor); Policeman (Ray Kellogg); Guard (Fred Waugh).

The Condemned
A little girl's fantastic story leads David to Morgan Tate. The businessman has faked his death after stealing a file that lists all of the important aliens on Earth. Wr: Robert Sherman. Dir: Richard Benedict.

Morgan Tate (Ralph Bellamy); Lewis Dunhill (Murray Hamilton); Carol Tate (Marlyn Mason); Carter (Larry Ward); Ed Tonkin (Wright King); Regan (Garry Walberg); John Finney (John S. Ragin); Victoria (Debbie Storm); Joey (Gordon Westcourt); Teenager (Geoffrey Deuel); Ed Peterson (Harlan Wade); Brock (Paul Bryar); Cabbie (Seymour Cassell); Coroner (Stuart Nisbet); Paul (Kevin Burchett); Cops (Randy Crawford, Bill White).

Season 2: 1967-68

Condition: Red
A country doctor's last words about a living corpse take David to the North American Defense Command. He discovers that a fleet of saucers are planning to sneak under the defense screens. Wr: Laurence Heath. Dir: Don Medford.

Laurie Keller (Antoinette Bower); Dan Keller (Jason Evers); Peter Stanhope (Simon Scott); Albertson (Forrest Compton); Dr. Rogers (Roy Engel); Arius (Mort Mills); Conners (Burt Douglas); Gen. Winters (Robert Brubaker); Technician (Jim Raymond).

The Saucer
David and another man capture a flying saucer, but they find a variety of obstacles when they try to turn it over to the authorities. Wr: Daniel B. Ullman. Dir: Jesse Hibbs.

Annie Rhodes (Anne Francis); Robert Morrison (Charles Drake); John Carter (Dabney Coleman); Alien (Sandy Kenyon); Sam Thorne (Kelly Thordsen); Joe Bonning (Robert Knapp); Boy (Christopher Shea); Alien pilot (John Ward); Maid (Tina Menard); Doctor (Glenn Bradley); Attendant (Robert Dulaine).

The Watchers
The horrible death of a hotel manager leads David to a tycoon whose business deals with the invaders could backfire and undermine America's defenses. Wr: Earl Hamner, Jerry Sohl, story by Earl Hamner, Michael Adams (Meyer Dolinsky). Dir: Jesse Hibbs.

Paul Cook (Kevin McCarthy); Margaret Cook (Shirley Knight); Ramsey (Leonard Stone); Danvers (Walter Brooke); Simms (Robert Yuro); General (John Zaremba); Alien #1 (Paul Sorenson); Alien #2 (Marlowe Jenson); Grayson (James Seay); Bowman (Harry Hickox).

Valley of the Shadow
When residents of a small town see an invader incinerate, the aliens move in to destroy the entire town. Wr: Robert Sabaroff, story by Robert Sabaroff, Howard Merrill. Dir: Jesse Hibbs.

Maria (Nan Martin); Sheriff Clements (Ron Hayes); Will Hale (Harry Townes); Fake Taft (Joe Maross); Major (Ted Knight); Taft (James B. Sikking); Dr. Larousse (Mark Roberts); Minister (Jon Lormer); Sergeant #2 (Wayne Heffley); Joe Manners (Hank Brandt); Deputy (Robert

Sorrells); Brother (Jimmy Hayes); Townspeople (Don Eitner, Claudia Bryar, Phil Chambers, Richard Gardner).

The Enemy

The alien survivor of a spaceship crash is helped by a compassionate human nurse. However, he's reverting back to his true alien form. Wr: John W. Bloch. Dir: Robert Butler.

Gale Frazer (Barbara Barrie); Blake (Richard Anderson); Vern Hammond (Paul Mantee); Sawyer (Gene F. Lyons); Sheriff (Russell Thorson); Lavin (George Keymas).

Trivia Alert: This is the second episode to show an alien losing its human form. Initially, Richard Anderson was placed in a big plastic bag of water to simulate a strange creature. The effect didn't work and Anderson's transformation was done with makeup.

The Trial

David knows that his friend killed an alien in self-defense, but the authorities believe he committed a murder and disposed of the body. Wr: David W. Rintels, George Eckstein. Dir: Robert Butler.

Charlie Gilman (Don Gordon); Janet Wilk (Lynda Day); Allen Salter (Harold Gould); Robert Bernard (Russell Johnson); Judge Symondson (Malcolm Atterbury); Fred Wilk (John Rayner); Bert Wisnofsky (Bill Zuckert); Wilk, Sir (Richard Hale); Mrs. Wilk (Amy Douglass); Clerk (Jason Wingreen); Brennan (James McCallion); John Lovell (Sid McCoy); Guard (Robert Duggan); Waitress (Selette Cole).

The Spores

A suitcase containing alien spores is found, in rapid succession, by a group of teenagers, a middle-aged couple and a group of children. Wr: David W. Rintels, George Eckstein, Ellis Kadison, Joel Kane, story by Alvin Ramrus, John Shaner, Ellis Kadison, Joel Kane. Dir: William Hale.

Tom Jessup (Gene Hackman); Ernie Goldhauer (John Randolph); John Mattson (Wayne Rogers); Jack Palay (Mark Miller); Sally Palay (Patricia Smith); Hal (James Gammon); Roy (Kevin Coughlin); Mavis (Judee Morton); Frank (Vince Howard); Mike (Brian Nash); Earl Garber (Joel Davidson); Elizabeth Garber (Christine Matchett); Waitress (Norma Connolly); Jerry Burns (Noam Pitlik); Archie (Stephen Liss); Sgt. Myons (Robert Johnson).

Dark Outpost

Hitching a ride on a saucer, David uncovers an alien medical center in the desert. By stealing an alien crystal, David puts the lives of college geologists in jeopardy. Wr: Jerry Sohl. Dir: George McCowan.

Vern Corbett (Andrew Prine); Eileen (Dawn Wells); Hal (Tim McIntire); Col. Harris (Whit Bissell); John Devin (William Sargent); Nicole (Kelly Jean Peters); Steve (Tom Lowell); Mrs. James (Susan Davis); Carr (William Wintersole); Thatcher (Sam Edwards); Sergeant (William Stevens); General (Walter Reed); Clerk (Ron Doyle); Driver (Bard Stevens); Attendant (Patrick Riley); Mechanic (Mark Allen); Alien (Robert Dulaine).

Memory Flash—Dawn Wells: "*The Invaders* was an imaginative show," says the actress best known as Mary Ann on *Gilligan's Island*. "It was the character of Eileen that really interested me in doing the show. After three years of comedy, I concentrated more on drama to avoid the inevitable typecasting which goes with being on series television. Eileen was quite a departure. We filmed it in the Mojave Desert during the summer of 1967. It was 120 degrees and there wasn't even the comforting shade of a tree. My tennis shoes couldn't take the heat and started to melt in the hot sand. The technicians put down a low platform on which I could walk safely!"

Summit Meeting, Part 1

David joins up with alien Ellie Markham, who is opposed to the aliens' plan to incinerate the human race with a belt of radiation. Wr: George Eckstein. Dir: Don Medford.

Ellie Markham (Diana Hyland); Mike Tressider (William Windom); Per Alquist (Michael Rennie); Thor Halvorson (Eduard Franz); Jonathon Blaine (Ford Rainey); Rosmundson (Ian Wolfe); Hypnotist (Vic Perrin); Hippie (Victoria Hale); Man (William Boyett); Detective (Ross Elliot); Lt. (Martin West); Colonel (Peter Hobbs); Emissary (Ben Wright); Newsman (Don Lamond); Man #2 (Dave Armstrong).

Summit Meeting, Part 2

David tries to stop a doomsday bomb from wiping out top heads of state during an international peace conference. Wr: George Eckstein. Dir: Don Medford.

Per Alquist (Michael Rennie); Ellie Markham (Diana Hyland); Mike Tressider (William Windom); Thor Halvorson (Eduard Franz); Cal Vanders (Richard Eastham); Aide (Jay Lanin); Guard (Morgan Jones); Newsman (Hank Simms); Man (Hal Riddle); Reporters (Don Ross, Gil Stuart, Troy Melton); Summit voice (Ted Knight); Aide (Lew Brown); Alien (John Mayo); Frenchman (Albert Carrier).

The Prophet

A glowing evangelist is used to fool people into thinking that salvation will "come from the skies." Wr: Warren Duff, story by Jerry de Bono, Warren Duff. Dir: Robert Douglas.

Brother Avery (Pat Hingle); Sister Claire (Zina Bethune); Bill Shay (Roger Perry); Brother John (Richard O'Brien); Brother James (Byron Keith); Reporter (Dan Frazer); Guard (Ray Kellogg).

Labyrinth

A fantastic series of events paint David as a paranoid after he obtains X-rays of an alien's body. Wr: Art Wallace. Dir: Murray Golden.

Laura Crowell (Sally Kellerman); Sam Crowell (Ed Begley); Harry Mills (James Callahan); Ed Harrison (John Zaremba); Mrs. Thorne (Virginia Christine); Darrow (Ed Peck); Henry Thorne (E. J. Andre); Lt. Eaton (Bill Quinn); Argyle (Martin Blaine); Miss Fox (Barbara Dodd); Patient (Wilhelm von Homburg); Cabbie (William Sumper).

The Captive

If David can't rescue an imprisoned alien from a Russian consulate, the invaders will destroy the building and trigger World War III. Wr: Laurence Heath. Dir: William Hale.

Dr. Katherine Serret (Dana Wynter); Peter Borke (Fritz Weaver); Wesley J. Sanders (Don Dubbins); Josef (Lawrence Dane); Martin (Doug Henderson); Conner (Jock Gaynor); Jim Royer (Dallas Mitchell); Dorian (Tom Palmer); Leo (Peter Coe); Foreman (K. L. Smith); Murphy (Robert Patten); Guard (Alex Rodine).

The Believers
The lives of David's new allies are threatened by young Elyse Reynolds. She's supplying the invaders with information in exchange for the release of her brother. Wr: Barry Oringer. Dir: Paul Wendkos.

Elyse Reynolds (Carol Lynley); Edgar Scoville (Kent Smith); Bob Torin (Anthony Eisley); Harland (Donald Davis); Prof. Hellman (Rhys Williams); Torberg (Than Wyenn); Mary Torin (Maura McGiveney); Lt. Sally Harper (Kathleen Larkin); Charles Russellini (Richard Karlan); Newcomb (Byron Morrow); Cabbie (Ed Barth); Arthur Singeiser (Warren Parker); Student (Tim Burns); Guard (Mark Tapscott); Friendly guard (Hal Baylor); Corridor guard (Ed Long); Library alien (Allen Emerson); Alien #1 (Frank Reinhard); Alien assassin (Robert Dulaine).

The Ransom
David captures an alien leader and holds him hostage in the wooded cottage owned by disillusioned poet Cyrus Stone. Wr: Robert Collins. Dir: Lewis Allen.

Leader (Alfred Ryder); Cyrus Stone (Laurence Naismith); Claudia Stone (Karen Black); Bob Torin (Anthony Eisley); Garth (Lawrence Montaigne); Edgar Scoville (Kent Smith); Lieutenant (Karl Held); Kant (John S. Ragin); Sentry (Ron Husmann); Gentry (John Graham); Policeman (Joe Quinn).

Memory Flash—Lawrence Montaigne: "I was in the Quinn Martin stock company. I did many of his shows. You never turned down anything from Quinn because you knew that every year you would get an X amount of dollars from the QM organization. In 'The Ransom,' I killed David Vincent [by throwing him into an electrical panel. He's later brought back to life by the aliens]. That was a unique experience. Not everybody gets to say, 'Yeah, I killed off the lead of the show!'"

Task Force
A weekly news magazine agrees to do an exposé on the aliens, but within hours, most of the staff is taken over by aliens. Wr: Warren Duff. Dir: Gerald Mayer.

Jeremy Mace (Linden Chiles); June Murray (Nancy Kovack); Eric Lund (Frank Marth); William Mace (Martin Wolfson); Edgar (Kent Smith); Bob Ferrara (John Lassell); John Niven (John Stephenson); Emmet Morgan (Barney Phillips); Leader (Walter Wolff King); Alien committeeman (Robert Dulaine).

The Possessed
David struggles to free a friend from an alien brain implant, which has turned him into a slave. Wr: John W. Bloch. Dir: William Hale.

Ted Willard (Michael Tolan); Adam Lane (William Smithers); Martin Willard (Michael Constantine); Janet Garner (Katherine Justice); Edgar (Kent Smith); Burt Newcomb (Charles Bateman); Coroner (Booth Colman); Nurse (Lyn Hobart); Housekeeper (Rose Hobart); Clerk (Matt Peno).

Counter-Attack
David's friends manage to blast an approaching saucer out of the sky, but David, ridiculed in the press, seemingly gives up the battle. Wr: Laurence Heath. Dir: Robert Douglas.

Joan Surrat (Ahna Capri); Jim Bryce (John Milford); Lucian (Donald Davis); Archie Harmon (Lin McCarthy); Edgar (Kent Smith); Lt. Connors (Ken Lynch); Earl (Warren Vanders); Elliot Kramer (Ross Elliot); Louise (Pamela Curran); Blake (Don Chastain); Robertson (Charles J. Stewart); Stan Leeds (Ed Prentiss); Custodian (Walter Baldwin).

The Pit
A professor's claim that he saw flying saucers landing in a college plaza leads David to a deadly dream machine. Wr: Jack Miller. Dir: Louis Allen.

Julian Reed (Charles Aidman); Patricia Reed (Joanne Linville); Jeff Brower (Don Harron); John Slaton (Simon Scott); Edgar (Kent Smith); Llewellan (Bartlett Robinson); Meyers (Noah Keen); Frank Reed (Johnny Jenson); Mrs. Fielding (Elizabeth Field); Guard (Michael Harris); Scientist (Pat O'Hara); Officer (Dort Clark).

The Organization
The aliens are unprepared for the fury of the Mafia when the Mob helps David search for a stolen drug crate containing saucer fragments. Wr: Franklin Barton. Dir: William Hale.

Peter Kalter (J.D. Cannon); Mike Calvin (Chris Robinson); Weller (Larry Gates); Dorcas (Barry Atwater); Edgar (Kent Smith); Court (Roy Poole); Perry (Ross Hagen); Dominic (John Kellogg); Second mate (Mark Allen); Chauffeur (Troy Melton); Amos Foster (Nelson Olmstead).

The Peacemaker
Alien and human military leaders begin peace talks to allow peaceful alien colonization. However, a fanatical general plans to destroy the alien leaders. Wr: David W. Rintels. Dir: Robert Day.

Gen. Sam ConCannon (James Daly); Sarah ConCannon (Phyllis Thaxter); Leader (Alfred Ryder); Archie Harmon (Lin McCarthy); Post (Jan Merlin); Edgar (Kent Smith); Cullenbine (Byron Keith); Bill ConCannon (Pat Cardi); Vance (Jack Bannon); Guard (Ed Deemer); Dr. Jacobs (Larry Thor); Willard (Craig Huebing).

Memory Flash—Jan Merlin: "It was special because I got to work with Alfred Ryder. He was a hell of a fine actor whom I knew from New York. After we did the show, Alfred went to Paris for a visit. He sent me a postcard of one of the Notre Dame gargoyles. He insisted it was my portrait as the alien from 'The Peacemaker.' He admitted that it really resembled himself—and it did!"

The Vice

The invaders make David look like a racist when he tries to block a black alien's confirmation to an important position in the space program. Wr: William Blinn, story by William Blinn, Robert Sabaroff. Dir: William Hale.

James Baxter (Raymond St. Jacques); Arnold Warren (Roscoe Lee Browne); Celia Baxter (Janet MacLachlan); Ollie (Lou Gossett, Jr.); Edgar (Kent Smith); William (Austin Willis); Casey (D'Urville Martin); TV man (James Devine); Horner Warren (Joel Fluellen); Mike Baxter (Pepe Brown); Attendant (Red Boyd Morgan); Policeman (John Ward); Newscaster (Robert Johnson).

The Miracle

David and a greedy bar owner try to get an alien crystal away from a troubled teenager. She was given the crystal by a dying alien. Wr: Robert Collins, story by Robert Collins, Norman Herman. Dir: Robert Day.

Beth Ferguson (Barbara Hershey); Harry Ferguson (Edward Asner); Father Paul (Arch Johnson); Johnny (Christopher Shea); Nun (Marion Thompson); Ricky (Robert Biheller); Deputy (Wayne Heffley); Courier (Rayford Barnes); Alien #1 (Phil Adams).

The Life Seekers

A wounded policeman's fantastic account leads David to two peaceful aliens. They will stop the invasion if they can escape alien assassins and reach a saucer rendezvous. Wr: Laurence Heath. Dir: Paul Wendkos.

Claire (Diana Muldaur); Keith (Barry Morse); Battersby (R.G. Armstrong); Trent (Arthur Franz); Joe Nash (Stephen Brooks); Edgar (Kent Smith); Leeds (Paul Comi); Rawlings (Morgan Jones); Dr. Stark (Herb Armstrong); Donner (Scott Graham); Dorsey (Barry Cahill); Newscaster (Robert Johnson).

The Pursued

Anne Gibbs, an alien woman given dangerous synthetic emotions, agrees to travel to Washington, D.C., with David as proof that aliens exist. Wr: Don Brinkley. Dir: William Hale.

Anne Gibbs (Suzanne Pleshette); Willis (Will Geer); John Corwin (Gene F. Lyons); Charles McCay (Richard O'Brien); Tom Holloway (Dana Elcar); Edgar (Kent Smith); Eddie McKay (Michael McGreevey); Antique owner (Eldon Quick); Newsboy (Barry Williams); Hattie Willis (Mary Jackson); Alien voice (Robert Johnson).

Inquisition

As the aliens prepare a final assault that will wipe out human life, David and the believers are framed for murder and hunted down one by one. Wr: Barry Oringer. Dir: Robert Glatzer.

Joan Seeley (Susan Oliver); Andy Hatcher (Peter Mark Richman); Hadley Jenkins (Stewart Moss); Jim Bouman (John Milford); Stan Frederickson (Robert H. Harris); Edgar (Kent Smith); Secretary (Mary Gregory); Robert Breeding (Alex Gerry); Security (Lincoln Demyan); George (Ernest Harada); Hotel engineer (George Robotham); Alien #1 (Burt Douglas); Also with Michael Harris, Bill Egan, Allen Joseph, Richard Merrifield).

Memory Flash—Art Director George Chan: "Right after the last scene of this episode was shot, I went to art-direct a film called *Gaily, Gaily*, for which I received an Oscar nomination. Under no circumstances would I return to *The Invaders* if it was renewed. Thankfully, it was not renewed. It had been a very long season of frustrations and hard work. Being so tired, I just went through the motions to complete my assignments. I had very little interest in the show. The only redeeming part of working on *The Invaders* was that I worked with some of the greatest talents of Hollywood."

The Invisible Man

September 1975–January 1976

When Dr. Daniel Westin becomes permanently invisible, he agrees to use his talents to spearhead dangerous government missions. Daniel uses a human mask and clothes, enabling him to interact with the outside world without revealing his unique condition.

Meanwhile, the Klae Research Corporation sponsors Westin's efforts to find a cure for his condition.

Cast: Dr. Daniel Westin (David McCallum); Dr. Kate Westin (Melinda Fee); Walter Carlson (Craig Stevens).

Based on the novel by H.G. Wells; *Created by:* Harve Bennett, Steven Bochco; *Producers:* Leslie Stevens, Robert F. O'Neill, Frank Telford; *Executive Producer:* Harve Bennett; *Music Theme:* Henry Mancini; NBC/Universal; 60 minutes.

"*The Invisible Man* was really a one-joke show," laments producer Robert O'Neill. "The minute you've taken the wrappings off his head, you've seen the joke."

The joke was met with sheer terror in 1933 when Claude Rains portrayed the invisible man in the Universal picture. Some theater patrons fainted as the sinister scientist unwrapped the

Cast of *The Invisible Man*, left to right: David McCallum, Melinda Fee and Craig Stevens. Copyright 1975 NBC/Universal.

bandages around his head to reveal … nothing. Rains' invisible man sets out on a campaign of terror before his footprints in the snow give him away and he's shot down.

David McCallum's invisible man was a decent fellow who worked with his wife to find a cure for his condition. The *Invisible Man* series first appeared as a 90-minute TV film in the spring of 1975. The film received good ratings, and a weekly series was announced for the fall. "The series coincided with new technology, a combination of film and video," recalls creator Harve Bennett. "By today's standards it was very crude, but in 1975 it allowed us tremendous opportunities. It was a very noble experiment, and I'm very proud of the series."

So is Melinda Fee, who played the wife of the invisible man, Kate Westin. "I wish I had a nickel for every time I wished I could be invisible," laughs Fee. "It's the greatest theme of all time. Talking to an invisible David McCallum was delicious. I'd practice a lot at home, jerking my body to simulate his grabbing my arm. Or cocking my head, listening to him talk, with my eyes focused on his direction. It's a skill that had to be learned." Kate Westin often pitched in to help her husband corner the bad guys. "I was thrilled to land the role," Fee says. "Kate Westin came along just about the time Women's Lib was making headway. She represented what women were striving for: separate professions, equality, recognition of intelligence and education. I loved Kate's brightness, intuition and humor. And I adored playing such a wide range of characters in disguises." Fee, however, was relieved that the series didn't follow the lead of the pilot movie. "The pilot was geared more to the lurking Feds scrambling to steal the formula of invisibility. It had the proverbial car chase, ending in a huge crash-and-burn sequence. The series centered on the relationship of Daniel and Kate. We traveled outside of that dreary lab, and I loved the personal scenes with David. It showed that scientists did have private lives."

The big challenge for the actress was the special effects. She was relating to a leading man who wasn't there. "Doing the effects today would be nothing. Back then, passing a syringe to an invisible David McCallum would take half a day's work. These effects would be checked right after shooting on a video recorder on the set. They had to be sure that the invisible man wasn't casting shadows or that shadows weren't falling on him. We'd often do a small piece of business over and over. It would take 75 takes at least. Forget acting! We were exhausted by the time the technical stuff was completed. It was frustrating, and the cost was astronomical."

Producer Robert O'Neill agrees. "Because of the mechanical and physical limitations, there were many disappointments. At first, it sounded like *The Invisible Man* was going to be a lot of fun. I thought we'd have a tremendous action show. We also had David McCallum, who had been popular on *The Man from U.N.C.L.E.*, and he wanted to recapture some of that magic. Problem was, unless you have a really big budget, science fiction shows are hard to produce. Networks generally don't want to pay the added expense for the technical things necessary. Back then, we used the blue screen process, which was very complex and time-consuming. It became a tremendous problem for the cameramen, directors and crew, especially on such a tight budget."

Working with special effects was nothing new for O'Neill. He had previously produced the ESP series *The Sixth Sense*. "Steve Bochco had written the 90-minute *Invisible Man* film, and someone got the notion to make it into a series. By this time, Bochco and Harve Bennett were busy on other things. Universal came after me and Leslie Stevens. We were the firemen they brought in at the ninth inning. Science fiction wasn't my forte, but since I had done *Sixth Sense*, Universal felt I could handle all of the trick things on *Invisible Man*."

The other challenge O'Neill faced was the basic concept. "It was very frustrating because we were dealing with a very narrow parameter. Since David was supposed to be wearing a mask to hide his invisibility, we were faced with, 'How do you make a mask react with sorrow, pain, grief and joy?' It wasn't that David, as a performer, wasn't being responsive to the audience. It was that when the mask came off, the joke was over. The audience is used to looking at someone's face. How can you show emotions on the face of someone who is invisible? We also faced the problem

of telling the audience where the invisible man was. We'd have him brushing up against furniture and bumping into potted plants. He ended up as the clumsiest guy in the world! We also found that invisibility made him invincible. Unless he was walking in the sand or snow, he was unbeatable. The very nature of the show deterred the action because he was really a superman. It was hard to work in jeopardy."

"The show never had a chance," claims story editor Seeleg Lester. "My objections were to the tenor of the plots, which approximated *The Six Million Dollar Man*. It was a shame because the invisibility theme could have been an intriguing element. Instead, it was a device used to capture a James Bond villain or an international terrorist. The original premise was subverted into ordinary melodrama with predictable plots. I asked for my release from the series before the year was over."

Melinda Fee, however, felt a special magic. "Sometimes we did get off the track with the hero vs. villains," she says, "and that did become predictable and boring. But the series had a lot of charm and wisdom."

As the series progressed, the humor flourished. As a guest on *The Mike Douglas Show* two weeks before *The Invisible Man* premiered, David McCallum commented with a hint of bewilderment, "We started out doing a very serious show, but it's turned into something of a comedy." The capper to the comedy turned out to be an episode titled "Pin Money." Inept bank robbers with Frankenstein monster masks give the invisible man some grief. The episode's writer, James Parriott, chuckles when he recalls the show. "*The Invisible Man* was my baptism by fire," he says. "I was writing *The Six Million Dollar Man* for Harve Bennett when he was having trouble with the *Invisible Man*. They were three weeks away from production, and they were getting behind schedule. He asked me to pitch some script ideas, and I started writing. So we were writing them and shooting them fast and furious.

"'Pin Money' turned out very funny. Toward the end, we felt that humor was working better than the other thing. But the premise of an invisible man is funny in itself. Look at the Chevy Chase film [*Memoirs of an Invisible Man*]. Rather than a spine-tingling drama, they made a comedy out of it. We realized that there was something very funny about invisible people."

The series was axed in January 1976 after 12 segments. Harve Bennett, who describes star

David McCallum as "one of the nicest actors with whom I have ever worked," feels that perhaps the audiences weren't ready for McCallum as a lead. "I loved David McCallum's work even before he did *The Man from U.N.C.L.E.*," Bennett says warmly. "David was also very caring, very considerate of the people who worked around him, very literate and very appreciative of material. He had been an enormous success as a supporting actor on *U.N.C.L.E.* He was the Mr. Spock on that show to Robert Vaughn's straight character. He added great color to the show. But when we put him in the role of a leading man on *Invisible Man*, it's conceivable that two things happened: First, people didn't want to see David as the leading man. They wanted him to be the 'color' man. Secondly—and this is a peculiar thing—we went in the face of an old saw in our TV industry. That is, British actors don't make it on TV as the leads. That was at the time. We felt the success of the Beatles had negated that old wives' tale."

Associate producer Richard Milton contends that McCallum was a scapegoat. "David got the blame when the network decided he was too foreign. It was the usual crap. David was a fine, talented actor. The failure of *The Invisible Man* had nothing to do with him. The format of the show just didn't work. They never got the concept down."

"The ratings weren't very good, but that could have been the time slot," says James Parriott. "I respected David enormously, and I thought he was well cast."

"David was a fine actor," says Robert O'Neill. "The format just didn't happen."

Melinda Fee believes the series fell victim to several factors: "The competition on the other networks, preemptions and politics at the network," she says. "Ironically, right after we were canceled, the ratings jumped. We were catching on—and we were dead in the water." She has fond memories of acting with her co-star. "David was an absolute joy to work with," she says. "He was inventive, smart and funny. Many times he'd be on the set working out a script or technical problem. It was if he really were Dr. Westin. He helped without stepping on anybody's toes. He was never late or demanding. The entire cast and crew loved him. David was also marvelous in the humorous scenes with that dry British wit."

Less than a year later, *The Invisible Man* returned (with the same production team) as *The Gemini Man*, starring Ben Murphy as a secret agent who can become invisible. "I was in Europe promoting *The Invisible Man* at the time," Fee recalls. "I never saw *Gemini Man*, but from what I understand, it was a direct rip-off of our show."

The Invisible Man hasn't faded entirely from TV screens. The series is occasionally rerun on cable and has enjoyed success in Europe. "My real regret was that the show didn't survive longer," says Fee. "It was a wonderful experience. I'd give anything to do it again!"

CAST NOTES

David McCallum (Dan): Born 1933. This Scottish-born actor was popular as secret agent Illya Kuryakin on *The Man from U.N.C.L.E.* (1964–68). In the 1970s, he starred in the British series *Sapphire and Steel*.

Melinda Fee (Kate): This Los Angeles–born actress was busy in daytime TV in the 1970s (*The Guiding Light*) and in TV movies of the 1980s (*The Aliens Are Coming*).

Craig Stevens (Carlson): Born 1918. Stevens is best known as TV's Peter Gunn (1958–1961). "Craig Stevens was a true gentleman," says Melinda Fee. "He had a dry wit, and he'd make subtle cracks which were appreciated by all."

EPISODE GUIDE

The Invisible Man (1975 TV movie)
Having made himself invisible, Dan tries to keep his secret away from the pursuing military. Wr: Steven Bochco. Dir: Robert Michael Lewis.

Walter Carlson (Jackie Cooper); Nick Maggio (Henry Darrow); Gen. Turner (Arch Johnson); Rick Steiner (Alex Henteloff); Blind man (John McLiam); Gate Guard (Ted Gehring); Chief (Paul Kent); Guest (Richard Forbes); Doctor (Milt Kogan); Lobby guard (Jon Cedar); Clerk (Lew Palter).

Season Episodes

The Klae Resource
Dan searches for an American scientist who is rumored to be helping a Middle Eastern country with an energy system. Wr: Steven Bochco. Dir: Robert Michael Lewis.

Lionel Parks (Barry Sullivan); James Fielder (Robert Alda); Homer (Conrad Janis); Brian Kelly (Paul Kent); Stern (Dick Balduzzi); Hotel man (James Karen); Boone (Richard Geary); Limo driver (Chuck Courtney); Drunk

(David Knapp); Operator (Jackie Russell); Guard (Scott Walker); Tech expert (Dennis Robertson); Bellman (Jack Frey); Croupier (Gary Paggett).

The Fine Art of Diplomacy
A web of diplomacy complicates Dan's efforts to get the goods on a thieving ambassador. Wr: James D. Parriott. Dir: Sigmund Neufeld, Jr.

Diego DeVega (Ross Martin); Wood (Paul Stewart); Vittorio Gregario (Vincent Beck); Tandy (Michael Pataki); Manuel (Pepe Callahan); Guards (Nicholas Lewis, Raymond O'Keefe); Capital guard (Gwil Richards).

Man of Influence
A senator is emotionally crippled when a fake spiritualist summons up the spectre of his dead wife. Dan poses as a ghost to expose the fake medium. Wr: Seeleg Lester, Rick Blaine, story by Rick Blaine. Dir: Alan J. Levi.

Ernest Gide (John Vernon); Sen. Hanover (Gene Raymond); Williams (Jack Colvin); Margaret Hanover (Shirley O'Hara); Andrea Hanover (Loni Anderson); Sen. Baldwyn (Alan Mandell); Dr. Theophilus (Robert Douglas); Woman (Dorothy Love); Policemen (Don Gentry, Jim Standifer).

Eyes Only
A mysterious killer and a young woman forced to work for an enemy country endanger Kate when she goes undercover. Wr: Leslie Stevens. Dir: Alan J. Levi.

Paula Simon (Barbara Anderson); Tony Bernard (Bobby Van); Ken Maynard (William Prince); Jack Pierson (Thayer David); Kirk (John Kerr); Joe Palanzi (Vince Martorano); Nick Palanzi (Frank Christi); Worker (Robert Hackman); Marty (William Bronder); Guard (Tony Swartz); Cabbie (Vern Rowe); Dino (Gregory Bach).

Barnard Wants Out
Dan tries to help an old friend return to America after spending years in Russia, but he's under the watchful eyes of a Russian major. Wr: James D. Parriott. Dir: Alan J. Levi.

Leon Barnard (Nehemiah Persoff); Anna Barnard (Jane Actman); Alexi Zartov (Paul Shenar); Guard (Cliff Osmond); Consul (Macon McCalman); Yuri (George Fisher); Petra (Peter Colt); Man (Charles J. Stewart); Soldier (Joe Rainer); Swedish woman (Inga Neilsen); Bellboy (Ralph Anderson).

Sight Unseen
The blind daughter of a businessman is kidnapped and threatened with death if her father testifies against the Mob. Wr: Brian Rehak, story by Brian and Kandy Rehak. Dir: Sigmund Neufeld, Jr.

Neroda Kappas (David Opatoshu); Laurie Kappas (Jamie Smith Jackson); Griggs (Richard X. Slattery); Jimmy James (Harry Davis); Mannie Hallman (Al Ruscio); Wells (Rod Colbin); Agent #1 (Brett Hadley); Guard #1 (Richard Reed); Pedestrian (Jack Garner); Gateman (Ken Del Conte); Guard #3 (Tom Gees).

Go Directly to Jail
Dan goes to jail to rescue a man, but discovers that he's blown the man's undercover status. Wr: Steven Bochco. Dir: Sigmund Neufeld, Jr.

Leland McCallister (James McEachin); Conor (John Crawford); Warden Stone (Pat Harrington); Senor Robles (Eric Mason); Cop (Gregory Walcott); Mrs. McCallister (Paulene Myers); Prisoner (Ed Call); Prisoners (Tony Burton, Gus Peters); Bunker guard (George Flower); Farmer (Jason Johnson); Guard (Nick Worth).

Stop When Red Lights Flash
A crooked cop and judge imprison Dan and Kate on a phoney traffic violation. Wr: Seeleg Lester. Dir: Gene Nelson.

Armistead Jones (Roger C. Carmel); Deputy Bentley (Scott Brady); Charles Hooten (Frank Aletter); Pop (Eddie Firestone); Benoit (Dean Santoro); Craig (Ted Hartley); Gert (Kasey Rogers); Jeo (Harold Ayer); Compositor (Donald Elson); Riley (John Furlong); Ethel (Pearl Shear); Girl (Kristin Larkin).

Pin Money
Carlson's aunt wants to return stolen money to a bank, but robbers wearing Frankenstein monster masks complicate her efforts. Wr: James D. Parriott. Dir: Alan J. Levi.

Margaret Carlson (Helen Kleeb); Sanders (James Blendick); Sgt. Mersky (Thom Carney); John Arnold (John Zee); Big Nose (Wayne Taylor); Lawyer (Jim Mills); Teller (Arline Anderson); Baldy (Wayne Grace); Tex (Larry French); Carter (G. J. Mitchell); Truck driver (Karl Lukas); Cabbie (Gene Borkan); Poker player (Ray Ballard); Driver #2 (Mickey Gatlin); Bruiser (James Whitworth).

Memory Flash—Cast member Melinda Fee: "'Pin Money' was a bit absurd but a real gas to play. *The Invisible Man* did become more comedic, and I liked that better. It became more Nick-and-Nora than *Star-Trek*-in-the-city."

The Klae Dynasty
Caroline Klae, one of the owners of Klae Corporation, refuses to take kidnapping threats seriously, forcing Daniel to shadow her. Wr: Philip DeGuere, Jr. Dir: Alan J. Levi.

Caroline Klae (Nancy Kovack); Julian Klae (Farley Granger); Morgan Klae (Peter Donat); Ryan (Joe Maross); Capt. Scopes (George Murdock); Pierce (Rayford Barnes).

Power Play
Carlson is held hostage by a criminal who shoots and wounds the invisible man. Wr: Leslie Stevens. Dir: Alan J. Levi.

Pike (Monte Markham).

An Attempt to Save Face
Dr. Nick Maggio, who made Dan's human mask, needs Dan's help: He needs to surgically alter an Eastern leader's face, and Dan agrees to exchange places with the leader and lure in two assassins. Wr: James D. Parriott, Leslie Stevens, story by Leslie Stevens. Dir: Don Henderson.

Nick Maggio (Charles Aidman); Katrina Storoff (Ina

Balin); Petra Kolchak (Terry Kiser); Chairman Rojin (Oscar Homolka); Vasil Brovnick (Gene Dynarski); Wendy (Julie Rogers); Sergei (W. T. Zacha); Anesthesiologist (Sid McCoy); Nurse (Karen Cobb).

Kolchak: The Night Stalker
September 1974–August 1975

Carl Kolchak, reporter for the rickety news outfit INS (Independent News Service), investigates supernatural happenings in Chicago. This puts the intrepid reporter on the trail of werewolves, vampires, zombies and other strange phenomena.

Cast: Carl Kolchak (Darren McGavin); Tony Vincenzo (Simon Oakland); Ron Updyke, reporter (Jack Grinnage); Miss Emily Cowles, advice columnist (Ruth McDevitt).

Based on the novel by Jeff Rice; **Producers:** Paul Playdon (early segments) (Cy Chermak); **Executive Producer:** Darren McGavin; ABC/Universal; 60 minutes.

"It was a nightmare!" Those are the first words out of unit production manager Ralph Sariego's mouth. In a nutshell, *Kolchak: The Night Stalker* was one of the most difficult shows, production-wise, to pull off every week. There was never any comfort from the ratings. From the word go, the series was doomed to drag around the lower echelons on the ratings pole.

The origins of *Kolchak: The Night Stalker* were much more successful. The Kolchak story first appeared in 1972 as a 90-minute *ABC Movie of the Week*. Produced by Dan Curtis (*Dark Shadows*) and scripted by novelist Richard Matheson, *The Night Stalker* became, at the time, the highest rated TV movie in history.

As played by Darren McGavin, Carl Kolchak was a rumpled, eccentric, exasperatingly tenacious reporter who tracked down a modern-day vampire in Las Vegas. The original film set the formula for the subsequent series: Kolchak destroys the vampire, but a lack of evidence and a surfeit of pressure from the authorities means his story can never be published.

ABC immediately asked for a second *Night Stalker* movie. The 1973 sequel, *The Night Strangler*, took Kolchak to Seattle to hunt down a fiendish immortal (played by Richard Anderson). This outing did almost as well in the ratings. A series was quickly put together.

Allen Baron was one of the first directors assigned to the show. "The first producer was Paul Playdon," he recalls. "We got along very well, but it was a strange situation. When I was directing the episode 'UFO'[about a hostile alien that sweeps through Chicago], I was still shaken up from a car accident. I came on the set and found an argument going on between Paul and Darren McGavin. They were debating whether this thing from outer space was visible or invisible. Paul wanted to have a creature, but Darren felt a creature would be like a cheap Japanese movie. There was merit to both arguments. Meanwhile, I was wandering around, not realizing that I was still in shock from the accident. At one point, I almost fainted. Meanwhile, these two guys kept at each other, and they weren't any closer to resolving the issue. Finally, I called one of the Universal executives and explained my dilemma. He said, 'Well, do the best you can.' So I arranged for a Ritter machine to be brought on the set. This is a large propeller that blows air, and I used it to create an effect of this space creature attacking people. It was a totally improvised monster and seemed like a good direction to go in. In retrospect, it needed more planning, but we got some good effects out of it."

Paul Playdon left the show, and Cy Chermak stepped in to produce. "Cy and I didn't get along at all," says Baron. "I couldn't stand him. There was a scene in 'UFO'where we blew up this wall. We used slow motion to show the alien spitting these cops through the air, and it was spectacular. I was very pleased when I saw the dailies. When the lights came up, Mr. Chermak said that he noticed that one of the cops had dark sunglasses on. I said, 'So?' Chermak thought that was a major error, and he made an issue out of it. I couldn't believe it. Here was a great scene, and he's angry about a cop's sunglasses? I said, 'Is that all you have to say?' I told him where to go, and that was one of the reasons I stopped doing the show. The quarreling was a strain, and the long hours were exhausting. I worked on 'The

Werewolf' show for 24 hours straight. I was getting, literally, a half-hour's sleep every night."

Baron's more pleasant memories of the show include working with the demonic dog in "The Devil's Platform." "I auditioned a bunch of dogs for that role. The dog we used was a Rottweiler. His trainer called him Bum. The trainer said to the dog, 'All right, Bum, walk down the alley.' The dog walked down the alley. Then he said, 'Follow that man leaving the studio.' The dog followed the man. 'Now go over to that post and lean against it.' The dog trotted over to the post and got up on its hind legs and leaned against the post. I was amazed. It was done totally through vocal commands. The trainer didn't raise his hands once. Then he said, 'Jump inside that truck!' The dog jumped into the truck. 'Now drive!' The dog put both paws on the steering wheel, looked over at me and waved. I said, 'He's got the job!' It was incredible. He was a great dog, but he was very docile. In one scene, he had to growl at McGavin. We put wires over his teeth to make him look ferocious. The sound guys added a growl later. At one point, McGavin asked the trainer, 'Listen, would it hurt the dog if you threw him at me?' The trainer said no, and one of the handlers literally tossed the dog through the air and it landed on McGavin. We used little tricks like that throughout the episode."

Another episode, "Jack the Ripper," required extensive stunt work. Possessing superhuman strength, the Ripper takes on the entire Chicago police force. "That show had a lot of good special effects," says Baron. "We also got some great reviews. The guy playing Jack the Ripper [Mickey Gilbert] was a stuntman. All of the scenes where he was running along the top of the building were filmed at night. We used a building that was under construction, and we shot 15 pages that night. I ran into *Night Stalker's* story editor David Chase recently. He said, 'Geez, Allen. I still can't believe you shot that sequence in one night!' We did, and it turned out great."

Baron, a former actor ("I starred in a cultish film called *The Big Blast* in 1961") praises the *Night Stalker* cast as "a very good group of people. Darren McGavin was a very inventive person, but sometimes he went overboard. He was very enthusiastic and at times he went crazy, in a creative way."

The serio-comic scenes in the INS newspaper office particularly impressed Baron. "Those were always great little scenes. Simon Oakland [who played Kolchak's long-suffering boss Vin-

Kolchak (Darren McGavin) is on the trail of a ghostly creature (Richard Kiel) in "Bad Medicine." Copyright 1974 ABC/Universal.

cenzo] was wonderful. I hired the little old lady, Ruth McDevitt, for a one-shot appearance on the 'Jack the Ripper show.' They loved her so much that they made her a regular [as Miss Emily]. The young, fat newspaper girl with the New York accent [Carol Ann Susi, who appeared in several early episodes] was a waitress when she was discovered by McGavin. He hired her for the show."

With the complicated night shooting, the special effects and makeup, as well as limited production time and budgets, meeting the show's production schedule was a back-breaking challenge.

"*The Night Stalker* was enormously hard on everyone because it was a night show," says production manager Ralph Sariego. "We shot day and night footage five days a week. The schedule was a killer." Although the series was shot primarily in Los Angeles, it needed some establishing shots in Chicago to bring authenticity to its setting. Says Sariego, "I went with the producer [Paul Playdon], Darren McGavin and his wife, actress Kathie Browne, to Chicago, where we shot a lot of second unit stuff. Then we hopped back on a plane and returned to Los Angeles."

The menacing monsters on the series were restricted on two fronts: network concerns that

Kolchak (Darren McGavin) enters the lair of "The Demon in Lace" (Teddie Blue). Copyright 1974 ABC/Universal.

some creatures might be too intense for audiences, and a budget that diminished the monsters themselves. "The series just ran out of material and money," claims Sariego. "We had a terrible time with the lizard creature ["The Sentry"]. It was a disaster. The lizard suit kept popping loose in the back. It looked awful. Another time, we literally had no money to make a monster. We used a wind machine instead. Again, it looked awful."

To counteract the sinking production values, there was the charm of Darren McGavin. "He was a very good actor," says Sariego, "but he wanted to control everything. He wanted to be involved with every aspect of production." However, that desire only served to frustrate McGavin, and he became disenchanted with the series. He had originally envisioned *Night Stalker* as a suspense show with a bare minimum of monsters. He was interested in placing Kolchak in more realistic situations with deeper layers of subtext in the stories. He bristled whenever the series was categorized as "a monster show." Despite the fact that he owned 50 percent of the show (with his Francy Productions), he couldn't change its formula. Although the emphasis on monsters made the show an unhappy experience

for the actor, he still considers Carl Kolchak one of his best roles.

Kolchak: The Night Stalker was canceled in early 1975. Reruns of the series popped up on the CBS late night movies in 1979 and racked up high ratings. Despite the continued cult status of the series, there have been no concrete plans to bring it back. "There were about eight really good episodes," says Sariego. "They were all at the beginning. It's a common problem in TV production. By mid-season, everything starts to collapse. It's very difficult to keep it up. Everybody gets tired. In terms of production, none of the *Night Stalker* episodes were fun to do. By the end of the season, everybody was completely exhausted by working day and night. When it was announced that we had been canceled, the whole company applauded."

CAST NOTES

Darren McGavin (Kolchak): Born 1922 in Spokane, Washington. McGavin is an Emmy award winner as Candice Bergen's father on television's *Murphy Brown*.

Simon Oakland (Vincenzo): Born 1922. A character actor who played the boss on TV shows such as *Toma* (1973–74) and *The Black Sheep Squadron* (1976–78), Oakland died in 1983.

Ruth McDevitt (Miss Emily): Born 1895. This character actress died in 1976.

Jack Grinnage (Updyke): One of Grinnage's earliest roles was as one of the performers on *Bob Newhart's Variety Show* (1961).

EPISODE GUIDE

Kolchak: The Night Stalker (1972 TV movie)
Kolchak pursues a vampire who is loose in Las Vegas. Wr: Richard Matheson. Dir: John Llewllyn Moxey.
 Gail Foster (Carol Lynley); Warren Butcher (Claude Akins); Janos Skorzeny (Barry Atwater); Bernie Jenks (Ralph Meeker); Ed Masterson (Charles McGraw); Thomas Paine (Kent Smith); Mickey Crawford (Elisha Cook); Fred Hurley (Stanley Adams); Ralph Mokurji (Larry Linville); O'Brien (Jordan Rhodes); Policemen (Hal Needham, Eddie Rice, Ronnie Rondell).

The Night Strangler (1973 TV movie)
Seattle's old underground city houses a centuries-

old scientist who needs young victims to replenish his youth. Wr: Richard Matheson. Dir: Dan Curtis.

Dr. Richard Malcolm (Richard Anderson); Louise Harper (Jo Ann Pflug); Roscue Schubert (Scott Brady); Llewellyn Crossbinder (John Carradine); Titus Berry (Wally Cox); Prof. Crabtree (Margaret Hamilton); Tramp (Al Lewis); Charisma Beauty (Nina Wayne); Christopher Webb (Ivor Francis); Wilma Frankheimer (Virginia Peters); Janie Watkins (Kate Murtaugh); Sheila (Anne Randall); Melissa (Regina Parton); Stacks (George Tobias); Joyce Gabriel (Diane Shalet); Woman (Francoise Birnheim).

Season Episodes

The Ripper
A superhuman version of Jack the Ripper has broken free from the police and is terrorizing Chicago. Wr: Rudolph Borchert. Dir: Allen Baron.

Jane Plum (Beatrice Colen); Capt. Warren (Ken Lynch); The Ripper (Mickey Gilbert); Det. Susan Cortazzo (Roberta Collins); Mrs. Englewyler (Ruth McDevitt); Policeman (Donald Mantooth); Masseuse (Marya Small); Driver (Clint Young); Mailboy (Robert Bryan Berger); Cheryl (Gwyn Karon); Driver's wife (Dulci Jordan); Ellen (Cathey Paine); Debbie (Denise Dillaway); Policeman (Ike Jones).

Zombie
Gangsters are being ripped apart by a giant zombie, and Kolchak is targeted as the creature's next victim. Wr: David Chase, story by Zekial Marko. Dir: Alex Grasshoff.

Capt. Leo Winwood (Charles Aidman); Ben Sposato (Joseph Sirola); Victor Friese (Val Bisoglio); Uncle Fileman (Scatman Crothers); Gordy the Ghoul (John Fiedler); The Monk (Ben Frommer); Bernard Welden (Antonio Fargas); Monique Marmelstein (Carol Ann Susi); Mamalois Edmonds (Paulene Myers); Francois Edmonds (Earl Faison); Caretaker (J. Pat O'Malley); Willie (Gary Baxley); Poppy (Roland Bob Harris); Jerry (Chuck Waters); Al Berg (Hank Calia).

They Have Been, They Are, They Will Be (aka UFO)
An invisible creature from space begins a path of death and destruction. Wr: Rudolph Borchert, story by Dennis Clark. Dir: Allen Baron.

Capt. Quill (James Gregory); Dr. Bess Weinstock (Mary Wickes); Alfred Brindle (Dick Van Patten); Woman (Maureen Arthur); Keeter Hudson (Gary Glanz); Monique Marmelstein (Carol Ann Susi); Crowley (Len Lesser); Howard Gough (Phil Leeds); Stan Wedemyer (Rudy Challenger); Gordon Spangler (John Fiedler); Rich (Fritz Feld); Riley (Dennis McCarthy); Leon van Heusen (Tony Rizzo).

Vampire
Kolchak antagonizes the L. A. police when he becomes obsessed with capturing a female vampire. Wr: David Chase, story by Bill Stratton. Dir: Don Weis.

Kathryn Rawlins (Kathleen Nolan); Lt. Matteo (William Daniels); Faye Kruger (Suzanne Charny); Jim the Swede (Larry Storch); Ichabod Grace (Jan Murray); Sample (John Doucette); Gingrich (Milt Kamen); Hooker (Anne Whitfield); Man (Army Archerd); Woman (Selma Archerd); Chandra (Noel de Souza); Reporter #1 (Bill Baldwin); Linda Courtner (Betty Endicott); Reporters (Scott Douglas, Alyscia Maxwell); Andrew Garth (Tony Epper); Stacker Schumaker (Rand Warren); Elena Munoz (Biene Blechschmidt); Hotel manager (Stuart Nisbet); Bellboy (Howard Gray); Talkative fellow (Jimmy Joyce).

The Werewolf
Kolchak discovers that a passenger on an ocean liner is a murderous werewolf. Wr: David Chase, Paul Playdon. Dir: Allen Baron.

Bernhardt Stieglitz (Eric Braeden); Paula Griffin (Nita Talbot); Capt. Wells (Henry Jones); Mel Tarter (Dick Gautier); Dr. Alan Ross (Barry Cahill); Hallem (Bob Hastings); Wendy (Jackie Russell); Gribbs (Dort Clark); George Levitt (Lewis Charles); Jim Hawkins (Jay Remy); Radioman (Heath Jobes); Lyn Prysock (Lyn Guild); Sailor (Steven Marlo); Bernie Efron (Ray Ballard).

Memory Flash—Allen Baron: "Eric Braeden is a terrific actor and a good friend. I showed him a videotape of this episode recently and he got a big kick out of seeing it again."

Fire Fall
Flaming deaths are tied in with a symphony conductor, who is being stalked by a restless, flaming spectre. Wr: Bill S. Ballinger. Dir: Don Weis.

Ryder Bond (Fred Beir); Maria (Madlyn Rhue); Sgt. Mayer (Philip Carey); Cardinale (David Doyle); Mrs. Shropell (Alice Backes); Doctor (Lenore Kasdorf); Mrs. Sherman (Carol Veazie); Stage manager (Gary Glanz); Felicia Porter (Patricia Estrin); George (Joshua Shelley); Mrs. Markoff (Virginia Vincent); Man (Marcus Smith); Woman (Martha Manor).

The Devil's Platform
An ambitious politician makes a devilish deal that results in his opponents dying in grisly accidents. Wr: Donn Mullally, story by Tim Maschler. Dir: Allen Baron.

Robert W. Palmer (Tom Skerritt); Lorraine Palmer (Ellen Weston); Susan (Julie Gregg); Dr. Kline (Jeanne Cooper); Louie (Stanley Adams); James Talbot (John Myhers); Officer (Robert Do Qui); Stephan Wald (Dick Patterson); Hale (William Mims); TV newsman (Bill Welsh); Bernie (Sam Edwards); Reporter (Keith Walker); Policemen (Bruce Powers, Ross Sherman); Engineers (John Dennis, Ike Jones).

Bad Medicine
Gems are being stolen by a towering Indian who seems to vanish into thin air. Wr: L. Ford Neale, John Huff. Dir: Alex Grasshoff.

Capt. Joe Baker (Ramon Bieri); Charles Rolling Thunder (Victor Jory); Indian (Richard Kiel); Dr. Agnes Temple (Alice Ghostley); Belloy (David Lewis); Albert Delgado (Marvin Kaplan); Schwartz (James Griffith); Guard (Morris Buchanan); Ballistics man (Dennis McCarthy); Hostess (Madilyn Clark); Policeman (Alex Sharp); Reporters (Keith Walker, Bill Deiz); Auction guard (Richard Geary); Detective (Bob Golden); Chauffeur (Ernie

Robinson); Desk officer (Troy Melton); Cop #2 (Walt Davis); Oriental man (Art Wong); Mrs. Marsky (Lois January); Mrs. Addison (Barbara Morrison); Mrs. Van Piet (Riza Royce).

The Spanish Moss Murders

A green swamp creature is on the loose after being dreamed into reality by a research project. Wr: Al Friedman, David Chase, story by Al Friedman. Dir: Gordon Hessler.

Capt. Siska (Keenan Wynn); Dr. Aaron Pollack (Severn Darden); Monster (Richard Kiel); Natalie (Elisabeth Brooks); Dr. Hollenbeck (Virginia Gregg); Fiddler (Randy Boone); Superintendent (Ned Glass); Record producer (Brian Avery); Pepe La Rue (Johnny Silver); Henri Villon (Maurice Marsac); Sleeper (Donald Mantooth); Michelle Kelly (Roberta Dean); Villaverde (Rudy Diaz); Johnson (James La Sane); Reporters (Frieda Rentie, Bill Deiz).

The Energy Eater

A new hospital is invaded by a sinister force that absorbs energy. Wr: Arthur Rowe, Robert Earll, Rudolph Borchert. Dir: Alex Grasshoff.

Jim Elkhorn (William Smith); Walter Green (Michael Strong); Janice Eisen (Elaine Giftos); Don Kibbey (Tom Drake); Capt. Webster (Robert Yuro); Dr. Hatfield (Robert Cornthwaite); Diana (Joyce Jillson); Frank Wesley (Michael Fox); Ralph Crane (John Alvin); Laurie (Barbara Graham); Janitor (John Mitchum); Receptionist (Ella Edwards); Policeman (Bob Golden); Girls (Melissa Greene, Dianne Harper).

Horror in the Heights

A creature that gnaws its victims to death has the ability to change its appearance. Wr: Jimmy Sangster. Dir: Michael T. Caffey.

Harry Starman (Phil Silvers); Indian (Abraham Sofaer); Lane Marriot (Murray Matheson); Jo (Ned Glass); Julius Buck Fineman (Benny Rubin); Barry (Barry Gordon); York (Shelly Novack); Sol Goldstein (Herb Vigran); Mrs. Goldstein (Naomi Stevens); Boxman (Eric Server); Thomas (Robert Karnes); Frank Rivas (James Goodwin); Charlie (John Bleifer); Prodman (Paul Sorenson).

Mr. R.I.N.G.

A robot murders its creator and seeks refuge with Dr. Leslie Dwyer. The doctor is convinced that the robot has gained human emotions. Wr: L. Ford Neale, John Huff. Dir: Gene Levitt.

Mrs. Walker (Julie Adams); Dr. Leslie Dwyer (Corinne Michaels); Mr. RING (Craig Baxley); Capt. Atkins (Bert Freed); Duncan Stephens (Henry Beckman); Col. Wright (Myron Healey); Guard (Donald "Red" Barry); Policeman (Vince Howard); Bernard Carmichael (Robert Easton); Librarian (Maidie Norman); Peters (Bruce Powers); Man (Read Morgan); Barham (Gail Bonney).

Primal Scream

Prehistoric cells hatch carnivorous ape-creatures who go on a rampage in Chicago. Wr: Bill S. Ballinger, David Chase. Dir: Robert Scheerer.

Dr. Helen Lynch (Katherine Woodville); Capt. Maurice Molnar (Keenan Wynn); Tom Kitsmiller (Pat Harrington); Jack Burton (Jamie Farr); Dr. Fisk (Lindsay Workman);

Policeman (Vince Howard); Cowan (Byron Morrow); Secretary (Barbara Rhodes); Dr. Peel (Regis J. Cordic); Landlady (Sandra Gould); Rosetta (Jeanie Bell); Nils (Al Checco); Creature (Gary Baxley); Woman (Barbara Luddy); Man (Paul Picerni); Barney (Arnold Williams); Jules Copenick (Paul Baxley); Robert Gurney (Craig Baxley); William Pratt (Chuck Waters).

The Trevi Collection

A beautiful witch is using living mannequins to vanquish her enemies. Wr: Rudolph Borchert. Dir: Don Weis.

Madelaine (Lara Parker); Mme. Trevi (Nina Foch); Doctor (Bernie Kopell); Lecturer (Marvin Miller); Superintendent (Douglas V. Fowley); Griselda (Priscilla Morrill); Ariel (Diane Quick); Photographer (Peter Leeds); Hoods (Dick Bakalyan, Henry Slate); The Figure (Dennis McCarthy); Melody Sedgewick (Beverly Gill); Man (Henry Brandon); Mickey Patchek (Chuck Waters); Manager (George Chandler).

Chopper

A headless corpse springs out of its coffin and decapitates former motorcycle gang members. Wr: Steve Fisher, David Chase, story by Robert Zemeckis, Bob Gale. Dir: Bruce Kessler.

Lila Morton (Sharon Farrell); Capt. Jonas (Larry Linville); Herb Bresson (Jim Backus); Henry Spake (Art Metrano); Dr. Eli Strig (Jay Robinson); Norman Kahill (Frank Aletter); Neil (Steve Franken); Watchman (Jesse White); Nurse (Brunetta Barnett); Electric Larry (Joey Aresco); Beaner (Jimmy Murphy); Otto (Jack Bernardi); Snow White (Jim Malinda); Watchman #2 (Jimmy Joyce); Rider (Steve Boyum); Rita Baker (Fern Barry); Claude (Ralph Montgomery).

Memory Flash—Bruce Kessler: "Darren McGavin called me up and said that [the script] was a piece of crap and that we weren't going to shoot it. I thought it was a good script, and in the end, we did the show. It was different and fantastic and I enjoyed doing it. Darren has a reputation for being difficult, but I had no problems with him. The cast was remarkable."

Demon in Lace

Cadaverous ghouls, disguised as beautiful women, are scaring young men to death. Wr: Stephen Lord, Michael Kozoll. Dir: Don Weis.

Prof. C. Evan Spat (Andrew Prine); Rosalind Winters (Kristina Holland); Capt. Jonas Siska (Keenan Wynn); Registrar (Carolyn Jones); Toomey (Jackie Vernon); Dr. Mozart (Milton Parsons); Spanish woman (Carmen Zapata); Maria Vanegas (Maria Grimm); Mike Thompson (Ben Masters); Coroner (Davis Roberts); Betty Walker (Margie Impert); Don Rhiner (Hunter von Leer); Mark Hansen (John Elerick); Craig Donnelly (Steve Stafford); Girl (Iris Edwards); Demon (Teddie Blue); Attendant (Snag Werris); Tim Brennan (Donald Mantooth); Landlord (Carlos Molina).

Legacy of Terror

A giant eagle has been killing people and Kolchak's investigation leads him to an Aztec mummy. Wr: Arthur Rowe. Dir: Don McDougall.

Capt. Webster (Ramon Bieri); Tillie Jones (Pippa Scott); George Andrews (Carlos Romero); Vicky (Sondra Currie); Pepe Torres (Erik Estrada); Mr. Eddy (Sorrell Booke); Jamie Rodrigues (Victor Campos); Rolf Anderson (Craig Baxley); Rita Torres (Mina Vasquez); Madge Timmins (Udana Power); Prof. Jones (Robert Casper); Medical examiner (Pitt Herbert); Mummy (Mickey Gilbert); Smith (Ron Stein); Olson (Gene Le Bell); Mrs. Torres (Alma Beltran); Taylor (Scott Douglas); Lona (Dorrie Thomson); Nina (Merrie Lynn Ross); Attendant (Cal Bartlett); Andrew Gomez (Ernesto Macias).

The Knightly Murders
A medieval knight comes to life and goes on a killing spree. Wr: Michael Kozoll, David Chase, story by Paul Magistretti. Dir: Vincent McEveety.

Capt. Vernon W. Rausch (John Dehner); Mendel Boggs (Hans Conried); Roger (Robert Emhardt); Minerva Musso (Lieux Dressler); Maura (Jeff Donnell); Brewster Hocking (William O'Connell); Roger Stenvold (Shug Fisher); Charles Johnson (Byran O'Byrne); Lester Nash (Don Carter); Bruce Krause (Sidney Clute); Sgt. Buxbaum (Gregg Palmer); Reporter (Ed McCready); Leo J. Ramutka (Jim Drum); Reporter #2 (Alyseia Maxwell).

The Youth Killer
A goddess is achieving immortality by sapping the youth of her victims. Wr: Rudolph Borchert. Dir: Don McDougall.

Helen (Cathy Lee Crosby); Sgt. Orkin (Dwayne Hickman); Bella Sarkof (Kathleen Freeman); Cabbie (Demosthenes); Gordy the Ghoul (John Fiedler); Lance Mervin (Michael Richardson); Lance's mother (Benny Santon); Conventioneer (Eddie Firestone); Manager (James Murtraugh); Secretary (Joss White); Young men (James Ingersoll, Reb Brown).

The Sentry
A prehistoric lizard goes on a rampage after a geologist steals its eggs. Wr: L. Ford Neale, John Huff. Dir: Seymour Robbie.

Lt. Irene Lamont (Kathie Browne); Col. Brady (Frank Marth); Jack Flaherty (Tom Bosley); Dr. James Verhyden (Albert Paulson); Dr. Lamar Beckwith (John Hoyt); Ted Chapman (Frank Campanella); Arnie Wisemore (Cliff Norton); Ruth Van Galen (Margaret Avery); Detective #1 (Lew Brown); Creature (Craig Baxley); Receptionist (Kelly Wilder); Dr. Phillips (Greg Finley); Dr. Gordon (Tom Moses); Brian (Keith Walker); Ed (Bill Deiz).

Land of the Giants
September 1968–September 1970

A spaceliner in 1983 is pulled into a space warp and crash-lands on an Earth-like planet where everything is gigantic. The earthlings, hunted by the giants, try to repair their spaceship and return to Earth.

Cast: Captain Steve Burton (Gary Conway); Copilot Dan Erickson (Don Marshall); Stewardess Betty Ann Hamilton (Heather Young); Mark Wilson (Don Matheson); Valerie Ames Scott (Deanna Lund); Alexander B. Fitzhugh (Kurt Kasznar); Barry Lockridge (Stefan Arngrim).

Created by: Irwin Allen; *Associate Producers:* Jerry Briskin, Bruce Fowler; *Developed for television by:* Anthony Wilson; *Special Effects:* L.B. Abbott, Art Cruikshank, Emil Kosa, Jr.; *Music Theme:* John Williams; ABC/Twentieth Century–Fox Television; 60 minutes.

Producer Irwin Allen awoke from a nightmare with a shout. He lay there in the darkness, his mind replaying the incredible adventure his mind had just put him through. He dreamed he was a little person, being chased by giants. Allen smiled and picked up the phone to call writer William Welch. There was a TV series in this idea!

Welch subsequently turned in a script about two American space pilots whose rocketship crashes on a mysterious planet of giants. The pair are befriended by a race of Robin Hood–type little people who are native to this strange world. The network liked the idea but rejected the script.

Anthony Wilson did a rewrite, introducing a varied group of people trapped on this alien planet: There was a courageous captain, an easygoing black co-pilot and a sensitive young stewardess. The passengers included a gruff tycoon, a spoiled jet-setter, an orphan boy and a con man. There was also the orphan boy's dog, Chipper. A ten-minute demonstration film won executives over.

"Artwork sold the series to ABC," says costume designer Paul Zastupnevich. "Many people in the industry are not very bright. Unless they have some pretty pictures to look at, they're lost. Irwin's demonstrated lecture included 10 to 18 sketches, which helped [the executives] visualize the series' concept."

On the surface, it appeared that the timing for a series about a planet of giants was off.

Trapped! The cast of *Land of the Giants*, left to right: Don Matheson, Heather Young, Kurt Kasznar, Deanna Lund, Gary Conway and Don Marshall. Copyright 1968 ABC/Twentieth Century–Fox.

Movies featuring little people in a giant world, such as *The Incredible Shrinking Man* (1957) and *Dr. Cyclops* (1940), were ancient history. The TV world had changed radically since Allen's previous successful series, *Voyage to the Bottom of the Sea* and *Lost in Space*. Fantasy and action-adventure formats were being discarded for more realistic shows such as *Mod Squad, Medical Center* and *The Bold Ones*. Giants hunting down little people seemed out of sync with audiences who were demanding more sophisticated programming.

A couple of the show's cast members expressed concern about doing such a far-out show. Their fears were allayed by their agents, who assured them that *Land of the Giants* wouldn't last more than 13 weeks.

After Allen saw the rushes of the first episode, he proclaimed *Land of the Giants* his best work. The first 13 episodes were filmed during 1967 and 1968, with ABC planning to unveil the show for a January 1968 debut on Friday nights.

At the last minute, however, *Land of the Giants* was held over until the fall, where it would replace Allen's tiring *Voyage to the Bottom of the Sea* on Sundays. Meanwhile, the National Home Testing Institute reported that the series might pay off big dividends: Out of the 25 new TV series for the fall, test audiences ranked *Land of the Giants* number five in the category of best series.

The cast was an attractive group of fresh faces, with one long-time veteran in the cast, Kurt Kasznar. Kasznar's devious Mr. Fitzhugh began as a bumbling clone of the Dr. Smith character from *Lost in Space*. Kasznar quickly imbued the roguish con-man with his own personality. Unlike Dr. Smith, Fitzhugh was willing to lay his life down for his comrades and displayed a likable if inept nature. More importantly, *Lost in Space* had been burned out by its emphasis on Dr. Smith. *Land of the Giants* featured its seven cast members equally.

Casting director Larry Stewart says, "I cast all of the folks for the series. I suggested casting [a black man] for the role of Dan Erickson because I was sensitized to those needs. I suggested Don Marshall for the part. He was a good actor and a friend. *Land of the Giants* was one of the first TV series that had a major continuing role for a black actor. It was a breakthrough for Twentieth Century–Fox Television and a breakthrough for Irwin Allen. It was also a fair battle with the network. We had to convince them to use Don. They weren't sure they were ready for this: 'But what if we lose the audience in Mississippi?' I had also cast the series *Julia,* with [black actress] Diahann Carroll. Once that bullet was bitten by Fox, it was a little easier getting Don Marshall on *Land of the Giants.* It wasn't easy, but it was easier."

For his own part, Don Marshall says that "the character of Dan reminded me of me. Like Dan, I had run track in high school, and I also liked jazz. I was very shy, and through acting I found a way to express myself."

Early trade papers reported actress Barbara Hershey was a front-runner for the stewardess role. "I don't recall Barbara Hershey," says Stewart, "but there was conversation about Sam Elliot for the role of the captain. Sam was under contract at Twentieth Century–Fox at the time. At one point, we felt Sam was going to do it."

Stewart feels the cast "worked out fine. Physically, they could handle the show. However, none of them really got any good moments to perform and show their acting ability."

Don Marshall agrees: "We had a good cast on *Land of the Giants.* Had the show's writers been given a freer hand to deal with the characters' human emotions, fear and humor, the show would not have been taken off the air."

When *Land of the Giants* premiered, it was touted as the most expensive series in TV history (a quarter of a million dollars per episode). However, this publicity was not entirely true. The budget for many later episodes was actually much lower. The early ratings for *Land of the Giants* were strong, and more importantly, the series picked up a broad family audience. This pleased Allen, who told columnist Cynthia Lowry weeks before the series aired, "It must be a big hit to survive. It's so expensive that it will have to attract the whole family. We know the kids will watch it and they will identify with the little people. Our job was to write stories that will attract the adults."

Many of the reviews were encouraging. *Newsday* said, "Visually, this show is a gas."

Singer Frank Sinatra called up *Land of the Giants* co-star Deanna Lund and congratulated her on "a groovy show."

The early episodes presented the land of the giants as a mysterious world where the giants were speechless. To be caught by the towering humanoids meant life in captivity or dissection. "Keeping the giants mute was a scary and effective way to add an alien dimension to the series," says writer Ellis St. Joseph. "It gave the giants' world a wonderful atmosphere of mystery."

When the giants did get voices, they were at first "deep and rumbling," says writer Esther Mitchell. "Later, we were told to ignore this scaling of sound in our scripts. The producers wanted the giants and earthlings to interact with each other. It was the right decision. It opened up the scope of the stories."

The show provided young viewers with adventure, likable characters and an occasional moral message. Using the giant world as a mirror of our own, the writers incorporated themes of freedom, justice and the futility of judging other life forms through prejudicial eyes. Indeed, the earthlings were feared and hated by many giants simply because they were different. The authorities, thinking the earthlings were invaders, used hate propaganda to inspire citizens to capture little people.

The giants' planet was an aesthetically pleasing world where the earthlings could walk fantastically long distances and not get winded, and trudge through the jungle still looking fresh in ironed clothes and immaculate hairstyles. Irwin Allen's brand of storytelling was to sell fantasy, not reality.

The cast themselves were put through rugged paces. Not only did they have to pretend that a spotlight on the studio ceiling was a giant; they had to do their own stunts. "That cast really labored for their pay," marvels Esther Mitchell. "They got fantastic workouts, scrambling up strings, slithering out of drains, dialing giant telephones, hiding in pencil holders. It was a real athletic feat, often difficult and even dangerous."

The show's most striking asset was the special effects. Howard Schwartz, director of photography for the series' first season, recalls, "We had a standard procedure in filming the series. Whenever we shot down at little people, we were on a big crane, shooting with a wide-angle lens to make the earthlings look really small. By contrast, when we were shooting the giants, we were on the floor, holding a hand-held camera. By using a wide angle lens, we made them look extremely tall."

Irwin Allen directed the pilot film, and Schwartz says, "He did things exactly as he wanted them. He had a favorite expression: 'Rock, Roll and Return!' That was to cue the actors as they fell from side to side in the spaceship."

During night scenes on Fox's backlot, Schwartz recalls, "We were setting up a shot when this huge bank of Los Angeles fog rolled in. It interfered with the shooting, and Irwin got very frustrated. He turned to his production manager and said, 'Get that fog outa here!' They brought out a couple of big wind machines, aimed them at the fog and turned them on. The result was hilarious. It didn't make a bit of difference. It was like turning on two tiny fans. The fog kept rolling in, and Irwin was jumping up and down. The crew was dying with laughter."

Schwartz had a good working relationship with Allen, saying, "He was a fine producer and a very creative guy. The crew loved to work with him because he was so loyal to everyone. He was a big job provider in the business, and I never had any problems with him. He allowed me to do some interesting things on the show. Like everyone, he had his phobias. He didn't like being up on the crane. Heights really bothered him. He also liked it cold in his production room. During the winter he had the air conditioners running on maximum. Once, as a gag, I walked into a production meeting wearing a heavy overcoat, a muffler, gloves and a hat. Irwin didn't say a word!"

Schwartz also enjoyed working with the cast. "We held up a broom for them to look at when they talked to a giant. I'm sure it was tough on them. They were all pleasant people. Gary Conway was the hardest member of the cast to get to know. The others were more outgoing and friendly. Gary wasn't unfriendly, he was just more of a loner. Kurt Kasznar was an old pro and a fine actor."

Bill Neff, a lighting technician on *Land of the Giants,* had worked on Walt Disney's *Babes in Toyland* (1961), "and that required a lot of overscale props, so *Land of the Giants* was a familiar kind of job for me. But it was an interesting series." A clash between Irwin Allen and Neff early on worked to Neff's advantage. "He respected me after that because nobody else ever stood up to him—nobody. As a dreamer of science fiction, he had a good imagination. But he

liked to get people stirred up. He would come on a set and say, 'I'm the boss. You'll listen to me and do what I say!' He thought it was a good idea to get people mad at him. After getting everybody worked up, he would walk off the set and chuckle to his production assistant, 'I sure told them!' We had good people, but generally, it was not a congenial, happy set because of this behavior. Irwin felt people did a better job riled up. He was always yelling, 'Time is money' at the directors."

Neff recalls the cast as "nice people. Gary Conway was very gung-ho. He wanted the series to be at its best. Don Marshall got a little aggravated once in a while because of Gary's sense of perfection. Gary occasionally tried to get a hold of the directing reins. He wasn't nasty, he was just over-zealous. He had all kinds of suggestions. The directors would say to Irwin, 'This guy's got too many ideas. We can't keep up with him.' Irwin had to tone Gary down a couple of times, and Gary would pout. Overall, though, his dedication was part of the reason for *Giants'* success.

"Heather Young looked like an entirely different person out of makeup. She wasn't the least bit glamorous off the set, but on the show, she was very attractive. Kurt Kasznar was the most professional of the cast. He did his job very well. I didn't think the boy [Stefan Arngrim] was that great in his role. I can only give him an E for effort."

Actor Don Matheson has good memories of his co-stars and enjoys telling tales on Heather Young: "Heather was a Mormon, and I was always trying to get her to say bad things. Once I begged her to say the F word. She would go, 'FFFFF...' and blush. She told me that she couldn't say bad words. She was a doll."

Paul Zastupnevich recalls, "The cast was terrific, even though they bitched and hollered sometimes because it wasn't an easy life. They had to report to the studio at five a.m. five days a week. Additionally, they all had to be in good physical shape because they climbed ladders, got tossed around in the spaceship and had to shimmy up ropes. It was like G. I. training every week. They got rope burns but they were troupers."

Actor Kevin Hagen appeared in nine episodes as Inspector Kobick, the giant police official determined to capture the little people. Hagen, who later played Doc Baker on the *Little House on the Prairie* series, recalls, "I liked Kobick's professionalism and dedication. He was frustrated by being outsmarted by these little creatures. I

The little people face two giant thieves (Willard Sage and Lane Bradford) in "Double Cross." Copyright 1968 ABC/Twentieth Century–Fox.

tried to portray a certain grudging admiration for them, and tried for a little lightness and humor whenever I could find it, which wasn't often." Sometimes little dolls would be supplied for the "giant" actors to look at, but Hagen doesn't recall that advantage. "Whenever I talked to a little person, I looked at the cameraman's knees, elbows or crotch. I saw whatever my imagination could come up with."

Guest star Lee Meriwether, who played a giant woman in the episode "Rescue," recalls that in her scenes with little people, "I was really talking to a twig and some grass. I asked the prop folks if they had something to help me out. Lo and behold, out came a couple of Barbie-like dolls. What a blessing those were. They helped tremendously."

From the other angle, Don Matheson recalls talking to non-existent giants. "We were relating to people who weren't there," says Matheson. "Sometimes we got Steve Marlo, our dialogue

coach, to go up a 16-foot ladder and read the giants' dialogue for us. All we had to do was find out Steve hated heights. We'd say to the director, 'Gee, you know, it would really help us in this scene if Steve would get waaaaay up there and relate to us.' So he got on the ladder, and he began sweating and turning the pages and hanging on for dear life. We didn't do it to him often, only when he gave us a bad time."

Despite efforts to appeal to a wide audience, *Land of the Giants* became known as another Irwin Allen children's show. Kurt Kasznar, for one, was exasperated by the lack of adult interest in the series, though he found it understandable. "Nobody I knew ever watched the show because it was so awful," he told *Movie Life* magazine in 1970. "I finally forced a friend to watch an episode. He never forgave me."

"The series was pure escapism," counters writer Esther Mitchell, "but we didn't write it for children. Many adult friends of ours watched the

Left to right: Kurt Kasznar, Deanna Lund and Don Matheson on the set of *Land of the Giants.* Copyright 1969 ABC/Twentieth Century–Fox.

compete with the show's special effects. "It would be a losing battle. You just give it your best shot. The whole concept of *Land of the Giants* was more of a star than any one of us."

Matheson admits the series needed to open up more. "There was a sameness to the show. One of us would get captured, and the rest of us would have to rescue that person. Too many of the shows were that way. I would read a script and turn to Deanna and say, 'It's your turn in the barrel this week.'"

Land of the Giants became known as the "getting captured and being rescued" kind of show. The novelty of the little people climbing up and down ropes quickly wore off. Occasionally, however, the writers had fun with the premise. In "Collector's Item," Steve rides the bumper of a giant's car; in "The Crash," a huge car roars out of a mist and passes over Steve and Dan; and in "Brainwash," the earthlings escape from a flooding cave by hitching a ride on a giant's foot.

show with their children. People loved to lose themselves in that fantastic land, rooting for the lovable little people. Viewers were never hammered by messages, never made ill by offensive violence and never caused to squirm by unwanted sexual scenes."

Actor Don Matheson found out how sensitive Irwin Allen was to the label "kids' show." "I gave an interview where I said, '*Land of the Giants* is especially entertaining to kids.' Irwin called me up and said, 'What are you saying? Stop telling people it's a kids' show. It's not a kids' show!' He gave me all of this psychological mumbo-jumbo about how adult women really dug us. I said, 'Jesus Christ! I didn't say it was just a kids' show. It's for the whole family.' He said, 'Well then, say that!'"

Matheson says the cast knew they couldn't

Writer Richard Shapiro, who later created TV's *Dynasty,* got his first break on *Land of the Giants.* "My writing career was not exactly soaring when I did the series," he says. "I needed the credit, I needed the money and frankly, I would have worked for anyone who offered to hire me. But it turned out to be a rather special experience."

Shapiro joined the series in the second year, and his stories occasionally had barbs of satiric insight. "I approached the show with a sense of fun," he says. "There was a charming innocence about *Land of the Giants.* Irwin felt that trying to be genuinely satirical would have destroyed that. However, looked at another way, *Land of the*

Giants does send up more serious science fiction. Maybe that's why the interest in the show has persisted. However, it was certainly more of a children's show than serious drama. Neither was it real science fiction. But the stories were good. They made moral points from which young people could profit. It was fun to watch for grownups, too, if they weren't too stuffy."

Shapiro recalls the show had a cooperative team. "Dick McDonagh, who died some years ago, was a very good story editor. Irwin and his production people always felt the story was most important. The effects served the story. There was a sign up in the production office that read, 'The quality will be remembered long after the cost is forgotten.' Except one day we came in to find the sign had been changed to read, 'The cost will be remembered long after the quality is forgotten.' It was a joke, of course. Irwin was always concerned about the quality of everything he did."

Shapiro was delighted by the guest stars used in his shows. "They cast my episodes with fine character actors like John Carradine and Ben Blue. I remember that shooting on "Giants and All That Jazz" almost shut down one day because Sugar Ray Robinson had to work with a boa constrictor. It turned out the middleweight champion of the world was terrified of snakes!"

Writers Robert and Wanda Duncan found some restrictions writing for *Land of the Giants*. "The strengths and weaknesses of the series were the special effects," Robert Duncan says. "They were often more important than the story. In 'Seven Little Indians,' we moved the plot around so that the little people could escape through the paws of a giant snow leopard. In other words, we manipulated the story for a startling visual. This sacrificed legitimate drama."

Duncan tried in vain to prevent the destruction of one of his giants. "In "Collector's Item," the conclusion has a house blown to smithereens. We asked that the housekeeper be shown getting away safely from the explosion. She had done nothing to require her obliteration. We wrote in the housekeeper's escape, and Irwin crossed it out. We wrote it in again, but once more, Irwin crossed it out. This went on until the filming where, of course, the housekeeper was demolished along with the house. Wanda and I were against gratuitous violence, and we explained that to Irwin. But he was a megalomaniac with extremely high control needs. This was his show, and we were not to forget it."

When *Land of the Giants* went into its sec-ond season, the series had peaked in the ratings. To liven up the format, stories of time travel, space travel, cloning, invisibility and lost islands were written. Music maestro John Williams composed a thrilling new title sequence. At the same time, however, "the show's budget became very important during the second season," says Esther Mitchell. "[My husband Robert and I] had written a story where the little people are swallowed by a giant fish. Irwin was enthusiastic about it, but the money wasn't there for such a production."

Regardless of any changes, ratings for a second year were poor, and the series was soon canceled.

"We were hoping for a third season when we were cut," says Paul Zastupnevich. "We were told we weren't getting the right demographics. You'll never convince me that the demographics and Nielsen ratings are as reliable as they say. It's a lot of hooey-balooey and we got stuck with it."

"We read about the series' cancelation in the trades," says Matheson. "I think Irwin found out the same way. He called me later, and we both felt it shouldn't have been canceled. I heard that it was canceled because it was too expensive to make."

The series had only marginal success in syndication for the next 20 years. *Land of the Giants* was nearly forgotten until it was dusted off for a national broadcast on America's USA channel in 1989. The series enjoyed a retroactive interest as a new generation discovered the show.

Land of the Giants writer Mann Rubin thinks the show's message still applies to today's world. "It showed these little people facing and overcoming towering obstacles. The series' message was that humans can endure. It confirmed our durability."

CAST NOTES

Gary Conway (Steve): Born 1936. Conway had the title role in 1957's *I Was A Teenage Frankenstein*. He starred in and produced the controversial film *The Farmer* (1977). He also guest-starred in such series as *Columbo*, *Police Story* and *Circle of Fear*. His wife is Miss America of 1957, Marian McKnight. As a producer, he co-founded the Ambush Entertainment Corporation in the 1980s.

Don Marshall (Dan): Born 1934. Marshall starred in the films *Cycles South* (1971) and *Terminal*

Island (1973). He also had a critically acclaimed guest role as a black doctor on *Little House on the Prairie* (1981). He continues to act in theater and is an engineering inventor.

Heather Young (Betty): Born 1945 in Bremerton, Washington. Heather was a singer and actress when she was nabbed for the part of Betty Hamilton on *Land of the Giants*. After the series, she devoted herself to raising five children.

In the mid–1970s, she wrote the novel *Debbie: Diary of A Mormon Girl*. As a singer, she released the 1979 album *Lioness and the Lamb*. She currently writes plays and children's books.

Don Matheson (Mark): This Dearborn, Michigan, native served in the Korean War and worked as an undercover narcotics detective before becoming an actor. He worked steadily in daytime TV in the 1970s (*General Hospital*) and was a regular on *Falcon Crest* (1983-84).

Deanna Lund (Valerie): Born 1937. Lund began her career as a Florida weathergirl. Her movie credits in the 1960s included *Tony Rome*, *The Oscar* and *Dimension Five*. She married *Giants* co-star Don Matheson in 1970. Their daughter, Michele, is an actress.

Deanna returned to acting after her divorce in the late 1970s. She also holds acting workshops around the country and acts in TV movies (*Red Wind*, 1991; *Obsessed*, 1992).

Stefan Arngrim (Barry): Born 1955 in Canada. Arngrim was the lead singer in a punk rock band in the 1970s. His TV appearances in the 1970s included *Switch* and *Police Story*. Today he's a screenwriter (*The Cold Front*, 1990) and musician.

Kurt Kasznar (Fitzhugh): Born 1913 in Vienna, Austria. Kasznar's first film role was in the silent film *Max, King of the Circus* (1920). He was a popular supporting actor in Hollywood during the 1950s and 1960s. He starred in a dinner theater production of *Fiddler on the Roof* that was an enormous success during 1977 and 1978. He died in 1979.

EPISODE GUIDE

Season 1: 1968-69

The Crash
When their spaceship crashes, Steve and Dan explore their mysterious world and are nearly run over by a giant car. Later, two of the earthlings are captured for study by a giant scientist. Featured: A giant dog, cat, spider and lizard. Wr: Anthony Wilson, story by Irwin Allen, William Welch. Dir: Irwin Allen.
   Woman giant (Anne Dore); Entomologist (Don Watters); Giant boy (Patrick Michenaud).

Trivia Alert: John Williams, who composed the exciting theme music for *Land of the Giants*, later went on to do the scores for such movies as *Star Wars*, *Jaws*, *ET* and *Raiders of the Lost Ark*.

Memory Flash—John Williams: "My kids really liked *Land of the Giants*. The series was very imaginative and original. That's why it's retained its popularity. Irwin Allen was an energetic, amusing man. I enjoyed working with him."

Ghost Town
The earthlings are terrorized by an inventor's sadistic granddaughter in a miniature city. Wr: Gilbert Ralston, William Welch, story by Anthony Wilson, Gilbert Ralston. Dir: Nathan Juran.
   Prof. Ackman (Percy Helton); Glendora (Amber Flower); Tramp (Raymond Guth).

Framed
Witnessing the murder of a young woman, the outraged earthlings invade the murderer's home and embark on a campaign to scare him into confessing. Wr: Mann Rubin. Dir: Harry Harris.
   Photographer (Paul Carr); Hobo (Doodles Weaver); Model (Linda Peck); Policeman #1 (Dennis Cross); Policeman #2 (Baynes Barron).

Underground
To help a giant break the totalitarian hold over the land, the little people sneak into a giant security complex to retrieve a top secret letter. Wr: Ellis St. Joseph, story by Anthony Wilson. Dir: Sobey Martin.
   Prof. Gorak (John Abbott); Policeman (Lance Le Gault); Guard #1 (Paul Trinka); Guard #2 (James Gosa); Sentry (Jerry Catron); Fugitive (Ivan Markota).

Terror Go Round
The earthlings build a hot-air balloon to escape from a sadistic gypsy who is going to turn them over to a circus. Featured: A giant bear. Wr: Charles Bennett. Dir: Sobey Martin.
   Carlos (Joseph Ruskin); Luigi (Arthur Batanides); Pepi (Gerald Michenaud); Policeman (Arch Whiting).

The Flight Plan
A shrunken giant, posing as a lost airplane pilot, befriends the earthlings with the intention of stealing their spaceship and flying back to Earth. Wr: Peter Packer. Dir: Harry Harris.
   Joe/Loka (Linden Chiles); 1st giant (William Bramley); Molloch (Myron Healey); Guard (John Pickard).

Memory Flash—Linden Chiles: "I played my role with tremendous ego and arrogance. That was the normal attitude of the giants. It was a decent job."

Manhunt
Dan tries to blast the spaceship and a giant out of a pit of quicksand. Wr: Jay E. Selby (Robert Lees), Stanley H. Silverman. Dir: Sobey Martin.
  Giant convict (John Napier).

Memory Flash—Robert Lees: "I handed our script over to associate producer Jerry Briskin for a script reading. He made a crack he thought was funny. 'Is this shit worth reading?' I didn't find that humorous. After a moment of supressed anger, I said, 'Is this reading worth shit?' That may be why Stan and I only did one episode of *Land of the Giants*."

The Trap
Igniting a precious hydrogen cell from the ship, which could maroon them forever, is the only option for the earthlings when Betty and Valerie are captured by two scientists. Featured: A giant praying mantis. Wr: Jack Bradford Turley, story by Anthony Wilson. Dir: Sobey Martin.
  Scientist (Stewart Bradley); Assistant (Morgan Jones); Hood #1 (George Robotham); Hood #2 (Carl Saxe); Old man (Gil Perkins).

The Creed
Steve is forced to operate on Barry when the boy is stricken with appendicitis. Wr: Robert and Esther Mitchell, story by Richard P. McDonagh. Dir: Sobey Martin.
  Dr. Brule (Paul Fix); Janitor (Henry Corden); Policeman (Wesley Lau); Cop #1 (Harry Lauter); Cop #2 (Grant Sullivan); Delivery boy (Gary Tigerman).

Double Cross
Giant thieves force an amnesiac Fitzhugh to steal a ruby from a museum. Featured: A giant cat. Wr: Robert and Esther Mitchell. Dir: Harry Harris.
  Lobo (Lane Bradford); Hook (Willard Sage); Curator (Howard Culver); Museum cop (Ted Jordan); Cabin cop (Joseph Ryan).

The Weird World
A stranded astronaut agrees to lead the earthlings to his captured spaceship, but their journey is fraught with danger: The giant spider that killed the astronaut's crew is lurking nearby. Featured: a giant gopher, spider and crow. Wr: Ellis St. Joseph, story by Anthony Wilson. Dir: Harry Harris.
  Major Kagan (Glenn Corbett); Watchman (Don Gazzaniga); Scientist (Tony Regan); Boy (Emmet Burke); Man with pipe (Art Reichle).

The Golden Cage
Mark falls for a mysterious Earth woman who was raised by the giants and has been conditioned to betray other earthlings. Featured: A giant turkey.

Wr: Jack Bradford Turley, story by Anthony Wilson. Dir: Sobey Martin.
  Marna Wayland (Celeste Yarnall); Scientist (Douglas Bank); Giant (Dawson Palmer); Giant #2 (Page Slattery).

Memory Flash—Celeste Yarnall: "I was emotionally exhausted by the end of the filming. I spent hours working up the same tears in my crying scene because they had to cover it from many angles. The crew was very supportive and the cast was great fun. *Gulliver's Travels* was one of my favorite stories as a child. I loved working on the series."

The Lost Ones
Four hostile, shipwrecked earthlings need Steve's help when one of their group is captured by a giant trapper. Wr: Robert and Esther Mitchell. Dir: Harry Harris.
  Nick (Zalman King); Joey (Jack Chaplain); Hopper (Lee Jay Lambert); Dolf (Tommy Webb); Trapper (Dave Dunlap).

Memory Flash—Cast member Don Matheson: "The guys playing the punks were weird. They struck us as being really strange, and they thought we were a bunch of squares. Zalman King was one hell of an actor. He really got into his role."

Brainwash
An underground radio base built by long-dead astronauts can contact Earth, but it's threatened by a brainwashed Steve. Wr: William Welch. Dir: Harry Harris.
  Capt. Ashim (Warren Stevens); Dr. Kraal (Leonard Stone); Policeman (Robert Dowdell); Prisoner (Len Lesser); Kentucky control voice (Bartell La Rue).

The Bounty Hunter
The earthlings intensify efforts to repair the ship and load a giant gun for protection when reward posters send a giant camper after them. Wr: Daniel B. Ullman, story by Anthony Wilson. Dir: Harry Harris.
  Girl (Kimberly Beck); Camper (Paul Sorenson).

On a Clear Night You Can See Earth
The earthlings try to save Steve from a fanatical scientist who has pinpointed Earth's location with infrared binoculars. Featured: A giant dog. Wr: Sheldon Stark, story by Anthony Wilson. Dir: Sobey Martin.
  Dr. Murtragh (Michael Ansara).

The Deadly Lodestone
Dan voluntarily banishes himself to a dangerous section of the jungle, filled with spiders and quicksand, after giants home in on a piece of metal embedded in his leg. Wr: William L. Stuart. Dir: Harry Harris.
  Dr. Brule (Paul Fix); Nurse Helg (Sheila Matthews); Dobbs Kobick (Kevin Hagen); Secretary (Robert Emhardt); Warden (Gene Dynarski); Karf (Bill Fletcher).

Night of Thrombeldinbar

Fitzhugh endangers his life when he tries to help two unwanted boys at an orphanage during the giant holidays. Featured: A giant monkey. Wr: Robert and Esther Mitchell. Dir: Sobey Martin.

Parteg (Alfred Ryder); Okun (Jay Novello); Tobek (Michael A. Freeman); Garna (Teddy Quinn); Housewife (Miriam Schiller).

Seven Little Indians

The little people embark on a dangerous journey through giant animal cages to rescue Barry and Chipper from a zoo. Featured: A giant hyena, leopard and bird. Wr: Robert and Wanda Duncan. Dir: Harry Harris.

Grotius (Cliff Osmond); Kobick (Kevin Hagen); SID Man (Garry Walberg); SID man #2 (Henry Rico Cattani); Arnak (Chris Alcaide); SID man #3 (Erik Nelson).

Target: Earth

A friendly scientist agrees to transport the earthlings to Earth if Mark will fix his invention. However, the scientist's wife is insanely jealous of the earthlings. Featured: Giant dogs. Wr: Arthur Weiss. Dir: Sobey Martin.

Dr. Franzen (Arthur Franz); Altha Franzen (Dee Hartford); Kobick (Kevin Hagen); Logar (Peter Mamakos); Guard (Ted Jordan); Sergeant (Denver Mattson); Sergeant #2 (Ivan Markota).

Genius at Work

Steve and Fitzhugh are turned into giants by a scientific formula. Steve has to pose as a fast-talking lawyer to spring Fitzhugh from prison. Wr: Robert and Esther Mitchell. Dir: Sobey Martin.

Jodar (Ron Howard); Zurpin (Jacques Aubuchon); Giant (Vic Perrin); Kobick (Kevin Hagen); Officer (Paul Trinka); Cop (Patrick Culliton); Boy (Rusty Jones).

The Return of Inidu

The earthlings spend a creepy night in a haunted mansion, inhabited by a friendly magician who has been falsely accused of murder. Featured: A snake and bird. Wr: Robert and Esther Mitchell. Dir: Sobey Martin.

Inidu (Jack Albertson); Enog (Peter Haskell); Cop (Steven Marlo); Torg (Jerry Davis); Grot (Tony Benson).

Rescue

Steve and Dan descend into a crumbling mine shaft to rescue two giant children. Wr: Robert and Esther Mitchell. Dir: Harry Harris.

Mother (Lee Meriwether); Father (Don Collier); Tedar (Buddy Foster); Leeda (Blair Ashley); Kobick (Kevin Hagen); Sgt. Gedo (Tom Reese); Newsman (Roy Rowan); Lt. Emar (Michael J. Quinn).

Memory Flash—Lee Meriwether: "The episode was filmed just before I went to Mexico to do the film *The Undefeated* with John Wayne. I had gotten a series of shots in both arms to ward off various diseases one gets when one goes into the interior of foreign countries. So my arms were very tender.

Well, 'Rescue' was a very emotional episode. My children had fallen down a hole, and rescue was dangerous. The actor playing my husband would grab my arms and squeeze. OOOch! It was painful, but it helped. I barely had to act in the crying scenes at all."

Sabotage

A giant politician uses a campaign of hate against little people to win votes. When the giant begins framing the earthlings for disasters, Steve decides to expose the politician. Wr: Robert and Esther Mitchell. Dir: Harry Harris.

Bolgar (Robert Colbert); Zarkin (John Marley); Obek (Parley Baer); Secretary (Elizabeth Rogers); Policeman (Douglas Bank); Newsboy (Keith Taylor).

Shell Game

The parents of a deaf-mute boy capture the spaceship and plan to turn it over to the authorities to gain reward money with which to cure their son. Featured: A giant lobster and weasel. Wr: Robert and Esther Mitchell, story by William Welch. Dir: Harry Harris.

Osla (Jan Sheppard); Talf (Larry Ward); Dal (Gary Dubin); Derg (Tol Avery).

The Chase

Steve and Mark endure giant creatures and poisonous chemicals as they travel through the city's storm drains to locate freedom fighters. Featured: A giant rat. Wr: William Welch, Arthur Weiss, story by William Welch. Dir: Sobey Martin.

Naylor (Robert F. Lyons); Trilling (Timothy Scott); Golan (Patrick Sullivan Burke); Kobick (Kevin Hagen); Sergeant (Norman Burton); SID man (Erik Nelson).

Season 2: 1969-70

The Mechanical Man

Mark agrees to fix a scientist's giant super-robot, which has been going on a violent rampage in the city. Featured: A giant ferret. Wr: William L. Stuart. Dir: Harry Harris.

Prof. Gorn (Broderick Crawford); Zoral (Stuart Margolin); Robot (James Daris); Secretary Mek (William Chapman); Policeman (Richard Carlyle); SID man (Erik Nelson); SID man #2 (Steven Marlo).

Memory Flash—Stuart Margolin: "I found myself in a strange role and in a strange costume. Broderick Crawford had been a great film actor. By this time, his career had diminished, and that saddened me. There were some interesting effects on *Land of the Giants* but the quality of the material was not fabulous."

Six Hours to Live

The earthlings join up with a reporter to clear an innocent man of murder, but his execution time is only hours away. Wr: Daniel B. Ullman. Dir: Sobey Martin.

Martin Reed (Sam Elliot); Joe Simmons (Richard Anderson); Martha Cass (Anne Seymour); Warden (Bill Quinn); Harry Cass (George Mitchell); Guard (Larry Pennell); Arnold (Michael J. Quinn); Pharmacist (Maxwell Power); Miller (Stewart Bradley).

The Inside Rail
The earthlings spend a harrowing day at the race track after Fitzhugh and a giant hobo place a bet on a winning horse. Featured: A giant chicken. Wr: Richard Shapiro. Dir: Harry Harris.

Moley (Ben Blue); Chief Rivers (Arch Johnson); Hood (Vic Tayback); Groom (John Harmon); Sergeant (Joseph Turkel).

The Deadly Pawn
Frozen, the earthlings thaw out on a giant chess board where they play a life and death game against a giant chess expert. Wr: Arthur Weiss. Dir: Nathan Juran.

Dr. Kronig (Alex Dreier); Dr. Lalor (John Zaremba); Technician (Steven Marlo); Guard (Charlie Briggs).

The Unsuspected
Poisoned by mushroom spores, a paranoid Steve captures his fellow earthlings one by one. Wr: Robert and Esther Mitchell. Dir: Harry Harris.

Eson (Leonard Stone); Kobick (Kevin Hagen).

Giants and All That Jazz
Dan teaches boxer Biff Bower how to play jazz but two giant loan-sharks threaten to kill Bower unless he pays off a debt. Featured: A giant snake. Wr: Richard Shapiro. Dir: Harry Harris.

Biff Bower (Sugar Ray Robinson); Hanley (William Bramley); Loach (Mike Mazurki); Nell (Diana Chesney).

Collector's Item
A spoiled nephew uses Valerie in a plot to murder his rich uncle. Featured: A giant dog and crow. Wr: Robert and Wanda Duncan. Dir: Sobey Martin.

Garak (Guy Stockwell); Mrs. Garak (Susan Howard); Uncle Tojar (Robert H. Harris); Goldsmith (George Sperdakos); SID man (Erik Nelson).

Every Dog Needs a Boy
A friendly giant operates on an injured Chipper, but his colleague tries to capture the little people and turn them over to the authorities. Featured: A giant dog, cat and ocelot. Wr: Jerry Thomas. Dir: Harry Harris.

Ben Carter (Michael Anderson, Jr.); Carl Howard (Tom Nardini); Clinton (Robert Shayne); Dr. Howard (Oliver McGowan).

Chamber of Fear
The earthlings agree to recover a stolen diamond from a spooky wax museum after a thief captures Fitzhugh. Featured: A giant dog. Wr: Arthur Weiss. Dir: Sobey Martin.

Deenar (Christopher Cary); Mara (Joan Freeman); Jolo (Cliff Osmond); Policeman (Don Kennedy); The Monk (Robert Tiedemann).

The Clones
The little people encounter strange, hostile duplicates of themselves. Wr: Robert and Esther Mitchell, Oliver Crawford, story by Oliver Crawford. Dir: Nathan Juran.

Dr. Arno (William Schallert); Dr. Greta Gault (Sandra Giles).

Comeback
The earthlings agree to star in a horror film, but the director's quest for realism nearly gets them killed. Featured: A giant gorilla. Wr: Richard Shapiro. Dir: Harry Harris.

Egor Krull (John Carradine); Max Manfred (Jesse White); Quigg (Fritz Feld); Baby (Janos Prohaska); Cameraman (Olan Soule); Gateman (James Jeter).

A Place Called Earth
Agressive time travelers from Earth, 5477 A.D., plan to wipe out the giants with advanced weapons. Wr: William Welch. Dir: Harmon Jones.

Olds (Warren Stevens); Fielder (Jerry Douglas); Bron (Jerry Quarry); Mezron (Rex Holman); Messenger (Scott Thomas); Mezron's brother (Gene Le Bell); Pharmacist (John Mooney).

Land of the Lost
A terrifying balloon ride across the sea deposits the earthlings on an island ruled by a fanatic dictator. Wr: William Welch. Dir: Sobey Martin and Nathan Juran.

Titus (Nehemiah Persoff); Andros (Clint Ritchie); Flight Man (Ron Husmann); Boy (Brian Nash); Vendor (Robert Braun); Slave #1 (Peter Canon); Sentry (Fred Villani).

Home Sweet Home
Steve and Fitzhugh return to Earth in a space capsule, but the year is 1900 and the New England townspeople mistake them for warlocks. Wr: William Welch. Dir: Harry Harris.

Wilson (John Milford); Emma Perkins (June Dayton); Homer (Mort Mills); Jack (William H. Bassett); Sloacum (Robert Adler); Guard (Pete Kellett); Peabody (William Benedict).

Our Man O'Reilly
A friendly Irishman, who believes the earthlings are leprechauns, helps them repair the spaceship. However, O'Reilly is framed for robbery by a crooked cop. Wr: Jackson Gillis. Dir: Sobey Martin.

O'Reilly (Alan Hale); Krenko (Alan Bergmann); Cunningham (Lindsay Workman); Jake (Michael J. Quinn); Harry (Billy Halop); Brynie (Edward Marr); Warner (Dusty Cadis).

Memory Flash—Alan Bergmann: "My memory of the actual show is dim, except for the kindness and sweetness of Alan Hale. Science fiction has always had its devotees, but radio was often more successful in this genre. *Lights Out* and *X Minus One*, which I acted on, are good examples. Radio allowed the imagination to run free."

Nightmare

An overdose of radiation from the spaceship's engine room plunges the earthlings and the giants into a nightmarish world of illusion. Featured: A giant lizard. Wr: William Welch. Dir: Nathan Juran.

Dr. Berger (Torin Thatcher); Andre (Yale Summers); Kobick (Kevin Hagen).

Pay the Piper

The little people fight off the Pied Piper of Hamelin. He's an alien who will go to any lengths to kidnap a senator's son. Featured: A giant badger. Wr: Richard Shapiro. Dir: Harry Harris.

Piper (Jonathan Harris); Senator (Peter Leeds); Timmy (Michael James-Wixted).

The Secret City of Limbo

The earthlings befriend the leader of an underground world. Giant geologists blasting from above may expose the secret city and begin an apocolyptic war. Featured: A giant lizard. Wr: Robert and Esther Mitchell. Dir: Sobey Martin.

Taru (Malachi Throne); Aza (Joseph Ruskin); Dr. Krane (Whit Bissell); Mylo (Peter Jason).

Panic

The earthlings try to free a giant inventor from jail and use his teleporter to return to Earth. Featured: A giant dog and cat. Wr: Robert and Wanda Duncan. Dir: Sobey Martin.

Prof. Kirmus (Jack Albertson); Mrs. Evers (Diane McBain); Marad (Peter Mark Richman); Willis (Patrick Culliton); Rogers (Edward G. Robinson, Jr.); Burns (Steven Marlo).

Memory Flash—Patrick Culliton: "Irwin regarded me as something of a good luck charm in his films. That was kind of amazing since we did great ones [*The Towering Inferno*] and weak ones [*Beyond the Poseidon Adventure*] together. Irwin was a genius. During the 1960s he would come up with fantastic ideas and sometimes people would laugh. When his shows were still a top ten hit three years later, people weren't laughing anymore. *Land of the Giants* did well for itself. It was a damn good show."

The Deadly Dart

Mark angrily leaves his fellow earthlings when evidence points to him as the killer of several giants. Wr: William L. Stuart. Dir: Harry Harris.

Bertha Frye (Madlyn Rhue); Lt. Grayson (John Dehner); Dr. Jelco (Kent Taylor); Zoral (Donald "Red" Barry); Barker (Christopher Dark); Swann (Willard Sage).

Doomsday

The little people and Inspector Kobick join forces to expose a ruthless woman scientist who has rigged the city with explosives. Featured: A giant chimp. Wr: Daniel B. Ullman. Dir: Harry Harris.

Dr. North (Francine York); Kobick (Kevin Hagen); Sergeant (Tom Drake); Kamber (Charles Dierkop); Warkin (Ed Peck); Driver (stunts) (Fred Lerner).

Trivia Alert: Actress and dancer Cyd Charisse was originally scheduled to play the role of the villainous Dr. North. She sprained her ankle a day before filming, and Francine York replaced her. Veteran actor John Dierkes (as Inspector Turner) was replaced at the last minute by Kevin Hagen.

A Small War

A vindictive boy launches his toy army against the little people. Wr: Shirl Hendryx, story by Anthony Wilson. Dir: Harry Harris.

Erdap (Charles Drake); Alek (Sean Kelly); Nurse (Miriam Schiller); Toys (Fred Lerner, Ralph Garrett, Ted Jordan).

The Marionettes

A greedy circus manager wants to capitalize on the singing talents of Betty and Fitzhugh. Featured: A giant gorilla. Wr: William Welch. Dir: Sobey Martin.

Lisa (Victoria Vetri); Brady (Robert Hogan); Goalby (Frank Ferguson); Dancer (Sandra Giles); Bo Bo (Janos Prohaska); Diane (Diane Krabbe); Fire eater (Al Lampkin); Knife thrower (Carl Carlson); Trainer (Martin Liverman); Puppet man (Robert Baker).

Wild Journey

Steve and Dan propel themselves back to Earth, 1983, where they try to change history by stopping the launch of the Spindrift. Featured: A giant dog. Wr: William Welch. Dir: Harry Harris.

Thorg (Bruce Dern); Berna (Yvonne Craig); Miss Collier (Sheila Matthews); SID man (Erik Nelson); Passerby (Marshall Stewart); Miss Smith (Louise Lorimer); Guards (William Hicks, Martin Liverman).

Memory Flash—Erik Nelson: "The brown Doberman pinscher that I used to chase down the little people was more disciplined than the majority of actors that I've worked with. I had always been cautious of Dobermans, but this one was a delight. He won me over."

The Graveyard of Fools

Transported to the other side of the planet, the earthlings face prehistoric creatures and a scientist who is exploiting a new energy source. Featured: A giant praying mantis and lizard. Wr: Sidney Marshall. Dir: Sobey Martin.

Melzac/Bryk (Albert Salmi); Tagor (John Crawford); Janitor (Marshall Stewart).

Logan's Run
September 1977–January 1978

In a utopian society all is not as it seems. Within the city's doomed walls are those who would refuse "renewal" and seek the mythical Sanctuary—those who would live beyond the age of 30. To stop these dissident "runners" is the job of the Sandmen. Logan 5 is a Sandman, and Jessica is the runner who convinces him that renewal is not rebirth, but really a death ritual, used to limit population growth. Together the fugitives, accompanied by the android REM, flee accross a post-nuclear America, always one step ahead of the Sandmen, who are led by Francis, Logan's one time partner.

Cast: Logan 5 (Gregory Harrison); Jessica 6 (Heather Menzies); REM (Donald Moffat); Francis 6 (Randy Powell).

Based on the novel by William F. Nolan and George Clayton Johnson; **Executive Producer:** Ivan Goff and Ben Roberts; **Producer:** Leonard Katzman; **Story Editor:** D.C. Fontana; **Theme:** Lawrence Rosenthal; CBS/MGM TV; 60 minutes.

In 1976, MGM asked you to run with Logan (Michael York) and his companion, Jessica (Jenny Agutter), in theaters. In the fall of 1977, they asked you to follow them on television. There would have been no series without the feature, and no feature without the controversial 1967 science fiction novel by William F. Nolan and George Clayton Johnson.

The premise of *Logan's Run* has changed with each incarnation. In the novel, a fledgling, futuristic society inside a large complex of domes is unaware of the existence of an outside world. No one in this society lives beyond 21; at that age, in a society-enforced population control device called Lastday, citizens engage in "life renewal," which is in truth voluntary death. Logan is a Sandman, a member of the police force that tracks down Lastday escapees, who are called runners. Logan is drawn into becoming a runner himself. He and companion Jessica escape from the domes to seek a haven for runners called Sanctuary. Another Sandman, Francis, is in pursuit.

In the film, for casting purposes, life ended at 30 instead of 21. Sanctuary was no longer an abandoned space station circling Mars, as in the novel; in the film, Sanctuary is never found. The film kept the basic society structure and several of the characters, but incorporated these into a different adventure for cinematic spectacle. Richard Jordan starred as the nemesis Sandman, Francis, while Peter Ustinov was a frail old man found among the ruins of Washington, D.C. (the character named Ballard in the novel). In the film, Logan and Jessica persuade the old man to return with them to the city of domes to prove that old age exists—that is, that life need not end at 30. In the end, the city of domes self-destructs, and life begins anew on the outside.

To help market the film, the novel was reprinted and has since gone through many printings. Nolan's two sequel novels, *Logan's World* and *Logan's Search*, have also been published. MGM released a soundtrack album of the film by composer Jerry Goldsmith, and the film also won an Oscar for best visual effects.

To adapt *Logan's Run* for television, producers Ivan Goff and Ben Roberts had to make changes to the premise. First, they recast the roles of Logan and Jessica (keeping the age limit of 30 years), which went to Gregory Harrison and Heather Menzies, with Randy Powell as the pursuing Francis. An original element, the Council of Elders, was added to explain who was running the society. (The council ordered Francis to retrieve Logan and his companion.) Next, the producers added an android named REM (the abbreviation for rapid eye movement, a phase of sleep), played by Donald Moffat, who accompanied them in an appropriated hovercraft in their search for Sanctuary. The resulting formula of the show was that Logan, Jessica and REM traveled across the post–nuclear holocaust Earth in search of a haven, encountering aliens, hunters, other Sandmen, ghosts, time travelers, and robots along the way. Francis, who traveled with a cohort of Sandmen, occasionally hampered their goals.

Gregory Harrison, star of *Logan's Run*, emphasizes that the notion of death at a young age "was a very popular concept at the time. Being over the age of 30 wasn't anything worth living; let's do those people in and start somebody over. There was a movie a few years before that called *Wild in the Streets* [1968] with Christopher Jones where these 20- to 25-year-old, young

Angela Cartwright (foreground) guest-stars in "The Collectors" with Heather Menzies (middle) and Gregory Harrison (back) in *Logan's Run*. Copyright 1977 CBS/MGM.

revolutionaries take over the government of the United States. It was the first major entertainment piece that perpetuated the idea that younger than 30 was the only valid age to be. And this is sort of the science fiction version of that concept.

"I remember sitting in the theatre at the Cinerama dome a year before the series, watching *Logan's Run* with Michael York, being absolutely fascinated. I've always been a huge science fiction fan, and watching the feature, I was thinking, 'This is wonderful, I love this,' but *never* imagining that I was going to be playing that part and wearing that costume and using the same gun. A lot of the stuff we used came directly from

the feature. It was quite a thrill when I got cast and screen tested."

Playing the lead in a prime-time hour television series can be a heady experience for an actor, especially when it's his first time, and the circumstances of *Logan's Run* made it all the more exciting. The show was constantly on the road filming at various locations in Southern California, and because it was science fiction, it involved creating new costumes, sets, and special effects for every episode. Also, with the involvement of MGM, the show drew on an impressive lineage including such science fiction and fantasy works as *Forbidden Planet* and the *Logan's* feature.

"At the time we were shooting," says Harrison, "it was pretty high-tech, top of the line in terms of special effects, opticals on film. ... While we were doing it, we were hearing stories about this other science fiction film called *Star Wars* which we didn't know. It came out after our first season was finished [filming], and it made everything we had done look like the old black-and-white Buck Rogers serials. It sort of made us obsolete almost immediately. Prior to the release of the movie, we thought we were high-end!"

Generally, *Logan's Run* was hampered by a format that encouraged many plots in which the main characters were either being captured, chased, threatened or forced to rescue others. It was a "road show" in a science fiction arena.

"We were always running away from the ugly fate that the Sandmen offered," says Harrison. "And we were looking toward Sanctuary, a place where we could be safe, where we could have a home, raise children. I remember the term 'renewal' was something we played a lot with on the set, because the series was always hoping for renewal. But we were running away from it. What they called 'renewal' was really death. [Renewal] was basically turning a slaughterhouse into a religion. Which has been done before—in real life. A lot of the evolution about religion throughout the world has been for the sake of control, to eliminate the chaos that comes without some kind of organized thought pattern."

Speaking of chaos, Harrison offers some recollections of one of his most physically challenging episodes, "Capture." "We shot that in Big Bear Lake, in Southern California. It was a very hectic show, a lot of running over hills, rocks, huge boulders everywhere up there. That show, we had a special effects man who didn't engender a lot of confidence. I remember I was supposed to get shot, [or] somebody was supposed to get shot, in that show. The special effects guy was doing a lot of drinking. I remember saying, 'No, I don't think we should put that squib on the person until we've tested it against the neoprene that will protect it.' So we put the neoprene on the rock and blew up the squib…, and there were pieces of rock that blew up behind it. That was one of my career lessons right there. I was careful enough to suggest a test and the test proved that the guy would have been disemboweled had he had the thing on."

Actually, it was earlier in the series that Harrison had an inkling to be more careful when performing stunts. In the pilot, Harrison had to use his weapon to blast a hole in a wall so he could appropriate a hovercraft for travel. Point the gun at the wall and I'll blow the explosives, the special effects man told Harrison. It's simple, he said. Not quite.

"The camera was behind me about 10 to 15 feet and I was about 20 feet away from the wall," explains Harrison. "The special effects guy—I think it was the same guy—said, 'OK, this is going to explode, not implode, so you can stand two feet from this wall and when we blow it, it's going to all blow in the *other* direction.

"I said, 'OK.' So I walk up to about 15 feet away from this wall, aim my gun—the camera is shooting over my shoulder—and fire. He pushes the button off camera, and the wall blows up entirely towards me and knocks me back, knocks the camera, and holes burn through my black outfit. I'm sure it's the same special effects guy, which is why I didn't trust him when he said,

'Yeah, you can hold this squib.' I don't think he stayed in the business for too long after that," laughs Harrison. The wall was rebuilt, the scene reshot, and the resulting film was shown under the main titles for every episode.

Other location memories included one fateful day that could have killed Harrison and ended the show on the spot. "I did a scene once where I was captured by a bunch of guys in white and they're riding on white horses," says Harrison, referring to the episode "Turnabout." "I think we shot up at Malibu Canyon. We're crossing far away from the camera. We're just slowly going along. While we're filming—this isn't in the show—my horse stepped on a squirrel hole that had become a beehive. And bees attacked. They came furiously out of this hole, and attacked my horse and me. There were hundreds of bees attached to my black wool Sandman outfit, pumping away, trying to get their stingers through there, and I ended up with 17 bee stings. Three or four in my head and hair and face, and several of them got through areas like elbows, knees, under my arms. I couldn't work for the rest of the day. I went into this sort of semi-coma for the day, as a reaction to the stings. Fortunately I wasn't allergic, or I would have died! It scared the hell out of everyone, and they shut down for the day, and the next day my ankle is the size of my thighs! It was so swollen up from the bee stings. All my blood had settled into my legs. For days I was miserable from all these bee stings, but we kept shooting. That was an interesting day."

As the show progressed, Harrison's life did not become any easier. "I remember one weekend," he says, "we were shooting a scene, crossing the desert. We were shooting up at Lancaster, the upper desert outside of Southern California. I went away for the weekend, they put us up at a hotel for each night. When I came back to my apartment, as I drove up there, the building is no longer there! It had burned to the ground!" Harrison laughs. "I lost everything I had owned in my apartment. I had only what I was carrying with me in the car. It was actually a blessing because my girlfriend and I were together for about six years at the time, we were in a miserable breakup mode for about a year and were trying to figure out how to divide up our stuff. We were still living there only because we didn't know who deserved to keep what. So, essentially, this ended that failed romance and there was no question anymore who kept what—there was nothing to keep."

The *Logan's Run* cast, left to right: Randy Powell, Heather Menzies, Donald Moffat and Gregory Harrison. Copyright 1977 CBS/MGM.

In the television incarnation of *Logan's Run*, Logan and Jessica were not the lovers they were in the book and film. Only twice in the series did they kiss—and one of those kisses came when Jessica was trying to seduce an amnesia-stricken Logan (in the episode "Carousel") so he would escape with her from the city of domes a second time.

"Well, that's the problem of television, especially in that era: No one believed you can have a leading man and woman in an ongoing series always stopping to do some hanky-panky and start running again," explains Harrison. "That was something reserved for a feature. They felt it would eliminate a good portion of the bible belt who would be offended by that concept. The problem with television in general, which I'm all too familiar with after five different series, is that they try to do the impossible. Trying to please everybody all the time, and offend no one. And you end up with such milk-processed kinds of plots and characters that *nothing* really gets said or accomplished, I feel, artistically or dramatically, because you're so afraid of offending someone about something. You have to homogenize everything so much to be inoffensive to *all* parties that you end up impressing no one or moving them emotionally. You've homogenized all the flavor out of it."

Working with co-star Heather Menzies was a delight for Harrison, and to this day, they remain close friends. "She had just married Robert Urich at that time," recalls Harrison. "They didn't have any children at the time, and now I think they have three children. One of them is 17 years old. I saw him the other day and

Playing Logan was fun for Harrison, but he does not recall any particular contributions he might have made to the character. This was his first leading role in a prime-time TV series, so his agenda was to be quiet and learn as much as he could. "I was developing opinions at that time," says Harrison. "I ended up working such tremendous hours on that show, I had walking pneumonia for the last six weeks of the season. Working 10 to 13 hours a day, every day, falling over on the weekend. There was no break for me. It was relentless. I recall it mostly being [more] a survival effort than an artistic effort for me. I did learn a lot about how television works—scheduling, technique, acting for camera, hitting marks, lines. It was basically my [film] school in that series."

I just had a heart attack, I couldn't believe it was that long since we had worked together. She is a wonderful woman and, I thought, a talented actress. But she pretty much finished her career with [*Logan's Run*] and opted for motherhood and wifehood and I think is very happily now living with Bob in Utah."

When asked for anecdotes of their working relationship, Harrison responds, "I remember Heather was always in this skimpy little pink outfit, she never wore a bra and you could always see her boobs underneath there and when it was cold, boy, you could tell! I was always wearing long-sleeved, wool with leather and a turtleneck. Shooting in the desert, Heather was just comfy as can be, and I was miserable. I would drink two gallons of water a day and be sweating like crazy all day long in 90 to 95 degree weather. When winter came around,

Francis (Randy Powell, left) and Logan (Gregory Harrison). Copyright 1977 CBS/MGM.

Heather was always freezing and I was always just great. We were opposing seasons, Heather and I."

REM was something of a magical character. His mastery of technological equipment helped the three escape from a number of binds during their travels. Harrison enjoyed working with the actor who played REM — "Donald is a wonderful, talented actor who's gone on to do some wonderful things since then"—but he confesses he never was pleased with how the character was used.

"The android character was sort of a cheat for the writers to not have to deal with the human limitation that I think makes drama so compelling. Here's an android that solves things when you get into a dilemma that the writers don't know how to get you out of. The android always

comes up with a solution because he wasn't limited by human frailties. ... That's probably my biggest gripe with the series right from the beginning. They always had that option available and unfortunately used it too often, instead of really challenging themselves to write the kind of stories ... where human beings with human frailties would have to find the means of survival on their own. And therefore make it something more relatable to present day. It was too much science, not enough human element. [The writers should have tried] to use human intellect and human emotion ... [not only as the] sentimental side of the story but survival side of the story."

D.C. Fontana, a *Star Trek* staff veteran who signed on as story editor agrees with Harrison's assessment of how REM was used. "Too many times REM (wonderfully acted by Donald Moffat, by the way) dominated a storyline or saved Logan and Jessica when, by all rights, they should have been saving themselves. REM had too many answers too often. Logan and Jessica should have been discovering answers for themselves."

But Fontana emphasizes that this is not commentary on the actors, who, she says, were all excellent in their roles. "It's merely an element in some scripts that I personally felt shouldn't have been there."

Concerning what else worked and didn't work on the show, Fontana says, "In my opinion, an important piece of the puzzle as to why Francis kept hunting Logan and Jessica was filled in, in the pilot, when he met the Council of Elders who really ruled the city and was promised that he, too, would live a long life if he captured runners and brought them back for punishment. This gave Francis a strong self-interest in continuing the pursuit at all costs. What became difficult to explain is how many of the other Sandmen Francis (or the Council) had to bring into the secret in order to get them to keep on going on the outside after the runners. (And how did Francis and the other Sandmen get all that equipment to keep on following as Logan and Jessica and REM progressed further away?)

"We had to work on the assumption that by necessity, a certain number of very dedicated Sandmen could be brought into at least partial knowledge of what was going on and that they, too, would be rewarded."

Working on *Logan's Run* gave Fontana some frustration. She and producer Leonard Katzman were hired on the show for their knowledge of the genre. Executive producers Ivan Goff and Ben Roberts publicly admitted they were novices in this area. So it was difficult for Fontana when her comments, along with Katzman's, were often ignored when it came to areas of science fiction. Goff and Roberts, says Fontana, were the ones who "ran scripts through the typewriter one last time. Frequently script and character emphasis was changed over our protests," she laments. "They were also the ones so in love with their character REM that at times the series threatened to be *REM's Run*, not *Logan's Run*. Unfortunately they were the ones with the final approvals."

Picking favorite episodes, Fontana cites her script "Carousel," because "Logan and Jessica were finally brought back to the city, and there was a strong hint of a much more important relationship between them." Fontana also liked "Futurepast," Katharyn Powers' love story between REM and a female android (played by Mariette Hartley).

Donald Moffat confesses that he remembers precious little of the show, adding, "I wasn't sorry when it was over. I got the part of REM the usual way—by auditioning for it—and I had some input as to what he looked like, etc. The open panel [on REM's body] with the wiring visible was my idea, and of course, his personality was mine. But actors, by and large, don't have much say in a thing—until it becomes a big success, and then they often have too much." Moffat got along well with his co-stars and muses the show's budget may have been too much for the network, noting that the special effects were very time-consuming.

Viewers might notice that occasionally, *Star Trek* sound effects were used whenever computer equipment processed data. This borrowing was only one of many practical distractions for discerning viewers. What about Logan's weapon, which has a number of settings like "blaster" and "stun" for freezing targets into stasis, yet never seems to run out of energy?

"There were a lot of questions like that. How come the vehicle bounced on a rock when it was supposed to be a hovercraft?" quips Gregory Harrison. "Lots of questions!"

The show remains popular via Turner network reruns, and Harrison reports that people still speak to him about the show today, particularly children. He himself remembers the series fondly, if modestly. "I was just an actor looking for a steady job, and was thrilled that I was doing science fiction. It was a venue I appreciated and enjoyed. I was glad to have my own series ... and I knew my career was going the right direction. I feel we have an A for effort and C for the show itself, for how it succeeded."

CAST NOTES

Gregory Harrison (Logan 5): Born 1950. Harrison co-starred for seven years (1979–86) in the popular *Trapper John M.D.* series as Gonzo Gates. His most recent series is *The Family Man*. His TV movies include *For Ladies Only* (1981), *Breaking the Silence* (1992) with Stephanie Zimbalist and *Duplicates* (USA Cable) with Cicely Tyson and Kevin McCarthy, shot in Oregon. With his production company, Catalina Production Group, Ltd., he's hosted *True Detectives* for CBS (1992).

Heather Menzies (Jessica 6): Born 1949. This Canadian-born actress played one of the Von Trapp children in the film *Sound of Music* (1965). She is married to actor Robert Urich. Before retiring from acting to raise a family, she appeared in *The Six Million Dollar Man*, the TV pilot *Captain America*, and Urich's series *Vegas* and *American Dreamer*.

Randy Powell (Francis): Born 1950. Powell appeared in *Dallas* in the early 1980s and, according to Gregory Harrison, has since moved to New Zealand.

Donald Moffat (REM): Born 1930 in Plymouth, England. Moffat's most recent work includes supporting roles in *Popeye* (1980) and John Carpenter's remake of *The Thing* (1982), as well as various TV movies and features.

EPISODE GUIDE

Logan's Run (90 minutes)
On Lastday, several hundred years in the future, Jessica meets policeman Logan and convinces him there is a world outside of their city of domes. As they become "runners" and escape, Logan's friend and colleague Francis is ordered by the Council of Elders to return Logan and Jessica to the city.

With Francis on their tail, Logan and Jessica, using an appropriated hovercraft, encounter a sheltered group of people who reveal to them the existence of old age. Leaving this society, they come across a mountain city where they meet Draco and Siri, robots who imprison them because they need someone to serve. REM, another robot saves them and joins them in their search for the mythic Sanctuary. Wr: William F. Nolan, Saul David, Leonard Katzman. Dir: Robert Day.

Draco (Keene Curtis); Siri (Lina Raymond); Jonathan (Wright King); Martin (E.J. Andre); Morgan (Morgan Woodward); Riles (Ron Hajek); Akers (J. Gary Dontzig); Ketcham (Anthony de Longis); Rider #3 (Cal Haynes); Marianne (Mary Hamill); Karlin (Ted Markland); Rider #4 (Sandy McPeak); Leanna (Kimberly LePage); David (Patrick Gorman); Man (Gilbert Girion); Paine (Marvin Dean Stewart); Sandman (Michael Biehn); Woman (Mary Ball); Barry (Gary Charles Davis).

The Collectors
Invaders from another planet capture Logan and Jessica via illusions—convincing them they have finally found Sanctuary. But REM, immune to illusions, sees through the deception. Wr: James Schmerer. Dir: Alexander Singer.

John (Linden Chiles); Joanna (Leslie Parrish); Karen (Angela Cartwright); Martin (Lawrence Casey); Sandman #1 (Perry Bullington); Sandman #2 (Ben Van Vactor); Sandman #3 (Stan Stratton).

Trivia Alert: Angela Cartwright, who starred in *Lost in Space*, appeared with Heather Menzies in *The Sound of Music*.

Capture
As Francis finally intercepts Logan, Jessica and REM, they are all captured by a professional hunter who has become bored with hunting animals. When the man accidentally kills his wife, he's doubly enraged, more than ever determined to kill Logan and Francis. Wr: Michael Edwards. Dir: Irving J. Moore.

James Borden (Horst Bucholz); Irene (Mary Woronov); Benjamin (Stan Stratton).

The Innocent
Cornered by their pursuers, the runners enter a minefield and find themselves in an unusual complex. A lonely woman who has never been in the outside world confronts them. She lives in a sterile, computerized world, and she falls in love with Logan. Wr: Ray Brenner and D.C. Fontana. Dir: Michael Preece.

Lisa (Lisa Eilbacher); Strong (Lou Richards); Jeremy (Barney McFadden); Patrick (Brian Kerwin); Friend (Gene Tyburn).

Man Out of Time
Logan, Jessica and REM encounter a time traveler who takes them to a place called Sanctuary. But it isn't their destination. Inhabitants are a very religious cult following the "old science." The stranger is looking for a way to prevent the holocaust that formed the domes. Wr: Noah Ward (David Gerrold). Dir: Nicholas Colasanto.

David Eakins (Paul Shenar); Analog (Mel Ferrer); Lab tech one (Woodrow Chambliss); Com tech four (Gene Tyburn); Gold (Hank Brandt); Fontaine (Betty Bridges); White (Wallace Chadwell); Martinez (Kenneth Martinez); Handley (Jeff Reese); Binary (Jeff Cotler); Katie (Sherril Lynn Katzman).

Half Life
The trio is attacked by a group of genetically duplicated humans: gentle and peaceful Positives, who live in the city, and animal-like Negatives, who are castouts from society living in the country. Jessica is "processed" and split into two people. Wr: Shimon Wincelberg. Dir: Steven Stern.

Patron/Modok (William Smith); Positive 14/Brawn (Len Birman); Rama II (Kim Cattrall); Rama I (Jeanne Sorel); Woman-Positive (Betty Jinnette); Engineer-Scientist (John Gowans).

Crypt
Six survivors of the holocaust are discovered frozen in an underground vault, but earthquakes hamper rescue and the serum to save them is dropped, leaving only enough to save three of them. Logan, Jessica and REM must decide which three will survive.

Complicating the picture, one of the six may be a murderer and an imposter. Wr: Al Hayes and Harlan Ellison. Dir: Michael Caffey.

David Pera (Christopher Stone); Rachel Greenhill (Ellen Weston); Dexter Kim (Soon Teck-Oh); Victoria Mackie (Neva Patterson); Frederick Lyman (Liam Sullivan); Sylvia Reyna (Adrienne LaRussa); Dr. Mildred Krim (Peggy McCay); Man on video (Richard Roat).

Memory Flash—Liam Sullivan: "The plot had six of us discovered in glass cases, like coffins. At one point, the doors were to open and we emerged as if from a deep trance. Except the lock on my coffin didn't work. They couldn't get me out. It looked as though they had to smash the glass, but at the last moment, one of the girls picked the lock and I staggered out.

"Logan's Run was a good series, but the premise of escaping from a tyrant city was hard to sustain over a period of time. Gregory Harrison was excellent. I recall *Man from Atlantis* was shooting on the next soundstage, and Patrick Duffy kept wandering over to our set, flapping his webbed feet and breaking us up. Wicked sense of humor, Patrick."

Fear Factor

Two scientists engaged in an unusual scientific experiment capture the travelers and use them to further their goals. The scientists want to remove emotions from subjects to create a race of docile followers. Wr: John Sherlock. Dir: Gerald Mayer.

Dr. Rowan (Ed Nelson); Dr. Emory Paulson (Jared Martin); Psychiatrist #1 (William Wellman, Jr.); Psychiatrist #2 (Peter Brandon); Psychiatrist #3 (Carl Byrd); The Woman (Jay W. Macintosh); Guard A (Sean Fallon Walsh); Guard #1 (Tim Gillin); Guard #2 (Thomas Brunelle).

Judas Goat

The fugitives meet up with a Sandman disguised as a runner, Hal 14, who persuades them to return to the city of domes to recruit more runners. But first they encounter a "Provider," who wants to serve their needs via electronic means. REM rescues them from the trap, but not before they visit the city of domes again. Wr: John Meredyth Lucas. Dir: Paul Krasny.

Hal 14 (Nicholas Hammond); Matthew (Lance LeGault); Jonathan (Wright King); Garth (Spencer Milligen); Morgan (Morgan Woodward); Joseph 8 (Gary Tomlin); Carlos (Andrew Masset); Elna (Diane Lander); Mark (Patrick Skelton); Theo (James Poyner).

Trivia Alert: Nicholas Hammond starred in *Spiderman*, and he also appeared in *The Sound of Music* with Heather Menzies.

Futurepast

Encountering a green-domed building, the travelers discover a female android named Ariana. Ariana hooks Logan and Jessica up to a dream analysis machine that can kill them. To complicate matters, Francis arrives before REM can free his friends. Wr: Kathryn Michaelian Powers. Dir: Michael O'Herlihy.

Ariana (Mariette Hartley); Clay (Michael Sullivan); Sandman #2 (Ed Couppee); Sandman #1 (Joey Fontana); The Woman (Janis Jamison).

Carousel

Logan is shot with a memory-erasing dart, causing him to forget his year as a runner. Francis finds Logan and takes his amnesia-stricken friend back to the city of domes for Lastday and "renewal"— voluntary death. Jessica and REM must retrieve Logan before too late. Wr: D.C. Fontana and Richard L. Bree, Jr. Dir: Irving J. Moore.

Diane (Rosanne Katon); Michael (Ross Bickell); Jonathan (Wright King); Morgan (Morgan Woodward); Sheila (Melody Anderson); Darrel (Regis J. Cordic); Peter (Gary Swanson); First man (Burton Cooper); Second man (William Molloy).

Night Visitors

The travelers encounter a "haunted house" inhabited by three spirits who can travel from their world into Earth. One, Gavin, chooses Jessica as a vessel to resurrect his wife. Captives Logan and REM find a way to turn the ghostly presences against themselves. Wr: Leonard Katzman. Dir: Paul Krasny.

Gavin (George Maharis); Marianne (Barbara Babcock); Barton (Paul Mantee).

Turnabout

Logan and company are captured by desert horsemen and are condemned to death. Francis arrives with his troops and realizes he must save Logan. Wr: Michael Michaelian and Al Hayes. Dir: Paul Krasny.

Asa (Nehemiah Persoff); Gera (Gerald McRaney); Samuel (Hari Rhodes); Mia (Victoria Racimo); Philip (John Furey); Aretha (Anina Minotto); Cell guard one (Arell Blanton); Second woman (Sherril Lynn Katzman); Uncredited: Horseman (Lou Elias).

Stargate

On a warm, sunny day, the travelers find a man who is freezing. They help him to his home and find aliens who come from a much hotter planet and who covet REM's electronic parts to repair their spaceship. Logan and Jessica must repair and rescue REM. Wr: Dennis O'Neil. Dir: Curtis Harrington.

Timon (Eddie Firestone); Morah (Paul Carr); Pata (Darrell Fetty); Arcana (Ian Tanza).

Lost in Space
September 1965–September 1968

In 1997, a family blasts off from Earth on a five-year journey to colonize a planet located in the Alpha Centauri solar system. Their ship, the Jupiter 2, *veers off course when a stowaway sabotages the ship's controls. The spaceship crash-lands on a remote and hostile planet where the family and their unwanted passenger, Dr. Smith, must struggle for survival.*

During the series' third year, the Robinsons repair their spaceship and travel to various planets in their efforts to reach Alpha Centauri.

Cast: Prof. John Robinson (Guy Williams); Dr. Maureen Robinson (June Lockhart); Major Don West (Mark Goddard); Dr. Zachary Smith (Jonathan Harris); Judy Robinson (Marta Kristen); Penny Robinson (Angela Cartwright); Will Robinson (Billy Mumy); The Robot (Bob May); The Robot's Voice/Narrator (Dick Tufeld).

Created by: Irwin Allen; *Developed for television by:* Shimon Wincelberg, Anthony Wilson; *Associate Producers:* Anthony Wilson, William Faralla; *Executive Producer:* Irwin Allen; *Music Theme:* John Williams; *Art Director:* Bob Kinoshita; CBS/ Twentieth Century–Fox; black and white (year 1), color (years 2 and 3); 60 minutes.

The original pilot film of *Lost in Space* sent a family of explorers into outer space, where they slammed into a meteor shower, crash-landed on a desert planet, and were subsequently doused by a tidal wave, blitzed by a lightning storm, trapped in an ancient city, and attacked by a giant cyclops. Producer-director Irwin Allen felt the $600,000 pilot was some of his best work. He was furious when, during the screening of the pilot by CBS executives in 1964, the brass began laughing hysterically. Allen got up and demanded the film be stopped. Story editor Anthony Wilson pulled Allen back into his chair, explaining that, laughter or not, the executives were enjoying the film. Wilson was correct, because the pilot immediately sold to CBS. This original pilot, which wasn't aired until 1993 on the Science Fiction cable channel, was a space-age version of Johann Wyss's *Swiss Family Robinson.* The idea was to call the series *The Space Family Robinson.* Legalities forced Allen to retitle his series *Lost in Space.*

Missing from the 1964 pilot were two characters who would be key to the series: the family robot, and a villainous stowaway, Dr. Zachary Smith. Wilson suggested adding Dr. Smith as a foil for the family. A new pilot, directed by Tony Leader, was filmed in 1965 with the addition of Smith, an enemy agent who programs the robot to destroy the ship en route to Alpha Centauri. When Smith gets trapped aboard the *Jupiter 2,* he has to awaken the Robinson family from their state of suspended animation to save himself. The character of Dr. Smith was originally intended as an evil spy. In Shimon Wincelberg's original script, Smith displays his cruelty by conning a young girl to walk into a forcefield, where she's incinerated. He later poisons a security guard with his deadly ring. CBS, feeling the show would be aimed at a family audience, had this violence cut from the script. Nevertheless, Dr. Smith, for the first few episodes of the series, was an evil villain who tried to kill the Robinsons.

Actors Roger C. Carmel, Jack Elam and Carroll O'Connor were considered for the role, but Broadway actor Jonathan Harris was finally selected. As the first season progressed, the hard edge of Dr. Smith faded, and Harris imbued the character with a bumbling, comical nature. Soon Dr. Smith became more of a scaredy-cat than a killer.

As Jonathan Harris explained it at a Boston convention in 1990, "I knew the Dr. Smith character better than any other writer because I created him. Irwin wanted a deep, dark villain, but there's no longevity in that kind of villain. He's boring." Dr. Smith became the series' most popular character. Harris received thousands of letters per week, most of them from children. This didn't surprise Harris, who admitted at the time, "I based Dr. Smith on every kid I have ever known."

The other big draw of *Lost in Space* was the special effects. However, once the Robinsons crash-landed on a desolate planet in the third episode, CBS and Twentieth Century–Fox marooned them there so that visual effects could be used sparingly. The series retained the most impressive hardware ever put on the television screen. In addition to the spaceship, which cost $350,000 to build, there was a futuristic all-terrain car called the chariot; a jet pack that allowed Professor Robinson to scout the planet; a surplus of laser guns and forcefields; and the Robinsons' talking robot, whose oft-repeated phrase was, "Danger! Danger!"

The most eye-catching weekly gimmick was the freeze-frame, cliffhanger endings. Each episode ended with a close call that would be resolved in the following segment.

The series' director of photography, Gene Polito, recalls that in the early episodes, the show needed out-of-this-world locations to convey a spooky planet. "We had a wonderful art director named Bill Creber, who had worked on George Stevens' film *The Greatest Story Ever Told*. I said to Bill, 'Gee, we need a location that's really unusual.' Bill remembered a location they had scouted for George Stevens that wasn't used. It was called the Trona Pinnacles in Red Rock Canyon, out in the Mojave desert. Creber and I drove out to this place, and it was a restricted area for naval bombardment practice. It was fantastic. I said to Bill, 'If you wanted to recreate a moonscape, this is it!' We went back to the studio and told the production manager that we had found a great location for filming. This threw him a curve because they already had another place set up. Word of the change got back to Irwin. Irwin called me and said, 'I'm getting a helicopter and flying out to this place tomorrow. If it isn't everything you and Bill say it is, I'm firing the two of you.' The next morning, the whole cast and crew was out at Red Rock Canyon, and by God, here comes a helicopter on the horizon. The helicopter landed, Irwin got out, ran over to the camera, and looked in it. He didn't say a thing. Finally, he looked at me and Bill. 'I gotta hand it to you guys,' he said. 'This is pretty fantastic.' He got back in the helicopter and off he went. We breathed a sigh of relief."

Polito was directly involved in supervising many of the special effects scenes in the desert locations. "We also had a guy there from Bell Aircraft who flew the jet pack. He could stay up in it for about a minute, and it looked wild." For Polito, a science fiction show was a terrific experience. "It was an interesting show to do, and it had a good following. The young generation, including my children, loved it." However, Polito found his job hanging by a thread when a photographic snafu developed. "We were working

inside the spaceship and Irwin came on the set: 'I want everybody's attention!' Irwin looked at me and said, 'Gene, I saw the dailies from yesterday. You have ruined me!' With that, he walked out. I thought, 'What the hell is he talking about?' I ran after him and said, 'What's wrong, Irwin?' He replied, 'Everything on the dailies is so dark I can't see anything.' Well, I knew I'd better call my agent because I was gonna have to be looking for another job by lunch time. Then I asked my second assistant cameraman to show me the camera reports from yesterday. It said, 'Day Interior Effect.' I asked the cameraman why he had written this. He said, 'Well, weren't you trying to create a 'day' effect in the spaceship?' I said, 'Sure, but the word *effect* on a camera report tells the lab boys that it needs a special effect shot. That means they'll print it down 6/8 points on the printer and it'll turn out as a real dark print.' The cameraman said, 'Oh my God!' I ran up to Sol Halprin, head of the camera department, and explained the situation. 'Solly, unless you can do a real fast reprint of all of yesterday's dailies, I think I'm out of a job!'"

"The next morning, Irwin came on the set and said, 'I want everybody's attention! I want to apologize to Gene about yesterday. I just saw the stuff and it's beautiful. Thank you very much. Now get back to work.' And he took off. After that, Irwin and I got along pretty well."

Polito praises his mentor, Oscar-winning cinematographer Winton Hoch, for teaching him about his craft. "Winnie was a brilliant guy who passed away years ago," says Polito. "He was a terrific, logical man who graduated from Cal Tech."

Polito, who filmed most of *Lost in Space*'s first year, strove to make his cinematography feature-film quality. "We had one of the biggest soundstages at Twentieth Century–Fox. I was an absolute stickler for making my photography look believable. When I filmed somebody walking along the sand, I only wanted to see one shadow. In lousy photography, you see four or five shadows and you know it was filmed on a soundstage. Once I was in a bar and—I think it was Joel August—one of the top cameramen at Columbia came over and asked, 'Are you Gene Polito? I was watching your *Lost in Space* show the other night and it was a pleasure. It was first-rate photography.' I said, 'Coming from you, that's an Emmy award in itself,' because this guy was an Oscar winner."

Another member of Allen's team was Paul

Zastupnevich, who created the human and creature costumes for *Lost in Space*. "I had to parade the various space monster costumes across the lot to have them approved by Irwin," Zastupnevich says. "People gave me funny looks as I walked by, carrying the cyclops or the lobster man. They'd ask me how I got my inspiration. I'd say, 'I eat a sandwich late at night, go to bed and have a nightmare!'" One of his favorite costumes was the giant cyclops monster in "There Were Giants in the Earth." "I didn't know how I was going to make it with our budget restrictions. I went for a walk, and I saw a group of firemen peeling bark from a palm tree. I picked up a piece of bark. It had an interesting texture, and it looked intriguing. I thought to myself, 'Hmm … I wonder what I could do with this?' I took a bunch of it back to my office, and that's what I used to make the cylops costume. I had it fireproofed, and it turned out to be a great monster."

Zastupnevich was also adept at turning animals into creatures. "Irwin was an animal lover, and in *Lost in Space,* we took a chimp and turned her into Penny's pet, the Bloop. We also had a tortoise which became an alien creature."

With each new season, Zastupnevich designed new costumes for the Robinson family. "By the time you had done a full season, even though you had triples of every costume, they were raunchy and threadbare. Also, the actors would ask me for a change—'I can't stand orchid anymore!'—and you couldn't blame them."

Seeing the series today, Zastupnevich is still impressed with the work that went into the show. "At the time, you're going back and forth, under enormous pressure, and you take the shows for granted. I see episodes today and say, 'How did we possibly do that costume or that effect?' I tried to make the Robinsons' costumes timeless, and I'm amazed that they still look current. … *Lost in Space* tried to teach a moral while entertaining and having fun. It was a wonderful show."

Even before the series premiered, audiences agreed. Test audiences gave *Lost in Space* a thumbs-up. The ratings began solidly, and went higher as the first year progressed, occasionally rocketing into the top ten.

Former *Twilight Zone* producer Buck Houghton was the producer of the first dozen segments before departing. "Basically, I didn't get along with the executive producer [Irwin Allen]," he says. "We both decided we'd be happier if we parted. There was no bad blood between us. It was just one of those things."

Houghton felt the series' concept was restrictive. "It was a very difficult premise to sustain. It later seemed to confine itself around the characters played by Billy Mumy and Jonathan Harris."

When Guy Williams and June Lockhart signed up for *Lost in Space*, it was understood that they would be the stars, and their show would be a serious adventure series. With the last-minute addition of Dr. Smith, however, writers found Harris's character a lot more fun to write for. The dailies in which Dr. Smith would kibitz with the temperamental robot, or play mind games with the trusting young Will Robinson, worked better for the brass than the family scenes. The more Harris hammed it up, the more Irwin Allen loved it. As a result, by the end of the first year, Harris dominated the storylines. The other actors, with the exception of Billy Mumy, were often superfluous to the story.

Prof. Robinson (Guy Williams). Copyright 1967 CBS/Twentieth Century–Fox.

It didn't set well with Williams or Lockhart. The result was ill feelings between the cast members. "It isn't so much that Harris steals the show," Williams told *TV Guide* in 1966. "It's that they [the producers] give it to him." However, as Lockhart conceded, Smith's character was largely responsible for the series' increased popularity. Love him or hate him, Dr. Smith was an original character for television, and Harris wasn't shy about taking full credit for making *Lost in Space* a success. Nevertheless, Harris realized the

Major West (Mark Goddard). Photo copyright 1967 CBS/Twentieth Century–Fox.

awkward position this had put Williams into. When Harris approached Williams with some conciliatory words, Williams walked away.

Irwin Allen had to pacify the unhappy cast members throughout the series' run. When Williams threatened to leave the series at the end of the first season, he was enticed back with a raise and promises of better storylines. It wasn't revealed to Williams that, starting with the second year, Harris would be the highest paid cast member.

Director Sutton Roley found Harris "a very professional actor. He was always prepared, and he did anything you asked of him. You just had to take him down a little. If you let him go full steam as Dr. Smith, he'd go absolutely ape! But I preferred that to somebody that you had to keep pumping up all of the time. Billy Mumy was an exceptionally talented actor. He was terrific. Angela Cartwright was a lovely little girl. Marta Kristen was okay. But Guy Williams and June Lockhart were so pretentious. They always wanted to hold hands in scenes and play it lovey-dovey. I'd say, 'Come on, June. Leave Guy alone!' Whenever one of the children was lost, they wanted to reach for each other first. I'd say, 'Forget that! Let's just be concerned about the kids for a moment.'"

Gene Polito found Guy Williams the most difficult cast member to work with. Realizing his part was now secondary to Jonathan Harris's, Williams demanded a certain number of close-ups per show. "He was, quite frankly, a pain in the butt," says Polito. "Whenever we did a shot of him from over the back of his shoulder, he would deliberately lean out of the frame. He did this two or three times. The director would finally say, 'Okay, let's forget the over the shoulder shot, Guy. We'll give you a close-up,' which is what Guy wanted. It was a little manipulation going on."

Billy Mumy and Jonathan Harris established a good working relationship, but Polito says, "I felt Jonathan was really gonna wreck Billy. He had this kid in the palm of his hand and tried to mold him into somebody that he wasn't. Billy just wanted to throw the baseball around between takes."

For some of the writers, *Lost in Space* offered a creative arena to script imaginative stories. Robert Duncan wrote six scripts for the series with his wife, Wanda. "Our children enjoyed watching the show, and we were invited by our friend, Tony Wilson, to write for it," says Duncan. "Wanda and I had a natural affinity for the characters. We came up with 50 story ideas offhand."

The Duncans regard the series fondly. "*Lost in Space* had one of the pleasantest sets in Hollywood," says Robert Duncan, "and the friendliness of the cast came through on screen. It was a remarkable show. Jonathan Harris would serve cookies to Wanda's mother when she visited the set; June Lockhart was always even-tempered, sweet and professional; Billy Mumy would ride his bike around the set; and there was an episode where our guest star showed up skunk drunk. He stayed that way all the days he worked. Being drunk gave him a swagger and character he wouldn't have had sober. He did his lines perfectly."

Duncan concedes the series had its limitations. "The cast of *Lost in Space* fought for better scripts. Irwin had a strong dislike for what I call 'relationship scenes.' Sometimes you could write an emotional scene for a guest star, but never for the regulars. All of Irwin's shows were basically the same. The heroes were put in jeopardy, from which they had four acts to extricate themselves."

Jack Turley tried his best to duck out of writing for the series. "Tony Wilson called me while he was on vacation in San Diego. He pleaded with me to write an episode of *Lost in Space*. I refused. I was considered a hot writer and had my pick of projects. I wasn't interested in writing anything for Irwin Allen. His reputation among writers was not inspiring, especially since he paid a lower scale per episode than other producers. I argued with Tony, but he knew how to work me. He patted me on the head and said I'd give it 'Turley quality.' I reluctantly submitted."

Turley's story, "Hunter's Moon" pits Professor Robinson against an alien hunter. "The role of the hunter, Megazor, was given to a guy who appeared a little light in the boots," says Turley. "He pranced around and minced his threats with a cute little lisp. I complained about this to Tony. He shrugged and said it gave the show 'another dimension.' How's that for mollifying an irate writer?" Turley was asked to write further episodes for the show, "but I ran as if my pants were on fire. *Lost in Space* would be perfect for the Saturday morning slots for the six-and-under set. Older kids are too sophisticated for that hokey, exploding-control-panel stuff."

Joey Tata supplied many of the alien voices for the series, and finds that the popularity of *Lost in Space* has extended to his current high school series, *Beverly Hills 90210*. "To the kids on this show, I'm a hero for working on *Lost in Space*," he laughs. "Luke Perry asked me, 'You worked with Dr. Smith? Man, when I was a kid I loved that show!' Luke always quotes lines from it."

The series provided Tata with one of his most embarrassing moments. "I was playing a crewman on *Voyage to the Bottom of the Sea*, which was filmed next door to *Lost in Space*. I had on my blue *Voyage* overalls, and during a break, I was playing a game of poker with Richard Basehart and the other *Voyage* actors. I had in my hand four kings. I knew it was a wonderful hand, but I didn't have any money on me. I said to them, 'Give me five minutes and I'll get some bread.' So I dashed off to the *Lost in Space* set, where I knew one of the guest stars, Ronnie Gans. Ron, who has this very deep voice, was playing a purple frog. He was operating this alien console when I walked in. His costume was so ridiculous I've called him Froggy ever since. I ran up to him and screamed, 'Ronnie, you can't believe this. I got four fucking kings. How much money have you got on you?' He looked at me and said, in this stilted, mechanical voice, 'Look … into … my … right … pocket.' So I tried to get the money out of his pocket, which is under this foam rubber. I pulled out 150 bucks. Ronnie said, 'You … will … pay … me … back … right … away.' I said, 'Why are you talking like a mechanical frog?' He said, 'Because … you've … walked … right … into … the … middle … of … a … scene!' I turned around and the entire *Lost in Space* cast and crew are there. Here I am, a *Voyage* crewman bugging

Penny (Angela Cartwright). Photo courtesy 1967 CBS/Twentieth Century–Fox.

a purple frog for a few bucks and they have it all on film. They ran the film in the dailies the next day, thinking it would be funny for Irwin. A memo was immediately issued: 'There will be no more gambling on the sets!'"

Actor Ted Lehmann played a glowing, disembodied head in the episode "Invaders from the Fifth Dimension." "That turned out to be the most inquired-about part I have ever done in my forty years as a Hollywood actor," he says. "It was the most elaborate makeup I have ever worn."

Lehman remembers Jonathan Harris's method of handling studio stuffiness. "During shooting, a couple of young studio executives appeared on the set. They caused a stir by announcing that there would be a visit from the crown prince and princess of a Third World country. The self-important attitude of these execs irritated Jonathan. He proceeded to cut them down to size with his formidable, sarcastic wit. He ordered them from the set and they made a hasty withdrawal. We were all in stitches. He was a delightful man."

The most arduous aspect of filming for Lehman was his ghostly white makeup. "My alien character had no mouth. All of my dialogue was done as a voice-over later in the recording studio. When it came to lunch time, the makeup people adamantly insisted that they would not remove their makeup masterpiece to allow me to eat. At the same time, there were Screen Actor Guild rules. An actor has to eat! A compromise was struck. My makeup would be cut, with a razor

Cast of *Lost in Space*, left to right: Guy Williams, June Lockhart, Billy Mumy, Bob May (inside the robot), Angela Cartwright, Jonathan Harris, Marta Kristen and Mark Goddard. Copyright 1965 CBS/Twentieth Century–Fox.

blade, allowing an opening where nourishment could be carefully guided. I was sent off to the commissary and after locating my mouth, I managed a sandwich. On the way back to the stage, I met an old friend of mine. I said, 'Hello, George.' He stared a second, then recognized my voice. 'Good God! Ted, is that you in there? What have they done to you!'"

Lost in Space enjoyed good ratings during its first two seasons. The first year, in black and white, began as a relatively serious adventure show as the Robinsons struggled for survival in a hostile environment. The second year, in color, quickly developed into the Dr. Smith comedy show, with a bare minimum of special effects.

The emphasis on Dr. Smith and his campy adventures was overkill, and the ratings dipped as the second year closed. Many viewers who loved Dr. Smith as a supporting ingredient during the first year reacted negatively to having him served as the main course. The mainstream family audi-

ence was eroding, and the series audience was now mainly children.

Several of the cast members continued to be resentful of Dr. Smith's grip on the series. To lessen the tensions and regain a bigger audience, the third season underwent a format change. The Robinsons blasted off from their desert world and frequently landed on other planets. The third season boasted excellent special effects, heavy doses of action and much more emphasis on the family cast members.

"We had been told that there had been too much whimsy in the second year," says Robert Duncan, who had mixed feelings about the shift. "We were given new guidelines for the third year. The result was less interplay between Dr. Smith and the robot and more action. Ironically, this was at a time when the networks were trying to reduce the amount of violence on television."

The cliffhanging endings were also gone. In the third year, each episode began with a freeze frame that led into John Williams' exciting new theme music.

It was a gallant attempt, but the more serious storylines didn't improve the ratings. After a dozen episodes, the series quietly slipped back into the comedic approach. Ironically, these last episodes were the highest rated.

As the leading television network, CBS pruned not only series with poor ratings, but those with mediocre ratings as well. *Lost in Space* finished its third year with a barely adequate rating. CBS felt that a fourth season would be a bust. Storywise, the series had gone from the *Swiss Family Robinson*–type adventures to whimsical comedy to special effects–laden action-adventure and finally to space camp. *Lost in Space* was huffing and puffing from creative exhaustion. When the series ended, the Robinson family were still lost in space.

"The real reason *Lost in Space* was canceled was because Bill Paley, the head of CBS, hated the show," says writer Robert Hamner. "He didn't understand its appeal and didn't want it on his network."

Irwin Allen admitted to TV columnist Cynthia Lowry in 1968 that *Lost in Space*'s audience consisted mainly of kids. "Frankly, *Lost in Space* was aimed at them," he admitted. "The problem was, kids don't buy many of the sponsors' products."

The series was put into syndication, where it did very well in afternoon time slots in the early 1970s. It was later eclipsed by the phenomenal success of another post-network space show, *Star Trek*. By the late 1970s, *Lost in Space* was airing in just 20 independent stations across America, compared to over 140 for *Star Trek*.

The fortunes of *Lost in Space* changed in 1981, when former star Bill Mumy tried to relaunch the show as a reunion movie. He hoped to resolve the premise and use the original cast. However, Mumy found Irwin Allen totally unreceptive to the idea.

CBS and Twentieth Century–Fox expressed interest in a reunion, but without Allen's legal go-ahead, the project was stillborn. *Lost in Space* fans campaigned on Mumy's behalf, sending in thousands of petitions and letters to Allen. In 1985, Allen conceded to long-time friend Merv Griffin that he was pleased by the fans' enthusiasm but thought it was too late for a reunion or revival of the show—something he said he wished he'd done ten years before.

Meanwhile, *Lost in Space* blossomed into cult status. Many of the cast reunited for a 1983 *Family Feud* special and appeared on many national talk shows and conventions; the USA Cable network aired *Lost in Space* in 1989 and 1990 to high ratings; and in 1991, Innovation Comics began its popular *Lost in Space* comic book series, with Bill Mumy as consultant and sometimes as writer. Irwin Allen died in 1991, and Irwin Allen Productions was officially disbanded a year later. But his series may live on in new cinematic adventures: In 1993, New Line Cinema obtained the rights for a *Lost in Space* feature film, which may provide the saga of the Robinsons with a conclusion.

CAST NOTES

Guy Williams (Professor Robinson): Born 1924. Williams soared to success as Walt Disney's Zorro on TV in the late 1950s. He was also featured as cousin Will Cartwright on *Bonanza* (1963-64). After *Lost in Space* ended, Williams moved to South America. "In America, I'm as unknown as a doormat," Williams told the *National Enquirer* in 1973. "In Argentina, I'm a smash. Everyone knows me as Zorro."

Financially secure through land investments, Williams made only two American TV appearances in the 1980s: First, he reunited with *Lost in Space* co-stars June Lockhart, Marta Kristen and Angela Cartwright for the game show *Family Feud* in 1983. That same year, he was a guest on *Good Morning, America* where he discussed Zorro. He died in 1989.

June Lockhart (Mrs. Robinson): Born 1925. The daughter of actors Gene and Kathleen Lockhart,. June made her film debut in *A Christmas Carol* (1938). June played the mother on the *Lassie* series (1958–64) and had a recurring role on daytime's *General Hospital* in the 1990s.

Mark Goddard (Major West): Born 1936. Goddard's first break was as one of Robert Taylor's TV *Detectives* (1960–62). He later became a theatrical agent and writer. His TV credits in the 1980s included *The Fall Guy*, *Barnaby Jones* and *Jake and the Fatman*. In the early 1990s, he taught high school in his home state of Massachusetts.

Marta Kristen (Judy Robinson): Born 1945. In addition to raising a family, she co-starred in the adventure films *Terminal Island* (1973) and *Battle*

Beyond the Stars (1980). She worked in Los Angeles theater during the 1990s.

Bill Mumy (Will Robinson): Born 1954. Mumy devoted time to his musical career in the 1970s, playing with the band America and forming his own band, Barnes and Barnes. His post–*Lost in Space* movie credits included the films *Bless the Beasts and the Children* (1971) and *Papillon* (1973). He co-starred in the 1975 series *Sunshine* and guest-starred on such shows as *Rockford Files* and *Matlock*. In the 1990s, he wrote several of the *Lost in Space* comic books for Innovation Comics. He became a regular on the TV series *Babylon 5* in 1994.

Angela Cartwright (Penny Robinson): Born 1952. Cartwright played Danny Thomas's youngest daughter on *Make Room for Daddy* (1957–64). She was also one of the Von Trapp children in *The Sound of Music* (1965). As an adult, she raised a family and wrote a children's book called *A Child's First Journal*. Her post–*Lost in Space* TV credits included *Love Boat* and *Airwolf*.

Jonathan Harris (Dr. Smith): Born 1914. This Broadway actor has done hundreds of voice-overs for commercials and cartoons. He starred in the long-running Saturday morning show *Space Academy*, in the 1970s. He retired from film acting in favor of voice-over work.

EPISODE GUIDE

Season 1: 1965-66

The Reluctant Stowaway
Sabotage by an enemy agent careens the *Jupiter 2* into a meteor shower. The robot, programmed for destruction, hinders the Robinsons' efforts to return to Earth. Wr: S. Bar David (Shimon Wincelberg), story by Shimon Wincelberg. Dir: Tony Leader.
President (Ford Rainey); General (Hal Torey); Newsman (Don Forbes); Technician (Tom Allen); Administrator (Fred Crane); Sentry (Brett Parker); Countdown voice (Bartell La Rue); Reporter (Paul Kremin); Space walk doubles (Donna Garrett, Chuck Couch).

The Derelict
The *Jupiter 2* enters a huge alien spaceship, where the Robinsons try to communicate with a race of bubble-like creatures. Wr: Peter Packer. Dir: Alex Singer.
Newsman (Don Forbes); Creature (Dawson Palmer); Alien voice (Dick Tufeld).

Trivia Alert: In a scene where Penny is listening to a tape of Shakespeare, the storyteller's voice is that of *Voyage to the Bottom of the Sea* star Richard Basehart.

Island in the Sky
Crash-landing on a desert world, Maureen and the others use the chariot to explore the strange landscape for the missing Prof. Robinson. Wr: Norman Lessing, story by Shimon Wincelberg. Dir: Tony Leader.
No guests.

There Were Giants in the Earth
While migrating south to avoid an ice age, the Robinsons travel through a valley filled with giant cyclops creatures. Wr: Carey Wilbur, story by Shimon Wincelberg. Dir: Leo Penn.
Cyclops #1 (Lamar Lundy); Cyclops #2 (Robert "Buck" Maffei); Parajet stunts (J. Courtney, John Garr).

The Hungry Sea
After escaping from an earthquake in an ancient city, the Robinsons use the chariot to navigate across a raging sea. Wr: William Welch, story by Shimon Wincelberg. Dir: Sobey Martin.
No guests.

Welcome, Stranger
The Robinsons get a visitor from Earth, astronaut James Hapgood. Although his spacecraft is in working order, he refuses the responsibility of taking Will and Penny back to Earth. Wr: Peter Packer. Dir: Alvin Ganzer.
Jim Hapgood (Warren Oates).

My Friend, Mr. Nobody
A lonely echo voice develops a friendship with Penny. Its over-protectiveness of the girl threatens the rest of the family. Wr: Jackson Gillis. Dir: Paul Stanley.
Mr. Nobody (William Bramley).

Invaders from the Fifth Dimension
The Robinsons desperately try to rescue Will from glowing humanoids. The aliens need the boy's brain to navigate their ship back to their home planet. Wr: Shimon Wincelberg, story by Shimon Wincelberg. Dir: Leonard Horn.
Luminary (Joseph Ryan); Alien (Ted Lehmann).

Memory Flash — Ted Lehmann: "The script was a good adventure yarn with no particular subtle or esoteric 'message.' After working on *Lost in Space*, I became a regular viewer. I'm proud to have been a part of one of the true pioneers of the space opera genre."

The Oasis
Dr. Smith is banished from camp after using the last of the drinking water for a shower. Smith plots revenge when an alien substance turns him into a giant. Wr: Peter Packer. Dir: Sutton Roley.
Giant bloop (Janos Prohaska).

The Sky Is Falling

Mistrust replaces friendship between the Robinsons and a telepathic alien family when Will and an alien boy disappear. Wr: Herman Groves, Barney Slater, story by Herman Groves. Dir: Sutton Roley.

Retho (Don Matheson); Moela (Francoise Ruggieri); Lunon (Eddie Rosson).

Memory Flash—Don Matheson: "I played a mute alien father who communicates through telepathy. The original idea was that you would hear my voice as I communicated through telepathy. Irwin Allen looked at the rushes and said, 'We don't need to add his voice. Don is conveying everything without words.' So I guess he was a little impressed."

Wish Upon a Star

Greed consumes several family members when they find an alien device that grants material wishes. Wr: Barney Slater. Dir: Sutton Roley.

Creature (Dawson Palmer).

The Raft

Efforts to launch the *Jupiter 2* fail. When the men build a two-man spaceship, Smith and Will accidentally launch it into space. Wr: Peter Packer. Dir: Sobey Martin.

Bush creature (Dawson Palmer).

One of Our Dogs Is Missing

A meteor shower deposits an old Earth satellite containing a monstrous creature that stalks the family. Wr: William Welch. Dir: Sutton Roley.

Creature (Charles Dierkop).

Attack of the Monster Plants

Banished from camp after leaving John and Don in quicksand, Smith steals the fuel for the *Jupiter 2*'s lift-off. Meanwhile, cyclamen plants manufacture a sinister duplicate of Judy. Wr: William Read Woodfield, Allan Balter. Dir: Justus Addiss.

No guests.

Return from Outer Space

Time portals return Will to Earth, but the townspeople in Vermont don't believe his fantastic stories. He's forced to live with a foster family. Wr: Peter Packer. Dir: Nathan Juran.

Clara (Reta Shaw); Ruth Templeton (Sheila Matthews); Lacy (Robert Easton); Davey Sims (Donald Losby); Rachel (Helen Kleeb); Sheriff Baxendale (Walter Sande); Woman (Anne Dore); Theodore (Keith Taylor); Grover (Harry Harvey, Sr.); Boy (Johnny Tuchy).

Memory Flash—actor and dialect coach, Robert Easton: "I had always been fascinated with science fiction. I was Sparks in the *Voyage to the Bottom of the Sea* movie. Later I worked in England doing multiple voices for the puppet series *Stingray*, where I played a Southern radio man named Phones. I was pleased to do *Lost in Space*. It gave me the chance to do a New England character. Producer Irwin Allen was a master of the genre and as gadget-happy as any child with new Christmas toys."

The Keeper, Part 1

An alien zookeeper threatens to destroy the Robinsons unless Will and Penny are turned over to him. Wr: Barney Slater. Dir: Harry Harris.

Keeper (Michael Rennie); Lighted head (Wilbur Evans); Creature (Mike Donovon).

The Keeper, Part 2

The Keeper's creatures, including a giant lizard and spider, overrun the planet. He refuses to withdraw the monsters unless his demands are met. Wr: Barney Slater. Dir: Harry Harris.

The Keeper (Michael Rennie); Lighted head (Wilbur Evans); Creature (Mike Donovon); Monsters (Dawson Palmer, Janos Prohaska).

The Sky Pirate

The Robinsons offer refuge to a pirate who was kidnapped from Earth in the 1800s by aliens. He's now being pursued by a creature that threatens the family. Wr: Carey Wilbur. Dir: Sobey Martin.

Alonzo P. Tucker (Albert Salmi); Izralun (Dawson Palmer).

Ghost in Space

An explosion awakens an invisible creature that goes on a destructive rampage. Wr: Peter Packer. Dir: Don Richardson.

No guests.

War of the Robots

A evil robotoid enslaves the family and plans to take them back to its master's planet. Wr: Barney Slater. Dir: Sobey Martin.

Robotoid voice (Ollie O'Toole); Master (Harold John Norman); Robotoid (Eldon Hansen).

The Magic Mirror

Penny enters another dimension after falling through a mirror and meets a lonely alien boy. Wr: Jackson Gillis. Dir: Nathan Juran.

Boy (Michael J. Pollard); Creature (Dawson Palmer).

The Challenge

John and Will accept an invitation to face an alien ruler and his son in several challenges that test strength and courage. Wr: Barney Slater. Dir: Don Richardson.

Quano (Kurt Russell); Ruler (Michael Ansara); Lizard creature (Dawson Palmer).

The Space Trader

A space wizard whips up a storm that destroys the Robinsons' food supply. They're forced to bargain with the alien. Wr: Barney Slater. Dir: Nathan Juran.

Trader (Torin Thatcher).

His Majesty Smith

Androids make Dr. Smith their king so that they can sacrifice him to primitive space gods. Wr: Carey Wilbur. Dir: Harry Harris.

The Master (Kevin Hagen); Nexus (Liam Sullivan); Android (Ronald Weber).

The Space Croppers

Space hillbillies bring grief to the Robinsons: Their pet is a dangerous werewolf; their daughter wants to marry Don; and their plants are carnivorous. Wr: Peter Packer. Dir: Sobey Martin.

Sybilla (Mercedes McCambridge); Effra (Sherry Jackson); Keel (Dawson Palmer).

All That Glitters

Smith makes off with a magic disc which makes everything he touches turn to platinum, including Penny. Wr: Barney Slater. Dir: Harry Harris.

Bolix (Werner Klemperer); Ohan (Larry Ward); Alien voice (Ted Lehmann); Creatures (Mike Donovon, Dawson Palmer).

Lost Civilization

Escaping from a valley of volcanoes, John, Don and Will explore a mysterious cave. They find a secret civilization of people frozen in suspended animation. Wr: William Welch. Dir: Don Richardson.

Major Domo (Royal Dano); Princess (Kym Karath); Soldier (Dawson Palmer).

A Change of Space

Will uses a spaceship to fly through the sixth dimension, and returns a genius; Dr. Smith uses the ship and returns an old man. Wr: Peter Packer. Dir: Sobey Martin.

Amphibian (Frank Graham).

Follow the Leader

Possessed by the spirit of an alien mummy, John becomes obsessed with getting the *Jupiter 2* ready for launch. Wr: Barney Slater. Dir: Don Richardson.

Canto (Gregory Morton).

Season 2: 1966-67

Blast Off into Space

The family has 24 hours to make emergency preparations for lift-off after an engineer sets off a series of chain reactions that disintegrates the Robinsons' planet. Wr: Peter Packer. Dir: Nathan Juran.

Nerim (Strother Martin); Statue (Dawson Palmer).

Wild Adventure

Space-borne, the Robinsons head for Earth, but their journey is imperiled by a variety of space dangers. Wr: William Read Woodfield, Allan Balter. Dir: Don Richardson.

Athena (Vitina Marcus); Alpha control voice (Bartell La Rue).

The Ghost Planet

The Robinsons land on a planet run by cyborgs who try to enslave the earthlings. Wr: Peter Packer. Dir: Nathan Juran.

Robot voice (Sue England); Prototype voice (Michael Fox); Cyborg (Dawson Palmer).

Forbidden World

Exploding missiles propel the *Jupiter 2* onto a planet where the family meets an unfriendly space captain. Wr: Barney Slater. Dir: Don Richardson.

Capt. Tiabo (Wally Cox); Bird (Janos Prohaska).

Space Circus

The Robinsons are entertained by a traveling circus troupe. The circus's owner cons Will into running away with them. Wr: Bob and Wanda Duncan. Dir: Harry Harris.

Dr. Andreas Marvello (James Westerfield); Fenestra (Melinda Fee); Nubu (Michael Greene); Vicho (Harry Monty); Monster (Dawson Palmer).

Memory Flash—Melinda Fee: "I remember that horrible first day of shooting. It was my first big role, and I was extremely nervous. A friend gave me a Valium. I had never taken one before, but I didn't think it would do any harm. My first scenes were going to be long shots and relatively important. But they changed the shooting order. The close-ups of my long monologue were now going to be shot first at 8 a.m. I had taken the Valium pill on an empty stomach, and I was feeling strange. My mouth got so dry I could barely speak. Luckily, I got through it, but it was awful. Never again!"

The Prisoners of Space

The Robinsons are put on trial one by one in an intergalactic courtroom for crimes they've committed in space. Wr: Barney Slater. Dir: Nathan Juran.

Judge Iko (Gregory Morton); Creature (Dawson Palmer).

The Android Machine

Penny befriends a female android who has developed emotions. She's been consigned for destruction by the aliens who built her. Wr: Robert and Wanda Duncan. Dir: Don Richardson.

Verda (Dee Hartford); Zumdish (Fritz Feld); Guard (Tiger Joe Marsh); Creature (Dawson Palmer); Voice (Ray Didsbury).

The Deadly Games of Gamma Six

Dr. Smith loses a boxing match and condemns Earth to destruction. John has to risk his life in a deadly showdown to save the planet. Wr: Barney Slater. Dir: Harry Harris.

Myko (Mike Kellin); Leader (Peter Brocco); Gromack (Ronald Weber); Boxer (Chuck Roberson); Geoo (Harry Monty).

The Thief of Outer Space

Dr. Smith and Will are swept up in a chieftain's efforts to find his missing princess. Wr: Jackson Gillis. Dir: Don Richardson.

Sheik Ali Ben Bad (Malachi Throne); Slave (Ted Cassidy); Princess (Maxine Gates).

Curse of Cousin Smith

Smith's cousin arrives and plots to kill Smith for their aunt's inheritance money. Wr: Barney Slater. Dir: Justus Addiss.

Jeremiah Beauregard Smith (Henry Jones); Little Joe (Allan Melvin).

West of Mars
Smith faces hanging on a western planet when he's mistaken for an outlaw. Meanwhile, the Robinsons are faced with a ruthless gunslinger who is posing as Dr. Smith. Wr: Michael Fessier. Dir: Nathan Juran.
Cladius (Allan Melvin); Bartender (Eddie Quillan); Pleiades Pete (Ken Mayer); Dee (Mickey Manners); Zeno Double (Charles Arthur).

Memory Flash—Allan Melvin: "It was a different character that seemed fun to play, and it was. It was a good script and a professional, happy group. *Lost in Space* was an outstanding series that appealed to adults as well as children. That's something that is not easily accomplished."

A Visit to Hades
A political rebel, banished to the Robinsons' planet, romances Judy while plotting another revolution. Wr: Carey Wilbur. Dir: Don Richardson.
Morbus (Gerald Mohr); Monster (Mike Donovan).

The Wreck of the Robot
Aliens use the robot to develop an army of indestructible machines. Wr: Barney Slater. Dir: Nathan Juran.
Saticon leader (Jim Mills); Aliens (John Hunt, Paul Kessler).

The Dream Monster
The Robinson family is rendered useless when their emotions are drained. Don is left to battle Dr. Sesmar, who has transferred the family's emotions into an android. Wr: Peter Packer. Dir: Don Richardson.
Dr. Sesmar (John Abbott); Radion (Dawson Palmer); Golden dwarf #1 (Harry Monty); Dwarf #2 (Frank Delfino).

The Golden Man
Maureen and the girls try to mediate a dispute between two alien leaders: a golden man and a misunderstood frog. Wr: Barney Slater. Dir: Don Richardson.
Keema (Dennis Patrick); Frog alien (Ronald Gans); Prince (William Troy).

The Girl from the Green Dimension
When Will is turned bright green, the boy's color can only be returned to normal if Smith fights an alien warrior to the death. Wr: Peter Packer. Dir: Nathan Juran.
Athena (Vitina Marcus); Urso (Harry Raybould).

Memory Flash—costume designer Paul Zastupnevich: "Vitina Marcus loved the green jumpsuit I made for her. She even made *Time* magazine the week this episode debuted. There was a picture of her floating around space, wearing the costume."

The Questing Beast
Penny develops a friendship with an intelligent dragon who is being hunted by a space knight. Wr: Carey Wilbur. Dir: Don Richardson.
Sir Sagramonte (Hans Conried); Gundemar voice (June Foray); Gundemar (Jefferson County).

The Toymaker
John enters a fourth-dimension toyshop and finds an old toymaker who has been banished from society because of his age. Wr: Robert and Wanda Duncan. Dir: Robert Douglas.
Toymaker (Walter Burke); Zumdish (Fritz Feld); Guard (Tiger Joe Marsh); Soldier (Larry Dean); Monster (Dawson Palmer).

Memory Flash—Robert Douglas: "*Lost in Space* was one of the most outstanding wastes of time I have ever encountered. Directing one segment was more than enough."

Mutiny in Space
Dr. Smith and Will blast off with an obsessed space admiral who wants to capture his mutinous first mate. Wr: Peter Packer. Dir: Don Richardson.
Admiral Zahrk (Ronald Long).

The Space Vikings
Dr. Smith and Will are transported to the valley of Thor, where they must help the Norse god battle green giants. Wr: Margaret Bookman Hill. Dir: Ezra Stone.
Brynhilda (Sheila Matthews); Thor (Bern Hoffman); Elf (Harry Monty); Elf #2 (Frank Delfino); Creature (John Hunt).

Rocket to Earth
Dr. Smith and Will take off for Earth in a magician's spaceship, unaware that the ship has been rigged to explode. Wr: Barney Slater. Dir: Don Richardson.
Zalto (Al Lewis); Puppet (Joey Tata).

Cave of the Wizards
The *Jupiter 2*'s launch is threatened when ancient computers transform Dr. Smith into an alien creature. Wr: Peter Packer. Dir: Don Richardson.
Computer brain (Michael Fox); Eye voice (Joey Tata); Mummy (Larry Dean); Rock monsters (John Hunt, Paul Kessler).

Treasure of the Lost Planet
Capt. Tucker returns with a motley band of pirates to search for a hidden treasure on the Robinsons' planet. Wr: Carey Wilbur. Dir: Harry Harris.
Alonzo P. Tucker (Albert Salmi); Deek (Craig Duncan); Smeek (Jim Boles); Izrulan (Dawson Palmer).

Revolt of the Androids
The android Verda returns and seeks protection against IDAK, a super-android programmed to destroy her. Wr: Robert and Wanda Duncan. Dir: Don Richardson.
Verda (Dee Hartford); IDAK Alpha 12 (Don Matheson); IDAK Omega 17 (Dawson Palmer); Creature (Dawson Palmer).

Memory Flash—Don Matheson: "It was a lot of fun. I looked on it as a job and thought, 'What the hell. Nobody's going to see this show,' and of course, everybody did!"

The Colonists
A space queen sentences the Robinson men to slave labor while indoctrinating the Robinson women against men. Wr: Peter Packer. Dir: Ezra Stone.
Niolani (Francine York); Slaves (Dave Dunlap, Erwin Niel, Orwin Harvey, Seymore Konic).

Memory Flash—costume designer Paul Zastupnevich: "Francine looked smashing in her purple jumpsuit, cape and spiked headdress. Francine said, 'I wish I could walk around wearing this every day. It makes me feel so powerful.'"

Trip Through the Robot
Dr. Smith and Will try to repair the robot, who has grown to the size of a skyscraper. Wr: Barney Slater. Dir: Don Richardson.
No guests.

The Phantom Family
An amphibian scientist creates duplicates of the Robinson family. He gives Will 24 hours to teach them to act like human beings. Wr: Peter Packer. Dir: Ezra Stone.
Lemnoc (Alan Hewitt).

The Mechanical Men
An army of tiny robots exchanges the personalities of the robot and Dr. Smith. Wr: Barney Slater. Dir: Seymour Robbie.
Robot leader's voice (Joey Tata).

The Astral Traveler
Will returns to Earth, 1998, where he's trapped in a Scottish castle inhabited by a sea creature and a friendly ghost. Wr: Carey Wilbur. Dir: Don Richardson.
James Stuart Hamish McPherson (Sean McClory); Angus (Dawson Palmer).

The Galaxy Gift
An asteroid is turned into a recreation of San Francisco's Chinatown in an effort to get a powerful amulet from Penny. Wr: Barney Slater. Dir: Ezra Stone.
Arcon (John Carradine); Saticon (Jim Mills); Saticon #2 (John Hunt); Saticon #3 (Paul Kessler); Fly creature (Harry Monty).

Season 3: 1967-68

The Condemned of Space
A rogue comet forces the *Jupiter 2* to make an emergency lift-off. The travelers land on a space station filled with frozen convicts. Wr: Peter Packer. Dir: Nathan Juran.
Phanzig (Marcel Hillaire); Robot Guard (Eldon Hansen); Judge (Bart La Rue); Convict (Dave Dunlap).

Visit to a Hostile Planet
A time warp propels the *Jupiter 2* back to 1947 Earth. Michigan residents have mistaken the Robinsons for alien invaders. Wr: Peter Packer. Dir: Sobey Martin.
Joe Cragmire (Robert Foulk); Stacy (Claire Wilcox); Craig (Robert Pine); Grover (Pitt Herbert); Charlie (Norman Leavitt); Newscaster (Bartell La Rue).

Kidnapped in Space
The *Jupiter 2* is drawn into a space station by aliens who need the robot to repair their clock leader. Wr: Robert Hamner. Dir: Don Richardson.
1220 (Carol Williams); 764 (Grant Sullivan); Young Smith (Joey Russo); Aliens (Jerry Traylor, Maritza Elsen, Rita Frabotta, Craig Chudy).

Hunter's Moon
John lands the space pod on a planet where he becomes the quarry of an alien hunter. Wr: Jack Bradford Turley. Dir: Don Richardson.
Megazor (Vincent Beck); Robot judge (Joey Tata); Invisibo (Fred Krone).

The Space Primevals
John has to cap a raging volcano that threatens to destroy the spaceship. He also must rescue Don and Dr. Smith, who have been sealed underground by hostile cavemen. Wr: Peter Packer. Dir: Nathan Juran.
Rongah (Arthur Batanides).

Memory Flash—Arthur Batanides: "I had to do a little impromptu dance and that was a little silly, but I liked the basic story. The cavemen discover that they can't look to a machine for salvation. When my character transforms himself into a golden Greek man at the end, that symbolizes his decision to think for himself. I liked the episode."

The Space Destructors
Dr. Smith goes berserk with power after creating an army of androids which threaten the Robinson family. Wr: Robert Hamner. Dir: Don Richardson.
Cyborg voice (Bartell La Rue); Cyborg (Tommy Farrell).

The Haunted Lighthouse
Rescuing the last survivor of an alien colony, the Robinsons blast off a storm-swept planet. They land on a manned Earth station in space. Wr: Jackson Gillis. Dir: Sobey Martin.
J-5 (Lou Wagner); Silas J. Fogey (Woodrow Parfrey); Zaybo (Kenya Coburn).

Flight into the Future
The Robinsons travel 300 years into the future and meet their descendants on a world where illusions are transformed into reality. Wr: Peter Packer. Dir: Sobey Martin.
Fletcher (Lew Gallo); Horatio Smith (Don Eitner); Alien machine (Bartell La Rue); Cyclops (Lamar Lundy); Stone man #1 (John Hunt); Stone man #2 (Paul Kessler); Spike monster (John Hunt).

Collision of the Planets

Efforts to lift off a planet are hampered by four space hippies who have orders to destroy the Robinsons' planet. Wr: Peter Packer. Dir: Don Richardson.

Ilan (Daniel J. Travanti); Girl (Linda Gaye Scott); Biker (Joey Tata); Alien #4 (Steve Marganian); Leader (Gene Dynarski); Strongman double (Paul Stader).

Memory Flash—Joey Tata: "That was fun. Dan Travanti was very nice, but we didn't have too much in common. Linda and I had worked before on *Batman* and had a lot of giggles. The big hippie with the muscles was a grip at the studio. They thought he was perfect for the role. That's Hollywood! You train and go to acting school for years. Here's a guy on the set with a hammer: 'Hey, you look good. Get in there!' Jonathan Harris [Dr. Smith] was absolutely charming and very funny."

The Space Creature

The family encounters a giant space creature and a sinister blue mist while traveling through space. It's all linked to a creature that feeds on fear. Wr: William Welch. Dir: Sobey Martin.

Voice (Ronald Gans); Creature (Fred Krone).

Deadliest of the Species

An agonizing decision for Robot: Marry a female robot, or turn her over to the authorities for her crimes. Wr: Robert Hamner. Dir: Sobey Martin.

Lady robot voice (Sue England); Leader (Ronald Gans); Android #1 (Lyle Waggoner); Android #2 (Ralph Lee).

Memory Flash—Lyle Waggoner: "The gun I was supposed to fire didn't go off. I pulled the trigger and nothing. So I went, 'Bang, Bang!' and everybody got a big laugh out of that. The special effects guy came in and fixed the gun. Between scenes, the guy inside the robot would pinch the girls with his mechanical claws!"

A Day at the Zoo

Put on display at a zoo, the Robinsons try to escape from their captors. Wr: Jackson Gillis. Dir: Irving J. Moore.

Farnum B. (Leonard Stone); Oggo (Gary Tigerman); Mort (Ronald Weber).

Two Weeks in Space

Dr. Smith turns the *Jupiter 2* into a hotel resort where his first customers are four escaped convicts. Wr: Robert Hamner. Dir: Don Richardson.

NON (Edy Williams); Zumdish (Fritz Feld); MXR (Richard Krisher); QZW (Eric Matthews); TAT (Carroll Roebke); QZW voice (Ronald Gans).

Castles in Space

Don and Judy to try protect an ice princess who is on the run from a space bandit. Wr: Peter Packer. Dir: Sobey Martin.

Princess Reyka (Corinna Tsopei); Chavo (Alberto Monte).

Trivia Alert: A major California TV station removed this episode from its package of *Lost in Space* reruns when the hispanic community objected to the stereotype of Chavo, the Mexican space bandit.

The Anti-Matter Man

John is kidnapped and taken to an alternate world. His evil duplicate returns to the family and poses as Prof. Robinson. Wr: K.C. Alison (Barney Slater, Robert Hamner). Dir: Sutton Roley.

Creature (Fred Krone); Doubles (Harper Carter, Joseph Canutt).

Target Earth

Shapeless beings assume the form of the Robinsons and travel through space to conquer Earth. Will and Dr. Smith are left to defeat the aliens. Wr: Peter Packer. Story: Allan Balter. Dir: Nathan Juran.

Gilt Proto (James Gosa); Family doubles (Sandy Gimpel, Harper Carter, John Hunt, Harry Carter); Proto #2 (Ralph Madlener); Proto #3 (Jerry Traylor).

The Princess of Space

Penny poses as a long-lost princess to quell a computer uprising. The real princess has been safely stored on a computer disc. Wr: Jackson Gillis. Dir: Don Richardson.

Fedor (Arte Johnson); Kraspo (Robert Foulk); Aunt Gamma (Sheila Matthews).

Memory Flash—casting director Larry Stewart: "I had cast Arte Johnson, and he was as nervous as hell. I said, 'Arte, what's the matter?' He replied, 'I had an audition today. I don't know if I'm going to get it or not. It's a really wild-ass show. It's like a series of 1,000 black-outs in one hour. It's called *Laugh-In.*' And Arte went directly from *Lost in Space* to *Laugh-In,* and it made him a star."

The Time Merchant

A time traveler sends Dr. Smith back to 1997, hours before the lift-off of the *Jupiter 2.* Wr: Robert and Wanda Duncan. Dir: Ezra Stone.

Dr. Chronos (John Crawford); General Squires (Byron Morrow); Rogers (Hoke Howell); Creature (Fred Krone).

The Promised Planet

The Robinsons think they've landed on an Earth colony, but it's actually inhabited by humanoid creatures who need Will and Penny. Wr: Peter Packer. Dir: Ezra Stone.

Bartholomew (Gil Rogers); Edgar (Keith Taylor).

Fugitives in Space

Don and Dr. Smith are sentenced to hard labor on a hot planet. They become caught up in the escape plans of a gorilla convict. Wr: Robert Hamner. Dir: Ezra Stone.

Creech (Michael Conrad); Warden (Tol Avery); Guard (Charles Horvath); Prisoner #1 (John Hunt); Prisoner #2 (Ralph Madlener).

Space Beauty
Judy enters an intergalactic beauty contest but finds that the other contestants are monsters. Wr: Jackson Gillis. Dir: Irving J. Moore.

Farnum B. (Leonard Stone); Nancy (Dee Hartford); Miss Teutonium (Miriam Schiller); Dictator (Ronald Weber); Knight (Jim Mills); Knight #2 (Bartell La Rue).

The Flaming Planet
Efforts to burn a giant plant off the ship's hull are hampered when an alien warrior fires a hail of missiles at the spaceship. Wr: Barney Slater. Dir: Don Richardson.

Sobram (Abraham Sofaer); Small plant (Harry Monty); Plant creature (Jerry Traylor); Plant #2 (John Hunt).

The Great Vegetable Rebellion
Living vegetables attack the Robinsons after Dr. Smith picks a flower. Wr: Peter Packer. Dir: Don Richardson.

Tybo (Stanley Adams); Willoughby (James Millhollin); Plant (Jerry Traylor).

Junkyard of Space
The *Jupiter 2* lands on a planet of flaming junk, where a junkman hijacks the spaceship. Wr: Barney Slater. Dir: Ezra Stone.

Junkman (Marcel Hillaire).

The Man from Atlantis
September 1977–July 1978

Washed ashore by a fierce storm, a dying humanoid amphibian is taken to the Naval Underwater Center. Revived, the well-spoken but amnesiac manfish is given the name "Mark Harris" by Dr. Elizabeth Merrill. She suspects that Mark is from the lost world of Atlantis. Mark agrees to join up with Elizabeth on underwater explorations aboard the submarine Cetacean.

Cast: Mark Harris (Patrick Duffy); Dr. Elizabeth Merrill (Belinda J. Montgomery); C.W. Crawford (Alan Fudge); *Crew of the* Cetacean: Jomo (Richard Williams); Chuey (J. Victor Lopez); Jane (Jean Marie Hon); Alan (Anson Downes).

Created by: Mayo Simon; *Producer:* Herman Miller; *Executive Producer:* Herbert F. Solow; NBC/Herbert F. Solow Productions; 60 minutes.

"If we had been able to include a laugh track on *The Man from Atlantis,* we could have let the audience know that, 'Hey, this is a comedy!'" says producer Herman Miller. He's serious. Miller contends that the audience couldn't relate to the comedic thrust of the series. "They needed permission to laugh," he says. "People didn't know what to make of it, and it confused them."

The initial four *Man from Atlantis* movies were played straight and pure. The 1977 pilot film took a serious look at what could happen to an underwater "Mr. Spock" if he were thrown into mankind's midst. When the weekly series debuted, the format had undergone a transformation. Tongue-in-cheek adventures prevailed as amphibian Mark Harris faced giant jellyfish, mermaids, gunslingers and sea elves. The capper was Oscar, the friendly two-headed seahorse in the episode "Scavenger Hunt." Misunderstood and lonely, the amiable animal plays with explosive fuel canisters on the ocean floor.

"It was actually a very funny series," notes Miller. He admits, however, that there was nothing funny about the mail from angry science fiction fans who felt the comical edge was a sinister development. "We got indignant letters from viewers who wrote, 'What have you done to this show?'" says Miller. "Or, 'This is supposed to be science fiction. How dare you do this kind of stuff.' The people we heard from seemed to prefer the pilot film."

"There was a science fiction magazine at the time that wrote us a brutal, nasty letter," recalls *Man from Atlantis* story editor Larry Alexander. "It said, 'We were considering giving your show coverage. After seeing your show, we're not going to give you any coverage. You have treated science fiction with disrespect.' I was stunned. I thought we had a nice, light show. If people want to blame the tongue-in-cheek for the show's failure, they can place the blame on my door completely."

The first TV movie dealt more with the question of Mark Harris's background. Was he from Atlantis? How would he fit with the human culture? Mark, a polite, gentle creature, couldn't recall his past. With Dr. Elizabeth Merrill's help, he tried to piece together his history. The storyline never resolved the question of Mark Harris's origin, and in the series, the question was moot.

"Herbert Solow saw it as an underwater *Star Trek*," notes Alexander. "Since the seas are a mysterious place, you could find all kinds of planets and interesting characters underwater. It was a reasonable, viable premise. It's a bit of a stretch to presume that there are civilizations beneath the sea, but if you accept that premise, it worked. The submarine was like the starship *Enterprise* from *Star Trek*."

The *Man from Atlantis* pilot film was a huge success. The ratings were a smash, and the response from viewers was strong. NBC followed this with three TV movie sequels. "My field is mainly doing pilots," says Herman Miller. "Herbert Solow asked me to do a quick rewrite of two of the TV movies following the pilot, and they turned out well. The

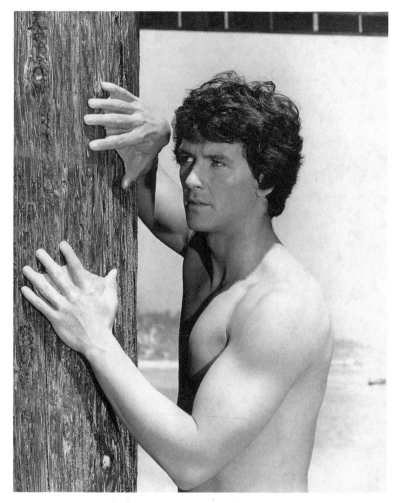

Patrick Duffy as Mark Harris, the *Man from Atlantis*. Copyright 1977 NBC/Solow Productions.

pilot in particular was a very good science fiction vehicle."

When the network expanded Mark Harris's adventures into a weekly series, Herman Miller accepted Solow's invitation to produce the show. "I immediately hired Larry Alexander as story editor. He's a good guy, and he was the best story editor I had had in years."

As the series took shape, Miller recalls, "We had a lot of conferences with the people at the network. They wanted to know what we planned to do with the series. We kicked around some ideas. Although the pilots had been terribly serious, we reached the notion of, 'Let's have some fun with this series.' That idea worked as far as we were concerned. NBC agreed to doing the show this way."

"The network executives were not science fiction fans," claims Alexander. "One of their main concerns was that women don't like science fiction. How could we attract that large portion of the audience?" Maintaining a serious approach to the series didn't interest Alexander. "The TV films were well produced, but they were too depressing. Too dull. There was nothing interesting about them."

Two weeks before the series premiered, Alexander saw red when he read *TV Guide*'s fall preview issue. "Their write-up of *The Man from Atlantis* basically excoriated the series," he says. "[The editors] hadn't seen a frame of film or read a script. They made it up. I read this and said, 'Oh, really? How can they say that?'"

Although Alexander took the brickbats from

Artwork introducing Mark Harris (Patrick Duffy), the humanoid amphibian from the mythical underwater continent. Copyright 1977 NBC/Solow Productions.

to the East River. In other words, we're the *New Yorker* of science fiction shows.' I knew that in terms of ratings and audiences, we were doomed. It was too witty. We had a perfectly workable format, but the audience wouldn't pick up on the tongue-in-cheek humor."

Alexander is quick to admit that a previous TV adventure, *Voyage to the Bottom of the Sea,* played an important part in shaping the series. "That was one of my problems with *The Man from Atlantis*," he says. "When they hired me, I said to Herb Solow, 'You realize, of course, that what we're doing is *Voyage to the Bottom of the Sea* with an alien.' Herb replied, 'Well, yes … but no.' Which meant that's exactly what we were doing. *Voyage to the Bottom of the Sea* was a very strange show. I thought it was written for infants. On *Man from Atlantis,* we tried to be witty. That didn't turn out to be the key to suc-

some science fiction fans for the show's content, he reveals that he was no stranger to the genre. "As a kid I was a big buff. I read Isaac Asimov and Arthur C. Clarke. I was even a member of the Science Fiction Book Club." Although he had high hopes for *The Man from Atlantis,* he heard the death knell long before the ratings came in. "The *New York Times* reviewed an episode I had written that featured the villainous Dr. Schubert. They said, 'What a wonderful, witty show.' I took the review to Herb Solow, and he said, 'This is a rave review. We're home free!' I said, 'No, Herb. It's all over. We're a bomb.' He looked at me, stunned, and said, 'What are you talking about?' I said, 'We're a hit in New York from 59th Street to 80th Street, from Central Park West

cess, but we *knew* that we had to play the stories straight. If you wink at an audience and let them in on the joke, you're through."

Alexander's favorite character on the show was the portly Dr. Schubert, played by Victor Buono. His weekly plans to dominate the world always went belly-up, but he was back the next week. "Victor Buono was wonderful. Before we were canceled, I wanted to do an episode where Schubert loses all of his money and ends up on skid row. He plots his revenge on the man from Atlantis from a flophouse. I always threw in Schubert jokes. There's one episode where he's plotting a nefarious scheme while playing Schubert's unfinished symphony on an organ. He's interrupted by his assistant, and Schubert looks up to heaven and says, 'One day I'm going to finish this!' That's an example of the things I did that people missed. This may sound terrible to science fiction buffs, but I wrote *The Man from Atlantis* as if it were *The Harvard Lampoon*. The show assumed that people had a college education." To Alexander's regret, Dr. Schubert was phased out of the series during the middle of its run. "The original idea was that he was going to be in every episode. That got tiring. It got to be like, 'Is he the only villain in the world?' So it was a conscious decision. It's unfortunate. The character was the best thing about the show."

Alexander had mixed feelings about Patrick Duffy's interpretation of the role, feeling that the man from Atlantis came across as too dry. "He was a nice guy, though, and very much into transcendental meditation. He would sit on a rug each day and hum.

"[One day] Herb Solow and I were watching the dailies and Herb suddenly yelled at the projectionist, 'Stop the film! Turn on the lights!' Herb ran over to the phone and said, 'Will somebody tell Patrick Duffy to shave his armpits! He's supposed to be an undersea creature. Undersea creatures don't have hairy arms!'"

Belinda J. Montgomery, who added the feminine touch as Dr. Merrill, vanished from the series toward the end of its run. "Belinda was a terrific person and a good actress," says Alexander. "She didn't quit. She was dropped from the last two episodes. She was very upset about it. It was a decision by the brass. I don't know what that was all about. I do remember somebody saying that [her Elizabeth Merrill character] was slowing the show down and making it too soft. Keep in mind, this was when the show was in deep trouble. We all knew that it wasn't going to last and [the studio and network] were doing everything they could to keep it going."

One thing they might have tried (but didn't) was changing the time slot. "*Man from Atlantis* was up against *Happy Days* and *Laverne and Shirley*," says Herbert Solow. "Those two series were so tough that we actually got better ratings up against the 1977 World Series."

For as long as the show lasted, though, writer Stephen Kandel had a blast. "I loved that series," he says. "It was a hoot. Whatever I pitched, they bought. "C.W. Hyde" was *Dr. Jekyll and Mr. Hyde*. We played it sideways, skewed. "The Naked Montague" was *Romeo and Juliet*. I not only carefully misquoted and requoted Shakespeare, I used the man from Atlantis to save

the two lovers. He created a long and happy life for them. If the series had continued, I was planning to write "19,000 Leagues Below the Surface," "S. Panza and Friend," "Whore and Piece," "Napoleon and Charlotte Russe" and anything else I could get away with. In other words, *Man from Atlantis* was a fantasy adventure with a sense of humor. A rare and happy combination."

The series sank from NBC's schedule in 1978. It bobbed to the surface many years later in the form of a big residual check in Larry Alexander's mailbox. "It was a huge hit in Communist China," he says. "That was around 1984. I found this $25,000 check staring at me in the face." Financial perks aside, Alexander says, "I enjoyed doing *The Man from Atlantis* tremendously. I would have watched it even if I hadn't written for it. Let's face it. How many witty science fiction programs does one come across?"

CAST NOTES

Patrick Duffy (Mark): Born 1949. Duffy starred (as Bobby Ewing) on *Dallas* (1978–91) and in the 1990s comedy series *Step by Step*.

Belinda J. Montgomery (Elizabeth): Born 1950 in Winnipeg. Montgomery played the title character's mother on the 1990s TV series *Doogie Howser*.

Alan Fudge (C.W.): Born 1944. "Alan used to play a lot of villains on Quinn Martin's detective shows during the 1970s," says writer Larry Alexander. "He's a fine actor." Fudge continues to work in guest roles on TV series such as the new *Columbo*.

EPISODE GUIDE

The Man from Atlantis (1977 TV movie)
After Mark washes ashore with amnesia, Elizabeth brings him to the attention of the Navy. Exploring the deep, Mark finds an underground laboratory where kidnapped missing scientists are working with the evil, eccentric scientist Dr. Schubert. Wr: Mayo Simon. Dir: Lee H. Katzin.

Schubert (Victor Buono); Cmdr. Phil Roth (Lawrence Pressman); Ernie Smith (Dean Santoro); Lt. Cmdr. Johnson (Allen Case); Ad. Dewey Pierce (Art Lund); Lt. Ainsley (Mark Jenkins); Doug Berkley (Joshua Bryant); Doctor (Steve Franken); Scientist (Virginia Gregg); Emil (Curt Lowens); British scientist (Charles Davis); French scientist (Lilyan Chauvin); U.S. scientist (Vincent Duke Milana); Russian scientist (Alex Rodine); George (Philip Baker Hall); Receptionist (Marguerite DeLain); Woman (Trudy Marshall); Popeye (Michael J. London); Divers (Robert Dore, Michael Watson); Nurse (Connie Izay); Intern (Judd Laurance); Man on beach (James Chandler); Receptionists (Pat Anderson, Akemi Kikumura); Ambulance driver (Larry Holt); Lab tech (Peter Weiss); Nurse #2 (Maralyn Thomas); Intern #2 (Phillip Roye); X-Ray tech (Cheryl Robinson); Beach boy (Scott Stevenson); Phone booth boy (Philip Tanzini).

The Death Scouts (1977 TV movie)

Creatures from an ocean world possess the bodies of two dead divers and go on a rampage in the city. Mark believes they could be the key to his true identity. Wr: Robert Lewin. Dir: Marc Daniels.

Lioa (Tiffany Bolling); Zos (Burr DeBenning); Miller Simon (Kenneth Tigar); Doctor (Russell Arms); Ginny Mendoza (Annette Cardona); Grant Stockwood (Alan Mandell); Herb Wayland (Vince Deadrick); Wes (Hank Stohl), Officer (Arch Archambrult); Crewman (Michael J. London); Boy (Stanley Clay); Lou (Maurice Hill); Manager (Joel Lawrence); Myrtle (Maralyn Thoma); Clerk (Dick Winslow).

Killer Spores (1977 TV movie)

Alien spores take over Mark's body in an effort to return to their home planet. Wr: John D. F. Black. Dir: Reza Badiyi.

Miller Simon (Kenneth Tigar); Captain (Fred Beir); Edwin Shirley (Ivan Bonar); Col. Manzone (James B. Sikking); Also with Lawrence Casey, Carole Demas, Brad David, Erik Holland, James Parkes.

The Disappearances (1977 TV movie)

Elizabeth is kidnapped and brainwashed by a woman scientist, whose sophisticated island complex threatens the submarine. Wr: Jerry Sohl, Luther Murdoch (Herman Miller). Dir: Charles Dubin.

Dr. Mary Smith (Darleen Carr); Dick Redstone (Dennis Redfield); Captain (Fred Beir); Miller Simon (Kenneth Tigar); Dr. Medlow (Ivor Francis); Jane (Pamela Peters-Solow); Clara (Ruth Manning).

Season Episodes

Melt Down

The evil Dr. Schubert will melt down the polar ice caps unless the government turns over Mark Harris. Wr: Tom Greene. Dir: Virgil W. Vogel.

Dr. Schubert (Victor Buono); Brent (Robert Lussier); Trubshawe (James E. Brodhead).

Mudworm

A highly advanced underwater probe is attacking ships. When Mark confronts the mechanical marvel, he learns the device has taken on human characteristics. Wr: Alan Caillou. Dir: Virgil W. Vogel.

Dr. Schubert (Victor Buono); Brent (Robert Lussier).

The Hawk of Mu

Mark finds an ancient stone hawk from an under-sea cave but the artifact, which can cause worldwide power blackouts, is snatched by Dr. Schubert. Wr: David Balkan, Luther Murdoch (Herman Miller). Dir: Harry Harris.

Dr. Schubert (Victor Buono); Brent (Robert Lussier); Juliette Schubert (Vicky Huxtable); Vicki (Carole Mallory); Smith (Sydney Lassick).

Giant!

Millions of gallons of water are leaking out of the ocean. Mark must team up with a giant gold prospector to battle a greedy conman. Wr: Michael Wagner. Dir: Richard Benedict.

Thark (Kareem Abdul-Jabbar); Muldoon (Ted Neeley); Dichter (Gene Le Belle); Bartender (John Dennis).

Man o' War

Schubert unleashes a giant jellyfish on swimmers at an international meet, forcing Mark to battle the monster. Wr: Larry Alexander. Dir: Michael O'Herlihy.

Dr. Schubert (Victor Buono); Dashki (Harvey Jason); Announcer (Gary Owens); Brent (Robert Lussier).

Shoot Out at Land's End

An undersea time warp propels Mark to the Old West, where he meets his double: Billy Jones, a notorious gunslinger and former amphibian. Wr: Luther Murdoch (Herman Miller). Dir: Barry Crane.

Clint Hollister (Pernell Roberts); Bettina Washburn (Jamie Smith Jackson); Artemus Washburn (Noble Willingham); Virgil (Bill Zuckert); Also with Tony Epper.

Crystal Water, Sudden Death

An underwater civilization is being exploited by Dr. Schubert, whose mining of energy crystals threatens to destroy their world. Wr: Larry Alexander. Dir: David Moessinger.

Dr. Schubert (Victor Buono); Havergal (Rene Auberjonois); Conrad (Rozelle Gayle); Click one (Tina Lenert); Click two (Flip Reade); Click three (Whitney Rydbeck).

The Naked Montague

An undersea time warp propels Mark into the fourteenth century, where he tries to arrange a happy ending for Romeo and Juliet. Wr: Stephen Kandel. Dir: Robert Douglas.

Romeo (John Shea); Juliet (Lisa Eilbacher); Friar Laurance (Lewis Arquette); Mercutio (Scott Porter); Tybalt (Norman Snow); Also with Ahna Capri.

C.W. Hyde

Undersea enzymes turn C.W. into a Dr. Jekyll/Mr. Hyde character. Wr: Stephen Kandel. Dir: Dan Cahn.

Belle (Michele Carey); Lew Calendar (Val Avery); Sarah (Pamela Peters-Solow); Bartender (Frank Bonner).

Scavenger Hunt

A playful two-headed seahorse is using nerve gas canisters as toys, unaware of their destructive force. Wr: Peter Allen Fields. Dir: David Moessinger.

Jack Muldoon (Ted Neeley); Oscar, the friendly sea

horse (Tony Urbano); Canja (Ted Cassidy); Toba (Yabo O'Brien); Trivi (Eugenia Wright); Also with Peter Kwong.

Imp
A playful sea elf accidentally causes a research team to drown themselves after his touch makes them revert to childhood. When the elf gets loose in the city, Mark tries to stop the imp before tragedy strikes again. Wr: Shimon Wincelberg. Dir: Paul Krasny.
   Moby the imp (Pat Morita); Duke (Dick Gautier); Clavius (Lyman Ward); Buddy O'Toole (Larry Breeding); Bert Davis (Mel Scott); Proprietor (Allen Joseph); Guard (William Benedict); Officer (James Ingersoll); Man (Harvey J. Goldenberg); Airlock officer (Anson Downes).

Siren
Pirates capture a mermaid and force her to stop Mark's pursuit of them. Wr: Michael Wagner. Dir: Ed Abroms.Jenny Reynolds (Lisa Blake Richards); Stringer (Neville Brand); Hugh Trevanian (Michael Strong); Mermaid (Carol Miyaoka); Amanda (Colleen Camp); Caine (Timothy Scott); Helmsman (Gary Tomlin).

The Deadly Carnival
Mark must infiltrate a group of renegade circus performers who are planning to steal an Egyptian artifact. Wr: Larry Alexander. Dir: Dennis Donnelly.
   Charlene Baker (Sharon Farrell); Moxie (Billy Barty); Summersday (Anthony James); Student (Donna Garrett).

Max Headroom: 20 Minutes into the Future
March 1987–October 1987

In the twenty-first century, Edison Carter, investigative reporter for the mega-station Network 23, is near death when, trying to stop an 'evil plot,' his ego is merged with an artificial intelligence program, creating the somewhat bizarre and thoroughly eccentric A.I., Max Headroom. Together Edison and Max fight for truth, liberty, and a better ratings share, in a world dominated by the images of television.

Cast: Edison Carter/Max Headroom (Matt Frewer); Theora Jones (Amanda Pays); Ben Chiviot (George Coe); Bryce Lynch (Chris Young) Murray (Jeffrey Tambor); Mrs. Formby (Virginia Kiser); Ashwell (Hank Garrett); Edwards (Lee Wilkof); Blank Reg (William Morgan Sheppard); Dominique (Concetta Tomei); Martinez (Ricardo Gutierrez).

Created by: Peter Wagg, Rocky Morton, Annabel Jankel, George Stone; *Executive Producer:* Philip DeGuere (American pilot), Terry Ellis (British pilot); *Line Producer:* Chris Griffin (British pilot); Peter Wagg; *Producer:* Brian Frankish; *Co-Producer:* Steve Roberts; *Supervising Producer:* Andrew Adelson (year 2); *Associate Producer:* Bruno George (year 1); Laurina Jean Adamson (year 2); ABC/ Lorimar; 60 minutes.

   A mass media phenomenon often springs from unlikely roots. In the case of *Max Headroom*, the phenomenon began with music videos. From there, it blossomed into talk shows, books, commercials and a prime-time dramatic television show.
   It was in 1981 that Peter Wagg, then head of Creative Services for Chrysalis Records in London, received a call from Andrew Park of England's newest television station, Channel Four, asking for a half-hour show for rock videos. Chrysalis Records agreed and arranged financing, but who would be the host? Seeking some-

thing interesting and innovative, Wagg went to a friend, advertising copywriter George Stone, for advice. Stone suggested a computer-based format. It was Stone who suggested the title *Max Headroom*, an abbreviation of "maximum headroom," the street-sign warning for tall trucks entering tunnels or underpasses.
   By 1983, Wagg had pulled in the video/animation directing team of Rocky Morton and Annabel Jankel for more nourishment and inspiration. (They directed the 1993 feature *Super Mario Brothers.*) Believing that just computer graphics and animation were not enough, they decided that Max needed personification. All four of these individuals—professionals in the fields of music, advertising and video—realized what they really desired was a "paranoid conspiracy movie." By this time, they had settled on an image: an investigative reporter who bashed his head against a lifting car barrier—with the words "Maximum Headroom 2.3" emblazoned in yellow and black—while trying to escape villains on a motorcycle.
   Channel Four was interested in a video series but just didn't have the financial clout for a one-hour TV movie. So, in 1984, Wagg took the concept to the HBO/Cinemax offices in New York. Intrigued by the ideas and images, within 48 hours the three-piece suits in the board room at HBO/

Cinemax decided they were willing to gamble and forked over half a million dollars to Wagg.

By summer George Stone was no longer involved, so Steve Roberts, a writer, penned a screenplay. The rough story of *Blipverts* was sketched out. In this tale of subliminal advertising via television in the twenty-first century, it was Network 23's investigative reporter, Edison Carter, who discovered the harmful effects their commercials were having on viewers. People were actually exploding when they overdosed on the ads! It was up to Carter to expose this insidious plot that had brought his network to the top of the ratings war. But when he got too close, Carter ran for his life and accidentally brought about the birth of Max Headroom.

Even while the team fine-tuned the script, Wagg continued work on a *Max Headroom* video version. Before the project could go any further, *somebody* had to portray Max. An extensive casting search led them to a Canadian, Matt Frewer. An early decision was not to use a British actor because Wagg wanted Max "to travel," to break the international boundaries and not have a Brit get in the way of that.

In October 1984, a script was finalized, and shooting commenced in November at Wembley, at an abandoned gasworks. In early 1985, *Max Headroom* premiered on Channel Four and was well received. This premiere served as a prelude to the video series. From here, the intensive media interest and the rumblings of a worldwide phenomenon began. By fall 1985, the film and video series began running on the Cinemax cable channel in the U.S. Steve Roberts added fuel to the forthcoming frenzy when he slapped together a pictorial novelization of the film and a second book; a humorous *Max Headroom's Guide to Life* was released.

Dubbed "the ultimate talk show," *The Max Headroom Show* on Cinemax was witty and flashy, with state-of-the-art jokes. It pulled in such guests as musician Sting, actors Jack Lemmon, Michael Caine and William Shatner, and hairstylist Vidal Sassoon, plus a variety of other entertainers.

How much further was this computer-generated video character going to go? A media phenomenon usually involves spinoffs such as lunch boxes, greeting cards, watches, t-shirts, skateboards, computer software games, and tons of copies of the film on videotape—and *Max Headroom* was no exception.

Flirting with the danger of overexposing an already widely recognized cult and pop figure,

Wagg signed on a major corporate sponsor, Coca-Cola. *Max Headroom* would do commercials for their brand new product, the new Coke. The slogan fit into the character's predilection for stuttering—"C-C-Caaatch the wave!" *Alien* director Ridley Scott directed two of the commercial series. The impact was amazing—stuttering became "in" at schools and colleges across America.

When Wagg approached NBC and CBS with the idea of an ongoing one-hour dramatic series built around Max Headroom, they turned him down, perhaps sensing the short lifespan of the gimmicky, smarmy talk-show-host-*cum*-soft-drink-pitcher. But ABC, then the third place network, gave him a free hand and said he could do it his way.

At this point, *Simon and Simon* producer Philip DeGuere climbed aboard. "I thought it was hysterical that an American television network wanted to take *Max Headroom* and put it in front of the American audiences," says DeGuere. "I was given a script of the one-hour British pilot that was done. I was told that ABC wanted to do this on American television, would I be interested in doing it? I was really quite astonished. I had never seen anything like it before, and I thought it was wonderful. It was obviously a biting satire on television. I also thought that there was no conceivable way that the show would work for any length of time on American television because it was obvious to me that the people involved in putting Max on American television didn't understand the show. Putting *Max Headroom* on American television is a little like George Bush saying he's going to vote for Bill Clinton. Everything about *Max Headroom* was diametrically opposed to American network television issues. And we could spoof. Therefore, it was apparent to me that the only reason they wanted to put it on the air was because they were familiar with the cult-like appeal of the character. I would never have taken a project like *Max Headroom* to a network based on a concept or a script." DeGuere says that it was very dangerous for him to become involved with something that he believed the producing network did *not* understand. Alarm bells were ringing in DeGuere's ears over potential disagreements and creative differences because of the very nature of the subject: a television series satirizing network programming and network manipulation of viewing audiences.

But the existing British pilot was the ace up his sleeve. "I said, 'Look, here's this film. Here it is! It's 60 minutes long. You want that on

The cast of the short-lived, but critically acclaimed *Max Headroom*, from left to right: Jeffrey Tambor (Murray), Chris Young (Bryce Lynch), Amanda Pays (Theora Jones), George Coe (Ben Cheviot), Virginia Kiser (Mrs. Formby), William Morgan Sheppard (Blank Reg), and Matt Frewer (Edison Carter/Max Headroom.

American television, correct?' And they say, 'Yes!' So I said, 'Ok, I'll put that on American television for you.'" says DeGuere. "Every time I would get into trouble, I would just go back to that and say, 'Wait a minute! Look! Here's the original film. This is what you said you wanted. This is what I'm doing. Now, get off my back!'"

That was the position he adopted to produce the American pilot. "I made it very clear that I had no interest in actually doing the series," points

out DeGuere. "All I was going to do was be executive producer of the pilot. I knew that doing the series would be a nightmare beyond belief. Especially when you get into the grind of series television, and you have a network on your case, and you're talking all the time, and you're dealing with something that they are absolutely incapable of understanding—you'd never be able to keep the show on track! It would just be an unpleasant experience. As a consequence I have to say I did not have *any* vision for the stories. It was not my job, and I didn't have to worry about it. All I did was see to it that the original show was cleaned up and made a bit more comprehensible and rendered more palatable for American viewers."

Of the premise and the intended audience, DeGuere says, "The style of the series was to see stories on film from Edison Carter's camera viewpiece. It was done well and imaginatively, and I think the setting was fabulous. I think stories could have been told in that setting, but I don't think that was a show that ever should have been on American network television. That show would have been better if it was done like *Dr. Who*, or the new *Star Trek*. That might have been better if it had been done directly for syndication."

The show's avant garde nature categorized it as "an experiment as far as ABC was concerned. [I felt there would be] certainties of having the same kinds of network interference [on this show] as I did on *Twilight Zone*. I wasn't directly involved with it, so I can't say whether it was similar to those experiences. All I can say is that the network insisted on trying to kick over the show into production and that cannot have a beneficial effect on them."

Director Thomas J. Wright had a much closer involvement with *Max Headroom* than did his friend DeGuere. "Phil wanted me to do the pilot and I wasn't available to do it. But as soon as I was available, I came in. It really was a lot of fun. But again, a very expensive show as you can tell by looking at it."

Responsible for three episodes of the series, "Rakers," "War" and "Dieties," Wright remembers the show fondly and says, "The shoot was probably 14 to 15 hours a day for an eight-day shoot. It was very complicated in putting it together. There was lots of video playback, lots of live feed, lots of action, lots of technical stuff. Coordination and everything had to be well thought out. But it was also a lot of fun. Great people. They were very tough shows, and I learned a lot."

Evaluating his work, Wright says, "I did two out of three very good shows for them. I gave them a really good cinematographer, and the shows I did are very, very good. A lot of style, good acting, worked very well. I had a lot of fun. The cast and crew were really into it. But they were very difficult shows."

Shooting on-site was one of the staples of the show, giving it a rundown, dirty and decrepit, futuristic look. Wright remembers the show's field trips. "When we did 'War,' we went on location for five to six days in Fontana at the old steel plant they were tearing down, near San Bernadino. 'Rakers' was done at an old building at Long Beach that was going to be torn down. We shot a lot there and built sets in this building and on the stage in L.A. But we would look for different places, and they liked what I was doing. For instance, when I got ready to do 'War,' they let us stay on location for six days. On TV this is not something that's done. You just don't do it. But we did it, and it was one of the best shows and one of my favorite shows. 'Rakers' and 'War' are very complex and full of so much style. Imagewise, scenes, acting, special effects, costumes— everything. 'War' is like a little movie. When I look at it—and I usually don't look at the stuff I've done—I can't even believe what was in 'War'! Some of *The Running Man* was also shot at the Fontana steel plant before it was torn down. It was very otherworldly looking."

Max Headroom, says Wright, "was a whole new concept for TV and was supposed to be a big breakthrough and a lot of new inventive stuff. But that was one of the problems. If you are going to do a show like that, then you go all out, which they did at first. It was always over-budget because it was a big, big deal. But after the first season they decided they couldn't keep doing this, so they started trimming. New people came in, and money and time was cut and the scripts changed to accommodate that and it's not the show it was any more. It was taken out of their hands."

What made the show's lifespan so short, according to Wright, was, "when it became so expensive to make and the audience started dropping off because they started cutting the money, which meant they cut stories, and the quality started going down compared to the first ones, it just didn't make it."

One of the difficulties of a show like *Max Headroom* was to try not to lose focus of the title character, given the many elements installed in the show. DeGuere and Wright readily acknowledge this problem.

"It became something of a gimmick," agrees DeGuere. "And it wasn't an easy gimmick to incorporate. Television works according to formulas. Take, for example, *The Incredible Hulk*. The formula of *The Incredible Hulk* was very simple. Twice on every fifteen-minute segment, the guy had to Hulk out. The theory is to construct a story that allows that to happen. Some very successful television series have been built around that kind of basic gimmick. So, just because there's a gimmick involved doesn't mean it isn't going to work.

"*Max Headroom* as a character tended to be something of a gimmick because it didn't really have a lot to do in a lot of the shows."

"That's right," says Wright. "People got tired of the same old thing over and over, and it was the fight against the [ABC] network. Again, according to what you want to do, and what input you give the writers, and so forth, it starts. And if you start being limited it reflects all the way down the line. It's like dominoes. It's very true, everything gets affected once you start pulling out certain things."

Matt Frewer, the star of the show as Edison Carter/Max Headroom, says that in the end, when the show got pulled from ABC's schedule, "It was really tragic. I went out and got drunk and all I was worried about was my headache!" Frewer's practical reaction was, "*Okay, on to the next thing.* It wasn't too bad because that kind of thing happens. I think it got canceled because the ratings were so bad. Also, because I think it became a sort of culty thing, and I think we bit the hand that fed us a few times when we probably should have nibbled. I think we were also guilty in the end of style over content. There was so much time spent on trying to get the bright-white-light-through-smoke look of the show. As great as it was, it made the characters and the plots suffer a bit."

"Yes, it did," agrees producer DeGuere. "Although I don't know if that was necessarily part of the problem. A lot of the successes during the eighties were often style over content. Specifically, *Miami Vice* and *Moonlighting*. I don't think style over content is necessarily a bad thing in TV in terms of success. But I agree with all of the other things that Matt said. And I think that in context, just from my own experience, let me explain this way: The premise that *Max Headroom* was based on is very difficult to include in storylines. It was very hard to work in the Max Headroom character in all the stories and give Edison Carter something to do and [have] all the other characters bouncing around. And because they didn't want to sacrifice any of those elements that were stylistic, I think the evolution of the stories undoubtedly suffered in some regard. I wasn't close enough to the process to really know that well."

Wright says, "I don't know why the show would suffer because of style—but what I saw was ... the D.P. [director of photography] kept a really good style and good look to the show, then after so many episodes he wanted to leave and do other things. I don't know. It depends on the director. You always want to create a style on the show you do, but still, it shouldn't inhibit your storytelling at all. Matt was great and was in it one thousand percent, but when you start seeing it happen, there's nothing that you can do."

Asked if he accomplished what he set to do with his character, Frewer is philosophical. "Not really. The Edison Carter character ended up being a fairly sort of strait-laced, lantern-jawed hero. I wanted to do more than that, but I was discouraged from doing that, and in a way that was okay because it was a real contrast to the way I played Max—a sort of wacky, let-your-rubber-hair-down kinda guy. It was unsatisfying to do it the way I was encouraged to do it. ... But Max was a great calling card for me. There are plenty of actors out in Los Angeles who don't have anything, and here I was playing two leads in a TV series, so it was a fantastic springboard. I'm not bitter about it at all."

In the end, Wright notes with a grin that there was a lot of irony attached to the show because it was a series that spoofed network programming and politics. "I think one of the inside jokes was we would do a scene and the network will never get it, you know, and it would be a sort of a turnabout on what was happening with the real network and the production company. Sometimes we'd write an off-sided scene to that and it went and the real network thought it was great. That happened quite a few times."

Looking back, DeGuere feels that in the end the show "turned out very well. In fact, I personally liked the American version better than the British version. I think it makes more sense. There were some things in the British version that were left hanging. Oh, I think the series turned out very well. I was quite impressed. However, I never expected it to be a success. Based on my experience in television, I had a pretty good idea of how much unusual entertainment television audiences could sit through. And Max was way too much for everyone. It was fast moving, it didn't give you a chance to go to the bathroom in the middle of the show, you really had to pay attention to it to follow it. On top of that, it was very, very funny in a very unique kind of way, and there wasn't anything quite like it on television. I just didn't think there was any possibility of it finding an audience. I couldn't resist putting something that outrageous on TV."

CAST NOTES

Matt Frewer (Edison Carter/Max): Born 1958. After this show, Frewer landed two sit-coms, *Doctor, Doctor* (1989) on CBS and *Shaky Ground* (1992) on Fox. He also guest-starred in *Star Trek — The Next Generation*'s "A Matter of Time." He's also been busy with comedy features like *Short Time* (1990) with Dabney Coleman.

Amanda Pays (Theora Jones): Born 1959. After *Max*, Pays, who is married to *L.A. Law*'s Corbin Bernsen, returned to prime time in 1990 with a role in *The Flash* as Dr. Tina McGee. She's also appeared in the Fox series *The X-Files* (1993).

EPISODE GUIDE

Max Headroom: 20 Minutes into the Future (British pilot)
Suspicious of a new advertising concept called Blipverts (used to increase ratings), investigative reporter Edison Carter breaks into a lab where experimental results show that viewers explode. When he's captured by a teenage scientist, his mind is copied and Max Headroom is born. When a woman scientist, Theora, helps him escape, he vows to expose Big Time Television. Wr: Steve Roberts, story by George Stone, Rocky Morton and Annabel Jankel. Dir: Rocky Morton and Annabel Jankel.
     Grossman (Nickolas Grace); Dominique (Hilary Tindall); Blank Reg (Morgan Shephard); Bryce (Paul Spurrier); Bruegal (Hilton McRae); Mahler (George Rossi); Murray (Roger Sloman); Gorrister (Anthony Dutton); Ben Cheviot (Constantine Gregory); Edwards (Lloyd McGuire); Ms. Formby (Elizabeth Richardson); Ashwell (Gary Hope); Body bank receptionist (Joanne Hall); ENG reporter (Howard Samuels); Helipad reporter (Roger Tebb); Eyewitness (Val McLane); Exploding man (Michael Cule).

Season 1: 1987

Blipverts
Investigative reporter Edison Carter discovers his employer is using a deadly form of TV advertising. This episode is an American reworking of the original British pilot. Wr: Joe Gannon, Steve Roberts and Philip DeGuere, from a screenplay by Steve Roberts. Dir: Farhad Mann.
     Grossberg (Charles Rocket); Florence (Billie Bird);
Gorrister (Ken Swofford); Breughel (Jere Burns); Mahler (Rick Ducommon); Apt. woman (Viola Kates Stimpson); Also with Irene Olga Lopez, Pearl Shear, Skip O'Brien, Matt Roe, , John Davey, Taylor Presnell, Heath Jobes.

Rakers
Theora is amazed to learn that her brother Shawn is involved in a gladiatorial combat game where youths on motorized skateboards score points by "raking" steel spiked gloves against each other. Network 23 wants to televise the illegal game. Carter needs to expose the game and save Shawn. Wr: James Crocker and Steve Roberts, story by James Crocker. Dir: Thomas J. Wright.
     Shawn (Peter Cohl); Jack Friday (Wortham Krimmer); Chip (J.W. Smith); Simon Peller (Sherman Howard); Promoter (Joseph Ruskin); Ped Xing (Arsenio "Sonny" Trinidad); Coach (Lee deBroux); Doc Willis (Wynn Irwin); Researcher (B.L. Collins); Dawn (Kimberly Delfin); Spivvy (Ron D. Ross); Fedora (Brian Libby); Fringe Kid (Bobby Brett); Winnie (Kawena Charlot); Grace (Kedren Zadikov); Newscaster (Doug Hale); Also with Tain Bodkin, Jeffrey Weisman, Tabi Cooper, David Preston, Lorilyn Huckstep, Heath Jobes.

Body Banks
Carter races against time to save a woman kidnapped to a "body bank" for experimentation. For help, he turns to Blank Reg at Big Time TV. Wr: Steve Roberts. Dir: Francis De Lia.
     Breughel (Jere Burns); Mahler (Rick Ducommon); Rik (J W Smith); Mel (Scott Kraft); Ped Xing (Arsenio "Sonny" Trinidad); Plantaganet (John Winston); Doctor Mason (Claude Earl Jones); Broadcaster (Fred Holliday); Dr. Moon (Robert Dowdell); Presenter (James "Gypsy" Haake); Pancho (Jenny Gago); Rayna (Peri Kaczmarek); Kyoku (Michael Paul Chan); Anaesthetist (Grace Simmons); Researcher #1 (B.L. Collins); Researcher #2 (Jay Arlen Jones); Tom Cowan (Rick Deats); Paula (Juliette Cummins).

Security Systems
While investigating a security company, Carter is bewildered to discover he's been accused of credit fraud. Wr: Michael Cassutt Dir: Tommy Lee Wallace.
     Valerie Towne (Carol Mayo Jenkins); Rik (J.W. Smith); First Operator (David Allyn); Second Operator (Peter Mins); Voice of A-7 (Sally Stevens); Mrs. Rivas (Julia Calderon); Mr. Rivas (Santos Morales); Security Guard (Mark Voland).

War
Network 23 loses ratings when a citywide guerilla war breaks out. A rival network is climbing in the numbers. Carter investigates a possible conspiracy between terrorists and the network. Wr: Michael Cassutt and Steve Roberts, from a story by Martin Pasko and Rebecca Parr Dir: Thomas J. Wright.
     Braddock (Gary Swenson); Hewett (Richard Lineback); Croyd Hauser (Robert O'Reilly); Janie Crane (Lisa Niemi); Lucian (J Michael Flynn); Ped Zing (Arsenio 'Sonny' Trinidad); Chief (Yana Nirvana); Also with Michael Colin Ward, Spencer Allan, Tom Miller.

The Blanks
When "blanks," unregistered computer people, are rounded up by the metrocops, computer hackers threaten to crash the city's computers. Wr: Steve Roberts. Dir: Tommy Lee Wallace.

Bruno (Peter Crook); Peller (Sherman Howard); Janie Crane (Lisa Niemi); Traker (Brian Brophy); Brenda (Elizabeth Gorcey); Ronald (Tom Everett); Joel (Rob Narita); Jacksy (Lycia Naff); Meg (Cynthia Stevenson); Fortune teller (Sandra Sexton); Also with Kenneth White, John Durbin, John Fleck.

Season 2: 1987-88

Academy
Blank Reg is accused of hijacking network frequencies, but Edison and Theora think Bryce is the real culprit. Wr: David Brown. Dir: Victor Lobl.

Sidney Harding (James Greene); Lauren (Sharon Barr); Shelley Keeler (Maureen Teefy); Announcer (Dick Patterson); Nicholas (Christopher Burton); Mr. Weeks (Barry Pearl); Prosecuting attorney (Bill Dearth); Zik Zak Girl (Sue Marrow); Also with Mya Akerling, Melissa Steinberg, Paul Marin, Joe Hart, Tom Fitzpatrick.

Dieties (aka Resurrection Vanna)
Carter is ambivalent about investigating the practices of the Church of Entropic Science, which is offering immortality via storing personalities on computers. The leader is Carter's old friend. Wr: Michael Cassutt. Dir: Thomas J. Wright.

Vanna Smith (Dayle Haddon) Lauren (Sharon Barr); Angela Barry (Rosalind Chao); Official (Gregory Itzin); Researcher (Michael Margotta); Jennifer Marx (Peg Stewart); Researcher (Brenda Hayes); Humphrey Marx (Gary Ballard); Churchgoer (Dale Raoul); Also with Clarence Brown, Ron Ray, Larry Spinak.

Grossberg's Return
Arch-villain Grossberg works for Network 66 now, and a politically corrupt ratings scheme is determined to bring down Network 23. Wr: Steve Roberts. Dir: Janet Greek.

Grossberg (Charles Rocket); Harriet Garth (Caroline Kava); Lauren (Sharon Barr); Chairman Thatcher (Stephen Elliott); Peller (Sherman Howard); Bartlett (Andreas Katsulas); Angela Barry (Rosalind Chao); Kersler (Brett Potter); Chubb (James F. Dean); Religious leader (John Hamelin); Also with Karen Hensel, Donald Burda, Lisa Peders, Rachelle Ottley, Brian Little, J. Jay Smith, Saida Pagan.

Dream Thieves
The death of an old reporter friend leads Carter to thieves who sell stolen dreams to the highest bidder. Wr: Steve Roberts, from a story by Charles Grant Craig. Dir: Todd Holland.

Paddy Ashton (Mark Lindsay Chapman); Breughel (Jere Burns); Greig (Ron Fassler); Bella (Jenette Goldstein);

Finn (Vernon Weddle); Deskman (Robin Bach); Joel (Rob Narita); Technician (Vince McKewin); Customer (Stephen Pershing); Also with Steven Rotblatt, Timothy Dang, Peter DeAnello, Patricila Veselich, Gary Dean Sweeney, Dalton Younger.

Whacketts (aka The Addiction Game)
Edison investigates an old-style game show that becomes addictive for viewers, while networks 23 and 66 vie to buy the game. Wr: Arthur Sellers, from a story by Dennis Rolfe. Dir: Victor Lobl.

Grossberg (Charles Rocket); Lauren (Sharon Barr); Ziskin (Bert Kramer); Haskel (Bill Maher); Biller (Richard Frank); Bartlett (Andreas Katsulas); Chubb (James F. Dean); Network 66 salesman (Lawrence Lott); Lt. Rico (Morgan Walsh); Also with Craig Schaeffer, Edward Beimfohr.

Baby Grobags
A new test tube baby-making facility has sprung up, and Carter investigates a claim by a couple that their baby has been stolen. Wr: Chris Ruppenthal. Dir: Janet Greek.

Grossberg (Charles Rocket); Breughel (Jere Burns); Lauren (Sharon Barr); Helen (Amanda Hillwood); Cornelia Firth (Millicent Martin); Bartlett (Andreas Katsulas); Joel (Rob Narita); Nurse (Leigh Kelly); Chubb (James F. Dean); Also with Carl Steven, David Hess, Paula Marchese, Tom McGuire, Robert Kerman, Kim Ameen, Mike Narz, Mary Kay Swedish.

Neurostim
Advertising is now sent directly to the customers' minds, thanks to Zik-Zak's bracelets. Customers think they are getting wonderful fantasies, but when Carter attempts to expose them, a special bracelet is prepared just for him. Wr: Arthur Sellers and Michael Cassutt. Dir: Maurice Phillips.

Lauren (Sharon Barr); Edison's dream girl (Joan Severance); Bryce's dream girl (Julie McCullough); Costumer (Frank Kahlil Wheaton); Chairman (Sab Shimono); Newscaster (Saida Pagan); Housewife's dream man (Jim Piddock); Aide (Evan Kim); Housewife (Jacque Lynn Colton); Sully's friend (Edward Wiley); Researcher (Michael Margotta); Sully (Martin Azarow); Bartender (Billy Beck); Sgt. Compton (Roger Hampton); Also with Michael Strasser, Tom Dugan, Michael Dobo.

Lessons
Carter and Theora witness a raid by Network 23 censors. Meanwhile, metrocops raid a fringers school when the Network instructional programming is pirated. Wr: Adrian Hein, Steve Roberts, from a story by Colman Dekay and Howard Brookner. Dir: Victor Lobl.

Lauren (Sharon Barr); Frances (Laura Carrington); Traker (Mike Preston); Dragul (John Durbin); Bruno the Blank (Peter Crook); Mink (Ainslie Currie); Also with Rick Lieberman, Guy Christopher, Lewis Dauber, Richard Lion, Jason Zahler, Melissa Behr, Ed Trotta, Larry Cortinas.

Men into Space

September 1959–September 1960

The adventures of Col. Edward McCauley and his dramatic efforts to probe the unknown reaches of space.

Cast: Col. Edward McCauley (William Lundigan); Mary McCauley (Joyce Taylor); Pete McCauley (Charles Herbert).

Producer: Lewis J. Rachmil; *Associate Producer:* Mel Epstein; *Technical Advisor:* Lawrence D. Ely, Col. USAF; *Space Paintings by:* Chesley Bonestell; *Music Theme:* David Rose; CBS/ZIV; 30 minutes; black and white.

When the economy-minded studio ZIV spent over $3,000 on astronaut garb for its new space series, insiders knew the little studio was serious about sending *Men into Space* into the ratings stratosphere. "All of this stuff is authentic," said a ZIV spokesman. Even William Lundigan's magnetic space shoes cost $75 apiece.

As the space race between the United States and the Soviet Union took off in the late 1950s, CBS decided to launch a series that reflected manned space flight. The most prestigious backing for the show came from the Department of Defense—which furnished technical advice, research and its facilities for the series—and the U.S. Air Force. Great effort went into ensuring that *Men into Space* was as accurate as possible. There would be no monsters or time warps or visitors from other worlds. The series format was projected just a few years ahead of real space accomplishments. McCauley rescued trapped astronauts, piloted space shuttles and repaired orbiting space stations. Occasionally he went to the moon, and once to Mars.

Technically, the series presented the best special effects for TV at the time. However, the characters and human drama often failed to reach orbit, thanks to the dry plots.

Writer Robert Hecker recalls that when he submitted his story, "Earthbound" (starring Robert Reed as a stowaway), the technical concerns outweighed the plot. "In one story

Men into Space: Col. Ed McCauley (William Lundigan) blasts off into space. Copyright 1959 CBS/ZIV–United Artists.

conference, their primary concern was, 'You can't have a stowaway because of the weight. Even an extra 100 pounds would abort the mission.' I told them that in the near-future time of the series, weight wouldn't be so critical. A stowaway could be possible. Besides, we should be allowed a little literary license. After all, half of the things depicted on *Men into Space* were highly problematic." Hecker convinced the producers but says, "We had at least three conferences on how much weight could we get away with. Nothing about character or plot. They were so bound up in the technical details, they tended to lose sight of the story."

Nevertheless, Hecker admired the technical integrity of the series. "*Men into Space* was ahead of its time, but not by much. Most of the events, such as moon landings and space walks, were already being investigated by scientists and the Aeronautics Institute, which later became NASA."

Hecker, who is a Lt. Col. USAF (retired), was well versed in what he wrote. "When I wrote for the series, I was writing scientific and technical audio-visual reports for North American Aviation, Lockheed, Hughes, Douglas Aircraft and various government agencies. I had an inside track on the latest technology."

While the series aimed at the future, its treatment of women was strictly primeval. An entertaining example, "The First Woman on the Moon," cast Nancy Gates as a housewife who agrees to spend three months on a moonbase. The less-than-progressive James Clavell script has the female astronaut bursting into tears the minute she walks into her lunar living room. The male astronauts snicker that the psychiatrists predicted such behavior. While the men wear helmets clearly stating their rank, the housewife has a helmet reading "Mrs. Hale." At first moody and irritable (because there are no shopping centers on the moon, states the sympathetic narrator), Mrs. Hale recovers with a sense of humor and passes her space test.

Actress Nancy Gates-Hayes, who retired from acting in the early 1970s to raise her four children, chuckles about the experience now. "At the time they were all male chauvinistic pigs!" she laughs. "Thankfully, things have changed." She was intrigued by the real-life science of the episode. "It was not your usual TV fare," she says. "People ask me about westerns I've done and all I remember is that we rode horses. A show like *Men into Space* put us on a lunar landscape. There was also someone from NASA on the set. He explained to us that within ten years they would be going to the moon, and we were fascinated. This was 1960, and man walked on the moon nine years later." She was also required to fly through space, recalling, "They lifted us up on wires and floated us around. It was such an unusual show I brought my son, Jeff, who was seven at the time, to the set. He loved it. He was a big science fiction fan. He went on to produce the series *Time Trax*."

Another guest star, Don Eitner, recalls that while ZIV was a small operation, "it was a very active TV studio. The other major studios were saying, 'Oh, TV is beneath us. We're not going to get involved.' ZIV was one of the leading producers of syndicated shows, and I was one of their stock players. "On *Men into Space*, they did the space scenes against a black backdrop. There wasn't any process work like they do today. They literally wired us and suspended us up in space. It wasn't dangerous because they only hung us up a few feet. It was fun to do."

Walter Doniger, a director of several episodes, also enjoyed his stint with the series. "It gave me the opportunity to do something that hadn't been done before, particularly dealing with the technical problems. We filmed the pilot at Lancaster, California, at Edwards Air Force Base, where they had all of this space equipment." Doniger fondly recalls star William Lundigan as "a very nice man. He was not a star or a man with a magic about him, but he was competent in the role. He was pleasant to work with and took instructions."

Writer Jerome Bixby provided the story for the segment "Is There Another Civilization?" in which the explorers try to reconstruct an alien spaceship by using the piece of an alien ship as a guide. "I cringed a little when I watched it," notes the science fiction novelist. "Such detailed reconstruction of an alien craft based on examination of a shard is, to put it mildly, unlikely. But I had written it!" Bixby had another story idea that didn't reach filming stage. "It concerned a guy stranded in a lifeboat. He's spotted by a manned satellite. The Defense Department nixed it. They said that was impossible. Preposterous, they said." Bixby, however, knew that such technology was possible. "They probably didn't want a satellite's spy potential emphasized on network television," Bixby reasons. Bixby, however, classifies *Men into Space* as a valiant attempt to realistically depict space travel. "As I recall, the production staff knew little about science, but they did care, [and] had a technical consultant. The science used on the series seemed sound. The series was ahead of its time. Bill Lundigan was also an asset: competent, easy to work with and a very funny guy. The one weakness was the special effects. They were toothpick, hairpin and bubblegum, due to a limited budget."

Despite the cast and crew's determination, the series' initial strength in the ratings faded quickly. The series ended after one full season. However, Robert Hecker feels it left its own legacy. "*Men into Space* was an enjoyable show," he says, "and it helped to pave the way for other space adventure series to follow."

CAST NOTES

William Lundigan (Col. McCauley): Born 1914. A former radio announcer who turned to TV after his movie career waned in the 1950s, Lundigan made his last TV appearance on *Marcus Welby, M.D.* (1970). He died in 1975.

EPISODE GUIDE

Moon Probe
During a lunar reconnaissance flight, McCauley is accidentally thrown clear from his spaceship. His shipmates must rescue him before his air supply runs out. Wr: Arthur Weiss. Dir: Walter Doniger.

Angie Dickinson, Paul Burke, H.M. Wynant, Paul Richards, John Vivyan, Robert Cornthwaite, James Anderson, William Phipps, Edward Kemmer, Charles Maxwell, Stacy Harris, Susan Dorn, Ashley Cowan, John Bleifer, Jacques Gallo, Robert Kino, Sam Capuano, Moody Blanchard.

Moon Landing
A moon landing is an apparent success, but one of the crew, severely injured, tries to hide his wound from the others. Wr: James Clavell. Dir: Walter Doniger.

Joe Maross, Paul Lambert, Dean Harens, Karl Swenson, Ernestine Barrier, Don Oreck, Andrew Glick, Edward Paul.

Building a Space Station
During construction of a space station, McCauley has little time to rescue a rookie spaceman trapped between two adjoined sections. Wr: Meyer Dolinsky. Dir: Otto Lang.

Don Dubbins, Christopher Dark, Nancy Hadley, Bartlett Robinson, Don Kennedy, Jack Mann, Michael Galloway, Walter Stocker.

Water Tank Rescue
When an astronaut has a heart attack on the moon, the crew has to build a water acceleration shield to safely return him to earth. Wr: Ib Melchior. Dir: Otto Lang.

Joan Taylor, Jon Shepodd, Paul Langton, Gar Moore, Stephen Talbot, Richard Travis, Peter Walker, Barry Brooks.

Lost Missile
McCauley must disarm a wayward nuclear missile before it strikes a group of lunar astronauts. Wr: Michael Plant. Dir: Walter Doniger.

Harry Townes, Marcia Henderson, Ken Lynch, Jeremy Slate, Gavin MacLeod, Jim Stockton.

Moonquake!
McCauley's moon expedition is imperiled when a moonquake destroys their spaceship. Wr: William Templeton. Dir: Lee Sholem.

Arthur Franz, Denver Pyle, Ross Elliot, Bek Nelson, Britt Lomond, Ann Doran, Robert Karnes, Mike Keene, Leonard Graves, Sumner Williams.

Space Trap
McCauley races to intercept a returning spaceship, whose unconscious crew is heading for a collision course with the Earth. Wr: Marianne Mosner, Francis Rosenwald. Dir: Charles Haas.

Peter Hansen, Robert Gist, Ron Foster, Russ Conway, Dallas Mitchell, Michael Chapin, Joe Haworth.

Asteroid
A time bomb is set to destroy a rogue asteroid, but McCauley must rescue one of his men, who remains blinded and trapped on the asteroid's surface. Wr: Ted Sherdeman. Dir: Lee Sholem.

Bill Williams, Herbert Rudley, Joyce Meadows, Walter Reed, Richard Crane, Richard Bull, Lionel Ames.

Edge of Eternity
McCauley and two crewmen try to stretch their dwindling air supply so that they can reach a nearby space station. Wr: Kalman Phillips. Dir: Nathan Juran.

Corey Allen, Kem Dibbs, Mary Webster, Louis Jean Heydt, Sue Carlton, Clark Howat, Hal Hamilton.

Burnout
McCauley agrees to repeat a controversial space-flight to discover if a pilot bailed out due to mechanical failure or cowardice. Wr: Donald Duncan. Dir: Alvin Ganzer.

Robert Clarke, John Sutton, Lance Fuller, Donna Martell, Barbara Bestar, Ken Drake, Tom McNamara.

First Woman on the Moon
Renza Hale agrees to be the first woman on the moon, where she must spend three months on moonbase. Wr: James Clavell. Dir: Herman Hoffman.

Nancy Gates, H.M. Wynant, Tyler McVey, Harry Jackson, Norman Leavitt, Danny Niles, Max Huber.

Christmas on the Moon
During Christmas on the moon, McCauley's team is tracking a new comet when one of the astronomers suffers an appendicitis attack. Wr: David Duncan, story by Lawrence Goldman. Dir: Richard Carlson.

Whit Bissell, Keith Larsen, Patricia Manning, Paul Langton, Del Russel, Sean Bartlett.

Quarantine

Two antagonistic space specialists are forced to work together to defeat a crippling space virus on a space station. Wr: Stuart James Byrne. Dir: Walter Doniger.

Warren Stevens, Simon Oakland, John Milford, Guy Stockwell, Ray Teal, Donald Freed.

Tankers in Space

Colliding with an explosive tanker, McCauley and his men try to get their damaged ship away from the leaking tanker. Wr: Arthur Weiss. Dir: Alvin Ganzer.

James Drury, Murray Hamilton, Philip Terry, Robert Brubaker, Mary Newton, Helen Mowery, Jennifer Lea, Jack Emrek.

Sea of Stars

Faulty rockets put a spaceship on a collision course with the sun. McCauley tries to save the two-man crew. Wr: Marianne Mosner, Francis Rosenwald, Kalman Phillips, story by Marianne Mosner, Francis Rosenwald. Dir: Lee Sholem.

Fred Beir, Jack Ging, Nan Peterson, Audrey Clark, Tom Brown, Angus Duncan, Jim Cody.

A Handful of Hours

Stranded on the moon's surface, an expedition's only chance for survival is to open a spare oxygen tank, but the only wrench available is inside astronaut Kelly's spacesuit. Wr: Michael Plant. Dir: Alvin Ganzer.

Peter Baldwin, Mark Dana, William Schallert, Logan Field, William Lundmark, Del Russel, Scott Davey, Wade Cagle, Robert O'Connor.

Earthbound

A stowaway on a training flight turns out to be the key to saving the ship from a rapidly decaying orbit. Wr: Robert L. Hecker, David Duncan, story by Robert L. Hecker. Dir: Nathan Juran.

Robert Reed, Anne Benton, Byron Morrow, John Garrett, Don Edmonds.

Caves of the Moon

McCauley must search lunar caverns for a lost space researcher. Wr: Meyer Dolinsky. Dir: Lee Sholem.

John Howard, Paul Comi, Donald May, Lillian Campbell.

Dateline: Moon

Newsmen accompany McCauley to the moon, where one reporter tries to sensationalize the discovery of a long-dead civilization. Wr: Robert Warnes Leach, story by Michael Adams (Meyer Dolinsky). Dir: Alan Crosland, Jr.

Harry Lauter, Lisa Gaye, Ray Montgomery, Brad Forrest, King Calder, Patrick Waltz, Rand Brooks, Dennis Moore, Dana Enlow.

Moon Cloud

When a geochemist falls into a moon crevice, his colleague wrestles with a dilemma: save him, or leave him to die and gain the fame of an energy discovery. Wr: Michael Plant, story by Sidney Kalcheim. Dir: Otto Lang.

Robert Vaughn, Allison Hayes, Douglas Dick, John Cliff, Bill Masters.

Contraband

To nab the culprit who sold a lunar crystal, McCauley reassembles the moon expedition and tries to trick the guilty party into revealing himself. Wr: David Duncan, story by Stuart James Byrne. Dir: Alvin Ganzer.

James Coburn, Robert Osterloh, Robert Christopher, Don Ross, John Close, Pat McCaffrie.

Dark Side of the Moon

A woman and two men are assigned to help McCauley study a solar eclipse, but the three are beset by feelings of competition and tension. Wr: David Duncan. Dir: Alvin Ganzer.

Carol Ohmart, Manning Ross, William Lechner, Dennis McCarthy, John McNamara, Robert Darin.

Verdict in Orbit

McCauley's son is injured by a hit-and-run driver. McCauley learns that the driver is a physicist who is aboard the space station Astra. Wr: Michael Plant, story by Sidney Kalcheim. Dir: Nathan Juran.

Peter Adams, Tod Griffin, Norman DuPont, John McCann, Robert Dornan.

Is There Another Civilization?

McCauley investigates when his shuttle crew begin to die one by one in mysterious accidents. It coincides with the discovery of a piece of alien debris. Wr: William Templeton, Robert Warnes Leach, story by Jerome Bixby. Dir: Nathan Juran.

Paul Carr, Tyler McVey, John Compton, John Bryant, Joe Flynn, Mike Rayhill, David Bedell, Howard Vann.

Shadows on the Moon

A geophysical expedition encounters several bizarre events on the moon, including vanishing instruments, untraced footprints and the sighting of a lunar creature. Wr: David Duncan. Dir: Alvin Ganzer.

Gerald Mohr, Mort Mills, Harry Carey, Jr.

Flash in the Sky

A satellite sent to Venus has veered into deep space. McCauley races to track down the vital probe. Wr: David Duncan. Dir: Walter Doniger.

John Lupton, Joan Marshall, William Hudson, Mark Houston, Robert O'Connor.

Lunar Secret

To solve the fate of a tragic moon expedition and to locate the source of a strange glow, McCauley and a photographer climb a lunar plateau. Wr: Michael Plant. Dir: Franklin Adreon.

John Hudson, Sally Bliss, Kort Falkenburg, Mimi Gibson, Robert Courtleigh.

Voice of Infinity

A rocket malfunction increases the spin of the space station, endangering the lives of the crew aboard. Wr: Ib Melchior. Dir: Alan Crosland, Jr.

Myron Healey, Ralph Taeger, Charles Cooper, Charles J. Stewart, Rand Brooks, Barnaby Hale.

From Another World
McCauley is certain that he saw a life form on an asteroid, but his superiors think that he's been over-worked. Wr: Beirne Lay, Jr. Dir: Herman Hoffman.

Edward C. Platt, Russ Conway, Alan Dexter, Rand Harper.

Emergency Mission
An untested X-1000 supercraft is used by McCauley to race after a manned spaceship that is heading out of control for deep space. Wr: Kalman Phillips. Dir: Alvin Ganzer.

Donald Woods, William Leslie, John Baer, Edson Stroll, Anne Neyland, Wayne Mallory, Taldo Kenyon.

Beyond the Stars
A signal from a distant star is the key to saving an injured lunar astronaut who has fallen down a rock crevice. Wr: David Duncan. Dir: Jack Herzberg.

James Best, Gene Nelson, Sally Fraser.

Mission to Mars
International competition to reach Mars takes an ironic twist when McCauley abandons his mission to save the Russian flight from disaster. Wr: Lewis Jay. Dir: William Conrad.

John Van Dreelan, Jeremy Slate, Jack Hogan, Don Eitner, Tyler Mcvey, Ted Roter, David Janti, Will Huffman.

Moon Trap
Marooned 200 miles away from moonbase, two astronauts must devise a temporary shelter as they await rescue from Earth. Wr: Lewis Jay. Dir: Otto Lang.

Dan Burton, Don Burnett, Robin Lory, Mike Keene, Richard Emory, Jim Cody.

Flight to the Red Planet
McCauley desperately searches the Martian moon Phobos for a missing astronomer before his crew is forced to leave without him. Wr: Lewis Jay. Dir: David Friedkin.

Marshall Thompson, Michael Pate, John Zaremba, Tom Middleton, Harry Ellerbe.

Flare Up
A Russian major, the only survivor of a crash-landing on the moon, intends to blame the crash on the Americans to hide his own failure. Wr: Donald Duncan, story by Sidney Kalcheim. Dir: Herman Hoffman.

Werner Klemperer, James "Skip" Ward, Eric Feldary, Edgar Barrier, Preston Hanson, Jay Warren, Larry Thor, Lee Raymond.

Into the Sun
A mission to send radioactive waste into the sun is imperiled by a former astronaut who has been emotionally scarred by a previous accident. Wr: Lewis Jay, story by Fred Freiberger. Dir: Jack Herzberg.

Paul Picerni, Harp McGuire, Nelson Leigh, Mack Williams.

The Sun Never Sets
Two British astronauts are marooned in space with a disabled capsule. McCauley, serving as a technical advisor for England's space program, must come up with a rescue plan. Wr: Lewis Jay. Dir: Alvin Ganzer.

John Sutton, Robin Hughes, David Frankham, Mavis Neal, Roy Dean, Sydney Smith.

Mystery Satellite
A mysterious UFO has caused a manned shuttle to burn up in the atmosphere. McCauley is determined to track down the origin of the UFO. Wr: Lewis Jay. Dir: William Conrad.

Edward Mallory, Brett King, John Archer, Charles Maxwell, Mike Steele, George Diestel, Mel Marshall.

The Misfits of Science
October 1985–February 1986
Dr. Billy Hayes recruits three young people with super powers to work with him at his science institute, Humanidyne. Hayes and the misfits conduct research and volunteer their services to people in need.

Cast: Dr. Billy Hayes (Dean Paul Martin); Elvin Lincoln (Kevin Peter Hall); Johnny B (Mark Thomas Miller); Gloria (Courteney Cox); Jane Miller (Jennifer Holmes); Richard Stetmeyer (Max Wright); Miss Nance (Diane Civita).

Created by: James D. Parriott; *Producer:* Morrie Ruvinsky; *Coordinating Producer:* Dean Zanetos; NBC/Universal; 60 minutes.

Misfits of Science has become something of a misfit in TV history. Its mere mention brings unbridled laughter and occasional groans. Even creator James Parriott's first reaction is to laugh, but with affection. "Let's face it, it had a dopey man," he says. "It had people running around with super powers. It was a funny series, and there are some episodes that are a riot."

The idea began with NBC president Brandon Tartikoff. "To this day, he's disowned *Misfits of Science*," says Parriott. "He won't admit it, but it was Brandon who wanted a gathering of misfit superheroes. He typed the idea on a piece of paper and tried to get Stephen Cannell to do it. Cannell said, 'Are you crazy? Forget it!'" Parriott first heard of the project when Tartikoff came to Universal. "I told him, 'It's either going to be a big hit or it'll fail miserably.'"

The main character is the eccentric, fun-loving Dr. Billy Hayes, who is constantly scraping up money to keep his science research lab going. Into his life come three young people who are trying to deal with their respective superpowers: Elvin Lincoln, who can shrink to a size of 8 inches; Johnny B., who shoots lightning from his fists; and Gloria, who uses her telekinetic ability to knock the bad guys over like bowling pins.

Once the characters were cast, Parriott felt more confident about the premise. "I loved our cast. They were delightful. We also had good, fun writers. It turned out to be the most fun that I've had on a show." Critics, however, didn't

Guest star Mickey Jones (left) poses with the *Misfits of Science* cast. Front row, left to right: Jennifer Holmes and Courteney Cox. Back row, left to right: Mark Thomas Miller, Dean Paul Martin and Kevin Peter Hall. Copyright 1985 NBC/Universal.

share Parriott's enthusiasm. "We got raked over the coals," he admits, "and people disowned it. But we had a great time doing it."

"It was a fun concept show," agrees coordinating producer Dean Zanetos, "but it was more contained than it should have been. The edict going in was to make it the most unbelievably far-out, imaginative show that had ever been done. Once we started dealing with a specific network representative, it became an issue of, 'Can you make it more like *The A-Team*?' That restricted us. In spite of that, it was still fun. Dean Paul Martin was truly a star. He was an incredible guy."

Executive story consultant Donald Todd says, "The year after *Misfits of Science* went off,

Brandon Tartikoff was telling people that it had been an embarrassment. He mentioned it as sort of a reference point for bad television shows. That makes me feel bad because it was a good show. On the surface it sounds like a ridiculous concept. It was also at a time when shows like *Manimal* and *Knight Rider* were around. Those shows were very 'high concept,' and *Misfits of Science* got lumped in with them. NBC wanted a superhero show, but Jim Parriott turned it into something more than that. The stories may have been bizarre, but they dealt with human values."

Todd had to hit the ground running when he was assigned to work on what was his first weekly TV series. "I had just come off a [new]

Twilight Zone when I was hired by Jim. *Misfits of Science* was fun because we could just let our minds go. The scripts had silly premises that we could do in a fun way."

One of Todd's scripts was about an intelligent dolphin who joins the misfits to expose dope smugglers. "The dolphin had discovered a cache of illegal drugs inside plastic pink flamingoes under the sea. I have no idea where these ideas came from," he laughs. "I was 25 years old at the time. I read somewhere that your most creative work is done in your twenties. The rest of your life is spent refining it. I thought of *Misfits of Science* when I read that because it did represent my most creative writing."

When it came to Todd's talking pig, however, Parriott laid down the law. "Jim wouldn't let me do an episode about an intelligence hormone that is used on a pig. The experiment goes amok and the pig becomes extremely intelligent. He can communicate with people. The more intelligent he becomes, the more he wants to take over! Every time Jim saw the talking pig in my typewriter, he pulled it out. His instincts were absolutely correct. There were boundaries. It was like an electric fence. You had to touch the fence to find out what you're not supposed to do. The intelligent pig was my electric fence."

The ideas that did reach filming were realized by "a terrific cast," says Todd. "They were brand new and happy to be working. They trusted the writers completely. Dean Paul Martin was a delight, and he became a good friend. Kevin Peter Hall also became a good friend. It's hard to believe that they're both gone. I still have a picture of the cast that I keep with me. They were the most wonderful, open-minded people." They were also courageous. Todd remembers their dedication once extended beyond safety. "On the very first day of shooting the first episode, after the pilot, we had a scene where debris falls from a building. The special effects guys put a loaded charge in the junk and shot it out of a cannon. The flaming debris came down on the actors. They had wireless microphones on, and I heard them saying, 'Hey, my jacket's on fire!' and 'We're on fire—what do we do?' Everything ended up okay, but we almost incinerated Mark Thomas Miller and Courteney Cox on the very first day. Their reaction was, 'Oh, sorry. Did we screw up the scene by yelling?'"

Todd reveals that the series had a minimum of staff writers: James Parriott, Morrie Ruvinsky and himself. "And that was absurd! Most TV series have twice that number. I think we started with a six-episode order. That's why we had such a small staff. We worked thirteen hours a day, seven days a week." Although Todd had a firm grasp of writing, he was thrown for a loop when Parriott got him into the show's production. "Jim's technique is to throw you right into the middle. He told me to sit in on a production meeting for one of my scripts. I didn't even know what a production meeting was. I sat there and listened. The line producer said, 'We have a man running through the jungle. He's wearing a hat.' He turned to me and said, 'What kind of hat?' I said, 'I don't know.' Then I realized that my job was to know. I said, 'A hat like Indiana Jones.' Everyone said okay. That's what they needed to know. Then the producer asked, 'He's running through bushes. Are they thick bushes?' I said, 'Yes.' Then it was, 'What kind of car is following them?' I said, 'A Volkswagen,' and so on. I made it up as I went along."

Todd's developing production skills came in handy when he produced the last episode, "Three Days of the Blender." "Jim had been pulled away to do a pilot and Morrie was doing something else. Universal studios didn't want to complete the episode. They knew the show was dead and they didn't want to spend the money. I insisted we do it. We did bring it in for much less money than the others."

Scripted by Todd, "Three Days of the Blender" remains one of his favorite episodes. "Billy is thrown into jail for refusing to say where he had gotten a blender. It contained a top secret microchip for a nuclear guidance system. The government had discovered their mistake and recalled all of the blenders, but one had gotten lost in the mail. It had been sent to Billy from his mother. When he gets it three years later, the authorities arrest him for having classified material. Billy won't give up the blender, and he goes to jail. The story was about standing up to the government when they play hardball. It was also good because all of the misfits were interviewed about their feelings towards Billy. It brought them together. It was a nice way to close the series." Although the episode wasn't aired on NBC, it is included in the syndication package.

As the series wound down, Todd had to think about finding another job. "I was standing with *Misfits of Science* director Burt Brinckerhoff on location one day. We were waiting for the sun to go down, and we were freezing. Burt and I turned to each other at the same time and said,

'Sitcoms!' The next year, he was directing *Newhart*, I was writing for *Alf*."

Reflecting on the series, Todd says, "Some episodes weren't successful. Some were plain dull. But the series had a sense of experimentation and fun that's missing on TV today. It also had one of the most exciting main title sequences of any show that year. It had a great, silly theme song. Considering our Friday night time slot, our ratings were okay. I think we had a 21 to 23 share. NBC was looking for a lesson-oriented show, and Jim was excited about doing something more than that. It was a special show executed in a fairly standard style. It never really reached its script potential." By season end, the series had finished fifty-fourth out of 74 shows.

"The numbers that *Misfits of Science* was pulling in [against *Dallas*] weren't strong enough for NBC," says Dean Zanetos. "We felt we were getting a different kind of audience and doing pretty well. We had very loyal viewers."

"I don't think we were allowed to be hip enough," says James Parriott. "It would have been a riot to have the misfits of science deal with Los Angeles traffic or put them into more adult situations. NBC wanted it to be like *The Incredible Hulk*. They wanted five heroes going on missions every week. That was a mistake. You can't deal with this premise straight. You've got to put a spin on it."

Donald Todd remains a champion of the series. "It was a terrific show," he says. "My favorite jacket is my *Misfits of Science* jacket. I wear it proudly!"

Cast Notes

Dean Paul Martin (Billy): Born 1951. Martin, a former tennis pro, was the son of singer Dean Martin. He died in 1987 when his Air National Guard jet crashed.

Kevin Peter Hall (Lincoln): Born 1956. Hall gained fame as the creature stalking Arnold Schwarzenegger in the film *Predator* (1989). He was playing Bigfoot in the TV series *Harry and the Hendersons* when he died in 1991.

Courteney Cox (Gloria): Born 1964. Cox had a recurring role on TV's *Family Ties* from 1987 to 1988. Cox was known as "the girl" who dances with Bruce Springsteen in his video "Dancing in the Dark" (1984). She later starred in the 1990s TV series *Friends*.

Mark Thomas Miller (Johnny B): Miller continues to make TV guest appearances.

Max Wright (Mr. Stetmeyer): Wright later played Mr. Tanner, the father of the household that hosted *Alf* in the late 1980s.

Episode Guide

Misfits of Science (1985 TV movie)
Billy assembles a group of teenage misfits with special powers. Their first case is Arnold Biefneiter, a man cryogenically frozen for 45 years. He escapes and goes on a rampage, freezing anyone he touches. The Misfits also deal with a scientist who has developed a doomsday neutron beam. Wr and Dir: James D. Parriott.

Gen. Thiel (Larry Linville); Dr. Strickland (Edward Winter); Sen. Donner (Kenneth Mars); Arnold Biefneiter (Mickey Jones); Dr. Maumquist (Eric Christmas); Gomez (Bert Rosario); Newsman (Preston Hanson); Stenker (Robert Starr); Donna (K.C. Winkler); Scanlon (Boyd Bodwell); Attendant (Eric Fleeks); Technicians (Wendy Oates, Ralph Brannen); Adie (Gerald Berns); Ballplayer (Dawan Scott); Guard (Tobie Norton); MP (Richard Camphuis); Officer (Walt Hunter); Mrs. Hayes (Kathleen O'Malley); Counterwoman (Courtenay McWhinney); Woman (Mimi Kinkade); Farmer (Al Dunlap); Also with Tawny Schneider, Leslie Easterbrook.

Season Episodes

Your Place or Mayan?
The Misfits go on an expedition to prove a murdered scientist's claim that a Mayan treasure is buried under Beverly Hills. Wr: Donald Todd. Dir: Alan J. Levi.

Angel (Dean Devlin); Stephan (Nicholas Hormann); Ramon (Tony Acierto); Old man (Ted Lehmann); Augie (Bob Larkin); Explorer (Rob Fitzgerald); Driver (Shane McCaney); Maitre d' (Matthew Faison); Clerk (David Blackwood); Rich man (Michael Blue).

Guess What's Coming to Dinner?
The Misfits' friend claims to have made radio contact with creatures on Mars. The worried authorities try to shut him down. Wr: Morrie Ruvinsky. Dir: Burt Brinckerhoff.

Harry McCarthy (James Sloyan); Judy (Janice Kent); Jeffries (Tom Bower); Jessica (Ashley McLean); Missile officer (Steve Antin); Josh (Gary Riley); Technician (John Mahon); MP (Roy Fegan); Old man (Carl D. Parker); Kelp (John Zarchen); Investigators (Michael Crabtree, Reid Smith); Man with children (Lewis Dauber); Old woman (Virginia Keppel); Sergeant (Bill Dearth).

Lost Link
A wild jungle boy, unable to communicate with the Misfits, escapes and runs amok in Hollywood. Wr: Mark Jones. Dir: Christopher Leitch.

Dr. Deanna Walter (Stephanie Faulkner); Dr. Komack (Allan Rich); Link (Jesse Dizon); Major Lauger (Billy Green Bush); Officer (Richard Foronjy); Bully (Richard Brose); Pusher (S.A. Griffin); Guard (Paul Roache); Man (Branscombe Richmond); Worker (Allan Graf); Manager (Leslie Morris); Agonized man (Ellis Levinson); Policeman (Mic Rodgers); Tourist (Patrika Darbo).

Sort of Looking for Gina
Mystery men and rumors of a shadowy monster haunt a museum where a $30 million exhibit has been set up. Johnny B's investigation is perked by the appearance of a strange, vanishing woman who apparently hails from the city's tunnels. Wr: Michael Cassutt, James D. Parriott, Morrie Ruvinsky. Dir: Jeffrey Hayden.

Gina (Rhonda Aldrich); Bucher (Michael Halsey); Zack (Greg Martin); Syl (Christopher Murray); Smitty (Marc Silver); Doorman (Richard Balin); Nick (Curtiss Marlowe); Hilly (Kimberley Pistone); Band guy (Michael Aaron); Royce (Rob Zapple); Valet (Kent Stoddart); Nurse (Elizabeth Reiko Kubota); Woman (Kacey Cobb).

Sonar ... and Yet So Far
The Misfits protect Donald, a talking dolphin who witnessed an undersea cocaine smuggling operation. Wr: Donald Todd. Dir: Burt Brinckerhoff.

Eddie (Gary Frank); Sherri (Sondra Currie); Chuck (Robert Donavan); Lietch (Michael Flynn); Smuggler #2 (Jorge Cervera, Jr.); Sailor Sam (Alice Nunn); Bartender (Phil Redrow); Guard (Jerry Boyd); Man (John H. Gamber).

Steer Crazy
Glowing hamburgers, contaminated by a meteor's radiation, turn three senior citizens into superhumans. The Misfits try to stop the radioactive trio before someone is hurt. Wr: James D. Parriott. Dir: John Tracy.

Barney (Ray Walston); Bessie (June Allyson); Irma (Eda Reiss Merin); Project manager (Dan Lauria); Taggart (Dennis Stewart); Governor (Lou Felder); Technician (Rodney Saulsberry); Cusak (David Selburg); Aide (John Stinson); Les (Robert Covarrubias); Fredo (Carlos Lacamara); Woman (Catherine Paolone); Newswoman (Mary Ingersoll); Manager (Tom Albert Clay); Demonstrators (Kerry Noonan, David Ashrow).

Fumble on the One
A secret agent, made of steel, has his arm sawed off by an enemy agent, and his briefcase is stolen. The Misfits travel to France to help the steel man recover the top secret data. Wr: Blaze Forrester. Dir: Bob Sweeney.

Brick Tyler (Dale Robinette); Alexis (Greta Blackburn); Bill (Tige Andrews); Swarthy man (Sid Haig); Bernard (Marius Mazmanian); Croupier (Clement St. George); Dealer (Alain St. Alix); Bellman (Yvon Benard); Guard (Gilles Savard).

Twin Engines
Johnny B's telepathic friend has a double whose life is threatened by people who want his new gas-saving carburetor. Wr: Donald Todd, R. Timothy Kring. Dir: Burt Brinckerhoff.

Lonnie/Dwayne (Joel Polis); Skinner (Paul Koslo); Didi (Joan Sweeney); Melnick (Warren Munson); Keith (Roy Firestone); Rice (James Hornbeck); Bart (Rick Brinkley); Miss Speedway (Brenda Strong); Byron (Joe Cala); Mechanic (Courtney Gains); Reporter #2 (Paunita Nichols); Reporter (Julie Inouye).

Grand Theft Bunny
An animal crusader sets Billy up as a thief by using him to steal experimental animals from a lab, unaware the animals are carrying a plague. Wr: Pamela Norris. Dir: Michael Switzer.

Sarah (Robin Riker); Vincent (Robin Thomas); Hunter (Mark Hutter); Dr. Moyer (Jordan Charney); Dr. Levine (Michael McGuire); Deputy (Gene Whittington); Edwards (Robert Benedict); Tom (Joe Colligan); Desk clerk (Colin Hamilton); Maid (Perla Walter); Guard (Charles Bazaldua); Prisoner (Jim McKeny); Ranger (George Bauer).

Grand Elusion
The Misfits reunite a Russian defector with his daughter, but their relationship is marred by past guilts and by KGB agents who are shadowing them. Wr: Morrie Ruvinsky. Dir: Bernard McEveety.

Nikolai (James Laurenson); Tatyana (Christie Houser); Galenkov (John Schuck); Connell (Tom Dahlgren); Galenkov's agents (Arthur Taxier, Waldemar Kalinowski); Natasha (Lena Pousette); Lydia (Denise Cheshire); Ludmilla (Jennifer Hairn Smith); Director (Conni Marie Brazelton); Lapinsky (Nick Lewin); Mrs. Willi (Patricia Wilson); Guard (Andrew Divoff); Manager (Frank Holms); Young Tatyana (Erinn Canavan); KGB agent (John Alden).

Once Upon a Night
It's no fairy tale as missing jewels, thugs and government agents surround a princess who needs Gloria's help. Wr: M. Shelby-Moore, Linda Campanelli. Dir: Barbara Peeters.

Jae (Elaine Wilkes); Casatti (Andrew Masset); Davis (Robert Alan Browne); Agent Jeff (Joseph Brutsman); The king (George Skaff); Henchmen (Arnie Moore, Sandy Ignon); Waitress (Sue Rihr); Butler (Mark Harris); Ride operator (Frank Biro); Diner waitress (Myra Turley).

Center of Attention
Elvin poses as a basketball player to get the goods on a crooked owner who is throwing games and ruining the confidence of one of the players. Wr: Sara Parriott. Dir: Burt Brinckerhoff.

Fly Avery (Wolfe Perry); Sonny (Warren Berlinger); Chairman (Liam Sullivan); Eddie Buxton (Barry Sattels); Ornette (Brian Mann); Linda (Zetta Whitlow); Wendy (Twyla Littleton); Sticky (Dawan Scott); R.J. Chapman (Paul McCracken); Guards (Roger Hampton, John Sherrod); Salesman (Larry Margo); Older fan (Viola Kates Simpson); Fan (Charlee Williams).

Memory Flash—Liam Sullivan: "I got a call from Universal studios to put on a blue suit and get over there as fast as possible. I was to be in a scene as the chairman of the board. I mostly asked questions of one of the Misfits, who was trying to do a presentation with story boards that kept falling off the easel.

We shot the scene, but two days later I was called back to redub all of my dialogue. They wanted me to make it angrier. I did. A few days later I was called back to redo the dialogue a little less angry! *Misfits of Science* was a wacky comedy. It had a funny premise."

Against All Odds
Trying to beat the record of staying awake is having a devastating effect on Billy. He's having chaotic flashbacks to past adventures. Wr: Morrie Ruvinsky. Dir: Michael Switzer.

Mrs. Willis (Patricia Wilson).

The Avenging Angel
When Gloria's telekinetic powers save a wrestler from thugs, the wrestler thinks he's the one with the power. Wr: Daniel DeStefano. Dir: Bernard McEveety.

Milt (Vic Polizos); Albert (Wolf Muser); Mr. Rogers (Dave Shelley); Rovich (Ric Mancini); Bates Motel (Jack Armstrong); Nate (Jimmy Lydon); Heddy (Ivy Bethune); Headsman (Gene Le Belle); Announcer (Bobby Ramsen); Connie (Dave Cass); Mrs. Willis (Patricia Wilson); Roy (Elven Havard); Kid (Bobby Jacoby); Joe (Carl Ciarfalio); C.J. (Caroline J. Silas); Bystander (Cam Clarke); Sam (Jonathan Hugger); Mr. Nice Guy (Tim Patterson).

Three Days of the Blender
Billy, on trial for his life for selling top military secrets, mystifies the Misfits with his strange behavior: He refuses to defend himself against the charges. Wr: Donald Todd. Dir: Michael Switzer.

Jerry McDermitt (Doug Hale); Chicken Jimmy (Erik Holland); Ruth Hayes (Meg Wyllie); Sergeant (Greg Lewis); Odor Williams (Julius Carry III); Chaplain (Peter Elbling); Guards (Michael McGuire, Frederic Tucker); Bouncer (Faith Minton); Miss Jobs (Nomi Mitty); Mrs. Bone (Patience Cleaveland); Moose (Charles Hoyes); Schlepp (Joe Nesnow); Older man (Gordon Clark); Also with Joe Dorsey, Doug Warhit.

The New People
September 1969–January 1970

Forty American college students, part of a Southeast Asia cultural exchange tour, are marooned on a lost island in the South Pacific after their plane crashes. The island is Bomano, once designated as the site for an atomic bomb test.

The students find a makeshift city, left behind by the Atomic Energy Commission. The castaways, realizing that they're thousands of miles away from the nearest shipping lanes, must now build their own world. For them, it's Year One.

Cast: Susan Bradley (Tiffany Bolling); Eugene "Bones" Washington (David Moses); George Potter (Peter Ratray); Robert Lee (Zooey Hall); Ginny Loomis (Jill Jaress); Stanley Gabriel (Dennis Olivieri).

Created by: Aaron Spelling, Larry Gordon; *Developed by:* Rod Serling; *Producer:* Harold Gast; *Executive Producer:* Aaron Spelling; *The New People theme sung by:* The First Edition; ABC/Danny Thomas/Aaron Spelling Production; 45 minutes.

"Can young people, having experienced a bad start in the old society, make things better if they're free from old pressures to start over again?" asks *New People* director Corey Allen. "I thought it was a terrific question for a TV series to ask."

The question was framed during the turbulent 1960s, when many young people were questioning their government and its power over them. Without question, *The New People* was aimed directly at a youthful audience.

"We are enormously excited over the challenge to create meaningful, quality programming that will make young people feel, 'This is our show,'" stated a press release from the producers in 1969. To ensure that the students wouldn't have to spend their time foraging for food and seeking shelter each week, they were supplied with an abandoned city. "The locale of an island with a city was chosen so that the young inhabitants will not become savages," the press release stated. "This is not primarily a struggle for physical survival."

Instead, the students grappled with more philosophical conflicts. "We wanted them to deal with social and moral dilemmas," recalls story editor Earl Booth. "Religion, ethics, morality, crime, justice, marriage, monogamy."

The ABC press release concluded, "While a few of the students will be preoccupied with leaving the island, most will accept the reality that they will never go home."

As depicted in the pilot film, most of the

The *New People* cast, left to right: Zooey Hall, Jill Jaress, Peter Ratray, Dennis Olivieri, Tiffany Bolling and David Moses. Copyright 1969 ABC/Spelling-Goldberg Productions.

the island in favor of morality plays. The science fiction angle *was* played up in the 1969 novelization of the series, written by Alex Steele, in which the castaways battled radioactive sea creatures. The closest the series came to science fiction was the segment "Panic in the Sand" in which a mysterious illness fells the islanders. The series' main focus was on the students as they tried to shape their world without repeating the mistakes of the old one. The character of Susan Bradley proclaims early on, "We can have instant peace!"

This naivete fades as their society begins to mirror the old one. Some blacks separate themselves from the whites; some men demand power over women; and some students find the island a perfect sanctuary for immorality.

students were totally self-centered. The only adult survivor of the crash, an injured government man named Hannichek (Richard Kiley), and one student, George Potter, are left to bury the nine plane crash casualties while the other youths go gallivanting off to party in the city.

With Hannichek's death, however, comes the end of fun and games. "These young rebels now had to come to terms with being on their own," notes David Moses, who played the young black man, Gene Washington. "We realize we had been criticizing our society from a very safe place—inside our fathers' mansions. When our parents die, as represented by Richard Kiley's character, a tremendous fear grips us. Now we have to take charge and make this society work."

More properly an allegorical fantasy than an adventure or science fiction series, *The New People* dispensed with the inherent mysteries of

The actors in *The New People* had their own challenge: to make the series a success. "It was my first professional job," recalls David Moses. "When Aaron Spelling called me, I was a riveter at Northrup Corporation at Aerospace. I was raising a family and waiting for my big break. Aaron said, 'We've been testing every black actor in town for this role. We might as well see you.'" Moses got the part.

Moses quickly took an interest in the series. "It had more potential than any other series I'd seen," he says. "It was an opportunity for young kids to demonstrate that they could do at least as well, if not better than the previous generation. Rod Serling and I got together a couple of times and talked about the character."

Moses' character of Gene Washington began as a bitter, hostile young man. He mellowed as he realized he had equal say in the development of the new society. "He was on his way to becoming a man," explains the actor. "Like all of the young people, Gene was testing who he was, what he was made of, where he had been, and where he was going."

Cast member Jill Jaress was also new to TV acting. "It was my first job, ever," she says. "On the first day of filming, I went to the director and said, 'Would you look out for me?' He said, 'What do you mean?' I said, 'The only camera I've been in front of was my father's Brownie Hawkeye.'"

Jaress was a last-minute addition to the cast, as the affable Ginny Loomis. "Ginny was the comedic relief," Jaress says. "A free spirit. I wasn't in the pilot. They originally planned ten regulars and ended up firing six of them. They hired me and Dennis Olivieri (Stanley) to fill out the series' cast. I had come out from Detroit a year earlier, when I was 18 years old. I didn't know a soul here. I went to acting class for a year and then I got *The New People*. I thought that happened to everybody!"

As the actors explored their characters, the writers and producers went to work fashioning believable scenarios for their stars. Although Rod (*The Twilight Zone*) Serling had scripted the pilot (under the pseudonym of John Phillips), producer Harold Gast confirms that Serling was not involved in the actual series. According to the show's early publicity, Serling was to have remained as series consultant. "I was engaged to produce *The New People* after the pilot was made," recalls Gast. "I know for a fact that Serling had nothing whatsoever to do with the series."

"The characters were all fairly representative, if somewhat shallow, of the 1960s," says Earl Booth. "Harold Gast and I were excited about the prospect of showing these young people building a new society. Early on, everyone was eager and cooperative. It was during the last half of production that distinct displeasure came to the forefront. The network was unhappy with the way the show was developing, and it led to bitter battles. ABC wanted to make it, purely and simply, an adventure show."

"The show had almost nothing to do with 1960s people," claims writer Stephen Kandel. "There was an attempt to fit things into a 1950s mold. There was friction [from the network] from the beginning. The original premise was that the students would experiment with social ideas. Communism. Fascism. Forced breeding to maintain a viable genetic stock. Pacifism. Hedonism. Gay/lesbian/hetero sexuality. You can imagine how ecstatic the network was at seeming to promote lesbian commie geneticism. The pilot, by Rod Serling, was striking. For the weekly series, the network wanted a cross between *Gilligan's Island* and *Beverly Hills, 90210. The New People* was postulated upon ideas, and that's always risky. With the best and the worst of intentions, it foundered quickly."

Two of Kandel's three *New People* scripts were filmed. The writer particularly remembers "Murderer," dealing with a student on trial for pushing another student off a cliff. "In the original script, the castaways had to recreate the Rule of Law," says Kandel. "The conflict dealt with the question of society's right to execute or to imprison, or to understand and forgive. The problem was, the network didn't want to deal with that. They wanted it softened. I refused, on the whimsical theory that they had agreed to the story I had written. Harold Gast, a remarkably decent man, finally made the changes, and I retained a scrap of my illusions. I believe the ending was solved by a *force majeur* gimmick: the alleged killer was actually innocent. The victim had slipped and fallen."

"The series was sort of like *Lord of the Flies,* except with college-educated people [instead of children]," notes Jill Jaress. "It could have been a wonderfully futuristic show. I felt, though, that by having the city come complete with electricity and everything, it defeated the intriguing part of the situation. I would have had the kids start from scratch, without any conveniences. We could have shown them using solar energy and building windmills or burning garbage to create energy."

One of the charges leveled at the series was that it was created by older people for younger people and that the students came off as Hollywood stereotypes. "It did deal with the issues from a middle-aged perspective," says Jaress. "It turned into, 'Oh, the new people fucked up again this week!' If a student had to handle an issue in a radical way, it was usually in a negative manner, or a violent one. We'd mess up and learn it was better to do things the old way." Considering the premise, however, Jaress admits the series was a challenge to write for. "I'm not blaming all of this on the writers," she says. "What *The New People* required was visionary writing. That's kind of hard to do when you're trying to beat a deadline. The series was a wonderful venue that they kinda missed the boat on."

"I'm afraid *The New People* was too on the

nose for TV at that time," reflects David Moses. "We didn't let up on the message. Rather than allow the audience to come to terms with, 'Hey, these kids are really making it,' we hit it on the nose every week. But we wanted to demonstrate that these kids could rise above their limitations and make a new society. It wouldn't be based on money value or skin color or ethnicity. It was based on 'Do unto others as you would have them do unto you.' The basic premise was terrific."

Looking back on the series, the actor says, "The pilot episode was great. We also did an episode called *The Prisoner of Bomano* with Billy Dee Williams and Judy Pace. It was about the power struggle between the blacks on the island. They take me prisoner and accuse me of being an Uncle Tom. It was a dilemma that was very life-like because many minorities find themselves in that situation, especially if they've risen to a level of prominence in an otherwise white society. I didn't have to manufacture any character motivation for that. In the series, Gene was friends with the white characters played by Jill, Dennis, Tiffany Bolling, Peter Ratray and Zooey Hall. On the other hand, *was* my allegiance to the characters played by Billy Dee and Judy because we're the same color? My character had to do what was right. His enemies turned out to be Billy and Judy's characters. The people I loved, and who cared for me, were the white kids. It was an incredible issue to deal with. It was an outstanding episode."

Aside from the dramatic nature of the episodes, the actors faced the challenges of a physically demanding series. Most of the beach exteriors for *The New People* were filmed in Malibu. "We filmed one episode at Paradise Cove," says Moses. "Zooey and I were on the side of a mountain having a fight. It was really kind of dangerous. They had put netting along the sides of the mountain so if we fell we wouldn't get killed. Zooey was supposed to piss me off, and I take a swing at him. We had the fight choreographed. Well, I took two steps instead of three and accidentally knocked the shit out of him. I almost knocked him over the cliff edge. But we just kept going, wrestling to the ground with the cameras rolling. I could see the look in my friend Zooey's eyes: 'Why you Mother------!' Another time, actress Brenda Scott was supposed to be stuck out on this raft. When it cracks up, she yells for help and I'm called in to save her. Well, I don't know why they picked me, because I can't swim. We filmed this in a watertank with wind machines blowing at us. I'm pretending to swim through the water. I could touch the bottom, so I felt fine. But I drifted over my head and down I went. Brenda saw me gulping for air, and she jumped off the raft and pulled me to the surface. Talk about being put in your place. I was too busy spitting water to thank her for saving my life!"

"One guest star who stands out in my mind is Richard Dreyfuss," recalls Jill Jaress. "He was wonderful. He played this biochemist named Owen Rudd. Richard was so cocky. When he walked on that set, he commanded attention. I was really upset that I didn't get any scenes with him." Jaress did get an episode to herself, but the results weren't rewarding. "Ginny was beaten up, thrown off a cliff, pushed into the ocean, and dragged up the side of a mountain. Just another day in the life of the new people! They had a courtroom scene where I'm telling everybody what happened, and I was really crying. The crew applauded after it was over, and everybody hugged me. But nobody had bothered to tell me that my scene had been shot in an extreme close-up. When people cry, their nostrils flare, and they don't look good. So when I saw the scene on TV, I looked like Dumbo, ready for the big jump!"

Former actor Corey Allen directed three segments of the series and recalls, "*The New People* was one of the first shows I had done as a director. The students were like the starship *Enterprise* crew. You had a community living in an experimental location. They were flawed people in a compacted situation so you could see what their interactions are. I'm not sure why the series didn't take off. It could have been a matter of casting chemistry. The production values in my episodes, particularly in 'Comes the Revolution, We Use the Girls' Shower' were terrific."

When *The New People* was canceled, "the ignorance of youth served us well," says Moses. "We all felt cocky enough to think we were gonna become big stars. It was like, 'I'd better get back to the phone because it's gonna be the big call.' Underneath all of that, I was heartbroken. We were opposite *Laugh-In*. We were coupled with a lead-in called *The Music Scene*, and we came on at 8:15. I mean, nobody was going to switch off *Laugh-In* to watch us. I was hard pressed not to watch *Laugh-In* myself. It was the biggest show on TV. I wish the network had moved us around."

"We were up against *Lucy, Gunsmoke* and *Laugh-In*," says Jill Jaress. "It was a time slot we couldn't win. Those were the three biggest hits on TV at the time."

Susan (Tiffany Bolling) and George (Peter Ratray) survey their new surroundings after the plane crash. Copyright 1969 ABC/Spelling-Goldberg Productions.

"I felt *The New People* turned out pretty well, artistically," says producer Harold Gast. "Practically, however, the outcome was disappointing because we were canceled in mid-season. That left an empty feeling." According to Gast, the 45-minute length was detrimental to the series. "The network strategists somehow figured out that this was the best way to capture a young audience. *The Music Scene* was also 45 minutes, which the network felt was certain to hook the kids. When *The Music Scene* ended, the audience would stay tuned to us [at 8:15] because we would be the only show airing at that time. Trouble was, nobody watched *The Music Scene* in the first place. So we were coming on at a weird time, virtually without a lead-in. Under the circumstances, our ratings weren't bad, but neither were they good enough to guarantee a pick-up. There were several people at the network who liked what we were doing. They were rooting for us, but it came down to the ratings. A lot of hard work was put into the show by all of us."

Unfortunately, *The New People* has not been screened in North America since its cancelation. "I can see why the series has never been repeated," says Gast. "How can you program a 45-minute episode?"

However, *The New People* did emerge briefly, according to Jaress, who says, "The series was shown in Australia the year after it left ABC." She's also found that people still remember the show. "When I met my husband on our very first date, he asked me what I'd done. I said my first series was called *The New People*. He said, 'I used to watch that when I was in grade school!' I thought, 'Whoa! He really knows how to flatter a woman—he's cool!'"

There was an aborted effort to make a space-age version of *The New People* in the early 1970s. Writer Hal Sidowitz was asked to come up with a theme of young people marooned on the moon. It didn't go beyond the outline stage.

"Nothing has changed over the years," says David Moses. "In *Melrose Place* and *Beverly Hills 90210* [both Aaron Spelling productions] I see the same characters: the Gene Washington, the Susan

Bradley, the Ginny Loomis … it's just more contemporary. The forerunner to *The New People* was another show by Aaron, *The Mod Squad*. In terms of acting on *The New People*, it was an honor to work with the producers, Rod Serling, Richard Kiley and all of the cast. It was a tremendous opportunity."

The new people were never rescued from their world, but Jaress ponders, "It would make an interesting movie-of-the-week to go back to that island and see what became of these people 20 years later."

Perhaps the final word on *The New People* comes from Aaron Spelling himself, who declares simply, "I never enjoyed doing a show more. It should have been a breakaway in television. Today, it would be."

CAST NOTES

Tiffany Bolling (Susan): A frequent TV guest star during the 1970s, Bolling co-starred with William Shatner in the film *Kingdom of the Spiders* (1977). She devoted much of the 1980s to raising her family.

David Moses (Gene): Now a writer, Moses was nominated for an Emmy award for a 1992 After School Special. He also works in television as a post-production coordinator, and in theater as a director.

Jill Jaress (Ginny): A Broadway singer and a writer, Jaress has made numerous appearances on TV and film since *The New People*, including the films *S.O.B.* (1981) and *Universal Soldier* (1992).

Zooey Hall (Bob Lee): Although he left acting, he began a singing career under the name of David Hall.

Peter Ratray (George): According to Jill Jaress, this Canadian-born actor is "living in New York and doing Broadway." He was on daytime's *Another World* during 1994-1995.

Dennis Olivieri (Stanley): An actor who seemingly disappeared from the acting scene, "Dennis vanished long before our youth did," says David Moses.

EPISODE GUIDE

The New People
After crashing on an island, efforts to summon help

are threatened by Bull. He's determined to sabotage rescue efforts so that Gene will never be rescued. Wr: John Phillips (Rod Serling). Directed: George McCowan.

Hannichek (Richard Kiley); John Pilgrim (Parley Baer); Bull (Lee Jay Lambert); Stanley (Kevin O'Neal); Gloria (Nancy DeCarl); Barbara (Brenda Sykes); Dexter (Kevin Michaels); Student (Jerry Strickler).

Panic in the Sand
A mysterious epidemic sweeps the island. Biochemist Owen Rudd needs a volunteer for a hazardous experiment that may cure or kill. Wr: Harold Gast. Dir: William Wiard.

Dr. Owen Rudd (Richard Dreyfus); Jack (Clive Clerk); Laura (Elizabeth Berger); Boyer (Lee Stanley); Carl (Tim Burns); Vicky (Marcy Brown); Phil (Steve Cory).

The Tin God
Bob Lee restores a dune buggy, but he faces the wrath of the students when his hot-rodding injures Wendy. Wr: Charles McDaniel. Dir: George McCowan.

Wendy (Donna Baccala); Jack (Clive Clerk); Laura (Elizabeth Berger); Fred (Jack Lange); Myra (Ellen Moss); Lou (Paul Ehrmann); Student (Patty Elder).

Murderer!
When one of the students dies from a fall from a cliff, Dan Stoner is the prime suspect. He had the motive and opportunity, but there's a lack of hard evidence. Wr: Stephen Kandel. Dir: Nick Webster.

Dan Stoner (Carl Reindel); Phil Peters (Mark Jenkins); Jack (Clive Clerk); Laura (Elizabeth Berger); Boyer (Lee Stanley); Louella (Beverly Atkinson); Gradis (A. Martinez); Ned Bender (Chris Erickson); Nellie (Sherry Miles).

Comes the Revolution, We Use the Girls' Shower
Stanley's campaign against an all-women's aqueduct is sidelined when he falls in love with a black woman. Wr: George Kirgo. Dir: Corey Allen.

Elisa Rhodes (Susan Batson); Caffey (Phil Chapin); Don (Jerry Diez); Sally (Elaine Princi).

Lifeline
Some of the islanders build a huge raft to leave the island despite warnings that their scheme is suicidal. Meanwhile, Christine Miller convinces George to use his army skills to make a more seaworthy boat. Wr: John W. Bloch. Dir: Nick Webster.

Christine Miller (Brenda Scott); Jack (Clive Clerk); Will (Steve Cory); Millie (Pamela Bekolay).

Marriage, Bomano Style
Cara's love affair on the island brings the Catholic girl guilt and confusion when she becomes pregnant with the island's first baby. Wr: E. Arthur Kean. Dir: Charles Dubin.

Cara (Kate Heflin); Toky (Robert Cannon); Rube (Dennis Redfield).

Is This Any Way to Run an Island?
The social structure of the island falls apart. George

and Ginny decide to live a hedonistic life on the beach. Wr: E. Arthur Kean. Dir: Charles Dubin.

Harry (Tim O'Kelly); Margo (Jan Sherman); Jack (Clive Clerk); Laura (Elizabeth Berger); Max (Richard Anthony).

The Dark Side of the Island
An expedition uncovers a skeleton on the far side of the island. Sinister events that follow convince the islanders that someone else is on the island. Wr: Gwen Bagni, Paul Dubov. Dir: Nick Webster.

Heather (Melissa Murphy); Ralph (Michael Hardstark); Patty (Joyce Ames); Marc (Dan Ferrone); Lorna (Valerie de Camp); Steve (Lee Stanley).

A Bride in Basic Black ("The Courtship"), Part 1
The women rise up and demand laws of protection: Bob Lee has apparently attacked a woman, and Ben Geary, obsessed with Susan, has demanded that she live with him. Wr: Harold Gast. Dir: Charles Dubin.

Ben Geary (Jim McMullan); Carrie (Pat Stich); Nedda (Peggi Boucher); Meg (Mary Gail Hobbs); Rube (Dennis Redfield); Jack (Clive Clerk); Laura (Elizabeth Berger); Walter (Harvey Fisher); Secondari (Danny Spelling); Freddie (Gordon Hoban).

A Bride in Basic Black ("The Surrender"), Part 2
Susan's law of protection fails, and when George falls critically ill, Susan must convince Ben to save him. Wr: Harold Gast. Dir: Charles Dubin.

Ben Geary (Jim McMullan); Carrie (Pat Stich); Nedda (Peggi Boucher); Jack (Clive Clerk); Laura (Elizabeth Berger); Walter (Harvey Fisher); Freddie (Gordon Hoban); Meg (Mary Gail Hobbs); Rube (Dennis Redfield); Nat (Judd Laurance).

The Pied Piper of Pot
Steppenwolf plants a field of pot and is determined to take the islanders on a mind blowing trip. Wr: Edwin Blum. Dir: Charles Dubin.

Steppenwolf (Richard Evans); Watson (Zack McWiggins); Bender (Chris Erickson); Fisher (Renny Roker); Sally (Elaine Princi); Secondari (Dan Spelling).

Speed Kills
Warren turns into a dangerous paranoid and turns his rage toward George. Wr: Lou Shaw. Dir: Harry Harvey, Jr.

Warren (Robert Drivas); Student (Frank Orsatti).

The Guns of Bomano
Gun control is the issue. All of the guns are locked away except for the one given to a selected policeman. Wr: Edward J. Lakso. Dir: George McCowan.

Bricker (Soloman Sturges); Davis (Aron Kincaid); Phil Peters (Mark Jenkins); Willard (Jeff Cooper); Judy (Cynthia Hull); Crissy (Beverly Cromwell); Caffey (Philip Chapin); John (Renny Roker); Millie (Pamela Bekolay).

The Prisoner of Bomano
Black students form their own society and imprison Gene when he expresses an allegiance to his white friends. Wr: Anthony Terpiloff, E. Arthur Kean, story by Anthony Terpiloff. Dir: Corey Allen.

Heath (Billy Dee Williams); Della (Judy Pace); Davey (Christopher Joy); Hap (Jim Iglehart).

The Siege of Fern's Castle
Fern, who lives in the wrecked plane, asks George to dispose of a dangerous mine that has washed ashore. Wr: Unknown. Dir: Harry Harvey, Jr.

Fern (Susan Howard); Rube (Dennis Redfield).

On the Horizon
A fishing trawler on the horizon can rescue the islanders, but Paul doesn't want to be rescued, and he disables the boat. Wr: Stephen Kandel. Dir: Corey Allen.

Kathy (Tyne Daly); Paul (Benjamin Archibek).

Otherworld

January 1985–March 1985

Hal Sterling and his family are touring one of the Egyptian pyramids when they get lost and tumble through another dimension. They find themselves on an Earth-like planet made up of different provinces. They travel through the provinces to find Imar, a land where they can be transported home. They are also pursued by the vengeful Kommander Kroll, leader of the Zone Troopers, who is determined to punish the Sterling family for violating a law in his province.

Cast: Hal Sterling (Sam Groom); June Sterling (Gretchen Corbett); Trace Sterling (Tony O'Dell); Gina Sterling (Jonna Lee); Smith Sterling (pilot) (Brandon Crane), (series) (Chris Hebert); Kommander Nuveen Kroll (Jonathan Banks); Main Title Narrator (Roderick Taylor).

Created by: Roderick Taylor; *Producer:* Lew Hunter; *Supervising Producer:* Alex Beaton; *Executive Producer:* Roderick Taylor; *Creative Consultant:* Philip DeGuere. CBS/Universal; 60 minutes

Otherworld was inspired when creator Roderick Taylor picked up a book on inter-dimensions.

Cast of *Otherworld*, left to right: Tony O'Dell, Gretchen Corbett, Chris Hebert, Sam Groom and Jonna Lee. Copyright 1985 CBS/Universal.

"It got me thinking about what might be in other dimensions," says Roderick Taylor. "Then it was a case of combining that with something similar to *Star Trek*. That was a great show that traveled from one culture to another, reflecting an aspect of our own world. The Sterling family did what Captain Kirk did. Instead of planet to planet, the family went from province to province. It was a family adrift in an alien world."

In creating the series, Taylor wanted to present

an identifiable family. "We tried to reconstitute the nuclear family of *The Waltons* and earlier TV families like *Father Knows Best* and *Leave It to Beaver* and bring them to a 1980s level. The name of the family, Sterling, was an allusion to Rod Serling [*Twilight Zone's* creator]."

Helping with the show's development was Taylor's son, Bruce. "Bruce was born when I was 16," says Taylor. "Bruce became a very good writing partner."

Bruce Taylor grew up on science fiction TV. "Shows like *Outer Limits, Star Trek* and *Twilight Zone* are timeless classics," he says. "I've always liked anthology series, but they've been unpopular with the networks. So we tried to do an anthology with a continuing cast. We came up with a family traveling through different states and encountering a new situation every week. It was a way to do *Star Trek* on Earth."

The series also had trappings of *Lost in Space,* which Bruce Taylor acknowledges. "There are similarities, but I wanted *Otherworld* to be more serious and deal with political and social problems. I liked *Lost in Space,* but it was kind of campy. *Star Trek* was more of a model."

Universal studios was instantly interested in a science fiction project. "Robert Harris was president of Universal at the time," recalls Roderick Taylor. "He was enthusiastic about a family oriented, 8 p.m. show. We pitched it to CBS, and they liked it." Next, Roderick Taylor cast his family. "Universal asked us to bring in three actors for each character. So we brought in three dads, three moms, etc. We were looking for actors who had that indefinable quality of riveting your attention and being charismatic. We changed the actor who played Smith Sterling after the first couple of episodes. The first boy wasn't working out. Nobody noticed!"

Initially, *Otherworld* got off to a promising start with CBS. "When the network executives screened the pilot, they loved it. The chairman of CBS in New York stood up and applauded. They said, 'We're definitely going to order it.' We went right into production."

Those good feelings hit snags early on. "We had a tremendous amount of interference from the network," says Roderick Taylor. "CBS never understood the show. Each episode turned out to be a huge problem for them. They'd say, 'What is this? We don't understand it. Is it funny or serious?' We'd say, 'It's both.' I spent 90 percent of my energy dealing with the network and 10 percent on the show.

"An example was the episode 'I Am Woman, Hear Me Roar.' It dealt with a province where men are treated as sex objects and sold at auctions. Networks get very concerned when you do satire. I had to fight for one thing in particular. The woman auctioneer brings out an old guy named Ollie. She says, 'What do you like to do, Ollie?' He says, 'I like to whittle and repair small appliances.' Unbelievably, the network demanded it be cut. I said 'Absolutely not!' They wanted me fired. They said it was making fun of old people. I said, 'It would be making fun of him if he just shuffled around and said nothing. This way, he's being funny and clever. We're making fun of this whole pretense of being auctioned off. It's comedy.' CBS didn't understand that kind of comedy, and they remained suspicious of the show. There was a kind of debate between me and the network in the *L.A. Times* at the time. CBS referred to us as 'a guerilla band operating in the hills of Universal.' I found that incredibly complimentary."

"It was an uphill battle all the way," recalls Bruce Taylor of their dealings with CBS. "The network was very square when it came to science fiction. It was a constant struggle between our vision and their lack of vision. It created a lot of tension."

Eight episodes of *Otherworld* were produced. As a midseason replacement, the series materialized in Saturday's 8:00 p.m. time slot. "We had an extremely small staff on the show," recalls Roderick Taylor. "A good friend and writer, Coleman Luck, served as story editor. Between Bruce, Coleman and myself, we wrote or developed most of the stories. At one point, we got together with some of the writers who had written for *Star Trek. Otherworld* never got far enough [to use them]."

The Sterling family's journey took them to various cultures and adventures. Where *Otherworld* was located wasn't made clear, but the Sterlings learned more about this dimension with every episode. The family did know that if they reached a place called Imar, they could be transported home.

The pilot film, "Rules of Attraction," reflected the best of the series for the elder Taylor. "It turned out very well. Amanda Wyss played an android, and she was very magnetic and beautiful in that. Trace Sterling falls in love with her, and there was the question of the android's humanity. She had been created to be exactly like a human being. She felt Trace could never really love her because she knew, deep down, he didn't believe she had a soul. It was a tragic love story. Both of them were young and idealistic. Trace had to leave with his family because the radiation in that province would eventually destroy him. Amanda Wyss got something like 30,000 letters for that episode. She was incredibly popular. Had we survived long enough, we would have brought her back in a sequel. I also liked the title of the episode, 'Rules of Attraction.' It resonated to the world of science. It also related to the relationship between Trace and Nova."

Taylor had to fight to keep "Village of the Motorpigs," a story of rough bikers, from being integrated into the pilot. "After we did the pilot, CBS loved it so much they said, 'Why not extend it to two hours?' I didn't want to dilute it with padding. I pressured the hell out of them to leave it the way it was." "Village of the Motorpigs" turned out to be something of a compromise. "It was conceived as a continuation of the pilot, but it stood on its own as well," says Taylor.

Taylor, who is also a rock singer, found the episode "Rock 'n' Roll Suicide" close to his heart. "That episode and the pilot were my two favorites," he says. "It was about the Sterling kids introducing rock 'n' roll music to the otherworld. It ended up having the same explosive impact that rock 'n' roll had in America in the 1950s. I had to teach Jonna Lee and Tony O'Dell [the Sterling children] how to play the instruments and lip synch. They're not really playing or singing, but it looked that way. Also, you see them playing to this vast crowd. I actually only had 16 extras. I moved them around a lot and intercut it with real concert footage."

In "Mansion of the Beast," mother June Sterling is held captive by a powerful creature who has fallen in love with her. The episode details the family's efforts to retrieve her. "There were great shots of the family riding their wagon through the mountains. It looked like we had gone to Oregon to film it. Actually, it was all shot on Universal. The forest was actually painted in with mattes."

Bruce Taylor offers his own rundown on the segments. "In the pilot, we tried to do a lot in that one hour. *Otherworld* had a fairly complicated set-up for a series. We added a voice-over on subsequent episodes [during the title sequence] to explain the premise because it was the kind of show that took viewers a few weeks to really understand what it was about. We also had to do a pilot that wasn't too far out. It had to appeal to the network. We wanted it to be science fiction but in some sense, also traditional, so the network would like it."

The story of "Zone Troopers Build Men" has Trace drafted into the zone troopers army. The only way he can resign is to advance in rank, and that means to kill innocent people. The plot was inspired by a real headline. "Trace was punished for bad school grades by being drafted," says Taylor. "The genesis of the idea was an article about a country where punishment for failing grades is to be put in the army."

"I Am Woman, Hear Me Roar" had trouble with its original title. "We wanted to call it 'You've Come a Long Way, Baby,'" says Taylor. "The network informed us we couldn't call it that because that was the Virginia Slims cigarette trademark. The story showed a matriarchal province carried to the ultra-feminist extreme. It was a political satire where men are reduced to almost slave-like status and auctioned off like cattle."

In "Princess Metra," Gina Sterling poses as a princess. "There was a Sean Connery film called *The Man Who Would Be King*. That gave us the idea. Gina resembles a former ruler of a province. She's thought to be Princess Metra, who was prophesied to return. After it was shot and edited, we found out the segment was six minutes too short. We wrote four minutes of additional material, and added two minutes of a dream montage. We got lots of letters from viewers who thought the montage was great. I was unhappy with its music score. It was repetitive and monotonous. It made the montage seem excessively long. But we were on a tight, rushed schedule and we had no time to change the music."

Some of the Taylors' favorite scripts were never shot. Roderick Taylor describes Coleman Luck's "Seeing Double" as "an incredibly tense story. It was carted by the network. They didn't want to do it. The family visits a province where everyone's worst fears come upon them. You saw each of the family's fears: the mother had a fear of being abandoned, the father had a fear of failing, Gina got fat and ugly which is a classic fear for a young girl, and so on. The network said, 'No, it's too intense.' It would have been a frightening episode, but they do triumph over their fears."

Also never filmed was the Bruce Taylor script "The Judge," which the elder Taylor calls "probably the best plotted story we ever had. The family encounters a Judge Roy Bean character.

They violated his rules, and he gives them a choice: remain in jail, or they can play a little game with him. If they lose, they lose everything. In one instance, they're walking down a road and come to a fork. They don't know which way to go and they have to be very smart about every decision they make.

"Unfortunately, 'Seeing Double' and 'The Judge' weren't shot. CBS was in a very hostile mood towards us by this time. We had also planned to do a story about a Jeopardy-like game show in *Otherworld*, where the family are contestants."

Otherworld was canceled after eight episodes in the spring of 1985. Although the ratings for the pilot had been adequate, the series slipped to the lower echelons of the ratings poll for the next seven episodes. Roderick Taylor points out, however, that the ratings didn't tell the whole story. "One of the most remarkable things was that *Otherworld* had the highest TVQ ratings than any other show on CBS. That meant that viewers who watched it considered it their favorite show. Obviously more people watched CBS's *Dallas*, but if you asked ten of its viewers if it was their favorite show, three would say yes. With *Otherworld*, five out of ten viewers would say it was their favorite show. It had a small but passionate following. It probably would have continued had there not been so much turmoil with CBS. The series also had a poor time slot. For a show that teenagers would watch, Saturdays was really bad."

"The ratings were marginal," says Bruce Taylor. "If we had been on a weeknight we would have done much better. According to the mail we received, a lot of people liked the show. It had great word-of-mouth. CBS received many letters protesting its cancellation."

Looking back on the series today, Bruce Taylor feels, "It succeeded in combining a lot of elements: a family show, social satire, science fiction. But since we were dealing with other dimensions, you're constantly restrained by the network, who wants it to be as 'normal' as possible. That's my biggest regret: *Otherworld* didn't get to be as good as it could have been. I'm proud of the series, but the best was yet to come. We never got to develop the subtext of the otherworld."

Taylor was gratified by the eight episodes' popularity on the USA Cable network recently. "Viewer response was great," he says, "and USA was extremely interested in producing more episodes for syndication. They were unable to work that out with Universal."

"*Otherworld* has done very well for an eight-episode show," says Roderick Taylor. "We tried to break away from what TV too often is, which is horrible and monotonous. We tried for something that was moving, sometimes funny and a little irreverent. It did ignite a spark in people because the later USA Cable broadcasts got very good ratings. Most shows that last only eight episodes wouldn't be the subject of a discussion ten years later. *Otherworld* will live again. For now, it's only sleeping."

CAST NOTES

Sam Groom (Hal Sterling): From 1971 to 1974, Groom starred in the Canadian TV series *Police Surgeon*. He continues making TV guest appearances.

Gretchen Corbett (June Sterling): Born 1947. This Oregon-born actress had a recurring role as Beth on *The Rockford Files* (1974–78).

Jonna Lee (Gina Sterling): Lee appeared in TV movies during the late 1980s.

Jonathan Banks (Kroll): Banks later had a recurring role in the 1980s series *Wiseguy*.

Tony O'Dell (Trace Sterling): O'Dell played one of the students in the 1980s situation comedy *Head of the Class*.

Chris Hebert (Smith Sterling): This young actor's first weekly series was *Boone* (1983–84).

EPISODE GUIDE

Rules of Attraction
After their tumble into another world, the Sterling family flee a province inhabited by androids and where the atmosphere is deadly to humans. Wr: Roderick Taylor. Dir: William Graham.

Gad-Ben Sirrah (Ray Walston); Nova (Amanda Wyss); Fred Roach (James Hampton); Mrs. Roach (Barbara Stuart); The Praetor (Peter Bromilow); Ahmed (Gokul); Prof. Kroyd (James Costy); Gov. Litton (Conrad Bachmann); Officer (Michael Rider); Grocery clerk (Michael Sharrett); Milton (Frank Birney); Lt. (Wayne Alexander); Monitor (Gary Pagett); Mrs. Mob (Barbara Beckley); Miss Wanda (Anita Jesse); Frabrique (Dan Lewk); Corporal

(Rodger LaRue); Woman (Janet Rasek); Student (Robert Vinson); Bo (Zachary Baker).

Memory Flash—creative consultant Philip De-Guere: "My creative consultant credit on the show was actually misleading. I was the executive producer on the pilot but I had no interest in being involved with the series. I didn't get any clear sense of the reasoning for the gateway between the two worlds. The premise was too much of a fantasy. I was also surprised to see that zone troopers in an alternative universe were driving Toyota mini-vans!"

The Zone Troopers Build Men

Trace is drafted into the Zone trooper army. His only way out is to be promoted to Officer, and then resign, but to do so, he must kill draft resisters. Wr: Coleman Luck, story by Roderick Taylor, Bruce A. Taylor. Dir: Richard Compton.

Comm. Peril Sightings (Mark Lenard); Hilbird Racks (Dominick Brascia); D.I. (Robert O'Reilly); Brindle (Kevin Scott Allen); Sergeant (Bryan McGuire); Aide (Wayne Alexander); Girl (Nadine van der Velde); Trooper (Michael McGrady); Teacher (Robert L. Gibson); Christopher (Greg Elliot); Map instructor (Kay Tornborg); Brax (Bill Covert); Instructor (Dale Butcher); D.I. #2 (Brian Thompson); Flight instructor (Steven Whiteford).

Paradise Lost

The family sails to a resort island, where its residents have discovered the fountain of youth. The life force is harvested from guests and the Sterlings are next in line. Wr: Josef Anderson, story by Roderick Taylor, Bruce A. Taylor. Dir: Thomas Wright.

Scarla (Barbara Stock); Bunny (Cindy Eilbacher); Miro (Ian Abercrombie); Osa (Hal England); Gibby (Arnold Turner); Bingo (Chad Hayes); Technicians (John Gowans, Walter Cox).

Rock and Roll Suicide

Trace and Gina decide to bring the youth of "otherworld" rock and roll music. Their newfound popularity brings them fame, fortune … and Kommander Kroll. Wr: Roderick Taylor, Bruce A. Taylor. Dir: Roderick Taylor.

Billy Sunshine (Michael Callan); Zetta (Sarah Buxton); Dr. Claxxon (Warren Munson); Baxter Bromo (Michael Ensign); The praetor (Peter Bromilow); Host (Joyce Little); Students (Todd Hollowell, Susan Isaacs); Woman trooper (Janet Rasak); Salesman (Robert Redding); Engineer (Walter Klenhard); Musician (Joel S. Rice); Receptionist (Maureen Lavette).

Village of the Motorpigs

Hal tries to free his family from a group of drug-abusing cyclists. Wr: Roderick Taylor, Bruce A. Taylor. Dir: Paul Michael Glaser.

Chalktrauma (Marjoe Gortner); Pango (Vincent Schiavelli); Rev (Jeff East); The Praetor (Peter Bromilow);

Officer (Michael Rider); Motoface (Donald Gibb); Lt. (Wayne Alexander); Motorpig (Jerry Potter); Motech girl (Estee Chandler); Corporal (Rodger LaRue); Trooper #2 (Michael John Meyer); Woman (Cynthia Steele); Pigseye (David Katims); Grunt (Tiny Wells); Men (Jeremy D. Lawrence, Martin Clark, David Wells).

I Am Woman, Hear Me Roar

The Sterlings visit a city where women rule and men are slaves. Wr: Bruce Taylor, Coleman Luck, story by Roderick Taylor, Bruce Taylor, Coleman Luck. Dir: Thomas Wright.

Belisama (Elaine Giftos); Sam (Dennis Howard); Gretchen (Susan Powell); Host (Earl Boen); Auctioneer (Beverly Todd); Counselor (Linda Hoy); Desk Sgt. (Kellye Nakahara); TV teacher (Barbara Townsend); Racquel (Toni Nero); Lieutenant (Wayne Alexander); Obnoxious woman (Ivy Bethune); Captain (Dallas Cole); Officer (Andrea Aal); Male shopper (Raymond Lynch); Girls (Jill Whitlow, Rosemarie Thomas); Patrol woman (Tina Blum); Woman (Pamela Bach); Ollie (Peter Macpherson); Ahjay (Merritt Yohnka); Counselor #1 (Faye Marie Baker); Photographer (Rea Simon); Muscular girls (Denise Gallup, Dian Gallup); Crowd voices (Melissa Lambert, Christina Schwimer).

Memory Flash—Thomas Wright: "*Otherworld* was an interesting, fun concept. It was an ambitious show to do for television but it turned out pretty well. Rod Taylor was very determined on what the concept was and who the characters were. The cast was very good and they liked the project. They made a good team. It was sad not to see it succeed because everybody was so dedicated to it."

Mansion of the Beast

While traveling through a forest, the Sterlings meet a man-beast. He gives them a choice: Leave June behind as his companion, or die. Wr: Roderick Taylor and Coleman Luck, story by Roderick Taylor, Coleman Luck, Bruce A. Taylor. Dir: Corey Allen.

Vorago (Alan Feinstein); Aiken (John Astin).

Princess Metra

Mistaken as a former ruler, Gina is made princess of a city where the people have been horribly exploited. Gina is determined to use her newfound title to make social changes. Wr: Douglas Lloyd MacIntosh, story by Roderick Taylor, Bruce A. Taylor. Dir: Peter Medak.

Prime manager (Carolyn Seymour); Capt. Valdor (Hunt Block); Manker (Byron Morrow); Vertleena (Joan Foley); Kort (Drake Hogestyn); Princess Metra (Kristi Somers); Tech #1 (Douglas Alan Shanklin); Head supervisor (Ellen Crawford); Lt. (Charles Walker); Girls (Robin Klein, Gigi Vorgan, Kathy Spitz); Men (Larry Cedar, Will Nye); Sector chief (Tom Harrison); Officers (Ted Richards, Alex Daniels); Peace guard (David Lloyd Nelson); Zal (Philip Simone); Microworker (Marneen Fields); Servant #1 (Nora Masterson); Guard #1 (Daniel McVicar); Lt. #2 (Mark Burke); Small boy (Christopher Walker).

The Outer Limits

September 1963–January 1965

Science fiction anthology series. Stories included themes of time travel, space travel, and creatures from other worlds.

Narrator: The Control Voice (Vic Perrin).

Created by: Leslie Stevens; *Producers:* Joseph Stefano (year 1); Ben Brady (year 2); *Executive Producer:* Leslie Stevens; *Music:* Dominic Frontiere (year 1); Harry Lubin (year 2); ABC/United Artists; 60 minutes, black and white.

Joseph Stefano, producer of *The Outer Limits'* first season, recalls an event that occurred in 1975, ten years after the series' demise. He characterizes it as "one of the strangest, most wonderful experiences I've ever had." Formally invited to a New York science fiction convention, Stefano was "surprised when they offered to pay not only my fare, but my wife's. They also provided a first class hotel room. I thought, 'What the hell is this?' We got there and found a huge audience. I told them, 'I don't really make speeches, but I'll answer questions.' I was truly shocked: they not only knew about *The Outer Limits*, they knew all about me! If I couldn't answer a question, somebody in the audience could. I thought, 'We're talking about a ten-year-old show here!'"

Stefano's initial arrangement was to spend one day at the convention, but "I couldn't get enough of these marvelous people. I returned for a second and third day. I looked at my wife, Marilyn, and said, 'I don't believe this is happening! *When* did it happen?'"

It all began much more quietly in 1962, when ABC-TV commissioned writer Leslie Stevens (whose previous series was Jack Lord's *Stoney Burke*) to set up a science fiction anthology

Fiendish space insects attack a small town in "The Zanti Misfits." Copyright 1964 ABC/United Artists.

An astronaut (James Shigeta) encounters one of the Ebonites (John Anderson) in "Nightmare." Copyright 1963 ABC/United Artists.

At the end of every episode, at least one character, whether human or monster, had gained some degree of insight.

As the first year went into production, Stefano went to work. "I spent a great deal of my time writing scripts or commissioning scripts, trying to get the next show on for the following week," he recalls. "If scripts didn't come in, I'd go home and write them, which is why I wrote so many. In my contract, I agreed to write four scripts. I think I ended up writing 12. I also rewrote many others, not because they were all bad but because many didn't fit our vision."

The most identifiable trademark of *The Outer Limits* was the Control Voice. The program opened with a white dot in the center of a black screen. An unseen voice would announce that for the next hour, "we are controlling transmission." At the program's close, the Control Voice returned with a soothing, "We now return control of your television to you ... until next time ... when the Control Voice will take you to the Outer Limits." It was a gripping, inventive device.

"The Control Voice was (and is) a peculiar phenomenon," says its creator, Leslie Stevens. "It first came to me at a pitch meeting with ABC. The network executives were asking me about the format for *The Outer Limits*. Rod Serling had been a success with *Twilight Zone*, and ABC felt the need for a host. I had no prepared answer, but I heard myself saying that the home viewers' TV set would turn off, leaving a glowing dot. A Control Voice would take over. I quite literally heard myself reciting the introductory speech about 'rolling, fluttering, focus,' etc."

The Control Voice also offered bits of

series. To help ensure commercial success, ABC wanted the emphasis to be on terror. This meant the guarantee of one monster per show.

Because *The Twilight Zone* was more of a gentle fantasy, *The Outer Limits* was truly the first big-budgeted science fiction series aimed at an adult audience. Stevens immediately contacted writer Joseph Stefano (who had scripted the 1960 film *Psycho*) to take on the producing reins. The working chemistry between the two was unbeatable. Stevens, a science fiction buff, was fascinated by the frontiers of science and its effect on society; Stefano was more interested in suspense and Gothic horror. It was his vision that provided most of the shudders. He also insisted on the thoughtful stories that depicted many of the monsters as intelligent and often misunderstood beings. In Stefano's world, mankind was still a groping child whose heart was in the right place.

thoughtful commentary at the close of the episodes. Joseph Stefano says this allowed him to express some of his most personal thoughts to the audience. "The Control Voice wasn't supposed to be God or some great sage," Stefano says. "It was really the voice of Leslie Stevens and Joe Stefano. It was our chance to say what we felt without putting it into a characterization."

At the time, Stefano had a lot to say. "I had just had a son, my first child, and I cared tremendously about what was going on in the world. I realized I had been rather inattentive the previous ten years, politically, because I had been struggling to get somewhere as an artist. I was coming out of that. In *The Outer Limits*, I meant just about everything I wrote. I'll see an episode today and think, 'I wonder if I still feel that way? Do these truths still hold up in my life?' Often they do, which is amazing. I've changed in so many ways since then. So the show even works for me in that respect. It gives me an opportunity to consider where I am as a human being today as opposed to then."

When *Newsweek* profiled *The Outer Limits* in January 1964, the magazine quoted Stefano as saying, "If there's one underlying message on the show, it's a strong preachment against violence, bigotry and prejudice." *Newsweek* credited Stefano's monsters for often pushing the series into the ratings' top twenty.

However, in some reviews *The Outer Limits* was actually criticized for its use of monsters. Some critics claimed the series was nothing more than a fancy creature-feature for television. *TV Guide* critic Cleveland Amory's snide review of the show ended with the grouchy reviewer seeking out a child to explain an episode that had left Amory thoroughly befuddled. As with most TV shows that were ahead of their time, the reviews say more about the critics, who were unable to look past the monsters to see the show's subtext.

"We did pretty much what we wanted to do," says Stefano. "In fact, it's hard to imagine being able to do today what we did then. Today, a network has too much executive control of TV and movies. *The Outer Limits* gave me the opportunity to communicate to the audience what I was thinking and feeling at the time."

Stefano not only crafted well-motivated monsters into the show, he also made strong political and social statements under the guise of science fiction. To the network's credit, Stefano was left alone. "The executives at ABC were pretty hip as to what we were doing," he says.

"They were not stupid people. Danny Melnick, who is a brilliant producer today, was head of ABC's programming development. They knew who we were and what our thinking was like. They knew what we were going to do with *The Outer Limits*. They also knew that we had the subtlety not to get everybody into trouble. They trusted us."

However, Leslie Stevens says that if he had been creatively unshackled by the network, there would have been differences in *The Outer Limits'* content. Stevens was intrigued by the new developments in science. "Digital computers were on the horizon, and I would have enjoyed exploring cyberspace," he says. "Hallucinogens are intriguing, and I'm all for a scientific probe of Nagual. My hobby is arcane math, and I love the realms of the Verhulst process. For sheer sci-fi excitement, nothing beats Kaluza-Klein, Banach and Tarski, Bell and non-local phenomena. But try to discuss this with network execs!"

Within the limitations of having a monster (nicknamed a "bear" by the producers), Stevens could still have some fun. One of his most daring monsters, however, never reached the screen. "I proposed a 'Sound Monster' to Dan Melnick. I found that a decibel oscillator, rising from pedal-tones to dog's hearing, made things like cups, saucers and ashtrays vibrate. I thought it would be fascinating to have the audience involved in a little viewer participation. We could have stuff in their living rooms suddenly buzz and clink as though some strange creature were loose in their house. The ABC legal department turned pale. They were thinking of things falling off shelves onto the heads of millions of viewers, with consequent lawsuits. Needless to say, the 'Sound Monster' was DOA."

Although the monsters on *The Outer Limits* often received the fan mail, today Stefano gets letters about the show's themes. "One fan asked me about my script *The Invisibles* (where parasitic beings control key men in government)," recalls Stefano. "He asked, 'It seems you were referring to the CIA in that. It seems odd you would be allowed to do that in 1963'—because we had just come out of a repressive society with the Eisenhower administration. My response was, 'I would never have been able to do that had it not been called science fiction.' I couldn't have done a *Playhouse 90* or a two-hour movie condemning or doubting the CIA. It would have been refused."

The quality of *The Outer Limits'* scripts and

A man-made alien is set loose to scare the world's leaders into peaceful co-existence in "Architects of Fear." Copyright 1963 ABC/United Artists.

as having a mechanical voice. I presumed they would do this technically by putting a special mike over my throat. Just before filming, I said, 'How are we gonna make my voice sound mechanical?' They said, 'You're going to do that.' I said, 'You mean I have to create this sound? It isn't exactly your average, conversational dialogue.' They told me to do the best I can. I shook my head. 'Damn! I wish that you had warned me earlier.' I went off into a corner and practiced. I managed this electronic-sounding voice. It must have worked because no one said, 'Jesus Christ! We can't use that.' Fans have told me that they had no idea it was me ... of course, I was hidden under this weird makeup that weighed about 800 pounds!

"It was very complicated. They attached this rubber head with glue and blended it onto my skin with liquid rubber. It took about an hour and a half." Legend has it that the cast, including Anderson in full Ebonite makeup, stopped traffic one day when they went out for lunch. "Never happened!" laughs Anderson. "I never left the studio with the makeup on. I couldn't even get into my car with that pointed head I was wearing. But a strange thing did happen on the first day of filming. I felt really odd. I thought I was coming down with something. I finally figured it out: with all this stuff glued to my face, I was suffering from claustrophobia and didn't even realize it. My whole body was encased in a wetsuit and rubber gloves with attenuated fingers. Once I understood it was claustrophobia, I was okay. And after two hours in makeup, I found that whenever I walked, I heard this eerie sloshing sound. I went to my stuntman [Paul

production attracted many talented actors and actresses to the series. Actor John Anderson says, "I wasn't a science fiction fan, but the few episodes I had seen of *The Outer Limits* were remarkable." Anderson signed up to play an alien in "Nightmare." As an Ebonite, Anderson was one of the extra-terrestrials helping the U. S. military perform mind games on a group of unwitting soldiers, with tragic results. "My role was certainly unique," says Anderson. "and we had an incredible cast, including Ed Nelson and James Shigeta. It was Martin Sheen's first good TV role, and there were wonderful character actors, including my dear friend Whit Bissell. A fabulous cast."

Anderson grappled briefly with the alien characterization. "The script described the alien

Stader], who had the same rig on, and said, 'Geez, whenever I take a step, it's like I'm wading in water. What's going on?' He said, 'You're sweating. As you sweat, it can't evaporate.' I said, 'Jesus Christ! You mean I'm walking around in two inches of my own sweat?' He said, 'Yep.' That made all the sense in the world."

Anderson was impressed with the episode. "It made a strong anti-war statement. It was several levels above your typical TV. The episode didn't change the world because since 1963 we've had nothing but bloodshed and fighting, but you've got to keep trying."

The popularity of *The Outer Limits* has even trickled down to its guest stars. Anderson recalls, "I came home one day and there was a bunch of people in my driveway. It turned out they were *Outer Limits* freaks. I call them that because they had a camera and 12 photos of me in that weird makeup. They asked me to sign all 12 of them and asked me all sorts of questions. I thought, 'Geez, they're nice people, but is this all they have to do?' Especially when they said that every weekend they went around looking for *Outer Limits* people!"

Joey Tata was another actor who found himself in the bizarre world of *The Outer Limits*. As one of the soldiers in "The Zanti Misfits" he battled deadly space ants. The one-foot ants, known as Zantis, had human faces and delivered nasty bites. They were some of the scariest and most unusual creatures ever depicted on television. "We shot the interiors at a Los Angeles TV station called KTTV," recalls Tata. "The soldiers' control outpost was about as big as a living room. When director Leonard Horn walked in with the ants we'd be fighting, we all looked at each other and tried not to laugh. We had a couple of actors from New York who looked down on us Hollywood guys, and they just looked down at their belly buttons as Leonard passed these rubber ants around. Lenny saw my face and he said, 'Tata! If you say one word about these ants…' I said, 'Well, they're too big to step on. How are we supposed to get rid of them?" Leonard said, 'You're gonna shoot them. If you can believe that an ant can talk, you can believe you can shoot them, right?' and we all laughed."

Tata counts the episode as one of his favorite experiences. "The episode turned out great," he says. "During the battle scene, the ants were everywhere: running down the sides of walls, climbing up desks, biting people's feet … and we were all shooting guns off like crazy in this little room. I'm talking 12 carbines with blanks going off. We were going deaf from the noise. Some of the ants were animated through stop-motion photography. Others were rigged with squibs and when we shot 'em, they blew apart. Man, it was great! I gave one of the ants to my niece as a gift."

Tata jumped at the chance to be in the series. "Lenny Horn and I had worked at CBS on *The Red Skelton Show*. When he asked me if I wanted to fight ants on *The Outer Limits*, I said, 'Absolutely!' I loved the series. Joe Stefano and his style were terrific. Today, it's a cult show. The makeup and direction on the series were dynamite."

One of the most haunting *Outer Limits* episodes was "The Man Who Was Never Born." Written by Anthony Lawrence, the story was about people making great personal sacrifices to save the Earth's future. An astronaut and a mutant from the year 2148 head back to 1963 to prevent the birth of a man who will be responsible for Earth's biological destruction.

Karl Held played the doomed astronaut, Joseph Reardon, who lands in Earth's future and finds it a desolate landscape populated by sterile, misshapen humanoids. "My challenge was to convey a believable reaction to the incredible circumstances," says Held. "Fortunately, Joe Reardon was a thinking man. He was literate, intelligent and quick-witted."

Held recalls the planet scenes were played out "in a small studio, under hot lights. My spacesuit didn't 'breathe,' and I was roasting. The makeup people would dry my face right up to 'Action!' I never got through a take without director Leonard Horn wincing as perspiration started on my face. He finally said, 'I guess we'll have to skip your close-ups, Karl.' I said, 'Hey, I just stopped sweating. I wonder why?' Leonard was a very easy man to work with. He saw I had a good grasp of the character and left me alone. He'd explain how the special effects would appear outside the spaceship viewport so that I could put myself in the physical context of the scene. He usually made a sincere, encouraging comment after a final take."

One of the most powerful moments in *The Outer Limits* is Reardon's death scene. The astronaut is dematerialized while passing through a space barrier to return to present-day Earth. "The scene's sense of fright was augmented by the special effects," Held says, "but also in my choice of playing his death with disbelief rather than fear."

Held has also received praise from viewers

for his role. "A stranger recognized me and said that my line, 'A microbe destroyed humanity?' was handled beautifully. Another person said, 'You made it believable with your sense of reality.' It was a strong episode. The special effects were pretty good for that kind of budget."

"When Joe Stefano sent me the script for 'The Man Who Was Never Born,' I loved it on the first read," says actor Martin Landau, who played Andro, the tragic, gentle mutant from the future. He falls in love with the Earth woman (played by Shirley Knight) who is destined to give birth to the child who will destroy the future. "I saw Shirley Knight in the role of the leading lady. She had been an acting student of mine in the 1950s. When Joe asked me if I wanted to do the episode, he coincidentally mentioned that they were trying to get Shirley Knight to played Noelle. I knew we were on the same wavelength! I immediately agreed to play Andro."

Because Andro could use hypnosis to alter his repelling appearance, Landau had something of a dual role. "I was playing both Andro and myself," he says. "Freddie Phillips, the makeup artist, devised a mask that was attached at my eyes and mouth in such a way that I could put it on or take it off in five minutes' time. The mask's nose holes had to be enlarged so I could breathe easier, although I did most of my breathing through my mouth. The misshapen feet were put on like boots, and the gnarled hands were donned like gloves."

The exciting chase scene, as Andro and Noelle are pursued through the woods, "was beautifully filmed by Conrad Hall, the director of photography, and his camera operator, Bill Fraker," says Landau. "Bill laid on his back, on carriage wheels, holding the camera on his chest. He was pulled by ropes to film the chase. The whole *Beauty and the Beast* love story, as well as the time travel aspect, caught everyone's attention. Dick Van Dyke called me up after the show aired and raved about it. I still get mail about the show. As a six-day shoot, we made a damned good little movie. It was a special episode and I'm very proud of it."

Landau's second *Outer Limits* appearance was in "The Bellero Shield," where he played a scientist who accidentally captures a space traveler. Sally Kellerman played his scheming wife. "It was an interesting episode, although I liked it less than "The Man Who Was Never Born." The director, John Brahm, was a great old pro out of World War II cinema. Sally Kellerman was a 17-year-old waitress at a 'beatnik' coffee house named Cosmo Alley when I first arrived in Hollywood. It was a place where people read poetry, sang folk songs and hung out."

Robert Justman, who was the assistant director on *The Outer Limits* "part of the time and also a unit production manager part of the time," thinks the series "introduced a lot of viewers to science fiction." His work on the series included "The Sixth Finger," starring David McCallum as a Welsh miner transformed into a man of the future. "As filming went on, it became clear to me and director James Goldstone that the segment's running time was going to come up short," recalls Justman. "So we wrote a sequence where David, who had some pianistic abilities, played two-part Bach. Since his character had six fingers, that made it interesting! David consulted with us, and together we picked out what music he would play. It was a lovely piece, and we derived enough footage to deliver the show."

The Outer Limits had a successful first season. In a ratings jungle where a 16.0 rating was needed for renewal, *The Outer Limits* ended the year with a respectable 19.0. The series was especially popular with teenagers. ABC granted the series a renewal, but moved *The Outer Limits* from its popular Monday night berth to Saturday nights. Joseph Stefano felt the new time slot, opposite the mighty Jackie Gleason show, was a mistake. Stefano protested the change by leaving the series at the end of its first year. *The Outer Limits*, one of the most popular shows of the 1963-64 season, was among the least-watched shows of the 1964-65 season. It was canceled in the middle of its second season.

"When I left," says Stefano, "it was simply because I felt *The Outer Limits* should not be moved to Saturdays. Monday night had been just great. Our ratings weren't sensational, but they were healthy. If we had stayed in that slot, I think the ratings would have increased in the second year. We could have run five or six years. I think what happened was that somebody at the top said, 'I think *The Outer Limits* has a chance to knock off Jackie Gleason on Saturday nights.' Two or three executives ended up deciding what an audience will watch and when. So they moved the series, and I moved on. I didn't see any of the second season. When *The Outer Limits* was canceled, it was exactly what I expected."

Robert Justman worked on both seasons. "I thought the first year, when Joe was involved, was much better than the second year. It was a monster show in the second season, which is what ABC wanted. It certainly didn't have the quality of writing the first season had. Joe's writing was extremely poetic. The themes of the first season were also more engrossing. The fellow who came in to replace Joe [producer Ben Brady] was not a writer. He didn't have the sensitivity Joe had. I didn't think the second season was going to be successful, especially when I saw the product we were being commissioned to churn out. In fact, I was unhappy enough that I seized the opportunity to go and prepare the first *Star Trek* pilot before the second season was over."

As the second year began production, however, the new producers issued a statement that the new *Outer Limits* would emphasize science over monsters. According to new story editor Seeleg Lester, "The first season, which I reviewed,

Agent Lou Mace (Robert Duvall) gets the drop on a friendly space creature (William O'Connell) in "The Chameleon." Copyright 1964 ABC/United Artists.

never satisfied Leslie Stevens' original concept. The first year was principally concerned with horror, a.k.a. bug-eyed monsters. I suspect ABC had a heavy hand on the producer's till. Whether the producer [Joseph Stefano] agreed or disagreed with the bug-eyed-monster concept, I don't know. Ben Brady and I were assured by the network there would be no intrusion of that kind of thinking in the second year. Their assurance was a lie. We were leaned on continuously to put horror into the scripts."

However, the second year did feature some unusual segments, including Harlan Ellison's "Soldier" and "Demon with a Glass Hand." There was also Seeleg Lester's and Sam Neuman's "The Inheritors," a two-part story about benevolent aliens who give afflicted children a second chance

for life on an alien planet. "'The Inheritors' was conceived because I wanted at least one show without monsters," says Lester. "I tried as story editor to make the show more imaginative and intriguing. The second year began to illustrate the imaginative kinds of stories that science fiction promises. The network, however, despite the huge success of the anthology series *One Step Beyond*, never understood or appreciated *The Outer Limits*. The networks still don't understand the underlying appeal of imaginatively different concepts or stories. *The Outer Limits* endures today because it was an opportunity for unusual, literate and intriguing television. There have been several other efforts since to cash in on science fiction TV, but they've been, aside from *Star Trek*, less than mediocre."

"Bobby Justman is correct, but then, so is Seeleg Lester," notes Leslie Stevens of *The Outer Limits'* content during its two-year run. "Dan Melnick, the ABC programmer, insisted that we 'bring on a bear' in every episode to grab disinterested audiences. We tried to take his command and run with it in imaginative ways. In the second year, Seeleg added wonderful elements, but he was shackled even worse than the first year. Both Lou Morheim [*The Outer Limits'* first season story editor] and Seeleg Lester wanted to accomplish the impossible and almost did. We dreamed of integrity, and we wanted every show to be great, but the business affairs of TV is a hard taskmaster. *The Outer Limits* had zero sex, so we were required to pump in the adrenalin (violence) by 'bringing on the bear' in the first five minutes. It's interesting to note that in the hostile, murderous world of TV drama, commercials suggest that to consume something will bring relief. It's always, 'Have a Coke or a Bud or a Rolaid or be part of the gusto group by consuming something.' The secret theme of 50 threatening years of mass TV drama might well be, 'Consume or die.'"

Stevens has a definite favorite of the two seasons. "The first season was very near and dear to me. The second year, the network clipped our wings, and I was limited to being executive producer. I admired Seeleg's valiant efforts, but in my view Ben Brady was miscast as boss of an imaginative series."

The cancellation of *The Outer Limits* in 1965 was the beginning of its rebirth. Before production of the show's second season, the series had already been sold to 25 foreign TV markets. In 1965, independent American stations quickly snapped up all 49 episodes for syndication. By the late 1960s, *The Outer Limits* was a huge hit in syndication. As early as 1966 there was talk of reviving the series. "I think it was ABC that expressed interest in doing the series again at that time," says Joseph Stefano. "I can't tell you how many companies and network people have talked to me over the years, wanting to do another *Outer Limits*–like show. But they've always hedged their bets. In the mid–1980s, Leslie Stevens and I had a meeting with ABC. They said, 'We want you to do *The Outer Limits* again, but we don't want you to have the power that you had on the original.' I feel the original has lasted because Leslie and I did what we wanted to do. Or they'll say, 'We want to do it again but this time add continuing characters.' At that point I always politely excuse

myself. I still feel the only way to do it is as an anthology. The problem with a lot of science fiction today is that the networks and studios think special effects are the key. I talked to a network guy, and he said, 'The kind of things you want to do would cost a fortune today.' I said, 'Why's that?' He replied, 'Because special effects are so expensive now.' I said, 'But I'm not talking about special effects!' That's part of the Steven Spielberg legacy. It's like, 'How are we going to know it's set in the future unless we have all this special effects stuff going on?' Those kinds of TV series haven't worked. They've had weak stories and characters without depth."

Today, Stefano relishes the attention still lavished on *The Outer Limits*. "It's fantastic. Whenever TNT [the cable network] does its *Outer Limits* marathons, the ratings are very good." Ironically, the marathons are broadcast Saturday nights.

"You're not going to see 1990s special effects," Stefano says. "If you know that some of the effects are going to look a little corny, then you'll realize that they're not what the show was about anyway." The writer acknowledges that he's primarily known for his *Psycho* screenplay and his *Outer Limits* work. "I'm grateful to be one of the few writers to get to write a TV series and a movie that have become classics," he says.

A new *Outer Limits* series, produced by Atlantis Films, debuted in syndication in 1995, with Stefano and Leslie Stevens serving as executive story consultants.

Today, Stefano gets mail from the kids of people who watched the series originally. "It's well into its second generation of viewers," he marvels. "It's wonderful. I get all kinds of philosophical questions: 'Is this really what you believed in at the time?'

"We had just enough episodes to make it viable in syndication, where it went wild," continues Stefano. "In a strange way, I wonder, if we had lasted five years on ABC, would the series be as popular today? Perhaps because we lasted such a short time, the episodes have become jewel-like."

All 49 episodes, which were filmed in black and white, are selling well on MGM/UA home video. "There have been very few things on TV that have captured the fancy of young people," says Stefano. "I think *The Outer Limits* was ahead of its time. I get 17-year-olds who write to me, asking, 'Was there really a time when you could see this kind of show on television?'"

CAST NOTES

Vic Perrin (The Control Voice): Born 1916. Perrin began his career as a senior NBC announcer. He also supplied countless voices for commercials, movies and cartoon series. He died in 1989.

EPISODE GUIDE

Season 1: 1963-64

The Galaxy Being
A radio engineer accidentally transports a glowing, friendly creature from Andromeda to Earth. Wr and Dir: Leslie Stevens.

Allan Maxwell (Cliff Robertson); Carol Maxwell (Jacqueline Scott); Gene Maxwell (Lee Phillips); Eddie Phillips (Bert Metcalfe); Loreen (Allyson Ames); Alien being (William O'Douglas, Jr.); Trooper (James Frawley); Major (Bill Catching); Policeman (Allan Pinson); Collins (Roy Sickner); Being #2 (Charles MacQuarry); Also with William Stevens, Joseph Perry, Mavis Neal, Peter Madsen, May Boss, Polly Burson, Donald C. Harvey.

One Hundred Days of the Dragon
The vice-president of the U.S. discovers that the president is actually a deadly Oriental agent who has the ability to change his appearance. Wr: Allan Balter, Robert Mintz. Dir: Byron Haskin.

William Lyons Selby (Sidney Blackmer); Ted Pearson (Phillip Pine); Carol Carter (Nancy Rennick); Robert Carter (Mark Roberts); Li Chin Sung (Richard Loo); Frank Sommers (Bert Remsen); Ann Pearson (Joan Camden); Su Lin (Aki Aleong); Wen Lee (James Hong); Marshall (Henry Scott); Byron (Robert Brubaker); Li Kwan (James Yagi); Ho Chi Wong (Clarence Lung); Hotel Oriental (Eugene Chan); Carter (Dennis McCarthy); Schumacher (Vic Perrin); Briggs (Richard Gittings); Election announcer (Leslie Stevens).

The Architects of Fear
A scientist is turned into a space monster to scare the world's leaders into peaceful coexistence. Wr: Meyer Dolinsky. Dir: Byron Haskin.

Allan Leighton (Robert Culp); Yvette Leighton (Geraldine Brooks); Philip Gainer (Leonard Stone); Paul Fredericks (Doug Henderson); Dr. Herschel (Martin Wolfson); Carl Ford (Lee Zimmer); The Thetan (Janos Prohaska); Fred (Clay Tanner); Bert Bolsey (Hal Bokar); Tom (William Bush).

Trivia Alert: Some of ABC's affiliate stations found the alien's appearance so frightening that they blacked out Act IV's monster scenes.

The Man with the Power
A college instructor volunteers for mind-control experiments for a space agency. He's unaware that his subconscious mind is creating a cloud-like force that destroys anyone in its way. Wr: Jerome Ross. Dir: Laslo Benedek.

Harold J. Finley (Donald Pleasance); Steve Crandon (Fred Beir); Keenan (Frank Maxwell); Sigmund Hindemann (John Marley); Vera Finley (Priscilla Morrill); Dean Radcliffe (Edward C. Platt); Dr. Henschell (Paul Lambert); Detective (Paul Kent); Emily Radcliffe (Anne Loos); Dr. Tremaine (James McCallion); Doctor (Harry Ellerbe); Secretary (Diane Strom); Tree pruner (Saul Gross); Nurse (Jane Barclay); Surgeon (Pat O'Hara).

The Man Who Was Never Born
A mutant from Earth's future travels back in time to prevent the birth of a man who will destroy humanity. Wr: Anthony Lawrence. Dir: Leonard Horn.

Andro (Martin Landau); Noelle Andresen (Shirley Knight); Bertram Cabot (John Considine); Joe Reardon (Karl Held); Mrs. McCluskey (Maxine Stuart); Minister (Marlowe Jenson).

Trivia Alert: In a scene filmed but deleted from the original ending, Jack Raine played a man who welcomes Noelle to Earth's beautiful future in 2148.

Memory Flash—Anthony Lawrence: "I've seen it many times since. The director did a really good job and added things that weren't in the script. It holds up very well."

The Sixth Finger
A small Welsh town is faced with destruction after a good-hearted miner volunteers for an experiment that transforms him into a dangerous man of the future. Wr: Ellis St. Joseph. Dir: James Goldstone.

Gwilliam Griffith (David McCallum); Cathy Evans (Jill Haworth); Prof. Mathers (Edward Mulhare); Mrs. Ives (Nora Marlowe); Wilt Morgan (Robert Doyle); Gert Evans (Constance Cavendish); Darwin (Janos Prohaska); Policeman (George Pelling); Deputy (Chuck Hayward).

O.B.I.T.
While investigating the death of a technician who was killed by a strange creature, a senator discovers alien beings have infiltrated American security. Wr: Meyer Dolinsky. Dir: Gerd Oswald.

Jeremiah Orville (Peter Breck); Byron Lomax (Jeff Corey); Clifford Scott (Harry Townes); Barbara Scott (Joanna Gilbert); Creature (William O'Douglas, Jr.); Col. Grover (Alan Dexter); Clyde Wyatt (Sam Reese); Fred Severn (Jason Wingreen); Dr. Anderson (Lindsay Workman); Phil Fletcher (Konstantin Shayne); James Harrison (Robert Beneveds); Armand Younger (Chuck Hamilton).

The Human Factor
Major Brothers claims he's being stalked by a strange creature. A scientist exchanges minds with Brothers to learn more about the spectre. Wr: David Duncan. Dir: Abner Biberman.

Dr. Jim Hamilton (Gary Merrill); Roger Brothers (Harry Guardino); Ingrid Larkin (Sally Kellerman); Harold Giles (Ivan Dixon); Bill Campbell (Joe de Santis); Peterson (John Newton); Dr. Soldini (Shirley O'Hara); Orderly (James B. Sikking); Nurse (Jane Langley); Sergeant (Art Alisi); Sentry (Matty Jordan); Voice (Vic Perrin); Private Gordon (William O'Douglas, Jr.).

The Corpus Earthling

A doctor and his wife are on the run from two alien creatures, which engulf and possess human bodies. Wr: Orin Borsten, story by Louis Charbonneau. Dir: Gerd Oswald.

Dr. Paul Cameron (Robert Culp); Laurie Cameron (Salome Jens); Jonas Temple (Barry Atwater); Ralph (David Garner); Caretaker (Ken Renard); Creature's voice (Robert Johnson).

Nightmare

Six astronauts are held captive on an alien planet and forced to participate in a series of war games. Wr: Joseph Stefano. Dir: John Erman.

Luke Stone (Ed Nelson); Major Jong (James Shigeta); Arthur Dix (Martin Sheen); Interrogator (John Anderson); Terence Ralph Brookman (David Frankham); General (Whit Bissell); James P. Willowmore (Bill Gunn); Ersa Krug (Bernard Kates); Chief of staff (Willard Sage); Gen. Benton (Ben Wright); Krug's grandfather (Sasha Harden); Krug's governness (Lisa Mann); Dix's mother (Lillian Adams); Dr. Whorf (Martin Brandt); Alien guard (Paul Stader).

It Crawled Out of the Woodwork

Investigating strange deaths, a detective discovers the staff of an energy plant is harboring a black cloud of destructive energy. Wr: Joseph Stefano. Dir: Gerd Oswald.

Jory Peters (Scott Marlowe); Thomas Siroleo (Edward Asner); Gaby Christian (Barbara Luna); Dr. Block (Kent Smith); Stuart Peters (Michael Forest); Dr. Stephanie Linden (Joan Camden); Coroner (Tom Palmer); Sentry (Ted de Corsia); Warren Edgar Morley (Gene Darfler); Cleaning Lady (Lea Marmer); NORCO voice (Robert Johnson).

The Borderland

Convinced that his dead son is trapped in another dimension, a tycoon sponsors a team of scientists in their efforts to cross over into the fourth dimension. Wr and Dir: Leslie Stevens.

Dr. Ian Frazer (Peter Mark Richman); Dr. Eva Frazer (Nina Foch); Lincoln Russell (Philip Abbott); Mrs. Palmer (Gladys Cooper); Edgar Price (Alfred Ryder); Dwight Hartley (Barry Jones); Benson Sawyer (Gene Raymond); Dr. Sung (Noel de Sousa); Scientist (Vic Perrin).

Memory Flash—Peter Mark Richman: "We had a wonderful cast. Nina Foch is a good friend. The producer, Joe Stefano, wrote the film *The Black Orchid* [1959]. I was in that with Sophia Loren and Anthony Quinn. *Outer Limits* was an excellent series. It was imaginative and they had the courage to do good stuff."

Tourist Attraction

A businessman captures a giant lizard-fish creature in South America. He plans to put the monster on display in the States. Wr: Dean Riesner. Dir: Laslo Benedek.

John Dexter (Ralph Meeker); Lynn Arthur (Janet Blair); Juan Mercurio (Henry Silva); Tom Evans (Jerry Douglas); Mario (Henry Darrow); Prof. Arivello (Jay Novello); Reporters (Edward Colmans, Willard Sage);

Skipper (Stuart Lancaster); Oswaldo (Jon Silo); Woman (Shelley Morrison); Paco (Martin Garralega); Fortunato (Francis Ravel); Man (Noel de Sousa); Butler (Marco Antonio); Fish creature #1 (Roger Stern); Fish creatures (Paul Stader, George Robotham).

The Zanti Misfits

An army outpost in the Death Valley desert is attacked by deadly space insects that resemble ants with human faces. Wr: Joseph Stefano. Dir: Leonard Horn.

Steve Graves (Michael Tolan); Ben Garth (Bruce Dern); Lisa Lawrence (Olive Deering); Max R. Hart (Robert F. Simon); Roger Hill (Claude Woolman); Radar man (Joey Tata); Radioman (Lex Johnson); Computer man (George Sims); Air sergeant (Michael Mikler); Corp. Delano (Bill Hart); Newscaster (Robert Johnson); Zanti voices (Vic Perrin, John Elizalde).

The Mice

A convict agrees to take part in an interplanetary exchange program, but the aliens are actually planning an invasion of Earth. Wr: Joseph Stefano, Bill S. Ballinger, story by Lou Morheim. Dir: Gerd Oswald, Alan Crosland, Jr.

Chino Rivera (Henry Silva); Dr. Julia Harrison (Diana Sands); Dr. Tom Kellander (Michael Higgens); Robert Richardson (Ron Foster); Haddon (Don Ross); Goldsmith (Gene Tyburn); Williams (Dabney Coleman); Warden (Francis de Sales); Chromoite (Hugh Langtry); Chromo voices (Vic Perrin, Robert Johnson).

Controlled Experiment

When a woman shoots her cheating husband, two Martians use a time converter to replay the murder in an effort to understand aggressive behavior. Wr and Dir: Leslie Stevens.

Phobos one (Barry Morse); Deimos (Carroll O'Connor); Carla Duveen (Grace Lee Whitney); Bert Hamil (Robert Fortier); Frank Brant (Robert Kelljan); Arlene Schnable (Linda Hutchins); Martian voice (Leslie Stevens).

Don't Open till Doomsday

While honeymooning in a Gothic mansion, a newlywed couple discovers a mysterious box containing an alien lizard creature. Wr: Joseph Stefano. Dir: Gerd Oswald.

Mary Kry (Miriam Hopkins); Gerd Hayden (Buck Taylor); Viva Hayden (Melinda Plowman); Emmett Balfour (John Hoyt); Harvey Kry (David Frankham); Justice of the peace (Russell Collins); Wife (Nellie Burt); Mordecai Spazman (Anthony Jochim); Creature (Frank Delfino); Voice (Robert Johnson).

ZZZZZ

A queen bee, transformed into a human being, sabotages a scientist's efforts to communicate with a bee colony. Wr: Meyer Dolinsky, Joseph Stefano. Dir: John Brahm.

Benedict Fields (Philip Abbott); Francesca Fields (Marsha Hunt); Regina (Joanna Frank); Howard Warren (Booth Colman); Mr. Lund (Robert Johnson); Bee voices (John Elizalde).

The Invisibles

An undercover agent finds that slug-like parasites from another world have taken over key men in government. Wr: Joseph Stefano. Dir: Gerd Oswald.

Luis B. Spain (Don Gordon); Larry K. Hillerman (George McCready); Mrs. Clarke (Dee Hartford); Recruiter (Walter Burke); Hilary J. Clarke (Neil Hamilton); Genero Planetta (Tony Mordente); Oliver Fair (Richard Dawson); Johnny (William O'Douglas, Jr.); GIA agent (Len Lesser); Henry Castle (Chris Warfield); Supervisor (John Graham); GIA chief (Vic Perrin); Invisibles voice (Robert Johnson).

The Bellero Shield

A scientist intercepts a traveling space creature. The friendly alien's life is endangered by the scientist's greedy wife. Wr: Joseph Stefano, story by Joseph Stefano, Lou Morheim, based on a story by Arthur Leo Zagat. Dir: John Brahm.

Richard Bellero (Martin Landau); Judith Bellero (Sally Kellerman); Mrs. Dame (Chita Rivera); Bifrost alien (John Hoyt); Richard Bellero, Sr. (Neil Hamilton).

The Children of Spider County

An alien returns to Earth to claim his half-human son, but the young man rejects his father after seeing the alien use violence against humans. Wr: Anthony Lawrence. Dir: Leonard Horn.

Ethan Wechsler (Lee Kinsolving); Aabel (Kent Smith); John Bartlett (John Milford); Anna Bishop (Benneye Gatteys); Bishop (Dabbs Greer); Sheriff Simon Stakefield (Crahan Denton); Deputy (Joey Tata); General (Robert Osterloh); Officer (Roy Engel); Alien (William O'Douglas, Jr.); Greenbane (Joseph Perry); Man (Burt Douglas).

Specimen: Unknown

A space shuttle brings back deadly plants that grow at an astonishing rate and emit deadly spores. Wr: Stephen Lord. Dir: Gerd Oswald.

J.T. MacWilliams (Stephen McNally); Mike Doweling (Richard Jaeckel); Clark Benedict (Russell Johnson); Janet Doweling (Gail Kobe); Ken Galvin (Arthur Batanides); Gordon Halper (Peter Baldwin); Rupert Lawrence Howard (Dabney Coleman); Nathan Jennings (John Kellogg); Sergeant (Walt Davis); Intercom voice (Robert Johnson).

Memory Flash—Russell Johnson: "The spores that the plants shot out were Kix cereal," says the actor best known as the Professor on *Gilligan's Island*. "But it was a fine script and a good series."

Second Chance

An alien forces a group of people to go on a space journey to his planet, where he needs their help in saving his world. Wr: Lin Dane (Sonya Roberts), Lou Morheim, story by Lin Dane. Dir: Paul Stanley.

Empyrian (Simon Oakland); Dave Crowell (Don Gordon); Mara Matthews (Janet de Gore); Buddy Lyman (Yale Summers); Arjay Beasley (John McLiam); Donise Ward (Mimsy Farmer); Sue Ann Beasley (Angela Clarke); Tommy Nebbs Shadbury (Arnold Merritt).

Moonstone

A moonbase crew tries to protect helpless aliens from a huge creature from another galaxy. Wr: William Bast. Dir: Robert Florey.

Prof. Diana Brice (Ruth Roman); Clint Anderson (Tim O'Connor); Lee Stocker (Alex Nicol); Dr. Philip Mendl (Curt Conway); Lt. Ernie Travers (Hari Rhodes); Grippian voice (Ben Wright); Unit voice (Vic Perrin).

Memory Flash—Tim O'Connor: "It was the first interesting science fiction series for television. It picked up a big audience that year. [Creator] Leslie Stevens was a good writer and a classy guy. I remember Ruth Roman said to Alex Nicol between takes, 'Isn't it wonderful to be a star!'"

The Mutant

A scientist on another planet is turned into a bug-eyed mutant by a silvery rain. His fellow explorers discover that he can read minds and destroy with a single touch. Wr: Allan Balter, Robert Mintz, story by Joseph Stefano, Jerome Thomas, Ellis St. Joseph. Dir: Alan Crosland, Jr.

Reese Fowler (Warren Oates); Evan Marshall (Larry Pennell); Dr. Julie Griffith (Betsy Jones-Moreland); Dr. Fred Riner (Walter Burke); Peter Chandler (Robert Sampson); Philip Griffith (Richard Derr); Henry LaCosta (Herman Rudin).

Memory Flash—Jill Sherman-Donner: "You don't get any better than *The Outer Limits*," says the writer/producer who later worked on *The Incredible Hulk* and *Voyagers!* "*Outer Limits* is timeless. The Robert Culp episodes were the best, but I remember another episode about these people trapped on an alien planet ["The Mutant"]. This silverly rain made one guy horribly bug-eyed. I remember it as being absolutely chilling."

The Guests

In a house where time stands still, a drifter finds escape blocked by a sinister creature who is experimenting with human beings. Wr: Donald S. Sanford, story by Charles Beaumont. Dir: Paul Stanley.

Florida Patton (Gloria Grahame); Wayde Norton (Geoffrey Horne); Theresa Ames (Luana Anders); Randy Latimer (Vaughn Taylor); Ethel Latimer (Nellie Burt); Dr. Ames (Burt Mustin); Alien's voice (Robert Johnson).

Fun and Games

Two earthlings are transported to a jungle asteroid where they must save Earth by defeating two lizard creatures. Wr: Robert Specht, Joseph Stefano, based on the short story "Arena" by Fredric Brown. Dir: Gerd Oswald.

Mike Benson (Nick Adams); Laura Hanley (Nancy Malone); The senator (Robert Johnson); Detective (Ray Kellogg); Creature (Bill Hart); Poker dealer (Read Morgan); Poker player (Theo Marcuse); Sharpie (Harvey Gardner); Players (Charles Horvath, Jack Perkins, Buzz Henry); Female creature (Charles MacQuarry).

Memory Flash—Robert Specht: "My original story [for "Fun and Games"] was called 'Natural Selection.' My original story was all action. It was rewritten as a rather talky show."

The Special One

A father learns that his son's tutor is an alien invader. Wr: Oliver Crawford. Dir: Gerd Oswald.

Roy Benjamin (MacDonald Carey); Agnes Benjamin (Marion Ross); Zeno (Richard Ney); Kenny Benjamin (Flip Mark); Joe Haydn (Bert Freed); Terrence (Edward C. Platt); Bill Turner (Jason Wingreen).

A Feasibility Study

The residents of six neighborhood blocks are transported to a planet by creatures who need humans for slave labor. Wr: Joseph Stefano. Dir: Byron Haskin.

Simon Holm (Sam Wanamaker); Ralph Cashman (David Opatoshu); Andrea Holm (Phyllis Love); Rhea Cashman (Joyce Van Patten); Voice of authority (Ben Wright); Father Fontana (Frank Puglia); Teenager (Glenn Cannon); Being (Robert Justman).

The Production and Decay of Strange Particles

Globs of blue light from another dimension take over technicians at a nuclear power plant. Wr and Dir: Leslie Stevens.

Dr. Marshall (George McCready); Laurel Marshall (Signe Hasso); Collins (Joseph Ruskin); Griffin (Rudy Solari); Paul Pollard (Robert Fortier); Konig (Leonard Nimoy); Arndis Pollard (Allyson Ames); Terrell (Barry Russo); Coulter (Willard Sage); Official (Paul Lukather).

The Chameleon

Louis Mace volunteers to be turned into an alien creature. He infiltrates the crew of a disabled spaceship to find out what the aliens' motives are. Wr: Robert Towne, story by Robert Towne, Lou Morheim, Joseph Stefano. Dir: Gerd Oswald.

Louis Mace (Robert Duvall); Leon Chambers (Howard Caine); Alien (William O'Connell); Gen. Crawford (Henry Brandon); Dr. Tillyard (Doug Henderson); Gunman (Roy Jenson); Alien #2 (Dean Smith); Pilot's voice (Robert Johnson); Army voice (Vic Perrin); Guitarist (Tony Olvera).

Memory Flash—William O'Connell: "The alien makeup fitted around my whole head. It was not just a facial mask. I felt claustrophobic. But the results were excellent. I used a slightly theatrical way of moving my body and turning my head. Robert Duvall was a very quiet, unassuming person. When we rehearsed the scene where he meets the aliens, he said, 'Let me listen to you and I'll adjust my voice to match yours.' There wasn't one false move in that episode. Usually, aliens are depicted as a threat to humanity. They're horrible. Here, there was an element of hope in the unknown."

Forms of Things Unknown

Two murderesses take refuge in a cottage, where they meet a man who has used time travel to resurrect their victim. Wr: Joseph Stefano. Dir: Gerd Oswald.

Kassia Paine (Vera Miles); Leonora Edmond (Barbara Rush); Tone Hobart (David McCallum); Andre Pavan (Scott Marlowe); Colas (Sir Cedric Hardwicke); French people (Wolfe Barzelle, Madeline Holmes, Gabrielle Rossillon).

Season 2: 1964-65

Soldier

A soldier from the future, trained only to kill, is befriended by a family in the twentieth century. Wr: Harlan Ellison, story by Harlan Ellison. Dir: Gerd Oswald.

Tom Kagan (Lloyd Nolan); Quarlo Clobregnny (Michael Ansara); Paul Tanner (Tim O'Connor); Abby Kagan (Catherine McLeod); Toni Kagan (Jill Hill); The Enemy (Allen Jaffe); Loren Kagan (Ralph Hart); Sgt. Berry (Marlowe Jenson); Doctor (Ted Stanhope); News vendor (Jamie Forster); Woman (Mavis Neal).

Cold Hands, Warm Heart

An astronaut returns from Venus and discovers that he's changing into a scaly, Venusian-like creature. Wr: Milton Krims, story by Daniel B. Ullman. Dir: Charles Haas.

Jeff Barton (William Shatner); Ann Barton (Geraldine Brooks); Mike (Malachi Throne); Matt Claiborne (Lloyd Gough); Medicine tech. (Dean Harens); Botany (James B. Sikking); Construction (Lawrence Montaigne); Electronics (Henry Scott); Reporter (Julian N. Burton); Reporter #2 (Peter Madsen); Guard (Lou Elias); Chief (Hugh Jensen); Chairman (Tim Huntley); Attendants (Patrick Riley, Ray Kellogg); Newsman (Vic Perrin).

Behold, Eck!

A friendly two-dimensional being, which has sawed a skyscraper in half and caused mass havoc in its frenzied attempts to get home, is befriended by a scientist. Wr: John Mantley, story by William R. Cox, based on the story by Edwin Abbott. Dir: Byron Haskin.

Jim Stone (Peter Lind Hayes); Elizabeth Dunn (Joan Freeman); Bernard Stone (Parley Baer); Lt. Runyan (Doug Henderson); Eck (Lou Elias); Miss Willett (Marcel Hebert); George Wilkerson (Sam Reese); Grayson (Paul Sorenson); Sgt. Jackson (Jack Wilson); Newsman (Richard Gittings); Rogers (Taggart Casey); Eck's voice (Robert Johnson).

The Expanding Human

Drug experiments that advance the mind and body are linked to a series of brutal murders at a university. Wr: Francis Cockrell. Dir: Gerd Oswald.

Roy Clinton (Skip Homeier); Peter Wayne (Keith Andes); Lt. Branch (James Doohan); Henry Akata (Aki Aleong); Mark Lake (Robert Doyle); Dean Flint (Vaughn Taylor); Mrs. Merrill (Mary Gregory); Leland (Jason Wingreen); Lee Morrow (Peter Duryea); Sgt. Alger (Troy Melton); Receptionist (Shirley O'Hara); Susan Wayne (Barbara Wilken); Student (Michael Falcon); Watchman (Owen McGiveney); Bellaire (Sherwood Keith); Elevator man (Bill Cort).

Demon with a Glass Hand

Trent awakens in a city without a memory. He has a glowing glass hand that helps him elude humanoid aliens who want to kill him. Wr: Harlan Ellison. Dir: Byron Haskin.

Trent (Robert Culp); Consuelo Biros (Arlene Martel); Arch (Abraham Sofaer); Battle (Rex Holman); Budge

(Robert Fortier); Breech (Steve Harris); Durn (Bill Hart); Kyben (Wally Rose, Fred Krone).

The Cry of Silence
Trapped in a canyon filled with moving rocks and hostile frogs, a couple tries to communicate with an unseen alien. Wr: Robert C. Dennis, story by Louis Charbonneau. Dir: Charles Haas.

Andy Thorne (Eddie Albert); Karen Thorne (June Havoc); Lamont (Arthur Hunnicut); Stunts (Richard Farnsworth, Helen Thurston).

The Invisible Enemy
Investigating the deaths of a Mars expedition, astronauts find the Martian sands crawling with sand serpents that feed on blood. Wr: Jerry Sohl. Dir: Byron Haskin.

Charles Merritt (Adam West); Jack Buckley (Rudy Solari); Gen. Winston (Joe Maross); Jerome (Ted Knight); Paul Lazzari (Peter Marko); Frank Johnson (Robert Doqui); Hal Danvers (Christopher Alcaide); James Bowman (Anthony Costello); Fred Thomas (Michael Mikler); Technician (James Tartan).

Wolf 359
A scientist creates a miniature world in a glass dome. By speeding up its evolutionary process, he hopes to see the future of mankind. Wr: Seeleg Lester, story by Richard Landau. Dir: Laslo Benedek.

John Meredith (Patrick O'Neal); Ethel Meredith (Sara Shane); Peter Jellicoe (Peter Haskell); Philip Exeter Dundee (Ben Wright); James Custer (Dabney Coleman).

Memory Flash—Richard Landau: "I had read something about the big bang theory long before it came into vogue. That was the springboard for my idea. I never saw the finished episode. In my original story, I had a scientist recreate a planet. This put him in the position of the almighty. In doing so, it led to his own destruction. You can't play God. That was my basic thought. It's amazing how *Outer Limits* keeps going. It was far ahead of its time."

I, Robot
A friendly robot goes on trial for murdering its creator. A lawyer knows the death was accidental, but unless he can prove it, the robot will be destroyed. Wr: Robert C. Dennis, story by Otto Binder. Dir: Leon Benson.

Thurman Cutler (Howard da Silva); Nina Link (Marianna Hill); Adam Link (Read Morgan); Thomas Coyle (Ford Rainey); Judson Ellis (Leonard Nimoy); Charles Link (Peter Brocco); Prof. Hebbel (John Hoyt); Fred (Robert Sorrells); Evie Cooper (Christine Matchett); Sheriff Barclay (Hugh Sanders); Mrs. Macrae (Mary Jackson); Judge (Ken Drake); Truck driver (John Hudkins); Adam's voice (John Caper, Jr.).

The Inheritors, Part 1
Four soldiers, recently wounded in Vietnam, return to the States and find themselves under the control of an alien force that directs them to build a giant spaceship. Agent Ballard is determined to find out what their motives are. Wr: Seeleg Lester, Sam Neuman, story by Seeleg Lester, Sam Neuman, idea by Ed Adamson. Dir: James Goldstone.

Adam Ballard (Robert Duvall); Ngo Newa (James Shigeta); Arthur Ray Harris (Don Harron); Philip J. Minns (Steve Ihnat); James Conover (Ivan Dixon); Robert Renaldo (James Frawley); Francis Hadley (Dee Pollock); E. F. Larkin (Dabbs Greer); Randy E. Branch (Ted de Corsia); Andy Whitsett (William Wintersole); M.P. (Sy Prescott); Jessup (Robert Cinder); Nurse (Linda Hutchins); Superintendent (Leon Askin); Soldier (Yoneo Iguchi); Surgeon (Robert J. Nelson); John (Kim Hector).

The Inheritors, Part 2
As the soldiers get closer to completing the spaceship, Ballard and his team close in. Wr: Seeleg Lester, Sam Neuman, story by Seeleg Lester, Sam Neuman, idea by Ed Adamson. Dir: James Goldstone.

Adam Ballard (Robert Duvall); Philip J. Minns (Steve Ihnat); Arthur Ray Harris (Don Harron); Robert Renaldo (James Frawley); James Conover (Ivan Dixon); Francis Hadley (Dee Pollock); Randy E. Branch (Ted de Corsia); Mrs. Suberon (Jan Shutan); Miss Steen (Joanne Stuart); Minerva Gordon (Suzanne Cupito); Johnny Suberon (Kim Hector); Grainger (Jon Cedar); Boy (Charles Herbert); Danny Newton Masters (David Brady); Child (Michel Petit); Nurse (Paulle Clark); Kids (John Harding, Earl Brown).

Trivia Alert: Suzanne Cupito later changed her name to Morgan Brittany and became one of the stars of TV's *Dallas*.

Keeper of the Purple Twilight
An alien exchanges his intellect for a scientist's emotions. When alien assassins arrive to destroy the Earth, the alien tries to block their invasion. Wr: Milton Krims, story by Stephen Lord. Dir: Charles Haas.

Ikar (Robert Webber); Eric Plummer (Warren Stevens); Janet Lane (Gail Kobe); Frank Carlin (Curt Conway); David Hunt (Edward C. Platt); Alien Ikar (Mike Lane); Creatures (Hugh Langtry, Fred Stromsoe, Gene Wiley, LeRoy Ellis).

The Duplicate Man
In 2025, a scientist accidentally lets a dangerous monster loose in the city. He makes a clone of himself to hunt down the creature. Wr: Robert C. Dennis, story by Clifford D. Simak. Dir: Gerd Oswald.

Henderson James (Ron Randall); Laura James (Constance Towers); Karl Emmett (Sean McClory); Basil Jerichau (Steven Geray); Megasoid (Mike Lane); Murdock (Konstantin Shayne); Miss Thorson (Ivy Bethune); Pedestrian (Jonathon Hole); Policeman (Jeff Scott); Zoo guide (Alan Gifford).

Counterweight
A simulated flight to another world is disturbed by a plant-like creature who doesn't want its world exploited by human beings. Wr: Milton Krims, story by Jerry Sohl. Dir: Paul Stanley.

Joe Dix (Michael Constantine); Dr. Alicia Hendrix (Jacqueline Scott); Prof. Henry Craif (Sandy Kenyon);

Keith Ellis (Larry Ward); Harvey Branson (Stephen Joyce); Margaret O'Hara (Shary Marshall); Michael Lint (Charles Hradilac); Matthew James (Crahan Denton); Voice (Robert Johnson).

Memory Flash—Michael Constantine: "I finally got to say a line I had heard in every scary movie since I was a kid: 'No, no, aaaaagh!' I loved it!"

The Brain of Colonel Barham

A dying astronaut volunteers his brain for a space journey but the brain becomes stronger and vindictive during testing. Wr: Robert C. Dennis, story by Sidney Ellis. Dir: Charles Haas.

Doug McKinnon (Grant Williams); Alec Barham (Anthony Eisley); Jennifer Barham (Elizabeth Perry); Dr. Rahm (Wesley Addy); Leo Hausner (Martin Kosleck); Gen. Dan Pettit (Doug Kennedy); Ed Nichols (Paul Lukather); Maj. Locke (Peter Hanson); Guard (Robert Chadwick); Scientist (Randy Crawford).

The Premonition

A test pilot and his wife find everyone frozen in time, including their daughter, who is in the path of an oncoming truck. Wr: Ib Melchior, Sam Roeca, story by Sam Roeca. Dir: Gerd Oswald.

Jim Darcy (Dewey Martin); Linda Darcy (Mary Murphy); Baldy Baldwin (William Bramley); Jane Darcy (Emma Tyson); Limbo being (Kay E. Kuter); Matron (Dorothy Green); Gate sentry (Coby Denton).

The Probe

Survivors of an airplane crash are plucked from a raging sea and deposited inside a giant alien space probe. Wr: Seeleg Lester, story by Sam Neuman. Dir: Felix Feist.

Jefferson Rome (Peter Mark Richman); Amanda Frank (Peggy Ann Garner); Frank Coberly (Ron Hayes); Beeman (William Boyett); Dexter (William Stevens); The Mikie (Janos Prohaska); Engineer (Richard Tretter).

Memory Flash—Peter Mark Richman: "We all got very sick. The temperature on the set was kept at 55 Fahrenheit so that the smoke pots could create the fog. Then we were doused with spray water before each take because we were supposed to be at sea. Bronchitis and hacking colds were the result! There was also a sadness that such a good series was dead. I've been through that many times."

The Phoenix

March 1982–September 1982

In an ancient sarcophagus, archaeologists discover Bennu, an alien from the distant past. Revived, he escapes and is pursued. The government becomes involved, and Preminger, an agent, is determined to capture him. Meanwhile, Bennu searches the lands for his wife Mira, entombed somewhere in an Indian burial ground.

Cast: Bennu (Judson Scott); Justin Preminger (Richard Lynch).

Created by: Anthony and Nancy Lawrence; *Executive Producer:* Mark Carliner; *Producers:* Anthony and Nancy Lawrence (pilot), Leigh Vance (series); *Supervising Producer:* Bob Birnbaum; *Associate Producer:* Julia Crosthwait; ABC; 60 minutes.

Two of the most difficult things to do in television series production (things that become even more difficult in a science fiction series) are (1) present original ideas and concepts and win network acceptance for them, and (2) broadcast anything that hints of a religious nature that may potentially offend viewers.

The Phoenix, at least initially, took on both of these challenges, and it is a tribute to its creators, the husband-and-wife screenwriting team of Anthony and Nancy Lawrence, that the series got off the ground at all.

The show did not evolve as they intended, but the genesis of the idea for *The Phoenix* was "done on a spec basis," says Nancy Lawrence. Lawrence says that she and her husband had read a number of books that discussed the theories of ancient astronauts visiting Earth in the distant past. Most notable were Von Daniken's theories. Armed with this research, they drew up a treatment for a series idea. "We thought it was a fascinating concept," says Nancy Lawrence. "We thought it might be interesting. Tony told Mark Carliner about it, and Mark said, 'Well, if it's not right for now, it'll be right for later.' So, Mark told Jonathan Axelrod, the head of ABC at the time, and Jonathan read it, and it happened very quickly! It was 24 hours. My husband and I went in, stayed at ABC until 9:00 in the evening, and we went with this. Everybody got behind it. We wrote a script [from the treatment] in six and a half days, and turned it in. They didn't change a line. All they said was, 'We need an antagonist.' That was the network mentality—everything has to be like *The Fugitive*. We turned the script in, and they liked it, and it went into production."

The pilot was close to what the Lawrences had hoped for. From there, as usual, the network tried to include elements derived from various hit series in an effort to capitalize on their success. In this case, *The Fugitive* was the template. *The Phoenix* also bore resemblance to *The Incredible Hulk, Starman, The Immortal*, and to a certain extent *Logan's Run*—but then, all these were derivative of *The Fugitive* as well.

"The network was so concerned that there would only be a cult audience," says Lawrence. "They wanted to appeal to everybody, and as it turned out, the pilot received a good rating. The network was very respectful, but they didn't understand the show's nature. It was a big disappointment. What they said they wanted, ultimately, they did not want—they were too scared. When we screened the pilot [with ABC head Tony Tomopulous], at the end of it, Tomopulous stood up and applauded. 'We've never had a pilot like this!' But there were too many cooks stirring the broth at ABC. We got many concessions because the network was under the gun, they needed the show immediately. Tony and I wrote five scripts. We let a lot of people in the science fiction business read it [the prospectus], and they said they liked it, but the network began to have second thoughts."

That's when the tide turned between the production of the pilot and the series. When ABC "had more time to think about the series," says Lawrence, "what they wanted was more comic book."

Carliner took over as executive producer of the series and introduced the couple to potential staff writers and editors. In the end, because the Lawrences had access to such good literature on ancient astronauts, "we felt we'd be safer going with what had been documented," says Lawrence.

The man who took over as story editor, Earl Booth, recalls his brief tenure with this show as "a sorry experience. None of the original material the Lawrences wrote was ever accepted by ABC. The four scripts filmed were completely new scripts. While I was working on *The Phoenix*, everyone was trying to decide what they wanted to do with the pilot. It was an unsettling period of constant change. There was never a definite direction. I suspect the network was groping for another version of *The Fugitive*."

"It was one of the most horrible experiences of my career!" declares Larry Alexander, a writer who tried pitching stories to *The Phoenix*. "Not because of the show itself. It was a horrible experience for almost everybody. My boss, Mike Sullivan, when he first started, was an ABC executive, that's how I met him. One of the shows he was shepherding was *The Phoenix*, which he considered to be the single worst show he had seen in his entire life. He thought it was *so* terrible that he has parodied it in about three episodes of the sitcoms *Growing Pains* and *Just the 10 of Us* [both of which Sullivan produced]. Earl Booth was a terrific guy. He was one of the few story editors who *didn't* write. He literally was a *story* editor. He called me in and gave me an assignment. I turned in the story, and he called me up and said, 'It's wonderful—go to script.' And ten minutes later he called me back and said, 'Cancel that!' I said, 'You just gave me a script commitment.' He said, 'I'll deny it.' I said, 'What? What's going on?' He said, 'I can't tell you.' I said, 'Excuse me?' He said, 'Larry, please … don't make an issue of it. I can't tell you. I'm in a very bad position. The powers that be don't like the story and I was unauthorized to give you a go-ahead. Blame me if you want. I can't help it.' And I said, 'OK.' And I didn't talk to him for *ten* years, needless to say. And I was working on another ABC show at the time, *Breaking Away* [1980-1981]. I also got cut off on a story with *Breaking Away*, and both of these stories were very good. It took me ten years to find out that an executive at ABC, who, when we were kids, I had punched in the face, had taken vengeance. He was able to cut me out of both assignments, which I found fascinating."

When it comes to the Lawrences' goals in creating the show, Nancy says, "We tried to be provocative to the extent that it opened minds to look at things that happened long ago. We wanted people to at least think. We took that point of view. We weren't peddling our philosophy. We were saying, 'This is a possibility. This is the evidence discovered that we have no answers to.'"

The protagonist, Bennu, as played by actor Judson Scott, was meant to be a reversal of many characters presented in *Twilight Zone*, who tended to be ordinary people in extraordinary circumstances. Bennu was an expression of the reverse: an extraordinary being transplanted into the ordinary life of modern-day Earth.

Bennu was a compassionate, charismatic and benevolent man in search of his wife, Mira, ("our one-armed man," says Nancy Lawrence),

Shelley Smith guest-stars with Judson Scott in *The Phoenix*'s 90-minute pilot. Copyright 1982 ABC.

they were when he went to sleep," points out Lawrence. "In other words, we have not progressed or improved. It was a tough thing because we didn't want him preachy. We talked to Judson about the character a lot. Judson was passed by the network. They wanted someone to look all-American, which I don't think he did. Judson had a very interesting oddness about him. He did certain things during his screen test that the network didn't like, and they said, 'He can never do this again.' The taboos began to mount up. For example, Judson would wave his hands or move them as he tried to explain something. He was trying to get beyond the words. The network said, 'Tell him to keep his hands to his side.' They were frightened of the messianic imagery in the gestures. Also, there was a scene [in the pilot] where he's at the ocean and he runs into the water and disappears.

who he believed was buried somewhere in North America at an Indian burial site. His only lead to her location was a small Indian stone symbol.

This ancient astronaut had powers beyond those of mortal men, aided by a golden medallion on his neck. This medallion was the centerpiece—quite literally—of the character and of the show. With it, Bennu's body soaked in solar rays, which could be released as energy from his fingertips. In times of danger, when earthlings would aim guns or swing chains at him, he would grasp the medallion with one hand and aim the other against his enemy. Bennu could also read other people's minds, communicate with animals and levitate.

"He simply went to sleep many years ago, woke up and [found] things much worse than

Bennu, being from a different time, has no hang-ups. Judson was wearing these green surgical rags, the clothes the doctors were using when he got out of the hospital. At the beach, he became ill, so he goes into the water to re-oxygenate. We showed clips of him taking off his shirt, dropping his pants. He was stark naked, and from a long shot from the cliffs we photographed him running toward the water. We got it at a perfect time of day. The sun was going down and it made him a backlit silhouette, and the network, which had initially approved of it, nearly had a stroke. Mark Carliner told us, 'Cut it!'"

Lawrence wanted the scene to emphasize that this was a person "just joining the Earth. He was childlike and wanted to keep that quality."

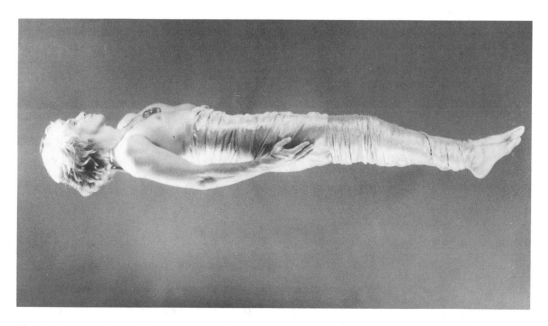

Floating in space, Bennu (Judson Scott) will reawaken in a new world and embark on a mission to find his wife. Copyright 1982 ABC.

Lawrence confesses that the series eventually bore little resemblance to original intent. "In the pilot, we took a lot of time to keep anything from being pretentious, a disaster in science fiction. We told the network, 'You have a series here, but it has little to do with an ancient astronaut.' There are certain political things that are always in place. And you can't fight them. It's not the network's fault, because they don't understand science fiction or didn't at the time."

The idealized vision of *The Phoenix* was quite different from what appeared on television, according to Nancy Lawrence. She says, "This was a man who was looking to contact his people. He was very homesick. The network had already decided it had to be a road show, i.e., *The Fugitive*, so he roamed from town to town. That brought a different flavor. The network wanted someone chasing Bennu, and we said, 'Not the police, not the CIA,' and we came up with a character that Tony and I liked very much who was somebody who had been sent to terminate Bennu [Justin Preminger, played by veteran villain actor Richard Lynch]. He was like the dark side of this planet, but the network [softened him]. Tony and I wrote five scripts, we were paid for them [but they were never used]. The network felt they were too risky, or maybe they just hated them."

One of the original scripts "had to do with the South. There was one with Bennu breaking the law in the South and being in a chain gang. That's what the network wanted, but we added something to it which brought out his whole difference in philosophy. We wanted him always to make that difference."

Synopses of the unfilmed scripts bear out the Lawrences' original version. One of them, "Trial by Fire," is credited to Richard Christian Matheson and Thomas Szollosi. According to the synopsis, Bennu, "nearly disabled by solar flares, and in extreme pain … stows away on a small plane, hiding in the cargo bay. When it then crashes in the desert he and the five passengers (and crew) must work together to stay alive. Bennu helps them all survive while at the same time helping to heal the emotional breach between a father and son."

Another one, titled "The Face of an Angel," which bears no author credit, had Bennu "receiving a psychic message from his home planet (Eldobran). Bennu sickens. With scientist Frazier's help he learns of Mira and also about 'people' from his own planet who mean them harm. Bennu goes to Tullner, Texas, to find Mira only to discover she's been kidnapped by the evil people. While he tries to find her he becomes involved in drugs and murder."

But two scripts credited to Anthony and Nancy Lawrence brought other shades of Bennu to the surface.

In "Deadly Cargo," "Bennu covertly climbs on board a truck hauling toxic waste in Georgia. Thrown from the truck, he hits his head and wakes with amnesia. Taken prisoner as a hijacker, he ends up on a work farm where he comes to the aid of the Warden's too-young and questionably-retarded young wife—Willow. Freeing himself from the prison, he and Willow attempt to dispose of the toxic waste that is killing people … and causing Bennu's continuing amnesia and health problems."

In "The Star Needle," Bennu is found "wandering near a Kansas City zoo, and becomes involved with a young mother-to-be, Regan, and her special baby. When her drunken husband is murdered, Bennu must protect both of them from the killer. Preminger sweeps upon Bennu and captures him. He escapes their trap, though, to again rescue Regan from her would-be-murderers."

When the swift ax of cancellation fell down, "Judson was in a lot of pain," recalls Lawrence. "Once I got a call from him at 2 a.m. from New York. He was knocked out by its cancellation."

Describing Bennu's goals on Earth, Lawrence notes that "Bennu was a man who came from a different culture. We didn't want a talky thing where he imparted his culture and was a Jesus figure. We did episodes where he was mistaken about our culture. We can only speculate on why these people came to Earth, and maybe they're still here, and that scared the hell out of everybody." Perhaps that fear inspired ABC network's second thoughts about this series.

Lawrence goes so far as to say that Bennu's mission changed from its original goal.

"Tony and I wrote a whole prospectus on it, but I don't think the network even read it. They wanted more of a simplistic children's show, and then The Fugitive thing came in. We felt it had to be more of an anthology, to have the latitude to bring in other characters from this planet and from his. But the network put it within stricter bounds and it didn't work."

The aftermath of The Phoenix's debut on television didn't end the interest in the show, Lawrence recalls. "We had people writing to us saying they were from certain planets, and they said Judson was from that planet also. They truly believed they were from another planet."

Sometimes, people forget the enormous power of television.

Cast Notes

Judson Scott (Bennu): After a notable part in *Star Trek II: The Wrath of Khan* (1982), Scott kept busy with guest roles, many in science fiction television shows like *Powers of Matthew Star, Greatest American Hero, Star Trek: The Next Generation* and *Babylon 5.*

Richard Lynch (Preminger): Lynch has almost always appeared as a villain. He's known for many TV and feature roles. He was the main baddy in *Invasion USA* (1985) with Chuck Norris. TV appearances include *Serpico, Streets of San Francisco, Buck Rogers, The A Team, Hunter,* and *Starsky and Hutch.* He also played Xavier in *Galactica 1980*'s premiere episodes.

Episode Guide

The Phoenix (1982 TV movie, 90 minutes)
Uncovering a tomb in Peru, archaeologists discover a chamber containing the sarcophagus of an ancient Egyptian astronaut, Bennu. Sent to Earth during the tenth century, Bennu is to be awakened in a time when he's needed by mankind. The scientists accidentally erase his instructions upon opening the coffin. Awakening alone in the lab, Bennu stumbles into the street, where he's picked up by young female photographer named Noelle. Shot by a policeman, Bennu recontacts the scientist who discovered him. Wr: Anthony and Nancy Lawrence. Dir: Douglas Hickox.
     Dr. Ward Frazier (E.G. Marshall); Justin Preminger (Richard Lynch); Diego De Varga (Fernando Allende); Noelle Marshall (Shelley Smith); Dr. Clifford David (Daryl Anderson); Lynn (Hersha Parady); Tim (Jimmy Mair); Howard (Lyman Ward); Kingston (Carmen Argenziano); Murray (Stanley Kamel); Surgeon (Angus Duncan); Patrolman (Wayne Storm); Hood (Terry Jastrow); Technician (Bret Williams); Anesthesiologist (Paul Marin); Nurse (Patricia Conklin); Croupier (James Malinda).

Season Episodes

In Search of Mira
Bennu, having witnessed a drug-related murder, seeks refuge from the killers when he befriends a farming family. Wr: Leigh Vance. Dir: Douglas Hickox.
     Dr. Ward Frazier (E.G. Marshall); Harry Atkins (John Vernon); Hal Massey (Bert Remsen); Sheriff (Britt Leach); Woods (Terry Wills); Darlene (Jenny Parsons); Unger (Sandy Ward).

One of Them
Preminger is close on the heels of Bennu. Meanwhile,

the ancient astronaut believes Mira, his long-lost wife, is still in suspended animation in an Indian burial site. Wr: Mark Carliner. Dir: Reza Badiyi.

Delancey Coleman (Andrea Marcovicci); The Professor (Peter Michael Goetz); Aide (Lawrence Casey); Police chief (Gene Ross); Co-ed (Debbie Richter); Sheriff (Marshall Teague); George (Josh Cadman); Dog handler (John Zenda); Carmelita (Carmen Zapata); Bart (Behrouz Vossi); Sheriff (Marc Alaimo); Also with Sheila Frazier; Uncredited: Little girl (Shannen Doherty).

A Presence of Evil

Terrorists plotting to transport stolen uranium threaten Bennu and the family who runs the horse stables where Bennu is working. Wr: David Guthrie. Dir: Douglas Hickox.

Cindy Houghton (Lee Purcell); Jack Houghton (Kaz Garas); Roddy (Jeremy Licht); Freda (Joan Foley); George

(Jim Staskel); Buck (Tobias Anderson); Mrs. Carpenter (Carol Vogel); 1st cop (Bill Dearth); Preminger's aide (Rudy Daniels); Penny (Lisa Morton); Dolfo (Robert O'Reilly); Holly (Nancy Grahn).

The Fire Within

Seeking Mira's burial site at a state park, Bennu gets a job at a construction site, where he learns his boss may be the victim of a swindle. Wr: David Guthrie. Dir: Reza Badiyi.

Harry Cartwright (John Milford); Jan (Tracey Gold); Ellie (Eileen Davidson); Fred Barford (Peter Iacangelo); Dave (Carmen Argenziano); Mr. Fast (Nacona Aranda); Aide (Woody Eney); Newsstand lady (Karen Anders); Robby (Bret Shryer); Det. Barford (Rick Grass); Electrician (Ned Bellamy); Fire captain (Noel Conlon); Tardoff (Fred Franklin); Albert (Sam Laws); Doorman (Nelson Mashita).

Planet of the Apes

September 1974–December 1974

Three astronauts from 1988, Virdon, Burke and Jones, are propelled through time by a space warp. Their spaceship crash-lands, and Jones is killed. Virdon and Burke recover and find that they're on Earth, but the year is 3085 A.D.

Apes now rule the world, and humans are slaves in farming villages. The two astronauts, whose ideas of freedom are a threat to the ape culture, are sentenced to be executed. Escaping with their ally, a friendly chimpanzee named Galen, they begin a life as fugitives on the planet of the apes.

Cast: Galen (Roddy McDowall); Alan Virdon (Ron Harper); Pete Burke (James Naughton); Urko, the Chief Gorilla (Mark Lenard); Dr. Zaius, Orangutan Council Chief (Booth Colman).

Based on characters created by: Pierre Boulle; *Developed for television by:* Anthony Wilson, Art Wallace; *Producer:* Stan Hough; *Executive Producer:* Herbert Hirschman; *Makeup:* Dan Striepeke; CBS/Twentieth Century–Fox; 60 minutes.

An entire planet of the apes was wiped off the TV screen after a scant fourteen episodes. Before the series was launched into network orbit, CBS executives believed the *Planet of the Apes* TV series couldn't miss. There had already been five successful *Apes* motion pictures made between 1968 and 1973. When the first movie aired on CBS in 1973, the film grabbed an astronomical 60 share in the ratings. That's when CBS decided to spin off a weekly series based on the popular films. Industry analysts predicted *Planet of the Apes* would be one of the biggest hits of the season. *TV Guide* said *Planet of the Apes* "won't monkey around."

The optimistic word-of-mouth was reassuring to star Ron Harper. He had already had several TV series shot out from under him (including *87th Precinct* and *Garrison's Gorillas*). "*Planet of the Apes* was my fifth TV series," says Harper. "Just before the series aired, I did an interview and they said, 'Well, you've finally got one that's gonna go. It can't miss.' The motion pictures made something like 160 million dollars, and everybody expected the series to be a shoo-in. I thought we were going to be for at least a couple of years. It didn't work out that way. It was very disappointing."

The cinematic history of *Planet of the Apes* began in 1968. The first film, scripted by Michael Wilson and Rod Serling, starred Charlton Heston as an astronaut who crash-lands on a futuristic world where apes rule and men are mute, primitive animals. The film's surprise ending revealed that the planet was Earth, two thousand years in the future. Mankind had destroyed itself in a nuclear holocaust, and apes had risen to power.

Beneath the Planet of the Apes (1970) continued the saga with James Franciscus as an astronaut who encounters underground human mutants and their doomsday bomb. The film ends with the H-bomb destroying the world. However, box office receipts demanded another sequel, and *Escape from the Planet of the Apes* (1971) had three superintelligent chimpanzees use Heston's spaceship to travel back to Earth, 1973. The chimps are eventually killed by paranoid humans, but they leave behind an offspring, Caesar. Caesar begins *The Conquest of the Planet of the Apes* (1972), inciting his fellow apes to rebel against mankind. The last and least successful sequel, *Battle for the Planet of the Apes* (1973), dealt with the apes fighting more mutants just after the ape takeover.

Actor Roddy McDowall, who had played the ape Cornelius in *Planet* and *Escape*, and Caesar in *Conquest* and *Battle*, eagerly signed up to play a new chimpanzee character, Galen, for the series.

One important person missing from the TV series was Arthur P. Jacobs, producer of the *Apes* motion pictures. He was preparing an outline for the series when he died of a heart attack in 1973. Writers Anthony Wilson and Art Wallace were brought in to lay down the series concept. While the films had taken a misanthropic view and laced their cynicism with a satiric edge, the TV series was played softer. Instead of a weekly condemnation of mankind, the storyline gave humans the benefit of the doubt. If man were to ever regain control of his planet, perhaps he would be of a better, more tolerant breed.

"I had to be careful not to repeat what the movies had done," says Art Wallace as he shaped the series. "I wanted an entirely different approach. I wrote the first script and laid out the characters for the other writers." Wallace developed a respect for the format as it took shape. "At first I thought the idea was kind of silly. But then Herb Hirschman [executive producer] and I felt this would be an interesting way to make comments on contemporary society. We were particularly concerned with commenting on racial violence. The apes were dealt with as if they were another race, separate but equal. The idea was that it was the white man getting stepped on. There was very little science fiction, although we added the gimmick of the astronaut trying to decipher the spaceship's computer disk and find a way back home."

Although he felt the series got off to a good start, "it gradually developed into hoke. The apes had to be realistic to be taken seriously, but they started to look silly. In terms of acting, what can you do with that ape makeup on? They also had

the astronauts beating up the apes on a regular basis. In addition, the series had to be done relatively cheaply. It was too expensive for television."

Wallace also felt the series was hurt by the casting. "Roddy McDowall was okay, but he was playing an ape. How much could he do? I felt that [Ron Harper and James Naughton] didn't have the charisma that the show needed. The whole show turned out to be a jinx for the network."

"Some people felt, and maybe they were right, that the series was a one-joke show," admits Ron Harper. "The first movie was a big hit because everyone was surprised by the concept. Once you're over the shock of, 'Man, those are talking apes!' it becomes progressively downhill. Unless you have really good stories, you lose the suspense and the humor. You can't keep toasting on that one situation."

Harper's character of Alan Virdon had several goals: As a humanitarian, the astronaut was determined to reignite the self-esteem of the humans he encountered. His more personal quest was to find a civilization that could provide a way back home. Unlike Burke, who was a bachelor and resigned to his fate, Virdon had a wife and son back home in 1988. "Virdon was a confirmed optimist," notes Harper. "He felt that as long as he's alive, there's a chance he could build a spaceship. Or maybe a rescue expedition would find them. As long as he had that computer disk from the spaceship, he felt he could get home. So he kept plugging away. "There are a lot of people like that, particularly actors!" he laughs. "And I think that he did get home. It might have taken him ten years, but I think he made it."

One segment that stood out for Harper was "The Legacy." Virdon is held captive with a young mother and her son who remind him of his family. "That was an interesting idea. I had just been married [to actress Sally Stark], and there was a photograph Virdon carried around of his wife and son. The photo was actually of my wife, Sally, and the producer's son. But when we filmed "The Legacy," they had cast a blonde actress, Zina Bethune, as the mother. Sally had dark hair, and to reinforce the story's point, they had to reshoot the photograph with a blonde actress."

Although many fans of the *Planet of the Apes* movies were disappointed that the weekly series set its sights so low, on its own undemanding level, the series was a reasonably entertaining mixture of adventure and humor. Harper admits to having mixed feelings about the show's content.

"Personally, I liked the more humanistic stories. In "The Good Seeds," we taught a farming family of apes about human values. They were saving all of the good corn and planting the bad corn. Virdon explains, 'No, you plant the good seeds. This way the generations improve themselves.' It didn't take us long to realize that our young audience wasn't terribly interested in this. They wanted to see more action. They liked the fights with the sharks and the bulldogging off horses. While we weren't geared primarily as a children's show, we did have a mostly young audience. They were disappointed that there wasn't more action-adventure. We may have got too caught up in the humanistic-morality stories. It's a cliche to say, 'Well, it was the writing,' but the truth is, if you analyze some of the stories, we had one basic plot: One of us gets captured by the apes; the other two have to rescue

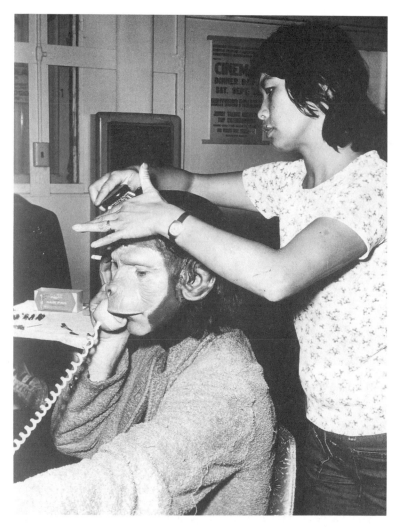

Roddy McDowall gets a last-minute brush from the makeup woman. Copyright 1974 CBS/Twentieth Century–Fox.

him. We took turns getting captured. They needed to break out of that. In that regard, the stories weren't that interesting."

Harper draws a parallel with his later series, *Land of the Lost*. The Saturday morning series featured a family trapped in a prehistoric world. Harper played Uncle Jack during the 1976-77 season. "Even though it was a Saturday morning show, the stories were more interesting than on *Planet of the Apes*. Our producer loved writing for it. He would spend weekends writing scripts. He experimented with ancient myths and fables, like the Flying Dutchman and Medusa. The stories were much more than getting captured every week."

However, Harper found the working atmo-sphere on *Apes* more satisfying. "We had a lot of good actors on the show. The producer [Stan Hough] said he thought he'd cast the show perfectly. I wish we had run a little longer run to bear that out. Roddy McDowall was wonderful. He gave Jim Naughton and me our own directors' chairs. When mine arrived, my name was misspelled as Rin. Roddy had done it as a gag."

Despite the rigorous makeup ritual McDowall had endured for the feature films, he was anxious to reprise his ape role for television. "I was surprised that he agreed to do the series," comments Harper. "It took him three and a half hours in that makeup chair. He couldn't sleep while they applied it because he had to keep his face set in a certain way. So he listened to classical music. After

Burke (James Naughton), Galen (Roddy McDowall) and Virdon (Ron Harper) discover a science center in "The Legacy." Copyright 1974 CBS/Twentieth Century–Fox.

four or five episodes, though, his face looked like raw hamburger because of the rubber appliance. He had to take a week off to heal his skin."

Harper's relationship with James Naughton was more casual. "Jim and I worked very hard together on the show, but we weren't as close as we could have been. There was a funny moment when we had to sneak into a gorilla guard house. Jim was supposed to whisper, 'No noise.' So Jim knocks out a gorilla with a judo chop and yells at the top of his lungs, 'No noise!' I cracked up and fell to the floor. I said, 'Jim, I think you've just defeated the purpose of your line!'"

Visually, *Planet of the Apes* rarely inspired a sense of the fantastic. One notable exception was in the first episode, "Escape from Tomorrow." A hunted villager is caught in a fierce gust of wind as the sounds of a roaring engine bear down on him. The unseen spaceship makes a splintering crash nearby.

The first glimpse of the smoking spaceship, sprawled in the middle of a mountain valley, is stunning. "To the young people in the audience, it was probably fascinating," admits Harper, "but in reality, the spaceship wasn't much of anything. It was a wooden, hollow shell. The scenes with us

at the controls were shot on a soundstage. What looked impressive was the way they dug that burning burrow behind the spaceship to make it look like it took it about half a mile to land."

Booth Colman had the recurring role of the great ape sage, Dr. Zaius, the orangutan who presided over Ape City. His duty was to make certain that his ape culture didn't discover that mankind had once ruled the planet. Colman recalls, "When they asked me if I would feel claustrophobic in the makeup, I said that Lon Chaney's spirit would look down and protect me. I got the laugh—and the part!" Colman found a startling coincidence as he prepared for the role. "Maurice Evans had played Dr. Zaius in the motion pictures. I had been in his Broadway company in *Hamlet* during 1944-45. He was a wonderful actor and coincidentally, I wore the same ape costume he had worn in the features. It had been carefully preserved at the studio. I found an old British lotto ticket in an inner pocket and returned it to Maurice by mail. He was living in England and wrote back, wishing me luck with the series and hoping that they had washed and ironed everything for me!"

To prepare for the role, Colman first went to

the nearby zoo to study ape behavior. "I tried to develop a personality for Zaius that would be believable. I saw him as an extraordinary elder, high in the council. He was all-knowing and decided what was best for everyone. He had an arrogance of authority and a one-track mind of determination."

Like Roddy McDowall and Mark Lenard (Urko the gorilla), Colman had to undergo the rigors of makeup. "I left home at 4 a.m. to be in makeup man Frank Westmore's chair by 5:30 a.m. I had to be ready for shooting by 8:30. At the end of the day, my solidified mask was carefully removed and used on an atmosphere extra the next day."

Colman enjoyed working on *Planet of the Apes*, but he was not impressed with the way the series evolved. "The first feature had an originality and eeriness. They also had the advantage of shock. A TV series couldn't maintain that without highly ingenious stories. I would have gone after a writer like Ray Bradbury, who has a creative ability for the weird and unworldy. I preferred stories that said something and had a point of view rather than the usual claptrap. The props, costumes and actors were superior; the material was decidedly inferior. It was rushed into production before stories could be properly prepared. It was just as quickly and mistakenly canceled. It could have built a solid audience under other circumstances."

Director Ralph Senensky, who directed the segment "The Tyrant," says, "Originally, the series was about the relationship between the two cultures. The tyranny of the apes over the humans. That's what played best on the series. The minute you had the apes wrangling with each other or talking, it got dreadfully boring. It's also hard to do anything like *Planet of the Apes* on a seven-day schedule."

Although *Planet* had the ideal opportunity for drawing social parallels with twentieth century Earth, Senensky feels that "it kind of copped out. It became more of an adventure series. Their options seemed to have gotten a little screwed up. They set up a premise that didn't leave them much room to maneuver. In hindsight, wouldn't it have been more interesting if they had looked at the Civil War in the 1800s for story material? They could have used those parallels about slavery in the series. The white population are the slaves and the gentry are the apes. That's what the first movie was about. That's what got lost in the series."

Nevertheless, the director enjoyed his stint. "Roddy was marvelous. He was very dedicated to the show. Because of the glue and rubber used in the masks, there was no way he could work a 14 to 18 hour day. Twelve hours was his maximum." Senensky also had respect for the producers, including the late Stan Hough. "Stan was a marvelous producer. The main thing with Stan was to get the job done. When you work in TV, a lot of it is getting it committed to film. It's something of an artistic assembly line. You don't wait around until you get the inspiration. Looking back on *Planet of the Apes,* it was a terribly ambitious project for the economics and scheduling of series television."

"The makeup factor killed the show," notes writer Arthur Brown, Jr. "It was a doomed series. Anytime you translate from the motion picture screen to television, you lose a certain punch." Browne recalls the plight of the actors who played gorillas on the show. "Most of the exteriors were shot at the Fox ranch at Malibu. The temperatures were hitting over 100 degrees. Apes were falling down and passing out from the heat."

Tom McDonough, a gorilla stand-in and extra, admits, "The makeup was miserable. We carried umbrellas for shade. It was especially hard for me because I have blue eyes, requiring me to wear contact lenses to make my eyes brown. With the dust kicked up by the horses, it was terrible. The makeup took three and a half hours to apply. Your head was completely enclosed in hair, rubber and glue. We had to drink through straws."

Assistant director Bill Derwin adds, "*Planet* was physically the toughest TV series ever made. How the actors and extras playing the apes handled it, I'll never know. Imagine what it would be like to be even slightly claustrophobic and to wear heavy, hot, scratchy uniforms. And to work at the Fox ranch where it always seemed to be 110 degrees. You're on a horse you can't ride, and you have to hit your marks and remember your dialogue. Most of them could manage, but for those who couldn't, it was impossible to fake it. A couple of actors literally fell apart. They ripped off their makeup and tore off their uniforms."

Veteran stuntman George Robotham pleads guilty. Robotham had tackled everything from dangerous explosions to underwater stunts, but he could not face the demands of being a gorilla. "In a mishmash of 5,000 fights and 5,000 falls in my career, *Planet of the Apes* is one show I don't want to remember," he says. "I spent two hours with that makeup on my face. Paul Stader was

The spaceship mock-up used in the original *Planet of the Apes* movie (1968) was reused for the first episode of the TV series. Copyright 1968 Twentieth Century–Fox.

the stunt coordinator, and I went to Paul and said, 'Paul, I don't need this crap. Let somebody else do it. See you later!' The makeup was miserable."

Art Wallace got a kick out of watching apes milling around the studio, and recalls, "Right across the street Mel Brooks was making the film *Young Frankenstein*. One guy in an ape costume was standing by the building when Mel walked outside. The ape went up to Mel and said, 'Hey, Mel! Remember me? We worked on such and such a show.' Mel just looked at him and said, 'Are you working now?' I thought that was funny."

What wasn't funny was how quickly *Planet of the Apes* got skewered by the network after months of hype. Originally scheduled to play Tuesday evenings, the series was shifted to Friday nights. The premiere episode grabbed a 34 share. It was a decent showing, but hardly comparable to the 46 share scored by its competitor on NBC, *Sanford and Son*. From then on, the ratings dipped. Although the series ranked as the second most popular show with the 2-11 age group, it was not getting a wide enough audience. A month after its premiere, CBS began making noises about scuttling the show.

TV Guide reported that *Planet's* biggest disappointment was its inability to attract older viewers. According to Art Wallace, CBS programming wizard Fred Silverman hailed the first episode of *Planet* as "the best first episode of a TV series I've ever seen." He was considerably less enthusiastic when he was quoted by *TV Guide* that fall. "Of people 50 and over, apparently only four are watching," Silverman noted sarcastically. "Two old ladies in Iowa and a couple who own a zoo."

In addition, the president of CBS, William Paley, didn't want the series on his network to begin with. The decision to end the series was swift, and after four months on the air, *Planet of the Apes* silently vanished.

Bill Derwin felt that the series may have stepped on some toes. "Some people thought the series was racist. The power and cruelty of the apes was toned down. The series soon became *Planet of the Benevolent Apes*."

"I wasn't surprised by the cancellation, though naturally I was disappointed," says Booth Colman. "I had hopes of a long run. I got no formal notice from the studio that we were over, but their long faces told me the tale. With the right stories and time slot, it could have lasted. Universal studios, after all, got a lot of mileage from a couple of monsters in a cape and neck screws!"

"Two episodes before the end, we were waiting for word from CBS to pick us up," recalls Ron Harper. "It didn't happen. I asked Stan Hough, 'What are we going to do?' He said, 'I'm going to make several more episodes. Maybe they'll change their minds.' We shot two more episodes. On a Monday morning, Stan called Jim and me in and said, 'This is going to be the last episode.' So Jim and I took our stunt friends out to a four-hour lunch!"

Although a dud by American ratings standards, all 14 episodes were run in England the following year. The series was a smash. It also proved popular in other foreign countries. In 1980, Fox studios released ten episodes in the form of TV movies for syndication.

Although the series' cancellation was a disappointment to Harper, he can chuckle over the series' afterlife. Occasionally, he's invited to return to the Planet of the Apes, but in a more leisurely form. "I was invited to a telethon in Australia with Mickey Dolenz of *The Monkees* a few years ago. *Planet of the Apes* had just started running down there. When I got off the plane in Sydney, I was greeted by a guy dressed up like an ape! It's very nice that people still remember the show."

CAST NOTES

Roddy McDowall (Galen): Born 1928. The English-born McDowall was already a child actor when his family moved to America in 1940. He made the transition to adult star, including appearances in the films *Cleopatra* (1963), *The Poseidon Adventure* (1972) and the *Fright Night* films in the 1980s. He's also a noted photographer.

Ron Harper (Virdon): Born 1935. One of Harper's most memorable TV series was the World War II action show *Garrison's Gorillas* (1967-68). He went into daytime TV (*Love of Life*, *Capital*) in the 1970s and continues making guest appearances on prime-time TV.

James Naughton (Burke): Born 1945. A successful Broadway actor, Naughton was one of the stars of the acclaimed 1992 *Brooklyn Bridge* series.

Mark Lenard (Urko): Born 1927. Well known as Mr. Spock's father on *Star Trek* and as a regular on TV's *Here Come the Brides* (1968–70). Lenard is active on stage and does TV commercial voice work.

Booth Colman (Dr. Zaius): Born 1923. This Oregon-born actor received his education at the University of Washington. A veteran actor with hundreds of TV credits, every winter he appears in Michigan to do the play *A Christmas Carol*.

EPISODE GUIDE

Escape from Tomorrow
Astronauts Virdon and Burke are captured and their spaceship confiscated by gorillas. Wr: Art Wallace. Dir: Don Weis.
Farrow (Royal Dano); Veska (Woodrow Parfrey); Arno (Bobby Porter); Grundig (William Beckley); Ullman (Biff Elliot); Proto (Jerome Thor); Turvo (Ron Stein); Man (Alvin Hammer).

The Gladiators
Burke escapes from gladiatorial games where humans are pitted against each other. However, he has to rescue Virdon, who is scheduled for the next game. Wr: Art Wallace. Dir: Don McDougall.
Tolar (William Smith); Dalton (Marc Singer); Barlow (John Hoyt); Jason (Pat Renella); Gorilla sgt. (Eddie Fontaine); Gorilla #1 (Ron Stein); Gorilla (Nick Dimitri); Gorilla #2 (Jim Stader); Man (Andy Albin).

The Trap
Earthquakes trap Burke and Urko in a subway, where the two must forge an uneasy alliance to survive. Wr: Edward J. Lakso. Dir: Arnold Laven.
Miller (John Milford); Lisa Miller (Cindy Eilbacher); Zako (Norman Alden); Olam (Eldon Burke); Jick Miller (Mickey LeClair); Mary Miller (Wallace Earl); Old woman (Gail Bonney); Mema (Ron Stein).

The Good Seeds
The earthlings work at a gorilla farm, but when a chimp believes the humans have cursed his prize cow, he plans to turn them over to the gorillas. Wr: Robert W. Lenski. Dir: Don Weis.
Anto (Geoffrey Deuel); Zantes (Jacqueline Scott); Polar (Lonny Chapman); Remus (Bobby Porter); Jilla (Eileen Dietz Elber); Gorilla officer (Dennis Cross); Police gorilla (John Garwood); Patrol rider (Michael Carr); Gorilla (Fred Lerner).

The Legacy
A scientific bunker in a ruined city could provide the answer to returning home, but Virdon is captured and imprisoned with a woman and boy. Wr: Robert Hamner. Dir: Bernard McEveety.

Arn (Zina Bethune); Kraik (Jackie Earle Haley); Gorilla capt. (Robert Phillips); Scientist (Jon Lormer); Human (Victor Killian); Gorilla sgt. (Wayne Foster).

Tomorrow's Tide

The astronauts are forced to work in shark-infested waters as fishermen, and Galen's well-meaning efforts to free them make matters worse. Wr: Robert W. Lenski. Dir: Don McDougall.

Hurion (Roscoe Lee Browne); Bandor (Jay Robinson); Soma (Kathleen Bracken); Romar (James Storm); Gahto (John McLiam); Human (Frank Orsatti); Drayman #2 (Larry Ellis).

The Surgeon

Critically injured, Virdon is taken to Galen's ex-fiancee, a surgeon. She can save him with an experimental blood transfusion, but Urko is closing in. Wr: Barry Oringer. Dir: Arnold Laven.

Kira (Jacqueline Scott); Leander (Martin E. Brooks); Travin (Michael Strong); Arna (Jamie Smith Jackson); Dr. Stole (David Naughton); Brigid (Diana Hale); Jordo (Phil Montgomery); Haman/Lafer (Ron Stein); Human (Raymond Mayo).

The Deception

While trying to expose the leader of a renegade gorilla band that terrorizes human villagers, the trio meets a blind chimp. She falls in love with Burke. Wr: Anthony Lawrence, Ken Spears, Joe Ruby, story by Anthony Lawrence. Dir: Don McDougall.

Fauna (Jane Actman); Sestus (John Milford); Perdix (Baynes Barron); Zon (Pat Renella); Jasko (Hal Baylor); Macor (Tom McDonough); Chilot (Eldon Burke); Krona (Ron Stein).

Memory Flash—Anthony Lawrence: "Everyone laughed when I said, `What about a blind chimp?' Gradually, I got them to go along with it."

The Horse Race

Virdon rides against a gorilla in a horse race to save a boy from execution. But Urko has instructed his gorillas to shoot Virdon during the race. Wr: David P. Lewis, Booker Bradshaw. Dir: Jack Starrett.

Barlow (John Hoyt); Martin (Morgan Woodward); Zandar (Richard Devon); Gregor (Meegan King); Kagan (Wesley Fuller); Prefect (Henry Levin); Zilo (Joe Tornatore); Damon (Russ Marin).

The Interrogation

Flashbacks to Burke's life on Earth highlight this story of a female chimp who uses ancient brain-washing techniques on the astronaut. Galen tries to free Burke with the help of his parents. Wr: Richard Collins. Dir: Alf Kjellin.

Wanda (Beverly Garland); Ann (Anne Seymour); Yalu (Normann Burton); Dr. Malthus (Harry Townes); Susan (Lynn Benesch); Gorilla officer (Lee Delano); Peasant ape (Eldon Burke); Gorilla leader (Ron Stein); Gorilla lt. (Wayne Foster).

The Tyrant

Aboro the gorilla is extorting wheat from local farmers, and is plotting to kill Urko. Wr: Walter Black. Dir: Ralph Senensky.

Aboro (Percy Rodrigues); Daku (Joseph Ruskin); Janor (Michael Conrad); Augustus (Tom Troupe); Mikal (James Daughton); Gorilla driver (Gary Coombs); Gola (Arlen Stuart); Gorilla (Ron Stein); Sam (Klair Bybee).

Memory Flash—Ralph Senensky: "It was the twelfth show shot, and the studio wasn't happy about spending extra money on a series that wasn't going to be picked up. We shot 15 pages in one day. When you're shooting talking apes, it doesn't necessarily make the best of drama. Percy Rodrigues, however, was sensational."

The Cure

The trio enters a village swept by malaria and tries to help a chimpanzee doctor develop a cure before Urko and his gorillas arrive. Wr: Edward J. Lakso. Dir: Bernard McEveety.

Amy (Sondra Locke); Zoran (David Sheiner); Kava (Ron Soble); Talbert (George Wallace); Oranguatang (Biff Elliot); Mason (Albert Cole); Inta (Eldon Burke); Neesa (Ron Stein); Man (Charles Leland).

The Liberator

Mercenary humans who worship a temple are capturing other humans and turning them over to gorillas. Wr: Howard Dimsdale. Dir: Arnold Laven.

Brun (John Ireland); Miro (Ben Andrews); Talia (Jennifer Ashley); Clim (Peter G. Skinner); Villager (Mark Bailey); Gorilla (Ron Stein); Gorilla #2 (Tom McDonough).

Up Above the World So High

A human's hang glider is exploited by a female chimp who plans to drop fragmentation bombs on Ape City. Wr: Arthur Brown, Jr., S. Bar David (Shimon Wincelberg), story by S. Bar David. Dir: John Meredyth Lucas.

Leuric (Frank Aletter); Carsia (Joanna Barnes); Konag (Martin E. Brooks); Council orang (William Beckley); Human driver (Glenn Wilder); Gorilla guard (Ron Stein); Gorilla trooper (Eldon Burke).

Memory Flash—Frank Aletter: "The first couple of movies were really good. It was a great concept. The only uncomfortable thing about the episode was that they shot it on the Pacific Ocean. Since my character's hang glider crashes into the ocean, we had to be in the water and it was cold! We wore wetsuits underneath our costumes."

Powers of Matthew Star
September 1982–September 1983

A young prince from the planet Quadris comes to Earth to hide from assassins. With his mentor, Walter Shepherd, he learns of his responsibilities and how to manage his strange psychic powers while studying in school.

Cast: Matthew Star (Peter Barton); Walt Shepherd (Louis Gossett, Jr.); Pam Elliott (Amy Steel); Bob Alexander (Chip Frye); Coach Curtis (Barry Van Dyke); General Tucker (John Crawford); Wendell Wymore (James Karen).

Created by: Steven deSouza; *Developed by:* Daniel Wilson, Harve Bennett, Robert Earll, Allan Balter; *Supervising Producer:* Bruce Johnson, Robert Earll, Allan Balter; *Producer:* Carl Pingitore, Martin Goldstein, Fran Sears, Steven E. DeSouza; *Executive Producer:* Daniel Wilson, Harve Bennett, Bruce Lansbury; *Co-Producer:* Gil Grant; *Associate Producer:* Christopher Chulack and Mervin B. Dayan, Jay Scherberth, Scott Winant, Karl Epstein, Linda Feitelson; *Executive Story Consultant/Editor:* Judy Burns, Richard Christian Matheson and Thomas Szollosi, Gregory S. Dinallo; NBC/Paramount; 60 minutes.

The basic idea behind *Powers of Matthew Star* was to tell the story of a super-powered teenager, growing up on Earth but not a celebrity. Creator and producer Steven deSouza remembers the NBC television network asking for a teenage Superman.

"The *Superman* movie had [just] come out. I came up with this concept, and [the network] liked the element of Superman as a high school student and he had problems with football teams and couldn't join because he was too good." The inspiration comes largely from a segment of the *Superman* film when young Clark Kent laments his problems in high school, with girls and with the difficulty of hiding his powers while playing football. "That's what they were looking for," says deSouza.

"When we went to cast the show, the network insisted on an actor [Gerald O'Loughlin] to play the mentor character which is completely miscast. He used a heavy accent, he talked in 'dis' 'dem' and 'dose'. We ended up making him the janitor because you couldn't believe he was anything else. There was just no sophistication to the character. He's a very common-cut type of guy. There's no way this character could be Obi-Wan Kenobi."

But "Starr Knight" was the premise pilot of the show. DeSouza explains that in television filmmaking, there are actually two kinds of pilots. A premise pilot sets up for the viewer the premise of the show and the characters he will be seeing in the episodes to follow. The episode pilot is simply the first episode; it is typical of the series and could just as easily air in the seventh week as in the first.

In "Starr Knight," written by deSouza, then-named *David* Starr does not know his heritage or his powers. His mentor, Max, played by O'Loughlin keeps the knowledge from him so he can grow up "normal" on Earth. In the course of the story, his powers are needed, and David has to activate them in order to save some lives.

"I thought it was a great idea," remembers star Peter Barton fondly. "Matthew was the kind

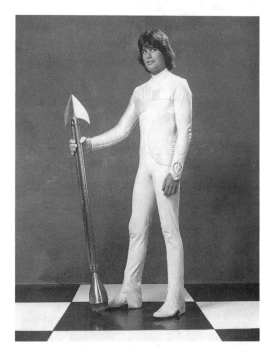

Peter Barton stars as Matthew Star, who seems to be an ordinary 16-year-old, but is in reality a prince from a distant planet with special powers: telekinesis, telepathy, and clairvoyance. Copyright 1981 NBC/Paramount.

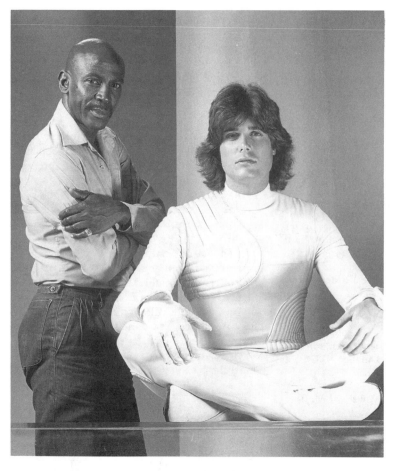

Matthew Star (Peter Barton) with his guardian, Walt Shepherd (Emmy Award winner Lou Gossett, Jr.). Copyright 1981 NBC/Paramount.

Earth. Let's find another clever way of doing a premise pilot.' So I said, 'Ok, let's do the one where he discovers for the first time he's not human.' Again, we borrowed from Superman, because in the original *Superman* comic he's not told when he's a young man that he's from another planet."

NBC liked the pilot, but before going to series, a few changes were needed. Louis Gossett, Jr., replaced O'Loughlin as the mentor, now named Walt Shepherd, and the lead was renamed *Matthew Star*. Now well aware of his own powers, with Walt's guidance Matthew would shape his strengths and weaknesses so that when called to return to his home planet, he would be ready to reclaim the throne. Meanwhile, Matthew had high school and a girlfriend to keep him busy.

of character that basically I've played a lot in life—characters who are trying to do what's right in life, and fight the forces of evil—and I felt very strongly about Matthew being that type of individual. So it was a very good role for me at that time of my life.

"I thought the first pilot was what the character was all about. I thought it was a very good episode, but then [the network] wanted to fine-tune things. But I thought it was a very nice, sensitive story. It goes deeper than just a prince from another planet who's going to go back some day and save his people. It's the story of a young man growing into manhood and accepting responsibility for himself and other people."

DeSouza says that while he was writing the premise pilot, the network said to him, "'We don't want a science fiction show. We don't want a show where the spaceship lands the little boy on

"The second pilot was really not a new pilot at all. It was exactly the same rules as the first one," says deSouza. "It was a reconceptualization of the premise of the show. And he was the rightful leader of the government of his planet. He was brought here to be safe. He was living in hiding because there might be assassins coming after him some day. That was my original premise!"

Unfortunately, *Powers of Matthew Star* had some bad luck in its evolution on television. During the filming of "Jackal," the second pilot, Barton had a fire-related accident. Ron Satlof, a director of two *Powers* episodes, recalls the incident vividly. "Peter was a young actor who was always trying to do something extra," he remembers. "That's why he got burned. He was trying to do more than he was asked to do, and that cost him."

The scene was this: Louis Gossett was tied

up in a chair, surrounded by lit magnesium flares in a junkyard set. Barton was supposed to come into the scene and drag Gossett out of the circle of flares while avoiding some falling debris. Stuntmen had already done the important bits of action for the actors. But, for close-up purposes, Barton and Gossett did portions of the scene to match with the stunt segments. "What Peter was instructed to do was come in and get to the chair, and say dialogue," explains Satlof. "It was just a close-up. He didn't have to repeat any of the moves because the stunt had already been done. Basically, he just steps into the shot, says a few words to Lou and starts making motions of moving the chair back, from which we'd cut to the stuntman doing all that. Instead of that, he leaned the chair back and he *actually* dragged it past the circle of flares. He tripped. He fell on one of the flares."

"Lou was very smart," says Barton, remembering the incident. "They were talking about tying his hands, and he said, 'You're not tying my hands.' If he was tied in the chair he wouldn't have been able to ... I mean, he rolled off me very quickly. He fell on top of me, and I fell on top of the flare. Because he wasn't tied, he was able to maneuver out of there very fast, which allowed me to roll off the flare just as fast."

"It's horrible that it did happen, and thank god he's okay," remarks Satlof.

With Barton out of commission for several months, the production was shut down. Because the network had faith in the series, filming restarted as soon as Barton was able.

"I was very happy when we came back to start filming the series [after the pilot], and I felt we were on the right track," continues Barton. "But after the accident—and I think there were four months of recuperating—I had to come back and wear all of the burn garments ... It's kind of sad. I was still enthusiastic, but something had shifted in me. It wore on me to have gone through that trauma. We still had some pretty good episodes after that, but I felt there was a whole spontaneity and enthusiasm before the accident, and after the accident, something changed."

When Hollywood shoots episodic television, often the filming order is different from the airing order. "The dolphin ["Experiments"] and football ["Winning"] episodes—those were done before I was burned," notes Barton. "We were maybe a quarter of the way into the filming of "Jackal" [when the accident occured]. You can even see the difference. If you look at the footage

of where ... I get into the junkyard, and I hop the fence, and I'm running around, and my hair's longer, that's *before* I was burned. And as soon as poles are about to fall over and the flares are lit, that's where I got burned, and then they picked up the footage of me rescuing Lou five months later. And the scenes where I'm meeting people on the bus, that was filmed *after* I was burned."

Two other factors may have also contributed to the show's difficult startup. A writer's strike occurred during the period, and one of the early producers, Allan Balter, died from a heart attack—during a board meeting while excitedly pitching the premise of the show to network executives.

The show ran the first completed episodes, but someone on the decision-making level still wanted to fine-tune the show. Matthew Star changed from a young boy growing up and learning about life to a young boy becoming a secret agent for the U.S. government. Harve Bennett, the second producer, went out, and in came Bruce Lansbury, well known for *Mission Impossible*, *Wild, Wild, West* and many other fan favorites.

"And what was Bruce's claim to fame?" says Barton. "*I, Spy.* He was brought in to sort of fix it again. It was too much. There was too much tension. I loved Danny Wilson, the first producer; I loved Harve Bennett, the second producer. There was one episode with Jeff Corey and Julie Newmar, where they come from my planet, and that was one of the better episodes that I enjoyed. It had a nice direction there. It was more Star Trekky, and we were getting into that. Now, all of a sudden, it's *I, Spy* and here we are. I'm supposed to be Robert Culp and Lou's supposed to be Bill Cosby. It went too far. It became *I, Spy* with science fiction. In the beginning it was like family science fiction, and now we're doing *I, Spy*, which is not what it's supposed to be, and it got too confusing."

DeSouza wasn't around to follow through on his pet project. After Barton's accident, he jumped studio to Universal, even though the network tried to get him back.

"They went off track in the last nine episodes of the season," complains deSouza. "They brought in a government character and created missions for our government. I think that was the mistake for the series because they severed all their ties to what made the series unique."

DeSouza believes that *Powers* would have had better success "if the show had dealt with the problems of a superhuman kid fitting in, his normal life, with periodic danger, excitement, and mystery due to his special nature. The show would have worked. They showed the lighter approach with *My Secret Identity*, a Universal studios show that lasted four or five years in syndication. It was comedic, not quite a sitcom, it had a lighter touch but it was exactly that idea."

On a happier note, Barton remembers working with Amy Steel and Lou Gossett as a highlight of his experience with the show. "I still am so fond of Amy," he says. "She'll always be a real special person in my mind. The same way that Pam, her character, had that tremendous strength for Matthew, Amy had that strength for Peter. I really just loved Amy Steel. She was the greatest. And Lou was a fantastic person. He made me look so good. Working with the man, all you had to do was be around the guy and he was so charismatic, he gave so much positive energy. I can't say enough about either of them. I wish that they kept us all together rather than splitting us up and taking Amy out of there and making us *I, Spy*."

Two actors had the opportunity to direct episodes: Leonard Nimoy and, for the final episode, Lou Gossett. Barton says, "It's always nice to work with an actor who's directing because they come from more of an actor's point of view. It doesn't mean that the project is going to come out any better than if it's a regular director, but they're a lot more understanding and sensitive to an actor's processes. There are directors who are sensitive too, but an actor who is a director is just logically going to have more of that. It was nice working with Leonard and Lou."

Some TV critics complained that Barton looked too old to be playing a high school teenager. Barton disagrees. "I was 24, and I think I looked pretty much 16 or 17 years old," he insists. "I mean, it's the same thing with Ralph Macchio [in the *Karate Kid* feature films]. He was 25 playing 16. Same difference. If the illusion is bought, who cares? It's like *Beverly Hills 90210*. Those kids are *old*. I thought in *Matthew Star* I was more like a teenager as they really are—confused, don't know where they are going, don't know who the hell they are—and *Beverly Hills 90210*, *these* guys are really *together*. Even though I was 24, I thought the portrayal of a confused teenager was more believable than what they're portraying on *Beverly Hills 90210* … but it's an illusion. Acting's an illusion."

In summary, Barton looks back at *Powers of Matthew Star*'s strengths and shortcomings and what would have been if the show had continued. "What worked for me," he says, "was when they were dealing with the science fiction and I was the prince from another planet and I got involved in the lives of my classmates. I liked that. That's the way 13 of our episodes were. And when they changed stream and made us CIA agents and we were going to tackle these big *I, Spy* sort of things, that didn't work for me."

Barton also discounts a revival TV movie to resolve the premise. "I wouldn't think so. The whole premise was that he was here for training. I was here to grow into a man and someday go and take back the planet. It was like Luke Skywalker, having the Force training and going back to deal with one's self. All in all, it was a well-intentioned show and a wholesome thing, and I'm happy I was able to be a part of it."

Cast Notes

Peter Barton (Matthew Star): Born 1958. Barton graduated to daytime television with a popular role on the *Young and the Restless* in the early 1990s. During spring 1994, he co-starred with Gene Barry in the prime-time CBS show *Burke's Law*.

Louis Gossett Jr. (Walter Shepherd): Born 1936 in Brooklyn. Gossett won an Emmy for his role as Fiddler in *Roots* (1977) and an Oscar as a drill instructor in *Officer and a Gentleman* (1982). Gossett has kept busy in films with *Iron Eagle* (1986), the science fiction actioner *Enemy Mine* (1985), and *Diggstown* (1992).

Amy Steel (Pam Elliott): After this show, Steel continued acting in roles on *Matlock*, a Perry Mason TV movie, *Quantum Leap* and *Space Rangers*. She's also a fashion designer.

Episode Guide

Jackal

Matthew Starr and Walt Shepherd, two aliens living in southern California, are hiding from assassins from the planet Quadris. Unknown to Matthew, two assassins have arrived on Earth and are after him. Meanwhile, General Tucker of the U.S. Air Force approaches them and tells them he knows who they are. This was the second pilot for the series. Wr: Robert Earll and Allan Balter. Dir: Ron Satlof.

Float (Judson Scott); Cindy During (Maylo McCaslin); Brian (John Laughlin); Mr. Heller. (Michael Fairman); Nan (Adrienne Grant); Richard Lopez (Justin Mastro); Dawn (Betsy Russell); Bus driver (Susan Ruttan); Sergeant (Terrance Beasor); Air woman (Jessica Hoyt); First student (Thom Ford).

The Accused
Walt's arrested for a murder that his drug-pushing double is responsible for. His only hope to prove his innocence lies with Matthew. Wr: Gregory S. Dinallo. Dir: Ron Satlof.

Howard (John Aprea); Brancato (Carmen Argenziano); Crawford (Phil Hamilton); Judge Condon (Lynn Hamilton); April (Margaret Avery); Bret (Fred Lerner); Sarkis (Chuck Hicks); Williams (Terry Burns); First guard (Vincent Duke Milani); Smith (Dick Durock); Ticket agent (Jerry Martin); Engineer (Kenneth Phillips); Operator (Martin Dolciamore); Carson (Bob Minor); Danny (Cameron Smith); Frank (Martin Brumer); Bill Chambers (Stuart Pankin); Tom (Thomas Byrd).

Daredevil
When a film is being shot at Crestridge High, Matthew runs into an old friend who aspires to be a stuntman. Wr: Jeffrey Allen Scott. Dir: Bruce Bilson.

Frank Trenton (Bill Daily); Pete (Paul Regina); Mr. Heller (Michael Fairman); Burt Garner (Kaz Garas); Girl #1 (Verda Marie Bridges); Crewman (Ralph Steadman); Cheerleader (Kimberly Sands); Cheerleader (Corinne Bohrer).

Genius
During a science fair, a classmate has invented a revolutionary new paint that nullifies Matthew's powers. On closer examination, Walt and Matthew realize the paint's formula can be a highly dangerous explosive. Wr: Tom Greene. Dir: Bob Claver.

Mr. Hansley (Earl Boen); Mrs. Kraft (Fay DeWitt); Jerry (David Wallace); Monica Kraft (Margaret Fitzgerald); Mr. Kraft (Alan North); Mr. Heller (Michael Fairman); Weatherman (Larry Carroll); Security guard (Dan Barrows); Construction foreman (Reid Cruickshanks); Gardener (Ernie Fuentes); Computer operator (Randolph Dreyfuss).

Prediction
During an illegal road race, Matthew discovers a new power of telepathy and learns that a classmate has also gained powers of precognition. Those powers fortell Walt and Matthew's death! Wr: Richard Christian Matheson and Thomas Szollosi. Dir: Guy Magar.

Becky Vance (Suzanne Adkinson); Vance (Arthur Roberts); Kay (Lenora May); Shawn (Joseph Taggart); Nick (Brian Kale); Charlie (Steven Apostle Peg); Richard Lopez (Justin Mastro); Policeman #1 (Tom Gagen); Coach (Peggy Kaye); Policeman #2 (Gene Ryals); Male driver (Merritt Olsen).

The Italian Caper
When a secret weapon is stolen in Italy, General Tucker sends Walt and Matthew to Rome to retrieve it. But the stakes are raised when General Tucker is kidnapped. Wr: James M. Miller. Dir: Guy Magar.

Giancarlo (Michael Constantine); Zealotta (Robert Davi); Adrianna (Donna Cyrus); Pileggi (Michael Tucci); Praeger (Alex Rodine); Mr. Heller (Michael Fairman); Bowen (James O'Sullivan); Woman on bus (Renata Vanni); Catania (E.M. Margolese); Monica (Carrie Cavalier); Ned (Andrew Ethier); Grandpa (Cesare Buia).

Winning
Interested in joining the football team, Matthew finds an obstacle in Tony, who is making moves on the field ... and with Pam. Wr: Gregory S. Dinallo. Dir: Ron Satlof.

Tony Garcia (David Labiosa); Football player (Tojo Fairman); Second referee (Douglas Johnson); Third referee (Dave Adams); First student (Gene Pietragallo); Collins (Sandra Friebel); Second student (Michelle LaMar); Lopez (Justin Mastro); Radio announcer (Jay B. Larson).

Endurance
While on a mountain survival hike, Pam sprains her leg. A ranger warns her and her fellow hikers about escaped mental patients in the area. Wr: Ruel Fischmann. Dir: Paul Krasny.

Fletcher (Mike Chieffo); Ted (Grant Wilson); Lisa (Krista Errickson); Bill Campbell (Spencer Milligan); Jackie (John Dennis Johnston); Anne (Jenny Parsons).

Triangle
When Pam's treasure-hunting uncle disappears in the Bermuda Triangle, Matthew hops on a plane with Pam on a search to find him. Wr: Richard Christian Matheson and Thomas Szollosi. Dir: Leonard Nimoy.

Vohll (Jeff Corey); Nian (Julie Newmar); Ron Elliot (Robert Sampson); Nicky O'Keefe (Rudy Solari); Caroline Elliott (Susan Bjurman); Stewardess (Patti Cohenour); Helicopter clerk (John Wyler); Party kid (Andrew Ethier); Grandma (Merie Earle).

Mother
A fortune teller gives a ring to Matthew, and Walt realizes the ring belongs to Matthew's mother. Wr: Walter Koenig. Dir: Ron Satlof.

Fortune teller (Tricia O'Neil); Vate (Jeff Cooper); Garn (Don Stroud); Zond (Jeff Davis); Little girl (Jennifer George); Wheel vendor (Allan Wisch); Balloon vendor (Irwin Simon).

Experiment
Matthew discovers he can read the minds of other species when he communicates with a dolphin. Fearing scientists are unduly experimenting on the dolphin, Matthew breaks into the lab to investigate. Wr: Thomas Szollosi and Richard Christian Matheson. Dir: Gunnar Hellstrom.

Dr. Simon Bernard (John Reilly); Dana Eastland (Amanda McBroom); Lee (Clyde Kusatsu); Ms. Johnson (Meredith Duncan); Park guard (John Herzog); Gate guard (Ed Call).

The Fugitive
When Matthew is accidentally scanned while at the

hospital, Walt becomes upset and dashes to the hospital to remove any evidence that might expose Matt as an alien. But Walt suddenly falls ill. Wr: Judy Burns. Dir: Jeffrey Hayden.

Dr. Stewart (Sam Weisman); Dr. Jerry Linsey (Danny Goldman); Dr. Baker (Ray Vitte); Bubba (Wyatt Johnson); Police officer (Jack Yates); Police sergeant (Michael Griswold); Technician (Christine Avila); Guard (Hank Robinson); E.R. nurse (Constance Ball); Nurse on elevator (Louise Heath); Surfer (Michael Peterson).

Matthew Star: D.O.A.

Walt and Matt are summoned by the government to investigate a series of deaths of underworld mobsters at a hospital. Wr: Bruce Shelly. Dir: Leslie H. Martinson.

Dr. Braff (Nicholas Pryor); Donzelli (Pat Corley); Dr. Benson (David Paymer); Clegg (Luke Askew); Kerri Saxon (Amanda Wyss); Second brother (Phil Brock); Fiske (Matthew Tobin); Foreman (Wendell W. Wright); First brother (Demetre Phillips); Nurse (Starletta DuPois); Marla Evans (Molly Cheek); Mr. Stein (George Sawaya).

Racer's Edge

The government once again calls on Walt and Matthew, this time to protect the life of a motorcycle racer. Her father is an important politician and is engaging in top-secret negotiations that might threaten her life. Wr: Luciano Comici. Dir: Corey Allen.

Daughter (Doran Clark); Lloyd Strickland (Don Gordon); Anthony Garcia (Ron Joseph); Ed Hernandez (Alex Colon); Desk clerk (Dennis Robertson); Terri (Katherine Kelly Lang); Stewart (Tom McDonald); Cliff Delancey (Gerard Prendergast); Burnside (Joel Brooks).

Dead Man's Hand

Wymore calls upon Walt and Matthew to curtail the gambling activities of a ruthless career criminal after all other agents have failed. Wr: David Bennett Carren. Dir: Vincent McEveety.

Dave Wellman (Richard Herd); Gregorian (Jack Somack); Wolfson (Raymond St. Jacques); Dan Veetz (Richard Kuss); Dalco (Arthur Taxier); Alice Wellman (Peggy McCay); Lisa Wellman (Judie Aronson); Craddock (Louis Quinn); Waiter #2 (Eric Trules); Technician (Joe Howard); Man in audience (Ed McCready); Woman player (Patty Regan).

36 Hours

Astronauts have 36 hours to live when terrorists steal electronic gear that is needed to land the space shuttle. Wr: David Bennett Carren, story by William Mageean and Gil Grant. Dir: Barry Crane.

Col. Ezra Conlan (Scott Hylands); Lara Boston (Penny Peyser); Martin Ragland (Joshua Bryant); Dr. Paul Autry (Bruce French); Rudolph Beckman (Jan-Ivan Dorin); Naughton (Colin Hamilton); Hook (Michael Lemon); Manager (Hal Floyd); Guard (Charles Walker); Henchman (Buddy Farmer); Also with Raleigh Bond.

The Quadrian Caper

Walt and Matthew run into thieves who are plotting to steal diamonds while helping Wymore to return a necklace that was illegally borrowed by Wymore's nephew. Wr: Bruce Shelley. Dir: Guy Magar.

Deke Griffin (Dennis Lipscomb); Donna Tait (Laura Johnson); Cliff Miller (Ron Max); Gary Wymore (Gary Imhoff); Guard #1 (Karl Johnson); Tattooed man (Lex Winter); Frank Lund (Felice Orlandi); Tattoo artist (Shirley Stoler).

Brain Drain

The United States is experiencing a brain drain of important scientists. Wymore wants Matthew and Walt to investigate a suspicious dating service called "Heart's Desire" that may be linked to the disappearing men. Wr: George McIdowie, story by William Mageean and Gil Grant. Dir: Leslie H. Martinson.

Weston (John Vernon); Evita (Sharon Acker); Pierce Benton (Richard Venture); Christianne (Lisa Lucas); Lenore (Lynn Longos); Roxanne (Anne Marie Martin); Kerry (Sheila De Windt); Receptionist (Janit Baldwin); Donald Emmett (David Moses); Omar Mustafa (Carl Strand); Reporter (Joe Horvath); General (Don Eitner).

The Great Waldo Shepherd

When a plane containing top-secret NATO plans is stolen from an air show, Walt and Matthew go undercover as a pilot and wing walker. Wr: Bill Taub, story by Gil Grant and William Mageean. Dir: Barry Crane.

Terry (Terrence McNally); Ryan Wilson (Byron Thames); Lou Daggot; Christopher Goutman; Sheldon Pinsky (Floyd Levine); Saunders (John La Fayette); Latimer (Scott Marlowe); Gracie Harrington (Nancy Holmes).

Road Rebels

Laser crystals are being stolen from Silicon Valley and sold to foreign agents. Walt and Matthew must infiltrate a road-racing punk group to find out who the thieves are and where the crystals have been hidden. Wr: Mark Jones. Dir: Barbara Peeters.

Brad (Jonathan Gries); Hanks (Beau Starr); Penny (Felicia Landsbury); Harriett (Dana Freeman); Simonson (Don Knight); Corey (Barry Berman); Stella (Marguerite De Lain); Policeman (Jay Lomack); Van Dyke (Byrne Piven).

Swords and Quests

Matthew joins a sword-and-sorcery game, which is a ploy by a toy company to steal top-secret information from a scientist. Meanwhile, Matthew is in danger of dying and Walt must find him quickly. Wr: Lee Sheldon. Dir: Lou Gossett, Jr.

Steven Mason (Kevin Hooks); Mandy Tucker (Michele Tobin); Keating (Hari Rhodes); Katya (Martine Beswick); Hugh Travis (Charley Lang); Bill (Tim Wead); Dr. Tucker (John H. Fields); Herb (Jimmy Greenleaf); Security guard (Will Hare); Fred (Leif Green).

Starr Knight

In this slightly different concept of the series, David Starr is living in Southern California with his mentor, Max. David doesn't realize he's capable of strange powers and that he's from Quadris. But when a school bus nearly falls over a cliff, he begins to realize he's very different from other school children. When David meets Pam's parents, he's able to hear their thoughts, frightening him into the city streets. This is the first pilot for the series. Wr: Steven DeSouza. Dir: Ivan Nagy.

Principal (Maxwell Caufield); Fleming (Priscilla Morrill); FBI agent (Dick Anthony Williams); Student (Steve Beauchamp); Student (Tom Heinsohn); Max (Gerald O'Loughlin); Mrs. Elliot (Cynthia Harris); Mr. Elliot (Jack Knight); Eve Brice (Barbara O); Louise (Belita Moreno); Fire officer (Tony Lorea); Rosita (Perla Walter); Little girl (Amy Nicole); Giant (Steven Waxman); Elfin creature (Peter D. Risch).

The Prisoner

October 1967–January 1968 (ATV)
June 1968–September 1968 (CBS)

When a man resigns from an important top-secret government job, he's whisked to a bizarre, idyllic resort called The Village. Names are meaningless, and numbers are a means of identification. Now known as Number 6, the man discovers he has been imprisoned with no exit until his captors learn why he has resigned. Pitting his wits in every episode against an ever-changing roster of individuals who lead The Village as Number 2, Number 6 vows to escape and never to reveal his secrets.

Cast: Number 6 (Patrick McGoohan); The Butler (Angelo Muscat).

Created by: Patrick McGoohan; *Executive Producer:* Patrick McGoohan; *Producer:* David Tomblin; CBS/ITC; 60 minutes.

SURREALISM: A modern movement in the arts
—trying to depict the workings of the unconscious mind.
—*Webster's New World Dictionary of the American Language*

"What the series is about is creative people for once running the asylum. We were doing what we wanted and showing what the medium was capable of … showing what a marvelous tool television is for surrealistic expression. Surrealism is always the counterpoint of two totally disparate and surprising images and television is superbly equipped to do this."

Speaking is screenwriter Terence Feely, who wrote two of *The Prisoner*'s scripts, "The Schizoid Man" and "The Girl Who Was Death."

"That last episode ["Fall Out"] is, I think, one of the best examples of total surrealism. No prisoners taken.

"This was a series built to last. It is only just beginning to be properly appreciated, and I wouldn't be surprised if it is still going strong as a cult thing in another 20 years. I can't think of any other series you would put against it, really, and say, 'Well, that's a match for *The Prisoner* in that genre.' I mean, what would you put against *The Prisoner*, with that kind of mesmeric, time-warp, out-of-this-world atmosphere, at the same time filled with tension and questions and problems, with a totally contemporary theme of freedom of the personality against control by the State? That's utterly twentieth, twenty-first century theme, and it is going to be even more appropriate after the year 2000 than it is now. You can see the seeds being sown at this moment. It is the seminal series which turns an intelligent and moral problem into pure entertainment, and the fact that it has been such a success does not surprise me."

The Prisoner is like a Rorschach ink blot: It is what the viewer makes of it. *The Prisoner* has been called one of the most enigmatic series ever created. A dramatic, allegorical treatment of how society imprisons its inhabitants. The show was about how one man, forever nameless, resigned from an important intelligence position and was secretly whisked to the mysterious Village. "I will not be pushed, filed, stamped, indexed, briefed, debriefed or numbered! My life is my own! I resigned!" said Number 6.

Patrick McGoohan launched his idea for *The Prisoner* while he was in the heat of his hit TV series *Secret Agent*. (This is the American title of the show, which aired in the U.S. 1965-1966. In England, it was known as *Danger Man* and aired in 1959-1960 and 1964-1966.) McGoohan was restless and showed up one day at the office of Lew Grade, president of the television production company ITC. Under his arms were detailed plans and descriptions of *The Prisoner*. Grade paced through his large, plush office, listening to

As Number 6 (Patrick McGoohan, on chair) looks on, Number 2 (Leo McKern, stretched out by guards) pleads his case to the court in the final episode, "Fall Out." Copyright 1969 ITC.

McGoohan's series pitch. He thought it was such a crazy idea that, "It just might work!" and asked, "How soon can you start?" With a handshake, McGoohan went on his way.

Producer David Tomblin recalls Patrick McGoohan speaking with him just after meeting with Grade and saying, "'We've got the money for the series,' so I said, 'Oh, great!' I wasn't sure what he was about, you know, so he said, 'Sit down and write the first episode.' So I said, 'I haven't written anything before!' I mean, I had scratched out ideas occasionally. So I locked myself in a room with George Markstein for one month, and we came out with the first episode, which Patrick took and embellished. The style of the series was really his baby. I can't take too much credit for that, because I was used to action-adventure things, which I liked very much, and with his more imaginative ideas, it came into *The Prisoner*. It was a combination of thoughts, really."

Tomblin, after *Prisoner*, went on to *Space:*

1999 and *UFO*; much later, he worked for George Lucas on virtually all of his major films. Tomblin says McGoohan "is a very secretive man, in a way, so he would come up with these weird and wonderful ideas and never explain them—so you just had to work them into the context of the stories.

"He is a very talented man." recalls Tomblin. "Haven't seen him for some years. ... I think he was a bit disappointed with the reaction to *The Prisoner*, so he went to Geneva, and from there to America. I hoped great things for him then, but he hasn't seemed to have done very much. I don't know why."

"He was an amazing man—he *is* an amazing man," recalls Peter Howell, who played the Professor in "The General." "I think one of the most interesting things about how the series develops is clearly the personality of Pat McGoohan, because you were interested in knowing, I think, what sort of effect he had on the other actors and what they felt about him. He was extraordinary to work with. From the moment you went into that makeup room early in the morning for the day's filming, there was something about this man's amazing electricity, this kind of burning dedication, which is pretty unique, I think."

Asked if he felt remote from McGoohan, Howell responds, "Yes, of course you felt remote from him because he had so many things he was involved with. In fact, if ever you could see a man burning himself up, it was Patrick McGoohan, because the speed and the pressure of the work of this series was such that there he was ... he was writing, he was directing, he was acting. He was the star. And it wasn't so much that he was not easy to get to know—there was no time to get to know him. You were astonishingly aware of this immense dedication and precision and energy, and there are few actors who have that. And if I can just expand on that for a moment, one of the reasons for the success of the series, the way it has become a cult, must be to do with the ability and panache and the flair of this extraordinary man."

Camera operator Jack Lowin reinforces Tomblin and Howell's views on Patrick McGoohan, and he says, "Patrick was very heavily involved with *everything*. It was, in a sense, a one-man band. The idea was Pat's, and only Pat really had this particular *concept* of the thing. He found it very, very difficult to get everybody else to have the concept.

"They started off with directors who had worked on *Danger Man*, but Pat had laid down very strict rules as to what he wanted done, and later on he had even more say in what happened. Later on, to some extent, the directors became simply figureheads and Pat was doing it all himself.

"It was enormous strain to act in a series like that—a show where most of the stuff, after all, includes him—*and* to direct it, *and* to be concerned with everything else ... it was an enormous strain."

Filmed in the MGM British Studios in Borehamwood, England, *The Prisoner* also took advantage of exteriors at a North Wales resort known as the Hotel Portmeirion, which proved an integral aspect of the show's popularity. It gave a unique, physical location to the Village. The show's filming at Portmierion was actually kept a secret during the show's production as the producers did not want *Prisoner* fans trampling the grounds and interfering with their production schedules. It was not until the very last episode,

"Fall Out," that the main titles revealed the use of the hotel.

The resort first came to the attention of McGoohan while there for an episode of *Danger Man*. "Portmierion impressed Pat very much," says Jack Lowin, "and I think he was looking for an opportunity to use it for something in the future. It is an unusual place, an outstanding place—not a place you could go to and not comment about. It was a weird and fantastic series of pieces of architecture ... it was ideal because you had little corners which were Italy, corners which were Austria ... you could use it for almost any country in Europe, so it was an ideal location."

Peter Howell concurs, noting that "one of the achievements of the series is the location ... because of the bizarreness of it ... you've got everything there, haven't you? It's slightly strange and other-worldly, and also these great masses of beach you can use. It's a very good idea to use that."

Jack Lowin reveals that the genesis of *The Prisoner* came during the last days of *Danger Man*. "Pat got the idea for *The Prisoner* because he read a book published in America. ... It was about what happens to agents when they eventually retired, and it actually proposed the theory that an agent who obviously had a vast amount of information was not a safe person to allow to roam about, because he could be kidnapped by enemy agents to extract the information. It mentioned the idea that somewhere in North America was a 'village' or 'town' or an area where these people were sent for security reasons.

"And I think this impressed Pat very much, and it put the idea in his head as to what would have to happen when agents [like John Drake, his character] in *Danger Man* finally left the service. They would have to be incarcerated for their own protection and to ensure that no sensitive material could ever be extracted from them," says Lowin.

"And that was his original idea—just a pure follow-up to *Danger Man* about the same character and what would happen to him after he left the service. And I think he started writing scripts, or having scripts written, on that basis. Then, the idea obviously evolved. Quite where it changed from being a straightforward piece to this much more way-out, extraordinary thing, I don't know. When we started to do *The Prisoner*, I think it was an enormous surprise to everybody, the way it was being done ... this way-out, weird way of doing it was a complete surprise to everybody."

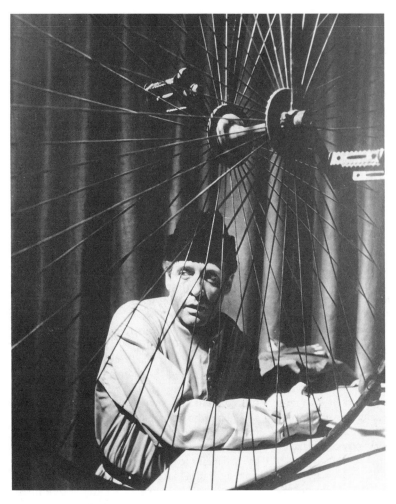

Patrick McGoohan hides out behind a pennyfarthing bicycle in *The Prisoner*. Copyright 1969 ITC.

Allegedly, in McGoohan's eyes the definitive seven episodes for the show are as follows in the preferred order: "Arrival," "Free for All," "Dance of the Dead," "Checkmate," "The Chimes of Big Ben," "Once Upon a Time" and "Fall Out."

"Checkmate" was written by Gerald Kelsey. Having watched the episode again recently after so many years, he says that "it is virtually timeless and has stood up like a surrealist painting. The filmic quality is outstanding. Few watching for the first time would imagine this was now over 20 years old. ... Does 'Checkmate' fit well with the series as a whole? I think it fits very well. ... The chess game with human pieces was an idea that I introduced in my script. It captured the imagination of the aficionados, who seem to regard it as a significant element in the series. I am always questioned about it when viewers talk of the series."

McGoohan originally intended the show to run for only seven episodes, but the CBS network wanted 26. Grade also asked for more, but McGoohan felt the premise could not sustain such lengths, so they compromised at the 17 episodes produced.

"Originally we were going to do quite a few," says Tomblin. "But it came to a point where [episodes] were so complex, and we tried to make them so well—trying to make them like feature films—that the schedule suffered somewhat for various reasons. So the number was eventually 17.

"*The Prisoner* was such an involved, complex subject that you couldn't really take the short cuts—you had to see the story through. So that's why there were 17."

"Number 2" for this episode was actor Peter Wyngarde. His recollection of his time with McGoohan was that "he was a perfectionist and, like all professionals, didn't suffer fools gladly. On the contrary, he behaved impeccably, and I had nothing but admiration for the originality, artistic economy and command of his material. The continuing success of the series is proof of this. Any series succeeds through the personality and ability of the main protagonist, and he brought a style which made it the best series around at the time."

Wyngarde confesses that upon arriving on the set, he had no idea what the show was about.

"I was excited by its ambiguity," he says. "The standard was comparable to most feature films made at the time, at a quarter of their budgets."

Wyngarde is one of two Number 2's who claim that in the show's burgeoning days, a permanent Number 2 was contemplated and he was to fill the role. The other actor making this claim is Derren Nesbitt, who played "New Number 2" in "It's Your Funeral."

Wyngarde says, "Pat particularly wanted me to do it—he asked me himself. He was very hazy about the whole thing in the beginning, but he had considered a permanent Number 2. ... He really didn't know which direction the program was going to go in, but finally decided that a change of Village administration added to the air of mystery."

Producer Tomblin confirms such speculations. "Originally, we were going to have one Number 2. I thought it would be a good idea if we had a different one each week—not so that you have a guest appearance of a good actor, but because the idea of the Village would be that you could never form a relationship, you never had security, you could never hatch plots, you can never escape, because you could never trust anybody. So, therefore, if you had a different Number 2 each week, you could keep people apart from each other."

The enigmatic nature of *The Prisoner* comes out when one considers that the tantalizing questions raised by the series have *remained* unanswered to this day. A catchphrase used on the show was "Questions are a burden to others; answers, a prison for oneself."

Why did Number 6 resign from his intelligence post? Was Number 6 supposed to be *Danger Man*'s John Drake? Who runs the Village? Where is the Village? And just who is Number 1? Did Number 6 truly escape in the final episode?

The first question has never been adequately answered, although there has been a suggestion that "vacation" was on Number 6's mind (revealed in "A, B, and C"). Story editor George Markstein states emphatically that Number 6 *is* John Drake from *Danger Man*, but McGoohan says he is not. Perhaps one reason McGoohan cannot acknowledge Number 6's true identity is that *Danger Man* is owned by a man named Ralph Smart and McGoohan does not own rights to the character.

The Village is allegedly run by "both sides" of the world's intelligence corps, but no one really knows who is in charge. The Village's location is mentioned two times during the series, but each time the purported location is different. Finally, in "Fall Out," it's established that the Village is within driving distance of London via a tunnel that leads to the A20 highway (or "motorway", the English term) in Kent.

Number 1, some viewers joked, was probably the mute butler (played by Angelo Muscat) who appeared in every episode but three. But it is revealed in "Fall Out" that Number 1 was Number 6. In the opening titles, when Number 6 asks, "Who is Number 1?" the reply is, "You are Number 6." But if a comma is added, the reply changes meaning. That is, "*You* are, Number 6."

And finally, did the Prisoner ever escape? As McGoohan has stated for the record: "No! That was the point of the whole thing. We are all prisoners of something." The cycle repeated itself, and Number 6 never truly escaped the Villagers.

Adding to the surrealism was Rover, a white, bouncing balloon ball that guarded against escape attempts. It was never explained just what Rover was. Many viewers over the years wondered if Rover was a sentient being, but certainly he was not a mechanical construction. Rover was always nameless except for a reference in "The Schizoid Man." Originally, a mechanical contraption was created to be Rover in "Arrival." However, the contraption failed miserably. The story goes that a gigantic weather balloon had passed by the beach set, and McGoohan—his passion for surreal images surfacing once again—wondered, "Can we get one of those?"

The final two episodes are unusual entries into the show. "Once Upon a Time" was a tour de force in which Patrick McGoohan and Leo McKern (appearing for the second time as Number 2) lock themselves in a simple black set for a battle of wits in the procedure called Degree Absolute. Number 2 psychologically pummels Number 6 for the information he wants. To survive, Number 6 must win. The filming was an intense time between McGoohan and McKern, so much that McKern experienced a nervous breakdown. Propsman Mickey O'Toole confirms McKern disappeared from the set at one point and needed three weeks' rest on completing his work.

David Tomblin remembers filming "Once Upon a Time" as "very tough. But Leo was a professional actor, and ... a tough old guy, and he does what he thinks is good. He is a wonderful man. ... He's not a commercial actor, he doesn't do it for the money, he does it for the things that he thinks are interesting."

Jack Lowin also remembers the shoot. "The scripts would appear minute by minute, almost," he says. "Fresh pages would appear during the day, and that was very traumatic because it was a terrific interplay of dialogue between the two of them and it created a tense atmosphere. The whole thing was a weird ... sort of thing—and this actually got through to Leo McKern. He practically had a nervous breakdown over it. The taut repartee was really very wearing, particularly on Pat and Leo but also on the whole crew, really. It was like watching a private argument, in a sense. That was one of the most difficult episodes to work on."

"Once Upon a Time" is inextricably linked with the subsequent episode, "Fall Out," yet the two episodes were filmed almost a year apart. Part of the original 13 episodes, "Once Upon a Time" was not initially intended as the first of a two-parter that would conclude the show. However, when the time came to film four more segments ("Do Not Forsake Me Oh My Darling," "Living in Harmony," "The Girl Who Was Death," and "Fall Out") McGoohan increased the episode's importance by moving its air date and adding a new ending. Presumably, that ending is when the Supervisor walks in and asks, "What do you desire?" and Number 6, in disgust with the proceedings, throws down the glass of wine and mutters, "Number 1!"

It is interesting to note that although the four episodes just named were created principally to complete a package for CBS, the network declined to air one of the four, "Living in Harmony." In this episode, Number 6 turned down the job of Sheriff and refused to carry a gun. Vietnam was raging at the time, so Number 6's refusal to take up a gun was seen as sympathetic to those who were protesting the war.

Between the filming of "Once Upon a Time" and "Fall Out," so much time had passed that when McKern was invited back, he refused to regrow his beard and his hair to match his appearance in "Once Upon a Time." McGoohan had to devise a solution in the script so McKern could appear again, but look different.

McGoohan wrote "Fall Out" over a weekend by locking himself into a room until he was finished. It was the script everyone was waiting for, and no one, not even David Tomblin, knew what McGoohan had in mind to resolve the story.

"It was sort of a fragmented idea—things that we had discussed over a long period of time that obviously stuck in Pat's head," says Tomblin. "And there was a lot of sense in it—there was a reason, there was a theme, in his own sort of

thinking. It may have escaped some people. *I* understood it. It was completely his episode, but I understood it better than most because I knew Patrick and the way he thinks. But I'm not surprised that other people found it oblique."

Might McGoohan have had the entire adventure plotted out from the beginning? Tomblin responds, "For my part, I never get into an adventure unless I have plotted it out in my mind. I know the beginning, the middle and the end. And I used to discuss with Patrick possible endings as to how we would finish it. But we never sat down and had a detailed conversation, so we never agreed or resolved things at that stage. And so ... we just had to have faith that when we got to the end, the ideas that we had talked about to conclude it, plus the experience that we had in making it, would become an ending. But, as I say, this was Patrick's own thing at the end. Normally, I suppose, you would sit down and discuss it—plot it and polish it and round it and change it. And eventually, the final episode may have been—would have been—very different, and it may have made more obvious sense at the end. But it was oblique, because Patrick is an oblique person. But I thought it was extremely interesting."

Kenneth Griffith, who played the President in "Fall Out," remembers the part fondly and says that "all serious artists are very particular that everyone gives his utmost. If Patrick trusted anyone's ability, he would freely delegate. He was monstrously overworked. Patrick strives for perfection."

On the final script, which would give him the opportunity to write a major speech because McGoohan was pressed for time during shooting, Griffith says, "I understood Patrick's mind. The meaning of life and death is essentially—for us humans—ambiguous. No, I wouldn't have ended it differently; it was Patrick's mind."

Reaction to "Fall Out" from the British television audience was fierce, to say the least. Angry viewers tied up the broadcaster's ATV switchboard because the episode did not resolve all the questions that were posed throughout the series, particularly Number 1's identity. Legend has it that McGoohan had to leave town until emotions got cooler.

Not many television series have "lost scripts" but *The Prisoner* is an exception. Writer Moris Farhi claims he wrote a script titled "The Outsider." The plot featured a plane crash-landing near the Village and Number 6's efforts to repair it and fly to freedom. The script would also have Number 6 studying the migration of birds to determine the location of the Village. But McGoohan stepped in and quashed the idea by saying, "Heroes don't birdwatch!"

Since the show went off the air in the late 1960s, fans have raised it to cult status. They are in awe of McGoohan's use of surrealism, social commentary and symbols in an unexpected juxtaposition. These symbols, although often baffling to the casual viewer, are nevertheless heavily laden with meaning to the artist himself, and can become clearer as one gets to know more about the mind of its creator, Patrick McGoohan.

This show is one of the few completely available on home video and aired occasionally on PBS stations uncut.

The Prisoner has an appreciation society of fans, The Six of One Club, based in England with several thousand members worldwide. Warner Books has published *The Official Prisoner Companion.*

Looking closer, we can see a number of elements predicted in the late 1960s that have already come to pass. Today, any time we go to the bank or a department store, we are under silent surveillance by remote cameras "for our safety." When we make a commercial transaction, we tender a plastic card whose unique string of numbers personally identifies us. Our drivers' licenses and our vehicles likewise have letters and numbers on them. The age of cordless telephones has also come upon us.

The Prisoner also spawned a four-part "graphic novel" in 1988 by D.C. Comics. The story takes place 20 years after the events of "Fall Out" and concerns a female agent winding up in the destroyed and barren Village that has only one inhabitant: Number 6.

So rabid was the cult factor that in 1986 media columnists from the *Chicago Sun-Times* to *Electronic Media* magazine announced CBS and ITC were working together to bring back the show in some form. Of course, it never happened, but there was an attempt to "pick up the show where it left off" as a continuation or a remake. There was even a report of an Americanized rendition of the show. From other quarters, the new series would be about Number 6's *son.* Writing in *Electronic Media*, Carl H. Weiner of New York said, "*The Prisoner* was a literate, complex, multifaceted series which appealed to viewers on different levels. There had never been a series like it. … *The Prisoner* was the quirkiest series to hit the airwaves. Had not Michael Dann (then vice-president of programming at CBS) been able to purchase it at a bargain-basement price, it might never have been seen by American viewers."

Patrick McGoohan had no involvement in any of these revival attempts. Whether a new incarnation of *The Prisoner* will ever ride the airwaves depends solely on McGoohan.

CAST NOTES

Patrick McGoohan (Number 6): Born 1928 in New York. Raised in England, McGoohan first made his mark as John Drake in *Secret Agent* in the 1960s and acted in feature films, including *Ice Station Zebra*, *Kings and Desperate Men*, and *Baby*. He's also received two Emmys for his work acting and directing on *Columbo*.

EPISODE GUIDE

Arrival
After resigning from his sensitive government position, a man is abducted and brought to a strange town known as "the Village," actually a spy prison camp for retired spies. Stripped of his identity, he's tagged as Number 6 and is introduced to the leader of the Village, Number 2. At all costs, Number 6 is determined to escape. Wr: George Markstein and David Tomblin. Dir: Don Chaffey.

Woman (Virgina Maskell); Number 2 (Guy Doleman); Cobb (Paul Eddington); New Number 2 (George Baker); Taxi driver (Barbara Yu Ling); Maid (Stephanie Randall); Doctor (Jack Allen); Welfare worker (Fabia Drake); Shopkeeper (Denis Shaw); Gardener/Electrician (Oliver MacGreevy); Ex-Admiral (Frederick Piper); Waitress (Patsy Smart); Labour exchange mgr. (Christopher Benjamin); Supervisor (Peter Swanwick); Hospital attendant (David Garfield); Croquet player (Peter Brace); Croquet player (Keith Peacock).

The Chimes of Big Ben
Finding an ally in a woman, Number 6 plans an escape by sea. He winds up in what appears to be his London office. Wr: Vincent Tisley. Dir: Don Chaffey.

Number 2 (Leo McKern); Nadia (Nadia Gray); General (Finlay Currie); Fotheringay (Richard Wattis); Colonel J. (Kevin Stoney); No. 2's asst. (Christopher Benjamin); Karel (David Arlen); Supervisor (Peter Swanwick); Number 38 (Hilda Barry); Judge (Jack Le-White); Judge (John Maxim); Judge (Lucy Griffiths).

A, B & C
Using medical technology to explore Number 6's dreams to find out why he resigned, Number 2 takes Number 6 through a number of trials and tribulations. Wr: Anthony Skene. Dir: Pat Jackson (Patrick McGoohan).

Engadine (Katherine Kath); Number 14 (Sheila Allen); Number 2 (Colin Gordon); A (Peter Bowles); Blonde (Georgina Cookson); B (Annette Carol); Flower girl (Lucille Soong); Maid at party (Bettine Le Beau); Thug (Terry Yorke); Thug (Peter Brayham); Henchman (Bill Cummings).

Free for All
To Number 6, the upcoming elections are yet another sham, but when he's asked to run for Number 2, he begins to wonder what the game is. Wr: Patrick McGoohan. Dir: Patrick McGoohan.
Number 2 (Eric Portman); Number 58 (Rachel Herbert); Labour exchange mgr. (George Benson); Reporter (Harold Berens); Man in cave (John Cazabon); Photographer (Dene Cooper); Supervisor (Kenneth Benda); Waitress (Holly Doone); Mechanic (Peter Brace); Mechanic (Alf Joint).

The Schizoid Man
A double of Number 6 is brought to the Village in an attempt to break him by convincing him he's Number 12. Wr: Terence Feely. Dir: Pat Jackson (Patrick McGoohan).
Alison (Jane Merrow); Number 2 (Anton Rodgers); Supervisor (Earl Cameron); Number 36 (Gay Cameron); Doctor (David Nettheim); Nurse (Pat Keen); Guardian (Gerry Crampton); Guardian (Dinney Powell).

The General
Everyone in the Village takes speedlearn lessons, attaining a university degree. But Number 6 has a better idea to curtail the scheme. Wr: Lewis Greifer. Dir: Peter Graham Scott.
Number 2 (Colin Gordon); Number 12 (John Castle); Professor (Peter Howell); Announcer (Al Mancini); Professors' wife (Betty McDowall); Supervisor (Peter Swanwick); Doctor (Conrad Phillips); Man in buggy (Michael Miller); Waiter (Keith Pyott); Man in cafe (1st top hat) (Ian Fleming); Mechanic (Norman Mitchell); Projection operator (Peter Bourne); Corridor guard (George Leech); Corridor guard (Jackie Cooper).

Many Happy Returns
Waking up one morning, Number 6 finds the Village totally deserted. Dumbfounded, he assembles a raft and escapes. Arriving in London, he discovers someone has taken over his flat. Wr: Anthony Skene. Dir: Patrick McGoohan.
Colonel (Donald Sinden); Thorpe (Patrick Cargill); Mrs. Butterworth/Number 2 (Georgina Cookson); Group Captain (Brian Worth); Commander (Richard Caldicot); Gunther (Dennis Chinnery); Ernest (Jon Laurimore); Gypsy girl (Nike Arrighi); Maid (Grace Arnold); Gypsy man (Larry Taylor).

Dance of the Dead
When death strikes a carnival, Number 6 is brought on trial for trying to smuggle out a message in a corpse. Wr: Anthony Skene. Dir: Don Chaffey.
Number 2 (Mary Morris); Doctor (Donald MacRae); Girl Bo-Peep (Norma West); Town crier (Aubrey Morris); Psychologist (Bee Duffell); Day supervisor (Camilla Hasse); Dutton (Alan White); Night supervisor (Michael Nightingale); Night maid (Patsy Smart); Maid (Denise

Huckley); Postman (George Merritt); Flowerman (John Frawley); Lady in corridor (Lucy Griffiths); Second doctor (William Lyon Brown).

Checkmate
Participating in a bizarre game of human chess, Number 6 tries to discover who are the agents and who are the prisoners. Wr: Gerald Kelsey. Dir: Don Chaffey.
Rook (Ronald Radd); First psychiatrist (Patricia Jessel); Number 2 (Peter Wyngarde); Queen (Rosalie Crutchley); Man with stick (George Coulouris); Second psychiatrist (Bee Duffell); Supervisor (Basil Dignam); Painter (Danvers Walker); Shopkeeper (Denis Shaw); Asst. supervisor (Victor Platt); Nurse (Shivaun O'Casey); Skipper (Geoffrey Reed); Sailor (Terence Donovan); Tower guard (Joe Dunne); Tower guard (Romor Gorrara).

Hammer into Anvil
Wanting to avenge the death of a girl, Number 6 plays cat-and-mouse with Number 2, in a plan to convince him that *he* is the one being spied on. Wr: Roger Woddis. Dir: Pat Jackson (Patrick McGoohan).
Number 2 (Patrick Cargill); Bandmaster (Victor Maddern); Number 14 (Basil Hoskins); Psychiatric director (Norman Scace); New supervisor (Derek Aylward); Number 73 (Hilary Dwyer); Control room operator (Arthur Gross); Supervisor (Peter Swanwick); Shop asst. (Victor Woolf); Technician (Michael Segal); Shop girl (Margo Andrew); Female code expert (Susan Sheers); Guardian (Jackie Cooper); Guardian (Fred Haggerty); Guardian (Eddie Powell); Guardian (George Leach).

It's Your Funeral
Number 6 becomes embroiled in an assassination plot against Number 2 during a change-of-guard ceremony. Wr: Michael Cramoy. Dir: Robert Asher.
New Number 2 (Derrin Nesbitt); Watchmaker's daughter (Annette Andre); Number 100 (Mark Eden); Retiring Number 2 (Andre Van Gyseghem); Watchmaker (Martin Miller); Computer attendant (Wanda Ventham); Number 2's asst. (Mark Burns); Supervisor (Peter Swanwick); Artist (Charles Lloyd Pack); Number 36 (Grace Arnold); Stallholder (Arthur White); MC councillor (Michael Bilton); Koshu opponent (Gerry Crampton).

A Change of Mind
Number 6 is subjected to drugs and soundwaves to force him to reveal why he resigned from his top-secret job. Wr: Roger Parkes. Dir: Patrick McGoohan.
Number 86 (Angela Browne); Number 2 (John Sharpe); Doctor (George Pravda); Number 42 (Kathleen Reck); Supervisor (Peter Swanwick); Lobo Man (Thomas Heathcote); Committee chairman (Bartlett Mullins); Number 93 (Michael Miller); Social group member (Joseph Cuby); Social group member (Michael Chow); Number 48 (June Ellis); Woodland Man (John Hamblin); Woodland Man (Michael Billington).

Do Not Forsake Me Oh My Darling
The mind of Number 6 is transferred into the body of another man. Number 6 is then able to escape

the Village but returns to claim his body. Wr: Vincent Tisley. Dir: Pat Jackson (Patrick McGoohan).

Janet (Zena Walker); Number 2 (Clifford Evans); The Colonel (Nigel Stock); Seltzman (Hugo Schuster); Sir Charles (John Wentworth); Villers (James Bree); Minister (Kynaston Reeves); Stapelton (Lloyd Lamble); Danvers (Patrick Jorgan); Camera Shop mgr. (Lockwood West); Potter (Frederick Abbott); Cafe waiter (Gertan Klauber); Old guest (Henry Longhurst); First new man (Danvers Walker); Young guest (John Nolan).

Living in Harmony
In an unusual and controversial story, Number 6 finds himself in a Wild West town. He's tricked into becoming the Sheriff, which he refuses. Is this town real or fantasy? Wr: David Tomblin, story by David Tomblin and Ian L. Rakoff. Dir: David Tomblin.

Kid (Number 48) (Alexis Kanner); Judge (Number 2) (David Bauer); Kathy (Valerie French); Town elder (Gordon Tanner); Bystander (Gordon Sterne); Will (Michael Balfour); Mexican Sam (Larry Taylor); Town dignitary (Monti De lyle); Horse dealer (Douglas Jones); Gunman (Bill Nick); Gunman (Les Crawford); Gunman (Frank Maher); Horseman (Max Faulkner); Horseman (Bill Cummings); Horseman (Eddie Eddon).

The Girl Who Was Death
Number 6 faces a lethal woman who calls herself "Death." She believes they were made for each other, as he is a survivor and she is a killer. Wr: Terence Feely, from an idea by David Tomblin. Dir: David Tomblin.

Schnipps (Number 2) (Kenneth Griffith); Sonja (Justine Lord); Potter (Christopher Benjamin); Killer Kaminski (Michael Brennan); Boxing M.C. (Harold Berens); Barmaid (Sheena Marsh); Scots Napoleon (Max Faulkner); Welsh Napoleon (John Rees); Yorkshire Napoleon (Joe Gladwin); Bowler (John Drake); Little girl (Gaynor Steward); Little boy (Graham Steward); Little boy (Stephen Howe).

Once Upon a Time
Disgusted with the lack of progress in obtaining information from Number 6, a previous Number 2 returns and declares it's time for Degree Absolute— a one-on-one confrontation between the two men until one cracks! Wr: Patrick McGoohan Dir: Patrick McGoohan.

Number 2 (Leo McKern); Supervisor (Peter Swanwick); Umbrella Man (John Cazabon); Number 86 (John Maxim).

Fall Out
Defeating Number 2 in the emotionally and psychologically tasking Degree Absolute, Number 6 demands to see Number 1. He's taken to an underground court where his future will be decided, once and for all. Wr: Patrick McGoohan Dir: Patrick McGoohan.

Former Number 2 (Leo McKern); The President (Kenneth Griffith); Number 48 (Alexis Kanner); Supervisor (Peter Swanwick); Delegate (Michael Miller).

Probe
March 1988–June 1988

Austin James, a young genius and creator of the scientific corporate empire Serendip, conducts scientific experiments in his huge warehouse dubbed "the Batcave." With his secretary, Mickey Castle, Austin uses his intellectual wizardry to solve strange mysteries.

Cast: Austin James (Parker Stevenson); Michelle "Mickey" Castle (Ashley Crow).

Created by: Isaac Asimov, Michael Wagner; **Producers:** Stephen Caldwell, Michael Piller; **Executive Producers:** Michael Wagner, Alan J. Levi; **Executive Story Consultant:** William Link; ABC/Universal; 60 minutes.

"Austin James was not the kind of character that you saw very often on television," says actor Parker Stevenson. "He was intelligent but eccentric. He was much more comfortable being alone in his warehouse, creating and thinking. I saw him as kind of a Howard Hughes recluse."

Only real-life mysteries could lure Austin away from his warehouse: Why did a TV host die

after a supposed witch put a curse on him? Did an orangutan really commit murder? Did an anti-smoking cure turn everyone in a neighborhood block into zombies?

While Austin James was not intended to be Tom Swift, the teenage inventor created in a book series by Edward Stratemeyer, the resemblance is close enough to say that Tom Swift is James's literary ancestor. Both create inventions, solve mysteries and embark on fantastic adventures—and both have a corporation working for them.

Probe's respect for science was no surprise to those familiar with the writings of science writer Isaac Asimov. The late novelist created *Probe*'s basic concept. His original treatment was for a series to be called *Isaac Asimov's Probe*. As it

The stars of *Probe*, Ashley Crow and Parker Stevenson. Copyright 1988 ABC/MCA.

turned out, the New York–based Asimov had little to do with the resulting series.

"The original idea was that the stories would be guided by Asimov," recalls Stevenson. According to the actor, one reason for Asimov's minimal participation was his fear of flying. "He didn't fly anywhere. This meant he couldn't attend the story meetings or script consultations or even visit the set. That was something the producers hadn't anticipated. When I found out he didn't fly, I had second thoughts about flying myself. He was a pretty smart guy. I thought, `What does he know that I don't know?'"

While the series took a different direction from his original treatment, Asimov liked the results and called the series "delightful." The title of the project was changed simply to *Probe* because "the network's research showed that *Probe* tested better as a title," says Stevenson. "Unless you were a science fiction fan, the name Isaac Asimov may not have been familiar."

Michael Wagner scripted a two-hour film introducing the series, which aired in December 1987. A six-episode run followed on ABC in the spring of 1988.

"Michael Wagner was one of the keys to the show," notes Stevenson of the young writer who died shortly after the series. "He basically took over after Asimov's treatment and wrote some wonderful scripts. I used to watch Michael on the set, and I patterned a lot of Austin's physical behavior after him. [Executive producer] Alan Levi was another key element to the show. Alan was very comfortable with the technical stuff: computers, machinery, visual graphics. He was the main drive of the show's physical production."

New York actress Ashley Crow played Austin's hyper, non-scientific secretary, Mickey Castle. "The long hours on a series are grueling, and it was nice to be in the company of Ashley," says Stevenson. "She gave her character the right balance of innocence, spirit and fire. She was wonderful for the show and we worked well off each other."

Crow's character was an emotional counterpoint to Austin's coolness. Her unshackled emotional nature gave Austin more to contemplate than his dials and vials. "The character of Mickey was a good foil for Austin," notes Stevenson. "It provided some conflict. Mickey was often irritated, confused and perplexed by Austin. At the same time, she was fascinated by him. There was also an unstated attraction between them. A lot of time you end up being closest to the people you have friction with."

Mickey's openness also gave Austin some insight into his own humanity. "Austin lived alone in this warehouse because he didn't get along with people. Mickey is the one person who begins to understand him. There was no doubt that Austin was a brat, an irritating guy. Anybody who works with this particular man would go nuts. In the pilot, Mickey keeps quitting because he's driving her crazy. He keeps manipulating her to get her back. Deep down, he wants her to stay around because there's a part of him that doesn't want to be left alone. He also thinks she's a lot more capable than she thinks she is, and he's determined to show her that. Between the two of them, you see these dynamics being played out."

Playing a genius meant Stevenson had to spew long lines of scientific dialogue. "That was my greatest challenge. The writers had an over-inflated estimate of what I was capable of. We often shot 16 hours a day, and I'd go home every night and learn 10 pages of dialogue. Most of the time I had no idea what I was saying. Partly out of laziness and probably lousy education, I often mispronounced nuclear. I'd say nu-cu-ler. I'd get mail from viewers correcting me that it was nu-clee-er. A lot of times I would look up words in the dictionary to find out what they meant and how they were pronounced. We had dictionaries and science books all over the set!"

The pilot of *Probe* was filmed in South Carolina to take advantage of a facility needed for a set backdrop. The subsequent series was filmed in Phoenix, Arizona. "When we shot in South Carolina, we shot at an abandoned nuclear power plant. It made me think twice about whether or not I'd go home glowing. A series like *Probe* puts you in those kinds of situations."

Stevenson was impressed by the myriad of hardware that filled Austin's warehouse. "We had some incredible props. We even had an airplane hanging from the roof, a big yellow crop duster. We also had generators, electron microscopes, everything. The set was brilliant, and just being there was an adventure!"

The series gave Stevenson the opportunity to act with an unusual guest star: a female orang-utan. "Rob Bowman was the director of a show called 'Metamorphic, Anthropoidic, Prototype Over You.' I don't know what that means. We just called it the MAPE show. The story was about interspecies intelligence and communications. Rob had a show that was, logistically, impossible to shoot. He also had to work with the orang-utan. Her name was Sunshine, and her trainer had taught her to do several things in sequence. In one scene, she was in a big cage where she was supposed to go under a couch, retrieve a wallet, pull out a credit card, go to the cage door, jimmy the lock open with the card, put the card back in the wallet, put the wallet away and leave the cage. This was done without giving her independent cues. But from a filming perspective, it was a very complicated shot.

"Sunshine was good for only two or three takes and then she got bored. By the fourth take, she was all pissed off, like, 'Hey, I want my banana!' She wanted to move on to the next scene. In a TV show, there are so many things that can go wrong, it doesn't work that way. So we had to do scenes quickly to accommodate her. It turned out to be my favorite show. Rob Bowman, who is a brilliant director, did an amazing job."

Probe premiered in March 1988, but despite a publicity blitz, it was unable to attract a large audience. "We were opposite *The Cosby Show* at its height," recalls Stevenson. "*Cosby* was pulling a 44 share and we were in our mid-teens. In hindsight, those were terrific ratings against *Cosby*, but the network had a lot of pressure on them. They wanted to find something that would do better. Had they stuck with *Probe*, or moved it to another time, I think it would have done better."

Stevenson also thinks the show's very nature may have required more time to promote. "I loved *Probe*, but it was a difficult show to put a label on. That's good because it was a unique show, but possibly people didn't know what we were about. An original show is hard to sell. Series like *Hill Street Blues* and *Northern Exposure* took time to find their audience. But I want to be clear: I don't blame the network. I understood their decision when we were canceled. I knew how strong *Cosby* was and the pressure that was on ABC for counter-programming. I just regret that they didn't stay with it a little longer."

Stevenson likes hearing from fans who enjoyed the show. "It did have a loyal following of people who watched it. Every couple of months someone will say, `I loved that show. It was great!' Maybe they're being polite and making conversation, but I tend to think that if they remember the show, and make it a topic of conversation, they probably did enjoy it. That means a lot to me. We really put our hearts into that show."

CAST NOTES

Parker Stevenson (Austin James): Born 1952. Stevenson, who is married to actress Kirstie Alley, was one of TV's *Hardy Boys* (1977–79).

Ashley Crow (Mickey Castle): She was a regular on the New York daytime series *As the World Turns* in the 1980s. Her recent film roles include *The Good Son* (1993).

EPISODE GUIDE

Computer Logic (1987 TV movie)
Austin becomes the target of a sophisticated computer named Crossover. It has killed its creator and is now determining who lives and dies in the city. Wr: Michael Wagner. Dir: Sandor Stern.

Howard Milhouse (Jon Cypher); Miles (William Edward Phipps); John Blaine (Andy Wood); Maid (Jan Sandwich); William Stevens (Scott Feraco); Manager (Raymond Guth); Old man (Fred Schiwiller); Truck driver (Bill Lane); Preacher (Gene Johnson); Personnel (Judy Scovern); Secretary #1 (Diana Baynes); Secretary #2 (Carol Weston); Customer (Sandy Elias); Old woman (Gertrude Nicholls).

Season Episodes

Plan 10 from Outer Space
A famous science fiction author summons Austin,

claiming he's made contact with an electromagnetic alien called Pretzel. Austin believes it's all part of a plan to kill the author. Wr: Michael Wagner. Dir: Vigil Vogel.

　　Truman J. Smith (Michael Constantine); Helga (May Britt); Tish Smith (Sam Currie).

"Now You See It…"

Austin's technology gets the blame when two executives fall to their deaths. Austin discovers that someone is using holographic images as a deadly weapon. Wr: James Novack. Dir: Rob Iscove.

　　Rand McKinley (Clive Revill); John Bolt (Severn Darden); Randolph (Nicholas Hormann); Jordan (Mickey Jones); Paul Watkins (Gary Clarke); Driver (Michael Waltman).

Black Cats Don't Walk Under Ladders (Do They?)

A skeptical TV host dies on air, apparently from a witch's spell. Austin searches for the true cause of death. Wr: Lee Sheldon. Dir: Alan J. Levi.

　　Angela Little (Gretchen Wyler); Sabrina Stillwater (Lina Raymond); Marty Corrigan (Stanley Kamel); Roman Drauchavitch (Eric Christmas); Jennifer (Heather McNair); Drake (Larry Stoller); Nichols (Bob Sorenson); Waiter (Jackson Douglas Fisher); Frank (Joel Kennedy); Bulwer (Ron Briskman); Guest (Randy Harris); Woman (Liz Romero).

Metamorphic, Anthropoidic, Prototype Over You

An intelligence-boosting experiment results in an orangutan shooting a woman to death. Austin, believing the ape was framed, comes to a surprising conclusion. Wr: Tim Burns, story by Robert Bielak. Dir: Rob Bowman.

　　Dr. Deena Hardwick (Kathryn Leigh Scott); Rand McKinley (Clive Revill); Louise Ellen Boken (Tata Windsor); Judge Parker (Tom Downs); Sgt. Greenwald (John M. Jackson); Decker (Michael Pniewski); Walt (Michael McNab); Eric (Arthur Cybulski); Josephine's voice (Frank Welker); Animal officer (Joe Corcoran); Mrs. Parker (Carolyn Pain); Officer (Andy Hill); Officer (Marc Madnick).

Memory Flash—Rob Bowman: The orangutan was incredibly well trained. We had to clear the set and rehearse with her for an hour so that she wouldn't be distracted. Then we brought in the crew and actors. It took a long time but she did a very good job. She was a lovable little creature too!"

Quit It

Austin investigates a neighborhood where the people are too perfect. Possibly they've been affected by a smoking remedy that has severe side-effects. Wr: Philip Reed. Dir: Vince McEveety.

　　Ted Strawn (Jim McMullan); Karen Strawn (Eileen Seeley); Lou McNally (Philip R. Allen); Sheri (Darleen Carr); Abby Strawn (Deborah Slaboda); Julie Cutler (Connie Kranz); Chris Cutler (Lance Harpham); Barry, Jr. (Josh Arnold); Barb McNally (Polly Chapman); Elaine Boxell (Linda Jurgens); Barry Boxell (Fred Nelson); Robert Black (Paul Mancuso); Wayne Laudormil (Danny Sullivan).

　　Memory Flash—Jim McMullan: "You couldn't have asked for a better lead actor than Parker Stevenson. He was also very helpful. The episode reminded me of *The Stepford Wives*—the concept of people acting weird and nobody knows why. It was a good show. I enjoyed working with director Vince McEveety. I worked with him on *Wagon Train* back in 1962!"

Untouched by Human Hands

Puzzling Austin are a nuclear explosion, a radioactive corpse and a 2.5 million dollar insurance policy that benefits the victim's maid. Wr: Lee Sheldon, story by Howard Brookner, Colman deKay. Dir: Kevin Hooks.

　　Liz Leyton (Katherine Moffat); Howard Milhouse (Jon Cypher); Rebecca Kingsley (Eileen Barnett); Harold Putnam (Christopher Thomas); Val Kennedy (Emily Ragsdale); Matson (Frank Sprague); Housekeeper (Hope Silvestri); Secretary (Carol Weston); Elder (Nick Young).

Project UFO
February 1978–August 1979

Two Air Force officers roam the country investigating UFO encounters. Based on the real-life cases documented in Project Blue Book, a declassified project that concluded that UFOs were not a threat to national security, the show boasted the help of a retired U.S. Air Force colonel as a producer.

Cast: Maj. Jake Gatlin (year 1) (William Jordan); Sgt. Harry Fitz (Caskey Swaim); Capt. Ben Ryan (year 2) (Ed Winter).

Executive Producers: Jack Webb, Gene Levitt; *Producers:* Robert Leeds, Col. W. Coleman, Gene

Levitt, Robert Blees; NBC/Mark VIII Production; 60 minutes.

　　Hollywood likes trends. When *Star Wars* blasted across film screens in 1977, *Battlestar Galactica* was television's answer. When *Superman* flew through the theaters of America in 1978, the three TV networks answered with their own superhero programs in *Greatest American Hero, Powers of Matthew Star, Spiderman, Wonder Woman* and *The Incredible Hulk.* But when *Close Encounters of the Third Kind* made us look to the skies in 1977, Jack Webb, a producer most famous for *Dragnet*, was clever to recognize that Project Blue Book's declassification by an act of Congress was an opportunity to dramatize the cases in a one-hour television format.

Actor William Jordan, who played Maj. Jake Gatlin on the show's first season, recalls that *Project UFO* was not the show he hoped it would be.

"What was unfortunate was Jack was a very bright, innovative mind, but he was unable to go in any other direction other than his success with *Dragnet*," explains Jordan. "Most of his storytelling cramped

David Yanez (left), William Jordan, Caskey Swaim (right) in *Project UFO.* Copyright 1978 NBC/Mark VIII Productions.

in terms of his dimensions. My character, Maj. Jake Gatlin, had no other life other than just being with his sergeant and traveling around and interviewing people. He had no family life, he had no dimension. I think that was the fault of the show. There was never any further dimension. It made them out to be cardboard characters.

"We were the number-one rated show for a season. This was about the same time that *Close Encounters of the Third Kind* came out. It was very timely, and people were very curious. The first several shows were very promising of what might be revealed that the Air Force perhaps covered up for years. [But] Jack, even though he was a very talented man ... didn't want input into his ideas."

Jordan candidly reveals that "Jack and I parted in that series after about a year, because he was intolerant, not wanting suggestions. What about showing that we have a life of some kind other than just Air Force staff? Don't I have a wife? Don't I have a family? Don't I have friends? If you give people the same thing every week, in that same tone of voice like *Dragnet*, for two, three or four years, that's pretty boring stuff."

Jordan is kinder to his co-star on the show, Caskey Swaim. "Caskey was a very pleasant, cooperative actor ... He did a very nice character that he developed, and he had a very nice quality."

To properly adapt casefiles for a prime-time TV series, it was necessary to "dramatize" the events and structure them to be entertaining and accessible. As Jordan explains, "It's not so much fictionalized as Jack chose to put them together in a fashion that fit his purposes at the time. There were some liberties taken. The way they compiled, so to speak, the story construction. It's part of television to be aware of the constraints of time and the needs for the hour to fill. I never got to be a contributor in the sense of seeing the original Project Blue Book stories. I was never given that opportunity."

Jordan laments that if the producers had been more creative and allowed the show wider parameters, "we would have been a much more profound experience for everyone." Jordan also wanted stories that were more pointed about the phenomenon of UFOs. "I felt there was more to be learned had we sought the direction of trying to be bold in storytelling. In the outcome of the episodes, a lot of the resolutions were very matter-of-fact and there were no abstractions. In my way of thinking, it would have been better had there been more mysterious stories rather than the indirect reference to balloons and gases. In many cases, we had open-and-shut cases."

As to his own thoughts about UFOs, Jordan wonders if Air Force personnel know more than they are revealing, "and don't quite know how to disseminate to people. I think they don't know how to make them palatable."

Lots of viewers thought Jordan did know all about the Project Blue Book. He reports that fans assumed he knew much more than he ever revealed on the show, and they would write to him asking for more information.

"If I wrote back and told them I didn't know, a lot of them would be disappointed or be angry that I would not be forthcoming with information. There was a resentment sometimes that I would not be able to answer their questions about the phenomena. Because I'm on television playing an Air Force officer doing this, I must have knowledge of a lot more than I would be able to tell them."

If Jordan looked official and well cast in the role of Maj. Gatlin, it was because he did serve in the Air Force and served time in the Korean War in 1959. "It was not like I needed training to be an Air Force officer," he says. "I spent three years and nine months as an officer." As a result of Jordan's background, he rightly could call himself an authority in the portrayal of such military men. "I used to have a lot of differences [with Webb] about military bearing and behavior I would have as an Air Force officer, as opposed to nuts-and-bolts, stilted kind of *Dragnet* qualities that were sometimes imposed on me. I felt I had a beam on the character and what this character might think as opposed to military bearing imposed on certain projects like this. After all, these characters are people first."

When Jordan left the show at the end of its first year, actor Edward Winter took over as Capt. Ben Ryan, while Caskey Swaim carried on. The show was canceled after 13 episodes.

In the end, Jordan remarks that "Every time I run into someone who was at NBC and knew the show, they would say, 'We're sorry we didn't listen to you more closely, and that we let Mr. Webb influence us so drastically.'"

CAST NOTES

William Jordan (Maj. Jake Gatlin): Born in Milan, Indiana, Jordan has acted in many TV movies and series. He's well known for *The Disappearance of Aimee* (1976), *The Trial of Lee Harvey Oswald* (1977), *King* (1978) and *Friendly Fire* (1979). Series appearances include *Lou Grant*, *The Rockford Files*, *The Magician* and *Mannix*. Today, Jordan continues to be active with books-on-cassette narrations and TV movies.

Ed Winter (Capt. Ben Ryan): This Ventura, California–born actor is most memorable as the crazed CIA agent Col. Flagg in *M*A*S*H*. His guest roles on television have been varied. TV movie appearances include *Eleanor and Franklin*, *Perry Mason: The Case of the Notorious Nun*, *Stranded* and *The Christmas Gift*.

Caskey Swaim (Sgt. Harry Fitz): Born in Lexington, North Carolina. Only six months prior to landing *Project UFO*, Swaim was a starstruck bellhop at Hyatt House on the Sunset Strip. His first motion picture was a role in Henry Winkler and Harrison Ford's vehicle, *Heroes*. Acting was his dream since childhood; he saw his first play when he was seven years old, and by nine he was imitating Elvis Presley. After an 18-month tour of duty in the Army, including service in Okinawa, Swaim moved to Los Angeles to pursue an acting career.

EPISODE GUIDE

Season 1: 1978

Sighting 4001: The Washington D.C. Incident
A Virginia farm woman reports a strange object in her yard, and a robot-like creature descends from the craft and communicates with her. Also, a U.S. Air Force pilot sights a UFO and gives chase ... to his death. Wr: Harold Jack Bloom. Dir: Richard Quine.

Helen McNair (Anne Schedeen); Operations director (Len Wayland); Martha Carlyle (Frances Reid); Senior controller (Linwood McCarthy); Burke (Hoke Howell); Lt. Gary McNair (John Findlater).

Sighting 4002: The Joshua Flats Incident
When prominent citizens of a town report seeing a UFO, investigators can't get information from them, so they turn to a frightened 11-year-old. Wr: Harold Jack Bloom. Dir: Robert Leeds.

Earl Clay (Jim Davis); Helen Ramirez (Barbara Luna); Barney Tomlinson (Mills Watson); Pauley Ramirez (David Yanez); Jim (Colby Chester); George La Tourette (Olan Soule); Tom Fairly (Parley Baer).

Sighting 4003: The Fremont Incident
A police officer sees a strange alien craft land and two astronaut-type figures exit. The sighting brings ridicule upon the officer from family and friends. Wr: Donald L. Gold and Lester Wm. Berke. Dir: Sigmund Neufeld.

Robert Lee Armstrong (Rod Perry); Milton Short (Frank Aletter); Marsden (Herbert Rudley); Diane Armstrong (Kim Hamilton); Maynard Timmons (Gary Crosby); Chief Gaffrey (Rod Cameron); Sam Carver (Paul Tuerpe); Frank Marco (Don Ross).

Sighting 4004: Howard Crossing Incident
Creatures attack a rancher and his family, and in a recreation of an actual sighting by series producer Col. William T. Coleman, Gatlin recalls the time he chased a UFO and nearly caught it. Wr: Donald L. Gold and Lester Wm. Berke. Dir: Robert Leeds.

Frederick Carlson (Leif Erickson); Jeannie Carlson (Maggie King); Martin Carlson (Claude Johnson); Prof. Hollander (Ezra Stone); Greta Marshall (Virginia Gregg); Alex Marshall (Lou Frizzel); Dr. Forrest (Malachi Throne); Darryl Cochran (Richard Derr); Capt. Roy Gordon (Jack Ging); Helen Carlson (Peggy Webber).

Sighting 4005: The Medicine Bow Incident
A boomerang-shaped vehicle chases a commercial airliner, and a would-be politician says he was almost "barbecued." Wr: Sean Baine. Dir: Dennis Donnelly.

Ed Mason (Paul Picerni); Brad Everett (Ed Winter); Gus Shaftner (Kenneth Mars); Charles Lundman (Anthony Eisley); Danny Peterson (Darrell Larson); Peggy Williams (Joan Freeman).

Sighting 4006: The Nevada Desert Incident
An Air Force lieutenant sees four metallic flying objects and a mothership, risking his career and his marriage when he reports it. Wr: Robert Blees. Dir: Robert Leeds.

Lt. Paul Staley (Scott Hylands); Dr. O'Neill (Andrew Duggan); Cynthia Staley (Adrienne La Russa); Maj. Birnham (Buck Young); Co. Fox (Hank Brandt); Wendy (Donna Douglas); Capt. Selvidge (Robert Patten).

Sighting 4007: The Forest City Incident
High school kids parked in the woods with their dates see a UFO, and a duck hunter claims to have a photo of a UFO. Wr: Donald L. Gold. Dir: Dennis Donnelly.

Jerry Daniels (Stephen Hudis); Clay Munson (Michael Francis Blake); Stu Hadley (Tim Donnelly); Mr. Mathis (Stacy Keach Sr.); Lt. Ed Coogan (Skip Homeier); Marcy Corning (Cynthia Eilbacher); Ellie Hammond (Deborah Donnelly); Lt. Carmichael (Christopher Woods); Charles Hamlin (Don Dubbins); Herb (Sam Edwards); Pete (Vic Perrin); Eddie (Radames Pera).

Sighting 4008: The Desert Springs Incident
A gigantic UFO pursues an agent and a film writer as they ride down a tram in a California resort at Desert Springs. Meanwhile, an elderly woman claims she was visited by aliens who offered a trip to Venus. Wr: Donald L. Gold. Dir: Robert Leeds.

Dave Chapman (Buckley Norris); Mike Kirby (Jack Sheldon); Emma Smith (Peggy Webber); Gist (Joseph Ruskin); Cindy Carroll (Darlene Duralia); Francine Roth (Dana House).

Sighting 4009: The French Incident
A son of a presidential envoy is kidnapped by a UFO in France. Gatlin and Fitz are ordered by the White House to investigate. Wr: Donald L. Gold. Dir: Sigmund Neufeld.

Marchand (Jacques Aubuchon); Paul Gerard (Eric Braeden); Michelle Tanner (Maria Grimm); Carlton Tanner (Morgan Woodward); John Tanner (Kip Niven).

Sighting 4010: The Waterford Incident
Boys at a military school become involved with a strange web-like substance from an unidentified flying object, and a hunter is attacked by a robot. Wr: Michael Donovan. Dir: Dennis Donnelly.

Col. Delany (Craig Stevens); Darryl Biggs (Anthony Geary); Timmy Delany (Shane Sinutko); Jim Croft (S. Newton Anderson); Dr. Paulson (Dr. Joyce Brothers); Dr. Bensinger (Howard Culver); Paul Radcliffe (Winter Horton).

Sighting 4011: The Doll House Incident
Alien beings offer a strange, lotus-shaped loaf of bread to an elderly man in exchange for a jug of water. Wr: Robert Blees Dir: Robert Leeds.

Carl Youngstrom (Alf Kjellin); Frederick Flanagan (David Hedison); Kristie Shields (Linda Foster); Anita (Marta Kristen).

Sighting 4012: The Rock and Hard Place Incident
Gatlin and Fitz witness a flying saucer leaving a trail of exploding colors over a restaurant. Later, they find themselves under investigation. Wr: Michael Donovan and Robert Blees. Dir: Dennis Donnelly.

Theresa Ball (Elaine Joyce); Max Stacey (Jack Hogan); Arley McCoy (Paul Brinegar); Annie Butler (Ann Doran); Jeff Peters (Robert Ginty); Col. Davis (Robert Patten); Andy (Scott Garrett).

Sighting 4013: The St. Hillary Incident

Two nuns report a UFO sighting and a cryptic message about their return. Wr: James E. Moser. Dir: Robert Leeds.

Sister Lucy Ryker (Pamela Franklin); Sister Anne (Amzie Strickland); Sister Superior (Virginia Gregg); Monsignor Killian (David Watson); Sheriff Daiz (Val De Vargas).

Season 2: 1978-79

Sighting 4015: The Underwater Incident

A charter boat is rammed by a UFO and crashes into the ocean. Wr: Steve Downing, Margaret Armen, Alf Harris, Robert Blees. Dir: John Patterson.

Paul Marshall (Scott Thomas); Eve Summers (Caroline McWilliams); Linda Collins (Laurette Spang); Cmdr. Bell (Allen Case).

Sighting 4016: The Pipeline Incident

A cargo plane navigator mysteriously changes his reported UFO story of an incredible encounter in the Yukon. Wr: Andrew Burke. Dir: Robert Leeds.

Tim Jenkins (Randolph Mantooth); Donald Worth (Cameron Mitchell); Richard McLane (Donald May); Lew Perrino (Brad Dexter); Aileen Jenkins (Melodie Johnson).

Sighting 4017: The Devilish Davidson Lights Incident

A trio of college professors sights a pair of V-shaped UFOs, and later, residents of the town witness the second appearance. Wr: Robert Blees. Dir: John Patterson.

Dr. Samantha Klein (Kim Hunter); Dr. Jon Robinson (Jared Martin); Dr. Linda Robinson (Jenny Sullivan); Capt. Harlan (Bob Delegall); Capt. Calvin Harlan (Isaac Ruiz); Bill Gillette (Allan Miller).

Sighting 4018: The Incident on the Cliffs

A young woman with a history of mental illness films bright blue and white UFOs as evidence for Project UFO. Wr: Greg Heffernan. Dir: Robert Leeds.

Lisa Forman (Trish Stewart); Roger Forman (William Reynolds); Amy Forman (Kim Richards); Lt. Col. Hutton (Miles Shearer).

Sighting 4014: The Wild Blue Yonder Incident

A student pilot spots a UFO and recklessly dives to Earth trying to chase it. But later, when she's about to be expelled from her school, she doesn't realize her boyfriend is keeping information from her and the school officials. Wr: Robert Blees. Dir: Rich Greer.

Kay Galloway (Rebecca York); Doug Deweiler (W.K. Stratton); Roland Highbie (Thomas A. Stewart); Capt. Moran (Fred Holliday); Jonathan Ames (Lloyd Alann).

Sighting 4019: The Believe It or Not Incident

An engineering student says he was warned by lasers and musical notes that the aliens will take over Earth unless pollution is cleaned up. Wr: Donald L. Gold and George Slavin. Dir: John Patterson.

Roy Layton (Mark Slade); Cara Layton (Marie Windsor); Ann Booth (Anne Lockhart); Prof. Diedler (Olan Soule).

Sighting 4022: The Camouflage Incident

When a UFO attacks three businessmen, one of them manages to film the craft. But the filmmaker refuses to part with the evidence. In a related search, a man claims to have pieces of the UFO in his garage. Wr: Robert C. Dennis. Dir: Robert Leeds.

Charles Robinson (Michael Strong); Ed Norwood (Gary Crosby); Dr. Phil Greiner (Normann Burton); Mrs. Robinson (Elaine Devry); Harold Moon (Henry Jones); Terry Robinson (Bradley Greene); Don Barry (Barry Cahill).

Sighting 4020: The Island Incident

A doctor and three natives of a South Pacific island see a small UFO fly out of a mothership, but the islanders later deny the incident occurred. Wr: Donald L. Gold, Andrew Burke and Ben Masselink. Dir: Robert Leeds.

Dr. Ted Sanders (James Olson); Donna Sanders (Marlyn Mason); Peter Ucki (Cal Bellini); Manuku (Ken Renard); Timi (Sam Tampjoya).

Sighting 4021: The Superstition Mountain Incident

A young student from South Dakota finds two artifacts of pure magnesium left in a mine by a UFO. But a gypsy warns the boy not to tell anyone about their visit. Wr: Larry Alexander and George F. Slavin. Dir: Larry Dobkin.

Charlie (Josh Albee); Clara (Anna Karen); Laurie Pawling (Leslie Ackerman); Timothy Hooper (William Bogert); Dr. Siginaw (Dr. Joyce Brothers).

Sighting 4023: The I-Man Incident

On a beach, a large UFO hovers over a 10-year-old, who says it played her a message that was sent from Earth into space 15 years ago. Wr: Buck Houghton. Dir: Richard Moder.

Cindy Harper (Pamelyn Ferdin); Harper (Whit Bissell); Prof. Lazlo (Malachi Throne).

Sighting 4024: The Scoutmaster Incident

A Vietnam veteran has an encounter with a UFO. Scouting with kids in the hills, the Scoutmaster receives burns from the encounter. Wr: Albert Aley, George F. Slavin, story by Robert Leeds. Dir: Robert Leeds.

Andy McMurtry (Russell Wiggins); Chief Morton (Jim B. Smith); Luke Primrose (Lou Frizzel); Ella Primrose (Joyce Jameson); Sgt. Eddie Larkin (Scott Mulhurn); Ron Denby (Kenneth Tigar); Chris Sherwood (Steve Patrick); Sam Robbins (Brian Part).

Sighting 4025: The Whitman Tower Incident

After an L.A. Airport traffic controller spots a UFO on his scanner, residents of an apartment are startled by the appearance of a UFO outside their windows. Wr: T.S. Cook. Dir: Rich Greer.

Chuck Ryerson (Fred Holliday); Janet Ryerson (Linda Foster); Felix Webster (Robert Patten); Emerson Keyes (Olan Soule); Tom Pederson (Christopher Woods); Rashoon (Vic Perrin).

Sighting 4026: The Atlantic Queen Incident
An officer aboard the luxury liner *Atlantic Queen*

makes a UFO sighting while crossing the Atlantic. The ship's captain says his officer has invented the story to further his career. But someone else also is a witness. Wr: Donald L. Gold. Dir: Robert Leeds.

Steve Rollins (Peter Brown); Capt. Bergstad (John Anderson); Ollie Hyers (Morey Amsterdam); Marlene Baker (Jayne Meadows); Helmsman (Raymond Mayo); Mrs. Ferrell (Donna Douglas); Radar operator (Ed Deemer).

Quantum Leap
March 1989–August 1993

While working on Project Quantum Leap in 1999 New Mexico, Dr. Samuel Beckett accidentally trips himself into a never-ending bounce through history, "leaping" into the bodies of other people within his lifetime (from the early 1950s to the present) and hoping one day he will make the leap home to the Waiting Room. Sam's accompanied by a hologram figure seen only by him—Al, a welcome companion because with Al is Ziggy, the hand-held computer link to Quantum Leap's computer. Together, on each leap, they set things right for the individuals that Sam leaps into. They must correct any anomalies that exist and hope the next leap will allow Sam to return home, to his own body.

Cast: Dr. Samuel Beckett (Scott Bakula); Admiral Al Calavicci (Dean Stockwell).

Created by: Donald P. Bellisario; *Executive Producer:* Donald P. Bellisario; *Co-Executive Producer:* Deborah Pratt, Michael Zinberg; *Supervising Producer:* Paul M. Belous, Scott Shepherd (year 1), Robert Wolterstorff, Harker Wade, Tommy Thompson; *Producer:* Robin Jill Bernheim; *Co-Producer:* Chris Ruppenthal, Paul Brown, Jeff Gourson (years 1–3); *Narrator Main Title:* Deborah Pratt; NBC/Universal; 60 minutes.

"People take that attitude that if it's science fiction it cannot be serious, or it cannot touch you or move you, or can't be good drama," says Donald P. Bellisario. With his successful and very popular dramatic program *Quantum Leap*, Bellisario proved that attitude wrong. As proof, he says, "I have enough nominations. But more than that, I have enough letters from people who have been touched by episodes of this show. Lives have been changed by it."

Bellisario points out that, "throughout the country, schools—grade schools especially—are using episodes of *Quantum Leap* to teach kids about racial violence, about things in our society. We deal with a show about blacks, or animal rights, or we deal with bigotry in any form.... Schools pick them up and use them! We get calls all the time for episodes from schools."

Bellisario also pointed to an encounter with a female journalist. "She was very upset with the 'Oswald' episode," he says. "And I said, 'Why?' and she said, 'Well, it's such a serious subject, the killing of President Kennedy, on a show like *Quantum Leap*, a science fiction show, to treat that.' And I said, 'Well, what does that have to do with it? You thought *JFK* was right on the nose,' and she said, 'Yes. Obviously.' I said, 'There's more fiction in *JFK* than in this episode of *Quantum Leap*.'" In *JFK*, director Oliver Stone postulated that the assassination was the result of a conspiracy, but Bellisario's treatment gave an interesting counterpoint to the assumption that Lee Harvey Oswald was the sole assassin.

When Bellisario created *Quantum Leap*, he was working on *Magnum P.I.* with Tom Selleck. He was also looking for a way to do an anthology show. "Shows of that structure do not sell to networks," says Bellisario. "Studios wouldn't allow me to do that. I thought, if I can come up with a time-travel show with a star, that leaped each week, I could get viewers interested in the star and the era we visited each week. We could keep changing the stories and I could do whatever I wanted every week. We wouldn't be locked into that action-adventure, cop format."

Amazingly, in his pitch to the networks, Bellisario had not yet invented Al. "It's hard for me to look beyond the two of them now," admits

Bellisario. "It's difficult for me to see any other two characters playing the part. It's a give-and-take partnership. It works very well for the show. Al's being able to give him information but not being able to physically help him at any time is a big asset. It allows me to get out any kind of information I need to get out of the show. Ziggy comes up with information, and Al relates it, and what Ziggy comes up with and doesn't come up with is purely at our whim. It allows us to tell the kinds of stories we need to do."

So complicated was *Quantum Leap* that Bellisario calls it the only show that needs an instruction manual before you watch it. NBC president Brandon Tartikoff was a fan, but in meetings he would beg Bellisario to "tell me that again in less than 20 seconds and so my mother understands it." And Bellisario says, "I believe his mother understands it, but I'm still trying to explain it to Brandon."

To avoid any pitfalls that may have befallen other time-travel shows, Bellisario set out to entrench the show with certain crucial rules that establish the show's unique identity. As a result, the *Quantum Leap* "bible" allegedly is two or three inches thick and has been dubbed "Don's Rules of Quantum Leaping."

"One [rule] was a decision to make the show only within his lifetime," notes Bellisario. "That was done so the show had some sense of reality to it. I felt that if I did a time-travel show and he would be leaping anywhere in time, the temptation is to have him zipping back to feudal times, or forward into the future, all of those things. The show would not have had quite the appeal. I didn't want the show to be a time-travel show, to be honest with you. I wanted a show that told warm, humanistic stories ... and if I was suddenly leaping back to Julius Caesar or Napoleon, it just wasn't what I wanted to make. So I limited it to his lifetime."

Even within Sam's lifetime, the opportunities for diverse stories were practically unlimited. Sam leapt into a NASA chimp about to be sent into space, a soldier in the heat of the Vietnam war, a baseball player, a homeless man, a Klan member, a rape victim, a paraplegic, a co-pilot of a doomed flight and many others. So broad were the parameters of the show that Bellisario even considered, at one point, allowing Sam to leap into an animated character.

"The next thing I limited it to was stories about little people, not famous people," says Bellisario. "[During] our fifth season, we broke that." The first rule-breaking episode was the two-hour "Lee Harvey Oswald," in which *Quantum Leap* dealt with the assassination of President John F. Kennedy. Sam leaped into Lee Harvey Oswald himself. Another episode had Sam leap into Marilyn Monroe's chauffeur to examine the true nature of Marilyn's death. Later, Sam explored the origins of Elvis Presley. The rule was broken primarily for ratings, plus the creative challenges it offered. Nevertheless, "we went four seasons maintaining this rule," points out Bellisario. "And I did it for a reason. I wanted to tell stories of the average guy."

But brushes with history or historical figures were cleverly incorporated into the show via tiny vignettes. Co-executive producer Deborah Pratt calls this "kisses with history," For example, Sam implores a young Buddy Holly to change "Piggy Sue, Piggy Sue" to "Peggy Sue." "Kisses with history have to be immediately recognizable, they have to be funny, they have to come out of left field and kiss the story, and then you move on. They're very tough to do," says Pratt.

The show's producers approached a number of celebrities for permission to have Sam encounter them in moments before fame and fortune. Madonna declined, but Stephen King agreed to an actor portraying him in such a small moment. A young Woody Allen also appears on the show, and in an early episode, a young Michael Jackson.

The third parameter set for the show was directed at writers. "People [were complaining], especially writers I was hiring for the show, 'He can't change this and he can't change that ... because of the ripple effect that'll change time,'" explains Bellisario. " 'God knows what'll happen?' I [told the writers], 'Forget it. You can change anything you want to change! Throw the time travel out! What difference does it make? As long as [Sam] doesn't change history that we know.'"

Bellisario does not see *Quantum Leap* as a science fiction show. For him, the show uses science fiction as a device to tell a dramatic story. "I see it as a drama, I see it sometimes as a comedy, sometimes as a fantasy drama, sometimes as an action-adventure, and yet sometimes as a romantic story."

This view is reinforced in the show's press kit, which states that "[*Quantum Leap*] is erroneously described as a science fiction series. In reality, it uses the conventions of the genre to its own ends, and goes beyond them. *Quantum Leap* uses the concept of time travel, but the show is not about time travel. It's a show about the

The many guises of Dr. Sam Beckett. Each week scientist Beckett bounces back and forth in time, entering the bodies of people he never knew or heard of—and righting a wrong in the lives he assumes. Copyright 1989 NBC/Universal.

amazing changes in our society and our world over the past three decades, and how they affected the ordinary people of our time. It's history given flesh, sociology blended into drama, a look at who we were and how we became what we are."

The series' clever premise and complex machinations inspired many questions among viewers. During a series of question-and-answer sessions with fans at U.C.L.A., Universal studios and the Museum of Broadcasting, the staff and stars of *Quantum Leap* answered some of those queries.

One fan wanted to know what happens to the people whom Sam leaps into. What do they do when they, in turn, leap into Sam's body and must wait to return where they belong?

"They're under observation," replied Bellisario. "They have the same Swiss-cheesed brain that Sam had when he leaped. They're observed, probed, looked at by people in masks, and they come back and write books about their UFO experiences."

Another person wanted to how the imaging chamber works and who Al sees when he visits Sam in the imaging chamber. Does Al see the person leaped into, or Sam?

"It sounds complex," replied Bellisario. "It's very simple. Where Dean [Stockwell] is standing in an imaging chamber—it's a vast chamber, miles across, empty, nothing there. And when he tunes in, or the computer tunes him in to Sam, everything, Sam and everything around Sam appears as a hologram in that chamber. And to Sam, Al appears as a hologram. There's nothing else in the chamber." When Al joins Sam, he sees the leaped character, but knows it's Sam.

"That's another rule of time travel according to Don Bellisario," added Dean Stockwell. "That certain individuals—kids under five, because they're on an alpha wave and are very pure, they can sense or spot the hologram. And animals. And I think it should be blondes with low IQs!" Discussing his character, Stockwell said that "the definition of Al's character is this, he interacts solely with Sam. And that's a challenge in itself. I found that I got very fortunate when I got into this show in being blended with Scott, because we get along beautifully and he's wonderful to work with. He's great. He really is. Plus, he has to work 12, 14 hours a day, every scene, five days a week, every show.

"Al seems to have a hell of a past, a very widely varied experience in his life. A lot of that

comes up in the show, and those are interesting things to deal with and to act. So I'm very happy. I like the concept."

The initial premise of the show was that in every episode, Sam's memory would be "Swiss-cheesed." He knew he was leaping around time, but the entire contents of his memory just wouldn't be available. (Hence the need for Al as a guide.) But as the show progressed, this wasn't dealt with so closely, making some viewers wonder just how much Sam knew. Scott Bakula explained: "We don't deal with this very often any more because so many of the viewers know the rules now that we don't go back into the Swiss-cheese thing. But we mention it periodically. I think there's a little Swiss-cheesing that happens all the time. I think [Sam] remembers certain things. We've never leapt from one show and brought him into another and had him dealing with that last memory exactly." Continuity between episodes is dangerous to consider because often episodes are not aired in the same order, said Bakula.

One of the panelists at the Q and A sessions was technical advisor and sometime actor Rich Whiteside. For the episode "The Leap Home, Part II," in which Sam joined his brother during the Vietnam War, Bellisario went to Whiteside for technical advice to make the episode as authentic as possible. "When Don was preparing to do the Vietnam episode, he had about four months before they were actually going in to shoot, which is unusual," recounts Whiteside, who also made an appearance in the episode as a doctor. "He had contacted me, given me the thumbnail sketch of what the show was going to be about and asked me to provide him background information. Unfortunately, he didn't know what he was asking for, 'cause I flooded him with stuff for about four months. I gave him pictures from guys on the teams in Vietnam."

Because Whiteside himself never toured Vietnam, it was necessary for him to fly to Virginia and expand on the research by talking with veterans. "I interviewed guys that were commanders in Vietnam, that did POW repatriation missions, and brought that information back to him," says Whiteside. "There was a SEAL Team Two 20-year picture album that came out, so I sent that back to him. I got hold of books that were written by members who served there that detailed missions, highlighted what it was like to be in a firefight on the recipients' standpoint. What was it like to be on a POW repatriation mission. What were the different basic character types that exist in the teams.

"Coming from an acting standpoint, I kinda knew what he was looking for, and I tried to feed him things he could digest and put into the story. And so ... on top of that, he layered the story. And I have to give Don and everybody on the staff a lot of credit, because they took the time under an incredibly busy schedule to sit back and listen to what I had to say, and then they incorporated it. And that was from costumes, to props, to makeup, all the way down the line. And when we were shooting it, Michael Zinberg, who was directing it, would call me up and he would say, this is the way I see the scene developing. I would tell him where there were inconsistencies, just from a military standpoint. If he could make a correction and use it, then he did. ... When it came down to artistic license, he made the decision."

Looking back at the work accomplished, Bellisario says, "I think it was a wonderful show. I'm not as happy with some of the [stories] we made fifth season." Some of those later episodes—the ones Bellisario liked least—were affected by the circumstances of the series' last days. Those circumstances, Bellisario says, included budgets that were "reduced and reduced and reduced," making the show more difficult to produce, and the unwelcome change to an 8:00 time slot. "That was not the right slot for us. With an attempt to attract new viewers, we did some things that came out just fine, but they weren't the old show." Despite support from a loyal audience, Bellisario says, "when we got to our 8 p.m. Tuesday time slot, we crawled down to an 11 share, which is not enough to get picked up. ... It's really a show that plays best at 10 p.m."

In fact, Quantum Leap had its own "leaping" crisis. The network bounced the show around various days and times, making it difficult for viewers to find it.When the show was moved, in the middle of the fourth season, from a successful 10 p.m. Wednesday viewing period to the "death slot" period of Friday at 8 p.m., NBC was inundated with letters and FAX bombs. Advocacy groups such as Viewers for Quality Television (2500 strong) and fan clubs who subscribe to the fanzine newsletter Quantum Quarterly joined the fray and sent some 50,000 letters protesting the move. The campaign was successful, and Warren Littlefield, then NBC president, recanted. In a show of support in the summer of 1991, NBC aired one episode a night for five nights running,

repeating a similar stunt from 1990. Only twice before in the history of television has a science fiction show been so broadly accepted as a quality program. Before Quantum Leap, The Twilight Zone and Star Trek were the only two science fiction shows ever nominated for Emmys by the Academy of Television Arts and Sciences in the category of best dramatic series. Quantum Leap joined that august company. Furthermore, for three consecutive years, between 1990 and 1992, Quantum Leap received Emmy nominations for acting (Scott Bakula and Dean Stockwell), as well as cinematography, costume and art direction nominations and awards.

"It's very satisfying that the show was produced and written, directed, and acted well enough to garner the nominations and awards that it has," says Bellisario, but he also is incredulous that scripts have never been nominated. "I'm always amazed how shows get nominated for best drama series on TV and none of the writers get nominated!" he laughs. "You gotta make a quality show to get those things. You gotta make a show that's hot. Quantum Leap was never that. Quantum Leap was always a quality show that was well made and garnered nominations, but it was a show that never was the darling of the [industry]." Only Rod Serling, with his work on The Twilight Zone, has won Emmys for writing science fiction on television.

Working with Scott Bakula and Dean Stockwell was always a treat for Bellisario. "Those two guys are the best," he attests, noting that after five years on the series they remained "as professional, as helpful, as excited, as dedicated to the show as they were when they did the pilot. Usually when you make shows like this, by the time you get to the fifth season, your stars get tired and grumpy and don't want to do what they did in the first season. They don't want to go through the physical strain. Making a show is very difficult. Everybody works long hours. And these two guys [stayed] just the same as the first show." Bellisario speculates that the nature of the show may have kept the actors fresh. Bakula, he says, often called his role "the best acting job in television. Because every week, he becomes a different person. You know, he's not the same guy who has a detective job every week!"

The storylines presented on the show were often controversial, dealing with such topical and sensitive issues as homosexuality, race, or rape. Did Bellisario have a difficult time with the NBC network as a result? No, he says, "they've been

Sam (Scott Bakula, left) leaps into the life of a Vietnam-era soldier with ex-admiral Al Calavicci (Dean Stockwell) by his side, April 7, 1970, on NBC's *Quantum Leap*. Copyright 1991 NBC/Universal.

says Bellisario, were those that dealt with injustice, such as one episode where Sam leapt into a black man in the South of the 1950s. "We did episodes where Sam leaps into a chimp. We had Sam leaping into a woman dealing with aggressive sexual harassment on the job. He leapt into an older person, an American Indian battling with dignity to die ... [We did] one about the Watts riots.... We did one on a gay man in a military school—or was he gay? We never really did say if he was or not. He was presumed to be.... Those episodes all touch people.

"And it doesn't have to be things like that. I can recall writing episodes in which the theme of the episode might have been, no matter how dark or black your life becomes, there's always hope. You just gotta keep fighting and you will come through it. You will come through the worst of times. I had people write me after episodes like that and say, 'I was down, I was on the verge of committing suicide, or I was depressed, or I have a cancer child, and we were giving up and after we had seen that episode, we picked ourselves up, and we went on.' I get letters like that all the time."

Actor James Whitmore, Jr., star of *Baa Baa Black Sheep*, guest star of many episodes of *Magnum, P.I.*, and *The Rockford Files*, directed 13 episodes of *Quantum Leap*, including the controversial fifth season opener, "Lee Harvey Oswald."

"*Quantum Leap*'s premise is a rather esoteric one," notes Whitmore. "We sat down many times, Don Bellisario and I, and I asked him to explain to me how the show works. And quite

extremely supportive. We've had times where we've [clashed] over shows because of subject matter, where advertisers had to pull out of the show. That's purely business. They've been very supportive. They've never interfered with the show. We've had the usual discussions and the conflicts you have with standards and practices, but they were minimal on this show. They never said to me, 'You can't make that show,' or, 'We don't like this script.' They did say, on a show about homosexuals, that advertisers were upset about that. And they went [with the show]. And they lost a lot of advertising."

Viewer response to the stories was often emotional. The ones that particularly hit a nerve,

frankly, all I [got was] a vague, general description every time! The great thing about the premise is Don [could] really do almost anything ... within the limits of what the audience [had] come to expect."

Asked whether the show is science fiction with dramatic elements or a drama show only using science fiction as a device to tell stories, Whitmore responded, "It's both. I think the science fiction elements are a device to explore the sociology of the mid-twentieth century, the various things that are going on at different times. It's a device. Don has been very specific about creating this device, and there are very specific elements to it. But I think it's a device to tell stories—to take a character anywhere he wants to take him."

Whitmore calls *Quantum Leap* "the most exciting, pleasurable show I've ever worked on because of the creativity involved. Each episode is a completely different movie." Even when plots were similar, says Whitmore, the ideas behind them were "always new and fresh and kind of interesting." The structure was very exciting for "an actor and a person who likes *ideas*. And I think that's how Donald Bellisario feels about it."

Whitmore has worked very closely with Bellisario over the years on many other TV shows. When asked to describe the man, Whitmore initially demurs, but then says, "He's an absolute unique individual in television. He has a strong commitment to his own intuition. It's very hard to get Don to compromise. It's very hard to get Don to do something for the sake of demographics or for an audience segment. He wants to tell his stories and hopes other people respond to it. What the networks want and what they need, he'll deal with that to get a show on the air. But Don mostly wants to express his feelings, ideas and world view. That's what he's all about. A lot of things in television are part of the *pecking* order. They're trying to find a way in and stay in and keep the networks happy."

Whitmore echoes Bellisario's sentiment that Dean Stockwell and Scott Bakula are two very hard-working and committed actors who relish their craft. "They're extraordinary. I've worked with a lot of folks as an actor and as a director, but their commitment to the work ... [goes] above and beyond the craft. Sometimes there's some ego-twisting and that stuff with actors in a series [that] has to do with how they as people are versus how important the product is," says Whitmore. "That gets in the way often, but in the case of Scott and Dean, that *never* gets in the way. ... I can't say enough nice things about Scott and Dean. They're always professional. Impeccable."

Whitmore admired how diligently Bakula researched his role for each segment, even while working on a current show. For an actor, says Whitmore, the show had to be "a never-ending battle. You have to go home to bed at the end of the show that he finishes now; get up in the next morning and be in a totally different world. A totally different setup."

As for Dean Stockwell, one of the few actors alive who has literally grown up with the film industry, Whitmore makes it clear that he was no second banana to Bakula. On the set, the actors were equals. Whitmore adds that "Dean Stockwell is a natural phenomenon. Dean Stockwell is an actor who's done more acting and films than you and I have seen! He's an extraordinary man to have on set. His work is forever inventive, new and fresh and real, and quite magical. His awareness of what works and what doesn't in terms of a scene is a wonderful gift. [He's] a bonus to have when you're shooting these pictures. He can figure a way to help you if you need something in the scene that's not working. I'll give Dean a line, and [ask], 'Give me this or give me that, or how about this or that?' and he'll do it better. An awful lot of actors," Whitmore confides, "are not trained actors. [Many] are just guys who are walking down Venice Beach or somebody sitting at Schwab's and somebody says, 'You look great!' A lot of actors get a big film role before they get a chance to explore the craft!" Stockwell is emphatically *not* in this category.

When it comes to specific episodes of the show that he's directed, the segment closest to Whitmore's heart may be the three-part episode "Trilogy." In fact, he calls the episode "one of my favorite shows I've ever done in my life ... a really spooky, crazy gothic show about a woman in Louisiana. It goes three different generations in Louisiana. It's all about a curse on a lady's family. Every other generation, a woman in the family kills her children, and ... it's a really kind of a spooky, gothic thing. And a very beautiful love story right in the middle of it. In the end, Sam leaps into a sheriff of this Louisiana town. The sheriff's daughter is being charged with murder. It's a very neat story. Sam winds up saving the daughter's life in the first episode in a fire. In the second half, it's twelve years later, he leaps into the arms of the daughter's lover. Sam falls desperately in love. Unbeknownst to himself, he gets this woman pregnant. And then in the third hour, which is thirteen years later, he meets his young daughter."

Whitmore emphasizes that while the characters believe it's the lover who sired the daughter, Sam's own genes are transmitted to the woman he loves. It's actually Sam's own daughter.

Of "Oswald," Whitmore says, "[Don] wanted to tell who Oswald was, and when I started working on the damn thing, I realized it hadn't really been done much. Who is this guy? We don't really know much about Oswald. What kind of a guy he was and what his life was all about. I think it's very important to know whether or not he acted alone. *I'm* not sure he acted alone."

Candidly, Whitmore evaluates his work and admits, "I'm not sure that picture worked. I don't think we ever really plotted this out together. There are some very interesting sequences that weren't really going anywhere. We knew we were going to Dallas eventually. We knew that somehow we would see what happened in the depository. Don's position is that Oswald acted alone and he fired the shot that killed Kennedy.

"I thought it was too diffuse and didn't work together as a whole. I thought the element was fascinating, and I had a lot of fun doing it! It's just that I didn't know if it was Sam or Oswald or who the hell it was. I think it was very confusing, and the response I got from the show was no one knew what the hell was going on. If you are a conspiracy buff, [the show] pissed you off. If you are *not* a conspiracy buff, or just a general viewer, I think you'd be interested in it."

An almost incredible coincidence is that Bellisario and Lee Harvey Oswald served together as Marines in the mid–1950s, stationed at Santa Ana, California. Indeed, Don worked a character named "Sgt. Bellisario" into the show.

For Whitmore, the directing stamp he leaves on the show does not involve the science fiction elements at all. "The thing that matters to me are the people, the stories, the emotional situations and how people react to the given situations." That's the core, he says. "It's about how we survive, how we live, how we deal with each other. That's what I think is exciting about *Quantum Leap*. I don't mind cop shows, bizarre shows, all kinds of garbage; it's pat, it's formula." In *Quantum Leap*, however, each week presented "a very different situation. And a very different human quandary to deal with. And that's the beauty of making films for me."

Whitmore recognizes, however, that the science fiction elements are important. "I know people are drawn to them. There are a whole bunch of them out there, 'Leapers,' who love it. Dean popping in and out, walking through walls, that kind of stuff. It's kind of fun to do, neat to watch, but it's not what the story is about for me."

Describing the last episode of *Quantum Leap* ("Mirror Image, August 5, 1953"), Bellisario says, "Sam leaps into a small tavern bar in a coal mining town of Pennsylvania in 1953. He comes face to face with himself in the mirror. Back in Project Quantum Leap, there's no one in the Waiting Room. Al doesn't know where or how to find him. Sam's deciding that this bartender behind the bar is really God, or time or fate. Sam comes face to face with what's really leaping him around. He thinks he does. It has a very surprising, tender ending. But I will say that Sam does not go home at the end of it. And where he goes, nobody knows. Until the next *Quantum Leap*....."

Many viewers have noticed that Sam's leaping and doing good deeds in different time periods suggests religious overtones and that Sam just might be doing God's work.

"Well, it could be God's work, or he's doing someone else's work," quips Bellisario. "We never say it quite. We say God, time or fate. In this episode, Sam even says, 'Or maybe something we never knew about.' Well, the implication is it's obviously a higher being. God or some sort."

Whitmore has fond memories of directing "Mirror Image." "It was great, it was mysterious, one of the best-looking and most fun shows we ever made. It created a very interesting final episode. It was very emotional. We all knew it was the last show we were going to do. The way it was finally cut, it was pretty much the end. We weren't sure it was going to be the end when we were shooting it. But we all felt it was."

Can he provide a definitive answer to what Bellisario was trying to say in "Mirror Image"? Can he reveal the identity of the bartender? Whitmore just chuckles. "There's a lot of ideas. The fact of the matter is, we all shot up with ideas. I have my ideas, Scott has his ideas, and Don has his ideas. Don was very specific—that God, time or fate did not exist. It was Sam choosing his own fate. The kind of person that he was, he kept going from place to place to help people. Scott and I decided that's what it was."

But beyond that explanation, Whitmore refuses to say anything more, feeling that to do so would defeat the purposely enigmatic nature of the script.

"I have my own beliefs, but I don't even want to tell you. It simplifies it too much. It takes all the ramifications out of it and all the interest out of it. Useful art is good because it makes you think. In a way, I hate to tell you what's really going on in there because the fact of the matter is, it's a metaphor for anything you want it to be."

As for the man behind the counter in Al's Tavern, Whitmore says, "The bartender was a pretty powerful guy. He had a lot to do with what's going on everywhere. He was actually patterned after Don's father. Bruce McGill, the actor, was almost a spitting image of Don's father."

Will Sam Beckett ever leap again? Don Bellisario insists that Quantum Leap "won't end. It's a kind of a show that's much like Star Trek in that it's got great viewer appeal. It's running on USA cable and they're finding that it's doing very well, getting stronger and stronger. They're delighted with it. So, Quantum Leap will go on in some form. I'm sure what will happen is we can make a movie of some kind, theatrical release, for television, whatever. There will be some form of the show coming back. It does have too loyal a following. Too many people love it. It's too interesting a show to disappear."

Co-executive producer, writer and actress Deborah Pratt agrees. According to Pratt, Sidney Sheinberg, the president of Universal TV, thinks Quantum Leap's potential as a feature film is very high. He believes so strongly in the property that he wants to develop the show as a series of feature films similar to the Star Trek features treatment.

So, don't be surprised if one day the person standing next to you, in a moment of emotional or physical strain, stops momentarily, looks around confusedly and mutters under his breath, "Oh, boy!"

CAST NOTES

Scott Bakula (Dr. Sam Beckett): Born 1955. For his role in Quantum Leap, Bakula received four Emmy nominations and a Viewers for Quality Television award for best actor in a drama series. He's appeared in the Paramount comedy Necessary Roughness (1991), Carl Reiner's Sibling Rivalry (1990) with Kirstie Alley, and an NBC Movie of the Week, An Eye for an Eye. Before making his mark on Quantum Leap, Bakula was already a well-known actor in the theater circuit, acknowledged by a Tony nomination for Romance/Romance.

Born in St. Louis, Bakula originally planned on following his father's footsteps by becoming a lawyer. Moving to New York in 1976, he made his Broadway debut as Joe DiMaggio in Marilyn: An American Fable. An accomplished singer, dancer, pianist and composer, Bakula currently resides in Los Angeles with his wife and children.

After Quantum Leap, he joined the cast of Murphy Brown in the fall of 1993 and completed several TV movies, such as Mercy Mission (1993) and State of Terror (1994).

Dean Stockwell (Adm. Al Calavicci): Born 1936. A former child star, Stockwell is still one of the busiest actors in Hollywood. He gained raves for his performances in the hit feature films Married to the Mob (Academy Award nomination) and Tucker: The Man and His Dream (NY/LA Film Critics Award). His career is being called the major comeback of the decade. For Quantum Leap, he's received a Golden Globe award as best supporting actor.

Stockwell's film appearances as a child actor include Anchors Aweigh (1945), The Boy with Green Hair (1948), Kim (1950) and, as a young man, Compulsion (1959). He's rendered memorable performances in Dune (1984), Paris, Texas (1984), To Live and Die in L.A. (1985), Blue Velvet (1986), Gardens of Stone (1987) and Beverly Hills Cop II (1987).

Stockwell was six years old when his father, Harry—the voice of Prince Charming in the film Snow White—took him to an audition. The next thing he knew, he was playing the lead onstage in Innocent Voyage.

But no one asked him if he wanted to be an actor. "I quit the business when I was sixteen, I cut my hair off, changed my name and disappeared into the countryside," he says. "I did odd jobs for five years, then when I ran out of things to do, I went back into the business to try again." It wasn't until 1984, after marrying his wife, Joy, starting a family (son Austin, daughter Sophia) and moving to New Mexico, that he found himself in demand again.

Stockwell lives in Los Angeles, where he spends his free time educating the public about saving the environment and preventing the depletion of the ozone layer.

Episode Guide

Season 1: beginning March 1989

Genesis, September 13, 1956 (2-hour pilot)
Although the Project isn't ready yet, Sam hops into the Accelerator and leaps for the first time. As Tom Stratton, an Air Force test pilot, Sam finds his memory Swiss-cheesed, with only enough left to know that he is not where or when he belongs. Al explains that the Project has gone awry and that the only way Sam can leap out is by flying the X-2 to Mach 3. Instead, Sam leaps after saving his wife and child, only to find that rather than leaping home, he's leapt into Ken Fox, a minor league baseball player in Texas, at the end of the 1968 season, where he must make the winning play in order to leap. Wr: Donald P. Bellisario. Dir: David Hemmings.

Peg Stratton (Jennifer Runyon); Capt. "Bird Dog" Birdell (John Allen Nelson); Dr. Burger (W.K. Stratton); John Beckett (Newell Alexander); Baseball coach (Lee DeBroux); Capt. Tony LaMott (Larry Poindexter); Weird Ernie (Bruce McGill); Tina (Barbara Horan); Capt. Doug Walker (David Trent); Dr. Blaustein (James F. Dean); Lucy (Lela Ivey); Gooshie (Dennis Wolfberg); Sally (Lydia Cornell); Jeanie (Christine Poor); Sportscaster (Doug Cox); Mikey Stratton (Christian Van Dorn); Umpire (Hank Robinson); Old man (Patrick Crenshaw); Bat boy (Brent Chalem); Young Sam (Adam Affonso); Matt (Mike Greenwood); Clyde (Dave Duensing); Barnes (Dave Dawson); Pepper (Kevin Johnson); Ken Martin/Mirror (Tim Fox); Tom Stratton/Mirror (Layne Beamer).

Star-Crossed, June 15, 1972
As Dr. Gerald Bryant, a literature professor at the Ohio college attended by his one-time fiancee, Sam has to prevent an amorous coed from attaching to him and ruining her life. Despite threats to his job, Al gives Sam the information he needs to reunite his star-crossed lover with her father and, maybe, give himself a second shot at marriage. Wr: Deborah Pratt. Dir: Mark Sobel.

Donna (Teri Hatcher); Jamie Lee (Leslie Sachs); Col. Wojohowitz (Michael Gregory); Oscar (Michael Mc-Grady); Frank (Charles Walker); Harry (Ken Gibbel); Gerald Bryant (John Tayloe); Waitress (Anne Leyden); Gas attendant (Kort Falkenburg); Student (Afro) (Tonya D. Pullman); Student (pragmatic) (Mary Boessow); Student (headband) (Lisa Meddin); Space cadet student (Stacey Adams).

The Right Hand of God, October 24, 1974
Having leapt into Kid Cody, a boxer on the take, Sam has to win the championship to fund a new church for his trainers, a group of nuns. Sam must face the bookie who counts on him to take a dive in the final bout, and, with the help of several trainers, and Al's appearance in the ring to guide his punches, Sam wins the bout and finances the chapel. Wr: John Hill. Dir: Gilbert Shilton.

Jake (Guy Stockwell); Sister Angela (Michelle Joyner); Dixie (Teri Copley); Gomez (Alex Colon); Sister Sarah

(Nancy Kulp); Roscoe (Jonathan Gries); Fr. Muldooney (Lewis Arquette); Chalky (James Cavan); Bartender (Rocky Giordani); Black boxer (George King); Referee (George O'Mara); Clarence Cody (Michael Strasser).

How the Tess Was Won, August 5, 1956
As a veterinarian in rural Texas, Sam's mission appears to be winning the love of an heiress to a large ranch. Sabotaged by another suitor, Sam fails and finds that his true goal was to save the life of a sick piglet, and to help an unnamed cohort with a task he's performing. Wr: Deborah Arakelian. Dir: Ivan Dixon.

Chance/Werewolf (Lance LeGault); Tess (Kari Lizer); Wayne (Marshall R. Teague); Buddy (Holly) (Scott Fults); Orly (Tommy Bush); Doc/Mirror (Sloan Fischer).

Double Identity, November 8, 1965
Though his goal as a Mafia hitman named Frankie is unclear, Sam follows a list of instructions, supplied by Ziggy in an effort to bring Sam back to the Project. These instructions result in the Great East Coast Blackout, and rather than leaping home, Sam finds himself in the life of the Mafia don who's been jealously preventing a romance between Frankie and the don's girlfriend. Wr: Donald P. Bellisario. Dir: Aaron Lipstadt.

Teresa (Terri Garber); Geno (Michael Genovese); Tony (Joe Santos); Segundo (Tom Silardi); Frankie La Palma (Page Moseley); Primo (Nick Cassavetes); Angela (Patricia Veselich); Al (Ric Mancini); Momma (Harriet Medin); Adriano (Mark Margolis); Father Sebastian (Dean Fortunato); Student (Joseph Svezia); Burt (John Hostetter); Charlie (Michael Franco).

The Color of Truth, August 8, 1955
In the life of Jesse Tyler, an aging black man, Sam must face discrimination in the South while trying to prevent the death of an elderly white woman. Actions motivated by his own belief in equality cause violent reactions, as Sam tries to convince one of the pillars of the community to change her views on racism. Wr: Deborah Pratt. Dir: Michael Vejar.

Miz Melanie (Susan French); Sheriff Blount (Royce D. Applegate); Willis Trafford (Michael D. Roberts); Clayton (James Ingersoll); Nell (Kimberly Bailey); Billy Joe Bob (Michael Krueger); Toad (Jeff Tyler); Miz Patty (Jane Abbott); Nurse Ethel (Elyse Donalson); Jesse Tyler/Mirror (Howard Johnson); Doctor (Christopher J. Keane); Effie (J.T. Solomon).

Camikazi Kid, June 6, 1961
As a high school nerd, Sam is required to prevent the marriage of his sister to an abusive drinker, with the wedding only three days away. By drag racing the prospective husband, beating him with a car that couldn't have won without nitrous oxide, Sam shows the groom's true tendencies. Wr: Paul Brown. Dir: Alan J. Levi.

Cheryl (Romy Windsor); Bob (Kevin Blair); Chuck (Robert Costanzo); Jill (Holly Fields); Pencil (Jason Priestley); Dad Wilson (Richard McGonagle); Janie (Janet

Carroll); Mrs. Thompson (Mary Pat Gleason); Marty (Johnny Lage); Cameron/Mirror (Scott Melville); Minister (Edmund Shaff); Impala (Tom Verica); Older brother (Brandon Adams); Little boy (Michael Bellisario).

Play It Again, Seymour, April 14, 1953

With looks that could double for Humphrey Bogart, Sam is Nic Allen, a private investigator looking for the murderer of his partner—and, if he doesn't find the answer in time, of himself. The case is solved with a number of Casablanca references as Sam launches a new pulp novelist along the way. Wr: Scott Shepherd and Donald P. Bellisario, story by Tom Blomquist, Scott Shepherd, and Donald P. Bellisario. Dir: Aaron Lipstadt.

Allison (Claudia Christian); Seymour (William Garson); Lionel (Paul Linke); Nick Allen (Tony Heller); Crooner (Don Keith Opper); Lt. Lannon (Richard Riehle); Old lady (Jeannette Miller); Policeman (Don Maxwell); Little Woody Allen (Kevin Mockain); Mama (Barbara London); Band leader (Ron Ulstad); Bartender (Hap Lawrence).

Season 2: Beginning September 1989

Honeymoon Express, April 27, 1960

As Tom McBride, a New York City cop on his honeymoon, Sam must save himself from a jealous and sociopathic ex-husband. To make matters worse, the Project's funding will be cut off, stranding Sam alone in the past, unless he can prevent the U2 flight from being shot down over Russia. Wr: Donald P. Bellisario. Dir: Aaron Lipstadt.

Diane (Alice Adair); Roget (Mathieu Carriere); Porter (Hank Rolike); Senator (Warren Frost); Henri (James Mastrantanio); Black senator (Fitzhugh G. Houston); Southern senator (King Moody); Woman senator (Virginia Paris); Yankee senator (Kirk Scott); Grey-haired lady (Donna Hardy); Conductor (William McDonald); Engineer (James Clark); Asst. engineer (Stan Garner); Tom McBride/Mirror (Ron Chabidon).

Disco Inferno, April 1, 1976

As a stuntman, Sam is to save the life of his younger brother, while trying to convince the pair's obsessive father to let the younger son go his own way, even if it means going into country-western music, rather than following the family tradition of stuntwork. Wr: Paul Brown. Dir: Gilbert Shilton.

Ray (Michael Greene); Chris (Kris Kamm); Shannon (Kelli Williams); Director (Peter Onorati); Traci (Arnetia Walker); Female extra (Maureen Fletcher-Evans); Stuntwoman (Michelle Costello); Cinematographer (Joe Farago); Chad Stone (Kevin Light); Dancer (Tobi Redlich); Country singer (Helena Buscema).

The Americanization of Machiko, August 4, 1953

As a sailor returning from Japan, Sam brings a foreign wife to a small town. He then has to fight against the prejudice of both a scheming ex-girlfriend and his mother in order to gain acceptance of his new bride. Wr: Charlie Coffey. Dir: Gilbert Shilton.

Lenore (K. Callan); Henry (Wayne Tippit); Machiko (Leila Hee Olsen); Naomi (Elena Stiteler); Rusty (Patrick Massett); Rev. Felcher (Chuck Walling); Betty Fletcher (Marjorie Stapp); George O'Bannon (Clive Rosengren); Delores (Pat Ast); Deputy Herman (Cary Pitts); Lionel/Mayor (Keith R. Mills); Eugene (James Oden Hatch); Charlie (Bill Arnold).

What Price Gloria? October 16, 1961

Sam is shocked when he learns he's leaped into a woman, Samantha Stormer. As a gorgeous secretary for an automobile company, Sam has to cope with sexual harassment by the boss, a suicide attempt by a roommate, and the effect his looks have on Al's lecherous tendencies. Wr: Deborah Pratt. Dir: Alan J. Levi.

Gloria (Jean Sagal); Buddy Wright (John Calvin); Parker (Gregg Berger); Richard (Matt Landers); Samantha/Mirror (LaReine Chabut); Johnny (Jack Armstrong); Gail Wright (Laurel Schaefer); Ted Hartman (Ryan MacDonald); Miss Bramford (Joy Stockwell); Gloria Collins/Mirror (Katie Sagal).

Blind Faith, February 6, 1964

Although the concert pianist he leaps into is blind, a fact which bothers his girlfriend's disapproving mother, Sam can still see. At least until an exploding flashbulb blinds him at the crucial moment: when he must rescue his girlfriend from a serial killer. Wr: Scott Shepherd. Dir: David J. Phinney.

Michele (Cynthia Bain); Agnes (Jennifer Rhodes); Pete (Kevin Skousen); Stage manager (Sloan Fischer); Waitress (Judy Kam); French woman (Hilla Moll); Andrew Ross (Billy Burdin); Girl (Cynthia Mann).

Good Morning, Peoria, September 9, 1959

Rock 'n' roll is about to become big, but not in Peoria. That is, unless Sam, as DJ Howlin' Chick Howell, can manage to keep the radio station where he's employed from being shut down by overly conservative town elders. Wr: Chris Ruppenthal. Dir: Michael Zinberg.

Rachel (Patricia Richardson); Fred (Richard McKenzie); Brian (Todd Merrill); Chubby Checker (Himself); Leland (Steve Bean); Mayor (Hal England); Sheriff Jake Foley (E.R. Davies); Theora (Barbara Perry); Businessman/Councilman (J. Frank Stewart); Man in suit (Kurt Andon); Reporter (Steve Whiteford); Chick (Doug Ibold).

Thou Shalt Not..., February 2, 1974

Sam's task as a rabbi is to keep his sister-in-law from falling for a sleazy author and ruining her life. In the process he also helps the family recover from the death of their son. Wr: Tammy Ader. Dir: Randy Roberts.

Joe Basch (James Sutorius); Irene Basch (Terri Hanauer); Karen Basch (Lindsay Fisher); Bert Glasserman (Russ Tamblyn); Shirley Winnick (Jill Jacobson); Hannah (Twink Caplan); Mrs. Miriam Dalwitz (Magda Harout); Maxine (Freyda Thomas); Woman (Joie Magidow); Rabbi (David K. Basch); Rabbi David K. Basch (John J. Reiner);

Mr. Harold Dalwitz (Milt Hammerman); Cantor (Jay Frailich); Singer (Patti Pivaar).

Jimmy, October 14, 1964
Since mainstreaming the mentally retarded is not yet a popular concept, Sam must help Jimmy LaMotta, the "slow" young man he's leaped into, get a job and gain his co-workers' acceptance, to prevent his brother from returning Jimmy to the institution. Wr: Paul M. Belous and Robert Wolterstorff. Dir: James Whitmore, Jr.

Frank (John D'Aquino); Connie (Laura Harrington); Charlie Samuels (Michael Alldredge); Corey LaMotta (Ryan McWhorter); Blue (Michael Madsen); Mrs. Kirksey (Elaine Hausman); Peter Kirksey (Josh Peden); Jimmy (Brad Silverman).

So Help Me God, July 29, 1957
Though he can't remember much more than habeas corpus, Sam finds himself the defense attorney for a young black woman accused of murdering the son of the most powerful man in a small Louisiana town. Wr: Deborah Pratt. Dir: Andy Cadiff.

Captain Cotter (Byrne Piven); Lila (Tyra Ferrell); Sadie (Kathleen Noone); Myrtle (Ketty Lester); Sheriff Dixon (John Apicella); Sugee (Stacy Ray); Bo Parsons (John Shepard); Judge Haller (William Schallert); Chigger (Robert Dryer); Clerk (Scotch Byerley); Woman gossip (Heather Lee); Travis Michael Holder (Leonard Dancey); Coroner (Philip Parsons); Gardener (Cal Gibson).

Catch a Falling Star, May 21, 1979
Sam leaps into Ray Hutton, the understudy for the role of Cervantes, just seconds before curtain time. His mission: Prevent the drunken star from falling and seriously injuring himself during a benefit performance of *Man of La Mancha*. Sam isn't helped by the presence of his former piano teacher, on whom he once had a crush, and who now appears to have caught the star's eye as well. Wr: Paul Brown. Dir: Donald P. Bellisario.

John O'Malley (John Cullum); Nicole (Michele Pawk); Michelle (Janine Turner); Manny (Ernie Sabella); Charlie (Paul Sand); Dolores (Myra Turley); Anita (Maria Lauren); Ray Hutton/Mirror (Michael Carl); Dr. Carrasco (Marshall Borden); Padro (Rand Hopkins); Muleteer (Michael DeMarlo); Muleteer (Jay Horton); Muleteer (Dafidd McCracken); Muleteer (Sam Rapp); Innkeeper (John Huffman); Housekeeper (Ruth Miller).

A Portrait for Troian, February 7, 1971
Sam leaps into a renowned parapsychologist, and he must prevent a young widow from joining her husband at the bottom of a lake, while proving that she's not crazy, despite her claims of hearing her dead husband calling to her. Wr: Scott Shepherd and Donald P. Bellisario, story by John Hill and Scott Shepherd. Dir: Michael Zinberg.

Troian (Deborah Pratt); Jimmy (Robert Torti); Miss Stoltz (Carolyn Seymour); Mrs. Little (Bette Ray); Coroner (Bill McLaughlin); Timothy Mintz (Don P. Bellisario); Julian Claridge (Paul Brown).

Animal Frat, October 19, 1967
Trapped in the body of Knut Wileton, better known as "Wild Thing," the typical frat jock, Sam must win the confidence of an attractive campus radical before she bombs the college's chemistry building as a protest against the war in Vietnam. Wr: Chris Ruppenthal. Dir: Gilbert Shilton.

Elisabeth Spokane (Stacy Edwards); Will (Raphael Sbarge); Duck (Darren Dalton); Guna (Brian Haley); Hags (Stuart Fratkin); Scooter (Robert Petkoff); Prof. Davenport (Edward Edwards); Knut "Wild Thing" Wileton (Jeff Benson); Emily (Jacqueline Citron); Cindy (Kriston Citron); Woman #1 (Hope Marie Carleton); Woman #2 (Shannon Terhune); Frat boy (Michael Giambone); Frat boy (Brian Leckner); Frat boy (David Pressman).

Another Mother, September 30, 1981
As a divorced mother of three, Sam's job of preventing his teenage son from running away, never to be seen again, is made more interesting by the fact that his youngest daughter can see both him and Al. Wr: Deborah Pratt. Dir: Joseph L. Scanlan.

Kevin (Michael Stoyanov); Susan (Olivia Burnette); Teresa (Troian Bellisario); Jackie (Allison Barron); Teddy (Andrew Held); Ox (Larron Tate); David (Kevin Telles); Paul (Eric Welch); Stick (Terrence Evans); Lemule (Michael Kemmerling); Rafaella (Alina Cenal); Linda (Molly Meeker).

All-Americans, November 6, 1962
Keeping his best friend from throwing the high school championship football game, costing both of them their scholarship offers, Sam must also get their families to consolidate. Wr: Paul Brown and Donald P. Bellisario. Dir: John Cullum.

Chuey (Richard Coca); Celia (Ruth Britt); Manuel (Pepe Serna); Ruben (Fausto Bara); Coach (Robert Benedetti); Hal (Ralph Monaco); Otto (Otto Coelho); Carla (Maria Caldare); Maria (Christi Alvarez); Eddie Vega (Corey Smith).

Her Charm, September 26, 1973
Protecting a female member of the witness protection program from a Mafia hitman proves difficult for Sam, since the FBI appears to have an informant confounding his attempts to hide her. Wr: Deborah Pratt and Donald P. Bellisario, story by Paul M. Belous, Robert Wolterstorff, Deborah Pratt, and Donald P. Bellisario. Dir: Chris Welch.

Dana Beringer (Teri Austin); Richardson (Stanley Brock); Nick (John Snyder); Andy (Rene Assa); Thomas (John Shepard); Professor Sebastian LoNigro (James Hardie); Peter Langly (Mark Harigian).

Freedom, November 22, 1970
Rather than saving his grandfather's life, Sam has to escape from jail and elude the police long enough to get them both to the reservation, where the old man can die in peace, at home. Wr: Chris Ruppenthal. Dir: Alan J. Levi.

Joseph Whitehorse (Frank Sotonoma Salsedo); Taggart (Leon Rippy); Suzanne (Gloria Hayes); Deputy Sheriff Hazlitt (Tom Everett); Proprietor (D. Hooks); George Washukio (Jim Jaimes).

Good Night, Dear Heart, November 9, 1957
Rather than saving the damsel of the episode, who supposedly committed suicide, Sam is the coroner trying to prove that she was murdered, and find out by whom. Wr: Paul Brown. Dir: Christopher T. Welch.

Roger (William Cain); Stephanie (Marcia Cross); Greg (Robert Duncan McNeill); Aggie (Deborah Strang); Lyle (W.K. Stratton); Groundskeeper (Hal Bokar); Hilla (Suzanne Tegman); Melvin (Marvyn Berkett).

Pool Hall Blues, September 4, 1954
In order to help his granddaughter save a small bar from the slimy loan shark holding a note on the place, Sam has to play pool like a pro ... with a little help from Al and Ziggy. Wr: Randy Holland. Dir: Joe Napolitano.

Violet (Shari Headley); Eddie (J.W. Smith); Grady (Teddy Wilson); "The Brush" (Eddie's sidekick) (Ken Foree); Charles Griffin (Robert Gossett); Lester Brown (Alton Blair Carter); Miss White (Annie Wasterman); Magic (Robert 'Rags' Woods).

Leaping in Without a Net, November 18, 1958
Sam remembers he's afraid of heights when he leaps into a trapeze artist, whose sister wants him to catch her as she does a triple without a net. Dad is less than pleased, since his wife died a few years earlier while attempting the same stunt. Wr: Tommy Thompson. Dir: Christopher T. Welch.

Laszlo (Jan Triska); Eva (Fabiana Udenio); Vargas (Richard Riehle); Big Moe (Phil Fondacaro); Sybil (Roya Megnot); Benny Skyler (Jan Eddy); Ringmaster (Kristopher Antekeier); Stripper (Vivian Paxton); Carmenina (Maria Lauren); Victor Panzini (Ted Nordblum).

Maybe Baby, March 11, 1963
Babysitting a kidnapped tot and a flaky, compulsively lying stripper keeps Sam busy as they cross Texas, on the run from the legal father and a squad of cops. Wr: Paul Brown and Julie Brown. Dir: Michael Zinberg.

Bunny McBride (Julie Brown); Sheriff Barnes (Jimmy Ray Weeks); Deputy Sutton (Travis McKenna); Baby Christy (Cathy McAuley); Reed (Charles Frank); Big Bob (Ray Young); Leon (Byrne Offutt); Officer Montero (Garrett Pearson); Margaret Cole (Maggie Egan); Farmer (Carmen Filpi); Madeline (Eve Brenner); Buster (Jay Boryea).

Sea Bride, June 3, 1954
Aboard an ocean liner, Sam must stop the marriage of a young man's ex-wife to a mobster. In the process, he finds himself in one heck of a mess in the ship's garbage compartment. Wr: Deborah Pratt. Dir: Joe Napolitano.

Catherine (Beverly Leech); Weathers (John Hertzler); Vincent (James Harper); Marian (Patricia Harty); Jennifer Farrington (Juliet Sorcey); Tony (Tony Maggio); Alfonso (Louis Guss); Head steward (Ralph Brunea); Captain Sheffield (Kurt Knudson); Philip Dumont (Kent Phillips); Carlo Monte (Rick Buche).

M.I.A., April 1, 1969
When Sam leaps into the life of an undercover cop, Al explains that his mission is to convince a Navy nurse that her M.I.A. husband is still alive, and to prevent her from marrying a lawyer she meets on the day Sam leaps in. But a series of coincidences causes Sam to wonder about the true nature of his mission. Wr: Donald P. Bellisario. Dir: Michael Zinberg.

Skaggs (Jason Beghe); Beth (Susan Diol); Dirk Simon (Norman Large); Sergeant Riley (Dan Ziskie); Tequila (Pat Skipper); Carol (Sierra Pecheur); Boner (William Shockley); Rosalie (Leticia Vasquez); Pusher (Gregory Millar); Hippie girl (Cyndy Strittmatter); Taco man (Javi Mulero); Hippie guy (Rob Mendel); Jake Rawlins (Doug Bauer).

Season 3: Beginning September 1990

The Leap Home, November 25, 1969
As himself at the age of 16, Sam has the opportunity to both win the high school basketball championship and save his family from their sad fates. Wr: Donald P. Bellisario. Dir: Joe Napolitano.

John Samuel Beckett (Scott Bakula); Tom Beckett (David Newsom); Sis (Olivia Burnette); Cheerleader (Hannah Cutrona); Cheerleader (Mai-Lis Kuniholm); Mom (Caroline Kava); Coach Donnelly (Mik Scribba); Dr. Berger (Miles Brewster); Herky (Matthew John Graeser); Sibby (Ethan Wilson); No Nose Pruitt (John L. Tuell); Sam (Adam Affonso).

The Leap Home, Part 2, April 7, 1970
As a Navy SEAL in his own brother's squad, Sam must determine whether he is there to save Tom's life or ensure the success of the mission on which his brother was killed. Wr: Donald P. Bellisario. Dir: Michael Zinberg.

Tom Beckett (David Newsom); Maggie (Andrea Thompson); Col. Deke (Ernie Lively); Dempsey (David Hayward); Titi (Tia Carrere); Preacher (Adam Nelson); Blaster (Patrick Warburton); Shamo (Ryan Reid); Doc (Rich Whiteside); Choo Choo (Rodney Kageyama); Herbert "Magic" Williams (Christopher Kirby).

Leap of Faith, August 19, 1963
Sam finds himself in one holy mess as a priest in Philadelphia, trying to help an alcoholic priest deal with a killer and the death of a young parishoner. Wr: Tommy Thompson, story by Nick Harding, Karen Hall, and Tommy Thompson. Dir: James Whitmore, Jr.

Father John MacPherson (Sandy McPeak); Tony Pronti (Danny Nucci); Joey Pronti (Davey Roberts); Rose Monticello (Erica Yohn); Rita Monticello (Penny Stanton); Woman (Pat Crawford Brown); Young Sly (Todd Raderman); Allen, old man in church (Robert Beecher); Policeman (Bo Sabato); Cab driver (Dominic Oliver); Mrs. Dellisio (Lisa Passero); Tony's girlfriend (Amy Tritico); Father Frank Pistano (Bud Sabatino).

One Strobe Over the Line, June 15, 1965
Sam is a photographer who must protect a fashion model from a growing dependency on amphetamines

and a predatory manager's ambitions. Wr: Chris Ruppenthal. Dir: Michael Zinberg.

Helen LeBaron (Marjorie Monaghan); Edie (Susan Anton); Byron (Kristoffer Tabori); Mike (David Sheinkompf); Frank (Robert Trumbull); Irv (John Achorn); Waiter (Nigel Gibbs); Karl Stone (Dan McCoy); Nubian guard (Lawrence McNeal III).

The Boogieman, October 31, 1964

Things do more than go bump in the night when Sam leaps into Joshua Raye, a horror novelist, on Halloween. Although Ziggy claims he's there to prevent the death of a church deacon, things get even stranger when two more people die without warning. Wr: Chris Ruppenthal. Dir: Joe Napolitano.

Mary (Valerie Mahaffey); Sheriff (Paul Linke); Dorothy (Fran Ryan); Stevie (David Kriegel); Tully (Donald Hotton); Joshua Rey (Chris Ruppenthal).

Miss Deep South, June 7, 1958

As Darlene Monte, a contestant in the "Miss Deep South" beauty pageant, Sam must come to the aid of an innocent contender who faces disgrace when she poses for naughty pictures taken by a sleazy pageant photographer. As if things weren't bad enough, Sam must ensure that Darlene finishes third, so that she'll go on to become a doctor. Wr: Tommy Thompson. Dir: Christopher Welch.

Connie (Heather McAdam); Peg Myers (Nancy Stafford); Clint (David A. Brooks); Vicky (Julie Ann Lowery); Judge (Hugh Gillin); Arlene (Linda Hoy); Woman judge (Marte Boyle Slout); Master of Ceremonies (Martin Clark); Cheryl Lynn (Karina Moore); Beauty contestant (Janeen Rae Heller); Darlene Monte/Monty (Theresa Ring).

Black on White on Fire, August 11, 1965

Sam leaps into a black med student engaged to a white woman in order to ensure that he and his fiancee survive the Watts Riot together. Wr: Deborah Pratt. Dir: Joe Napolitano.

Nita Jordan (C.C.H. Pounder); Lonnie Jordan (Gregory Millar); Susan Bond (Corie Henninger); B.B. (Sami Chester); Papa Dee (Ron Taylor); Capt. Paul Bond (Marc Alaimo); Sheri (Laverne Anderson); Matty (Montrose Hagins); Young woman (Cheryl Francis Harrington); Police sniper (Jon Berry); Ray Harper (Garon Grigsby).

The Great Spontini, May 9, 1974

Leaping into magician Harry Spontini, Sam has to prevent his estranged wife from taking their daughter away from him as she files for divorce so she can marry her sleazy divorce attorney. Wr: Christy Dawson and Beverly Bridges. Dir: James Whitmore, Jr.

Maggie (Amy Steel); Steve (Erich Anderson); Jamie (Lauren Woodland); Judge (Michael Fairman); Elaine (Robin Greer); Mrs. Futrell (Jean Adams); Harry Spontini (Dan Birch).

Rebel Without a Clue, September 1, 1958

As "Bones," a member of a motorcycle gang, Sam is an uneasy rider who has to prevent a Kerouac-inspired young woman from meeting her death on the road. Wr: Randy Holland and Paul Brown, story by Nick Harding and Paul Brown. Dir: James Whitmore, Jr.

Becky (Josie Bissett); Dillon (Dietrich Bader); Ernie Tyler (Teddy Wilson); Jack Kerouac (Michael Bryan French); Mad dog (Scott Kraft); Biker (Mark Boone, Jr.); Biker (Joshua Cadman); Shane "Funny Bone" Thomas (Kristopher Logan).

A Little Miracle, December 24, 1962

On Christmas Eve, Sam leaps into Reginald Pierson, valet to a wealthy contractor who is in danger of losing his soul in an attempt to demolish a Salvation Army mission so he can build his "Blake's Plaza." Seeing a similarity to the Dickens character, Sam and Al decide to "Scrooge" the greed out of the man. Wr: Sandy Fries and Robert A. Wolterstorff, story by Sandy Fries. Dir: Michael Watkins.

Blake (Charles Rocket); Laura (Melinda McGraw); Max (Robert Lesser); Calloway (Tom McTigue); Lt. Porterman (Michael Dan Wagner); Newscaster (Dale Harimoto); Mickey (Christopher Fleming); Tiny boy (Jarrett Lennon); Charlie (Dan Hareimonto Brown); Maintenance man (Duane Whitaker); Reginald Pierson (Milan Nicksic).

Runaway, July 4, 1964

On a cross-country car trip, Sam, as 13-year-old Butchie, must contend with a sadistic older sister and a mother on the verge of running away from an unfulfilling marriage in search of the feminine mystique. Wr: Paul Brown. Dir: Michael Katelman.

Emma (Sandy Faison); Hank (Sherman Howard); Bill (Joeseph Hacker); Alex (Ami Foster); Beth (Amber Susa); Butchie (Buff Borin)

8 1/2 Months, November 15, 1955

Billie Jean Crockett is a pregnant teenager who will make the second biggest mistake of her life—giving her baby up for adoption—unless Sam, as Billie Jean, can convince someone to help her raise her child ... before he goes into labor himself! Wr: Deborah Pratt. Dir: James Whitmore, Jr.

Dotty (Lana Schwab); Bob (James Whitmore, Jr.); Keeter (Hunter von Leer); Effy (Tasha Scott); Mrs. Thailer (Anne Haney); Rogers (Parley Baer); Willis (Philip Linton); Nurse Denton (Peggy Walton-Walker); Mrs. Suffy (Molly McClure); Billie Jean Crockett (Priscilla Weems).

Future Boy, October 6, 1957

Sam leaps into Kenny Sharp, better known as "Future Boy," sidekick to Moe Stein, host of the kid's show Time Patrol, who also happens to be building a time machine in his basement. Unless Sam can prevent Moe's daughter from attempting to have her father committed, Moe is destined to be killed as he tries to hop a freight train. Wr: Tommy Thompson. Dir: Michael Switzer.

Moe Stein/Capt. Galaxy (Richard Herd); Irene Kiner (Debra Sticklin); Ben Harris (George Wyner); Dr. Sandler (Alan Fudge); Judge (David Sage); Roger (Nicholas Schaffer); Caped futurite (Jason Kincaid); Boy (John Christian Grahs); Kid (Jesse Switzer); Kenny Sharp (Matt Marfoglia).

Private Dancer, October 6, 1979
An aspiring dancer working as a waitress in a strip club is in danger of being led into a life of prostitution unless Sam, as "Rod the Bod," can convince her to audition for a spot in a professional dance group. But she is deaf, and the choreographer doesn't believe she has the time to give the young lady the attention she'll need. Wr: Paul Brown. Dir: Debbie Allen.

Joanne Chapman (Debbie Allen); Mario (Louis Mustillo); Valerie (Heidi Swedberg); Otto (Robert Schuch); Female dancer (Marguerite Pomerhn-Derricks); Diana Quinna (Rhondee Beriault); Martin (Henry Woronicza); Winnie (Melinda Cordell); Officer Arden (Charles Emmett); Lou (Frank Novack); Louie (Harry Cohn); Rod (Christopher Solari).

Piano Man, November 10, 1985
Joey Dinardo is a lounge lizard on the run from Mob hitmen. When Sam leaps in, he's been found by his ex-girlfriend and former musical partner, and now both are on a run for their lives from a killer who seems to know their every move. Wr: Ed Scharlach. Dir: James Whitmore, Jr.

Lorraine (Marietta DePrima); Carl Morgan (Angelo Tiffe); Frank (John Oldach); Janelle (Denise Gentile); Heetor (Frank Roman); Thelma (Cherry Davis); Chuck/Joey (Sam Clay).

Trivia Alert: Scott Bakula's lyrical debut: "Somewhere in the Night."

Southern Comforts, August 4, 1961 (aka Love for Sale)
It's the best little cathouse in New Orleans. No, it's the Gilbert Labonte Sewin' and Quiltin' Academy. As the proprietor of this worthy establishment, Sam must prevent the mysterious death of a resident who doesn't belong there. Wr: Tommy Thompson. Dir: Chris Ruppenthal.

Marsha (Rita Taggart); Sheriff (David Graf); Gina (Georgia Emelin); Jake Dorliac (Dan Butler); Sophie (Lauren Tom); Ruby, prostitute #1 (Minnie Summers Lindsey); Prostitute #2 (Diane Delano); Luther (David Powledge); Warren (Walter Sylvest); Sailor (J. Marvin Campbell); Paulette (Stacey Cortez); Abby (Monica McMurtry); Reese (Jeffrey Concklin); Carl (David Alan Graf); Gilbert La Bonte (Richard White).

Glitter Rock, April 12, 1974
Sam is a glitter rock star in danger of being stabbed to death after a performance, unless Sam can determine who, from a growing list of people, the real killer is. Wr: Chris Ruppenthal. Dir: Andy Cadiff.

Flash McGrath (Jonathan Gries); Dwayne (Peter Noone); Philip Silbar (Christian Hoff); Nick (Michael Cerveris); Wilder (Robert Bauer); Sandy (Liza Whitcraft); Whittler (Jan Eddy); Blonde (Sharon Martin); Heather (Dorrie Krum); Chase (Bob Cady); Tonic/Mirror (Bruce Michael Paine).

A Hunting We Will Go, June 18, 1976
It's the leap from hell as Sam, a bounty hunter handcuffed to a wiley embezzler who will stop at noth-

ing to get away from him, has to deal with his captive, as well as his attraction towards her. Wr: Beverly Bridges. Dir: Andy Cadiff.

Diane Frost (Jane Sibbett); Rodney (Ken Marshall); Sheriff Michaels (Cliff Bemis); Jack (Michael McCarty); Bill (Dale Swann); Luke (Jeffrey King); Clive (Warren Harrington); Edwine (Maxine Elliott); Cashier (Dorothy Blass); Gordon O'Reilly (Ken Kells).

Last Dance Before an Execution, May 12, 1971
"Just think of someplace far away" is the advice Sam hears as he leaps into Jesus Ortega, a Cuban-American being strapped into an electric chair. A last-second stay of execution gives Sam just 48 hours to either prove himself innocent or fulfill his mission so that he can leap before the switch is pulled. Wr: Deborah Pratt, story by Bill Bigelow, Donald P. Bellisario, and Deborah Pratt. Dir: Michael Watkins.

Teresa (Jenny Gago); Raoul (Julio Oscar Mechoso); Ripley (Christopher Allport); Theodore Wallace Moody (James Sloyan); Officer Little (Leonard C. Lightfoot); Officer Hudson (Jack Jozefson); Herb Steain (Michael Holden); Maria (Krista Muscare); Father Raftery (Charles Woolf); Tia (Irene Olga Lopez); Burl Manners (A.J. Freeman); Reporter (Wendy Jill Gordon); Reporter (Andrew Amador); Older man (Harry Fleer); Black man (Neil Baron); Jesus/Mirror (Stephen Dominga).

Heart of a Champion, July 23, 1955
The heart of a champion belongs to Ronnie, a professional wrestler, who will die if he competes in the title match. Sam, as his brother and new partner, Terry, must convince him of his hidden health problem, while avoiding his own health problem—the jealous wrestler husband of a woman who has taken an amorous interest in Sam. Wr: Tommy Thompson. Dir: Joe Napolitano.

Ronnie (Jerry Bossard); Lamar (Don Hood); Sherry (Deborah Wakeham); Lotty (Angela Paton); Dr. Griggs (Rance Howard); Myra (Susan Isaacs); Carl Shilough (Terry Funk); Stan (Tim deZarn); Referee (Don Dolan); Terry (Jeff Hochendoner); Executioner I (Jay S. York); Hank (John Kidwell).

Nuclear Family, October 26, 1962
Sam finds himself the brother of a fallout shelter salesman during the Cuban Missile Crisis. He must defuse a potentially explosive situation as panic sets in on the night of John F. Kennedy's speech to the nation. Wr: Paul Brown. Dir: James Whitmore, Jr.

Matt (Timothy Carhart); Burt (Kurt Fuller); Kate (Kim Flowers); Stevie (Robert Hy Gorman); Kimberly (Candy Hutson); Mrs. Klingman (Delia Salvi); Eddie (Patrick M. Bruneau).

Shock Theater, October 2, 1954
Leaping into Sam Bederman, a mental patient who is suffering from acute depression, Sam receives an overloaded electroshock treatment, which causes his Swiss-cheesed memory to be replaced by personae from previous leaps. Al, who is visible to the mentally ill, must try to complete Sam's mission and

convince him to take another shock treatment, in order to leap Sam out before contact is lost forever. Wr: Deborah Pratt. Dir: Joe Napolitano.

Dr. Masters (David Proval); Butcher (Bruce A. Young); Tibby Johnson (Scott Lawrence); Dr. Wickless (Robert Symonds); Dr. Beaks (Candy Ann Brown); Freddie (Nick Brooks); Nurse Chatam (Lee Garlington); Mortimer (Frank Collison); Oswald (Ralph Marero); Young doctor (Kevin Page); Older doctor (Harry Pugh); Jesse Tyler (Howard Matthew Johnson); Samantha Stormer (LeReine Charut); Jimmy (Brad Silverman).

Season 4: Beginning September 1991

The Leap Back, June 15, 1945
Struck by lightning, Sam and Al find their roles reversed, as Sam returns to the future and to a long-lost love, while Al leaps back to 1945 to prevent the death of a returning World War II hero and his former girlfriend. Wr: Donald P. Bellisario. Dir: Michael Zinberg.

Donna Elissi (Mimi Kuzyk); Suzanne (Amanda Wyss); Mike (Douglas Roberts); Clifford (Robert Prescott); Dr. Beeks (Candy Ann Brown); Kelly (Jeanine Jackson); Gooshie (Dennis Wolfberg); Tina (Gigi Rice); Naval admiral (Susan Ann Connor); Capt. Tom Jarret (Dean Denton); The voice of Ziggy (Deborah Pratt).

Play Ball, August 6, 1961
A pitcher on a minor league baseball team, Sam must decide if he's there to help a fellow team member get his host back into the major leagues, or babysit the porcine team mascot, all while resisting the amorous advances of the women in his life. Wr: Tommy Thompson. Dir: Joe Napolitano.

Chucky (Neal McDonough); Margaret Twilly (Maree Cheatham); Manager (Don Stroud); Bunny (Courtney Gebhart); Warren Monroe (Peter Jason); Talent scout (Casey Sander); Radio reporter (Royce D. Applegate); Billy (Michael Bellisario); Jorge (Juan Garcia); Ryker (Chuck Fick); Eagle mgr. (Russel Lunday); First umpire (Hank Robinson); Immigration officer (David B. Maccabee); Doc (Owen Rutledge).

Hurricane, August 17, 1969
Sam meets Camille, and possibly a killer, when he leaps into a deputy sheriff in a small Mississippi town lying in the path of a deadly hurricane. Wr: Chris Ruppenthal. Dir: Michael Watkins.

Cissy Davis (Marilyn Jones); Lisa (Tracy Kolis); Mr. Lejeune [man at party] (James Morrison); Joe Deever (Bill Erwin); Ma Maw (Barbara Townsend); Mark (Richard Grove); Unabelle (Marjorie Lovett); Sitter (Stephanie Shroyer); Deputy Sheriff Archie Necaise/Mirror (Bob Hamiton).

Justice, May 11, 1965
Sam must don the robe of a Ku Klux Klansman in order to save the life of an ambitious young civil rights leader who is trying to register black voters. Wr: Toni Graphia. Dir: Rob Bowman.

Lilly (Lisa Waltz); Nathaniel Simpson (Michael Beach);

Ada Simpson (Fran Bennett); Tom (Dirk Blocker); Grady (Glenn Morshower); Cody (Lee Weaver); Mr. Thompson (Jacob Gelman); Gene/Grand Dragon (Noble Willingham); Sheriff Otis (Charlie Holliday); Leon (Steve Blackwood); Jim (Michael Craig Patterson); Clyde/Mirror (Glenn Edden); First child (Jullian Roy Doster); Second child (Ashley Woolfolk); Third child (Jesshaye Callier).

Permanent Wave, June 2, 1983
Sam leaps into Frank Bianca, a hairstylist in leather pants, to prevent the death of a young murder witness and his mother. Wr: Beverly Bridges. Dir: Scott Bakula.

Laura (Doran Clark); Chloe (Lela Ivy); Kyle (Joseph Gordon-Levitt); Det. Ward (Harry Groener); Ralph (Stephen Kay); Mimi (Christine Cattell); Elsa (Candi Brough); Lisel (Randi Brough); Frank Bianca (Robert Jacobs).

Raped, June 20, 1980
It's up to Sam to try to bring a rapist to justice when he leaps into the victim, a young woman who may have been unwilling to press charges against the young man—the son of the pillar of the community. Wr: Beverly Bridges. Dir: Michael Zinberg.

Nancy (Penny Peyser); Colleen (Nancy Lenehan); Jim (Arthur Rosenburg); Kevin Wentworth (Matthew Sheehan); Libby (Amy Ryan); Katie McBain (Cheryl Pollak); Judge Bowers (Aaron Lustig); Officer Shamway (Eugene Lee); Paula Fletcher (Liz Vassey); Glenn (Eric Bruskotter); Brian Chadwick (John Petlock); Dr. Samuel (Michael Griswold); Randy (Pat O'Neal); Nurse (Nora Masterson); Baliff (Mark Conley).

The Wrong Stuff, January 24, 1961
The fates make a monkey out of Sam when he leaps into Bobo, an astrochimp who must avoid succumbing to the experiments of an Air Force neurologist. Wr: Paul Brown. Dir: Joe Napolitano.

Dr. Leslie Ashton (Caroline Goodall); Dr. Winger (Gary Swanson); Dr. Tucker (Albert Stratton); First military officer (Kim Robillard); Second military officer (Peter Murnik).

Dreams, February 28, 1979
It's more like a nightmare when Sam leaps into a detective investigating a gruesome murder. He may be next if he doesn't find out who eviscerated the victim, and his only hope is the victim's catatonic son and her husband's psychiatrist. The horrific flashbacks he's experiencing don't help matters much. Wr: Deborah Pratt. Dir: Anita Addison.

Pamela Roselli (Jocelyn O'Brien); Dr. Crane (Alan Scarfe); Capt. Vincent (Bill Marcus); Peter DeCaro (Tim Ahern); Lea DeCaro (Noley Thornton); P.J. DeCaro (Michael Patrick Carter); Officer Talbot (Anthony Pena); Coroner (Wycliffe Young); Jack Stone (David Gene Garrison).

A Single Drop of Rain, September 7, 1953
A devastating drought will be the ruin of a small town unless Sam, as Billy Beaumont, "purveyor of precipitation and maker of rain," can find a way to make it rain, while keeping his family together in the

process. Wr: Richard C. Okie, story by Richard Stanley and Ralph Mayering, Jr. Dir: Virgil W. Vogel.

Annie [Mrs. Beaumont] (Phyllis Lyons); Ralph Beaumont (Patrick Massett); Clinton (Carl Anthony Payne II); Vern Coutis (Britt Leach); Davison (R.G. Armstrong); Grace Beaumont (Anne Haney); Velma Waters (Lesly Kahn); Bill Beaumont (Ted Baader); Norm (Hal Landon, Jr.).

Unchained, November 2, 1956
Sam and a fellow convict named Boone are the defiant ones when Sam has to rescue his companion from a 15-year sentence on a chain gang. Wr: Paris Qualles. Dir: Michael Watkins.

Jasper Boone (Basil Wallace); Boss Cooley (J.C. Quinn); Warden B.T. Elias (Claude Earl Jones); Old Convict (Robert V. Barron); Jake Wiles (Don Sparks); Mr. Monroe, guard (Jed Mills); Chance Cole/mirror (Mark Kemble).

The Play's the Thing, September 9, 1969
May meets December when Sam leaps into a young actor in love with an older woman, who is also an aspiring singer. If he can't boost her confidence and help her get her career on track, she will face a "fate worse than death": returning with her son to Cleveland. Wr: Beverly Bridges. Dir: Eric Laneuville.

Jane Lindhurst (Penny Fuller); Ted (Robert Pine); Neil Lindhurst (Daniel Roebuck); Liz Lindhurst (Anna Gunn); Director (Craig Richard Nelson), Rob Jackson (Paul Collins); Petra (Eva Loseth); King [band leader] (Deem Bristow); Joe Thurlow/Mirror (Wil Schaub).

Running for Honor, June 11, 1964
As a track star in a Navy college, Sam must prevent the death of his ex-roommate, who was expelled because he was gay, and who is slated to die at the hands of a group of bigoted cadets. Wr: Robert Harris Duncan. Dir: Bob Hulme.

Admiral Spencer (John Finn); Philip (Sean O'Bryan); Ronnie Chambers (Anthony Palermo); Coach Martz (John Roselius); Karen (Lisa Lawrence); Plebe guard (Jake Price); Waitress (Roz Witt); Cadet (Martin Hansen); Plebe (Brian Selbert); Tommy H. York (Beau Windham).

Temptation Eyes, February 1, 1985
A serial killer stalks San Francisco while Sam, as TV reporter Dillion Powell, protects a beautiful psychic who's working on the case from becoming the next victim. The young lady is very clear of sight, as Sam and Al soon discover. Wr: Paul Brown. Dir: Christopher Hibler.

Tamlyn Masuta (Tamlyn Tomita); Collins (Kent Williams); Ross (James Handy); Tony Beche (Rob LaBelle); Dylan Powell (Harker Wade).

The Last Gunfighter, November 28, 1957
Sam finds himself in the life of Tyler Meanes, a teller of tall tales who faces death at the hand of an old friend in a shootout at high noon. Wr: Sam Rolfe and Chris Ruppenthal, story by Sam Rolfe. Dir: Joe Napolitano.

Pat Knight (John Anderson); Lucy (Susan Isaacs); Ben

Stiner (Kenneth Tigar); Stevie (Sean Baca); Otis (Joseph Burke); Cindy (Bonnie Morgan); Tyler Means (Paul Bordman); Also with O'Neal Compton, Jerry Potter.

A Song for the Soul, April 7, 1963
As a backup singer in a black amateur girl group, Sam finds himself caught between the 15-year-old lead singer and her father as he attempts to rescue the girl from a sleazy nightclub owner's clutches. Wr: Deborah Pratt. Dir: Michael Watkins.

Rev. Walters (Harrison Page); Lynell (Tamara Townsend); Paula (T'Keyah "Crystal" Keymah); Bobby Lee (Eric LaSalle); JoJo (Richard McGregor); Rainey (G. Smokey Campbell); Cheree/Mirror (Tiffany Jameson); Raghead teen #1 (Clyde R. Jones); Raghead teen #2 (Tommy Morgan); Raghead teen #3 (Christopher M. Brown).

Ghost Ship, August 13, 1956
Flying over the Bermuda Triangle, Sam, as the co-pilot, must get a seriously ill passenger to a doctor before she dies. Flying through the triangle is riskier than it seems, and Sam, deprived of Al's help when the hologram fades out, must get them through alive. Wr: Paris Qualles and Donald P. Bellisario. Dir: Anita Addison.

Capt. Cooper (Scott Hoxby); Wendy (Kimberly Foster); Craig Cutter Jr. (Kurt Deutsch); Michelle Temple (Carla Gugino); Francis Edward "Eddie" Brackett (Mark McPherson).

Roberto! January 27, 1982
Sam, as Roberto! is a tabloid talk show host à la Geraldo who, with an asthmatic rival and co-worker, tries to uncover a mystery at a local chemical plant, a mystery which may prove deadly to his co-worker. Wr: Chris Ruppenthal. Dir: Scott Bakula.

Jenny Eisenberg (DeLane Matthews); Earl (Alan Oppenheimer); Saxton (Jerry Hardin); Tim (Michael Heintzman); Rick Upfield (Marcus Giamatti); Esther (Barbara Tarbuck); Herself (Laura Schlessinger); Jetters (Charles Daughtery); Red Norton (Dennis Fimple); Hank (Victor Talmadge); Dawn (Sherri Lyn Rotham); Deputy (Gregg Binkley); Ernesto (Paul Felix Montez); Roberto Gutierrez (Andrew Roa); Also with Don Gibb.

It's a Wonderful Leap, May 10, 1958
Sam finds himself behind the wheel of a New York taxicab, in the life of Max Greenman, a driver striving to win his own tag, a license to drive his own cab. His mission is aided by a woman who claims to be a guardian angel. Wr: Paul Brown, story by Danielle Alexandra and Paul Brown. Dir: Paul Brown.

Angelita Carmen Guadalupe Cecelia Jimenez (Liz Torres); Lenny (Jerry Adler); Frank (Peter Iacangelo); Elizabeth (Robin Frates); Lucky (Milt Kogan); Tony (Jack R. Orend); Moe (Douglas McHugh); Father (Vaughn Armstrong); Sgt. McCann (Frank Girardeau); Executive (Ed Wasser); The son (Justin Thomas); Max/Mirror (Ross Partridge).

Moments to Live, May 4, 1985
Sam is a soap opera heart surgeon and the obsession of a lovestruck, if somewhat deranged, fan. He must

escape from the woman and her husband, who kidnap him for reproductive purposes. Wr: Tommy Thompson. Dir: Joe Napolitano.

Norma Jean Bate (Kathleen Wilhoite); Hank (Pruitt Taylor Vince); Mildred (Frances Bay); Ben (Brian George); TV husband (Matthew Ashford); Roger (James Gleason); Woman (Ellen Gerstein); Nurse Kidman (Krista Mione); Waitress (Julie Lloyd); Policeman (Mark Fauser); Vendor (Richard Merson); Kyle Hart (Patrick Lowe).

The Curse of Ptah-Hotep, March 2, 1957
It's almost as though Sam were on vacation when, as Egyptologist Dale Conway, he gets to read hieroglyphics, search lost tombs, and, of course, visit Egypt. But between an encroaching sandstorm, computer glitches back at the Project, the suspicious deaths of the guides, and a 3000-year-old curse to round things off, Sam has very little time to play in the sand. Wr: Chris Ruppenthal. Dir: Joe Napolitano.

Ginny Will (Lisa Darr); Mustafa (John Kapelos); Ali (Chaim Jeraffi); Gamal (Ali Dean); Dale Conway/Mirror (Rodger LaRue).

Stand Up, April 30, 1959
Sam, as the singing half of a comedy team, soon finds that trying to convince two people that they're truly in love is no laughing matter, especially when one of them is the object of a sleazy casino owner's desire. Wr: Deborah Pratt. Dir: Michael Zinberg.

Mark McKay (Bob Saget); Frankie Warsharsky (Amy Yasbeck); Carlo De Grigorio (Robert Miranda); Joey (Tom LaGrua); Charlie (Wil Albert); Trucker (Pete Schrum); Emcee (Jon Melichar); Waitress (Martha Jane); Davey Parker (Rafe Battiste); Maria Rose (Rosemary Tarrquino); Also with Mark Lonow.

A Leap for Lisa, June 25, 1957
Sam leaps into one Al "Bingo" Calavicci to prevent the death of his married lover. But when Sam accidentally alters history, and finds out too late about the lover's untimely demise, it could mean the gas chamber for Al … and a whole new situation at the Project. Wr: Donald P. Bellisario. Dir: James Whitmore, Jr.

Comm. Riker (Charles Rocket); Chip (Jeffrey Corbett); Comm. Hugh Dobbs (Larry Brandenburg); Bingo (James Walters); Lisa (Terry Farrell); Judge (Anthony Peck); Edward St. John V (Roddy McDowall); Pollack (Steve Carlisle); Stacker (Jeff Nowinski); Marci (Debbie L. James); Plumber (Ivan Gueron); Flight surgeon (Jack Stauffer); Marine guard (Rich Whiteside).

Season 5: Beginning September 1992

Lee Harvey Oswald, October 5, 1957 and November 22, 1963 (aka Leaping on a String; Leap to Judgement) (2 hours)
As a result of leaping again before he had a chance to complete his original mission, Sam finds himself leaping back and forth through the life of Lee Harvey Oswald. Following the sole assassin theory,

Sam and Al attempt to prevent Oswald's attack on John F. Kennedy. But, with each leap giving Oswald more control over Sam's body, history seems doomed to repeat itself. Wr: Donald P. Bellisario. Dir: James Whitmore, Jr.

Sgt. Lopez (Reni Stanton); Lee Harvey Oswald (Willie Garson); Marina (Natasha Pavlova); Maj. Kosenko (Elya Baskin); Mariska (Donna Magnani); Gooshie (Dennis Wolfberg); Corp. McBride (Michael Rich); PFC Briggs (Philip McNiven); Lt. Obrigowitz (Ward C. Boland); Joda (Rodney Kageyama); Bar girl (Patty Toy); Carlos (James Medina); New Orleans policeman (Chris Kinkade); Sgt. Bellisario (Charles Nelson); Lt. Guri (Erika Amato); Guard (Lazar); Frasier (Nathan Lisle); Ruth Paine (Becky London); Jackie Kennedy (Karen Ingram).

Leaping of the Shrew, September 27, 1956 (aka Washed Away; When Venus Smiles)
It's Robinson Crusoe with a twist when Sam leaps into a Greek sailor stranded on a deserted island with a beautiful young rich woman who appears to be less than fond of both him and their stranded situation. Wr: Richard Okie and Robin Jill Bernheim. Dir: Alan J. Levi.

Vanessa (Brooke Shields); Socrates Alafouzos (Nikos Stathatos).

Nowhere to Run, August 10, 1968
As a Marine captain whose legs were amputated after a mishap in Vietnam, Sam finds himself in a veteran's hospital, where he must prevent the suicide of a fellow patient who would rather be dead than face life paralyzed from the neck down. Making matters worse, his wife seems incapable of accepting the fact that she and Sam's host can still lead a normal life, in spite of his condition. Wr: Tommy Thompson. Dir: Alan J. Levi.

Sgt. William "Billy" Johnson (Michael Boatman); Kiki Wilson (Jennifer Aniston); Comm. Hartig (Norman Snow); Holt (Gene Lythgow); Carol (Simone Allen); Young nurse (Kendra Booth); Baxter (Joseph M. Hamilton); Hippie (David Marshall); Vet (David McSwain); Capt. Ronald Miller/Mirror (Michael Carpenter); Julie (Judith Hoag).

Killin' Time, June 18, 1958
Sam leaps into a tricky situation as an escaped killer holed up in a house with a mother and daughter as hostages. Escape isn't going to be easy for either Sam or his hostages when the real killer breaks out of the Waiting Room, stranding Sam in the past, destined to die at the hands of a vengeful sheriff. Wr: Tommy Thompson. Dir: Michael Watkins.

Carol Pruitt (Connie Ray); Leon Styles (Cameron Dye); Sheriff John Hoyt (Jim Haynie); Deputy (Joseph Malone); Hooker (Carolyn Lowry); Becky Pruitt (Beverly Mitchell); Reporter (Lewis Dauber); Gooshie (Dennis Wolfberg).

Star Light, Star Bright, May 21, 1966
Sam leaps into a 79-year-old man whose son wants to have him committed when he claims to have seen UFOs. Sam is kept busy as he tries to keep the family

together, prevent the future drug overdose of "his" grandson, and avoid the sinister plans of the military. Wr: Richard C. Okie. Dir: Christopher Hibler.

Tim Stoddard (Morgan Weisser); Dr. Hardy (H. Richard Greene); Maj. Meadows (Michael L. Maguire); Mrs. Stoddard (Anne Lockhart); John Stoddard (Guy Boyd); Officer Milardi (Joshua Cox); Max Stoddard (Douglas Stark).

Deliver Us from Evil, March 19, 1966

Things are already on their way downhill when Sam leaps back into Jimmy LaMotta (see "Jimmy," Season 2). Despite Sam's inaction, history continues to change for the worse. The cause is unknown until Sam discovers another time traveler on the scene, one who's determined to destroy Jimmy's family, as well as Sam's. Wr: Robin Jill Bernheim, Tommy Thompson, and Deborah Pratt. Dir: Bob Hulme.

Zoey (Carolyn Seymour); Frank (John D'Aquino); Alia (Renee Coleman); Connie (Laura Harrington); Shirley Constantine (Kristen Cloke); Mr. Samuel (Ryan Mc-Whorter); Jimmy (Brad Silverman); Corey (Michael Alldredge).

Trilogy, Part 1, August 8, 1955 (aka One Little Heart)

A pair of unsolved murders marks just the tip of the iceberg when Sam leaps into a sheriff in a small Louisana town. Rumors of a history of family insanity, the suspicions surrounding his daughter Abigail's involvement in the murders, and ghostly visions of his institutionalized wife just make matters worse. Wr: Deborah Pratt. Dir: James Whitmore, Jr.

Leta Ada (Mary Gordon Murray); Doc Kinman (Max Wright); Deputy Bo Loman (Stephen Lee); Marie (Fran Bennett); Will Kinman (Travis Fine); Attorney Lawrence Stanton III (W.K. Stratton); Sammy Jo (Kimberly Cullum); Laura Fuller (Meg Foster); Abigail Fuller (Melora Hardin); Denton Waters (James Greene); Judge Shiner (Parley Baer); Sherlinda Stanton (Diana Bellamy); Mrs. Takin (Wendy Robie); Mr. Takin (Christopher Curry); Clayton Fuller (James Whitmore, Jr.).

Trilogy, Part 2, June 14, 1966 (aka For Your Love)

Finding himself back in the same small Louisiana town, in the arms of Abigail, now 21, Sam must prevent an angry crowd of townspeople from lynching his fiancee, following the disappearance of a young boy whom she had been babysitting.

Trilogy, Part 3 (aka The Last Door)

Sam is an aging lawyer, recruited by Abigail, now 33, to defend her when she is put on trial for the murder of Lita Aider, the woman whose daughter Abigail was accused of killing almost 25 years earlier. Wr: Deborah Pratt. Dir: James Whitmore, Jr.

Abigail Fuller (Melora Hardin); Lita Aider (Mary Gordon Murray); Doc Kinman (Max Wright); Denton Waters (James Greene); Deputy Bo Loman (Stephen Lee); Judge Shiner (Parley Baer); Marie (Fran Bennett); Mrs. Takin (Wendy Robie); Mr. Takin (Christopher Curry); Laura Fuller (Meg Foster); Attorney Lawrence Stanton III (W.K. Stratton); Sammy Jo (Kimberly Cullum); Towns-

woman (Beth Peters); Townsman (R. Leo Schreiber); Bailiff (Lanier Edwards); Violet Aider (Heather Lauren Olson); Will Kinman (Travis Fine); Sherlinda Stanton (Diana Bellamy).

Promised Land, December 22, 1971

Sam leaps to Elk Ridge, Indiana, to help save the lives of the Walters boys as they try to save their farm from a banker with designs on getting rich from foreclosure. Wr: Gillian Horvath and Tommy Thompson. Dir: Scott Bakula.

Neil Waters (Dwier Brown); Sheriff (Clyde Mundy); Sheriff Mundy (Arlen Dean Snyder); John Walters (Chris Stacy); Gus Vernon (Jonathan Hogan); Beth (Elizabeth Dennehy); Carl Wilkens (James C. Victor); Stan Pierce (Charles Dugan); Lila Pierce (Marion Dugan); Deputy (Jim Townsend); Willie Walters Jr. (Daniel Engstrom); Carrie (Kellie Overbey); Mary Walters (Lorinne Dills-Vozof); Cindy Wilkens (Elizabeth Rainey); John Beckett (Scott Bakula); John Beckett photo double (Kurt Andon); Sam photo double (Gregory Paul Jackson).

A Tale of Two Sweeties, February 25, 1958

As a horse-playing traveling brush salesman, Sam finds himself with two wives and two families. Although Ziggy predicts that Sam's mission is to choose between the two lives, the choice is made more difficult by the fact that there's only a 50/50 chance that he'll choose the right one. Sam finds that his penniless host owes a pair of bookies some big bucks. Wr: Robin Jill Bernheim. Dir: Christopher Hibler.

Ellen (Mary Lou Childs); Rachel (Jill Tracy); Jessica (Ashley Peldon); Josh (J.D. Daniels); Mary (Shay Astar); Martin, Jr. (Michael Bellisario); Vic, the Bookie (Larry Manetti); Receptionist (J.C. Wendel); Gus (Jack Yates); Gina, wife #3 (Kristie Transeau); John Beckett photo (Kurt Andon).

Liberation, October 19, 1968

Leaping into a housewife and mother of two on the verge of women's lib, Sam must prevent the death of his daughter during a sit-in, while convincing the girl's father that his marriage can survive a liberated wife and daughter. Wr: Chris Abbott and Deborah Pratt. Dir: Bob Hulme.

George (Max Gail); Diana St. Cloud (Deborah Van Valkenburgh); Suzi (Megyn Price); Chief Donald Tipton (Stephen Mills); Peter Tipton (Bill Calvert); Flanners (Bill Cort); Evy (Jordan Baker); Red (Eric Bruskotter); George Jr. (Elan Rothschild); Photographer (Matt Kirkwood); Dora (Mary Elizabeth Murphy).

Dr. Ruth, April 25, 1985

While Sam is in 1985, running her radio talk show, playing matchmaker to her producers, and trying to help a young secretary who's being sexually harassed by her boss, Dr. Ruth Westheimer spends her time in the Waiting Room, counseling Al on his feelings towards his five wives and his relationship with Tina. Wr: Robin Jill Bernheim. Dir: Stuart Margolin.

Herself (Dr. Ruth Westheimer); Doug (Peter Spears); Debbie (Anita Barone); Jonathan (James McDonnell);

Annie Wilkins (Robyn Lively); Grandma (Ellen Albertini Dow); Cabbie (Paul Roache); Other woman (Mary Scheer); Anita's friend (Doreene Hamilton); Anita (Bridget Morrow); Vampire (Robert MacKenzie).

Blood Moon, March 10, 1975

As an eccentric, possibly vampiric, artist just outside of London, Sam must bear with Al's superstitions, while trying to prevent the death of his host's young wife at the hands of a couple who are taking a sacrificial ceremony in honor of the "blood moon." Wr: Tommy Thompson. Dir: Alan J. Levi.

Victor (Ian Buchanan); Claudia (Deborah Maria Moore); Alexandra (Shae D'Lyn); Horace (Rod Loomis); Detective (Garth Wilton).

Return, October 8, 1956 (aka And Forgive Us Our Sins; The Evil Men Do)

As Arnold Watkins, better known as The Midnight Marauder, Sam has to persuade a fraternity to stop using chicken races as a part of their hazing ceremonies, while Al tries to convince Arnold to stop trying to get himself killed in retaliation for his parents' deaths twelve years earlier. When Alia, the evil leaper, appears on the scene, Sam becomes determined to take her with him when he leaps. Wr: Richard C. Okie. Dir: Harvey Laidman.

Alia (Renee Coleman); Zoey (Carolyn Seymour); Arnold Watkins (Tristan Tait); Jack (Paul Scherrer); Sophie (Katherine Cortez); Frank (Bojesse Christopher); Jerry (Michael Manasseri); Masterson (Maggie Roswell); Warden Myers (Sam Scarber); Vivian (Barbara Montgomery); Mike Hammond (Neil Patrick Harris); Officer Miller (Philip O'Brien); Liz Tate (Cynthia Steele); Angel (Laura O'Laughlin); Dawn Taylor (Raquel Krelle).

Trivia Alert: This episode and "Revenge" aired together as a two-hour episode.

Revenge, September 16, 1987

Having simo-leaped, both Sam and Alia find themselves trapped in a women's prison, accused of murdering a fellow inmate. Their efforts to unmask the real killer are not their top priority as the two attempt to keep Alia's location hidden from her observer, Zoey, who leaps into the same place and time, determined to make Alia pay for her betrayal. Wr: Deborah Pratt. Dir: Debbie Allen.

Alia (Renee Coleman); Zoey (Carolyn Seymour); Thames (Hinton Battle); Fiddler (Rosana DeSoto); Arnold Watkins (Tristan Tait); Jack (Paul Scherrer); Sophie (Katherine Cortez); Frank (Bojesse Christopher); Jerry (Michael Manasseri); Masterson (Maggie Roswell); Warden Myers (Sam Scarber); Vivian (Barbara Montgomery).

Goodbye Norma Jean, April 4, 1960

As chauffeur to Marilyn Monroe, Sam must try to prevent Marilyn's tragic death. But when a well-meaning plan backfires, it could mean the end of Marilyn's career, even if her life is saved. Wr: Richard C. Okie. Dir: Christopher Hibler.

Marilyn Monroe (Susan Griffiths); Barbara (Liz Vassey); Peter Lawford (Joris Stuyck); John Huston (Tony Young); Clark Gable (Larry Pennell); John Tremaine, Jr. (Stephen Root); Rocky (Eric Scott Woods); Jane (Elizabeth Jane Coffee); Dennis Boardman (Stephen Bowers).

The Beast Within, November 6, 1972

Sam leaps into Henry Adams, one of a trio of friends who fought in Vietnam and came home with their own personal scars and the memory of a lost buddy. He has to save the life of a friend, Roy, as well as a young boy, Daniel, who ventures into the woods of Washington looking for proof of Bigfoot. Wr: John D'Aquino. Dir: Gus Trikonis.

Luke (Pat Skipper); Karen (Eileen Seeley); Roy (Sean Gregory Sullivan); Daniel (David Tom); Deputy (David Denney); John Worful (John Burke); Henry Adams (Mike Jolly).

The Leap Between the States, September 20, 1862

In a bizarre twist of a genetic coil, Sam leaps into his great-grandfather, Captain John Beckett, during the Civil War. He must not interfere with his ancestor's romance with a riled southern belle named Olivia. He must also avoid being hanged as a Yankee dog by some home-guard Confederate soldiers. Wr: Richard C. Okie. Dir: David Hemmings.

Mrs. Olivington (Kate McNeil); Lt. Richard Montgomery (Geoffrey Lower); Isaac (Michael D. Roberts); Pvt. Ryder (Neil Giuntoli); Wounded soldier (Paul Wittenberg); Capt. Beckett (Rob Hyland); Young soldier (Robby Sutton).

Memphis Melody, July 3, 1954

Sam swivels his hips into Elvis Presley, mere days before he is discovered. Along with making sure that Elvis does become the King, Sam must keep Sue Anne, a local songbird, from being trapped in a not-so-gilded cage of marriage. Wr: Robin Jill Bernheim. Dir: James Whitmore, Jr.

Sue Ann (Mary Elizabeth McGlynn); Frank (John Scott Clough); Marion (Lisa Jane Persky); Gladys (Garn Stephens); Mr. Phillips (Gregory Itzin); Red West (John Boyd West); Beau (Eric Bruskotter); DJ (Frazer Smith); Julie (Melissa Bernheim); Cute girl (Stephanie Scott); Elvis Presley (Michael St. Gerard).

Mirror Image, August 8, 1953

Sam lands in a not-so-ordinary bar in a coal mining town, where strange things are happening and familiar people don't know him. With the help of another Al, he still has something to set right … or is there more than one thing he needs to change? Wr: Donald P. Bellisario. Dir: James Whitmore, Jr.

Al, the bartender (Bruce McGill); "Tonchi" (John D'Aquino); "Ziggy" (Richard Herd); Bearded Gooshie (W. Morgan Sheppard); "Stawpah" (Stephen McHattie); Mr. Collins (Mike Genovese); Beth (Susan Diol); "Mutta" (Dan Butler); Gooshie (Dennis Wolfberg); Kruger (Kevin McDermott); Ghee (Ferdinand Carangelo); Pete (Brad Silverman); Kid #1 (J.D. Daniels); Kid #2 (Michael Bellisario); Police captain (James Whitmore, Jr.).

The Ray Bradbury Theater
1986–1992

An anthology adapting the many short stories written during the lifetime of this grand-master of science fiction and fantasy. Half-hour flights of "magic realism," dreams of life on Mars, and childhood memories.

Developed for television for Wilcox Productions Inc: Mark Massari; *Executive Producer for Atlantis Films:* Michael MacMillan; *Executive Producers for Wilcox Productions:* Larry Wilcox, Ray Bradbury; *Executive Producers:* Ray Bradbury (#1–65); Michael Macmillan (#1–6); John Ross (#4–6); Peter Sussman (#7–65); Larry Wilcox (#1–65); *Co-Executive Producers:* Bill Allan (#7–18); Pierre Bertrand Jaume (#7–18); Stephane Sperry (#7–18); *Supervising Producers:* Tom Cotter (#19–65); Jonathan Goodwill (#37, 39–41); Mary Kahn (#43–50); Seaton McLean (#11–36, 38, 42); Don Reynolds (#51–65); *Producers:* Chris Bailey (#51–65); Randy Bradshaw (#43–50); Tom Cotter (#12, 13, 15, 17); Tom Dent-Cox (#37, 39–41, 43–50); Jonathan Goodwill (#19–36, 38, 42); Arvi Liimatainen (#27–30); Mary Kahn (#51–65); Doug MacLeod (#37, 39–41, 43–50); Grahame McLean (#19–26); Seaton McLean (#1–10); Pamela Meekings-Stewart (#31–42); Hubert Niogret (#11, 14, 16, 18); Don Reynolds (#43–50); *Line Producers:* Narelle Barsby (#19–26); Janine Dickins (#51–65); Jonathan Goodwill (#7–10); Gillian Richardson (#1–3); *Produced in association with the following participants:* HBO (#1–6); Avalon Television Centre (#1–65); Bradshaw, MacLeod, and Associates Ltd. (#30–42); Ellipse Programme (#37, 39–41, 43–50); Grahame McLean Associates Limited (#7, 8, 10–18); Granada Television International (#19–30); South Pacific Pictures Limited (#7, 8, 10–18); In Association with Allarcom (#43–65); Kicking Horse Productions Limited (#19–42); WIC Western International Communications Ltd. (#27–30); Wilcox Productions, Inc. (#43–65) Produced in Co-operation with Dune (#1–65); USA Network (#19–30); Produced with Participation of The Alberta Motion Picture Development Corp. (#7–65); The Global Television Network (#19–65); Telefilm Canada (#1–6); Produced in Association with First Choice Canadian Communications Corp. (#1–3); The Global Television Network (#7–65); Superchannel (#7–65); Super Ecran (#19–65); Developed for Television for Wilcox Productions, Inc. by Mark Massari (#19–65); Executive in Charge of Production for WIC Western International Communications Ltd. Nicolas Wry (#1–6); Production Executive for USA Network Rick Weaver (#43–65); Co-Produced by T.F.1 (#43–65); *Host/Opening Narrator:* Ray Bradbury; 30 minutes.

For author Ray Bradbury, having a television show of his very own, a show that cinematically adapted his favorite short stories, was an idea so repellent that it took producers Larry Wilcox and Mark Massari two solid years to convince him to do it. Why would Bradbury—an author whose lifetime of writing short stories had produced a large bank of material from which to draw for adaptations—be so reluctant to see his stories televised? A little history may offer some explanation.

When *Twilight Zone* was in production in the early 1960s, Rod Serling had adapted Bradbury's short story "I Sing the Body Electric" for the series. When the episode aired, a crucial scene had been removed. Bradbury was so shocked that he refused to do any further work for Serling.

In 1969, *The Illustrated Man* was produced, starring Rod Steiger. The script was done without Bradbury's participation, which upset him. While he liked the music and photography, he was not happy with the fact that the script began the story midway through the novel.

At one time filmmaker François Truffaut was going to do *The Illustrated Man*, but he couldn't get financing. So he turned to another Bradbury work, *Fahrenheit 451*, in 1967. Writing the script himself, Truffaut created a film that Bradbury found very touching. Truffaut even improved on his ending when it started snowing on the set and he continued filming when he should have stopped. However, Bradbury admitted that the film is full of flaws—even he hasn't counted them all—and that technical shortcomings and various acting qualities make this film not the masterpiece he had hoped for.

In 1980, NBC proposed a six-hour mini-series of Bradbury's collection of short stories about life on the planet Mars. Starring such acting vets as Darren McGavin, Rock Hudson, Roddy McDowall and Nicholas Hammond, *The Martian Chronicles* was adapted by *Twilight Zone* scripter Richard Matheson and directed by Michael Anderson, who helmed the feature *Logan's Run*. While Bradbury liked certain stories or certain acting performances, he largely blames the director for an overall "disappointing and boring" result.

Yet another brush with filmmaking came with *Something Wicked This Way Comes* (1982), starring Jonathan Pryce and directed by Jack Clayton, Bradbury's old friend from the days of working with director John Huston. While very pleased with the final outcome of the film (for which he wrote the screenplay) Bradbury disagreed with Clayton on the way the ending was executed and argued with him about the fact that Clayton was cutting story elements without consulting him. Consequently, the experience soured him on filmmaking.

So, as Bradbury describes it, when Wilcox and Massari approached him about doing a project together, promising him control over casting and editing and, for quite probably the first time in the history of television, the opportunity to be the sole screenwriter, he remained skeptical. "They'd take me to lunch and dinner. They'd say, 'Come on, Ray! Don't be afraid!' I said, 'I don't want to be hurt any more. I'd rather not do it than be disappointed.' 'Look, we'll protect you, we're quality people, we want to put on a *Ray Bradbury Theater*, not the Larry Wilcox Theater or Mark Massari Theater.' Over a period of two years they convinced me, and I got started. I said, 'OK, I trust you, let's do it!' And it turned out, they were right, they were good. It manifested itself as an excellent series. So, the first couple of years there were four [producers], and then later, other people took over. Massari and Wilcox had other things to do. But they got me started. And I'm deeply grateful."

Describing the show, Bradbury calls *The Ray Bradbury Theater* "a fantasy anthology show, which combines science fiction, fantasy, magic realism—whatever that is. The story of 'Colonel Stonesteel [and the Desperate Empties'], that's fantasy—magic realism. [He's] a man, an ordinary everyday magician who had the ability to make a young boy fall in love with life. That little boy is me. [It's the kind of] imagination that changed my life. So, in a way, Colonel Stonesteel was like Mr. Electrico"—the carnival showman impresario Bradbury met when he was a child, who provided the inspiration for the stories told in "The Black Ferris" (which served as the basis for the novel *Something Wicked This Way Comes*).

Proposing a television series is one thing, but to actually produce, edit and broadcast it and hope fervently of finding an audience is another. Wilcox and Massari "shopped" the show around to various networks, but amazingly, no one was interested! It wasn't until 1986 that Wilcox landed at Home Box Office and produced an initial three episodes: "The Crowd" (with Nick Mancuso), "Marionettes, Inc.," (with Leslie Nielsen), and "The Playground" (with William Shatner). Suddenly the Bradbury name became an interesting property to contend with. The next year, a further three episodes were produced and filmed in Toronto, Canada. "The Screaming Woman" featured Drew Barrymore; "The Town Where No One Got Off," Jeff Goldblum; and "Banshee," the legendary Peter O'Toole. But then, abruptly, HBO canceled *The Ray Bradbury Theater*.

The show was provoking good critical and audience reaction. It was seen in 42 countries, and producers felt the show was too good to expire. But money was needed. Producers opened negotiations with a number of international production companies, and ultimately, a French and English company joined forces with USA Cable, a national open cable company who needed a companion with their revival of *Alfred Hitchcock Presents*. Off and running once again with the same production crew, *Ray Bradbury Theater* expanded to a more ambitious 12 episodes, this time filming in Canada, the United Kingdom and France, which embellished the show with a lavish international flavor that's rare for television.

To Bradbury, HBO's cancellation after six episodes was ironic. "We got 17 nominations by the ACE Cable Awards. And we won seven or eight that year. Can you believe that? Seven awards out of 17 nominations—at which point HBO canceled the series! Now, if you can figure that. I was so glad that USA bought the show. It's been a fascinating history."

Bradbury recalls predicting Harold Gould's ACE Cable award in 1991 for his performance in "Into the Chicago Abyss." "I'm very proud of my relationship with an actor like Harold Gould," said Bradbury. Previous to this win, Gould had received an Emmy nomination for the same role in 1990.

Ultimately, *Ray Bradbury Theater* completed 65 individual segments, using the talents of many directors, actors and production personnel from four different countries (Canada, New Zealand, England, France) in three different continents. *Ray Bradbury Theater's* reputation as a quality show attracted high-powered talent recognizable all over the world. Some of them have been attracted to the show simply because they were fans of the Master's stories. Canadian playwright, producer and actor Gordon Pinsent was one of them. In 1958, as a young actor starting out in the business, Pinsent was recruited by a fellow actor to perform in a local radio play in Winnipeg, Manitoba. The production? A classic collection of short stories portraying man's conquest of and life on the planet Mars, titled *The Martian Chronicles.*

"I would do different characters each week for each show," recalls Pinsent fondly. "I loved the Bradbury stuff. That was the first and last time I was in touch with his writing and so on until this particular situation. When I was asked to take part in ["The Earthmen" episode of *Ray Bradbury Theater*], I recognized immediately that this was probably one of those shows I had done on radio. I recognized immediately the textures and the type of people involved."

Coming full circle with Bradbury because of that long-ago radio series, Pinsent was tapped as the lead Martian in "The Earthmen,"

Ray Bradbury, host/narrator of his very own show, *The Ray Bradbury Theater.* Mr. Bradbury adapted many of his classic short stories for the series. Copyright 1986 USA/Atlantis Films.

opposite David Birney as the arriving astronaut. "I liked it," says Pinsent. However, "When I arrived [to film the episode] I was looking mainly for story. I wondered how faithful it would be to Bradbury. It was fine. From a standpoint of story, where it was coming from and all that, I thought, 'Well, can you really go wrong with Ray Bradbury?' And certainly, he scripted it. And all that was reason enough to do it. But certain production qualities were not where they should have been. Whatever production values missed or whatever other things that might be missed, there was not that much concern of

mine afterwards because I was such a fan of Bradbury.

"I don't know what I expected. When they say 'Martian,' you never know which way they're going to go with that. But knowing Bradbury, it's probably not going to be too extreme. Through his writing, he suggests something fairly normal. Of course there would be things to separate the Martians from the Earthmen, but at the same time, there was nothing too extreme in facial changes and so on. It had this terrific audacity to be dry and satiric. I just found it to be highly interesting."

In the end, the episode was completed to everyone's satisfaction. "You come away with some joy out of it, because it was Ray Bradbury and he was going to give you something before you left," says Pinsent. "It wasn't going to be a cheap experience. Again, my interest in Ray Bradbury himself kept me aware and alert."

Admirers of Bradbury for the series alone (not even counting his many books) are worldwide, because at this writing, the show is seen in 40 countries—Spain, France, England and Italy are among a few—and episodes will probably continue running for many years to come.

For Canadian directors Randy Bradshaw and Brad Turner, working on *Ray Bradbury Theater* was a creatively enriching and productive experience. Bradshaw recalls that one segment he directed, "And the Moon Be Still as Bright" (a *Martian Chronicles* story starring David Carradine and Kenneth Welsh), was "almost like a Western. It had very little action. Ray's dialogue is so unique. It's like a stream-of-consciousness poetry sometimes. I found it quite enchanting. I'm so glad things like that get broadcast, so people who might not ordinarily be exposed to writing of that kind do get a chance to look at it."

Brad Turner's first episode was "Gotcha." "Basically it was about a couple that were falling in love," he explains. "The woman [played by Kate Lynch, starring opposite Saul Rubinek] mentions a game called 'Gotcha,' and he doesn't know what she's talking about. They go to a sleazy hotel, they check in, and she starts playing the game, it's very odd. But really, [she's] playing on his personal paranoia and psyche ... and what Ray Bradbury was going for was the fact that you're your own personal paranoia and your own personal strengths and weaknesses.... The game has nothing to do with the player who initiates it. It's all got to do with your own inner self, playing games upon itself, and what ends up happening is he's just completely wiped out by this game because of his own personal fears. It takes him to the brink. It sends him over the edge. And he imagines things that aren't happening. And she basically turns into someone that scares him, and he never recovers.

"It's an interesting piece because it really has no ending. And although we tried to give it an ending, Ray Bradbury wasn't all that interested in us making an ending. He wanted it to be dot, dot, dot. And most audience members, after they watch it, go, 'What was that?' Which is good filmmaking in my opinion. Really, there should

be a message or there should be something at the end that makes you go back and reflect upon the entire story rather than dwell on what's ... ambiguous. It's a very good show. It was also good because it helped my career a lot. I did three *Bradbury*'s, and you couldn't have three [more] different shows if you tried. They are so unique and so different in every way."

The other two were "Exorcism" and "The Veldt," the latter a story from *The Illustrated Man*. When Turner completed "Exorcism," Bradbury wrote to Turner expressing how pleased he was with the show.

"Finally!" says Turner. "We had a film he felt really worked. [It was] what he imagined the story was. It's very different than anything else I would have imagined he would've liked. It's totally opposite. It was fascinating."

"The Veldt" tells the story of a family of the future living in a magical house where the nursery is a holographic projection room. In this nursery, the family's two children have conjured up an African veldt containing lions—with which they will wreak a terrible revenge on the parents who have showered them with material goods instead of love.

Malcolm Stewart, who played the father of the family opposite *Lou Grant*'s Linda Kelsey, remembers being on set of the segment. "I really liked the idea of a futuristic abode that we're all put in. As far as actually doing it, it was technically very difficult for both Linda and myself, as you can well imagine; the lions and all those things weren't really there, and they had to superimpose that on a blue screen. So we had to imagine in our performances all of that happening. I thought it was a terrific treatment of his short story.

"Bradbury always writes that imagination is a very, very powerful thing," adds Stewart. "Anything is possible with the imagination. I think Bradbury is a great believer that you can get there in the mind if you can't get there physically!"

One interesting thing about this segment is that we never see the outside of the Hadley's home. All the drama takes place inside the house.

"That's true," laughs Stewart. "It was probably written that way for a reason. It has ... a lot to do with how we did the shooting. We got everything we needed. Everything electronic was taken care of, and everything was computerized."

"The Veldt" was filmed previously as part of the 1969 feature *The Illustrated Man* with Rod

Steiger. It's known that Bradbury was unhappy with that incarnation, suggesting a reason why this segment was filmed again.

Evaluating Brad Turner's direction of "The Veldt," Stewart says, "Brad is good at visually imagining what he wants, as most good directors do. Before the camera ever starts filming, he has a really solid idea of what he wants the finished product to look like. In that respect he's a very good director for getting it done on time and getting a good quality product. ... He hires actors that he knows will give him a performance in the right role. He's not going to spend a lot of time giving direction to the actor. If there's a problem, he certainly knows how to give a performer direction. Some directors don't know how to do that. I call them traffic cops. They just tell you where to move, where to go, and if there's a problem with a particular interpretation, they don't know how to push the right button to make you change that interpretation or get what they want. Brad makes you think about what you're doing."

Another one of *The Ray Bradbury Theater*'s many directors is a familiar name to television audiences who remember *The Rockford Files*: Stuart Margolin. Not only did Margolin act in one of the New Zealand–filmed segments titled "Sun and Shadow," he directed the earlier "Utterly Perfect Murder," starring the actor veteran Richard Kiley, who was nominated for an Emmy in 1992 for his role in this episode.

"[Ray Bradbury] was extremely fond of the segment I directed," recalls Margolin. "I'm aware of his plays and a great many of his short stories, and I had a good time directing the segment in Edmonton. It was funny. A lot of the crew, when they read the script, thought this one was going to be a weak one. [But when we finished filming] they thought the show turned out to be one of the better ones. So, I'm very proud of it."

"Utterly Perfect Murder" is about Doug Spalding, a man reaching his forty-eighth birthday, who remains haunted by childhood memories of fighting with a bully. He becomes determined to lay the images to rest by returning to his hometown. As Spalding reaches the bully's home, ideas of committing the perfect murder come to mind. I thought it was simple and to the point," says Margolin of "Murder's" script. "This man was blaming a lot of his own personal spiritual failure on a relationship he had when he was a child, a bully that had broken his heart in not letting him run around with the gang and also pushing him around. Then, at the moment when it

becomes time for revenge, he realizes this man has grown up much more pathetic than he has. So he becomes thankful that he has the position he's in.

"Richard Kiley is a good actor and a very underrated one. People who saw *Man of La Mancha* will tell you that was one of the great theatrical experiences they ever had."

Giving final thoughts on "Murder," Margolin says, "We accomplished dramatizing a story that, on paper, didn't seem to be as fulfilling as it turned out to be. It's one of the things I directed that I did a lot with."

Richard Flower is an assistant director who had the unique opportunity, on the episode "Banshee," to work with the famed *Lawrence of Arabia* actor, Peter O'Toole. Flower paints O'Toole as something of an arrogant, over-the-top fellow not unlike the character he was portraying, a character loosely based on director John Huston.

"Peter O'Toole is quite an incredible actor. He really impressed me," says Flower. "He used to do this warm-up routine. And the first time he did it he scared half of the crew to death! He would come in and just before we were about to roll, he would make this incredible roaring sound, sort of like a lion's roar. He did it to warm up and get his throat ready."

Flower also describes what he calls a "power play" that O'Toole put on the crew. "The first scene we did, involved him walking straight toward the camera, and the camera was supposed to pull back and pan to the left as he walked into another room," explains Flower. "We rehearsed it, and and it went fine. Then, when it came time to shoot it, all of a sudden, when he was coming toward the camera, he came at an incredible pace, much faster than he did in rehearsal. He zoomed right by us, and we missed the shot. When the cameraman told him he walked past too quickly, Peter O'Toole said to him, 'I'm the actor in the scene, you have to follow me!' He said it very directly, and we got the idea that we'd better be on our guard."

One of the *Ray Bradbury Theater* producers was Jonathan Goodwill. Attached to Atlantis Films, one of the series' financial partners, Goodwill assisted the show by developing the scripts to the point where pre-production could start.

"I supervise the production, the editing, listen to the music; I look at everything from the inception of a particular episode through to its

Stars of three very different tales from *The Ray Bradbury Theater*: James Coco ("Marionettes, Inc.,"), Drew Barrymore ("The Screaming Woman") and William Shatner ("The Playground"). Copyright 1986 USA/ Atlantis Films.

delivery," says Goodwill. "The interesting thing about [this job] is it's never the same thing twice. There's always fresh challenges.There's always something interesting to do. What we do on various levels is that we're storytellers. Bradbury is a storyteller, and when you produce, direct, or act in a show, you're a storyteller. And everything is subserving to tell that story."

Goodwill admits that sometimes a lot of juggling is required to satisfy both an audience and an author looking over his shoulder. However, he says, "to a certain degree the author is more important than the audience and the needs of the network. This is an unusual case because it's a famous living author and he requires certain approvals to the content of the series, and to satisfy him, contractually, to keep him onboard, to keep the series going perfect. [But] he also satisfies the audience in telling stories. There's always ... a balancing act."

Goodwill says that sometimes everyone will agree on an approach, but in other efforts, they may not. "It requires some diplomacy on this particular kind of adaptation," he notes.

Before any stories are drawn from Bradbury's large storehouse of fantasy and science fiction shorts, all parties have to agree which ones

qualify for a filmed, half-hour adaptation. "We make lists at the start of each season," explains Bradbury. "I make a list of 12 stories. My wife makes one. My best friend makes one. My agent makes one. Atlantis Films makes one. And USA makes one. We put together these six or seven lists and we all agree. We don't just list 12, we do 18 as well. We all agree on most of the stories. Automatically, good stories are bound to come up. "Toynbee Convector" was one. There have been no fights."

Goodwill points out another unusual aspect of being involved in an anthology series with a literary giant: "We come from different point of views. I may find a compelling story, but that may not be the most interesting thing for Bradbury. When you don't have a famous living author involved, the director's point of view might be different from the producer's, or the writer's, or the actors might have a different take on a role in the way you envisioned it. It [goes] to another level when you have a famous living author. That's another one of the challenges."

Goodwill confesses to having been intimidated in the beginning because of this "other level," and admits, "It gets complicated. On the other hand, you have this great author, and his fabulous stories are source material. That comes with the territory. You have to make it work.

"The interesting thing about Bradbury is that his stories are so visual. It's not like *Twilight Zone* or *Alfred Hitchcock Presents* where stories are always linear. Bradbury's stuff is always very evocative. It has to do with emotions, memories. Television at large is driven more by linear status, rather than character. All good drama is character driven. You get into something like "The Day It Rained Forever," which is absolutely, truly character driven. That's the Bradbury world: provocative, moody, childhood memories, fears, and the subconscious. The challenge is to make that compelling."

Adapting from the printed page to the screen has its own unique problems, but the transition can be easier than usual when the source material is strong.

"And some of it is our skill at selecting the stories and adapting them," notes Goodwill. "Finding the right characters to play them, finding the right directors to shoot them, it's all part of making a television show; [finding] art directors, cinematographers, editors, composers, all these people. It could also be pure luck, being at the right place at the right time. [The series] has really grown with the cable evolution in the United States. Suddenly there is a demand for more product. And product that's different from conventional cable. And this kind of fit the bill—it was literary and it has a certain element of high-brow; at the same time it was tremendously popular literature."

Success of this show, explains Goodwill, is not defined by ratings. "It's very respected. It gets its share of critical acclaim and nomination of awards. It's an attraction for the broadcasters."

Ray Bradbury found the experience of working on his very own show to be an interesting one; it was an opportunity to take advantage of certain things technology had to offer. Never before had filmmaking been so easy.

"I worked alone and I worked away from everybody, and they were all in Canada, and the productions were done—four in Paris and four in London and a number in Alberta and New Zealand," says Bradbury. "The whole enterprise is science fiction. ... We communicated across the world with my scripts, and we could make changes in a few minutes because of the FAX machine. Just a few years ago, you would have to wait three or four days from the other side to go

back and forth. They send me video cassettes of every show so that I go to the nearest studio and run the pictures and call them and criticize them. And I say, 'This needs changing or that needs some work,' etc. But this is one of the few times in history where someone has produced a film across the world."

Explaining why the show had to end after 65 episodes, Randy Bradshaw says that producing a television series requires financing and that it is "a question of how far out [do you want to finance]? It's their bank account that determines whether they stop or go." Producer Jonathan Goodwill blames it on burnout: "After 65 shows, we're all exhausted. There's a limited number that works as television dramas of which rights are available to." But Bradbury responds more to the point: "Well, how how long do you want the series to go? I've got other things to do. I've got a screenplay for an animated film to finish, I have a novel to complete, short stories, two articles to write."

In the end, does Ray Bradbury feel vindicated after all these years of having his work maligned by other artists and by critics who say his works are not adaptable to film? Perturbed, Bradbury responds: "They've always been wrong! Because I'm the most cinematic of writers living today! I love film! I love cinema! A lot of these people don't understand motion pictures! ... My mother was in love with motion pictures, so she took me to the movies two or three times a week. When I was three years old, five years old, then when I was older, then I went at least twice a week. And I saw anywhere from six to 15 films a week. I swam in them, I drowned in them. So, it shows in my writing. My short stories, my novels, if you take a single page of one of my novels and look at it, each paragraph is a shot, an angle. When I had a meeting with Sam Peckinpah 20 years ago when I first met him, he wanted to do *Something Wicked This Way Comes* and I said, 'Sam, how are you going to do it?' And he said, 'Tear a few pages of your book and stuff it in the camera.' And he was exactly right. If you do that, you can adapt my stories. These people who think I can't be adapted, just haven't read me. Because I deal in metaphors. It's part of my life and style. But if you shift the metaphors, they say you can't do this way because it's too subliminal. Well, this is not true.

"When I give you an action, beautiful and metaphorically, as you might say, you're writing haiku for the screen. And that's what we have with my series, and the series really works. It's out of a page and right to the screen."

Having received so little satisfaction from film adaptations of his works in the past, Bradbury particularly relishes the success of *The Ray Bradbury Theater*. "Wherever I go," he says, "people tell me how much they like them. There's plenty of room out there; there's Hitchcock, Serling and myself. The average is very high, out of 65 shows, only four were outright clinkers. But that's got to be expected. No series that I know has ever been perfect. Sometimes it's the casting, sometimes it's the directing. But you say, 'Well, there it is! Let's look at all the good stuff.'"

EPISODE GUIDE

All episodes based on an original story and written by Ray Bradbury except "The Town Where No One Got Off," which was written for the screen by Ray Bradbury.

1986: Three episodes produced by Atlantis and filmed in Canada

The Crowd

As Joe Spallner lies on the pavement after being thrown from his car in a near-fatal crash, he watches a group of onlookers quickly gather. Days later he witnesses another accident; the same crowd appears. With the help of a friend, he investigates a series of accidents. News footage shows the same crowd at every scene. What's more, their faces match the photographs Spallner has at the city morgue. Dir: Ralph L. Thomas.

Spallner (Nick Mancuso); Morgan (R.H. Thomson); Doctor (David Hughes); Paramedic (Victor Eeartmantis).

Marionettes, Inc.

Charles Braling, a bored computer salesman, one morning receives an odd message on his computer screen: "Marionettes, Inc. We shadow forth." The same cryptic message turns up in his newspaper and on his luncheon bill. Curious, he tracks them down and meets a man who offers to sell him a robot replica of himself. Dir: Paul Lynch.

Braling (James Coco); Fantoccini (Leslie Nielsen); Mrs. Braling (Jayne Eastwood); Crane (Kenneth Welsh); Buyer (Pixie Bigelow); Buyer (Rex Hagon); Buyer (Michael Fletcher); Secretary (Laura Henry); The other Braling (Tom Christopher).

The Playground

As a child, Charles Underhill was tormented by neighborhood kids. Now his son wants to play in the local playground, but Charles is apprehensive. Relenting, Charles sees a bully from his youth. All the childhood memories come flooding back. Charles is jolted out of his trance as he sees his son moving further into the nightmare world of his youth. Dir: William Fruet.

Charles Underhill (Willam Shatner); Steve (Keith Dutson); Carol (Kate Trotter); Ralph (Mirko Malish); Charlie (Steven Andrad); Robert Peerless (Barry Flatman).

1987: Three episodes produced by Atlantis and filmed in Canada

The Screaming Woman

Heather Leary has an active imagination. One day in the woods near her home she hears a faint moaning underground. Her skeptical parents won't believe her but later Heather finds her friend and neighbor, Mrs. Nesbitt, is missing. That night, she returns to the woods to bid her friend farewell. She comes home humming a melody she heard in the forest. As he tucks Heather into bed, her father recognizes the tune. It's a melody, he realizes, that he shares with only one special neighbor. Dir: Bruce Pittman.

Heather Leary (Drew Barrymore); Mother (Janet Laine Green); Father (Roger Dunn); Dippy (Ian Heath); Old Man Kelly (Ken James); Charles Nesbitt (Alan Scarfe); Policeman (Michael Copeman); Mrs. Kelly (Jacqueline McLeod); Screaming woman (Mary Anne Coles); Construction worker (Dick Callahan); Neighbor (Fran Gebhard).

The Town Where No One Got Off

On a train moving across the Midwest, Sam Cogswell meets a cynical salesman. An aspring writer, Cogswell argues that there's a special innocence about small-town people. The salesman dares him to get off at the next stop, so he does. Wandering about the town, Sam notices an old man following him. The old man says he's waited a long time for a stranger. Now he can fulfill his life-long dream: murder. Dir: Don McBrearty.

Cogswell (Jeff Goldblum); Old man (Ed McNamara); Salesman (Cec Linder); Conductor (Errol Slue); Store owner lady (Clare Coulter); Little boy #1 (Jason Forbes); Little boy #2 (Trevor Forbes); Boarding house woman (Samantha Langevin); Girl on swing (Rachel Gemmell); Gent in store (Wayne Robson).

Banshee

Douglas Rogers is invited to the Irish manor of his friend, John Hampton, a compulsive womanizer and practical joker. Of course, Hampton decides to play a prank on his guest. An eerie moan is heard over the moors, and Hampton dares his friend to investigate. Douglas finds a beautiful, ghostly maiden in the blackened night and returns, a little shaken, to a gleeful Hampton. Douglas challenges his friend to face her and Hampton's curiosity is piqued. He eagerly rushes out to the moors ... but will he return? Dir: Doug Jackson.

John Hampton (Peter O'Toole); Douglas Rogers (Charles Martin Smith); Banshee (Jennifer Dale); Taxi driver (Michael Copeman).

1988: 12 episodes produced by Atlantis in Canada, Granada (UK), and Ellipse (France). Four filmed in each country.

The Emissary

Martin lies in his sickbed, waiting for his dog to bring company. One day, he shepherds in a special guest: Miss Haight, a beautiful teacher who brightens Martin's dismal days until she dies tragically in a car accident. And then Dog disappears. Martin is inconsolable. When Dog returns, the boy is overjoyed. Burying his face in the dog's fur, he is repulsed by the putrid smell of decay. "Where've you been diggin, Dog?" The creak of a door opening startles the boy. Martin has company. Dir: Sturla Gunnarsson.

Miss Haight (Helen Shaver); Martin (Keram Malicki-Sanchez); Mother (Linda Goranson); Father (Neil Munro); Big boy (Eric Hebert); Neighbor (Stuart Kenney).

Punishment Without Crime

George so loves his wife that he wants to kill her. She's been unfaithful, you see, and now he must find a way to purge his anger. Desperate, he turns to Facsimilies Ltd., an illegal firm offering the satisfaction of murder without legal consequences. A replica of his wife is created, but George falls in love all over again and can't bring himself to do it. Finally he is provoked and fires a pistol at the replica. Why, then, is he arrested for the murder of his wife? Dir: Bruce MacDonald.

George Hill (Donald Pleasence); Katherine (Lynsey Baxter); The judge (Peggy Mount); Prosecuting counsel (Ian Cuthbertson); Defense counsel (Frank Williams).

On the Orient, North

Traveling on the Orient Express, Nurse Minerva is called to comfort a passenger, a man she quickly realizes is a ghost. He's traveling to a castle in the north of England, and Minerva, in her sixties and ailing herself, decides to escort him. They become inseparable. Upon reaching England she finds it difficult to part. As the ghost turns to say goodbye, he is startled by a crowd hovering over a collapsed body. A hand touches him; Minerva is by his side and eager to share his afterlife. Dir: Frank Cassenti.

Minerva Halliday (Magali Noel); The ghastly passenger (Ian Bannen); Train official (François Clavier); Priest (Herve Pauchon); Nun (Sylvie Novak); Policeman (Tim Holm); Doctor (Jean Gluck).

The Coffin

Charles Braling's inventions have made him rich. With death approaching, he works on the final creation: a coffin, a masterpiece of invention and gadgetry. A visit from his despised brother, Richard, results in Charles' death of a heart attack. The will leaves Richard nothing. Furious, he ransacks his brother's house and finally finds the money in the lining of the coffin. As Richard gleefully lies in the coffin to count his reward, his brother's genius becomes apparent. The lid slams and the coffin, which bears the name "Richard Braling," begins its slow descent. Dir: Tom Cotter.

Richard Braling (Denholm Elliot); Charles Braling (Dan O'Herlihy); St. John Court (Clive Swift).

The Fruit at the Bottom of the Bowl

William Acton, reluctant hero and anxious cuckold, knocks on the door of the man he has come to murder. Donald Huxley welcomes his guest with a smile. He gives Acton a tour of his elegant home, urging him to handle and enjoy all his precious artifacts. Unwilling to be patronized any longer, Acton tells his host of his dark plan. Huxley's mockery provokes his guest into action. With Huxley dead, Acton's elation turns to terror as he realizes that he's left a trail of incriminating fingerprints throughout the house. Dir: Gilbert Shilton.

Acton (Robert Vaughn); Huxley (Michael Ironside).

The Small Assassin

Alice Leiber feels her baby's heart beating frantically within her womb and is gripped with fear. When the child is finally born, her world becomes a nightmare. The child seems to watch her every move as if waiting for the moment to strike. Her husband attributes his wife's irrational fears to stress. The child, meanwhile, is already planning its first deadly move. Dir: Tom Cotter.

Alice Lieber (Susan Wooldridge); David Leiber (Leigh Lawson); Dr. Jeffers (Cyril Cusack); Nurse (Lottie Ward).

Gotcha!

They meet at a party; he's dressed as Laurel, she as Hardy. Their love affair blossoms into a steady relationship until one day John wonders aloud how long it might last, commenting that "good times never last forever." Then the game begins. Alicia takes him to a cheap motel in a dangerous part of town, telling him that they are going to play a game called "Gotcha!" "It'll scare you to death," she promises. Sometimes games can be taken too seriously ... and too far. Dir: Brad Turner.

John Griffiths (Saul Rubinek); Alicia Hart (Kate Lynch); Hotel clerk (James Kidnie); Party person #1 (Olwyn Chipman); Party person #2 (Sharolyn Sparrow); Stockbroker (Bear) (Michael Healy); Stockbroker (Bozo) (Adrian Paul).

Skeleton

Bert Harris is a hypochondriac. His latest problem: His bones hurt. His doctor dismisses his complaints, so Bert seeks out a specialist, Dr. Munigant. Munigant tells him: "There are actually two of you—bone and flesh both fighting for survival. ... The cure starts with your belief in my abilities." How unfortunate that the cure is so much more ghastly than the complaint. Dir: Steve DiMarco.

Bert Harris (Eugene Levy); Clarisse (Diane D'Aquila); Munigant (Peter Blais); Dr. Burleigh (Sean Hewitt); Fat man (Thick Wilson).

The Wonderful Death of Dudley Stone
Who killed Dudley Stone, the most famous writer of his day? A surprise confession reveals Stone to have been the consummate artist—even in the execution of the ultimate work of fiction: his own death. Dir: David Copeland.

Dudly Stone (John Saxon); John Oatis Kendall (Alan Scarfe); Sara Stone (Susan Wilson); Dudly Stone's Publisher (Lewis Rowe).

The Veldt
George and Lydia Hedley are model parents of the future. Their house is a miracle of inventions created to facilitate the perfect human existence, and the jewel of the house is the children's nursery. Here, young Wendy and Peter can look at the walls and fantasize. The walls "deliver" with incredible realism. When Wendy and Peter become preoccupied with a fantasy of the Veldt and its man-eating lions, the nursery becomes a place of terror. Dir: Brad Turner.

Lydia Hadley (Linda Kelsey); George Hadley (Malcolm Stewart); Peter Hadley (Damien Atkins); Wendy Hadley (Shana Alexander); David McLean (Thomas Peacocke); Mechanical voice (Del Mehes).

Hail and Farewell
Will looks 12, but his birth certificate says he's 43. He's frozen in innocent youth and must miss forever the joys and miseries of growing up. He moves from town to town, offering himself up for adoption. But when his secret is discovered it's time once again to move on. Dir: Alan Kroeker.

Willie (Josh Saviano); Old woman (Georgie Collins); The bully (Trevor McCarthy); Charlotte (Mary Day); Charlotte's mother (Christine McInnis); Emma Webley (Judith Haynes); John Webley (Frank C. Turner); Tiny Tim (Mark Parr); Ice cream man (Frank Bueckert); Little woman (Ann Allen); Big kid, orphanage (Chad Cole); 2nd kid, orphanage (Joel Dacks); Bully's sidekick (Donovan Workun).

Boys! Raise Giant Mushrooms in Your Cellar
It is a harmless hobby—growing mail-order mushrooms. Tom gets his seeds through the post. His friend, Roger, already has his. In fact, all the boys in the neighborhood are growing mushrooms in their cellars. Then Roger's father mysteriously disappears. Maybe Mrs. Goodbody, with her spray gun zapping "Marasmius Oreades," has the right idea. And maybe the alien mushrooms know the place to begin their plot for world domination is down in the cellar. Dir: David Brandes.

Hugh Fortnum (Charles Martin Smith); Tom Fortnum (Marc Reid); Cyntha Fortnum (Patricia Phillips); Mrs. Goodbody (Judy Mahbey); Roger Willis (Frank C. Turner);

Dorothy Willis (Dorothy Anne Haug); Joe Willis (Michael Leskow); Mailman (David Mann).

1989: 12 episodes produced by Atlantis in Canada, and Avalon Television in New Zealand (four in Canada, eight in New Zealand)

A Sound of Thunder
Time Safari offers safaris to any period in history. Eckles joins a safari hunting party under the command of Travis, 60 million years into the past, to hunt Tyrannosaurus Rex—the deadliest dinosaur of all time! Rules of the hunt are strict: "Stay on the path, never step off," or you could affect the future. "Step on a mouse and you leave your print across eternity." Eckles disobeys—and the party returns to a modern world utterly changed. Dir: Costa Botes.

Eckles (Kiel Martin); Travis (John Bach); Agent (Michael McLeod); Hunter (Michael Batley); Hunter (John McDavitt).

And So Died Riabouchinska
A murder is committed in the theater. A detective interrogates the likely suspects: a ventriloquist, his wife and the agent. But then an unlikely witness is introduced: the beautiful marionette Riabouchinska, who provides an ongoing commentary on the investigation. Things become more clear when the detective finds a photo that greatly resembles Riabouchinska. The ventriloquist admits that the woman was his assistant who disappeared long ago. Dir: Denys Granier-Deferre.

John Fabian (Alan Bates); Lt. Krovitch (Jean Pierre Kalfon); Alyce Fabian (Pati Layne); Ilyana Riamonova (Annabelle Mouloudji); Mr. Douglas (Hilary Staunton); Ockham (Jacques Berrocal).

The Man Upstairs
Douglas is visiting his grandmother in Paris. During dinners the curious boy notices a new boarder: Mr. Koberman, a strange man who eats with wooden cutlery and agonizes over the sound of silver rattling. He sleeps days and wanders the street at night. Is it a coincidence that young women in the area are being murdered? Armed with a carving knife and a jar of coins, Douglas creeps up the stairs. It's time to get to know Mr. Koberman. Dir: Alain Bonnot.

Douglas (Adam Negley); Mr. Koberman (Fedodor Atkins); Grandma (Micheline Presle); Miss Treadwell (Kate Hardie).

There Was an Old Woman
Four men in dark suits carry a long wicker basket into a old woman's home. Matilda soon realizes who the leader is: Death has come to visit. But she is unwilling to die and tells the party to leave. When she awakes from a nap she is alone, but her relief is short-lived. Her niece soon appears in the doorway,

sobbing uncontrollably. Matilda reaches to comfort her and realizes that her fight with Death has only just begun. Dir: Bruce MacDonald.

Matilda (Mary Morris); The listener (Ronald Lacey); Funeral director (Sylvestra Le Touzel); Father (Robin Soans); Mortician (Finetime Fontayne); Listener's assistants: Peter Barton, Stephen Boyes, Louis Emerick, Ken Kitson.

Tyrannosaurus Rex
Joe Clarence, movie director and tyrant, has a passion for prehistoric beasts. Enter John Terwilliger, a sensitive and honorable craftsman with a rare ability to sculpt miniatures. He is hired to recreate a Tyrannosaurus Rex for Clarence's new movie. Clarence is dissatisfied with John's work and continues to scream for more horrific and shocking characteristics. John's hatred for the man becomes evident when he begins sculpting oddly familiar features into his prehistoric beast. Dir: Gilles Behat.

Terwilliger (Cris Campion); Glass (Daniel Ceccaldi); Joe Clarence (Jim Dunk); Glass' niece (Julie Reitzman).

The Dwarf
"That dwarf, you see him? Every night, pays his dime, runs in the mirror maze..." Ralph Banghat, showman, runs a hall of mirrors. When he takes Aimee to see the dwarf, she shares in the secret joy the man experiences dancing before the "larger than life" image of himself. But Ralph plays a trick on the little man, a trick that only a warped and jealous mind could conceive. Even as the dwarf flees in despair, the mirrors exact a fitting revenge on his tormentor. Dir: Costa Botes.

Aimee (Megan Follows); Ralph Banghart (Miguel Fernandes); Mr. Bigelow (Machs Colombani); Magazine vendor (David Cameron).

A Miracle of Rare Device
Old Robert and William can't shake off Ned Bartlin, a man as mean as they are generous. Every scheme, every piece of luck, every attempt to make an honest dime is ruined by Ned. One day Robert and William see the Mirage, a city of wondrous spheres shimmering in the desert. They set up a makeshift car park and viewing facilities for "a quarter a time" and are doing fine, until Ned arrives. But maybe mirages don't work for the mean-spirited, and the Miracle of Rare Device can only be seen by the pure at heart. Dir: Roger Tompkins.

Robert (Pat Harrington, Jr.); William (Wayne Robson); Ned Bartlin (William Kircher); Old man (Des Kelly); Old woman (Barbara Laurenson); Woman (Helen Jarroe); Young man (Ben Vere-Jones); Old man #2 (Roy Wesney); Xanadu young man (Stephen Lovatt); Farmer (Peter Dennett); Farmer's wife (Annie Ruth); Farmer's son (Baden Campbell); Farmer's daughter (Sarah McLaughlin).

The Lake
When Harold was twelve he loved Tally, but one day Tally, with the long blond pigtails, went swimming out from shore, never to return. Harold built half a sand castle: "Tally—if you hear me—come in and build the rest." For Harold, life goes on: adulthood, marriage and a return to the lake for his honeymoon. A little girl's body is brought ashore, and a new half-finished castle is waiting for Harold to complete. Dir: Pat Robins.

Douglas (Gordon Thomson); Young Douglas (Eli Sharplin); Young Tally (Jessical Billingsley); Tally's mother (Sylvia Rands); Douglas' mother (Prue Langbein); Margaret (Tina Regtien); Lifeguard (Jim Moriarty).

The Wind
Allin has trespassed into the Valley of the Winds. Now he's terrified the Wind will exact its revenge. His friend Herb Thompson thinks Allin's imagination is playing tricks on him. At Thompson's house, the evening is calm; a game of cards is in progress. At Allin's place the lonely man is experiencing the nightmare of the Wind's invasion: smashed windows, slamming doors and, ultimately, the destruction of the man who knows its secret ... and anyone with whom he's shared that confidence. Dir: Grahame McLean.

John Colt (Michael Sarrazin); Herb Thompson (Ray Henwood); Susan Thompson (Vivienne Labone); Keith Parkinson (Keith Richardson); Anne Parkinson (Anne Pacey).

To the Chicago Abyss
It is the twilight after A.D.—Annihilation Day, that is—and one old man can't help remembering. The "gospel" he recalls is the details of our consumer society—the smell of coffee beans, the feel of a packet of cigarettes. This "Prophet of Memory" is a danger to the State, which now possesses none of these treasures. They want him dead, but they have to catch him and the small band of rebels who are helping him flee to a place where he can share his memories with others. Dir: Randy Bradshaw.

Old man (Harold Gould); The stranger (Neil Munro); Woman in the park (Doreen Ibsen); Stranger's wife (Arne MacPherson); The policeman (Bill Meilen); The betrayer (Ronald Rault); Joseph (Chad Krowchuk).

The Pedestrian
In the world of the future, some simple pleasures we take for granted are forbidden. Mead is a criminal because he likes to take an evening walk and breathe the sweet night air. He encourages his friend Stockwell to join him in this "deviant" behavior. As they stroll the silent streets, television watchers, police cars and helicopters combine to hunt them down. Dir: Alun Bollinger.

Leonard Mead (David Ogden Stiers); Stockwell (Grant Tilly); Voice (out of view) (Stig Eldred); Man on TV (Matt Murphy).

The Haunting of the New
Grynwood is a house with a spirit of its own. Its wild, decadent parties ended when the house decided it had had enough and burnt itself to the ground. Nora rebuilds the mansion to start the

merry-go-round once more, but Grynwood isn't so sure it will allow the past to be repeated. Dir: Roger Tompkins.

Nora (Susannah York); Charles (Richard Comar); Duchess (Sheila Hammond).

1990: 12 episodes produced by Atlantis in Canada, and South Pacific Pictures in New Zealand (four in Canada, eight in New Zealand)

Touched with Fire
It is hot in the city, and the mercury climbs toward 92 degrees, the temperature at which most murders are committed. Retired insurance assessors Mr. Foxe and Mr. Shaw try to prevent Mrs. Shrike, a woman so obnoxious she is the classic "murderee," from achieving her seemingly inevitable grisly destiny. Dir: Roger Tompkins.

Mrs. Shrike (Eileen Brennan); Mr. Shaw (Barry Morse); Mr. Foxe (Joseph Shaw); Also with Michael Noonan, Paul Nadas.

Mars Is Heaven
As the first successful mission to Mars touches down, the men stare through the mists of the Martian dawn and find they are looking at a small town straight out of the American Midwest. Long-lost loved ones of the crew greet the space travelers. The question is, "Is this heaven or a Martian-built hell?" Dir: John Laing.

Capt. Black (Hal Linden); Skip (Paul Gross); Also with Helen Moulder, Patrick Smythe, Wendy McFarlane, Eddie Campbell, Brian Sergent, Stephen Papps.

Here There Be Tygers
"Here there be tygers," stated the old maps wherever terror was thought to lurk in uncharted wilderness, but the world where Driscoll and Chatterton and other members of the planetary exploration team arrive seems a veritable paradise. Smooth grass, shady trees, crystal streams afford all the delights of a beautiful lady waiting to be loved. But hell hath no fury like a woman scorned, and when Chatterton abuses the body of this perfect planet, it reveals another, deadly, force. Dir: John Laing.

Forrester (Timothy Bottoms); Chatterton (Peter Elliot); Driscoll (George Henare); Koestler (Lorae Parry).

The Murderer
Arthur Brock is a killer ... of sounds. In a world of boom boxes, Walkmen, portable phones, wrist radios, chattering faxes and all-pervasive muzak, he desires the delights of perfect silence. His destruction of sound-infested environments at work and at home lands him in a psychiatric cell. Will his therapy cure him of being a minority, or will he pass his noiseless message on? Dir: Roger Tompkins.

Brock (Bruce Weitz); Dr. Fellows (Cedric Smith); Also with Donna Akerston, Michael Haigh.

A Touch of Petulance
Jonathan Hughes has the perfect marriage. He anticipates the joy of returning home to his beautiful wife, Alice, as he rides the evening commuter train out of the city. Opposite Hughes an old man reads a newspaper—from the future. A headline tells of a woman's murder and the search for her missing husband, Jonathan Hughes. Who is the old man, and can he change the future? Dir: John Laing.

Man (Eddie Albert); Jonathan Hughes (Jesse Collins); Alice Hughes (Dulcie Smart).

Usher II
Stendahl lives for the world of fantasy and imagination epitomized in Edgar Allan Poe's "The Fall of the House of Usher." Garrett, Chief Investigator for Moral Climates, represents the world's government, which has arranged that imagination should die. Stendahl's library is destroyed, all works of fantasy proscribed. In defiance, Stendahl builds a second House of Usher and invites Garrett and his colleagues to a party to celebrate its destruction. Dir: Lee Tamahori.

Stendhal (Patrick MacNee); Pikes (Ian Mune); Garrett (Stewart Devinie).

The Black Ferris
The carnival comes to town, and with it the mysterious Mr. Cooger. At the same time a little boy takes up residence with a rich and lonely Miss Foley. Hank tries to convince his friend Pete that there is a connection between the sinister carnival man and the strange boy. Is that connection the Black Ferris that Mr. Cooger rides as it gyrates backwards in the night sky? Dir: Roger Tompkins.

Peter (Zachary Bennett); Hank (Nathaniel Moreau); Also with Frank Whitten, Jonathan Marks, Pat Evison, Duncan Smith, Stephen Gledhill, Kathy Downes.

The Toynbee Convector
It is the future and it works. The world is clean, the atmosphere pure, and man lives in harmony with man. Perfection has been achieved because 100 years ago Craig Bennett Stiles traveled in his time machine—the Toynbee Convector—to the future. The world embraced the message and brought it to pass. Now the grateful millions and the world's media wait for the historic moment when the young Stiles as time traveler will meet his old self. The young man doesn't appear, but a secret is safe and the future secure. Dir: John Laing.

Craig Bennett Stiles (James Whitmore); Shumway (Michael Hurst); Also with Perry Piercy, Michael Galvin.

The Long Years
Twenty years after the great war, Mars is a tomb deserted by Earth settlers. But Hathaway, a brilliant scientist with the fourth expedition, has remained on the planet. With him are his wife, two daughters and a son. Capt. Wilder and his space crew return. Hathaway's family makes the Earthmen welcome, but there is something wrong. Dir: Paul Lynch.

John Hathaway (Robert Culp); Capt. Wilder (George Touliatos); Cora (Judith Buchan); Margurite (Donna Larson); Tom (Bruce Mitchell); Bill Williamson (Jason Wolff).

The Day It Rained Forever

At Joe Terle's Desert Hotel, three dried old husks wait for the day when it always rains. The rain doesn't come, and as the old men quarrel, a dust cloud appears on the horizon. It is Miss Blanche Hillgood in her jalopy. She is as old as the men, but a free spirit now, on the move with her music to a new life. A harp is played in the dusty hotel and, as the notes cascade, so does the rain. Life-giving water is all around and the 50 years of drought are over. Dir: Randy Bradshaw.

Vincent Gardenia, Gerard Parkes, Robert Clothier; Blanche Hillgood (Sheila Moore).

And the Moon Be Still as Bright

Jeff Spender is different from the other men in the Martian expedition. While exploring a ruined Martian city, Spender disappears. When he returns, he brings death amongst the Earthmen, an avenging Martian who would destroy these polluters of his ancient civilization. A manhunt amongst the red rocks of the ancient planet leaves Capt. Wilder facing the dreadful prospect of having to act as an Earthman and destroyer of life. Dir: Randy Bradshaw.

Spender (David Carradine); Capt. Wilder (Kenneth Welsh); Also with James Purcell, Ben Cardinal, Brian Jensen, Warren Perkins.

Exorcism

Why is Clara Goodwater reading the works of Albertus Magnus? Elmira Brown knows. Clara is a witch and has used her powers of sorcery for years to keep Elmira from the presidency of the Ladies Honeysuckle Harmony Lodge. Annually Elmira has suffered strange injuries which prevent her campaigning as the vote draws near. This year, with only one day to go, she cuts her thumb, trips over a lawnmower and nearly gets run down by a car! Enough is enough, so Elmira brews herself an anti-witch potion and plans to exorcise Clara at the election. But as Elmira gives her speech, she thinks she can see a wax doll and a long hat pin in Clara's hand. Dir: Brad Turner.

Clara Goodwater (Sally Kellerman); Elmira Brown (Jayne Eastwood); Sam Brown (Bartley Bard); Tom (Jordan Singer).

1991-92: 23 episodes produced by Atlantis in Canada, and South Pacific Pictures in New Zealand (8 in Canada, 15 in New Zealand)

The Earthmen

The third expedition from Earth, commanded by Capt. Jonathan Williams, lands on Mars in search of the two previous expeditions that have vanished without a trace. Williams and his crew soon encounter some Martians who have two things in common: They are telepathic, and they treat Earthmen as though they were all crazy. Can Williams and his crew prove they are Earthmen from a distant planet, or are they all merely suffering from powerful delusion? Dir: Graeme Campbell.

Capt. Williams (David Birney); Mr. X (Gordon Pinsent); Lt. Wilson (Larry Musser); Lt. Young (David Sivertsen); Mrs. TH (Patricia Phillips); Mr. Aaa (Jim Shepard); Mr. Iii (Raul Tome).

Zero Hour

All eight-year-old children are talking about Invasion and a mysterious, invisible leader called Drill, even Mary Morris' daughter, Mink. If Mink and the other kids help Drill build his "entry apparatus," Drill promises that the kids will run the world. But since eight year olds are so impressionable, who listens to them, or takes them seriously, thinks Mrs. Morris. So what are those explosions, and whose heavy footsteps are coming up the stairs with Mink? Dir: Don McBrearty.

Mary Morris (Sally Kirkland); Minx (Katherine Isobel Murray); Helen (Jill Dyck); Henry Morris (Brian Taylor); Eddie (Kurtis Brown); Joseph (Ronan Cahill).

Colonel Stonesteel and the Desperate Empties

Nothing ever happens in Green Town, Illinois, and 12-year-old Charlie is bored to death. That is, until his elderly friend Colonel Stonesteel devises a little entertainment for them both. Soon the discovery of Ramses Tut the Third in a farmer's field has all of Green Town buzzing with the news that Ancient Egyptians lived and died in Illinois 3,000 years ago! Dir: Randy Bradshaw.

Colonel Stonesteel (Harold Gould); Charlie (Shawn Asmore); The sheriff (Wayne Robson); Mayor (Walter Kaasa).

The Concrete Mixer

Ettil Vyre, a Martian, is horrified when the planet's military devises a plan to invade Earth. Don't they know that Earth is populated by muscular, blond-haired Earthmen, usually named Rick, who cripple Martian invaders and destroy them? Ettil knows from some comic books that his grandfather brought back from an earlier Earth expedition. Forced to accept the duty that has been assigned to him, Ettil joins the invasion team, only to see his worst fears come true. Dir: Eleanore Lindo.

Ettil (Ben Cross); Van Plank (Howard Jerome); Assignor (John Gilbert); Tylla (Jan Smith); Mayor (Grant Reddick).

The Jar

In rural Louisana, Charlie wants to impress his neighbors, and he has just the thing: a mysterious jar he bought at a nearby carnival. Inside the jar, something moves listlessly in a hazy liquid. Everyone has a different opinion what it is. The jar is the talk of the town until Charlie's wife, Thedy, ridicules him. Now, Thedy disappears and the jar contains one or two more unidentifiable items. Dir: Randy Bradshaw.

Charlie (Paul LeMat); Thedy (Jennifer Dale); Tom Carmody (Earl Pastko); Gramps Medknowe (John Dee); Juke Marmer (Billy Morton); Jahdoo (Bill Meilen); Carneyboss (Randall Payne).

The Utterly Perfect Murder

Doug Spalding is celebrating his forty-eighth birthday but he still can't shake the nagging memory of Ralph Underhill, a childhood bully who pushed him around when he was 12. As boyish voices of "Mine! Mine! Gimme! Gimme!" fill his head, Doug decides to return to his hometown to seek revenge for these traumatic childhood events, to commit the utterly perfect murder. Dir: Stuart Margolin.

Doug (Richard Kiley); Ralph (Robert Clothier); Young Doug (David Turri); Young Ralph (Eric J. Johnson).

Let's Play Poison

Mr. Howard always prided himself on his appearance and strict, concise teaching style. He does not fear his class of 11- and 12-year-olds even though he believes they are the enemy, invaders from another dimension, and it's his job to reform their uncivilized little minds. These children scream and yell, punch and kick, and play "poison" on a sidewalk under construction. Dir: Bruce Pittman.

Mr. Howard (Richard Benjamin); Michael (Shane Meier); Charles (Adam Derges); Donald (Warren Graves).

The Martian

Rene and Anna La Farge move to Mars for a new life and forget their painful past. But one rainy night, Rene is awakened by whistling from outside his house. Dimly seen in the night is the shadow outline of a young man … Tom, their son who died five years ago on Earth. Welcoming the return of his son, Rene suspects this is not really his son, but a Martian. Dir: Anne Wheeler.

La Farge (John Vernon); Tom (Paul Clemens); Anna (Sheila Moore); Saul (Paul Coeur); Lavinia (Janne Mortil).

The Dead Man

For years people in town have made fun of Odd, the town eccentric who claims to have been "dead" for years. Lonely Miss Weldon befriends Odd, who is inspired overnight to prepare for marriage. But walking at dusk toward their new house just outside of town, Miss Weldon finds not a house, but a cemetery! Dir: Costa Botes.

Miss Weldon (Louise Fletcher); Odd (Frank Whitten); Mr. Simpson (Ross Duncan); Mr. Gilpatrick (Gilbert Goldie); Sheriff (Peter McCauley); Radney Bellows (David Taylor); Mrs. Bellows (Irene Drake); Customer (Alistair Douglas); Rev. Polk (Peter Morgan); Henry Scott (David Telford).

The Happiness Machine

Leo Auffmann is inspired to build a Happiness Machine in the garage—one that gives you the illusion of being anywhere in the world, at any time in history. The task consumes him. To his surprise, the Happiness Machine creates unhappiness, and Auffman realizes that the real miracle happens with his family every day in his own living room. Dir: John Laing.

Leo (Elliott Gould); Lena (Mimi Kuzyk); Saul Auffmann (Paul McIvor); Naomi Auffmann (Tania Mason); Aaron Auffmann (Matthew Brennan); Rosalyn Auffmann (Claire Chitham).

The Lonely One

The serial killer nicknamed "The Lonely One" has been stalking and murdering the town's women. The dark outdoors aren't safe. Lavinia boasts that she isn't afraid. And one night, she gets the scare of her life. Dir: Ian Mune.

Lavinia (Joanna Cassidy); Francine (Shiela McCarthy); Helen (Maggie Harper); Officer Kennedy (Stephen O'Rourke); Druggist (Peter Rowley); Frank Dillon (David Perrett); Theatre manager (Chic Littlewood); Pale man (Patrick Smith); Miss Roberts (Elizabeth Pendergrast); Miss Fern (Kathleen Kelley).

The Long Rain

What kind of planet is this? It rains and rains. Always, forever. And creepy rain creatures attack, invade and dissolve all life forms—especially human ones! One by one, members of the expedition from Earth are picked off as they desperately attempt to get to the Sundome. Dir: Lee Tamahori.

Trask (Marc Singer); Simmons (Michael Hurst); Boltz (Brian Sergent); Cooper (Mark Raffety).

The Anthem Sprinters

In an Irish pub, the patrons place bets on a very strange race: who can get out of the cinema before the national anthem starts! Douglas, an American writer, finds himself a contestant and realizes the Irish will give up the game when confronted by the sheer poetry of film. Dir: Wayne Tourell.

Douglas (Len Cariou); Doone (Robert Ball); Timulty (Ken Blackburn); Heeber Finn (Ian Watkin); Fogarty (Terry Hayman); O'Gavin (Bruce Allpress); Cinema mgr. (Karl Bradley); Phil, projectionist (Grant Bridger); Nolan (Alister Babbage); Kelly (David Baxter); Bookstore owner (Maurice Keene).

Fee Fie Foe Fum

Tom Barton comes home with a "garburator," a machine that eats garbage. Grandma is nervous and is sure her son-in-law is trying to scare her to death. If she dies, he gets all her money. Dir: John Reid.

Grandma (Jean Stapleton); Tom (Robert Morelli); Liddy Barton (Lucy Lawless); Postman (Patrick Smith).

Downwind from Gettysburg

Will history repeat itself? Abraham Lincoln has been assassinated—again. Not the real Lincoln, but Norman Llewellyn Booth has shot and destroyed an exact replica of the famous American president. And Bayes, manager of the theatre, denies the assassin the reward of immortality for the crime. Dir: Chris Bailey.

Bayes (Howard Hessman); Booth (Robert Joy); Phipps (Kelly Johnson); Lincoln (Roy Bonnell); Attendant (Jim Rawdon); Boy (Timothy Dale).

By the Numbers

For 30 years, the Ambassador Hotel pool has been tended by an old drill sergeant and his ten-year-old son. Thirty years later, the boy, now a man, drinks a martini on a train. What happened to his father, and what kind of a man grows from such a cold and calculating upbringing? Dir: Wayne Tourell.

The father (Ray Sharkey); Douglas (Geordie Johnson); The boy (Ciaran Pennington); Sid (Marton Csokas); Young man (Erik Thomson); Hotel waiter (Bruce Tegart); Train waiter (Nii Hammond).

Tombstone

Traveling four days in their Model T Ford, Leota and Walter reach an old brick town. There, they find a room at a hotel that contains a tombstone. Shaken, Leota fears the rising of the dead to haunt them. Soon, groaning from below and crashing sounds bring even more terror to their lives. Dir: Warrick (Waka) Attewell.

Leoth Bean (Shelley Duvall); Walter Bean (Ron White); The landlord (Desmond Kelly); Mr. Whetmore (John Smythe); The woman (Mrs. White) (June Bishop); Couch potato (Paul Royce); Man [Mr. White] (Lyndon Peoples); Young lady (Jocelyn Brodeur).

Tomorrow's Child

Peter and Polly eagerly await the birth of their first child. But the amazing new machine assisting in the birth malfunctions, creating a baby unlike any other ever born. It lives, breathes, cries and resembles a blue pyramid with six snakelike appendages and three eyes blinking from long projecting structures. Not a mutant, they name him/her "Pi." A difficult choice awaits them: raise the "freak" or have the machine transport them into the other dimension so they, "freaks" themselves, can be united with their baby. Dir: Costa Botes.

Polly (Carol Kane); Peter (Michael Sarrazin); Dr. Wolcott (Peter Bland); Workman (Mark Clare); Mary (Lisa Tapley-Bale); Bill (Mike Daly); Sheila (Mandy McMullin); Don (John Kerr).

Sun and Shadow

Model photography in Mexico becomes complicated when Ricardo, a simple Mexican man, doesn't allow the camera to capture what is his—his house and his wall. But when the photographer persists, Ricardo finds a different, shocking way to stop him. Dir: Larry Parr.

Ricardo (Gregory Sierra); Lazlo (John Bach); Vincent (Stuart Margolin); Maria Reyes (Vicky Haughton); Policeman (Ken Blackburn); Tomas Reyes (Lee Mete Kingi); Jorge (Jose Bribiesca); Andrew (James Roberts).

Silent Towns

Walter is the last man on Mars. All settlers have returned to Earth. When Walter, off wandering in the Martian wilderness, returns to the Martian town, he finds it silent and empty—until he hears the phone ringing. Someone else is on the planet. Soon, Walter desperately tries to lose the person he so desperately tried to find. Dir: Lee Tamahori.

Walter (John Glover); Genevieve (Monica Parker).

Some Live Like Lazarus

For half a century Roger looked after his mother. Year after year, summer after summer, Roger has denied his own happiness in unselfish service to the old woman in the wheelchair. And Anna, his teenage sweetheart, has waited year after year so he could marry her. But when the old woman dies, was it nature, or did Roger try to help nature along? Dir: Peter Sharp.

Anna (present day) (Janice Rule); Roger (Yannick Bisson); Mother (Yvonne Lawley); Roger (60) (Noel Trevarthen); Anna (18–22) (Katie Wolfe); Anna (10–12) (Kristin Darragh); Roger (10–12) (Leon Woods); Paul (Andrew Thurtell); Carol (Greer Robson); Hotel maid (Deborah Katherine).

Great Wide World Over There

Cora lives a lonely life with her husband, Tom, in a remote wilderness area. But Cora is curious about the "great wide world over there," and she learns about it when her nephew Benjy visits them. Through Benjy, a door is opened to the rich variety of people and places of which she has been so long deprived. But when Benjy leaves, life returns to desolation. Dir: Ian Mune.

Cora Gibbs (Tyne Daly); Benjy (David Orth); Tom Gibbs (Bill Johnson); Mrs. Brabbam (Helen Moulder); Mailman (Frank Whitten).

The Handler

Mr. Benedict, the town mortician, gets back at all the people who have ridiculed and belittled him over the years by making a few "adjustments" to the faces of his dead clients. But Benedict himself is victimized when all those corpses return from the grave to exact their revenge. Dir: Peter Sharp.

Mr. Benedict (Michael J. Pollard); Mr. Merriwell Blythe (Henry Beckman); Mr. Stuyvesant (John Sumner); Mr. Flinger (Peter Rowley); Mrs. Rogers (Lee Grant); Mrs. Shellmund (Lynne Skinner); Mr. Wren (Johnny Crews); Edmund Worth (Steve Cleary); Small boy (Casey Anstiss); Skateboarding boy (Christopher Brodeur); Mrs. McNamara (Jocelyn Brodeur).

Rod Serling's Night Gallery

December 1970–August 1973

In this anthology series, Rod Serling presents an art gallery where frightening paintings represent stories of the occult and the bizarre.

Host: (Rod Serling).

Created by: Rod Serling; *Producer:* Jack Laird; *Executive Producer:* Rod Serling; NBC/Universal; 60 minutes, years 1 and 2; 30 minutes, year 3.

A villain opens a box and finds a living doll whose lips curl into a wicked smile. A Mission Controller finds that a giant lunar rat devoured members of a moon expedition. A scientist searches a graveyard for a missing colleague and finds him dead, his throat in the clutches of a grinning skeleton. These were some of the visual images that embedded themselves in the imaginations of an enthusiastic teenage audience during the early 1970s. Rod Serling was perceived as "cool," *Night Gallery* as "hip," and many parents and PTA members were outraged over *Night Gallery's* supernatural content.

Unlike Rod Serling's *Twilight Zone*, which celebrated mankind, *Night Gallery* reflected the host's darker nature. Yet it was a difficult show to categorize. "People compared *Night Gallery* to *The Twilight Zone*," says story editor Gerald Sanford, "but it never found its identity. It was a bastard child."

The origins of *Night Gallery* go back to 1964. As *Twilight Zone* was going off the air, Serling came up with a suspense anthology titled *Rod Serling's Wax Museum*. Producer William Sackheim expressed interest in doing a TV movie based on Serling's three *Wax Museum* scripts. Serling agreed, and the pair came up with *Night Gallery*. The sinister waxworks were replaced by bizarre paintings.

The 1969 TV film was a ratings success. Its associate producer, John Badham, says, "It was an exciting project to do. We had to come up with three different directors for each story, and three casts. Bill Sackheim was asked if he'd be interested in having a 20-year-old kid named Steven Spielberg direct the Joan Crawford segment. It was Spielberg's first directing job. I was 27 at the time, and my job was to help Steven in any way I could." Crawford played a blind woman who ruthlessly strikes a bargain with a debt-ridden man (Tom Bosley) to buy his eyes. "Steven was terrified of Crawford," recalls Badham. "She was a very formidable woman. When you're 20 years old and confronted with a legend, it's intimidating. The two of us took her out to dinner to break the ice."

Spielberg, a *Twilight Zone* fan, wasn't thrilled by the script. "Steve was kinda at war with himself on how to approach it. He said, 'This is really just an old-fashioned Rod Serling script.' He insisted on doing something inventive with it. In the dailies, we were knocked out by what he was doing. It was very elegant, visually. Steven's best shots were those that made a point about what the movie was about. He wasn't going for just nifty shots."

NBC and Universal studios went ahead with a limited *Night Gallery* series for the 1970-71 season. It was one of four series airing under the title *Four in One* (*McCloud, The Psychiatrist* and *San Francisco International Airport* were the three other series that alternated with *Night Gallery*). Six hour-long episodes were made of each program.

For Serling, the *Four in One* segments represented *Night Gallery's* zenith. "I worked very intently on the series during that first year," Serling told writer David Johnson of *Planet of the Apes* magazine in 1974. "Then I got kind of aced out. Universal sort of took it over, creatively and completely."

One of the series' highlights for Serling was the Emmy-nominated "They're Tearing Down Tim Riley's Bar." William Windom starred as a middle-aged executive who seeks solace from life's realities by escaping into the happier memories of his past. "It was the best script I have ever been offered," says Windom. "The character and story were incisive and believable. After it aired, I got a most welcome phone call from Rod Serling."

However, when Universal executives read the script, Windom's marquee value didn't satisfy the studio. "Universal didn't want me for the role," says Windom. "I felt forced down their throat. Director Don Taylor told them, 'Use Windom or lose me!' They relented. Don had been an actor, and his directorial skills were built in. He was hands-on with the crew, hands-off with the actors. He was loud, direct and fair. He was open to ideas and closed to bullshit."

The resulting episode was an exceptionally thoughtful drama that was compromised only by "a happy, mushy ending," says Windom. "It's the only piece of film I've bought since I moved to Hollywood in 1961. I wanted to show my children their old man at his best. When it originally aired, a power failure in L.A. blacked out the last couple of minutes. Because of viewers' phone calls, they ran the ending on the local news the following night!"

Night Gallery's good ratings on *Four in One* convinced NBC to graduate the series to full-time status for the 1971-72 season. Former *Peyton Place* writer Gerald Sanford was brought in as story editor and helped producer Jack Laird prepare the scripts.

"Jack Laird was the strangest human being who ever lived," recalls Sanford of the late producer. "I was told, 'No one can work for Jack. He's impossible.' He would get into these violent, dark moods and scream and throw things. He never hurt anybody, but he was a total loner. He didn't relate to the people at Universal, but he loved working on *Night Gallery*. He did everything—wrote, directed, acted and picked costumes—but he rarely left his office. He even slept overnight there. In the morning I'd find him asleep on the couch."

One contribution Laird made to the series was the quick, comical blackouts. These included such bits as a skeleton getting lessons in elevator manners, and a babysitter meeting Count Dracula. Serling hated the blackouts, feeling they cheapened the show, but his control over *Night Gallery* was limited. As he said in 1974, "The blackouts would have been great in bad nightclubs but they were as destructive as hell for the show."

"Laird was a talented writer," says Sanford. "It wasn't his show, but he had total control. NBC was in awe of Rod, but Jack simply tolerated him. He often used Rod as a cover to get things done. The executives at Universal considered Jack a genius, and they left him alone."

For Serling, the series became a frustrating experience: His scripts were often rewritten by Sanford. "Universal has turned *Night Gallery* into a supernatural suspense thing with action," he said during the second season. "You don't walk past the graveyard, you're chased." When the PTA protested the show's content, Serling couldn't dismiss their grievances. "*Twilight Zone* may have been a little scary but it was never physically violent," he said. "I never heard from any PTA group that we lent sizable or meaningful damage to young people who watched the show. This show is called *Rod Serling's Night Gallery* but it's not remotely Rod Serling."

The unhappy Serling was bound by contract to host the show, but he continued to write scripts. "Rod was a great idea man," says Sanford. "But his scripts were often overwritten. His script for a 15-minute show might run 70 pages. He would write them overnight. Whatever came out of his typewriter, that's what he turned in the next day. Rod would have ten scripts delivered to us Monday morning, and the basic ideas in them were very good. It was the dialogue that needed changing. Jack and I would read them, and Jack would say, 'Well, what do you think?' I would say, 'Well, Jack...' He'd say, 'I agree. Let's go to work on 'em,' and we rewrote them. Rod hated rewrites. The first time I rewrote one of his scripts, Universal said to me, 'You realize if you try to get credit for this, we'll have to let you go. You can't take credit from Rod.' I said, 'I wasn't even thinking of it.' I wasn't interested in taking credit for scripts that weren't totally mine."

Sanford recalls Serling as "the way you saw him on TV. He was very clenched-mouthed and uptight. He was rather feisty. I always felt he really wanted to be an actor."

Jack Laird did become an actor on the series. "Jack acted in some of the episodes," says Sanford. "He was also one of the ghouls in the main title sequence. He said, 'Hey, Gerald, why don't you play a ghoul?'" Sanford declined and concentrated on writing scripts. "Many of the episodes were based on old novels. We'd buy the rights for a small fee and give story credit to the author. This way we could use some interesting ideas and not get sued."

One of the series' most popular episodes was "The Caterpillar," written by Rod Serling and directed by Jeannot Szwarc (*Jaws 2*, *Supergirl*). The segment starred Lawrence Harvey as an Englishman who arranges to have a flesh-eating earwig placed in the ear of his rival. A mix-up results in Harvey's character getting the earwig placed in his ear instead. He goes through excruciating anguish until the earwig, miraculously, tunnels out his other ear. His relief is short-lived when he learns the earwig has laid millions of its eggs in his brain.

"It's the episode of *Night Gallery* people

seem to remember most," says Szwarc. "We shot it in three days and the atmosphere and setting (a plantation in the Borneo jungles) was very successful. It was the first appearance of Lawrence Harvey on American TV. We became very close friends."

Assistant director Ralph Sariego recalls, "Universal had these ratty dressing rooms. Lawrence Harvey walked in, looked at his room and said, 'Now I know that I've reached the bottom.' But he went on and did the show. He was enormously professional."

Harvey's co-star, Don Knight, offers chilling testimony to Harvey's dedication to the role. "Larry was dying of cancer when he did *Night Gallery*," says Knight. "He deliberately went off his pain killers so he could feel the pain of the earwig. His horrendous agony in the episode was real. I was astonished by the difference between what Larry had done in rehearsals and what was coming down during filming. When I saw a doctor on the set, I asked Larry what was going on. That's when he told me. We remained friends for the little time he had left."

Szwarc's favorite episode was "The Sins of the Fathers," which dealt with the Welsh custom of sin eating. Richard Thomas played a nineteenth-century youth who pretends to be a sin-eater (to cleanse corpses of their sins by feasting in their presence) so he can steal food for his starving family. The segment ends with Thomas finding that, in the interim, his father has died. The young man goes into a screaming frenzy as he eats the food to cleanse his father's corpse.

"The network was petrified by the script," recalls Szwarc. "They found the content too strong. Jack Laird kept the script in reserve until I was available to direct it. When we filmed it, Jack still didn't have an official okay from the network. If Universal had known that, Jack and I would have been in trouble. That took an enormous amount of courage for Jack. We were both nervous when we showed it to the NBC brass. We were relieved when all they asked for was a little less screaming. My aim in the episode was to show hunger. I think we succeeded."

Writer Alvin Sapinsley wrote six scripts for *Night Gallery*, including "The Ghost of Sorworth Place," about a woman (Jill Ireland) being terrorized by the ghost of her husband. "Rod Serling called me after it aired and said how much he liked it. He said, 'This is how *Night Gallery* should be.'"

Sapinsley, who had known Serling from the live TV days, recalls, "The guiding hand of *Night Gallery* was not Rod's but that of Jack Laird. Rod was the creator and host, and he read all of the scripts, but he had very little control or influence. Laird once said to me, 'My biggest job on the show is to persuade Rod not to write any scripts.'"

The writer remembers Laird as "one of the most creative, knowledgeable, critical and interesting people I've ever met. After reading my scripts, he'd come back with pages and pages of the most precise, intelligent notes I have ever read. After I'd rewrite a script, he'd say, 'It's different but it's no better. Do it again!' He was a man who was largely unappreciated."

As a young contract player at Universal, actor Darrell Larson was cast as a student pursued by a monster in "There Aren't Any More Mac-Banes." "I was a big fan of *Twilight Zone*," says Larson, "and I was thrilled to be doing a Rod Serling show." At one point, Larson's character is chased down a staircase by a demonic creature. "The director, John Newland, was a wonderful, courtly gentleman who had been the host of *One Step Beyond*," says Larson. "He coached me in my screaming when the monster corners me. During rehearsals, I had to do ten variations of that scream. The monster breaking into the basement was actually just a stunt guy thrusting two claws through the window. Newland expertly growled for me [as the monster] off-camera."

Larson's other highlight was acting with Joel Grey, who played the eccentric student who dreams up the monster. "Joel is a consummate performer. He had reams of dialogue in the last scene and most of it was fairly unintelligible. In TV, there's a common practice of trimming an overwritten script on the set to get it to an actable level. Joel was certain this script would be cut for filming. It wasn't, and poor Joel hadn't bothered to learn all of this dialogue. I just had reaction shots, so the burden was on Joel. He was contrite and charming about it, and we pressed on. Ellen Blake [who played the monster] had to stand around in that ridiculous green-eyed monster get-up. She got a little miffed."

Night Gallery finished the 1971-72 season with modest ratings against *Mannix* on CBS. Although *Night Gallery* was unable to hold onto the huge audience provided by its lead-in, the *NBC Mystery Movie* series, it did have a loyal audience in the 12 to 25 age group. Nevertheless, NBC and Universal felt the ratings didn't justify the series cost.

"Anthologies never work," says Gerald Sanford. "That was *Night Gallery*'s main problem. It would have done much better if someone like Vincent Price had played a recurring character. Or if Rod Serling had appeared as a detective or writer each week, trying to track down the source of these stories. As a pure anthology, it wasn't that successful."

Sanford says the series had another problem. "Universal didn't care for the series. It was very expensive for them because you usually had three stories per show. You had to have three to six big-name stars, three directors, three writers, etc. The 15–20 minute stories added up in cost.

"We were always going over budget. Once, in the middle of a show, Universal pulled the plug. We took the footage we had and edited it to make an episode."

Creator/writer Rod Serling stands among the strange, eerie paintings of the Night Gallery. Copyright 1970 NBC/Universal.

"The ratings were not great but generally good for its time slot," says Jeannot Szwarc. "The demographics were excellent, and the audience it attracted was very loyal."

As the second season came to a close, Sanford decided to pursue other writing assignments. "I didn't like what *Night Gallery* had become," he says. "They started doing a lot of ugly and weird shows. I couldn't watch it anymore. They got away from doing human interest stories."

NBC renewed *Night Gallery* for a third season, 1972-73. Cut to a half-hour length, each episode contained only one story per show, reminiscent of *The Twilight Zone*. The third season would also be less horrific, with an emphasis on suspense. "*Night Gallery* had used a lot of old English and Welsh ghost stories for material," says Ralph Sariego. "There was a decision to move away from that in the third year and do contemporary stories. I didn't agree with that change."

Neither did Jeannot Szwarc. "Some of *Night Gallery*'s previous material had come from some of the best authors of the genre. The shortening of the format hurt, and there were no more interesting mixtures. The whole thing became monochromatic."

"*Night Gallery*'s original format was to do short stories, in varying lengths," says director John Badham. "It wouldn't be the same canned formula every week." Badham speculates the third year tried to cut some losses. "The network probably said, 'The series isn't doing that well. Maybe it's this weird, variable format.' Also, people tended not to like the one-minute comedy blackouts, so they were dropped. The show was changed to a safer, half-hour format. This also saved money since we were on terrifyingly tight budgets."

Director Ralph Senensky felt that the multisegmented format may have been confusing. "The series hurt itself by chopping itself into very short and long pieces per episode. The more time you put on a screen, the more complete an audience's reaction is going to be. The blackouts were probably a concept that sounded better than they played."

Serling's reaction to the new half-hour format was, at the time, uncharacteristically mild. "I'm more resigned than angry," he said. Two years later, however, he told writer David Johnson, "It was a very destructive change. You can't suddenly cut an hour show in half and expect audiences to accept it as the same animal."

The new *Night Gallery* was an animal trapped in a dead-end time slot, Sundays at 10 p.m. Buried in the schedule with scant publicity and often preempted, with a softer style that lacked the charisma of the previous seasons, the series failed to pull in a strong audience.

John Badham recalls the third year still offered some challenges. "It was a wonderful idea to cast Ozzie and Harriet Nelson in "You Can Come Up Now, Mrs. Millikan" [a Rod Serling tale of a bumbling scientist who brings back the dead]. It gave people a chance to see that the Nelsons had a nice dramatic talent. Ozzie was a very nervous man. He made up his own cue cards for all of his dialogue and planted them around the set. Harriet told me, 'Yes, he did that on *The Ozzie and Harriet Show* too!'"

Badham recalls Ozzie Nelson getting caught up in a minuscule plot point. "He was a very precise, exact man. He came to me about a rather innocuous line like, 'We're going to have a wonderful time today!' Ozzie said, 'Gee, I wonder if I should say, "We're going to have a nice time today" instead? Which do you like better?' I'm thinking, 'What's going on in this guy's mind?' I said, 'Well, I think the writer wrote "wonderful time" because your character is excited to show off his invention to all of these scientists.' Ozzie said, 'Yes, but maybe he's nervous about showing off his invention. If he's feeling cautious, he may want to say, "nice time" instead of "wonderful."' I said, 'Well, is this something you'd rather say?' He said, 'I dunno. What would you say?' I said, 'Part of my job is to defend the author. Since we're doing his work, I understand why he wrote "wonderful."' Ozzie replied, 'Yes, but...' and he continued arguing his point. Finally I said, 'Okay, fine! Why don't you say "Nice time?" He said, 'No, that's okay.' You couldn't win for losing! He was actually very funny."

Filming Badham's "The Doll of Death," a tale of voodoo magic, was another matter. "I got fired on that show," he says. "We were filming a shot where Barbara Parkins and Alejandro Rey ride a horse past the camera in their wedding outfits. The day before filming, I said to both actors, 'Do you ride well enough to ride bareback? We can get riding doubles, but it sure would be nice if you can do it.' Both Parkins and Rey said they would.

"The next morning, they rode past us on the horse. They were supposed to pull to a halt 50 yards down the road on the Universal lot. The horse stopped dead, but I saw Parkins grabbing for Rey, and they both plunged off the horse and went *bonk*! Everyone yelled, 'Oh my God!' We raced over there, and Parkins was okay but shaken. When you fall six feet onto hard-packed dirt, you take a good hit. We ran her over to St. Joseph's hospital in Burbank. They X-rayed her, and she was okay. Jack Laird went over to see how she was doing.

"Well, I presume she told Jack, 'The director made me get up on that horse,' because my name was suddenly Mud Badham. I continued filming the show with doubles, and Susan Strasberg replaced Barbara Parkins. After filming was over, I was told that I was not to do any more *Night Gallerys*. I always felt bad about Barbara Parkins. I haven't seen her since. But it was a great lesson for me. Being a relatively new director at the time, I didn't know how much you could get away with by using doubles."

Rod Serling's Night Gallery was canceled at the end of the 1972-73 season. "They were three great years," says Ralph Sariego of the experience. "The calibre of material was terrific. It had good stories and attracted wonderful talent."

"Perhaps its weakness was that it tried to embrace too wide a range," says Jeannot Szwarc. "It never found its specific *Zone* like *Twilight* did." Szwarc felt the show's uniqueness contributed to its cancellation. "It was too different and too original. Neither the network nor the studio ever understood it. Although the people who worked on it were passionate about the show, its very sophistication and literary quality turned the people in power off. The series never had any champions among the network or studio executives."

John Badham notes, "*Night Gallery*'s failure was caused by the unwillingness of American audiences to be the least bit experimental. They'd rather watch their old buddy *Roseanne*. Kids are much more experimental, and their willingness to watch *Night Gallery* was tremendous. They found it exciting and imaginative. As people get older, they take less risks."

Universal studios realized that placing *Night Gallery* into syndication wouldn't be easy. The studio decided to cut all of the hour episodes into half-hours. Stories that originally ran 45 minutes long, such as "They're Tearing Down Tim Riley's Bar," "A Question of Fear" and "The Messiah on Mott Street," had to be edited to a half-hour. The 20-minute segments had to be stretched to 30 minutes by adding stock footage from old movies.

"The Different Ones" was expanded from 20 minutes to 26 minutes by adding footage from the films *Silent Running* and *Fahrenheit 451*. Another episode, "Logoda's Heads," had its story radically altered by adding 10 minutes of a 1956 Beverly Garland jungle film called *Curucu, Beast of the Amazon*. To explain the old footage, "Logoda's" star, Tim Matheson, was brought in to loop new narrative dialogue.

Despite some inventive editing, the syndicated *Night Gallery* is frequently inferior to what aired originally on NBC. Its creative values were sacrificed by the studio's practical needs to make a profit.

One of John Badham's episodes, "Camera Obscura," was another casualty. "They padded it by adding a series of repetitive shots of ghostly faces floating out of a wall. Once or twice is fine, but they did it over and over to kill time. They turned what was a tight, fast-moving story into something flabby. Originally, it was one of my favorite episodes. Watching it now, it's dreadful. They slowed it to a crawl."

Jeannot Szwarc also grimaces at the editing. "Once a series has been canceled, it's like carrion. The vultures do what they want. I never saw the episodes in syndication, but I'm sure the overall result was awful."

When the editing knives were put away, *Night Gallery* consisted of 75 half-hour segments. It wasn't enough. "There had been another series at Universal called *The Sixth Sense*, starring Gary Collins," says Badham. "Universal decided to combine the *Night Gallery* syndication package with *The Sixth Sense*. Harry Katleman, a wonderful man at Universal, had the difficult job of taking the 25 episodes of *Sixth Sense* and editing them down.... He made them into very tight and exciting half-hours. I had directed a couple *Sixth Senses*, and I said to Harry, 'They're

much better now! Originally, they were deadly boring.'"

Artist Jaroslav Gebr was recruited to paint 25 new paintings, and Rod Serling agreed to host the extra narration for a cool $250,000. "I did the narration because I wanted out," said Serling in 1974, "but some of what they gave me to say was incredible."

Night Gallery wasn't a big succcess in syndication, but the original series is still fondly remembered for chilling a generation. John Badham recalls, "I went on a date with a young woman, and she found out I had directed the *Night Gallery* episode "Green Fingers." She had been in school when it aired and said everyone loved this wonderful series called *Night Gallery*." Badham married the woman shortly afterward.

For Jeannot Szwarc, the series represented some of his most creative work. "*Night Gallery* was one of the best things to happen on television," he concludes. "It had an aesthetic and poetic quality which, sadly, has been missing from TV ever since."

CAST NOTES

Rod Serling: see **Twilight Zone.**

EPISODE GUIDE

Night Gallery (1969 TV movie)
1.The Cemetery
A greedy nephew is tormented by a painting that shows his dead uncle crawling out of his grave. Wr: Rod Serling. Dir: Boris Sagal.
  Jeremy Evans (Roddy McDowall); Osmond Portifoy (Ossie Davis); William Hendricks (George McCready); Carson (Barry Atwater); Doctor (Richard Hale); Gibbons (Tom Bascham).

2. Eyes
A ruthless woman buys a man's eyes for 12 hours of sight, but her vision is made short-lived by a cruel twist of fate. Wr: Rod Serling. Dir: Steven Spielberg.
  Claudia Menlo (Joan Crawford); Dr. Frank Heatherton (Barry Sullivan); Sid Resnick (Tom Bosley); Lou (Fred Sadoff); Packer (Byron Morrow); Nurse (Shannon Farnon).

3. Escape Route
A German war criminal projects himself into a peaceful painting to elude authorities. Wr: Rod Serling. Dir: Barry Shear.
  Josef Strobe (Richard Kiley); Bleum (Sam Jaffe); Gretchen (Norma Crane); Agent (George Murdock); Louis (Garry Goodrow).

Season 1: 1970-71

1.1. The Dead Man
The tapes of a failed experiment reveal that a sinister corpse in a nearby mausoleum has the ability to rise again. Wr: Doug Heyes, Sr., story by Fritz Leiber. Dir: Doug Heyes, Sr.

Max Redford (Carl Betz); Miles Talmadge (Jeff Corey); Velia Redford (Louise Sorel); John W. Fearing (Michael Blodgett); Minister (Glenn Dixon).

1.2. The Housekeeper
A magical frog has the power to transfer the kind soul of an old woman into the body of a man's selfish wife. Wr: Matthew Howard (Doug Heyes, Sr.) Dir: John Meredyth Lucas.

Cedric Acton (Larry Hagman); Carlotta Acton (Suzy Parker); Miss Wattle (Jeanette Nolan); Miss Beamish (Cathleen Cordell); Maurice (Howard Morton).

2.1. Room with a View
An invalid manipulates a cheerful young nurse to kill his unfaithful wife. Wr: Hal Dresner, story by Hal Dresner. Dir: Jerrold Freedman.

Mr. B. (Joseph Wiseman); Nurse (Diane Keaton); Lila B. (Angel Tompkins); Charles (Morgan Farley); Vic (Larry Watson).

Memory Flash—Hal Dresner: "Unhappy marriages and murders were a staple of the *Alfred Hitchcock* magazines. That's where this story was first published. Most of the writers that I knew—happily married or not—used a variation of this formula. It's probably no longer politically correct."

2.2. The Little Black Bag
When a twenty-first century medical bag is accidentally transported to 1970, a discredited doctor uses the kit to perform miraculous cures of the city's poor people. Wr: Rod Serling, story by C.M. Kornbluth. Dir: Jeannot Szwarc.

Dr. William Fall (Burgess Meredith); Heppelwhite (Chill Wills); Gillings (George Furth); Charlie Peterson (E.J. Andre); Mother (Eunice Suarez); Dr. Nodella (Robert Terry); First doctor (Lindsay Workman); Second doctor (Matt Pelto); Girl (Marion Yal); Ennie (Arthur Malet); First man (Ralph Moody); Second man (William Challee); Pawnbroker (Johnny Silver).

2.3. The Nature of the Enemy
Astronauts were eaten alive by something on the moon. The key to the tragedy is a strange device the astronauts were making when they died. Wr: Rod Serling. Dir: Allen Reisner.

Simms (Joseph Campanella); Astronaut (Richard Van Fleet); Reporter (James B. Sikking); Reporter #2 (Jason Wingreen); Reporter #3 (Albert Popwell); Man (Jerry Strickler).

3.1. The House
A woman is terrorized by a ghost that knocks on the door of her dream house. Wr: Rod Serling, story by Andre Maurois. Dir: John Astin.

Elaine Latimer (Joanna Pettet); Peter Mitchell (Steve Franken); Peugot (Paul Richards); Nurse (Jan Murrell); Old woman (Almira Sessions).

3.2. Certain Shadows on the Wall
The lingering shadow of a dead woman haunts her murderous brother. Wr: Rod Serling, story by Mary E. Wilkins-Freeman. Dir: Jeff Corey.

Stephen Brigham (Louis Hayward); Emma Brigham (Agnes Moorehead); Rebecca Brigham (Rachel Roberts); Ann Brigham (Grayson Hall).

4.1. Make Me Laugh
A guru gives a failing comedian the ability to make people laugh. Soon everything he says is met with hysterical laughter. Wr: Rod Serling. Dir: Steven Spielberg.

Jackie Slater (Godfrey Cambridge); Jules Kettleman (Tom Bosley); Chatterje (Jackie Vernon); Myron Mishkin (Al Lewis); David Garrick (Sidney Clute); Bartender #2 (Gene Kearney); Bartender #1 (Sonny Klein); Heckler (John J. Fox); Director (Tony Russel); Miss Wilson (Michael Hart); Flower lady (Georgia Schmidt); First laugher (Sid Rushakoff); Second laugher (Don Melvoin).

4.2. Clean Kills and Other Trophies
Col. Dittman demands that his peace-loving son kill a deer. His request leads to a gruesome conclusion. Wr: Rod Serling. Dir: Walter Doniger.

Archie Dittman (Raymond Massey); Pierce (Tom Troupe); Tom (Herb Jefferson, Jr.); Archie Jr. (Barry Brown).

5.1. Pamela's Voice
A man kills his nagging wife—or so he thinks, until she shows up with some surprising gossip. Wr: Rod Serling. Dir: Richard Benedict.

Pamela (Phyllis Diller); Jonathon (John Astin).

5.2. Lone Survivor
The crew of an ocean liner rescues a *Titanic* survivor three years after the sinking. Wr: Rod Serling. Dir: Gene Levitt.

Survivor (John Colicos); Captain (Torin Thatcher); Doctor (Hedley Mattingly); Wilson (Charles Davis); Richards (William Beckley); Captain #2 (Edward Colmans); Quartermaster (Brendon Dillon); Helmsman (Terence Pushman); Officer #2 (Pierre Jalbert); Quartermaster #2 (Carl Milletaire).

5.3. The Doll
Col. Masters has to outwit the deadly gift sent to him by an enemy: a living doll with poisonous fangs. Wr: Rod Serling, story by Algernon Blackwood. Dir: Rudi Dorn.

Col. Masters (John Williams); Miss Danton (Shani Wallis); Pandit Chola (Henry Silva); Monica (Jewel Blanch); Indian (Than Wyenn); Butler (John Barclay).

Memory Flash—Rudi Dorn: "We had only two days to shoot this. I was pulled aside by the producers, who suggested I get all of Miss Shani Wallis's performance on film as fast as possible. She had to fly to Israel the next day. On the second day, I finished the show by using over-the-shoulder shots of a double. The episode turned out first rate. The living doll's effectiveness on screen must go to a German special effects man, whose name I unfortunately don't recall."

6.1. They're Tearing Down Tim Riley's Bar
Executive Randy Lane faces a mid-life crisis until he confronts the ghosts of his past. Wr: Rod Serling. Dir: Don Taylor.

Randy Lane (William Windom); Lynn Alcott (Diane Baker); Pritkin (John Randolph); Doane (Bert Convy); McDermott (Henry Beckman); Tim Riley (Robert Herrman); Blodgett (David Astor); Bartender (Gene O'Donnell); Father (Frederic Downs); Policeman (John S. Ragin); Intern (David Frank); Katy (Susannah Darrow); Miss Trevor (Mary Gail Hobbs); Operator (Margie Hall); Workman (Don Melvoin); Workman #2 (Matt Pelto).

6.2. The Last Laurel
Invalid Marius Davis plans to use astral projection to murder his wife's supposed lover. Wr: Rod Serling, story by Davis Grubb. Dir: Daryl Duke.

Marius Davis (Jack Cassidy); Susan Davis (Martine Beswick); Dr. Armstrong (Martin E. Brooks).

Season 2: 1971-72

7.1. The Boy Who Predicted Earthquakes
A small boy becomes a sensation with his ability to predict the future. But one day, he mysteriously stops predicting. Wr: Rod Serling, story by Margaret St. Clair. Dir: John M. Badham.

Wellman (Michael Constantine); Herbie Bittman (Clint Howard); Dr. Peterson (Ellen Weston); Reed (Bernie Kopell); Godwin (William Hansen); Secretary (Rosary Nix); Cameraman Rance (Rance Howard); Director (Gene Tyburn); Grip (John Donald); Pilot (Jim Gavin).

Memory Flash—Story editor Gerald Sanford: "It was a good episode, but watching the dailies was sheer torture. We had to watch that little kid go on and on. His speeches were endless and they were repeated over and over. It just about drove us nuts!"

7.2. Miss Lovecraft Sent Me
A hip babysitter splits when she learns the baby is a three-legged werewolf and his father is Count Dracula. Wr: Jack Laird. Dir: Gene Kearney.

Betsy (Sue Lyon); Count (Joseph Campanella).

7.3. The Hand of Borgus Weems
A man pleads with surgeons to chop off his hand, which has a murderous mind of its own. Wr: Alvin Sapinsley, story by George Langelaan. Dir: John Meredyth Lucas.

Peter Lacland (George Maharis); Archibald Ravadon (Ray Milland); Susan Douglas (Joan Huntington); Nico Kazanzakis (Peter Mamakos); Dr. Innokenti (Patricia Donahue); Brock Ramsey (William Mims); Everett Winterreich (Robert Hoy).

Trivia Note: Changed radically for syndication, this episode was padded with LSD dream sequences from the Darren McGavin movie *The Forty-Eight Hour Mile* (1968). One scene includes a man battling a giant tarantula.

7.4. Phantom of What Opera?
A masked Phantom terrorizes his beautiful captive until she reveals her secret. Wr and Dir: Gene Kearney.

Phantom (Leslie Neilsen); Singer (Mary Ann Beck).

8.1. A Death in the Family
A fugitive finds a morgue where the dead have been preserved by a lonely funeral director. Wr: Rod Serling, story by Miriam Allen DeFord. Dir: Jeannot Szwarc.

Mr. Soames (E.G. Marshall); Doran (Desi Arnaz, Jr.); Driver (Noam Pitlik); Trooper (James B. Sikking); Trooper #2 (John Williams Evans); Trooper #3 (Bill Elliot); Grave digger (Bud Walls).

Memory Flash—Desi Arnaz, Jr.: "It was a very unusual story with a wonderful director. I played a guy who escaped from prison and found a place that was even more horrible. This mortician, instead of burying bodies, is keeping them around as family. Since my character is dying, the mortician is looking at him like the next family member! It was almost too much. It was a weird, black comedy. E.G. Marshall was perfect: so proper as the mortician, but underneath the calm exterior was a crazy man."

8.2. The Merciful
A woman's effort to end her husband's misery backfires. Wr: Jack Laird, story by Charles L. Sweeney, Jr. Dir: Jeannot Szwarc.

Wife (Imogene Coca); Husband (King Donavon).

8.3. The Class of '99
A student in 1999 rebels against a course that teaches racial bigotry. Wr: Rod Serling. Dir: Jeannot Szwarc.

Professor (Vincent Price); Johnson (Brandon de Wilde); Elkins (Randolph Mantooth); Barnes (Hilly Hicks); Miss Wheeton (Lenore Kasdorf); Clinton (Frank Hotchkiss); Miss Fields (Suzanne Cohane); Miss Peterson (Barbara Shannon); Bruce (Richard Doyle); Templeton (Hunter von Leer); McWhirter (John Davey).

Memory Flash—Jeannot Szwarc: "It was one of my favorite episodes. It had to be done in a day and a half. The production designer, Joe Alves, loved the idea of a white-on-white set and did it brilliantly. The cameraman, Lionel Linden, did some incredible lighting. It was also my first gig with Vincent Price. The moment when all of the students froze was done live; no slow motion, no trick photography. It was also the first script by Rod Serling that I did. He loved it, and thanks to this episode, I got to do many of his scripts."

8.4. Witches Feast
Three witches try to cook up a new brew, but when

the recipe goes poof! they order out. Wr: Gene Kearney. Dir: Jerrold Freedman.

Main witch (Agnes Moorehead); Hungry witch (Ruth Buzzi); Old witch (Fran Ryan); Flying witch (Allison McKay).

9.1. Since Aunt Ada Came to Stay

A young teacher tries to prevent a withered old witch from taking over the body of his wife. Wr: Alvin Sapinsley, story by A.E. van Vogt. Dir: William Hale.

Craig Lowell (James Farentino); Joanna Lowell (Michele Lee); Aunt Ada (Jeanette Nolan); Nick Porteus (Jonathan Harris); Frank Heller (Eldon Quick); Caretaker (Charles Seel); Housekeeper (Alma Platt); Boy (Arnold Turner).

9.2. With Apologies to Mr. Hyde

A hunchbacked assistant bungles a new formula for his master, Dr. Jekyll. Wr: Jack Laird. Dir: Jeannot Szwarc.

Mr. Hyde (Adam West); Assistant (Jack Laird).

9.3. The Flip Side of Satan

A DJ finds a radio station where the hit songs are all playbacks of his past crimes. Wr: Malcolm Marmorstein, Gerald Sanford, story by Hal Dresner. Dir: Jerrold Freedman.

J.J. Wilson (Arte Johnson).

Memory Flash—Gerald Sanford: "For years I thought it was Regis Philbin who starred in this segment. I met Regis a few years ago and I complimented him on the excellent job that he did. He didn't know what I was talking about! Arte Johnson was terrific in the show."

10.1. A Fear of Spiders

A cruel gourmet battles a spider, which gets bigger every time it's washed down the drain. Wr: Rod Serling, story by Elizabeth Walter. Dir: John Astin.

Justus Walters (Patrick O'Neal); Elizabeth (Kim Stanley); Boucher (Tom Pedi).

Memory Flash—Story editor Gerald Sanford: "We always had good parts for actors, which is why we attracted such talented people. We sent this script to Kim Stanley and she said, 'I'll do it!' It was one of my favorite episodes; a two-character tour de force told with wit and humor."

10.2. Junior

A Frankenstein monster–like baby demands a glass of water from its parents. Wr: Gene Kearney. Dir: Theodore J. Flicker.

Father (Wally Cox); Mother (Barbara Flicker); Junior (Bill Svanoe).

10.3. Marmalade Wine

A storm forces a braggart to seek shelter at the house of a strange plastic surgeon. Wr: Jerrold Freedman, story by Joan Aiken. Dir: Jerrold Freedman.

Roger Blacker (Robert Morse); Dr. Francis Deeking (Rudy Vallee).

10.4. The Academy

An exasperated father checks out a military academy where the cadets never leave. Wr: Rod Serling, story by David Ely. Dir: Jeff Corey.

Holston (Pat Boone); Director (Leif Erickson); Sloane (Larry Linville); D.I. (Edward Call); Bradley (Stanley Waxman); Simmons (Robert Gibbons); George (E.A. Sirianni); Cadet (John Gruber).

11.1. The Phantom Farmhouse

A doctor befriends a female werewolf whose ravenous family has been tearing people apart. Wr: Halstead Welles, story by Seabury Quinn. Dir: Jeannot Szwarc.

Joel Winter (David McCallum); Mildred Squire (Linda Marsh); Gideon (David Carradine); Pierre (Ivor Francis); Sheriff (Ford Rainey); Tom (Bill Quinn); Betty (Trina Parks); Mrs. Squire (Gail Bonney); Mr. Squire (Martin Ashe); Grouch (Ray Ballard); Shepherd (Frank Arnold).

11.2. Silent Snow, Secret Snow

A boy's relationship with falling snow draws him into a strange world. Wr: Gene Kearney, story by Conrad Aiken. Dir: Gene Kearney.

Narrator (Orson Welles); Paul Hasserman (Radames Pera); Father (Lonny Chapman); Mother (Lisabeth Hush); Doctor (Jason Wingreen); Mrs. Buel (Francis Spanier); Deidre (Patti Cohoon).

12.1. A Question of Fear

Special effects highlight this story of a fearless colonel who makes a bet that he can survive a night in a haunted house. Wr: Theodore J. Flicker, story by Bryan Lewis. Dir: Jack Laird.

Denny Malloy (Leslie Nielsen); Dr. Mazi (Fritz Weaver); Al (Jack Bannon); Fred (Ivan Bonar); Walter (Owen Cunningham).

12.2. The Devil Is Not Mocked

Nazi soldiers face a family of vampires when they try to take over a Balkan castle. Wr: Gene Kearney, story by Manly Wade Wellman. Dir: Gene Kearney.

General (Helmut Dantine); Dracula (Francis Lederer); Kranz (Hank Brandt); Hugo (Martin Kosleck); Radioman (Gino Gottarelli); Gunner (Mark de Vries)

13.1. Midnight Never Ends

A hitch-hiking Marine and a young woman discover they're characters in a novel. Wr: Rod Serling. Dir: Jeannot Szwarc.

Ruth (Susan Strasberg); Vincent Riley (Robert F. Lyons); Joe Bateman (Joseph Perry); Sheriff (Robert Karnes).

Trivia Alert: Production designer/artist Tom Wright did over 100 paintings for *Night Gallery*. In this segment, the painting is that of Rod Serling.

13.2. Brenda

A lonely teenage girl develops a friendship with a misunderstood blob during her summer vacation. Wr: Matthew Howard (Doug Heyes, Sr.), story by Margaret St. Clair. Dir: Allen Reisner.

Brenda Alden (Laurie Prange); Richard Alden (Glenn

Corbett); Flora Alden (Barbara Babcock); Jim Emsden (Robert Hogan); Elizabeth Emsden (Sue Taylor); Creature (Fred Carson); Francis Anne Emsden (Pamelyn Ferdin).

14.1. The Diary
A cruel gossip columnist is given a diary that predicts horrifying events. Wr: Rod Serling. Dir: William Hale.
Holly Schaeffer (Patty Duke); Dr. Mill (David Wayne); Carrie Crane (Virginia Mayo); Jeb (Robert Yuro); Maid (Diana Chesney); Nurse (Lindsay Wagner); Receptionist (Floy Dean); George (James McCallion).

14.2. A Matter of Semantics
Count Dracula discusses a transaction at the local blood bank. Wr: Gene Kearney. Dir: Jack Laird.
Count Dracula (Cesar Romero); Nurse (E. J. Peaker); Candy Striper (Monie Ellis).

14.3. The Big Surprise
An old farmer promises three boys that if they dig in a certain spot, they'll get a big surprise. Wr: Richard Matheson, story by Richard Matheson. Dir: Jeannot Szwarc.
Hawkins (John Carradine); Chris (Vincent Van Patten); Jason (Marc Vahanian); Dan (Eric Chase).

14.4. Professor Peabody's Last Lecture
When a professor scoffs at ancient gods, the gods get even by turning him into a monster. Wr: Jack Laird. Dir: Jerrold Freedman.
Prof. Peabody (Carl Reiner); Miss Heald (Louise Lawson); Lovecraft (Johnny Collins, III); Bloch (Richard Annis); Derleth (Larry Watson).

15.1. House with Ghost
A conniving husband strikes a deal with an English ghost to kill off his wife. Wr: Gene Kearney, story by August Derleth. Dir: Gene Kearney.
Ellis Travis (Bob Crane); Iris Travis (Jo Anne Worley); Canby (Bernard Fox); Sherry (Trisha Noble); Chichester (Eric Christmas); Doctor (Alan Napier).

15.2. A Midnight Visit to the Neighborhood Blood Bank
A thirsty vampire gets a unique reaction from his intended victim. Wr: Jack Laird. Dir: William Hale.
Vampire (Victor Buono); Girl (Journey Laird).

15.3. Dr. Stringfellow's Rejuvenator
A con man in the Old West promises to save a dying girl. When she dies, he finds himself haunted by her spirit. Wr: Rod Serling. Dir: Jerrold Freedman.
Stringfellow (Forrest Tucker); Snyder (Murray Hamilton); Rolpho (Don Pedro Colley); Man (Lou Frizzell).

15.4. Hell's Bells
A hippie dies in a car crash and finds himself in the waiting room for hell. Wr: Theodore J. Flicker, story by Harry Turner. Dir: Theodore J. Flicker.
Hippie (John Astin); Devil (Theodore Flicker); Tourist (John J. Fox); Lady tourist (Ceil Cabot); Big lady (Jody Gilbert); The bore (Hank Worden); Demons (Ted Flicker, Jack Laird, Gene Kearney).

16.1. The Dark Boy
A young teacher in the late 1800s tries to communicate with the shy ghost of a boy. Wr: Halstead Welles, story by August Derleth. Dir: John Astin.
Mrs. Timm (Elizabeth Hartman); Tom Robb (Michael Baseleon); Abigail Moore (Gale Sondergaard); Lettie Moore (Hope Summers); Joel Robb (Michael Laird); Ed Robb (Steven Lorange); Boy (Ted Foulkes).

16.2. Keep in Touch—We'll Think of Something
Obsessed with finding the beautiful woman who appears in his dreams, a man gives her description to the police. Wr and Dir: Gene Kearney.
Erik Sutton (Alex Cord); Claire Foster (Joanna Pettet); Joe Brice (Richard O'Brien); Cop (Paul Trinka); Hruska (Dave Morick); Alfred (Mike Robelo).

17.1. Pickman's Model
Scaly creatures living under the city kidnap and mate with human women. One of their off-spring is a sensitive painter named Pickman. He tries to prevent a young student from being snatched by the creatures. Wr: Alvin Sapinsley, story by H.P. Lovecraft. Dir: Jack Laird.
Richard Pickman (Bradford Dillman); Mavis Goldsmith (Louise Sorel); Uncle George (Donald Moffat); Larry Rand (Jack Livingston); Elliot Blackman (Joshua Bryant); Mrs. DeWitt (Joan Tompkins); Creature (Robert Prohaska).

17.2. The Dear Departed
Phony spiritualists find themselves haunted by a departed partner. Wr: Rod Serling, story by Alice-Mary Schnirring. Dir: Jeff Corey.
Mark (Steve Lawrence); Joe Casey (Harvey Lembeck); Angela Casey (Maureen Arthur); Mrs. Harcourt (Patricia Donahue); Mr. Harcourt (Stanley Waxman); Mrs. Hugo (Rose Hobart); Cop (Steve Carlson).

17.3. An Act of Chivalry
A living skeleton gets a lesson in elevator manners. Wr and Dir: Jack Laird.
Woman (Deidre Hudson); Spectre (Ron Stein); Passenger (Jimmy Cross).

18.1. Cool Air
A woman falls in love with a scientist who must stay in a refrigerated room to avoid decomposing. Wr: Rod Serling, story by H.P. Lovecraft. Dir: Jeannot Szwarc.
Agatha Howard (Barbara Rush); Dr. Juan Munos (Henry Darrow); Mrs. Gibbons (Beatrice Kay); Crowley (Larry Blake); Iceman (Karl Lukas).

Memory Flash—Henry Darrow: "The final scene was originally going to be shot with my face fizzing out on camera. Alka Selzer was used on my makeup. When they fired a mist of water from a spray gun, my face would melt and disappear. But it was rejected as much too gory!"

18.2. Camera Obscura
A magical camera hurls a greedy businessman into a town of ghouls. Wr: Rod Serling, story by Basil Copper. Dir: John Badham.

Gingold (Ross Martin); Sharsted, Jr. (Rene Auberjonois); Abel Joyce (Arthur Malet); Lamplighter (Milton Parsons); Drucker (Brendon Dillon); Driver (Philip Kenneally); Sharsted, Sr. (John Barclay).

18.3. Quoth the Raven
An obnoxious Raven helps Edgar Allan Poe compose his poem. Wr: Jack Laird. Dir: Jeff Corey.
Edgar Allan Poe (Marty Allen); Raven's voice (Mel Blanc).

19.1. The Messiah of Mott Street
A young boy tries to save his grandfather from the angel of death and searches the ghetto for the angel of life. Wr: Rod Serling. Dir: Don Taylor.
Abraham Goldman (Edward G. Robinson); Buckman (Yaphet Kotto); Dr. Levine (Tony Roberts); Mikey Goldman (Ricky Powell); Fanatic (Joseph Ruskin); Santa Claus (John J. Fox); Miss Moretti (Anne Taylor).

19.2. The Painted Mirror
A woman enters a strange mirror and finds a prehistoric world. Wr: Gene Kearney, story by Donald Wandrei. Dir: Gene Kearney.
Mrs. Moore (Zsa Zsa Gabor); Frank Standish (Arthur O'Connell); Ellen Chase (Rosemary de Camp).

20.1. The Different Ones
In 1993, a deformed young man who has been ostracized by his peers agrees to fly to an alien planet in hopes that he'll find some peace. Wr: Rod Serling. Dir: John Meredyth Lucas.
Paul Koch (Dana Andrews); Victor Koch (Jon Korkes); Official (Monica Lewis); Woman (Peggy Webber); Woman #2 (Mary Gregory).

Memory Flash—story editor Gerald Sanford: "I rewrote Rod Serling's original script. It turned out to be our best show. A disfigured teenager is put on a spaceship by his father and taken to a planet where everybody looks like him. It was the thoughtful story of a kid who can't find happiness on Earth because he looks different."

20.2. Tell David
A woman travels into the futuristic world of 1992, where she meets her grown-up son. She learns she killed the boy's father 20 years earlier. Wr: Gerald Sanford, story by Penelope Wallace. Dir: Jeff Corey.
Ann Bolt (Sandra Dee); Tony Bolt/David Blessington (Jared Martin); Pat Blessington (Jenny Sullivan); Jane Blessington (Jan Shutan); Yvonne (Françoise Ruggieri); Julie (Anne Randall); David Bolt (Chris Patrick); Announcer (Jeff Corey).

20.3. Logoda's Heads
Shrunken African heads that eat flesh are controlled by a voodoo chief. Wr: Robert Bloch, story by August Derleth. Dir: Jeannot Szwarc.
Henley (Tim Matheson); Major Crosby (Patrick Macnee); Kyro (Denise Nicholas); Logoda (Brock Peters); Emba (Zara Cully); Sgt. Imo (Albert Popwell); Askari (Roger E. Mosley).

21.1. Green Fingers
A greedy land developer has an old woman killed so that he can take over her ranch, but she grows back again in her garden. Wr: Rod Serling. Story: R.C. Cook. Dir: John Badham.
Mrs. Bowen (Elsa Lanchester); Michael J. Saunders (Cameron Mitchell); Ernest (Michael Bell); Crowley (George Keymas); Doctor (Bill Quinn); Sheriff (Harry Hickox); Deputy #2 (Jeff Burton); Deputy #1 (Larry Watson).

Memory Flash—John Badham: "Cameron Mitchell was a lot of fun. He accidentally cut his finger at one point while crawling out of a grave. He waved it in front of me and said, 'See what I've done? I've cut my finger for you!'"

21.2. The Funeral
Special effects highlight this tale of a vampire who invites a bunch of rowdy monsters to his funeral. Wr: Richard Matheson, story by Richard Matheson. Dir: John Meredyth Lucas.
Ludwig Astor (Werner Klemperer); Milton Silkline (Joe Flynn); Morrow (Harvey Jason); Count (Charles Macauley); Jenny (Laura Lacey); Vampire (Diana Hale); Ygor (Jack Laird); Vampire #2 (Leonidas P. Ossetynski); Werewolf (Jerry Summers).

21.3. The Tune in Dan's Cafe
A song linked to a tragic romance gives a bickering couple a second chance. Wr: Gerald Sanford, Garrie Bateson, story by Shamus Frazier. Dir: David Rawlins.
Joe Bellman (Pernell Roberts); Kelly Bellman (Susan Oliver); Red (Brooke Mills); Dan (James Nusser); Roy Gleason (James Davidson); Singer (Jerry Wallace).

22.1. Lindemann's Catch
A sea captain falls in love with a captured mermaid. His efforts to turn her into a human being result in disaster. Wr: Rod Serling. Dir: Jeff Corey.
Lindemann (Stuart Whitman); Suggs (Harry Townes); Mermaid (Anabel Garth); Dr. Nichols (Jack Aranson); Granger (John Alderson); Bennett (Jim Boles); Phineas (Matt Pelto); Ollie (Ed Bakey); Charlie (Michael Stanwood).

22.2. A Feast of Blood
A strange man gives a woman a mouse-like brooch that feeds on blood. Wr: Stanford Whitmore, story by Dulcie Gray. Dir: Jeannot Szwarc.
Sheila Gray (Sondra Locke); Henry Mallory (Norman Lloyd); Mrs. Gray (Hermoine Baddeley); Frankie (Patrick O'Hara); Gippo (Barry Bernard); Girl (Cara Burgess); Chauffeur (Gerald S. Peters).

Memory Flash—Stanford Whitmore: "I'm not fond of the supernatural or science fiction. Producer Jack Laird asked me to write a couple of *Night Galleries*. He caught me at a time that I was grinding out rewrites and needed a change of pace. Jack was a brilliant, eccentric producer. He did it all. Rod Serling had virtually nothing to do with the series. 'A Feast of Blood' was lucky to have Norman and Sondra. It was just a trick little story."

22.3. The Late Mr. Peddington

A funeral director is confused by a woman who is making arrangements for her living husband. Wr: Jack Laird, story by Frank Sisk. Dir: Jeff Corey.

Cora Peddington (Kim Hunter); Thaddeus Conway (Harry Morgan); John (Randy Quaid).

23.1. The Miracle at Camefeo

A con man tries to pull off another job at a Mexican shrine but gets a terrible punishment instead. Wr: Rod Serling, story by C.B. Gilford. Dir: Ralph Senensky.

Rogan (Harry Guardino); Gay Melcor (Julie Adams); Joe Melcor (Ray Danton); Reverend (Richard Yniguez); Bartender (Rodolfo Hoyos); Woman (Margarita Garcia); Blind boy (Thomas Trujillo).

Memory Flash—Ralph Senensky: "It was a two-day shoot. It was a pretty thin story with a trick ending that telegraphs. Harry Guardino was masterful. He's one of those underrated actors who is capable of doing so much more than he's given."

23.2. The Ghost of Sorworth Place

A Scottish woman begs an American traveler to protect her from the corpse of her husband, who has vowed to kill her at midnight. Wr: Alvin Sapinsley, story by Russell Kirk. Dir: Ralph Senensky.

Ralph Bain (Richard Kiley); Ann Loring (Jill Ireland); Alistair Loring (John Schofield); Mrs. Ducker (Mavis Neal); MacLeod (Patrick O'Moore).

Memory Flash—Ralph Senensky: "Ghost stories are always fun to do, and this one had some substance. There was some controversy over the semi-nude scene at the end. They [the studio] wanted Jill to be nude from the waist up. She didn't want to do it. I sided with her. I figured they wouldn't be able to air it, so why shoot it? We settled on covering up her front with a sheet."

24.1. The Waiting Room

A gunslinger encounters five ghostly figures who know his past and future. Wr: Rod Serling. Dir: Jeannot Szwarc.

Sam Dichter (Steve Forrest); Dr. Soames (Buddy Ebsen); Bartender (Gilbert Roland); Joe Bristol (Albert Salmi); Charlie McKinley (Lex Barker); Abe Bennett (Jim Davis); Max Auburn (Larry Watson).

24.2. The Last Rites of a Dead Druid

A satanic statue terrorizes a young couple in its bid to possess the husband's body. Wr: Alvin Sapinsley. Dir: Jeannot Szwarc.

Jenny Farraday (Carol Lynley); Bruce Farraday (Bill Bixby); Mildred McVane (Donna Douglas); Bernstein (Ned Glass); Marta (Janya Brannt).

Memory Flash—Alvin Sapinsley: "I based the story on a statue of a monk that I still have standing in my backyard. It turned out both funny and scary. *Night Gallery* was a solid show. Technically, it was flawless."

25.1. Deliveries in the Rear

A nineteenth-century doctor pays two murderers to secure bodies for medical research, but the consequences are tragic. Wr: Rod Serling. Dir: Jeff Corey.

John Fletcher (Cornel Wilde); Barbara Bennett (Rosemary Forsythe); Bennett (Kent Smith); Jameson (Walter Burke); Dr. Shockman (Peter Brocco); Hannify (Larry D. Mann); Dillingham (Ian Wolfe); Tuttle (Gerald McRaney); Graverobber (Peter Whitney); Graverobber #2 (John Maddison); Mrs. Woods (Marjorie E. Bennett).

Trivia Alert: This was Gerald McRaney's acting debut. The actor later starred in TV's *Simon and Simon* and *Major Dad*.

25.2. Stop Killing Me!

A police sergeant is intrigued by a terrified woman's claim that her husband is trying to scare her to death. Wr: Jack Laird, story by Hal Dresner. Dir: Jeannot Szwarc.

Frances Turchin (Geraldine Page); Sgt. Stan Beverlow (James Gregory).

Memory Flash—Jeannot Szwarc: "I had to do this in one day. Gerry Page was incredible. It was because of this episode that she came back to do more. The big hurdle for the episode was to avoid being static."

25.3. Dead Weight

A cruel gangster tries to escape to South America, but he ends up as excess baggage. Wr: Jack Laird, story by Jeffry Scott. Dir: Timothy Galfas.

Landau (Bobby Darin); Bullivant (Jack Albertson); Delivery boy (James Metrople).

26.1. I'll Never Leave You—Ever

A woman uses a living doll to kill her husband. The doll then turns on her. Wr: Jack Laird, story by Rene Morris. Dir: Daniel Haller.

Mrs. Owen (Lois Nettleton); Ianto (John Saxon); Owen (Royal Dano); Witch (Peggy Webber).

26.2. There Aren't Any More MacBanes

A student of the occult conjures up a huge, fanged monster to kill his uncle, but the creature continues its killing rampage. Wr: Alvin T. Sapinsley, story by Stephen Hall. Dir: John Newland.

Andrew (Joel Grey); Arthur Porter (Howard Duff); Elie Green (Darrell Larson); Mickey Standish (Barry Higgens); Monster (Ellen Blake); Francis (Mark Hamill); Servant (Vincent Van Lynn).

Memory Flash—Darrell Larson: "The script ... was definitely not one of their better ones. Barry Higgens is the brother of Colin Higgens, who directed the films *Harold and Maude* and *Foul Play*. The guy who delivered the telegram is Mark Hamill, Luke Skywalker in *Star Wars*."

27.1. The Sins of the Fathers

In order to get food for his starving family, a young Welsh boy agrees to perform a traditional ritual to cleanse the sins of an old man: eating food in the presence of the body. Wr: Halsted Welles, story by Christianna Brand. Dir: Jeannot Szwarc.

Ian Evans (Richard Thomas); Miss Evans (Geraldine Page); Widow (Barbara Steele); Servant (Michael Dunn); Old man (Cyril Delevanti); The man (Alan Napier); Men (Terence Pushman, John Barclay).

27.2. You Can't Get Help Like That Anymore
A female android is abused and humiliated by a rich couple until she rebels. Wr: Rod Serling. Dir: Jeff Corey.

Joe Fulton (Broderick Crawford); Mrs. Fulton (Cloris Leachman); Maid (Lana Wood); Malcolm Hample (Henry Jones); Dr. Kessler (Severn Darden); Foster (Christopher Law); Mrs. Foster (Pamela Susan Shoop); Miss Charmin (A' Leshia Lee); Android (Roberta Carol Braham).

28.1. The Caterpillar
Flesh-eating earwigs that devour people's brains are used as a weapon by an Englishman who wants a rival dead. Wr: Rod Serling, story by Oscar Cook. Dir: Jeannot Szwarc.

Steven Macey (Laurence Harvey); Rhona Warwick (Joanna Pettet); Tommy Robinson (Don Knight); Doctor (John Williams); John Warwick (Tom Helmore).

Memory Flash—Don Knight: "One of the makeup men thought I was too young and clean-cut for the part. I scruffed myself up, grew a stubble beard and grew my hair longer. When Jean Szwarc saw me, he said, 'My God, you're exactly right!'"

28.2. Little Girl Lost
A brilliant scientist keeps his grip on sanity by pretending that his daughter, who died a year ago, is still alive. Wr: Stanford Whitmore, story by E.C. Tubb. Dir: Timothy Galfas.

Dr. Putnam (William Windom); Tom Burke (Ed Nelson); Dr. Cottrell (Ivor Francis); Col. Hawes (John Lasell); Man (Sandy Ward); Waiter (Nelson Cuevas).

Memory Flash—Stanford Whitmore: "Producer Jack Laird gave me six story ideas and I picked this one. The story attracted me because of its anti-war sense. Vietnam was emerging as a huge tragedy. The episode turned out very well."

29.1. Pay Now, Die Later
A funeral director drums up business with the help of a black cat. Wr: Jack Laird, story by Mary Linn Roby. Dir: Timothy Galfas.

Walt (Will Geer); Ned (Slim Pickens).

Trivia Alert: *Pay Now, Die Later* and the following two segments were not aired on NBC during the show's original run. They are included in the syndication package.

29.2. Room for One Less
A space creature materializes on a crowded elevator. Wr and Dir: Jack Laird.

Alien (Lee Jay Lambert); Elevator operator (James Metrople).

29.3. Satisfaction Guaranteed
A finicky customer wants to find the perfect woman to devour. Wr: Jack Laird. Dir: Jeannot Szwarc.

Customer (Victor Buono); Mrs. Mount (Cathleen Cordell); Miss Caraway (Eve Curtis); Miss Blodgett (Cherie Franklin); Miss Ransom (Leigh Christian); Virginia Walters (Marion Charles).

Season 3: 1972-73

Return of the Sorcerer
A man is stalked by the pieces of his dead brother. Wr: Halsted Welles, story by Clark Ashton Smith. Dir: Jeannot Szwarc.

Noel Evans (Bill Bixby); Carnby (Vincent Price); Fern (Tisha Sterling).

Memory Flash—Unit production manager Ralph Sariego: "This episode had crawling hands and feet. The key for that kind of show was to give the art director several weeks notice to design them and for the special effects guys to make them work."

The Girl with the Hungry Eyes
A young model's fiery eyes are responsible for several mysterious deaths. A photographer endangers his life to expose the seductive creature. Wr: Robert Malcolm Young, story by Fritz Leiber. Dir: John M. Badham.

Girl (Joanna Pettet); David Faulkner (James Farentino); Munsch (John Astin); Harry Krell (Kip Niven); Man (Bruce Powers).

Memory Flash—John Badham: "That was a lot of fun because Joanna Pettet was such a turn-on. She was beautiful, and we got to make all of these wonderful photos of her half-naked."

Fright Night
A couple moves into a cottage and finds a trunk that moves by itself, along with a note promising that a long-dead relative will be back to collect it. Wr: Robert Malcolm Young, story by Kurt van Elting. Dir: Jeff Corey.

Tom Ogilvy (Stuart Whitman); Leona Ogilvy (Barbara Anderson); Miss Patience (Ellen Corby); Zachariah Ogilvy (Alan Napier); Mover (Larry Watson); Goblin #1 (Michael Laird); Goblin #2 (Glenna Sergeant).

Rare Objects
A gangster, betrayed at every turn, seeks refuge with a scientist who collects objects from the past. Wr: Rod Serling. Dir: Jeannot Szwarc.

Augie Koloney (Mickey Rooney); Dr. Glendon (Raymond Massey); Molly Mitchell (Fay Spain); Joseph (Victor Sen Yung); Blockman (David Fresco); Doctor (Regis J. Cordic); Tony (Ralph Adano).

Spectre in Tap Dancing Shoes
A dancing ghost tries to protect her sister from a killer. Wr: Gene Kearney, story by Jack Laird. Dir: Jeannot Szwarc.

Millicent/Marion (Sandra Dee); Sam (Christopher Connelly); Jason (Dane Clark); Dr. Coolidge (Russell Thorson); Andy (Michael Richardson); Michael (Michael Laird); Policeman (Stuart Nisbet).

The Ring with the Red Velvet Ropes
A boxing champion, imprisoned in a mansion, must fight an immortal who hasn't lost a match in over 100 years. Wr: Robert Malcolm Young, story by Edward D. Hoch. Dir: Jeannot Szwarc.

Roderick Blanco (Chuck Connors); Jim Figg (Gary Lockwood); Sandra Blanco (Joan Van Ark); Dan Anger (Ji-Tu Cumbuku); Hayes (Charles Davis); Referee (Frankie Van); Max (Ralph Manza); Reporter (James Bacon).

1. You Can Come Up Now, Mrs. Millikan
Serio-comic story about an eccentric scientist who uses his trusting wife in an experiment to bring back the dead. Wr: Rod Serling, story by J. Wesley Rosenquist. Dir: John M. Badham.

Henry Millikan (Ozzie Nelson); Helena Millikan (Harriet Nelson); George Beaumont (Roger Davis); Burgess (Michael Lerner); Coolidge (Don Keefer); Mrs. Steinhem (Margaret Muse); Stacy (Lew Brown); Kimbrough (Stuart Nisbet).

2. Smile, Please
An adventurous photographer sneaks into a castle to photograph a sleeping vampire. Wr and Dir: Jack Laird.

Vampire (Cesare Danova); Photographer (Lindsay Wagner).

Memory Flash—Story editor Gerald Sanford: "I wrote a story along the lines of 'The Portrait of Dorian Gray.' It was about a count who stays young while his portrait ages. A young woman searches his castle for the painting and finds that it's all disfigured. It was one of Lindsay Wagner's first roles. They shot it for the second season [the episode was later reshot to make the count a mischievous vampire]."

The Other Way Out
Bradley Meredith is trapped in a house surrounded by man-eating dogs. His only chance for escape lies with a mysterious person named Sonny. Wr: Gene Kearney, story by Kurt van Elting. Dir: Gene Kearney.

Old man (Burl Ives); Bradley Meredith (Ross Martin); Potter (Jack Collins); Estelle Meredith (Peggy Feury); Miss Flanagan (Elizabeth Thompson); Sonny (Adam Weed); Cop (Paul Micale).

Finnegan's Flight
A convict is hypnotized into thinking he can fly, but the sensation takes on a very real and dangerous dimension. Wr: Rod Serling. Dir: Gene Kearney.

Tuttle (Cameron Mitchell); Finnegan (Burgess Meredith); Dr. Simpson (Barry Sullivan); Warden (Kenneth Tobey); Prisoner (Dort Clark); Prisoner #2 (Roger E. Mosley); Guard (Michael Masters); Infirmary man (John Gilgreen); Prisoner #1 (Raymond Mayo).

She'll Be Company for You
After killing his wife, a man finds himself being stalked by a black cat. Wr: David Rayfiel, story by Andrea Newman. Dir: Gerald Perry Finnerman.

Henry Auden (Leonard Nimoy); Barbara (Lorraine Gary); June (Kathryn May Hays); Minister (Bern Hoffman); Willy (Jack Oakie).

Memory Flash—David Rayfiel: "I've been accused of writing 'foreign films,' which may explain the moodiness in my *Night Gallery* scripts. It's true of everything I do. Sometimes it results in a lack of clarity or confusion. The acting in my *Night Galleries* was good, but I was disappointed that both segments were hard to follow. I suppose it's my fault, with a possible assist from the director."

Something in the Woodwork
A sad ghost reluctantly agrees to scare a woman's husband to death, but it proves to be the woman's undoing. Wr: Rod Serling, story by R. Chetwynde Hayes. Dir: Edmund M. Abroms.

Molly Wheatland (Geraldine Page); Charlie Wheatland (Leif Erickson); Julie (Barbara Rhodes); Joe Wilson (Paul Jenkins); Jamie Dilman (John McMurty).

Death on a Barge
A lonely fisherman carries on a romance with a female vampire who has been responsible for several deaths. Wr: Halsted Welles, story by Everill Worrell. Dir: Leonard Nimoy.

Hyacinth (Lesley Ann Warren); Jake (Lou Antonio); Phyllis (Brooke Bundy); Ron (Robert Pratt); Father (Jim Boles); Coastguardsman (Arthur Spain); Customer (Dee Dee Young); Woman (Dorothy Conrad).

Trivia Alert: This was Leonard Nimoy's directorial debut. He later directed several of the *Star Trek* motion pictures and the popular comedy film *Three Men and a Baby*.

Whisper
A husband struggles to free his wife from the spirits in an old cottage. Wr: David Rayfiel, story by Martin Waddell. Dir: Jeannot Szwarc.

Irene (Sally Field); Charlie (Dean Stockwell); Doctor (Kent Smith).

Memory Flash—David Rayfiel: "Jack Laird asked me to write a couple of scripts for *Night Gallery*, but science fiction has never interested me much. The rules aren't strict enough. It's like having an insane protaganist. You don't have to think about his motivation because he's crazy and he can do anything. Science fiction is similar. Anything can happen."

The Doll of Death
A woman struggles to defeat a spurned Englishman, who is exacting revenge on her husband through a voodoo doll. Wr: Jack Guss, story by Vivian Meik. Dir: John M. Badham.

Sheila (Susan Strasberg); Raphael (Alejandro Rey); Brandon (Barry Atwater); Dr. Strang (Murray Matheson); Andrew (Jean Durand); Vereker (Henry Brandon).

1. Hatred Unto Death
A writer captures a ferocious gorilla and fights a life-and-death battle with the beast. Wr: Halsted Welles, story by Milton Geiger. Dir: Gerald Perry Finnerman.

    Grant Wilson (Steve Forrest); Ruth Wilson (Dina Merrill); Ramirez (Fernando Lamas); N'gi the Gorilla (George Barrows); Native #1 (Caro Kenyatta); Native #2 (Ed Rue); Native #3 (David Tyrone).

2. How to Cure the Common Vampire
Vampire hunters track a vampire to its lair but debate over an effective way to dispatch the creature. Wr and Dir: Jack Laird.

    Hesitant man (Richard Deacon); Man #2 (Johnny Brown).

Salvage One

January 1979–November 1979

Junkman Harry Broderick builds a homemade, 33-foot rocketship to salvage junk from the moon. In later episodes, he uses the spaceship, the Vulture, *to explore lost islands, oceans and deserts for salvageable material.*

Cast: Harry Broderick (Andy Griffith); Addison "Skip" Carmichael (Joel Higgins); Melanie Slozar (Trish Stewart); Mack, the mechanic (J. Jay Saunders); Jack Klinger, FBI agent (Richard Jaeckel); Michele Ryan (year 2) (Heather McAdam).

Created by: Michael Lloyd Ross; *Producer:* Ralph Sariego; *Executive Producer:* Harve Bennett; *Science Advisor:* Isaac Asimov; ABC/ Columbia; 60 minutes.

As a modern day fantasy, *Salvage One* tapped into the "boys of all ages" dream of building your own spaceship and traveling to the stars. No government grants, no red tape; just a hammer, nails and imagination.

Harry Broderick, owner of a salvage business, takes his dream into his workshop and comes out with the *Vulture*, a homemade rocket. In the lighthearted two-hour pilot film, Broderick goes through painstaking scientific research, confronts bothersome legalities and blasts off for the moon. His mission: salvage all of the junk there and return to Earth to hawk his lunar wares. Harry was a one-man billboard for the free enterprise system.

In subsequent episodes, Broderick and his two friends, Skip (a former astronaut) and Melanie (a scientist), use the spaceship to salvage things from all over the world.

The successful TV movie was, as executive producer Harve Bennett points out, the beginning of the end for the series.

"The pilot film stands with anything that I've ever done," says Bennett. "If you can accept the basic premise, then the actors will win your heart. It was a marvelous two-hour show about a junkman going to the moon and facing the entire establishment. He proved that a man's dream can be attained. Problem was, once you've gone to the moon, what do you do next? Frankly, we couldn't top the pilot. Only the charm of the characters carried the show for two seasons."

The origins of *Salvage One* began cleanly and simply. "The idea and script were by Michael Lloyd Ross," says Bennett. "My business partner at the time, Harris Katleman, said to me, 'I've got this wonderful, imaginative fellow who has a terrific idea.' I met Mike, and he was a terrific guy with a wonderful script."

ABC was excited over the unusual premise and gave the go-ahead for the film. When it went to series, Ralph Sariego was handed the producing reins. Having already been a production man for *The Six Million Dollar Man* and *The Bionic Woman*, Sariego was ready for the challenge. "Mike Ross, the creator, had done commercials and documentaries, but he had no real industry experience," explains Sariego. "Since I had a heavy episodic experience, I was put in charge of the show's physical production. Mike was essentially the writer for the show." Ross, who died in the 1980s, is characterized by Sariego as, "A nice young fellow, but he was a chain smoker. He went through three packs a day and it eventually caught up with him."

Sariego didn't bother fine-tuning the show's format. "It had been dictated by the pilot. The real challenge was to produce what was on the printed page. In the second season, we did a show about an iceberg being towed from Alaska ["Hard Water"]. It was a grand adventure. I flew up to

Alaska for a week with our art director, Jack Wickman. He was about 83 at the time and kept working until his 90s. After scouting locations for Alaska, I looked up stock footage. We also built a 120-foot-long by 20-foot-high glacier." The producer found out, though, that the art department and stock footage made the filming in Alaska unnecessary. "By the time I got all of the stock footage together, we had everything we needed. We hardly used any of our Alaskan footage." The episode also used a great many special effects to create its iceberg illusion. "The way special effects were done back then was so primitive. We had matte paintings and traveling mattes. However, the overall effect turned out very well."

Although Mike Ross wanted science fiction to be secondary to the adventure, one early storyline, never filmed, had the salvagers catapulted back in time to the prehistoric era.

The series also allowed actors to play some unusual roles. Portraying a stranded astronaut on a malfunctioning spaceship in the two-part episode *Golden Orbit* remains a memorable experience for actress Ellen Bry. Her main memory is sweating inside a spacesuit. "It was extremely awkward and bulky," she recalls. "It made me feel fat. It was not my favorite wardrobe. In the episode they used tons and tons of smoke because the spaceship was suppose to have a leaky valve that contained freezing gasses. The funny thing was, although we were supposed to be freezing, the spacesuits were so incredibly hot we were actually dying from the heat."

Bry says humor salvaged the technical challenges. "Joel Higgins [Skip] has a great sense of humor. Between shots we were cracking a lot of jokes. If everybody hadn't been so good-natured, we would have had some very cross people. We spent nine days in that bloody space capsule!"

Salvage One was a success in its first year. The series had an unlimited format, a intriguing dose of science fiction (with impressive shots of the spaceship roaring through the skies) and offbeat plots that involved the salvagers meeting alien beings and strange creatures. "We also had a good cast," says Harve Bennett. "Anytime you work with Andy Griffith, you're in for a treat. *Salvage One* lasted as long as it did because of the charm of Andy Griffith and Joel Higgins. Joel's had a couple of series since and they were big successes by him just being there. He has a very unique brand of open charm."

"The cast was one of the most delightful groups of people that I've ever worked with," says Sariego. "Andy, Joel and Trish Stewart were exceptionally nice people."

Frequent director Ron Satlof agrees. "It was a good crew, with good actors and good producers. Andy Griffith was a joy to work with."

The series entered its ill-fated second year with high hopes and a new cast member. Heather McAdam was now aboard as Melanie's adopted child, Michele. "Heather was added in an effort to draw in a younger audience," notes Sariego. The once fantastic plots gave way to generally more conventional themes, including two segments dealing with wayward horses. The spaceship, for the most part, was left in dry dock. The story changes didn't have a chance to express themselves. After the two-part opener, dealing with the giant iceberg, ABC abruptly pulled the plug. Four episodes were never aired. The network felt the show had run out of steam.

"We were pulled off the air because we were pulling a 26 share," says Sariego. "Today, a 26 is an enormous hit. ABC wanted a 30 share. We made a total of 20 episodes, so it wasn't as if ABC hadn't given the show a chance. It just didn't produce the numbers the network wanted."

"They put us in a strange death slot called Monday Night Football," notes Bennett. "We came on just before the football games. It was a terrible place to be until *MacGyver* [the Richard Dean Anderson action series] came along years later. That was the right kind of programming, and it lasted seven years in that weird slot."

Time slot aside, Bennett is realistic as to why *Salvage One* couldn't keep its audience. "We milked the material as much as we could. Mike Ross did his mightiest, as did we all, to keep topping going to the moon. There was the wonderful episode we did about solving California's drought by moving an iceberg from Alaska. That two-parter had the size and the scope of the pilot. The other episodes didn't. But *Salvage One* was one of my neatest experiences. It was an exercise in whimsey, and whimsey isn't something you see a lot in TV. That was probably the series' ultimate, fatal flaw."

CAST NOTES

Andy Griffith (Harry): Born 1926. He is best known as Andy Taylor in *The Andy Griffith Show* (1960–68) and as television's *Matlock* in the 1990s series.

Cast of *Salvage One*, top to bottom: Andy Griffith, Joel Higgins and Trish Stewart. Copyright 1979 ABC/Columbia.

Joel Higgins (Skip): Born 1943. Higgins later starred in the situation comedy *Silver Spoons* (1982–1986).

Trish Stewart (Melanie): Stewart studied literature and philosophy at the Sorbonne in Paris, where she was also a nightclub singer. Her career took off in 1973 while playing Chris Brooks on daytime's *The Young and the Restless*. Little has been seen of her since 1980.

"She was a very sensitive, exceptionally nice woman," recalls producer Ralph Sariego. "I haven't seen her in years. She may have left the business."

Richard Jaeckel (Klinger): Born 1926. Oscar-nominated for his performance in *Sometimes a*

Great Notion (1971), Jaeckel became a regular in the 1980s series *Spenser for Hire* and the 1990s series *Baywatch*.

EPISODE GUIDE

Season 1: 1979

Salvage (1979 TV Movie) Harry Broderick attempts to launch a rocket to the moon. He hires Skip and Melanie, and together they encounter a variety of hazards. Wr: Mike Lloyd Ross. Dir: Lee Philips.

Lorene (Jacqueline Scott); Bill Kelly (Peter Brown); Commentator (Richard Eastham); Fred (Raleigh Bond); Hank Beddoes (Lee De-Broux).

Dark Island
The Salvage One crew is stranded on an African island, where they encounter a lone scientist and a giant ape creature. Wr: Ruel Fischmann. Dir: Gene Nelson.

John Goodwin (Henry Jones); Creature (Ray Young); Brinks (Richard Eastham); Kramer (Howard Mann); Husband (John Mooney); Wife (Jeanne Kallan).

Shangri-La-Lil
On a mission to the Burmese jungles, Harry finds the B-25 bomber he flew in World War II during the Doolittle raid. He also encounters a Japanese soldier who is still fighting the war. Wr: Mike Lloyd Ross, Judy Burns. Dir: Ron Satloff.

Tishiro (Mako); Morse (Dane Clark); Lee Chow (James Hong); Fong (Byron Chung); Street (Larry Pennell); Newscaster (Larry Carroll); Tuan (George Kee Cheung); Insurgent #2 (Richard Lee-Sung).

Shelter Five
The salvagers are threatened by earthquakes as they try to rescue a major's young daughter who is trapped in a bomb shelter. Wr: Gerald K. Siegel, story by Geoffrey Fischer. Dir: Jim Benson.

Maj. Phil Burke (Sam Groom); Susan Burke (Michelle Stacey).

The Haunting of Manderly Mansion (aka Ghost Trap)
The travelers befriend a space creature from Andromeda who has assumed Harry's form. Trapped in a mansion, the alien needs the earthling's spaceship to burn an escape corridor into the atmosphere. Wr: Mike Robe. Dir: Ray Austin.
Sam Bishop (Bert Freed); Kramer (Howard Mann); Auctioneer (Henry Sutton); Also with Bob Hoy, Keith McConnell.

The Bugatti Treasure
A map from 1543 may lead the salvagers to an ancient treasure of Cortez, buried in the Mojave desert. Wr: Richard Chapman, Ruel Fischmann, story by Mike Lloyd Ross. Dir: Ed Abroms.
Max Jacoby (David Opatoshu); Wilbur (Ron Soble); Casper Beckman (Severn Darden); M.P. (Bill Schreiner); Gate M.P. (Ralph Wilcox); G.I. (James Burr Johnson); Range officer (John Markanton); Auctioneer (Don P. Britt); Junkman (Jim Kingsley); Lila (Mary Louise Rogers).

Golden Orbit, Parts 1 and 2
Harry fights red tape to launch the *Vulture* to salvage a communications satellite. Meanwhile, Skip rejoins NASA and finds himself and his crew threatened by freezing cold during a space mission. In part 2, a meteor storm threatens the *Vulture* when it blasts off to save Skip's crew. Wr: Robert Swanson. Dir: Ron Satlof.
Vanessa Ashley (Ellen Bry); Buck Fulton (Edward Winter); Dr. Singleton (Barry Nelson); Jim Webster (Gary Stephen Swanson); Also with Jon Vanness, Joel Lawrence, Lloyd Bremseth.

Operation Breakout!
When their FBI friend Klinger faces a firing squad in Africa, Harry buys time by turning the spaceship over to a dictator. Wr: Gerald Siegel. Dir: Gerald Perry Finnerman.
Yaffert Boratu (Moses Gunn); Sanders (John Crawford); Pierre (Hari Rhodes); Also with Peter Maclean.

Mermadon
An army robot escapes and is befriended by the salvagers. Almost human, the mechanical marvel has an ingratiating personality but has also been programmed to kill at the first sign of danger. Wr: Mike Lloyd Ross. Dir: Ron Satlof.
Gen. Macklin (Ed Nelson); Dr. Marvin (Philip Abbott); Receptionist (Lauren White); Also with Katherine Woodville, Julie Anne Haddock, Cliff Emmich, Jeff Schafrath.

Up, Up and Away
Harry and plane-crash survivors in a canyon learn that smugglers are coming after them to retrieve counterfeit bills. Wr: Bob Swanson. Dir: Leslie Greene.
Milo (Christopher Connelly); Spiro (Adam Roarke); Agamemnon (Al Ruscio); Bassett (George Furth); Street (Larry Pennell); Basil (Aharon Ipale).

The Energy Solution
Melanie's dangerous method of creating crude oil works well until the oil drill catches fire and rages as an underground inferno. Wr: Ruel Fischmann, Richard Chapman. Dir: Ron Satlof.
Dawson (Peter Donat); Sanborne (Ben Piazza); Brinks (Richard Eastham); Also with Stanley Brock.

Confederate Gold
While trying to find confederate gold, the salvagers are captured by greedy townspeople who are determined to get the treasure. Wr: Jack Bradford Turley, story by Robert E. Swanson. Dir: Ray Austin.
Sheriff Moss (R.G. Armstrong); Melba (Fran Ryan); Shorty (Dub Taylor); Buster Wakefield (Med Flory); Billy Wakefield (Dirk Blocker); Phil (Kenneth White); Frank Edwards (Del Hinkley).

Season 2: 1979-80

Hard Water, Part 1
Harry's rival, Sam Bishop, is towing an iceberg from the North Pole when it breaks away. Wr: Mike Lloyd Ross. Dir: Leslie L. Green.
Sam Bishop (Bert Freed); Kress (Philip Charles Mackenzie); Brinks (Richard Eastham); Cameron (Warren Kemmerling); Flora (Rosemary Prinz); Capt. Barlow (Frank Campanella); Also with Paul Sorenson; Cal Bowman; Richard Dix; Michael Horsley; Ralph Montgomery; Hank Underwood; Newton Anderson; Cameron Young; Dolores Albin; Norman Alexander Gibbs; Ned Mohell.

Hard Water, Part 2
Harry desperately tries to change the direction of the wayward iceberg, but the Navy is moving in to destroy it. Wr: Mike Lloyd Ross. Dir: Leslie L. Green.
Sam Bishop (Bert Freed); Kress (Philip Charles MacKenzie); Flora (Rosemary Prinz); Cameron (Warren Kemmerling); Capt. Barlow (Frank Campanella); Gentry (David Pritchard); Brinks (Richard Eastham); Also with Cal Bowman, Richard Dix, Paul Sorenson, Michael Horsley, Ralph Montgomery, Hank Underwood, Newton Anderson, Cameron Young, Dolores Albin, Norman Alexander Gibbs, Ned Mohell.

Dry Spell
Harry and Skip devise a rain-making device to help drought-stricken farmers. The salvagers fly a biplane into the clouds and use a giant device to heat up the atmosphere. Wr: Jeri Taylor. Dir: Ray Austin.
Hutchinson (Morgan Woodward); Aunt Adah (Irene Tedrow); Truman Boone (Art Lund).

Harry's Doll
A scientist saves Michelle's injured race horse with laser surgery, and the girl rides the animal in the upcoming race. Wr: R.K. Pierce, story by Ruel Fischmann. Dir: Ed Abroms.
Willie Shoemaker (Himself); Dr. Mott (Allan Arbus); Vet (Peter Hobbs); Burton (Jack Somack).

Round Up
The salvagers try to round up wild horses before they're destroyed by local ranchers. Wr: Jeri Taylor, story by Walter Bloch. Dir: Ron Satlof.

Carson (John Ireland); Coburn (Colby Chester); Crandall (Stanley Brock); Crowder (John Calvin); Officer (Scott Perry).

Diamond Volcano
Harry and Skip tunnel their way through the base of a Hawaiian volcano to salvage a corridor of raw diamond. Wr: Geoffrey Fisher. Dir: Dana Elcar.

Flannery (Ron Rifkin); Karl Miller (William Bogert); Steve (Derek Wells); Doris (Olive Dunbar); Takata (Yuki Shimoda); Also with Frank Maxwell.

Science Fiction Theater
1955–1957

Anthology series dealing with science and its impact on human beings. Themes included time travel, ESP, space travel and robots.

Host: Truman Bradley.

Producer: Ivan Tors; *Story Supervisor:* Jon Epstein; Syndicated/ZIV Productions; 30 minutes; color, year 1; B/W, year 2.

Science Fiction Theater represented genuine science fiction. Its stories dealt with advancements in science that could affect society. Episodes took the latest scientific advancements and postulated what could happen with the next level of invention. *Science Fiction Theater* examined advanced pacemakers, mind control and animal behavior; in its wilder moments, it leaped into the world of extra-terrestrials and time travel. Every episode was anchored by the presence of host Truman Bradley, a former news commentator.

"The maturity of *Science Fiction Theater*'s stories was due to Ivan Tors' intelligence," says director Herbert L. Strock of the series' producer. "Ivan wouldn't accept junk such as aliens attacking Earth or giant insects on the loose. He wasn't interested in that. He was interested in weird things that could happen. He wasn't into space battles, and he would turn down any story along those lines."

Writer Lou Huston agrees. "Ivan rejected stories involving horrible-looking aliens for two reasons. One, Ivan looked for the good in nature, including human nature. A more practical reason was that ZIV studios had very low budgets. That made creating believably scary aliens rather risky. Laughter rather than chills could have been the result."

Tors was fascinated by true science, and Huston notes, "Ivan's vision of *Science Fiction Theater* was a show where science played a positive role for humanity. Even in stories in which characters suffered harm, Ivan used the wrap-up narration by Truman Bradley to point to possible progress for scientific research."

Tors had come to America to make his fortune as a movie writer and producer. "Ivan, a Hungarian by birth, served in America's OSS, a forerunner of the CIA," says Huston. "He had a thick Hungarian accent and a pleasant, direct manner of speaking. There was no pretense about him. Ivan died [in 1983] while searching out locations for a new series in South America." Tors, who was married to actress Constance Dowling, was born in Budapest, Hungary, in 1916. He later made a career in the 1960s with family films such as *Namu, the Killer Whale* (1966) and animal series that included *Daktari, Flipper* and *Gentle Ben.*

Herbert Strock, who began his career as a writer and producer, was anxious to do *Science Fiction Theater.* "I had done the first TV series ever made, in 1946, called *The Cases of Eddie Drake.* It was a half-hour show that we made for $7500 a piece. That led to work on *I Led Three Lives, Men of Annapolis* and *Harbor Command*—all ZIV shows. *Science Fiction Theater* was the ZIV series I enjoyed the most. It broke new ground in science fiction and it got good reviews. Ivan Tors was always deep into science fiction," continues Strock. "He gave me my first job as director. I co-directed his film *Riders to the Stars* [1954] and later directed *Gog* [1954]. I thoroughly enjoyed working for him. *Science Fiction Theater* was Ivan's first TV series. He would get his basic ideas from *Scientific American* magazine. He came up with very intelligent story approaches and then got writers to do the screenplays. There were no scientific advisors on the show. Ivan was the science guide. He knew people involved in science and had friends at universities. He provided all of the science facts for the writers. As directors, once we got the scripts, we didn't double-check the science. We, personally, didn't have to be convinced that the scientific devices in the story could actually work. But I was amazed by the letters we got from people. The show had a very good following. Ivan had that knack of getting into scientific advances on the horizon, including ESP, computers and mind-tapping. He had a prolific mind and read lots of science magazines. Jon Epstein, our executive story editor, was also constantly attempting to upgrade and improve stories."

Science Fiction Theater's science frequently took precedence over the characters and plot. "Sometimes the science took out the drama," admits Strock. "I tried to show things rather than explain them. I demanded intelligent, coherent scripts with speakable dialogue. I didn't want any story holes. Ivan was a nut for getting stock footage and using it to explain scientific principles. The scientific approach worked well, but sometimes Ivan had a bad habit of explaining things with specific details and the story would stop. I had to find ways to make those stories work dramatically. Once in a while, we got a story that was really crappy. I would try to get Ivan to shove off that story and get something else, but it wasn't done. It was always money, money, money. That was ZIV's main concern. Ivan really did his best with *Science Fiction Theater* and was very easy to work for. He never lost his temper, and everyone on the series had great respect for him."

"He was a kind and honest man with a positive outlook," says Lou Huston. "He took a chance on me, giving me my first TV writing assignment. Ivan gave writers oral directions for their scripts. One day I turned in a second draft and Ivan said, 'You did exactly what I told you to do. But it doesn't work. I was wrong. Will you try it a different way?' I came back with a new version, which he accepted. To my surprise, I received an extra check for my work. He could have taken advantage of me, an inexperienced TV writer, but he didn't. He was one of the finest men I knew."

Huston had spotted an announcement in a Hollywood trade paper advertising a new show called *Science Fiction Theater*. "From the age of ten, I had been interested in science fiction, starting with the Jules Verne novels and later H.G. Wells. I was enthralled with Hugo Gernsback's magazine *Science and Invention*. I also found his *Amazing Stories* magazine fascinating."

Like most of the writers on the series,

Huston didn't have a strong background in science. "My formal education in science consists of one year in Freshman Biology at the University of Southern California in 1931," he says. "My scientific discipline was illustrated when our class was dissecting frogs and making a drawing of their internal organs as we performed an autopsy. The Professor's assistant passed by, looked at my drawing and said, 'Hmmm ... a hermaphroditic frog!' Not being able to discern much from my specimen, I had copied from the young woman's drawing beside me. I still don't know which of us had the male or female specimen, but my sketch had included the organs of both."

When he pitched ideas to Ivan Tors, Huston recalls, "I had picked up enough science through my reading to spark ideas. I didn't know enough to keep me from going astray into the improbabilities. My impression was that while we [the writers] shared an intense interest in science, we didn't have any real scientific background."

Huston notes several of the pluses and minuses of this early anthology series. "Our stories presented examples of science fiction that didn't rely on strange monsters from Zorg or absurd melodrama involving mad scientists. Our characters were everyday people doing everyday things, until something unusual happened. The series helped to give an impression that science wasn't something to be afraid of. It could excite wonder, not terror, and expand the imagination. Truman Bradley would tell viewers, 'What you've just seen is fiction, but research indicates that the basic idea could, in the future, benefit mankind.'"

As an example of how Tors' stories fit into real life, Huston cites the episode "The Killer Tree." "Ivan Tors wanted to make the point that science can obtain facts that dispel harmful or useless superstition. In this story, several people, on different occasions, are found dead under a tree. Conclusion: the tree must have killed them. A scientist couple investigates and learns that carbon dioxide is seeping up from the ground. Anyone sleeping by the tree will fill their lungs with the gas and suffocate. The source is coming from volcanic action unusually near the surface. A year or two after the episode aired, some animals and, I think, several people died near the shores of an African lake. Cause: Deep waters in the lake 'burped' pockets of gas."

Huston felt one weakness of the series was its lack of budget. "The budgets limited the stories from the standpoint of sets and special effects," he says. "ZIV was under a variety of restrictions and limitations. This limited the writers and yet made us focus on characters and motive instead of relying on startling phenomena."

More inhibiting were the taboos that applied to all television at the time. "Clergymen, for example, were to appear utterly without sin or suspicion," says Huston. "They were confined to performing marriage ceremonies and consoling the bereaved. If a doctor had to be portrayed as an incompetent or evil, the writer had to insert a 'typical' doctor to show the rotten one was a rarity. Taboos of that era were prudish to the point of absurdity. Unmarried males and females over 12 years old could not be shown in a bedroom together. If they were married, only one could be shown in bed. Bad men and women couldn't be from a specific country, lest the viewers of that descent threaten to boycott the sponsor's product. Also, on-camera TV was not an "equal opportunity employer." While the effect was racist, I believe the intent was merely 'don't make waves.' From a practical viewpoint, the policy, whether spoken or unspoken, was not directed at minorities. It was a means of avoiding trouble from super-sensitive members of all ethnic groups, including WASPs."

Obsequious regard for sponsors led to even more restrictions that Herbert Strock calls "ridiculous. There was a script where a character puts his foot up on a coffee table. We were screamed at: 'You must take the word coffee out because we may have tea sponsors!' We had to cover up the word FORD on the backs of trucks because we might upset a sponsor."

Science Fiction Theater was one of the few 1950s programs that was shot in color (during its first year). "The color film was very expensive, and it was a test to our cameraman," says Strock. "We had fringe cameramen. They weren't the best, but *Science Fiction Theater* gave them an opportunity to became the best. Many left ZIV to go into features, and they did very well. The main thing with the series was budget. You had to shoot fast. You couldn't fool around and waste film. Since I had been a film editor, I was able to shoot much less footage than most other directors. My films always came in or under budget. Today, some of *Science Fiction Theater* is pretty corny, but at the time, we tried to make dramatic, well-constructed shows with good actors and interesting themes. It turned out to be a really good series. Getting the actors we wanted was

tough because of the salary ZIV paid them. We had a terrible time casting the shows because of money and because many actors didn't do TV at the time. I was thrilled when we'd get people like Gene Lockhart and DeForest Kelley. We also had great character actors like Michael Fox, who was an old standby. Anytime you were in trouble, call Mike! He never blew a line."

Special effects had to be kept at a minimum because of budget. "As a syndicated show, we had a much lower budget than a network show. A little more money was spent on *Science Fiction Theater* because it was in color and the stars demanded more money. With a science fiction show, it's difficult because you can't just take sets out of storage. You've got to build new things. We had to execute our ideas inexpensively. One time I didn't have the money to build a futuristic set. Jack Collis [the special effects man] went out and got a bunch of cardboard egg crates from a market, stapled them together and sprayed them gold and silver. We displayed colored lights over them, and we had the darndest set you ever saw for $1.98."

On other occasions, however, a set presented unexpected problems. Strock particularly remembers the episode "Dead Reckoning," which concerned the crew of an Air Force plane trapped in a magnetic storm. "I had all of our shots planned out. ... I walked onto the stage that morning and looked at the plane. I said, 'I don't get it. It's the wrong plane.' The story was written for a B-29. We had been sent a B-25. Therefore, the pilot could not talk to the navigator. I stood there with my mouth open. How am I gonna rewrite this? I can't keep having a person run back and forth between the pilot and navigator, relaying messages. So I had to rewrite. I took dialogue away from some actors and gave it to actors who sat closer to the pilot. It was a terrible, terrible chore. We got it done. I said to Ivan Tors, 'You got me the wrong plane!' He said, 'What do I know about a B-25 or B-29!' The segment turned out very well and was very well received."

Sometimes there were problems with actors—especially the nonhuman variety. In "Conversation with an Ape," a scientist (Hugh Beaumont) finds his experiments on a chimp save his life from a robber. "The chimp was supposed to come down the stairs and give Beaumont a gun so that he could overcome the heavy. The chimp did everything perfectly during rehearsals. But the minute I rolled the camera, she would refuse to give Beaumont the gun. She took off and jumped into the scaffolding. Her trainer and I were beside ourselves because we were short on time and money. The trainer used a BB gun and shot pellets near the chimp, scaring her into coming back down. We rehearsed the scene again, this time with the chimp on a tether. She seemed fine, so we started filming. Off she went again! I was about to rewrite the scene and eliminate her from the action when she finally did it right, much to our collective delight!"

"Living Lights" forced Strock to create an unusual life form. "We had to divide these lights through an arc light on stage. The light had to grow smaller and go underneath doors, and all of this took hours. It was a real tough show to do because of the planning. It worked only because of Maxwell Smith's engineering expertise. Today you could do those kinds of opticals with a computer. Back then, we had to do all of it on stage. I

Host Truman Bradley presents a mechanical guest star, Garco the Robot. Copyright 1955 ZIV.

don't recall ever using any special optical effects in any of my episodes."

Lou Huston's scripts included "The Barrier of Silence," about enemy agents using total silence as a psychological weapon. "The story sprang from Ivan Tors' visit to the Bell Telephone Company's laboratory which contains a silent room. It's acoustically dead. The walls reflect no sound. When anyone speaks in the room, their words just fall out of their mouths, lifeless. The room is also heavily insulated from outside vibrations, including traffic and even seismic tremors. Bell's scientists would test new equipment in that

room, and Ivan was intrigued by the room's effect on the technicians. They couldn't remain in the room very long without experiencing physical and psychological effects that interfered with their objectivity. In that utter silence they could hear their own digestive processes, their heartbeats and even their own blood flowing!"

On this foundation, Tors commissioned Huston to write a script. "We built a story around this phenomenon. Perhaps such silence, prolonged, could speed up a brainwashing process in the hands of enemy scientists. We came up with an electronic device that could emit frequencies that cancel out any other vibration within the beam."

"Project 44" took the series into outer space. "Ivan felt that this tale, of preparing astronauts for the first flight to Mars, might be too far-fetched for viewers," recalls Huston. To bring some respectability to the premise, Tors contacted a noted astronomer, Dr. Robert Richardson. He agreed to be interviewed by Truman Bradley and thus give his blessing to the idea of space travel. "Ivan and I hoped Dr. Richardson would be optimistic about when interplanetary voyages could take place. However, when I met him, to write up the brief interview between him and Bradley, he was unyieldingly conservative. He was not about to make any statement that would make him look foolish to his scientific colleagues. He wouldn't predict the remotest possibility of space travel in less than twenty years. So we had to go with that. At least Richardson didn't call our story preposterous! This was two years before *Sputnik* went beeping over our heads, telling America that the space age had arrived."

"Project 44" also posed a curious challenge. "The story described the problems of a crew on a flight to other planets. Since Ivan and I were ahead of our time in that we were not sexual chauvinists, we included female scientists among our astronauts. We were so occupied with the technical atmosphere inside the ship we gave no thought to the moral atmosphere pervading television at the time. We were putting unmarried men and women in a sealed spaceship together for four years. My God! In TV at the time, you couldn't even show a married couple in the small bed. Ivan understood that either the top studio executive would scream in panic or prudish viewers would write outraged letters to our sponsors. Ivan's solution: 'We'll make one of the technicians a divinity student.' This way, if the hormones got out of hand, the divinity student could perform a marriage ceremony and prevent the astronauts from committing fornication. It must have worked because the TV stations and the studio received no shocked protests!"

Science Fiction Theater wound down after a solid two-year run. Neither Herbert Strock nor Lou Huston felt any sense of a tragic, premature cancellation. The series had apparently run its course.

"The ratings were still high," says Strock. "I think they either ran out of material or they only planned to do so many."

"The ratings may not have been high enough to justify the budget," speculates Huston. "But it's also possible Ivan Tors wanted to put his energies into his new series, *Sea Hunt*. Possibly Ivan had said everything he wanted to say with *Science Fiction Theater*."

At one point, the series was re-named *Beyond the Limits* for syndication in the 1960s. Much of its "science fiction" has become reality in today's world.

CAST NOTES

Truman Bradley (Host): Born 1905. "Truman came into television from radio. He was an announcer on KMTR in L.A.," says writer Lou Huston. "He was an exceptional announcer: distinctive and yet natural and likeable."

"Truman was a great character," says director Herbert Strock. "He could make you believe something that sounded far-fetched. He helped to give *Science Fiction Theater* authenticity. He was a very bright and charming guy." Bradley died in 1974.

EPISODE GUIDE

Season 1: 1955-56

Beyond
A jet pilot claims that his plane nearly collided with a UFO. The resulting investigation leads to a peculiar conclusion. Wr: Robert Smith, George Van Marter, story by Ivan Tors. Dir: Herbert L. Strock.
　　Fred Gunderman (William Lundigan); Helen Gunderman (Ellen Drew); Gen. Troy (Bruce Bennett); Dr. Carson (Basil Ruysdael); Dr. Everett (Tom Drake); Col. Barton (Doug Kennedy); Also with Michael Fox, Robert C. Carson, Mark Lowell.

Memory Flash—Herbert L. Strock: "William Lundigan was a great guy and a wonderful conversationalist. I had done two documentaries on UFOs, and Dr. Frank Stranges was one of the UFO-ologists I worked with. I saw actual photographs of phenomena that could not be explained. I also interviewed dozens of sighters and abductees."

Time Is Just a Place
A man discovers that his neighbors are fugitives from 500 years in the future. Wr: Lee Berg, story by Jack Finney. Dir: Jack Arnold.
　　Al Brown (Don DeFore); Ted Heller (Warren Stevens); Nell Brown (Marie Windsor); Ann Heller (Peggy O'Connor).

No Food for Thought

A synthetic nutrient prolongs the life span of human beings, but a deadly virus has been created by the process. Wr: Robert M. Fresco. Dir: Jack Arnold.

Dr. Paul Novak (John Howard); Emmanual Hall (Otto Kruger); Jan Corey (Vera Miles); Lee Suyin (Clarence Lung); Simpson (Stanley Andrews); Also with Hank Patterson, Hal K. Dawson.

Out of Nowhere

Dr. Osbourne is amazed when bats crash into the side of a building. He discovers that a radar-disrupting device is being used by enemy agents. Wr: Donn Mullally. Dir: Herbert L. Strock.

Dr. Osbourne (Richard Arlen); Dr. Jeffries (Jess Barker); Kenyon (Carlyle Mitchell); Dr. Milton (Jonathon Hale); Fleming (Hal Forest); Superintendent (Irving Mitchell); Robb (Craig Duncan); Also with Elsie Baker, Robert Templeton.

Y. O. R. D.

An alien spaceship, in distress over the earth's atmosphere, is sending an SOS to personnel at an Arctic outpost. Wr: George Van Marter and Leon Benson, story by George Van Marter and Ivan Tors. Dir: Leon Benson.

Dr. Lawton (Walter Kingsford); Edna Miner (Judith Ames); Lt. Dunne (Kenneth Tobey); Col. Van Dyke (Louis Jean Heydt); Capt. Hall, MD (DeForest Kelley); Also with John Bryant, Clark Howat.

Strangers in the Desert

After encountering a radioactive eagle and a vanishing botanist, two prospectors find a strange energy source in the desert. Wr: Curtis Kenyon, Robert Fresco, story by Ivan Tors. Dir: Henry S. Kesler.

Gil Collins (Marshall Thompson); Bud Porter (Gene Evans); Ballard (Lowell Gilmore); Also with John Mitchum, Ray Bennett.

The Sound of Murder

A scientist finds that he's been framed for murder by a man who has constructed a voice-sound synthesizer. Wr: Stuart Jerome, story by Ivan Tors. Dir: Jack Arnold.

Dr. Tom Mathews (Howard Duff); Grayson (Whit Bissell); Van Kamp (Wheaton Chambers); Wilkins (Olan Soule); Also with Russ Conway, Charlotte Lawrence, Paul Peters, Julie Jordan, Christine Larson, Ruth Perrott, Edward Earle, Charles Maxwell.

The Brain of John Emerson

A police sergeant discovers that his mind has all of the knowledge from a brilliant, now deceased scientist. He tries to continue the man's work. Wr: Rik Vollaerts. Dir: Leslie Goodwins.

John Emerson (John Howard); Joan (Joyce Holden); Mrs. Tunrer (Ellen Drew); Dr. Franklin (Michael Fox); Damon (Robert F. Simon); Nurse (Jackie Blanchard); Also with Charles Maxwell.

Spider, Inc.

A giant spider fossil leads a geologist to the secret of synthesizing petroleum. Wr: Jerome Sackheim. Dir: Jack Arnold.

Joe Ferguson (Gene Barry); Ellie Ferguson (Audrey Totter); Also with Ludwig Stossel, Robert Clarke, Herbert Rudley, Frank Hanley, Phil Arnold, George Meader.

Death at 2 a.m.

A professor uses a serum that produces great strength to carry out the murder of an ex-con who has been blackmailing him. Wr: Ellis Marcus, story by Ivan Tors. Dir: Henry Kesler.

Sam Avery (John Qualen); Bill Reynolds (Skip Homeier); also with Ted de Corsia, Doug Henderson, Virginia Hunter.

Conversation with an Ape

A telepathic chimp is the key to saving a scientist and his wife when they're confronted by a killer. Wr: Rik Vollaerts. Dir: Herbert L. Strock.

Nancy Stanton (Barbara Hale); Guy Stanton (Hugh Beaumont); Pete Lane (Paul Birch).

Marked "Danger"

A mysterious green gas in a space capsule is released and alters a young woman's metabolism. Wr: Jerome Sackheim, Stuart Jerome, story by John Bennett. Dir: Leigh Jason.

Lois Strand (Nancy Gates); Werner Engstrom (Otto Kruger); Fred Strand (Arthur Franz); Also with Steve Pendleton, John Pickard, John Alvin, Phyllis Cole.

Hour of Nightmare

A husband and wife discover the dead body of an alien creature in the desert. They learn that strange lights in the Mexican skies are caused by aliens looking for their fallen comrade. Wr: Lou Huston. Dir: Henry Kesler.

Mel Wingate (William Bishop); Verda Wingate (Lynn Bari); Ramon Sanchez (Christopher Dark); Ed Tratnor (Charles Evans); Velasquez (Tony Barrett).

Memory Flash—Lou Huston: "Ivan Tors and I were in agreement that we should not show the tiny alien's dead body. Rather, let the audience's imagination provide the details. The corpse is placed in a sack and loaded on a burro for the trip back to a Mexican town. The propmen conceived a chilling touch. Whatever they put in the sack—probably sponge rubber, shaped to humanoid contours—provided an eerie effect. As the burro walked, the sack jiggled."

The Strange Dr. Lopez

A doctor discovers that a honey formula temporarily cures physical ailments. He works to increase the honey's effectiveness. Wr: Norman Jolley. Dir: Leigh Jason.

Dr. Fred Garner (Donald Curtis); Dr. Lorenz (Edmund Gwenn); Helen (Kristine Miller); Also with Hank Patterson, Charles Waggenheim, Madge Cleveland.

One Hundred Years Young

A chemist's claim that he's over 200 years old spurs an effort to perfect a serum that can create immortality. Wr: Jerome Sackheim, story by Arthur Fitz Richard. Dir: Herbert L. Strock.

Bernice Knight (Ruth Hussey); John Bowers (John Abbott); Mike Redding (John Archer); Also with Charles Meredith, Larry Hudson.

The Frozen Sound
A doctor is charged with espionage. A physicist learns the man was a victim of a synthetic crystal that records private conversations. Wr: Norman Jolley, story by Norman Jolley, Ivan Tors. Dir: Leigh Jason.

David Masters (Marshall Thompson); Linda Otis (Marilyn Erskine); Dr. Gordon (Michael Fox); Milton Otis (Ray Collins); Also with Elizabeth Patterson.

The Stones Began to Move
An Egyptologist works to prove that the ancient pyramids were constructed through levitation. Wr: Doris Gilbert, story by Doris Gilbert, Ivan Tors. Dir: Lew Landers.

Victor Berenson (Basil Rathbone); Virginia Kinkaid (Jean Willes); Morton Archer (Jonathan Hale); Ahmed Abdullah (Richard Flato); Also with Russ Conway, Robin Short, Carol Thurston, Helen Van Camp.

Memory Flash—Writer Lou Huston: "Ivan Tors referred to Doris Gilbert as one of the best writers on his series. I was invited to a party at Doris's home in Bel Air in 1960. She is the daughter of L. Wolfe Gilbert, one of the top songwriters of the 1920s. Among his many hits was *Waiting for the Robert E. Lee*. Doris was a very pleasant, gracious woman."

The Lost Heartbeat
A scientist, on the verge of a socially progressive experiment, will die unless he gets a mechanical heart. The procedure must be done in record time or the scientist will die. Wr: Stuart Jerome, story by R. DeWitt Miller, Anna Hunger. Dir: Henry Kesler.

Dr. Richard Marshall (Zachary Scott); Dr. John Crane (Walter Kingsford); Joan Crane (Jan Sheppard); Also with John Mitchum, Thomas McKee, Ted Thorpe, Gordon Wynn, Pierce Lyden.

The World Below
The survivors of a submarine disaster claim that they saw a city on the sea floor, but they're ridiculed by the investigators. Wr: Lee Hewitt. Dir: Herbert L. Strock.

Capt. Forrester (Gene Barry); Prof. Weaver (Tol Avery); Jean Forrester (Marguerite Chapman); Also with Paul Dubov, John Phillips, George Eldredge, William Stout, James Waters, George Mather.

Barrier of Silence
A barrier of silence is constructed to help a top scientist recover his mind, which was brainwashed by enemy agents. Wr: Lou Huston. Dir: Leon Benson.

Prof. Sheldon (Warren Stevens); Karen Sheldon (Phyllis Coates); Dr. Elliot Harcourt (Adolphe Menjou); Thornton (Charles Maxwell); Neilson (John Doucette).

Negative Man
A blast of lightning jolts a man's IQ into the genius range. He begins to solve the world's problems. Wr: Thelma Schnee, story by Ivan Tors. Dir: Henry Kesler.

Vic Murphy (Dane Clark); Sally Torens (Beverly Garland); Pete (Carl Switzer); Also with Robert F. Simon, Joe Forte, Pat Miller, David Alpert, Tom Daly, Peter Davis.

Dead Reckoning
An Air Force plane is trapped in a magnetic storm, forcing the crew to use Earth's magnetic fields to chart a course to safety. Wr: Gene Levitt. Dir: Herbert L. Strock.

Capt. John Berry (James Craig); Lt. Bookman (Adam Williams); Evelyn Raleigh (Arlene Whelan); David Kramer (Steve Brodie); Dr. Millard (Everett Glass); Sgt. Cooper (Arthur Lewis); Also with Tom Anthony, Frank Gerstle.

A Visit from Dr. Pliny
A scientist from the future travels back in time to help a scientist in the twentieth century build an "eternal power machine." Wr: Sloan Nibley. Dir: Henry Kesler.

Dr. Pliny (Edmund Gwenn); Dr. Brewster (John Stephenson); Thomas (William Schallert); George Halsey (Morris Ankrum); Also with Howard Wright, Juney Ellis, Marilyn Saris, Victoria Fox.

The Strange People at Pecos
A radar expert suspects that a girl who is immune to pain is an alien being. Wr: Doris Gilbert. Dir: Eddie Davis.

Jeff Jamison (Arthur Franz); Celia Jamison (Doris Dowling); Terry Jamison (Andrew Glick); Arthur Kern (Dabbs Greer); Laurie (Beverly Washburn); Amy Kern (Judith Ames); Junior Jamison (Barry Froner); Also with James Westerfield, Paul Birch, Hank Patterson.

Dead Storage
A prehistoric mammoth, awakened from suspended animation after 500,000 years, is brought back to health. It gives scientists vital clues on freezing living tissue. Wr: Stuart Jerome, story by Ivan Tors. Dir: Jack Herzberg.

Dr. Myrna Griffith (Virginia Bruce); Dr. Robinson (Robert H. Harris); Dr. Avery (Doug Henderson); Warren Keith (Walter Coy); Dr. McLeod (Booth Colman).

The Human Equation
A doctor discovers that savage murders are being caused by a wheat fungus experiment that produces violent side-effects. Wr: Norman Jolley. Dir: Henry Kesler.

Dr. Lee Seward (MacDonald Carey); Nan Guild (Jean Byron); Dr. Clements (Peter Adams); Dr. Upton (Tom Mckee); Also with Marjorie Bennett, Michael Winkelman, George Meader.

Target Hurricane
A hurricane, caused by a meteor's plunge into the ocean, sweeps toward Florida. A weatherman desperately tries to locate his son before the storm hits. Wr: Robert Schaefer, Eric Freiwald, story by Ivan Tors. Dir: Leigh Jason.

James Tyler (Marshall Thompson); Bobby Tyler (Gary Marshall); Julie Tyler (Margaret Tyler); Walter Bronson

(Robert Griffin); Hugh Fredericks (Ray Collins); Also with John Doucette, John Bryant, Will J. White.

The Water Maker
A scientist conducts an experiment to create water by chemical means. It was a project his friend was working on when he was murdered by greedy associates. Wr: Stuart Jerome, story by Jerome Sackheim. Dir: Herbert L. Strock.

    David Brooks (Craig Stevens); Sheila Dunlap (Virginia Gray); Norman Conway (William Talman); Also with Elmore Vincent, John Mitchum.

The Unexplored
A wife's telepathic abilities lead her and her husband to a missing biologist. Wr: Arthur Weiss. Dir: Eddie Davis.

    Prof. Alex Bondar (Kent Smith); Julie Bondar (Osa Massen); Henry Stark (Harvey Stephens); Mrs. Canby (Madge Kennedy); Also with George Eldredge, Ruta Lee, George Crise, Paul Hahn.

The Hastings Secret
A scientist is killed by deadly termites in the Peruvian jungle. A young couple tries to complete his experiments on the termites, which devour solid rock. Wr: Lee Hewitt. Dir: Jack Herzberg.

    Bill Twinning (Bill Williams); Pat Hastings (Barbara Hale); Dr. Clausen (Morris Ankrum).

Postcard from Barcelona
A dead scientist's papers reveal that he had made a deal with aliens inhabiting an artificial asteroid to help mankind's progress in science. Wr: Sloan Nibley, story by Ivan Tors, Tom Gries. Dir: Alvin Ganzer.

    Edward Burton (Kneefe Brasselle); Nina Keller (Christine Larsen); Dr. Cole (Walter Kingsford); Also with Cyril Delevanti, Charles Cane.

Friend of a Raven
A social worker grows interested in a deaf-mute boy who can communicate with animals. The boy rebels against her when his speech and hearing are restored. Wr: Richard Joseph Tuber. Dir: Tom Gries.

    Tim Daniels (Richard Eyer); Jean Gordon (Virginia Bruce); Walter Daniels (William Ching); Dr. Hoster (Bernard Phillips); Frank Jenkins (Charles Cane); Also with Isa Ashdown.

Beyond Return
A serum cures a dying woman, but the side-effects turn her into a cold, calculating killer who can change her physical appearance at will. Wr: Doris Gilbert, story by John Jessel. Dir: Eddie Davis.

    Dr. Erwin Bach (Zachary Scott); Dr. Dan Scott (Peter Hansen); Kyra Zelas (Joan Vohs); Also with James Seay, Tom De Graffenried, Alan Reynolds, Dennis Moore, Lizz Slifer, Kay Faylen, Toni Carroll.

Before the Beginning
A scientist uses a Photon Gun to cure his assistant of a hand injury and his wife of a mysterious disease. Wr: Arthur Weiss, story by Arthur Weiss, Ivan Tors. Dir: Alvin Ganzer.

Ken Donaldson (Dane Clark); Kate Donaldson (Judith Ames); Norman Heller (Phillip Pine); Also with Ted de Corsia, Emerson Treacy.

The Long Day
A neighborhood, already disrupted by the arrival of an ex-con on the block, is frenzied when an experimental rocket creates artificial daylight and nights no longer exist. Wr: George and Gertrude Fass. Dir: Paul Guilfoyle.

    Sam Gilmore (George Brent); Laura Gilmore (Jean Byron); Robert Barton (Steve Brodie); Also with DeForest Kelley, Raymond Bailey, Brad Jackson, Michael Winkelman, Michael Garth, Addison Richards, Carol Thurston.

Project 44
A crew is selected for the first flight to Mars, but the project is continually sabotaged by an astronaut. Newly married, the astronaut is reluctant to go on the mission. Wr: Lou Huston. Dir: Tom Gries.

    Arnold Bryan (Bill Williams); Janice Morgan (Doris Dowling); Ed Garrett (Biff Elliot); Also with Mary Munday, Mack Williams, Toni Carroll, Amanda Webb, Vicki Bakker, Ken Drake, Robert Nelson, Tom Bernard.

Are We Invaded?
A student, in his effort to prove that a fireball in the sky was a flying saucer, comes across a photograph that could only have been taken in another solar system. Wr: Norman Jolley. Dir: Leon Benson.

    Walter Arnold (Pat O'Brien); Barbara Arnold (Leslie Gaye); Seth Turner (Richard Erdman); Galleon (Anthony Eustral); Also with Paul Hahn.

Operation Flypaper
A thief uses a sonic paralyzer to freeze people while he steals valuable scientific documents. Wr: Doris Gilbert. Dir: Eddie Davis.

    Philip Redmond (Vincent Price); David Vollard (George Eldredge); John Vollard (John Eldredge); Alma Ford (Kristine Miller); MacNamara (Dabbs Greer); Also with Mauritz Hugo, William Vaughn.

The Other Side of the Moon
A scientist believes that the moon is being used as a nuclear dumping ground by creatures from other worlds. Wr: Robert Fresco, Richard Joseph Tuber. Dir: Eddie Davis.

    Larry Kersten (Skip Homeier); Katey Kersten (Beverly Garland); Carl Schneider (Philip Ober); Also with Paul Guilfoyle, Bill Henry, Mack Williams, Paul Hahn, Peter Davis, Peter Dunne.

Season 2: 1956-57

Signals from the Heart
When a policeman, wearing an electronic heart transmitter, suffers a heart attack in the city, a doctor helps the police find the stricken officer. Wr: Stuart Jerome, story by Ivan Tors. Dir: Herbert L. Strock.

    Prof. Tubor (Walter Kingsford); Dr. Warren Stark (Peter Hansen); Tom Horton (Gene Roth); Alma Stark

(Joyce Holden); Also with Riza Royce, Grey Moffet, Gordon Barnes, Larry Kerr, Michael Garth.

The Long Sleep

A desperate father forces a scientist to put his dying son into a deep freeze in the hopes that one day he can be cured. Wr: Arthur Weiss, story by Ivan Tors. Dir: Paul Guilfoyle.

Dr. Sam Willard (Dick Foran); John Barton (John Doucette); Ruth Taney (Nancy Hale); Also with Helen Mowery, Barry Froner, Bill Erwin, Eddie Gallagher.

Who Is This Man?

An experiment in hypnosis veers off course when a young man adopts the personality of a murderer who was hanged in 1882. Wr: Charles B. Smith. Dir: William Castle.

Dr. Hugh Bentley (Bruce Bennett); Tom Cooper (Charles Smith); Karl Krauss (Harlow Wilcox); Also with Lisa Davis, Don Eitner, David Alpert, Tom Pittman, Tom Bernard, Maureen Cassidy, Sam Scar.

The Green Bomb

A scientist uses stolen material to create an atomic bomb in his house. Wr: Tom Gries, story by Ivan Tors. Dir: Tom Gries.

Maxwell Carnaven (Whit Bissell); Frank Davis (Kenneth Tobey); Ralp Scott (Robert Griffin); Also with Melville Ruick, Charles Maxwell, Robert Sherman, Eve McVeagh, Leo Needham, George Huerts.

When a Camera Fails

A doctor's sanity is suspected when he claims he can see perfectly preserved images from the past by using special eyeglasses. Wr: Norman Jolley, story by Ivan Tors. Dir: Herbert L. Strock.

Dr. Richard Hewitt (Gene Lockhart); Dr. Johnston (Mack Williams); Dr. Herbert (Than Wyenn); Also with Byron Kane, Opal Euard, Lewis Auerbach.

Memory Flash—Herbert L. Strock: "Gene Lockhart was a very sensitive man. He had come from stage and had done many movies. We did a long shot, and I didn't like it. I asked Gene to pick it up from the middle. Gene came up to me and said, 'Would it be all right if we started the entire scene from the beginning? For me to pick it up in the middle will be very difficult.' I said, 'Fine,' but I knew I couldn't afford to waste 800 feet of color film. So I let him do the scene from the top. I pretended to look like I was shooting. I kept my hand on the camera switch and didn't turn it on until Gene reached the part I wanted. He never knew the difference."

Bullet Proof

A resistant metal left behind by an alien spaceship is used as a shield by a bank robber. Wr: Lee Hewitt. Dir: Paul Guilfoyle.

Jim Connors (Marshall Thompson); Ralph Parr (Christopher Dark); Prof. Rudman (John Eldredge); Jean Rudman (Jacqueline Holt); Also with Gene Roth, John Mitchum.

The Flicker

Two police inspectors try to prove that a killer murdered his victim because of a hypnotic effect caused by a movie-screen flicker. Wr: Lou Huston, story by Robert E. Smith. Dir: Herbert L. Strock.

Lt. Kiel (Victor Jory); Dr. Kinkaid (Michael Fox); Steve Morris (Brad Jackson); Also with Judith Ames, Irene Bolton.

The Unguided Missile

A young woman finds herself a security risk when her ESP abilities pick up top-secret defense formulas. Wr: Arthur Weiss. Dir: Herbert L. Strock.

Janice O'Hara (Ruth Hussey); Henry Maxon (Peter Hansen); Prof. Bernini (Francis McDonald); Also with Morris Ankrum, Thomas B. Henry, Lizz Slifer.

End of Tomorrow

A defecting scientist has a gift for the western world: a serum that will destroy all viruses. However, a doctor believes the serum is actually a weapon designed to cause mass sterility. Wr: Peter R. Brooke. Dir: Herbert L. Strock.

Keith Brandon (Christopher Dark); Jane Brandon (Diana Douglas); Rudyard Parker (Walter Kingsford); Prof. Reimers (Dabbs Greer); Also with Arthur Marshall, Michael Garth.

The Mind Machine

A dying scientist is able to transmit his knowledge through a brain-transmitting machine. Wr: Ellis Marcus. Dir: Paul Guilfoyle.

Alan Cathcart (Bill Williams); Dr. Lewis Milton (Cyril Delevanti); Mark Cook (Brad Trumbull); Also with Sydney Mason, Lonnie Blackman, Jim Sheldon, Fred Coby, Helen Jay.

The Missing Waveband

A scientist admits that numerous scientific formulas came to him from a prisoner on a totalitarian world, millions of light years away. Wr: Lou Huston, story by Ivan Tors. Dir: Jack Herzberg.

Dr. Milhurst (Dick Foran); Prof. van Doorne (Stafford Repp); Dr. Maxwell (Michael Fox); Dr. Lawrence (Gene Roth); Also with George Leigh, Tom McKee.

The Human Experiment

Three people who are given a serum adopt the same social pattern as a colony of bees. Wr: Doris Gilbert, story by Ivan Tors. Dir: Paul Guilfoyle.

Dr. Tom MacDougall (Marshall Thompson); Dr. Ellen Ballard (Virginia Christine); Jean Richardson (Claudia Barrett); Also with Gloria Clark, Julie Van Zandt, George Barrows, Alan Paige.

The Man Who Didn't Know

After his plane crashes, a test pilot recovers with no memory of his recent past. He's unaware that he's been implanted with an enemy spying device. Wr: Rik Vollaerts. Dir: Herbert L. Strock.

Mark Kendler (Arthur Franz); Peggy Kendler (Susan Cummings); Al Mitchell (Bruce Wendell); Also with Paul Lukather, Voltaire Perkins, Guy Rennie, Granville Dixon, Joe Hamilton, Bill Erwin.

The Phantom Car

A sheriff and a geologist desperately try to stop the rampage of a radio-controlled car. Wr: Lee Hewitt. Dir: Herbert L. Strock.

Arthur Gress (John Archer); Peggie Gress (Judith Ames); Barney Cole (Tyler McVey); Also with Herbert Lytton, Patricia Donahue, Troy Melton, William Fawcett, Joe Colbert.

Beam of Fire

Top scientists are being killed by an alien beam. A scientist discovers that space scouts are determined to stop mankind's progression into space. Wr: Stuart Jerome, story by Ivan Tors. Dir: Herbert L. Strock.

Steve Conway (Wayne Morris); Lindstrom (Harlan Warde); Dr. Davis (Frank Gerstle); Also with Leonard Mudie, John Dennis, Paul Harber, William Vaughn, Bruce Payne, George Pembroke.

Legend of Crater Mountain

A teacher in a small Arizona town finds herself up against malevolent, telepathic schoolchildren. Wr: Lue Hall, Bill Buchanan. Dir: Paul Guilfoyle.

Marion Brown (Marilyn Erskine); Jim Harris (Brad Jackson); Rosellen Avitor (Jo Ann Lilliquist); Bobby Avitor (Freddy Ridgeway); Susan Avitor (Nadene Ashdown); Also with Paul Guilfoyle.

Living Lights

A scientist creates a synthetic version of Venus, but he accidentally creates creatures that threaten the Earth. Wr: Ellis Marcus, story by Ellis Marcus, Ivan Tors. Dir: Herbert L. Strock.

Bob Laurie (Skip Homeier); Grace Laurie (Joan Sinclair); Charles Irwin (Michael Garth); Also with Darlene Albert, Jason Johnson, Robert Weston.

Jupitron

A scientist and his wife are transported to a moon of Jupiter, where a long-missing Earth scientist gives them a formula for creating syntheic food. Wr: Arthur Weiss. Dir: Paul Guilfoyle.

John Barlow (Bill Williams); Nina Barlow (Toni Gerry); August Wykoff (Lowell Gilmore); Dr. Norsted (Michael Fox); Also with Arthur Marshall, Paul Guilfoyle.

The Throwback

A biologist believes he can predict people's lives by researching their ancestors. Wr: Thelma Schnee. Dir: Paul Guilfoyle.

Norman Hughes (Peter Hansen); Joe Castle (Ed Kemmer); Anna Adler (Virginia Christine); Also with Jan Sheppard, Tris Coffin, Bill Welsh.

The Miracle of Dr. Dove

The FBI tries to find three nutrition experts who vanished. Evidence suggests they've found the key to a longer life. Wr: George Asness, story by George Asness, Ivan Tors. Dir: Herbert L. Strock.

Edward Dove (Gene Lockhart); Ed Gorman (Charles Wagenheim); Sean Daley (Rhodes Reason); Jeff Spencer (Robin Short); Alice Kinder (Kay Faylen); Also with Cyril Delevanti, Virginia Pohlman.

One Thousand Eyes

A scientist is murdered and the most likely suspect dies soon afterward. A police scientist uses a revolutionary camera that reconstructs the crime and reveals what really happened. Wr: Stuart Jerome. Dir: Paul Guilfoyle.

Gary Williams (Vincent Price); Ada March (Jean Byron); Lt. Moss (Bruce Wendell); Also with David Hillary Hughes, Tom Dillon.

Brains Unlimited

A pilot is forced to bail out at 50,000 feet while testing an anti-black-out serum. He tries to recreate the event by speeding up his brain. Wr: Sloan Nibley, story by Sloan Nibley, Ivan Tors. Dir: Tom Gries.

Jeff Conover (Arthur Franz); Elaine Conover (Diana Douglas); Ralph Marken (Doug Wilson); Also with Thomas B. Henry, George Becwar, Melinda Plowman, Burt Mustin, Bob Wehling.

Death at My Fingertips

A student is framed for murder by fingerprint evidence. It turns out the real killer knows how to transfer fingerprints through plastic skin grafts. Wr: Joel Malcolm Rapp. Dir: Tom Gries.

Eve Patrick (June Lockhart); Dr. Don Stewart (Dick Foran); Mark Davis (John Stephenson); Also with Michael Granger, David Alpert, William Vaughn, Lonnie Blackman, Charles Postal.

Sound That Kills

The creator of an ultrasonic weapon is blamed for the murder of a scientist. He tries to clear himself by locating the real killer. Wr: Meyer Dolinsky. Dir: Herbert L. Strock.

Dr. Richard Wissman (Ludwig Stossel); Dr. Paul Sinclair (Ray Collins); Ed Martin (Charles Victor); Also with Larry Hudson, Jean G. Harvey, David Dwight, Paul Hahn, Delores Michaels, Cynthia Baer.

Survival in Box Canyon

A rescue operation is underway to locate a pilot whose plane crashed in an atom bomb test area. Wr: Lou Huston, story by Ivan Tors. Dir: Herbert L. Strock.

Dr. Milo Barton (DeForest Kelley); Sorenson (Bruce Bennett); Ellen Barton (Susan Cummings); Also with Paul Birch, Harlan Warde, Freddy Ridgeway, Dale Hutchinson, Robert Sherman, Bing Russell.

Memory Flash—DeForest Kelley: "I loved working with Herb. I was not a science fiction fan. Many times during the production I wondered what the hell we were doing! But we were well ahead of our time."

The Voice

An ESP skeptic discovers new evidence that will save a man sentenced to die in the electric chair. When his plane crashes in a forest, he must resort to ESP to transmit the crucial evidence to prison authorities. Wr: Doris Gilbert. Dir: Paul Guilfoyle.

Roger Brown (Donald Curtis); Anna Brown (Kristine Miller); Mendoza (Anthony Eustral); Also with William

Phipps, Morris Ankrum, Julian Burton, Billy Griffith, Anne Navarro, Hal Hoover, Beverly Barnes, Roland Varno, Bruce Payne.

Three Minute Mile

A football star is given a serum that increases his strength, enabling him to lift 1000 pounds and run a mile in three minutes. Wr: George Asness. Dir: Eddie Davis.

Brit (Martin Milner); Nat Kendall (Marshall Thompson); Jill (Gloria Marshall); Also with Robert Bice, Bill Henry, John Eldredge.

The Last Barrier

A satellite is sent to photograph the dark side of the moon. Photographic evidence suggests alien interference. Wr: Rik Vollaerts. Dir: Paul Guilfoyle.

Robert Porter (William Ching); Dan Blake (Bruce Wendell); Wayne Masters (Tom McKee); Also with Sydney Mason, Lee Millar, Jason Johnson, Jim Sheldon, George Barrows.

Signals from the Moon

A diplomat from an eastern country is critically injured by an assassin's bullet. A doctor must supervise the delicate operation by bouncing a video signal off the moon. Wr: Tom Gries. Dir: Paul Guilfoyle.

Gen. Frank Terrance (Bruce Bennett); Dr. Edwards (Michael Fox); Dr. Robert Werth (Bob Schield); Also with Don Brodie, Alfred Linder, Steven Ritch, Bhupesch Ch.Guha.

Doctor Robot

A computer holds the key to helping a scientist's wife, who must undergo a tricky medical procedure. Wr: Ellis Marcus. Dir: Eddie Davis.

Dr. Ed Barnes (Peter Hansen); Fred Lopert (Whit Bissell); Doug Hinkle (Doug Wilson); Also with John Stephenson, Elizabeth Flourney, Robert Weston, Esther Furst.

The Human Circuit

A dancer's vision of a stranded pilot at sea is electronically reproduced, leading to a rescue operation. Wr: Joel Malcolm Rapp. Dir: Eddie Davis.

Dr. Albert Neville (Marshall Thompson); Nina Lasalle (Joyce Jameson); Dr. George Stonehman (Bill Ching); Also with Phil Arnold, Gretchen Thomas, Thomas Anthony, James Waters, Renee Patryn, Leo Needham.

Sun Gold

In Peru, explorers discover the lost world of the Incas and evidence of colonization by space explorers long ago. Wr: Peter R. Brooke. Dir: Eddie Davis.

Susan Calvin (Marilyn Erskine); Howard Evans (Ross Elliot); Tawa (Paul Fierro).

Facsimile

Three top scientists are felled by a mysterious disease, which delays a satellite project. Wr: John Bushnell, Stuart Jerome, story by John Bushnell, Ivan Tors. Dir: Eddie Davis.

George Bascombe (Arthur Franz); Barbara Davis (Aline Towne); Hugh Warner (Donald Curtis).

The Killer Tree

An odd-looking tree, with the power to kill, is actually a natural chimney for a deadly underground volcano. Wr: Lou Huston, story by Robert E. Smith. Dir: Eddie Davis.

Paul Cameron (Bill Williams); Barbara Cameron (Bonita Granville); Clyde Bishop (Keith Richards); Also with Hank Patterson, Terry Frost.

Gravity Zero

Two scientists manage to extend their science project grant when they neutralize the effects of gravity. Wr: Donald Cory. Dir: Paul Guilfoyle.

Dr. John Hustead (Percy Helton); Elizabeth Wickes (Lisa Gaye); Kemn Waring (Bill Hudson); Also with Walter Kingsford, Lizz Slifer.

The Magic Suitcase

A little boy and his grandfather find a mysterious suitcase containing tremendous energy. Wr: Lou Huston, story by William P. Epperson. Dir: Paul Guilfoyle.

Grandpa Scott (Charles Winninger); John Scott (William Vaughn); Eileen Scott (Judith Ames).

Bolt of Lightning

An investigation reveals that a scientist died and his entire building was atomized when he tried to build a flying saucer under controlled conditions. Wr: Meyer Dolinsky. Dir: Eddie Davis.

Dr. Sheldon Thorpe (Bruce Bennett); Cynthia Blake (Kristine Miller); President Franklin (Sidney Smith); Also with Lyle Talbot, Bruce Payne, Connie Buck, Steve Mitchell.

The Strange Lodger

A strange little man is sending signals to a bright light 1,000 miles away. He mysteriously disappears before authorities can grab him. Wr: Arthur Weiss. Dir: Eddie Davis.

Dr. Jim Wallaby (Peter Hansen); Maggie Dawes (Jan Sheppard); Bill North (Charles Maxwell); Also with John Zaremba, Cyril Delevanti, Daniel White, Frances Pasco, Hugh Lawrence, George Gilbreath, Troy Melton.

The Miracle Hour

A scientist works to restore a young boy's sight using a new light technique. Wr: Stanley H. Silverman. Dir: Paul Guilfoyle.

Jim Wells (Dick Foran); Cathy Parker (Jean Byron); Tommy Parker (Charles Herbert); Also with Donald Curtis, Riza Royce, Ken Christy.

The Six Million Dollar Man

October 1973–March 1978

Astronaut Steve Austin, critically injured in the crash of an Air Force jet, is rebuilt with bionic limbs by government scientists. His new legs, one arm and an eye are bionic prostheses that give him tremendous strength and vision. Steve works with the government's intelligence agency on top secret missions.

Cast: Steve Austin (Lee Majors); Oscar Goldman, his boss (Richard Anderson); Dr. Rudy Wells (1974–75) (Alan Oppenheimer), (1975–78) (Martin E. Brooks).

Based on the novel Cyborg *by Martin Caidin; Producers included:* Kenneth Johnson, Lionel Seigel, Fred Freiberger, Richard Landau; *Executive Producer:* Harve Bennett; ABC/Universal; 90 minutes (1973 segments); 60 minutes.

"We can rebuild him. We have the technology. We can make him better than he was. Better, stronger, faster." That was Oscar Goldman's vow as surgeons put Steve Austin back together again with artificial limbs after a plane crash. The 1974 pop rock single "The Six Million Dollar Man," sung by Dusty Springfield, proclaims Steve Austin as "one of a kind."

This modern-day superman did what few TV heroes have done: cheated the noose of cancellation twice within one year. When it was reprieved the second time, *The Six Million Dollar Man* found its footing and blasted off as one of America's favorite shows.

The series first appeared as a successful 90-minute TV movie. Two TV movies followed, and the *Six Million Dollar Man* nearly died in the process. The show was then revamped as a 60-minute show and rocketed into the top 15. In its second year, the series sank in the ratings and was given up for dead until miraculous creative surgery (and a new time slot) propelled it into a major hit.

Author Martin Caidin, whose novel *Marooned* was turned into a 1969 feature film, had a lively background that included being a war correspondent and working with the Air Force on its early bionics program. Universal studios was interested in turning his novel *Cyborg* into a TV film after Warner Brothers didn't pick up its option. "Richard Irving, who was vice-president of Universal, flipped over it," recalls Caidin. "A screenwriter wrote it as a TV movie, and I served as technical advisor. No one was expecting to make a series out of it."

Lee Majors was cast as Steve Austin, who is torn apart in the crash of an experimental plane. (Footage of an actual crash of an X-15 was used for the scene. The real pilot of that 1967 crash suffered severe injuries which ended his test pilot career. The TV movie followed Steve Austin's difficulty in adjusting to being a bionic man. He reluctantly becomes an agent for the government's Office of Strategic Intelligence (O.S.I.). Darren McGavin played Steve's boss, Oscar Goldman, in the film. "Oscar Goldman was based on a real person, who shall go unnamed," says Caidin. "Dr. Rudy Wells [who spearheads the bionic surgery] was also a real person. He was my flight surgeon in the Air Force. We did the bionic research together. Rudy loved being portrayed in the series."

Caidin recalls, "The director, Dick Irving, wanted as much reality as possible, and he was a very tough taskmaster. That was marvelous because I'm a pretty nasty S.O.B. myself when it comes to work! I don't believe in putting up with somebody who can't do a job."

The TV movie, in Caidin's eye, got the job done as speculative science and good entertainment. Steve Austin's bionic arm was based on an experimental prosthetic arm being tested at the UCLA Medical Center.

Caidin's first candidate to play the bionic man was actor Monte Markham. "I knew Monte's brother quite well. He was a top navy pilot. Monte is one of the finest actors in the world. But he was doing a lawyer show at the time [*The New Perry Mason*]. They picked Lee because he was an ex–football player and was good for action. He's pretty dull as an actor, but he fit the part perfectly. He appealed to that 12- to 14-year-old audience."

The Six Million Dollar Man TV movie was a success. "There was an incredible reaction to the show," says Caidin. "Mail, calls, telegrams, and an avalanche of favorable reviews." The result was two more 90-minute *Six Million Dollar Man* movies for ABC in the fall of 1973, produced by Glen Larson.

This time, Richard Anderson was recruited to play Oscar Goldman. "I cast Richard," says Larson, "because when you're doing what I call a bullshit premise, you need to surround it with as much honesty and reality as you can. Richard brought us that credibility. It was less likely that the series was going to end up as a cartoon. Frank Price asked me to redevelop [the premise] and make a new pilot. I wrote the first 90-minute episode, 'Wine, Women and War.'"

Larson's TV movies gave a James Bondian twist to the series. Steve Austin was a suave, sophisticated bionic man surrounded by beautiful women. "I don't know if I would side it with James Bond," says Larson, "but Frank Price did write a two-page treatment delineating where the 90-minute movies would go. I believe his treatment did point out the success of other heroes, including James Bond. The chief adversary in 'Wine, Women and War' was sort of a Bondian bad guy."

The ratings of the two TV films were disappointing. "The 90-minute episodes almost killed the whole thing," says Caidin. "They were the worst pieces of shit I had seen in years. Austin was a James Bondian guy, and that's crappo! Larson is a very successful producer, but we didn't get along. When he turned it into James Bond, I raised holy hell with Dick Irving. I said, 'Dick, you're gonna kill the damn thing. We've got a great thing going here and you're gonna blow it completely with this bullshit.' I was so displeased that I had my name removed from the credits of those shows."

With the future of Six Million Dollar Man in limbo, Universal called in producer Harve Bennett. "I've kinda been the doctor who comes in and saves the dead patient," muses Bennett, who resuscitated the Star Trek movie series with The Wrath of Khan [1982] after the disappointing first film. Initially, Bennett wasn't excited over saving The Six Million Dollar Man. "I was exhausted from having done The Mod Squad for five years," he says. "Universal said, 'Look, only you can make a series out of this.'"

Bennett agreed to revitalize the project. He, too, saw the James Bond style as a mistake. "It may have been right for Sean Connery, but Lee Majors is Lee Majors. So the ratings dropped, and ABC wasn't interested in continuing it as a series."

ABC finally agreed to consider one more shot. "Frank Price asked me to watch the pilot and see what I could do," says Bennett. "The pilot had presented Lee as a kind of old-fashioned western hero. There's a marvelous scene where he's walking off into the desert, just before his near-fatal flight, chewing a match. He reminded me of Gary Cooper. I told Frank, 'Let's go back in that direction. Let me make this character a salt-of-the-earth Gary Cooper.' They said, 'Fine.' They also said, 'Do it in six weeks!' That part they hadn't told me about! I accepted the series commitment in November 1973, and we were on the air in mid–January. We returned Lee to that monosyllabic, shy-with-ladies, aw-shucks kind of hero. That, to me, is what made it work. He was a modest, kind of western man amidst all of this technology, which he used well. I've worked with the military on films, and I admire military people who keep cool when worlds collide around them. Lee portrayed that wonderfully."

Series producer Lionel Siegel agrees. "The casting of Lee Majors eventually determined the personality and character of The Six Million Dollar Man. Majors is a reactor, and his responses are often cryptic and sometimes clever. He was perfect for the part. Lee had a preference for a minimum of dialogue, and that fit his southern background. Lee is a country boy, smart as a fox for business, a tough competitor and a loyal friend. He postures sometimes as a country bumpkin, but inside he's slick."

Ralph Sariego, who worked in production on The Six Million Dollar Man, recalls, "Lee, during the first season, was a very affable, warm and open fellow. By the second year, he became kinda distant and kept to himself. He developed a small circle of friends. That's a very common thing to happen to a leading actor when his show becomes a hit."

The Six Million Dollar Man premiered in January 1974 as a Friday night action show for ABC and immediately zoomed into the top ten. The oft-repeated action sequences included Steve running 60 miles an hour, bending steel beams and leaping to great heights. "We could have gone into a more science fiction direction and thereby produced some very theatrical pieces," says Siegel, "but the cost was prohibitive. The cost and time necessary to build a robot, for instance, made that impractical."

Siegel viewed the series as "in its own way, a morality play. It was also the forerunner of using disabled people in contemporary drama. Steve Austin had various prosthetics attached to his body which enabled him to be normal. The fact that this gave him super strength was a bonus. For me, if the action didn't keep you tuned, if the humor didn't work, if you didn't get a lump in your throat, and if you couldn't follow the plot, we failed. If most of the above did work, we succeeded."

With the series on track as an hourly show, Martin Caidin had his name put back on the credits. "I'd say the weekly series got within 90 percent of what I felt was the perfect kind of show," he says. "Obviously, a man cannot run 60 miles an hour without leaning into his own path of run because of the center of gravity. A man cannot pick up a 4,000-pound car without counter-bracing himself for leverage. We all understood that. This was made to entertain. They kept it as technically accurate as possible, but they didn't want to be too inhibited."

Lee Majors as *The Six Million Dollar Man.* Copyright 1973 ABC/Universal.

The series began its 1974-75 season as a ratings disaster. ABC's entire Friday night line-up, which included Clint Walker's *Kodiak* and *The Night Stalker,* collapsed. *Six Million Dollar Man,* stuck in the middle of the line-up, crashed to the bottom of the ratings. For the first time in TV history, ABC suspended its Friday night programming and ran old movies until the schedule could be reworked. "We were close to being canceled," confirms Siegel. "ABC was the more 'nervous' of the networks at the time. The power of Universal and ABC's lack of enthusiasm for their new pilots resulted in a renewal. New story editors were hired, more promotion in the markets was scheduled and bigger budgets were allotted for guest stars."

Two changes saved the series: a move to Sunday nights—where the battered show slowly came out of its ratings stupor—and a decision to do a love story that would ignite into a TV phenomenon.

Writer Kenneth Johnson picks up the story. "A close friend of mine in college, writer Steven Bochco, introduced me to Harve Bennett. *The Six Million Dollar Man* was sort of flagging. They were desperate for new scripts. Harve and I hit it off, and one of our ideas was *The Bride of Frankenstein.* I said, 'Doesn't it make sense to give Steve Austin a mate?' Harve smiled and said, 'You know, Frank Price and I have been talking about the same thing. You wanna write it?'

"I wrote a script in a week, called 'Mrs. Steve Austin.' We later called it 'The Bionic Woman.' While everyone liked it, Fred Silverman [in charge of programming] thought it was too dense for an hour script. I said to Harve, 'What does that mean?' He said, 'It means you've got too much in there. Let's make it a two-hour script.'"

Cast as the love interest was Lindsay Wagner, a Universal contract player. As Steve Austin's high school sweetheart, Jaime Sommers, she's critically injured in a parachuting accident and restored with bionic limbs. "My original script ended with the bionic woman, Jaime Sommers, being put in a cryogenic deep freeze because I didn't want to kill her," says Johnson. "Frank Price and Fred Silverman said, 'No, no! We want her dead. We don't want a lot of bionic people running around. We're doing *Love Story*. She's got to die.' I told them it was a big mistake. They wanted her dead, so I killed her with a cerebral hemorrhage. The episode turned out to be the highest-rated *Six Million Dollar Man* ever. The letters started coming in. People were upset that we had killed the bionic woman. We even had a letter from the head of the Psychology Department at Boston University: 'How dare you create such a splendid archetype for women to admire and pattern themselves after and then so brutally kill her!'

"Frank Price and Fred Silverman were going, 'Yeah, Ken! Why did you have to kill her off? Bring her back to life!'" It took Johnson less than two weeks to devise a way to return the bionic woman to life. Johnson used his original cryogenics theory as the solution. After suffering the hemorrhage, Jaime is put in cold storage until she can be cured.

"Bringing her back to life actually worked to my advantage," he says. "In the process of being revived, she had lost her memory of her love for Steve. You felt sympathy for Steve ever after because of his unrequited love for her. It also gave the characters an opportunity to strike sparks and start over again."

The Six Million Dollar Man was renewed for a third season, and Johnson wrote the season opener, "The Return of the Bionic Woman." "The ratings were phenomenal," says Johnson. "It took *The Six Million Dollar Man* into the top ten, where it stayed for a long time. Everybody loved it. Fred Silverman looked at the ratings and said, 'Gee, we gotta spin-off "The Bionic Woman" and make it a separate show!'"

Johnson wrote a spin-off pilot for *The Bionic Woman,* which debuted in January 1976. It immediately joined *The Six Million Dollar Man* in the top ten.

Meanwhile, as *The Six Million Dollar Man* began its third year, there was an important cast change. Martin Brooks replaced Alan Oppenheimer as Dr. Rudy Wells. "ABC wanted a younger, more vigorous guy," says Lionel Siegel. "It was the early wave of the network's apathy for older actors in TV series."

The third year took itself less seriously. Johnson feels this helped pave the way for the show's popularity. "When I joined the show it was very stiff and straight. I brought a sense of humor. In one of my early scripts, Steve's pulling tree stumps out by hand. He pulls one stump out so hard he goes flying across the lawn and falls flat on his ass. He also mows the lawn bionically. Somebody said, 'No, you can't do that.' I said, 'Bullshit! If you were bionic, wouldn't you mow the lawn that way?' I showed that the bionic people could laugh at their abilities and use them in ways that were funny, not just saving people from Arab terrorists and knocking walls down. We started doing what I referred to as 'pocket bionics' where Jaime would open a can of tuna with her bionic thumbnail. George Burns told me a long time ago that if you're gonna tell a lie, put as much truth as you can into it. I tried to do that here. What would *I* do if I were bionic? I think the humor is why *The Six Million Dollar Man* became a lot more successful."

The series also had fun with its casting. While its plots were often out of Cold War storage, its guest stars represented mainstream Americana: Gymnast Cathy Rigby, pro football player Larry Csonka, Hamburger chomper Rodney Allen Rippy, announcer Frank Gifford, and comedians Flip Wilson and Sonny Bono.

One of the most popular guest characters for the series was Bigfoot. Steve encounters the legendary creature while investigating reports of alien activity. "Bigfoot had fascinated me for a long time," says Johnson. "I thought, 'Suppose Bigfoot isn't what we think he is? What if he's a robotic entity created by extra-terrestrials?' *Six Million Dollar Man* had already done an episode with Meg Foster as an alien ["Straight On Till Morning"]. So an alien Bigfoot wasn't out of line."

Johnson made sure the far-out plots didn't tax the show's budget. "In my script, Bigfoot beats up Steve and carries him through an ice tunnel. Production manager Ted Schills called me, saying, 'Ken, are you outta your mind? We can't build anything like that.' I said, 'Ted, have you been on the Universal tours lately? The train drives through an ice tunnel.' In all the time I was at Universal, I used every damn thing on tour! My production designer, Chuck Davis, and I would look for sets to steal. We literally wrote those sets into scripts so we wouldn't have to spend money making them. Today, there's hardly any of the backlot left. The place where Steve and

Bigfoot had their battle is now all restaurants and parking lots!"

Johnson enjoyed working with Lee Majors, recalling, "He was a terrific guy. When I first started doing the show, he was holding out for more money. He was very whimsical about it. He said to me, 'Kenny, don't think I don't know how lucky I am. If I hadn't lucked into this show, I'd be coaching high school football somewhere.' He was a solid pro and very easy to work with. He always knew his lines. We only had a couple of tiffs, which he later apologized over. He also knew his limitations. He knew he wasn't an Al Pacino. Then again, neither was Steve McQueen or Gary Cooper. Lee could play that strong, silent type very well. He also had a whimsy about him, and he was pleased when I'd inject some humor into the series. We did one episode where he's down south and there are guys smuggling moonshine. It wasn't saving the world, but it was a funny show."

Johnson eventually had to make a decision regarding his bionic future. "For awhile, I was writing and producing both *The Six Million Dollar Man* and *Bionic Woman*. *Six Million Dollar Man* was number one in the ratings, *The Bionic Woman* was number three." To ease the work load, Johnson had to choose between the two series. "I elected to leave *Six Million Dollar Man*, and went to work full time on *Bionic Woman*. Lindsay's acting gave me a little more latitude to work with. It turned out to be the right way to go."

With *The Bionic Woman*'s success, Universal began to ponder the possibility of other bionic spin-offs. Majors was already unhappy about *The Bionic Woman* series, feeling it might affect his show's popularity. Individual episodes featured bionic dogs, a bionic boy and a seven million dollar man, played by Monte Markham. "Monte did two appearances as the seven million dollar man," says Martin Caidin. "I thought it was a stupid idea. Monte did a good job, but the show was pretty hackneyed. The bionic boy was purely puke time."

Writer Richard Landau came in to produce, with Fred Freiberger, the last season of *The Six Million Dollar Man*. Going into the 1977-78 season, the series was now beginning its descent in the ratings. "We knew this might be its last year," says Landau. "We tried to goose the show up with more two-parters and some location filming in Hawaii. We had one story set on the dark side of the moon and brought back the Death Probe [a

wayward land rover from space]. We also tried to get Steve romantically involved."

Landau enjoyed his first meeting with Lee Majors and recalls his sly sense of humor. "I went up to his trailer outside the studio," recalls Landau. "I'm post-polio, and I use a cane for walking. Getting into the trailer was like climbing Mt. Everest. A couple of Lee's bodyguard characters offered to help me up and I said no, I can do it myself. After a lot of struggling, I hoisted myself up into the trailer and half-collapsed on the couch. There was Lee. I introduced myself as the new producer. He looked at me with a straight face and said, 'Tell me something. If I invited you to play tennis, would you do it?' I knew he was putting me on. I said, 'Well, shit, Lee—only if I can hop back and forth over the net to warm up first.' That broke the ice. He was a friendly, down-to-earth guy. He was great with the crew."

There was some question, going into the fifth and final year, whether Majors would sign with the show again. "Lee's contract hadn't been renegotiated," says Landau. "He wanted more money, so the studio asked us to come up with other actors as possible replacements. Harrison Ford's name came up. This was just before *Star Wars*. Believe it or not, Universal said, 'No, no. He's not right for an action show.' Of course, Ford went on to do the *Indiana Jones* movies."

"Lee was a holdout," continues Harve Bennett. "Universal felt it was terribly important to hold the line. There was a protracted period of holdout negotiations. We were asked by the studio to test five actors for the part. Since I wasn't head of the studio, I did what I was asked to do. Gil Gerard [the future *Buck Rogers*] was one of the actors. He got the most attention because he was a contract player at Universal and he was the most physical. We also tested Bruce Jenner. It was all for naught, because Lee eventually signed back on."

By 1978, the bionic saga was over. *The Six Million Dollar Man* (as well as *The Bionic Woman*) was retired. Martin Caidin feels there were two major factors that contributed to the show's cancellation. "Harve Bennett was a damn good producer," says Caidin, "but both Bennett and Universal studios refused to update the science on the series. There had been great advances made in bionics, but for some reason, they didn't want to reflect that. I said, 'Unless you change the basic bionic stuff, you're gonna be old hat before much longer.' The other problem was that Lee Majors

Lee Majors and Lindsay Wagner meet again in the TV movie *The Bionic Showdown* (1989). Copyright 1989 NBC.

America hurt *The Six Million Dollar Man*'s syndicated sales domestically, but there was enough interest for the making of two *Six Million Dollar Man/ Bionic Woman* TV films in the 1980s. Lee Majors and Lindsay Wagner reprised their roles. In 1990, Richard Anderson discussed a new *Six Million Dollar Man* project with Martin Caidin. "He was interested in reviving the series on a weekly basis," recalls Caidin. Those plans didn't materialize. Majors and Wagner *did* reunite for a third TV film, *Bionic Ever After* (1994).

The series was a big smash in the international market. "A few years ago, my wife and I went to Caracas, Venezuela," says Caidin. "We were front page news. I was known as the creator of *The Six Million Dollar Man*. At the airport were these big mobs of kids. I felt like the Pied Piper of Hamelin. The series is now showing in 72 countries."

was saying to the press, 'I'm gonna get out of this show. To hell with it!' and he began to lose his faithful fans. That helped to kill the show. Majors wanted to do motion pictures. He went on to do a Viking movie afterward. It was set 2,000 years ago. When a Viking comes ashore, you see a Coca-Cola can on the beach. Right! Terrific! Great technical work!" says Caidin wryly.

The Six Million Dollar Man was still in the top 40. "There was talk of continuing the series without Majors," says Caidin. Actor Gil Gerard was again brought up as a possible replacement, but the plan was abandoned.

"We hoped that the series would have a last-minute reprieve," says Richard Landau, "but the series had run its course. There wasn't much more you could do with it. It had a good life." Harve Bennett agrees. "There are very few hour-long shows that go five years."

The dwindling demand for hour shows in

felt like the Pied Piper of Hamelin. The series is now showing in 72 countries."

Caidin also is gratified by how the series popularized the concept of bionics. "When I wrote the novel *Cyborg*, nobody really believed in bionics. Now bionics has become a byword throughout the world. It's changed the way people think in terms of their own health, and the ability [science has] to repair their bodies. When I wrote the book, it was a dream. Now there's a whole generation growing up in a world where bionics is a reality."

CAST NOTES

Lee Majors (Steve Austin): Born 1939. Majors is a veteran of several TV series (including *The Big Valley*, *Owen Marshall* and, later, *The Fall Guy*). He later co-starred in the 1990s CBS series, *Raven*.

Richard Anderson (Oscar Goldman): Born 1926. A veteran character actor who decided to become an actor right after high school, Anderson began working in the mail room at MGM studios. He went on to star in the classic 1956 film *Forbidden Planet*. Producer Glen Larson cast Anderson for *The Six Million Dollar Man*. "Richard's a solid actor," Larson says. "He's been eternally grateful because the series made him very rich!"

EPISODE GUIDE

The Six Million Dollar Man (1973 TV movie)
With his body reconstructed after a plane crash, test pilot Steve Austin rebels against the government's plans to use him as a super agent, and copes with the psychological trauma of living with bionic powers. Based on the novel *Cyborg* by Martin Caidin. Wr: Henry Simoun, Howard Rodman and Steven Bochco. Dir: Richard Irving.
    Oliver Spencer (Darren McGavin); Rudy Wells (Martin Balsam); Jean Manners (Barbara Anderson); Mrs. McKay (Dorothy Green); Prisoner (Charles Knox Robinson); Dr. Ashburn (Robert Cornthwaite); Geraldton (Ivor Barry); General (George Wallace); Saltillo (Olan Soule); Man (Richard Webb); Woman (Anne Whitfield); Woman #2 (Norma Storch); Aide (John Mark Robinson); Nudaylah (Maurice Sherbanee).

Season 1: 1973-74

Wine, Women and War (90 min.)
Steve's mission to locate stolen missiles in the Bahamas involves him with ruthless killers and beautiful women. Wr: Glen A. Larson. Dir: Russ Mayberry.
    Arlen Findletter (Eric Braedon); Alexi Kaslov (David McCallum); Cynthia Hollan (Michele Carey); Harry Donner (Earl Holliman); Katrina Volana (Britt Eklund); Masaha (Lee Bergere); Dawson (Simon Scott); Walker (Robert F. Simon); Commander (George Keymas); Meade (Dennis Rucker); Passenger (Don Hamner).

The Solid Gold Kidnapping (90 min.)
Dead brain cells from hostile kidnappers point Steve toward the location of a missing statesman. Wr: Larry Alexander, story by Alan Caillou, Michael Gleason, Larry Alexander. Dir: Russ Mayberry.
    Dr. Erica Bergner (Elizabeth Ashley); Julian Peck (John Vernon); William Henry Cameron (Leif Erickson); Contessa (Luciana Paluzzi); Chairman (Maurice Evans); Scott (David White); Mel Bristol (Terry Carter); Inspector (Marcel Hillaire); Roger Ventriss (Craig Huebing); Skier (Leigh Christian); Secretary (Polly Middleton); Clerk (Maurice Marsac); Man (Jan Arvan).

Population Zero
The entire population of a town is killed, apparently by an embittered scientist, who demands a 10 mil-

lion dollar payment to keep him from killing another town. Wr: Elroy Schwartz. Dir: Jeannot Szwarc.
    Dr. Stanley Bacon (Don Porter); Chris Forbes (Penny Fuller); Joe Taylor (Paul Fix); Joe Hollister (Colby Chester); Paul Cord (Paul Carr); Gen. Harland (Walter Brooke); Mrs. Nelson (Virginia Gregg); Phillips (Morgan Jones); Edward Presby (John Elerick); Harry Johnson (Stuart Nisbet); Frank (Mike Santiago); Technician (Bob Delegall); Teletype man (David Valentine).

Survival of the Fittest
Crash-landing on a desolate island, Steve must protect Oscar from two assassins. Wr: Mann Rubin, story by Lionel Siegel, Harve Bennett. Dir: Leslie Martinson.
    Ted Maxwell (William Smith); Lt. Colby (Christine Belford); Lt. Ralph Cromewell (James McEachin); Mona (Jo Anne Worley); Barris (Randall Carver); Roberts (W.T. Zacha); Helen (Laurette Spang); Captain (Dale Johnson); Navy Lt. (Reed Smith).

Operation: Firefly
Steve Austin and Susan Abbott encounter quicksand, crocodiles and murderous henchmen as they slog their way through the Everglades to rescue Susan's kidnapped father. Wr: Sy Salkowitz, story by Ric Hardman. Dir: Reza Badiyi.
    Susan Abbott (Pamela Franklin); John Belson (Jack Hogan); Sam Abbott (Simon Scott); Charles LeDuc (Joseph Ruskin); Rawlins (Erik Holland); Frank (Joe Kapp); Eddie (Vic Mohica); Hobbs (Bill Conklin).

Day of the Robot
Steve drives Major Sloan across the country, not realizing that Sloan is an android programmed to kill him. Wr: Del Reisman, story by Harold Livingston, Lionel Siegel. Dir: Leslie H. Martinson.
    Fred Sloan (John Saxon); Gavern Wilson (Lloyd Bochner); Dr. Jeff Dolenz (Henry Jones); Parnell (Charles Bateman); Tanhill (Noah Keen); Roy (Lou Elias); Al (Robert Rothwell); Driver (Mike Alaimo).

Memory Flash—Les Martinson: "It was a very interesting episode where John Saxon played a robot with bionic strength. There's an eight-minute fight in slow motion at the end. The episode got the highest rating of that season. Some months later, I was in a theater and there was a tap on my shoulder. It was John Saxon. 'Thank you, Leslie,' he said, 'for destroying my career. Here I've done all of this theater and for the last two months, everyone refers to me as being the robot on "The Six Million Dollar Man!"'"

Little Orphan Airplane
Steve must repair a plane to save himself and pilot Josh Perkins before an African major and his men kill them for top-secret film. Wr: Elroy Schwartz. Dir: Reza Badiyi.
    Josh Perkins (Greg Morris); Sister Annette (Marge Redmond); Maj. Chooka (Scoey Mitchell); Braco (Lincoln

Kilpatrick); Datara (Ji-Tu Cumbuka); Sister Terese (Susan G. Powell); Sergeant (Arnold Turner); Gen. Magoffin (Paul Bryar); Farmer (Dave Turner); Bajad (Stack Pierce).

Doomsday and Counting
Steve burrows furiously into an underground Russian installation to save the fiancee of a Russian colonel from a nuclear blast. Wr: Larry Brody, story by Jimmy Sangster. Dir: Jerry Jameson.

Irina Leonova (Jane Merrow); Col. Vasily Zhukov (Gary Collins); Koskenko (William Smithers); Voda (Bruce Glover); General (William Boyett); Operator (Walker Edmiston); Pilot (Jim Gavin); Technician (Henry Rico Cattani); Technician #2 (Anne Newman).

Eyewitness to Murder
Steve, nearly killed by a sniper, is confounded by the hitman's alibi: He was on a live talk show at the time of the shooting. Wr: William Driskill. Dir: Alf Kjellin.

John Hopper (Gary Lockwood); Lorin Sandusky (William Schallert); Tanner (Leonard Stone); Sebastian (Richard Webb); Henley (Ivor Barry); TV host (Regis J. Cordic); Cabbie (Lew Palter); Clerk (Donna Mantoan); Tom Windom (Sal Ponti); Guido (Nicky Blair); Dorsey (Allen Joseph); Doorman (Al Dunlap).

The Rescue of Athena One
Steve tries to rescue a woman astronaut, but the weightlessness of space affects Steve's bionics. Wr: Dorothy C. Fontana. Dir: Lawrence Doheny.

Maj. Kelly Wood (Farrah Fawcett); Jules Bergman (Himself); Wolf (Paul Kent); Capcom (Quinn Redeker); Flight director (John S. Ragin); Osterman (Dean Smith); Retro (Doug Collins).

Dr. Wells Is Missing
Rudy is kidnapped and taken to an isolated castle where terrorists demand that he create an indestructible bionic man. Wr: Elroy Schwartz, story by Lionel Siegel, Bill Keenan, Krishna Shah. Dir: Virgil Vogel.

Alfredo Tucelli (John Van Dreelan); Julio Tucelli (Michael Dante); Fraulein Krueger (Cynthia Lynn); Clerk (Than Wyenn); Yamo (Jim Shane); Porter (Norbert Schiller); Anton Brandt (Curt Lowens); Vincent (Terry Leonard); Kurt (Dave Cass); Operator (Inez Van Holt).

Memory Flash—Writer Kenneth Johnson: "Before I wrote for the series, I watched a few episodes with my kids. I thought, 'Gee, that's odd. Steve Austin is running in slow motion but he's supposed to be running fast.' Once I accepted that, it was okay."

The Last of the Fourth of Julys
Steve makes a hazardous trek to the Norwegian mountains to reach a fortress protected by a deadly laser beam. Wr: Richard Landau. Dir: Reza Badiyi.

Quail (Steve Forrest); Root (Kevin Tighe); Violette (Arlene Martell); Joe Alabam (Tom Reese); Ives (Ben Wright); Captain (Barry Cahill); Balsam (Hank Stohl); Hurst (H. Alan Degin); Sonarman (Tom Hayden).

Burning Bright
An astronaut returns to Earth with special powers, but he soon becomes a threat to the community. Wr: Del Reisman. Dir: Jerry London.

Josh Lang (William Shatner); Tina Larsen (Anne Schedeen); Calvin Billings (Quinn Redeker); Ted Haldane (Warren Kemmerling); Ernesto Arruza (Rodolfo Hoyos); Millie (Mary Rings); Soldier (Ron Stokes).

The Coward
Stalked by killers, Steve travels to the Orient to clear his father's name of accusations of cowardice during World War II. Wr: Elroy Schwartz. Dir: Reza Badiyi.

Garth (George Montgomery); Marnu (France Nuyen); Chin Ling (George Takei); Quang-Dri (Ron Soble); Helen (Martha Scott); Kai Sing (Fuji); Prokar (Kim Kahana); Johara (Ken Endosa).

Run, Steve, Run!
Steve is captured by Dr. Dolenz, who intends to create an army of super-robots and raid Ft. Knox. Wr: Lionel E. Siegel. Dir: Jerry Jameson.

Dr. Jeff Dolenz (Henry Jones); Rossi (George Murdock); Suzie Lund (Melissa Greene); Tom Molson (Noah Berry, Jr.); Cliff Platt (Mike Henry); Smitty (Bill Conklin); Bill Wooters (Fred Lerner); Art Ramirez (Victor Millan).

Season 2: 1974-75

Nuclear Alert!
Imprisoned on an enemy plane, Steve and a scientist try to stop terrorists from dropping an atomic bomb. Wr: William Driskill. Dir: Jerry London.

Dr. Clea Broder (Carol Lawrence); Ted Swenson (Fred Beir); Gen. Wiley (George Gaynes); Cal (Felice Orlandi); Major (Stewart Moss); General #2 (John Stephenson); Zeb (Gabriel Walsh); Carson (Thomas Bellin); Farmer (Charles Wagenheim); Farmer's wife (Irene Tedrow); Tome (Stuart Nisbet); Menger (Phillip Adams); Passenger (Michael Kane); Elaine (Savannah Bentley); Passengers (Sig Haig, Noel de Souza, Ben Frommer).

The Pioneers
A superhuman astronaut awakens from suspended animation and goes on a rampage after his spaceship crashes. Wr: Bill Svanoe, story by Katey Barrett. Dir: Christian Nyby, II.

David Tate (Mike Farrell); Nicole Simmons (Joan Darling); Sheriff (Robert F. Simon); Walker (Vince Howard); Men (Milt Kogan, Bill Sorrells); Campers (Angelo de Meo, Justin Wilde).

Pilot Error
Temporarily blinded, Steve must take over the piloting of a small plane. Wr: Edward J. Lakso. Dir: Jerry Jameson.

Senator Hill (Pat Hingle); Joe Lannon (Alfred Ryder); Jill Denby (Suzanne Zenor); Cole (Hank Brandt); Doctor (Dennis McCarthy); Greg Hill (Stephen Nathan); Reporter (Chet Douglas); Phillipe (Hank Stohl).

The Pal-Mir Escort
Madame Pal-Mir must travel across the country to

receive a bionic heart. Steve accompanies her and fights off her would-be assassins on the way. Wr: Margaret and Paul Schneider. Dir: Lawrence Dobkin.

Salka Pal-Mir (Anne Revere); Stellen (Denny Miller); Linda (Jamie Donnelly); Dr. Avni (Leo Fuchs); Michael (John Landis); Sarah (Virginia Gregg); Kern (Don Pulford); Johnson (Robert Rothwell); Philip (Everett Creach); Shahvid (Nate Esformes).

The Seven Million Dollar Man

Barney Miller is the world's second bionic man, but Steve is opposed to him becoming an OSI agent because Miller is having psychological trouble adapting to superman status. Wr: Peter Allen Fields. Dir: Richard Moder.

Barney Miller (Monte Markham); Maggie Sullivan (Carla Peterson); OSI man (Fred Lerner); Guard (Marshall Reed).

Straight On till Morning

A family of golden-skinned aliens, hunted by the authorities, need Steve's help to rejoin their mothership. Wr: Dorothy C. Fontana. Dir: Lawrence Doheny.

Minonee (Meg Foster); Sheriff Bob Kemp (Cliff Osmond); Jeff Lohman (Donald Billett); Dr. Matt Waters (Jimmy Lydon); Cockrell (Kurt Grayson); Project director (John Calvin); Eymon (Christopher Mears); Keron (Vincent Chase); Ilea (Frances Osborne); Frank Packer (Lucas White); Ed Hermon (Al Dunlap); Technician (Robert Bruce Lang).

The Midas Touch

A frame-up implicates Oscar as a gold thief, but the real culprit is Oscar's old friend. Wr: Donald L. Gold, Lester William Berke, Peter Allen Fields, story by Donald L. Gold, Lester William Berke. Dir: Bruce Bilson.

Bert Carrington (Farley Granger); MacGregor (Noam Pitlik); Pop (Woodrow Chambliss); Julie Farrell (Kate McKeown); Conlan (Dave Morick); Lt. Evers (Gary Cashdollar); Conners (Rick Hurst); Eric (Lou Elias); George (Jim Connors); Sentry (Marcus Smith).

Deadly Replay

Evidence suggests sabotage caused the crash that nearly killed Steve years ago. Steve agrees to flush out the saboteurs by flying the rebuilt plane. Wr: Wilton Denmark. Dir: Christian Nyby II.

Andrea Collins (Lara Parker); Ted Collins (Jack Ging); Walter Burns (Clifton James); Jay Rogers (Robert Symonds); Carl Amison (Jack Manning); Simcon (William Scherer); Man (Regis J. Cordic).

Act of Piracy

When hostile countrymen from Santa Ventura capture a U.S. patrol boat, Steve ends up trapped on the sea floor in a diving bell. Wr: Peter Allen Fields, story by Dave Ketchum, Bruce Shelley. Dir: Christian Nyby II.

Louis Craig (Stephen McNally); Sharon Ellis (Lenore Kasdorf); Fernando Ferraga (Carlos Romero); Lt. (Jorge Cervera, Jr.); Jed Hall (Hagan Beggs); Julio (Frank Ramirez); Guard (David Dominiquez); Officer (Joe LaDue).

Stranger in Broken Fork

Stricken with amnesia after a plane crash, Steve is befriended by psychologist Angie Walker, who is being harassed by local townspeople. Wr: Bill Svanoe, Wilton Denmark, story by Bill Svanoe. Dir: Christian Nyby, Sr.

Angie Walker (Sharon Farrell); Dr. Wayne Carlton (Arthur Franz); Horace Milsner (Robert Donner); Jody (Kristine Ritzke); Mother (Sally Yarnell); Thrumond (Bill Henry); Corley Weems (Troy Melton); Major (Eric Mason); Trooper (Paul LeClair).

Peeping Blonde

After an ambitious newslady catches Steve making a bionic jump on film, her boss makes a deal with a foreign country to capture Steve. Wr: William T. Zacha, Sr., Wilton Denmark, story by William T. Zacha, Sr. Dir: Herschel Daugherty.

Victoria Webster (Farrah Fawcett); Charles Colby (Roger Perry); Karl (Hari Rhodes); Victor (W.T. Zacha); Billy Jackson (Chris Nelson); Flightcom (Martin Speer).

Cross Country Kidnapping

A horse-riding champion is threatened by kidnappers who want to exploit her computer skills. Wr: Ray Brenner, Stephen Kandel, story by Ray Brenner. Dir: Christian Nyby, Sr.

Lisa Leitman (Donna Mills); Arnold Blake (Tab Hunter); Ross Borden (Frank Aletter); Dirk Shuster (John Gabriel); Benno (Ben Wright); Davis (Robert Forward); Veneman (Jerome Guardino).

Lost Love

A mystery ensues when Steve reunites his old flame with her missing husband, who has been working for a foreign country. Wr: Richard Carr, story by Mel and Tom Levy. Dir: Arnold Laven.

Barbara Thatcher (Linda Marsh); Orin Thatcher (Jeff Corey); Markos (Joseph Ruskin); Prof. Kosoyin (Than Wyenn); Emil (Wesley Lau); Waiter (Harry Pugh).

The Last Kamikaze

An atomic bomb falls into the hands of a Japanese World War II pilot who is still fighting the war on a Pacific island. Wr: Judy Burns. Dir: Richard Moder.

Kuroda (John Fujioka); Tomas Gabella (Robert Ito); Hayworth (Edmund Gilbert); Richmond (Jimmy Joyce); Radioman (Paul Vaughn); Lorraine (Jane Goodnow Gillett).

Return of the Robot Maker

Dr. Dolenz returns. This time he replaces Oscar with an android duplicate. Wr: Mark Frost, story by Del Reisman and Mark Frost. Dir: Phil Bondelli.

Chester Dolenz (Henry Jones); Gen. Stacey (Ben Hammer); Amy (Iris Edwards); Barney Barnes (Troy Melton); Aide (Judd Laurance); Miss Wilson (Sarah Simmons); Denise (Jean Lee Brooks).

Taneha

Steve uses his bionics to protect a rare golden

cougar, on the run from angry hunters. Wr: Margaret Armen. Dir: Earl Bellamy.

E.J. Haskell (Jess Walton); Will Long (James Griffith); Bleeker (Bill Fletcher); Rafe Morris (Paul Brinegar); Bob Elliot (Jim Smith); Attendant (Trent Dolan).

Memory Flash—Margaret Armen: "I went in to pitch a story to the show's story editor. As I sat there, I noticed a woman's hand coming up from under my chair. This young story editor thought it was screamingly funny. It was a plastic hand that he used to scare people. He thought it was a good ice breaker."

Look Alike
Steve discovers a duplicate of himself who has been spying on OSI files. Steve must also battle a fighter in the boxing ring. Wr: Richard Carr, story by Gustave Field. Dir: Jerry London.

Marcus Garvy (George Foreman); Breezy (Robert Do Qui); Freddie (Eddie Fontaine); Ed Jasper (Jack Colvin); LaSalle (Robert Salvio); Molly (Mary Rings); Carrathurs (Arthur Space); Secretary (Susan Keller).

The ESP Spy
Spies are using telepathy to steal secrets from a scientist's mind. Steve joins up with a young girl with ESP to find the culprits. Wr: Lionel Siegel. Dir: Jerry London.

Audrey Moss (Robbie Lee); Harry Green (Dick Van Patten); Charles Lund (Alan Bergmann); Mike Randolph (Philip Bruns); Pierce (Paul Cavonis); Jarecki (George Patten); George Vant (Bert Kramer).

The Bionic Woman, Part 1
Steve's renewed romance with Jaime Sommers falls apart when she's critically injured in a parachute accident and fitted with bionics. Steve opposes Oscar's plan to use Jaime to crack a counterfeit ring. Wr: Kenneth Johnson. Dir: Richard Moder.

Jaime Sommers (Lindsay Wagner); Joseph Wrona (Malachi Throne); Timberlake (Paul Carr); Helen Elgin (Martha Scott); Jim Elgin (Ford Rainey); Schwartz (Sidney Clute); Jon Ellerton (Harry Hickox).

Memory Flash—producer Lionel Siegel: "Lee Majors wanted to do a two-part love story where he would sing several songs. I wanted Lindsay for the part of his mate, and she got it."

The Bionic Woman, Part 2
Jaime agrees to break into the villains' vault, but the mission is imperiled when her body rejects her bionic limbs. Wr: Kenneth Johnson. Dir: Richard Moder.

Jaime Sommers (Lindsay Wagner); Joseph Wrona (Malachi Throne); Timberlake (Paul Carr); Helen Elgin (Martha Scott); Jim Elgin (Ford Rainey); Nurse (Elisabeth Brooks); Nurse #2 (Margie Impert); Schwartz (Sidney Clute); Attendant (Richard Jannone); Lomax (Walt Conley).

Outrage in Balinderry
Steve battles ruthless revolutionaries who plan to kill a kidnapped ambassador's wife unless their fellow members are released from prison. Wr: Paul Schneider, story by Paul and Margaret Schneider. Dir: Earl Bellamy.

Julia Flood (Martine Beswick); Slayton (Richard Erdman); Abbott (David Frankham); Carmichael (Alan Caillou); Fred Collins (William Sylvester); Breen (Richard O'Brien); Mrs. Collins (Margaret Fairchild); Jessica (Diana Chesney); Dan (Gavan O'Herlihy); Crewman (Michael Regan).

Steve Austin, Fugitive
Framed for murder, Steve breaks away from police custody and searches for the truth. Wr: Mark Frost, Richard Carr, story by Wilton Denmark, William Gordon and James Doherty. Dir: Russ Mayberry.

Hopper (Gary Lockwood); Charlie Taylor (Andy Romano); Peggy Callahan (Jennifer Darling); Dobbs (Bernie Hamilton); OSI guard (Jesse Nichols); Portez (Marco Lopez); Atkins (Reb Brown); Old lady (Amzie Strickland).

Season 3: 1975-76

Return of the Bionic Woman, Parts 1 and 2
Steve discovers that Jaime didn't die: She was cryogenically frozen and is about to be revived with new bionics. In Part 2, the bionic duo tries to stop terrorists in the Caribbean. Wr: Kenneth Johnson. Dir: Richard Moder.

Jaime Sommers (Lindsay Wagner); Carlton Harris (Dennis Patrick); Jim Elgin (Ford Rainey); Mike Marchetti (Rick Lenz); Chester (Al Ruscio); Abe Collins (Tony Giorgio); Arkoff (George Keymas); Mrs. Raymond (Virginia Gregg).

The Price of Liberty
A scientist steals the Liberty Bell, rigging it with explosives. Steve asks convict Neils Lindstrom to disarm the bomb, but Lindstrom has his eyes on escaping. Wr: Kenneth Johnson, story by Justin Edgerton, Ken Johnson. Dir: Richard Moder.

Neils Lindstrom (Chuck Conners); Robert Meyer (Henry Beckman); Doug Witherspoon (Sandy Ward); Tom (Bill Quinn); Bill (George Jordan); Doorman (Joe Brooks); Man (Scott B. Wells).

The Song and Dance Spy
Oscar suspects that Steve's friend is stealing top government secrets. Wr: Jerry Devine. Dir: Richard Moder.

John Perry (Sonny Bono); Buckner (Bruce Glover); Louise (Jayne Kennedy); Lee Michaels (Vic Mohica); Damon (Robin Clarke); Crawford (Fred Holliday); Laura (Susan McIver); Linda (Susie Coelho).

The Wolf Boy
Steve discovers an orphan boy in Japan's wilderness. Raised by wolves, the boy is mistrustful of human beings. Wr: Judy Burns. Dir: Jerry London.

Wolf boy (Buddy Foster); Kuroda (John Fujioka); Bob Masters (Quinn Redeker); Shige Ishikawa (Teru Shimada); Toshio (Bill Saito); Rollin Moriyama.

The Deadly Test
Steve poses as a prince to flush out would-be assassins. Wr: James D. Parriott. Dir: Christian Nyby II.
Col. Joe Gordon (Tim O'Connor); Winslow (Frank Marth); Lt. Jan Simmons (Leigh Christian); Prince Sakari (Erik Estrada); Levy (Martin Speer); Pratt (Harry Pugh); Jim Barrows (Bill Scherer); Also with Helen Magee.

Target in the Sky
Steve poses as a lumberjack to short-circuit a plan to blow up presidential cabinet members. Wr: Larry Alexander, Kenneth Johnson. Dir: Jerry London.
Kelly Wixted (Barbara Rhodes); Thaddeus Jones (Rafer Johnson); Jeremy Burke (Denny Miller); Morton Craig (Ivor Francis); Charlie Two Feathers (Skeeter Vaughn); Ben Cosgrove (Hank Stohl).

Memory Flash—Kenneth Johnson: "Universal had done a Paul Newman logging movie called *Sometimes a Great Notion*. So we wrote a show where Steve poses as a lumberjack. We used leftover footage from the movie. The result was terrific. It looked like we had gone on location to Oregon for two months. Jerry London, the director, couldn't believe it. When he saw the episode, he said, 'Kenny, you're a magician!' A lot of shows were created in the editing room by using stock footage of rocket launches and stuff."

One of Our Running Backs Is Missing
Superstar Larry Bronco is kidnapped before a big football game by a jealous teammate. Wr: Kenneth Johnson, story by Elroy Schwartz. Dir: Lee Majors.
Larry Bronco (Larry Csonka); Pam Bronco (Pam Csonka); Bob Laport (Dick Butkus); Tatashore (Mike Henry); Stolar (Carl Weathers); Rick Laport (Lee Josephson); George Yokum (Al Checco); Coach Ailes (Earl Faison); Kibbee (Tom Mack); Quarterback (George Clifton).

Memory Flash—Kenneth Johnson: "We wanted to call it 'One of Our Csonkas Is Missing' but the network wouldn't let us. Lee Majors said to me, 'Kenny, I think it's time I directed something,' and he did a fine job. We were flying by the seat of our pants: How do we show a football game on our budget? Obviously, we couldn't fill a stadium with 50,000 people. We did a lot of it with sound effects."

The Bionic Criminal
Barney, the seven million dollar man, is reactivated against Steve's warnings, and decides to embark on a life of crime. Wr: Richard Carr, story by Peter Allan Fields. Dir: Leslie H. Martinson.
Barney Miller (Monte Markham); Carla Peterson (Maggie Sullivan); Shatley (John Milford); Lester Burstyn (Donald Moffat).

The Blue Flash
Posing as a longshoreman to find smugglers, Steve's investigation is compromised by a young black boy. Wr: Sheridan Gibney, Sidney Field. Dir: Cliff Bole.
Ernest Cook (Rodney Allan Rippy); Mrs. Cook (Janet MacLachlan); Jimbo (Michael Conrad); Tony Anderson (Eddie Fontaine); Logan (Jason Wingreen); Olmstead (Barry Cahill); Charlie (Benny Nickelberry); Harold (Garrison True); Fred (Virgil Charles Frye).

The White Lightning War
Death by a poisonous snake is the fate awaiting Steve when he investigates corruption in a small town. Wr: Wilton Denmark. Dir: Phil Bondelli.
Middy (Katherine Helmond); Kermit (Robert Donner); Charles Quinten (Austin Stoker); Bo Willis (Ben Hammer); Sheriff Weems (Hugh Gillin); Owner (Red West); Johnny (Randy Kirby).

Divided Loyalty
Steve tries to escort a scientist and his rebellious son out of a communist country, but soldiers are closing in. Wr: Jim Carlson, Terry McDonnell. Dir: Alan Crosland, Jr.
Alex Jackson (Radames Pera); Leon Jackson (Michael McGuire); Ednar Jackson (Johana de Winter); Sergeant (Ralph Taeger); Boris (Ned Romero); Captain (Curt Lowens); Gottke (Larry Levine); Lt. (Rod Haase).

Clark Templeton O'Flaherty
Either Steve's old janitor friend has broken into an underground spy organization, or he's playing Steve for a fool. Wr: Frank Dandridge, story by Frank Dandridge, Dennis Pryor. Dir: Ernest Pintoff.
Clark Templeton O'Flaherty (Lou Gossett, Jr.); McAdams (H.M. Wynant); Ms. Hallaway (Louise Latham); George van Rensselaer (Ryan McDonald); Landlady (Lillian Randolph); Technician (Susan Quick); Woman (Linda Nesbit).

The Winning Smile
Oscar's secretary, Callahan, is being set up for a fall when her boyfriend begins stealing government secrets. Wr: Gustave Field, Richard Carr, story by Gustave Field. Dir: Arnold Laven.
Gene Finney (Stewart Moss); Peggy Callahan (Jennifer Darling); Emil Losey (Milton Selzer); Tom Dempster (Bob Delegall); Hector (Harry Lewis); Agee (Ben Andrews); Ted Harter (James Ingersoll); Agent (Rick Podell).

Welcome Home, Jaime
Steve helps Jaime settle down in Ojai, California, where she begins teaching an unruly classroom and considers a future with the OSI. Concluded on *The Bionic Woman*. Wr: Kenneth Johnson. Dir: Alan Crosland, Jr.
Jaime Sommers (Lindsay Wagner); Carlton Harris (Dennis Patrick); Tom Holloway (Roger Davis); Mike Marchetti (Rick Lenz); Karen Stone (Dee Timberlake); Gwen (Alicia Gardner); Lydia (Alexa Kanin); Joey (Kraig Metzinger).

Hocus Pocus
Teenager Audrey Moss puts on a show with her ESP powers to trap a group of spies. Wr: Richard Carr, story by Richard Carr, James Schmerer. Dir: Barry Crane.
Mark Wharton (Pernell Roberts); Audrey Moss (Robbie Lee); Will Collins (Jack Colvin); Jack (Chris Nelson); George (W.T. Zacha); David (Mark Wilson); Dinallo (Richard Geary).

The Secret of Bigfoot, Parts 1 and 2
Alien beings conducting underground tests use an android Bigfoot to capture Steve. In Part 2, Steve helps the aliens prevent an earthquake that could destroy northern California. Wr: Kenneth Johnson. Dir: Alan Crosland, Jr.

Shalon (Stefanie Powers); Apploy (Severn Darden); Bigfoot (Andre the Giant); Marlene Beckley (Penelope Windust); Faler (Charles Cyphers); Ivan Beckey (Hank Brandt); Tom Raintree (Donn Whyte); Captain (Ford Lile); Guard (Chuck Bowman); Technician (Alan Mandell).

The Golden Pharaoh
Steve enters a trap when he tries to recover a statue from a foreign diplomat's office. Wr: Margaret and Paul Schneider. Dir: Cliff Bole.

Trish Hollander (Farrah Fawcett); Gustav Tokar (Joe Maross); Joe (Gary Vinson); Skorvic (Mike Lane); Wheel Jackson (Gordon Connell); Dave Martino (Rudy Challenger); Secretary (Lyndel Stuart); Croupier (Joe LaCava); Chauffeur (Peter Ashton).

Love Song for Tanya
To heat up relations between the two superpowers, agents are trying to kill Soviet gymnast Tanya Breski. Wr: David H. Balkan, Alan Folsom. Dir: Phil Bondelli.

Tanya Breski (Cathy Rigby); Jaime Sommers (Lindsay Wagner); Alexsi (Terry Kiser); Uri Gargon (Kurt Grayson); Andre (Alan Manson); Waitress (Elizabeth Treadwell); Ivan (Walker Edmiston); Director (Curtis Credel); Saleslady (Sheila Wills); Guard (Michael Cartel).

The Bionic Badge
The odd behavior of a policeman baffles Steve as he tries to stop a hostile country from building an atomic bomb. Wr: Wilton Denmark. Dir: Cliff Bole.

Greg Banner (Noah Beery, Jr.); Burman (Alan Bergmann); Cindy Walker (Susan G. Powell); Gerry Martin (Thomas Bellin); Clint (Mike Santiago); Randolph (Stack Pierce); Man (Tom Morgan).

Big Brother
Steve joins Big Brothers and helps a young street kid by defusing the hostilities of a gang. Wr: Kenneth Johnson. Dir: Cliff Bole.

Jaime Sommers (Lindsay Wagner); Carlos Pelgado (Michael A. Salcido); Smiley (Carl Crudup); Larry Hamlin (Ralph Wilcox); Phil (John Hesley); Chico (David Yanez); Boy (Jorge Cervera, III); Secretary (Renie Radich); Margarita Delgado (Maria Elena Cordero).

Season 4: 1976-77

The Return of Bigfoot
Steve is framed for gold robberies when aliens program Bigfoot to plunder the Earth's resources. The friendly alien Shalon helps Steve battle the invaders. Concluded on *The Bionic Woman*. Wr: Kenneth Johnson. Dir: Barry Crane.

Shalon (Stefanie Powers); Nedlik (John Saxon); Gillian (Sandy Duncan); Jaime Sommers (Lindsay Wagner); Bigfoot (Ted Cassidy); Dallett (Stephen Young); Apploy (Severn Darden); Faler (Charles Cyphers).

Nightmare in the Sky
Steve discovers an artificial Bermuda Triangle after a pilot claims her plane was shot down by a Japanese Zero. Wr: Jim Carlson, Terence McDonnell. Dir: Alan Crosland, Jr.

Kelly Wood (Farrah Fawcett); Dr. Martin Davis (Donald Moffat); Larry Stover (Dana Elcar); Mike (Hank Stohl).

Double Trouble
Steve learns that an American comedian is being controlled by a foreign power. Wr: Jerry Devine. Dir: Phil Bondelli.

Billy Parker/Prime Minister (Flip Wilson); Dr. Barto (Simon Scott); Susan (Mira L. Waters); Niko (Rick Podell); Cabbie (Jerome Guardino); Doorman (Borah Silver).

The Most Dangerous Enemy
Island experiments on chimpanzees accidentally infect Rudy, who is turned into a crazed superman. Wr: Judy Burns. Dir: Richard Moder.

Dr. Cheryl Osborne (Ina Balin).

H + 2 + O = Death
Steve infiltrates a criminal organization to recover an energy-producing device. Wr and Dir: John Meredyth Lucas.

Dr. Ilsa Martin (Elke Sommer); Omega (Linden Chiles); Matheson (John Van Dreelan); Walker (Robert Hogan); Kirov (Todd Martin); Ed (Frank Parker); Guard (Lawrence Bame); Officer (Frank Farmer).

Kill Oscar
Jaime hovers near death after female androids attack her. Dr. Franklin then orders his androids to kill Steve and Oscar. Parts 1 and 3 of this segment were on *The Bionic Woman*. Wr: W.T. Zacha, story by Arthur Rowe, Oliver Crawford. Dir: Barry Crane.

Dr. Franklin (John Houseman); Jaime (Lindsay Wagner); Hanson (Jack Ging); Comm. Gordon (Jim McMullan); Admiral Ricter (Sam Jaffe); Lynda (Corinne Michaels); Callahan (Jennifer Darling); Katy (Janice Witby); Newsman (Howard K. Smith); Gen. Williams (Eugene Peterson); Admiral Wilkins (Byron Morrow); Rawlins (John Dewey-Carter).

The Bionic Boy
A bionic teenager investigates his father's mysterious death. Wr: Tom Greene, story by Lionel Siegel, Wilton Schiller. Dir: Phil Bondelli.

Andy Sheffield (Vincent Van Patten); Valerie Sheffield (Joan Van Ark); Palmer (Dick Van Patten); Savannah (Woodrow Chambliss); Vernon (Richard Erdman); Judy Grant (Carol Jones); Coline Lightfoot (Kerry Sherman); Dr. Penny (George Martin); Dr. Melville (Jack Bannon); Frank Gifford (Himself); Joe Hamilton (Greg Evigan); Charlie (Nick David).

Vulture of the Andes
America's defenses are being blackmailed with threats of destruction unless the military helps a

sportsman invade San Lorenzo. Wr: Ben Masselink. Dir: Cliff Bole.

Leslie Morales (Barbara Luna); Byron Falco (Henry Darrow); Pete (Bernie Kopell); Raul (Zitto Kazann); Reynolds (Dallas Mitchell); Air policeman (Joe Haworth).

The Thunderbird Connection (2 hours)
Steve joins a U.S. Air Force squad to protect a young prince whose life is threatened by countrymen planning a coup. Wr: Jim Carlson, Terrence McDonnell. Dir: Christian Nyby, II.

Mahmud Majid (Robert Loggia); Shali Giba (Martine Beswick); Paul Miller (Jim McMullan); Akhmed Khadduri (Ned Romero); Jan Lawrence (Susanne Reed); Prince Hassad (Barry Miller); Col. Raman (Jeff David); Sgt. Young (Erik Holland); Arafa (Joe LoPresti).

A Bionic Christmas
A miser working with the Mars landing project is making his employees miserable during Christmas. Steve is brought in to bring some Christmas cheer and change the miser's ways. Wr: Wilton Schiller. Dir: Gerald Mayer.

Horton Budge (Ray Walston); Bob Crandall (Dick Sargent); Nora Crandall (Antoinette Bower); Charlie (Sheldon Allman); Elsie Crandall (Quinn Cummings); Cissy Crandall (Natasha Ryan); Dr. Hendricks (Noah Keen); Joe (Barry Cahill); Secretary (June Dayton); Clerk (Ann Dusenberry); Bob Jr. (Adam Rich); Worker (Howard McGillin).

Task Force
Steve infiltrates an organization which is planning to steal a missile. Wr: Robert C. Dennis, Wilton Schiller. Dir: Barry Crane.

Harraway (Alex Cord); Callahan (Jennifer Darling); Nicolini (Taylor Lacher); Maj. Sid Pell (Edmund Gilbert); General (Robert Forward); M.P. (Gary Cashdollar); Sheriff (Scott B. Wells); Henchmen (Glenn Wilder, Chuck Hicks, Tony Brubaker).

The Ultimate Imposter
Steve's friend Joe Patton is turned into a super-agent when his mind is given direct access to computer information. Wr: Lionel Siegel, William T. Zacha, story by William T. Zacha. Dir: Paul Stanley.

Joe Patton (Stephen Macht); Jenny Nicholas (Pamela Hensley); Stenger (David Sheiner); Lorraine Stenger (Kim Basinger); Lily Stenger (Margaret Fairchild); Wilkins (Harry Pugh); Mark (Mark Thomas); Mal (George Ball).

Death Probe, Part 1
A Russian Venus probe crashes in Wyoming and threatens to destroy a small town. Wr: Steven de Souza. Dir: Richard Moder.

Major Popov (Nehemiah Persoff); Irena Leonova (Jane Merrow); Secretary (Beverly Garland); Zach Meesham (Don Dubbins); Mechanic (Bill Fletcher); Captain (Austin Stoker); Russian general (Phillip Pine); Gen. Wiley (Walter Brooke); Sheriff (Ross Elliot); Photographer (Ryan McDonald).

Death Probe, Part 2
Weapons have no effect on the Probe's destructive rampage, forcing Steve to lure it into a trap. Wr: Steven de Souza. Dir: Richard Moder.

Major Popov (Nehemiah Persoff); Irena Leonova (Jane Merrow); Russian Gen. (Phillip Pine); Captain (Austin Stoker); Medic (John DeLancie); Technician (Judd Laurence).

Danny's Inferno
A teenager who creates an explosive formula is endangered by a land developer who wants to exploit the formula's power. Wr: Tom Greene. Dir: Cliff Bole.

Dr. Monica (David Opatoshu); Bill Bruner (Frank Marth); Glennis (E.J. Peaker); Danny Laswell (Lanny Horn); Dr. Spruger (John Hoyt); Lazarus (Mills Watson).

Fires of Hell
Disguised as an oil driller, Steve's life is threatened by a devious trio who are trying to mine uranium near an OSI drilling site. Wr: Orville Hampton. Dir: Ed Abroms.

Bertram Lomax (Charles Aidman); Alison Harker (Heather Menzies); Sheriff Burgess (Bruce Glover); Roy Palmer (Ken Swofford); Howie (Donald "Red" Barry); Susie (Melinda Naud); Firefighter (Larry Watson); Driver (Robert Neill); Worker (Nat Christian).

The Infiltrators
Steve gets into the ring as a boxing champ to kayo a group of assassins who are targeting foreign athletes who have defected. Wr: Sam Ross, Wilton Schiller. Dir: Phil Bondelli.

Wally (Jerry Quarry); Boris Retsky (Michael Conrad); Lena Bannister (Yvonne Craig); Cooper (Joe Kapp); Tollombe (Harold Sylvestor); Duclaire (Cliff Carnell); George Mason (Pervis Atkins).

Carnival of Spies
Steve discovers that a carnival site houses a missile designed to destroy a new B-1 bomber. Wr: Robert C. Dennis, story by Robert C. Dennis, Richard Carr. Dir: Richard Moder.

Rau (Lloyd Bochner); Kim (Cheryl Miller); Herman Lower (Michael Strong); Shira (Gloria Manon); General (H. M. Wynant); Hercules (Bob Minor); Walden (Wes Parker); Schmidt (Peter Weiss).

U-509
Submariners use an abandoned Nazi U-boat and a cache of nerve gas to extort 20 million from America. Wr: Michael Wagner. Dir: Phil Bondelli.

Henry Bulman (Guy Doleman); Prescott (William Sylvester); Covell (Steve Sandor); Lewis (Peter Canon); Captain (Morgan Jones); Shoemacher (Ian Abercrombie); Jaffe (Ted Hamilton).

Privacy of the Mind
Steve, posing as a scientist, is exposed as a fake after being subjected to an enemy mind-reading machine. Wr: Vanessa Boos, Wilton Schiller. Dir: Jimmy Lydon.

Dr. Batalova (Suzanne Charny); Dr. Berman (Roger Perry); Terry Campbell (Paul Mantee); Kulikov (Curt Lowens); Carlson (Robert Neill); Bob Kemps (Leslie Moonves).

To Catch an Eagle

Trapped scientists can't be rescued until Steve defeats a renegade Indian's powerful hold on his people by catching a wild eagle. Wr: Judy Burns, story by Peter R. Brooke. Dir: Phil Bondelli.

Silver Cloud (Peter Breck); Little Bear (Kathleen Beller); Iron Fist (Dehl Berti); Bob Marsh (Gerald McRaney); Ian Swanson (Jim Stathis); Lone Bear (George Loros).

Ghostly Teletype

Telepathic twins who are aging at an incredible rate steal a formula that will extend life, but Steve is accused of the theft. Wr: Wilton Schiller. Dir: Tom Connors.

Brenner (Robert H. Harris); Madame Marka (Jodean Russo); Margaret Waggner (Christina Hart); Davey Waggner (Les Lannom); Mrs. Waggner (Elizabeth Kerr); Angela (Linda Dano); Murdock (Larry Anderson).

Season 5: 1977-78

Sharks, Parts 1 and 2

Held captive in an underwater cave surrounded by sharks, Steve encounters a sub captain and his daughter, who plan to hijack a sub. In Part 2, Steve and the captain join forces to stop enemy agents from using the sub for crime. Wr: Arthur Weingarten. Dir: Alan J. Levi.

Cynthia Grayland (Pamela Hensley); Capt. Morgan Grayland (Stephen Elliot); Admiral Prescott (William Sylvester); Alex Parker (Gregory Walcott); Williams (Marc Alaimo); Ed (Larry Delaney); Man (William Whitton); Crewman (Buster Jones).

Deadly Countdown, Parts 1 and 2

Steve puts his life on the line to stop enemy agents from stealing American missile secrets. In Part 2, the daughter of a key space official is kidnapped by the enemy. Wr: Gregory S. Dinallo. Dir: Cliff Bole.

Dr. Leah Russell (Jenny Agutter); Gordon Shanks (Lloyd Bochner); Dave McGrath (Philip Abbott); Melissa McGrath (Sherry Hursey); Julian Richman (Crofton Hardester); G.H. Beck (Martin Caidin); Edgar Webster (Mills Watson); Ed Pierce (Bill Schere).

Memory Flash—author and pilot Martin Caidin: "I've been flying planes all of my life. I learned to fly a B-25 by taking it across the Atlantic through a blizzard. By the time I landed, I was an expert. On this *Six Million Dollar Man*, I played a real bad ass. They shot some of the episode in my house at Cocoa Beach, Florida. There's a scene where Steve Austin is driving a car along the river and he goes out of control. It was actually a stunt double for Lee Majors who was driving. I was flying a big bomber above him at 1200 feet. I took the bomber and, per instructions, dove the damn thing about three feet off the water, went full bore and went through that TV set like a hurricane. I knocked over all of the lights and reflectors and even blew Lee Majors into the river!

The crew threw a party that night, and that's the day I was made a member of the stuntman's association in California."

Bigfoot V

Steve is mystified by Bigfoot's behavior: The once friendly creature is on a rampage. Wr: Gregory S. Dinallo, Richard Landau. Dir: Rod Holcomb.

Bigfoot (Ted Cassidy); Charlie Wynn (Geoffrey Lewis); Hope Langston (Katherine de Hetre); Jason O'Neal (Tony Young); Explorer (Regis J. Cordic); Higbee (S. Newton Anderson).

Killer Wind

Steve must defeat bank robbers and save children trapped on a mountain tramway. Wr: Gregory S. Dinallo, story by Richard Landau. Dir: Richard Moder.

Dr. Jenny (Sylvia Walden); Nash (Adam Roarke); Garth (James McEachin); Rhonda Allen (Sheila Wills); Falco (Fred J. Gordon); Also with Madlyn Cain.

Rollback

Steve's on wheels when he joins a roller derby team to expose an international syndicate that threatens OSI security. Wr: Steven de Souza. Dir: Don McDougall.

Niles (Rick Springfield); Rand Hendricks (Robert Loggia); Maureen Wright (Suzanne Charney); Brady (Paul D'Amato); Men (Jim Connors, Matt Cord).

The Dark Side of the Moon, Part 1

Steve goes to the moon to stop mining operations which have shifted the moon's orbit and created havoc on Earth. Wr: John Meredyth Lucas, story by Richard Landau. Dir: Cliff Bole.

Bess Fowler (Simone Griffeth); Dr. Charles Leith (Jack Colvin); Ted Harmon (Skip Homeier); Dr. Jellman (Walter Brooke).

The Dark Side of the Moon, Part 2

Steve is forced to mine the moon with his bionics, or else Dr. Leith will mine it with nuclear explosives. Wr: John Meredyth Lucas, story by Richard Landau. Dir: Cliff Bole.

Dr. Charles Leith (Jack Colvin); Ted Harmon (Skip Homeier); Bess Fowler (Simone Griffeth); Frank Tracy (Quinn Redeker); Hal (James Ingersoll); Eric (Robert Neill).

Target: Steve Austin

Steve and a woman agent take a cross-country trip to trap agents who are making an A-Bomb. Wr: Donald L. Gold, Lester W. Berke, story by Richard Landau. Dir: Ed Abroms.

Joan (Lynette Mettey); Frank Stacy (Quinn Redeker); Hellerman (Curt Lowens); Jessica (Paula Victor); Rabbitt (Tony Epper); Cristo (Walter P. Robles); Alfred (Boris Aplon); Van driver (Larry Levine); Men (Ian Abercrombie, Carl Reindel).

The Cheshire Project

Steve's girlfriend vanishes while flying a top-secret plane. Wr: John Meredyth Lucas. Dir: Richard Moder.

Jenny Fraser (Suzanne Somers); Vail (John Larch); Hal (Robert Hogan); Gen. Meyers (Barry Cahill); Wilfred Damien (Stan Waxman); Blake (Fred Lerner); Stoner (Terry Leonard); Arthur (Jim Begg).

Walk a Deadly Wing
Dr. Cheraskin's wife will die unless he turns over a device to enemy agents. He created the device for peace, but it can also be used for war. Wr: Jim Carlson, Terrence McDonnell, story by Richard Landau. Dir: Herb Wallerstein.

Viktor Cheraskin (Eric Braedon); Frank Sullivan (Eddie Fontaine); Vera Cheraskin (Lanna Saunders); Edmund Dimitri (John Devlin); Ritter (Steve Eastin).

Just a Matter of Time
Steve's space capsule is apparently propelled six years into the future, where he faces charges of treason in 1984. Wr: Neal J. Sperling, Gregory Dinallo. Dir: Don McDougall.

Donna Hoffman (Leigh Christian); Ed Barris (Charles Cioffi); Gen. Winston Hayden (John Milford); Rev. Michael Essex (Paul Carr).

The Return of Death Probe, Part 1
Steve's bionics are no match for the reactivated Death Probe. Wr: Howard Dimsdale. Dir: Tom Conners.

Mahmoud (Than Wyenn); Arnold Blake (David Sheiner); Dan Kelly (Ken Swofford); Bates (Robert Lussier); Foreman (Jimmy Joyce); Kidnapper (John DeRose).

The Return of Death Probe, Part 2
Death Probe burrows underground and heads for a city. Wr: Howard Dimsdale. Dir: Tom Connors.

Arnold Blake (David Sheiner); Mahmoud (Than Wyenn); Dan Kelly (Ken Swofford); Bates (Robert Lussier); Foreman (Jimmy Joyce); Kidnapper (John De Rose); Sgt. Warren (Marlena Giovi).

Lost Island (2 hours)
While searching an island for a downed satellite, Steve befriends an alien woman. Her people are being terrorized by a power-crazed alien leader named Torg. Wr: Mel Goldberg, story by Lou Shaw. Dir: Cliff Bole.

Da-nay (Robin Mattson); Torg (Jared Martin); Arta (Anthony Geary); Gerro (Alf Kjellin); Zandor (Terence Burk); Jensen (Robert Symonds); Riga (Don Pulford); Ed (Paul Deadrick); Dr. Vrettass (Kwan Hi Lim).

The Madonna Caper
Steve pursues a stolen painting containing a top-secret microdot. Wr: Gregory S. Dinallo. Dir: Herb Wallerstein.

Countess Lysandra Korischeva (Bibi Besch); Viktor Bellushyn (Bruce Glover); Chilton Kane (Len Birman); Talbott (Robert Hoy); Boyle (Dominic Barto); Richard Tynan (Rudy Challenger); Sims (Michael McManus); Russell (Frank Parker); Undersecretary (Diana Webster); Armand (James Nolan).

Dead Ringer
Steve is being haunted by a shadowy apparition that appears to be a ghost of himself. Wr: Robert I. Holt,

story by Charles Mitchell, Robert I. Holt. Dir: Arnold Laven.

Dr. Margaret Winslow (Linda Dano); Fire captain (Robert Karnes); Delivery man (Mel Allen); Also with Leonard Stone, George Wilbur.

Date with Danger, Part 1
While trying to clear a friend of charges of espionage, Steve locates a master computer that has gained control of America's power base. Wr: John Meredyth Lucas, Wilton Schiller, story by Wilton Schiller. Dir: Rod Holcomb.

Cloche/Bell (Robert Walker); Emily Patterson (Elaine Giftos); Banner (Luke Askew); Fowler (Hank Brandt); Joe Canton (Noah Keen); Ralph (Paul Tully); Foreman (Robert Hackman); Pete (Raymond Davis); Guard (Eric Lawrence).

Date with Danger, Part 2
Emily Patterson, creator of the super-computer, and Steve become the machine's next targets as it tries to control America. Wr: John Meredyth Lucas, Wilton Schiller. Dir: Rod Holcomb.

Cloche/Bell (Robert Walker); Emily Patterson (Elaine Giftos); Dr. Ellis (Peter Mark Richman); Banner (Luke Askew); Fowler (Hank Brandt); Joe Canton (Noah Keen).

Moving Mountain
Steve is unaware that a plan to recover a rocket launcher will forfeit his life. Wr: Stephen Kandel. Dir: Don McDougall.

Gorbokov (John Colicos); Andrea Mestrova (Lisa Farringer); Erhardt (Michael Ebert); Walter (Paul Coufos); Ishihara (Beverly Kushida); Santos (George Clifton); Mishkin (Keith Langsdale); Lorie (Susie Fleming).

TV Movies

The Return of the Six Million Dollar Man and the Bionic Woman (1987)
Steve Austin is reunited with Jaime Sommers, and they rekindle the flame. Steve also meets his estranged son, who is soon in need of bionic limbs after a plane crash. Together, the bionic trio battles a criminal's army. Wr: Michael Sloan, story by Michael Sloan, Bruce Lansbury. Dir: Ray Austin.

Steve Austin (Lee Majors); Jaime Sommers (Lindsay Wagner); Oscar Goldman (Richard Anderson); Rudy Wells (Martin E. Brooks); Lyle Stenning (Martin Landau); Michael Austin (Tom Schanley); Jim Castillian (Lee Majors II); Nick (Scott Kraft); Shepherd (Bryan Cransteon); Jim Matlon (Keith Farrell); Christopher (Phil Nordell); Girl (Pamela Bryant); Secretary (Cathy McGhoohan); Sally (Deborah White); Magen (Kewena Jensen); Holly (Michele Minailo); Hostess (Julie H. Morgan); Also with William Campbell, Robert Hoy, Will Bledsoe, Cheryl McMannis, Patrick Pankhurst, Bob Seagren, Susan Wollen.

The Bionic Showdown (1989)
Steve and Jaime are on the run from the government after they're blamed for sabotaging security installations at OSI. The two also face a bionic foe and must foil an assassination plot aimed at the president

of the Soviet Union during his Montreal visit. Wr: Michael Sloan, Robert DeLaurentis and Ted Mann. Dir: Alan J. Levi.

Steve Austin (Lee Majors); Jaime Sommers (Lindsay Wagner); Oscar Goldman (Richard Anderson); Rudy Wells (Martin E. Brooks); Gen. McAllister (Robert Lansing); Jim Castillian (Lee Majors II); Katie (Sandra Bullock); Jimmy

Goodman (Jeff Yagher); Alan Devlin (Geraint Wyn Davies); Sally (Carolyn Dunn); Larry (Jack Blum); Kellagvn (Andrew R. Dan); Tanya (Marcia Levine); Williams (Robert McClure); Peter (David Nerman); Russ (Steve Pernie); Announcer (Steve Morris); Also with Lawrence Dane, Josef Sommer.

Something Is Out There

October 1988–December 1988

In the middle of his everyday routine, Los Angeles cop Jack Breslin arrives at a juncture that changes his life forever. He runs into T'Ara, an extraterrestrial female, who has come to Earth to hunt an evil, shape-changing monster called the Xenomorph. This monster escaped from its prison aboard T'Ara's ship, stole a shuttle and fled to Earth. Now the Xenomorph is on a gleeful killing spree in the City of Angels. Jack and T'Ara join forces against the monster. When they succeed in destroying the Xenomorph, T'Ara, stranded on Earth, helps Jack deal with L.A.'s strangest police cases.

Cast: Jack Breslin (Joe Cortese); T'Ara (Maryam d'Abo); Lt. Victor Maldonado (Gregory Sierra).

Created by: Frank Lupo; *Executive Producer:* Frank Lupo, John Ashley; *Associate Producer:* Bernadette Joyce; NBC/Columbia TV; 60 minutes.

It's very difficult for a TV series to live up to the promise of an exciting four-hour mini-series debut, especially when that debut introduces something the viewers want to see again—and don't. *Something Is Out There* fell into that trap. As it developed into episodic format, it abandoned the shape-changing evil creature from space that viewers had hoped would be a staple of the show.

The expensive mini-series boasted the talents of two Oscar-winning wizards: makeup designer Rick Baker to create the shape-changing Xenomorph alien, and special effects artist John Dykstra to add visual panache to the alien spaceships. Even after the failures *V*, *Manimal*, and *Misfits of Science*, NBC still wanted science fiction to work, so they developed this show.

For budget purposes, the mini-series was filmed partly in Sydney, Australia. Twenty-one days were devoted to exterior filming in and around Los Angeles, and 20 days were interiors in Australian studios.

Critics characterized *Something Is Out There* as a cross between *The Hidden*, *Starman* and *Aliens*, with a dash of *Moonlighting*. Reviews were mixed. However, ratings for the mini-series,

which aired in May 1988, were stellar, lending support for the notion of continuing the concept as a full-fledged series.

Now the producers faced the challenge of somehow designing a show that wasn't too hard-core for the fans and could attract a broad audience. There was also the problem of how to follow through with the exciting promises the mini-series offered. Costs were prohibitive; Rick Baker's bills for creating the Xenomorph ran as high as $700,000. Perhaps for this reason, the network, according to story editor Paul Bernbaum, "didn't want the series to revolve around the Xenomorph, nor did it want us to do the 'monster of the week.' They wanted to focus on the relationship between Jack and T'Ara and get them involved in paranormal cases." So the pulpish hunting-the-alien theme was sidelined in favor of a *Moonlighting*-style relationship between Jack and T'Ara—much to viewers' dismay.

"Looking back," says Bernbaum, "I think if we'd stuck with the Xenomorph-vs.-the-World stories, we may have had a better shot at staying on the air. After the mini-series, it was what people expected and we didn't deliver it for them."

The series debuted in October of 1988, and while eight episodes were filmed, only six made the air.

"Our first show, 'Gladiator,' did very well. But after that, we just died. There was no interest in the show we were doing. Our ratings were so low at that point, NBC just decided to pull us off the schedule," says Bernbaum.

Joe Cortese and Maryam d'Abo played the leading roles. Bernbaum says, "I thought both Joe and Maryam were fine in the pilot. When we got to series, however, it just didn't seem to work out. What I remember most is they both tended to mumble so much. I could never understand what they were saying. [But] Joe and Maryam had some nice moments together."

Gregory Sierra played Police Lieutenant Maldonado, the only character on the show who recognized that T'Ara was from space and that Jack was helping her hunt for the killing machine that had been released from the mothership. "Any time Gregory was on screen as Jack's lieutenant was a plus," says Bernbaum. "He's just a terrific actor."

Bernbaum's memories of the show seem laden with disappointment and discontent. "I remember going to the set to tell one of our directors that dailies were weak, he was missing the point," he sighs. "He blew up and quit on the spot. Came back, though."

A running gag on the show was that every now and then, T'Ara did not understand Earthly customs and mores, despite Jack's exasperated attempts at explaining them. These moments added humor and social commentary to their relationship and hinted at the influence of the prime-time hit *Moonlighting*. However, Bernbaum says that in *Something Is Out There*, "any attempt at humor fell completely flat. I remember laughing out loud at the opening scene of Lupo's 'Gladiator,' where Jack tries to explain to T'Ara what a joke was. But on screen, it just died. We also used traditional, dramatic episodic directors who maybe didn't have the feel for this kind of show we could have used. We ... probably told the wrong type of stories that we needed to draw an audience."

Towards the end of the show, Bernbaum says, they "tried to make the show harder-edged, more science fiction. On a script level, I think 'The Keeper' was our best. Lupo, as usual, came up with a great story. I always enjoyed working with Frank Lupo, who is a certifiable genius in this business, as well as being a great guy, and very, very funny." In an effort to return the show to its intended direction, Bernbaum reveals, production began on a two-parter that brought back the Xenomorph. "We knew we had to do something different at this point, and were several days into prep with our director when NBC pulled the plug." The episode, written by Bernbaum and Burt Pearl, was never filmed.

Maryam d'Abo and Joe Cortese star in *Something Is Out There*, about a beautiful alien woman who joins forces with a Los Angeles cop to track down a murderous, shape-changing monster. Copyright 1988 NBC.

Joe Cortese, as the L.A. cop Jack Breslin, recalls the mini-series as "terrific" because it blended the gritty Los Angeles police life with the science fiction aspects of hunting and finding a shape-changing monster, plus a relationship with a female extraterrestrial. Playing Jack Breslin gave Cortese an opportunity to portray a hard-nosed, gritty cop with an edge of humor that came up in moments of high tension, complicated by an increasing attraction to T'Ara. Cortese once described his character as "a regular guy. A stumblebum cop. He's confused by the set-up. He's all hung up on why the Dodgers lost last night, things like that."

Today, Cortese remembers the show as a fun time because he was among friends. Maryam d'Abo was "very nice to work with," he says, and he particularly appreciated the opportunity to experience the makeup artistry of Rick Baker. "I also enjoyed working with Kim Delaney [in the mini-series]." As for actor George Dzundza, who played his partner, Frank Deleo, Cortese says, "I've known him for a long time from New York. It made [the project] doubly enjoyable."

As much as he enjoyed the work, however, Cortese has a confession to make: "I don't even like science fiction. I don't relate to it at all. I'm more into humans. Do I think there's an evil power out there? I look on the Xenomorph as the devil."

The network's desire to concentrate on the relationships instead of a monster-of-the-week format was a good idea, acknowledges Cortese, but "it didn't work! I wish the show worked, but it didn't. I guess they needed a combination of other things than the monster." Cortese suggests that "it should have been like *The Fugitive*," with the pair continuing to play cat-and-mouse with their prey. Cortese points out that there was a threat of the Xenomorph returning at the end of the mini-series when the mothership crash-landed in the Earth's ocean. He feels that might have boosted continued interest in the show.

In summary, Cortese says he's happy with the work. "I thought it was a good character for me, and I felt pretty good about it. It's too bad it didn't continue."

CAST NOTES

Joe Cortese (Officer Jack Breslin): Has done several films, including *Cat Squad* (1986) and *Cat Squad II: Python Wolf* (1988), about a terrorist-bashing counter-spy team.

Maryam d'Abo (T'Ara): Her most notable role prior to this show was in *The Living Daylights* (1987) with Timothy Dalton. D'Abo also appeared in *Master of the Game* (1984).

Gregory Sierra (Lt. Victor Maldonado): One of his most popular roles was as Chano, a cop of the Twelfth Precinct in *Barney Miller*.

EPISODE GUIDE

Something Is Out There (1988 TV mini-series, 4 hours)
When a jogger gets beaten brutally by an alien shapeshifter who's arrived on Earth, Officer Jack Breslin takes charge of the case. He encounters a woman who convinces him she's from outer space and is in pursuit of the Xenomorph. Together, they fight for their lives against the ruthless assassin on Earth. Wr: Frank Lupo Dir: Richard Colla.

Jack Breslin (Joe Cortese); T'Ara (Maryam D'Abo); Lt. Victor Maldonado (Gregory Sierra); Frank DeLeo (George Dzundza); Commissioner Estabrook (Robert Webber); Mandy Estabrook (Kim Delaney); Creature (Jack Bricker); Roger (Joseph Cali); Remar (John O'Hurley); Coroner (Earl Billings); Lisa Oliver (Anne Elizabeth Ramsay); Doorman (Hank Rolike); Valez (Daniel Moriarty); Maitre'd (Christopher Carroll); Jogger (Hope North); Arnie McKura (Mickey Jones); Prisoner Y-50 (Jack Bircher); Prisoner X-90 (Kristoffer Greaves); 1st officer (Robert Taylor); Prisoner #2 (David Jobling); Guard #1 (Ian Mortimer); Claire Riggs (Melanie Jones); Ron Cobb (Matthew Faison); Professor Dietrich (Ray Reinhardt); McReady (Michael Cutt); Kelly Simon (Lori Michaels); Andrew Brockhurst (Dean Scofield); Enriquez (Hector Mercado); TV Interviewer (Andi Chapman); Driver (Richard Burns); Passerby (Doug McHugh); Cabbie (Cal Gibson); Lab technician (Tyler Coppin); Harv (Roger Eagle); Also with John Putch, James Emory, Clive Rosengren, Jack Scalici.

Season Episodes

Gladiator
Stranded on Earth after her spaceship crash-landed into the ocean, T'Ara joins with Jack to set up a laboratory in the hope she can find a way to return home. Meanwhile, a heat- and fire-resistant vest has been stolen. T'Ara and Jack have to get it back before a psychotic killer uses it for misdeeds. Wr: Frank Lupo. Dir: Richard Colla.

Eddie Ringeman (Brian Thompson); Tina (Elena Stiteler); Eddie's ex-boss (Richard Portnow); Sally Boy (Angelo Tiffe); Angelo (Rocky Giordani); Dr. Wilcher (Gregory Itzin); Night nurse (Jeanne Mori); First officer (Dante Di Loreto); Night nurse (Kathleen Bailey); Blond (Linda Hoffman).

Don't Look Back
Investigating a murder, Jack meets the victim's daughter, who's being pursued by a killer. But the CIA demands Jack turn her over to them when they learn she's the result of telekinetic experiments. Wr: Burt Pearl. Dir: Richard Colla.

Torry (Jandi Swanson); Agent Simon (Dakin Matthews); Agent Winters (Richard Holden); Laura Davis (Cheryl Anderson); Mrs. Gardener (Kate Williamson); Agent Simon (Gary Sloan); Counselor (Susan Anders); Dr. Davis (Buddy Joe Hooker).

In His Own Image
An axe murderer escapes from an asylum and is determined to get revenge against the jury that put him away. Wr: Burt Pearl. Dir: Larry Shaw.

Julian/Andrew Pike (Mitchell Laurance); Sandy (Lise Hilboldt); Vincent Pike (J.E. Freeman); Donny (Lee Arenberg); Maxie (Ritch Brinkley); Horowitz (Gerald Hiken); Abe (Jack Murdoch); Guard (Ron Taylor).

Good Psychics Are Hard to Come By
When a boy is kidnapped, Jack becomes frustrated because he's always one step behind. He asks T'Ara for her help. Wr: Paul Bernbaum. Dir: Lyndon Chubbuck.

Alex Boyer (Steve Inwood); Chick Marelli (Gerald Castillo); Mickey (John Durbin); Young (John Doolittle); Charley Moore (Vito D'Ambrosio); Eric Young (Spencer Vrooman); Mrs. Young (Catherine McNeal); Anchor woman (Mary Hale); Reporter #1 (Joel Hershman); Reporter #2 (Jan Munroe); Patrolman Randolph (James Arnone); Pretty girl (Monique Gabrielle).

Night of the Visitors

A science fiction writer has written a book about his alien abduction. On reading the book, T'Ara says the information is consistent with a race known as the Zantoreans. She's convinced the author could be the lead she needs to return home. Wr: Christian Darren. Dir: James Darren.

Charles Calvin (Frederick Coffin); Ted Quinn (Nestor Serriano); Paula (Kitty Swink); Det. Buchalter (David Dunard); Dr. Howard Goff (Richard Fancy); Doctor (Eric Poppick); Lester (Matt O'Toole); Trish (Catherine Christianson); Grey (Dave Efron).

A Message from Mr. Cool

When attractive blonde women are being killed, the only link appears to be a ventriloquist's show. Jack finds out that the ventriloquist's father was killed and the murderer has been released from the hospital. Wr: Paul Bernbaum. Dir: Don Medford.

Ronny Traynor (Jay Johnson); Benjamin Kelsey (David Wilson); Dr. Harmon (Deborah May); Det. Buchalter (David Dunard); Officer Jameson (Charles Walker); Manager (Mark Drexler); Megan Carter (Mary Ann Dorward); Bartender (Stephen Landis); Receptionist (Marta Miller); Murphy (Gary Epper); Woman (Lessa Lee); Laughing woman #1 (Nikki Kollins); Laughing woman #2 (Debbie Young).

A Hearse of Another Color

Jack's cousin, a flaky guy who drives a hearse, calls him for help when he's lost a body from the casket. Jack and T'Ara soon become involved in a drug-smuggling operation. Wr: Paul Bernbaum Dir: Richard Colla.

Ricky (Tommy Hinkley); Mike Preston; Lora (Lisa Wilcox); Jimmy (Michael Margotta); Tony (John Del Regno); Mr. Mulligan (F. William Parker); Cindy (Beverleigh Banfield); Det. Dusty McFarlane (Al Pugliese); Manuel (Kevin Sifuentes); Bishop (Patrick Kilpatrick); Mrs. Lawrence (Patti Gallagher); Philip (Charlie Holliday); Teller #2 (Susan O'Sullivan).

The Keeper

Two kids at the beach find a canister with a hand attached to it. Jack and T'Ara learn that it's the area where the alien prison ship crash-landed, and it could be linked to the recent disappearances of several ships. The two are quickly put on the trail of an alien intelligence. Wr: Paul Bernbaum. Dir: Jorge Montesi.

Joey (Brandon Call); Mr. Stewall (Dennis Howard); Eddie Mizell (Sean Six); Chaney (Neil Barry); Cliff Burgess (Michael DeLuise); Walter Canfield (Hal Bokar); Daniel Burak (Terrance Evans); Sheriff Dowling (Thom McFadden); Rudy (M.C. Gainey); Leanne Healy (Joely Fisher); Mr. Farber (Dabbs Greer); Dr. Geller (Bill Smillie); Trevor (Eric Fry); Mrs. Dowling (Ann Gee Byrd); Little girl (Kaitlyn Walker).

Space: 1999

1975–1977

On September 13, 1999, the moon is blown out of Earth's orbit by a nuclear explosion. The 311 inhabitants of Moonbase Alpha, led by Commander John Koenig, head off into the far reaches of space, encountering aliens, monsters and other planets. Their goal: Find a way to return to Earth, or colonize another planet.

Cast: Commander John Koenig (Martin Landau); Dr. Helena Russell (Barbara Bain); Professor Victor Bergman (year 1) (Barry Morse); Paul Morrow (year 1) (Prentis Hancock); David Kano (year 1) (Clifton Jones); Sandra Benes (Zienia Merton); Dr. Mathias (Anton Phillips); Alan Carter (Nick Tate); Maya (year 2) (Catherine Schell); Tony Verdeschi (year 2) (Tony Anholt); Yasko (year 2) (Yasuko Nagazumi); Fraser (year 2) (John Hug); Voice of Moonbase computer (Barbara Kelly).

Created by: Gerry and Sylvia Anderson; *Executive Producer:* Gerry Anderson; *Producer:* Sylvia Anderson (year 1) Fred Freiberger (year 2); *Costume Design by:* Rudi Gernreich; *Special Effects by:* Brian Johnson; *Music by:* Barry Gray (year 1) and Derek Wadsworth (year 2); Syndicated/ITC; 60 minutes.

In the early 1970s, when Gerry Anderson was hard at work on *UFO* and another series, *The Protectors*, he was called into the offices of ATV for a meeting with owner Lord Lew Grade. Grade asked Anderson for a television series. He didn't want a continuation of *UFO*; he wanted something new. It could not be just any other series. It had to be big. Grade offered seven million dollars for a show aimed at the American market. And here was the kicker: The story had to take place anywhere but on Earth! Space was the ticket to success.

When an excited Anderson left the office, it speedily dawned on him that such a series had to be done totally from scratch, meaning costumes, sets, models—everything.

It was Abe Mandell, president of ITC, who had pitched the idea of a spectacular, blockbuster British series to the American market, and who worked with the Andersons on creating that show. Legend has it that while he and Gerry Anderson were discussing what the concept was going to be, Anderson had quipped, "We'll blow up the Earth," but Mandell found that to be "too insecure" for Americans. In reply, Anderson said, "Okay, we'll blow up the moon." That rang the bells in Mandell's brain, and off they went.

Not well known is that *Space: 1999*'s working title, for several months, was *Menace in Space*.

Gerry Anderson refined his suggestion to Abe Mandell: "What happens if the moon breaks orbit around Earth, and if a moonbase full of people on it have to survive every week while they're flung into the dark ravages of space?"

Anderson and his wife, Sylvia, were no strangers to science fiction. They had created and produced a string of successful puppet (or Super Marionation) shows such as *Captain Scarlet, Stingray*, and *Thunderbirds* prior to *UFO*. Sylvia Anderson enjoyed the new challenge of *Space: 1999*. As co-creator and producer of the first season, she "had a big hand in the futuristic look of the wardrobe and general design," she says, adding proudly, "I felt that the look of the show was above-average for a TV production."

Americans Martin Landau and Barbara Bain, the husband-and-wife team made famous in *Mission: Impossible*, signed on as Commander John Koenig and Dr. Helena Russell. Together, they would lead the men and women of Moonbase Alpha through space. A stable of British actors provided the supporting cast. Amazingly, other casting permutations were considered. "During our trip to Hollywood in the setting up of the show, we did indeed, see, among many others, Robert Culp, who I personally felt would be a more interesting lead than Martin Landau,"says Sylvia Anderson. "Katharine Ross was one of the names put forward, but it was a decision by the financiers to cast the Landaus as a more commercial piece of casting."

Space: 1999 is often regarded as England's answer to *Star Trek*. In both shows, the main characters comprised a highly advanced group engaging in adventures from one central base, fighting hostile aliens and discovering new planets every week. Also, both shows can be referred to as "space operas," enhanced by state-of-the-art special effects. However, Sylvia Anderson continues to believe that *Star Trek* did not play any part in

the creation or planning of *Space: 1999*. "The media hype in the States for *Star Trek* may have got in the way of our program's identity, but that did not apply in the U.K," she says.

The mid-seventies was a daring age to be doing big-budgeted science fiction. At that time, the genre was considered bad business and did not have the respect it enjoys today. Yet, "we felt in late 1973, when we picked up and left for England to do *Space: 1999*, that it was a perfect time for a science fiction show," says star Martin Landau. "I felt it in my bones, that this type of entertainment format was about to be popular in the near future. Mind you, *Star Wars* was not on the horizon yet ... and *Star Trek* had not been at all successful during its network run."

Landau remembers the Andersons as very creative people who complemented each other well. "Sylvia was a charming and gregarious person, always ready for a good laugh, but very bright and serious when necessary. Gerry was more introspective, excepting when he had a couple of drinks, after work, when he'd open up a bit. He, too, was very bright, often very studious, and was much quicker to rise to anger than his wife."

Unbeknownst to the stars, the Andersons' collaboration was about to end. Landau says, "Although things must have been getting somewhat strained at home, they never gave us an indication during that entire first year of filming at Pinewood that their marriage was about to break apart. Considering the amount of time we spent at the studio with them, it was quite amazing, to say the least!

"When it came time to do production on the second season," says Landau, "Sylvia's absence was very strongly felt by me, as I liked dealing with her openness and her sensibilities. I found it much harder getting through to our new American producer, Freddie Freiberger, who now had settled into her office. He had much less respect for actors and their input and contribution. I'd say, 'Koenig wouldn't do that!' referring to a script in which the Alphans, on Koenig's orders, execute a preemptive strike at a possible foe. 'It's not within his character, nor his style.' Fred would just shrug and say, 'It doesn't matter, it's a good script and the audience won't notice if it's inconsistent with his character.' 'Of course they will!' I'd argue, for hours and hours ... usually losing the battle."

Landau goes on to say that often there wasn't time to fix script problems that were held up in writing stages, so they would receive pages or changes very late into shooting. Modifications were sometimes possible on the stage, but, "It was never easy," he sighs.

Fred Freiberger says he got involved with producing *Space: 1999* in the second season because of an earlier discussion with the Andersons about working on *UFO*. When Sylvia decided to bow from her duties for the second season, Gerry Anderson called him again.

Freiberger's first challenge was deciding what to wear for the interview. "I have lousy taste in clothes," he admits. "My wife dresses me in a sense—she inspects me. So, she dressed me for this interview with Gerry. I got a callback and he said, 'Would you be able to go to England for four weeks? We'd love you to come over. You've got the job.' So I said to my wife, 'Let's take a chance.' I asked Gerry, 'How did I get it? I'm the same guy you interviewed for *UFO*.' And he said that his secretary was impressed by how well color-coordinated my clothes were. So, I didn't get the *Space: 1999* job because of my experience or my charm or anything—I got the job because I was color-coordinated!"

Freiberger says he had a good time with Gerry Anderson and has a lot of respect for him. Anderson directed Freiberger to "Americanize" the show to bolster its appeal in the United States. And Freiberger was given the reins to do whatever he wanted.

"That was very refreshing," says Freiberger. "There were no studios, no networks; Gerry gave me carte blanche on the whole thing. So we started putting things together. Lord Lew Grade said, 'You do it your way.' So we had three weeks to do it. And we screened the first-year episodes and made suggestions." Freiberger contends the show needed resuscitation and was near collapsing at that stage. "Before I was offered the series, it was offered to [American producer] Allan Balter. According to Allan, Abe Mandell asked for suggestions on how to improve the show. Allan said, 'Fire Marty Landau and Barbara Bain.' When I arrived in England, Mandell suggested that I keep Marty and Barbara in the background and go heavy with the other characters. I said, 'Either fire them or let me handle them as stars.' He let me handle them as stars."

This decision still didn't ensure that *Space: 1999* would see a second year. "After three weeks, it was very shaky, and they were still undecided about the show's future. I wanted to leave and return to the U.S. My wife said, 'Let's stay another

week and see.' I looked at the show again and said to Gerry, 'Let me try to do something.' I wrote an analysis of what was wrong with the show, and I also introduced the new character, Maya—an alien who could transform into different life forms. That sold it. We got the go-ahead to do 24 episodes."

When Gerry Anderson asked him to analyze the first year, Freiberger charged that "there was no emotion in the show. Also, the [Moonbase Command Center] looked like a used living room." He observed that stories were nonexistent and characters were just standing around talking. He wanted emotion, action and humor.

When it came to characters, Freiberger wanted specific changes. "I said, 'If you're going to have a professor, then have a young kid with a beard in there, as the professor,'" says Freiberger. "[Anderson and Lord Grade] were very nervous about this change, and they brought in a good-looking kid, Tony Anholt, to bring in some romantic situations."

Originally, Teresa (*Get Christie Love*) Graves was sought for the role of Maya, but she was not available. Someone brought Catherine Schell to Freiberger's attention. Schell was not unknown to the production of the show. She had earlier guested in the episode 'Guardian of Piri.'

"Catherine Schell was a lovely, lovely girl. I wanted her to transform into a leopard. But they were afraid something like a panther would rip everybody apart, so they used a lion, which I thought was the wrong kind of animal."

In Barbara Bain, Freiberger thought he had found the light comedy relief he was looking for. "I had never met her, but I was familiar with her work. I realized she had a fine sense of humor, so I tried to do some comedy stuff for them and put some more humor into the series. And more action. They kept saying, 'Sell the American market!' That's what we tried to do. We streamlined the Moonbase, cut it way down." Freiberger's dedication to aiming at the North American market went so far as to make sure all signs on the base were spelled in the American, not the British, style.

In a drastic cast change, Barry Morse went out as the older Professor Bergman and Tony Anholt came in as the younger first officer, Tony Verdeschi. Despite Freiberger's suggestion regarding a young actor, the reason for this change wasn't as much a creative decision as a business one: Morse's agent asked for more money, during a time when producers were trying to keep tight reins on the show's budget.

The *Eagle* spacecraft blasts off from the Earth's moon as it careens throughout the cosmos with inhabitants of the moonbase Alpha aboard as passengers. Copyright 1975 ITC.

"Gerry was really reluctant to fire anybody," says Freiberger. "We called Martin and Barbara in California, and they were anxious to return. But, of course, everybody wanted raises. We said, 'Look, we can't raise anybody—we're lucky if we can get this show on!' We really wanted a young person in place of the professor, but Gerry felt terrible about letting anyone go."

When the show's renewal was announcd, all participating performers assumed they would return to work. "Barry's agent called and said, 'We want so much more.' I said to Gerry, 'This agent isn't saying that he has to go back and check with Barry. He's laying it on the line,'" recounts Freiberger. "'Now, if it's not us making the decision, and we can't afford it, let's just say no, and then we're out of this.' So we just said no to the agent, that it wasn't in our budget. And we hired Tony."

But Morse's agent called back and said, "We'll take the money that was there." But it was too late—Anholt had already been hired.

"You feel terrible about not using an actor again, but that's a case where an agent made a dumb mistake," says Freiberger. "I consider myself a writer, and a writer will say to his agent, 'Get me 20 million dollars for the deal, but don't screw it up. If it comes back to 10 million, I'll take it if I have to.' So, that was unfortunate. I have great respect for his acting ability. Gerry would have gone with Barry except for this mistake."

Nick Tate, who played *Eagle* pilot Alan Carter, almost got the ax, too. ITC wanted him out, but Freiberger refused.

As the show progressed through its second season, its popularity grew. In fact, says Freiberger, so well known did the show get during the heyday of its run that the public got to know him by name. He would walk through English Customs and an agent would recognize him. "The fans were amazing. They knew more about it than I did." It was a whole life for a lot of people, he says.

Sylvia Anderson says she is "surprised about the media criticism that stories in the first [season] were hard to follow. I would like to think that they were reasonably intelligent stories and therefore required a little more depth to the subject." However, Anderson notes that "some of the interesting support cast were not given sufficient opportunities to develop their characters" and that the show "worked better when subsidiary characters were given a little more action than merely walking several paces behind the lead."

Martin Landau actually prefers the first season episodes, citing more interesting, intriguing scripts and plot conventions. ("The Black Sun" and "War Games" remain favorites.) The second season, he charges, was more of a comic strip show. "I felt if we had stayed on the direction of the first season, we might've stayed on for several more years. But changes that came in with Freiberger changed the entire essence of the series."

Among his co-stars on the show, both first and second season, Landau points to Nick Tate as one "who became a very good friend of mine. He now lives in Hollywood with his wife and family." They speak on the phone occasionally and get together for lunch every few years. Catherine Schell, whom a television critic once called "the only woman who looked sexy in sideburns," often visits the U.S. and usually gives Landau a call when she's in Los Angeles.

For Barry Morse, so regrettably deposed after the first season, Landau has nothing but the highest praise. "Barry is a wonderful man. Kind, gentle, intelligent. He was born in the East End of London, which means he spoke like a Cockney when he was growing up. He worked like hell to get rid of that heavy dialect. He has since become a Canadian citizen. The English think he's English, Canadians think he's Canadian and, yes, Americans who know him from *The Fugitive* think he's one of us. Amazing, considering his handicap in having a thick, gutteral Cockney accent as a kid. Barry's brother, a London law enforcement officer, visited the set one day. I chatted with him and could barely understand him, as his accent was so thick. It allowed me to understand what Barry had overcome. Mind you, he can still *do* a great Cockney character should he have reason to. Barry Morse is one of the sweetest, gentlest souls in the world ... and one hell of an *actor!*"

Landau adds that he was quite close to Tony Anholt during filming but has not seen him for 15 years. "I liked Tony a lot. Same with Prentis Hancock. I haven't seen him in years. Barry Morse was here in Hollywood a few years ago at a *Space: 1999* convention. We saw each other, hugged, laughed, and chatted for a few hours."

Landau says that the United States is the only country in the world where *Space: 1999* did not go network. The show has proven to be more popular overseas than in the United States.

Director Ray Austin recalls his days with *Space: 1999* quite fondly: "I was very proud of my work on *Space: 1999*. It was a fun show to do at a fun studio. It's my favorite studio in the world," says Austin of Pinewood studios, where the show was filmed. Austin (who has most recently spent his time with Family Channel's *Zorro* and the syndicated series *Highlander—The Series*) felt that the show's innovation was the attempt to attract a prime-time American audience. Although *The Avengers*, another British show on which Austin worked extensively, at one point reached a worldwide audience of about 100 countries, the episodes were always aired late at night. *Space: 1999* was specifically for prime-time audiences.

Austin found Gerry Anderson to be a very professional and experienced producer. "He worked very hard to get *Space: 1999* made in England, because when he first showed it, they wanted to make it in America. They knew more about science fiction and wanted to go for it over there like they had with *Star Trek*. [Anderson] was very knowledgable on the subject, and he's a very good storyteller. Then, we had an American scripter, Fred Freiberger—he was a genius with scripts."

Austin says he thinks he was the first to develop an innovative technique for filming spacesuited astronauts walking on the sands of the moon. "We would shoot that in high speed, at 72 frames per second, and we did it two, three or four times to get it right," says Austin. Shooting at high speed gave the actors' movements a slow-motion, floating quality when the film was shown at normal speed. The purpose was to simulate the lower gravity on the moon. No wire work was ever involved. Even with actors jumping up and down in those bulky, plastic suits, the high speed was successful in getting the illusion across.

"It really looked very good," says Austin, "although they looked ridiculous running across the soundstage bouncing up in the air. It was very peculiar until you realized how it would work."

Austin remembers that the spacesuits were very hot and uncomfortable for the actors, with no ventilation. "Everybody suffered from the heat, every day, even in the winter, in those things," he chuckles. "They had to take the helmet off or turn the flap up whenever they had the chance. A take on film would be about two or three minutes; then they'd lift it up and they could breathe again. They could still breathe, but it was just very uncomfortable."

For Austin, the most memorable shoot on *Space: 1999* was the episode "Collision Course," with guest star Margaret Leighton. "Margaret's a friend of mine. She knew she was dying. I shot, I think, 15 pages in two days with her, which was unheard of. 'You'd better get [this shot], because I'm not going to last long...,' she said near the end of shooting. Sure enough, we did, and she died a few days later. She was very good. She sat on the throne all the time. She couldn't move, so we had to put her on a wheelchair."

Martin Landau echoes Austin's fondness for Leighton. "Margaret was an exceptionally talented actress, having been one of Laurence Olivier's leading ladies when quite young in several Shakespearean productions," he recalls. However, Landau disagrees with Ray Austin's memory, saying that Leighton did not die "a few days later" but eight or nine months after working with him. "Her husband, Michael Wilding, who at one time had been married to Elizabeth Taylor, died a year or so after Maggie did. I visited them in the countryside outside of London one time after she'd guested on the show. Michael was very grateful that I'd looked after her on the set and run the lines with her, as she found all the science fiction jargon a bit difficult to learn, insisting that it was just a lot of gobbledy-gook and ... that she hadn't a clue as to what it was she was saying. I liked her a lot. She was a real trouper, especially in her condition."

Asked to distinguish between the two seasons of the show, since he directed seven of the first season and two of the second, Austin says, "I liked the first season better. I thought the stories were more identifiable, and you could do more things with them."

Aside from state-of-the-art British special effects, to add futuristic flavor and interesting visuals, costumes were specially created by a top-ranking designer, Rudi Gernreich (now deceased), with a unisex concept. "The sleeve allowed one to recognize in what department any Moonbase Alpha inhabitant worked," says Landau. "Barbara's sleeve was white (medical); Main Mission workers, red; pilots, yellow; and so on. Mine was a charcoal grey, with a grey raised collar, as commander and chief officer, the only one of its kind on the base. The costumes were

changed the second year, and modified slightly, for economic reasons and expediency."

During the second year, says Landau, more colorful outerwear was introduced to give the show a greater variety of color. Someone at ITC's New York office, Landau remembers, thought the show looked too drab in its overall beige color scheme in the first season. Landau regretted the changes. "I loved the original look from an artistic and production design point of view. I felt it unique and original, and unlike anything else on the air, in the best artistic sense, but that was another battle I lost."

Austin notes that the show's budget was allocated very liberally on art and set decoration. "Everything was built on platforms so all the parts could be movable," he says. "And the ship was movable, so you could dismantle the ship entirely to new clampings and new sections."

The wild walls and pieces came in very handy when the story asked for multiple Eagle ships. Mixing and matching different pieces of the same set gave an illusion of many space vehicles.

"It was ... quite a revolution for the stage," says Austin, who, as a director, probably appreciated the flexibility for camera angles. The only drawback was that the angles on the Eagles were usually from one side only. "A lot of visitors in the industry used to come to see those sets."

The cancellation of *Space: 1999* was not a result of the usual ratings game, as the show was syndicated in the U.S. "Lord Lew Grade, producer and head of ITC Entertainment, had ventured into feature films," explains Martin Landau. Having produced some highly budgeted features like *Raise the Titanic!* (1980), "he found himself with cash flow problems. He needed to advertise and market these big theatrical ventures, and his ad budget, it seems, was about the *same* amount that was needed to produce another season of *Space: 1999*, and even though all parties involved [agreed that] another season would enhance the value of the show in syndication and other areas as a 72-hour package ... the plug was pulled on our show so he could effectively merchandise the features." And Landau sighs that after the show was out of production, "all the features were disastrous. All failed dismally at the box office. That period in ITC's history was a blemish. As a result of all this, Grade was deposed as head of the company (ATV and ITC) and new people took charge."

Space: 1999, says Landau, "might have gone

for at least another season," had ITC's money held out and had "these shenanigans not gone on."

CAST NOTES

Martin Landau (Commander John Koenig): Born 1928. Landau is perhaps best known for his work on *Mission: Impossible* as Rollin Hand, master of disguises. Most recently he's been acclaimed with Oscar supporting actor nominations for roles in *Tucker: A Man and His Dream* (1988) and *Crimes and Misdemeanors* (1989). Recently, he completed roles in the feature *Intersection* (1993) and the TV movie *12:01* (1993) for Fox Television. He won an Oscar for his portrayal of Bela Lugosi in the film *Ed Wood* (1994).

Barbara Bain (Dr. Helena Russell): Born 1931. The former wife of Martin Landau, Bain starred as Cinnamon in *Mission: Impossible* from 1966 to 1969, earning three consecutive Emmys for her work on that show. Prior to *Mission*, she appeared in *Richard Diamond, Private Detective* (1959) as Karen Wells.

Barry Morse (Professor Victor Bergman): Born in London in 1919, Morse become known as Lt. Gerard of *The Fugitive* fame from 1963 to 1967. He continues acting on stage in England and Canada. One of Morse's most visible appearances lately was a guest shot on William Shatner's TV movie adaptation of his novel *TekWar* (1994).

Catherine Schell (Maya): Born 1946. An accomplished Swiss actress, Schell worked with Peter Sellers in *The Return of the Pink Panther* (1975) and much later in *The Return of the Saint* with Ian Ogilvy.

Prentis Hancock (Paul Morrow): Television credits include *Return of the Saint*, *Doctor Who* ("Planet of Evil") *Danger UXB*, *Armchair Theatre* and *Secret Army*. Film appearances include *39 Steps* (1978) and *The Nativity* (1978).

EPISODE GUIDE

Season 1: 1975-76

Breakaway

As Commander Koenig arrives on Moonbase Alpha ready to prepare a deep space probe, a nuclear blast occurs on the far side of the moon. The moon is ripped from Earth's orbit and into the blackness of space. Wr: George Bellak. Dir: Lee H. Katzin.

Commissioner Simmonds (Roy Dotrice); Commander Gorski (Philip Madoc); Ouma (Lon Satton); Collins (Eric Carte).

Earthbound

An alien spaceship lands on the moon, and the captain says their destination is Earth. Commander Simmonds, who was accidentally on the moon during its breakaway, wants to get back in a hurry. Wr: Anthony Terpiloff. Dir: Charles Crichton.

Simmonds (Roy Dotrice); Zandor (Christopher Lee).

Dragon's Domain

The mythical story of deep space astronaut Tony Cellini's encounter with a terrifying monster aboard a spaceship graveyard gets the test when the moon drifts into the same space coordinates. Wr: Christopher Penhold. Dir: Charles Crichton.

Cellini (Gianni Garko); Commissioner Dixon (Douglas Wilmer); Dr. Monique Fauchere (Barbara Kellermann); Dr. King (Michael Sheard); Dr. Mackie (Susan Jameson).

Death's Other Dominion

Discovering an iced planet, the Alphans are invited by its inhabitants to share in an immortal life with members of a space expedition from 1986. Wr: Anthony Terpiloff and Elizabeth Burrows. Dir: Charles Crichton.

Rowland (Brian Blessed); Jack Turner (John Shrapnel); Freda (Mary Miller).

The Testament of Arkadia

The moon halts in space. Traveling to the nearby planet Arkadia, Koenig discovers that this may very well be the planet from which Earth life came. Complicating matters, some Alphans want to colonize there. Wr: Johnny Byrne. Dir: David Tomblin.

Luke Ferro (Orso Maria Guerrini); Anna Davis (Lisa Harrow).

The Troubled Spirit

A botanist is banned from continuing his experiments. But he's haunted by a ghost who wants to avenge a death that has not yet happened. Wr: Johnny Byrne. Dir: Ray Austin.

Dan Mateo (Giancarlo Prette); Dr. James Warren (Anthony Nicholls); Laura Adams (Hilary Dwyer).

Matter of Life and Death

Helena's husband, believed dead from years before, appears and warns everyone that the planet approaching is made of anti-matter. Wr: Art Wallace, Johnny Byrne. Dir: Charles Crichton.

Lee (Richard Johnson); Parks (Stuart Damon).

Force of Life

A technician is possessed by an alien force craving heat. Everything he touches becomes frozen. In order to destroy him, Alphans must deprive him of heat and light. Wr: Johnny Byrne. Dir: David Tomblin.

Anton Zoref (Ian McShane); Eva Zoref (Gay Hamilton); Mark Dominix (John Hamill); Jane (Eva Rueber-Staier).

Alpha Child

After the first birth on Alpha, it's discovered that the child ages rapidly and is an alien escaping extinction by taking over other people's bodies. Wr: Christopher Penfold. Dir: Ray Austin.

Cynthia/Rena (Cyd Hayman); Jarak (Julian Glover); Jackie (Wayne Brooks).

Another Time, Another Place

A weird accident creates duplicates of the moon. The Alphans encounter a duplicate moon orbiting the Earth again and confront their future selves. Wr: Johnny Byrne. Dir: David Tomblin.

Regina Kesslan (Judy Geeson).

The Black Sun

A collision course with a black sun is imminent. The Alphans' only hope for survival is in Professor Bergman's force field. Wr: David Weir. Dir: Lee H. Katzin.

Ryan (Paul Jones); Smitty (Jon Laurimore).

Guardian of Piri

A beautiful woman offers a peaceful, idyllic life on a planet, but Commander Koenig is skeptical. Wr: Christopher Penhold. Dir: Charles Crichton.

Guardian (Catherine Schell); Irving (Michael Culver); Davis (John Lee-Barber); Johnson (James Fagan).

The Last Sunset

A planet holds the prospect of a new Eden for everyone on Moonbase Alpha, but hopes are dashed when a new alien life appears. Wr: Christopher Penhold. Dir: Charles Crichton.

None.

The Last Enemy

The moon drifts into a war between two planets, and Alphans position themselves as mediators for a ceasefire before the moon gets in the way. Wr: Bob Kellett. Dir: Bob Kellett.

Dione (Caroline Mortimer); Talos (Kevin Stoney); Theia (Maxine Audley).

End of Eternity

When Koenig accidentally frees an immortal, psychopathic killer, he must risk his own life to defeat him. Wr: Johnny Byrne. Dir: Ray Austin.

Balor (Peter Bowles); Baxter (Jim Smilie).

Space Brain

When a space entity takes over the mind of a crewman, an explosives-laden Eagle aimed right at the entity seems to be the only solution—but the risks are high. Wr: Christopher Penhold. Dir: Charles Crichton.

Kelly (Shane Rimmer); Wayland (Derek Anders); Melita (Carl Romanelli).

Voyagers Return

When Moonbase Alpha discovers an old Voyager probe, it is emitting deadly radiation. Koenig wants to destroy it, but Bergman wants to salvage the information from it. Wr: Johnny Byrne. Dir: Bob Kellett.

Linden (Jeremy Kemp); Jim Haines (Barry Stoke); Aachon (Alex Scott); Abrams (Lawrence Trimble).

War Games

The Alphans are under attack and 129 people are dead. The base is no longer habitable. Koenig and Russell go to the enemy planet to seek terms and a new life. Wr: Christopher Penfold. Dir: Charles Crichton.

Alien man (Anthony Valentine); Alien woman (Isla Blair).

The Infernal Machine

A living machine and an aged companion arrive on Alpha. When the companion dies, the machine demands that Koenig and Helena thereafter become its lifelong companions. Wr: Anthony Terpiloff and Elizabeth Burrows. Dir: David Tomblin.

Companion (Leo McKern); Winters (Gary Waldhorn).

The Full Circle

Two Eagle crews accidentally enter a time warp, enter the Cro-Magnon period and become separated. They must find each other and a way back to the moon. Wr: Jesse Lasky, Jr., and Pat Silver. Dir: Bob Kellett.

Spearman (Oliver Cotton).

Missing Link

Injured in an Eagle crash, Koenig has been snatched in time and space to a planet where an anthropologist studies him, while the anthropologist's daughter falls in love with him. Wr: Edward Di Lorenzo. Dir: Ray Austin.

Raan (Peter Cushing); Vana (Joanna Dunham).

Ring Around the Moon

An ages-old probe imprisons Alpha, and Helena is an unwilling captive. To free everyone, Koenig must convince the probe its home planet is dead. Wr: Edward Di Lorenzo. Dir: Ray Austin.

Ted Clifford (Max Faulkner).

Collison Course

On a collision course with the planet Astheria, Bergman suggests placing a series of mines in space to avoid the terrible impact. But Arra, the planetary leader, insists they do nothing, in order to fulfill a prophecy. Wr: Anthony Terpiloff. Dir: Ray Austin.

Arra (Margaret Leighton).

Mission of the Darians

Responding to a distress call, Alphans find a spaceship that has been drifting through space for 900 years. Its survivors have reverted to cannibalism. Wr: Johnny Byrne. Dir: Ray Austin.

Kara (Joan Collins); High priest (Aubrey Morris);

Neman (Dennis Burgess); Hadin (Robert Russell); Lowry (Paul Antrim).

Season 2: 1976-77

The Metamorph
When an evil alien scientist covets the brains of Alphans to restore the biological computers that run his civilization, his daughter, Maya, helps them escape. Wr: Johnny Byrne. Dir: Charles Crichton.

Mentor (Brian Blessed); Annette Fraser (Anouska Hempel); Ray Torens (Nick Brimble); Petrov (Peter Porteous).

All That Glisters
The moonbase is attacked by deadly, telepathic, teleporting rocks who are in desperate need for water. Wr: Keith Miles. Dir: Ray Austin.

Dave O'Reilly (Patrick Mower).

The Exiles
Alphans find two cylinders floating in space. Inside, they find young aliens who apparently are killers and who want to return to their home planet. Wr: Donald James. Dir: Ray Austin.

Cantar (Peter Duncan); Zova (Stacy Dorning); Mirella (Margaret Inglis).

Journey to Where
Alphans receive a message from Earth's future and have an offer to return home via a transference device. But when Koenig, Alan and Helena jump in, they're transported to 1339 Scotland, where barbarians think they're plague carriers. Wr: Donald James. Dir: Tom Clegg.

Dr. Logan (Freddie Jones); Carla (Isla Blair); MacDonald (Roger Bizley); Dr. Ben Vincent (Jeffrey Kissoon); Jackson (Laurence Harrington).

The Mark of Archanon
Deep within the moon lie two aliens in suspended animation. But when one of them revives, a medical emergency affecting all Alpha erupts. Wr: Lew Schwartz. Dir: Charles Crichton.

Pasc (John Standing); Etrec (Michael Gallagher); Maruna (Veronica Lang); Dr. Nunez (Raul Newney); Carson (Anthony Forrest); Johnson (John Alkin).

One Moment of Humanity
Helena and Tony are kidnapped by an alien who wants to use their emotional makeup as a model for a race of androids so the instinct to kill can be taught. Wr: Tony Barwick. Dir: Charles Crichton.

Zamara (Billie Whitelaw); Zarl (Leigh Lawson); Number Eight (Geoffrey Bayldon); Coreographer (Lionel Blair).

The Rules of Luton
When the Alphans go berry picking on an alien planet, the judges of Luton declare them murderers and pit Koenig and Maya against three powerful alien beings. Wr: Charles Woodgrove (Fred Freiberger). Dir: Val Guest.

"Strong" (David Jackson); "Transporter" (Godfrey James); "Invisible" (Roy Marsden).

The Taybor
An interstellar slave trader offers the Alphans a ride home via a jump-ship drive device in exchange for Maya. Wr: Thom Keyes. Dir: Bob Brooks.

Taybor (Willoughby Goddard); Arkaren (Laraine Humphreys); Slatternly woman (Rita Webb); Andrews (Mel Taylor).

The Beta Cloud
A gigantic space cloud attacks Moonbase Alpha. It's impervious to laser fire and seems impossible to destroy until Maya realizes it's a robot. Wr: Charles Woodgrove (Fred Freiberger). Dir: Robert Lynn.

Creature (Dave Prowse); Space animals (Albin Pahernik).

Brian the Brain
A super-robot from an early space probe kidnaps Koenig and Helena, but Tony and Maya mount a rescue mission. Wr: Jack Ronder. Dir: Kevin Connor.

Capt. Michaels (Bernard Cribbins); Brian/Robot (Michael Sharvill-Martin); Operative (Annie Lambert).

The A-B Chrysalis
A powerful energy beam is projected from a planet, pummeling the moon, and when Alphans investigate they realize it is a planetary defense system. Wr: Tony Barwick. Dir: Val Guest.

A (Ina Skriver); B (Sarah Douglas); Sphere voice (Robert Rietty).

The Catacombs of the Moon
An engineer has visions of Moonbase Alpha's destruction, and as Dr. Russell fights to save his life, fire breaks out. Wr: Anthony Terpiloff. Dir: Robert Lynn.

Osgood (James Laurenson); Michelle (Pamela Stephenson); Engineer (Lloyd McGuire); Engineer (Saul Reichlin); Nurse (Karen Ford).

Seed of Destruction
Inside an alien asteroid, an evil Koenig is created and returns to Alpha with seeds to use the moon's energy to restore life to the asteroid. Wr: John Goldsmith. Dir: Kevin Connor.

Dr. Vincent (Jeffrey Kissoon).

Space Warp
The moon falls into a space warp. Koenig and Tony, left behind in an Eagle, desperately seek the way home. Meanwhile, on the base, Maya's sick, and her transforming powers have gone wild. Wr: Charles Woodgrove (Fred Freiberger). Dir: Peter Medak.

Security guard (Tony Osoba); Petrov (Peter Porteous).

New Adam, New Eve
An impressive, powerful alien comes on Moonbase Alpha and declares himself as the creator offering a new Eden. He appoints Koenig, Helena, Tony and

Maya as the new Adams and Eves. Wr: Terence Feely. Dir: Charles Crichton.

Magus (Guy Rolfe); Humanoid (Bernard Kay); Beautiful girl (Barbara Wise).

A Matter of Balance

The keeper of an alien temple wants to replace members of Moonbase Alpha with members of his own race. Wr: Pip and Jane Baker. Dir: Charles Crichton.

Shermeen (Lynne Frederick); Vindrus (Stuart Wilson); Eddie Collins (Nicholas Campbell).

The Bringers of Wonder, Part 1

A spaceship from Earth arrives on the moon and brings old friends of the Alphans. But Koenig sees them as horrifying aliens waiting to take over. Wr: Terence Feely. Dir: Tom Clegg.

Guido (Stuart Damon); Jack Bartlett (Jeremy Young); Joe Ehrlich (Drewe Henley); Louisa (Cher Cameron); Sandstrom (Earl Robinson); Dr. Shaw (Patrick Westwood); Peter Rockwell (Nicholas Young); Lizard animal (Albin Pahernik).

The Bringers of Wonder, Part 2

With no one believing him, Koenig takes desperate measures to convince everyone on Alpha that the friends from Earth are not who they say they are. Wr: Terence Feely. Dir: Tom Clegg.

Same cast as Part 1.

The Lambda Factor

A cosmic cloud transforms one of the women into a megalomaniac who attains strange super-powers. Wr: Terrance Dicks. Dir: Charles Crichton.

Carolyn Powell (Deborah Fallender); Mark Sanders (Jess Conrad); George Crato (Anthony Stamboulieh); Carl Renton (Michael Walker); Peter Garforth (Gregory de Polnay); Sally Martin (Lydia Lisle).

Devil's Planet (aka Devil's Moon)

Commander Koenig is captured and held by a race of cat women in a penal colony. Wr: Michael Winder. Dir: Tom Clegg.

Elizia (Hildegard Neil); Crael (Roy Marsden); Blake Maine (Michael Dickinson); Sares (Cassandra Harris); Interrogator (Dora Reisser).

Dorzak

An evil criminal from Maya's home planet catches up with the Alphans and threatens destruction. Wr: Christopher Penhold. Dir: Val Guest.

Dorzak (Lee Montague); Sahala (Jill Townsend); Yesta (Kathryn Leigh Scott).

The Seance Spectre

Again, the moon is on a collision course with a planet. Wr: Donald James. Dir: Peter Medak.

Sanderson (Ken Hutchinson); Eva (Carolyn Seymour); Cernik (Nigel Pegram); Sevens (James Snell).

Immunity Syndrome

Exploring another planet, a reconnaissance team finds a being composed of blinding light and sound. Any efforts to communicate result in insanity. Wr: Johnny Byrne. Dir: Bob Brooks.

Zoran (Nadim Swalha); Joe Lustig (Roy Boyd); Travis (Karl Held); Voice (Hal Galili).

The Dorcons

A huge spaceship appears above the moon. The ship's crew demand Maya be given to them, as they believe she can give them immortality. Refusing to turn her over, the base is attacked. Wr: Johnny Byrne. Dir: Tom Clegg.

Archon (Patrick Troughton); Varda (Ann Firbank); Malic (Gerry Sundquist); Alibe (Alibe Parsons); Medical officer (Hazel McBride).

(The Amazing) Spiderman

April 1978–July 1979

College student Peter Parker, bitten by a radioactive spider, becomes endowed with strange powers. He can climb walls, and he has heightened senses of danger as well as super agility and strength. Parker's photographer job at the Daily Bugle *newspaper allows him to fight crime as Spiderman.*

Cast: Peter Parker (Nicholas Hammond); J. Jonah Jameson (pilot) (David White); J. Jonah Jameson (Robert F. Simon); Rita (Chip Fields); Captain Barbera (year 1) (Michael Pataki); Julie Masters (year 2) (Ellen Bry).

Spiderman created by: Stan Lee; *Executive Producers:* Charles Fries, Daniel Goodman; *Producers:* Robert Janes, Ron Satlof (year 1), Arnold F. Turner (year 2); *Supervising Producer:* Lionel E. Siegel;

Theme and Music: Stu Phillips (year 1) Dana Kaproff (year 2); *2nd Unit and Stunt Coordinator:* Fred Waugh; CBS/Fries Entertainment; 60 minutes.

During the filming of the *Spiderman* two-part episode "The Deadly Dust," stuntman Fred Waugh, as our intrepid superhero, almost went *splat* against a concrete skyscraper. For a brief instant in mid-air, hanging by a wire under a

Stunt coordinator Fred Waugh prepares a shot from the roof of a building so he can climb down the wall as Spiderman. Copyright 1978 CBS/Columbia.

flying helicopter, Waugh almost hit the side of a building because the helicopter pilot did not know he was still attached. The production crew and director on the rooftop stood by and watched in horror.

The plot of this episode involves villains who plant an atomic bomb on the roof of a building and try to escape by helicopter. Spiderman spins a web to catch a ride. Flying over Los Angeles with Spiderman hanging under them, the villains engage in aerial acrobatics to shake him off, depositing him onto the very building they are trying to escape.

To film the scene where Spiderman drops down from his hanging web to the rooftop, stuntman Waugh grabbed the wire hanging from the helicopter landing strut and lifted off with the chopper. The helicopter moved some 30 or 40 feet away from the building, then flew back toward the cameras. However, Waugh found his positioning was erratic and not good for the

planned jump, so he just hung on. The pilot continued further out and then came back for a landing. Not knowing that he and Waugh were still connected, he flew low. Waugh could have ended up as a squashed bug unless that pilot moved *up* in a hurry.

"We were able to communicate to this pilot just in time!" recalls director Ronald Satlof vividly. "My god! I must say, he pulled up just in time to save his life. We're talking about a matter of within two or three feet [before hitting the building], I think. So, it was a very exciting little day we had when we shot that. It gave us all heart attacks."

Reminded of this pulse-pounding day, stunt coordinator and on-camera Spiderman Fred Waugh, who operates a camera company today, recalls the events slightly differently. While he readily acknowledges this was "the stunt that I almost got killed on," he says the danger was not almost hitting the skyscraper, but hanging over the city by only one arm. The bad part was I was only hanging on with one hand on the cable because I had injured the other hand about a week before—I caught a stick through my hand—so I really couldn't hold on to it with my left hand at all. I was just hanging onto the cable with my right hand. At the bottom of the cable was a little loop. Previously, I had hooked my harness into it as we were flying around the city. So, all I was hanging onto was a very, very small loop with my one hand."

As Waugh recalls it, the stunt was successfully completed in the first take. "The helicopter lifted me up about six or seven feet off the ground, and we flew towards the camera. Just before I got to the camera, I let go, and I just rolled into the camera. We did that one time, and everything was fine." However, Satlof asked for another take.

"This time, when the helicopter lifted me up, he lifted me about 20 feet off the deck," explains Waugh. "The pilot's assistant down on the ground was signaling him to come back down. But as he was bringing him down, he wasn't watching me, and I was beginning to twist with my back towards the camera; when we got low enough he told the pilot to come ahead, and when the pilot started flying forward, my back was to the camera, so I couldn't let go because it would flip me right over my head."

And this was the dangerous part: "He thought I was off, but I wasn't, and we were out over the city. It was my mistake, and there I was hanging over the city with one hand and the pilot didn't realize it. And you know, he could have turned the helicopter very sharply and ripped me right off."

Waugh believes he hung by one hand with no roof under him for about a minute, with only about 15 or 20 seconds reserve time, before he returned to safety.

"They radioed and told him I was still underneath, and got me back," Waugh says matter-of-factly. "I'm still here."

Spiderman first spun his web on television in 1977 with a TV movie exploring how Peter Parker got bitten by the radioactive spider at his physics laboratory. Starring Nicholas Hammond as Peter Parker and David White as J. Jonah Jameson, the film garnered enough viewer interest that CBS commissioned five episodes as a programming filler. When those did well, eight additional hours were requested and aired in the fall of 1978, bringing *Spiderman* to a total of 13 episodes.

Nicholas Hammond remembers that when *Spiderman* was starting up, the feature film *Superman* with Christopher Reeve had just come out. Many people were worried about doing a superhero show. They were afraid that it would be a campy, laughable affair in the same vein as the 1960s *Batman* TV show.

"I liked the idea of taking a fantasy hero and making him believable as a person. I made it clear going into it that I was not interested in doing something that was just a camp joke," says Hammond. "I was given an opportunity here to do some good work and tell some good, interesting stories."

Hammond feels that the show lost an ally in failing to consult with Spiderman's creator, Stan Lee, during production.

"I thought Stan Lee was an enormously talented man. I was always tremendously impressed by Stan. I always wished we could have worked more closely with him. We could have tapped into a larger market if we'd used more of Stan's ideas." Instead, says Hammond, "My early feeling was that, maybe [network and producers] thought, 'Stan's background is comic books and we want to get away from that here—a comic book feel. What we want to do here is make it more an adventure-drama series.' I feel that his input would have been very, very useful."

Stan Lee, too, regrets the lack of a working relationship. "After I read the scripts, I called a meeting at CBS," he says. "The director was there, the producer was there, and the network executives were there. I spent 20 minutes telling them what was wrong with the show, they listened politely and then they left and paid no attention to what I had told them!"

Producer Daniel Goodman says, "I was at all the meetings with Stan. Somehow the writers could not agree on many of his suggestions. His input was good, but unfortunately, there was evident frustration on his part and a sympathetic reaction on mine. You can't satisfy *all* parties *all* the time. Perhaps we could have had a longer run on CBS if we had heeded his suggestions, but one never knows.

"You see, my concept was to make *Spiderman* more acceptable to a general audience than just to kiddies, and perhaps there was a clash of ideologies. We had to compromise as CBS was sold on my original sales presentation of a prime-time, *general* audience show. Stan will always have my deepest respect and admiration."

Lee believes that the network's concept of

Spiderman affected Nicholas Hammond's portrayal. "He's a good actor," Lee says sincerely. "He was *directed* badly. He came across as a very uninteresting character, and I don't think it was his fault. I think it was the way the director and the producer conceived of the show and the character. He came across as very square, very humorless, and, I thought, very dull. But it wasn't his fault."

Hammond felt strongly about doing his best because after several episodes had aired, he started getting interesting, provocative mail from minority communities across America.

"The show was terribly popular with ghetto kids. But I'd also get a lot of letters from their mothers and fathers who'd say, 'You are the only positive role model in my child's life! When

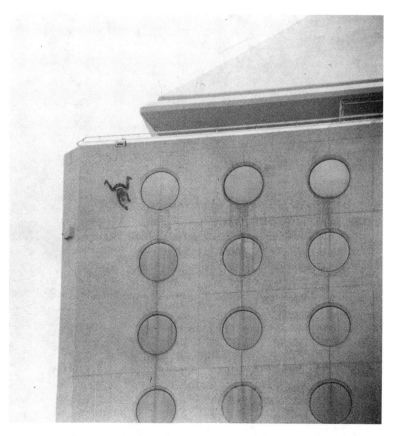

Stuntman Fred Waugh hangs on the side of a building in Hong Kong for the final 2-hour *Spiderman* episode, "The Chinese Web." Copyright 1979 CBS/Columbia.

he's out in the streets, all he sees are drug pushers, pimps, prostitutes. And the only message he gets from the streets is the only way you make it is outside the law. And Peter Parker each week is telling him that there's a better way.' Peter is given this power, and he has to make a moral choice, do the difficult thing, not to use his powers to rob banks but to use his power to try to help people. I always thought, 'Gee, there's a tremendous potential here.'

"I used to speak quite often to inner city schools. The first time was during National Book Week or something when I was asked to give a speech and stress the importance of reading and books. I guess this was 1979. The school was in east L.A., mainly black and Mexican kids. I was warned they were very unruly and poorly disciplined, but the staff was shocked to see them all sit spellbound when Peter Parker got up to talk. Afterwards, teachers wrote me to say it had a more profound effect on them than anything that

year. So I realized the potential for using Peter Parker's 'prestige' among these kids as a positive force.

"As you probably know, series stars are asked to do endless public appearances for all sorts of charities and social groups, and it is impossible to do them all. But from then on, I never turned down the opportunity to speak to inner city kids. Even if they weren't interested in reading conventional books, it was good to keep them reading *Spiderman*. By the way, during the Gulf War, it was reported that because of the low reading skills of so many GI's a lot of training manuals were being printed in comic book form. Probably my ex-students!" laughs Hammond.

"*Spiderman* always had a huge, huge following among the black community, I don't know why. Some people say it's because when you're in that suit, your skin has no color and everybody can identify with you. I used to go to the producers and say, 'Hey, let's use this! Let's do stories

The cast of *Spiderman*, year two, clockwise from front: Nicholas Hammond, Ellen Bry, Robert F. Simon, Chip Fields. Stuntman Fred Waugh hangs out in the background as Spiderman. Copyright 1978 CBS/Columbia.

sorry we never got the chance to do it because I think it would have been useful."

Goodman has no recollections of Hammond approaching him with these suggestions. "I personally never heard any comments of this nature from him. As for teenage pregnancy—in 1979 no one took up this subject in an 8 p.m. time slot!"

While schoolchildren worshipped him, Spiderman in full regalia sometimes came as a shock to the general public. Hammond learned this lesson during the filming of the 90-minute pilot. With Los Angeles doubling for New York, a house in Pasadena was used for the Parker home. Hammond recalls that "early in the morning, there would be all these derelicts and winos, stumbling around our equipment. I'd be walking around wearing a spider suit, and these guys were just waking up out of the gutter, won-

about drugs in Harlem. Let's do stories about teenage pregnancy. Let's do stories where Spiderman and Peter get involved.' And *not* bashing people over the head, in the context of a highly entertaining show. Let's very gently just try to get the message across that you can make a moral choice, you can do the right thing. That's really using television to its best purpose. My greatest disappointment is not going to a third season. Not for the fame, for the money, or having my own TV series, but I felt we were on the *verge* of getting into those kinds of stories. I was hoping that we could sit down and say, 'Ok. Let's look at six issues and in the next 13 episodes, in a *very* delicate way, let's touch on them.' So that we're doing shows that we're proud of and we feel we're using television in a constructive way. I'm just

dering 'What the…?!' It was probably enough for them to swear off the cheap wine!"

Ninety percent of *Spiderman* was filmed in Los Angeles. The remainder of the footage was shot in New York, and it was there that Fred Waugh would perform his incredible stunts for the action scenes. Remembering those stunts, Nicholas Hammond, Ellen Bry and supervising producer Lionel Siegel all use the same word to describe Waugh: *fearless*.

"He was absolutely fearless about heights," attests Hammond. With a background as a wire artist in the Ringling Brothers–Barnum and Bailey Circus, Waugh possessed astonishing physical abilities. "He was an extraordinary guy. He was obviously very, very good, because he'd walk right to the edge of the tallest building in New

York and just lean over and start to climb off the side of it. Terrifying. He developed this helmet camera. If you remember, in some of the shows, you see Spiderman's point of view. Freddie invented that camera. It was like a football helmet, and he had a small camera mounted inside of it. And he would just pop it on his head and wear it while he was hanging, literally, 69 to 70 stories in the air on the side of the Empire State Building. ... Those wall-climbing shots, they were so well done that most people don't believe they're real. I always have people after the series, to this day, come up to me, and say, 'What did you do? Were you just lying flat on the ground and did they turn the film sideways?' or, 'Was it a superimposed effect or something against a painted building?' It's so extraordinary that he's that high up in the air. Everybody just assumes that it must be a trick! That it can't really be a man that high on the side of a building! But it is! It's all real!"

Fred Waugh responds that it *had* to be real; the studio couldn't afford special effects. "The TV series was limited on money, and they needed more optical effects on it, but they were prohibited because they were very, very expensive," he says. "If they were made now, with the cost of optical effects coming down, especially with digital visual effects, we could have done a lot of wonderful things. But the way it was, we had to do everything physically—what you saw on the side of a building was *me*! We used cable to hold me up. One was called a pull cable; the other was a travel cable. I'd set that travel cable real tight against the building, and I'd anchor that into a little pulley I had on my harness, and that would keep me stuck on the building. Otherwise, I'd drift away. The pull cable had seven or eight men on top of the building who would pull it. I had radio communication with them where I could tell them to stop or speed up."

Co-star Ellen Bry, who joined the show during its second season as a rival newspaper photographer, echoes Hammond's praise of Waugh. "I thought that Fred Waugh was and continues to be one of the best stuntmen in the business," she says. "I've worked with a lot of stuntmen, and I think Freddie is incredible. Some of the stunts he pulled were just amazing. The one I remember very clearly was [when] a core group of the company went back to New York to shoot some location stuff to be included into a lot of different episodes. He swung out of a window of the Empire State Building and climbed up and down

outside of the building. He really did it—that was not trick photography. It was incredible."

The climbing stunts, says Waugh, were the most fun. Describing his daring stunt on the outside of one of the world's tallest skyscrapers, he recalls that a woman in one of the offices stuck her head out the window and saw him in the red and blue suit, crawling up and down—a moment that's preserved on film as a shot in the main titles of the show and used for the episode "Photo Finish."

"That wasn't planned," chuckles Waugh. "When we rigged the building for the stunt, there wasn't anyone in that office. But when we did the stunt three hours later, I went across, and as I passed the window, I saw this woman coming into the room. I climbed to the top and turned around and came back down, and as I passed the window, she was standing there saying, 'What are you doing out there? Who are you?' and I just kept going down. I yelled, 'I'm Spiderman, lady!' I went back up and talked to her after the scene was over, and she laughed. That was the only time that happened."

"Fred was, to my mind, fearless," says Lionel Siegel. "And intelligent. I enjoyed working with him."

And yet more praise from producer Daniel Goodman: "Freddy remains my *very good* friend. I shall always admire his stunt work and his courage. His work was meritorious. He added much to the program's excitement. There were times I feared for his life!"

The most complicated stunt, according to Waugh, "was in the pilot where I jumped on the ceiling, and walked down from the ceiling"— while battling Japanese assassins—"which was all done on cables and piano wire. It was very time-consuming."

The near-catastrophe with the helicopter is not the only stunt Waugh remembers from the episode "The Deadly Dust." He describes one scene in which a bad guy throws a stunned Spiderman from the rooftop. "I shot a web out of my hand and landed in a spider net. The net was made out of yarn to look like a spider net spread out between the alley. It was ten feet by ten feet, and we had people holding it so it would stretch across the alley."

For the pilot, in a stunt performed only once, Spiderman did his trademark swinging from one building to another. Waugh reports that it was a very intricate job and took two days to rig. It was only in the pilot where crews cheated a little by employing video effects and the put-the-building-on-the-floor trick to create the illusion of a man climbing walls. But this trick tended to look fake on film. "That's why they never did it again, says Hammond. "They said, 'Well, this is ridiculous! It's not nearly as good as having him out there, and he can do it, so let's have him do it.'"

Hammond himself donned the red and blue suit for key scenes. It's easy, he says, to figure out who's in the suit: "If it was a stunt, Freddie wore it. If it was a scene that involved dialogue, I wore it. Obviously if it was a moment where the suit had to come off, and it revealed to the audience or other characters that it was actually Peter Parker who was Spiderman, that would be me as well. Because we were turning out these shows every seven days, we had a second unit filming Fred doing his stunts. And Fred would go out with his little crew of stunt people, and they would do a long climb or jump or whatever he was doing that day. And so he'd have a second camera crew working with him while the first unit with the director would be working with me. If you see the show, it breaks down pretty much 85 percent Peter, and 15 percent Spiderman. That's how we divided the workload throughout the week.

"The character was so popular in New York that it became difficult to film on the streets," continues Hammond. "After the first season had aired, and I had played the character for a while, when we went back the second time, we just got mobbed everywhere we went! And it just made it much more difficult to film. In the first year, we had scenes of me just walking down Fifth Avenue, mingling with the crowd, going into the Empire State Building, wandering around in Central Park. It wasn't possible to do that in the second year because Peter Parker had gotten fairly recognizable to the public by then and, you know, I'd walk down the street and an awful lot of people would turn around and start chasing after me. So we weren't able to get the same kind of feeling of reality in the streets of New York as we had in the first year."

Ratings at first looked promising. "The pilot scored a 39 share, which was the highest rated show CBS had that year," remembers Hammond. "They put [the series] against *Eight Is Enough*, and we beat them consistently every week we were on, so the show was doing extremely well. I think CBS got a little cocky, and they had no luck at all against *Happy Days* and *Laverne and Shirley* which, at that time, were the number one and number two shows in America. Because we had

done so well, and we had knocked *Eight Is Enough* off its perch, they thought, 'Well, this is going to appeal to the same age group that watches *Happy Days* and *Laverne and Shirley*, we'll put *Spiderman* up against that.' I begged them not to! I said, 'There's no way we can take on the Fonz and *Happy Days*!' At that point it was an absolute American institution! And sure enough, we didn't! We did very badly against them. And it was kind of the beginning of the end of the show, which was a pity, but for the time we were on, we did enjoy a great deal of popularity and success in the first year."

That popularity has caught up with Nicholas Hammond. He was doing a play in Melbourne, Australia, recently when a fan came backstage with a strange present.

"A passionate writer fan came backstage to see me, and he's written a treatment to redo another pilot to show Peter, now, ten years later, where he's completely renounced all of his powers. He's now married with a child. And the child is abducted or threatened, and Peter has to go back to being Spiderman again, something he said he would never do because … he wanted to lead a normal life. It's like the story of the old western gunslinger, who has to come back for one last time! He's written this marvelous story about Peter Parker, and he's now a middle-aged guy with a job, living in the suburbs. And one more time, he has to go out there to fight the good fight, this time to protect his children. Suddenly, Peter realizes the boy is starting to do things that Peter did all those years ago when he got bitten by the spider. He realizes it's been passed on genetically to the boy. And now Peter's got to teach the boy how to use his powers responsibly. Almost against his will he has to reenter the world of superheroes. I actually think it's a charming idea."

Hammond brings up an interesting point: Peter Parker never really had a girlfriend. Ellen Bry's portrayal of Julie Masters was an attempt at that, but, Hammond says, "He could never be clearly living with a woman, or clearly sexually involved with a woman, because it would put her at risk. Because if the bad guys found out there was a woman Peter had an emotional attachment to, of course she would become a target. That's why we had to keep him just on the *verge* of getting involved with someone, and then he would have to gently push away."

Told that Peter Parker in the current comics is married to a lovely red-haired Mary Jane, a surprised Hammond responds, "Oh, well, there you go! I think that's better."

At one point during *Spiderman* production, Hammond lit on the idea of a crossover story between the *Incredible Hulk* and his show. But it never happened, largely because *Spiderman* got canned too quickly to develop the idea.

"To be honest with you," says Hammond, "it was my idea, but I stole it from years before. I was working on a series called *Owen Marshall, Counsellor at Law*, with Lee Majors and Arthur Hill. Universal was doing two series at the same time, *Marcus Welby* and *Owen Marshall*. So they did a two-hour story where Welby was sued for malpractice and Owen Marshall had to come and defend him. So you've got the stars of one series appearing in the other series. So I thought, why don't we do a story where David Banner comes to my university and looks for some research, or whatever, but there's a reason why we're at the same place at the same time. And then there's some kind of terrible outside threat, I'm in jeopardy, or he's in jeopardy, and I need to get my Spider powers to save him, or he needs to use his Hulk qualities to save me, but we end up having to work together to resolve the crisis. We were definitely going to do it because we were on the same network. Well, it never happened, because we never got that far! They said, 'Oh, yeah! Great! Let's do that next year!' But we never got a next year. Maybe one of these days we'll go back and do it again."

For Ellen Bry, *Spiderman* was an exciting introduction to prime-time television. "It was an *incredibly* exciting time in my life, coming from New York," she says. "This was my first introduction to L.A. and to doing a starring role in a TV series. ... I was very happy. People are paying a lot of attention to you, you're making good money. It's very glamorous. And of course, for me, coming out to Los Angeles, I was star-struck and working non-stop. It was a very happy time for me. Everything was new and different and exciting.

"I was walking two feet off the ground. I was just in ecstasy! You have to understand that this is a young actress's dream come true! She's struggling away in New York; all of a sudden, bong! She gets plucked up and gets put into a high-paying, fabulous nighttime TV series and moved from the bowels of New York and into glorious Los Angeles. I was just so thrilled. I just felt they were family to me."

The swift relocation from the East Coast to the palm trees of California meant that Bry didn't know anyone in town. "And so, I latched onto the people I worked with. It was intense work. We were working non-stop for a number of months. I just felt it was a very warm, very nurturing group of people. I just have very happy memories of it! It was a time of discovery."

Bry has since become so experienced as a television actress that she looks upon *Spiderman* as her "early work" and says, "You cringe a lot. I've gotten a lot better. I feel I was just very new, and I tried hard. It's not that I'm embarrassed by it. At the time I was very happy with the work accomplished. Now, when I watch myself, I realize how differently I could have played a scene."

Working with Nicholas Hammond was part of that experience. "Nick was very nice," says Bry. "I enjoyed working with him, and yet I felt ... that in a way, there was a little bit of resentment that the network or production company or whoever had decided that he couldn't carry the show alone. That they needed a female co-star and that they needed a romantic foil. ... I was having to share the limelight a little bit. The show was *Spiderman*, and *he* was Spiderman. He was the star of the show, so that was exciting for him.

"In terms of his attitude about his playing a superhero, did he have concerns about being typecast? Yes! He was *extremely* nervous about it. He was very concerned that playing Spiderman would typecast him."

Bry speculates on why the show didn't last longer. "I think the show failed for a couple of reasons. Firstly, there were a lot of superhero shows around at the time. I think CBS was not really behind *Spiderman*. I think they had a lot of superhero shows on their plate [e.g. *Wonder Woman*, *Incredible Hulk*, plus TV movies *Dr. Strange* and *Captain America*] and this was just another one. ... I think they weren't pushing it. The ratings weren't good.

"I think the main flaw of the show was ... it was geared too much for young kids. I don't think it had enough general appeal." Bry admits that the second season was intended to be more appealing to an adult audience, but "I don't think it succeeded," she says. "Whatever efforts were made to make it a more adult show basically failed because I felt we had a very young audience, based on the feedback I did get. It came from kids anywhere from 6 to 8 and from 14 to 15. I think the audience it appealed to was too young for it to get good demographics for sales and advertising. From 5- to 15-year-olds, I got

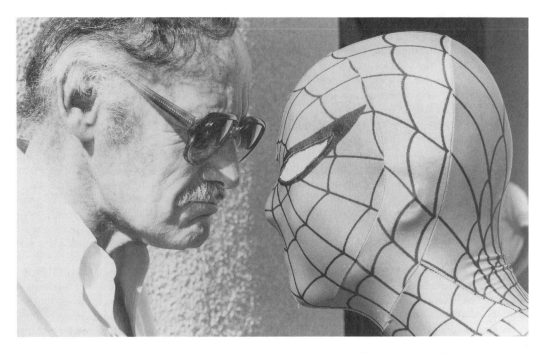

Stan Lee faces his most popular comics creation, Spiderman. Photo courtesy of Stan Lee.

tremendous feedback. I got lots of letters. Kids absolutely adored it. They started fan clubs and stuff like that. But unfortunately, I don't think most advertisers are aiming at 5- to 15-year-old audiences. My fan letters from adults were few and far between. Ninety to 95 percent of my fan mail was from kids. Which is fine, but, you know, it doesn't sell soap. So, I think it was geared for too young an audience. It didn't have enough mass appeal. But this is just speculation. I'm not in a position to say definitively why it didn't have enough adult interest."

Producer on the second season for *Spiderman* was Lionel E. Siegel. Bry says, "I owe him a lot of thank-yous. He really gave me a break. I was doing commercials and soaps and off-Broadway theatre, and I was brought out to do *Spiderman*, so he really changed my career and brought me into doing prime-time television series."

Was Siegel in some way dissatisfied with his Peter Parker/Spiderman? Regarding the casting of Hammond, Siegel says, "Tough call. He was OK. Worked very hard and was extremely conscientious, but his very nature, his personality (same on screen as off) lacked the toughness, the rough-edgeness that most of the male stars of TV series of the day ... had. Most of these guys weren't actors, they were personalities."

And what kind of stories did Siegel hope to

bring to the second season? "Action, heart, mysteries, humor," he says, "all woven together in a compelling way."

Siegel's major contribution to the show was its final two-hour episode, "The Chinese Web," filmed on location in Hong Kong. "He wrote that based on experiences he had as a Marine during World War II when he had been over in Asia," says Hammond. "He's a fascinating guy! I was very impressed by him. I think, far and away, he was the most thoughtful person we ever had associated with the show. ... He told me a story about some Marines who shot a Chinese man's water buffalo, which in those days was a terrible crime because the animals were a source of income for the man's family. He used the basis of this incident that he remembered as the kernel of information which he developed into this whole story that became 'The Chinese Web.' He was a great guy. I'd actually very much like to work with him again. I really liked him."

Ralph Sariego, on the production crew as a location scout, recalls using the Connaught Tower in Hong Kong for a wall-climbing sequence at the end of this story. "We were supposed to shoot on one side of the building," he says, "and we were on the roof of the building. But coincidentally, it was [an anniversary of some sort], they had bloody, bloody riots out there. It was on this particular day in October, and we were afraid that a man in a red suit climbing a building might cause a riot. So we had to switch to the other side of the building so that the Chinese would not cause an international incident with the man in the red suit climbing up the side of the building.

"It was a tense time in Hong Kong. I remember scouting along the Chinese border in a helicopter, being afraid that they were going to send a missile up and shoot me down. I was very nervous about that. I was sort of fantasizing being shot down by the Chinese along the border."

Sariego was not the only one who found something to be scared of in that shoot. It was during this episode that Fred Waugh's fearlessness finally faltered. Actor Hagan Beggs, who appeared in "The Chinese Web" as the main bad guy's right-hand man, tells the story.

"He had no trouble climbing down building walls in Hong Kong, but he had some reluctance about jumping into the water at the Aberdeen harbor because the water was so polluted. He didn't want to do it. He just thought, 'Oh, it's so polluted, I just don't want to get a mouthful of it. I don't mind going down walls on cables, but I don't want to throw myself off into that water!'"

Nick Hammond adds, "Not only did Fred refuse to do it, he very wisely refused to do it. It was absolutely poisonous, filthy water! We had a lot of these really, really tough kung fu stuntmen, working with us, these chinese boys. These guys were as tough as nails! There was nothing they wouldn't do! When we got to the Aberdeen harbor and suddenly, someone had to take a fall into the water, no one would do it. Absolutely no one! The camera crew finally got it, but we were totally flat out!"

Reminded of the story, Fred Waugh says, "One look at that harbor and you wouldn't do it. It would be like jumping into a cesspool."

Ultimately, a local fellow was recruited to take the fall that the script asked for.

Beggs recalls the wall-crawling Connaught Tower sequence: "That particular night when Waugh was going down that large building, I know it was quite a complicated affair because they had their stunt coordinator people and a Hong Kong team working together. They were very concerned everything would go very well. They were nervous about it, but everything did work out OK. But they did have some problem there about making sure that the Hong Kong workers holding the ropes were tying off correctly. They were concerned because sometimes they had to use an interpreter. Fred said, 'Make sure these guys are tied to me so if I go, they go—that way I'm sure I'll be safe!'"

The conclusion of "The Chinese Web" has Spiderman tracking a kidnapped professor to a penthouse at the tower. After quickly disposing of some guards on the balcony, he breaks his way into the boardroom. Inside, Beggs and actor Richard Erdman are conversing. Erdman is closer to the camera, while Beggs is down the long boardroom table in the distance. As soon as Spiderman flips the drape curtains, Erdman dashes for a nearby door, while Beggs tries pulling a gun. To stop him from firing, Spiderman leaps head-first across the long boardroom table and uses his momentum to tackle Beggs.

Of this scene, Beggs remembers the belt buckle on the Spiderman costume. Waugh "banged his back on that, and it was quite painful. Isn't it ironic—that a simple dive across a table with a belt on hurt him. It's typical of the business. You find things that look so dangerous, and yet it just takes a dive across a table to give yourself a 'thump.' … It's amazing sometimes that the most simple things give you a problem."

With filmmaker James Cameron signed to write and direct a *Spiderman* feature for the 1990s, Nicholas Hammond notes, "I've been hearing for ten years about a preparation of a *Spiderman* feature film. Good luck to them. It would be great with the special effects. That, unfortunately, was our limitation, being a TV series where every seven days you had to turn out a one-hour episode. And also with TV budgets being much lower than movie budgets, we were very limited with our special effects, with what we could do. It would be fantastic if they could do a feature film."

Stan Lee also agrees that a Cameron-filmed *Spiderman* would be exciting. "James Cameron is a brilliant man, and he has all the digital computer experience he needs to do a movie like that. They'll do a wonderful job," says Fred Waugh.

Collecting his thoughts on his days as the web-slinger, Waugh says, "It was an easy show for me. I had a lot of fun doing it. I had to create a lot of nice effects. If they had the money and the time, there's nothing a stuntman can't do. The writers would ask me what I wanted to do, and they'd incorporate them [into stories]. I've been in the business 38 years, and I recently did the Arnold Schwarzenneger film *The Last Action Hero*, so I'm happy."

Cast Notes

Nicholas Hammond (Peter Parker/Spiderman): Born 1950. The actor who first found fame as one of the children in *The Sound of Music* now lives and works in Australia, doing stage and television. "I love it out here, which is why I've stayed. I worked a great deal after the show." He also appeared in "*The Manions of America* (with Pierce Brosnan), which was about two Irish boys moving to the United States. I've worked a great deal in the theatre, which is what I've done before *Spiderman*. I've been working with the Center Theatre group in Los Angeles for years. I went back and did more plays with them, and then I went to New York to do a play called *Noises Off*, and it was during the play I became interested in going off to Australia. I did four mini-series in Australia the first two years I was here. Then I went to London for another play, so I go back and forth. But my base now is here."

Hammond also had a role in the 1980 mini-series of Ray Bradbury's *The Martian Chronicles*.

Robert F. Simon (J. Jonah Jameson): This gruff, veteran character actor appeared in *The Outer Limits'* "The Zanti Misfits." He died in 1992 at 83 years old.

Ellen Bry (Julie Masters): After *Spiderman*, Bry appeared as Shirley Daniels in *St. Elsewhere* (1982–85). Television films include *Indestructible Man* (or *I-Man*) in 1986 with Scott Bakula. She has had recurring roles in *Dallas* and in *Riker* (with Michael Shannon), and TV movie roles in *Starflight One* (1983) and *Dallas Cowboy Cheerleaders* (1979). Most recently, she guest-starred on *Star Trek: The Next Generation*.

Chip Fields (Rita Conway): A New York actress whose daughter Kim garnered a claim to fame with a regular role in *The Facts of Life*.

Episode Guide

Spiderman (1977 TV movie, 2 hours)
New York City is under siege by a terrorist who demands $50 million dollars from the city or he will use mind control to kill important individuals throughout the city.

Meanwhile, university physics student Peter Parker is bitten by a radioactive spider at his lab. To his surprise, he develops newfound powers. As Spiderman, his first mission is to vanquish the evil terrorist. Wr: Alvin Boretz. Dir: E.W. Swackhamer.

Edward Byron (Thayer David); Captain Barbera (Michael Pataki); Monahan (Robert Hastings); Aunt May (Jeff Donnell); Judy Tyler (Lisa Eilbacher); Professor Noah Tyler (Ivor Francis); Robbie Robinson (Hilly Hicks); Purse snatcher (Barry Cutler); Also with Mary Ann Kasica, Len Lesser, Jim Storm, Ivan Bonar, Norman Rice, Harry Cesar, George Cooper, Roy West, James E. Brodhead, Carmelita Pope, Kathryn Reynolds, Robert Snively.

Season 1: 1978

The Deadly Dust, Parts 1 and 2
A reporter from Florida joins a nervous Peter Parker in search of a Spiderman story, but when plutonium is stolen from the university lab and Spiderman is the prime suspect, the stakes get high. Peter and reporter Gale must travel to Los Angeles to retrieve the plutonium, which has been transformed into a bomb. Wr: Robert Janes. Dir: Ron Satlof.

Gale Hoffman (Joanna Cameron); Mr. White (Robert Alda); Greg (Randy Powell); Sid (Lawrence Casey); Dr. Baylor (Simon Scott); DiCarlo (Sidney Clute); Carla (Anne Bloom); Ted (Steven Anderson); LeBeau (Herbert S. Braha); Benson (Emil Farkas); Angel (Dick Kyker); Linda (Leigh Kavanaugh); Asst. cameraman (Gino Ardito); Cameraman (Steve Goodwins); Salesman (Ron Hajek); Girl (Kerrie Cullen); Singer (David Somerville); Singer (Gail Jensen); Intern (Bonnie Johns); Guard (George Barrows); Cop (Orin Kennedy); N.Y. cabbie (Barry Roberts); Helicopter repairman (Walt Davis); Waitress (Barbara Sanders); Doorman (Jerry Martin); Arachnologist (Will Albert).

The Curse of Rava
Assigned to cover the Rava exhibit from Kalastan, Peter discovers there's a curse on the statue. When Jameson is accused of murder, Spiderman must clear him and find out who is orchestrating seemingly supernatural incidents. Wr: Robert Janes, story by Dick Nelson and Robert Janes. Dir: Michael Caffey.

Mandak (Theodore Bikel); Trina (Adrienne LaRussa); Rusten (Byron Webster); Dr. Keller (David Ralphe); Museum guard (John Clavin).

Night of the Clones
While attending a press conference, Peter discovers a bitter scientist's breakthrough in cloning. The scientist manages to get a genetic sample of Parker's blood, creating an evil Spiderman. Parker must outwit himself to win. Wr: John W. Bloch. Dir: Fernando Lamas.

Lisa Benson (Morgan Fairchild); Dr. Moon (Lloyd Bochner); Dr. Reichman (Rick Traeger); Aunt May (Irene Tedrow); Dr. Benson (Karl Swenson); Elevator inspector (Vince Howard); Dr. Ketya (Alex Rodine); Girl reporter (Debi Fries); Desk clerk (Larry Levine); Reporter #2 (Terrence McNally); Reporter #1 (Erik Stern); Reporter #3 (John Finnegan).

Escort to Danger

Assigned to chaperone a foreign president's daughter at a beauty contest, Peter soon realizes that she is the next victim of opponents of the president's political party. Wr: Duke Sandefur. Dir: Dennis Donnelly.

President Calderon (Alejandro Rey); Lisa Alvarez (Barbara Luna); Maria Calderon (Madeline Stowe); Matsu (Harold Sakata); Sauti (Michael Marsellos); Kim Barker (Lachelle Price); Curt Klein (Bob Minor); Chaperone official (Danna Hansen); Pageant official (Selma Archerd); Ted Arthur (Mark Baxley); Emcee (Bruce Hayes); Bodyguard (Michael Santiago).

Season 2: 1978-79

The Captive Tower

A new, electronically controlled building is under siege by terrorists. Spiderman must stop them and their threats to blow up the building. Wr: Gregory S. Dinallo, story by Bruce Kalish, Philip John Taylor. Dir: Cliff Bole.

Maj. E.W. Forster (David Sheiner); Farnum (Todd Susman); Hammer (Warren Vanders); Duke (Fred Lerner); Deputy Mayor Edward Nuget (William Mims); Police officer (Michael Bond); Lt. Ramirez (Ed Sancho-Bonet); Police officer (Norman Rice); Barry (Barry Cutler); Terrorist (Bill Dearth); Police officer (Harry Pugh).

A Matter of State

When Julie accidentally photographs thieves stealing top-secret government documents at the airport, they pursue her to retrieve the film. Spiderman must protect her and find the men responsible for the robbery. Wr: Howard Dimsdale. Dir: Larry Stewart.

Andre (Nicholas Coster); Evans (John Crawford); 2nd henchman (Michael Santiago); Martin (James Victor); Jim McGann (FBI) (Don Gazzaniga); 1st henchman (Erik Stern); Airport spokesman (John Dewey Carter); Also with Tony Miller.

The Con Caper

A paroled politician is seeking the *Bugle*'s endorsement. The man's covert goals include the robbery of $50 million from a security vault. Wr: Gregory S. Dinallo, story by Brian McKay. Dir: Tom Blank.

James Colbert (William Smithers); Cates (Ramon Bieri); McTeague (Andrew Robinson); Warden Rischer (Fred Downs); Guard (W.T. Zacha); Convict (Paul Wexler); Carlos (Pat Corley).

Kirkwood Haunting

Jameson sends Peter to investigate reports that his late friend's estate is haunted. Wr: Michael Michaelian. Dir: Don McDougall.

Lisa Kirkwood (Marlyn Mason); Dr. Anthony Polarsky (Peter McLean); Ganz (Paul Carr); Dr. Davis (Peggy McCay); Thug (Del Monroe); Gatekeeper (Jamie DeRoy).

Photo Finish

Working on a story about rare coins, Peter is hit from behind while interviewing collector Welden Grey. A fugitive from the police after trying to clear an innocent woman of the crime, Peter tries to find the real culprits. Wr: Howard Dimsdale. Dir: Tony Ganz.

Mrs. Gray (Jennifer Billingsley); Police lieutenant (Charles Haid); Weldon Gray (Geoffrey Lewis); Wiley (Milt Kogan); Cork (Kenneth O'Brien); Prison guard (Ed Walsh); Judge (Davis Roberts); Police officer (Chip Johnson); Also with Wendy Oates, Livia Genise.

Wolfpack

A mind-controlling drug is accidentally created at the university by a classmate of Peter's. The man from a chemical company takes advantage of this by using it for criminal purposes. Wr: Steven Kandel. Dir: Joe Manduke.

David (Gavan O'Herlihy); Art (Wil Selzer); George Hansen (Allan Arbus); Ben Sorgerson (Dolph Sweet); Dr. Stillwell (Joe Medalis); Soldier (Robert Miano); Brandon (Ted Noose); Also with George Petrie, Tom Stewart, Terrence McNally, William Georgio.

The Chinese Web (2 Hours)

To help an old friend of Jameson's, Peter must find Marines who can clear the man of espionage charges. When one is found, Peter travels to Hong Kong and faces ruthless criminals who will go to any lengths to prevent the witness from testifying. Wr: Lionel E. Siegel. Dir: Don McDougall.

Emily Loo T'ao (Rosalind Chao); Evans (Hagan Beggs); Zeider (Richard Erdman); Jonathan Fleming (John Milford); Min Lo Chan (Benson Fong); Quinn (Anthony Charnotta); Dr. Pai (George Cheung); Joe (Tony Clark); Major Collings (Ted Danson); Lt. Olson (Myron Healey); Bertino (Michael Mancini); Lou (Robert Mayo); Abbott (Arnold F. Turner); Hot Dog vendor (Herman Tweeder); Hong Kong cast: Zara Brierley, Peter Wong, Joel Laykin, Michael Chan, W.K. Lam, Suzanne Vale, Hudson Leung, Eric Wile.

The Starlost

September 1973–April 1974

To ensure mankind's survival in the face of planetary destruction, the giant spaceship Ark is built. People representing various cultures around the world board the vessel for a generational space voyage to a habitable star system.

One hundred years after the launch, the spaceship's crew mysteriously perishes, and the ship's 60 environmental domes, containing various communities of people, are sealed off from each other. The future generations of human beings lose the knowledge that their worlds are housed aboard a spaceship.

Five hundred years later, in the year 2790 A.D., an inquisitive young man named Devon, his lover, Rachel, and her former fiancé, Garth, discover that their farming community, Cypress Corners, is a space biosphere.

Devon learns the Ark has veered off course and is on a collision course with a star, but he's unable to convince the village elders of his discovery. Leaving their repressed society, Devon, Rachel and Garth embark on a journey through the various domes to find the ship's control room and save the Ark.

Cast: Devon (Keir Dullea); Rachel (Gay Rowan); Garth (Robin Ward); Mulander 165, the Computer (William Osler).

Created by: Cordwainer Bird (Harlan Ellison); *Producer:* William Davidson; *Science Consultant:* Ben Bova; *Art Director:* Jack McAdam; CTV/A Glen Warren Production Syndicated by Twentieth Century–Fox for NBC affiliates; 60 minutes.

Although it had one of the most ambitious concepts in TV history, the producers of *The Starlost* were forced to bring it to life with restricted technology and limited production values.

Twentieth Century–Fox executive Robert Kline asked writer Harlan Ellison to come up with an idea for a science fiction series. Kline liked Ellison's idea of a space-age Noah's Ark and tried to sell the idea to England's BBC network. When the BBC rejected the idea, Kline sold it to Canada's CTV network. The show would also air over 40 of NBC's affiliate stations in America. However, *The Starlost* was dogged by problems. Ellison, who left the show early on because of creative differences, was so unhappy with the final product that he put his pen name, Cordwainer Bird, on the screen.

One summary of the birth and death of *The Starlost* is offered by the show's producer, William Davidson. A graduate of Canada's Lorne Greene Academy of Radio Arts in 1948, he was immediately hired by the National Film Board of Canada, and with writer friend Norman Klenman, he later produced documentaries, drama series and features.

"Arthur Weinthal of CTV and Ted Delaney of CFTO–Glen Warren called me in to discuss producing *The Starlost*," recalls Davidson. "I thought it was a terrific concept and offered strong dramatic possibilities and popular appeal. I knew Harlan, by reputation, as a kind of science fiction guru. When I met him, I was equally impressed by his ideas and his incredible energy.

I brought about 34 Canadian writers in to meet him, and he chose some of them to begin working with him. Meanwhile, his U.S. contacts began to show an interest in the series."

Ellison, initially excited over the project, contacted such science fiction novelists as Philip Dick, A.E. Van Vogt, Joanna Russ and Frank Herbert to write for the show.

The technical advantage for *The Starlost* was using Doug Trumbull's new technology, Magicam, to film the series. Trumbull's special effects credits included *2001: A Space Odyssey* (1968) and *Silent Running* (1972). Trumbull's revolutionary new process would allow the actors to be transposed into miniature models and lavish landscapes to convey their travels through the domes (each of which was supposed to be 50 miles in diameter). It would give the series incredible visual leeway at an economical cost.

"I appreciated the opportunity to work with Doug Trumbull and to introduce his Magicam process to television production," says Davidson. "Doug is a genius and one of the nicest people you could work with. He was full of enthusiasm and energy. He brought his family up with him and rented a cottage north of Toronto. Then there was CFTO–Glen Warren. As a videotape production facility, they were as good as any facility in the world. Managing to get their senior production staff man, Ed Richardson, as associate producer and director was icing on the cake. The potential for something great was there."

The promise of great things soon fizzled. "As we went into production, a couple of unexpected things happened," recalls Davidson. "Harlan quit on us. The full story of his 'deserting the ship' is very complex. He's written, in very harsh terms, about his involvement with the project." (Ellison's description of his *Starlost* experience appears as a supplement to his book *Phoenix Without Ashes*, a novelization of his original *Starlost* pilot script.)

"I'm sure Harlan's rage and indignation are

genuine and deep. Whatever the complete story, he made no attempt whatsoever to understand our budget and production problems. He wrote scripts and story ideas that called for Spielberg-like production budgets. Then he had his lawyers give us the 'bird' with his nom-de-plume, Cordwainer Bird.

"The other major event was that Doug Trumbull's Magicam system didn't work in time. We went into production with an overnight switch back to the standard technique of electronically joining images of static background settings, and having the performers working in front of blue curtains.

"We all felt very sorry for Doug. He had problems in delivering his system on time, and it was very unfortunate for everyone. I lost a valuable associate."

Associate producer Ed Richardson says, "Initially, we had Keir Dullea, Harlan Ellison and Doug Trumbull, and that gave it a science fiction marquee of three people who knew about science fiction. I directed a promotional piece for the show with Trumbull, and we tried a number of effects with Keir in the studio. We were trying to create a video technology as we went along. The special effects device that should have worked, didn't. If it had, it would have enabled us to take miniature models and put our actors into them. We could have created all kinds of hills and valleys and monsters and blended our live actors into that. The process, however, only worked sparingly and quickly fell down. We had to film the series static, and it turned out flat."

Davidson retains a modest nostalgia and some regret about The Starlost. As the seams began to unravel, he says, "there were a few handicaps, but we thought we could handle everything."

When Kline's efforts to sell to the BBC were unsuccessful, the production venue was changed to Toronto. "CFTO–Glen Warren studios agreed to mount the production at a fraction of the budget estimates," says Davidson. "We had a budget of $100,000–125,000, less than many one-minute commercials. We went right into program one, 'Voyage of Discovery,' cold. We ended up with a budget overage of 50 percent or more. Immediately, we had to tighten up costs.

"There were no scripts at all; Doug's Magicam process wasn't working yet; studio space was very tight for such an ambitious project and the completion schedule was frightening. There was no time for rehearsal for the performers. We had a four-day shoot, seven days for complex video-tape editing, laying music and effects, and turning out a two-inch master completed program for the U.S. three days later. We knew we would be working 24 hours a day, seven days a week. The lights never went out in the Starlost offices."

For casting, NBC wanted a recognizable star for the series. Actor Keir Dullea was living in London and agreed to move to Toronto for the series' duration. Canadian newcomers Gay Rowan and Robin Ward were recruited as co-stars.

"Keir Dullea had been contracted before I signed on," recalls Davidson. "I had a high regard for his acting skills. He was a nice, enthusiastic person. He was very intense, and intrigued by the character of Devon. He found the pressure of television series production, and videotape in particular, to be very stressful, but he gave it everything he had. Robin Ward was perfect in the role, and the complete professional. Gay Rowan was intelligent, charming and although lacking a little in experience, I felt she could become a big star. A second season would have given more attention to Gay's role. She was full of creative ideas on how to develop her character."

Norman Klenman, a Canadian writer who had worked extensively in American episodic TV, recalls, "Arthur Weinthal told me the Americans wouldn't do a show in Canada unless it had an American star and American head writer. I had done a lot of work at Fox, so they zeroed in on me. There had never been any major Canadian series done from here [Canada] to there [U.S.]."

Klenman's dealings with Ellison were rocky at best. "When I read his bible for The Starlost and his first draft of the opening episode, I nearly gave birth to a cow. Bad is one thing. Boring is another. I regretted having to give Harlan a call and introduce myself to him. I knew him to be an egotistical son of a bitch. I said to him, 'Harlan, I'm on my way to Toronto to work on the show. I haven't had any experience in science fiction. I gather you wrote the pilot?' He was snarky on the phone. I said, 'Well, then, to hell with you!'

"When I got to Toronto, they gave me his pilot to read, and it was dreadful biblical nonsense. The idea of people stranded on a sphere on a spaceship wasn't bad, but everything else was boring. I rewrote it and tried to lighten it up and make the characters more three-dimensional. Ellison later went moaning and groaning around the country, advertising his disappointment with the Starlost series. The strange thing was, Harlan later won a Writer's Guild of America award for his [original] script."

Keir Dullea as Devon in *The Starlost*. Copyright 1973 CTV/Twentieth Century–Fox.

Associate producer Ed Richardson says, "Harlan Ellison is an incredible writer. Most of my dealings with him were on the phone when he was in a Toronto hotel room, writing. I have a great deal of respect for Ellison. He stuck to his guns and knows damn well what he wants. He's a feisty guy—the Muhammad Ali of science fiction."

Right after Ellison left, it became clear *The Starlost* was imbued in technical problems. "[Doug Trumbull's] new process would have made the shooting of the spaceship model much more realistic," says Klenman. "But they didn't have the technology ready. All the technical work was eventually done by CFTO in Toronto, and they did a fairly good job. CFTO was a huge production facility and was one of the early videotape producers in North America."

It remained a disappointing compromise. Instead of a vibrant and innovative-looking show, *The Starlost* emerged as a static series, with its actors confined to peculiar-looking sets and claustrophobic direction. For audiences expecting the technical equivalent of a *Star Trek*, *The Starlost* fell a planet short.

"There's a Paula Abdul commercial where she's dancing with the late Fred Astaire," says Klenman. "You can do that with today's film technology. All we could do in 1973 was to film a spaceship model in a black studio, with pinpoints of light in the background as stars. We moved the camera to give the illusion of the ship traveling through space. Because of the lack of special effects, the scripts had to be more character-oriented.

"We had a great bunch of people. Bill Davidson was a superb producer, and Ed Richardson was an excellent director. They put together a good team. But I was the only one in the writing department. There were no writers or scripts prepared. Of the 16, I wrote four, did four massive rewrites of others, and on four more I did minor rewrites. There were four others that came in pretty good shape. There were a lot of good Canadian writers, but almost nobody had been trained in writing American kind of drama. Unless you stood over them, or did it yourself, it didn't work."

With Harlan Ellison and Doug Trumbull gone, that left Ben Bova as science consultant. "Harlan had asked me to be science advisor for the series," says Bova. "I was living in New York, and I shuttled back and forth to Toronto.

"My job was to read scripts and find if there were any scientific goofs and find a way around them without totally destroying the scripts. There were plenty of goofs, and I did figure ways around them. I was paid rather handsomely as a consultant, and praised by everybody ... and my advice was totally ignored. They shot the scripts as originally written.

"It was very embarrassing because at the end of these idiotic shows there's a full screen credit: 'Ben Bova, Science Consultant.' I was shocked and dismayed to see all the work I did was absolutely for nothing. It was very disappointing to me, personally. The show was just bad. I was not involved in writing the scripts nor the creative aspects of the show. They were so hard-pressed to get the show done they paid lip service to have a science advisor. I don't just blame the people working on *The Starlost*. The general TV audience neither knows or cares about scientific accuracy. [However] science fiction fans are very knowledgeable and very critical of scientific inaccuracy. The inept acting, the poor plots, the very poor production values made the show ridiculous, but the scientific goofs just added to the poor quality of the series."

Writer Norman Klenman defends the *Starlost* team's decisions. "Ben Bova was a nice guy and a big name in science fiction," he says. "But what has science fiction got to do with drama? Stories are stories. Characters are characters. As head writer, I never found anything Mr. Bova had to say germane to our task. It was all sort of intellectual mumbo jumbo. He couldn't reduce it to clear, precise instructions.

"TV viewers are interested in the characters, not scientific theory or accuracy. We used very little of the latter two, and no one missed them. Bova was a talented man with a sure reputation. He was too courteous to cause a problem. He was just misplaced on this series."

"Ben tried to be helpful and continued working with us even after his buddy Harlan had jumped ship," observes William Davidson. "I am not suggesting that Ben was happy with the outcome, but I was satisfied with the contributions he made. As it was, we had to use the phone and the mail service. He was a novice about television production, and he never really got to know us and understand our production problems."

Nevertheless, Bova found the show's original format inspiring. "The basic idea was of a generational starship that had gone wrong. The people inside believe their ship is their universe. The ship had broken down and was falling into the gravity well of a star. Unless something was done, the ship and everybody aboard were going to perish. That premise is capable of all kinds of themes and stories. It had tremendous flexibility and had the possibilities of very good drama.

"One of the things Harlan wanted to do was to write the show like a novel where each episode was another chapter, so each episode had to be shown in sequence. The pilot of *Starlost* was very good. Harlan's [original] script was also very good. He's an excellent writer. Whether you love him or hate him, he's one of the best writers in the United States, but by the time they started shooting the scripts, Harlan had left."

Bova found a creative way to vent his spleen over the experience. "The show got so ridiculous that I wrote a satirical novel about it called *The Starcrossed*. It's based on what really happened during production of *The Starlost*. Only the names have been changed to protect the guilty.

"The people involved were trying to do their best, but that wasn't good enough. What came out was undoubtedly the worst television series ever. A lot of time was spent staring into the camera."

Bova felt the budget problems could have been circumvented. "The less money you have, the more creative you have to be. The budget of *The Starlost* did not make it a lousy show. It was that the people didn't know what they were doing. The people in the script department were tearing their hair out, trying to get decent scripts. The production people were trying to get the show videotaped and in the can. The problem was that these people didn't understand that what they were doing was bad. They were just concerned with shooting a number of script pages per day and getting the tape done."

Among those laboring under this demanding schedule was Canadian film and stage actor Robin Ward, who nabbed the role of Garth. In the pilot, the elders have promised Rachel in marriage to Garth. When Rachel falls for Devon, Garth becomes her protector and an uneasy ally of Devon as they set out on their journey.

"Just about every actor in Canada had been auditioned for the role of Garth," says Ward. "In desperation, they came around to me. I did a screen test, and suddenly I was Garth.

"As an actor who was doing theater in Canada, I would have accepted a series called *Pharmacists in Space*. Even so, I loved the concept and my character, whom I saw as a 'Mennonite in space' with an attitude."

However, that early attitude was too sharp for Ward's taste. "Garth was too negative as originally conceived. I felt he needed to build sympathy with the audience by a gradual relationship with the others. I attempted to do this, but I disliked his lack of humor.

"As actors we had some input in improving some dreadful scripts, and lots of input into character, but it really depended on who was directing. Keir, Gay and I became great friends, held together by incredibly long days, sometimes working 20 to 22 hours in a day.

"We developed a group sense of humor, and in a sly way—and sometimes not so subtle—we sent up the whole thing when we felt it was becoming a bit silly."

For Ward personally, the silliest moment was a stunt gone awry. "We were all wired up to fly in space. After the others took off, it was my turn. Unfortunately, I'm top heavy. I turned over and flew upside down. They ended up leaving that in the show."

Looking back on the series, Ward notes, "The first episode was the best, from a special effects point of view. In general, the series was severely restricted by budget as far as production goodies, but it was a good experience for a young actor. Over the years, it has clearly established a cult following. It was a great concept by Ellison and had a quirky and unusual atmosphere that was partly intended and partly accidental, with some eccentric acting. The weaknesses were bad

Rachel (Gay Rowan) and Garth (Robin Ward) in a reflective moment. Copyright 1973 CTV/Twentieth Century–Fox.

scripts and a great lack of imaginative and convincing special effects."

During its brief run, *The Starlost* managed to attract many recognizable actors for its guest stars.

"We had some very good guest actors," says Norman Klenman. "Lloyd Bochner was a real charmer and kept us in stitches. He collects jokes, and he was a wonderfully witty man. Walter Koenig was a funny guy. He wanted to work on the show each week. If we had been picked up, I would have fought for him as a regular because he was a terrific, very bright fellow." Had the series continued, several other well-known stars were set for guest appearances, including Richard Basehart, Leslie Nielsen, Patrick MacNee, William Shatner and Gordon Pinsent.

Klenman did have some reservations about the regular cast. "The star, Keir Dullea, was a nice man, but he was the most wooden actor I've ever met, although he was wonderful in *2001*. Gay Rowan was pure wood. Robin Ward was fine."

Robin Ward stands out in Ed Richardson's

mind as well. "He was heaven to work with. He was one of the nicest and most cooperative actors I've worked with. He was a talented fellow."

When the series debuted, the atmosphere looked promising. It was the most ambitious project ever attempted by a Canadian network. In its first four weeks on the air, it was number one in its time slots in both New York and L.A. *The Starlost* was also the recipient of many favorable reviews. "It's carried science fiction television a galactic step forward," *Toronto Star* columnist Jack Miller wrote about the pilot. "In depth of plot and sincerity of acting and staging, it was a world ahead of *Star Trek*.... This is the best science fiction series ever to come to television."

Joan Irwin of *The Montreal Star* noted, "*The Starlost* shows every sign of inheriting the mantle of the phenomenally successful *Star Trek*." In Canada, where the highest rated series on CTV was the American series *Ironside* (with 250,000 viewers a week), *The Starlost* followed with a healthy 200,000 viewers.

When a Tom Jones special preempted an

episode of *The Starlost,* CFTO studios received 147 phone calls from angry viewers who protested the bumping of the show. Only one lone viewer called in to rave about the Tom Jones special.

However, the production headaches continued. "There were a lot of problems," says Klenman. "While the stories were sound, the special effects technology wasn't advanced enough. In that regard, there was a little lack of imagination. They did very well with what they had. Occasionally, I would wince over how the episodes were produced."

He admits he campaigned for changes during the production. "I used to object to scenes where Keir and Robin would pull Gay along by her elbows whenever they were chased. My argument was, 'Women are some of the best athletes in the world. It's not like she's in high heels.' And that was kind of accepted."

Klenman also pushed for finding the *Ark*'s control center. "I wanted them to find a remote part of the ship where the central computers were, where you could steer the ship. I wanted a three-floor set, 50 feet high, and to have a steering wheel on top that would be from an old sailing ship. I thought it would be a wonderfully out-of-time thing, but nobody got the joke."

The Starlost was a success in Canada and attracted a sizable audience in America, but Davidson recalls that NBC felt the show's sluggish pace needed improving. "The only major criticisms (actually, suggestions) made by NBC, were: 'The program's slow, pick up the pace, more action, more cuts, faster cuts, fuller music and effects … and Keir seems to lack energy.' We did the creative alternative. We concentrated on the story, on the characters, on the performances and on the up-front drama. Keir's kind of internal, intense, low-key acting style carried a kind of conviction and honesty that no amount of running around would convey."

During the last few weeks of production, the producers were unsure if the series would be picked up for an additional eight segments by NBC. "Many great television programs have taken several weeks, months, even an entire first season to shake down and develop their true potential," says Davidson. "The initial reaction in Los Angeles, New York and other U.S. cities was excellent. Then [in following weeks] it was a matter of the ratings up one week, down the next. They were never downhill all the way. We were down to the wire. Will we get a pick up from NBC? Twentieth Century–Fox still wanted to go

ahead. CTV also wanted to continue since the show was doing well in ratings and with sponsors in Canada.

"But the ultimate decision came down to one man: Wes Harris at NBC. He wavered back and forth, then pulled the plug. It was devastating. To the key people who worked on *The Starlost* it was never a failure. We delivered it on time and on budget. In the final programs, we were trying to get control over what we hoped to do in the future, so my executives moved into the front line: Ed Richardson directing, Norman Klenman writing scripts. Had we been asked back for a second season, we would have made serious overtures to established science fiction writers to create story ideas, if not complete scripts."

"NBC was looking for immediate results and an instant hit," says Klenman. "Sixteen episodes was very little to judge it on. They probably killed it because of its technical quality. But it was well shot, beautifully edited and had good music. These series take years to catch on, just as Mr. Spock's ears took years to catch on. But their attitude is they have to make their money tomorrow or they're dead. If they had stayed with it, *The Starlost* might have been one of the greatest success stories that they ever had.

"The ratings in Canada were never a problem. If it had only been Canadian audiences, *The Starlost* could have run indefinitely. But while Fox was keen to keep the show going to a point, they weren't going to finance the whole thing. They had to have a [financial] commitment from NBC. NBC looked at the ratings and didn't think it was gonna make it, so they let it go. On the fifteenth episode, we got the cancellation notice. An embarrassed executive at CFTO said to me, 'Do you mind if we fire you today instead of next week?' so they could save money on the sixteenth show. I said, 'No, let me out.' I had a lot of other work piling up in L.A. Personally, the cancellation was not a big disappointment. I just felt NBC was depriving itself of the show."

"In Canada, you only needed an audience of 200,000 people to be a success," notes Richardson. "We did OK because there was a science fiction audience out there. We were very close to being renewed. We thought we would do okay in America because we were delivering a show for a lot less the cost than Americans could deliver a show. But simply, if the ratings had been higher, we would have been renewed."

In retrospect, Richardson says, "Harlan Ellison's concept was an incredibly good one. It had unlimited story potential. But when you watch the show, it falls short of your expectations. One problem was that it was on videotape and nobody was used to looking at a prime-time drama on videotape unless it was something from the BBC, where it was expected to look a little strange. The reason it was on video was to limit the cost of the special effects. On film, you'd have to create them in post-production and it would be a lot more expensive.

"When you watch the effects today, you ask, 'Why weren't they better?' It's difficult to put yourself back into that stone-age technology. It was a tough schedule, and there were budgetary constraints. We made those shows in five days. You can see by the effects how crazy they were. But there were a lot of people trying to make the show better. If you look at an editing facility today, you can animate the hell out of everything. Back then, we were on two-inch tape. It was the stone-age version of videotape. Had we had advanced technology, we could have concentrated more on the script and acting and not the effects, which were always short of the mark. But nobody should apologize for what they did. It was a damn good try."

Davidson thinks the lack of technology contributed significantly to The Starlost's woes. "The videotape methods were the show's biggest restrictions. If we had known Magicam wasn't going to work, we would have used different techniques from the beginning. The few visual effects we were able to put together were makeshift, costly and time-consuming, and did little for the visual impact. At times, we had up to a dozen small sets crammed into one studio, with barely enough room to turn around, let alone stage major action scenes. Those were the conditions we worked under. These aren't excuses. We thought we could handle the situation. I in particular have no excuses because I made all of the major decisions on a day-to-day basis with the full support of [executives] Arthur Weinthal of CTV and Ted Delaney of CFTO–Glen Warren. Robert Kline had provided an experienced and dedicated associate in Preston Fischer from New York, and we worked closely together. You only have my word for it, but a second season of programs would have been very good indeed. We never got the chance."

According to Klenman, The Starlost hasn't been left adrift in syndication. "Talk about cult shows," he says. "The series has been shown around the world. I've been dragooned to speak in San Francisco to Starlost fans. My daughter was in New Orleans and called to say she had met a bunch of nuts who watched Starlost and remembered it. I was in England once and somebody came up and shook my hand, saying, 'You're Norman Klenman from The Starlost. That was the greatest TV series ever made!' The Starlost could be revived today, using modern technology but with the same scripts. I still consider it a successful show in that it took off in syndication."

"To put The Starlost in perspective, it is useful to know that science fiction was a hard sell in those years," concludes Davidson. "The genre was considered death on network TV. Leave it to the 'syndicaters,' they said. The rebirth of science fiction in features and TV came later. Maybe all of our expectations were too high for the times."

CAST NOTES

Keir Dullea (Devon): Born 1936. Dullea is best known as the star of *2001: A Space Odyssey* (1968). He enjoyed success on the London stage after the series and continues to work in theater.

Gay Rowan (Rachel): Born 1948. This Toronto-born actress moved to Hollywood right after *The Starlost*, turning up in occasional TV guest roles including *Time Express* (1979) and *The Greatest American Hero* (1982).

Robin Ward (Garth): Born 1944. Ward came from a show business family. He hosted several Canadian game shows in the 1980s. In the 1990s he hosted a Canadian cooking program, *The Light Gourmet*, and was the weather and show biz commentator on Toronto's CFTO newscasts.

William Osler (Mulander 165, the computer): Osler's character, a computer image who often frustrated the travelers with his convoluted advice and direction, was both sinister and comical. "William Osler was for many years one of the finest character actors on the Toronto scene," says producer William Davidson. "He worked for me many times, although I have not spoken to him in several years now."

EPISODE GUIDE

Voyage of Discovery
Shunned by their small community after discovering that their world is on a spaceship, a young couple

embarks on a journey through the other spaceship biospheres. Wr: Cordwainer Bird (Harlan Ellison). Dir: Harvey Hart.

Jeremiah (Sterling Hayden); Jubal (George Sperdakos); Rachel's parents (Sean Sullivan, Aileen Seaton); Abraham (Gillie Fenwick); Garth's parents (Jim Barron, Kay Hawtrey); Boy (Scott Fisher).

Memory Flash—producer William Davidson: "I regretted that the late Harvey Hart was unable to direct more than two episodes because of prior commitments. Keir Dullea, Gay Rowan and Robin Ward felt comfortable working with Harvey, who had a marvelous way with performers and a knack of getting the very best out of them."

Lazarus from the Mist
A revived scientist claims he can avert the *Ark*'s collision course. His mission is threatened by a tribe of savage cavemen. Wr: Doug Hall, Don Wallace. Dir: Leo Orenstein.

Dr. Gerald Aaron (Frank Converse); Sergeant (Doug McGrath); Mrs. Aaron (Vivian Reis); Dwellers (Alan Bleviss, Mel Tuck).

The Goddess Calabra
Rachel is forced into a wedding by a governor who plans to capitalize on her resemblance to a goddess named Calabra. Wr: Martin Lager, story by Ursula K. LeGuin. Dir: Harvey Hart.

Governor (John Colicos); Shalith (Barry Morse); Priest (Dominic Hogan); Captain (Michael Kirby); Deputy (George Naklowych).

Memory Flash—John Colicos: "There was a scene where Keir and I had a sword fight. We didn't have any stunt doubles. We thought we could handle it ourselves. Keir got a little carried away, and he bonked me on the head and knocked me unconscious. You could hear the bonk echoing throughout the studio! I was rushed off to the hospital, and there wasn't any permanent damage. The next day, I went back to work, and Keir was most apologetic. That shot was left in the final cut. *The Starlost* was a technically innovative series, particularly for Toronto television."

The Pisces
A spaceship returns to the *Ark* after 409 years. The *Ark*'s atmosphere causes the crew to age at an accelerated rate. Wr: Norman Klenman. Dir: Leo Orenstein.

Col. Garroway (Lloyd Bochner); Janice (Diana Barrington); Teale (Carol Lazare); Old woman (Lillian Graham); Old man (Ted Beatie); Young women (June Stacey, Donna Stacey); Technician (Susan Fleming).

The Children of Methuselah
The trio find an *Ark* training center manned by 500-year-old children. Devon tries to draw the youngsters out of their fantasy world. Wr: Jonah Royston, George Ghent. Dir: Joseph L. Scanlan.

Captain (David Tyrell); Supervisor (Gina Dick); Prosecutor (Scott Fisher); Number 5 (Susan Stacey).

And Only Man Is Vile
A scientist uses the trio in an experiment to test human nature. He's determined to prove that mankind is too selfish and emotional to colonize the stars. Wr: Shimon Wincelberg. Dir: Ed Richardson.

Dr. Asgard (Simon Oakland); Lethe (Trudy Young); Dr. Diana Tabor (Irene Mayeska); Village elder (Tim Whelan); Villager A (John Bethune).

Memory Flash—Shimon Wincelberg: "*The Starlost* involved a very pleasant trip to Toronto and working with some nice, bright people. But the end result, which I could only view in someone's office at Twentieth Century–Fox, showed the seams of an ultra–low budget production."

Circuit of Death
Devon and an engineer are miniaturized to stop the *Ark*'s self-destruct mechanism. Wr: Norman Klenman. Dir: Peter Levin.

Sakharov (Percy Rodrigues); Valerie (Nerene Virgin); Cort (Calvin Butler).

Gallery of Terror
The trio become pawns of Magnus, a super-computer who creates people from their past. Devon asks the machine to conjure up the *Ark*'s long-dead captain. Wr: Alf Harris. Dir: Ed Richardson.

Daphne (Angel Tompkins); Admiral Austin (William Clune); Garth's father (Jim Barron).

Mr. Smith of Manchester
A biosphere leader plans to attack and conquer the *Ark*'s other domes. Wr: Arthur Heinemann. Dir: Joseph L. Scanlan.

Mr. Smith (Ed Ames); Trent (Pat Galloway); Nurse Green (Doris Petrie); Girl (Nina Weintraub).

The Alien Oro
A stranded alien cons the travelers into fixing his spaceship. He soon meets an alien woman who will die unless she's returned to her native planet. Wr: Mort Forer, Marion Waldman. Dir: Joseph L. Scanlan.

Oro (Walter Koenig); Ydana (Alexandra Bastedo).

Memory Flash—William Davidson: "We thought highly of Walter Koenig. It's possible that Oro might have become a regular character on later episodes."

Astro-Medics
A father-son medical team must choose between saving Devon, who is stricken with radiation sickness, or aliens on a plague-ridden planet. Wr: Paul Schneider. Dir: George McCowan.

Dr. Chris (Stephen Young); Dr. Jean (Meg Hogarth); Dr. Martin (Budd Knapp); Commander (Michael Zenon); Also with William Kemp.

The Implant People
A dying life form on a mountaintop and a scheming advisor in the village below, who is controlling people with implants, pose dangers to the trio. Wr: John Meredyth Lucas, story by Alan Spraggett,

Helen French and George Ghent. Dir: Joseph L. Scanlan.

Roloff (Donnelly Rhodes); Serina (Pat Collins); Brant (Leo Leyden); Jardy (Jeff Toner); Domal (Dino Narizzano).

The Return of Oro

Oro returns and promises to change the *Ark*'s destructive course by taking it to his home planet. Devon learns Oro's planet will be disastrous for human life. Wr: Norman Klenman. Dir: Francis Chapman.

Oro (Walter Koenig); William (Henry Beckman); Tau Zeta (Philip Stevens).

Farthing's Comet

A meteor storm threatens to destroy the *Ark* unless Devon endures a hazardous space walk and pilots the ship to safety. Wr: Norman Klenman. Dir: Ed Richardson.

Linus Farthing (Ed Andrews); McBride (Linda Sorenson); Computer voice (Alan Stewart Coats).

Memory Flash—Ed Richardson: "The scenes of Keir floating around in space were accomplished by putting Keir in a black chair against a blue screen and moving the chair around with little rods. When we keyed in the star background, it looked like he was floating in space. The meteors were little pieces of styrofoam that we threw past the camera lens."

Beehive

Giant telepathic bees are directing attacks to keep a zoological biosphere under their control. Wr: Norman Klenman. Dir: William Davis.

Heather (Antoinette Bower); Pete (William Hutt); Callisher (Alan McRae); Keebie (John Friesen).

Space Precinct

Joining the intergalactic police, Garth investigates hijacking incidents that could plunge two planets into war. Wr: Martin Lager. Dir: Joseph L. Scanlan.

Chief Masters (Ivor Barry); Reena (Nuala Fitzgerald); Mike (Richard Alden); Also with Diane Dewey.

Starman

September 1986–September 1987

Starman, an alien being who previously crash-landed and spent three days on Earth, returns to find a teenage son. Together, they travel across the country, fleeing from government agent George Fox while searching for Jenny Hayden, Scott's mother. Hitchhiking or driving across the byways of the United States, Starman and Scott develop a relationship and learn about the world around them.

Cast: Paul Forrester/Starman (Robert Hays); Scott Hayden, Jr. (C.B. Barnes); George Fox (Michael Cavanaugh); Wylie (also Wiley) (Patrick Culliton).

Based on characters created by Bruce A. Evans and Raynold Gideon; *Developed for television:* James Henerson and James Hirsch, and Mike Gray and John Mason; *Executive Producers:* James Henerson, James Hirsch, Michael Douglas; *Supervising Producer:* Leon Tokatyan; *Producers:* Mike Gray, John Mason; *Consulting Producers:* Deborah Ellis Leoni, Joel Chernoff; *Associate Producers:* Stephanie Austin, Jeanne Marie Byrd; ABC/Columbia TV; 60 minutes.

"The eyes of an innocent. The wisdom of the universe."—An ABC-TV network ad for *Starman* in *TV Guide*.

In the feature film *Starman* (1984) starring Jeff Bridges, Karen Allen and Richard Jaeckel, an alien crash-landed on Earth and took on the guise of Jenny Hayden's dead husband, Scott. He kidnapped her, and from Wisconsin they headed for Arizona where the spacecraft would retrieve him. They were pursued by a desperate government agent, Fox. Along the way Starman discovered love for the first time, and before he left, he gave Jenny the gift of a son.

The series came to be when producers James Henerson and James Hirsch saw the film and thought, 'We should do something with this!' They approached film producer Michael Douglas about the idea of a series. The initial thought was to develop it as a mid-season replacement, but when ABC heard the notion of a series and liked it, the show was slotted as a prime-time September entry.

Henerson and Hirsch hired producers Mike Gray and John Mason to write what's known in the business as a "promo" or "demo" film to pitch the premise. In this promotional video, the character Jenny Hayden is killed in a car crash. But that was changed later to allow the series characters to be *in search of* Jenny Hayden. The new face of Starman (actor Robert Hays) was easy to explain: The alien had simply taken on a new guise, this time the body of photographer Paul Forrester.

"Although I was hesitant because Jeff Bridges had done such a wonderful job in the film, I realized that this was 14 years later and upon returning to Earth, Starman would have to find a new body," says Robert Hays. "After 14 years, even he must have realized Jeff's body wouldn't be smelling too good—a bit ripe! It seemed like a wonderful opportunity. Like Michael Douglas said to me, 'It's completely open—you can do anything with this character.'" And with that in mind, Hays grabbed the leather jacket and lens and hit the road.

"I've been involved in metaphysics for some years, and [I was intrigued about] the idea of someone possessing the powers that [Starman] had," says co-star Michael Cavanaugh, who played the federal security agent Fox. "If you remember, at the end of the movie, there was [going to be] a son, and he said the son was going to be the second coming. I don't mean that in the religious sense, but it would mean this son would be an embodiment of that idea. That really impressed me. I thought Jeff Bridges did a great job. So when I heard about the series, I was very enthusiastic about it."

"I thought it was very novel. We were all looking for [a] flower [to bloom]," says supervising producer Leon Tokatyan.

The basis of the show's appeal, according to Tokatyan and Cavanaugh was the relationship between Scott Hayden—a somewhat rebellious growing son—and his extraterrestrial father, a very strange, compassionate alien who saw the world naively and struggled to be a good parent.

"He's not us," says Tokatyan. "He's a role model for his son. Once, he sat in the desert with his son and pointed to the sky and said, 'That's where I come from.'"

Tokatyan says the basic foundation of a show is the chemistry between the leading characters. Without good chemistry, the show doesn't work. In *Starman*'s case, [Hays and Barnes] "had something very nice together."

This chemistry was the very foundation of the show's appeal. "It's a father and son communicating together and resolving conflicts together, with a little patience and understanding," says Cavanaugh. "And I think that's something very appealing to people."

As evidence, says Cavanaugh, "during the filming of the show, I was in California, and I walked into a hotel lobby. A burly-looking man,

a Texan, was there and he looked at me and said, 'You're that guy on *Starman*, ain'tcha?' He said to me he loves the show because of the relationships between Bob and C.B., which is really delightful. I was quite surprised and quite pleased to see the show touched him."

The humanity of the relationships depicted in *Starman* is rare for television, says Cavanaugh. "The thing that sealed it for me, in terms of my enthusiasm for the show, was what I tend to know and understand: The powers that are in [Starman] are within all of us."

But conveying such a message begins with the right words. Supervising producer Tokatyan, who was responsible for hiring, gathering all the stories for the season and giving Starman his direction, describes how carefully scripts were constructed.

"We worked out the entire script, scene by scene, before they started. We made notes and then did a second draft. Sometimes I had to take over; either I did it or [executive story editors] Geoff Fischer or Tom Lazarus did it. I was responsible for the final draft," he explains.

To develop a story, all major parties involved in the show would gather around a table and analyze the script. "We had readings every week of the scripts we were going to shoot, so all the actors gathered around, with the exception of the [one-] day players," says Tokatyan. "The three or four major people. From that, we can go off and do a final polish. We could see what works or didn't work. ... Sometimes there would be tongue twisters. We would sit there and check off parts that didn't play or were repetitive or too long or not clear. We never get enough time to fine-tune them. I remember people dashing in and saying, 'We're two minutes short.' Aaaghh! I have to write a whole new scene. I have to find out where to put it and what does it consist of. Sometimes it's two minutes over and they cut like hell and then they say, 'My mistake!'

Michael Cavanaugh gained the role of FSA agent George Fox by becoming, not unlike his character, obsessed with the part. "I don't think I ever wanted something as much as I did with that series," he says. "There were several people in the office, producers, and I was supposed to go in and read for the part. I went in and did my audition, and left. Later, from several different people—producers and other actors sitting outside the room—I heard that producers walked out and said, 'We're not seeing anyone else.' That's how well it went. That day I happened to

Starman/Paul Forrester (Robert Hays) and Scott Hayden (C.B. Barnes) travel across the country seeking Jenny Hayden and avoiding their nemesis, FSA agent Fox. Copyright 1986 ABC/Columbia.

be the first on the audition list. I was so zeroed in to doing this part, that in my mind, there was no one else. I was absolutely convinced I was going to do that part."

Of course, the producers accommodated the other would-be Foxes in the outer room, but their minds were set on Cavanaugh. "So, later I had to read for the network. Normally, there's three, four, five or six different people they take to the network. They didn't bring anyone but me. The producers were that convinced. Fortunately, the network was convinced, too. So, there's the story. … I had no question in my mind that I wanted to be involved with something of this stature, [this] metaphysical nature."

Some say villains' roles are always the most interesting. The truth of the matter is, Cavanaugh did not see Fox as a villain. Not even as an antagonist. "He was a man who was absolutely dedicated to his job," explains Cavanaugh. "He had absolute conviction that the world and the nation was at stake at every moment. I don't think he was ever interested in killing Starman; I think he

was interested in removing him from circulation. He did not have the understanding of Paul Forrester that the audience has. He perceived him as a threat to the nation. I guess you could call him an absolute company man. Somebody who's got a job to do, and he's willing to do it virtually at all costs."

It was important to Cavanaugh that Fox's character be consistent. In the episode "Grifters," which detailed Fox and Starman's first face-to-face encounter, Fox was supposed to tell Forrester, "If I could kill you now, I'd do it." Both Hays and Cavanaugh objected to that line and implored the producers to change it. They did. "That was a *big* bone of contention between me and the producers. I must say, though, the producers were very receptive to our ideas."

Again, Cavanaugh returns to the idea of *Starman* as a show with a message. "With a little intensity, drive and conviction on your part, you can get [Starman's] ability! He was not judgmental. That's a tremendous, subtle message of the show.

"Forrester was almost a naive individual. His naivete allowed him to see the good in people and not have his vision clouded by appearances. He went to the heart and soul of people, not their appearances. His basic goodness allowed him to see the basic goodness in other people. A good example of that was saving George Fox's life."

Cavanaugh refers to a scene in the only two-parter of the series, "Starscape." Confronting Forrester, Fox suffers a heart attack. "Just as I'm ready to shoot him in the back, he turns around and recognizes a man is about to die, and he heals me! It's the most amazing thing. I get the chills just thinking about it. It's a tremendous, loving, non-judgmental way of doing things.

"I would have liked to have seen in another season where Fox starts to get confused with this man."

In the scene where Forrester heals the agent, Fox is unconscious. Cavanaugh says it was important that Fox be unaware of the deed in order to ensure (if the show had continued into further years) that the conflict between the two would continue.

"If, in the first season, I love the man, there's no show!" Cavanaugh exclaims. "So you have to maintain that conflict and over a period of time, drop in some hints" that Fox is beginning to have doubts about his mission.

Starman stories were *about* something. Episodes addressed species preservation, literacy, family estrangements and even illegal (earthly) aliens crossing the border. "I don't think hard-edged stories would have worked," says Tokatyan. "It's not what [Starman] was about. It's not what the series was."

Tokatyan's favorite story was Michael Mark's "Appearances." "A blind farming girl realizes [Starman] has magic powers. She says, 'Heal me! Let me see you!' And he tries to tell her he couldn't do that. Stories like that I think were worthwhile. We wanted to get into talking about the fundamentalists on the show. Everyone was against the religious aspects. In my head, it was the parents saying, 'That's the way God wants it, that you can't see. You can't change that.' They were very harsh about that. It gets convoluted. There's a lot going on in there. The problem was I wanted to make it more religion-oriented."

Another script Tokatyan found remarkable was "The Probe," by Syrie Astrahan James. In his 25 years in television, never has a script passed

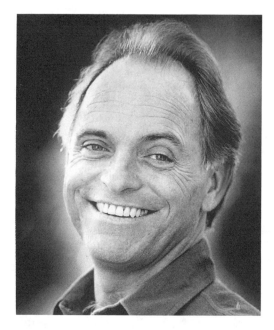

Michael Cavanaugh played FSA agent George Fox. Photo courtesy Michael Cavanaugh.

his desk that didn't need tinkering—except this one.

"I didn't have to cut it! I didn't have to touch a word! She's a very interesting woman. She had written a romance novel and it was published. She wrote another one and it was published. She got bored and wrote a feature screenplay, which [*Starman* producers] Henerson and Hirsch optioned! So, she decided, 'Well, this is kind of fun, maybe I can do television too!' Everything she touched became gold. Nothing had to be done with it. The second one ["Fathers and Sons"] needed work, but we worked on it together."

Tokatyan says if he could go back and make one change in the series, he would add more of the wry adult humor that Hays did so well as the character. "By adult, I don't mean archaic cursing or of the sexual innuendo variety, but more sly humor. There was a limit to how much we could play the alien aspects," he notes. "Doing a show in a week is madness. You never have enough time to do anything. I remember going to Bob's place one morning with a script that had to be out *that day*."

The achievement of *Starman*, says Tokatyan, was that although the show was typically filled with compromises, when he stood back and looked at the finished product, he was happy with what he saw. "In any collaborative effort, compromise is necessary, so one has to be satisfied with the end product because it's as close as possible to the concept. It was like a sausage factory. And the fact it turned out as well as it did, is a miracle."

Despite his overall satisfaction, Tokatyan longed for more stories that provided "a mirror to contemporary society. That was our original intent and conception. That's one of the reasons I wanted to do religious stuff in 'Appearances.' The pressures of getting the show on—you can't ask a crew to stand by while you think of a script—went against some of the ideals you want for the show."

Although Tokatyan acknowledges that the Starman character was a good foundation for examining society, "I don't think we were that successful. We were successful in bits and pieces, but you gotta look fast. Just the pressures of getting the show out. For example, if we had the opportunity to do all 22 shows before we started shooting show number one, we can look at number two and say, 'Aha! This should be shifted this way, and that should be shifted that way. We can take this one out and get another one.' We didn't have that luxury."

Starman was stronger in telling stories about Paul and Scott's relationship than about his extraterrestrial adventures. Viewers never really learned about Starman's life in space.

"We went around and around about that," confesses Tokatyan. "What do they do? How are they born where he is? Is there death where he comes from? He cloned himself from another living human and from the blood of the real Paul Forrester." After hours of discussion, producers decided not to dwell on the details of Starman's otherworldly existence, "because we felt we weren't really a science fiction show per se. It's not a science fiction show except for the sphere." Tokatyan refers to a mysterious, glowing blue sphere Starman carried with him. The sphere had magical powers (in the film, Jeff Bridges had several spheres, which spent their energy by being used). "We kept wondering, what's inside that sphere? We had many, many meetings about the limits of that sphere." Tokatyan says they made a conscious effort to use the sphere judiciously. "We didn't want this to turn into a magic show where he'd take the sphere and have them taken out of a forest fire or something."

Starman shared with many other shows the premise of a protagonist pursued by an antagonist. Perhaps the first to ride this premise into megahit status was *The Fugitive*, followed over the years by *The Incredible Hulk* (Banner was chased by reporter McGee), *The Immortal* (a millionaire wanted Ben Richards' blood), *The Phoenix* (federal agent Preminger dogged the Egyptian Bennu), *Otherworld* (a family transported into a different universe were sought by a high-ranking military man), and *Logan's Run* (Logan and Jessica with REM ran from fellow Sandman Francis).

Cavanaugh, presented with brief descriptions of each of these shows, is amazed at the common theme. "I haven't heard of 80 percent of them, or think I've seen any of them," he says. "I don't really watch television. I'm not very familiar with drama television, so it's a revelation to me, this chase premise. It seems to have been necessary to create conflict in this way. There has to be something to create tension."

Cavanaugh adds that even in Starman's neighborhood, conflict is necessary to life. "The nature of life is to move forward, and what makes us move forward with wisdom and intelligence is conflict. It makes you think. It makes you expand."

"Networks aren't brilliant thinkers. They wanted jeopardy," Tokatyan says succinctly.

Robert Hays' portrayal of Paul Forrester garnered high marks from Tokatyan, who liked how Hays played the character very openly and gave him enough of a "clean slate" that he would react naively to ordinary occurences. "In the pilot when [Starman] steps into the elevator, when the door starts to close, that is something he's never seen before. A lot of actors might have just stood there, but Bob did it being very startled. It was a small moment, but he did a marvelous job."

Robert Hays describes Starman as "basically a void waiting to be filled, and during this process he reacted quizzically to the world around him—while taking it in he questioned it all. This made for potentially a blank and therefore bland performance if I wasn't careful. It was also hard to keep from jumping ahead of ourselves. Once Starman learned something, you could never have him go back to where he didn't know it, for a story point."

"Robert Hays is one of the nicest men I've ever met in the business," says Tokatyan. "If there was a meeting and a stranger walked in, he does everything he can make this person feel at home."

Working with Robert Hays and C.B. Barnes was a delight for Cavanaugh, who characterizes

Hays as "a very generous, outgoing, warm man. C.B. was only 14 at the time. And the three of us got along really well. And that connection spread throughout the whole production and even to guest stars coming aboard. It was an extraordinary experience. We seemed to get the message of the show out—the interaction, kindness, teachings. Those ideas seemed to permeate the whole atmosphere of the set, the production offices; everyone loved the project. I think it comes across on the screen because it was a genuine atmosphere on the set."

And the further miracle of the show for Cavanaugh is that "we're all still friends. The friendships have continued beyond the show." They do not necessarily see each other as frequently as all would like because everyone is occupied with projects, but whenever reunions or birthday parties are arranged, Cavanaugh says, those friendships continue.

Starman/Paul Forrester (Robert Hays) with a falcon in the episode "Peregrine." Copyright 1986 ABC/Columbia.

Tokatyan says C.B. Barnes also brought excellent performances to his role as Scott. Barnes, in interviews, said the show was so popular that he received letters from all over the world, including West Germany, Japan, Taiwan, Hong Kong and Chile. Occasionally, he had to get those letters translated.

Cavanaugh excitedly relates personal experiences that demonstrated the international scope of Starman's popularity. For example, while visiting Paris in 1990, he was recognized for *Starman* in streets, subways and restaurants. But it was while doing a film in Lima, Peru, that Cavanaugh had his most rewarding encounter. In this

moment, language was a barrier, but no language was needed to exchange the mutual delight.

"We had a day off, so we went shopping," describes Cavanaugh. "We went to this market and in a long lineup of stalls selling wares, we went into this one stall and there was a television, and on the television is *Starman*. I'm in a scene with a kid with a broken arm asking about Scott [Hayden]. There I am, speaking in perfect [dubbed] Spanish. Of course, it's not me! It was hysterical! Behind the counter there were these two little boys, about 10 or 12. They saw and recognized me, and their faces just lit up. Those kids will probably never forget that day. There's the guy on the TV screen and in front of them at the same time! It was an incredible, amazing experience!"

Starman ran against *L.A. Law, Miami Vice, The Cosby Show* and *Falcon Crest*. It lagged in ratings and was canceled in May 1987. Immediately, an organization called Spotlight Starman sprang up, representing fans and admirers from all over the United States and Canada. They tried very hard, with a letter-writing campaign to pressure ABC into renewing the show. Failing, they have since channeled their energies to creative or charitable endeavors, and the organization has been elevated to an international level.

"I thought it was wonderful that they tried," says Tokatyan. "It's very difficult. We weren't even borderline [in the ratings]. Of course today, it might be a different story. In those days, the network was arrogant. People love this show. I get letters. I still get newsletters from the national club. They love the father-son relationship. They love the childlike innocence that [Starman] has that turns into so much wisdom."

Robert Hays says, "They are a remarkable bunch of people, from all walks of life and from many countries around the world. *Starman* really touched a lot of people in a wonderful, positive way."

Spotlight Starman literature obtained by the authors indicated mailing lists for admirers of the show were, initially, in the thousands. Fans were in North America and several foreign countries, with active chapters in Australia, Germany, New Zealand and South Africa.

One of the members of the Spotlight Starman group is a woman named Jean Laidig, and in a nod to the ABC promo quote used in the beginning of this chapter, Laidig invented her own. She describes the Starman's qualities as "naive wisdom, stubborn flexibility, humorous gravity and awkward grace."

Spotlight Starman appears to be different from typical fandoms. Although members network among themselves and produce a "newsletterzine" called Blue Lights as well as calendars, songbooks, cookbooks and audiotapes, Spotlight Starman also endeavors to focus its energies towards raising money for charities.

"They have weekend conventions where auctions are held. They give money to particular charities," explains Cavanaugh. "To me that's a very good effort on their part. It carries on a tradition of doing good for others that Starman epitomized in the series. To me, that speaks volumes about their dedication to the theme of the show."

Active since 1987, the organization has held eight conventions over the years and has raised more than $13,000, distributed to organizations such as Literacy Volunteers of America, the Cousteau Society, Alzheimer's Association, the Society for the Preservation of Variety Arts, the Nature Conservancy, and Greenpeace.

Every two years in Los Angeles, Spotlight Starman organizes a reunion of the cast, crew and staff of the series. Other fandoms seldom engage in such efforts.

"I was incredibly impressed by their organization and their determination and their love of the show," announces Cavanaugh. "It's very gratifying. So many people were touched. It's nice to know that something I was involved in meant so much to so many people. I think they're a very impressive group of people."

Addressing the possibility of a *Starman* reunion movie to reveal whether Paul Forrester and son ever reunite with Jenny Hayden and escape the clutches of Fox, Robert Hays says, "I don't know about any of the other people. *Starman* was such a special show to all of us, it would be wonderful to get together to do it again, even if it were just a one-shot TV movie. And when I say all of us, I mean cast and crew both. It was such a great group of people. But I think the reality of it is that it's been so long and people have gone off to other things." The fact that the producing team of James Hirsch and James Henerson has since dissolved might also present problems.

Hays says, "Although getting the go-ahead so quickly put us a bit behind the eight ball, I felt Jim Hirsch, Jim Henerson, Leon Tokatyan, Mike Gray, John Mason (the list goes on!) all created wonderful shows. We were all very proud of the shows.

"I think I could always be happy with any work I've ever done, but all in all, *Starman* is something I am very proud of. Having been able to work with that cast and crew was one of the best experiences in a life that has been lucky enough to have had a bunch of good'ns!"

CAST NOTES

Robert Hays (Paul Forrester/Starman): Born 1947. Hays, a comedy-drama actor who starred in the features *Airplane* and *Airplane II* and the TV series *Angie* (1979-80), remains busy with TV movies like *Murder by the Book* and *Running*

Against Time, and features such as *50/50* and *Homeward Bound*.

Christopher Daniel (C.B.) Barnes (Scott Hayden, Jr.): After *Starman*, Barnes starred in *Day by Day* (1988-89), a sitcom with Linda Kelsey. He made guest appearances in *The Golden Girls* and *Herman's Head* and starred in the specials *Testing Dirty* and *Just Perfect*. He had supporting roles in the TV movies *Frankenstein: The College Years* (1991) and *Murder Without Motive: The Edmund Perry Story* (1992). Barnes had two appearances on *Blossom*, and he also appeared in *Time Trax* (1993).

Michael Cavanaugh (FSA agent George Fox): Starting out on stage in *Oh, Calcutta!* Cavanaugh gradually made his way through episodic television on *Charlie's Angels* and *Streets of San Francisco*, and appeared in features such as *The Enforcer* (1976) and *Gray Lady Down* (1978). In the 1980s he appeared in *Airwolf*, *Cagney and Lacey*, *MacGyver*, *Star Trek: The Next Generation* and *The A-Team*, and during the 1990s, *Dark Shadows*, *Dr. Quinn—Medicine Woman*, *The X-Files* and *Lois and Clark: The New Adventures of Superman*.

EPISODE GUIDE

The Return
Starman returns to Earth when a signal from his son's sphere calls out to him. He takes the body of photojournalist Paul Forrester, who dies in a helicopter crash. Starman traces his son, Scott, to a Seattle orphanage. A reporter who once knew Forrester meets Starman and believes him to be Paul. Meanwhile, George Fox investigates Scott's escape from a car crash. Reporter Baynes tells Fox about Paul. Together, Starman and Scott vow to find Jenny Hayden. Wr: James Henerson and James Hirsch. Dir: Charles S. Dubin.
Liz Baynes (Mimi Kuzyk); Fay Tomarkin (Ruth Manning); General Wade (Jason Wingreen); Wiley (Patrick Culliton); Clerk (Lou Cutell); Photo technician (Mark Burke); Waiter (Charles Davis); Darcy (Lydie Denier); Kent (Christopher Kriesa); Eileen (Julie Mannix); Bellman (Richard Molnar); Aide (John Otrin); Woman in elevator (Mavis Neal Palmer); Wes, the pilot (Joseph Phelan); Boy #1 (Marcello Krakoff); Boy #2 (Ryan Bollman); Boy #3 (Brad Kesten).

Like Father, Like Son
Scott's bitter over his father's return and believes they have nothing in common. Later, Scott and Paul help a mother and her daughter when the car breaks down. Fox continues in his hunt for Starman. Wr: Geoffrey Fischer. Dir: Nancy Malone.
Shannon McGovern (Candy Clark); Beth McGovern (Robyn Lively); Vic (Jeremy Slate); Dana McGovern (Paul Tuerpe); John (Alan Haufrect); Pat (Diana Webster); Jay (Kurt Smildsin); Officer (Seth Mitchell); Hunter #1 (Charles Quertermous); Hunter #2 (Josh Gordon); Roy (Marco Hernandez); Glenn (Tom Kindle); Waitress (Joy Ellison).

Fatal Flaw
While photographing at a motorcycle meet, Starman saves a biker from being killed. Moving on so Fox won't find them, Scott and Paul become involved with a woman who's trying to save the family aircraft design company. Wr: Mike Gray and John Mason. Dir: Robert Chenault.
Joe Foss (Sam Melville); Jessica Bennett (Patricia McPherson); Conrad Bennett (Kenneth Tobey); Sam (Timothy Jecko); Sheriff (Herb Armstrong); Frank (Bill Shick); Randy (Shannon Sinutko); Boy (Anthony Barton).

Blue Lights
Accidentally creating blue lights in the sky while camping, Scott and Starman are captured by the local law. Wr: Tom Lazarus. Dir: Claudio Guzman.
Charlie Ewing (Rick Hurst); Laurie (Margot Rose); Wiley (Patrick Culliton); Buddy (Lawrence Bame); Vern (Richard Fullerton); Kelly (Sharon Madden); Louie (Michael Griswold); Lizard #1 (J. Omar Hansen); Lizard #2 (Walter Caldwell); Waitress (Diane Vincent).

Best Buddies
In Phoenix to complete a photography assignment, Starman runs into Paul's Vietnam buddy and learns Paul was having an affair with his buddy's wife. Scott wants to leave, but Starman wants to finish the photo assignment. Wr: Leon Tokatyan. Dir: Charles S. Dubin.
Jake Lawton (Cliff Potts); Kathy Lawton (Suzanne Lederer); Rayfield (John Anderson); Barker (Jason Ronard); Milton (Barbara Beckley); Cindy (Tamara Mark); Dave (Tony Miller); Man #1 (Biff Elliot); Burgess (Eduardo Ricard); Arnold Davidson (Ric Mancini); Maryanne (Michelle Casey); Asian businessman (Rob Narita); Woman with dog (Kathryn Fuller); Man #2 (Scott Martin); Mother (Elyse Donalson).

Secrets
Scott and Starman see a TV report that Jenny escaped from a mental hospital. But it's an elaborate trap set by Fox. Wr: Randall Wallace. Dir: Bob Sweeney.
Angela (Lisa Blount); Bobby (Jonas Marlowe); Dr. Schuyler (Michael Prince); Anne Nishakura (Mie Hunt); Mr. Romero (Frank Lugo); Wiley (Patrick Culliton); Sportscaster (David Bowman); Newscaster (Pete Gonneau); Orderly (Eddie) (Peter Jolly); Young man (Kim Strauss); Patient (Sam Temeles).

One for the Road
Settling into a small town, Scott enters high school and looks forward to a slower life—and he meets a

girl who interests him. But when Starman photographs a councilman sleeping in chambers and the photo goes national, it's time to move again. Wr: Michael Marks. Dir: Claudio Guzman.

Joe Connell (Robert Donner); Mrs. Madison (Ellen Regan); Kelly Jordan (Ami Dolenz); Coach Carl Newman (Henry G. Sanders); Justin Wright (Terry Burns); Ric Baker (Keith Coogan); Editor (Ed Hooks); Police sergeant (Robert Moberly); Wiley (Patrick Culliton); Photo editor (Glenn Robards); Reporter (Roger Scott); "Totally" Jordan (Jane Kehl).

Peregrine
Rescuing an injured falcon brings Scott and Starman new jobs with a veterinarian. Wr: Geoffrey Fischer. Dir: Robert Chenault.

Casey Flynn (Margaret Klenck); Brian Willis (David Hayward); Chief Harold Galley (Jason Bernard); Carrie (Waitress #1 and Owner #2) (Deborah Rose); Waitress #2 (Lee Arnone); Owner #1 (Hartley Silver); Owner #3 (Joe Clarke).

Society's Pet
Starman discovers that Scott has inherited $10,000 from his foster father, but they learn from the foster aunt that she wants to keep her nephew. Wr: Ross Hirshorn. Dir: Claudio Guzman.

Antonia Weyburn (Janet Leigh); Samantha (Katherine Moffat); Wiley (Patrick Culliton); Mitchell (Jack Fletcher); Seymour McGillis (William Ian Gamble).

Fever
Starman becomes sick after a photography assignment and lands in the hospital, where he slips into a coma. Fox knows how to find him. Wr: Tom Lazarus. Dir: Bill Duke.

Dr. Ellen Dukow (Marta DuBois); Nurse Corona (Virginia Capers); Ralph Woolery (Dabbs Greer); General Wade (Russ Marin); Nardo (Angus Duncan); Samuel Traynor (Mike Muscat); Grey lady (Courtenay McWhinney); Spring (Pamela Roylance); Motel manager (Sam Nudell); Nervous man (Daniel Verdin); Lab tech (Brad Zerbst); Psychiatric Ward Attendant #1 (Benjamin Jurand); Psychiatric Ward Attendant #2 (Larry Turk); Orderly (Jeris L. Poindexter).

The Gift
Starman receives a letter from Paul's mother asking him to come home for Christmas. But later, he discovers that a friend wrote the letter and that Paul's mother is actually dying. Wr: Peggy Goldman. Dir: Mike Gray.

Stella Forrester (Jane Wyatt); Hal Walker (Jeff Corey); Dave Winfield (Don Sparks); Milt Linden (Joe Nesnow); Hawkins (Nick Shields); Sam (James O'Connell); Antique store mgr. (Mary Gregory); Council president (Lynn Seibel); Art councilman (Charles Olson); Fire chief (Terence Marinan); Vera (Judy Jean Berns); Gas station attendant (Ritchie Montgomery); Bystander (Dave Alverson); Minister (John Marshall); Officer Pinella (Michael George-Benko); Man talking to sheriff (Adam Taylor).

The System
Scott and Starman become entangled in the justice system when Starman gets thrown in jail. Fox wants them, but the Constitution blocks his way. Wr: Steven Hollander. Dir: Bill Duke.

Charlotte Hart (Jessica Harper); Judge Arthur Richardson (Raymond St. Jacques); Tyrone Washington (Tim Russ); Wiley (Patrick Culliton); Desk sgt. (Troy Evans); Les Martin (Arthur Burghardt); Murray (Jack Bernardi); Cashier (Alan Koss); Eddie Benton (Kerry Stein); Thompson (Nathan Haas); Patrolman (Laurence Braude); Guard #1 (Spike Sorrentino); Bailiff (Dale Reynolds); Meter maid (Abbe Kanter); Edna, George's secretary (Toni Lamond); Pizza lady (Stephanie Rose).

Appearances
When their truck breaks down, Scott and Starman meet a religious family with a blind daughter who wants Starman to heal her with his strange powers. Wr: Michael Marks, story by Michael Marks and Joe Goodson. Dir: Nick Marck.

Frank Radin (Don Dubbins); Mary Radin (Carol Vogel); Julie Radin (Nadine Van Der Velde); Driver (Buck Taylor); Sheriff (Wayne Grace); Man (Ed Corbett).

The Probe
Seeking money, Starman becomes a subject in a psychology experiment and slowly falls in love with the woman administering the tests. Meanwhile, Scott's science experiment becomes more accurate than necessary when Starman adds a couple of classified satellites to the demonstration. Wr: Syrie Astrahan James. Dir: Mike Gray.

Dr. Katherine Bradford (Kay Lenz); Dr. Dan Willet (David Spielberg); Major Holmes (James Ingersoll); Jim Johnson (David J. Partington); Government worker (Mark Costello); Science fair director (Paula Slade); Controller #1 (David Michael Sterling).

Dusty
When a stranded young woman steals their car with all their belongings (including their spheres), Starman and Scott track her to Reno, where Starman discovers the concept of gambling. Wr: Peggy Goldman. Dir: Claudio Guzman.

Dusty (Joanna Haley) (Lori Lethin); Joe Dinata (Joseph Hacker); Henry Bridges (Ron Masak); Little old lady (Billie Bird); Ron (Ben Frank); Gold Chain #1 (Ned Bellamy); Gold Chain #2 (Tony Borgia); Bellman (Bruce Winant); Salesman (J.P. Bumstead).

Barriers
Fleeing from Fox and Wylie in San Diego, Scott and Starman become separated. Starman winds up in Mexico and looks for a way back home. Wr: Michael Marks. Dir: Mike Gray.

Tonita de Cordova (Danelle Hand); Ida Schwartzman (Alice Hirson); Richard Billings (Radames Pera); Ruiz (Castulo Guerra); Pepe (Julio Medina); Wylie (Patrick Culliton); Senora Lopez (Gloria Manos); Don Miguel de Cordova (Harold Cannon-Lopez); Counterman (Roger Hampton); Mike (Ted Gehring); Man (Paul Tauger); Mexican woman (Marabina Davila); Mexican man (Mark Morante); Armand (Ernesto Hernandez); Henchman #1

(Gregory Norman Cruz); Henchman #2 (Fernando Negrette); Neighbor (John Houy).

Grifters
To earn money, Scott and Starman deliver a Rolls-Royce to Beverly Hills. Unbeknownst to them, the car contains $10 million in treasury notes. Wr: Steven Hollander. Dir: Claudio Guzman.

Artemus Guiness (Artie) (David Doyle); Agent Howard (Eric Server); Agent (Burke Byrnes); Naughton Wells (Bill Macy); Wylie (Patrick Culliton); Harry (Alec Murdock); Police officer (Dominick LaRae); Man in crowd (John Platt); Victim (John Houy); IRS agent (Brian Kinsley).

Trivia Alert: This is the first and only episode where Fox and Starman have a conversation.

The Wedding
When an old acquaintance of Paul's tries to stop his daughter's wedding, he manipulates Paul so that the wedding will not happen. But someone realizes that Paul and Scott are on the run from the Federal Security Agency. Wr: Geoffrey Fischer. Dir: Nick Marck.

Matteo Gionetti (Al Ruscio); Anna Gionetti (Christine Healy); Henry Kimble (Timothy Stack); Aunt Rose (Penny Santon); Wylie (Patrick Culliton); Father Sullivan (Malachy McCourt); Deliveryman (Joseph Romeo); Bridesmaid #1 (Kathie Gibboney); Bridesmaid #2 (Karen Huie); Olga (Irene Olga Lopez); Cake (Blonde) (Bobbi Pavis); Fisherman (Jay S. York); Eddie (Tony Travis).

Fathers and Sons
In Santa Barbara, Starman discovers that Paul has a biological son. That son wants to escape from his mother and stepfather and travel with Paul, complicating Starman's relationship with Scott. Wr: Syrie Astrahan James. Dir: Ted Lange.

Joanna Daniels Kendall (Julie Cobb); Eric Kendall (Rodney Eastman); Bill Avery (David Haskell); Tom Kendall (Barry Jenner); Christina (Kat Sawyer-Young); Michael Goodman (John Lafayette); Dennis Lambert (Dennis Romer); Reporter #1 (Carmen Hayward); Reporter #2 (Deck McKenzie); Vendor (Louise Claps); Receptionist (Debra Christofferson); Mrs. Haverty (Ernestine Mercer).

Starscape, Part 1
A painting in Portland finally provides Starman a lead to finding Jenny Hayden. Starman tracks her down in Arizona. But Scott's trapped in the desert with her brother, Wayne, who is injured in an accident. Wr: James Henerson and James Hirsch. Dir: Claudio Guzman.

Jenny Hayden (Erin Gray); Wayne Geffner (Joshua Bryant); Lainie Fine (Marilyn Lightstone); Phyllis Geffner (Brooke Bundy); Dr. Costigan (Robert Benedetti); Foreman (Steve Eastin); Bartender (Richard Balin); Tech #1 (Paul Tompkins); Tech #2 (Charles Randolph-Wright); Major (Dennis Crabbe); Worker (Robert Sutton); Tech #3 (Philip Weyland); Tech #4 (Michael Kelly).

Starscape, Part 2
After Starman and Jenny share a night together, Fox manages to capture Starman and holds him at an air force facility. Meanwhile, Scott and Wayne attempt survival in the desert. Wr: James Henerson and James Hirsch. Dir: Claudio Guzman.

Jenny Hayden (Erin Gray); Wayne Geffner (Joshua Bryant); Lainie Fine (Marilyn Lightstone); General Elliott (Peter Hansen); Tom (Tom Jackman); Tech #1 (Paul Tompkins); Tech #2 (Charles Randolph-Wright); Medic (Phil Poulos); Tech #3 (Philip Weyland); Tech #4 (Michael Kelly); Nurse (Stephanie Rose).

The Test
Losing contact with Jenny, Starman and Scott return to California. There, as a dishwasher, Starman discovers a co-worker who's illiterate and encourages tutoring to increase his reading skills. Meanwhile, Scott needs to take an equivalency test so he can enter the tenth grade. Wr: Laurie Newbound. Dir: Robert Hays.

Lorraine Michaels (Madge Sinclair); Gus (Jerry Hardin); Murphy (Dub Taylor); Stan (Buck Taylor); Bo (Courtney Gains); Mr. Hubbard (Robert DoQui); Alex (Richard Coca); Principal Kevin Altman (Richard Fancy); Wylie (Patrick Culliton); J.B. (Phill Lewis); Mr. Gimble (Gary Waynesmith); Landlady (Olive Dunbar); Sid (Rick Williamson); Norman (Don Kennedy); Jessica (Tina Erickson); Student (James Lunsford).

Star Trek
September 1966–September 1969

Two hundred years in the future, the starship Enterprise *(one of 12 starships in the United Federation of Planets and manned by 430 men and women) explores the galaxy. Her five-year mission is "to seek out new worlds and new civilizations."*

Cast: Captain James T. Kirk (William Shatner); Mr. Spock (Leonard Nimoy); Dr. Leonard McCoy (DeForest Kelley); Montgomery Scott (Engineer) (James Doohan); Lt. Uhura (Communications) (Nichelle Nichols); Mr. Sulu (Helmsman) (George Takei); Pavel Chekov (Navigator, 1967–1969) (Walter Koenig); Nurse Christine Chapel (Majel Barrett); Computer voice (Majel Barrett); Theme music singer (Loolie-Jean Norman).

Created by: Gene Roddenberry; *Producers:* Gene Roddenberry (year 1); Gene Coon (years 1 and 2); John Meredyth Lucas (year 2); Fred Freiberger, Robert H. Justman (year 3); *Executive Producer:* Gene Roddenberry; NBC/Paramount; 60 minutes.

Star Trek's history has been analyzed from all angles—by historians, writers, fans, sociologists and critics. They've poked and prodded the phenomenon, unfastening *Trek's* dramatic hinges to see what made it run. Was it a magical chemistry of the cast? Imaginative plots? Or the optimistic portrayal of mankind as it reached out to other worlds?

Star Trek's legendary origins have been well documented. Gene Roddenberry, former airline pilot and policeman, wanted to make social and political statements on television without being crucified by the censors. Science fiction offered him the chance to comment on his world by setting his stories in other worlds. Although similar to the 1956 film *Forbidden Planet* (which also featured a United Star Cruiser in the far future), *Star Trek* was unique for television.

CBS rejected Roddenberry's proposal in favor of *Lost in Space,* but NBC expressed interest. The 1964 pilot, titled "The Cage," cast Jeffrey Hunter as *Enterprise* captain Christopher Pike and Leonard Nimoy as the half-human, half–Vulcan science officer, Mr. Spock. Majel Barrett played the female first officer, Number One. The story told of the *Enterprise's* encounter with an alien, telepathic race which snatches Pike for breeding purposes.

"After NBC watched it, they said, 'We like it, we believe it, we don't understand it. Do it again,'" remembers director Robert Butler. The brass felt the pilot was "too cerebral" for audiences and wanted another pilot to demonstrate the format's action-adventure potential.

Even while filming "The Cage," Butler had had his own reservations. "It was a complicated story," he admits, "and I wondered if audiences would respond to it. While rehearsing the pilot, Howard Hawks' film *The Thing* was very much on my mind. That film was very dry and underplayed, naturalistic and quiet. I tried that with the *Star Trek* cast for a couple of days, but it didn't work. It turned out flat, so I said, 'I was wrong. Let's go back to our traditional style,' which is slightly melodramatic, slightly alarmed and aroused. It worked better."

While generally satisfied with "The Cage," Butler says that his vision of the future, on both

a visual and a dramatic level, was different from Roddenberry's. "*Star Trek* supposedly conveys interesting ideas and philosophies. I found it more preachy and spoken than dramatic. The technical effects were great, but the drama was stand-around. Occasionally, a few guns went off, but at its best and worst, there was a lot of thinking, postulating and reasoning. It was walking radio—thoughts, ideas, words—theatrical space opera. I wanted to get into something more vivid."

He also preferred a visual style that was more realistic. "I respected the way the movie *Star Wars* took the future and wore it down. I wanted to do that with 'The Cage.' I wanted to wear down the ship's hardware and bring in some wear and tear and naturalism. I was told, wrongly I think, that the brand spanking new ship was the wave of the future. For me, that cleanliness robbed *Star Trek* of realism. There's more realism in unrest and disorder. When I directed *Hill Street Blues,* I got into that seamy side of reality."

NBC asked for several character changes after screening the pilot. Test audiences had not been receptive to seeing a woman in a position of command. Roddenberry reluctantly agreed to drop the Number One character. The network was also uneasy about the Satanic appearance of Mr. Spock. They asked for the character to be removed. Roddenberry fought to keep the pointeared alien, feeling that the Vulcan's constant struggle with his suppressed human emotions would provide the series with a major dramatic thrust. Roddenberry won the battle, and Spock became one of the show's biggest draws.

As for the starship captain, Jeffrey Hunter decided not to go ahead with the series. "Jeff was a decent, professional guy," recalls Butler. "He liked the overall integrity that went into *Star Trek,* but as I vaguely recall, his wife wasn't all that happy with him doing a science fiction series. I think there was also a commercial sense of getting a clean start with the second pilot. They changed as much as possible within reason. That included re-casting." Some of the actors considered for the role of *Enterprise* captain included James Coburn, Roy Thinnes, Jack Lord and Lloyd Bridges.

The second pilot, "Where No Man Has Gone Before," was directed by James Goldstone in 1965. William Shatner was cast as the new starship captain, James T. Kirk. This pilot sold the series to NBC. "The Cage" would later be used in the two-hour *Star Trek* episode "The Menagerie" as flashback footage. "Gene asked me to come back and direct the new footage for 'The Menagerie,' but I was busy, which was OK," recalls Butler. "I'd already been there and wasn't interested in coming back. But I enjoyed working with Gene. He was a very unpretentious, basic guy. He was a man's man, with a lot of enthusiasm, leadership and strength."

As *Star Trek* neared its first air date for the 1966-67 season, it was publicized as the first adult space series. However, the first episode aired was about a salt-sucking creature loose on the *Enterprise*. It didn't get the show's image off to a good start. "NBC chose 'The Man Trap' to open the season because it had a monster," says co-producer Robert Justman. "I stood up in the projection room when the network people were trying to decide which episode to open the season with. I strongly objected to showing 'The Man Trap' as the premiere. Not only did it lack the quality of some of the other shows we had done, but it would give the audience a mistaken idea of what we were attempting to do. However, I lost. I felt the network, aside from a few people, never understood what we were trying to do with the series."

Many critics certainly didn't. After "The Man Trap" aired, *Daily Variety* sniffed that "*Star Trek* won't work," while the *L. A. Times* groaned, "The stars take a trek into a real mess."

It didn't take long, however, for subsequent episodes of the series to win over a modest but loyal following. This included real-life space scientists, astronauts and even writer Isaac Asimov, who proclaimed it "the first good science fiction series."

Writer Margaret Armen was a faithful viewer who recalls that she instructed her agent to "keep hounding Gene Roddenberry until he asked to see me. At that time, women writers were subject to suspicion as to their ability to write hard stories. Gene was open-minded, especially after his one-time secretary, Dorothy Fontana, exhibited such writing ability as a *Star Trek* writer. Gene agreed to a story conference with me, and liked my 'Gamesters of Triskelion' story. The first day I walked into the *Star Trek* office, I was greeted by this huge, life-sized cutout of one of the show's monsters. It was a shock … but a nice touch!"

Armen recalls, "There was sort of a competition between William Shatner and Leonard Nimoy. Actors' egos are very fragile. They're always on guard against somebody taking over from them. They were both wonderful, however,

and played their characters beautifully. Nimoy could be a little temperamental, but he was also very charming and very sexy. He had a very magnetic personality."

One of the ribbings *Star Trek* has endured over the years has been its treatment of the unknown crewmen. When a landing party consisted of Captain Kirk, Mr. Spock, Dr. McCoy and a guard named Smith, it was a sure bet Smith would get blasted by Act 1.

Jay Jones was one of the main stuntmen on the show, and he made his living dying on *Star Trek*. "In the first episode I did, 'Catspaw,' I was dead the minute you saw me," he laughs. "They needed an actor who could do his own falls. In 'Catspaw,' I beam up as a zombie, fall flat on my face and as Kirk holds me, evil voices come out of my mouth. That was my introduction to *Star Trek*." Jones, whose father was also a stuntman, had gained his own reputation by doing stunts for Robert Vaughn on *The Man from U.N.C.L.E.* He left that series for *Star Trek*.

"Gene Roddenberry took a liking to me and the word came down I was to get as much work as I could handle," explains Jones. "I started by doubling for James Doohan, and later for Leonard Nimoy." But it was his hazardous security duty that got him the most attention. "The big joke on the set was how hard it was for a guard to live past the first half-hour." At the time, Jones regarded the show as just a job. "My father thought the series was great, but I didn't like science fiction. It wasn't until the reruns that I realized what a terrific show it was. When I got my 'Catspaw' script, my only line was, 'One to beam up.' I had no idea what that meant. The next day, a neighborhood kid went by on a bicycle. I asked him, 'Do you watch *Star Trek*?' He said, 'Yeah!' I asked, 'Do you know what beam up means?' This kid explained it all to me."

Getting beamed up was a breeze compared to the stunts Jones did for several episodes. In "Who Mourns for Adonais," the Greek god Apollo expels his wrath on Scotty several times. The stuntman was Jones. "Apollo backflips me over a table, but I hit the corner, so they chained it down and I did it again. This time I caught the table's edge in the kidneys. By the end of the day, I was pretty sore. Then they wanted to do the wire gag known as a neckbreaker. You wear a vest under your clothes, and it's attached to a pulley. Three 200-pound guys jump off a six-foot ladder and it takes up the slack. It jerked me across the stage. We thought it would take me 10 to 12 feet

The cast of *Star Trek* on the bridge of the starship *Enterprise*. Left to right: James Doohan, Walter Koenig, DeForest Kelley, Majel Barrett, William Shatner, Nichelle Nichols, Leonard Nimoy and George Takei. Copyright 1968 NBC/Paramount.

and it took me 18. I flew right over Shatner's head. My head snapped against the floor, and I went through a wall, although that was cut from the print. I was out cold. They rushed me to the hospital with a concussion. I was banged up, but nothing major."

In the episode "The Apple," Jones played crewman Mallory, one of the landing party who finds a planet ruled by the computer god Vaal. Although he was supposed to sneak silently up to a village, Mallory inexplicably blows his cover by trying to alert Captain Kirk. "The director wanted me to run over a hill and scream, 'Captain! The village is over there!'" laughs Jones. "Looking back on it now, it sounds pretty silly!"

When Mallory stepped on an exploding rock, it was stunt time. "I had to lobby director Joe Pevney for that scene," recalls Jones. "He was a dear man and refused to let me do it. He felt it was too dangerous. I held out. I said, 'I don't want

to do this stunt the Mickey Mouse way.' He finally said okay. Well, I was wrong. I got hurt.

"There was a jumper trampoline buried in the ground. When I hit the trampoline, the explosive was supposed to go off. Well, the timing had to be perfect, and it wasn't. The special effects guy was a hundredth of a second too late. I was directly over it when the blast hit me. In the episode, you can see me literally blown toward the camera. The force hit me in the stomach, burned my side, blew the skin off my rib cage and impacted all of this dirt into my sinuses. I couldn't open my eyes or breathe. They rushed me to the hospital emergency room." Still, Jones says cheerfully, "It was nothing major. It could have been a lot worse."

Jones's father was less stoic. "Dad had been a stuntman all of his life. When he saw that stunt on TV, he knew I really ate it. He literally got sick to his stomach. They had filmed the explosion from another angle as well, and it was incredible. I looked like a human fireball. It wasn't used because NBC felt it was too violent. I was really the stunt coordinator for the show," he continues. "I'd dream up stunts and work with the directors and cameramen on how we could use them in scenes. I've been on some shows where the directors are trying to get you killed. I've done other shows where the directors really care about your safety. On *Star Trek*, the same stunt guys were called back regularly. It was a great group of people."

In his appraisal of the cast, Jones notes, "Leonard Nimoy was very quiet and shy. He was a nice guy, but he seldom said anything. Dee Kelley and Jimmy Doohan were the greatest guys in the world. The toughest guy was Shatner. He loved to relate to the stunt guys because he thought he was a jock. The first fight I had with him he got caught up in the adrenalin. He busted me in the mouth a couple of times. We weren't the best of friends during the show, although we grew closer towards the end. The cast was very interested in learning how we did stunts. They were our biggest fans because they knew the stunts made them look good. The actors always wanted to do stunts. The stuntmen always wanted to act!"

Jones figures that he maneuvered himself out of a recurring role on the series. "I was asked if I could do accents. They were trying to write in some new characters, but they hadn't decided on a dialect. I had just done a play where I had a French accent, and I butchered it. So when they asked me if I'd do a test scene in 'Catspaw' with an accent, I said, 'No way. I won't embarrass myself again.' I found out later they were considering me for the role of Chekov. Walter Koenig has been riding the crest ever since."

Jones notes that the morale during *Star Trek's* third year was low. "There seemed to be a problem between Gene and the actors. Gene was marketing everything related to the series—buttons and stuff. He was just being a businessman, but some of the cast didn't feel that was correct. They were in it for the art."

After *Star Trek*, Jones went on to do stunts in *Bonanza* and *The High Chaparral*. He later became a professional racquetball player. Today, he's an actor and a private investigator.

Canadian actor John Colicos had the privilege of introducing the hostile Klingons to *Star Trek* audiences. In "Errand of Mercy," Commander Kor (Colicos) and his men invade what seems to be a primitive, push-over planet. "My first thought was, 'What the hell should a Klingon look like?'" says Colicos. "Then I thought of a futuristic Ghengis Khan, and the makeup suggested a Mongolian warrior, hell-bent on the destruction of the planet. But we should have had spines growing out of the top of their heads to make them look like mutants!"

The episode brings the Klingons and the Earth Federation to the edge of all-out war. Their battle is abruptly halted by the peace-loving villagers, who are actually highly advanced life forms. They force the two sides to arrange a long-standing truce known as the Organian Peace Treaty. "When the aliens told Kirk and Kor, 'Get the hell off our planet. We don't want your war,' it was the beginning of a new generation," says Colicos. "The show's message was to let there be peace and harmony in the world for a change."

Colicos, an avid viewer of the 1987–94 *Star Trek: The Next Generation*, was surprised by the changes made in the Klingon Empire. "Now they're the good guys," he says. "The Klingon makeup is entirely different from what we did in the series. It would be very interesting to bring back Kor, who's been living on top of a mountain for the last 100 years, and have him cursing and screaming, 'Why the hell has everyone become so nice!'"

Actor Lawrence Montaigne had been a top stuntman in Europe before embarking on a successful acting career in America. It was his role as Stonn, the Vulcan in love with Spock's fiancee in "Amok Time," that brings back a memory. "Gene Roddenberry was a phenomenon. I can also say, of all the people I've worked for in show business, he was the most vicious. I hated the man. The role of Stonn had only three lines, and I wasn't interested. To pacify me, they offered to give me guest star billing and to pay my price. I still didn't want to do it.

"Roddenberry called me direct and told me if I didn't do the part, I would never work at Paramount again. What could I do? Acting was how I made my living. Gene was a very imposing man. What he wanted, he got. He had been a cop and behaved like one."

Reluctantly, Montaigne did the role, but then there was another controversy. "They wanted me to be bare-chested as Stonn. I didn't think that was something you ask somebody to do unless it's pre-arranged. You don't wait until a guy is in his costume and say, 'Oh, by the way, shave your chest.' I called my agent and said,

'They want me to shave my chest. Are they out of their minds? Do they expect me to stand around for the next two months and itch? I'm not gonna do it.' I went to my dressing room, and suddenly Gene knocks on the door. 'What is this shit?' he says. 'You're holding up production.' We already had this wonderful rapport going because of our earlier clash. I told him I wasn't going to shave and I didn't care what he did. Well, my agent came down, Gene was there, and guess who was the heavy? They finally came up with the idea of a black turtleneck sweater. The outcome was that I never worked for Gene or for Paramount again."

All the same, the actor says, "Gene was a genius in his own right. He created a unique show. I didn't have to agree with or like the man. Hell, personality conflicts happen in every bloody business in the world. It's only because it's in show business that it becomes high profile."

Montaigne's experiences with the cast were on the lighter note. "Leonard Nimoy didn't have a sense of humor. During lunch we were in the commissary and a bus pulled up. A bunch of tourists came out and rushed over to Leonard, 'Mr. Nimoy! Mr. Nimoy!' So after lunch, we were on the set and I said to Leonard, 'You know, Leonard, a funny thing happened in the commissary after you left. Another busload of people arrived and they mistook me for you. They came up and began yelling, "Mr. Nimoy, can you sign our autographs?" I told them to go fuck themselves.' Well, if you wanna give somebody shock therapy, that would have done it. Leonard blanched, and his jaw fell to his chest. It was so typical of Leonard. He would never have thought for a minute that maybe I was kidding. I feel that when we take ourselves too seriously, it's time for a little introspection. On *Star Trek*, you had to work your ass off, trying to make it believable, but after awhile, you've got to laugh. That was the good thing about Shatner. He enjoyed it and played it tongue-in-cheek. Leonard took the whole thing very seriously."

Montaigne says (and co-producer Robert Justman confirms) that he was under serious consideration to replace Leonard Nimoy after *Star Trek*'s first year. "Leonard's agent was negotiating for a new contract, and it looked like Leonard wouldn't be back," says Montaigne. "My agent called and negotiated a deal for me to take over the role. Leonard changed his mind and went back for a second season."

Actor Booker Bradshaw, who played *Enter-*

prise doctor M'Benga in two episodes, recalls that occasionally the space-age dialogue gave everyone the giggles. "There's a scene in 'A Private Little War' where Dr. McCoy says, 'Thank God his heart is where his liver is or he'd be dead now.' That scene took us 50 takes. We couldn't get through that line without laughing. When we finally got it together and stopped laughing, the cameraman laughed and jiggled the camera on the 50th take. So we had to do it again."

Bradshaw notes that the laughs between Shatner and Nimoy became more subdued as the series went on. "When *Star Trek* began, William Shatner was supposed to be the next Laurence Olivier of America," says Bradshaw. "Most of the salary went to Bill, and Leonard was an afterthought. Then, the show took a strange turn. Leonard started pulling in 10,000 fan letters a week. So a certain envy began to develop with Shatner, but it never took the form of a healthy discussion. It was subliminal."

It was when Nimoy had to appear at the Texas State Fair during the filming of "A Private Little War" that Bradshaw got into his own trouble. "We had to film a scene in sickbay, where Spock is comatose and I'm supposed to revive him by slapping him. Leonard wanted to get the scene done so he could fly to the Texas State Fair. Leonard said, 'Booker, I only want to do this scene once. When you hit me, make it realistic. I don't want a stage slap. I want you to slap the shit out of me.' I said, 'I gotcha!'

"We began filming and I walked over to Leonard and I slapped him. I've never slapped anyone as hard as I slapped him—and his ears flew off! There was mass hysteria on the set. The cameraman was in convulsions, and people were rolling on the floor. Leonard was totally pissed off. He chased me around the set, yelling, 'I'm gonna kill this guy!' I'm yelling, 'Please! I did what you told me to do.' The director's yelling, 'What the hell's going on here? Don't you understand what a stage slap is, Bradshaw? Now we have to cover up the bruise marks on Leonard's face and he wants to beat you up because you slapped the piss out of him.' I said, 'Look, all I ever wanted to be was a classical actor. I don't need this shit. I'm going home!' Well, Leonard grabbed me and said, 'In a pig's ass you are. We're going to do it again—this time, use a stage slap.' So we did, and the scene was fine, and Leonard hugged me and said, 'I'm not gonna beat you up, Booker,' and off he went to the Texas State Fair."

Star Trek developed a small, loyal audience,

but the ratings were a constant concern. The first season of *Star Trek* finished number 52 out of nearly 100 shows. It finished just behind *Mission Impossible*, and ahead of *The Wild, Wild West* and *Run for Your Life.*

At the end of the 1966-67 season, NBC reported *Star Trek's* chances for renewal were iffy. Several thousand TV viewers wrote in, helping to secure the series for a second season. However, the show was moved from its Thursday night slot to Friday nights. According to Robert Justman, that hurt *Star Trek*. "By the time we had built up an audience during the summer of 1967 in that Thursday slot, NBC moved us to Fridays at 8:30. That was tough because part of our audience was young people and that was their night to go out."

"There was never any strong general audience support for *Star Trek* after the first year," says Herbert Solow, who was vice-president of Desilu studios at the time.

When the series completed its second season with weaker ratings, cancellation was definitely in the offing, and NBC confirmed the show was borderline. This time, fan reaction was intense. For the first time in TV history, viewers actively campaigned to save a TV series. Fans picketed NBC headquarters. Petitions and letters flooded the network. Newspapers and magazines publicized the reaction.

Although Roddenberry claimed that he had little to do with the letter campaigns, Solow contends, "It was a manufactured campaign that Roddenberry waged, using students at several engineering universities, including Cal Tech and MIT." NBC made an unprecedented on-air announcement in March 1968, following the broadcast of the episode "The Omega Glory," that the series would continue for a third year.

When Roddenberry didn't get the 7:30 p.m. Monday slot that NBC had originally promised for 1968-69, he reversed his decision to personally produce the series' third season. He felt the 10 p.m. Friday time slot was certain death for the series. Producer Fred Freiberger was brought in.

"The ratings were falling, and NBC wasn't happy with the show or Roddenberry," recalls Freiberger. "If it hadn't been for the loyalty of the fans, *Star Trek* would have definitely ended after the second season." The new producer was given the daunting task of turning *Star Trek* into a ratings success.

"Usually, when a new producer comes in, he wants to scrap everything. I wanted to keep doing what they had been doing. A network researcher told me that one reason the ratings were poor was that women were afraid of something as infinite as space. Although we had female fans, the network hoped to boost ratings by getting more women to watch. I tried to get more romance into the series. I also wanted to give the subsidiary actors more meaningful things to say than just 'warp 3.' We made it more of an ensemble show.

"Because of budget, we had to set every fourth show aboard the *Enterprise*. However, that didn't necessarily mean we couldn't do good shipboard stories. It gave us the opportunity to do some morality plays and make some nice statements."

As the third season struggled in the ratings, Freiberger found the budget tightening. "The studio was watching every nickel. At one point, a production guy said to me, 'Look at William Shatner's breakfast charge. He's charging 15 dollars every morning for meals.' At that time, that was a lot of money. They asked me to talk to him about it. I said, 'Bill, what do you eat for breakfast?' He said, 'Ham, bacon, eggs, coffee and juice.' I said, 'That comes out to only seven bucks!' He replied, 'It's my dog—he eats the same thing for breakfast.' I said, 'Bill, if you don't tell anyone about this, I'll forget we had this conversation.'"

As the series reached its end, relations between the network and Roddenberry didn't flourish. "It's true that NBC didn't like *Star Trek*," notes Freiberger. "When Roddenberry first introduced me to the network staff, I was shocked by the contempt with which Roddenberry treated them. That's when I realized they didn't like Roddenberry or the show and he didn't like them."

"NBC resented Roddenberry for the way he painted them as losers and as the enemy," agrees Herbert Solow.

Nevertheless, there were those at NBC who regularly defended *Star Trek*. Throughout its run, the late Mort Werner (NBC's vice-president of programming) and NBC programming research executive Paul Klein publicly praised the show. As Klein told *TV Guide*, "It's the only science fiction show with a scientific base."

"Mort Werner was very supportive of the show, and I know Gene Roddenberry thought very highly of him," says Robert Justman. "But he was in New York. Mort wasn't one of the people we dealt with on the West Coast. Paul Klein, who was a very bright man, was also supportive, but his position at NBC was such that all he did was deliver research to the people at programming."

"Mort Werner and Grant Tinker were staunch supporters of *Star Trek*," adds Herbert Solow. In the end, however, it was the ratings that ditched the series after three years on NBC.

"I don't think *Star Trek* ever got into the top 40," says Freiberger. "Today, if you have a 22 or 25 share, you're a smash hit. In those days, we ran a 25 to 29 share. After the first year, the ratings kept going down, and historically, that slide continues."

"That third season was a rough year," says DeForest Kelley. "We lost Roddenberry's touch because he was at war with NBC. We knew this would be our last year."

"We knew darn well we wouldn't continue in that 10 p.m. time slot," adds Robert Justman.

However, only two years earlier, the infamous 10 p.m. time slot had turned another slow starter, *The Man from U.N.C.L.E,* into a top ten smash. Moreover, *Star Trek's* competition in its last year was the buckling *Judd for the Defense* on ABC and an unusually weak package of CBS movies. In addition, *Star Trek* had a good lead-in, the pseudo-intellectual *Name of the Game.* Furthermore, *Star Trek* had received months of free publicity created by the historic letter-writing campaign. Yet *Star Trek* still lagged with a 25 share.

Margaret Armen offers perhaps the most practical explanation. "Many people didn't watch *Star Trek* because they were firmly anchored in the Earth," she says. "My husband, a high school teacher, never watched *Star Trek,* not even my episodes. He'd say, 'I can't relate to something about a spaceship warping out of the solar system. It's like a fairy tale.' I think many other intelligent people felt the same way. Engineers I knew always watched it, perhaps because an engineer's mind is always thinking of the mechanics of the future. I always felt the series was rooted in a future reality and that it was certainly within the realm of possibility. The network executives, as well as some people at Paramount, thought the show was a fluke. I felt they were crazy not to recognize *Star Trek's* virtues."

Star Trek left NBC in the fall of 1969, but many people felt there was more to come. "That's true," says Al Francis, *Star Trek's* director of photography. "When we had a wrap party in 1969, Gene said, 'One thing we're not gonna do is take anything apart. We're going to keep the sets standing because I think we're going to be back.' The sets remained for sometime." Mort Werner actually tried to launch a 90-minute TV movie version of *Star Trek,* with the original cast, for the fall of 1970. "Although Gene called me, Jim Rugg (special effects) and Matt Jeffries (art director) in later, saying Paramount was going to do a film, we never heard anything else. I know Gene wanted to do a *Star Trek* feature as early as 1968. He was a terrific writer and a real brain."

In syndication, *Star Trek* gained momentum like a rolling snowball. In January 1972, organizers of the first *Star Trek* convention in New York anticipated 300 fans. Over 3,000 showed up. *TV Guide's* feature article on the convention in March 1972 made millions of other fans aware of the show's popularity. From this point on, there was more talk of reviving *Star Trek* as a TV movie. Talks constantly stalled, although NBC did air a 1973–75 Saturday morning animated version of *Star Trek.* The show, featuring the voices of the original cast, won an Emmy in 1975 as best children's show.

"Kids were *Star Trek's* audience," says Freiberger. "On the network it had been a failure. In syndication, kids got it at 5 and 6 p.m. and made it a smash."

As conventions, reruns and fan clubs continued to thrive, Paramount announced a new *Star Trek* series for 1978, with most of the original cast. "Paramount called in various writers, and they wrote about 30 scripts," recalls Margaret Armen, who co-wrote one script with partner Alf Harris.

"We were signed up for the TV pilot when suddenly Paramount decided to go with *Star Trek—The Motion Picture,*" recalls DeForest Kelley. The 1979 film was followed by five sequels: *The Wrath of Khan* (1982); *The Search for Spock* (1984); *The Voyage Home* (1986, the most successful of the film series to date); *The Final Frontier* (1989); and *The Undiscovered Country* (1991).

Meanwhile, the 79 TV episodes continued to break syndication records. Although some critics, infuriated by the series' cult status, have directed super-critical slaps at the shows' plots and 1960s sexism, the fact remains that most of *Star Trek's* stories have withstood the test of time.

The torch was passed to a new TV *Enterprise* in 1987. The new cast set off in the series *Star Trek: The Next Generation,* which proved a ratings smash in first-run syndication. Roddenberry died in 1991, but his legacy continued with a *Next Generation* spinoff titled *Deep Space 9.* This saga debuted in 1993 to good ratings. Another spinoff, *Voyager,* premiered in 1995.

Even after twenty years, the original *Star Trek* reruns continue to be popular in syndication. Although it has typecast some of the actors, they're still popular speakers at conventions around the world. Asked about the convention circuit, DeForest Kelley replies, "The question I'm asked most is what was my favorite episode. That would be 'City on the Edge of Forever.' And I've been asked, 'If I had to do it over again, would I choose to do *Star Trek*?' The answer is YES."

CAST NOTES

William Shatner (Captain Kirk): Born 1931. Canadian-born actor who became one of TV's busiest actors after *Star Trek*. In the 1980s he starred in *T.J. Hooker* (1982–86) and in the 1990s hosted the series *Rescue 911*. He's also an author (The *Tek War* series and *Star Trek Memories*).

Leonard Nimoy (Mr. Spock): Born 1931. One of his earliest roles was as a Martian in the film *Zombies of the Stratosphere* (1953). Nimoy spent two years as agent Paris on *Mission: Impossible* (1969–71). An acclaimed stage actor (Sherlock Holmes, Vincent Van Gogh), Nimoy also found success as a motion picture director in the 1980s (*Three Men and a Baby*, *The Good Mother* and two of the *Star Trek* films, *The Search for Spock* and *The Voyage Home*).

DeForest Kelley (Dr. McCoy): Born 1920. Had it not been for acting, Kelley claims, he probably would have become a doctor. (He has, however, contributed much to the world of medicine: "I am constantly receiving letters from physicians who went into medicine as a result of watching *Star Trek*.") Kelley was usually cast as a villain in numerous films and TV shows in the 1950s and 1960s. His post–*Star Trek* TV appearances in the 1970s included *The FBI*, *The Virginian*, *Room 222* and *Ironside*.

Nichelle Nichols (Lt. Uhura): Born 1936. As *Star Trek*'s first season came to a close in 1967, Nichols was poised to leave the show. It was Martin Luther King who convinced her to stay on the series and provide a role model for young black women. Nichelle worked closely with NASA in the 1970s and 1980s on their recruiting program.

James Doohan (Scotty): Born 1920. This Vancouver-born actor admits his career slowed down considerably after being typecast as the starship's engineer. Since *Star Trek*, he's done guest shots on *Magnum P.I.*, *Fantasy Island* and *MacGyver*. He's a frequent guest speaker at *Star Trek* conventions.

George Takei (Sulu): Born 1939. One of Takei's earliest jobs was to dub English dialogue over Japanese science fiction films. He also branched off into L.A. city politics. His many TV appearances include *Miami Vice*, *MacGyver*, *Hawaii 5-0*, *Baa Baa Black Sheep* and *Magnum P.I.*

Walter Koenig (Chekov): Born 1935. Frustrated by his stalled acting career following *Star Trek*, Koenig turned to writing TV scripts and novels. In 1990, he received acclaim (along with co-star Mark Lenard) for the play *The Boys in Autumn*.

Majel Barrett (Nurse Chapel): Born 1935. She married *Star Trek* creator Gene Roddenberry in 1969. She held a recurring role as Lwaxana Troi (Deanna's mother) in *Star Trek: The Next Generation*.

EPISODE GUIDE

Season 1 : 1966-67

The Man Trap
A creature that feeds on salt hunts down *Enterprise* crew members. Wr: George Clayton Johnson. Dir: Marc Daniels.
 Nancy Crater (Jeanne Bal); Robert Crater (Alfred Ryder); Yeoman Janice Rand (Grace Lee Whitney); Darnell (Michael Zaslow); Black crewman (Vince Howard); Blonde (Francine Pyne); Green (Bruce Watson); Guard (William Knight); Creature (Sharon Gimpel); Crewmen (Larry Anthony, Garrison True); Plant puppeteer (Robert Baker).

Charlie X
A young space orphan rescued from a planet after 14 years threatens the *Enterprise* with his telepathic powers. Wr: Dorothy C. Fontana, story by Gene Roddenberry. Dir: Lawrence Dobkin.
 Charlie Evans (Robert Walker); Thasian (Abraham Sofaer); Janice (Grace Lee Whitney); Tina Lawton (Patricia McNulty); Ramart (Charles J. Stewart); Tom Nellis (Dallas Mitchell); Navigator (Don Eitner); Crewman #1 (John Bellah); Crewman #2 (Garland Thompson); Old lady (Laura Wood); Chef's voice (Gene Roddenberry); Sam (Beau Vandenecker); Crewmen (John Lindesmith, Robert Herron).

Where No Man Has Gone Before
Kirk must maroon his friend Gary Mitchell on a desolate planet after Mitchell is turned into a dangerous

telepath. Wr: Samuel A. Peeples. Dir: James Goldstone.

Gary Mitchell (Gary Lockwood); Dr. Elizabeth Dehner (Sally Kellerman); Lee Kelso (Paul Carr); Dr. Mark Piper (Paul Fix); Lloyd Alden (Lloyd Haynes); Yeoman Smith (Andrea Dromm); Guard (Eddie Paskey).

The Naked Time
As the starship hurtles toward a frozen planet, the crew is caught in the grip of a virus that strips away all inhibitions. Wr: John D.F. Black. Dir: Marc Daniels.

Kevin Riley (Bruce Hyde); Joe Tormolen (Stewart Moss); Janice (Grace Lee Whitney); Leslie (Eddie Paskey); Harrison (John Bellah); Singing man (William Knight); Brent (Frank da Vinci); Crewmen (Chris Dureau, Woody Talbert, Bud da Vinca).

Memory Flash—Stewart Moss: "The day after I finished shooting, a friend asked me what kind of part I played. I said, 'A crew member who catches a space disease, goes bonkers and stabs himself with a butter knife.' My friend suggested that I go back to the theater in New York immediately!"

The Enemy Within
An evil duplicate of Captain Kirk is created by a transporter malfunction and begins a reign of terror aboard the ship. Wr: Richard Matheson. Dir: Leo Penn.

Janice (Grace Lee Whitney); John Farrell (Jim Goodwin); Fisher (Edward Madden); Wilson (Garland Thompson).

Memory Flash—Don Eitner: "I played the good/evil camera double for Bill Shatner. I'm kind of the King of B Movies. I fought the *Queen of Blood* with Dennis Hopper, and I was a soldier eaten by a giant grasshopper in *Beginning of the End*. But I never worked harder than I did on *Star Trek*. It was a very exacting schedule. I had to rehearse both 'characters.' Bill was very pleased with the results. The cast was very dedicated. Bill even challenged some of the logic of the scenes in 'The Enemy Within.' Things were worked out and it turned out to be a terrific show. [Creator] Gene Roddenberry was a brilliant writer. The original series is far superior to *The Next Generation*. The characters were much richer."

Mudd's Women
Harry Mudd makes a deal with three lonely miners: If they'll spring him from custody, he'll give them his cargo of beautiful women. Wr: Stephen Kandel, story by Gene Roddenberry. Dir: Harvey Hart.

Harcourt Fenton Mudd (Roger C. Carmel); Eve McHuron (Karen Steele); Ben Childress (Gene Dynarski); Magda Kovas (Susan Denberg); Ruth Bonaventure (Maggie Thrett); Farrell (Jim Goodwin); Gossett (Jon Kowal); Benton (Seamon Glass); Guard (Jerry Foxworth); Conners (Eddie Paskey).

What Are Little Girls Made Of?
Nurse Chapel finds her long-lost fiance on an ice planet. He's constructed androids and plans to introduce them into society. Wr: Robert Bloch. Dir: James Goldstone.

Dr. Roger Korby (Michael Strong); Andrea (Sherry Jackson); Ruk (Ted Cassidy); Brown (Harry Basch); Matthews (Vince Deadrick); Rayburn (Budd Albright).

Miri
On an Earth-like planet, the officers find a group of 300-year-old children. Wr: Adrian Spies. Dir: Vincent McEveety.

Miri (Kim Darby); Jahn (Michael J. Pollard); Janice (Grace Lee Whitney); Farrell (Jim Goodwin); Diseased man (Ed McCready); Blonde girl (Kellie Flanagan); Jahn's friend (Keith Taylor); Little boy (John Megna); Guard (David L. Ross); Redheaded boy (Steven McEveety); Crewman (John Arndt); Little girl (Lisabeth Shatner); Girls (Dawn Roddenberry, Melanie Shatner); Small boy (Scott Whitney); Kids (Phil Morris, Irene Sale, Jon and Scott Dweck, Darlene Roddenberry).

Dagger of the Mind
Dr. Tristan Adams has turned a medical center into a chamber of horrors. Wr: S. Bar David (Shimon Wincelberg). Dir: Vincent McEveety.

Tristan Adams (James Gregory); Simon Van Gelder (Morgan Woodward); Dr. Helen Noel (Marianna Hill); Lethe (Suzanne Wasson); Inmate (Ed McCready); Berkely (Larry Anthony); Crewman (John Arndt); Therapists (Eli Behar, Walt Davis); Guard (David L. Ross); Inmate guard (Lou Elias).

Memory Flash—Morgan Woodward: "Van Gelder was the most physically and emotionally demanding role that I have ever played. After we finished filming, I went home and spent four days just recovering. All of that screaming and struggling had exhausted me. The first time I saw the episode, I was terribly disappointed. I felt the director had let me go crazy, so to speak, and my acting seemed overdone. Since then, I've had people congratulate me on the performance. Actors are never good at evaluating their own performances."

The Corbomite Maneuver
The *Enterprise* is confronted by a giant spaceship, whose commander gives the *Enterprise* crew 10 minutes to prepare for their execution. Wr: Jerry Sohl. Dir: Joseph Sargent.

Dave Bailey (Anthony Call); Balok (Clint Howard); Janice (Grace Lee Whitney); Alien voice (Ted Cassidy); Balok's real voice (Walker Edmiston); Crewwoman's voice (Majel Barrett); Crew (John Gabriel, Bruce Mars, Sean Morgan, Ena Hartman, Jonathan Lippe, Gloria Calomee, Mittie Lawrence, George Bochman).

The Menagerie, Part 1
Spock takes over the *Enterprise* to transport his former captain, Chris Pike, to a forbidden planet. Wr: Gene Roddenberry. Dir: Robert Butler (old footage), Marc Daniels (new footage).

("The Cage" footage): Christopher Pike (Jeff Hunter); Vina (Susan Oliver); Number One (Majel Barrett); Dr.

Phillip Boyce (John Hoyt); Yeoman Colt (Laurel Goodwin); Jose Tyler (Peter Duryea); Geologist (Edward Madden); Garrison (Adam Roarke); Chief Pitcairn (Clegg Hoyt); Theodore Haskins (Jon Lormer); Talosians (Georgia Schmidt, Serena Sands); Survivors (Anthony Joachim, Leonard Mudie); Voice (Tom Curtis).

("Menagerie" footage): Jose Mendez (Malachi Throne); Crippled Chris Pike (Sean Kenney); Miss Piper (Julie Parrish); Hansen (Hagan Beggs); Humbolt (George Sawaya); Guard (Brett Dunham); Crewmen (Ian Reddin, Tom Lupo).

Trivia Alert: This two-part episode incorporates footage from *Star Trek*'s original pilot, "The Cage." Jeff Hunter was creator Gene Roddenberry's first choice as starship captain. Hunter decided not to commit himself to a weekly series, and William Shatner stepped in. Hunter died tragically in 1969 after falling down a flight of stairs in his house.

The Menagerie, Part 2
On trial for his life, Spock uses flashbacks to show Captain Pike's visit to the Talosian planet years ago. Wr: Gene Roddenberry. Dir: Robert Butler (old footage), Marc Daniels (new footage).

("The Cage" footage): Christopher Pike (Jeff Hunter); Vina (Susan Oliver); Number One (Majel Barrett); Dr. Phillip Boyce (John Hoyt); The keeper (Meg Wylie); Keeper's voice (Malachi Throne); Yeoman Colt (Laurel Goodwin); Jose Tyler (Peter Duryea); Garrison (Adam Roarke); Geologist (Edward Madden); Talosians (Georgia Schmidt, Serena Sands); Officer (Robert Phillips); Orion trader (Joseph Mell); Theodore Haskins (Jon Lormer); Survivors (Leonard Mudie, Anthony Joachim); Chief Pitcairn (Clegg Hoyt); Creature (Randy Crawford); Alien (Janos Prohaska), Warrior (Mike Dugan).

("Menagerie" footage): Jose Mendez (Malachi Throne); Crippled Chris Pike (Sean Kenney); Miss Piper (Julie Parrish); Hansen (Hagan Beggs); Humbolt (George Sawaya); Guard (Brett Dunham).

Memory Flash—Susan Oliver: "*Star Trek* was one of my favorite roles in television. The producers had a choreographer work with me for a solid week before we filmed Vina's dance [as the green slave girl]. Often, after filming, we went to Gene Roddenberry's home to have coffee and talk about the script. He was like a nice poppa bear to us."

Conscience of the King
Kirk agrees to transport an acting troupe because he suspects the lead actor, Karidian, is the ex-governor who killed millions of people 20 years ago. Wr: Barry Trivers. Dir: Gerd Oswald.

Lenore Karidian (Barbara Anderson); Anton Karidian (Kodos) (Arnold Moss); Kevin Riley (Bruce Hyde); Dr. Tom Leighton (William Sargent); Martha Leighton (Natalie Norwick); Janice (Grace Lee Whitney); King Duncan (Karl Bruck); Hamlet (Marc Adams); Larry Matson (David Troy); Leslie (Eddie Paskey); Dailey (Frank Vince).

Balance of Terror
The *Enterprise* is forced into a cat-and-mouse game with a Romulan warship. It's been destroying Federation outposts with a new weapon. Wr: Paul Schneider. Dir: Vincent McEveety.

Romulan commander (Mark Lenard); Andrew Stiles (Paul Comi); Decius (Lawrence Montaigne); Janice (Grace Lee Whitney); Centurion (John Warburton); Hanson (Garry Walberg); Angela Martine (Barbara Baldavin); Robert Tomlinson (Stephen Mines); Fields (John Arndt); Crewman (Sean Morgan); Romulan (Robert Chadwick); Romulan crew (Walt Davis, Vince Deadrick).

Shore Leave
A landing party find themselves trapped on a sinister planet where wishes are instantly granted. Wr: Theodore Sturgeon. Dir: Robert Sparr.

Tonia Barrows (Emily Banks); Esteban Rodriguez (Perry Lopez); Finnegan (Bruce Mars); Caretaker (Oliver McGowan); Angela Martine-Teller (Barbara Baldavin); Ruth (Shirley Bonne); Alice in Wonderland (Marcia Brown); White Rabbit (William Blackburn); Don Juan (James Gruzaf); Samurai (Sebastion Tom); Black knight (Paul Baxley); Guard (John Carr).

The Galileo Seven
A shuttlecraft crash-lands on a hostile planet inhabited by Neanderthal creatures. The survivors work desperately to achieve a lift-off. Wr: Oliver Crawford, S. Bar David (Shimon Wincelberg), story by Oliver Crawford. Dir: Robert Gist.

Lt. Boma (Don Marshall); Ferris (John Crawford); Yeoman Mears (Phyllis Douglas); Gaetano (Peter Marko); Kelowitz (Grant Woods); Latimer (Reese Vaughn); Creature (Robert "Buck" Maffei); Transporter man (David L. Ross).

The Squire of Gothos
A spoiled alien, Trelane, transports Kirk and his officers to a seventeenth-century castle for fun and games. Wr: Paul Schneider. Dir: Don McDougall.

Trelane (William Campbell); DeSalle (Michael Barrier); Karl Jaeger (Richard Carlyle); Teresa Ross (Venita Wolf); Mother's voice (Barbara Babcock); Father's voice (James Doohan).

Arena
Kirk is forced to battle a lizard creature on a barren asteroid. Wr: Gene L. Coon, story by Frederick L. Brown. Dir: Joe Pevney.

Metron's voice (Vic Perrin); Lt. Harold (Tom Troupe); Metron (Carole Shelyne); Kelowitz (Grant Woods); DePaul (Sean Kenney); O'Herlihy (Jerry Ayres); Lang (James Farley); The Gorn (Gary Coombs, Bobby Clark); Gorn's voice (Ted Cassidy).

Tomorrow Is Yesterday
A time warp thrusts the *Enterprise* back to Earth, 1969, where the starship is mistaken for a UFO. Wr: Dorothy C. Fontana. Dir: Michael O'Herlihy.

Capt. John Christopher (Roger Perry); Col. Fellini (Ed Peck); Kyle (John Winston); Sergeant (Hal Lynch); Captain (Mark Dempsey); Webb (Richard Merrifield); Crewwoman (Sherri Townsend); Air police (Jim Spencer).

Memory Flash—Roger Perry: "I think my character could have used a little more humor, but overall, the episode holds up today. I was amazed by how easy it was for Leonard Nimoy to say all of those technical, complicated lines. *Star Trek* is a classic show and for good reason."

Court Martial
Kirk fights to save his reputation after computer records shows his negligence caused the death of a crewman. Wr: Don M. Mankiewicz, Stephen W. Carabatsos, story by Don M. Mankiewicz. Dir: Marc Daniels.

Commodore Stone (Percy Rodrigues); Sam T. Cogley (Elisha Cook); Lt. Areel Shaw (Joan Marshall); Ben Finney (Richard Webb); Jamie Finney (Alice Rawlings); Hansen (Hagan Beggs); Timothy (Winston DeLugo); Personnel officer (Nancy Wong); Capt. Chandra (Reginald Lalsingh); Capt. Krasnowsky (Bart Conrad); Lindstrom (William Meader); Corrigan (Tom Curtis).

Memory Flash—Elisha Cook: "Percy Rodrigues stands out as having a magnificent voice. People enjoy *Star Trek*, but for me it was another fast TV job. I didn't think I was very good. My favorite roles are drunks, informers, hot heads, etc. It's enjoyable when people recognize me for a role and say, 'Hey, you bum!' or 'Why, you no good...!'"

The Return of the Archons
Kirk and his crew land in a city ruled by a ghostly computer image called Landru. Wr: Boris Sobelman, story by Gene Roddenberry. Dir: Joe Pevney.

Marplon (Torin Thatcher); Reger (Harry Townes); Lindstrom (Karl Held); Landru (Charles Macauley); Tula (Brioni Farrell); Woman (Barbara Webber); Tamar (Jon Lormer); First lawgiver (Sid Haig); Lt. O'Neil (Sean Morgan); Hacom (Morgan Farley); Bilar (Ralph Maurer); Leslie (Eddie Paskey); Guard (David L. Ross); Townsperson (Bobby Clark).

Memory Flash—Karl Held: "I hated that experience. I was dressed in a hot, bulky jacket and felt physically uncomfortable [as one of Kirk's officers]. I did my best, but I don't think I was very good. *Star Trek* was a well-done and imaginative series. The premise made for good stories, and they were realized by the writers."

Space Seed
Khan, a superhuman from the 1990s, is awakened from suspended animation. He and his crew seize the *Enterprise*. Wr: Gene L. Coon, Carey Wilbur, story by Carey Wilbur. Dir: Marc Daniels.

Khan Noonian Singh (Ricardo Montalban); Lt. Marla McGivers (Madlyn Rhue); Joaquin (Mark Tobin); Angela (Barbara Baldavin); Kyle (John Winston); Spinelli (Blaisdell Makee); Female guard (Joan Johnson); Crewwoman (Kathy Ahart); Guard (Bobby Bass); Nurse (Joan Webster); Crewmen (John Arndt, Jan Reddin).

Trivia Alert: This episode inspired the feature *Star Trek II—The Wrath of Khan* (1982).

A Taste of Armageddon
The *Enterprise* is marked for destruction on a planet that has been fighting a 500-year-old computer war.

Wr: Robert Hamner, Gene L. Coon, story by Robert Hamner. Dir: Joe Pevney.

Anan 7 (David Opatoshu); Mea 349 (Barbara Babcock); Robert Fox (Gene F. Lyons); Sar 6 (Robert Sampson); Yeoman Tamura (Miko Mayama); Galloway (David L. Ross); DePaul (Sean Kenney); Eminiar guards (Eddie Paskey, William Blackburn, Ron Veto, Frank da Vinci, John Burnside).

This Side of Paradise
The *Enterprise* crew abandon their ship to live on a planet paradise after being exposed to plant spores. Wr: Dorothy C. Fontana, story by Nathan Butler (Jerry Sohl), Dorothy C. Fontana. Dir: Ralph Senensky.

Leila Kalomi (Jill Ireland); Elias Sandoval (Frank Overton); Kelowitz (Grant Woods); DeSalle (Michael Barrier); Leslie (Eddie Paskey); Mr. Paynter (Dick Scotter); Crewman (Bobby Bass); Crewmen (Fred Shue, Sean Morgan, John Lindesmith).

The Devil in the Dark
A creature has been killing miners, and Kirk agrees to help track down the monster. He discovers the creature is trying to protect its eggs from the miners' equipment. Wr: Gene L. Coon. Dir: Joe Pevney.

Vanderberg (Ken Lynch); Horta (Janos Prohaska); Giotto (Barry Russo); Ed Appel (Brad Weston); Schmitter (Biff Elliot); Engineer (George E. Allen); Sam (Dick Dial); Guard (John Cavett); Lewis (Davis Roberts).

Errand of Mercy
As the Federation and Klingon warships prepare for intergalactic war, Kirk and Spock try to save the peaceful villagers of Organia from a Klingon garrison. Wr: Gene L. Coon. Dir: John Newland.

Kor (John Colicos); Ayelborne (John Abbott); Claymare (Peter Brocco); Klingon Lt. (Vic Lundin); Trefayne (David Hillary Hughes); Klingon #2 (George Sawaya); Klingon soldiers (Walt Davis, Gary Coombs, Bobby Bass).

Memory Flash—Vic Lundin: "I had been called in when they were casting the role of Mr. Spock. I understood that it was between me, Leonard Nimoy and another actor a distant third. Byron Haskin, who had directed *Robinson Crusoe on Mars* [where Lundin played the slave, Friday] was working on *Star Trek*, and he tried to get me cast as Spock. But Gene Roddenberry and Nimoy had known each other since the 1950s, and Nimoy got the role."

The Alternative Factor
A time traveler enlists Kirk's aid to battle his sinister counterpart from the anti-matter world. Wr: Don Ingalls. Dir: Gerd Oswald.

Lazarus A and B (Robert Brown); Lt. Charlene Masters (Janet MacLachlan); Barstow (Richard Derr); Engineer (Arch Whiting); Technician (Christian Patrick); Leslie (Eddie Paskey); Security guards (Ron Veto, Tom Lupo, Vince Calenti, William Blackburn); Anti-Matter Lazarus beings (Al Wyatt, Bill Catching).

Trivia Alert: Actor John Drew Barrymore was originally cast as Lazarus. He was replaced by Robert Brown at the last minute.

City on the Edge of Forever

To find Dr. McCoy, Kirk and Spock must travel to 1930 New York. When Kirk falls in love with a social worker, he must choose between saving her life or not changing history. Wr: Harlan Ellison. Dir: Joe Pevney.

Edith Keeler (Joan Collins); Guardian of Forever (Bart La Rue); Policeman (Hal Baylor); Tramp (John Harmon); Kyle (John Winston); Galloway (David L. Ross); Driver (Carey Loftin).

Operation: Annihilate!

Jellyfish-like creatures have infected a planet's entire population and driven them insane. Wr: Stephen W. Carabatsos. Dir: Herschel Daugherty.

Aurelan Kirk (Joan Swift); Peter Kirk (Craig Hundley); Yeoman Zahra Jamal (Maurishka Taliferro); Kartan (Dave Armstrong); Denevans (Jerry Catron, Fred Carson); Leslie (Eddie Paskey).

Memory Flash—Craig Hundley: "I was a big fan of *Star Trek*. In fact, producer Gene Roddenberry wanted me as a regular on the series as Captain Kirk's nephew, Peter. Because of other commitments, I was unavailable. Gene did ask me back for the third season episode, 'And The Children Shall Lead.'"

Season 2: 1967-68

Amok Time

When Vulcan biology forces Spock to return to his home planet, his fiancee T'Pring pits Kirk against Spock in a violent, ancient Vulcan ritual. Wr: Theodore Sturgeon. Dir: Joe Pevney.

T'Pau (Celia Lovsky); T'Pring (Arlene Martell); Stonn (Lawrence Montaigne); Komack (Byron Morrow); Executioner (Russ Peek); Vulcans (Gary Wright, Mark Russell, Charles Palmer, Joseph Paz, Mauri Russell, Frank da Vinci).

Who Mourns for Adonais?

The *Enterprise* crew face the fantastic powers of the Greek god Apollo, who grabs the starship. He demands that they become his followers. Wr: Gilbert A. Ralston, Gene L. Coon, story by Gilbert A. Ralston. Dir: Marc Daniels.

Apollo (Michael Forest); Lt. Carolyn Palamas (Leslie Parrish); Kyle (John Winston).

Memory Flash—Michael Forest: "During filming, I was seated on my throne, and Leonard Nimoy, who wasn't working that day, was watching from behind the cameras. I 'commanded' him to approach me and pay homage. He played along, and groveled his way to my feet like a slave. It got a good laugh from cast and crew. Apollo is my favorite TV role. It was a well-written script."

The Changeling

The *Enterprise* is nearly destroyed by a small space probe called Nomad. Beaming it aboard, Kirk dis-covers Nomad has been programmed to destroy life forms that don't meet its standards of perfection. Wr: John Meredyth Lucas. Dir: Marc Daniels.

Nomad's voice (Vic Perrin); Singh (Blaisdell Makee); Astrochemist (Barbara Gates); Carlisle (Arnold Lessing); Engineer (Meade Martin); Leslie (Eddie Paskey); Jackson Roykirk (Marc Daniels).

Mirror, Mirror

A storm transports Kirk and three crewmembers onto a savage duplicate of the *Enterprise* where officers move up through assassination. Wr: Jerome Bixby. Dir: Marc Daniels.

Lt. Marlena Moreau (Barbara Luna); Tharn (Vic Perrin); Kyle (John Winston); Farrell (Pete Kellett); Wilson (Garth Pillsbury); Computer voice (John Winston); Guard (Paul Prokop); Chekov's thugs (Bobby Bass, Bobby Clark); Sulu's thug (Johnny Mandell).

The Apple

Poisonous plants, lightning bolts and exploding rocks threaten a landing party on a jungle planet inhabited by peaceful villagers. The natives are ruled by their computer god, Vaal. Wr: Max Ehrlich, Gene L. Coon, story by Max Ehrlich. Dir: Joe Pevney.

Akuta (Keith Andes); Yeoman Martha Landon (Celeste Yarnall); Makora (David Soul); Sayana (Shari Nims); Mallory (Jay Jones); Marple (Jerry Daniels); Hendorff (Mal Friedman); Kaplan (Dick Dial); Kyle (John Winston); Natives (Ron Burke, Vince Deadrick, Paul Baxley, Bobby Clark).

Memory Flash—Celeste Yarnall: "*Star Trek* had one of the most expansive concepts on television. That's why it has held up so well. Yesterdays's science fiction is today's science fact. My role could have been more challenging, but they did give me a little spice despite my silly hairdo! It will always be one of my favorite shows."

The Doomsday Machine

An obsessed starship captain uses the *Enterprise* to recklessly battle a huge robot ship that is destroying everything in its path. Wr: Norman Spinrad. Dir: Marc Daniels.

Matt Decker (William Windom); Lt. Palmer (Elizabeth Rogers); Kyle (John Winston); Washburn (Richard Compton); Montgomery (Jerry Catron); Elliot (John Copage); Russ (Tim Burns); Leslie (Eddie Paskey); Navigator (William Blackburn).

Memory Flash—William Windom: "The *Star Trek* fans are the most loyal group in the world. [But] my episode affects me with mild indifference. I've seen bits of it ... while changing channels. Marc Daniels was a good director. I admired his skill and amused detachment. We both shared the relief of knowing that we weren't regulars on the show. The cast got along so-so. They fought."

Catspaw

Giant cats, castles and three witches greet Kirk, Spock and McCoy when they investigate the disappearance of a landing party. Wr: Robert Bloch. Dir: Joe Pevney.

Sylvia (Antoinette Bower); Korob (Theodore Marcuse); DeSalle (Michael Barrier); Kyle (John Winston); Jackson (Jay Jones); First witch (Rhodie Cogan); Second witch (Gail Bonney); Third witch (Maryesther Denver).

I, Mudd

The *Enterprise* is hijacked and taken to Harry Mudd's planet, where they're imprisoned by his androids. Wr: Stephen Kandel, David Gerrold. Dir: Marc Daniels.

Harcourt Fenton Mudd (Roger C. Carmel); Norman (Richard Tatro); Alice androids (Rhea Andrece, Alyce Andrece); Lt. Rowe (Mike Howden); Jordan (Michael Zaslow); Stella Mudd (Kay Elliot); Herman androids (Tom LeGarde, Ted LeGarde); Barbara androids (Maureen Thornton, Colleen Thornton); Maisie androids (Tamara Wilson, Starr Wilson); Engineers (Bob Orrison, Bobby Bass).

Metamorphosis

A stranded shuttlecraft party is witness to a strange love affair between a long-lost astronaut and a shimmering creature called The Companion. Wr: Gene L. Coon. Dir: Ralph Senensky.

Zefrem Cochrane (Glenn Corbett); Nancy Hedford (Elinor Donahue); Companion's voice (Elizabeth Rogers).

Journey to Babel

While transporting alien delegates to a conference, the *Enterprise* is shadowed by an alien ship and beset by murder, sabotage and the illness of Spock's father. Wr: Dorothy C. Fontana. Dir: Joe Pevney.

Amanda (Jane Wyatt); Sarek (Mark Lenard); Thelev (William O'Connell); Shras (Reggie Nalder); Gav (John Wheeler); Lt. Josephs (James X. Mitchell); Nurse (Cindy Lou); Dwarf alien #1 (Billy Curtis).

Memory Flash—William O'Connell: "Dr. Huer from the Buck Rogers comic strips had been my hero as a boy. When I stepped onto the sets of *Star Trek*, I had a very hyper-critical eye. I wasn't impressed. After I saw the segment, my attitude changed and I valued the series. Thelev was absolutely committed to his cause of disrupting the conference. When he was caught, I tried to project his vulnerability. His mission of destruction ended with him taking the slow-acting poison. It was a nicely balanced episode."

Friday's Child

Kirk, Spock, McCoy and a pregnant woman marked for death flee across a mountain to escape hostile tribesmen and a Klingon. Wr: Dorothy C. Fontana. Dir: Joe Pevney.

Eleen (Julie Newmar); Kras (Tige Andrews); Maab (Michael Dante); Akaar (Ben Gage); Keel (Cal Bolder); Duur (Kirk Raymone); Grant (Robert Bralver); Warrior (Dick Dial).

Memory Flash—stuntman Jay Jones: "I doubled as the Klingon for Tige Andrews. One day I walked into the hospital with this weird Klingon makeup on

to see my wife, who worked as a nurse. When people saw me, they cleared the halls and backed up against the walls. They thought I was some crazy man. When I got to the nurse's station, my wife didn't even recognize me!"

The Deadly Years

Kirk and his officers are stricken with a disease that causes them to rapidly age. Wr: David P. Harmon. Dir: Joe Pevney.

George Stocker (Charles Drake); Dr. Janet Wallace (Sarah Marshall); Lt. Arlene Galway (Beverly Washburn); Robert Johnson (Felix Locher); Elaine Johnson (Laura Wood); Yeoman Doris Atkins (Carolyn Nelson).

Obsession

Kirk is determined to destroy a cloud creature that feeds on blood. Wr: Art Wallace. Dir: Ralph Senensky.

Garrovick (Stephen Brooks); Rizzo (Jerry Ayres); Leslie (Eddie Paskey); Guard (William Blackburn).

Memory Flash—Art Wallace: "I said to Gene Roddenberry, 'Why don't we do Moby Dick? Instead of a white whale, we can have a white cloud!' It was an interesting special effect. I liked the question of whether or not Captain Kirk was capable of command."

Wolf in the Fold

A crime-free planet is stricken with a series of Jack the Ripper–like murders. Scotty becomes the prime suspect. Wr: Robert Bloch. Dir: Joe Pevney.

Jaris (Charles Macauley); Hengist (John Fiedler); Sybo (Pilar Seurat); Morla (Charles Dierkop); Tark (Joseph Bernard); Lt. Karen Tracey (Virginia Aldridge); Yeoman Tankris (Judith McConnell); Nurse (Judi Sherven); Kara (Tania Lemani); Serving girls (Suzanne Lodge, Marlys Burdette).

The Trouble with Tribbles

While protecting a grain shipment on space station K-7, Kirk is faced with the proliferation of tribbles, balls of living fluff. Wr: David Gerrold. Dir: Joe Pevney.

Nilz Barris (William Schallert); Koloth (William Campbell); Lurry (Whit Bissell); Cyrano Jones (Stanley Adams); Korax (Michael Pataki); Arne Darvin (Charlie Brill); Bartender (Guy Raymond); Fitzpatrick (Ed Reimers); Freeman (Paul Baxley); Guard (David L. Ross); Leslie (Eddie Paskey); Klingons (Phil Adams, Bob Myles, Bob Orrison, Dick Crockett, Richard Antoni).

Memory Flash—Director of Photography Al Francis: "This was one of my favorite episodes. The propman was Irving Feinberg, and he was fantastic. He made all of these little tribbles move. *Star Trek* had many loyal fans. During the second year, I had a call from a fan from New York at 3 a.m. asking how I did a shot! I respect people's curiosity, but not at three in the morning!"

The Gamesters of Triskelion

Kirk, Uhura and Chekov are forced into gladiatorial

combat for the amusement of alien creatures. Wr: Margaret Armen. Dir: Gene Nelson.

Galt (Joseph Ruskin); Shahna (Angelique Pettyjohn); Lars (Steve Sandor); Jana Haines (Victoria George); Kloog (Mickey Morton); Tamoon (Jane Ross); Andorian Thrall (Dick Crockett); Voices (Bart La Rue, Walker Edmiston).

Memory Flash—Margaret Armen: "I wanted to illustrate Lt. Uhura's confidence as an officer. She's locked in a cell and suddenly the Thrall, Lars, comes in and says he's been chosen for her. She says, 'Sorry, you're not my type.' He makes a pass at her and persists. She uses karate and down he goes. The scene was filmed but cut. The young lady who typed my scripts said, 'Gee, that's a very sexy scene.' Someone else may have felt it was too sexy. But it was a cute exchange."

A Piece of the Action
Kirk and his officers land on a planet similar to Chicago, 1925, where mobs are trying to kill each other. Wr: David P. Harmon, Gene L. Coon, story by David P. Harmon. Dir: James Komack.

Bela Oxmyx (Anthony Caruso); Jojo Krako (Vic Tayback); Kalo (Lee Delano); Zabo (Steve Marlo); Tepo (John Harmon); Boy (Sheldon Collins); Krako's girl (Marlys Burdette); Girl #1 (Dyanne Thorne); Girl #2 (Sharyn Hillyer); Mirt (Jay Jones); Lt. Hadley (William Blackburn); Hood (Buddy Garion).

Trivia Alert: William Blackburn was the uncredited navigator who often replaced Chekov and Sulu at the console. For the first time, he was given a character name.

Memory Flash—DeForest Kelley: "Bill Blackburn was also my stand-in. He's the only [extra] I hear from occasionally. He is—and has been—a successful costumer on various shows."

The Immunity Syndrome
The *Enterprise* confronts a huge single-celled amoeba that has already destroyed one galaxy and is about to reproduce. Wr: Robert Sabaroff. Dir: Joe Pevney.

Kyle (John Winston); Leslie (Eddie Paskey); Starfleet voice (Robert Johnson).

A Private Little War
Kirk has to introduce warfare to a group of peaceful villagers who are being killed by a rival tribe that is being backed by the Klingons. Wr: Gene Roddenberry, Gene L. Coon, story by Judd Crucis (Don Ingalls). Dir: Marc Daniels.

Tyree (Michael Witney); Nona (Nancy Kovack); Dr. M'Benga (Booker Bradshaw); Yutan (Gary Pillar); Krell (Ned Romero); Apella (Arthur Bernard); Patrol leader (Paul Baxley); Mugato (Janos Prohaska); Villagers (Bob Orrison, Roy Sickner, Bob Lyon).

Return to Tomorrow
Kirk, Spock and Dr. Ann Mulhall agree to lend their bodies to formless beings who need to construct android bodies. The alien inside Spock's body decides to keep his Vulcan form. Wr: Gene Roddenberry, story by John Kingsbridge (John T. Dugan). Dir: Ralph Senensky.

Dr. Anne Mulhall (Diana Muldaur); Sargon's voice (James Doohan); Nurse (Cindy Lou); Guards (Roger Holloway, Eddie Paskey).

Patterns of Force
Kirk and Spock land on a planet identical to Nazi Germany. Wr: John Meredyth Lucas. Dir: Vincent McEveety.

Melakon (Skip Homeier); Isak (Richard Evans); John Gill (David Brian); Daras (Valora Norland); Abrom (William Wintersole); Eneg (Patrick Horgan); SS major (Gilbert Green); SS lt. (Ralph Maurer); Newscaster (Bart La Rue); Trooper #1 (Paul Baxley); Gestapo lt. (Peter Canon); SS trooper (Ed McCready); Davod (Chuck Courtney).

By Any Other Name
Aliens take over the *Enterprise* for a 300-year journey to the Andromeda galaxy. Wr: Dorothy C. Fontana, Jerome Bixby, story by Jerome Bixby. Dir: Marc Daniels.

Rojan (Warren Stevens); Kelinda (Barbara Bouchet); Hanar (Stewart Moss); Tomar (Robert Fortier); Yeoman Leslie Thompson (Julie Cobb); Lt. Shea (Carl Byrd); Drea (Leslie Dalton); Leslie (Eddie Paskey); Navigator (William Blackburn).

Memory Flash—Stewart Moss: "My only frustration on that show was striking out with Barbara Bouchet. After a delightful week in her company, I asked her out to dinner. She stared at me, smiled and answered, 'To what purpose? You're an attractive man but what can you do for me?' She later married the head of a film studio in Germany. Smart girl!"

Memory Flash—Barbara Bouchet: "When I was in Switzerland in 1988, I had people asking me all sorts of questions about the *Star Trek* sets. There wasn't much I could say. All I remember is that I had a crush on Bill Shatner!"

The Omega Glory
Kirk battles a starship captain who is using modern weapons to determine the outcome of the primitive planet's civil war. Wr: Gene Roddenberry. Dir: Vincent McEveety.

Ron Tracey (Morgan Woodward); Cloud William (Roy Jenson); Sirah (Irene Kelley); Galloway (David L. Ross); Dr. Carter (Ed McCready); Wu (Lloyd Kino); Marak scholar (Morgan Farley); Executioner (Frank Atienza); Leslie (Eddie Paskey).

The Ultimate Computer
The M-5 computer takes over the *Enterprise* for war games. When the computer malfunctions and begins killing, Kirk tries to deactivate the machine before more lives are lost. Wr: Dorothy C. Fontana, story by Laurence N. Wolfe. Dir: John Meredyth Lucas.

Dr. Richard Daystrom (William Marshall); Robert

Wesley (Barry Russo); Harper (Sean Morgan); M-5 voice (James Doohan).

Memory Flash—William Marshall: "It was an extremely thought-provoking story and a challenging role. Dr. Daystrom was a man of science and morality, but he's unaware that he's also a man of great arrogance. I've worked with no team as classy as *Star Trek*'s or participated in creating a product as memorable."

Bread and Circuses
Kirk struggles against a twentieth-century Rome that wants to use his crew in gladiatorial games. Wr: Gene L. Coon, Gene Roddenberry, story by John Kneubuhl. Dir: Ralph Senensky.
R.M. Merik/Merikus (William Smithers); Flavius (Rhodes Reason); Claudius Marcus (Logan Ramsey); Septimus (Ian Wolfe); Drusilla (Lois Jewell); Policeman (William Bramley); Master of games (Jack Perkins); Announcer (Bart La Rue); Maximus (Max Kleven); Policeman #2 (Paul Baxley); Policeman #3 (Bob Orrison); Slaves (Paul Stader, Tom Steele, Gil Perkins); Leslie (Eddie Paskey).

Assignment: Earth
While conducting research in 1968, the *Enterprise* crew encounters Gary Seven. Seven claims he's an earthling who has been trained by aliens to guide Earth through its nuclear age. Wr: Art Wallace, story by Art Wallace, Gene Roddenberry. Dir: Marc Daniels.
Gary Seven (Robert Lansing); Roberta Lincoln (Teri Garr); Isis's voice (Barbara Babcock); Cromwell (Don Keefer); Nesvig (Morgan Jones); Lipton (Lincoln Demyan); Security chief (Paul Baxley); Police officer (Ted Gehring); Charlie (Bruce Mars); Beta 5 computer voice (Majel Barrett); Mission control voice (James Doohan).

Memory Flash—Art Wallace: "It was a pilot for NBC's 1968-69 season. I had talked to Gene Roddenberry about the idea, and he said he had an idea just like it. 'Why don't we put them together?' he said. It was a good show. Paramount wanted it as a series, but NBC wasn't interested."

Season 3: 1968-69

Spock's Brain
A beautiful woman materializes on the *Enterprise* and steals Spock's brain. Kirk follows the thief to an ice-age planet, where a race of women have made Spock their leader. Wr: Lee Cronin (Gene L. Coon). Dir: Marc Daniels.
Kara (Marj Dusay); Luma (Sheila Leighton); Morg (James Daris).

The *Enterprise* Incident
To steal the Romulans' cloaking device, Kirk feigns madness while Spock courts the female Romulan commander. Wr: Dorothy C. Fontana. Dir: John Meredyth Lucas.

Romulan commander (Joanne Linville); Tal (Jack Donner); Romulan officer (Richard Compton); Romulan technician (Robert Gentile); Romulan soldier (Gordon Coffey); Romulan guard (Mike Howden).

The Paradise Syndrome
Stricken with amnesia, Kirk marries a young Indian woman on a planet that is threatened by a runaway asteroid. Wr: Margaret Armen. Dir: Jud Taylor.
Miramanee (Sabrina Scharf); Salish (Rudy Solari); Chief Goro (Richard Hale); Indian woman (Naomi Pollack); Engineer (John Lindesmith); Indian boy (Lamont Laird); Lumo (Peter Virgo, Jr.); Indian (Richard Geary).

Memory Flash—Margaret Armen: "Fred Freiberger was producer in the third year, and in my view, he concentrated too much on action and cut out character-driven scenes. I don't think he cared much for *Star Trek*. I was in the screening room when he saw the pilots, and his remark to me was, 'Oh, I get it. It's a show about tits and stars.' That didn't go over very well with me. He didn't care for 'Paradise Syndrome' and was amazed when the sponsors and their wives liked it. The episode is a favorite of mine, and Sabrina Scharf was lovely."

And the Children Shall Lead
The starship is taken over by five children who are being controlled by Gorgon, an evil angel. Wr: Edward J. Lakso. Dir: Marvin Chomsky.
Gorgon (Melvin Belli); Tommy Starnes (Craig Hundley); Prof. Starnes (James Wellman); Mary Janowski (Pamelyn Ferdin); Ray Tsingtao (Brian Tochi); Steve O'Connell (Caesar Belli); Don Linden (Mark Robert Brown); Engineer (Lou Elias); Engineer #2 (Jay Jones); Guard #1 (Dick Dial); Leslie (Eddie Paskey).

Is There in Truth No Beauty?
Kolos is a Medusan, a formless alien being transported by the *Enterprise*. Its escort is Miranda, a telepath who is extremely possessive of the alien. Wr: Jean Lisette Aroeste. Dir: Ralph Senensky.
Dr. Miranda Jones (Diana Muldaur); Larry Marvick (David Frankham); Guard (Richard Geary).

Spectre of the Gun
Kirk and his top officers are forced into a restaging of the gunfight at the OK Corral in 1881. Wr: Lee Cronin (Gene L. Coon). Dir: Vincent McEveety.
Wyatt Earp (Ron Soble); Sylvia (Bonnie Beecher); Morgan Earp (Rex Holman); Doc Holliday (Sam Gilman); Vigil Earp (Charles Maxwell); Johnny Behan (Bill Zuckert); Barber (Ed McCready); Ed (Charles Seel); Rancher (Gregg Palmer); Rider (Richard Anthony); Melkot voice (Abraham Sofaer); Melkot buoy voice (James Doohan); Cowboys (Paul Baxley, Bob Orrisson).

Memory Flash—Ron Soble: "I didn't think we could pull this show off. The sets were peculiar, and when I first read the script, I didn't think it was that good. Director Vincent McEveety told me to play Wyatt Earp as if he were dead! It turned out to be the key to my performance. It was one of my best roles and an excellent episode."

Day of the Dove

A sparkling alien that lives on hate transports Klingons aboard the *Enterprise*. Armed only with swords, both sides battle to the death. Wr: Jerome Bixby. Dir: Marvin Chomsky.

Kang (Michael Ansara); Mara (Susan Howard); Johnson (David L. Ross); Klingon (Mark Tobin).

Memory Flash—Jerome Bixby: "When I wrote this, the Klingon was supposed to be Kor, from the earlier segment 'Errand of Mercy.' When John Colicos was offered the chance to reprise the role, he was shooting a movie. They wouldn't let him go away for a week to do 'Day of the Dove.' Colicos was so distraught that he went out on a balcony and banged his head against the wall. It bugs him to this day. Michael Ansara got the role and he was very good."

For the World Is Hollow and I Have Touched the Sky

Dying of an incurable disease, McCoy marries the high priestess of a planet and learns their world is on a collision course with another planet. Wr: Rik Vollaerts. Dir: Tony Leader.

Natira (Katherine Woodville); Westervelt (Byron Morrow); Old man (Jon Lormer); Oracle's voice (James Doohan).

The Tholian Web

Efforts to rescue Captain Kirk from another dimension are threatened by hostile aliens, who encase the *Enterprise* in an energy field. Wr: Judy Burns, Chet Richards. Dir: Ralph Senensky (uncredited), Herb Wallerstein.

O'Neil (Sean Morgan); Tholian voice (Barbara Babcock); Dizzy crewman (Jay Jones); Crazed crewman (Lou Elias).

Memory Flash—Sean Morgan: "I took my acting seriously, but I didn't take *Star Trek* seriously. During the show's production, many unemployed actors shaved their sideburns to a point to make people think they had been working on *Star Trek*. *Star Trek* was a terrific show until they began doing stories about the gunfight at the OK Corral and space Nazis. Give me a break!"

Plato's Stepchildren

Kirk, Spock and McCoy are tormented by an arrogant telepath and his followers. Their only ally is a sympathetic dwarf, Alexander. Wr: Meyer Dolinsky. Dir: David Alexander.

Alexander (Michael Dunn); Parmen (Liam Sullivan); Philana (Barbara Babcock); Eraclitus (Ted Scott); Dionyd (Derek Partridge).

Trivia Alert: The episode "Plato's Stepchildren" made news headlines when it featured the first interracial kiss on network television (between Captain Kirk and the young, black Lieutenant Uhura). Guest star Liam Sullivan, who played the alien leader, says,

"The story had to do with tyranny, and as an anti-brutality message, I liked the script. I was this power-mad emperor who forces Captain Kirk and Lt. Uhura to kiss. I don't recall the scene being a big deal during filming. It took several takes to do because Shatner and Nichelle Nichols kept giggling during the sequence."

Wink of an Eye

Kirk battles aliens who need him for mating purposes to continue their race. Wr: Arthur Heinemann, story by Lee Cronin (Gene L. Coon). Dir: Jud Taylor.

Deela (Kathie Browne); Rael (Jason Evers); Ekor (Erik Holland); Compton (Geoffrey Binney); Scalosians (Richard Geary, Ed Hice).

The Empath

Kirk and his officers find a mute woman and two aliens who subject them to unexplained torture. Wr: Joyce Muskat. Dir: John Erman.

Gem (Kathryn May Hays); Lal (Alan Bergmann); Thann (Willard Sage); Linke (Jason Wingreen); Ozaba (Davis Roberts); Crewman (Roger Holloway).

Memory Flash—Alan Bergmann: "I was called in by director John Erman to do *Star Trek*, but the part sounded limited. The idea of appearing in the grotesque makeup disturbed me as well. I declined. John urged me to do it and promised to beef up the part. With much reluctance, I agreed. It took three hours every morning to get into the rubberized makeup. Willard Sage and I made a pretty picture drinking lunch through a straw in the Paramount commissary. Working with Ms. Hays was a pleasure. Mr. Shatner and Mr. Nimoy seemed to be in conflict. They struggled over better camera positions and made life difficult for the director. Given the minimal sets and the ludicrous pajama-like costumes of the regulars, the episode was quite successful in text and production."

Elaan of Troyius

Kirk tries to teach manners to the spoiled Elaan of Troyius before her wedding. Sabotage and a pursuing Klingon ship endanger his mission. Wr and Dir: John Meredyth Lucas.

Elaan (France Nuyen); Lord Petri (Jay Robinson); Kryton (Tony Young); Watson (Victor Brandt); Evans (Lee Duncan); Klingon (K.L. Smith); Elasian guards (Dick Durock, Charles Beck).

Whom Gods Destroy

Kirk and Spock are prisoners of Garth, a crazed space captain who can change his appearance. Wr: Lee Erwin (Irwin Lieberman), story by Jerry Sohl, Lee Erwin. Dir: Herb Wallerstein.

Garth of Izar (Steve Ihnat); Marta (Yvonne Craig); Donald Cory (Keye Luke); Andorian (Richard Geary); Tellarite (Gary Downey); Medical assistant (Frank da Vinci); Guard (Roger Holloway); Navigator (William Blackburn).

Trivia Alert: Along with "Plato's Stepchildren" and "The Empath," "Whom Gods Destroy" is one of the *Star Trek* episodes banned in England due to its excessive violence.

Let That Be Your Last Battlefield
Two aliens who have been fighting for thousands of years board the *Enterprise*. One demands sanctuary; the other demands that his prisoner be turned over for murder. Wr: Oliver Crawford, story by Lee Cronin (Gene L. Coon). Dir: Jud Taylor.
   Bele (Frank Gorshin); Lokai (Lou Antonio).

The Mark of Gideon
Kirk is transported to an empty *Enterprise* with a young woman for company. He learns it's all a plot to end the overpopulation problem on the planet Gideon. Wr: George F. Slavin, Stanley Adams. Dir: Jud Taylor.
   Odona (Sharon Acker); Hodin (David Hurst); Fitzgerald (Richard Derr); Krodak (Gene Dynarski).

That Which Survives
A stranded landing party faces a strange woman whose touch means instant death. Wr: John Meredyth Lucas, story by Michael Richards (Dorothy C. Fontana). Dir: Herb Wallerstein.
   Losira (Lee Meriwether); D'Amato (Arthur Batanides); Dr. M'Benga (Booker Bradshaw); Lt. Rahda (Naomi Pollack); John B. Watkins (Kenneth Washington); Wyatt (Brad Forrest); Guard (Roger Holloway); Navigator (William Blackburn).

The Lights of Zetar
Glowing life forms invade the *Enterprise* and take over the body of young Lt. Romaine. Wr: Shari Lewis, Jeremy Tarcher. Dir: Herb Kenwith.
   Lt. Mira Romaine (Jan Shutan); Kyle (John Winston); Technician (Libby Erwin); Crewman's voice (Bud da Vinci); Alien voice (Barbara Babcock).

Requiem for Methuselah
Kirk's mission to save his crew from a disease is jeopardized by an immortal named Flint. He needs Kirk to awaken the emotions of his innocent ward, Reena. Wr: Jerome Bixby. Dir: Murray Golden.
   Flint (James Daly); Reena Kapec (Louise Sorel); Orderly (John Buonomo); Navigator (William Blackburn).

The Way to Eden
Space hippies entice the crew with their music, but their sinister motive is to hijack the starship. Wr: Arthur Heinemann, story by Michael Richards (Dorothy C. Fontana), Arthur Heinemann. Dir: David Alexander.
   Dr. Sevrin (Skip Homeier); Irini Galliulin (Mary-Linda Rapelye); Adam (Charles Napier); Lt. Palmer (Elizabeth Rogers); Tongo Rad (Victor Brandt); Mavig (Deborah Downey); Girl hippie (Phyllis Douglas).

   Memory Flash—Elizabeth Rogers: "Lt. Palmer was first introduced in 'The Doomsday Machine.' I got the part when Uhura [Nichelle Nichols] had a singing engagement. I was used as an instant 'threat' replacement. It was a very pleasant experience. This was not as enjoyable. The director was a very rude little man. On the other hand, Leonard Nimoy was a joy to work with. He was very professional and extremely talented."

The Cloud Minders
Kirk gets involved in a class struggle between arrogant people living in a floating city and struggling mine workers. Wr: Margaret Armen, story by Oliver Crawford, David Gerrold. Dir: Jud Taylor.
   Plasus (Jeff Corey); Droxine (Diana Ewing); Vanna (Charlene Polite); Anka (Fred Williamson); Midro (Henry Evens); Prisoner (Garth Pillsbury); Guard #1 (Kirk Raymone); Guard #2 (Jimmy Fields); Guard (Harve Selsby); Miner (Ed Long); Troglytes (Jay Jones, Lou Elias, Marvin Walters); City guards (Richard Geary, Bob Myles, Walter Scott).

The Savage Curtain
Kirk and Spock are forced to join up with Abraham Lincoln to battle four of history's most evil villains. Wr: Gene Roddenberry, Arthur Heinemann, story by Gene Roddenberry. Dir: Herschel Daugherty.
   Abraham Lincoln (Lee Bergere); Surak (Barry Atwater); Col. Greene (Phillip E. Pine); Yarnek (Janos Prohaska); Yarnek's voice (Bart La Rue); Kahless (Robert Herron); Zora (Carol Daniels Dement); Genghis Khan (Nathan Jung); Lt. Dickerson (Lt. Arell Blanton).

   Memory Flash—Lee Bergere: "I must say, immodestly so, that my performance was good. I did not wish to canonize or sanctify Mr. Lincoln. I wished for immediate reality. Between takes, Bill Shatner's Doberman tried to eat my foot. Bill told me it was out of love. Hah!"

All Our Yesterdays
Kirk is accidentally transported to a land where he's accused of witchcraft. Meanwhile, Spock and McCoy are trapped in the ice age, where they meet an exiled young woman. Wr: Jean Lisette Aroeste. Dir: Marvin Chomsky.
   Zarabeth (Mariette Hartley); Mr. Atoz (Ian Wolfe); Prosecutor (Kermit Murdock); Constable (Johnny Haymer); Woman (Anna Karen); Fop (Ed Bakey); Fop #2 (Al Cavens); Jailer (Al Barrett).

Turnabout Intruder
Spock tries to prove that a woman scientist has forcibly exchanged bodies with Captain Kirk and is now in control of the *Enterprise*. Wr: Arthur H. Singer, story by Gene Roddenberry. Dir: Herb Wallerstein.
   Dr. Janice Lester (Sandra Smith); Arthur Coleman (Harry Landers); Guard (David L. Ross); Angela (Barbara Baldavin); Lemli (Roger Holloway); Guard #2 (John Boyer).

Star Trek: The Next Generation
September 1987–May 1994

The Galaxy Starship Cruiser U.S.S. Enterprise continues its adventures as it explores the far reaches of space in the twenty-fourth century. The United Federation of Planets has become a "United Nations" of the galaxy, allied now with the Klingon empire. The continuing threat to peace is the Romulans, who reside across a neutral zone, and the terrifying mind-collective, the Borg.

Cast: Captain Jean-Luc Picard (Patrick Stewart); Commander William Riker (Jonathan Frakes); Lieutenant Commander Data (Brent Spiner); Lieutenant Commander Geordi La Forge (LeVar Burton); Dr. Beverly Crusher (year 1; years 3–7) (Gates McFadden); Dr. Katherine Pulaski (year 2) (Diana Muldaur); Ensign Wesley Crusher (years 1–5), Beverly's son (Wil Wheaton); Counselor Deanna Troi (Marina Sirtis); Lieutenant Worf, Security Chief (Michael Dorn); Lieutenant Tasha Yar, Security Chief (year 1) (Denise Crosby); Guinan (years 2–7) (Whoopi Goldberg).

Created by: Gene Roddenberry; *Executive Producer:* Gene Roddenberry, Rick Berman (years 3–6), Michael Piller (years 4–7); *Co-Executive Producer:* Rick Berman (years 1–2), Maurice Hurley (year 2), Michael Wagner (year 3), Michael Piller (year 3), Jeri Taylor (year 6–7); *Co-Producer:* Robert Lewin (year 1), Herbert Wright (year 1), Hans Beimler and Richard Manning (year 3), Peter Lauritson (year 3–5), Joe Menosky (year 5), Ronald D. Moore (year 5–6), Wendy Neuss (year 6–7), Brannon Braga (year 7); *Line Producer:* David Livingston (years 2–3), Merri D. Howard (years 6–7); *Producer:* Maurice Hurley (year 1), David Livingston (years 1, 4–5), Burton Armus (year 2), Robert L. McCullough (year 2), John Mason and Mike Gray (year 2), Ira Steven Behr (year 3), Peter Lauritson (years 6–7), Ronald D. Moore (year 7); *Supervising Producer:* Robert H. Justman (year 1), Jeri Taylor (years 4–5), David Livingston (years 6–7); *Associate Producer:* Peter Lauritson (years 1–2), D.C. Fontana (year 1), Wendy Neuss (years 4–5); Syndicated/Paramount; 60 minutes.

During the 1970s and 1980s, whenever asked if *Star Trek* would be returning to television as a series, Gene Roddenberry would answer that if it ever did, he did not want to be a part of it. The three-year stint of the original series was exhausting for him. He hardly saw his family, network battles created scars, and creative problems with the show were difficult. Roddenberry just didn't want to repeat the experience.

While making a string of TV movies in the 1970s that included *Spectre*, *The Questor Tapes*,

Genesis II and its sequel, *Planet Earth*, Roddenberry made a living touring colleges and universities lecturing about space and *Star Trek*.

In 1977, when *Star Wars* hit the movie screens across America, Paramount realized they had a golden egg waiting to hatch on their own lot. A second series, dubbed *Star Trek II*, was developed, but this ultimately mutated into *Star Trek—The Motion Picture*. This was after a long period of flip-flopping by Paramount, who couldn't make up their minds in what form they wanted the show to be revived.

But in 1986, prompted by the success of *Star Trek IV—The Voyage Home*, Paramount fast tracked the notion of a another kind of *Star Trek*, a *Star Trek* with a totally different cast placed approximately 78 years into the future. Realizing they could not do this show without Roddenberry, the company asked if he would be interested in developing another *Trek* series. He grabbed at the chance. Although it might have seemed an unusual move, the reasons behind the quick decision were simple. Paramount presented several conditions that lured him in.

For starters, Roddenberry admitted that whenever someone said, *"Star Trek can't be done again!"* it served as an irresistible challenge. The additional incentives were the absence of a network censor and the promise that the show would be syndicated. There was also the excitement of developing new characters and a new starship using the advanced technology of the 1980s to pull off a show with higher production values.

Reassembling many of his original production crew, plus a collection of the finest contemporary production players Hollywood had to offer, Roddenberry rolled up his sleeves and went to work in the twenty-fourth century.

Writers David Gerrold and Dorothy Fontana; producers Eddie Milkis and Robert Justman; costumer William Ware Theiss; assistant director Charles Washburn and set decorator John Dwyer were some of the original guard that came back to create the next generation. Talented newcomers who joined the team included executive producer Rick Berman, production designer Herman Zimmerman, and design staffers Rick Sternbach, Andrew Probert and Michael Okuda. With a staff assembled, Roddenberry's tough task was to assemble an *Enterprise* crew who would have the same appeal and longevity as the original cast.

After Bob Justman discovered Patrick Stewart at a UCLA Shakespeare reading, and after arduous casting calls, other team members were assembled. The new crew of the starship *Enterprise* was born.

"Everybody was aware we were following a famous forefather. ... The fact [is] that there's nothing you can do to try to match to it," says *Next Generation* director Rob Bowman, who was responsible for 13 episodes over five seasons of the show. "Everybody was really intent that we're not going to be like those guys. We're going to make our own. They're too big. So basically, you slay the giant by throwing one rock at a time. Everybody was very open—all the actors, Gene—to starting fresh. I don't think anyone had any idea the show would be as successful as it did. We were all hoping that we would even be picked up again for a second season."

Another director, Paul Lynch, echoes Bowman's memory of the first season's atmosphere. "Nobody quite knew what was going to happen to the series when I directed my first episode," he remembers. "Jonathan [Frakes] and Patrick [Stewart] and I were standing around talking, and they were saying how they figured they'd be there for 13 [episodes] and maybe be there for a year but that'd be it. And I said, 'Five years.' I guessed it would run for five years, maybe six. So, I'm close to being correct."

As director of the two-hour pilot, "Encounter at Farpoint"—the first original *Star Trek* product to hit the airwaves since 1969—Corey Allen says that he didn't have any pretentions or misgivings about being the first director to take on a property that had classic status. "I really didn't feel that. It was a very easy, very fun project from the get-go. I was thrilled to do it. I had a definite vision, which I think coincided with Gene Roddenberry's." Allen is generally pleased with his work on the pilot. "I liked it very much. There was one sequence that didn't pay off very well, and I was frustrated with that. It was the tentacles coming out of the wall, when the other spaceship first comes alive. I don't think that

effect worked very well, and so I was frustrated."

Of the newly assembled crew for the starship, Allen says that the acting was excellent. "Patrick Stewart is one of my favorite actors. He's the epitome of what a professional actor is—he cares about what he's doing, he's invested in what he is doing—and John DeLancie, who plays Q, both of them were a delight to work with.

"Brent Spiner was a find. We cast far and wide to find that character and found Brent. Thank gosh. He was one of the final two [actors auditioning for the role—the other was Eric Menyuk, who would come aboard later as the Traveler in 'Where No One Has Gone Before']. The rest is history."

Rob Bowman says that the mantra chanted throughout the first season was, "'Let's just be ourselves. Let's make our own *Star Trek*.' When I was directing it, I tried to bring my own visual style to it and do as much storytelling with the camera as I could. [The show] was very straightforward in terms of camera work and lighting. We tried to be a bit more creative on the cinematic side. We also had incredible sets ... that the original did not have. It's amazing. Automatically, from the beginning, it was going to be visually more dynamic and believable. We had a vessel that was really inside the *Enterprise*."

Robert Justman, a member of the original production crew of the classic *Trek*, was a supervising producer in the first season of *The Next Generation*. "I thought it was the same show!" he says. "I loved it. I'm sure Gene Roddenberry felt the same way, too. It just had different faces in it. I think Rick Berman and [later producer] Michael Piller did an outstanding job. It's a marvelous show."

Justman lasted only one season on the new show before resigning, for a simple reason. "I left because I was tired," says Justman. "I didn't want to have to work that hard any longer. I figured I paid my dues. One season was good enough for me."

Others who were to resign over creative or professional reasons were Dorothy Fontana, David Gerrold and Maurice Hurley. Allegedly, the first season had a balky start-up because a revolving door in the writing staff accounted for uneven first season scripts.

The show's start-up problems also resulted in two casualties in the cast. Denise Crosby, as security chief Lt. Tasha Yar, decided she was more interested in a film career and felt her character

The world-famous Starship *Enterprise* was the Federation's vessel that transported its crew throughout the galaxy in search of peace, exploration and other alien life forms. Copyright 1991 Paramount Pictures.

was not used well enough. At her request, she was written out, in the notorious "Skin of Evil" segment. (A slag of oil stranded on a planet zapped Yar, and she died.) Another cast member, Gates McFadden as Dr. Beverly Crusher, was asked not to return in the second season. Producers did not like the direction the character was going and wanted someone else. During the second season, veteran actress Diana Muldaur appeared as Dr. Kate Pulaski. Oddly, she was dubbed only a "special guest star" and was not listed in the main titles along with the rest of the regulars.

The second season also allowed a longtime fan of the *Star Trek* saga to climb aboard as, of all things, a bartender. When comedienne Whoopi Goldberg heard of Denise Crosby's departure from the show, she told friend LeVar Burton that she would love to beam aboard. But the producers didn't believe Burton and laughed it off. It took a bold phone call from Goldberg to convince them that her desire was sincere. At the time, a new set was under consideration, so the producers merged the two. Goldberg signed on as Guinan, the bartender at the bar, Ten-Forward.

By the second season, Rob Bowman says, "we all had a great deal more confidence on the show ... and we were all very proud of the

amount of work we'd done. We'd take more risks in terms of storytelling, and, I think, very successfully so. I think everybody had settled into their characters, and I was more confident, and we had kind of jelled at that point."

For the actors, says Bowman, discovering their characters was an important journey, sometimes fraught with difficulty. "Sometimes the writers are pressed, or the actors are pressed, and there's not a marriage between the writing and the actors, and they say, 'Well, I would never do this.' It's not a negative thing, it's, 'Listen, there's a certain realm of believability for this character,' and the actor believes that this is something not part of it. There's usually a discussion between the writer and the actor: 'I've never done this before. I feel uncomfortable about doing this now. Explain it to me, or maybe we can rewrite it.' You always know that's going to happen. I would say *any* of those people, from my experience on *Star Trek*, are *total* professionals. They don't reduce the value of the characters by saying, 'I would never do this,' just to be negative."

As an example of how the actors never let personal opinions get in the way of a performance, Bowman recalls a story during the production of second season's "Elementary, Dear

Data." In this episode, Geordi and Data enter the holodeck as Sherlock Holmes and Dr. Watson, and they pit their wits against Professor Moriarity.

"The first time they entered [the foggy London streets inside the holodeck], Brent was having difficulty with the dialogue as written," recalls Bowman. "He was in his usual pre-creative mode of making comments about the script. We're sitting there, we roll cameras, he's disgruntled with the script, but when I said, 'Action!' he *immediately*, at the flick of a switch, turned into Data. He starts talking to Geordi, who's playing Watson. And then, flicks into Sherlock Holmes and then flicks back into Data vernacular and then I say, 'Cut! Print!' and then he's back complaining again, and it's one of the most brilliant things I've seen this guy do: go from complaining about the scene, to playing Data, playing Sherlock Holmes, 'Cut! Print!' and back to me. It was one of the moments I realized how brilliant he was. That's just the way he is; when the camera goes, he is just *out there*."

Bowman goes on to praise other members of the cast. "I had a highly creative experience with every single actor on that show. To me, when I direct, I go to have a good time and try to take some risks. Jonathan is the one who keeps the set smiling and laughing. Patrick is a polished Shakespearan actor. And Michael Dorn is an absolute rock. He's very steady. He's very creative about what we should be doing and really understands that Worf character. That was a lucky piece of casting. I was very fortunate to direct 'Heart of Glory,' the first Klingon/Worf episode. I know he was eager, but boy, he came through in shining colors in that show."

By the third season, Gates McFadden had returned as Dr. Crusher, and Dr. Pulaski was out. Diana Muldaur moved over to *L.A. Law.*

Bowman's fourth-season episode "Brothers," was significant for several reasons. It marked the return of Lore, not seen since first season's "Datalore," and introduced Data's creator, Dr. Noonian Soong. It was also executive producer Rick Berman's first script. "Brothers" also provided Brent Spiner quite probably one of his most challenging moments as an actor: he was required to play three roles (Data, Lore and Dr. Soong).

"Brent has to play scenes and act and react scenes against himself," says Bowman. "And he's not there to act against himself. So he has to do this scene as Data, and he's looking at a stand-in. The next day he has to come back and play the other side of the conversation as his father. And he has to work out the timing to make it sound like a natural conversation. It's a very difficult thing to do."

Early in the production, it was suggested that veteran actor Keye Luke should play Dr. Soong. But that idea got killed quickly, and Spiner got the part. Bowman says he would not have liked anyone other than Brent to play him because it provided such an acting challenge.

"When I came back for 'Brothers,' everybody was very streamlined in their characters," says Bowman. "The actors had *really* become those people. They were very at ease and very polished, and it was a really wonderful experience to go back and see everybody just working *so* smoothly! "Brothers" was a show very technically difficult to do; a lot of motion control, split screens, the pressures for Brent Spiner to memorize lines that had scenes with nobody on the other side. He was brilliant. I thought the camera work, the lighting, the screenplay, the whole thing was just a great experience."

Bowman stopped directing *Next Generation* episodes after "Brothers." He pleads a simple case of burnout, with a desire to work on other shows to help in his creative growth. "I love everybody there very much," he adds. "I miss them all very much." He has stellar reviews for the shows that followed his departure, calling them "incredible work" and "beautiful episodes."

Don't underestimate the difficulty of creating a good show, says Bowman. If a show is good, it is because the people behind it genuinely care about it.

"You have to thank Gene Roddenberry, Rick Berman, and the actors who [really kept] the enthusiasm in that show," insists Bowman. "People on *Star Trek* really love what they're doing. You watch those shows, and I don't care if you're not a Trekkie or if you've never seen it, you catch a great episode and you're blown away and people talk about it. When you get down to it, why [did we do] this show? Why do people like *Star Trek*? Because there's something about it that gives us a sense of hope and makes us feel good about who we are and what we're going to become. Even if we're down on ourselves right now, *Star Trek* gives you a sense of optimism, and I believe that's its core for each person working on the show. It was for me. That will never go away. That will *never* die in people. Hope and optimism is something we have to have in our lives. And I think that's what *Star Trek* is founded upon.

"I've done a lot of TV shows, but the ones people ask me about are *Star Trek*s. ... People on the street won't come up to me and say, 'Tell me about this show for this other network.' They'll just say, 'Did you enjoy *Star Trek*?' That makes me feel good."

There was a time, in the heat of filming various episodes, that Bowman was unhappy with his working relationship with those on the show. In published interviews for science fiction media publications, Bowman cited problems such as having a day chopped from his schedule for "Q Who" and "Elementary Dear Data," having episodes switched around, losing an opportunity to direct "The Big Goodbye" and receiving "an unshootable script" in "Datalore." And he declared that if he were ever to return to the show, it would be only under a supervising producer/director title.

But having been away from the *Enterprise* sets for some time, Bowman finds that his feelings have changed. "Let me follow this up by saying that any director—I still do the same thing—asks for more time. I think when I was asked some of those questions, I was probably an angrier person. I complained about that, and I shouldn't have complained. Anyone is going to want more time. The studio [executives] do what they have to do. I am *wholly* and singularly grateful to have ever worked on that show. ... Any complaints I had before were just ventilation and were not from me at all. I take back *every* complaint I ever had about that show. I was grateful for the opportunity. I think my biggest beef was on the Borg show, we were doing something brand new. It was a quite ambitious show. What I failed to point out, if I complained about that, was they had given me a very challenging script. They knew we could pull it off. The positive of that is to say, 'Thanks for trusting in me and giving me this script,' instead of saying, 'You took a day away from me!' Who doesn't want more time to make it better? And that's part of the creative process. I think the problem with 'Q Who' was I was not included in the scheduling and was held responsible for it. And I thought there may have been another way of working that out. Nevertheless, I'm glad I had a chance to direct that show."

Like Rob Bowman, Paul Lynch is a director who was on the show at the very beginning, then tuned out after a period of activity. But unlike Bowman, who started out as a young man new to the business, Lynch has credits going back to the 1970s, when he directed various feature films and a variety of episodic television, many of which were science fiction or fantasy related.

Lynch says that directing "11011001" was a challenge because for the show to be successful, both casting and post-production sound had to be perfect. "The Binars were actually small women," he reveals. "They were women of about 25, all who happened to be about four foot nine." Most of the difficulties in assembling the show came from "just to get them to all speak in synch all the time. They all had to speak together. Even though it came out of their mouths, they had to do it [again later] in post-production [dubbing]."

Later episodes that proved memorable for Lynch included "Unnatural Selection," because of the special effects, and "A Matter of Time" (guest-starring Matt Frewer) because "it was a very clever episode. Quite different. It was comedic." But a stronger highlight came from fifth season's "The First Duty," the episode that would finally give us a look at Ensign Wesley Crusher's tenure at Starfleet Academy.

"Wil Wheaton was terrific in it," says Lynch. "He really proved himself. I thought he was a good actor already, but I thought he did a great job in it. It was basically him."

By coincidence, Robert Duncan MacNeil, with whom Lynch had worked on *The Twilight Zone*'s "A Message from Charity," got cast as the antagonist Cadet Nick Locarno. Ray Walston, most famous for *My Favorite Martian* series in the 1960s played the gardener, Boothby. Lynch comments that Walston is "really like a gardener. He has an extraordinary amount of energy for a man his age."

Looking for favorite moments from his stint on the show, Lynch points to scenes in "11011001" and "The Naked Now." In the former, Lynch likes the holodeck sequence between Minuet and Commander Riker, and in the latter, the scene where Tasha Yar seduces Data.

As for why the show was so successful—some say even more than its progenitor—Lynch points to improvements in production quality. "Originally, when Gene was running [TNG], I don't think it was as strong .... I think he was too close to the original. He was, rightly or wrongly stuck in a time-warp that didn't quite measure up to today's world. I remember having a big discussion with Denise Crosby on 'Naked Now' because one of the things that Gene wanted was to see the girls' bodies. Gene seemed to have a very '50s attitude to women characters." According to Lynch, it was in the later seasons that the show "changed dramatically. And I think it was Rick Berman who brought the series up to date. I think the success of the show belongs to him. It was through him the show has become what it is.

"Gene's problem was that he would hold back. He would not progress nearly as fast as should have happened. But the guy responsible for that progress and the series is Rick Berman. It's probably the best television in recent memory. There's nothing in comparison. It's well acted, well written, and very compelling. It's also a family series and an entertaining fantasy series. I think that's why it's so popular."

Someone else who is happy to have been given the reins to direct the show, one of several *Next Generation* actors to become a director, is Jonathan Frakes. Frakes turned into a prodigious director, debuting with third season's "The Offspring." He followed with a pivotal Klingon story in fourth season's "Reunion," as well as Jean Simmons' guest appearance in "The Drumhead." After a season break as a director, Frakes returned with fifth season's intriguing "time causation loop" in "Cause and Effect." The sixth season gave him not one, but two episodes: "The Quality of Life" and "The Chase."

"In the first one I got to do, I felt really lucky to have Brent Spiner as the featured artist," says Frakes. "The Offspring" was Data's turn at being a parent, by constructing his child. "I think he is incredibly talented, probably the actor with the biggest range of anyone on the show. I was a nervous wreck, and he couldn't have been more helpful."

Directing "Reunion" was a considerable challenge. "I'm a huge Klingon fan, and a close friend of Michael Dorn's, so I got to do a totally different type of show, which was kind of exciting—to go from the sensitive quiet Lal, ['The Offspring'], a Data story to a rather large Klingon story. I was sad to have to kill the lovely K'Ehleyr (Worf's half human-half Klingon girlfriend), Suzie Plakson."

In "The Drumhead," Frakes says, "I had the privilege of having Jean Simmons, who is a two-time Oscar nominee and one of the great ladies of cinema and who also happens to be a big *Star Trek* fan. She watches the show every Wednesday in Los Angeles, then calls her friends on the phone and they discuss the episodes. So, we were blessed to get her."

Still another director, Winrich Kolbe, who directed at least two or three episodes of the show

every season since the second, heralds the *Enterprise*'s casting. In an interview before the show's final season, Kolbe called the actors "one of the finest ensemble casts in television. Considering, we have quite a lot of people. We have long scenes on the observation deck, and other scenes on the bridge and other locations. It's a very easy experience. Now, it's like doing a repertory theater. They're quite relaxed. They know their characters. It's very easy for a director who's in tune with the cast because you don't have to tell them what you want. They know it. They know better than you as a director. It's up to the director to get the staging going and get the movement coordinated and make sure everyone is on camera properly, etc. As far as acting is concerned, sometimes someone comes on a little slow because of the night before or whatever, and you have to spruce them up. But that's very easy. With one word, one movement with the finger pointing up..."

Kolbe attributed the show's success, as Lynch does, to executive producer Rick Berman, who held the seams of the show together. "I like Rick. He sometimes drives me up the wall because he's so deeply loyal. I became aware he was under tremendous pressure in a way, to be specific. Because the audience isn't just an audience that just watches the show—they live it. He has to make sure the continuity in various stories is very detailed and under close control. He keeps it all together."

Kolbe said his memories of working on the *Next Generation* stages would always be fun and full of music. That's right. *Music.*

"On pretty much most of the shows, we have an ongoing musical affair on the bridge," grinned Kolbe. "When most of the cast is on the bridge, and we're shooting the whole day on the same set, there's tension. So, after our tenth take, usually something turns on our music machine. Don't ask me how this got around. I think it started when Brent Spiner was coming into the bridge and suddenly Jonathan Frakes throws in something that looks like a microphone and the bridge now turns into a Las Vegas stage. Brent Spiner makes this elaborate show biz stage introduction of himself and suddenly, I don't know how this grew, but we're all singing 'Volare.' And I'm the only one who doesn't know the next lines to 'Volare'! I got suckered into that one. The moment that Jonathan Frakes plugs into 'Volare,' the whole crew and cast starts screaming 'Volare.' I ran down with a breaking voice. By that time,

I'm pretty tired, too. I don't know it now, but it comes to me when I'm singing it. By that time, we're swinging into our twentieth wind. We go through that pretty much on every show. Things need a little juicing up."

Being on *Star Trek* was often a spotlight for guest stars. Anyone familiar with the classic *Trek* series will recall memorable guests as villains or protagonists. *The Next Generation* was no exception.

One of the few guest stars who had the privilege of being directed by Jonathan Frakes was *Spiderman*'s Ellen Bry. Beamed aboard for the sixth season's "The Quality of Life" as a scientist, Bry says, "My real happiness was working with these people because it was one of the most pleasurable work experiences I've ever had. I've been on other long-running shows and shows that have never aired, where there's a lot of tension, people are sick of it and where people don't show up at work. But this show, you go on the set and you just feel good. Everyone is as nice as they can be to you, welcoming you, friendly, and because they've been together for six years, they really meshed. There's a lot of joking, a lot of fun. People are good-humored and there's a lot of fooling around and stuff."

"The Quality of Life" is a story about a dedicated scientist (Bry) working at a space station. She has invented a sophisticated tool, called the exocomps, to help in mining development. But after a malfunction, Data discovers the exocomps has the ability to repair itself, and he declares it a life form. The story was a rare opportunity, says Bry, because seldom did an episode center so strongly on a single female guest star.

"Even as a lead guest star, you rarely get the size of the role that I got on this show," remarks Bry. "And Jonathan Frakes said in his recollection this was the largest guest star role they'd ever had. I was almost in every scene."

Although a veteran of many episodic television shows including the long-running *St. Elsewhere*, Bry found that this episode provided many challenges. "Memorizing the dialogue was like trying to learn a foreign language! I had a whole wealth of technobabble to memorize and a large role on top of it. I tried to make her strong and determined. But a lot of that is in the writing. I feel I was able to pull off that technobabble with real sincerity. I think I was able to get familiar with it enough to get beyond the dialogue and start focusing on the acting. The dialogue was so lengthy and so tricky that I feel very proud about

getting beyond the memorization to present a character. Believe me, you can easily get hung up with the words!"

Thanks to a physician friend who watched the episode, says Bry, she developed new insights into the script and the character. "He said, 'You know, for all intents and purposes, this is an animal rights show.' In terms of the exocomps and life, it's almost about animal rights. I thought that was interesting. I thought, in thinking about the analogy, he's right! Brent Spiner's character goes on the line for these machines. What I thought was great about the script was it brought out a lot of philosophical issues about life and what is life and the definition of life."

Although Bry found the whole experience challenging and enjoyable, what really knocked her socks off was "being beamed! The idea of being able to beam. Not that it was a favorite in terms of content, but I must admit that I enjoyed beaming!" she laughs.

When veteran actor John Anderson appeared in third season's "The Survivors," it proved to be a difficult experience for him. For Anderson, the role of Kevin Uxbridge, a survivor of an alien massacre, was in fact a painful acting chore. In the story, Uxbridge is an alien who has blinked out the existence of the alien marauders because they have killed his human wife, and he has used his powers to recreate her for companionship. In real life, Anderson's own wife had died only a few months before the production of this episode. Emotions remained strong for Anderson, and he admits he almost rejected the role for that reason.

"This was the first job I had taken after [my wife's] death, and they knew about it," says Anderson solemnly. "The terrible part of it was that ... they originally scheduled a highly emotional sequence, talking about my great love and this wonderful woman (guest star Anne Haney playing Uxbridge's wife, Rishon), for either the last day or towards the end of the shooting schedule. Well, something happened and they had to do it the *first* day. My agent told them that this was my first job after my wife's death, so I was still in a state of grieving. When they told me that we had to switch scenes and shoot this on the first day, I just fell apart.

"I told the director, 'I don't know how I'm going to do this because it comes awfully close to my recent experience of marriage of 43 years to a very special woman who's now gone,' but we went into it, and it was very difficult for me, personally.

But it worked, and they were wonderful about taking the time I needed and saying, 'If you need to get away for a minute, we'll understand.'"

Regardless of any difficulties, Anderson was intrigued by the story. "It was a wonderful character and a wonderful story of these two people who were co-dependent and had this idyllic marriage," he says. "It was a people's story. The *Star Trek* crew couldn't figure out how these two people had survived the total obliteration of their planet, and they have to figure out how we survived this total holocaust. At the end of the story, when they pin me down and I reveal to them [that Kevin Uxbridge was an immortal superalien], it was a very touching, emotional scene."

Of working with the *Next Generation* cast, Anderson says that "Jonathan Frakes was an old friend. He played my son in *North and South*, a mini-series, and it was a pleasure to see him doing well. He's a terrific guy."

So successful has this show been in syndication that Paramount, always in search of money, entered into discussions with executive producer Rick Berman in 1992 and encouraged him to develop another show. Paramount head Brandon Tartikoff, who has been known to appreciate science fiction shows, said it did not necessarily have to be a *Star Trek* show. Berman and Piller's research found that yet another *Star Trek* spinoff would be exciting and viable. Together, they dreamed and assembled *Star Trek: Deep Space Nine*, which premiered in the fall of 1992, to an audience of 30 million viewers and respectable critical reviews.

Star Trek: The Next Generation ended its television run at the close of its seventh season in May 1994 and immediately graduated to a feature films debut with *Star Trek: Generations* in November 1994. With the *The Next Generation* on the big screen, Paramount decided they wanted a third ongoing series to replace the show on television to be concurrent with *Deep Space Nine*. *Star Trek—Voyager* premiered as the flagship show for the United Paramount Network (UPN) in January 1995. Never before in the history of television has one dramatic television series (*Star Trek*) spawned three spinoff television shows (*Next Generation, Deep Space Nine* and *Voyager*)!

CAST NOTES

Patrick Stewart (Capt. Picard): Born July 13, 1940. Prior to beaming on the *Enterprise*, Stewart appeared in BBC productions such as *I, Claudius*; *Smiley's People* and *Tinker, Tailor, Soldier, Spy*. He's also had roles in *Dune* (1984), *Lifeforce* (1985), *Excalibur* (1981), and *L.A. Story* (1990). Stewart made his directorial debut in *Next Generation*'s "In Theory" and refined his talent with "Hero Worship" and "A Fistful of Datas."

He performed in the acclaimed one-man play of Charles Dickens' *A Christmas Carol* and has recorded it for Simon and Schuster audio. Further use of his vocal talents beckoned for the PBS series *Shape of the World* and a home video describing *The Planets*.

Stewart grew up in the English town of Mirfield and for 25 years has been an associate artist of the Royal Shakespeare Company.

Jonathan Frakes (Cmdr. Riker): "Riker's job is to provide Capt. Picard with the most efficiently run ship and the best-prepared crew he can. As a result, he maintains a more military bearing than the other characters, despite the fact that salutes and other military protocols no longer exist in the twenty-fourth- century," says Jonathan Frakes.

Born August 19, 1952, and raised in Pennsylvania, Frakes has also appeared in *Falcon Crest*, *Paper Dolls*, *Twilight Zone*'s "But Can She Type?," and *Bare Essence*. He held roles in the miniseries *North and South*, its sequel *Heaven and Hell* and *Dream West*.

Frakes is married to actress Genie Francis.

Brent Spiner (Lt. Cmdr. Data): Born February 2, 1949, and raised in Houston, Texas, after college Spiner moved to New York, where he did numerous off–Broadway plays. He says, "The play that finally pushed me over into the serious actor category was a public theater production of *The Seagull*." After moving to Los Angeles in 1984, Spiner appeared in a theater production of *Little Shop of Horrors* and in Woody Allen's *Stardust Memories*. Television appearances include *Twilight Zone*, *Night Court*, and *Hill Street Blues*.

LeVar Burton (Lt. Cmdr. Geordi LaForge): Born February 16, 1957, Burton is best known for his role as Kunta Kinte in the smash miniseries *Roots*. The character Geordi LaForge is named after a disabled *Star Trek* fan who passed away, says Burton. Burton also served as host to the Emmy-winning PBS series *Reading Rainbow*, and he lent his voice to the environmentally conscious animated series *Captain Planet*.

Some of his many television and film credits

include *Dummy* (1979), *The Guyana Tragedy: The Story of Jim Jones* (1980), *Battered* (1978), *Billy: A Portrait of a Street Kid* (1977) and *The Hunter* (1980).

Michael Dorn (Lt. Worf): "I really enjoy playing a Klingon because the character is so totally different from the nice-guy roles I've done in the past," says Dorn. So successful was Dorn as a Klingon that the producers of *Star Trek VI—The Undiscovered Country* (1991) tapped Dorn to play Lt. Worf's grandfather, a defending lawyer for Capt. Kirk and Dr. McCoy.

Born in Texas on December 9, 1952, and raised in Pasadena, Dorn made his first appearance on TV in *W.E.B.* and later landed a three-year role on *CHIPS*.

Gates McFadden (Dr. Beverly Crusher): Born August 28, 1949. Prior to joining *Next Generation*, McFadden had a good career on the New York stage, both acting and directing. Film appearances include *The Muppets Take Manhattan* (1984) and a cameo in *The Hunt for Red October* (1989). She also has contributed choreographic work in *Labyrinth* (1986).

Diana Muldaur (Dr. Kate Pulaski): Born 1943. Best known to science fiction fans for her two appearances in the original *Star Trek* ("Is There in Truth No Beauty" and "Return to Tomorrow"), Muldaur has a long and rich history as a television actress, including a regular role in *McCloud* (1970–77). Subsequent to her second-season stint in *The Next Generation*, she appeared in *L.A. Law*.

Marina Sirtis (Counselor Deanna Troi): *Star Trek: The Next Generation* came to Sirtis just minutes before she was getting ready to fly back to England, believing she could not find work in Los Angeles.

"Deanna is a very wise person with extensive knowledge of philosophy, psychology and different religions and is called on to advise the captain in a variety of situations," says Sirtis.

Born in East London to Greek parents and brought up in North London, Sirtis performed in *Hamlet*, among other classical works. Film appearances include *The Wicked Lady* (1983) and *Waxwork II: Adventures in Time*.

Wil Wheaton (Wesley Crusher): Born March 29, 1972, Wheaton first came to screen with a critically acclaimed role in the feature *Stand By Me*

(1985). After leaving *The Next Generation* during the fourth season to pursue other acting assignments, Wheaton starred in *Toy Soldiers* (1992) with Sean Astin.

EPISODE GUIDE

Season 1: 1987-88

Encounter at Farpoint (2 hours)
In the twenty-fourth century, 78 years after the original *Enterprise* voyages, Captain Jean-Luc Picard and his new crew of the USS *Enterprise*, NCC-1701-D, journey to the mysterious Farpoint station on the planet Deneb IV. There, they pick up a new first officer, chief medical officer and her son along with Lt. LaForge. But before they get there, they encounter superbeing alien "Q," who places them on trial for the crimes of mankind. Wr: Gene Roddenberry and D.C. Fontana. Dir: Corey Allen.
   Adm. McCoy (DeForest Kelley); Q (John de Lancie); Groppler Zorn (Michael Bell); Battle bridge ensign (Colm Meaney); Mandarin bailiff (Cary-Hiroyuki); Main bridge security (Timothy Dang); Bandi shopkeeper (David Erskine); Female ensign (Evelyn Guerrero); Military officer (Chuck Hicks); Torres (Jimmy Ortega).

The Naked Now
While investigating mysterious deaths aboard another starship, Geordi becomes infected with a virus that spreads quickly to the rest of the crew of the *Enterprise*. The virus brings out deep-seated inhibitions from individuals. Wr: J. Michael Bingham, story by John D.F. Black and J. Michael Bingham. Dir: Paul Lynch.
   Chief engineer Sarah McDougal (Brooke Bundy); Asst. engineer Jim Shimoda (Benjamin W.S. Lum); Transporter chief (Michael Rider); Conn (David Renan); Engineering crewman (Skip Stellrecht); Kissing crewman (Kenny Koch).

   Trivia Alert: This is a remake of "The Naked Time" from the original *Star Trek*.

Code of Honor
When the crew visits Ligon II to obtain a rare and valuable vaccine, the leader kidnaps Tasha and forces Picard to abide by their code of honor to obtain her release. Wr: Kathryn Powers and Michael Baron. Dir: Russ Mayberry.
   Yarenna (Karole Selmon); Lutan (Jessie Lawrence Ferguson); Hagon (James Louis Watkins); Transporter chief (Michael Rider).

The Last Outpost
A sudden energy loss thwarts the *Enterprise* and a starship of the hostile Ferengi empire, prompting teams of each ship to search for its cause on a planet inhabited by the sentinel of an ages-old stellar empire. Wr: Herbert Wright, story by Richard Krzemien. Dir: Richard Colla.

Letek (Armin Shimerman); Mordoc (Jake Dengel); Kayron (Tracey Walter); Portal (Darryl Henriques); Daimon Tarr (Mike Gomez).

Where No One Has Gone Before
A glitch in the *Enterprise*'s propulsion system superwarps the ship into another galaxy, where mental powers become extraordinary and the crew find that their thoughts conjure immediate actions. Wr: Diane Duane and J. Michael Reaves. Dir: Rob Bowman.

Chief Argyle (Biff Yeager); Kosinski (Stanley Kamel); The Traveler (Eric Menyuk); Crewmember (Charles Dayton); Ballerina (Victoria Dillard); Picard's mother (Herta Ware).

Lonely Among Us
While escorting aliens to the planet Parliament, Picard and his crew are enveloped by an energy cloud that seizes control of their minds and alters their behavior. Wr: D.C. Fontana. Story by Michael Halperin. Dir: Cliff Bole.

Chief engineer Singh (Kavi Raz); 1st security guard (Colm Meaney); Ssestar (John Durbin).

Justice
Plans for vacation on the paradise planet Rubicam 3 are disrupted when Wesley breaks a planet law. Meanwhile, above the planet is an intelligence objecting to human colonization. Wr: Worley Thorne, story by Ralph Willis (John D.F. Black) and Worley Thorne. Dir: James L. Conway.

Liator (Jay Louden); Rivan (Brenda Bakke); Conn (Josh Clarke); 1st mediator (David Q. Combs); 2nd mediator (Richard Lavin); Edo girl (Judith Jones); 1st Edo boy (Eric Matthew); 2nd Edo boy (David Michael Graves); Medical technician (Brad Zerbst).

The Battle
When the Ferengi return Capt. Picard's old ship, the *Stargazer*, Picard finds himself under attack by a mind-altering apparatus, forcing him to relive the battle in which the Ferengi's son was killed. Wr: Herbert Wright, story by Larry Forrester. Dir: Rob Bowman.

Daimon Bok (Frank Corsentino); Kazago (Doug Warhit); Rata (Robert Towers).

Hide and Q
Q shows up again to play with the *Enterprise*. This time he offers Riker an opportunity to wield mighty powers and pits the crew against fanged creatures. Wr: C.J. Holland (Maurice Hurley) and Gene Roddenberry, story by C.J. Holland. Dir: Cliff Bole.

Q (John de Lancie); Female Klingon (Elaine Nalee); Older Wesley (William A. Wallace).

Haven
Deanna Troi's mother appears with news of impending marriage between Deanna and the son of an old family friend. Wr: Tracy Torme, story by Tracy Torme and Lan O'Kun. Dir: Richard Compton.

Lwaxana Troi (Majel Barrett); Wyatt Miller (Rob Knepper); Victoria Miller (Nan Martin); Steven Miller (Robert Ellenstein); Mr. Homn (Carel Struycken); Ariana (Danitza Kingsley); Electorine Valeda Innis (Anna Katarina); Wrenn (Raye Birk); Transporter chief (Michael Rider).

The Big Goodbye
Using the ship's holodeck technology, Picard, Data and Dr. Crusher enter the world of 1941 San Francisco to visit Picard's favorite fictional character: Dixon Hill, Private Eye. But when the system malfunctions, they're trapped inside the holodeck. Wr: Tracy Torme. Dir: Joseph Scanlan.

Felix Leech (Harvey Jason); Lt. Dan Bell (William Boyett); Lt. McNary (Gary Armagnal); Cyrus Redblock (Lawrence Tierney); Whalen (David Selburg); Desk sergeant (Mike Genovese); Vendor (Dick Miller); Jessica Bradley (Carolyn Allport); Secretary (Rhonda Aldrich); Thug (Erik Cord).

Trivia Alert: This episode won a Peabody Award.

Datalore
While exploring on Data's home planet, Geordi LaForge discovers a hidden entrance, revealing a sprawling laboratory that contains body parts for another android. When assembled, Data's double, Lore, has clandestine motivations and goals of his own. Wr: Robert Lewin and Gene Roddenberry, story by Robert Lewin and Maurice Hurley. Dir: Rob Bowman.

Lore (Brent Spiner); Argyle (Biff Yeager).

Angel One
On a female-dominated planetary society the crew discovers that survivors of a Federation freighter accident are now fugitives because they oppose the matriarchy. Wr: Patrick Barry. Dir: Michael Rhodes.

Beata (Karen Montgomery); Ariel (Patricia McPherson); Ramsay (Sam Hennings); Trent (Leonard John Crofoot).

11001001 (aka Unconditional Return)
When the computer evacuates the *Enterprise* at a starbase, the crew is unaware that computer-dominated alien technicians are really plotting the hijacking of the starship. Wr: Maurice Hurley and Robert Lewin. Dir: Paul Lynch.

Minuet (Carolyn McCormick); One Zero (Alexandra Johnson); Zero One (Katy Beyer); Zero Zero (Iva Lane); One One (Kelli Ann McNally); Piano player (Jack Sheldon); Bass player (Abdul Salaam el Razzac); Drummer (Ron Brown); Computer chief Quinteros (Gene Dynarski).

Too Short a Season
The *Enterprise* transports Admiral Mark Jameson, a renowned but ailing negotiator, to a planet held hostage by the governor. The startling nature of his illness places the mission in jeopardy. Wr: Michael Michaelian and D.C. Fontana, story by Michael Michaelian. Dir: Rob Bowman.

Adm. Mark Jameson (Clayton Rohner); Governor Karnas (Michael Pataki); Anne Jameson (Marsha Hunt).

Memory Flash—Director Rob Bowman on Adm. Jameson's wheelchair: "It didn't work! It wouldn't work at all. It would just turn left! The flexibility of moving that character around just went away! He could only come into the scene and turn left. Any movement I planned [had to be abandoned]. There's some great stuff in that show, stuff I love very much."

When the Bough Breaks
A hidden, technologically advanced but sterile race kidnaps children aboard the starship *Enterprise* for themselves. Capt. Picard must do everything in his power to retrieve them. Wr: Hannah Louise Shearer. Dir: Kim Manners.
Radue (Jerry Hardin); Rashella (Brenda Strong); Katie (Jandi Swanson); Melian (Paul Lambert); Duana (Ivy Bethune); Dr. Bernard (Dierk Torsek); Leda (Michelle Marsh); Accolan (Dan Mason); Harry Bernard (Philip N. Waller); Toya (Connie Danese); Alexandra (Jessica and Vanessa Bova).

Homesoil
While visiting Velara III, where terraformers are attempting to make a barren planet habitable, the crew of the *Enterprise* discover an unusual life form. Wr: Robert Sabaroff, story by Karl Guers, Ralph Sanchez and Robert Sabaroff. Dir: Corey Allen.
Kurt Mandl (Walter Gotell); Louisa Kim (Elizabeth Lindsey); Arthur Malencon (Mario Roccuzzo); Bjorn Benson (Gerard Prendergast); Female engineer (Carolyne Barry).

Coming of Age
While Wesley takes the Starfleet entrance exam, Capt. Picard's performance as a commander is evaluated by the Inspector General. Wr: Sandy Fries. Dir: Michael Vejar.
Lt. Cmdr. Dexter Remmick (Robert Schenkkan); Tactical officer Chang (Robert Ito); Adm. Gregory Quinn (Ward Costello); Jake Kurland (Stephen Gregory); Mordock (John Putch); T'Shanik (Tasia Valenza); Oliana Mirren (Estee Chandler); Tech. #1 (Brendan McKane); Tech #2 (Wyatt Knight); Rondon (Daniel Riordan).

Heart of Glory
Worf finds himself torn between two worlds when renegade Klingons ask him to join their cause to regain the strength of the warrior race. Wr: Maurice Hurley, story by Herbert Wright and D.C. Fontana. Dir: Rob Bowman.
Capt. K'Nera (David Froman); Korris (Vaughn Armstrong); Konmel (Charles H. Hyman); Kunivas (Robert Bauer); Nurse (Brad Zerbst); Ramos (Dennis Madalone).

Arsenal of Freedom
Approaching the planet Minos, the *Enterprise* intercepts a recorded message pitching super-weapons to starfaring passers-by. On the planet, Riker is frozen by a technologically advanced probe. In the meantime, Picard and Crusher disappear on the planet surface. Wr: Richard Manning and Hans Beimler, story by Maurice Hurley and Robert Lewin. Dir: Les Landau.
Salesman (Vincent Schiavelli); Capt. Paul Rice (Marco Rodriguez); Chief engineer Logan (Vyto Ruginis); Ensign Lian T-Su (Julia Nickson); Lt. Orfil Solis (George de la Pena).

Symbiosis
As the *Enterprise* encounters two vessels involved in a trading dispute, they learn that one society is addicted to a narcotic which the other supplies in exchange for goods. The Prime Directive leaves few choices for Picard. Wr: Robert Lewin, Richard Manning and Hans Beimler, story by Robert Lewin. Dir: Win Phelps.
T'Jon (Merrit Butrick); Sobi (Judson Scott); Romas (Richard Lineback); Langor (Kimberly Farr).

Skin of Evil (aka **The Shroud**)
After crashing a shuttlecraft on Vagra II, counselor Troi is held captive by an alien being, an oil slick, who revels in taunting the rescue team. Wr: Joseph Stefano and Hannah Louise Shearer, story by Joseph Stefano. Dir: Joseph Scanlan.
Armus (Mart McChesney); Voice of Armus (Ron Gans); Lt. Cmdr. Leland T. Lynch (Walker Boone); Nurse (Brad Zerbst); Lt. Ben Prieto (Raymond Forchion).

Trivia Alert: Lt. Tasha Yar dies in this episode.

We'll Always Have Paris
An old love of Picard's appears in his life again when her husband's experiments disrupt space and time. Picard must solve the problem before it runs wild, and at the same time must contend with memories. Wr: Deborah Dean Davis and Hannah Louise Shearer. Dir: Robert Becker.
Jenice Manheim (Michelle Phillips); Dr. Paul Manheim (Rod Loomis); Gabrielle (Isabel Lorca); Lt. Dean (Dan Kern); Edouard (Jean-Paul Vignon); Francine (Kelly Ashmore); Trans. chief Herbert (Lance Spellerberg).

Conspiracy
Picard investigates a plot to infiltrate the highest levels of Starfleet Command and returns to Earth to confront the conspirators. Wr: Tracy Torme, story by Robert Sabaroff. Dir: Cliff Bole.
Adm. Greg Quinn (Ward Costello); Adm. Aaron (Ray Reinhardt); Adm. Savar (Henry Darrow); Adm. Walker Keel (Jonathan Farwell); Lt. Cmdr. Dexter Remmick (Robert Schenkkan); Capt. Tryla Scott (Ursaline Bryant); Capt. Rixx (Michael Berryman).

Neutral Zone
The crew revives three cryogenically preserved bodies on a twentieth-century Earth satellite, just as the *Enterprise* is ordered to the Neutral Zone to confront the Romulans. Wr: Maurice Hurley, story by Deborah McIntyre and Mona Glee. Dir: James L. Conway.
L.Q. "Sonny" Clemonds (Leon Rippy); Ralph Offenhouse (Peter Mark Richman); Clare Raymond (Gracie Harrison); Cmdr. Tebok (Marc Alaimo); Sub-commander Thei (Anthony James).

Season 2: 1988-89

The Child
During a mission to rush samples of a disease organism to a research station, Deanna Troi suddenly announces she is pregnant—"by an alien presence." Wr: Jaron Summers, Jon Povill and Maurice Hurley. Dir: Rob Bowman.

Hester Dealt (Seymour Cassel); Ian (R.J. Williams); Miss Gladstone (Dawn Arnemann); Young Ian (Zachery Benjamin); Engineering ensign (Dore Keller); Chief O'Brien (Colm Meaney).

Trivia Alert: This script was originally written for the aborted *Star Trek II* television series in the 1970s before the first *Star Trek* film. The names were changed to protect the original cast!

Where Silence Has Lease
Enroute to the Morgana Quadrant, the *Enterprise* enters and becomes trapped in a starless void. There the crew discover a deserted spacecraft and once again encounter an alien being interested in the human species. Wr: Jack Sowards. Dir: Winrich Kolbe.

Nagilum (Earl Boem); Haskell (Charles Douglass); Chief O'Brien (Colm Meaney).

Elementary Dear Data
With a few days off for rest and relaxation, Geordi and Data retreat to the Holodeck for a Sherlock Holmes adventure that pits them against the ever-increasing powers of Professor Moriarity. Wr: Brian Alan Lane. Dir: Rob Bowman.

Professor Moriarity (Daniel Davis); Inspector Lestrade (Alan Shearman); Ruffian (Biff Manard); Prostitute (Diz White); Asst. engineer Clancy (Anne Elizabeth Ramsay); Pie man (Richard Merson).

The Outrageous Okona
Bumping across a space derelict introduces the crew of the *Enterprise* to a rogue named Okona who's accused of stealing jewels. In the meantime, Data tries to understand the meaning of humor. Wr: Burton Armus, story by Les Menchen, Lance Dickson and David Landsburg. Dir: Robert Becker.

Okona (William O. Campbell); Debin (Douglas Rowe); Kushell (Albert Stratton); Yanar (Rosalind Ingledew); Benzan (Kieran Mulroney); The Comic (Joe Piscopo); Guinan (Whoopi Goldberg).

Loud as a Whisper
A deaf-mute negotiator is picked up by the *Enterprise* to mediate a truce between two planets who have been fighting for generations. But the task is made more difficult when Riva's cohorts are killed before negotiations can even begin. Wr: Jacqueline Zambrano. Dir: Larry Shaw.

Riva (Howie Seago); Harmony (Marnie Mosiman); Scholar (Thomas Oglesby); Warrior/Adonis (Leo Damian); Alien warrior (Richard Lavin); Alien warrior (Chip Heller); Lieutenant (John Garrett); Chief O'Brien (Colm Meaney).

Trivia Alert: Marnie Mosiman is the wife of John ("Q") de Lancie.

The Schizoid Man
Dr. Ira Graves, a dying egomanical scientist, at the last moment of his life deposits his intellect into Data, creating a schizophrenic android. Wr: Tracy Torme, story by Richard Manning and Hans Beimler. Dir: Les Landau.

Dr. Ira Graves (W. Morgan Sheppard); Lt. Selar (Suzi Plakson); Kareen Brianon (Barbara Alyn Woods).

Trivia Alert: This was Suzi Plakson's first of three appearances, later as a Klingon.

Unnatural Selection
A genetic experiment at a Federation colony goes awry, and afflicted parties, including the *Enterprise*'s own Dr. Pulaski, suffer rapid aging. Wr: John Mason and Michael Gray. Dir: Paul Lynch.

Dr. Sara Kingsley (Patricia Smith); Capt. Taggart (J. Patrick McNamara); Transporter ensign (Scott Trost); Chief O'Brien (Colm Meaney).

A Matter of Honor
As part of an exchange program, Riker transfers to a Klingon vessel and undergoes a unique adventure with the Klingons. Meanwhile, Wesley and a Benzite conduct experiments. Wr: Burton Armus, story by Wanda M. Haight, Gregory Amos and Burton Armus. Dir: Rob Bowman.

Ensign Mendon (John Putch); Capt. Kargan (Christopher Collins); Lt. Klag (Brian Thompson); Tactics officer (Peter Parros); Vekma (Laura Drake); Chief O'Brien (Colm Meaney).

The Measure of a Man
A Federation commander wants authorization to disassemble Data for study. Picard and Data object, sparking a hearing that will settle the question: Is Data a sentient being? Wr: Melinda Snodgrass. Dir: Robert Scheerer.

Capt. Philipa Louvois (Amanda McBroom); Cmdr. Bruce Maddox (Brian Brophy); Admiral Nakamura (Clyde Kusatsu); Chief O'Brien (Colm Meaney); Guinan (Whoopi Goldberg).

The Dauphin
An alien princess comes aboard the *Enterprise* to learn and accept her regal responsibilities to mediate a planetary dispute. While on board, she develops an increasing interest in Wesley. Her protector and chaperone, a shape-changing creature, resists any contact she has with the crew. Wr: Scott Rubenstein and Leonard Mlodinow. Dir: Rob Bowman.

Anya (Paddi Edwards); Salia (Jamie Hubbard); Aron (Peter Neptune); Teenage girl (Madchen Amick); Furry animal (Cindy Sorenson); Ensign Gibson (Jennifer Barlow); Chief O'Brien (Colm Meaney); Guinan (Whoopi Goldberg).

Contagion
A deadly computer virus from another Federation vessel, the *Yamato*, threatens the *Enterprise*. The

secret to stopping it lies on the planet surface where an advanced civilization lies dormant. The Romulans make a guest appearance. Wr: Steve Gerber and Beth Woods. Dir: Joseph Scanlan.

Capt. Donald Varley (Thalmus Rasulala); Sub commander Taris (Carolyn Seymour); Communications officer (Dana Sparks); Doctor (Folkert Schmidt); Chief O'Brien (Colm Meaney).

The Royale
Hunting for clues to an Air Force vessel, the Away Team find themselves inside the Hotel Royale, where Riker, Worf and Data are trapped and can find no exit. Wr: Keith Mills (Tracy Torme) Dir: Cliff Bole.

Assistant manager (Sam Anderson); Vanessa (Jill Jacobson); Bell boy (Leo Garcia); Texan (Noble Willingham); Mickey D. (Gregory Beecroft); Chief O'Brien (Colm Meaney).

Time Squared (aka Time to the Second)
Capt. Picard finds his double in a shuttlecraft from a future time, where the *Enterprise* has entered a space anomaly. As time grows shorter, Picard grows more uncertain of his decision-making, concerned with mistakes he might make towards the *Enterprise*'s destruction. Wr: Maurice Hurley, story by Kurt Michael Bensmiller. Dir: Joseph Scanlan.

Chief O'Brien (Colm Meaney).

The Icarus Factor
Offered command of his own ship, Riker is briefed in his new duties by his estranged father. Meanwhile, Worf is experiencing a spiritual crisis. Wr: David Assael and Robert L. McCullough, story by David Assael. Dir: Robert Iscove.

Kyle Riker (Mitchell Ryan); Ensign Herbert (Lance Spellerberg); Klingon (John Tesh); Chief O'Brien (Colm Meaney).

Pen Pals
Data initiates an unauthorized communication with an alien girl, Sarjenka, who calls for help as her planet is stricken with earthquakes and volcanic eruptions. Wr: Melinda Snodgrass, story by Hannah Louise Shearer. Dir: Winrich Kolbe.

Sarjenka (Nikki Cox); Ensign Davies (Nicholas Cascone); Allison Hildebrand (Ann H. Gillespie); Alans (Whitney Rydbeck); Chief O'Brien (Colm Meaney).

Q Who
Picard's arch-nemesis, Q, tosses the *Enterprise* into the far end of the galaxy. There they engage in a deadly battle with the Borgs, whose collective mind overpowers the ship's defenses. Wr: Maurice Hurley. Dir: Rob Bowman.

Q (John de Lancie); Ensign Sonia Gomez (Lycia Naff); Chief O'Brien (Colm Meaney); Guinan (Whoopi Goldberg).

Memory Flash—Director Rob Bowman: "I don't know where that [title] came from. We can speculate that Q is a kind of a nuisance and always has a smile in your ear and he gets their attention on that show: 'You guys are complacent, you think you own the universe, that no one out there can match up to you, well, let me show you something. Let me show you something you don't know about. Maybe this will give you a little perspective and make you feel like you're not kings of the universe. Make the statement, "Q, Who?" well, let me tell you who!' And there, he gets their attention. That was basically the seed of that episode—bring a little perspective to the crew of the *Enterprise*."

Samaritan Snare
After Picard is taken to a starbase for a heart operation, the *Enterprise* aids a Pakled vessel, but Geordi is taken hostage. Wr: Robert L. McCullough. Dir: Les Landau.

Grebnedlog (Christopher Collins); Reginod (Leslie Morris); Surgeon (Daniel Benzali); Second doctor (Tzi Ma); Ensign Sonia Gomez (Lycia Naff).

Up the Long Ladder (aka Send in the Clones)
The *Enterprise* encounters two threatened cultures: the Bringloidis, descendants of colonists from Earth; and the Mariposans, clones in dire need of new genetic material. Wr: Melinda Snodgrass. Dir: Winrich Kolbe.

Danilo Odell (Barrie Ingham); Brenna Odell (Rosalyn Landor); Wilson Granger (Jon de Vries); Chief O'Brien (Colm Meaney).

Manhunt
En route to a Federation conference, the crew picks up two delegates from the planet Antede Three and gets a surprise visit from Troi's mother, who avidly pursues Capt. Picard. Wr: Terry Devereaux (Tracy Torme). Dir: Rob Bowman.

Lwaxana Troi (Majel Barrett); Mr. Homn (Carel Struycken); Slade Bender (Robert Costanzo); Rex, the bartender (Rod Arrants); Jimmy Kuzo (Robert O'Reilly); Madeline (Rhonda Aldrich); Transporter pilot (Wren T. Brown); Antedian (Mick Fleetwood); Chief O'Brien (Colm Meaney).

The Emissary
A half-Klingon woman from Worf's past boards the *Enterprise* as a special agent to intercept a Klingon vessel carrying a crew in cryogenic suspension. Wr: Richard Manning and Hans Beimler, story by Thomas H. Calder. Dir: Cliff Bole.

K'Ehleyr (Suzie Plakson); K'Temoc (Lance Le Gault); Admiral Gromek (Georgann Johnson); Ensign Clancy (Ann Elizabeth Ramsay); Tactical crewmen (Dietrich Bader); Chief O'Brien (Colm Meaney).

Peak Performance
Engaged in war games, the *Enterprise* is pitted against Riker, commanding the *Hathaway* starship. Wr: David Kemper. Dir: Robert Scheerer.

Sima Kolrami (Roy Brocksmith); Capt. Bractor (Armin Shimeran); Second Ferengi (David L. Lander); Ensign Burke (Glenn Morshower); Ensign Nagel (Leslie Neale).

Shades of Grey
Riker contracts a mysterious disease that attacks the

central nervous system. Dr. Pulaski with counselor Troi tries to save him with a potentially lethal course of treatment. Wr: Maurice Hurley, Richard Manning and Hans Beimler, story by Maurice Hurley. Dir: Rob Bowman.

   Guinan (Whoopi Goldberg); Chief O'Brien (Colm Meaney); Tasha Yar (Denise Crosby).

   Memory Flash—Director Rob Bowman: "I shot that in three days. I was very happy with what I shot. There's neat stuff in it. But that's part of television, to save some money and use existing footage. Okay, 'Shades of Grey' is my least favorite. We did the best we could."

Season 3: 1989-90

Evolution
En route to a stellar phenomenon, the main computers of the *Enterprise* malfunctions, and the ship is drawn toward the fiery remains of an exploding star. Wr: Michael Piller, story by Michael Piller and Michael Wagner. Dir: Winrich Kolbe.

   Dr. Paul Stubbs (Ken Jenkins); Guinan (Whoopi Goldberg); Nurse (Mary McCusker); Crewman #1 (Randall Patrick).

Ensigns of Command
The *Enterprise* is in a race against time: The alien Sheliaks have demanded that all humans living on their planet be evacuated within four days or the entire population will be annihilated. Data must convince the colonists of the impending danger. Wr: Melinda Snodgrass. Dir: Cliff Bole.

   Gosheven (Grainger Hines); Ard'rian Mackenzie (Eileen Seeley); Kentor (Richard Allen); Haritath (Mark L. Taylor); Sheliak (Mart McChesney); Chief O'Brien (Colm Meaney).

The Survivors
Responding to a distress call from a remote Federation planet, the Away Team discover the entire population has been killed except for an elderly couple. Wr: Michael Wagner. Dir: Les Landau.

   Kevin Uxbridge (John Anderson); Rishan Uxbridge (Anne Haney).

Who Watches the Watchers
Federation anthropologists studying the primitive culture of the Mintakans, Vulcan-like humanoids, are injured in an explosion, threatening the Observers' existence. Wr: Richard Manning and Hans Beimler. Dir: Robert Weimer.

   Nuria (Kathryn Leigh Scott); Liko (Ray Wise); Dr. Barron (James Greene); Oji (Pamela Segall); Fento (John McLiam); Hali (James McIntire); Dr. Mary Warren (Lois Hall).

The Bonding
An Away Team survey of a deserted planet results in an accident that kills an archaeologist. The crew tries to comfort her only son. Wr: Ronald D. Moore. Dir: Winrich Kolbe.

Marla Aster (Susan Powell); Jeremy Aster (Gabriel Damon); Teacher (Raymond D. Turner); Chief O'Brien (Colm Meaney).

Booby Trap
The *Enterprise* encounters a dead, thousand-year-old spaceship in an asteroid field. But they're in a booby trap that endangers the ship. Geordi LaForge must use the holodeck to conjure up propulsion expert Leah Brahms to help find a way out. Wr: Ron Roman, Michael Piller and Richard Danus, story by Michael Wagner and Ron Roman. Dir: Gabrielle Beaumont.

   Dr. Leah Brahms (Susan Gibney); Galek Dar (Albert Hall); Chief O'Brien (Colm Meaney); Guinan (Whoopi Goldberg); Christy Henshaw (Julie Warner).

The Enemy
Stranded in a hostile planetary environment with a Romulan, Geordi must use every means possible to survive. Wr: David Kemper and Michael Piller. Dir: David Carson.

   Centurion Bochra (John Snyder); Commander Tomalak (Andreas Katsulas); Pahtak (Steven Rankin); Chief O'Brien (Colm Meaney).

The Price
During negotiations over the rights to a stable wormhole, Deanna Troi falls in love with one Betazoid diplomat. Meanwhile, Data and Geordi use a shuttle to test the wormhole's potentials. Wr: Hannah Louise Shearer. Dir: Robert Scheerer.

   Devinoni Ral (Matt McCoy); Premier Bhavani (Elizabeth Hoffman); Daimon Goss (Scott Thompson); Dr. Arridor (Dan Shor); Dr. Mendoza (Castulo Guerra); Leyor of the Caldonians (Kevin Peter Hall); Chief O'Brien (Colm Meaney).

The Vengeance Factor
While negotiating between the Gatherers and the inhabitants of Acamar III, Riker falls for Yuta, but doesn't realize she has a deadly, covert agenda all her own. Wr: Sam Rolfe. Dir: Timothy Bond.

   Yuta (Lisa Wilcox); Sovereign Marouk (Nancy Parsons); Brull (Joey Aresco); Chorgan (Stephen Lee); Volnoth (Marc Lawrence); Temarek (Elkanah J. Burns).

The Defector
When a Romulan defects to the Federation, they investigate his claims that the Romulans are secretly preparing for war. Wr: Ron D. Moore. Dir: Robert Scheerer.

   Setal/Adm. Jarok (James Sloyan); Admiral Tomalak (Andreas Katsulas); Starfleet admiral (John Hancock); John Bates (S.A. Templeman).

The Hunted
On a trip to consider a planet for membership in the Federation, an escaped fugitive boards the *Enterprise* and causes much havoc that just might interfere with the ships' mission. Wr: Robin Jill Bernhein. Dir: Cliff Bole

   Roga Danar (Jeff McCarthy); Prime Minister Nayrok

(James Cromwell); Zayner (J. Michael Flynn); Wagnor (Andrew Bicknell).

The High Ground
Dr. Crusher is kidnapped by terrorists. Capt. Picard and crew must work with the planetary police force to retrieve her, and they must do so quickly. The *Enterprise* has also been targeted for terrorism. Wr: Melinda Snodgrass. Dir: Gabrielle Beaumont.

Kyril Finn (Richard Cox); Alexana Devos (Kerrie Keane); Waiter (Marc Buckland); Policeman (Fred G. Smith); Boy (Christopher Pettiet).

Deja Q
Stripped of his powers, Q drops into the *Enterprise* unannounced once again. Picard and crew must, to their dismay, deal with a whining, crowing and powerless Q. Wr: Richard Danus. Dir: Les Landau.

Q (John de Lancie); Guinan (Whoopi Goldberg); Q2 (Corbin Bernsen); Dr. Garin (Richard Cansino); Scientist (Betty Muramoto).

A Matter of Perspective
When a laboratory scientist is killed in an explosion aboard a space station, Commander Riker is accused of murder. A hearing is convened, and the holodeck is used to present evidence. Wr: Ed Zuckerman. Dir: Cliff Bole.

Dr. Nel Apgar (Mark Margolis); Manua Apgar (Gina Hecht); Chief investigator Krag (Craig Richard Nelson); Tayna (Juli Donald); Chief O'Brien (Colm Meaney).

Yesterday's Enterprise
A time warp sends the *Enterprise C* into the future, where it meets *Enterprise D* and, as a result, alters history. The revised history means the Klingons and the Federation never made peace. Tasha Yar is alive, and Guinan is the only one who realizes what's happening. Wr: Ira Stephen Behr, Richard Manning, Hans Beimler and Ronald Moore, story by Trent Christopher Ganino and Eric A. Stillwell. Dir: David Carson.

Lt. Tasha Yar (Denise Crosby); Lt. Richard Castillo (Christopher MacDonald); Capt. Rachel Garrett (Tricia O'Neil); Guinan (Whoopi Goldberg).

The Offspring
Data creates his "daughter," an android. When Starfleet hears this, they insist that she must be removed from the *Enterprise*, a move to which Data objects. Wr: Rene Echeverria. Dir: Jonathan Frakes.

Lal (Hallie Todd); Guinan (Whoopi Goldberg); Admiral Haftel (Nicolas Coster); Lt. Ballard (Judy Ann Elder); Android (John Leonard Crofoot); Ten Forward crew (Diane Moser, Wayne Bayle, Maria Leone, James G. Becker).

Sins of the Father
When Worf discovers he has a Klingon brother and learns that his late father is accused of treason, the *Enterprise* goes to the Klingon high command to clear the family name. Wr: Ronald D. Moore and W. Reed Moran, based on a teleplay by Drew Deighan. Dir: Les Landau.

K'mpec (Charles Cooper); Commander Kurn (Tony Todd); Duras (Patrick Massett); Kahlest (Thelma Lee); Transporter tech. (Teddy Davis); Assassin (B.J. Davis); Assassin (Chris Doyle).

Allegiance
The captain is kidnapped and held captive, unbeknownst to the crew, who believe he's still aboard, thanks to an imposter. Wr: Hans Beimler and Richard Manning. Dir: Winrich Kolbe.

Esoqq (Reiner Schöne); Mitena Haro (Joycelyn O'Brien); Tholl (Stephen Markle); Aliens (Jerry and Jeff Rector).

Captain's Holiday
Forced to take a holiday, Capt. Picard finds little peace when a Ferengi chases after a beautiful archaeologist who hides behind Picard. Wr: Ira Stephen Behr. Dir: Chip Chalmers.

Vash (Jennifer Hetrick); Ajur (Karen Landry); Boratus (Michael Champion); Sovak (Max Grodenchik); Joval (Dierdre Imershein).

Tin Man
On a race against time to reach a newly discovered alien entity traveling through space, the *Enterprise*, with a Betazoid on hand for communications, encounters the Romulans. Wr: Dennis Putnam Bailey and David Bischoff. Dir: Robert Scheerer.

Tam Elbrun (Harry Groener); Capt. Robert DeSoto (Michael Cavanaugh); Romulan commander (Peter Vogt); Chief O'Brien (Colm Meaney).

Hollow Pursuits
A socially inept engineer, Reginald Barclay, spends his time inside the holodeck creating difficulties for Geordi LaForge during an important medical mission. Wr: Sally Caves. Dir: Cliff Bole.

Lt. Reginald Barclay (Dwight Schultz); Lt. Duffy (Charley Lang); Chief O'Brien (Colm Meaney); Guinan (Whoopi Goldberg).

The Most Toys
When a shuttle containing Data is destroyed, the crew of the *Enterprise* believe him dead, when actually he's held captive by a collector of rare artifacts. Wr: Shari Goodhartz. Dir: Timothy Bond.

Kivas Fajo (Saul Rubinek); Varria (Jane Daly); Toff (Nehemiah Persoff); Chief O'Brien (Colm Meaney).

Sarek
Vulcan ambassador Sarek arrives aboard the *Enterprise* on an important mission, but when tempers start flying throughout the ship, suspicion falls on the ambassador, who is not himself. Wr: Peter S. Beagle, from an unpublished story by Marc Cushman and Jake Jacobs. Dir: Les Landau.

Sarek (Mark Lenard); Perrin (Joanna Miles); Mendrossen (William Denis); Sakkath (Rocco Sisto); Crewman (John H. Francis); Chief O'Brien (Colm Meaney).

Menage à Trois
Lwaxana and Deanna Troi, with Commander Riker, are kidnapped by the Ferengi. Wr: Fred Bronson and Susan Sackett. Dir: Robert Legato.

Lwaxana Troi (Majel Barrett); Daimon Tog (Frank Corsentino); Dr. Farek (Ethan Phillips); Mr. Homn (Carel Struycken); Nibor (Peter Slutsker); Rizan Grax (Rudolph Willrich).

Transfigurations

The *Enterprise* recovers a survivor of a shuttle accident who has no memory of who he is or why he has strange healing powers. But when a Zalconian ship appears, they demand the return of the man. Wr: Rene Echeverria. Dir: Tom Benko.

John Doe (Mark LaMura); Sunad (Charles Dennis); Christy Henshaw (Julie Warner); Chief O'Brien (Colm Meaney); Nurse Temple (Patti Tippo).

Best of Both Worlds, Part 1

The Borg destroy a colony. Aided by Commander Shelby, the *Enterprise* heads the Federation attack against them, but they must create new weapons to be effective in their assault. Wr: Michael Piller. Dir: Cliff Bole.

Lt. Commander Shelby (Elizabeth Dennehy); Admiral Hanson (George Murdock); Chief O'Brien (Colm Meaney); Guinan (Whoopi Goldberg).

Season 4: 1990-91

Best of Both Worlds, Part 2

Captain Picard is taken and becomes a Borg. Riker now must use every means possible to outwit the Borg before they head for Earth to "assimilate" the inhabitants there. Wr: Michael Piller. Dir: Cliff Bole.

Lt. Commander Shelby (Elizabeth Dennehy); Admiral Hanson (George Murdock); Chief O'Brien (Colm Meaney); Guinan (Whoopi Goldberg); Lt. Gleason (Todd Merrill).

Family

Recovering from the Borg attack, Picard returns somberly home to his brother and his family while Worf gives his foster parents a tour of the *Enterprise*. Wr: Ronald D. Moore, based in part on a premise by Susanne Lambdin and Bryan Stewart. Dir: Les Landau.

Robert Picard (Jeremy Kemp); Marie Picard (Samantha Eggar); Rene Picard (David Tristin Birkin); Sergi Rozenko (Theodore Bikel); Elena Rozenko (Georgia Brown); Louis (Dennis Creaghan); Chief O'Brien (Colm Meaney); Guinan (Whoopi Goldberg); Jack Crusher (Doug Wert).

Brothers

Activated by an internal homing signal, against everyone's wishes, Data alters the *Enterprise*'s course to a planet where he finds his long-lost creator, Dr. Noonian Soong. Wr: Rick Berman. Dir: Rob Bowman.

Dr. Noonian Soong (Brent Spiner); Lore (Brent Spiner); Jake Potts (Cory Danziger); Willie Potts (Adam Ryen); Ensign Kopf (James Lashly); Chief O'Brien (Colm Meaney).

Memory Flash—Director Rob Bowman: "'Brothers' came about because it was a Rick Berman script

and Rick and I were very good friends. And I told Rick earlier that 'Some time or other I would like to come back and direct a show for you.' When his script came up, the suggestion was made that I direct that show. I think Rick was happy with it."

Suddenly Human

A teenage boy is found on a wounded Tellerian ship and is brought aboard the *Enterprise*. The boy's identity is discovered, but he refuses to return to his own culture, while his adoptive father demands his return. Wr: John Welpley and Jeri Taylor, story by Ralph Phillips. Dir: Gabrielle Beaumont.

Jono (Chad Allen); Captain Endar (Sherman Howard); Admiral Rossa (Barbara Townsend).

Remember Me

Dr. Crusher becomes trapped in a parallel universe where the crew of the *Enterprise* are disappearing rapidly. Aboard the real *Enterprise*, the rest of the crew desperately seek to rescue her. Wr: Lee Sheldon. Dir: Cliff Bole.

Traveler (Eric Menyuk); Dr. Dalen Quaice (Bill Erwin); Chief O'Brien (Colm Meaney).

Legacy (aka Beyond Tomorrow)

When a Federation ship crash-lands on Tasha Yar's home planet, Ishara Yar, Tasha's sister, comes aboard to help the *Enterprise* free them. Wr: Joe Menosky. Dir: Robert Scheerer.

Ishara Yar (Beth Toussaint); Hayne (Don Mirault); Tan Tsu (Vladimir Velasco); Coalition lieutenant (Christopher Michael); Chief O'Brien (Colm Meaney).

Reunion (aka When Honor Is Lost)

A Klingon ship meets the *Enterprise*, and K'Ehleyr returns to the *Enterprise* with a son. K'Mpec, head of the Klingon High Council, fears someone is trying to kill him, so he seeks Picard's help. Wr: Thomas Perry, Jo Perry, Ronald D. Moore and Brannon Braga, story by Drew Deighan, Thomas Perry and Jo Perry. Dir: Jonathan Frakes.

K'Ehleyr (Suzie Plakson); K'Mpec (Charles Cooper); Duras (Patrick Massett); Gowron (Robert O'Reilly); Alexander (Jon Steuer); Security guard (Michael Rider); Transporter chief Hubbell (April Grace); 1st Klingon guard (Basil Wallace); 2nd Klingon guard (Mirron E. Willis).

Future Imperfect

After beaming down on a mysterious planet, Cmdr. Riker finds himself propelled into the future. He's now the captain of the *Enterprise*, but he's got no memory of the last 16 years. Wr: J. Larry Carroll and David Bennett Carren. Dir: Les Landau.

Tomalak (Andreas Katsulas); Jean-Luc Riker (Chris Demetral); Minuet (Carolyn McCormick); Nurse (Patti Yasutake); Gleason (Todd Merrill); Transporter chief Hubbell (April Grace); Transporter chief (George O'Hanlon, Jr.).

Final Mission

On a last mission before entering Starfleet Academy,

Ensign Crusher escorts Capt. Picard to an important diplomatic meeting, only to crash-land on a desert planet. Wr: Kasey Arnold-Ince and Jeri Taylor, story by Kasey Arnold Ince. Dir: Corey Allen.

Dirgo (Nick Tate); Ensign Allenby (Mary Kohnert); Sonji (Kim Hamilton).

The Loss

Counselor Troi loses her powers when the ship becomes entangled in a cloud. Her only recourse, she feels, is to resign. Wr: Hilary J. Badler, Alan J. Adler and Vanessa Greene, story by Hilary J. Badler. Dir: Chip Chalmers.

Janet Brooks (Kim Braden); Ensign Allenby (Mary Kohnert); Guinan (Whoopi Goldberg).

Data's Day

A day in the life of a starship, with Data up front. Chief O'Brien's getting married, and the female Vulcan ambassador is engaging in secret negotiations with the Romulans. Wr: Harold Apter and Ronald D. Moore, story By Harold Apter. Dir: Robert Wiemer.

Keiko Ishikawa (Rosalind Chao); T'Pel (Sierra Pecheur); Mendak (Alan Scarfe); Transporter chief Hubbell (April Grace); V'Sal (Shelly Desai); Chief O'Brien (Colm Meaney).

The Wounded

A starship commander is destroying Cardassian ships. Starfleet orders Picard to reel in Captain Maxwell. Wr: Jeri Taylor, story by Stuart Charno, Sara Charno and Cy Chermak. Dir: Chip Chalmers.

Capt. Ben Maxwell (Bob Gunton); Keiko (Rosalind Chao); Gui Macet (Marc Alaimo); Glinn Daro (Time Winters); Admiral Haden (John Hancock); Glinn Telle (Marco Rodriguez); Chief O'Brien (Colm Meaney).

Devil's Due

Ventax II is about to turn over its planet, after experiencing a thousand years of a prophecy, to Ardra, who claims to be the devil. Wr: Philip Lazebnik, story by Philip Lazebnik and William Douglas Lansford. Dir: Tom Benko.

Ardra (Marta DuBois); Acost Jared (Marcello Tubert); Dr. Howard Clark (Paul Lambert); Devil monster (Thad Lamey); Klingon monster (Tom Magee); Marley (William Glover).

Clues

The Enterprise crew is knocked unconcious when encountering a wormhole, and subsequent events leave many unanswered questions. Only Data seems to know what's going on. Wr: Bruce D. Arthurs and Joe Menosky, story by Bruce D. Arthurs. Dir: Les Landau.

Ensign McKnight (Pamela Winslow); Madeline (Rhonda Aldrich); Johnny (Thomas Knickerbocker); Nurse Ogawa (Patti Yasutake); Guinan (Whoopi Goldberg); Chief O'Brien (Colm Meaney).

First Contact

While on a first contact mission on a planet, Cmdr.

Riker is captured and identified as an alien. Picard and the Enterprise must explore their options before he comes to harm. Wr: Dennis Russell Bailey, David Bischoff, Joe Menosky, Ronald D. Moore, story by Marc Scott Zicree. Dir: Cliff Bole.

Chancellor Durkin (George Coe); Mirasta Yale (Carolyn Seymour); Krola (Michael Ensign); Berel (George Hearn); Krola (Michael Ensign); Nilrem (Steven Anderson); Tava (Sachi Parker); Lanel (Bebe Neuwirth).

Galaxy's Child

Geordi's overjoyed at the opportunity to finally meet the Enterprise's engines designer, Dr. Leah Brahms, but things are not what they seem. Meanwhile, a space creature dies, but not before the Enterprise helps it give birth—creating more problems when it thinks the starship is its mother. Wr: Maurice Hurley, story by Thomas Kartozian. Dir: Winrich Kolbe.

Dr. Leah Brahms (Susan Gibney); Ensign Estevez (Lanei Chapman); Ensign Pavlik (Jana Marie Hupp); Guinan (Whoopi Goldberg); Transporter chief Hubbell (April Grace).

Night Terrors

Strange nightmares and disturbances start affecting the crew after encountering a dead science vessel whose only survivor is a Betazoid counselor. Wr: Pamela Douglas and Jeri Taylor, story by Shari Goodhartz Dir: Les Landau.

Keiko (Rosalind Chao); Hagan (John Vickery); Gillespie (Duke Moosekian); Ens. Peeples (Craig Hurley); Ens. Lin (Brian Tochi); Ens. Rager (Lanei Chapman); Guinan (Whoopi Goldberg); Chief O'Brien (Colm Meaney); Capt. Zaheva (Deborah Taylor).

Identity Crisis

LaForge is disturbed to learn that former crewmembers who visited Tarchannen III five years ago are mysteriously drawn back to the planet for unknown purposes. Wr: Brannon Braga, story by Timothy De Haas. Dir: Winrich Kolbe.

Commander Susanna Leitjen (Maryann Plunkett); Nurse Ogawa (Patti Yasutake); Lt. Hickman (Amick Byram); Transporter tech. (Dennis Madalone); Ens. Graham (Mona Grudt).

The Nth Degree

Lt. Barclay gets hit by an alien beam, transforming him into a super-intellectual mind that directly links up with the Enterprise computers. Wr: Joe Menosky Dir: Robert Legato.

Let. Reginald Barclay (Dwight Schultz); Lt. Larson (Saxon Trainor); Einstein (Jim Morton); Cynterian (Kay E. Kuter); Ens. April Anaya (Page Leong); Ens. Brower (David Coburn).

Q-Pid

Wanting to do something "nice" for Capt. Picard, Q sends him and the command crew into the legendary Sherwood Forest so Picard can save his friend Vash from the clutches of Sir Guy. Wr: Ira Steven Behr, story by Randee Russell and Ira Steven Behr. Dir: Cliff Bole.

Q (John De Lancie); Vash (Jennifer Hetrick); Sir Guy (Clive Revill); Servant (Joi Staton).

The Drumhead
A witch hunt begins when Admiral Satie comes out of retirement to investigate who is responsible for an explosion in the *Enterprise*'s dilithium chamber. Wr: Jeri Taylor Dir: Jonathan Frakes.
    Adm. Satie (Jean Simmons); Sabin (Bruce French); Simon Tarses (Spencer Garrett); Admiral Henry (Earl Billings); J'Dan (Henry Woronicz); Nellen (Ann Shea).

Half a Life (aka Civil Wars)
When Lwaxana Troi meets and becomes attached to an aging alien scientist, then discovers his planet's ritual suicide, she is enraged and appalled. Wr: Peter Allen Fields, story by Ted Roberts and Peter Allan Fields. Dir: Les Landau.
    Lwaxana Troi (Majel Barrett); Dr. Timicin (David Odgen Stiers); Dara (Michelle Forbes); B'Tardat (Terrence McNally); Mr. Homn (Carel Strucyken); Chief O'Brien (Colm Meaney).

The Host (aka Paradise)
Dr. Crusher falls in love with an alien ambassador, but when he's injured, the parasite living inside his body must move to a different host. Commander Riker offers to serve as an interim host. Wr: Michael Horvath. Dir: Marvin V. Rush.
    Odan (Franc Luz); Leka (Barbara Tarbuck); Kalin Trose (William Newman); Kareel (Nicole Orth-Pallavicini); Nurse Ogawa (Patti Yasutake).

The Mind's Eye
After La Forge is kidnapped by Romulans, a plot to split the Federation-Klingon alliance is engaged. Someone has to discover Geordi's brainwashing. Wr: Rene Echeverria, story by Ken Schafer and Rene Echeverria. Dir: David Livingston.
    Ambassador Kell (Larry Dobkin); Governor Vagh (Edward Wiley); Commaner Taibak (John Fleck); Chief O'Brien (Colm Meaney); Computer voice (Majel Barrett).

In Theory (aka Breaking Up Is Hard to Do)
Data's in for a closer study of humanity when an ensign falls in love with him. Meanwhile, the *Enterprise* studies a dangerous nebula. Wr: Joe Menosky and Ronald D. Moore. Dir: Patrick Stewart.
    Jenna (Michelle Scarabelli); Keiko (Rosalind Chao); Chief O'Brien (Colm Meaney); Ens. McKnight (Pamela Winslow); Guinan (Whoopi Goldberg).

Redemption, Part 1
When Picard returns to the Klingon planet to oversee Gowron's installation as emperor, he encourages Worf to resolve his family's discommendation. Wr: Ronald D. Moore. Dir: Cliff Bole.
    Gowron (Robert O'Reilly); Kurn (Tony Todd); Lursa (Barbara March); B'Etor (Gwynth Walsh); K'Tal (Ben Slack); Gen. Movar (Nicholas Kepros); Toral (J.D. Cullum); Guinan (Whoopi Goldberg); Klingon first officer (Tom Ormeny); Romulan commander (Denise Crosby); Computer voice (Majel Barrett).

Season 5: 1991-92

Redemption, Part 2
Having rejoined his Klingon brothers, Worf suspects Romulan interference aided by the Duras family. Meanwhile, Picard has won consent for a blockade on the Neutral Zone. Wr: Ronald D. Moore Dir: David Carson.
    Commander Sela (Denise Crosby); Gowron (Robert O'Reilly); Kurn (Tony Todd); Lursa (Barbara March); B'Etor (Gwynth Walsh); Gen. Movar (Nicholas Kepros); Toral (J.D. Cullum); Capt. Larg (Michael G. Hagerty); Adm. Shanti (Fran Bennett); Lt. Cmdr. Hobson (Timothy Carhart); Guinan (Whoopi Goldberg); Kulge (Jordan Lund); Helmsman (Stephen James Carver); Ensign Craig (Clifton Jones); Chief O'Brien (Colm Meaney).

Darmok
While trying to communicate with an alien race, Captain Picard is abducted and beamed down to a planet where the leader, Dathon, tries to communicate in their language. Wr: Joe Menosky, story by Philip Lazebnik and Joe Menosky. Dir: Winrich Kolbe.
    Tamarian first officer (Richard James); Dathon (Paul Winfield); Ens. Robin Lefler (Ashley Judd); Chief O'Brien (Colm Meaney).

    Memory Flash—Winrich Kolbe: "'Darmok' was intriguing because story-wise it really stands out. It's probably the best show about the Prime Directive, in a way. Philosophically, it deals with two people who are forced to communicate with each other, without having the means to communicate. If I were to direct a show in Russia, it would be difficult for me. I need a translator. [Picard and Darmok] had no translator. They had to utilize totally different aspects of cooperation. Darmok knew, and Picard didn't know, of a general approach to dealing with danger. Either running or attacking. Communication was bare minimum. We could learn from that show. We got the basic cornerstone for communication. Two peoples who never really had contact because of the basic difficulties of communication."

Ensign Ro
A Bajorian, Ensign Ro, comes aboard the *Enterprise* after being pardoned of past crimes by a Starfleet admiral. Her mission: to convince her people to stop raids against the Federation colony and accept resettlement. Wr: Michael Piller, story by Rick Berman and Michael Piller. Dir: Les Landau.
    Ensign Ro Laren (Michelle Forbes); Admiral Kennelly (Cliff Potts); Keeve Falor (Scott Marlowe); Gui Dolak (Frank Collison); Orta (Jeffry Hayenga); Transporter officer (Harley Venton); Barber Mot (Ken Thorley); Guinan (Whoopi Goldberg).

Silicon Avatar
Assisting colonists in their new home, Riker and the Away Team encounter an old nemesis: the crystal creature from "Datalore." Data learns that a doctor

hates him because his brother, Lore, brought the crystal to a planet where her son died. Wr: Jeri Taylor, story by Lawrence V. Conley. Dir: Cliff Bole.

Dr. Kila Marr (Ellen Geer); Carmen Davila (Susan Diol).

Disaster

When the *Enterprise* is crippled and all systems are down, Troi is trapped on the bridge, and Picard in a turbolift with three children. Meanwhile, Keiko is about to give birth in Ten-Forward. Wr: Ronald D. Moore, story by Ron Jarvis and Philip Scorza. Dir: Gabrielle Beaumont.

Keiko O'Brien (Rosalind Chao); Ensign Ro (Michelle Forbes); Marissa (Erika Flores); Jay Gordon (John Christopher Graas); Patterson (Max Supera); Ens. Mandel (Cameron Arnett); Lt. Monroe (Jana Marie Hupp); Chief O'Brien (Colm Meaney).

The Game

Wesley Crusher (returning for a visit) and Ensign Lefler fight for their lives when an addictive "game" is brought onboard by Commander Riker. Wr: Brannon Braga, story by Susan Sackett, Fred Bronson and Brannon Braga. Dir: Corey Allen.

Wesley Crusher (Wil Wheaton); Ens. Robin Lefler (Ashley Judd); Etana Joi (Katherine Moffat); Nurse Ogawa (Patti Yasutake); Ensign (Diane M. Hurley); Chief O'Brien (Colm Meaney).

Memory Flash—Brent Spiner: "There's a moment where Dr. Crusher comes behind me and turns me off and I fall on the table. We rehearsed that first thing in the morning, 7:00 in the morning. Corey Allen said, 'OK, what I'd like to do, I'd like to start on the other side of the room with the camera, and we see Gates coming up behind you. She punches the button in your back'—and I fall forward on the table, and by the time I hit the table the camera would have gotten into a close-up.

"So I said, 'Gee, I don't know, Corey. I just *fall* on the table? Couldn't I just sort of start to fall, and you make a cut, and then we see me hit, and we do it in two pieces?' And he said, 'Well, I don't think so. It would be such a better shot.' And I said, 'OK, I'll try it.' And Gates pressed the button—there actually is a button, by the way—I fell forward and hit my chin on the corner of the table. And I raised up, because I recognized pain, and I saw this big gold patch on the corner of the table. And I said, 'Oh, that must be where I hit.' And then all of sudden, little drops of red started hitting it. I had just gashed my chin open. And they had to rush me to a clinic and have it sewn up.

"And I came back, and Michael Westmore, the genius that he is, put a bandage on it and made up over the bandage so you couldn't see it. We came back in to do it again. And Corey said, 'Would you mind doing it one more time?' And I did, and that's there. But if you look at that episode closely, you'll see something hanging from my chin, and that's my chin, actually!"

Unification, Part 1

Shocked to discover that Ambassador Spock has been sighted on Romulus, Starfleet sends Picard and Data on an undercover mission to the planet to discover if he has defected. Wr: Jeri Taylor, story by Rick Berman and Michael Piller. Dir: Les Landau.

Spock (Leonard Nimoy); Perrin (Joanna Miles); Sarek (Mark Lenard); Capt. K'Vada (Stephen D. Root); Klim Dokachin (Graham Jarvis); Senator Pardek (Malachi Throne); Proconsul Neral (Norman Large); Romulan #1 (Daniel Roebuck); B'ljik (Erick Avari); Admiral Brackett (Karen Hensel); Soup woman (Mimi Cozzens); Computer voice (Majel Barrett).

Unification, Part 2

Having found Spock at Romulus trying to further the notion of a reunification between Vulcans and Romulans, Picard and Data have the unenviable task of telling him his father has died. Meanwhile, Sela reveals a daring plan of an attack force to Vulcan. Wr: Michael Piller, story by Rick Berman and Michael Piller. Dir: Cliff Bole.

Spock (Leonard Nimoy); Senator Pardek (Malachi Throne); Proconsul Neral (Norman Large); Romulan #1 (Daniel Roebuck); Capt. K'Vada (Stephen D. Root); Omag (William Bastiani); Romulan #2 (Susan Fallender); Commander Sela (Denise Crosby); D'Tan (Vidal Peterson); Amarie (Harriet Leider).

A Matter of Time

While trying to save a planet from destruction, the *Enterprise* is visited by a time traveler who claims to be from the future, studying the critical events they are experiencing. Wr: Rick Berman. Dir: Paul Lynch.

Berlingoff Rasmussen (Matt Frewer); Dr. Hal Mosely (Stefan Gierasch); Ens. Felton (Sheila Franklin); Scientist (Shay Garner).

New Ground (aka Barriers)

While testing a new drive system that will change the ways of space travel, Worf is paid a visit by his foster mother, who brings Alexander to the *Enterprise*. Wr: Grant Rosenberg, story by Sara Charno and Stuart Charno. Dir: Robert Scheerer.

Helena Rozenko (Georgia Brown); Alexander (Brian Bonsall); Dr. Ja'Dar (Richard McGonagle); Kyle (Jennifer Edwards); Ens. Felton (Sheila Franklin); Computer voice (Majel Barrett).

Hero Worship

When a young boy survives and is traumatized by a terrible spaceship accident, Deanna encourages Data to further a friendship, resulting in the boy taking on Data's persona. Wr: Joe Menosky, story by Hilary J. Bader. Dir: Patrick Stewart.

Timothy (Joshua Harris); Transporter chief (Harley Venton); Ens. Felton (Sheila Franklin); Teacher (Steven Einspahr).

Violations

When telepathic historians board the *Enterprise* and want to probe the crew's forgotten memories, they encounter resistance, and various crewmembers are forced to relive emotional moments in their lives. Wr: Pamela Gray and Jeri Taylor, story by Shari Goodhartz, Michael Gray and Pamela Gray. Dir: Robert Weimer.

Keiko O'Brien (Rosalind Chao); Jev (Ben Lemon); Tarmin (David Sage); Dr. Martin (Rick Fitts); Inad (Eve Brenner); Lt. Cmdr. Jack Crusher (Doug Wert); Crewman Davis (Craig Benton); Computer voice (Majel Barrett).

The Masterpiece Society

While studying a neutron star, the *Enterprise* discovers a human colony on one of the planets, and the people there refuse to relocate. They believe they have created the perfect society and abhor outside contact. Wr: Adam Belanoff and Michael Piller, story by James Kahn and Adam Belanoff. Dir: Winrich Kolbe

Aaron Conor (John Snyder); Hannah Bates (Dey Young); Martin Benbeck (Ron Canada); Ens. Felton (Sheila Franklin).

Conundrum

When they're scanned by an unknown entity, everyone aboard the *Enterprise* is stricken with amnesia, but orders indicate they are on their way to a dangerous mission. Wr: Barry M. Schkolnick, story by Paul Schiffer. Dir: Les Landau.

Cmdr. Kieran McDuff (Erich Anderson); Ensign Ro (Michelle Forbes); Kristin (Liz Vassey); Crewman (Erick Weiss).

Power Play (aka Terror in Ten-Forward)

Deanna, Chief O'Brien and Data are taken over by entities long stranded on a planet, and they take hostages in Ten-Forward in a bid for freedom. Wr: Rene Balcer, Herbert J. Wright and Brannon Braga, story by Paul Ruben and Maurice Hurley. Dir: David Livingston.

Transporter tech. (Ryan Reid); Keiko O'Brien (Rosalind Chao); Ensign Ro (Michelle Forbes); Chief O'Brien (Colm Meaney); Computer voice (Majel Barrett).

Ethics

When Worf is crippled by a cargo deck accident, he believes he must take his own life now that he is useless. Wr: Ronald D. Moore, story by Sara Charno and Stuart Charno. Dir: Chip Chalmers.

Dr. Toby Russell (Caroline Kava); Alexander (Brian Bonsall); Nurse Ogawa (Patti Yasutake).

The Outcast

Cmdr. Riker falls in love with Soren, a member of an androgynous race. But her growing desires for Riker brands her as a sick person, and she is put on trial on her home planet. Wr: Jeri Taylor. Dir: Robert Scheerer.

Soren (Melinda Culea); Krite (Callan White); Noor (Megan Cole).

Cause and Effect

The *Enterprise* is caught in a time glitch just before the ship explodes. During the weekly poker game,

crewmembers begin to realize what's happening and make desperate attempts to release themselves from the loop. Wr: Brannon Braga. Dir: Jonathan Frakes.

Capt. Morgan Bateman (Kelsey Grammer); Ensign Ro (Michelle Forbes); Nurse Ogawa (Patti Yasutake).

The First Duty

Visiting Wesley Crusher at Starfleet Academy, Picard and Dr. Crusher find that Wesley has been involved in an accident while performing an illegal training maneuver with his cadet team. Wr: Ronald D. Moore and Naren Shankar. Dir: Paul Lynch.

Wesley Crusher (Wil Wheaton); Boothby (Ray Walston); Cadet Nick Locarno (Robert Duncan MacNeil); Lt. Commander Albert (Ed Lauter); Capt. Saltek (Richard Fancy); Admiral Brand (Jacqueline Brookes); Cadet Jean Hajar (Walker Brandt); Cadet Sito (Shannon Fill); Cadet (Richard Rothenberg).

Cost of Living

Mrs. Troi once again boards the *Enterprise* and announces she's getting married. Meanwhile, the rebellious Alexander finds a new ally in Mrs. Troi, who takes him under her wing against the wishes of Deanna and Worf. Wr: Peter Allan Fields. Dir: Winrich Kolbe.

Lwaxana Troi (Majel Barrett); Alexander (Brian Bonsall); Campio (Tony Jay); Mr. Homn (Carel Struycken); Young man (David Oliver); Juggler (Albie Selznick); Erko (Patrick Cronin); Young woman (Tracey D'Arcy); Poet (George Edie); First learner (Christopher Halste).

The Perfect Mate

When a beautiful and intelligent female ambassador is offered as a gift to the ruler of the warring planet in order to end an intergalactic war, Capt. Picard is surprised to find himself drawn to her. Wr: Gary Percante and Michael Piller, story by Rene Echevarria and Gary Percante. Dir: Cliff Bole.

Kamala (Famke Janssen); Briam (Tim O'Connor); Par Lenor (Max Grodenchik); Alrik (Michel Cottrell); Qoi (Michael Snyder); Miner #1 (David Paul Needles); Miner #2 (Roger Rignack); Miner #3 (Charles Gunning); Trans. chief Hubbell (April Grace); Computer voice (Majel Barrett).

Imaginary Friend

When a young girl aboard the *Enterprise* begins to exhibit signs that she has an "imaginary friend," Capt. Picard and Deanna investigate. Meanwhile, the ship's energy is being drained by stellar phenomena. Wr: Edithe Swenson and Brannon Braga, story by Ronald Wilderson, Jean Matthias and Richard Fliegel. Dir: Gabrielle Beaumont.

Clara Sutter (Noley Thornton); Isabella (Shay Aster); Ens. Daniel Sutter (Jeff Allin); Alexander (Brian Bonsall); Nurse Ogawa (Patti Yasutake); Ens. Felton (Shiela Franklin); Guinan (Whoopi Goldberg).

I, Borg

The *Enterprise* runs into the Borg again—one of them. Bringing him aboard, they learn what's happened to the collective since their last encounter. Wr: Rene Echevarria. Dir: Robert Lederman.

"Hugh" Borg (Jonathan Del Arco); Guinan (Whoopi Goldberg).

The Next Phase

When Picard offers to help a disabled Romulan ship, Ro and LaForge become "phased" in an accident, and no one onboard can see or hear them. Wr: Ronald D. Moore. Dir: David Carson.

Ensign Ro (Michelle Forbes); Mirok (Thomas Kopache); Varel (Susanna Thompson); Trans. chief Brossmer (Shelby Leverington); Parem (Brian Cousins); Ens. McDowell (Kenneth Messerole).

The Inner Light

When Capt. Picard is hit by a transmission beam from a probe, he's transported into the family life of a man on a planet suffering from drought. Meanwhile, on the bridge, the emission beams continue to be linked with Picard despite everyone's efforts. Wr: Morgan Gendel and Peter Allan Fields, story by Morgan Gendel. Dir: Peter Lauritson.

Eline (Margot Rose); Batai (Richard Riehle); Administrator (Scott Jaeck); Meribor (Jennifer Nash); Young Batai (Daniel Stewart); Nurse Ogawa (Patti Yasutake).

Time's Arrow, Part 1

The *Enterprise* crew travels between the nineteenth and twenty-fourth centuries in an attempt to prevent Data's death in nineteenth century San Francisco. Wr: Joe Menosky and Michael Piller, story by Joe Menosky. Dir: Les Landau.

Samuel Clemens (Jerry Hardin); Bellboy (Michael Aron); Doorman (Barry Kivel); Sea man (Ken Thorley); Joe Falling Hawk (Sheldon Peters Wolfchild); Beggar (John M. Murdock); Gambler (Marc Alaimo); Scientist (Milt Tarver); Guinan (Whoopi Goldberg); Roughneck (Michael Hungerford).

Season 6: 1992-93

Time's Arrow, Part 2

Trapped in the nineteenth century, Capt. Picard and members of the command crew join Data in an attempt to return home. Meanwhile, the author Mark Twain interferes when it is least expected. Wr: Jeri Taylor, story by Joe Menosky. Dir: Les Landau.

Guinan (Whoopi Goldberg); Samuel Clemens (Jerry Hardin); Young reporter (Alexander Enberg); Morgue attendant (Van Epperson); Mrs. Carmichael (Pamela Kosh); Jack the bellboy (Michael Aron); Dr. Appollinaire (James Gleason); Male patient (Bill Cho Lee); Policeman (William Boyett); Alien nurse (Mary Stein).

Realm of Fear

Our old friend Barclay is forced to confront his paralyzing fear of being transported. What he sees during the transporting process frightens him even more. Wr: Brannon Braga. Dir: Cliff Bole.

Reginald Barclay (Dwight Schultz); Chief O'Brien (Colm Meaney); Admiral Hayes (Renata Scott); Crew member (Thomas Velgrey); Nurse Ogawa (Patti Yasutake); Computer voice (Majel Barrett).

Man of the People

Troi is drastically transformed when a visiting ambassador secretly uses her to achieve his covert aims. Wr: Frank Abatemarco. Dir: Winrich Kolbe.

Alkar (Chip Lucia); Maylor (Susan French); Liva (Stephanie Erb); Jarth (Rick Scarry); Ensign (J.P. Hubbell); Ensign Janeway (Lucy Boryer); Admiral (George D. Wallace).

Relics

Trapped in limbo on a dead transport ship for 75 years, Captain Montgomery Scott awakens to join the Next Generation in the twenty-fourth century as they confront what appears to be a Dyson sphere. Wr: Ronald D. Moore. Dir: Alexander Singer.

Scotty (James Doohan); Ensign Rager (Lanei Chapman); Ensign Kane (Erick Weiss); Engineer Bartel (Stacie Foster); Waiter (Ernie Mirich); Computer voice (Majel Barrett).

Schisms

The *Enterprise* crew suffers bizarre physical and psychological consequences following a secret, unwelcome alien visit. Wr: Brannon Braga, story by: Jean Louise Matthias and Ron Wilkerson. Dir: Robert Wiemer.

Ensign Rager (Lanei Chapman); Mott (Ken Thorley); Lieutenant Shipley (Scott T. Trost); Crewman (Angelo McCabe); Kaminer (Angelina Fiordellisi); Medical technician (John Nelson); Computer voice (Majel Barrett).

True Q (aka Q and I)

A gifted young intern learns of her true heritage and must face the question, to Q or not to Q? Wr: Rene Echevarria. Dir: Robert Scherrer.

Q (John de Lancie); Amanda (Olivia d'Abo); Lote (John P. Connolly).

Rascals

A bizarre transporter mishap transforms Picard and three other staff members into children just as Ferengis invade and disable the ship. Wr: Allison Hock, story by Ward Botsford and Diana Dru Botsford and Michael Piller. Dir: Adam Nimoy.

Alexander (Brian Bonsall); Young Picard (David Tristan Birkin); Young Guinan (Isis Jones); Young Keiko (Caroline Junko King); Lurin (Mike Gomez); Berik (Tracey Walter); Morta (Michael Snyder); O'Brien (Colm Meaney); Ensign Ro (Michelle Forbes); Young Ro (Megan Parlen); Kid #1 (Morgan Nagler); Molly (Hana Hatae); Keiko (Rosalind Chao); Computer voice (Majel Barrett).

A Fistful of Datas

A holodeck fantasy goes awry, sending Worf and his son into a Wild West showdown with a villain who's a dead ringer for Data. Wr: Brannon Braga. Dir: Patrick Stewart.

Alexander (Brian Bonsall); Eli Hollander (John Pyper-Ferguson); Annie (Joy Garrett); Bandito (Jorge Cervera); Computer voice (Majel Barrett).

The Quality of Life

Data risks Picard and Geordi's lives in order to protect a living machine inadvertently created by a space station scientist. Wr: Naren Shankar. Dir: Jonathan Frakes.

    Dr. Farallon (Ellen Bry); Trans. chief Kelso (David Windsor); Computer voice (Majel Barrett).

Memory Flash—Ellen Bry: "On the first day of shooting, I recall, Jonathan and I were very excited to finally meet each other. We traded stories about friends we had in common. He's just a terrific director and was extremely friendly and works well with actors.

    "What I liked about Jonathan was that he knew exactly what he wanted. He left us alone unless we weren't giving him what we wanted. In that case, he gave suggestions, and gently guided us to get the results he wanted. What I liked most about him was he kept the cast and crew in good spirits and made the whole experience fun. He was a secure director in that he doesn't need 10 or 15 takes of everything. When he knows he has it, whether it's the first, third or tenth take, we move on. And I like that in a director. He's not insecure. When he gets his shot, we don't waste time, and that's nice."

Chain of Command, Part 1

After resigning his command to the tough-minded Captain Jellico in order to participate in a danger-ous secret mission, Captain Picard is taken hostage by the Cardassians. Wr: Frank Abatemarco, story by Ronald D. Moore. Dir: Robert Scheerer.

    Gul Madred (David Warner); Captain Jellico (Ronny Cox); Admiral Nechayev (Natalija Nogulich); Gul Lemec (John Durbin); Solok (Lou Wagner).

Chain of Command, Part 2

While under the command of an unfeeling new cap-tain, the *Enterprise* attempts to rescue Picard, who is being tortured by the Cardassians. Wr: Frank Abatemarco. Dir: Les Landau

    Captain Jellico (Ronny Cox); Gul Lemec (John Durbin); Gul Madred (David Warner); Jil Orra (Heather Lauren Olson).

Ship in a Bottle

A calculating Professor Moriarty (whom we last met in "Elementary Dear Data"), traps Picard and oth-ers in a holodeck simulation. Wr: Rene Echevarria Dir: Alexander Singer.

    Moriarty (Daniel Davis); Barclay (Dwight Schultz); Gentleman (Clement Von Franckenstein); Countess (Stephanie Beacham); Computer voice (Majel Barrett).

Aquiel

Geordi is enamored with a beautiful and mysterious Starfleet lieutenant accused of murder. Wr: Brannon Braga and Ronald D. Moore, story by Jeri Taylor. Dir: Cliff Bole.

    Aquiel (Renee Jones); Governor Torak (Wayne Grace); Morag (Reg E. Cathey); Computer voice (Majel Barret).

Face of the Enemy

Forced to impersonate a Romulan intelligence officer, counselor Troi plays a pivotal role in an elab-orate defection scheme. Wr: Naren Shankar, story by Rene Echevarria. Dir: Gabrielle Beaumont.

    N'Vek (Scott MacDonald); Toreth (Carolyn Seymour); DeSeve (Barry Lynch); Pilot (Robertson Dean); Alien cap-tain (Dennis Cockrum); Ensign McKnight (Pamela Winslow); Computer voice (Majel Barret).

Tapestry

After Picard loses his life in a surprise attack, Q gives him the chance to change his destiny. Together, they explore Picard's roots as a cadet just out of Starfleet Academy. Wr: Ronald D. Moore. Dir: Les Landau.

    Corey (Ned Vaughn); Marta (J.C. Brandy); Nausicaan #1 (Clint Carmichael); Penny (Rae Norman); Q (John de Lancie); Maurice Picard (Clive Church); Young Picard (Marcus Nash); Computer voice (Majel Barret).

Birthright, Part 1

Worf and Data embark on unusual journeys to seek out their fathers. Worf travels to a Klingon prison camp, while Data enlists the help of Geordi and Dr. Bashir in an experiment. Wr: Brannon Braga. Dir: Winrich Kolbe.

    Dr. Julian Bashir (Siddig El Fadil); Shrek (James Cromwell); Gi'ral (Cristine Rose); Ba'el (Jennifer Gatti); L'Kor (Richard Herd).

Birthright, Part 2

Imprisoned in a society of peaceful Klingons and Romulans, Worf risks his life to show the younger Klingons their lost heritage and inspire them to claim their honor. However, his interference may cost him his life. Wr: Rene Echevarria. Dir: Dan Curry.

    Gi'ral (Cristine Rose); Shrek (James Cromwell); Toq (Sterling Macer, Jr.); Tokath (Alan Scarfe); Ba'el (Jennifer Gatti); L'Kor (Richard Herd).

Starship Mine

While the *Enterprise* is bombarded with lethal rays during a maintenance stopover, Picard is trapped onboard an empty ship with a band of interstellar thieves. Wr: Morgan Gendel. Dir: Cliff Bole.

    Hutchinson (David Spielberg); Kelsey (Marie Mar-shall); Devor (Tim Russ); Orton (Glenn Morshower); Neil (Tom Nibley); Satler (Tim deZarn); Kiros (Patricia Tallman); Waiter (Arlee Reed); Pomet (Alan Altshuld).

Lessons

Picard is torn between love and duty when he is forced to send the woman he loves on a potentially deadly mission. Wr: Ronald Wilkerson and Jean Louise Matthias. Dir: Robert Wiemer.

    Nella Daren (Wendy Hughes).

The Chase

Picard finds himself in a race with Cardassians, Klingons and Romulans to solve a four-billion-year-old genetic puzzle. Wr: Joe Menosky, story by Joe Menosky and Ronald D. Moore. Dir: Jonathan Frakes.

    Humanoid (Salome Jens); Nu'Daq (John Cothran, Jr.); Romulan captain (Maurice Roeves); Gul Ocett (Linda Thorson); Professor Galen (Norman Lloyd).

Frame of Mind
Trapped in an alien mental hospital, with jumbled memories of the past, Riker is convinced he is going insane. Wr: Brannon Braga. Dir: James L. Conway.

Doctor Syrus (David Selburg); Administrator (Andrew Prine); Mavek (Gary Werntz); Inmate (Susanna Thompson).

Suspicions
A pioneering Ferengi scientist is found dead, and Beverly risks her career to prove he was murdered. Wr: Joe Menosky and Naren Shankar. Dir: Cliff Bole.

Ogawa (Patti Yasutake); Kurak (Tricia O'Neil); Dr. Reyga (Peter Slutsker); Jo'Bril (James Horan); Dr. Christopher (John S. Ragin); T'Pan (Joan Stuart Morris); Guinan (Whoopi Goldberg).

Rightful Heir
Worf finds his faith sorely tested when it appears that the greatest Klingon warrior of all time has returned from the dead to reclaim the empire. Wr: Ronald D. Moore, story by James E. Brooks. Dir: Winrich Kolbe.

Koroth (Alan Oppenheimer); Gowron (Robert O'Reilly); Torin (Norman Snow); Divok (Charles Esten); Kahless (Kevin Conway).

Second Chances
Returning to the site of an eight-year-old mission, Riker encounters a double of himself created during a transporter accident, who tries to rekindle a romantic relationship with Deanna. Wr: Rene Echevarria, story by Michael A. Medlock. Dir: LeVar Burton.

Ensign Palmer (Dr. Mae Jemison).

Timescape
The *Enterprise* is frozen in time on the brink of total annihilation, and Picard, Geordi and Deanna must figure out how to rescue it without destroying it. Wr: Brannon Braga. Dir: Adam Nimoy.

Romulan/Alien (Michael Bofshever).

Descent, Part 1
When the Borg return to do battle with the Federation, they boast a new individuality—and tempt Data when they help him feel his first emotion. Wr: Ronald D. Moore, story by Jeri Taylor. Dir: Alexander Singer.

Isaac Newton (John Neville); Albert Einstein (Jim Norton); Admiral Nechayev (Natalija Nogulich); Crosis (Brian J. Cousins); Professor Stephen Hawking (Himself); Lore (Brent Spiner).

Season 7: 1993-94

Descent, Part 2
Picard, LaForge and Troi are captured by Lore, who's now leading the Borg and has corrupted Data. Meanwhile, Dr. Crusher is in command of the ship and engaging a Borg ship. Wr: Rene Echevarria. Dir: Alexander Singer.

Hugh (Jonathan Del Arco); Barnaby (James Horan); Taitt (Alex Datcher); Crosis (Brian J. Cousins); Salazar

(Benito Martinez); Goval (Michael Reilly Burke); Lore (Brent Spiner).

Liaisons
Hosting ambassadors are Troi and Worf, but Picard crash-lands on a planet surface with his ambassador. She falls in love with him—but all is not as it seems. Wr: Jeanne Carrigan Fauci and Lisa Rich, story by Roger Eschbacher and Jaq Greenspon. Dir: Cliff Bole.

Anna (Barbara Williams); Voval (Eric Pierpoint); Loquel (Paul Eiding); Byleth (Michael Harris).

Interface
While attached to an experimental probe interface, Geordi sees his mother and she's in danger while on a mission hundreds of light years away. Wr: Joe Menosky. Dir: Robert Wiemer.

Captain Silva La Forge (Madge Sinclair); Admiral Holt (Warren Munson); Doctor La Forge (Ben Vereen).

Gambit, Part 1
Investigating what appears to be the captain's death, Riker infiltrates a mercenary ship and discovers Picard as one of the crew. Wr: Naren Shankar, story by Christopher Hatton and Naren Shankar. Dir: Peter Lauritson.

Baran (Richard Lynch); Tallera (Robin Curtis); Vekor (Caitlin Brown); Narik (Cameron Thor); Yranac (Alan Altshuld); Admiral Chekote (Bruce Gray); Ensign Giusti (Sabrina LeBeauf); Bartender (Stephen Lee); Lt. Sanders (Derek Webster).

Gambit, Part 2
Undercover in the mercenary's ship, Picard and Riker bring the crew close to mutiny to discover their goals in finding rare archeological artifacts. Wr: Ronald D. Moore, story by Naren Shankar. Dir: Alexander Singer.

Baran (Richard Lynch); Tallera (Robin Curtis); Vekor (Caitlin Brown); Narik (Cameron Thor); Koral (James Worthy); Ensign Giusti (Sabrina LeBeauf).

Phantasms
Data's dream program generates nightmares and alters his behavior. Meanwhile, Geordi becomes suspicious when strange events begin happening onboard. Wr: Brannon Braga. Dir: Patrick Stewart.

Ensign Tyler (Gina Ravarra); Sigmund Freud (Bernard Kates); Admiral Nakamura (Clyde Kusatsu); Workman (David L. Crowley).

Dark Page
While attending to a host of telepathic aliens, Lwaxana Troi suffers a nervous breakdown, and Deanna tries to discover what has caused it. Wr: Hilary J. Bader. Dir: Les Landau.

Lwaxana Troi (Majel Barrett); Maques (Norman Large); Hedril (Kirsten Dunst); Mr. Troi (Amick Byram).

Attached
Kidnapped during a diplomatic mission, Picard and Crusher become telepathically linked while they're on the run, and they discover their true feelings for

each other. Wr: Nicholas Sagan. Dir: Jonathan Frakes.

   Mauric (Robin Gammell); Lorin (Lenore Kasdorf).

Force of Nature
While searching for a missing vessel, an alien couple boards the ship and declares that the warp engines are destroying the very fabric of space. Wr: Naren Shankar. Dir: Robert Lederman.

   Rabal (Michael Corbett); Serova (Margaret Reed); Prak (Lee Arenberg).

Inheritance
Data meets a scientist who claims to be his mother, Dr. Soong's ex-wife, Juliana Soong. Wr: Dan Koeppel and Rene Echevarria, story by Dan Koeppel. Dir: Robert Scheerer.

   Juliana Tainer (Fionnula Flanagan); Pran (William Lithgow).

Parallels
As he returns from a Klingon combat competition, Worf discovers that the world around him is constantly changing, and his sanity is on the edge. Wr: Brannon Braga. Dir: Robert Wiemer.

   Ogawa (Patti Yasutake); Gul Nador (Mark Bramhall); Wesley (Wil Wheaton).

Pegasus
Riker's loyalties are divided when his former commanding officer comes aboard and embarks on a mysterious, secret mission to salvage their old ship. Wr: Ronald D. Moore. Dir: LeVar Burton.

   Admiral Pressman (Terry O'Quinn); Admiral Blackwell (Nancy Vawter).

Homeward
While on a planet where the atmosphere is quickly disintegrating, Worf meets his adoptive brother, who breaks the Prime Directive in a desperate bid to save the inhabitants. Wr: Naren Shankar, story by Spike Steingasser. Dir: Alexander Singer.

   Nikolai (Paul Sorvino); Dobara (Penny Johnson); Vorin (Brian Markinson); Kateras (Edward Penn); Tarrana (Susan Christy); Computer voice (Majel Barrett).

Sub Rosa
After attending her grandmother's funeral, Dr. Crusher discovers she has inherited the family ghost, who's been haunting for centuries. Wr: Brannon Braga, story by Jeri Taylor, based upon material by Jeanna F. Gallo. Dir: Jonathan Frakes.

   Maturin (Michael Keenan); Ned Quint (Shay Duffin); Ronin (Duncan Regehr).

Lower Decks
Four junior officers find themselves tested to the limit by the senior staff and are given a secret mission in place of their promotion evaluations. Wr: Rene Echevarria, story by Ronald Wilkerson and Jean Louise Matthias. Dir: Gabrielle Beaumont.

   Lavelle (Dan Gauthier); Sito (Shannon Fill); Taurik (Alexander Enberg); Ben (Bruce Beatty); Ogawa (Patti Yasutake); Joret (Don Reilly).

Thine Own Self
Data's stranded on a pre-industrial planetary society with amnesia. Back on the ship, Troi applies for the bridge officer's test. Wr: Ronald D. Moore, story by Christopher Hatton. Dir: Winrich Kolbe.

   Talur (Ronnie Claire Edwards); Garvin (Michael Rothhaar); Gia (Kimberly Cullum); Skoran (Michael G. Hagerty).

Masks
After a brush with a comet, Data begins exhibiting multiple personalities, and the *Enterprise* slowly transforms into an ancient alien city. Wr: Joe Menosky. Dir: Robert Wiemer.

   Eric (Rickey D'shon Collins).

Eye of the Beholder
As they investigate the mysterious suicide of a crewmember, Worf and Troi's relationship veers into a romantic one. Wr: Rene Echevarria, story by Brannon Braga. Dir: Cliff Bole.

   Walter Pierce (Mark Rolston); Lt. Nara (Nancy Harewood); Lt. Kwan (Tim Lounibos); Calloway (Johanna McCloy).

Genesis
When Picard and Data return to the *Enterprise* from a mission, they discover prehistoric creatures inhabiting the ship. Wr: Brannon Braga. Dir: Gates McFadden.

   Ogawa (Patti Yatusake); Barclay (Dwight Schultz); Ensign Dern (Robert Feero); Computer voice (Majel Barret).

Journey's End
Visiting the *Enterprise* while on vacation, Wesley interferes with the relocation of a planet colony of native Americans. Wr: Ronald D. Moore. Dir: Corey Allen.

   Lakanta (Tom Jackson); Admiral Nechevev (Natalija Nogulich); Anthwara (Ned Romero); Wakasa (George Aguilar); Gul Evek (Richard Poe); Traveller (Eric Menyuk); Jack Crusher (Doug Wert); Wesley Crusher (Wil Wheaton).

First Born
As Alexander grows, Worf begins to realize that his son may not become the warrior that he hopes. K'mtar, a "family friend," tries to convince him of this. Wr: Rene Echevarria, story by Mark Kalbfeld. Dir: Jonathan West.

   K'mtar (James Sloyan); Alexander (Brian Bonsall); B'etor (Gwynyth Walsh); Lursa (Barbara March); Yog (Joel Swetow); Gorta (Colin Mitchell); Quark (Armin Shimerman).

Bloodlines
Bok, the renegade Ferengi, swears revenge on Picard by declaring that he will kill the son Picard never knew. Wr: Nicholas Sagan. Dir: Les Landau.

   Jason (Ken Olandt); Bok (Lee Arenberg); Birta (Peter Slutsker).

Emergence
When the *Enterprise* develops its own intelligence,

the crew is in grave danger and must discover what is taking place. Wr: Joe Menosky, story by Brannon Braga. Dir: Cliff Bole.

Conductor (David Huddleston); Hitman (Vinny Argiro); Engineer (Thomas Kopache); Hayseed (Arlee Reed).

Preemptive Strike (aka The Good Fight)

Ensign Ro is assigned to infiltrate the vigilante Maquis to find out when and how they're going to strike against the Cardassians. Wr: Rene Echevarria, story by Naren Shankar. Dir: Patrick Stewart.

Ro Laren (Michelle Forbes); Gul Evek (Richard Poe); Kalita (Shannon Cochran); Macias (John Franklyn-Robbins); Santos (William Thomas Jr.).

All Good Things...

Picard believes he's bouncing back and forth in time between the ship's maiden voyage, the present and the far future, while Q returns him to court for crimes of mankind. Wr: Ronald D. Moore and Brannon Braga. Dir: Winrich Kolbe.

Q (John DeLancie); Tomalak (Andreas Katsulas); Admiral Nakamura (Clyde Kusatsu); Ogawa (Patti Yasutake); Tasha Yar (Denise Crosby); O'Brien (Colm Meaney); Jessel (Pamela Kosh); Lt. Gaines (Tim Kelleher); Ens. Chilton (Alison Brooks); Ensign (Stephen Matthew); Computer voice (Majel Barrett).

(The Adventures of) Superboy
October 1988–May 1992

The adventures of a younger version of Superman. The last survivor of the planet Krypton, Superboy fights supervillains and crime and stands as a testament to truth and justice everywhere. His alter-ego, Clark Kent, is a journalism student at Shuster University. Later, after graduating from the university, Kent and pal Lana Lang join the Bureau of Extranormal Affairs so he can be on the lookout for where he might be needed.

Cast: Clark Kent/Superboy (year 1) (John Haymes Newton); Clark Kent/Superboy (years 2–4) (Gerard Christopher); Lana Lang (Stacy Haiduk); T.J. White (year 1) (Jim Calvert); Andy McAlister (year 2) (Ilan Mitchell-Smith); Matt Ritter (years 3–4) (Peter Fernandez); C. Dennis Jackson (years 3–4) (Robert Levine); Jonathan Kent (Stuart Whitman); Ma Kent (Salome Jens); Lex Luthor (year 1) (Scott Wells); Lex Luthor (years 2–4) (Sherman Howard); Dr. Peterson (year 1) (George Chakiris).

Superboy created by: Jerry Siegel and Joe Shuster; *Series suggested for television by:* Peter R. Marino; *Executive Producers:* Ilya and Alexander Salkind; *Producers:* Robert Simmonds (years 1–2), Stan Berkowitz (year 4); *Co-Producers:* Stan Berkowitz (year 3), Gerard Christopher (year 4), Paul Stubenrauch (year 4); *Line Producer:* Barry Waldman (year 3–4); *Supervising Producer:* Julia Pistor (year 3); *Flying Effects:* Bob Harman, Steve Crawley, Roy Weatherley, Ray Hardesty; Syndicated/Viacom; 30 minutes.

"Look! Up in the sky! It's a bird! It's a plane! It's—" Whoops. Wrong show. While it has many similarities to its predecessor of the 1950s, *The Adventures of Superboy* has many elements that were never possible in those days. To start with, the show had a budget that allowed a young, first-

time-on-camera cast to go outside of studio soundstages. John Haymes Newton (and later Gerard Christopher), Stacy Haiduk and Jim Calvert had characters who were students at Shuster University.

The show witnessed the dramatic debuts of such comics supervillains as Metallo, Mr. Mxyzptlk, Lex Luthor and Bizarro. Original creations for the screen include Young Dracula, Nick Knack and Neila.

Modern-day special effects also allowed for more realistic flying sequences. For John Haymes Newton, *The Adventures of Superboy* was a chance at experiencing the fantasy of flight.

"The first time I flew was in a studio lot with a practice harness. It was pretty exciting because we had a crane that ejected me 60 to 65 feet in the air," says Newton who got to don the famous red and blue costume. The crane rig, handled by *Superman* films veteran Bob Harman, was versatile and mobile for filming. "It's pretty neat because of the way they were able to move it from location to location. You forget you're on wires after a while. Not in a psychotic way, but in a way that was very freeing. It's a neat feeling. There was one take during one of the early episodes where I actually left off the ground before the wires—I thought I could really fly. I went ahead of the wires," recalls Newton. "The nature of it is you don't do any leaping or jumping—the wires do all the work. You can't even help them. Otherwise, there's a jerk effect, or it's not smooth, or it doesn't look natural. There was a lot of effects involved into just doing it properly and making it believable. I did some research into that as far as weight and balance and [finding] different ways of how to turn, physics and stuff like that. I think the first few times I flew I was more involved in what I was doing … then really thinking, 'Wow, this is neat, I'm flying.'"

Newton doesn't recall any accidents during his tenure as the orphan from Krypton, but he does say that he almost hit a train once. And like Christopher Reeve before him, his wardrobe was varied for different scenes. There were walking and flying capes. "I felt safe at all times because the flying people had done all the *Superman* films, and they are some of the best people in the industry," attests Newton.

One stunt Newton particularly enjoyed was a motorcycle stunt in "Black Flamingo." "I got to break down some double doors, with a 50-pound snake around my neck and glasses and a beard. It was pretty interesting to do all that, and I got to ride my own motorcycle."

Newton also remembers an episode called "Hollywood." "That was a lot of fun, to do a period piece with the period garb and go against gangsters. … They're throwing guns at me, and I just grabbed the pistol, and because it was a rubber pistol, I bent it. We did that in rehearsal and it worked, so we did it for a take and they used it."

David Nutter, director of that episode, happily recalls this moment also as well. "I wanted to do the same kind of things they did in the original *Superman* TV series, a 1930s setting," he says. "And that's when the bad guys shot at Superboy at the old abandoned warehouse. After shooting at him, they throw their guns at him. And then he grabbed one and did the obligatory bending of the barrel. That was a fun thing we did."

Being cast as the Boy of Steel came about rather quickly. A native of North Carolina who had been working and studying in New York in an acting program for two years, Newton was on a vacation trip home when he got noticed by a casting director working on a film. The director's other chore was *Superboy*, and Newton immediately got tested.

"It was one of those fluke type of experiences," says Newton dreamily. "It was a pretty weird day!"

But, after a year's work, Newton left the show abruptly. Reports suggested he left because of a creative dispute between him and the producers, Ilya and Alexander Salkind, over how Clark Kent would be portrayed. But apparently, this was not the case. "Our salaries were very low," explains Newton. "I was doing a lot of stunts, I was doing two characters … so, when we came to negotiate at the end of the season, we asked for more money, and they said, 'No!' And it came down to who was going to call the other person's bluff. We came down to a significant amount, and it was between them and Viacom. Viacom and neither of those two would give in to pay us more money. Because they had been going through this back and forth all season long. I was determined not to give in another penny. So, the Salkinds didn't have the money to give. They were really caught in a bind, and so my agents chose to not go back."

As a result, the Salkinds had the unenviable task of recasting the lead role of a successful syndicated half-hour show. "They had plenty of time to recast the character, and that's what they did," says Newton.

Newton notes that he did spend some time going "back and forth" with the Salkinds concerning the portrayal of Clark Kent. Should Clark be a bumbling idiot (to cover his super identity while around friends) or a normal teenager? "I wanted him to be shy and a little insecure," Newton says. "They wanted me to do Chris Reeve's Clark Kent … not that I wouldn't do. It's just that it copied something that Chris was doing. I got a lot of positive response that I didn't do that. It's obvious that [Clark and Superboy] look very similar. But there's another force coming into play that prevents the audience or prevents people or friends from noticing that I'm this person—Clark Kent as Superboy. There's other things that affect people and how they see you as a person, and the nerdy thing doesn't disguise how you look. It portrays a different person. But I thought the insecure thing was better than the nerdy thing. It gets to be a caricature. If you play somebody really nerdy, it gets to be they're not even real anymore.

"I could have played him more insecure—I could have gone farther with it but the scripts were not written that way.

"There was a Lex Luthor episode where we saw more of it. There were certain episodes where it came out more. But as I say, it's all hindsight—20/20."

Newton claims that he's in possession of a letter from the Salkinds asking him to return to the show and offering a price—but a low one, he says. "Why would they send me a letter asking me to come back to the show, if they didn't like the way I was playing Clark Kent?" he asks. "We never had a dispute about this. It was always a friendly discussion. It was never anything vicious. If it came down that they were totally unhappy [with the portrayal], I would have played nerdy."

However, Newton adds, "I don't think the audience wanted to watch a caricature on television. I felt they wanted real people. And that's what I did, I thought. What Gerry [Christopher] did or didn't do, I don't know. I'm sure he did a good job, doing whatever choices he made."

Newton does not appear at all bitter about giving up the lead role in an exciting fantasy series. "I went on to do some of the most incredible work of my life after I left the show!" he says. "I went on to TV movies about American Indians; I've done three feature films. I mean, how can you do that if you're doing a TV series? It's very difficult. I've done some incredible regional theatre in New York. I've been doing some writing. I've been asked to do sequels to films that I've completed. I still have a long way to go."

Newton reports that his fan mail was stronger after his departure than when he was in the show. "People miss me. I'm not saying they'd rather have me on the show but I'm saying they miss seeing me. It's very nice, the amount of support I got once I left the show. It gradually tapered off because they don't really air the episodes. ... I still stayed with people who originally followed me with the show and keep up with my work."

Gerard Christopher was recast as Clark Kent/Superboy and Sherman Howard replaced Scott Wells as the recurring villain, Lex Luthor, from the second season on.

For co-star Stacy Haiduk, as for Newton, *The Adventures of Superboy* was an opportunity to flex newly developed acting muscles in front of cameras for the first time. "It was all so new to me. I was just so excited to be working," she says.

Being constantly saved by Superboy was fun at first, says Haiduk, but "after a year, I felt extremely frustrated because Lana was so predictable. Although it did change in the fourth year.... With Lana's characterization, I felt that, working with writers, Lana became a stronger and more independent woman towards the last two seasons."

Because she was so new to episodic television business, Haiduk says she was grateful for the opportunity to learn and become comfortable in front of the camera. She confesses to being very critical of herself and her acting. Looking back, she says, "I feel good about the work that was done, but I would have made some changes in my performances. Overall, I am satisfied with the end result."

Asked to point to a segment that she especially enjoyed, Haiduk cites "The Basement," "because I was able to create a whole new character, and an evil one at that. I also like a few of the earlier shows written by Cary Bates."

But for Haiduk, the most memorable moments working on the show came not from acting scenes or working with a tightly knit production cast and crew, but "watching the reaction of young children when they met Superboy—seeing their faces light up and how excited they would be."

Haiduk parts with a final memory of those four years as a fledgling actress. "From a personal point of view, I remember one scene I was really looking forward to. It was a very difficult, passionate scene. When we finally got to it, it was midnight, the crew was exhausted, tension was high because we were now into overtime. I got my orders from the director—'Do it in one take!' It was a lot of pressure, but I pulled it off, and I actually felt good about my performance.

"A week later, I found the scene ended up on the cutting floor," sighs Haiduk, adding philosophically, "That's show business!"

For David Nutter, *The Adventures of Superboy* was a chance to grow into his directing craft. He had completed a feature with Don Johnson (pre–*Miami Vice*) after graduating from college and had been exposed to the seedy world of *21 Jump Street* before moving into the Superboy universe. Thanks to an introduction to the Salkinds by an assistant director friend, Nutter would become one of the show's youngest directors (still in his early 20s) and the show's highest recurring director with 21 episodes.

"They showed me a couple of shows, and apparently what had happened was when the series first started they had worked with a lot of directors who had done a lot of television for many years," recalls Nutter. "They were very unhappy for the first 13 episodes. So they started down a new path of [hiring] younger people.

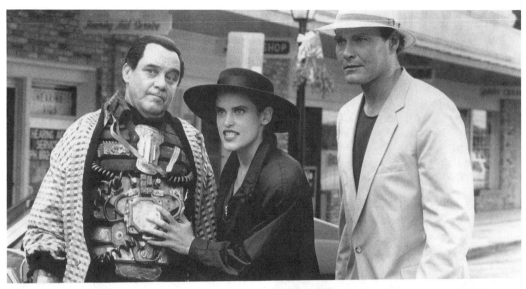

Top: Superboy faces off against a trio of villains: left to right, Metallo (Michael Callan), Odessa (Justina Vail) and Lex Luthor (Sherman Howard). *Bottom left:* Gerard Christopher as Superboy. *Bottom right:* Gerard Christopher as Clark Kent. Copyright 1992 Viacom.

They started with [fellow director] David Grossman, and they wanted to continue that trend, so they brought me in."

Nutter remembers *The Adventures of Superboy* as a show "that tried to do pretty big scripts and pretty big stories with no money. It's tough to write scripts in half-hour mode, in a sort of A-B-C storyline. I've spent many, many hours cutting scripts and having to cut down time. Scripts were too long. The problem is when you do a series like *Superboy*, in a half-hour mode, it's tough to develop three or four characters. You have to cut it down to 20 to 22 minutes. There's no time for 'B' stories."

Nutter remembers that the Salkinds "were looking for someone else, another person to play the role. Nutter, despite Newton's remarks, still insists that "basically, they didn't like the Clark

Kent characterization. John was a kid, rather young, and I'm not sure that series television was the type of thing right for him at the time. He was really good, physically, in stunts, and he was very strong. I think he was honest in his portrayal. [But] I think basically he was a young guy who didn't have a lot of experience.

"There's always a situation with actors and finances, and as far as the situation with the characterization, it was a situation they didn't feel worked."

Nutter was pleased to see Stacy Haiduk's growth as an actress. "She was very young at the time the show started, and I got to see her just blossom in the last couple of seasons," he says. "It was amazing. In the first couple of shows she was just a ditzy redhead. As the show developed, she became a very serious actress."

Gerard Christopher as the new Superboy was fresh, Nutter notes. "I think when he started out on the show, his Clark Kent was quite good, but he had problems with the strengths of Superboy. But then as the show went on, he got more comfortable with the character. He definitely had the facial look. He had the charisma that was necessary. There were areas where he could have had more depth, though..."

The keys to the show's success, says Nutter, were the writing, character scripting and casting. "In the second season, the introduction of [writer] Mark Jones would bring interesting characters that really added to the show. When *Superboy* came to third and fourth season, the show became more involved with the characters."

There were also many supervillains to contend with. Nutter says the show really came to life in the second season with the introduction of Sherman Howard as Lex Luthor. Howard saw (and played him) as Batman's nemesis, the Joker.

The show's gradual character development and increase in production quality happened, says Nutter, when the Salkinds stepped away from the project and Julia Pistor entered to produce. A new director of photography and some others below the line helped change the show's look and tone.

But *Superman*'s publisher, in Nutter's view, remained actively involved. "DC Comics always had an idea of how the show should be. It's a situation in which you have to go back and forth and get a lot of 'DC' notes. ...'He wouldn't do that, or she wouldn't do that.' They would really tell you how they want the show to be. We had to succumb to those things."

For "Paranoid," Nutter says, "Stan [Berkowitz] originally wanted it to be a situation in which the paranoia was real, with nothing artificial and nothing extraterrestrial involved. DC said there had to be some type of extraterrestrial to make this all copacetic."

Both Stan Berkowitz and David Nutter point to third season's "Road to Hell" with Ron Ely as particularly exciting. "He was a perfect choice for that character," says Nutter. "I thought he was wonderful. He made the character as someone with charisma and stature, someone of that nature. There wasn't better casting if we had a lot more money."

Ninety percent of acting is casting, Nutter says. To demonstrate the difficulties of matching character, actor, and circumstance, he offers this behind-the-scenes story about casting the episode "A Change of Heart": "I was working with Miguel Ferrer in Vancouver, Canada. I told him I also worked on *Superboy*. When I talk to directors about *Superboy*, they'll sigh and say, 'Yeah, what's that?' but with Miguel, he said, 'Oh my god! That's a great show!' He was a comic book writer, had been in movies, and he really appreciated it. 'I'd love to do that show sometime.' So we talked about the kind of characters he'd like to play in it. And I called Stan Berkowitz and Julia Pistor, and said, 'Listen, Miguel Ferrer would come down and do the show if you could write a character for him.' So, we wrote a character for him. What happened was Lex Luthor was trying to be a good guy. But there was a scheduling problem with Sherman Howard. He couldn't come in."

So, with a few keystrokes on a word processor, Luthor was out and new characters were created. In place of a villain turning good, "Miguel and I suggested Billy Mumy as this kind of demented character," says Nutter.

Bill Mumy, the carrot-topped kid in the 1960s series *Lost in Space*, happened to be a friend and partner of Miguel Ferrer.

"The Billy Mumy role [replaced] Lex Luthor," says Nutter. "But what happened was Miguel, who was going to play our lead villain, was shooting *On the Air*, the David Lynch [half-hour sitcom]. They were one day over schedule. So, that one day he couldn't come down to Orlando."

As a result, Michael DesBarres, known for a recurring role in *MacGyver* as the villain Murdoc, stepped in. "Michael DesBarres did a great job. He came in to do the show. Michael was great, and it was a great show."

The episode "Paranoid" featured two very familiar faces as guest stars. On the suggestion of someone at the show's distributor, Viacom, *The Adventures of Superboy* brought onboard two regulars from the 1950s predecessor *The Adventures of Superman*: Noel Neill and Jack Larson, who had played Lois Lane and Jimmy Olsen.

"There's one point when Jack's possibly the one who did the killing—'You're after me?'—and he was swiping pencils and papers, back when he was at the newspaper," says Nutter. "When Superboy flies up to the windowsill, Jack looks up and says 'Jeepers!' It was a lot of fun, and both of them were a real treat to work with. Noel hadn't acted in years. And Jack had been on the scene, but doing a lot of writing. We hoped it would work out, and it did."

Although the two acting veterans had not worked for a long time in front of cameras, Nutter reports that Neill and Larson were comfortable working with a stage setting, and the sophisticated shooting style of the 1980s was not too different or difficult for them.

"They were used to someone like myself who doesn't just set the camera down and treat it like a stage," says Nutter. After completing some 21 episodes over four seasons, Nutter found the show's demise an emotional and difficult time.

"It was like losing a family member," says Nutter somberly. "It was a very, very emotional time for me, and you know how they say the first time is something you always remember [although] you get bigger and better. There were a lot of people there, and when you do a series for that long, you really develop relationships with people. I'd love to do [a series] again in a situation like that. In the entertainment industry, it's very transitory. You can be a director for two or three weeks on a show and you're gone."

Over the four seasons, Nutter saw many changes in *Superboy*. At the end of the second season, with a desire to add new blood and find new directions for the show, the producers hired new writers, cinematographers, art directors and producers. By the third season, Clark Kent and Lana Lang graduated from Shuster University and together arrived at the Bureau of Extranormal Affairs. This change allowed the characters to escape the campus environment and interact more directly with unusual and extraordinary phenomena in the world—a perfect opportunity for Superboy to intervene. It was also an allusion to Kent's future job at the *Daily Planet*.

Stan Berkowitz was tapped as the head writer for seasons three and four, under the title of co-producer and later producer. "I was told by Viacom that they wanted to expand the audience for the show," recalls Berkowitz. "Basically, they felt children watched the show. So they wanted to expand it so adults could get into it. I was given examples of movies they liked—*Robocop, Die Hard*—models to follow. They wanted to know what kind of movies I liked. They wanted to make the show darker, more mysterious and adult. Darker visually and in terms of stories."

Looking back, Berkowitz says simply, "Nobody's work is ever perfect." He wishes he could erase some decisions made on individual episodes in the third and fourth year. But he adds, "I wish the show had gotten a little more credit. I think a lot of people didn't want to watch it because of the title *Superboy*. And, we were trying to get adults! I think adults were going, 'I don't care. It's about a *boy*.' I think if they had watched, they would have said, 'This isn't bad! There are some interesting themes here.' Instead of treating it as Super*boy*, we wanted to be Super*man* without actually saying Superman."

For legal reasons, the name Super*man* could not be used on the show. Never mind that he was the same character and only slightly younger; *man* was taboo and only *boy* was allowed.

"It's part of the original, confusing and complex deal the Salkinds had with DC Comics that means they only have the rights to a TV Superboy," says Berkowitz. "Now, there was a [two-part] episode called 'Road to Hell' where we see a full-grown man (played by Ron Ely). And we couldn't actually call him Superman. So, we just sort of avoided that word in the dialogue."

Sometimes, however, things leak out. "In the first version of the credits, which I actually have on tape, it came out as 'Ron Ely as Superman,'" attests Berkowitz. "The casting director had used it. But when the DC [Comics representatives] looked at that, they said, 'No! You can't use that word!' So, they simply deleted that from the copy that went out on the air. But I have a pre-air copy."

Critiquing the first two seasons, Berkowitz believes that "they were trying to be Superman. He would be the only anomaly in the universe. I saw a couple of them, and his adversaries were crooked real estate developers and the like. For superheroes, those aren't really very good adversaries. There's one where the adversary was an insane concentration camp victim. You needed bigger villains. Halfway through the season they started bringing in space creatures and things like that." Berkowitz found these stories more interesting but says, "The scripts were poorly thought out."

To produce the show, it was necessary for three partners—a publishing company who owned rights to a character, a production company that held the bank credit line and a French father-son production team—to achieve a mind-melding without emasculating the product they were all creating.

"The situation with Superboy is that it's owned by DC Comics, and it was rented out to Viacom so the Salkinds could make a TV series," explains Berkowitz. "They all have a stake in it, and they're all fighting and screaming at each other. And essentially, it was like Solomon's baby. It's like three mothers fighting over the baby. But if Solomon asked them, 'Ok, we're going to chop up the baby, which one of you wants to give in?' none of them gave in. The result was essentially what you saw on the air. By the time I came on the show, Salkind had pretty much dropped out of the equation. And the DC guys backed off a little"—which left Viacom to run the show.

Berkowitz's memories of his experiences on the show consist mainly of "bitching and fighting, screaming," with DC Comics over story particulars—"Can he do this or that?" and "Is this logical or not logical?" Nevertheless, "we got things done. We never lost a day of shooting or anything like that. We never had any major disasters. We were writing all the time."

Berkowitz felt that Gerard Christopher, as Clark Kent/Superboy, was "not very good in that [second] season. I thought he was wooden. Clark looked silly. "I think he was too nerdy. The first guy, who was fired, supposedly he was not nerdy enough as Clark, and they made Gerry *really* nerdy as Clark. And then, in season three, Clark became closer to what he is in the comic books. He was still a guy who got lost in a crowd of two. He was shy. He didn't fight back. In fact, we made a point of him showing him fighting back only once, and that was in "Cat and Mouse," where he goes against the psychiatrist and he stands up for himself. They eased back on [the nerdiness]. If you watch the show, he was maturing.

"I don't think he had much to work with at first," adds Berkowitz. "My initial opinion was that he was not a very good actor. [But] sometimes we can be fooled by that. A guy who seems to be a bad actor can turn out to be a good actor when he gets better scripts."

Later, as he got to know Christopher, Berkowitz found that "he was very ambitious about being a producer/director during the whole shoot. But he was so busy acting, there wasn't much time for that. He was best as an actor, I think, when he was playing a bad guy. He was also good as Clark when they gave him enough to do. He always felt awkward playing Superboy because of the costume. 'What do I do? Here's a character that's perfect.'

"I thought progressively, starting with season three, he got better and better. Some episodes like "A Day in the Double Life," I thought, 'This guy is really fun to watch!' There are also points where he plays villains. 'Roads Not Taken, Parts 1 and 2,' particularly ... as the dictator, he was *fun* to watch. That's why you write—to see your words become entertaining. There's also a 'body swap,' where he played Lex Luthor. He was wonderful. Supposedly Luthor's brain gets into Superboy's body."

Regarding Stacy Haiduk, as Kent/Superboy's friend Lana Lang, Berkowitz says, "You had to explain stuff from the scripts to her. What's going on, why the characters are doing stuff. The way she'd do best is if you sat down with her and go through everything Lana had to do. Here's why she's doing this, here's why she's doing that. Unfortunately, I didn't have much time for that. For 'Road to Hell,' I took her out to dinner and sat down with the script and went over it line by line. So if she seems special in that, it's because she was sitting down and actually talking about the script at length with the writer."

Because of the show's status as a syndicated show, feedback was bare, and ratings were spotty at best. "The ratings declined as the show got better," says an incredulous Berkowitz. "I don't know what to make of that. Perhaps it was a bad idea to try to move the show up to adults, because if you have a successful show that children are watching, it probably makes more sense to [leave it that way]."

In analysis of specific episodes created during his tenure on the show, Berkowitz cites the two-parters "Roads Not Taken" and "Road to Hell" as particularly satisfying.

"John [Francis] Moore was pitching ideas for the show," says Berkowitz. "He's a friend of Andy Helfer [a writer for the show as well as a DC Comics consultant]. So John said, 'Why don't you have the guy go into a different dimension?' 'What dimension?' 'Oh, it's this cold, weird place and there's this monster waiting for him.' I thought, 'Oh, too hard to shoot that!' But then I remembered an article about alternate worlds. Every time you make a choice, there's an alternate world created where you made the opposite choice. ... Each new world is triggered by you making a different choice. What about that, I said. So we sat down and worked on it. Before John got very far, almost immediately after that meeting, he got hired as story editor on *The Flash* [1990]. So it's a shared story credit on the scripts. I was pleased. I thought it worked out quite well. There was more humor in the scripts that sort of got deleted by the director during the shooting and cutting of the show."

Another interesting episode was "Obituary for a Super Hero," in which Superboy had supposedly died. The episode dealt with the media's reaction to his presumed death.

"It just came to me watching *Nightline* and being told we had one day to do a shoot," admits Berkowitz. "I thought, what can we shoot? A lot of creativity comes from desperation! A lot of my creativity comes when there's very limited parameters. 'You can't do this, you can't do that, you can't do that, you have only this amount of time to do it.' You start thinking, 'Let's see, what can we do, given those limits there?' I think that show is indicative of that."

After some 100 episodes of the show, with Viacom wanting to end their deficit financing and hoping to recover their investment in syndication, the show stopped filming. The last two-parter, titled "Rites of Passage," had an interesting genesis.

"Mike [Carlin] and Andy [Helfer] had pitched the idea of Superboy going through puberty for a long time, probably even before I got there," recalls Berkowitz. "I was saying, 'What are you talking about? Pubic hair and stuff like this?' and they'd answer, 'No, no, no! He's an alien! All these different weird things start happening to him. His powers go berserk.' How does it end, I asked. 'It ends with the punchline being that it's puberty.' I'm thinking, 'Great!' but you can't end the show that way. So that was put on hold for a while. And then we thought show 100 would be the final show, so we'd graduate him to be Superman. Stop calling a 32-year-old actor Superboy and start calling him Superman. We planned to use the puberty aspects of his powers going crazy and taking him back to the spaceship and all that as a prelude to making him Super-

man. The script is halfway done and Ilya Salkind says, "No, no, no! You can't do this. We may go another season, we may go back into production.' He wants to wait until he's 40 or something. It seemed like a foolish objection that Salkind had, but we had to obey them. We shaped the show where he went through these rites of passage—Kryptonian rites of passage—moving toward manhood, but not quite achieving it."

And that's how the show ended.

CAST NOTES

John Haymes Newton (Clark Kent/Superboy): *Superboy* was Newton's first television series. Afterwards, the actor remained very busy with a TV movie about the American Indians, and lead roles in films such as *Cool as Ice* (1991)—"I played the bad guy in that and it was good for me to break through the All-American stereotype as Superboy"—and Paramount's 1993 feature *Alive*. Most recently, he was one of the *Untouchables* on Fox television.

Gerard Christopher (Clark Kent/Superboy): Christopher has studied at the Juilliard School and appeared in the films *Dangerously Close* (1986) and *Tomboy* (1985). His television appearances include *Murphy's Law* and *True Confessions*, and he has done more than 60 commercials.

Christopher calls his role in *Superboy* "the opportunity that everybody dreams of. It's a unique experience where you carve out of a slice of Americana."

Christopher, in addition to becoming co-producer late into the series, penned two *Superboy* scripts: "Wish for Armageddon" and "Cat and Mouse."

Stacy Haiduk (Lana Lang): Haiduk appeared in a string of music videos prior to being cast in *Superboy*. She also had a recurring role on *Another World*. After four seasons of flying in Superboy's arms, she promptly moved to Aaron Spelling's TV series *The Roundtable* (1992), before landing a regular role in *seaQuest, DSV* (1993).

Peter Fernandez (Matt Ritter): "Superboy is the true enigma. He's the UFO that everyone talks about but he's real, he's here. You can touch him.

He's the reason for the Bureau of Extranormal Affairs. You can believe that other things are possible."

From Hanson, Massachusetts, Fernandez previously appeared in *The Cotton Club* (1984) and *One Life to Live*. A theatrically trained actor, he has appeared in dozens of New York Shakespeare Festival productions including *Macbeth*, *Julius Caesar* and *The Merchant of Venice*.

Robert Levine (C. Dennis Jackson): The veteran actor appeared in such classic movies as *Splendor in the Grass* (1961), *Up the Down Staircase* (1967), *The Hot Rock* (1972) and *All That Jazz* (1979). He also had roles in *Dominick and Eugene* (1988) and *Tootsie* (1982). On television, he has appeared in *L.A. Law, Thirtysomething, Barney Miller, Taxi* and *Kate and Allie*.

EPISODE GUIDE

Season 1: 1988-89

The Jewel of Techacal
Lana's father, an archeologist, arrives at the university with what he believes to be a cursed relic. But Lex Luthor and his henchmen steal the jewel so they can sell it to the highest bidder. Wr: Fred Freiberger. Dir: Reza S. Badiyi.
  Prof. Thomas Lang (Peter White); Leo (Michael Manno); Haines (Gregg Todd Davis); Dean Thompson (Forest Neal); Dr. Spencer (Bob Barnes).

A Kind of Princess
Clark falls for Sarah Danner, daughter of an important crime boss who visits the university for her birthday. A rival boss thinks he's moving in on his territory and orders Matt Danner shot. Wr: Howard Dimsdale and Michael Morris. Dir: Reza S. Badiyi.
  Sarah Danner (Julie McCullough); Matt Danner (Ed Winter); Casey (Harry Cup); Jake (Antoni Carone); Arnie (Steven Anthony); Detective Harris (Roger Pratto); Nancy (Rebecca Perle); Henry Oman (Dennis Michael); Bodyguard (Dennis Underwood); Cop (Paul J. Darby).

Back to Oblivion
When T.J. explores violence at a nearby scrap heap, he gets into danger with destructive machines constructed by Wagner, the owner, to protect himself against imagined Nazi horrors. Wr: Fred Freiberger. Dir: Colin Chilvers.
  Mr. Wagner (Abe Vigoda); Henry (Dennis Michael).

The Russian Exchange Student
When a Russian exchange student arrives at the university for a Soviet-American energy experiment, Professor Gordon holds Natasha responsible for a lab accident. Clark, T.J. and Lana don't believe it and try and clear her name. Wr: Vida Spears and Sava V. Finney. Dir: Reza S. Badiyi.
  Prof. Abel Gordon (Ray Walston); Natasha Pakovsky (Heather Haase); Jeff (Courtney Gains); Elena (Tania Harley); Detective Harris (Roger Pretto); Drake (Chase Randolph); Janitor (Ralph Rafferty); Policeman (Rick Defuria); Thug (Dennis Deveaugh); Thug #2 (Aley Edlin).

Countdown to Nowhere
During a protest over a dangerous laser weapon, four thieves dressed as football players steal the weapon and kidnap Lana along the way. Clark realizes the weapon is being used to sabotage the space shuttle launching later in the day. Wr: Fred Freiberger. Dir: Colin Chilvers.
  Roscoe Williams (Doug Barr); Theodore (Duriell Harris); Miller (Noah Meeks); Detective (Fred Broderson); Security chief (Jay Glick); Radio operator (Paul J. Darby).

Bringing Down the House
Accidents are occuring across the university while a rock star magnetizes Lana. Soon, she discovers he is driven to collect everything—including her. Wr: Howard Dimsdale and Michael Morris. Dir: Colin Chilvers.
  Judd Faust (Leif Garrett); Andy (Don Sheldon); Charles (Antonio Fabrizio); Henry (Dennis Michael); Betsy (Sabrina Lloyd); Umpire (Ed Montgomery).

The Beast and Beauty
A jewel heist is pinned on Superboy when a janitor swears it was the heat vision that melted the vault. Later, Superboy is arrested while saving some police officers. Wr: Toby Martin and Bernard M. Khan. Dir: Jackie Cooper.
  Hugo Stone (David Marciano); Jennifer Jenkins (Lonnie Shaw); Detective Harris (Roger Pretto); Rudy (Jeff Moldovan); Cop (Rick Higely); Security guard (Tom Nowicki); Emcee (Dan Barber); Announcer (Tal Millican); Woman (Cyndi Vicino).

The Fixer
Lex Luthor fixes the local basketball team to win bets. Clark, T.J. and Lana convince the star player to win despite Lex's threats to destroy his pro basketball career. Wr: Alden Schwimmer. Dir: Colin Chilvers.
  Stretch (Michael Landon Jr.); Leo (Michael Manno); Moose (Carl Jay Cofield); Coach (James Hampton); State coach (Curley Neal); Referee (Harry Burney III); Umpire (Ron Segall).

The Alien Solution
A gaseous creature comes down to Earth from space and wreaks havoc on the campus. It's up to Superboy to stop it, even as the creature inhabits Lana's body. Wr: Michael Carlin and Andrew Helfer. Dir: Colin Chilvers.
  Alien warrior (Jeff Moldovan); Henry (Dennis Michael); Dr. Howard (Christine Page); Paramedic (Ray Muennich); 1st student (Todd Sealey); 2nd student (Tom Bahr).

Troubled Waters

Pa Kent becomes the victim of a farm accident just when a land investor, Kenderson, bids to take farm land. Clark goes home to investigate, but Kenderson is determined to have his way. Wr: Dick Robbins. Dir: Reza S. Badiyi.

Ellen Jensen (Juli Donald); Cal Kenderson (Peter Palmer); Jarvis (John Zenda); Borkner (Daniel Kamin); Bennington (Norman Lund); Corbin (Joe Tomko).

Kryptonite Kills

Clark faints during Professor Peterson's demonstration in class of a glowing green rock, which Luthor promptly steals. Using the green rock's strange powers, Luthor plans to bring the city to its knees so he can cover for a robbery. Wr: Andrew Helfer and Mike Carlin. Dir: Jackie Cooper.

Veronica Lawlor (Pamela Bach); Leo (Michael Manno); Anges (Cyndi Vance); Oswald (Paul Cohn); Felix (Larry Francer).

Revenge of the Alien, Part 1

The gaseous creature from "The Alien Solution" is released from its frozen canister and now wants revenge against Superboy. Since Pa Kent has been visiting Clark, the entity takes over Pa's body, kidnaps Lana and holds her hostage. Wr: Andrew Helfer and Mike Carlin. Dir: Peter Kiwitt.

Johnson (Glenn Scherer); Henry (Dennis Michael); Crook (Mark Macaulay); Cop (Chick Bernhardt); Williams (Alan Jordan).

Revenge of the Alien, Part 2

Clark is in a real bind this time. The entity, using his father's body, wreaks havoc on the city and has access to the deadly Kryptonite that can kill him. Wr: Andrew Helfer and Mike Carlin. Dir: Peter Kiwitt.

Lt. Zeke Harris (Roger Pretto); Dean Lockhardt (Dana Mark); Newscaster (Jerry Eden).

Stand Up and Get Knocked Down

To investigate the mysterious death of his friend Michael, T.J. signs up at a local comedy club and learns drugs are involved. Wr: David Patrick Columbia and Toby Martin. Dir: David Grossman.

Dexter Linton (Gary Lockwood); Michael (Hayden Logston); Angel (Cindy Hamsey); Emcee (Lester Bibbs); Goon (Jack Spirtos); Goon #2 (Joe Hess); The Suit (Brett Rice).

Meet Mr. Mxyzptlk

An imp from the fifth dimension crosses over to our world and pesters for the affections of Lana Lang while posing as Clark Kent. Superboy must find a way to stop Mr. Mxyzptlk from taking Lana back with him to his world. Wr: Dennis O'Neil. Dir: Peter Kiwitt.

Mr. Mxyzptlk (Michael J. Pollard); Prof. Royer (Russ Wheeler); Lady (Cindy Vicino); Mugger (Steve Dash); Mugger (Jim Rios).

Birdwoman of the Swamps

A construction project starts having problems when an old Indian woman says the local animals are upset with the site and must not be disturbed. Clark, Lana and T.J. investigate and learn that the contractor, Hogan, is determined not to let the old woman stop his work. Wr: Bernard M. Khan. Dir: Reza S. Badiyi.

Birdwoman (Marlene Cameron); Mr. Hogan (James MacArthur); Woody (Mike Walters); Accomplice (Ted Science); Frank (Jack Swanson); Prof. Rogers (Kim Crow); Student (Liz Vassey).

Terror from the Blue

When Lana witnesses an attempted murder between two cops, she becomes a target of the antagonist. When she finally contacts Clark, a tapped phone line sends him straight to her. Wr: George Kirgo. Dir: David Grossman.

Lt. Harris (Roger Pretto); Detective Jed Slade (Cary-Haroyuki Tagawa); Oscar (Chase Randolph); Stone (Michael Stark); Gray (Jim Howard); Manton (David Hauser); Kinneran (Chick Bernhard); Baker (Eddie Edenfield).

War of the Species

A super-powered android goes awry at a scientific laboratory, and it's up to Superboy to stop it from multiplying and completing its programming to destroy humanity. Wr: Steven L. Sears. Dir: Peter Kiwitt.

Dr. Stuart (Kevyn Major Howard); Android (John Matuzak).

Little Hercules

While playing with computers and modems and delivering love notes, a young teenager triggers a secret code activating powerful military weapons. Unable to stop them from activating, the military contacts Superboy for help. Wr: Wayne A. Rice. Dir: David Grossman.

Billy Hercules (Leaf Phoenix); Lt. Redman (Allen Hall); Commander (Mal Jones); Amanda (Elizabeth Marion); Larry (Twig Tolle); Prof. Simon (Dean Drapin); Heywood (Robert Hollinger); Lenny (Brian Solako); Driggs (Jason Jacobs).

Mutant

During a scientific convention, Clark witnesses a prominent scientist being kidnapped by strange beings who turn out to be mutants from the twenty-fourth century seeking plutonium. Wr: Michael Morris. Dir: Joe Ravitz.

Val (Skye Aubrey); Hol (Bill Christie); Adio (Edgar Allen Poe IV); Prof. Lipcott (Jack Swanson).

The Phantom of the Third Division

While Clark is in Smallville to visit his parents with Lana and T.J., Pa Kent is abducted by a man seeking revenge for crimes Kent committed during the Korean War. Wr: Bernard M. Khan. Dir: David Nutter.

Phantom (Joe Campanella).

Black Flamingo

When a punk rocker attempts the assassination of a

senator, Clark goes undercover at a punk rock nightclub. He meets a mysterious figure named Snake-Man who uses hypnosis to force young people to do his evil bidding. Wr: Cary Bates. Dir: Chuck Martinez.

Snake-Man (Fernando Allende); Natasha (Ada Maris); Agar (Herbert Hofer); Senator (Ron Knight); Punk (Remy Palacios); Punk #2 (Reggie Pierre); Bouncer (Ron Russell); Bouncer (Scott Gallin).

Hollywood
When Superboy tries to help Professor Zugo's time machine, they're thrown back in time to 1939. Clark goes up against gangsters and meets a beautiful movie star while trying to repair the time machine. Wr: Fred Freiberger. Dir: David Nutter.

Prof. Zugo (Doug McClure); Victoria Letour (Gail O'Grady); Stoddard (Fred Buch); Willis (Nick Stannard); Gus (Stephen Geng); Hood (Jeff Moldovan); Asst. director (Bill Cordell); Lawyer (Gene Tate); Paper boy (Frank Cipolla); Truck driver (Emmet Fitzsimmons); Husband (Arnie Cox).

Succubus
A sexy romance author entrances T.J. and seduces him in order to entrap Superboy and drain his youth to become immortal. Wr: Stephen Lord. Dir: David Nutter.

Succubus (Sybil Danning); Prof. Myers (Rita Rehn); Executive (T.J. Kelly); Simon (Lee Stevens).

Luthor Unleashed
Luthor breaks into an army base to steal a laser weapon. The military, Clark and T.J. quickly suspect Luthor as the culprit. But later, Superboy saves Luthor during an explosion at the chem lab. The result is that Luthor becomes bald, and he vows revenge against Superboy for his deed. Wr: Stephen Lord. Dir: David Nutter.

Leo (Michael Manno); Harris (Roger Pretto); Colonel (Rance Howard); Guard (Steve Howard); Felix (Larry Francer); Oswald (Paul Cohn).

The Invisible People
Superboy saves the day for a group of homeless people when a firebomb threatens their tent city. The prime suspect is a real estate developer who has interest in the adjoining land and who is determined to keep the group from interfering with his goals. Wr: Mark Evanier. Dir: Jackie Cooper.

Gerold Manfred (Sonny Shroyer); Damon (Greg Morris); Alice (Cynthia Ann Roses); Gruber (Bill Orsini); Baker (Jack Malone); Cop (Rick Higlet); Alex (Bob Painter).

Season 2: 1989-90

Part 1: With This Ring I Thee Kill
Completing plastic surgery to protect himself from Superboy, Luthor steals a powerful military missile. He also kidnaps Lana Lang and forces her to marry him. Wr: Fred Freiberger. Dir: David Nutter.

Lex Luthor (Sherman Howard); Leo (Michael Manno); General (Douglas Brush); Security guard (Kevin Corrigan); Commander (Thom Scoggins); Secretary (Linda Perry); Doctor (David Cullinane); Minister (Jim Greene); Nurse (Janice Shea).

Part 2: Luthor Sentenced to Death
Hit by a missile and wounded, Superboy's in a wheelchair, but when Luthor taunts him with an audiotape, a grueling rehabilitation brings him back to fighting his arch-foe. Wr: Fred Freiberger. Dir: David Grossman.

Lex Luthor (Sherman Howard); Darla (Tracey Roberts); Wally (Clarence Thomas); Warden (Richard Lake); Journalist (Jerry Eden); Doctor (David Cullinane); Professor Peterson (George Chakiris).

Metallo
An escaped bank robber, in the hospital suffering from a heart attack, transforms into Metallo, a hulk of a man with a Kryptonite-powered heart. Wr: Mike Carlin and Andrew Helfer. Dir: David Grossman.

Metallo (Michael Callan); Schwartz (Paul Brown); Mayor (Dave Fennel); Doctor (Kurt Smildsin).

Young Dracula
A doctor by day is a vampire by night. When Clark meets him at a hospital, it's revealed that Dr. Shelly is being hounded by an older vampire who wants him to stay home. Wr: Ilya Salkind and Cary Bates. Dir: David Nutter.

Dr. Shelly (Kevin Berhardt); Old vampire (Lloyd Bochner); Doctor (Dennis Neal).

Nightmare Island
Clark and Lana go boating, but their beat-up raft sinks. They manage to land on an island. There, a stranded, hostile alien manages to negate Superboy's powers. Wr: Mark Jones. Dir: David Nutter.

Alien (Phil Fondacaro).

Part 1: Bizarro ...The Thing of Steel
Professor Peterson accidentally creates a bizarre duplicate of Superboy. "Bizarro" manages to escape study and takes on Clark's identity to court Lana Lang. Wr: Mark Jones. Dir: Ken Bowser.

Bizarro (Barry Meyers); Mom (Valerie Grant); Tod (Billy Flanigan); Girl (Christy Lyle); Cop (Kristin Truelson); Kid (Andrew Lamoureaux); Student (Chris Lombardi).

Part 2: The Battle with Bizarro
After Andy saves Superboy from Kryptonite, the Boy of Steel and Professor Peterson realize that Bizarro is a bad copy. Meanwhile, Bizarro holds Lana and tries to explain his love for her. Wr: Mark Jones. Dir: David Nutter.

Bizarro (Barry Meyers); Police sgt. (Tom Norwicki); Clown (Larry Lee); S.W.A.T. leader (John McLoughlin).

Mr. and Mrs. Superboy
The imp from the fifth dimension returns, and this time he's got a giant after him, seeking revenge for

a practical joke. The chase wreaks havoc all across town. The only way to stop the madness is if Superboy and Lana pretend to be married and adopt Mxyzptlk. Wr: Denny O'Neil. Dir: Peter Kiwitt.

Mr. Mxyzptlk (Michael J. Pollard); Vikabok (Richard Kiel).

Programmed for Death

Andy's dad comes to the university looking for help from Superboy, who encounters a robot that's the warped, evil side of Jack McAlister. Wr: Cary Bates. Dir: David Nutter.

Jack McAlister (George Maharis); Detective (Bruce Ward); Cop (Eric Whitmore); Security guard (Fred Ottaviano).

Superboy's Deadly Touch

Crafty Luthor sprays Superboy with a gas giving him deadly power. Luthor offers to reverse the process only if the governor grants him a full pardon. Wr: Mark Jones, story by Mark Jones and Cary Bates. Dir: Kenneth Bowser.

Darla (Tracey Roberts); Cop (Ken Grant); Governor (Robert Thompson); Government official (Barry Cutler); Nun (Janis Benson); Nun (Cay Fry); Technician (Denise Norgaras).

The Power of Evil

An evil gaseous monster escapes from his prison and searches for Superboy. Sensei travels to America to warn the Boy of Steel of the creature's destructive powers. Wr: Michael Prescott. Dir: Danny Irom.

Sensei (Keye Luke); Seth (Michael Champlin); Old man (Bret Cipes); Cop (Jim Becke); Voice of creature (Michael Marzello).

Superboy ... Rest in Peace

In the far-flung future, an android has escaped into the past and seeks to kill Superboy, unaware of his identity. But a scientist who knows Clark Kent is Superboy goes back to warn him. Wr: Michael Maurer. Dir: Danny Irom.

Serene (Betsy Russell); Android (Andreas Wisniewski); Prof. Henderson (John Swidels); Scientist (Lamont Lofton); Lab assistant (Judy Clayton); Gloria (Gayle Nadler); Debbie (Alison Dietz); Campus guard (Harry L. Burney III).

Super Menace!

The army accidentally creates red Kryptonite during experiments and makes Superboy evil. Metallo is recruited to contain the Boy of Steel, but together, they become a formidable pair. Wr: Michael Maurer. Dir: Richard J. Lewis.

Metallo (Michael Callan); General Swan (Jim McDonald); Warden Ordway (Richard Vaigts); 1st scientist (Barry W. Mizerski); 2nd scientist (Henry J.).

Yellow Peri's Spell of Doom

When a woman practicing black magic obtains Superboy's autograph, she uses it to make him fall in love with her. But Lana Lang's true love can break the spell. Wr: Mark Jones and Cary Bates. Dir: Peter Kiwitt.

Loretta/Yellow Peri (Elizabeth Keipher); Student (Georgia Sattele); Bartender (John Glenn Harding); Newscaster (Steve Latshaw); Gazook (Steve Hansen); Voice of Gazook (James Detmar).

Microboy

A would-be superhero creates a machine to give him remarkable powers in the hopes of gaining the favor of Lana Lang. But his efforts only creates dangerous situations. Wr: Cary Bates. Dir: Richard J. Lewis.

Microboy (Frank Military); Professor Peterson (George Chakiris); Mother (Kaye Stevens); Derelict (Tony Fabuzzi); Felix (Larry Francer); Orville Wright (Tim Powell); Wilbur Wright (Steve Kelly); Drama teacher (George Colangelo); Julie Ann (Stacy Haiduk).

Run Dracula, Run

When Dr. Shelly's serum to control his vampirism is stolen from him, he reverts to his evil ways. When Lana gets a call from him, he turns her into a vampire and later, Superboy as well. Wr: Ilya Salkind and Cary Bates. Dir: Richard J. Lewis.

Dr. Byron Shelly (Kevin Bernhardt); Sheriff (Louis Seeger Crune); Old man (Ivan Green); Lorraine (Leslee Lacey); Moe (Ed Amatrudo).

Brimstone

A powerful, insane magician scratches Andy during a sports event melee, and those scratches will hideously change him. Brimstone comes forward and offers him a cure. Superboy becomes overpowered by the evil magician Prodo, and it's up to Brimstone to save the Kryptonian. Wr: Mike Carlin and Andrew Helfer. Dir: Andre R. Guttfreund.

Brimstone (Philip Michael Thomas); Prodo (Carlos Gestero); Manic (Marc Macaulay); Cop (Antoni Carone); Security cop (Michael Leopard).

Abandon Earth

Jor-el and Lara, Clark's true parents, arrive on Earth. When Clark sees them via the media, he goes and meets them. They convince him it's time to return to Krypton. But Superboy is not totally convinced these are his true parents. Wr: Cary Bates and Mark Jones. Dir: Richard J. Lewis.

Lara (Britt Ekland); Jor-el (George Lazenby); Officer Campbell (Ken Grant); Officer Woods (Emily Lester); Police officer (Eric Whitmore); 2nd police officer (Michael Preston); FBI agent (D.J. Kaussar); Terrorist (Michael Mass); Newsman (Steve Latshaw); Newscaster (Bob Wells).

Escape to Earth

Arriving on an alien planet, Superboy quickly learns that Jor-el and Lara are not his true parents and that Andy and Lana have been brought along to become exhibits in a space zoo. Wr: Cary Bates and Mark Jones. Dir: Andre R. Guttfreund.

Lara (Britt Ekland); Jor-el (George Lazenby); Studd (Frank Tranchina).

Superstar

After Superboy saves a famous rock star from an auto accident, Clark becomes involved with the woman and learns that personas are not what they seem. Wr: Toby Martin. Dir: Kenneth Bowser.

Jessica (Ami Dolenz); Venus (Kimberly Bronson); Tucker (Kevin Quigley); Tiffany (Deborah DeFrancisco); Maitre d' (Joe Candelora); Security guard (Bradford Dunaway); Engineer (Steve Latshaw).

Nick Knack

A demented electronics genius, behind bars because of Superboy, breaks out and uses his genius to suck Superboy's powers into a mechanical suit he can wear. Wr: Mark Jones. Dir: David Nutter.

Nick Knack (Gilbert Gottfried); Daisy (Donna Lee Betz); Soldier (David Hauser); Security guard (Andrew Clark).

The Haunting of Andy McAlister

Paying a visit to an enormous mansion on the request of Andy, Clark and Lana become involved in a haunted house mystery. Wr: Andrew Helfer and Michael Carlin. Dir: David Nutter.

Billy the Kid (Thomas Shuster); Uncle Nate (Fred Ornstein); Bullet hole outlaw (Dan Kamin); Woman outlaw (Sandy Huelsman); Hangman outlaw (C. Rand MacPherson); Toothless outlaw (Ricardo Rogers).

Revenge from the Deep

Lana brings home an attractive piece of coral from the beach. Unbeknownst to her, it contains the spirit of a woman named Ariana. The mystical woman from the sea takes over Lana and seeks revenge against the man who put her there. Wr: Toby Martin. Dir: Andre R. Guttfreund.

Ariana (Jody James Donatello); Charlie (Michael Shaner); Announcer (Steve Latshaw); Heather (Judy Johns); Bartender (D. Christian Gotshail); Susie (Connie Adams); Beach patrol officer (Steve Zurk).

The Secrets of Superboy

Nick Knack escapes from jail again and uses a deadly brain scan to lure Lana and Andy to him so that Superboy can be a willing victim to his probe. Wr: T. Gilmour and Mark Jones. Dir: Joe Ravetz.

Nick Knack (Gilbert Gottfried); Daisy (Donna Lee Betz); Girlfriend (Roxie Stice).

Johnny Casanova and the Case of the Secret Serum

Using a secret chemical formula, a man named Johnny Casanova becomes captivating to women. But the man who created the formula wants it back at any cost. Wr: Ilya Salkind and Mark Jones. Dir: David Nutter.

Johnny Casanova (Mark Holton); Johnny Avonasac (Glenn Maska); Stanley (Robert Reynolds); Mr. Gore (Michael Marzella); Cabbie (Danny Haneman); Suited man 1 (Steve Dash); Suited man 2 (Nich Stannard); Manager (Gregory Ashburn); Bouncer (Conrad Goode).

A Woman Called Tiger Eye

A woman trying to complete a set of magical crystals wants Superboy to fuse them for her, so she kidnaps Lana to lure the hero to her. Wr: Michael Maurer. Dir: Andre R. Guttfreund.

Tiger Eye (Skye Aubrey); Peter (Erik Freeman); Denny

(Erik Lindshield); Philip (Tony Dimartino); Bobby (Danny Wynans); Asian man (Peter S. Paik); Teacher (Ilse Earl).

Season 3: 1990-91

The Bride of Bizarro, Part 1

Luthor convinces the defective copy of the Boy of Steel to defeat Superboy by exposing him to Kryptonite. Wr: Michael Carlin and Andrew Helfer. Dir: David Grossman.

Bizarro (Barry Meyers); Darla (Tracy Roberts); Wendy Leigh (Jody James Donatello); Mike (James Zelley); Bizarro Darla (Leith Audrey).

The Bride of Bizarro, Part 2

When a duplicate Lana is created, she convinces Bizarro not to kill Superboy but to go against Luthor. Wr: Michael Carlin and Andrew Helfer. Dir: David Grossman.

Artie (D. Christian Gotshail); Reporter (Bruce Hamilton); Bizarro Lana (Shanna Teare); Bartender (Eric Whitmore); Man (Bill Orsini).

The Lair

When Matt is kidnapped while investigating rumors of a creature near a forest, Lana and Clark investigate and find the monster. Wr: Stan Berkowitz. Dir: David Grossman.

Patrick Kenderson (Jordan Williams); Antoni Carone (Michael Pniewski); Bob (Tom Nowicki); Ed (Dennis Neal); Ron (Robert Small); Hal (Paul Vroom); Jerry (Buddy Staccardo); Mrs. Carter (Kathy Nell); Bartender (Joe E. Ring); Arnie (D. Christian Gotshail).

Neila

A powerful female alien lands on Earth seeking a mate and demands to see Superboy. But when she realizes he's devoted to Lana Lang, she threatens to destroy the planet unless Lana sacrifices herself. Wr: Gary Rosen and Stan Berkowitz. Dir: Mark Vargo.

Neila (Christine Moore); Lee (James Van Harper); Proprietor (Arnie Cox); Officer (Mike Goughn); Clothing store owner (Barry Mizerski).

Roads Not Taken, Part 1

Lex Luthor accidentally falls into a dimensional portal into alternate universes. He lands in a universe where Superboy is a criminal and has killed his counterpart. But in the "real" dimension, Darla wants Lex back and blackmails Superboy to return him. Wr: Stan Berkowitz, story by John Francis Moore and Stan Berkowitz. Dir: Richard J. Lewis.

Dr. Winger (Kenneth Robert Shippy); Darla (Tracy Roberts); Farmer (Robert Reynolds); Kid (Jason Padell); Fan (Brian Grant); Derelict (Edgar Allen Poe III); Mom (Maureen Collins).

Roads Not Taken, Part 2

Looking for Luthor in an alternate dimension, Superboy finds him as a messiah. When he attempts to bring him back to their world, he lands in another universe where his alterego reigns as a dictator with

Lana and Lex as freedom fighters. Wr: Stan Berkowitz, story by John Francis Moore and Stan Berkowitz. Dir: Richard J. Lewis.

Messenger (Robert Floyd); Advisor 1 (Jacob Witkin); Advisor 2 (Jack Swanson); Driver (Steve Demouchel); The Kid (Jason Padgell); Man (Tim Powell); Superboy double (Paul Matthew).

The Sons of Icarus
A flying man leads Superboy to Matt Ritter, who's being drawn into a group of African descendants who practice a ritual giving the power of flight. But each time, an imbalance in nature creates a fire creature. Wr: Paul Stubenrauch. Dir: Richard J. Lewis.

Teo (Brett Jennings); Joseph (Lou Walker); Marinda (Alice McGill); Artie (D. Christian Gotshail); Malcolm (Robb Morris); Jasmine (Annelle Johnson); John (Wayne Brady).

Carnival
When people begin disappearing, Lana's investigation leads to a mysterious carnival with a colorful cast of players. A plot is afloat to steal Superboy's soul. Wr: Toby Martin. Dir: David Grossman.

Samuels (Gregg Allman); Deville (Christopher Neame); Beth (Claudia Miller); David (George Colangelo); Bearded lady (Shavonne Rhodes); Dwarf (John Edward Allen); Fortune teller (Janice Shea); Cop (Billy Gillespie); Hostess (Elizabeth Fendrick); Shelley (Leslie Lacy).

Test of Time
As a mysterious tornado engulfs Lana and Clark, the Boy of Steel discovers her frozen in time. As he wanders into town, he learns everything else is also frozen. Soon, he understands they are not frozen, only that he has slowed down. Wr: David Gerrold. Dir: David Hartwell.

Alien #1 (Eric Conger); Alien #2 (Bryce Ward); Robot (Rex Benson); Driver (Danny Haneman).

Mindscape
When a mysterious rock is brought into the Bureau for study, Superboy's attempt at fusing it, causes an oozing entity to wrap itself around his neck and transports the Kryptonian into bizarre dreams. Wr: Michael Carlin and Andrew Helfer. Dir: David Nutter.

Superboy Mark II (Lex Luger); Stern (Judy Clayton); Staffer #1 (Sonya Mattox); Staffer #2 (Chris Calvert); Worker (Rod Ball); Man (Jacob Wilkin); Woman (Kathy Poling); Superboy double (Cliff O'Neal).

Superboy ... Lost
After trying to deflect a threatening comet on a collision course to Earth, Superboy lands on Earth with amnesia. A woman and her son living in the swamps discover him but do not recognize him. Wr: Michael Maurer. Dir: Richard J. Lewis.

Marissa (Sara Essex); Damon (Kevin Quigley); Jon (Juan Cejas); Ranger (Kevin Corrigan); Jeremy (Paul Sutera); Rosemary (Shaun Padgett).

Special Effects
Jackson sends Clark and Lana to interview a ten-year-old boy who says he witnessed the death of a film director. The boy claims the murderer was the monster Caliban created by a special effects man. Wr: Elliot Anderson. Dir: David Grossman.

Max Von Norman (Richard Marcus); Caliban (Barry Meyers); Andy McAlister (Ilan Mitchell Smith); Writer (Bill Cardell); Risa (Denise Locca); Lou Lloyd (Jim Cardes); Ajax (Rob Burman); Ingenue (Carla Kneeland); Robin Melville (Bodie Piecas); Mrs. Watson (Andrea Lively); Teddy (Danny Gura); Script girl (Candice Miller).

Neila and the Beast
Neila returns to Earth and seeks Superboy's help because the "commoners" of her planet have revolted and are looking to kill her, too. Lana and Clark try to help Neila learn about life on Earth. Wr: Lawrence Klaven and Stan Berkowitz. Dir: Jefferson Kibbee.

Neila (Christine Moore); Mitch (Terence Jenkins); Peter (Chris McCarty); Stern (Judy Clayton); Hank (Danny Dyer); First scientist (Christopher Oyen); Beast (Tom Akas).

Golem
An old Jewish man creates a creature from clay, a Golem, to defeat neo–Nazis, but when the creature accidentally kills his creator, the directive to kill remains. Wr: Paul Stubenrauch. Dir: Robert Weimer.

Daniel (Paul Coufos); Golem (Brian Thompson); Levi (Victor Helou); Mike (Darren Dollar); Jonah (Larry Bucklan); Darryll (Matt Battaglia); First kid (Chris Vance); Second kid (Kristopher Kazmarek).

A Day in the Double Life
Annoyed with Clark's "dashing emergencies," Jackson orders Kent to write a diary. Meanwhile, Clark observes agents Harris and Keller arguing with each other, but using his powers, he helps encourage their interest in each other. Wr: Stan Berkowitz and Paul Stubenrauch. Dir: David Nutter.

Agent Stephanie Harris (Allyce Beasley); Agent Frank Keller (Tom Kouchalakos); Leader (Jeff Maldovan); Cop#1 (Billy Gillespie); Traffic cop (Bill Painter); Eddie (Jessie Stone); Man #2 (Carl Campeon); Hunter (Jack Carrol); Doug (Barry Cutler); Sheriff (Dan Fitzgerald); Farm woman (Allison McKay).

Bodyswap
Luthor tricks Superboy into exchanging bodies with him. Now armed with Superboy's powers, Luthor in Superboy's body attempts to seduce Lana Lang. Meanwhile, Superboy in Luthor's body must convince Lana and the authorities of what has taken place. Wr: Paul Schiffer. Dir: David Grossman.

Dr. Oliver Deland (Nathan Adler); Artie (D. Christian Gotshail); Dad (Ken Grant); Mom (Valerie Grant); Girl (Carrie Ann Reiter); Bob (Ryan Porter); Burly man (Randy Helm); Warden (Bob Barnes); Governor (Joe Candelora); Cop (Lamont Lofton); Newswoman (Ann Morsella); Guard (Kurt Smildsin); Jailer (Shawn McAllister).

Rebirth, Part 1

While stopping a commando raid on military weapons, Superboy believes he accidentally caused the death of the gang's leader in a van. Morose, Superboy goes home and vows to give up the suit forever. Wr: Paul Diamond. Dir: Richard J. Lewis.

Desmond (Kevin Benton); Mayall (Michael Owens); Winston (Joseph Pickney); Llewellyn (Gregory Millar); Reporter (Bob Sakale); Hector (Robert M. Rodriguez); Lemont (W. Paul Bodie); Capt. Quentin (Paul Darby); Sergeant (Steve Roulerson); Woman (Rita Rehn); Lt. Fulton (Michael Balin).

Rebirth, Part 2

Saving his father's life and listening to advice from his parents convinces Clark that he cannot turn his back on his gifts, and he returns to Capitol City to finish the job he started. Wr: Paul Diamond. Dir: Richard J. Lewis.

Desmond (Kevin Benton); Mayall (Michael Owens); Winston (Joseph Pickney); Marshal (Roger Pretto).

Werewolf

A woman arrives at the Bureau with a videotape, claiming she has seen a werewolf. Clark's supervision finds something interesting, and he takes her case. Wr: Toby Martin. Dir: Bryan Spicer.

Christine Riley (Paula Marshall); Canaris (Robert Winston); Jeweler (Jay Glick); Doug (Barry Cutler); Security guard (Kelfus Matthews); Office guard (Ray Russell).

People vs. Metallo

In court for his crimes, Metallo manages to get Kryptonite smuggled to him just as Superboy takes the stand. Metallo then puts the weakened Boy of Steel on trial with Lana as defense counselor. Wr: Andrew Helfer and Michael Carlin. Dir: Richard J. Lewis.

Metallo (Michael Callan); Judge (Janis Benson); Nichols (Tim Powell); Prof. Schwartz (Paul Brown); Doctor (Kurt Smildsin); Gen. Swain (Jim McDonald); Scientist 1 (Barry Mizerski); Scientist 2 (Henry J.); Older woman (Doreen Chalmers); Greta (Joann Hawkins); Sloane, Def. attorney (Ric Reitz); Gunther (Greg Paul Meyers).

Jackson and Hyde

Drinking an elixir gives Dennis Jackson super-strength, but it also makes him wild and savage. Wr: Toby Martin. Dir: John Huneck.

Gail Peyton (Heather Ehlers); Elissa (Juice Newton); Hank (Barry Cutler); Brenda (Kelly Muilis).

Mine Games

Luthor, Superboy and Lana become trapped deep in a mine cave with Kryptonite on the premises to weaken the Boy of Steel. They taunt each other while oxygen slowly runs out. Wr: Sherman Howard. Dir: Hugh Martin.

Lex Luthor (Sherman Howard).

Wish for Armageddon

Clark's disturbing and horrifying dreams apparently are real, and he's shocked to discover he is the cause of them. A medieval man who has obtained Superboy's signature has used it to secretly control the Boy of Steel to bring armageddon. Wr: Gerard Christopher. Dir: Bob Wiemer.

Garrett Waters (Robert Miano); Lee Woods (Marc Macaulay); President (Peter Palmer); Russian officer (Gailna Loginova); Tortured woman (Rebecca Staples); Anatoil (Walter Hook); Judge (Lewis Crume); Dave (Frank Hilgenberg); Waitress (Angy Harper); Wife (Peggy O'Neal); Construction worker (Craig Thomas); Reporter (Bob Sakoler); Radar operator (Scott MacKenzie).

Standoff

Clark's held hostage in a crowded restaurant by a pair of escaped felons, unable to switch to his secret identity. Wr: Joseph Gunn. Dir: John Huneck.

Escaped convict #1 (Tom Schuster); Escaped convict #2 (Philip J. Celia); Fran (Frances Peach); Doug (Barry Cutler); Cop (Alan Landers); Screaming woman (Sharie Doolittle); Bartender (Jim Greene); Sgt. Barker (Ralph Wilcox); Lt. Riley (Lou Bedlord); Reporter (Bob Sokoler).

The Road to Hell, Part 1

Once again trapped in an alternate universe, Superboy visits Dr. Winger, the dimension portal inventor. Meanwhile, Luthor discovers a super-powered, newly landed baby in the forest and plots to use the child for his evil purposes. Wr: Stan Berkowitz, Michael Maurer and Matt Uitz. Dir: David Nutter.

Dr. Winger (Kenneth Robert Shippy); Darla (Tracy Roberts); Alternate Superboy (Joel Carlson); Serena (Carla Capps); Dr. Winger's assistant (Justina Vail); Man (James Zelly); Newspaper vendor (Jesse Stone).

The Road to Hell, Part 2

Trying to find a way home, Superboy becomes injured and finds himself in a world where Luthor is a doctor and his older self gives him a transfusion. Together, they battle an alternate Luthor and save a child version of themselves. Wr: Stan Berkowitz, Michael Maurer and Matt Uitz. Dir: David Nutter.

Superman (Ron Ely); Serena (Carla Capps); Dr. Winger's assistant (Justina Vail); Three-year-old Superboy (Arron Schnell); Second doctor (Manuel Depina); Short cop (Doug Dobbs); Reporter (Kent Lindsey).

Season 4: 1991-92

A Change of Heart, Part 1

Tired of waiting for Superboy, Lana starts dating a powerful man who uses giant TV screens and sub-liminal messages to further his evil schemes. The man who created the technology, Puck, warns Superboy of what's going on. In the course of events, Verrell frames Superboy for killing Lana Lang. Wr: Paul Stubenrauch. Dir: David Nutter.

Adam Verrel (Michael DesBarres); Tommy Puck (Bill Mumy); Deana (Carla Copps); Ernie (Frank Eugene Matthew, Jr.); Dr. Connelly (Bill Cordell); Lt. Walker (Jim

McDonald); Mayor (Don Fitzgerald); Priest (Jay Glick); Smiling woman (Kathy Poling); Security guard (Robert Reynolds); Prison guard (Danny Haneman); Man (Bob Norris); First reporter (Dennie Neal); Second reporter (Tricia Jean Matthews).

A Change of Heart, Part 2
Superboy's taken to jail for the "death" of Lana Lang. But as Verrel continues to use the monitors to further his hidden agenda, Superboy becomes angry and smashes all the monitors. Verrel then reveals that Lana is indeed alive and under his power. Wr: Paul Stubenrauch. Dir: David Nutter.
   Adam Verrel (Michael DesBarres); Tommy Puck (Bill Mumy); Deana (Carla Copps); Ernie (Frank Eugene Matthew, Jr.); Dr. Connelly (Bill Cordell); Lt. Walker (Jim McDonald); Prison guard (Danny Haneman); Gang leader (Chris Calvert).

The Kryptonite Kid
While trying to find a cure for Superboy's weakness by Kryptonite, a young man becomes blasted by the stuff and turns evil. Powerless against him, Superboy turns to a double to defeat the radiation-scarred villain. Wr: Michael Carlin and Andrew Helfer. Dir: Thierry Notz.
   Mike Walker (Jay Underwood); Babe (Sharon Camille); Reporter (David Carr); Reporter (Dawn McClendon).

The Basement
Investigating a report of basement ghosts, Lana discovers aliens, who take on her image and fool just about everyone at the Bureau except Clark, who becomes suspicious. Later, as Superboy, he's confronted by two identical Lanas. Wr: Toby Martin. Dir: Hugh Martin.
   Girl (Cassandra Leigh Abel).

Darla Goes Ballistic
Angry at Luthor's arrogance, Darla drinks an experiment which transforms her into a human supercomputer with psychokinetic powers. To lure Superboy, she kidnaps Clark and Lana. But Clark convinces Lex to free him so Superboy can create an antidote for Darla's powers. Wr: Sherman Howard. Dir: John Huneck.
   Darla (Tracy Roberts); Bank CEO (Ronald Knight).

Paranoid
Paranoia erupts at the Bureau when Jackson's superiors descend upon the place looking for someone who may have knowledge of national security secrets. Wr: Paul Stubenrauch. Dir: David Nutter.
   Lou Lamont (Jack Larson); Alexis Andrews (Noel Neill); Flynn (Jordan Williams); Mel Stuart (Kevin Corrigan); Margaret (Elizabeth Fendrick); Cop (Jeff Breslauer); Charlie (Tony Shepperd).

Know Thine Enemy, Part 1
Telling the entire city that they have only six hours to live, Luthor lures Superboy to a lab, where, upon putting on a headset contraption, Superboy plunges into Luthor's childhood memories. Wr: J.M. DeMatteis. Dir: Bryan Spicer.

Lena (12) (Jennifer Hawkins); Lena (23) (Denise Gossett); Lex's mother (Kathy Gustafson-Hilton); Lex's father (Edgar Allen Poe IV); Bully (Ryan Porter); Newscaster (Bob Sokoler).

Know Thine Enemy, Part 2
After Lana helps pull Superboy out of Luthor's mind, together they seek Luthor's sister, Lena. Meanwhile, Lex tells them there's no way to stop the bomb. Wr: J.M. DeMatteis. Dir: Bryan Spicer.
   Lena (12) (Jennifer Hawkins); Lena (23) (Denise Gossett); Newscaster (Bob Sokoler).

Hell Breaks Loose
Construction work at the Bureau reveals strange noises and lights. Further investigation shows that a clarinet and a human skeleton are hidden behind the walls of the office. In the 1930s, a man working for the Mob decided to go straight and promised his lady love that he would wait for her—forever. Wr: James Ponti. Dir: Robert Weimer.
   Johnny Carino (Gerard Christopher); Lisa (Phyllis Alexion); Construction worker (Beverleigh Banfield); Ben (James Delmar); Jeno (Fred Ottoviano); Officer (Michael Edwards); Henchman (Paul Vroom); Eddie (Frank Eugene Matthews Jr.); Young Eddie (Chris Labban); Band leader (Jim Candelora).

Into the Mystery
Superboy's haunted by the vision of Azrael, a woman who appears whenever disaster strikes. At the same time, he's haunted by the memory of his Aunt Cassandra and begins to suspect there is a relationship between the two women. Wr: J.M. DeMatteis. Dir: John Huneck.
   Azrael (Peggy O'Neal); Aunt Cassandra (Frances Peach); Young Clark (Edan Gross); Cody (Tina Dean Taylor); Andy (Andy Isaacs); Hardware store owner (Jack Carroll); Elderly beautician (Gayila Cole); Miss Cooper (Debra Ann Gay); Driver (Kurt Smildsin); Anchor (Bob Sokoler).

To Be Human, Part 1
While Chaos wreaks havoc on the city, Bizarro loses Bizarro Lana in a puff of smoke. Superboy counsels and with Dr. Lynn decides that it is possible to make Bizarro human. Wr: J.M. DeMatteis. Dir: John Huneck.
   Bizarro (Barry Meyers); Chaos (Paul McCrane); Dr. Lynn (Patricia Helwick); Bizarro Lana (Leith Audrey).

To Be Human, Part 2
When Chaos publicly brutalizes a weakened Superboy, Bizarro watches and realizes it's important for him to go back to being what he was and save the Boy of Steel. Wr: J.M. DeMatteis. Dir: John Huneck.
   Bizarro (Barry Meyers); Chaos (Paul McCrane); Dr. Lynn (Patricia Helwick); First policeman (Russ Blackwell); Second policeman (Michael Monroe).

West of Alpha Centauri
An extraterrestrial cube is brought into the Bureau, and when Superboy tries to break in, he's transported with Lana to a spaceship hovering over

Earth. Together, they wind up in jail with other intergalactic prisoners. Wr: Mark Jones. Dir: Jefferson Kibbee.

Ta-El (Gregory E. Boyd); Capt. Vladic (Andrew Clark); Sage (Kevin Quigley); First mate (Darren Dollar); Zoren (Angie Harper); Orek (Patrick Cherry); Bomb squad man (Michael Monroe).

Threesome, Part 1

A psychiatrist with revenge for Superboy springs Metallo and Luthor from prison, and together, they plot to destroy the Kryptonian. Wr: Stan Berkowitz. Dir: David Nutter.

Dr. Odessa Vexman (Justina Vail); Lex Luthor (Sherman Howard); Metallo (Michael Callan); Donnie (David Hess); Warden (Bob Barnes).

Threesome, Part 2

Barely escaping the plot against him by Metallo, Luthor and Dr. Vexman, Superboy retreats to Smallville, where he finds a despondent Lana. The fearsome threesome follow him home, and a final showdown is in the cards. Wr: Stan Berkowitz. Dir: David Nutter.

Dr. Odessa Vexman (Justina Vail); Lex Luthor (Sherman Howard); Metallo (Michael Callan); Trenton (Ed Amatruda); Ray (James Zelly).

Out of Luck

A thief lands on a good luck coin that passes on bad luck to everyone around him. Lana and Superboy become victims of his bad fortune. Wr: Sandy Fries. Dir: Robert Weimer.

Charlie Carmichael (Pat Cupo); Corrigan (Jack Swanson); Bob (Larry Bucklan); Andrew (Sam Ayres); Philip (Steve Oumothel); Bennett (Donald Ferguson); Mrs. Berger (Kathy Neff); Woman (Kathy Bronston); First nun (Trisha Colligan); Second nun (Kim Gabriel); Woman (Mindy Bronston); Director (Craig Thomas).

Who Is Superboy?

A super-computer is delivered to the Bureau, and Lana becomes intrigued about using the tool to find out Superboy's true identity. Wr: Stan Berkowitz. Dir: Robert Weimer.

Lex Luthor (Sherman Howard); Whitehead (Brett Rice); Darla (Tracy Roberts); Governor (Joe Candelora); Warden (Bob Barnes); Bizarro (Barry Meyers); Bizarro Lana (Shanna Teare); Llewelyn (Gregory Miller); Neila (Christine Moore); Police officer (Bill Painter); Security guard (Keifus Mathews); Werewolf (Kelly Erin Welton); Worker (Rod Ball).

Cat and Mouse

To ascend to a promotion at the Bureau, Clark Kent must endure a psychiatric evaluation, which includes

a lie detector test and a couch session with a psychiatrist. Wr: Gerard Christopher. Dir: Peter Kiwitt.

Dr. Samantha Meyers (Erin Gray); Mayall (Michael Owens); Capt. Quentin (Paul Darby); Lt. Fulton (Michael Balin); Desmond (Kevin Benton); Neila (Christine Moore); Garrett Woods (Robert Miano); Adam Verrel (Michael DesBarres); Anatoil (Walter Hook); Dave (Frank Hilgenberg).

Obituary for a Super Hero

When the media reports that Superboy may have perished in the midst of a yacht explosion, Lex Luthor starts celebrating. Wr: Stan Berkowitz. Dir: John Huneck.

Tommy Puck (Bill Mumy); Bizarro (Barry Meyers); Metallo (Michael Callan); Lex Luthor (Sherman Howard); Mandel (George Sarris); Female reporter (Elizabeth Rothan); Bureau worker (Lesa Thurman); Boy (Jesse Zelgler); Girl (Joanna Garcia); Scholarly type (Kristin Truelson); Coast guard captain (Jim Grimshaw).

Metamorphosis

When old people with young IDs start dying, Clark and Matt investigate. The trail leads to a health club run by a man named Adrian Temple. And when Lana is discovered as an old woman, Superboy studies the science of alchemy. Wr: Paul Robert Coyle. Dir: Robert Weimer.

Adrian Temple (Roddy Piper); Sasha (Robin O'Dell); Dr. Stern (Judy Clayton); Nathan Steeps (Bret Cipes); Receptionist (Stacey Black); Body builder (Valerie Basilone); Kid #1 (Roger Floyd); Old Jeff Olton (Joe Beadles); Pathologist (Billy Gillespie).

Rites of Passage, Part 1

As Clark reaches an important birthday, his hidden spaceship hums and glows, and suddenly, he loses control of his powers. Rushing home to Smallville, he receives a holographic projection from the ship that tells him to place a purple crystal—but there isn't one! Wr: Michael Carlin and Andy Helfer. Dir: David Grossman.

Jonathan Kent (Stuart Whitman); Martha Kent (Salome Jens); Thief (Buddy Stoccardo); Cop (Shawn McAlister); Superintendent (Key Howard).

Rites of Passage, Part 2

To regain his powers, Clark must locate the purple crystal and complete the rite of passage to adulthood. Having Jackson, Ritter and a very suspicious Lana hanging about isn't helping! Wr: Michael Carlin and Andy Helfer. Dir: David Grossman.

Jonathan Kent. (Stuart Whitman); Martha Kent (Salome Jens); Grace (Nancy Ouerr); Dick (Rob Richards); Elder (Richard Casey).

The Time Tunnel
September 1966–September 1967

Two American scientists from the year 1968 tumble through time and space and land in different eras. The scientists are part of project Tic Toc, a $12 billion tunnel that can send people into "past and future ages." Located miles beneath Arizona, the time tunnel staff try to return the scientists to 1968.

Cast: Dr. Tony Newman (James Darren); Dr. Doug Phillips (Robert Colbert); Dr. Ann MacGregor (Lee Meriwether); Gen. Heywood Kirk (Whit Bissell); Dr. Raymond Swain (John Zaremba); Narrator (Dick Tufeld).

Created by: Irwin Allen; *Developed for television by:* Shimon Wincelberg, Harold Jack Bloom; *Associate Producer:* Jerry Briskin; *Executive Producer:* Irwin Allen; *Director of Photography:* Winton C. Hoch; *Special Effects:* L.B. Abbott; *Music Theme:* John Williams; ABC/Twentieth Century–Fox; 60 minutes.

"Time Tunnel is destined to become the most ambitious, spectacular and expensive project in television." That's what Twentieth Century–Fox said weeks before the series premiered. *Time Tunnel* was rumored to be one of the biggest and most original TV series in years.

From a production viewpoint, *The Time Tunnel* seemed to fulfill the prophesy. The series featured a subterranean city under the Arizona desert. The 800-story complex housed over 12,000 people, all engaged in the effort to conquer time with a huge spiral drum called the time tunnel.

In reality, the time tunnel was a giant-sized prop capable of spitting out sparks. A 30-foot-high miniature was used to simulate the rest of the complex, complete with ramps, moving elevators, blinking lights and a stunning power core. Optical effects then placed real people on the walkways.

The most startling effect was the weekly tumble of Newman and Phillips through time's kaleidoscope of shimmering colors. Initially, producer Irwin Allen was going to have old movie footage superimposed over the actors as they fell through the centuries. Allen hated the result, which he said "looked like dirty soup." Colorful animation was substituted to represent time passages.

Inspired by a novel by Murray Leinster called *Time Tunnel*, Irwin Allen commissioned writer Shimon Wincelberg to script a pilot whose story had nothing to do with Leinster's novel. Wincelberg's script was later revised by Harold Jack Bloom. "There's no limit, either in space or time, as to how far we can go with *Time Tunnel*," proclaimed Allen. "We're planning stories built around Appomattox, Dunkirk, the American Revolution, Columbus' discovery of America, the storming of Troy, the Babylonian revels, the glory of Rome and the majesty of the Incas. We can go from the days of the early caveman to the height of the ancient Egyptian civilizations."

The premiere episode has a senator (Gary Merrill) threatening to cancel the time project unless a man can be transported back in time. Tony Newman uses himself as a test subject and ends up on the *Titanic* in 1912. Doug Phillips goes to his rescue, but since the tunnel hasn't been perfected, the science team can't retrieve them. They can only transfer them to one time zone after another.

The series began its run in a fiercely competitive time slot (Fridays at 8 p.m.). In its first few months, *Time Tunnel* proved surprisingly tenacious. A nationwide poll of high school students placed the series, along with *Star Trek* and *That Girl,* as the most popular new show of the season. Reviews were equally encouraging. *Daily Variety* found the pilot episode, "elaborately wrought and well scripted ... the sets and special effects are outstanding." The *World Journal Tribune* chimed, "tastefully made and suspenseful."

The lavish pilot, however, gave way to more conventional stories and production. Beyond their strong loyalty to each other, the characterization of the two time travelers was minimal. Tony became known for his trademark-green turtleneck sweater, and Doug for his 1912 business suit. Although peace-loving scientists, the pair demonstrated impressive fighting ability and rarely expressed scientific interest in the history that unfolded around them.

Each episode ended with a freeze-frame cliffhanger as the time travelers materialized in their next adventure. Thomas Moore, president of ABC at the time, was hopeful of *Time Tunnel*'s chances. "It was a very promising show. The writing, directing and acting were, perhaps, less important than the special effects," he says, "but it was amazing what Irwin Allen accomplished on his budgets. Sometimes he went over budget and Fox executives ran to us. They would cry and cry and cry. They thought he was going to break them!"

Moore reveals that *Time Tunnel* was deliberately aimed at younger viewers. While older viewers were attracted to CBS and NBC by personalities such as Ed Sullivan, Red Skelton and Bob Hope, ABC turned to "action, suspense and adventure as our niches," says Moore. "The early 1960s was a time to experiment, and

Cast of *The Time Tunnel*. Copyright 1966 ABC/Twentieth Century–Fox.

we felt that next to sports, nothing worked better in the medium than science fiction. We believed the genre was of interest to teenagers and viewers in their twenties." Moore points to *Voyage to the Bottom of the Sea* and the high-rated first seasons of *Outer Limits, The Invaders* and *Land of the Giants* as successful examples of ABC's strategy.

Not everyone was taken with the series. When the pilot was unveiled at the 1966 World Science Fiction Convention, science fiction novelist Jerry Sohl recalls many attendees booed at certain scenes. "The kids at that convention took their science fiction seriously," says Sohl. "In the pilot, you see the desert lift up and a car goes underneath. Then the desert closes up again. That scene was booed. The kids were thinking, 'Is that necessary?' The show had too many special effects. You didn't need such an elaborate set-up for a time travel series. In the movie *The Time Machine*, Rod Taylor had just a little machine. Here you had a desert that lifted up at a 45 degree angle and then slammed over you. That's

hokey. It turns you off if you're a science fiction fan."

Writer Ellis St. Joseph was far more impressed by the pilot but says that Twentieth Century–Fox's library of stock footage proved more important to *Time Tunnel*'s conception than creative inspiration.

"From a practical standpoint, it was a brilliant idea. The studio backlot had everything from ancient Babylon to the Hawaiian Islands. The centuries were built next to each other. Allen knew more about producing a series under budget than anyone else in Hollywood. He was extremely severe in his budget restrictions, but if you knew what he wanted, he was fine. If he didn't respect your talent, he could be arrogant and contemptuous."

Lee Meriwether played Ann MacGregor, one of the scientists dedicated to returning Tony and Doug to the tunnel. "I loved doing the show, but it was one of the most difficult acting jobs of my career. While Robert Colbert and Jimmy Darren were spinning around in time, Whit Bissell, John

Zaremba and I were at the tunnel, tracking their whereabouts and trying to bring them back."

Meriwether had to visualize what she was seeing on the tunnel's view screen. "We were really looking at little round dots placed on sticks in the tunnel. Since Robert and Jimmy's scenes were filmed before we shot ours, the director could tell us how close the pirate's knife was to Robert's throat or how close Jimmy was to stepping on a land mine. It wasn't the easiest acting job!"

Her most vivid memory is of the segment "Pirates of Deadman's Cove," where a pirate (played by Victor Jory) dangles her over the time tunnel's power core. "Ann was always getting into some kind of danger. In that episode, it was real! I still carry a small scar on my right thumb from Victor Jory's pirate knife. I got a scraped knee on that show, too."

James Darren insisted on doing many of his own stunts, and by mid-season, he had smashed his head on a rock, been burned in an explosion and taken some bruises in a spear fight.

One stunt that Meriwether wanted to do was floating through time. "I longed to do the time tunnel tumble," she says. "That would have been fun. It would also have been interesting to play one of Ann's ancestors, perhaps an evil one. Robert Colbert and I also thought that Doug and Ann should have had a romance, but it never came to be."

The actress saw Irwin Allen as a "witty man whose bark was worse than his bite. When he directed the pilot, he climbed a tall ladder and sat there banging a pail with a hammer. It made a horrendous noise, but that was his way of generating energy for everyone on the set. It worked! There was a method to his particular madness."

"Loyalty was very important to Allen," says Robert Mintz, who served as post-production coordinator, "and he rewarded it generously. He had a permanent staff of six people. He kept them on his payroll whether he was in production or not."

Mintz got first-hand knowledge of Allen's methods early on as assistant editor on Allen's 1960 film *The Lost World*. "There was an actors' strike, and rather than shut down production, Irwin brought in a dozen lizards and shot 'dinosaur' fights with them until the last lizard was dead from exhaustion. Irwin never missed a beat.

"Irwin also had a keen mind, which was never more evident than in the projection room

when he watched the dailies. God help you if you were not paying attention when Irwin asked you a question. During one screening, a sound effects man fell asleep. When the lights came up, he was snoring. Irwin played a little spider-and-the-fly game with him, much to everyone's amusement and much to the mortification of the effects editor. He woke up, sputtering all of the wrong answers to Irwin's questions. Irwin was a showman through and through."

Although *Time Tunnel* went everywhere from 1 million B. C. to 1 million A.D., the writers weren't required to study history or science. Weeks after it premiered, disappointed viewers wrote to *TV Guide* to complain about the series' lax historical and scientific standards. "Irwin had a favorite saying," says writer Bob Duncan, who scripted nine episodes with his wife, Wanda. "That was, 'Don't get logical with me!' There was absolutely no pressure on the writers to make their scripts historically accurate. For our scripts on "The Alamo" and "Devil's Island," we did considerable research to ensure the authenticity of the settings. When the series entered that strange combination of space aliens woven into historical stories, there was no longer a need for accuracy."

Like all of the writers, the Duncans were encouraged to use old movie footage to help plot their stories. "We sat through hours and hours of footage," recalls Duncan. "We selected clips that would work best in our stories. This gave the episodes millions of dollars worth of production value."

Some story ideas were rejected because of budget. Leonard Stadd's script dealing with the *Marie Celeste* (a sailing ship found adrift in the Atlantic in 1872 with its crew and passengers missing) was deemed too expensive to film. "My idea was that a giant squid had grabbed the people," says Stadd. "Tony and Doug explore the ship and end up battling the creature. During the story's pre-production meeting, the special effects guys were discussing how they could make a giant octopus tentacle. Irwin got very disturbed. Finally he said, 'No, it won't work. I used an octopus tentacle on *Voyage* and it cost me $30,000!' The production guys couldn't convince him that they could make one for just a few hundred dollars."

Ellis St. Joseph wrote one of the series' most popular segments, "The Day the Sky Fell In." The travelers land in Hawaii, 1941, hours before the Japanese attack on Pearl Harbor. Tony's father was listed MIA after the attack, and he tries to unlock the mystery of his father's disappearance. It ends with a tearful scene between Tony and his dying father. "I was thrilled by the concept of a son going back in time and trying to save his father," says St. Joseph. "The ending, where the father dies in his son's arms, was tremendously moving. I watched that scene with playwright William Inge. He was teary-eyed at the end. The episode was a big success with Irwin Allen, and he asked me to stay and write more."

St. Joseph went on to write "The Walls of Jericho." "I went to the Bible for inspiration, but my ambition got the better of me. I wrote an epic screenplay rather than a teleplay." St. Joseph found out, too late, that a TV budget couldn't accommodate his grandiose storyline. He was also disappointed in the guest cast. "The script was first-rate, but since many of the actors couldn't play it, it didn't move people. However, Rhodes Reason as Joshua was superb, and Abraham Sofaer as the father played his role with great dignity, intelligence and pathos."

St. Joseph's script left Jericho's miracles open to interpretation. Is it a cyclone or the hand of God that brings down the walls? The time tunnel staff draw different conclusions. "It was daring for TV to question the Bible," says St. Joseph. "You had General Kirk, Dr. Swain and Ann— fundamentalist, agnostic and atheist—contesting their convictions. I got away with it by leaving the matter unresolved. Dr. Swain reaches a compromise between Kirk and Ann by saying, 'Anything that creates faith is a miracle.'"

Time Tunnel also attracted a wide range of actors. Joey Tata, who had worked for Irwin Allen in the past, had to fight to play the role of Napoleon Bonaparte in *Reign of Terror*.

"Irwin put a big ad in the trade papers that read, 'Irwin Allen is looking for Napoleon!' says Tata. "I'm thinking, 'I gotta get a chance at this.' I asked Larry Stewart, the casting director, for the role, but Larry and Irwin didn't feel I was right for it. So I called up Larry using a French accent. He told me to come in. When he saw me, he said, 'Joey! it's you!' Larry called up Irwin and gave me the phone. I pretended I was an actor named Pierre and did my French accent for Irwin. He invited me to his office. When I walked in, he looked up from his desk and said, 'Tata? You were the actor doing the accent? You conned me! You crazy actor. Get outta here. You've got the part.'"

Actor Victor Lundin played a volcano-worshipping native on Krakatoa in "Crack of Doom."

"Jimmy Darren and I were going to have a fight scene. I said to Jimmy, 'Jimmy, I know you like doing your own stunts, but I'll use a stunt double.' Well, Jimmy was really swinging, and he splattered the stunt guy's nose all over the set. That could have been me! I had just had my nose broken on another show."

Lundin also recalls some directorial juggling during filming. "Our director, Bill Hale, was a nice young guy, an actor's director. Apparently he was taking too long because Irwin Allen came down and reamed Bill out in front of everyone. Irwin took over and almost kicked Bill off the set. Irwin was a very petulant guy. If you crossed him, that was it."

"Irwin Allen was not only a character, he was a genius," claims Australian actor Michael Pate, whose episodes included "The Last Patrol" and "The Walls of Jericho." "He was the one who made everything happen. He was kind and considerate to his staff but gently ruthless when it came to getting things done properly. He would allow his directors great liberties, but if they didn't get it right, he took over. Time was always money."

Another actor, Jan Merlin, was best known as the buddy of *Tom Corbett, Space Cadet* in the 1950s. In "Visitors from Beyond the Stars," he was an alien who takes over an Arizona town in 1885. "I had never heard of a science fiction western before," says Merlin. "It was weird to be out west as a silver-skinned alien. After they dabbed the makeup on me and Fred Beir, we noticed our eyeballs had changed to yellow-pink. I didn't care for the way we were told to play the aliens. It was the same tired version of aliens we've seen since the Saturday matinee days."

Time Tunnel began its run as one of the season's highlights. In November 1966, ABC categorized the series as "the network's unsung hero" for its competitive sparkle. But by January 1967, the series had lost its punch. The writers were encouraged to write aliens into the show to boost ratings.

"The series was running out of available stock footage, and the plots drifted into the alien invasion vein," says Bob Duncan. "It shifted from its original and better format. Personally, I found the alien episodes, including the ones we wrote, to be silly in the extreme."

Lee Meriwether agrees. "It weakened the series to take it into the future. The more far-fetched the premise, the less credible the episode."

Tony (James Darren) and a hostile alien prince (Kevin Hagen). Copyright 1967 ABC/Twentieth Century–Fox.

who said, "*Time Tunnel's* pseudo-scientific stories and complicated gadgetry and silly, involved plots make it unsuitable for children."

In an interview with the *L.A. Herald Examiner*, James Darren responded to the criticism by saying, "*Time Tunnel* is a service. We give youngsters lots of entertainment and pique their interest in history. We've tried to make the stories as logical as possible. With our budget, it's a little like re-making the Bible for a nickel per page. The youngsters don't mind. They like action first, read the story later."

When filming ended in 1967, Meriwether recalls, there was still hope that the series would be back. "On the final day of shooting, we had a cast and crew party. Instead of being sad, it was a joyous time because there was a rumor that we had been picked up. It was the perfect way to end the season. After the festivities, I was leaving the soundstage and heading to my car when an electrician yelled from the back of a passing truck, 'We're gonna miss you, Lee.' I assumed he meant until next season but no. I found out that we had been canceled. No one wanted to spoil our last days together with the bad news."

Meriwether claims the historical episodes got the best audience response. "We got letters from teachers who used *Time Tunnel* to stimulate history research in classes," she says. "To do more than just entertain with my acting was always my dream, and *Time Tunnel* gave me that chance."

By early February 1967, rumors were rampant that the series wouldn't be renewed for a second year. "My then-husband, Frank Aletter, was starring in a series called *It's About Time*," recalls Meriwether. "He had a ratings list framed on his dressing room wall. Both of our series were listed waaay down at the bottom of the page. We were not a ratings threat to any show that season."

Among young people, *Time Tunnel* still had a loyal audience. Network research showed viewers up to the age of 18 enjoyed the series. A poll by *TV Radio* magazine in January 1967 ranked *Time Tunnel* as number seven out of 40 shows as most popular new series of the season. The show's popularity among young viewers frustrated the National Association for Better Broadcasting,

The network was reluctant to cancel the series. When a list of ABC's casualties was released in March 1967, *Time Tunnel* was not among them. The series was slated to play its second season on Wednesdays opposite another Irwin Allen series, *Lost in Space*. It was a scheduling move that infuriated Allen. Two weeks later, the network decided its new *Legend of Custer* had a better chance in that slot. *Time Tunnel* was squeezed out of the line-up. "The day Irwin Allen got the call about *Time Tunnel's* fate, he was such a pro that he didn't display any disappointment," recalls Bob Duncan. "It was onward to the next project."

However, the show's cancellation remained a personal disappointment to Allen. In the years that followed, he tried to revive the format with the TV film *Time Travellers* (1976) and the script *Time Project* (1982). They failed to materialize as weekly series.

Time Tunnel went on to find several dozen markets in syndication, where its ratings were high. It continues to play around the world.

Lee Meriwether considers the prospect of a *Time Tunnel* film "fun" but says, "We've lost both Irwin Allen and John Zaremba," and concedes their deaths probably end the chance of a film reunion.

When asked what she thinks became of the characters, Meriwether phones Robert Colbert for his input. "Robert thinks Tony and Doug made it back to the tunnel. Doug and Ann got married and they had four children, two boys and two girls. The boys become scientists and are currently time traveling. The daughters are beautiful, but they're angry that they don't get to soar through space and time. They have to stay home. Hmmm … history has a way of repeating itself," she laughs. "As for Tony, he opened an Italian restaurant in Philly. He manufactures tight-fitting, green, scratchy sweaters for exports to any country with whom we are currently at odds."

CAST NOTES

James Darren (Tony): Born 1935. He began as a teenage singing idol and Gidget's boyfriend in the 1960s motion pictures. From 1983 to 1986, he co-starred on TV's *T.J. Hooker*. He's now a top TV director.

Robert Colbert (Doug): Born 1932. One of the stars of daytime's *The Young and the Restless* (1973–83), Colbert has also been a guest star on prime-time TV series such as *In the Heat of the Night, Hunter* and *Dallas*.

Lee Meriwether (Ann): Born 1935. This 1955 Miss America later co-starred in TV's *Barnaby Jones* (1973–80) and as Lily Munster in *The New Munsters* in the 1980s.

Whit Bissell (Gen. Kirk): Born 1909. A New York character actor with a vast number of film and TV credits, Bissell retired from acting in the mid-1980s. He died in 1996.

John Zaremba (Dr. Swain): Born 1908. In addition to being a judge in the *Owen Marshall* series (1971–74), Zaremba was seen as the Hills Brothers Coffee spokesman during the 1970s and 1980s. "John was a very good actor, with a gentle, easygoing nature," recalls co-star Lee Meriwether. "I'll always remember his warm, easy smile and witty personality." Zaremba died in 1986.

EPISODE GUIDE

Rendezvous with Yesterday
Tony lands aboard the *Titanic* in 1912, where he's imprisoned as a stowaway. Doug follows and tries to prevent the sinking of the ocean liner. Wr: Harold Jack Bloom, Shimon Wincelberg, story by Shimon Wincelberg, Irwin Allen, Harold Jack Bloom. Dir: Irwin Allen.
    Sen. LeRoy Clark (Gary Merrill); Althea Hall (Susan Hampshire); Capt. Malcolm Smith (Michael Rennie); Grainger (Don Knight); Marcel (Gerald Michenaud); Jiggs (Wesley Lau); George (Brett Parker); Guard (John Winston); Passenger (Dennis Hopper); Voice (Bart La Rue).

Trivia Alert: Dennis Hopper was originally cast as an Englishman aboard the *Titanic*. His English accent didn't satisfy producer Irwin Allen, and Hopper's character was written out. However, he can still be seen in the background aboard the ill-fated ship.

Memory Flash—Susan Hampshire: "I think it was my first American television appearance," notes the British actress. "I was thrilled to be working in Hollywood. I remember my makeup was very thick, as was the style in those days, and it was very hot. I was very proud to be on *The Time Tunnel* as there had been quite a buzz about it. It's become sort of a cult show. Curiously enough, I still get letters about it from time to time."

One Way to the Moon
Tony and Doug land on a rocket heading for Mars in 1978, but their added weight forces the ship to land on the moon. At the tunnel, personnel search for a double agent loose in the complex. Wr: William Welch. Dir: Harry Harris.
    Beard (James Callahan); Harlow (Warren Stevens); Nazzaro (Ben Cooper); Kane (Larry Ward); Brandon (Ross Elliot); Jerry Briggs (Sam Groom); Admiral Killian (Barry Kelley); Jiggs (Wesley Lau); Countdown voice (Dick Tufeld).

End of the World
Halley's comet imperils the travelers' efforts to rescue 200 trapped miners in 1910. Meanwhile, the time tunnel is nearly destroyed when it locks in on

the comet. This episode concludes with Tony visiting the time tunnel in 1958 when the tunnel was still under construction. Wr: William Welch. Dir: Sobey Martin.

Henderson (Paul Fix); Blaine (Paul Carr); Jerry (Sam Groom); Prof. Ainsley (Gregory Morton); Sheriff (James Westerfield); Preacher (Nelson Leigh); Man (Robert Adler); Jiggs (Wesley Lau); Soldier (Michael Haynes).

The Day the Sky Fell In

Tony's father was listed as MIA after the Japanese attack at Pearl Harbor, 1941. Days before the attack, Tony tries to unlock the mystery surrounding his father's disappearance. Wr: Ellis St. Joseph. Dir: William Hale.

Lt. Newman (Linden Chiles); Louise Neal (Susan Flannery); Yoku (Caroline Kido); Jerry (Sam Groom); Tom Anderson (Lew Gallo); Radioman (Patrick Culliton); Tony (Sheldon Golomb-Collins); Tasaka (Bob Okazaki); Brandt (Robert Riordon); Sumida (Shuji Nozawa-Fuji); Japanese Lt. (Jerry Fujikawa); Billy Neal (Frankie Kabott).

Memory Flash—Linden Chiles: "It was a terrific script and a very nice role. It also had a wonderfully historic storyline. We had an excellent director, Bill Hale. He gave us plenty of time to work through our scenes. One day, producer Irwin Allen came on the set and suddenly took over the directing. He was not a good director, and we were all relieved when Bill was allowed to return and finish the show."

The Last Patrol

Tony and Doug find themselves sentenced to death as spies during the war of 1812. At the tunnel, a dying general is granted his wish to travel back to 1812 to solve a historical mystery. Wr: Robert and Wanda Duncan. Dir: Sobey Martin.

Gen./Col. Phillip Southall (Carroll O'Connor); Hotchkiss (Michael Pate); Reynerson (David Watson); Jenkins (John Napier); British sentry (John Winston); Sergeant (Christopher King); Scout (John Burns); Soldier (Marshall Carter).

The Crack of Doom

The time tunnel's efforts to transport the travelers off Krakatoa, 1883, is hampered by the erupting volcano. Tony returns to the tunnel and finds everyone frozen in a time warp. Wr: William Welch. Dir: William Hale.

Dr. Ernest Holland (Torin Thatcher); Eve Holland (Ellen McRae); Karnosu (Victor Lundin); Jerry (Sam Groom); Native (George Matsui).

Trivia Alert: Actress Ellen McRae later changed her name to Ellen Burstyn and became a star in such films as The Exorcist and Alice Doesn't Live Here Anymore.

Revenge of the Gods

The travelers are hailed as gods when they become involved in the war between the Trojans and the Greeks in 1200 B.C. Wr: William Read Woodfield, Allan Balter. Dir: Sobey Martin.

Ulysses (John Doucette); Helen of Troy (Dee Hartford); Paris (Paul Carr); Sardis (Joseph Ruskin); Epeios (Abraham Sofaer); Greek leader (Kevin Hagen); Sentry (Patrick Culliton); Jiggs (Wesley Lau); Trojan (Anthony Brand); Greek (Paul Stader).

Memory Flash—Patrick Culliton: "Time Tunnel was my favorite Irwin Allen series. It had a clever premise, and the pilot with Michael Rennie was hot stuff. It was kind of based on Irwin's 1957 film The Story of Mankind. That was a rather brilliantly bizarre film and reflected Irwin's sense of humor. The time tunnel prop was fantastic. I've walked onto a lot of sets, but you don't see something like that every day."

Massacre

In 1876, Doug tries to stop Gen. Custer from reaching the Little Big Horn. Tony befriends Chief Sitting Bull and tries to change his mind about attacking the troops. Wr: Carey Wilbur. Dir: Murray Golden.

George Custer (Joe Maross); Yellow Elk (Lawrence Montaigne); Benteen (Paul Comi); Dr. Charles Whitebeard (Perry Lopez); Crazy Horse (Christopher Dark); Sitting Bull (George Mitchell); Major Reno (John Pickard); Tom Custer (Bruce Mars); Tim (Jim Halferty).

Memory Flash—Lawrence Montaigne: "The great thing about Time Tunnel was that it wasn't afraid to experiment with technology. We always think of TV as being the bastard child of motion pictures, but today's film technology came from wonderful shows like Star Trek, Time Tunnel and The Invaders."

Devil's Island

The travelers are sentenced to hard labor by a sadistic commandant on Devil's Island in 1895. Wr: Robert and Wanda Duncan. Dir: Jerry Hopper.

Commandant (Oscar Beregi); Lescoux (Theodore Marcuse); Boudaire (Marcel Hillaire); Perrault (Steven Geray); Alfred Dreyfus (Ted Roter); Claude (Alain Patrice); Man (Robert Adler).

Reign of Terror

As the travelers try to save Marie Antoinette, the tunnel accidentally brings Kirk's cruel ancestor, Querque, into the complex. Whit Bissell plays Querque. Wr: William Welch. Dir: Sobey Martin.

Blanchard (David Opatoshu); Marie Antoinette (Monique LeMaire); Napoleon Bonaparte (Joey Tata); Simon (Louis Mercier); Dauphin (Patrick Michenaud); Executioner (Tiger Joe Marsh); Voice (Howard Culver).

Memory Flash—Joey Tata: "Time Tunnel was a fabulous show. Producer Irwin Allen was the toughest SOB in the world. Ninety-nine percent of people were intimidated by him, but we hit it off. Whenever an actor went in for wardrobe, you had to walk across the Fox lot and let Irwin approve you."

Secret Weapon

Tony and Doug investigate a scientist in 1956 who has built a replica of the time tunnel as an enemy weapon. Wr: Theodore Apstein. Dir: Sobey Martin.

Anton Biraki (Nehemiah Persoff); Hruda (Michael Ansara); Jerry (Sam Groom); McDonnell (Kevin Hagen); Alexis (Gregory Gay); Gen. Parker (Russ Conway).

The Death Trap
The Gephardt brothers plan to kill Abe Lincoln in 1861 to speed up the Civil War. Wr: Leonard Stadd. Dir: William Hale.

Jeremiah Gephardt (Scott Marlowe); Matthew Gephardt (Tom Skerritt); Pinkerton (R.G. Armstrong); Lincoln (Ford Rainey); Carver (Richard Geary); David (Chris Harris); Scott (George Robotham).

The Alamo
The travelers land at the Alamo in 1836, where they try to convince Col. Travis that he's facing a hopeless battle. Wr: Robert and Wanda Duncan. Dir: Sobey Martin.

Col. Travis (Rhodes Reason); Capt. Reynerson (John Lupton); Col. Bowie (Jim Davis); Mrs. Reynerson (Elizabeth Rogers); Dr. Armandez (Edward Colmans); Capt. Rodriguez (Rodolfo Hoyos); Sgt. Garcia (Alberto Monte); Sentry (Orwin Harvey).

The Night of the Long Knives
Tony joins up with Rudyard Kipling in 1886 to free Doug from a sadistic Indian leader named Singh. Wr: William Welch. Dir: Paul Stanley.

Rudyard Kipling (David Watson); Singh (Malachi Throne); Jerry (Sam Groom); Major Kabir (Perry Lopez); Kashi (Peter Brocco); Col. Fettretch (Brendon Dillon); Gladstone (Dayton Lummis); Cabinet minister (Ben Wright); Ali (George Keymas).

Invasion
A Nazi scientist brainwashes Doug into becoming a killer. His first target is Tony. The place: Cherbourg, France, 1944. Wr: Robert and Wanda Duncan. Dir: Jerry Brisken.

Major Hoffman (Lyle Bettger); Mirabeau (Robert Carricart); Duchamps (Michael St. Claire); Verlaine (Joey Tata); Dr. Kleinemann (John Wengraf); Dr. Shumate (Francis de Sales); Soldier (Dick Dial).

Revenge of Robin Hood
The travelers help Robin Hood's men launch a rocket attack against King John's castle in the thirteenth century. Wr: Leonard Stadd. Dir: William Hale.

Robin Hood/Earl of Huntington (Don Harron); Baroness Elmont (Erin O'Brien); King John (John Crawford); Friar Tuck (Ronald Long); Dubois (James Lanphier); Little John (John Alderson); Engelard (John Orchard).

Kill Two by Two
An American-educated kamikaze pilot pursues the travelers on a Pacific island during World War II. At the tunnel, the pilot's elderly father uses a gun to force Kirk to retrieve his son. Wr: Robert and Wanda Duncan. Dir: Herschel Daugherty.

Lt. Nakamura (Mako); Sgt. Itsugi (Kam Tong); Dr. Nakamura (Philip Ahn); Medic (Vince Howard); Marine (Brent Davis).

Visitors from Beyond the Stars
The travelers unite townspeople against silver-skinned aliens, who have landed in Arizona, 1885. Meanwhile, the time tunnel is invaded by more aliens in 1968. Wr: Robert and Wanda Duncan. Dir: Sobey Martin.

Centauri (Jan Merlin); Taureg (Fred Beir); Sheriff (Ross Elliot); Alien leader (John Hoyt); Crawford (Tris Coffin); Williams (Byron Foulger); Deputy (Gary Haynes).

Memory Flash—Jan Merlin: "That was a lot of fun to do. Most of my Western cohorts and people at Western film festivals loved this particular episode. They considered a science fiction show set in the Old West a rare item."

The Ghost of Nero
An exploding rocket awakens the ghost of Nero in Italy, 1915. The travelers try to protect friendly Count Galba from the vengeful spirit. Wr: Leonard Stadd. Dir: Sobey Martin.

Mueller (Richard Jaeckel); Galba (Eduardo Cianelli); Neistadt (Gunnar Hellstrom); Dr. Steinholtz (John Hoyt); Benito Mussolini (Nino Candido).

Memory Flash—Leonard Stadd: "I like writing ghost stories. Since Time Tunnel was pure comic strip, I got away with combining science fiction and poltergeists. It turned out to be great melodrama and lots of fun."

The Walls of Jericho
Trapped inside Jericho, the travelers face death by torture until they're given refuge by a young prostitute, Rahab. Wr: Ellis St. Joseph. Dir: Nathan Juran.

Rahab (Myrna Fahey); Captain (Michael Pate); Joshua (Rhodes Reason); Malek (Arnold Moss); Father (Abraham Sofaer); Jiggs (Wesley Lau); Ahza (Lisa Gaye); Shala (Cynthia Lane); Torturer (Tiger Joe Marsh).

Memory Flash—Michael Pate: "The cast was really something for television. Arnold Moss and Abraham Sofaer were fine actors. Myrna Fahey was a delicious lady but not easy to get to know. She wasn't used to working in the TV format—brief rehearsals and set-ups, etc. She was a bit uptight so we helped her along in some of the scenes. Debra Paget's sister, Lisa Gaye, was an old friend. She was a very nice, gregarious girl."

Idol of Death
After witnessing a massacre, the time travelers vow to stop Cortez's bloody conquest of Mexico in 1519. At the tunnel, a crazed art collector demands that the tunnel retrieve a priceless artifact from 1519. Wr: Robert and Wanda Duncan. Dir: Sobey Martin.

Cortez (Anthony Caruso); Alvarado (Lawrence Montaigne); Castillano (Rodolfo Hoyos); Retainer (Peter Brocco); Qexcotl (Teno Pollick); Bowman (Abel Fernandez); Spaniard (Patrick Culliton); Spaniard #2 (Paul Stader).

Memory Flash—Lawrence Montaigne: "I had been a stuntman in Europe. When I had a sword duel in *Time Tunnel*, producer Irwin Allen said to stunt coordinator Paul Stader, 'You'd better get a stunt double for Lawrence.' Paul, who knew of my background, said, 'Irwin, that's the craziest thing I have ever heard!' Paul and I worked out a sword routine, and it turned out beautiful."

Billy the Kid

Billy the Kid is consumed with rage after Doug takes a pot shot at him in 1881. Meanwhile, Tony is mistakenly arrested as Billy and sentenced to hang. Wr: William Welch. Dir: Nathan Juran.

Billy (Robert Walker); Pat Garrett (Allen Case); Sheriff (John Crawford); Wilson (Harry Lauter); McKinney (Pitt Herbert); Marshall (Phil Chambers); Cowboy (Patrick Culliton).

Pirates of Deadman's Island

The travelers are pursued by pirates on the Barbary Coast, 1805. At the tunnel, a retired doctor convinces Kirk to send him back to 1805, where his medical skills are needed. Wr: Barney Slater. Dir: Sobey Martin.

Capt. Beal (Victor Jory); Dr. Benjamin Berkhart (Regis Toomey); Hampton (James Anderson); Capt. Stephen Decatur (Charles Bateman); Johnson (Harry Lauter); Spanish captain (Alex Montoya); Armando (Pepito Galindo).

Chase Through Time

The travelers chase a tunnel saboteur through three time epochs: 1547 Grand Canyon, A.D. 1 million, and 1 million B.C. Wr: Carey Wilbur. Dir: Sobey Martin.

Raoul Nimon (Robert Duvall); Zee (Vitina Marcus); Vokar (Lew Gallo); Magister (Joseph Ryan); Jiggs (Wesley Lau); Intercom voice (Bart La Rue).

The Death Merchant

An amnesiac Tony joins Confederate soldiers near Gettysburg. Meanwhile, Doug discovers that sixteenth-century philosopher Machiavelli is making a literal game out of the Civil War. Wr: Robert and Wanda Duncan. Dir: William Hale.

Michaels/Machiavelli (Malachi Throne); Major (John Crawford); Maddox (Kevin Hagen); Corporal (Kevin O'Neal).

Attack of the Barbarians

Tony decides to give up time traveling and marry a woman in thirteenth-century Mongolia. Mean-while, Doug helps Marco Polo defend his castle against hostile tribesmen. Wr: Robert Hamner. Dir: Sobey Martin.

Marco Polo (John Saxon); Batu (Arthur Batanides); Sarit (Vitina Marcus); Ambahai (Paul Mantee).

Merlin the Magician

The famous wizard asks the travelers to help him secure King Arthur's throne in sixth-century England. He uses his magical powers to help them battle Viking warriors. Wr: William Welch. Dir: Harry Harris.

Merlin (Christopher Cary); King Arthur (Jim McMullan); Guinevere (Lisa Jak); Wogan (Vincent Beck); Soldiers (Chuck Hicks, George Robotham, Paul Stader, Denver Mattson, Pete Peterson); Vikings (Gene Silvani, Paul Kessler).

Memory Flash—Jim McMullan: "A coach taught me how to do the sword fighting. *Time Tunnel* was a heck of a good show. I loved the whole concept of going back in time. It would be a good series to revive as a motion picture."

The Kidnappers

Ann is kidnapped by an android and taken to a star in the year 8433. She's imprisoned by an intergalactic zookeeper who collects famous people from Earth's past. Wr: William Welch. Dir: Sobey Martin.

Curator (Michael Ansara); Ott (Del Monroe); Hitler (Bob May).

Raiders from Outer Space

Tony and Doug battle an alien prince in Khartoum, 1883. The creature plans to destroy Earth to prove himself worthy of being a king. Wr: Robert and Wanda Duncan. Dir: Nathan Juran.

Capt. Henderson (John Crawford); Prince (Kevin Hagen).

Memory Flash—Kevin Hagen: "I almost went up in flames when my giant alien brain caught fire in a special effects stunt gone awry!"

Town of Terror

A young woman helps Tony and Doug to battle alien invaders. The creatures are draining the oxygen from a New England town, 1978. Wr: Carey Wilbur. Dir: Herschel Daugherty.

Joan (Heather Young); Sarah Pettinghill (Mabel Albertson); Pete (Gary Haynes); Alien leader (Vincent Beck); Alien Sarah (Kelly Thordsen).

The Twilight Zone

October 1959–September 1964

Anthology series dealing with ordinary people who encounter the fantastic and bizarre.

Host: (Rod Serling).

Created by: Rod Serling; *Producer:* Buck Houghton (years 1–3); Herbert Hirschman, Bert Granet (year 4); Bert Granet, William Froug (year 5); *Executive Producer:* Rod Serling; *Theme Music:* Bernard Herrmann (year 1), Marius Constant (years 1–5); CBS/Cayuga productions; 30 minutes (60 minutes during 1962-63); black and white.

Hammering together a set for a crime show is simple: Go to the studio's storage lockers and pull out a used table, desk and chair. In *The Twilight Zone,* set "between the pit of man's fears and the summit of his knowledge," the crew had to make not only their own props, but often their own worlds.

Producer Buck Houghton recalls when a *Twilight Zone* art director walked in with the script "Little Girl Lost." He showed Houghton a page where it said, "INTERIOR: LIMBO."

"He asked, 'What's that supposed to be, Buck?' I said, 'It's up to you.'"

The art director went off and created a fourth dimension for the episode (about a young girl who tumbles into a strange world). "He broke his neck to make a limbo set," says Houghton proudly. "That's challenge and response. That's what the scripts were full of."

When Rod Serling created *The Twilight Zone,* he was one of television's hottest writers. He had already won Emmy awards for his dramatic teleplays for *Patterns* (1955) and *Requiem for a Heavyweight* (1956). However, *The Twilight Zone* fulfilled a long-standing dream of Serling's. "I wanted to do a series of imaginative tales that weren't bound by time or space," he said at the time.

Rather than relying on gadgets and gizmos, *The Twilight Zone* illuminated the strengths and weaknesses of humanity. Man was generally conceded as being worthy of respect and full of potential. However, when his uglier traits rose to the surface in the twilight zone (often manifested as prejudice and greed), he was subject to a well-deserved and often ironic drubbing in that boundless realm.

The Twilight Zone was the first adult, prime-time fantasy series. In lieu of lavish special effects, the series told simple stories of ordinary people caught up in the bizarre. Concerned with the world around him, Serling made sure his stories had something to say about humanity and its environment.

Serling's unofficial pilot for *The Twilight Zone* was a one-shot drama titled "The Time Element." Broadcast on *Desilu Playhouse* in 1958, the story starred William Bendix as a man who dreams himself back to the Japanese attack on Pearl Harbor in 1941. Mail response from viewers was overwhelming, and CBS commissioned Serling to develop a weekly *Twilight Zone* series. Serling wrote an official pilot, "Where Is Everybody?" with Earl Holliman as a man trapped in a deserted town. The network was impressed and immediately put *The Twilight Zone* on the 1959-60 schedule.

Buck Houghton, producer of the series' first three seasons, was confident the series would find an audience. "The scripts I was handed were thoroughly entertaining and thought-provoking," he says. "That was my standard of what was going to please the average TV viewer. After all, I was a perfectly average fellow, minding my own business, when I was asked to read the first scripts. Fantasy or not, they were damn good."

One of the advantages *The Twilight Zone* offered to Serling was more freedom from censors. "It's true that Rod felt what could be said between two Martians couldn't be said between two senators," says Houghton. Using fantasy, Serling was able to slip in political and social themes without having them ravaged by nervous censors. However, it was the "what if" premise of the series that appealed to Houghton. "I wasn't a science fiction fan, although *Twilight Zone* wasn't science fiction. It was tales of imagination. There was no science hardware involved, no magic machines, no interstellar travel. It was about people with common problems who encountered fantasy. What would it be like if you could go back to the town where you were born and raised, and see that it's just the way it was at the time? That's something you can relate to very easily, and that was the key to the show's success."

During the first three seasons, Serling dedicated himself fiercely to the series. "The bulk of the episodes were written by Rod," notes Houghton, "and by the end of the third year, he was getting a bit pooped! We also had some fine scripts from people such as Richard Matheson and Jack Neuman. As a producer, I knew how lucky I was to be getting these kinds of scripts. You hardly ever ran into that calibre of writing."

The entire production crew of *Twilight Zone* also recognized that they were working on a quality show. "From the assistant propman to the cameraman, they worked their ass off," says Houghton. "They wanted to do the scripts justice,

A stranded astronaut (James Whitmore) faces an eternity on an asteroid in "On Thursday We Leave for Home." Copyright 1962 CBS/Viacom.

According to novelist Ray Bradbury, Serling was uneasy about doing *Twilight Zone* without input from science fiction writers. "Serling came over to the house one night and told me what he was doing," says Bradbury. "He said, 'Can you suggest some writers?' I said 'Sure!' I went down to my basement and came back with paperback copies by Richard Matheson, Charles Beaumont, George Clayton Johnson and John Collier. I said, 'These are good people. And you can use me, too.' The series went on shortly afterwards, and it's been running ever since."

Unfortunately, Bradbury's one script for the series, 'I Sing the Body Electric,' resulted in an episode that didn't meet his expectations. The story was about a robotic grandmother who raises a widower's three children. "Rod promised me that he would buy a couple of my scripts and that he wouldn't touch them. 'I Sing the Body Electric' turned out okay, but they took out the most important scene. In my script, the father asks the electric grandmother, 'Why are there electric grandmothers?' She gives him a moment of truth: She can do something no mother ever can. She can pay attention to all of the children equally. Only a machine could do that, and since the father may never find a new wife, somebody has to look after the children. The electric grandmother is the substitute for the mother that isn't there.

"When I saw that this scene was cut from the episode, I was furious! I called Rod the next day and said, 'For God's sake, why didn't you tell me?' He apologized and said that there hadn't been time to film it. I said, 'I had all of my friends come over to the house, and we sat down to watch the show, and the most important scene is gone! I

and that made a lot of difference in how the episodes looked. The crew was absolutely thrilled to see how the shows were going to come off."

Houghton recalls "Eye of the Beholder," with Maxine Stuart as a beautiful woman shunned in a world of pig-faced people. "Our director of photography, George Clemens, was delighted with the challenge of doing that show. You don't realize the faces of the doctors are hidden until you see their ugly mugs in front of you at the end. George and director Douglas Heyes worked that out together before filming."

Twilight Zone also attracted a wide range of top stars, including Ida Lupino, Ed Wynn, Robert Cummings and Mickey Rooney. "On occasion, an actor's agent would tell our casting director, 'Oh, he doesn't do TV.' We'd give him a copy of the script anyway, and the agent would call back, 'He'll do this one!' We got a lot of positive effect out of the first-rate scripts by Rod Serling."

don't want to work on the show anymore.' I told him that I couldn't trust him [as producer]."

The experience didn't get in the way of Bradbury's high regard for the series in general. "That series is going to run on forever," he says. "Wherever I go, people tell me how much they like *The Twilight Zone*."

The series became a critically acclaimed show early on, but it was never a mainstream hit. The sponsors were looking for weekly ratings in the 24.0 range. *Twilight Zone* managed a sturdy seasonal average of 19.0 in its first (and strongest) year. Its viewers included an enthusiastic audience in the 12–15 audience range. The late *Twilight Zone* writer Charles Beaumont said at the time, "Maybe that's because kids are hungry for the full play of their imagination while their elders are inclined to fear it."

"We were always on the edge of getting canceled," notes Houghton.

The directors of *Twilight Zone* ranged from veterans who had worked in the silent film era (Mitchell Leisen, John Brahm) to young directors who cut their teeth in live television (Don Siegel, Richard Donner). Ralph Senensky was relatively new to directing when he helmed "Printer's Devil," one of the hour-long episodes produced during the fourth year. Burgess Meredith played a sinister newsman whose headlines predict the future. "I was very proud of the way it turned out," says Senensky. "Burgess Meredith told me that director John Huston called him the day after the episode aired, commending him on the show."

Even as a TV viewer, Senensky was impressed. "The series was a true television classic. They're timeless morality plays. Each show was like an O. Henry short story. It'll continue to play on and on. I'm not sure that things that are being done today will be around in 30 years."

Another young director, Robert Butler, recalls meeting Rod Serling during the days of *Playhouse 90* in the mid-1950s. "Rod was a hardworking guy, willing to do anything to make his scripts better. However, he insisted on revising them himself. He was very paternal about his work. He was a fiercely principled, highly original guy. His sense of reality was a little quirky and ironic."

Butler directed one of the series' most controversial segments, "The Encounter" (written by Martin Goldsmith). The two-character story has an ex–Marine (Neville Brand) and a Japanese gardener (George Takei) dealing with their respective prejudices while cleaning out an attic. The episode wasn't included in *The Twilight Zone* syndication package, but was released on video in 1993.

"Some people thought that it was racist," says Butler. "The American-vs.-the-Japanese theme could have been too volatile. It wasn't your typical TV.

"Neville Brand was this beer-drinking Marine, getting a little smashed as he goes over his old World War II mementos. Throw into this environment a Japanese gardener who wants to borrow a pair of clippers. These two characters are drawn into the attic by the fates and relive World War II. It's dark, it's down, it's antagonistic and it's a very harsh show. Both of them die at the end. I'm sure it was considered too hot to handle."

Butler, however, doesn't feel the episode compromised itself. "It's raw conflict, and it gave both the actors and myself a terrific opportunity. We didn't have to spend time on any production linguistics. We spent time on developing the theme, the characters and the drama. For me, it conveyed a tragic circumstance. How unfortunate that these two people should meet in peacetime and rekindle that same volatility. Each of the individuals is a fine person, but the fates have thrown them together. Physically, it was a small show—two individuals in a small attic—but it was also huge because it dealt with the nature of fateful, inevitable conflict. These men had been stained by history, and they were unable to be harmonious with each other. That was the tragedy."

Butler recalls that a misunderstanding developed while shooting the show. "There was either something in the script or the character— I don't recall which—that I felt needed some clarity. I talked to producer William Froug about it. He got very impatient with my position, and we argued about it. He was left feeling that I simply didn't like the show, period. I simply wanted to be clear on a story point, but I remember being misunderstood. In any case, the episode turned out to be a terrific little piece."

Butler also directed "Caesar and Me," with Jackie Cooper as an unemployed ventriloquist browbeaten by his murderous dummy. "Jackie thought it would be interesting to play the character as a naive Irishman. He was very effective."

Butler's most challenging job was to bring the dummy to life. "We had him on a dolly so that when we filmed him from the hip up, we could

A couple (Peggy Stewart, Larry Gates) seek refuge from their desperate neighbors in "The Shelter." Copyright 1961 CBS/Viacom.

when atomic war appears imminent. He's the only person in the neighborhood with a bomb shelter, and his frightened friends turn into savages when try to force their way in.

"It was a first-rate script by Rod Serling," marvels Gates. "It dealt with the insanity of believing that one could escape from a nuclear holocaust. My character of Dr. Stockton believed he was doing the most reasonable thing with his shelter, but it turned out he had hopelessly misjudged the results of his actions. The story embraced the dilemma of trying to protect a few while others were going to be destroyed. It ended with the psychological destruction of all. A valid dramatic work must be formed around a dilemma from which there is no escape, and 'The Shelter' qualifies."

"We had a wonderful cast," Gates adds, "and an excellent director [Lamont Johnson], a happy company and crew and a fascinating script."

make the dummy pace back and forth across the room, weaving his spell over Jackie. I was aware that the episode was quite derivative of earlier *Twilight Zones*. There had been one with Cliff Robertson ["The Dummy"], and there had been the classic British film *Dead of Night* that also used the talking dummy theme. But on its own terms, the script was well written."

Actors on *Twilight Zone* found themselves acting in scripts that were not only entertaining but had a point of view. In a TV era where the most popular shows were westerns, *Twilight Zone* offered a refreshing switch. In the episode "The Shelter," Larry Gates played a doctor who ushers his family into their homemade bomb shelter

Surprisingly, Gates, who effectively portrays a decent man forced into an uncompromising situation to ensure his family's self-preservation, is critical of his own acting. "When I saw the episode years later, I didn't like my performance. I thought I had overacted. But the script, direction and cast made it work. *The Twilight Zone* in general was remarkable because it didn't rely on gimmicks. It was motivated by ideas and actions that involved and stimulated the audience. Rod Serling was a marvelously creative writer."

Actor John Anderson made several trips into *The Twilight Zone* and considers them among his career's highlights. "The series was highly touted because Rod already had an incredible track record. Everyone wanted to be on the show. It was like a feather in your cap. I was fortunate to do four episodes."

Anderson's first visit was as an airline pilot in "The Odyssey of Flight 33." A freak tailwind propels a commercial jet airliner back to the pre-historic era, and later to New York, 1939. The episode ends with the crew preparing for another time jump, hoping this time they'll return to their rightful era. "We looked damn serious doing that show," laughs Anderson, "but we had a blast filming that. The guys playing my co-pilots were great. The director [Justus Addiss] had trouble getting us settled because we were having so much fun. When you see me looking out at the dinosaur, I'm really looking at the poor director. As soon as he'd yell, 'Cut,' we were cracking jokes again."

The light-heartedness was one way for the actors to deal with their cramped environment. "We were confined to this little cockpit. Whenever the director said, 'There's a dinosaur,' we had to pretend that it was out there. I saw the episode recently, and I was amazed I was able to spew out that technical gobbledygook."

Anderson followed this up with "A Passage for Trumpet," where he played the musically oriented archangel Gabe, who gives a sad trumpeter (Jack Klugman) a second chance. "That was my favorite episode," he says. "It was a great script. The relationship between Klugman's character and Gabe was touching. There's a wonderful ending. I'm walking off into the shadows, and Klugman says, 'Hey! I didn't get your name.' I turn and say, 'Call me Gabe.'"

The episode required that Anderson and Klugman learn how to fake playing a trumpet. "They wrote a special music piece for the show. Neither Jack nor I played trumpet, so CBS went to the trouble of sending their musical director to my house with a cassette of the song and the sheet music. On the sheet, it told me what trumpet valves to press as the tape played. I worked my butt off, learning to play it by pantomime. Later, Jack and I, who are old friends, started rehearsing the scene, and I said, 'Jack, how did you do with the trumpet practice?' He said, 'What practice?' I said, 'Klugman! Are you telling me that you didn't even practice? You're gonna fake it?' He said, 'For Christ's sake, Anderson, who's gonna notice if we're hitting the right valves or not? If the audience is busy looking at our fingers, then we're really in trouble.' I said, 'Jack, you SOB! I worked my butt off to learn the finger-

ing!' and he laughed. But Jack was right. Fact was, you couldn't tell if I'm faking it or if he's faking it."

Anderson also did one of the hour-long segments, "Of Late I Think of Cliffordville." "All I remember was that Albert Salmi, who played this devilish character, had to laugh maniacally whenever he pulled a devious deed. However, Al couldn't laugh on cue. All David Rich, the director, could get out of him was a very heavy, totally unconvincing, 'HA! HA! HA!'

"David, a wonderful man, came up to me and said, 'John, what am I going to do with Al? I can't use that laugh.' I said, 'Jesus, David, I don't know, but it sure ain't working, is it?' I suggested that they lay down a sound track of somebody else's laughter. That's what they must have done, because you sure as hell couldn't use what ol' Al was giving 'em!"

Anderson remains gratified by having been a part of *The Twilight Zone*. "We had no idea that it would become a way of life for two generations of people. It elevated for a brief time the quality of TV. It still does. A week doesn't go by that somebody doesn't say, 'Hey, I saw you on *Twilight Zone*.' *Twilight Zone* was a very rare experience."

Actor Liam Sullivan starred in "The Silence," playing Jamie Tennyson, a compulsive talker. A fed-up tycoon (Franchot Tone) makes Jamie a wager: If Jamie can shut up for a whole year, the tycoon will pay him half a million dollars. Jamie accepts the offer. However, he wins the bet only because he has his vocal cords severed.

"Rod Serling was a short, tough ex-para-trooper with an extraordinary gift for offbeat plots that dealt with the human condition in a positive way," says Sullivan. "The long speech I had in the opening sequence was three pages. The day of shooting, Rod came up to me and asked if I could memorize an additional page of dialogue on the spot. It was going so well, he wanted to lengthen the scene. I said if he could write that fast, I could memorize it. He went off into a corner and started scribbling. He handed me the sheets off his notepad. I picked a corner and started memorizing. He was very pleased with the results.

"Rod was a very quiet fellow on the set," Sullivan adds. "He let the director take over in most things. He was a terrific writer, and after that experience, I was a *Twilight Zone* fan."

By the end of the third season, the network wanted to spice up the series. Their suggestion was to increase the show to 60 minutes, and initially Serling was excited over the prospect of fleshing out the stories and characters in an hour format. The resulting ratings, however, were barely passable, and the reviews mixed. Serling himself was not enamored with the final result. The fifth and final season returned to the half-hour length.

Larry Stewart was casting director for the final year. "*Twilight Zone* was a brilliant series," says Stewart, "and Rod was an incredible, prolific man. He'd come in at 9 a.m. and say, 'On my way over here, I was thinking, what would happen if everybody suddenly walked out of Boot Hill in an Old Western town?' He'd go in his office, close the door and by noon, he had completed a teleplay. We usually shot his first draft. I had never seen anybody write that fast." Stewart recalls that Serling's favorite actors included "Jack Klugman, and Royal Dano, who had a spooky persona. We generally had small casts on *Twilight Zone,* so actors knew they'd be getting a good part. It was the half-hour equivalent of *Playhouse 90.* It attracted what we'd call New York actors. Being a New York actor was a status symbol that didn't make a hell of a lot of sense. An actor is an actor, but at the time, Hollywood was impressed by actors who made the trek from New York."

Stewart was on hand when *Twilight Zone* got the ax from CBS. The final season had averaged a solid 18.4 rating, a dramatic improvement over the previous season's average of 16.3. Nevertheless, the brass wanted a change. When ABC expressed an interest in picking up the series for a sixth year, Serling met with network president Thomas Moore. "Moore wanted the show, but he wanted Rod to change it significantly," recalls Stewart. "He wanted it to be all science fiction and horror, and to have the name changed to *Witches, Warlocks and Werewolves.* Rod said no, and that was the end of it. Rod was a man of incredible integrity. He wasn't about to screw around with *Twilight Zone.*"

The series was canceled after 156 segments. CBS reran some of the episodes during the summer of 1965. The series then pole-vaulted into the lucrative world of syndication, where it has remained a fixture ever since. Several episodes have also been released on videotape. The very words "Twilight Zone" have seeped into everyday language as a reference to anything weird or bizarre.

Of the series' continued popularity, Buck Houghton says, "I'm delighted, for Rod's sake, that a good, quality show endures."

Serling remained interested in reviving *The Twilight Zone* long after its demise. Even after Serling's death in 1975, there was talk of updating the show. Without Serling, however, it would be in name only. The 1983 film *Twilight Zone— The Movie* opened to mediocre box office returns. In 1985, CBS launched a new, short-lived version of *The Twilight Zone* (see pages 486–503).

"I saw damned few of the new *Twilight Zones*," admits Houghton of the 1985 series. "I didn't want to be in the position of being asked what I thought of it. I did have an earlier experience when CBS wanted to revive the series. I talked to various writers about a new *Twilight Zone*–like show, which would have been under another title but touched the same nerve. I was surprised by how few of them got the point. They came in with scripts about things that you couldn't possibly imagine happening to the average person."

That ill-fated revival didn't come to pass, but Houghton was invited to make an appearance in the *Twilight Zone* film. "I had a cameo in the remake of one of our original episodes, 'It's a Good Life' [a young boy uses his mental powers to keep a small town under his control]. The set of the home had curved tops to doors, and the fireplaces were figure eights. It was unlike any house you've ever seen. Once again, I knew that they just didn't get the point of *Twilight Zone.*"

Actor John Anderson likes to relate a *Twilight Zone*-ish memory from 1974. "My wife and I used to make an annual trip out to Death Valley. A couple we knew from New York had opened up a little opera house. That night as I was preparing to go onstage, the husband, Tom, said to me, 'Oh, John, by the way, an old friend of yours is going to be out in the audience watching the show tonight—Rod Serling.' Well, I was delighted, and I looked forward to seeing him. But just before the show, we scanned the audience and no Rod. I was disappointed and went on with the show.

"During intermission, I went outside for a smoke. As I lit up my cigar, I could see Death Valley's bleak desert landscape in front of me. Suddenly, a guy 10 feet away lights up a cigarette. I thought, 'Who the hell is that?' He stepped out of the shadows and said, 'Hi, John.' It was Rod. He had arrived late. We chatted under the pale blue moon, looking out over the weird, forbidding landscape.

"He said, 'You know, the other night they showed one of my favorite *Twilight Zones.* It was the one with you as the airline pilot. It was so good.' I said, 'Rod, they were all good.' He asked me if I still received residual payment for them. I told him that I didn't. We rapped a while and Rod said, 'John, I'll talk to you after the show.'

"When the show was over, I said to my wife, 'Come on! We gotta get outside. Rod Serling was out there.' She said, 'He was?' I said, 'Yeah." So we went outside and no Rod. I ran around calling his name. Tom came out and asked what was going on. I told him about Rod. 'Well, where is he?' Tom asked. We all looked around, but there was nothing but the moon and the desert.

"The fact was, Rod was a very private man. He didn't like to be fawned over. My reading of the situation was that he had arrived late, sat down quietly in the back, and when the show was over, he left. After we had our talk, he probably thought, 'If I stay around and wait for John, the lights will come on and everybody will be all over me.' So he left. That's all I could figure. He died about six months later. I told Carol, his wife, about it and she was amazed. It was a very strange experience. No one else even saw Rod at the theater that night. It's my word that Rod and I had that quiet chat." John Anderson chuckles. "You know, it was just like *The Twilight Zone!*"

Cast Notes

Rod Serling (Host): Born 1924. Serling was one of the most prolific and acclaimed writers of live television drama in the 1950s. He later co-wrote the film *Planet of the Apes* (1968) and provided narration for many documentaries during the 1970s, including the *Undersea World of Jacques Cousteau* specials. Serling died from complications following heart surgery in 1975.

Episode Guide

Season 1: 1959-60

Where Is Everybody?
A man finds himself in an empty town and suspects he's being watched by unseen eyes. Wr: Rod Serling. Dir: Robert Stevens.
    Mike Ferris (Earl Holliman); General (James Gregory); Also with Paul Langdon, James McCallion, Garry Walberg, John Conwell, Jay Overholts, Carter Mullavey, James Johnson.

One for the Angels
A salesman manages to escape from Mr. Death, but then learns Death plans to take the life of a little girl in his place. Wr: Rod Serling. Dir: Robert Parrish.
    Lew Bookman (Ed Wynn); Mr. Death (Murray Hamilton); Maggie (Dana Dillaway); Truck driver (Merritt Bohn); Doctor (Jay Overholts); Boy (Mickey Maga).

Mr. Denton on Doomsday
A former gunslinger recovers his ability to quick-draw, but this brings a wave of new challengers. Wr: Rod Serling. Dir: Allen Reisner.
    Al Denton (Dan Duryea); Hotaling (Martin Landau); Liz (Jeanne Cooper); Henry J. Fate (Malcolm Atterbury); Pete Grant (Doug McClure); Charlie (Ken Lynch); Leader (Arthur Batanides); Doctor (Robert Burton); Man (Bill Erwin).

    Memory Flash—Martin Landau: "On the first day the cast sat around a table on MGM's Western street with director Allen Reisner and Rod Serling and read the script. It was just as we used to do in the theater or in the old "live TV" days. We made changes, worked and reworked stuff all morning until we felt it was right. Then and only then did we start to film it."

The 16mm Shrine
A former movie star finds a way to escape into her old movies. Wr: Rod Serling. Dir: Mitchell Leisen.
    Barbara Jean Trenton (Ida Lupino); Danny Weiss (Martin Balsam); Marty Sall (Ted de Corsia); Jerry Hearndan (Jerome Cowan); Sally (Alice Frost); Young Hearndan (John Clarke).

Walking Distance
A harried businessman goes back in time to his childhood, where he meets himself as a boy. Wr: Rod Serling. Dir: Robert Stevens.
    Martin Sloan (Gig Young); Sloan (Frank Overton); Mrs. Sloan (Irene Tedrow); Young Martin (Michael Montgomery); Charlie (Byron Foulger); Soda Jerk (Joe Corey); Mr. Wilson (Pat O'Malley); Boy (Ron Howard); Wilcox (Bill Erwin); Teen (Buzz Martin); Woman (Nan Peterson); Attendant (Sheridan Comerate).

Escape Clause
Walter Bedeker is granted immortality, but when he grows bored, he goes to extraordinary lengths to liven up his life. Wr: Rod Serling. Dir: Mitchell Leisen.
    Walter Bedeker (David Wayne); Cadwallader (Thomas Gomez); Ethel Bedeker (Virginia Christine); Doctor (Raymond Bailey); Adjuster (Dick Wilson); Adjuster #2 (Joe Flynn); Judge (George Baxter); Cooper (Wendell Holmes); Guard (Nesdon Booth); Subway guard (Allan Lurie); Janitor (Paul E. Burns).

The Lonely
A prisoner serving a life sentence on a barren asteroid is given a gift: a female android. Wr: Rod Serling. Dir: Jack Smight.
    James Corry (Jack Warden); Alicia (Jean Marsh); Allenby (John Dehner); Adams (Ted Knight); Carstairs (James Turley).

Memory Flash—Jean Marsh: "Death Valley was a very unique location. It was extremely hot. Even Rod Serling wore shorts! I was extremely impressed by his mental coolness. Jack Warden advised me to sleep outside my cabana because of the heat. He also said to leave a light on inside so all of the desert insects would gather in one room and leave me alone. Unfortunately, I chose to leave the bathroom light on. In the morning, there was a thick fog of insects, and a tarantula."

Time Enough at Last

A meek librarian finds that the world has been destroyed in a nuclear holocaust. He has time enough at last to catch up on his reading. Wr: Rod Serling, story by Lynn Venable. Dir: John Brahm.

Henry Bemis (Burgess Meredith); Carsville (Vaughn Taylor); Helen Bemis (Jacqueline DeWit); Customer (Lela Bliss).

Perchance to Dream

A sinister woman in Edward Hall's dreams is trying to scare him to death. Wr: Charles Beaumont, story by Charles Beaumont. Dir: Robert Florey.

Edward Hall (Richard Conte); Maya/Miss Thomas (Suzanne Lloyd); Dr. Rathmann (John Larch); Barker (Edward Marr); Rifle Barker (Russell Trent); Stranger (Ted Stanhope).

Judgment Night

A U-Boat captain during World War II is doomed to relive the events of the ship he torpedoed by being one of its passengers. Wr: Rod Serling. Dir: John Brahm.

Capt. Carl Lanser (Nehemiah Persoff); Capt. Wilbur (Ben Wright); First officer (Patrick Macnee); Mueller (James Franciscus); Potter (Hugh Sanders); Barbara (Diedre Owen); Devereaux (Leslie Bradley); Bartender (Kendrick Huxham); Steward (Richard Pell); Stewart #2 (Don Journeaux); Girl (Debbie Joyce); Engineer (Barry Bernard).

And When the Sky Was Opened

Three astronauts return from a space mission, but suddenly astronaut Harrington finds nobody on Earth remembers who he is. Wr: Rod Serling, story by Richard Matheson. Dir: Douglas Heyes.

Col. Clegg Forbes (Rod Taylor); Col. Ed Harrington (Charles Aidman); Maj. William Gart (Jim Hutton); Amy (Maxine Cooper); Nurse (Sue Randall); Officer (Oliver McGowan); Bartender (Paul Bryar); Woman (Gloria Pall); Investigator (Logan Field); Doctor (Joe Bassett); Harrington (S. John Launer); Nurse #2 (Elizabeth Fielding).

What You Need

Fred Lenard tries to exploit a salesman's ability to predict the future. Wr: Rod Serling, story by Lewis Padgett (Henry Kuttner, C.L. Moore). Dir: Alvin Ganzer.

Fred Renard (Steve Cochran); Pedott (Ernest Truex); Girl (Arline Sax); Lefty (Read Morgan); Bartender (William Edmonson); Woman (Judy Ellis); Man (Fred Kruger); Clerk (Norman Sturgis); Waiter (Frank Allocca); Photographer (Mark Sunday).

The Four of Us Are Dying

A con man with the ability to change his appearance assumes the identities of people with colorful pasts. Wr: Rod Serling, story by George Clayton Johnson. Dir: John Brahm.

Arch Hammer (Harry Townes); Foster (Ross Martin); Sterig (Phillip Pine); Marshak (Don Gordon); Maggie (Beverly Garland); Pop Marshak (Peter Brocco); Penell (Bernard Fein); Detective (Milton Frome); Trumpet player (Harry Jackson); Man in bar (Bob Hopkins); Second man (Pat Comiskey); Busboy (Sam Rawlins).

Third from the Sun

Two families plan to steal a spaceship and escape their planet before a nuclear war occurs. Wr: Rod Serling, story by Richard Matheson. Dir: Richard L. Bare.

William Sturka (Fritz Weaver); Jerry Riden (Joe Maross); Carling (Edward Andrews); Eve (Lori March); Jody (Denise Alexander); Ann (Jeanne Evans); Guard (Will J. White); Voice (John S. Launer).

I Shot an Arrow into the Air

Astronauts crash-land on a desert planet. With supplies running out, crewman Corey is determined to survive at any cost. Wr: Rod Serling, story by Madelon Champion. Dir: Stuart Rosenberg.

Corey (Dewey Martin); Col. Donlin (Edward Binns); Pierson (Ted Otis); Brandt (Leslie Barrett); Langford (Harry Bartell).

The Hitch-hiker

Nan Adams is plagued by a series of near-fatal accidents during her cross-country drive. The events are tied to a mysterious hitch-hiker. Wr: Rod Serling, story by Lucille Fletcher. Dir: Alvin Ganzer.

Nan Adams (Inger Stevens); Sailor (Adam Williams); Hitch-hiker (Leonard Strong); Mechanic (Lew Gallo); Gas station man (George Mitchell); Flag man (Dwight Townsend); Counterman (Russ Bender); Mrs. Whitney (Eleanor Audley); Waitress (Mitzi McCall).

The Fever

Franklin Gibbs develops an obsession for beating a Las Vegas slot machine that has a mind of its own. Wr: Rod Serling. Dir: Robert Florey.

Franklin Gibbs (Everett Sloane); Flora Gibbs (Vivi Janiss); Drunk (Art Lewis); P.R. Man (William Kendis); Manager (Lee Sands); Cashier (Marc Towers); Photographer (Lee Millar); Sheriff (Arthur Peterson); Girl (Carole Kent); Croupier (Jeffrey Sayre).

The Last Flight

A fighter pilot from 1917 lands at an air base, but he finds it's 1959. Wr: Richard Matheson. Dir: William Claxton.

Lt. William Terence Decker (Kenneth Haigh); Wilson (Simon Scott); Harper (Alexander Scourby); Mackaye (Robert Warwick); Corporal (Harry Raybould); Guard (Jerry Catron); Jeep driver (Paul Baxley); Truck driver (Jack Perkins); Stunt pilot (Frank Gifford Tallman).

The Purple Testament

During World War II, Lt. Fitzgerald discovers he can

predict which men are going to die in battle. Wr: Rod Serling. Dir: Richard L. Bare.

Lt. Fitzgerald (William Reynolds); Riker (Dick York); Gunther (Barney Phillips); Driver (Warren Oates); Smitty (Michael Vandever); Sergeant (William Phipps); Orderly (Paul Mazursky); Harmonica man (Ron Masak); Colonel (S. John Launer); Freeman (Marc Clavell).

Elegy
Three astronauts land on an Earth-like world where everyone is frozen and the only "living person" is an android. Wr: Charles Beaumont, story by Charles Beaumont. Dir: Douglas Heyes.

Jeremy Wickwire (Cecil Kellaway); James Webber (Kevin Hagen); Kurt Meyers (Jeff Morrow); Peter Kirby (Don Dubbins).

Mirror Image
Millicent Barnes is haunted by her exact double. Wr: Rod Serling. Dir: John Brahm.

Millicent Barnes (Vera Miles); Paul Grinstead (Martin Milner); Ticket man (Joe Hamilton); Woman (Naomi Stevens); Husband (Ferris Taylor); Old woman (Terese Lyon); Bus driver (Edwin Rand).

The Monsters Are Due on Maple Street
Neighbors turn against each other when they learn that aliens may have invaded the area. Wr: Rod Serling. Dir: Ron Winston.

Steve Brand (Claude Akins); Charlie (Jack Weston); Goodman (Barry Atwater); Don (Burt Metcalfe); Tommy (Jan Handzlik); Tommy's mother (Mary Gregory); Mrs. Brand (Anne Barton); Mrs. Goodman (Lea Waggner); Pete van Horn (Ben Erway); Charlie's wife (Lyn Guild); Neighbors (Joan Sudlow, Jason Johnson, Amzie Strickland); Alien (Sheldon Allman).

A World of Difference
A fictional TV character finds himself trapped in the "real world." Wr: Richard Matheson. Dir: Ted Post.

Arthur Curtis (Howard Duff); Marty (Frank Maxwell); Nora (Eileen Ryan); Brinkley (David White); Sally (Gail Kobe); Endicott (Peter Walker); Kelly (William Idelson); Marian (Susan Dorn).

Long Live Walter Jameson
A college professor discovers that his daughter's fiance is over two thousand years old. Wr: Charles Beaumont. Dir: Tony Leader.

Walter Jameson (Kevin McCarthy); Samuel Kittridge (Edgar Stehli); Laurette Bowen (Estelle Winwood); Susanna Kittridge (Dody Heath).

People Are Alike All Over
A stranded astronaut grows suspicious of friendly Martians who eagerly supply him with everything he wants. Wr: Rod Serling, story by Paul W. Fairman. Dir: Mitchell Leisen.

Sam Conrad (Roddy McDowall); Warren Marcusson (Paul Comi); Teenya (Susan Oliver); Martians (Byron Morrow, Vic Perrin, Vernon Gray).

Memory Flash—Susan Oliver: "That was lots of fun. Roddy used to take me to lunch at MGM. He had practically grown up there. He used to do all of these hilarious impressions of big movie moguls. Rod Serling was very special. He was a nice, gentle man, very modest and self-effacing. Mitchell Leisen had been a costumer as well as a film director. He picked my costume, a Greek gown, for me to wear as a Martian. He said, 'You can only be so futuristic and then it comes back to what the classic is.'"

Execution
A scientist's time machine accidentally snatches a killer from 1880 and deposits him in 1960. Wr: Rod Serling, story by George Clayton Johnson. Dir: David Orrick McDearmon.

Joe Caswell (Albert Salmi); Dr. George Manion (Russell Johnson); Johnson (Than Wyenn); Reverend (Jon Lormer); Judge (Fay Roope); Old man (George Mitchell); Bartender (Richard Karlan); Cowboy (Joe Haworth).

The Big, Tall Wish
A young boy makes a wish for boxer Bolie Jackson to win a match, but the prizefighter refuses to believe in magic. Wr: Rod Serling. Dir: Ron Winston.

Bolie Jackson (Ivan Dixon); Henry (Steven Perry); Frances (Kim Hamilton); Mizell (Walter Burke); Thomas (Henry Scott); Fighter (Charles Horvath); Announcer (Carl McIntire); Referee (Frankie Van).

A Nice Place to Visit
A thief, Rocky Valentine, finds himself in a world filled with gambling casinos, beautiful women, and a mysterious man named Mr. Pip. Wr: Charles Beaumont. Dir: John Brahm.

Rocky Valentine (Larry Blyden); Mr. Pip (Sebastian Cabot); Policeman (John Close); Croupier (Wayne Tucker); Girl (Sandra Warner); Dancer (Barbara English); Dealer (Peter Hornsby); Dwarf cop (Nels Nelson); Attendant (Bill Mullikin).

Nightmare as a Child
The appearance of a strange child opens up repressed memories for teacher Helen Foley, who now remembers who killed her mother. Wr: Rod Serling. Dir: Alvin Ganzer.

Helen Foley (Janice Rule); Markie (Terry Burnham); Peter Selden (Shepperd Strudwick); Doctor (Michael Fox); Lt. (Joseph Perry); Girl (Suzanne Cupito).

A Stop at Willoughby
An uptight businessman steps off a train and finds himself in the peaceful town of Willoughby, 1880. Wr: Rod Serling. Dir: Robert Parrish.

Gart Williams (James Daly); Jane Williams (Patricia Donahue); Misrell (Howard Smith); Conductor (Jason Wingreen); Conductor #2 (James Maloney); Helen (Mavis Neal); Boy (Billy Booth); Boy #2 (Butch Hengen); Trainman (Ryan Hayes); Man (Max Slaten).

The Chaser
A young man uses a love potion to gain the affections of a woman, but the result has him climbing the walls. Wr: Robert Presnell, Jr., story by John Collier. Dir: Douglas Heyes.

Roger Shackleforth (George Grizzard); Daemon (John McIntire); Leila (Patricia Barry); Homburg (J. Pat O'Malley); Woman (Barbara Perry); Big lady (Marjorie Bennett); Bartender (Duane Grey); Man (Rusty Wescoatt).

A Passage for Trumpet
Caught between life and death, a sad trumpet player is given another chance at life, courtesy of an angel. Wr: Rod Serling. Dir: Don Medford.

Joey Crown (Jack Klugman); Gabe (John Anderson); Nan (Mary Webster); Baron (Frank Wolff); Truck driver (James Flavin); Pawnshop dealer (Ned Glass); Woman (Diane Honodel).

Memory Flash—John Anderson: "Rod later told me this episode won as best short film at the Cannes Film Festival."

Mr. Bevis
A goofy eccentric named Bevis agrees to let a guardian angel bring him success. Wr: Rod Serling. Dir: William Asher.

James Bevis (Orson Bean); J. Hardy Hempstead (Henry Jones); Peckinpaugh (Charles Lane); Bartender (Horace McMahon); Policeman (William Schallert); Cop #2 (House Peters, Jr.); Woman (Colleen O'Sullivan); Margaret (Florence MacMichael); Peddler (Vito Scotti); Landlady (Dorothy Neuman); Boy (Timmy Cletro).

Memory Flash—Orson Bean: "I liked Rod Serling enormously. He was a regular guy. There was no bullshit about him. I wanted to work with Rod, *thinking* he was going to direct this show.
Twilight Zone is like *The Lucy Show* and *The Honeymooners*—its continued popularity is a pleasant mystery. It's a strange form of immortality to be on a *Twilight Zone*. It will be playing long after I'm dead. This episode played in L.A. during Thanksgiving 1993 as part of a traditional marathon. Twenty people spoke to me the next day of having seen it!"

The After Hours
A shopper finds terror in a department store when the mannequins come to life. Wr: Rod Serling. Dir: Douglas Heyes.

Marsha White (Anne Francis); Saleswoman (Elizabeth Allen); Armbruster (James Millhollin); Elevator man (John Conwell); Miss Pettigrew (Nancy Rennick); Sloan (Patrick Whyte).

The Mighty Casey
A baseball team goes straight to the top when they use a robot pitcher. Wr: Rod Serling. Dir: Robert Parrish, Alvin Ganzer.

McGarry (Jack Warden); Dr. Stillman (Abraham Sofaer); Casey (Robert Sorrells); Monk (Don O'Kelly); Doctor (Jonathan Hole); Beasley (Alan Dexter); Commissioner (Rusty Lane).

Trivia Alert: The late Paul Douglas was originally cast as coach McGarry.

A World of His Own
A writer finds he can turn his characters into living people. He promptly conjures up a beautiful woman, an elephant and host Rod Serling. Wr: Richard Matheson. Dir: Ralph Nelson.

Gregory West (Keenan Wynn); Victoria West (Phyllis Kirk); Mary (Mary La Roche).

Season 2: 1960-61

King Nine Will Not Return
Capt. James Embry awakens from the crash of his B-25 bomber in Africa, 1943. He searches frantically for his missing crew. Wr: Rod Serling. Dir: Buzz Kulik.

James Embry (Robert Cummings); Doctor (Paul Lambert); Psychiatrist (Gene F. Lyons); Nurse (Jenna McMahon); Officer (Seymour Green); British man (Richard Lupino).

Man in the Bottle
An elderly couple request three wishes from a genie, but each wish brings them more despair. Wr: Rod Serling. Dir: Don Medford.

Arthur Castle (Luther Adler); Edna Castle (Vivi Janiss); Genie (Joseph Ruskin); Mrs. Gumley (Lisa Golm); IRS man (Olan Soule); German officers (Peter Coe, Albert Szabo).

Memory Flash—Joseph Ruskin: "It was a fun show to do. We rehearsed that show for two days. It was wonderful. I never did a TV show that gave actors that much time for rehearsal."

Nervous Man in a Four Dollar Room
Jackie Rhodes is pressured by a gangster to carry out a murder, but a double of Jackie appears in the mirror and gives him the chance to think for himself. Wr: Rod Serling. Dir: Douglas Heyes.

Jackie Rhoades (Joe Mantell); George (William D. Gordon).

A Thing About Machines
Bartlett Finchely is thrust into all-out war with his household machines. Wr: Rod Serling. Dir: David Orrick McDearmon.

Bartlett Finchley (Richard Haydn); Repairman (Barney Phillips); Edith (Barbara Stuart); Intern (Jay Overholts); Policeman (Henry Beckman); Girl (Margarita Cordova); Lineman (Lew Brown).

The Howling Man
A traveler in Europe finds a strange, howling man locked behind a door. Wr: Charles Beaumont, story by Charles Beaumont. Dir: Douglas Heyes.

David Ellington (H.M. Wynant); Brother Jerome (John Carradine); Howling man (Robin Hughes); Christophorus (Frederic Ledebur); Housekeeper (Ezelle Poule).

Eye of the Beholder
In a world of pig-faced humanoids, surgeons try to repair a deformed woman's face. Wr: Rod Serling. Dir: Douglas Heyes.

Janet Tyler (Maxine Stuart); Janet Tyler (unmasked) (Donna Douglas); Doctor (William D. Gordon); Nurse

(Jennifer Howard); Leader (George Keymas); Receptionist (Joanna Heyes); Walter Smith (Edson Stroll).

Memory Flash—Donna Douglas: "I was a newcomer and thrilled to be working on *Twilight Zone*," says the actress best known as Elly-Mae on *The Beverly Hillbillies*. "The episode showed the great efforts that people go to be accepted by others. I had a great admiration for Rod Serling and for his writing ability."

Nick of Time
In a local diner, a young husband becomes obsessed with a fortune-telling device. Wr: Richard Matheson. Dir: Richard L. Bare.
Don Carter (William Shatner); Pat Carter (Patricia Breslin); Counter man (Guy Wilkerson); Mechanic (Stafford Repp); Couple (Walter Reed, Dee Carroll).

The Lateness of the Hour
A woman rebels against her parents' household, where androids cater to their every need. Wr: Rod Serling. Dir: Jack Smight.
Jana (Inger Stevens); Dr. Loren (John Hoyt); Mrs. Loren (Irene Tedrow); Nelda (Mary Gregory); Robert (Tom Palmer); Gretchen (Doris Karnes); Suzanne (Valley Keane); Jensen (Jason Johnson).

The Trouble with Templeton
When a lonely old man escapes back to 1927, he finds his memories of his wife are sweeter than she actually was. Wr: E. Jack Neuman. Dir: Buzz Kulik.
Booth Templeton (Brian Aherne); Laura Templeton (Pippa Scott); Barney Flueger (Charles S. Carlson); Willis (Sydney Pollack); Freddie (Larry Blake); Sid Sperry (King Calder); Marcel (Dave Willock); Ed Page (John Kroger); Eddie (David Thursby).

A Most Unusual Camera
Thieves fight over a camera that takes pictures of the future. Wr: Rod Serling. Dir: John Rich.
Chester Diedrich (Fred Clark); Paula Diedrich (Jean Carson); Woodward (Adam Williams); Waiter (Marcel Hillaire); Tout (Artie Lewis).

Night of the Meek
A drunken department store Santa finds a bag filled with an inexhaustible supply of gifts. Wr: Rod Serling. Dir: Jack Smight.
Henry Corwin (Art Carney); Dundee (John Fiedler); Sister Florence (Meg Wyllie); Burt (Burt Mustin); Flaherty (Robert Lieb); Bartender (Val Avery); Elf (Larrian Gillespie); Woman (Kay Cousins).

Dust
A peddler promises a convicted boy's family that a magic bag of dust will turn hate into forgiveness. Wr: Rod Serling. Dir: Douglas Heyes.
Sheriff Koch (John Larch); Sykes (Thomas Gomez); Gallegos (Vladimir Sokoloff); Luis Gallegos (John Alonso); Canfield (Paul Genge); Estrelita (Andrea Margolis); Mrs. Canfield (Dorothy Adams); Rogers (Duane Grey); Old man (Jon Lormer); Second man (Daniel White); Boy (Douglas Heyes, Jr.).

Back There
Can the past be changed? A man from 1961 asks that question when he's inexplicably transported to 1865, where he tries to stop the assassination of President Lincoln. Wr: Rod Serling. Dir: David Orrick McDearmon.
Peter Corrigan (Russell Johnson); William (Bartlett Robinson); Sergeant (Paul Hartman); Policeman (James Gavin); John Wilkes Booth (John Lassell); Jackson (Raymond Greenleaf); Millard (Raymond Bailey); Lt. (Lew Brown); Woman (Carol Rossen); Patrolman (James Lydon); Whittaker (John Eldredge); Attendant 1865 (Fred Kruger); Mrs. Landers (Jean Innes); Maid (Nora Marlowe); Attendant 1961 (Pat O'Malley).

The Whole Truth
A used car salesman finds that an old Model A car casts a spell on its owners and makes them tell the truth. Wr: Rod Serling. Dir: James Sheldon.
Harvey Hunnicut (Jack Carson); Luther Grimbley (Loring Smith); Irv (Arte Johnson); Nikita Khrushchev (Lee Sabinson); Old man (George Chandler); Man (Jack Ging); Woman (Nan Peterson); Translator (Patrick Woodward).

The Invaders
A woman finds her house has been invaded by tiny spacemen. Wr: Richard Matheson. Dir: Douglas Heyes.
Woman (Agnes Moorehead); Astronaut's voice (Douglas Heyes, Sr.).

A Penny for Your Thoughts
When he knocks a coin on its edge, Hector Poole finds that he can read people's minds. Wr: George Clayton Johnson. Dir: James Sheldon.
Hector B. Poole (Dick York); Miss Turner (June Dayton); Bagby (Dan Tobin); Smithers (Cyril Delevanti); Sykes (Hayden Roarke); Brand (Harry Jackson); Driver (Frank London); Newsboy (Anthony Ray).

Twenty Two
A woman tries to escape from a dream that keeps beckoning her toward a morgue. Wr: Rod Serling, based on a story in *Famous Ghost Stories*, edited by Bennett Cerf. Dir: Jack Smight.
Elizabeth Powell (Barbara Nichols); Doctor (Jonathon Harris); Nurse/Stewardess (Arline Sax); Barney (Fredd Wayne); Night nurse (Norma Connolly); Ticket clerk (Wesley Lau); Day nurse (Mary Adams); Ticket clerk #2 (Joseph Sargent); Voice (Jay Overholts).

The Odyssey of Flight 33
A freak tailwind propels a jet airliner back to the dinosaur age and then to 1939 New York. Wr: Rod Serling. Dir: Justus Addiss.
Capt. Farver (John Anderson); Craig (Paul Comi); Purcell (Harp McGuire); Wyatt (Wayne Heffley); Hatch (Sandy Kenyon); Paula (Nancy Rennick); Jane (Beverly Brown); RAF man (Lester Fletcher); Lady (Betty Garde); Passenger (Jay Overholts).

Memory Flash—Paul Comi: "That was one of my favorite TV episodes. Rod Serling was a marvelous writer and a warm, friendly person. There was a creativeness on everyone's part. That rarely happens in TV today and the results have been disastrous. I don't see much work being done today that will last in years to come."

Mr. Dingle, the Strong
A salesman named Dingle is given superstrength by two Martians. Wr: Rod Serling. Dir: John Brahm.

Luther Dingle (Burgess Meredith); Bettor (Don Rickles); O'Toole (James Westerfield); Callahan (Eddie Ryder); 1st Martian (Doug Spencer); Martian #2 (Michael Fox); Abernathy (James Millhollin); 1st Venusian (Donald Losby); Venusian #2 (Greg Irvin); Boy (Jay Hector); Man (Phil Arnold); Man #2 (Doug Evans); Man #3 (Frank Richards); Nurse (Jo Ann Dixon); Photographer (Bob Duggan).

Static
An old man finds that his radio is picking up live shows from the past. Wr: Charles Beaumont, story by OCee Ritch. Dir: Buzz Kulik.

Ed Lindsay (Dean Jagger); Vinnie Broun (Carmen Mathews); Ackerman (Robert Emhardt); Mrs. Nielsen (Alice Pearce); Roscoe Bragg (Arch Johnson); Boy (Stephen Talbot); Miss Meredith (Lillian O'Malley); Mr. Llewellyn (Pat O'Malley); Junkman (Clegg Hoyt); Singer (Jerry Fuller); Pitchman (Edward Marr); Commercial girl (Diane Strom); DJ (Bob Crane); TV announcer (Roy Rowan); Men (Bob Duggan, Jay Overholts).

The Prime Mover
Ace Larsen takes advantage of his friend, who has the ability to move objects with his mind. Wr: Charles Beaumont, story by George Clayton Johnson. Dir: Richard L. Bare.

Jimbo Cobb (Buddy Ebsen); Ace Larsen (Dane Clark); Kitty Cavanaugh (Christine White); Phil Nolan (Nesdon Booth); Sheila (Jane Burgess); Trucker (Clancy Cooper); Croupier (Joe Scott); Hotel manager (Robert Riordan); Desk clerk (William Keene).

Long Distance Call
A child's parents try to protect their boy from the spirit of his late grandmother. Wr: William Idelson, Charles Beaumont. Dir: James Sheldon.

Chris Bayles (Philip Abbott); Billy Bayles (Billy Mumy); Grandma Bayles (Lila Darvas); Sylvia Bayles (Patricia Smith); Shirley (Jenny Maxwell); Dr. Unger (Henry Hunter); Peterson (Reid Hammond); Attendant (Lew Brown); Firemen (Bob McCord, Jim Turley); Nurse (Jutta Parr).

A Hundred Yards Over the Rim
An 1847 wagonmaster suddenly finds himself in 1961. Wr: Rod Serling. Dir: Buzz Kulik.

Christian Horn (Cliff Robertson); Joe (John Crawford); Mary Lou (Evans Evans); Martha Horn (Miranda Jones); Doctor (Edward C. Platt); Charlie (John Astin); Sheriff (Robert McCord, III).

The Rip Van Winkle Caper
Four gold robbers place themselves in suspended animation and awaken 100 years later. Wr: Rod Serling. Dir: Justus Addiss.

Decruz (Simon Oakland); Farwell (Oscar Beregi); Brooks (Lew Gallo); Erbie (John Mitchum); Man (Wallace Rooney); Woman (Shirley O'Hara).

The Silence
Archie Taylor, a millionaire, makes a deal with a compulsive talker: If the talker can remain silent for one year, Archie will pay him half a million dollars. Wr: Rod Serling. Dir: Boris Sagal.

Archie Taylor (Franchot Tone); Jamie Tennyson (Liam Sullivan); George Alfred (Jonathon Harris); Franklin (Cyril Delevanti); Men (Everett Glass, Felix Locher, John Holland).

Shadow Play
A man scheduled for the electric chair tries to convince the DA that it's all a dream. If he dies, their world will vanish when he awakes. Wr: Charles Beaumont. Dir: John Brahm.

Adam Grant (Dennis Weaver); Henry Ritchie (Harry Townes); Paul Carson (Wright King); Jiggs (Bill Edmondson); Carol Ritchie (Anne Barton); Coley (Bernie Hamilton); Phillips (Tommy Nello); Priest (Mack Williams); Judge (Gene Roth); Attorney (Jack Hyde); Foreman (Howard Culver); Guard (John Close).

The Mind and the Matter
Archie Beechcroft makes everyone in the world disappear. Wr: Rod Serling. Dir: Buzz Kulik.

Archibald Beechcroft (Shelley Berman); Henry (Jack Grinnage); Rogers (Chet Stratton); Landlady (Jeanne Wood).

Will the Real Martian Please Stand Up?
Two policeman track a Martian to a diner, where the creature has assumed human form. Wr: Rod Serling. Dir: Montgomery Pittman.

Ross (John Hoyt); Haley (Barney Phillips); Avery (Jack Elam); Dan Perry (Morgan Jones); Bill Padgett (John Archer); Olmstead (Bill Kendis); Ethel McConnell (Jean Willes); Peter Kramer (Bill Erwin); Rose Kramer (Gertrude Flynn); George Prince (Ron Kipling); Connie Prince (Jill Ellis).

The Obsolete Man
In a future society, Romney Wordsworth is sentenced to die. His last request is to have the cruel chancellor visit his apartment for a chat. Wr: Rod Serling. Dir: Elliot Silverstein.

Romney Wordsworth (Burgess Meredith); Chancellor (Fritz Weaver); Subaltern (Joe Elic); Guard (Harry Fleer); Woman (Jane Romeyn); Men (Barry Brooks, Harold Innocent).

Season 3: 1961-62

Two
The last two people on Earth accidentally meet. Wr and Dir: Montgomery Pittman.

Man (Charles Bronson); Woman (Elizabeth Montgomery).

The Arrival
Authorities are perplexed by the arrival of an

airplane without crew or passengers, until FAA investigator Sheckly comes up with a chilling theory. Wr: Rod Serling. Dir: Boris Sagal.

Grant Sheckly (Harold J. Stone); Paul Malloy (Fredd Wayne); Bengston (Noah Keen); Official (Robert Karnes); Attendant (Bing Russell); Tower Operator (Robert Brubaker); Dispatcher (Jim Boles).

The Shelter

When nuclear war looks imminent, Dr. Stockton and his family find themselves besieged by terrified neighbors who want to use their bomb shelter. Wr: Rod Serling. Dir: Lamont Johnson.

Dr. Stockton (Larry Gates); Grace Stockton (Peggy Stewart); Jerry Harlowe (Jack Albertson); Marty Weiss (Joseph Bernard); Henderson (Sandy Kenyon); Paul Stockton (Michael Burns); Mrs. Henderson (Mary Gregory); Neighbor (John McLiam); Mrs. Harlowe (Jo Helton); Mrs. Weiss (Moira Turner).

The Passerby

Lavinia Godwin discovers that the Civil War soldiers walking past her mansion are dead. Wr: Rod Serling. Dir: Elliot Silverstein.

Lavinia Godwin (Joanne Linville); Sergeant (James Gregory); Charlie (Rex Holman); Abe Lincoln (Austin Green); Lt. (David Garcia); Jud (Warren Kemmerling).

A Game of Pool

Jesse Cardiff gets his wish to play a game of pool with the late Fats Brown. Wr: George Clayton Johnson. Dir: Buzz Kulik.

Jesse Cardiff (Jack Klugman); Fats Brown (Jonathan Winters).

The Mirror

Dictator Ramos Clemente finds a mirror that reveals his enemies. Wr: Rod Serling. Dir: Don Medford.

Ramos Clemente (Peter Falk); DeCruz (Will Kuluva); Tabal (Arthur Batanides); Cristo (Tony Carbone); D'Allesandro (Richard Karlan); Priest (Vladimir Sokoloff); Garcia (Rodolfo Hoyos); Guard (Val Ruffino); Voices (Robert McCord, III, Jim Turley).

Memory Flash—Arthur Batanides: "Peter Falk's character was based loosely on Fidel Castro. It was at the height of the Cuban Missile Crisis. At one point, we all had to leave the studio dressed in our Latin American outfits. Since there was a lot of anti–Castro bias at the time, we felt insecure walking around the streets in these uniforms. It was definitely not the time to be running around looking like one of Castro's men. I thought somebody might run us down!"

The Grave

A gunfighter visits the grave of a man whom he killed—and who promised to get even. Wr and Dir: Montgomery Pittman.

Conny Miller (Lee Marvin); Mothershed (Strother Martin); Johnny Rob (James Best); Ilone (Ellen Willard); Steinhart (Lee Van Cleef); Ira Broadly (Stafford Repp); Jasen (William Challee); Corcoran (Larry Johns); Pinto Sykes (Richard Geary).

It's a Good Life

The townspeople of Peaksville are terrorized by a six-year-old boy who can destroy with his thoughts. Wr: Rod Serling, story by Jerome Bixby. Dir: James Sheldon.

Fremont (John Larch); Mrs. Fremont (Cloris Leachman); Anthony Fremont (Billy Mumy); Dan Hollis (Don Keefer); Aunt Amy (Alice Frost); Ethel Hollis (Jeanne Bates); Pat Riley (Casey Adams); Bill Soames (Tom Hatcher); Thelma Dunn (Lenore Kingston).

Death's Head Revisited

Capt. Lutze returns to a concentration camp, where he finds the ghosts of his victims. Wr: Rod Serling. Dir: Don Medford.

Capt. Lutze (Oscar Beregi); Becker (Joseph Schildkraut); Innkeeper (Kaaren Verne); Doctor (Ben Wright); Cabbie (Robert Boone); Prisoner (Chuck Fox).

The Midnight Sun

People struggle against boiling temperatures as the Earth careens into the sun. Wr: Rod Serling. Dir: Tony Leader.

Norma (Lois Nettleton); Mrs. Bronson (Betty Garde); Burglar (Tom Reese); Husband (Jason Wingreen); Wife (June Ellis); Repairman (Ned Glass); Policeman (John McLiam); Doctor (William Keene); Announcer (Robert J. Stevenson).

Still Valley

After finding a group of Union soldiers frozen in time, a Confederate scout learns that a book of black magic can win the war for his side. Wr: Rod Serling, story by Manly Wade Wellman. Dir: James Sheldon.

Paradine (Gary Merrill); Dauger (Ben Cooper); Old man (Vaughn Taylor); Lt. (Mark Tapscott); Sentry (Addison Myers); Mallory (Jack Mann).

The Jungle

Witch doctors place a curse on an engineer after he builds a dam in Africa. Upon his return to New York, he finds himself stalked by sinister forces. Wr: Charles Beaumont. Story; Charles Beaumont. Dir: William Claxton.

Alan Richards (John Dehner); Doris Richards (Emily McLaughlin); Chad Cooper (Walter Brooke); Templeton (Hugh Sanders); Hardy (Howard Wright); Sinclair (Donald Foster); Cabbie (Jay Overholts); Tramp (Jay Adler).

Once Upon a Time

Comic episode about a janitor from 1890 who uses a time helmet to travel to 1962. Wr: Richard Matheson. Dir: Norman Z. McLeod.

Woodrow Mulligan (Buster Keaton); Rollo (Stanley Adams); Repairman (Jesse White); Gilbert (Milton Parsons); Store manager (Warren Parker); Cop (1890) (Gil Lamb); Cops (1962) (James Flavin, Harry Fleer); Fenwick (George E. Stone).

Five Characters in Search of an Exit

A major and four eccentric characters try to escape from a mysterious giant drum. Wr: Rod Serling, story by Marvin Petal. Dir: Lamont Johnson.

Major (William Windom); Clown (Murray Matheson); Ballerina (Susan Harrison); Tramp (Kelton Garwood); Bagpipe player (Clark Allen); Girl (Mona Houghton); Woman (Carol Hill).

A Quality of Mercy

Lt. Katell is prepared to kill trapped Japanese soldiers during World War II. Suddenly he's transformed into a Japanese officer and is ordered to kill trapped American soldiers. Wr: Rod Serling, idea by Sam Rolfe. Dir: Buzz Kulik.

Lt. Katell/Yamuri (Dean Stockwell); Causarano (Albert Salmi); Japanese officer (Jerry Fujikawa); Watkins (Rayford Barnes); Hansen (Leonard Nimoy); Japanese soldier (Dale Ishimoto); Hanacheck (Ralph Votrain); Driver (Michael Pataki).

Nothing in the Dark

Elderly Wanda Duncan lets a wounded policeman into her apartment, but she fears that he's really Mr. Death in human form. Wr: George Clayton Johnson. Dir: Lamont Johnson.

Wanda Dunn (Gladys Cooper); Harold Beldon (Robert Redford); Contractor (R.G. Armstrong).

Memory Flash—Robert Redford: "It was one of those shows where everything went smoothly. Everyone loved each other, the feelings were good and we knew we had a good script. I thoroughly enjoyed the experience. Only thing was, I had no idea it would end up being such a classic."

One More Pallbearer

Paul Radin confines three of his enemies in a bomb shelter and tries to convince them that there's been a nuclear war. Wr: Rod Serling. Dir: Lamont Johnson.

Paul Radin (Joseph Wiseman); Huges (Gage Clark); Mrs. Langford (Katherine Squire); Hawthorne (Trevor Bardette); Policeman (Ray Galvin); Electricians (Joseph Elic, Robert Snyder).

Dead Men's Shoes

A derelict puts on a murdered gangster's shoes and becomes possessed by the man's vengeful spirit. Wr: Charles Beaumont, OCee Ritch. Dir: Montgomery Pittman.

Nate Bledsoe (Warren Stevens); Wilma (Joan Marshall); Dagget (Richard Devon); Girlfriend (Florence Marly); Chips (Ben Wright); Sam (Harry Swoger); Maitre d' (Gene Borden); Ben (Ron Hagerthy); Jimmy (Joe Mell).

The Hunt

Killed in an accident, a hillbilly and his dog, Rip, find something amiss when the gatekeeper at Heaven's doors won't allow the dog to enter. Wr: Earl Hamner, Jr. Dir: Harold Schuster.

Hyder Simpson (Arthur Hunnicut); Rachel Simpson (Jeanette Nolan); Gatekeeper (Robert Foulk); Wesley Miller (Titus Moede); Tillman Miller (Orville Sherman); Rev. Wood (Charles Seel); Messenger (Dexter Dupont).

Showdown with Rance McGrew

An arrogant actor finds himself in the real Old West where Jesse James is not happy about the way he's been depicted on TV. Wr: Rod Serling, story by Frederic Louis Fox. Dir: Christian Nyby.

Rance McGrew (Larry Blyden); Jesse James (Arch Johnson); Director (Robert Cornthwaite); Jesse James (TV) (Robert Kline); Property man (Bill McLean); Bartender (Robert J. Stevenson); Old man (Hal K. Dawson); Cowboys (Troy Melton, Jay Overholts); Rance's double (Jim Turley).

Kick the Can

Placed in an old folks' home, Charles Whitley discovers that by acting young, he becomes young. Wr: George Clayton Johnson. Dir: Lamont Johnson.

Charles Whitley (Ernest Truex); Mr. Cox (John Marley); Ben Conroy (Russell Collins); Carlson (Burt Mustin); Mrs. Summers (Marjorie Bennett); David Whitley (David Truex); Frietag (Hank Patterson); Mrs. Wister (Anne O'Neal); Agee (Earle Hodgins); Mrs. Densley (Lenore Shanewise); Nurse (Eve McVeagh); Boys (Gregory McCabe, Marc Stevens).

A Piano in the House

A cynical theater critic buys a piano that makes people reveal their true selves. Wr: Earl Hamner, Jr. Dir: David Greene.

Fitzgerald Fortune (Barry Morse); Esther Fortune (Joan Hackett); Greg Walker (Don Durant); Marvin (Cyril Delevanti); Marge Moore (Muriel Landers); Throckmorton (Phil Coolidge).

The Last Rites of Jeff Myrtlebank

When Jeff Myrtlebank sits up at his own funeral, terrified townspeople believe that the young man is possessed. Wr and Dir: Montgomery Pittman.

Jeff Myrtlebank (James Best); Comfort Gatewood (Sherry Jackson); Dr. Bolton (Edgar Buchanan); Peters (Dub Taylor); Orgram Gatewood (Lance Fuller); Mr. Myrtlebank (Ralph Moody); Mrs. Myrtlebank (Ezelle Poule); Mrs. Gatewood (Helen Wallace); Liz Myrtlebank (Vickie Barnes); Rev. Siddons (William Fawcett); Strauss (Jon Lormer); Mrs. Ferguson (Mabel Forrest); Tom (Pat Hector); Jerry (James Houghton).

To Serve Man

Nine-foot space creatures called Kanamits arrive and profess peace. A scientist thinks they're here for a more sinister purpose. Wr: Rod Serling, story by Damon Knight. Dir: Richard L. Bare.

Michael Chambers (Lloyd Bochner); Pat (Susan Cummings); Kanamit (Richard Kiel); Gregori (Theodore Marcuse); Reporters (Will J. White, Gene Benton); Colonels (Bartlett Robinson, Carlton Young); General (Hardie Albright); Valdes (Robert Tafur); Leveque (Lomax Study); Scientist (Nelson Olmstead); Men (James Wellman, Charles Tannen); Women (Adrienne Marden, Jeanne Evans).

The Fugitive

A crippled young girl befriends a reluctant king from another planet. Wr: Charles Beaumont. Dir: Richard L. Bare.

Jenny (Susan Gordon); Old Ben (J. Pat O'Malley); Mrs. Gann (Nancy Kulp); Aliens (Wesley Lau, Paul Tripp); Howie (Stephen Talbot); Pitcher (Johnny Eiman); Doctor (Russ Bender).

Little Girl Lost

Desperate parents try to locate their young daughter, who has tumbled into another dimension. Wr: Richard Matheson, story by Richard Matheson. Dir: Paul Stewart.

Bill (Charles Aidman); Chris Miller (Robert Sampson); Ruth Miller (Sarah Marshall); Tina (Tracy Stratford); Tina's voice (Rhoda Williams).

Person or Persons Unknown

Imagine that you awaken one morning and no one knows who you are. That's David Gurney's problem as he retraces his life in an effort to prove his existence. Wr: Charles Beaumont. Dir: John Brahm.

David Gurney (Richard Long); Dr. Koslenko (Frank Silvera); Wilma (Shirley Ballard); Wilma #2 (Julie Van Zandt); Clerk (Betty Harford); Sam Baker (Ed Glover); Policeman (Michael Keep); Bank guard (Joe Higgens); Cooper (John Newton).

The Little People

Two astronauts are repairing their spaceship on a strange world when one of the men finds a city of little people. Wr: Rod Serling. Dir: William Claxton.

Peter Craig (Joe Maross); William Fletcher (Claude Akins); Spacemen (Michael Ford, Robert Eaton).

Four o' Clock

A man uses magic powers to shrink every evil person to the size of two feet. Wr: Rod Serling, story by Price Day. Dir: Lamont Johnson.

Oliver Crangle (Theodore Bikel); Mrs. Williams (Moyna MacGill); Mrs. Lucas (Phyllis Love); Hall (Linden Chiles).

Hocus Pocus and Frisby

A spinner of tall tales is taken aboard a spacecraft by aliens who can't comprehend the concept of lying. Wr: Rod Serling, story by Frederic Louis Fox. Dir: Lamont Johnson.

Frisby (Andy Devine); Aliens (Milton Selzer, Larry Breitman, Peter Brocco); Mitchell (Howard McNear); Scanlan (Dabbs Greer); Old man (Clem Bevans).

The Trade-Ins

An elderly couple plan to transfer their personalities into the bodies of youthful-looking androids, but they find they have enough money for only one transfer. Wr: Rod Serling. Dir: Elliot Silverstein.

John Holt (Joseph Schildkraut); Marie Holt (Alma Platt); Vance (Noah Keen); Farrady (Theodore Marcuse); Android (Edson Stroll); Gamblers (Terence de Marney, Billy Vincent); Receptionist (Mary McMahon); Attendant (David Armstrong).

The Gift

A Mexican orphan befriends an alien who has come to Earth with a gift of peace but whose actions have been misinterpreted as hostile. Wr: Rod Serling. Dir: Allen H. Miner.

Williams (Geoffrey Horne); Doctor (Nico Minardos); Pedro (Edmund Vargas); Manuelo (Cliff Osmond); Officer (Paul Mazursky); Guitarist (Vladimir Sokoloff); Rudolpho (Vito Scotti); Sanchez (Henry Corden); Women (Carmen D'Antonio, Lea Marmer); Men (Joseph Perry, David Fresco).

The Dummy

Ventriloquist Jerry Etherson becomes terrified of his sinister dummy, who has come to life. Wr: Rod Serling, story by Lee Polk. Dir: Abner Biberman.

Jerry Etherson (Cliff Robertson); Frank (Frank Sutton); Willie (George Murdock); Georgie (John Harmon); Noreen (Sandra Warner); M.C. (Rudy Dolan); Doorman (Ralph Manza); Chorus girls (Edy Williams, Bethelynn Grey).

A Young Man's Fancy

A woman finds that her husband is being drawn back to his childhood by the spirit of his dominating mother. Wr: Richard Matheson. Dir: John Brahm.

Virginia Walker (Phyllis Thaxter); Alex Walker (Alex Nicol); Wilkinson (Wallace Rooney); Mother (Helen Brown); Young Alex (Rickey Kelman).

I Sing the Body Electric

A widower purchases a robotic grandmother to care for his three children, but young Anne refuses to accept the robot. Wr: Ray Bradbury, story by Ray Bradbury. Dir: James Sheldon and William Claxton.

Grandma (Josephine Hutchinson); Anne (Veronica Cartwright); Father (David White); Karen (Dana Dillaway); Tom (Charles Herbert); Salesman (Vaughn Taylor); Nedra (Doris Packer); Adult Anne (Susan Crane); Adult Karen (Judy Morton); Adult Tom (Paul Nesbitt).

Cavender Is Coming

A comedy episode with a laughtrack: A bumbling angel tries to help an unemployed woman by rearranging her life. Wr: Rod Serling. Dir: Chris Nyby.

Agnes Grep (Carol Burnett); Cavender (Jesse White); Polk (Howard Smith); Field reps (William O'Connell, Pitt Herbert, John Fiedler, G. Stanley Jones); Stout (Frank Behrens); Frenchman (Albert Carrier); Bus driver (Roy Sickner); Girl (Norma Shattuc); Boy (Rory O'Brien); Women (Sandra Gould, Donna Douglas, Adrienne Marden); Truck driver (Jack Younger); Child (Danny Kulick); Man (Maurice Dallimore); Older woman (Barbara Morrison).

Changing of the Guard

Professor Fowler is forced to retire during Christmas, but his spirits are revived by the ghosts of his former students. Wr: Rod Serling. Dir: Robert Ellis Miller.

Prof. Ellis Fowler (Donald Pleasence); Headmaster (Liam Sullivan); Mrs. Landers (Philippa Bevans); Graham (Robert Biheller); Butler (Kevin O'Neal); Students (Jimmy Baird, Kevin Jones, Tom Lowell, Pat Close, Russell Horton, Buddy Hart, Darryl Richard, James Browning, Dennis Kerlee).

Season 4: 1962-63

In His Image

A malfunctioning android searches for his creator.

Wr: Charles Beaumont, story by Charles Beaumont. Dir: Perry Lafferty.

Alan Talbot/Walter Ryder (George Grizzard); Jessica Connelly (Gail Kobe); Sheriff (James Seay); Woman (Katherine Squire); Man (Wallace Rooney); Girl (Sherry Granato); Driver (George Petrie); Hotel clerk (Jamie Forster).

The Thirty Fathom Grave

A Navy destroyer finds a sunken American submarine from World War II. Something inside is tapping on the hull with a hammer. Wr: Rod Serling. Dir: Perry Lafferty.

Bell (Mike Kellin); Beecham (Simon Oakland); Doc (David Sheiner); McClure (John Considine); O.O.D. (Bill Bixby); Lee Helmsman (Anthony Call); Helmsman (Derrick Lewis); Marmer (Conlan Carter); Officer (Forrest Compton); Sonar (Charles Kuenstle); Jr. O.O.D. (Henry Scott); Sailors (Vincent Bagetta, Lou Elias).

Valley of the Shadow

A stranded newsman discovers a town where the inhabitants were given enormous power by an alien 100 years ago. Wr: Charles Beaumont. Dir: Perry Lafferty.

Philip Redfield (Ed Nelson); Ellen Marshall (Natalie Trundy); Dorn (David Opatoshu); Evans (Dabbs Greer); Father (James Doohan); Girl (Suzanne Cupito); Connelly (Jacques Aubuchon); Gas attendant (Sandy Kenyon); Men (Henry Beckman, Bart Burns, King Calder, Pat O'Hara).

He's Alive

A neo–Nazi begins to sway people when he's assisted by a shadowy creature that turns out to be Adolph Hitler. Wr: Rod Serling. Dir: Stuart Rosenberg.

Peter Vollmer (Dennis Hopper); Ernst Ganz (Ludwig Donath); Hitler (Curt Conway); Nick (Howard Caine); Frank (Paul Mazursky); Stanley (Barnaby Hale); Heckler (Bernard Fein); Gibbons (Jay Adler); Proprietor (Wolfe Barzell).

Mute

A child who can only communicate through telepathy is adopted by a couple who try to integrate the girl into society. Wr: Richard Matheson, story by Richard Matheson. Dir: Stuart Rosenberg.

Ilse Nielsen (Ann Jillian); Harry Wheeler (Frank Overton); Cora Wheeler (Barbara Baxley); Miss Frank (Irene Daily); Karl Werner (Oscar Beregi); Frau Nielsen (Claudia Bryar); Holger Nielsen (Robert Boon); Frau Maria Werner (Eva Soreny); Tom Poulter (Percy Helton).

Death Ship

Three astronauts see a vision of their deaths on an alien planet, and try to change their future. Wr: Richard Matheson, story by Richard Matheson. Dir: Don Medford.

Paul Ross (Jack Klugman); Ted Mason (Ross Martin); Mike Carter (Fred Beir); Ruth (Mary Webster); Kramer (Ross Elliot); Jeannie (Tammy Marihugh); Mrs. Nolan (Sara Taft).

Jess-Belle

A young man struggles to free himself from an enticing witch's power. Wr: Earl Hamner, Jr. Dir: Buzz Kulik.

Jess-Belle (Anne Francis); Billy-Ben Turner (James Best); Ellwyn Glover (Laura Devon); Granny Hart (Jeanette Nolan); Ossie Stone (Virginia Gregg); Luther Glover (George Mitchell); Mattie Glover (Helen Kleeb); Obed Miller (Jim Boles); Minister (Jon Lormer).

Miniature

Charley Parkes develops a friendship with a beautiful miniature doll that has come to life. Wr: Charles Beaumont. Dir: Walter E. Grauman.

Charley Parkes (Robert Duvall); The Doll (Claire Griswold); Myrna (Barbara Barrie); Dr. Wallman (William Windom); Mrs. Parkes (Pert Kelton); Buddie (Lenny Weinrib); Guard (John McLiam); Maid (Nina Roman); Diemel (Barney Phillips); Suitor (Richard Angarola); Harriet (Joan Chambers); Guide (Chet Stratton).

Printer's Devil

A sinister man writes headlines that predict the future. Wr: Charles Beaumont, story by Charles Beaumont. Dir: Ralph Senensky.

Smith (Burgess Meredith); Doug Winter (Robert Sterling); Jackie Benson (Patricia Crowley); Franklin (Ray Teal); Andy Praskins (Charles Thompson); Landlady (Doris Kemper); Molly (Camille Franklin).

No Time Like the Past

A scientist uses a time machine to go back in time and change terrible events in history. Wr: Rod Serling. Dir: Justus Addiss.

Paul Driscoll (Dana Andrews); Abigail Sloan (Patricia Breslin); Harvey (Robert F. Simon); Prof. Eliot (Malcolm Atterbury); Hanford (Robert Cornthwaite); Hornplayer (John Zaremba); Captain (James Yagi); Lusitania Capt. (Tudor Owen); Bartender (Lindsay Workman); Mrs. Chamberlain (Marjorie Bennett).

The Parallel

An astronaut passes through a space warp and awakens on a mirror-image of Earth. Wr: Rod Serling. Dir: Alan Crosland, Jr.

Robert Gaines (Steve Forrest); Helen Gaines (Jacqueline Scott); Eaton (Philip Abbott); Connacher (Frank Aletter); Psychiatrist (Paul Comi); Project manager (William Sargent); Maggie Gaines (Shari Lee Bernath); Captain (Morgan Jones).

I Dream of Genie

An ordinary man discovers a modern genie who grants his wishes to attain wealth and power. Wr: John Furia, Jr. Dir: Robert Gist.

George P. Hanley (Howard Morris); Genie (Jack Albertson); Ann (Patricia Barry); Roger (Mark Miller); Actress (Joyce Jameson); Sam (Bob Hastings); Watson (Loring Smith); Masters (James Millhollin); Clerk (Robert Ball).

The New Exhibit

A museum employee learns the wax figures of infamous killers have started their own killing spree. Wr: Jerry Sohl, story by Charles Beaumont, Jerry Sohl. Dir: John Brahm.

Martin L. Senescu (Martin Balsam); Emma Senescu

(Maggie Mahoney); Ferguson (Will Kuluva); Dave (William Mims); Henri Landru (Milton Parsons); Jack the Ripper (David Bond); Albert Hicks (Bob Mitchell); Burke (Robert L. McCord); Hare (Billy Beck); Gas man (Phil Chambers); Guide (Marcel Hillaire); Van driver (Lennie Breman); Sailors (Ed Barth, Craig Curtis).

Of Late I Think of Cliffordville

An old businessman travels back to 1910 to acquire a new fortune, with the help of a demon named Miss Devlin. Wr: Rod Serling, story by Malcolm Jameson. Dir: David Lowell Rich.

Bill Feathersmith (Albert Salmi); Miss Devlin (Julie Newmar); Deidrich (John Anderson); Hecate (Wright King); Gibbons (Guy Raymond); Joanna (Christine Burke); Clark (John Harmon); Cronk (Hugh Sanders).

The Incredible World of Horace Ford

A man returns to his childhood and finds it was not the happy time that he recalled. Wr: Reginald Rose. Dir: Abner Biberman.

Horace Ford (Pat Hingle); Laura Ford (Nan Martin); Mrs. Ford (Ruth White); Leonard O'Brien (Phillip Pine); Betty O'Brien (Mary Carver); Judson (Vaughn Taylor); Young Horace (Jim E. Titus); Hermy Brandt (Jerry Davis).

On Thursday We Leave for Home

Benteen has kept a stranded group of colonists alive on an asteroid for 30 years. When a rescue ship arrives, he tries to keep his control over the people. Wr: Rod Serling. Dir: Buzz Kulik.

William Benteen (James Whitmore); Col. Sloane (Tim O'Connor); Al (James Broderick); George (Paul Langton); Julie (Jo Helton); Joan (Mercedes Shirley); Engle (Lew Gallo); Jo Jo (Daniel Kulick); Hank (Russ Bender); Colonists (Shirley O'Hara, Madge Kennedy, John Ward, Anthony Benson).

Memory Flash—Tim O'Connor: "Jim Whitmore was nice to work with. We all worked long hours on that show. The mountain set for the asteroid was fantastic. The amount of money MGM spent to build it was extraordinary. It stood three stories high. When I did another show at MGM five years later, the damn mountain was still there! They rented it out to various productions to get their money back on it."

Passage on the Lady Anne

A troubled couple book a trip on a boat to England and find their shipmates are mysterious older couples. Wr: Charles Beaumont, story by Charles Beaumont. Dir: Lamont Johnson.

Allan Ransome (Lee Philips); Eileen Ransome (Joyce Van Patten); Mckenzie (Wilfrid Hyde-White); Millie McKenzie (Gladys Cooper); Burgess (Cecil Kellaway); Capt. Protheroe (Alan Napier); Spiereto (Don Keefer); Officer (Cyril Delevanti).

The Bard

A writer summons up William Shakespeare to help him write a TV show. Wr: Rod Serling. Dir: David Butler.

Julius Moomer (Jack Weston); Shakespeare (John Williams); Shannon (John McGiver); Rocky Rhodes (Burt Reynolds); Cora (Judy Strangis); Gerald Huge (Henry Lascoe); Branhoff (Howard McNear); Secretary (Marge Redmond); Bus driver (Clegg Hoyt); Sadie (Doro Merande); Dolan (William Lanteau).

Season 5: 1963-64

In Praise of Pip

With his son Pip dying in Vietnam, Max Phillips finds an amusement park and Pip as a young boy. Wr: Rod Serling. Dir: Joseph Newman.

Max Phillips (Jack Klugman); Pip (Billy Mumy); Adult Pip (Robert Diamond); Mrs. Feeny (Connie Gilchrist); Moran (John Launer); George Reynold (Russell Horton); Doctor (Ross Elliot); Surgeon (Stuart Nisbet); Lt. (Gerald Gordon); Guman (Kreg Martin).

Steel

In 1974, where boxers are robots, Max Steel pretends to be an android to battle a super-robot. Wr: Richard Matheson, story by Richard Matheson. Dir: Don Weis.

Steel Kelly (Lee Marvin); Pole (Joe Mantell); Maynard Flash (Chuck Hicks); Battling Maxo (Tipp McClure); Nolan (Merritt Bohn); Maxwell (Frank London); Voice (Larry Barton).

Nightmare at 20,000 Feet

An airplane passenger can't convince anyone that a gremlin is tearing apart the plane's wing. Wr: Richard Matheson, story by Richard Matheson. Dir: Richard Donner.

Bob Wilson (William Shatner); Ruth Wilson (Christine White); Engineer (Edward Kemmer); Stewardess (Asa Maynor); Creature (Nick Cravat).

A Kind of a Stop Watch

A man robs a bank after getting a stop watch that freezes people in their tracks. Wr: Rod Serling, story by Michael D. Rosenthal. Dir: John Rich.

Patrick T. McNulty (Richard Erdman); Potts (Leon Belasco); Cooper (Roy Roberts); Joe (Herbie Faye); Secretary (Doris Singleton); Attendant (Ray Kellogg); Announcer (Sam Balter); Charlie (Richard Wessel); Man (Ken Drake).

The Last Night of a Jockey

An ex-racing jockey gets his wish to be ten feet tall. Wr: Rod Serling. Dir: Joseph M. Newman.

Grady (Mickey Rooney).

Living Doll

A man battles for his life against his daughter's evil, living doll. Wr: Jerry Sohl, story by Charles Beaumont, Jerry Sohl. Dir: Richard C. Sarafian.

Erich Streator (Telly Savalas); Annabelle Streator (Mary La Roche); Christie Streator (Tracy Stratford); Talky Tina's voice (June Foray).

Old Man in the Cave

Townspeople obey an unseen man in the cave, but renegade soldiers plan to expose the mysterious man. Wr: Rod Serling, story by Henry Slesar. Dir: Alan Crosland, Jr.

Goldsmith (John Anderson); French (James Coburn); Jason (John Marley); Evelyn (Josie Lloyd); Harber (Frank Watkins); Douglas (Lenny Geer); Furman (Don Wilbanks); Townspeople (Natalie Masters, John Craven).

Uncle Simon
A woman is glad to be rid of her uncle, but his pet robot has taken on the dead man's mannerisms. Wr: Rod Serling. Dir: Don Siegel.

Uncle Simon Polk (Sir Cedric Hardwicke); Barbara Polk (Constance Ford); Schwimmer (Ian Wolfe); Policeman (John McLiam); Robot (Dion Hansen).

Probe 7, Over and Out
Stranded on a beautiful planet, an astronaut meets a strange, mute woman. Wr: Rod Serling. Dir: Ted Post.

Col. Adam Cook (Richard Basehart); Eve Norda (Antoinette Bower); Larrabee (Harold Gould); Blane (Barton Heyman).

The 7th Is Made Up of Phantoms
Three army officers are transported back to 1876, where they try to change the outcome of the battle between Gen. Custer and the Indians at the Little Big Horn. Wr: Rod Serling. Dir: Alan Crosland, Jr.

Conners (Ron Foster); Langsford (Warren Oates); McCluskey (Randy Boone); Captain (Robert Bray); Lt. (Greg Morris); Scout (Wayne Mallory); Sergeant (Lew Brown); Corporal (Jacque Shelton); Radioman (Jeffrey Morris).

A Short Drink from a Certain Fountain
An experimental youth drug threatens to return an old man to infancy. Wr: Rod Serling, idea by Lou Holtz. Dir: Bernard Girard.

Harmon Gordon (Patrick O'Neal); Flora Gordon (Ruta Lee); Dr. Raymond Gordon (Walter Brooke).

Ninety Years Without Slumbering
Sam Forstmann desperately keeps his grandfather clock running. He believes that if it stops, he will die. Wr: Richard deRoy, story by George Clayton Johnson. Dir: Roger Kay.

Sam Forstmann (Ed Wynn); Marnie Kirk (Carolyn Kearney); Doug Kirk (James Callahan); Mel Avery (William Sargent); Carol Chase (Carol Byron); Policeman (John Pickard); Movers (Dick Wilson, Chuck Hicks).

Ring a Ding Girl
A movie star hides a chilling motivation when she demands that people see her put on a show. Wr: Earl Hamner, Jr. Dir: Alan Crosland, Jr.

Bunny Blake (Maggie McNamara); Hildy Powell (Mary Munday); Bud Powell (David Macklin); Ben Braden (Bing Russell); Gentry (Hank Patterson); Trooper (Vic Perrin); Floyd (George Mitchell); Cci (Betty Lou Gerson); Pilot (Bill Hickman).

You Drive
After he kills a newsboy in a hit-and-run accident, Oliver Pope is pursued by his own car. Wr: Earl Hamner, Jr. Dir: John Brahm.

Oliver Pope (Edward Andrews); Pete Radcliff (Kevin Hagen); Lillian Pope (Hellena Westcott); Policeman (John Hanek); Woman (Totty Ames).

The Long Morrow
Placed in suspended animation for a space voyage, an astronaut realizes his girlfriend on Earth will be an old woman by the time he returns. Wr: Rod Serling. Dir: Robert Florey.

Doug Stansfield (Robert Lansing); Sandra Horn (Mariette Hartley); Dr. Bixler (George MacReady); Gen. Walters (Edward Binns); Technicians (Donald Spruance, William Swan).

The Self Improvement of Salvadore Ross
A man tries to win a woman's heart by using his ability to exchange physical characteristics with other people. Wr: Jerry McNeely, story by Henry Slesar. Dir: Don Siegel.

Salvadore Ross (Don Gordon); Leah Maitland (Gail Kobe); Maitland (Vaughn Taylor); Old man (J. Pat O'Malley); Albert (Doug Lambert); Halpert (Douglass Dumbrille); Jerry (Seymour Cassell); Bartender (Ted Jacques); Nurse (Kathleen O'Malley).

Number Twelve Looks Just Like You
A rebellious teenage girl refuses to be transformed into a ravishing beauty. Wr: John Tomerlin and Charles Beaumont. Dir: Abner Biberman.

Marilyn Cuberle (Collin Wilcox); Lana Cuberle (Suzy Parker); Dr. Rex (Richard Long); New Marilyn (Pamela Austin).

Black Leather Jackets
Three toughs on motorbikes invade a neighborhood. They're actually aliens who plan to poison Earth's water supply. Wr: Earl Hamner, Jr. Dir: Joseph M. Newman.

Ellen Tillman (Shelley Fabares); Scott (Lee Kinsolving); Steve (Michael Forest); Sheriff Harper (Michael Conrad); Stu Tillman (Denver Pyle); Martha Tillman (Irene Hervey); Fred (Tom Gilleran); Mover (Wayne Heffley).

Night Call
An old woman receives phone calls from her dead fiance when a phone line falls atop his grave. Wr: Richard Matheson, story by Richard Matheson. Dir: Jacques Tourneur.

Elva Keene (Gladys Cooper); Margaret Phillips (Nora Marlowe); Miss Finch (Martine Bartlett).

From Agnes, with Love
A shy computer programmer uses a computer's advice to fetch his dream girl, but the computer has a crush on him. Wr: Bernard C. Shoenfeld. Dir: Richard Donner.

James Elwood (Wally Cox); Millie (Sue Randall); Walter Holmes (Ralph Taeger); Supervisor (Raymond Bailey); Fred Danziger (Don Keefer); Secretary (Nan Peterson); Assistant (Byron Kane).

Spur of the Moment
Anne Henderson's marriage plans are marred by the appearance of a ghoulish woman on horseback. Wr: Richard Matheson. Dir: Elliot Silverstein.

Anne Henderson (Diana Hyland); Robert Blake (Robert Hogan); David Mitchell (Roger Davis); Mrs. Henderson (Marsha Hunt); Henderson (Philip Ober); Reynolds (Jack Raine).

An Occurrence at Owl Creek Bridge
A French film short-aired under the *Twilight Zone* mantle. A Civil War spy being hanged from a bridge seems to escape death when his noose breaks. He makes a desperate trip through the forest to reach his wife. Wr and Dir: Robert Enrico, story by Ambrose Bierce.

Confederate spy (Roger Jacquet); Wife (Anne Cornaly); Also with Anker Larsen, Stephane Fey, Jean-François Zeller, Pierre Danny, Louis Adelin.

Queen of the Nile
A reporter suspects a movie star is the immortal Queen of the Nile. She keeps her youth by draining it from others. Wr: Jerry Sohl, Charles Beaumont. Dir: John Brahm.

Pamela Morris (Ann Blyth); Jordan Herrick (Lee Philips); Viola Draper (Celia Lovsky); Krueger (Frank Ferguson); Jackson (James Tyler); Maid (Ruth Phillips).

What's in the Box?
Joe Britt tries to prevent the murder of his wife after he sees himself on TV as the killer. Wr: Martin M. Goldsmith. Dir: Richard L. Bare.

Joe Britt (William Demarest); Phyllis Britt (Joan Blondell); Repairman (Sterling Holloway); Saltman (Herbert Lytton); Woman (Sandra Gould); Judge (Howard Wright); Duke (John Sullivan); Panther man (Ted Christy); Salesman (Ron Stokes); Prosecutor (Douglas Bank); Announcer (Tony Miller).

The Masks
An old man tells his selfish heirs that they will inherit his riches if they'll wear monster masks until midnight. Wr: Rod Serling. Dir: Ida Lupino.

Jason Foster (Robert Keith); Wilfred Harper (Milton Selzer); Paula Harper (Brooke Hayward); Emily Harper (Virginia Gregg); Wilfred, Jr. (Alan Sues); Doctor (Willis Bouchy); Butler (Bill Walker).

I Am the Night—Color Me Black
A strange darkness pervades a small town on the eve of a murderer's execution. Wr: Rod Serling. Dir: Abner Biberman.

Sheriff Charlie Koch (Michael Constantine); Colbey (Paul Fix); Jagger (Terry Becker); Pierce (George Lindsay); Rev. Anderson (Ivan Dixon); Ella Koch (Eve McVeagh); Woman (Elizabeth Harrower); Townspeople (Douglas Bank, Ward Wood).

Memory Flashes—Michael Constantine, Terry Becker and George Lindsay: "I was pleased and surprised to see Rod Serling actually come down to the set and do his opening lines," recalls Constantine. "He had them all memorized. No teleprompters. A real professional. I admired him very much."

Says Lindsay, "I wanted to play a mean, mean man. I think I succeeded. We filmed the episode with fuller's earth being blown around the soundstage. When we were not on camera, we had to wear nose-mouth filters."

Concludes Becker, who played the man who kills a racist, "I had the flu during filming, and I was in very bad shape. The story had a terrific idea: Whether it's for good or bad, hate destroys. Killing is killing and hatred, either which way, is destructive."

Sounds and Silences
A man who lives like a Navy captain in his own home gets a taste of his own medicine. Wr: Rod Serling. Dir: Richard Donner.

Roswell G. Flemington (John McGiver); Mrs. Flemington (Penny Singleton); Psychiatrist (Michael Fox); Conklin (William Benedict); Doctor (Francis deSales); Secretary (Renee Aubrey).

Caesar and Me
A ventriloquist and his malevolent wooden dummy embark on a life of crime. Wr: Adele T. Strassfield. Dir: Robert Butler.

Jonathan West (Jackie Cooper); Susan (Suzanne Cupito); Mrs. Cudahy (Sarah Selby); Mr. Smiles (Olan Soule); Pawnbroker (Stafford Repp); Detective (Don Gazzaniga); Watchman (Sidney Marion); Miller (Ken Konopka).

The Jeopardy Room
A Communist defector is trapped in a booby-trapped room. Wr: Rod Serling. Dir: Richard Donner.

Ivan Kuchenko (Martin Landau); Vassiloff (John Van Dreelan); Boris (Robert Kelljan).

Memory Flash—Martin Landau: "We filmed this episode in sequence, which is rare in film but always fun and very creative. Rod Serling did his narrations right on the set as the camera panned off us and onto him. Between 1959 to 1972 I saw Rod perhaps 10 to 15 times. We appeared on panels together ... went to the same parties ... had dinner together ... and I noticed changes in him. He became much more cynical. He was annoyed with TV and the networks toward the end of his life. I was shocked and saddened by his untimely death. I think of him often, even now."

Stopover in a Quiet Town
A couple find themselves in a deserted town where they're watched by a giant girl. Wr: Earl Hamner, Jr. Dir: Ron Winston.

Bob Frazier (Barry Nelson); Millie Frazier (Nancy Malone); Mother (Karen Norris); Little girl (Denise Lynn).

The Encounter
A World War II veteran and a Japanese gardener find themselves trapped in an attic. Wr: Martin M. Goldsmith. Dir: Robert Butler.

Fenton (Neville Brand); Arthur Takamuri (George Takei).

Mr. Garrity and the Graves

A con man convinces townspeople that he can raise the dead. Wr: Rod Serling, story by Mike Korologos. Dir: Ted Post.

Jared Garrity (John Dehner); Gooberman (J. Pat O'Malley); Jensen (Stanley Adams); Sheriff Gilchrist (Norman Leavitt); Lapham (Percy Helton); Ace (John Mitchum); Zelda Gooberman (Kate Murtagh); Lightning Peterson (John Cliff); Man (Patrick O'Moore).

The Brain Center at Whipple's

To save money and increase production, Mr. Whipple replaces his employees with machines. Wr: Rod Serling. Dir: Richard Donner.

Wallace Whipple (Richard Deacon); Hanley (Paul Newlan); Dickerson (Ted de Corsia); Bartender (Shawn Michaels); Technician (Jack Crowder); Watchman (Burt Conroy); Robot (Dion Hansen).

Come Wander with Me

A singer tries to exploit a hillbilly girl's vocal talents, but must contend with her violent brothers. Wr: Anthony Wilson. Dir: Richard Donner.

Floyd Burney (Gary Crosby); Mary Rachel (Bonnie Beecher); Billy Rayford (John Bolt); Store owner (Hank Patterson).

The Fear

A state trooper and a woman are pursued in the wilderness by giant alien creatures. Wr: Rod Serling. Dir: Ted Post.

Robert Franklin (Peter Mark Richman); Charlotte Scott (Hazel Court).

Memory Flash—Peter Mark Richman: "Thirty years ago, television was better. There was some fresh, innovative and wonderful literary content. Today it's all crap. Who watches? And 30 years later, *Twilight Zone* is still a good, imaginative series. Rod Serling was a sweet gentleman and what a talent! Hazel Court is still a friend."

The Bewitchin' Pool

Two unhappy children follow a strange boy to a peaceful world inhabited by friendly Aunt T. Wr: Earl Hamner, Jr. Dir: Joseph M. Newman.

Sport (Mary Badham); Gloria (Dee Hartford); Jeb (Tim Stafford); Gil (Tod Andrews); Aunt T (Georgia Simmons); Whitt (Kim Hector); Announcer (Harold Gould).

The Twilight Zone (CBS revival)

September 1985–July 1987

A continuation (twenty years later) of a science fiction anthology created by Rod Serling that explores the darkest depths of an individual as he crosses over into "the twilight zone." Short tales of surrealism, morality plays, personal nightmares and flights of fantasy characterize the show.

Creator: Rod Serling; *Executive Producer:* Philip DeGuere; *Supervising Producers:* James Crocker, Anthony and Nancy Lawrence; *Producer:* Harvey Frand; *Line Producer:* Ken Swor; *Associate Producers:* James Heinz, Mark Michaels, Howard Brock, Hali Paul; *Executive Story Consultant:* Alan Brennert; *Story Editor:* Rockne O'Bannon, George R.R. Martin, Martin Pasko, Rebecca Parr; *Creative Consultant:* Harlan Ellison, James Crocker; *Narrator:* Charles Aidman; *Main Title Theme:* The Grateful Dead and Merl Saunders; CBS/MGM TV; 60 minutes.

Take a classic television series from the early 1960s—a series that happens to bear the indelible stamp of one very hardworking and creative genius named Rod Serling—and usher it into the 1980s. It could have been a very intimidating task for any producer. But when Philip DeGuere and James Crocker were handed the assignment of reopening that door into *The Twilight Zone*, they felt it was a wonderful idea.

"When the opportunity came, I was very happy it was offered to me," says DeGuere. "All TV producers at one point have a strong desire to do an anthology series. When you do a lot of TV series, you have the same cast, the same basic premise and the same kinds of stories, week after week. It's easy to become creatively tired of production. But an anthology show is a different set of characters and a different set of stories every week. And particularly a show like the way I envisioned the *Twilight Zone*, which was to have multiple stories with varying lengths begin every hour—it would be the ideal additive to that kind of standard form of television."

To update *Twilight Zone* for the 1980s television viewing audience, CBS chose a man who had been very successful in producing several shows for the network. Philip DeGuere had created *Whiz Kids* and *Simon and Simon* and had even forayed into fantasy with his 1979 mysterioso TV movie *Dr. Strange*, based on the Marvel

Comics character. The timing was ideal. Over at NBC, Steven Spielberg (who co-produced the feature *Twilight Zone* in 1983) had begun *Amazing Stories*, and *Alfred Hitchcock Presents* was revived for NBC. There was also *Tales of the Darkside* and HBO's *The Hitchhiker*. As a result, *Twilight Zone* suddenly had anthology competition to contend with.

Although the keeper of the *Twilight Zone* is no longer with us, DeGuere acknowledges his presence hung over the show. "Not only did we *feel* his shadow, we *put* his shadow in the main title!" quips DeGuere, referring to the quick insert of Serling's black-and-white figure in the surreal, kaleidoscopic opening credits. "Although I'm sure I felt intimidation from time to time, I thought it was a significant challenge. It was my feeling that *Twilight Zone* was very much a product of its time…. The stories we would deal with would be significantly different, considerably more modern, and we would have the benefit of technological advances in terms of special effects. No one would look on the new show unkindly and compare it to the old show."

DeGuere confesses that if anything troubled him, it was the competition he faced from other network shows. "As a producer I was considerably more intimidated by what was going on with *Amazing Stories*. It was a show that not only had the benefit of Steven Spielberg's truly astronomical budget from NBC and Universal; it was the understanding in the industry that Spielberg would be attracting feature people. I felt, therefore, that since we were operating under a considerably more normal television series budget, and since I didn't have the benefit of Mr. Spielberg's famous name, or his familiarity with other famous people in the industry, the most important thing for us to do at the outset of the show was to ground our credibility as securely as possible in the world of science fiction and fantasy literature. To try to create the best possible scripts and then go on the assumption that, competitiveness being what it was, the quality of our scripts would serve to attract the kinds of stars and directors and other personnel in town that would allow us to effectively compete for the audience against *Amazing Stories*." DeGuere believes he was successful. He feels he was able to attract people who were almost entirely established in features or in the literary field to work on the *Twilight Zone*. "Generally, in developing the first season, I don't think any better writing staff has *ever* been assembled for a television series!"

Assembling a writing staff that did not usually cater to television screenwriting was that first step towards recreating *The Twilight Zone's* unique style and trademark. In many cases he successfully coaxed well-known authors who had never written for television to sign aboard his ship, including the controversial and boisterous Harlan Ellison and novelists Steven Barnes and George R.R. Martin. Screenwriters also adapted works by horror novelists Robert McCammon and Stephen King and science fiction authors Robert Silverberg, Theodore Sturgeon, Arthur C. Clarke, Henry Slesar and Ray Bradbury. Rockne O'Bannon, who contributed many scripts, became the Boy Wonder discovered on *Twilight Zone*. (O'Bannon later would write *Alien Nation* for the big screen and return to television with *Sea Quest DSV*.) Other writers on the "dream team" included Alan Brennert and the duo of Martin Pasko and Rebecca Parr.

In the acting department, *The Twilight Zone* boasted an impressive first year, with seasoned performances from Melinda Dillon, Morgan Freeman, Elliot Gould, Danny Kaye, Donald Moffatt, Fritz Weaver, Bruce Willis and many others.

Being involved in a dramatic anthology show for network television puts any producer in an unusual position. Every script, cast, writer and director is *different* on each and every episode of the show. For *Twilight Zone*, even the terminology was changed: Because occasionally more than one story would be told in a given one-hour slot, each "mini-movie" created was not an episode, but a "segment" of the show.

"We were developing scripts to a certain level," explains DeGuere. "And when everybody determined that [a script] was ready to film, we'd shoot it. We would do it without being sure what episode of the series a particular segment would go into. We didn't know how segments would be combined to air on a particular night. It was a real jigsaw challenge when we edited the show. We had to come up with two or three segments that would make up an hour show. [We hoped] none would be too severely truncated. I can't think of any television series that's been done with a problem quite like that!"

Scenes and moments were frequently cut out to make a segment fit into a given slot time. "We were cutting our legs, throwing a lot of money into the cutting room floor—some segments were too long to fit into their slot on the hour." Scripts don't necessarily determine story length, says DeGuere. "You really can't tell until you've edited. The script is a guideline up to a point. A director will impose a pace on it, for example." DeGuere notes that the unpredictability of timing is another challenge that makes an anthology series more interesting to do. "On a formula show, if you've done them enough times to be aware of actors talking at a certain pace, that certain kinds of scenes play a certain way, then you have an idea what to shoot for. Sometimes you'll go over, but other times you'll get pretty close. But if you go into something entirely new, you have no idea how it's going to play until you get to the other end—the cutting and editing. It was really quite a challenge to get them all to fit into an hour."

With so many variables to keep track of, DeGuere admits he occasionally suffered memory overload. "After we had five to ten episodes in the can and we had five or six in pre-production, five or six in post-production and we would be actively writing five or six with ten or twenty in development stages, I began to discover I was having trouble remembering people's names!" he says with amazement. "I would have difficulty remembering the name of my secretary or the people working on the show, or people who were friends of mine! I made a comment about this to our writing staff and discovered the other members of the writing staff were having the same kind of trouble! We realized we had so many stories with so many characters with unique names in each story, while we were struggling to keep track of all these stories in our heads, the available memory for names in our heads was being used up! It became terribly embarrassing when you run into someone and you don't know who they are! I'd draw a blank on people's names. There was a weird kind of gymnastics involved to keep all that straight. You'd consistently find yourself in a situation when you say 'Hi!' to somebody but their name wouldn't come to the tip of your tongue!"

Out of the 80 stories produced for the two seasons from 1985 to 1987, DeGuere is happy to discuss examples of what he considers the show's finest offerings.

First, he cites his adaptation of Robert McCammon's short story "Nightcrawlers,"— directed by William Friedkin, who's best known for *The Exorcist*—as an example of stretching the envelope on television.

"The original story was quite graphic, violent and rather frightening," recalls DeGuere. "I

adapted it almost word for word from the short story and quite literally put it on screen. What resulted was, in my opinion, one of the scariest and one of the most realistically gripping and violent stories for network television that has ever been produced."

Despite the storyline of a Vietnam veteran (actor Scott Paulin) having a very violent flashback of the war, the network did not offer objections to the treatment because at the time CBS was very supportive of the project. "Although they were concerned about the graphic nature of the violence, the show we completed was the show I wanted!" DeGuere says proudly.

But on the next week, *Twilight Zone* was preempted. After that, DeGuere remembers, production of the show, for "completely arbitrary, meaningless reasons," was accelerated. As a result, there was a loss in viewers. "We went from a 30 share to a 22 share or something like that. From that point on, the series never achieved an audience level higher."

DeGuere feels that "Nightcrawlers" was a show designed for a 10 p.m. audience, and that the 8 p.m. airing may have contributed to the decline of audience. "What I think happened was that you get 8:00 or 8:30, it's family hour, people are watching shows and kids are still awake…. To have this very gruesome, violent, frightening thing come on and kind of grip you—I mean, there wasn't even a commercial in the middle of the show—was simply too much!" explains DeGuere. "The television audience wasn't properly prepared for it. It was considerably more graphic and disturbing … and it wasn't what they had come to expect. A significant portion of the audience simply didn't want to be challenged like that. It's the end of the week, and you're supposed to put your feet up and relax."

Nevertheless, DeGuere still loves to entertain people by turning off all the lights in a room and turning on "Nightcrawlers," especially if they haven't seen it before.

Actor James Whitmore, Jr., played the sheriff in "Nightcrawlers." He remembers the experience as "bizarre and spooky! I loved it!" With Friedkin on helm, and the prestige and budget of the team behind them, the episode was "wonderful to be in. It was like being in a big, multimillion dollar feature film!

"I'll never forget the first night [of filming]," Whitmore continues. "The opening shot of that episode was me driving along in the police car. They had rain machines set up for a quarter of a mile of the road. Rain towers. I can't see any-thing. The character I was playing doesn't wear glasses, so I couldn't wear my glasses. I'm driving down this road, and I thought, 'Now, this is not a TV show at all! This is a feature film! This is crazy!'

"It was a fun experience. I like the show. I've had a lot of folks since say that they thought it was a damn good show. It was a crazy, interesting shoot. I don't know if it was too intense! Stuff they put on TV nowadays, you just turn on the *news* and you see stuff that you wonder, 'How do they put this on TV?'"

Two other episodes, "A Message from Charity" and "Her Pilgrim Soul," DeGuere con-siders in many ways, "some of the very best we'd ever done. I thought Alan Brennert was one of our best writers."

William M. Lee's short story, "A Message from Charity" was first published in 1969. It's the tale of a modern-day teenage boy who, feverish with illness, finds himself in a psychic bond with a seventeenth-century New England girl who is also in the throes of a fever. The two share their senses of sight and taste, and communicate tele-pathically. It's the story of a boy and a girl explor-ing each other's worlds, centuries apart, only for her to be accused of being a witch because of his modern-day ideas and surroundings.

Kerry Noonan, the actress who played the young girl Charity, recalls working on *Twilight Zone* as an enriching experience. Getting the lead role was an exercise in speaking up. She was audi-tioning for a smaller part, but upon reading the script, she immediately wanted the lead.

"I'd always been a history buff and had sub-jected my younger sister to endless games of 'olden days' in which we'd be Puritans or pioneers or Amish. I'd read extensively about Puritan New England as a kid," says Noonan. "I plucked up my courage and asked the casting director, Gary Zuckerbrod, if I could read for the lead." Zucker-brod and another man hemmed and hawed, reluctant to allow her to audition for the role of Charity. To discourage Noonan, they begged off to a meeting for an hour. "I'll wait!" she said eagerly.

After reading for the part, Noonan remem-bers, she was anxious for a week, trying not to wait by the phone. When her agent finally called, the verdict was that she was too old for the part. "I was so depressed," she laments. "But a week later, I got a call from my agents that *Twilight Zone* had a casting emergency. How quickly could

I get to CBS Radford studios?" Noonan did an additional reading, for a group of people she didn't recognize except for Zuckerbrod. When Zuckerbrod gave her another page to be read, she noticed one man grimacing and remembers thinking that she had better be good. As she stud-ied the lines outside the room, the grimacing man came out and told her, "We don't need to hear any more—you're hired. Go get fitted in ward-robe, and you start Monday."

The emergency had arisen because the woman originally slated to play Charity, *Family Ties'* Justine Bateman, was fired. Producers dis-covered they were not satisfied with her as a girl from another century. "Charity" director Paul Lynch recalls Kerry Noonan as being "terrific" in this segment. "The big difference was that Kerry was a good actress and Bateman wasn't."

Noonan remembers pointing out dialogue inaccuracies to the writer and producer of the episode, Alan Brennert, who's since become a good friend. In turn, he gave her freedom to change any dialogue she found grammatically incorrect.

Noonan's first day of shooting involved three difficult sequences: a scene with a Squire (who accuses her of being a witch) in a cabin, a drunk scene and a goodbye scene to the boy Peter Wood (Duncan McNeill).

"The Squire scene was hard because it was the scene with the most at stake for my charac-ter," recalls Noonan. "Gerry Hiken was terrifi-cally slimy as the Squire—wonderful to work off. Gerry taught me a great deal by example while I worked with him that morning. I knew intellec-tually about the difference between master shots and close-ups, but it helped to watch him and match him as we shot. He got smaller and more intense as the camera got closer, and so did I. He really made my skin crawl in that scene.

"The drunk scene was hard for me because, although I was very familiar with playing comedy on stage, I had not done a comic scene on film yet, and was unsure of how 'big' to make it. Paul Lynch was encouraging of me, and so it went fine."

The goodbye scene, "was difficult to do in two ways; technically it was a difficult shot, and emotionally it was a big scene. Bradford May was circling the camera round me as I did the scene, shooting it all in one continuous shot, so I had to be aware of the camera and do things like hitting the pillow at a precise moment, in coordination with the camera, or the whole shot wouldn't have

Charity Paine (Kerry Noonan) confronts her nemesis, Squire Hacker (Gerald Hiken), as her father (James Cromwell) looks on in "A Message from Charity." Copyright 1989 MGM/UA.

worked. We did many takes, but finally it came out right. Also, I had my worst nightmare come true: Brad explained the complicated camera moves on where I had to be at each mark, and then said, 'And when your head hits the pillow, we'd like tears—out of the left eye, if possible.'"

Noonan reacted the way most of us would when asked to generate tears on demand: She began hyperventilating. "If I know I *must* be in tears at a certain moment, I panic!" says Noonan.

"I was off in a corner, trying to make sure I'd cry—and wondering how to do it 'out of the left eye!' and worrying that my emotional commitment to the scene wasn't good enough."

But whenver she was asked how she was doing, the response was, "Great! We love it. Keep it up!"

"A Message from Charity" was filmed at CBS Radford (now MTM Television) with exteriors at the Disney Ranch, with the exception of the town square scenes, which were done at Burbank studios. The only sets built especially for the episode were the interiors of Charity's house and an airplane wall for Peter Wood's view outside an airplane.

Filming outdoors was fun for Noonan, but the hardest aspect of an exterior segment was being body-miked for a gardening sequence. As she hoed away, she was telepathically communicating with Peter. The camera was at a distance, and MacNeil stood with the cameras and shouted his lines to her.

"My inclination, both naturally and as a stage actress, was to project my voice to reach him," says Noonan. "The sound man had to keep reminding me to talk in a low tone of voice…. It's odd to do a scene where your partner is far away, shouting to you, and you answer in a very quiet voice! But I got used to it."

After completing the principal photography of "A Message from Charity," Noonan later received a call to loop (redub) some dialogue. Airplanes that flew over the location had interfered with some dialogue from the outdoor scenes. Almost all of her exterior dialogue, as well as Gerald Hiken's, was looped.

Looking back, Noonan is very pleased with her work on "A Message from Charity." "I got some nice industry attention, and lots of fan mail for it. I felt I knew the character inside and out, and playing her was a joy, and easy from an emotional point of view. I always remind myself to take risks in casting sessions. The only reason I got to do this wonderful role was because I spoke up and asked to be considered for it. I think the script was probably one of the best I've worked on for television. I think most of the *Twilight Zone* scripts were very good, and Alan Brennert's were some of the best of the lot."

Director Paul Lynch cites conversations between Peter Wood and Charity Paine as his favorite scenes of all the *Twilight Zones* he's directed. "Peter and Charity, when they talk, it's a good time. She's back in New England, and he's in the present. I think they worked great." Lynch says that he gave Noonan little direction for the episode. "She was so good, she didn't need it. She just did the character on her own."

In transition from the original airing on CBS to syndication, "A Message from Charity," like another episode, "Her Pilgrim Soul," was expanded to fit into two half-hour segments. Director Paul Lynch believes four minutes were added for the syndicated version. The expansion included bits of scenes cut from the original air.

Another change that occurred on the way from network to syndication was made not just to "Charity," but to every CBS episode that entered syndication: Charles Aidman's narration was looped over by Canadian Robin Ward's. Many people, Brennert included, prefer Aidman's work as a narrator.

Robin Ward is the Canadian actor who starred with Keir Dullea in *The Starlost* (1973). Of his participation in *Twilight Zone*, Ward says, "About 500 actors sent in tapes, and I was asked to audition. To my amazement, I got the job! From what I saw of the series, it was terrific. With residuals coming from the show, I hope fervently that it lasts in syndication." The fact that Canadian actor union residuals were cheaper than those in the United States played a role in Ward's choice as a narrator.

Another episode on DeGuere's list of favorites is "Her Pilgrim Soul," a unique entry. It is a story without violence, conflict or even an antagonist. Unabashedly, it is a love story.

Wes Craven, director of seven episodes, calls "Her Pilgrim Soul" his favorite. "It certainly has gotten the widest, most positive audience response," says Craven. "It was particularly pleasing for me to direct something that was so far away from what I had directed in the past, since it didn't involve any threat, and was instead clearly a love story."

Written by producer and writer Alan Brennert, who earned a Writers Guild nomination for the script, "Her Pilgrim Soul" is said to be his tribute to a woman he once loved. Directed by Wes Craven, of *Nightmare on Elm Street* fame, and starring Kristoffer Tabori, *Midnight Caller*'s Gary Cole and Anne Twomey, "Her Pilgrim Soul" tells the story of young computer scientist Kevin Drayton and his partner, Daniel, who are tinkering with a three-dimensional holograph device. One day, a human fetus appears suddenly on the holograph. Unable to rid the holograph of the fetus from their computer, they shut down. Restarting, they are haunted again by the fetus, which grows into a young girl, Nola Granville. With some information they have learned about the girl, Daniel goes out and searches for the truth of young Nola, while Kevin stays, not only to study the rapidly growing and aging woman/hologram, but to fall in love with her.

"'Pilgrim' had the difficulty of being an intensely dramatic piece absolutely dependent on the chemistry between the two leads, and yet the technical problems associated with making the woman translucent initially called for the two never to be on the same set at the same time!" says Craven. "I refused to allow that, however. There was enormous difficulty in shooting her scenes. In almost all cases the camera had to be locked down when she was filmed. Then, once a take was attained that I liked, I was required to shoot the set again, this time with a green cylinder placed where she sat, and a third time with nothing there, for the film plate of what would be showing through her and her cone of light, from the set behind. If a second character had to pass through the area she occupied, well, that was a fourth pass. Therefore, three to four times as many takes were required for any single given take involving the woman. It was murderous on our schedule."

But Kristoffer Tabori, who had to act in those scenes with Anne Twomey, was grateful he wouldn't be acting to empty air space. "That's why Wes is a really good director," remembers Tabori. "He understood that there are incomparable things that happen and that are essential about the transactions of human beings that can't be calculated, and they must be given space for. And I always felt that with all the technical problems in that piece, the split screen and all that nonsense, he recognized that the story would work with people [in the scene]. To get that investment, you have to give them the space and time for them to do their work. I always felt that most TV directors neither know very much about human behavior nor do they know very much about the instrument of an actor, nor are they very concerned about it. They consider it a bit of a liability to deal with the actor. But a director like Wes really recognizes [that having two actors working with each other live on set] is crucial to the event coming off. I thought his respect for us, his care for us, his real interest in what we're bringing and how to use it, was great! I thought it was wonderful."

Tabori also remembers, "I was really happy when I got this episode. The story interested me. The movement of the protagonist was something I connected with, and I had a strong feeling for how to play the character. I felt the script had the danger of being sentimental, and the way to avoid it was to identify in the screenplay ... what the real germ of this story was. And when it went off that center, it tended to take refuge in sentiment instead of what I think was the interesting, painful and trenchant story."

Tabori says he felt "really invigorated! I recognized I had a part that had some real muscle to it, and it was something that was active, interesting, attractive and appealing. I worked very hard on the script. ... I connected with it very strongly, and I [wanted to provide] a healthy aspect of an actor's contribution to a project. I remember having a very good relationship with Wes. I would come up to him with specific suggestions and he would agree. I think that's really good. In the best of circumstances, that's what a director should do, facilitate the process of on-set changes.

"I'm always trying to think about what's the story really about? What's really the journey of the character? How do we keep protecting it? I get sidetracked by details."

This very creative atmosphere, while not unusual for television, was very new in Tabori's experience for one reason: "This is the only episodic show I can think in the entire memory of my career—and I've been an actor for 20 to 25 years—where it seemed to me that the pact was getting it *right* instead of getting it *done*. I was amazed!"

Long after completing "Her Pilgrim Soul," Tabori continues to be reminded of his stint inside the *Twilight Zone*. "People are *always* coming up to me," he says. "I'd forgotten about it, and people come up to me and praise it. 'It's my favorite *Twilight Zone* episode ever!' or, 'That's one of the best pieces of television!' And it's amazing, the impact that *little* show has had! People really like that episode. It's very emotional. It's a very personal love story. It's very immediate in how it addresses the problems in what [Kevin Drayton] is going through. People have responded very strongly. I must say, I'm more than amazed."

Wes Craven, in recalling his tenure on the *Twilight Zone*, said that "Her Pilgrim Soul" was not the only episode with technical difficulties. "Shatterday," with Bruce Willis, is another example.

"Bruce was required to play both sides of a split personality. Again there were complicated scenes requiring multiple passes, to film both sides of his conversation. Further, a second actor needed to be found to play opposite both of Bruce's characters, to give him someone to respond to dramatically in any given scene."

Craven believes that *Twilight Zone*'s unique stamp comes from the fact that "Western art looks at our human reality through tunnel-vision glasses, seeing almost exclusively what is experienced rationally, linearly and apparently. But the spectrum of human consciousness is phenomenally broader than that. The great thing about *Twilight Zone* was/is that it acknowledged that other area—the deeply subjective, 'acoustic' non-linear arena of our 'other realities': dreams, hallucinations, premonitions, daydreams, visions—and gave it voice. The final unique stamp in the original, of course, was Rod Serling." Craven's retrospective opinion of *Twilight Zone's* revival is that "it was a moment of fine quality, wrapped around a show that was at once experimental and firmly rooted in a great tradition.

"Serling was a unique and powerful presence for the original *Twilight Zone*—compelling to look at and hear, and a gifted writer too—so that the tremendous disparity of subject matter had a central anchor that the new *Twilight Zone* did not." So, how could the updated *Twilight Zone* have been better? "If Serling had been cryogenically preserved!" quips Craven.

Working on the show for Craven was a creatively satisfying and creative stint. "There were so many positives. I received the chance to work with actors and actresses I'd never had access to before, with truly gifted writers, and with a really fine crew—from Bradford May onward they were exceptionally committed and gifted, and were great to work with. I'll always have a warm spot for Philip DeGuere for giving me that chance."

Craven recalls that the most amusing moments on the set usually came during the last several days of any given episode's filming. "Almost always we were behind schedule," Craven moaned. "The *Twilight Zones* were filmed like small features. Much care was given to every detail, directors were encouraged to shoot at feature level—and then there was the matter of cinematographer Bradford May's smoke.

"Brad shot beautifully, and he loved the look smoke gave to his lighting, and so would routinely smoke every set. Heavily. That meant all the sets had to be closed, so there were no errant winds carrying away the atmosphere, and there was a very limited window of ideal smoke-time. The process went like this. First, all the doors to the stage would be closed. Then the entire stage was smoked—smokers chugging away in every corner until the whole stage looked like London during its foggiest. Then we would come in and rehearse (cough, cough), then prepare for the shots.

"Now, the set itself had to be resmoked, and then, we waited ... until the smoke thinned (you must never be able to see the smoke), but not too much. Then, if all was well, the take. But often, halfway through the take, the smoke would thin too much. We'd have to cut, or else the smoke wouldn't match. More smoke, then another take. After each take, we'd have to resmoke, then wait for the smoke to settle.

"The amusing part was watching the faces of the line producer and his staff as they'd line up on the last days, when we were out of time and money and still shooting—looking at their watches, chain smoking—waiting with all the rest of us for the smoke to be ... just ... right!"

"Paladin of the Lost Hour," shot from Harlan Ellison's teleplay of his short story "Paladin," was another important accomplishment for *Twilight Zone*. It starred the legendary Danny Kaye as well as Glynn Turman, an actor who's since starred as a regular on the NBC sitcom *A Different World*.

"Paladin of the Lost Hour" is a story of a lonely old man, Gaspar, paying respects to his deceased wife at an out-of-the-way cemetery. When he's assaulted by two hoods, a young man, Billy Kinetta, rescues him. Touched and grateful for Billy's help, Gaspar persuades his way into Billy's apartment. There, under a rainstorm, Gaspar learns of Billy's Vietnam experiences. A buddy had lost his life saving Billy from an explosion, leaving Billy filled with grief through the years. Billy's emotions touch Gaspar. In the end, Billy discovers Gaspar's old timepiece is not an ordinary watch. Set perpetually at eleven o'clock, the watch carries the 'the last hour' of time. Gaspar is the guardian, a paladin. Armageddon will never come as long as the arrows stay from midnight. And Gaspar is looking for someone to carry on his work.

Sadly, "Paladin of the Lost Hour" was Danny Kaye's last acting performance before he died. But the script earned Harlan Ellison a Writers Guild award, and the short-story form won the fan-voted Hugo award.

Glynn Turman recalls the experience as a good one. Ellison had written the roles specifically for him and Kaye. He thinks that "it was a fine script. It was a different project. As it goes for science fiction, it was a very touching story."

Turman says that Billy Kinetta, the tortured Vietnam veteran who eventually meets his war buddy thanks to Gaspar's watch, was a man who wished he could have done something differently, given time. "He wished he had a chance to make amends, and wondered what he could do if he had a chance to do it over again. And I think what Harlan was saying is that things are as they are. And for that reason, there's no way to change it."

Working with Danny Kaye was a delight for Turman. "It was wonderful. I was very fortunate to work with him. One of the true patriots of old Hollywood, so to speak. He was truly a gracious superstar. As a matter of fact, he was a star and a superstar in films before we had the term superstar now. He carried himself in that manner. He was very aware of his status and still very gracious. He was a very talented man. He had a very simple and patient approach."

What did Kaye think of the script? "Oh, he loved it," says Turman. "He was very happy to be a part of that exercise. He enjoyed it tremendously. You could tell he was happy doing it. Everybody was up and happy and very involved with the work process, so he was happy to be part of it."

Since completing that *Twilight Zone* segment, Turman has been continually amazed by people's remembrance of him and his role in it. "They're taken by it. I've gotten very positive feedback from it. [Because] it was Danny Kaye's last performance, that made it a very special episode."

Sadly, "Paladin of the Lost Hour" suffered deep cuts when it was packaged for syndication. The episode's 31 minutes couldn't be translated to a half-hour, so the scissors came out and it was cut *down* by nine minutes to a standard 22. Today, a videotape of "Paladin's" CBS broadcast is an item of historical significance owned by a lucky few.

The impressive achievements of the show's first season were in keeping with the atmosphere on the set and behind the scenes. Philip DeGuere says that initially, he and his staff were full of energy and excitement and looking forward to a long run on television. But halfway into the season, it stopped being fun.

"We had a wonderful writing staff assembled and over the course of time, virtually every key member of that staff quit in disgust over CBS's handling of the creative process," says DeGuere. "CBS ended up compromising the series by its inability to allow the people who they hired to produce the show to do their work. That, unfortunately, in the last decade or so, is a fact of life or has become a fact of life, in television. There wasn't anything I could do about it, although I tried mightily."

DeGuere responds indignantly when asked if he feels he accomplished what he wanted for *The Twilight Zone.* "No! I did not accomplish what I, or the other people, intended to do on the show. Our efforts were successfully thwarted by the shortsightedness of the executives of CBS. The purpose of *The Twilight Zone*, as I envisioned it, was to create a new franchise on television, to have a long-running series that would be a different kind of entertainment for the television audience and be on the air for a long time. That would be an ideal place for really creative people like me in Hollywood to come and do shows and really have time to do shows. The fact of the matter is, most of our shows required only about three days to shoot. Some required one or two, and the longest I think we ever shot was like six days, and that was unusual. If a director had three weeks between filming features or something, he could come in and do a show for us. If an actor had three days available, he could come in and do a show for us. Because the scripts were short, writers could get a script in a week or two, whereas it would take months for a regular series. It was meant to be kind of a revolving door for talent. The idea was to make *Twilight Zone* an idealized collaboration between writer and director. Every writer, especially those on the staff of the show, was given an opportunity to be entirely in charge of what I had considered to be producing functions on the series. In other words, the writer would work directly with the directors and the actors in the production of the show, and [with] the film editors who are cutting the show. And I, as supervising producer, would only come in to look over people's shoulders and make sure things were done right and solve problems. That was accomplished to a certain extent, although the cost of interference by CBS added a difficulty to it.

"It was supposed to be an institution—an opportunity to bring writers into the field of television for those who might not ordinarily have a chance to do. I think we accomplished that with George R.R. Martin, who had never written a television show or a movie before. He came into *Twilight Zone* and he went on to being a supervising producer for *Beauty and the Beast.*

"It fulfilled its promise to a certain extent on every level, but the fact of the matter is, the ship was leaking. It was bound to sink. It became obvious the network wasn't capable of producing the series and keeping the creative team necessary to do that together. Many times I've been sorry I didn't quit the damn show, as a protest of

Fritz Weaver (left) and Donald Moffat in an adaptation of Arthur C. Clarke's short story "The Star," directed by Gerd Oswald. Copyright 1989 MGM/UA.

the way the network was handling it. From a creative point of view, it was allowed to sink into a somewhat inglorious conclusion."

As the show was finishing its two-year run on CBS, a foot got into the closing door. Someone else picked up the show in 1988 and moved it, with a different production staff, to Toronto, where 30 episodes were filmed for syndication (see pages 504–513). CBS episodes were thereon remixed, recut, and in some cases eliminated, to form a package with syndicated episodes. Robin Ward's narration was mixed in "for uniformity," as an MGM executive put it. DeGuere says he has never seen any of the syndicated episodes and calls the repackaging the last indignity thrown upon him and his hard-working and idealistic staff.

EPISODE GUIDE

Season 1: 1985-86

1.1. Shatterday
Accidentally dialing his home phone from a bar, Peter Jay Novins hears himself answering the phone. He discovers that he must deal with the other man, who also calls himself Peter Jay Novins. Wr: Alan Brennert, based on the short story by Harlan Ellison. Dir: Wes Craven.

Peter Jay Novins (Bruce Willis); Bartender (Dan Gilvezan); Woman at bank (Murukh); Clerk (John Carlyle); Alter ego (Seth Isler); Bellboy (Anthony Grumbach).

Memory Flash—Philip DeGuere: "Bruce had a case of laryngitis, so we had to loop all of his dialogue. It was such an incredibly cumbersome job, under the time frame we were working on. The effectiveness of that show was vastly reduced. It was really a shame too, because he gave a really good performance. He looped it all later, and that's very difficult to do on a television schedule."

1.2. A Little Peace and Quiet
A housewife in a noisy, boisterous household one afternoon discovers a buried necklace that freezes time when she wears it around her neck. Wr: James Crocker. Dir: Wes Craven.

Penny (Melinda Dillon); Russell (Greg Mullavey); Susan (Virgina Kechne); Janet (Brittany Wilson); Russ Jr. (Joshua Harris); Bertie (Judith Barsi); Newscaster (Claire Nono); First shopper (Elma Beronda Jackson); Second shopper (Pamela Gordon); Third shopper (Laura Waterbury); Preppy man (Todd Allen); Preppy girl (Isabelle Walker).

Memory Flash—Wes Craven: "It had many of the elements that keep line producers awake and sweating in the middle of the night—kids, a dog, and special effects. We experimented with various high tech methods of producing the 'freeze frames' when the woman would say 'Be quiet!' but the simplest turned out to be the best: The actors—kids, dog and all—simply froze in place. To my surprise they all proved to be great at this. We furthered the illusion by a glass of half-spilled milk, and, in the climactic scene, half a dozen custom armatures to hold extras frozen in mid-sprint."

2.1. Wordplay

A salesman wakes up one morning and, to his horror, people around him slowly degenerate their talk into gibberish that he cannot understand. His ability to communicate is needed more than ever when his son becomes sick. Wr: Rockne O'Bannon. Dir: Wes Craven.

Bill Lowery (Robert Klein); Kathy Lowery (Annie Potts); Donnie (Adam Raber); Mr. Miller (Robert J. Downey); Hotshot (Brian Bradley); Older salesman (Bernard Behrens); Admitting nurse (Anne Betancourt); Man in elevator (Willard Peugh); Woman #1 (Helene Udy); Receptionist (Mimi Neyer-Craven); Secretary (Brynja Willis); Doctor (Russ Marin); Nurse #1 (Alexandra Morgan); Nurse #2 (Lee Arnone); Bearded man (Raye Birk); Doug Seaver (Joseph Whipp); Robbie (Dwier Brown).

2.2. Dreams for Sale

On a picnic with her husband and their twins, a woman becomes perplexed and disoriented when events begin to repeat themselves. Awakening, she discovers herself in a futuristic dream-making machine. But which is nightmare and which is reality? Wr: Joe Gannon. Dir: Tommy Lee Wallace.

Dreamer (Meg Foster); Mark (David Hayward); Dream technician (Vincent Gastaferro); Rescue technician (Lee Anthony); Twins (Kristi and Deanna Purdy).

2.3. Chameleon

Returning from a space shuttle mission, NASA discovers they've picked up something unusual along the way. They soon discover they have a shape-changing alien in their holding tank that poses danger to all. Wr: James Crocker. Dir: Wes Craven.

Curt Lockridge (Terrance O'Quinn); Dr. Vaughn Heilman (Ben Piazza); Chief Bradley Simmons (John Ashton); Gerald Tyson (Steve Howell Bassett); Annie (Iona Morris); Teresa Rojas (Alma Martinez); Peter Iverson (Chad Hayes); Woman in tank (Lin Shaye).

3.1. Healer

A cat burglar smashes his way into a museum's ancient artifacts and accidentally picks up a rare gem with strange healing powers. Wr: Michael Bryant (Alan Brennert). Dir: Sigmund Neufeld Jr.

Jackie Thompson (Eric Bogosian); Harry (Vincent Gardenia); Joseph Rubello (Robert Costanzo); Duende (Joaquin Martinez); Deaf boy (Adam Ferris); Deaf boy's mother (Joy Pankin); First neighbor (Ed Levey); Black woman (Vivian Bonnell); Guard (Anthony Johnson); Amanda's mom (Lauren Levin).

3.2. Children's Zoo

Depressed with her parents' arguments and behavior, young Debbie goes to the Children's Zoo, where she can make some special changes in her life. Wr: Chris Hubbell and Gerrit Graham. Dir: Robert Downey.

Sheila Cunningham (Lorna Luft); Martin Cunningham (Steven Keats); Debbie Cunningham (Jaclyn Bernstein); Melody (Sydney Walsh); Caged man #1 (Wes Craven); Caged man #2 (Don Paul); Caged man #3 (Jack Taloe); Caged man #4 (Al Alu); Caged woman #1 (Kerry Slattery); Caged woman #2 (Sandy Brown Wyeth); Caged woman #3 (Pamela Brown); Caged woman #4 (Virgina Morris).

3.3. Kentucky Rye

Drunk-driving, Bob Spindler crashes his way into the "Kentucky Rye" bar where the inhabitants are all victims of drunk drivers. Wr: Richard Krzemien and Chip Duncan. Dir: John Hancock.

Bob Spindler (Jeffrey DeMunn); Irving (Michael Greene); Old man (Philip Bruns); Stranger (Arliss Howard); Randy (Clarence Felder); Pete (Scott Jaeck); George (John DeMita); Larry (Brad Burlingame); Nancy (Rosemarie Thomas); Laura (Gloria Rusch); Debbie (Lisa Long); Officer #1 (John Davey); Officer #2 (Tim Russ).

4.1. Little Boy Lost

A young female photographer must decide between marriage and a big career break. The pivotal ramifications of her decision hit home when she meets a mysterious young boy at the zoo. Wr: Lynn Barker. Dir: Tommy Lee Wallace.

Carol Shelton (Season Hubley); Kenny (Scott Grimes); Greg (Nicolas Surovy); Housewife (Nancy Kyes); Gina Craig (Diane Summerfield).

4.2. Wish Bank

Janice finds a magic lamp at a garden sale, but restrictions apply for her three wishes—not to mention lots of paperwork! Wr: Michael Cassutt. Dir: Rick Friedberg.

Janice Hamill (Dee Wallace-Stone); Brent (Peter Land); Mary Ellen (Julie Carmen); Willoughby (Harvey Vernon); Clerk (Julie Payne).

4.3. Nightcrawlers

When a deputy trooper stops by a diner during a rainy, stormy evening, a Vietnam veteran's nightmares come to life. Wr: Philip DeGuere, based on a short story by Robert R. McCannom. Dir: William Friedkin.

Price (Scott Paulin); Dennis Wells (James Whitmore Jr.); Bob (Robert Swan); Waitress (Exene Cervenka); Lindy (Sandy Martin); Ray (Bobby Bass); Ricky (Matt Levin).

5.1. If She Dies

A year after his wife died, a man is involved in a car accident, leaving his young daughter in a coma. But a vision comes to him on the way home. Wr: David Carren. Dir: John Hancock.

Paul Marano (Tony Lo Bianco); Sarah (Jenny Lewis); Sister Agnes (Nan Martin); Cathy Marano (Andrea Barber); Dr. Brice (John Gowans); Nun (Donna-Jean Lansing); Nurse (Adele Miller).

5.2. Ye Gods

Cupid strikes in the modern world. But the spell for his target doesn't work well. Cupid's going to have to try a little harder. Wr: Anne Collins. Dir: Peter Medak.

Todd Ettinger (David Dukes); Cupid (Robert Morse); Magaera (Carolyn Seymour); Bacchus (John Myhers); Peter (Andrew Masset); April (Patti Karr); Woman (Ingrid Boulting).

6.1. Examination Day

In the far-flung future, 12-year-old Dickie must pass the mandatory government intelligence test. He's nervous and so are his parents. Wr: Philip DeGuere, based on the short story by Henry Slesar. Dir: Paul Lynch.

Dickie Jordan (David Mendenhall); Richard Jordan (Christopher Allport); Ruth Jordan (Elizabeth Normant); Clerk #1 (Ed Krieger); Clerk #2 (Myrna White); Clerk #3 (Jeffrey Allen Chandler).

6.2. A Message from Charity

Fever-stricken Peter Wood, in 1985, finds himself in telepathic contact with Charity Paine, a sick girl his age living in Puritan New England. Their new-found contact turns to horror when Peter's knowledge of the future endangers Charity's life. Wr: Alan Brennert, based on a short story by William M. Lee. Dir: Paul Lynch.

Charity Paine (Kerry Noonan); Peter Wood (Duncan McNeill); Aunt Beulah (Vanessa Brown); Squire Jonas Hacker (Gerald Hiken); Obediah Paine (James Cromwell); Tom Carter (Michael Fox); Ursula Miller (Jennifer Parsons); Dr. Maxwell (Jack Wells); Mr. Wood (Philip Proctor); Mrs. Wood (Barbara Lindsay).

7.1. Teacher's Aide

Arriving at a violent high school, a teacher becomes possessed by the spirit of a gargoyle—and wait'll the kids see her now! Wr: Steven Barnes. Dir: B.W.L. Norton.

Miss Peters (Adrienne Barbeau); Wizard (Adam Postil); Trojan (Miguel Nunez); Fury (Josh Richman); Hugh Costin (Fred Mosell); 12th grader (Brian Robbins); Student teacher (Sarah Partridge); Younger brother (Richard Brainard); Jennifer (Susanne Sasson); Security guard (Al Christy); Amanda (Noelle Harling).

Memory Flash—Steven Barnes: "I wanted to do a story where I could deal with some of my feelings about junior high school. My sister's a school teacher and it was just a thought of what it would take to deal with monsters. It was fairly simple.

"I didn't like it. I liked [Adrienne Barbeau] fine. But the original script was 20 minutes, and they wanted to expand it to 30, but it aired as 15 minutes because it was on the front end of a Harlan Ellison episode. They cut mine, and it comes out almost incomprehensible."

7.2. Paladin of the Lost Hour

As Vietnam vet Billy saves an old man from a mugging at a cemetery, he soon discovers this is no ordinary man—Gaspar holds the very future of time in his watch. Wr: Harlan Ellison, based on his short story "Paladin." Dir: Alan Smithee (Gilbert Cates).

Gaspar (Danny Kaye); Billy Kinetta (Glynn Turman); Punk #1 (John Bryant); Punk #2 (Corky Ford); Driver (Mike Reynolds).

Memory Flash—Philip DeGuere: "The Directors Guild decided to throw Gil Cates from the set and ban him from the show. Gil Cates and Harlan didn't get along very well. Gil was the president of the Directors Guild and thought he was pretty hot stuff. I think he thought he was doing us a favor. When it came time for us to complete his show on the production schedule, he was out of town at the time and certain decisions had to be made, and he got very hussy about the fact that these decisions were made [without his participation] so he wrote a letter to the president of the network about the whole thing. He took the standard directors guild pseudonym for his particular show."

8.1. Act Break

A landlord hounds a playright for his rent; his partner dies of a heart attack; oh, what is Maury going to do? But wait—when he wishes he could become the greatest playright that ever lived, Maury's transported back in time to Shakespeare, thanks to the stone that Harry gave him. Wr: Haskell Barkin. Dir: Theodore Flicker.

Maury Winkler (James Coco); Harry/Shakespeare (Bob Dishy); Landlord (Avery Schreiber).

8.2. The Burning Man

As a mother and her son enjoy a drive in the country during a heatwave in the 1930s, they encounter a strange man who wants a ride. Wr: J.D. Feigelson, based on the short story by Ray Bradbury. Dir: J.D. Fiegelson.

Aunt Neva (Piper Laurie); Doug (Andre Gower); The man (Roberts Blossom); Young boy (Danny Cooksey).

Memory Flash—Ray Bradbury: "That was terrific. It was done by a friend of mine, J.D. Feigelson. I got him a job directing it also. But he was reluctant to ask, but I said to him, 'Get on the phone.' I'm not going to tell him how to direct the story because he did the adaptation. I bullied him into calling people. And he got the job. It was fine work."

8.3. Dealer's Choice

A friendly, weekly game of poker turns into a fight for souls when players realize they are playing with the devil. Wr: Donald Todd. Dir: Wes Craven.

Nick (Dan Hedaya); Peter (M. Emmet Walsh); Jake (Garrett Morris); Tony (Barney Martin); Marty (Morgan Freeman).

9.1. Dead Woman's Shoes

When a sales clerk at a clothing store puts on the shoes of a dead woman, her personality is altered and becomes the deceased's. Immediately, she sets out to avenge her death. Wr: Lynn Barker, based on an original story by Charles Beaumont. Dir: Peter Medak.

Maddy Duncan (Helen Mirren); Inez (Theresa Saldana); Stephen Montgomery (Jeffrey Tambor); Man (Robert Pastorelli); Eileen (Sasha von Scherler); Hyatt (Hyatt Rawles); Maid (Tyra Ferrell); Girl (Julie Dolan); Girl (Leslie Bega); Lori (Nana Visitor); Cabbie (Lance Nichols); Susan Montgomery (Pia Gronning).

9.2. Wong's Lost and Found Emporium
Desperately in search for something he's lost, David Wong seeks the Lost and Found Emporium, where he finds others in search of their lost items. Wr: Alan Brennert, based on the short story by William F. Wu. Dir: Paul Lynch.

David Wong (Brian Tochi); Melinda (Anna Marja Poon); Mrs. Whitford (Carol Bruce); Elderly man (Stacy Keach Sr.); Cashier (Jack Jozefson); Customer (Marty Levy).

10.1. The Shadow Man
The smartest boy in school becomes a target for bullies. At home in bed after an an attack, the boy meets the "Shadow Man," who offers a solution. Wr: Rockne O'Bannon. Dir: Joe Dante

Danny (Jonathan Ward); Eric (Jason Presson); Peter (Michael Rich); Liana Ames (Heather Haase); Shadow Man (Jeff Calhoun); Mother (Kathleen Coyne); Redhead girl (Tricia Bartholome); Girl with braces (Julia Hendler); Janie (Melissa Moultrie); Boy #1 (Chris Gosch); Boy with glasses (Marc Bentley).

10.2. The Uncle Devil Show
Parents don't realize that the video their child is watching demonstrates wonderful magic tricks like turning parents into lizards, giving a dog four eyes and lots of other good things. Wr: Donald Todd. Dir: David Steinberg.

Uncle Devil (Murphy Dunne); Joey (Gregory Mier).

10.3. Opening Day (aka Duck Shoot)
A beautiful woman and her boyfriend plot to kill her husband on the first day of the duck hunting season. Wr: Gerrit Graham and Chris Hubbell. Dir: John Milius.

Sally (Elan Oberson); Joe (Martin Kove); Carl (Jeff Jones); Kerry (Molly Morgan); Joe Jr. (Shaun Donahue); Beverly (Andrea Hall-Lovell); Ned (Michael Nissman); Girl at party (Shelby Billington); Sheriff (Frank McRae); Guest (Gary Hollis).

Memory Flash—Martin Kove: "I love John Milius. He's married to the soundtrack of *The Wind and the Lion*. Sort of the John Ford of our day. I loved working with him because he loves film history. He's more of an old-time filmmaker. I've always wanted to work with him. He was in New York and called me and asked me, 'Come do this thing!' I said, 'All right!' *Time* magazine called it the best episode of *Twilight Zone*. John and I had a ball doing it. It was just heaven, you know, and John

loved shooting. It was prestigious to be in *Twilight Zone*."

11.1. The Beacon
When a doctor's car breaks down, he runs into an unusual town where visitors are disliked and townspeople are terrified of the lighthouse and where it might shine, spelling death. Wr: Martin Pasko and Rebecca Parr. Dir: Gerd Oswald.

Dr. Dennis Barrows (Charles Martin Smith); William Cooper-James (Martin Landau); Teddy (Vonni Robisi); Mary Ann (Cheryl Anderson); Trooper (Scott Lincoln); Katie (Hayley Taylor Block).

11.2. One Life, Furnished in Early Poverty
Angry with his adult life, a man returns to his childhood stomping grounds to find himself transported back to being the boy again. Wr: Alan Brennert, based on the short story by Harlan Ellison. Dir: Don Carlos Dunaway.

Harry Rosenthal (Peter Riegert); Gus Rosenthal (Chris Hebert); Lou (Jack Kehoe); Sarita (Barbara Tarbuck); The woman (Susan Wheeler Duff); Cab driver (Biff Yeager); Jack Wheeldon (Gary Karp).

12.1. Her Pilgrim Soul
Experimenting with a holographic device, two scientists are abruptly confronted one day with a fetus in their machine. Growing, it becomes a woman whose life story allures Kevin. As Daniel goes out to investigate her background, Kevin stays at the lab and falls in love with her. Wr: Alan Brennert. Dir: Wes Craven.

Kevin Drayton (Kristoffer Tabori); Nola (Anne Twomey); Daniel (Gary Cole); Carol (Wendy Girard); Susan (Katherine Wallach); Lester (Richard McGonagle); Nola, age 5 (Betsy Jane Licon); Nola, age 10 (Danica M. McKellar).

12.2. I, of Newton
Frustrated at failing to resolve a complicated mathematical formula, a professor is visited by a demon who offers solutions to his problems—for a price. Wr: Alan Brennert, based on the short story by Joe Haldeman. Dir: Kenneth Gilbert.

Sam (Sherman Hemsley); The demon (Ron Glass).

13.1. Night of the Meek
When a bum takes the department store Santa job, he's surprised to find an extraordinary garbage bag that delivers all the gifts that he ever needs on Christmas Day. Wr: Rockne O'Bannon, based on the teleplay and story by Rod Serling. Dir: Martha Coolidge.

Henry Corwin (Richard Mulligan); Mr. Dundee (William Atherton); Older cop (Bill Henderson); Mother (Shelby Leverington); Mrs. Beacham (Joanne Barron); Businessman (Thomas F. Duffy); Mr. Dobson (Hugo Stanger); Girl with glasses (Elizabeth Ward); Bartender (Charles Swiegart); Manager (Wayne Morton); Old man (Monty Ash); Younger cop (Jeff Kober); Woman caroler (Patricia Wilson); Man in yard (Wilson Camp); Little boy (Benjie Gregory); Baseball boy (Paul Stout); Wife (Georgia

Schmidt); Mother of little girl (Muriel Minot); Spinster (Enid Rodgers); Father (Brian Muehl); Little girl (Toria Crosby); Older brother (Larenz Tate); Man on roof (Harry Governick); Woman on phone (Phyllis Erlick).

13.2. But Can She Type?

An underappreciated secretary falls into another universe where her occupation is highly revered. Wr: Martin Pasko and Rebecca Parr. Dir: Shelley Levinson.

Karen Billings (Pam Dawber); Burt (Charles Levin); Marcy (Jeannie Elias); Single guy (Jonathan Frakes); Hostess (Deborah Harmon); Rehnquist (Michael Prince); Model (Jolina Collins); Limo driver (Douglas Blair); Workman (Ken Sagoes).

13.3. The Star

Onboard a spaceship, an astrophysicist and a priest learn they've discovered a planet long dead and a transmitter emitting a signal for eons. And the discoveries they make there are shattering. Wr: Alan Brennert, based on the short story by Arthur C. Clarke. Dir: Gerd Oswald.

Fr. Matthew Costigan (Fritz Weaver); Dr. Chandler (Donald Moffat); Captain Durant (Elizabeth Huddle).

14.1. Still Life

Finding an old trunk, a couple realize it's got a false bottom, and inside is a 70-year-old film from the Amazon. When they process the film, those in it come alive. Wr: Gerrit Graham and Chris Hubbell. Dir: Peter Medak.

Daniel (Robert Carradine); Becky (Marilyn Jones); Prof. Alex Stottel (John Carradine).

14.2. The Little People of Killany Woods

No one believes that the town braggart at a local Irish pub has discovered little people in the deep woods. They don't believe him until he produces gold coins. Wr: J.D. Feigelson. Dir: J.D. Feigelson.

Liam O'Shaughnessey (Hamilton Camp); Mike (Michael Aldridge); Kelly (James Scally); Eddie Donovan (Tim Donoghue); McGinty (Anthony Palmer); O'Dell (Hal Landon); Mrs. Finnegan (Pat Crawford Brown).

14.3. The Misfortune Cookie

A food critic ravages a Chinese restaurant in print, but when he receives a fortune cookie that reveals the future, he wants more. Wr: Steven Rae, based on a short story by Charles E. Fritch. Dir: Allan Arkush.

Harry Folger (Elliot Gould); Mr. Lee (Bennett Ohta); April Hamilton (Caroline Lagerfelt); Max (Frederick Coffin); Glamorous gourmette (Claire Carter); O'Malley (John G. Scanlon); Guard (Elven Harvard); Proprietor (Albert Leong).

15.1. Monsters!

A young boy, a monster-maniac, encounters a friendly vampire when he moves to a new town. Wr: Robert Crais. Dir: B.W.L. Norton.

Toby Michaels (Oliver Robins); Emile Francis Bendictson (Ralph Bellamy); Mrs. Michaels (Kathleen Lloyd); Mr. Michaels (Bruce Solomon).

15.2. A Small Talent for War

When an alien ship arrives at the U.N. and the representative declares his disapointment at earthlings' progress, ambassadors plead for 24 hours to resolve differences. When the alien returns, ambassadors realize they've misunderstood him entirely. Wr: Carter Scholtz and Alan Brennert. Dir: Claudia Weill.

Alien ambassador (John Glover); American diplomat (Peter Michael Goetz); Russian diplomat (Stefan Gierasch); UN chairman (Fran Bennett); U.S. aide (Jose Santana); British delegate (Gillian Eaton); British aide (Richard Brestoff).

15.3. A Matter of Minutes

A young married couple discover their home is being remodeled by blue-clad workers who are the ones stuck in time moving objects from one period to another. Wr: Rockne S. O'Bannon, based on the short story "Yesterday Was Monday" by Theodore Sturgeon. Dir: Sheldon Larry.

Michael Wright (Adam Arkin); Maureen Wright (Karen Austin); Supervisor (Adolph Caesar); First woman in accident (Marianne Muellerleile); Heavyset man (Alan David Gelman).

16.1. The Elevator

Brothers looking for their mad-scientist father find only a deserted laboratory and no sign of their dad. Wr: Ray Bradbury, based on his short story. Dir: R.L. Thomas.

Will (Stephen Geoffreys); Roger (Robert Prescott); Young Will (Brandon Bluhm); Young Roger (Douglas Emerson).

Memory Flash—Ray Bradbury: "It was a complete mess. I did the script, and they chopped it up. In the end, you can't tell what's going on. There's a big spider in that shaft. It comes to grab and then it goes back up. There should be a real shock there when you realize what it is. There is no feeling of weirdness in the factory. And the dead animals were the wrong size. Everything in that was El Cheapo. One of the boys was hysterical all the time. He made us all nervous."

16.2. To See the Invisible Man

A man is sentenced to a year of invisibility, which he believes he can survive with ease. Wr: Steven Barnes, based on the short story by Robert Silverberg. Dir: Noel Black.

Mitchell Chapman (Cotter Smith); Invisible woman (Karlene Crockett); Blind man (Peter Hobbs); Margaret (Mary Robin-Redd); Comic (Jack Gallagher); Maitre d' (Kenneth Danziger); Guard #1 (Richard Jamison); Businessman (Chris McCarty); Waitress (Karla Richards); Nurse (Rebecca Robertson); Tough #1 (Dean Fortunato); Server (Steve Peterson); Crying girl (Terri Lynn Wood); Young boy (Whitby Hertford).

Memory Flash—Steven Barnes: "The producers asked me what were some of my favorite science fiction stories and wanted to know if I had any science fiction stories I've always wanted to adapt for television. I mentioned Robert Sheckley's 'Love, Incorporated' and Robert Silverberg's 'To See the Invisible Man.' They got copies of both of those stories and read them and said 'Love, Incorporated' was inappropriate for the show. It was sexist. I suggested switching the genders of the characters and it was still sexist, which I don't quite understand! But, 'To See the Invisible Man' got the OK.

"I thought it was good. The thing you have to remember is 'To See the Invisible Man' is a very internal story. It's mostly what's going on inside [Mitchell Chapman's] head. So we had to figure out a way to ... turn it into a visual presentation."

16.3 Tooth and Consequences
A dentist hates his job and tries to hang himself, but arriving at his rescue is his tooth fairy, who grants him work and respect to last lifetimes. Wr: Haskell Barkin. Directed by Robert Downey.

Dr. Myron Mandel (David Birney); Tooth fairy (Kenneth Mars); Lydia Bixby (Teresa Ganzel); Pinkham (Oliver Clark); Mrs. Schulman (Peggy Pope); Mrs. Taylor (Mina Kolb); Receptionist (Jane Ralston); Mr. Frank (Ermal Williamson); Man (Martin Azarow); Middle aged woman (Mitzi McCall); Eating hobo (William Utay); Hobo #1 (Nat Bernstein); Hobo #2 (Jack Lindine); Hobo #3 (Ron Ross).

17.1. Welcome to Winfield
The grim reaper arrives at a hospital to take possession of a dying man, but his wife rescues him and they wind up at the western town of Winfield, where residents have been living for hundreds of years. The reaper has failed to collect those who are living here. Wr: Les Enloe. Dir: Bruce Bilson.

Weldon (Elisha Cook Jr.); Sherrif (Alan Fudge); Mayor Abe (Henry Gibson); Matt Winnaker (Jonathan Caliri); Lori Bodell (Joann Willette); Griffin St. George (Gerrit Graham); Ray Bob (Dennis Fimple); Elton (Chip Heller); Mamie (Sally Klein); Townsperson #1 (Claudia Bryar); Townsperson #2 (Davie Morick).

17.2. Quarantine
Awakening after a couple of hundred years of sleep, a man finds he's in a world where psychic powers abound, and they want him to complete a mission only he can accomplish. Wr: Alan Brennert, based on a story by Philip DeGuere and Steven Bocho. Dir: Martha Coolidge.

Matthew Forman (Scott Wilson); Sarah (Tess Harper); Joshua (Larry Riley); John (D.W. Brown); Irene (Jeanne Mori).

18.1. Gramma
Left alone with a dying grandmother during a dark and stormy night, a boy discovers she is a witch. Wr: Harlan Ellison, based on the short story by Stephen King. Dir: Bradford May.

Georgie (Barret Oliver); Mother (Darlanne Fluegel); Gramma (Frederick Long).

18.2. Personal Demons
A screenwriter is having the writer's block of his life when strange impish creatures start haunting him and only he can see them. Wr: Rockne S. O'Bannon. Dir: Peter Medak.

Rockne O'Bannon (Martin Balsam); Herman Gold (Joshua Shelley); Agent (Clive Revill); Widow (Marlena Giovi); Pam (Penny Baker); Gary (Stephen Flanigan); Creature #1 (Tommy Madden); Creature (Billy Curtis); Creature (Gary Friedkin); Creature (Kevin Thompson); Creature (Don Frishman); Creature (Lou Carry); Creature (Jerry Maren).

18.3. Cold Reading
An actor shows up at a radio station to perform in a radio play. When an old voodoo stick is accidentally activated, the play becomes more real than anything anyone expected. Wr: Martin Pasko and Rebecca Parr. Dir: Gus Trikonis.

Nelson Westbrook (Dick Shawn); Milo Trent (Lawrence Poindexter); Marilyn Cavendish (Janet Carroll); Jack Holland (Joel Brooks); Carla (Annette McCarthy); Sol (Ralph Manza); Announcer (Kevin Scannell); Page (Mike Pniewski); Paul Loomis (Paul Keith); Ed Winter (Thomas Bellin); Also with Jon Melichar.

19.1. The Leprechaun Artist (aka Three Irish Wishes)
Vacationing in the U.S., an Irish leprechaun is caught by three boys. To be freed, he must grant them three wishes. Wr: Tommy Lee Wallace, based on a story by James Crocker. Dir: Tommy Lee Wallace.

Leprechaun (Cork Hubbert); J.P. (Joey Green); J.P.'s mom (Marguerite DeLaine); Richie (Bradley Gregg); Richie's dad (Burr Middleton); Buddy (Danny Nucci); Buddy's dad (Chuck Stransky); Buddy's mom (Melinda Peterson); Sgt. Brewer (James Hess).

19.2. Dead Run
A truck driver wants a job so desperately, he lands the plum job of transporting people to hell! Wr: Alan Brennert, based on the short story by Greg Bear. Dir: Paul Tucker.

Johnny Davis (Steve Railsback); Executive (John DeLancie); Pete (Barry Corbin); Gary Frick (Ebbie Roe Smith); Merle (James Lashly); Gay man (John LeMay); Middle-aged man (Ritch Brinkley); Draft dodger (Brent Spiner); Addict (Nancy Lenehan); Employee #1 (Brian Libby); Employee #2 (Howard Mungo); Elderly woman (Gertrude Flynn); Bald man (David Wells); Fat woman (Pat Ast); Ferret (Brad Fisher); Mean-looking man (Jimmie F. Skaggs); Young woman (Andy Landis); Trucker #2 (John Barlow); Young girl (Virginia Lantry); Woman #1 (Lisa Cloud); Woman #2 (Donna Lynn Leavy); Man #2 (Gregory Wagrowski).

20.1. Profile in Silver
A time-traveler comes back from the future to study the assassination of JFK. But he gets so involved in the life of the president that he breaks the rules of time travel and saves his life. Wr: J. Neil Schulman. Dir: John Hancock.

Professor Fitzgerald (Lane Smith); President Kennedy (Andrew Robinson); Livingston (Louis Giambalvo); Dr.

Kate Wagner (Barbara Baxley); Lyndon B. Johnson (Jerry Hardin); Presidential aide (Ken Hill); Texan (Huck Liggett).

20.2. Button, Button
A married couple living on welfare are offered a box with a button on it. If they press the button, $200,000 will be given to them, but someone they do not know will be killed. Wr: Logan Swanson (Richard Matheson). Dir: Peter Medak.

Norma (Mare Winningham); Arthur (Brad Davis); Steward (Basil Hoffman).

21.1. Need to Know
When people start going insane at a small farming community, a federal investigator arrives and becomes totally baffled. But soon he realizes the truth of life is being transmitted from person to person. Wr: Mary Sheldon, based on a short story by Sidney Sheldon. Dir: Paul Lynch.

Edward Sayers (William L. Peterson); Jeffrey Potts (Robin Gammell); Amanda Strickland (Frances McDormand); Mr. Strickland (Harold Ayer); Dr. Benitz (Eldon Quick); Mrs. Hotchkiss (Ellen Albertini Dow); Dr. Fall (Shay Garner).

21.2. Red Snow
A KGB investigator is sent to Siberia to investigate the deaths of party officials. Later, he discovers that Stalin's exiles are alive and well and the bodies of the dead people are drained of blood. Wr: Michael Cassutt. Dir: Jeannot Szwarc.

Col. Yanof (George Dzunda); Valentina (Victoria Tennant); Minister (Rod Colbin); Vladimir (Andrew Divoff); Grishenko (Jack Ross Obney); Galya (Kimberly Ann Morris); Golodkin (Mike Kulcsan); Villager (Tom Maier); Povin (Barry Miller); Titov (Vladamir Skomarovsky).

22.1. Take My Life ... Please!
After stealing someone else's standup act, a comedian dies in a car crash struggling with the competitor. He winds up in Hell, and his eternal life depends on the quality of his next performances. Wr: Gordon Mitchell. Dir: Gus Trikonis.

Billy Diamond (Tim Thomerson); Max (Ray Buktenica); Dave (Xander Berkeley); Marty (Jim MacKrell).

22.2. Devil's Alphabet
A college group hold their "Devil's Alphabet" meetings every year. But when one of them dies, all the rest begin dying because of foul play. Wr: Robert Hunter. Dir: Ben Bolt.

Frederick (Ben Cross); Grant (Hywell Bennett); Andrew (Osmond Bullock); Creditor (Stuart Dowling); Chimney sweep (Christopher Carroll); Assistant (Christopher Grove).

22.3. The Library
Landing a new job at a vast private library, a girl is warned never to look at the books. Taking a peek, she learns there's a book for everyone alive. When a neighbor pesters her, she rewrites his biography. Wr: Anne Collins. Dir: John Hancock.

Ellen Pendleton (Frances Conroy); Gloria (Uta Hagen); Lori Pendleton (Lori Petty); Doug Kelleher (Joe Santos); Carla (Candy Azzara); Edwin (Alan Blumenfeld); Man (Jay Gerber); Woman (Mimi Monaco).

23.1. Shadow Play
When a man is sentenced to death for murder, he tries to convince everyone the trial is not reality but just another of his never-ending dreams. Wr: James Crocker, based on a story and teleplay by Charles Beaumont. Dir: Paul Lynch.

Adam Grant (Peter Coyote); Mark Ritchie (Guy Boyd); Erin Jacobs (Janet Eilber); Carol Ritchie (Deborah May); Father Grant (William Schallert); Flash (Ramon Bieri); Guard (William Smith); Jimmy (Earl Billings); Judge (George O. Petrie); Foreman (Ella Raino Edwards); Warden (Hank Garrett); Munoz (Gilbert la Pena).

23.2. Grace Note
An opera singer is having a hard time lately. Her sister is at the hospital dying. But the sick sister leaves a precious gift: a glimpse into the future, when the singer is a world-famous star. Wr: Patrice Messina. Dir: Peter Medak.

Rosemarie Miletti (Julia Migenes-Johnson); Mary Miletti (Sydney Penney); Angelina (Rhoda Gemignani); Maestro Barbieri (Kay E. Kuter); Dorothy at 35 (Catherine Paolone); Sam (Ross Evans); Angelini (Ruth Zakarian); Dorothy at 9 (Gina Marie Vinaccia); Joey (Elliott Scott); Old woman (Tony Sawyer); Cabbie (Tom Finnegan); Guard (Craig Schaefer); Woman (Sandy Lipton).

24.1. A Day in Beaumont
In the 1950s a flying saucer crash-lands on Earth. The crash is observed by a couple. They run into town, but no one there believes them. Wr: David Gerrold. Dir: Philip DeGuere.

Dr. Kevin Carlson (Victor Garber); Faith (Stacy Nelkin); Sheriff Haskins (Kenneth Tobey); Pops (John Agar); H.G. Orson (Jeff Morrow); Major Whitmore (Warren Stevens); Sergeant (Richard Partlow); Young man (Myles O'Brien).

24.2. The Last Defender of Camelot
In modern-day London, Sir Lancelot encounters Morgan, who convinces him that Merlin must be freed from his eternal sleep. Wr: George R.R. Martin, based on a short story by Roger Zelanzy. Dir: Jeannot Szwarc.

Lancelot (Richard Kiley); Morgan (Jenny Agutter); Merlin (Norman Lloyd); Tom (John Cameron Mitchell); Punk #1 (Anthony LaPaglia); Punk #2 (Don Stark).

Memory Flash—Philip DeGuere: "We made a significant error in judgment in how many special effects we could produce in time to put that show on the air. We had over 200 special effects frames that had to be done, and we simply ran out of time!" The final sequence, a battle between Lancelot and Merlin, didn't go as planned. "The actors were doing things and there were supposed to be rays and beams being thrown back and forth, but you don't see them! It's really embarrassing. I swore to myself

I would never do another episode with as much special effects as that one."

Season 2: 1986-87

25.1. The Once and Future King
An Elvis impersonator is abruptly transported to the 1950s. There he meets the real Elvis, who thinks he's his brother. Wr: George R. R. Martin, story by Bryce Maritano. Dir: Jim McBride.

Gary Pitkin/Elvis Presley (Jeff Yagher); Sandra (Lisa Jane Perskey); Boss (Red West); Sam Phillips (Paul Eiding); Marion Keisky (Banks Harper); Bill (Brian Hatton); Scotty (Mitch Carter); Waitress (Cynthia Sanders); Barmaid (Nancy Throckmorton).

25.2. A Saucer of Loneliness
A mousey waitress encounters a glowing UFO which gives her a message that everyone wants to know. But she refuses to reveal what it is. Wr: David Gerrold, based on a short story by Theodore Sturgeon. Dir: John Hancock.

Margaret (Shelly Duvall); Man on beach (Richard Libertini); Mother (Nan Martin); Psychiatrist (Myrna White); Clerk (Michael Zand); Boyfriend (Brick Karnes); Hank Charles (James Edward Thomas); Officer (Bruno Aclin); Waitress (Laura Harlan); Anchorman (Geoff Witcher); Reporter #1 (Mary Ingersoll); Reporter #2 (David Grant Hayward); Reporter #3 (Shannon Lee Avnsoe); Reporter #4 (Omar Hansen); Jill (Mari Gorman); Young man (Andrew Masset).

26.1. What Are Friends For?
A lonely young boy discovers a new friend in "Mike," whom he meets in the forest. But no one believes Mike exists, and the father realizes Mike was a friend he had when he was a child. Wr: J. Michael Straczynski. Dir: Gus Trikonis.

Alex Mattingly (Tom Skerritt); Jeff Mattingly (Fred Savage); Mike (Lukas Haas); Allyson Conrad (Joy Claussen); Ross Conrad (Michael Ennis); Tim (Mark-Paul Gosselaar); Larry (Johnny Green); Cindy (Jennifer Roach); Doctor (David Selberg).

26.2. Aqua Vita
An aging TV anchor becomes worried about her appearance, so she seeks out Aqua Vita, a youth-retaining water. Wr: Jeremy Bertrand Finch and Paul Chitlik. Dir: Paul Tucker.

Christie (Mimi Kennedy); Marc (Joseph Hacker); Shauna (Barbara Horan); Delivery man (Christopher McDonald); News editor (Martin Doyle); Sales manager (Bob Delegall); Ted (John Le May); Man (Harry Stephens); Woman (Cynthia Kania).

27.1. The Storyteller
An old woman remembers her first teaching job when a boy constantly read stories to his grandfather, keeping him alive for 141 years. Wr: Rockne O'Bannon. Dir: Paul Lynch.

Dorothy (Glynnis O'Connor); Micah Frost (David Faustino); Grandfather Frost (Parley Baer); Heather (Nike

Doukas); Old woman (Ellen Albertini Dow); Bus driver (Robert Britton); Mrs. Dockweiller (Patricia Allison); William (Morgan Saint John); Daniel (Tony Anton); Nathaniel (Billy Anton); Pig-tailed girl (Melissa Clayton); Farmboy (Billie-Joe Wright); Doctor (Bill Sak); Man with scar (Frank Moon).

27.2. Night Song
A young D.J. working the graveyard shift at a radio station rediscovers a record album by her boyfriend, who disappeared five years ago. But when he suddenly appears again, she's surprised and upset. Wr: Michael Reaves. Dir: Bradford May.

Andrea Fields (Lisa Eilbacher); Ace (Kenneth David Gilman); Simon Locke (Antony Hamilton).

28.1. The After Hours
Arriving very late at a shopping mall, a woman becomes trapped and falls into a cat-and-mouse game with mannequins that are coming alive. Wr: Rockne O'Bannon, based on a story and teleplay by Rod Serling. Dir: Bruce Malmuth.

Marcia Cole (Terry Farrell); Thin man (Ned Bellamy); Clerk (Ann Wedgeworth); Workman (Chip Heller); Mother (Lori Michaels); Boy (Edan Gross); Mannequin #1 (Albie Selznick); Mannequin #2 (Deborah Bennett).

28.2. Lost and Found
A young college student has been losing personal items for some time. The mystery is resolved when she finds two time-travelers in her closet. Wr: George R.R. Martin, based on a short story by Phyllis Eisenstein. Dir: Gus Trikonis.

Jenny Templeton (Akousa Busia); Kathy (Cindy Harrell); Raye Birk (Leslie Ackerman).

28.3. The World Next Door
An inventor finds a passageway in his basement that leads to another world, where his counterpart leads a successful life. Wr: Lan O'Kun. Dir: Paul Lynch.

Barney Schlesinger (George Wendt); Katie (Bernadette Birkett); Milt (Jeffrey Tambor); Lucille (Victoria Bass); Francine (Dinah Lenney); Butler (John Mennick).

29.1. The Toys of Caliban
A retarded boy's parents are frightened by his gift of conjuring anything he wants after seeing a picture of it, but when he gets food poisoning, they become even more terrified. Wr: George R.R. Martin, based on a story by Terry Matz. Dir: Thomas J. Wright.

Ernest Ross (Richard Mulligan); Mary Ross (Anne Haney); Mandy (Alexandra Borrie); Toby Ross (David Greenlee); Resident (Richard Biggs); Minister (Earl Bullock).

Memory Flash—Thomas J. Wright: "[David Greenlee, the lead child actor] was very interesting and much older than you thought he was. Working with Richard [Mulligan] was a pleasant experience. If you want to do a good show, you listen to everybody and particularly listen to actors, because I feel when they're doing a part, they get into the part and analyze it pretty well, whether their thoughts are right or wrong on it. At least you listened to them. Richard contributed lots to the show. His whole presence added a lot to the show. An overall good working experience."

30.1. The Convict's Piano

A man in prison who insists he is innocent of a crime discovers a piano that transports him to the olden days of gangsters. Wr: Patricia Messina, based on a story by James Crocker. Dir: Thomas J. Wright.

Frost (Joe Penney); Eddie O'Hara (Norman Fell); Mickey Shaughnessy (Tom O'Brien); Dr. Puckett (John Hancock); Ellen (Cristen Kauffman).

31.1. The Road Less Traveled

A man who dodged the Vietnam draft gets visions of his other life as a soldier during the war. Wr: George R.R. Martin. Dir: Wes Craven.

Jeff McDowell (Cliff DeYoung); Denise McDowell (Margaret Klenck); Megan (Jaclyn-Rose Lester); Susan (Clare Nono); Jock (John Zarchen); Grunt (Christopher Brown).

32.1. The Card

A compulsive spender accepts "The Card" to keep up her habit. But stringent penalties kick in for late payments. Wr: Michael Cassutt. Dir: Bradford May.

Linda Wolfe (Susan Blakely); Miss Foley (Virgina Kiser); Brian Wolfe (William Atherton); Salesman (Ken Lerner); Receptionist (Beverly Eilbacher); Evan Wolfe (Coleby Lombardo); Matthew Wolfe (Zachary Bostrom); Tow truck driver (Frank Mangano).

32.2. The Junction

Trapped in a mine shaft, a man finds another person also stuck inside, and the man is from the year 1912. Wr: Virgina Aldridge. Dir: Bill Duke.

John Parker (William Allen Young); Ray (Chris Mulkey); Schmidt (Michael Alldredge); Melissa (Tanya Boyd); Bobby (James Lashley); Les (John Walcutt); Mrs. Clark (Ann Doran); First rescuer (Joe Unger); Sarah (Karen Landry); Woman (Dianna Patton); Stretcher bearer (Boby Hosea); Second rescuer (Christopher Kriesa); Also with John Dennis Johnston.

33.1. Joy Ride

Two teenage boys and their girlfriends steal a recently deceased man's classic car, but while on a joy ride, they accidentally kill a policeman. Wr: Cal Willingham. Dir: Gil Bettman.

Alonzo (Rob Knepper); Gregory (Brooke McCarter); Deena (Heidi Kozak); Adrienne (Tamara Mark); Policeman (Burr Middleton); Patrolman (Danny Spear); Fireman (Randy Hall).

33.2. Shelter Skelter

A survivalist traps himself inside his bomb shelter when a blast finally comes. Wr: Ron Cobb and Robin Love. Dir: Martha Coolidge.

Harry Dobbs (Joe Mantegna); Sally (Joan Allen); Nick (Jonathan Gries).

33.3. Private Channel

A hyperactive, obnoxious kid accidentally tunes into another channel on his Walkman radio while onboard a plane flight. Lightning transforms the radio into a telepathic tuning device, and he learns that the man he's sitting next to has a bomb. Wr: Edward Redlich, based on a story by Edward Redlich and John Bellucci. Dir: Peter Medak.

Keith Barnes (Scott Coffey); Williams (Andrew Robinson); Gloria (Claudia Cron); Mrs. Feldman (Louise Fitch); Trish (Joan Foley); Yuppie man (Roger Nolan); Clerk (Rebeccah Bush); Host (Alex Daniels); Yuppie woman (Julie Araskoc); Paul (Jackson Hughes); Little girl (Juliette Sorci).

34.1. Time and Teresa Golowitz

The Prince of Darkness visits a composer who has just died of a heart attack. Given one wish, the man wants to relive a youthful encounter with the girl of his dreams, Mary Ellen Kasgrove. Wr: Alan Brennert, based on a short story by Parke Godwin. Dir: Shelley Levinson.

Prince of Darkness (Gene Barry); Bluestone (Paul Sand); Binki (Grant Heslov); Teresa Golowitz (Kristi Lynes); Laura (Gina Gershon); Bob (Beau Dremann); Mary Ellen Cosgrove (Heather Haase); Nelson (Wally Ward); Boy at party (J.D. Roth); Girl (Laurel Green).

34.2. Voices in the Earth

In the far future, an expedition returns to a desolate, barren Earth, where a scientist begins to see the ghosts of those who died years ago. Wr: Alan Brennert. Dir: Curtis Harrington.

Prof. Donald Knowles (Martin Balsam); Jacinda Carlyle (Jenny Agutter); Archer (Tim Russ); Ghost (Wortham Kimmer); Bledsoe (Dennis Haskins); Old man (Ted Lehmann); Old woman (Eve Brenner); Girl (Sandra Ganzer); Young woman (C'esca Lawrence); Middle-aged man (Christopher Lofton).

35.1. Song of a Younger World

In 1916, a young couple who are in love are prevented from being together by the girl's vengeful father. But with the help of a very special book, they can be together for the rest of their lives. Wr: Anthony and Nancy Lawrence. Dir: Noel Black.

Tanner (Pete Kowanko); Amy (Jennifer Rubin); Buchanan (Vincent Rebholz); The Hoakie (Paul Benedict); Mordecai Hawkline (Roberts Blossom).

35.2. The Girl I Married

An attorney and his wife have successful careers, but they feel something is lacking in their marriage. Soon, both begin encountering younger versions of their mates. Wr: J.M. DeMatteis. Dir: Philip DeGuere.

Ira Richman (James Whitmore Jr.); Valerie (Linda Kelsey); Younger Valerie (Andrea Aal); Marvin Weingrod (Dennis Patrick); Bartender (Robert Zappa)..

The Twilight Zone (Syndicated)
1988–1989

Further episodes from the 1980s version of the science fiction anthology created by Rod Serling that explores the darkest depths of an individual as he crosses over into "the twilight zone." Short tales of surrealism, morality plays, personal nightmares and flights of fantasy characterize the show.

Executive Producer: Michael MacMillian, Mark Shelmerdine; *Producer:* Seaton McLean; *Narrator:* Robin Ward; *Main Title Theme:* Grateful Dead and Merl Saunders; Syndicated/MGM-Atlantis Films; 30 minutes.

The only reason this *Twilight Zone* incarnation was produced was to create enough episodes to assemble a syndication package for sale to independent stations around the country.

Created for considerably less money than its recent predecessor (allegedly half of the CBS revival's budget) and filmed in Toronto, Canada, with an entirely different production crew and writers, the syndicated *Twilight Zone* consisted of 30 episodes. Produced in collaboration with CBS, MGM/UA, Atlantis Films, and London Films, this show's segments were integrated with the CBS episodes and sold as a single package.

Because much of the show was filmed in Canada, "Canadian Content" requirements were on order and were filled by experienced film directors, with the writing staff in Los Angeles. On the acting side, supporting players were usually Canadians playing off imported American "marquee" names. Some of the names that joined this production included Louise Fletcher, Anthony Franciosa, Harry Morgan, Timothy Bottoms, Eddie Albert, Deborah Raffin, William Sanderson, Dean Stockwell and many others.

For Canadian directors Randy Bradshaw and Brad Turner, who worked at other times on another Atlantis Films project, *The Ray Bradbury Theater*, *The Twilight Zone* was an opportunity to stretch their craft in telling meaningful stories that they hoped would move their viewers to think about what they were watching.

"It seems to me that watching television today … there's a tremendous amount of action," says Bradshaw. "Not much of television is about the human spirit, the human condition and humanity."

Bradshaw cites "The Trance," a script by Jeff Stuart and J. Michael Straczynski, as an entry he directed that explored the human spirit—literally. In "The Trance," Leonard Randall professes himself a trance-channeler, a man who becomes psychically connected to otherworldly beings, who speak through him.

"It was very internal, imagining what the other place would be," says Bradshaw. "There was no indication in the script this was a modern story. How successful was he? How grand could you make it? How much money did we have to spend on the show to make it grand? The actual trance-channeling room where he brought his guests in, what was that going to look like? His office, the place where he sold all his tapes, and all the other things…. The script allowed for real production creativity in dealing with those elements, which read very well and created images in your mind, but [which we] were not always capable of creating in five days."

Because all *Twilight Zone*s were filmed in Toronto, American actors had to be imported so American viewers would see a recognizable face. Bradshaw tapped *Newhart*'s Peter Scolari for the role of Leonard Randall, the trance-channeler.

"I thought it was a real performance episode. It's a very dialogue-heavy show and I like the technical challenge of being in the talk show"—the portion of the show where Randall talks to an interviewer about his channeling powers.

With fellow actor Neil Munro, Scolari and Bradshaw, in the name of research, visited a real channeler. "We went on a Saturday before we started shooting," recalls Bradshaw. "And, a young man went into a trance and we talked about why [this old man] had come back to Earth through this young man. He'd answer questions, whatever we'd wanted. Peter asked about his family, I asked about spirit guides. It was a remarkable experience for me. I would not say whether it's real or unreal, I don't know. But to see someone transform in front of you from a 25-year-old man into a 75-year-old man I thought was quite remarkable. The way he gripped the chair, his whole posture, his breathing, his face looked drawn, the color had gone from his face. So, that was on Saturday. We talked a lot about it afterwards. Then we had a rehearsal on Sunday. Peter and I spent a lot of time discussing what he would do. What's organic that Peter could utilize for his performance? I didn't want to do post-production on it, I wanted *him* to create the sound of the voice, and so we worked on that, and for the most part, that's what Peter was able to accomplish.

"He had to play three characters at once, slipping in and out of the real guy, the real guy who's faking the trance to make money, and really channeling for the demon. Very challenging for an actor to know how far to go, how far to swing. Everybody just doesn't all of a sudden go, 'Oh, my god!'

"It's remarkable how many people I talk to have a real predilection for accepting the idea of trance-channeling. There are those who have a strong belief and leaning towards the spiritual world. Going all the way from horoscopes, to being psychic, all that stuff. I found out there's a world out there who make money off it."

Regarding anecdotes connected to the production, Bradshaw grins and said, "We're shooting with Peter in the television studio with Jeanne, a real interviewer, a celebrity in her own right in Toronto. Peter's a very funny guy, so we thought, we gotta play a trick on him here. He was [elsewhere] doing something so we told the whole crew … if Peter screws up here, everybody was to walk right on stage, while he's doing this scene, and start applauding. So, we're shooting and he doesn't know what's going on, and all of a sudden, we've got 50 guys up on his stage applauding. Quite funny.

Timothy Bottoms stars in "The Helgrammite Method" as a man who can't stop drinking. He resorts to desperate measures, with startling results. Copyright 1988 Atlantis Films.

Shooting was … technically, very difficult … trying to figure out, 'He shouldn't go here' or 'Should he walk over here?' It's dialogue and choreography."

In another episode for *Twilight Zone*, a remake of George Clayton Johnson's "A Game of Pool," (a classic from Rod Serling's days) Bradshaw once again faced a technical challenge: "You talk about action films. We got two guys in one room for the whole show! How do you make that interesting so people would watch?"

The actors involved, Maury Chaykin and Esai Morales, replaced the classics' Jonathan Winters and Jack Klugman, respectively. Oddly, "A Game of Pool" wound up using Johnson's original ending—not used in the classic episode—in which the young pool challenger *lost*. *Twilight Zone* was in the midst of a Los Angeles writers' strike at the time, so this script was bought.

"I knew that the actors would be all-consumed by this game of pool, and by [the challenge of] making them look like they're real pool players," says Bradshaw. "Good enough; we played pool in downtown Toronto. Maury hadn't played much pool before, but I think he still had the knack for it. While Esai Morales didn't know how to play pool, he was quite good and quite excited."

As Bradshaw says, these stories primarily consisted of choreography and dialogue, and this episode was no exception. "We were able to get a pool expert. I'm no expert, [but] at least I was able to play a little bit to figure out where the balls would go, where he would stand, where I would want him to stand, what he would have to do. So, we did have two continuity people on that show because after every shot, we had to redo it. The balls had to be set up at the table again, exactly like they were, so we had to know in case we had to come back tomorrow or even one shot to the next."

Maury Chaykin, who played the legendary pool shark Fats Brown, says he had the flu throughout the production and doesn't remember much about it. "I was aware that it had been done before with Jonathan Winters and Jack Klugman," he says. "I did see it; it popped off the television before I did the segment. I watched it and was not intimidated by it at all. Primarily because I felt that it wasn't very good. The acting wasn't very good. I don't know if the acting in *ours* was very good either, but I was not very impressed by Jonathan Winters. I mean, I didn't think he was very good. It was early in his career. I guess he started out as an actor, and you can imagine someone with his talent, his enormous talent, confined within a script. A lot of incredibly talented people, when they're confined to doing scripts that aren't really suited specifically to them, don't really shine or they're not great in them."

Despite the fact that his mind "was somewhere else" during the shoot, Chaykin did get a chance to work on some moves on the table. "It's very funny. I remember learning some pool tricks, and there were some shots that were made on camera. I'm not a pool player. I play a little now, but I was surprised I got that good, making moves on camera. But no, I'm not a good pool player."

In contrast to Chaykin's opinion, director Bradshaw admires the original take on the story by Winters and Klugman. "Great performances. I really enjoyed that. I thought they did a great job. Performances were just great, and I thought, 'How in hell are we going to measure up to that?' I liked the original ending."

Brad Turner's stint in directing "Acts of Terror" gave him a rare opportunity to tell a story that could have deep meaning for viewers. "Acts" wasn't just entertainment. It was a gripping, emotional story of a man (played by Kenneth Welsh) frequently and willfully beating his wife (Melanie Mayron). One day the wife receives a gift from her sister: a small silver statue of a dog. In times of need, the dog comes alive to save her from the vicious husband. "It was a very classic *Twilight Zone* story. It was imaginative," says Turner. "Wife-beating is a very contemporary problem that's come to the surface. That part of it I really liked. The challenge was to make the story a compassionate story about one individual's tale. Technically, the challenge is to make it believable.

"What I wanted to happen was to have the compassion between the dog and her—the dog is really an extension of her—to be a part of her. What was really nice about it was that Melanie Mayron likes dogs and actually had a dog in New York at the time. She had a full-sized poodle. We talked at length about it during the first rehearsals. She felt she was relating more to her dog than her husband!" laughs Turner.

Turner says that the story (by J. Michael Straczynski) has two parts: "The first part is that a cousin needs her. The second part is, she loves this man. She somehow can't shake the fact that she loves him. And he still wants it to be war. And what we're trying to do is tell the audience that the reality is she loves this guy. So, why get beaten? The dog comes alive as part of her and says, 'You can't do this anymore!' My idea was that she found the internal strength to say, 'I'm leaving.' For many, many people that's a very hard thing to do. That's amazing: 'I'm leaving.' I hope one female audience member finds some strength from that show. I thought, maybe, 'Oh, I'm just telling a story for television. [But] I'd better believe there's somebody out there who found the strength from that show.' It's very strong in terms of subject. It's very strong in terms of how it's presented. But there are moments in there where you realize, this guy can actually be kind of nice." And that's chilling.

Director of photography Andreas Poulsson

remembers that in "Acts of Terror," Turner wanted a shot from the point of view of the dog as it approaches the truck; the viewer doesn't see that it's a dog until the camera reverse-cuts from inside the truck and he's barking against the window. "We had very little time," said Poulsson. "It was very simple. It was just myself, running with the camera through the woods, and I think given the fact that the technology of it was very simple … it was very effective in heightening the suspense of that sequence."

Turner says he has not received any feedback from viewers regarding this segment of *Twilight Zone*, but he remembers the crew's reaction in a private screening. Crews are normally cordial and somewhat boisterous during screenings. There may be shots that are funny to them but not to the average viewer. Because they're the ones who create the shows and are on set, crews usually have a different perspective than the television audience. "There's baggage that audiences never know about that happens and when something's funny," says Turner. "[But] the crew saw it, and … just after the first five minutes, they fell silent, and the whole entire screening was absolutely dead silent. It sucks you in. It's the kind of story that really affects you, because [the wife] is so badly affected by it."

When asked why *Twilight Zone* is such a cultish, famous and successful show, Turner says, "It's an anthology show that is based on an individual's strengths or weaknesses and how normal, average people are driven to limits and how they recover. It's how they've learned or grown from the experience. The audience relates to the neighbor down the street, or the person I work with, or the guy in government.

Christianne Hirt and Terence Knox star in "Cold Equation," a memorable *Twilight Zone* drama in which a young girl stows away on a spaceship and places the pilot in a deadly dilemma. Copyright 1988 Atlantis Films.

"I always felt that when you were going to sit down and watch *Twilight Zone* you would actually learn something from it, something about life. You might agree or disagree with it, but it would definitely cause a reaction."

The challenge for anyone on any new version of *Twilight Zone* is doing the show without the presence of the show's creator and spirit, Rod Serling. "It'll never be the same without Rod. It's definitely not as good without Rod. As a host, we definitely miss him. But there were shows, in terms of writing, that were just as good as his stuff."

With nine episodes to his credit, Paul Lynch has the distinction of having worked on more new *Twilight Zones* than any other director (that's if you count the CBS years and syndicated episodes together). Lynch's facility for working in either Toronto or Los Angeles certainly was an advantage in this regard.

Lynch remembers that a syndicated episode,

Frances Hyland and Eddie Albert star in "Dream Me a Life," written by J. Michael Straczynski. Copyright 1988 Atlantis Films.

Harlan Ellison's "Crazy as a Soup Sandwich," provided some substantial weights for his directing muscles to heft.

"It was the longest schedule of any of them," sighs Lynch. "Six days. It was based on a Harlan Ellison short story. It was very stylized; it was done like a comic book and shot like a comic book, with strange angles and multicolored lighting. Because it was that kind of story, and it was hyper-real in the sense that it wasn't like the '30s, '40s or the '90s. It was just in no-man's-time. So in effect, we were sort of the pre-runner of *Dick Tracy* in the sense of the wild colors and the kind of look that they got. We created our own world, with strange angles and camera moves and things like that, so it was great fun to do.

"Of course, it had this creature in it, this monster. I had worked with the actor Gerry Robbins before, and so we brought him in and he played this creature. He's huge. He's, like, seven feet tall. Anthony Franciosa was in it, and Wayne Robson, and they were wonderful. It was done like a combination of comic books and old '40s movies. It was great fun."

"Crazy as a Soup Sandwich" is a sell-your-soul-to-the-devil tale in which flaky, spineless Arky Lockner is fleeing from a demon to another man, Mr. Lancaster, for help. It's a story that reminds poor Arky that you just *can't* get out of selling your soul...

Before filming "Soup Sandwich," Lynch recalls, he met with Ellison for a consultation on the script. "We chatted a little bit about it. He was very specific. To Harlan, he wants it *exactly* the way he wrote it. And of course, we *couldn't* get it exactly the way he wanted because of production things. We had to drop a scene because we could not afford to do it, and he was rather upset about it. But it just wasn't possible in six days. We didn't really need it. But because he wrote it, he was really pissed off about the cutting of the scene.

"In the course of [the story], Mr. Lancaster is going to solve Arky's problem. He leaves his henchmen and girlfriend behind. The cut in the show is, he's back and he's got this box. The way Harlan wanted it was [to show] that he went outside and he dug up the box." A later suggestion was to have him retrieve the box from a safety deposit box at the bank, but this idea, too, was dropped. "There was no way to do it in the schedule we had. But I remember Harlan was pissed off.

"In the script, they go to a store that sold devices for doing dope—pipes and paraphernalia. I think, originally, when he wrote the script, it was a long time ago. It just dated the whole thing. We found a beauty parlor that was great and had the look and feel of a strange time period. A beauty parlor seemed like a better idea. But because it wasn't his idea, he didn't like it."

As a consequence, explains Lynch, Ellison did not completely like the finished product. "Because we didn't do the scene of his dope emporium and we didn't do the scene at the bank. You know Harlan: Unless you do it word for word, you can't do [it justice]. He didn't really hate it; he just didn't necessarily agree with all the things we did, because he wanted it his way, and we couldn't do it his way because of budget restrictions. In his world you should spend millions of dollars to do it exactly the way he wants it. But you just can't do that. But we came as close as we could, and we certainly kept it in the spirit of what he was trying to do."

In 1990, as the first issue in a series of original stories from the *Twilight Zone*, Now Comics created an adaptation of Ellison's "Crazy as a Soup Sandwich," drawn by well-known industry artist Neal Adams. Receiving a copy during his interview, Lynch—who had never seen or heard of the comic—is surprised and excited. "I used to be a cartoonist when I was a kid and I remember writing to Neal Adams," he says. "Being a cartoonist, I used to collect comics, and I have an original Neal Adams–signed *Ben Casey* strip. How strange! Small world!"

Lynch says that the comic is a reflection of the script "in every word and in every way." He believes Adams must have viewed the episode to do the adaptation because of various things that matched—despite the fact that Lancaster's fetching-the-box scene is restored here as a bank sequence, and the beauty parlor is once again a dope emporium.

"If you look at the comic book and the show, the design of the little room they're in, with the triangle on the floor, and all of that, it's very similar to my beauty salon," explains Lynch. "The way [the emporium sequence] was staged in the comic book and how I did it in the show was very, very similar, so it was kind of interesting. [You'll find] a lot of similarity if you see the show and you see the comic book."

Before getting cast in "Rendezvous in a Dark Place" as Janet Leigh's son, Canadian actor Malcolm Stewart was in Los Angeles acting in a CBS television series, *Almost Grown*. As Stewart tells the story: "I was at Universal and I happened to be doing a scene with a girl; I'm having a shower and she comes in the shower like the *Psycho* scene. Jokingly, with a sponge, she's singing the *Psycho* music to scare me. The minute we finished doing that scene, I got a call from my agent, who said, 'Would you like to fly up to do a *Twilight Zone*?' And I said, 'Sure!' [And my agent said,] 'You're working with Janet Leigh!' Amazing coincidence!"

When Stewart actually got to the Toronto soundstages, he told Leigh about the coincidence. Then, he says, he asked her "so many questions about what it was like working with Alfred Hitchcock. It took seven days and 70 shots to do that [*Psycho*] shower scene to get 30 seconds of film. Uncommon! Unbelievable! Nobody shoots like that anymore! So, that's what I remember about *Twilight Zone*. It's not the script, but working with Janet Leigh."

When told that *Twilight Zone* would be coming to Canada for production, Andreas Poulsson, an experienced cinematographer of many television shows and documentaries, was excited. "I was always a big fan of *Twilight Zone*," says Poulsson. As the director of photography on the show, Poulsson's job was "to serve in telling the story. In reading and analyzing the script, seeing the locations, and discussing with the director, we come up with an appropriate look for the film and if there's any special effects and that sort of thing. You know, we're in the business of storytelling, and the cinematography serves to tell the story as much as any other element that a director makes.

"I don't think that a cinematographer necessarily should put their own stamp on it as much as serving the needs of the story. My style, the things I prefer in myself, especially in the case of *Twilight Zone*, is that *Twilight Zone* is generally suspense and it has a spooky aspect to it. [You want to] shoot in a low-key, dark-contrasty look as opposed to a bright look. The normal situation before it builds up to the supernatural element, is you start out with very ordinary people in very ordinary circumstances, and then all of a sudden something extraordinary happens. So you start with a very normal, everyday look and suddenly everything turns strange, and the look should suggest and complement that."

As one of his favorite sequences from the 11 episodes he photographed, Poulsson cites a segment of "The Helgrammite Method." "It's a sequence where Miles Judson [played by Timothy Bottoms] has his nightmarish dream. I think [it] was very successful. I was quite pleased with that. It was very high, looking straight down at him." Poulsson refers to a sequence where, after having taken the alcoholism cure and having a tapeworm that absorbs alcohol grow inside of him, Bottoms is on the kitchen floor in sheer, screaming agony as the camera zooms in from high above. "We crane down and tighten up on the area of the stomach" where the worm was undulating and quivering, says Poulsson.

As for working with Bottoms, "He was fantastic. He's the kind of actor you talk baseball with one minute and then he gets into the role the next minute and he's in character. He's amazingly quick."

Another segment of note was "The Call," with William Sanderson. "[It's a story] about a lonely man who gets a call from a woman. And it turns out to be a sculpture in a museum. At the very end, she summons him, and he breaks into the museum in order to be with her. But he triggers the alarm, and by the time the guard finds him—and it's the final image of the story—he turns into a statue next to her. And love was finally found in the *Twilight Zone*. I think that was very, very effective and exciting, too."

What Poulsson admires about the syndicated version of *The Twilight Zone* is its emphasis on story over gimmickry. "You would think it would be very heavy on special effects. One of the amazing things about the series is there was relatively very *little* special effects. And of what special effects there were, they were very simple. It was really [no] more than shooting it in 35 [mm film] and locking down the camera so they could superimpose things on the film. Really, it was extremely simple, and yet very effective. The only one with sophisticated special effects ... was the last one filmed ["Crazy as a Soup Sandwich"].

"For me, that's one of the strengths of the *Twilight Zone*—the scripts and the characters. It didn't really need all that fancy special effects. One thing that impressed me about the scripts, when I first read them, was something that's always been true to *Twilight Zone* (the original series with Rod Serling): ... They're very, very strong in story, characters and situations. You know how, in the beginning narration, you can define and set up the story and characters with just a few simple sentences? That's always been one of the things I loved about the *Twilight Zone*. I think ... they've succeeded in continuing that tradition. I think that was one of the most satisfying and fun projects I've been involved with. I kept asking, 'We should do more!' We should have kept going! It was a wonderful concept. Each episode is one individual movie. It's not like series television where you shoot the same characters every week. Here, we're making a whole different movie every episode."

Episode Guide

Season 1: 1988-89

The Curious Case of Edgar Witherspoon
When a woman tries to get her uncle committed, believing he's becoming senile, the investigating doctor finds Edgar living in an apartment made of all kinds of junk ... all designed to keep the world in balance. Wr: Haskell Barkin. Dir: Rene Bonniere.
Edgar Witherspoon (Harry Morgan); Dr. Jeremy Sinclair (Cedric Smith); Mrs. Milligan (Barbar Chilcott); Cynthia (Eve Crawford); Secretary (Pixie Bigelow).

Extra Innings
An ex-baseball player is given a very special, 1909 baseball card of a player that looks just like him. It's so special that he becomes drawn into the card and lives out the life of the player. Wr: Tom Palmer. Dir: Doug Jackson.
Ed Hamler/Hanks (Marc Singer); Paula (Amber Lea Weston); Cindy (Tracey Cunningham); McIntyre (J. Winston Carroll); Umpire (James O'Regan); Receptionist (Lynn Vogt); Baseball announcer (Don Chevrier).

The Crossing
A stressed-out priest repeatedly encounters a station wagon containing a young girl, and the car keeps crashing and bursting into fire. Wr: Ralph Phillips. Dir: Paul Lynch.
Father Mark Cassidy (Ted Shackelford); Monsignor (Gerard Parkes); Billy (Setrge LeBlanc); Kelly (Shelagh Harcourt); Mrs. Maggie Dugan (Bunty Webb).

The Hunters
When a young boy falls into an undiscovered cave near a housing project, an archaeologist studies strange paintings on its walls, and then bizarre incidents begin happening. Cave items are moved around, and animals are killed and brought into the cave. Wr: Paul Chitlik and Jeremy Bertrand Finch. Dir: Paul Lynch.
Dr. Cline (Louise Fletcher); Sheriff (Michael Hogan); Steve (Andrade); Holsen (Les Carlson); Farmer (Bob Warner); Teaching assistant (Jonathan Potts); Also with Steve Andrade.

Dream Me a Life
A man at a retirement home has been having nightmares about a strange woman, but he's shocked when that woman becomes his next-door neighbor. Wr: J. Michael Straczynski. Dir: Allan King.
Roger Simpson Leads (Eddie Albert); Laura (Frances Hyland); Frank (Barry Morse); Husband (Joseph Shaw); Nurse (Michelyn Emile); Boarder #1 (Jack Mather); Boarder #2 (Warren Van Evera).

Memories
A hypnotist who specializes in helping people relive their past lives tries to find her own history, but when she awakens, everyone wants to forget their experiences. Wr: Bob Underwood. Dir: Richard Bugjaski.

Mary McNeil (Barbara Stock); Sinclair (Nigel Bennett); Vigilante (James Kidnie); Mrs. Gustin (Judy Sinclair); Mrs. Vivencore (Deidre Flanagan); Woman (Lucy Filippone); Man (Alan Rosenthal).

The Helgrammite Method
Desperate to rid himself of his alcoholism, a man receives a special pill that absorbs all the alcohol he drinks but with dangerous consequences—unless he stops immediately! Wr: William Selby. Dir: Gilbert Shilton.

Miles Judson (Timothy Bottoms); Dr. Eugene Murrich (Leslie Yao); Frannie (Julie Khaner); Jamie (Alec Willows); Chad (Illya Woloshyn); Stranger (Gerry Salsberg).

Our Sylena Is Dying
When a woman dying of old age grabs her niece's arm during a visit, the niece begins to age rapidly while the aunt recovers miraculously. Wr: J. Michael Straczynski, based on an unproduced story by Rod Serling. Dir: Bruce Pittman.

Dr. Burrell (R.H. Thomson); Martha (Aileen Taylor); Orville (Paul Betts); Susan (Patricia Idette); First nurse (Jackie McLeod); Second nurse (Ann Turnbull); Doctor (Rob McClure); Specialist (Tim Koetting); Officer (Ron Payne); Diane (Jennifer Dale); Deborah (Terri Garber).

The Call
A lonely young man accidentally phones the wrong number and finds an intriguing female to whom he grows attached. When she refuses to meet him, he investigates and finds the phone in a museum, right next to a statue of a woman. Wr: J. Michael Straczynski. Dir: Gilbert Shilton.

Norman Bane (William Sanderson); Voice of Mary Ann (Julie Khaner); Richard (Dan Redican); Museum patron (Jill Frappier); Information lady (Djanet Sears); Museum attendant (Ian Nothnagel).

The Trance
A third-rate con artist who professes to be a dimensional channeler is suddenly confronted by the true demon. Wr: Jeff Stuart and J. Michael Straczynski. Dir: Randy Bradshaw.

Leonard Randall (Peter Scolari); Don (Neil Munro); Gerry (Ted Simonett); Dr. Greenberg (Hrant Alianak); Daphne Blake (Jeanne Beker); Believer #1 (Glynis Davies); Julia (Mona Matteo).

Acts of Terror
A loving wife who's constantly beaten by her husband receives a porcelain dog from her sister. To their amazement, whenever he becomes abusive, the dog comes alive to protect her. Wr: J. Michael Straczynski. Dir: Brad Turner.

Louise Simonson (Melanie Mayron); Sister (Kate Lynch); Brother-in-law (Lee J. Campbell); Jack Simonson (Kenneth Welsh); Postman (James Barron).

20/20 Vision
When a bank loan officer breaks his glasses, he discovers the next time he wears them that they give him a glimpse into the future. Wr: Robert Walden. Dir: Jim Purdy.

Warren Cribbens (Michael Moriarty); Horace Cutler (David Hemblen); Sandy Wheeler (Cynthia Belliveau); Vern Slater (Grant Roll); Teller (Diane Douglas); Farm wife (Evelyn Kaye); Farm boy (Calum McGeachie).

There Was an Old Woman
A famous children's book writer visits a sick boy and reads him one of her stories. Later, at home, she's disturbed by children's voices throughout her house, and learns from his parents that the boy has died. Wr: Tom J. Astle. Dir: Otta Hanus.

Hallie Parker (Colleen Dewhurst); Nancy Harris (Maria Ricossa); Man (Alf Humphreys); Brian (Zachary Bennett); Librarian (David Hughes); Real estate agent (Marilyn Smith); Martin (Karl Pruner); Page (Ferne Downey).

The Trunk
A young man at a rundown hotel discovers an empty trunk that grants any wishes, but during a party he realizes who his true friends are. Wr: Paul Chitlik and Jeremey Bertrand Finch. Dir: Steve DiMarco.

Willy Gardner (Bud Cort); Candy (Lisa Schrage); Danny (Milan Cheylov); Old man (Rummy Bishop); Young woman (Kelly Denomme); Mrs. Kudaba (Elena Kudaba); Cap (Gerry Quigley); Rocco (Mark Danton).

Appointment on Route 17
After completing a heart transplant, a man finds his personality has changed, and he has a strange attraction to a waitress at a road diner. Wr: Haskell Barkin. Dir: Rene Bonniere.

Tom Bennett (Paul LeMat); Mary Jo (Marianna Pascal); Elise (Rosemary Dunsmore); Spence (Chris Bondy); Julie (Lori Hallier); Tom's secretary (Tannis Burnett); Secretary #2 (Lucinda Nielsen).

The Cold Equations
A shuttle pilot on the outer fringes of space finds a stowaway aboard his ship. Because of the extra weight, he does not have enough fuel for his journey and faces a dilemma forcing him to consider jettisoning her into space. Wr: Alan Brennert, based on a short story by Tom Godwin. Dir: Martin Lavut.

Thomas Bartin (Terence Knox); Marilynn (Christianne Hirt); Gerry (Barclay Hope); Commander (Michael J. Reynolds); Clerk (Nicky Guadagni).

Strangers in Possum Meadows
A young boy playing in the fields encounters an older man, an alien, who is scouting for specimens to bring back to his planet. Wr: Paul Chitlik and Jeremy Bertrand Finch. Dir: Sturla Gunnerson.

Scout (Steve Kanaly); Danny Wilkins (Benjamin Barrett); Mother (Laura Press).

Street of Shadows
While taking a walk in a wealthy neighborhood, a chronically unemployed man living in a shelter experiences a most unusual transformation. Wr: Michael Reaves. Dir: Richard Bugjaski.

Steve Cranstan (Charles Haid); Elaine Cranstan (Angela Gei); Perry (Shawn Lawrence); Butler (James

Mainprize); Counselor (Marla Lukofsky); Lisa (Lisa Jacob); Repairman (Philip Williams); Also with Reiner Schwarz.

Something in the Walls

When a doctor arrives at his new job at a sanitarium, he discovers the case of a woman who is terribly frightened of something, but they are unable to understand her fears. Wr: J. Michael Straczynski. Dir: Allan Kroeker.

Sharon Miles (Deborah Raffin); Dr. Mallory Craig (Damir Andrei); Rebecca Robb (Lally Cadeau); Maid (Kate Parr); Wall person (Douglas Carrigan); Wall person (Janice Green); Wall person (Aaron Ross Fraser); Wall person (Martha Cronyn).

A Game of Pool

A young man who has devoted his life to pool suddenly finds himself pitted against the ghost of the greatest pool player who has ever lived, and the stakes are quite high—his life. Wr: George Clayton Johnson. Dir: Randy Bradshaw.

Fats Brown (Maury Chaykin); Jesse Cardiff (Esai Morales); Customer (Paul Jolicoeur); Owner (Guy Sanvido); Player (Elliot McIver).

Trivia Alert: This is a remake of the original episode from the 1960s, and the ending is different.

The Wall

At a research laboratory, a dimensional portal appears, and Major McAndrews is assigned to go through the portal and learn what's on the other side. Wr: J. Michael Straczynski. Dir: Atom Egoyan.

Maj. Alex McAndrews (John Beck); Berenn (Patricia Collins); Phillips (George R. Robertson); Kincaid (Eugene Clark); Perez (Robert Collins); Technician (Sharon Corder); Adviser (Jack Blum); Military adviser (Steve Atkinson).

Room 2446

A man is confined to a special room for acts and thoughts against the state. They want the formula for a weapon he does not want to reveal to the world. But escape, for Martin Decker, comes from the mind. Wr: Jeremy Bertrand Finch. Dir: Richard Bugajski.

Martin Decker (Dean Stockwell); Joseph (Brent Carver); Ostroff (Peter Boretski); Professor (Walter Massey); Orderly #1 (Nicholas Pasco); Orderly #2 (Al Therrien).

The Mind of Simon Foster

Desperate for money, a man sells his memories to a pawn broker and pays a terrible price for survival. Wr: J. Michael Straczynski. Dir: Doug Jackson.

Simon Foster (Bruce Weitz); Pawnbroker (Geza Kovacs); Counselor (Ilse Von Glatz); Manager (Rafe MacPherson); Principal (Reg Dreger); Carolyn (Jennifer Griffin); Beverly (Alyson Court).

Cat and Mouse

A plain, shy, secluded girl longs for her Prince Charming and one day finds him—in the form of a cat, who transforms into the man of her dreams. Wr: Christy Marx. Dir: Eric Till.

Andrea Moffitt (Pamela Bellwood); Prince Charming (Page Fletcher); Elaine (Gwynyth Walsh); Carl (John Blackwood); Asst. vet (Peg Christopherson).

Many, Many Monkeys

An epidemic breaks out, and many people begin arriving at a hospital, stricken blind. But there's something more going on: People have become cold and heartless towards each other. Wr: William Froug. Dir: Richard Bugajski.

Nurse Claire Hendricks (Karen Valentine); Mrs. Reed (Jackie Burroughs); Dr. Friedman (Ken Pogue); Dr. Peterson (Jan Filips); Susan (Norah Grant); Elderly man (Warren Van Evera); Mr. Reed (John Gardiner).

Rendezvous in a Dark Place

An older woman has an obsession with death and attends funerals for entertainment. But one night when an injured thief breaks into her home, she allows him to die and waits for Mr. Death to collect him. Wr: J. Michael Straczynski. Dir: Rene Bonniere.

Barbara LeMay (Janet Leigh); Mr. Death (Stephen McHattie); LeMay's son (Malcolm Stewart); Trent (Todd Duckworth); Minister (Lorne Cossette); Detective (Michael Miller); Thief (Eric House).

Special Service

A man suddenly discovers that his entire life has been filmed and there is a special network channel just for him. Wr: J. Michael Straczynski. Dir: Randy Bradshaw.

John Selly (David Naughton); Repairman (Keith Knight); Network manager (Elias Zarou); Mrs. Selly (Susan Roman); Receptionist (Marion McGann); Fan (Barbara Von Radicki).

Love Is Blind

When Jack Haines learns his wife is meeting a man at a road nightclub, he goes there with a plan to kill them both. But the strange country and western singer seems to know everything he is planning. Wr: Cal Willingham. Dir: Gilbert Shilton.

Jack Haines (Ben Murphy); Blind singer (Sneezy Waters); Bartender (Eric Keenleyside); Taylor (Steve Adams); Elaine (Cindy Girling); Man in bar (John Novak).

Crazy as a Soup Sandwich

A cowardly two-bit thief is running for his life. He owes money to a demon, Volkerps. Asking for Mr. Lancaster's help, as Arky will find, is a very expensive proposition. Wr: Harlan Ellison. Dir: Paul Lynch.

Mr. Lancaster (Anthony Franciosa); Arky Lockner (Wayne Robson); Girlfriend (Laurie Paton); Cassandra Fishbine (Susan Wright); Gus (George Buza); Bork (B.J. McQueen); Volkerp's voice (Thick Wilson); Volkerps (Garry Robbins).

Father and Son Game

A 79-year-old man wants to keep on living, so he transplants his brain into a younger body, but his son resents his father's continued life and tries to wrest power from him. Wr: Paul Chitlik and Jeremy Bertrand Finch. Dir: Randy Bradshaw.

Darius Stevens (Ed Marinaro); Michael Stevens (Eugene Robert Glazer); Anita Stevens (Patricia Phillips); Dave (George Touliatos); Dr. Wilson (Richard Monette); Larry (Mark Melymick).

UFO

1969–1970

In 1980, a secret organization called SHADO (Supreme Headquarters Alien Defense Organization) battles hostile alien creatures from a dying world. SHADO's control center is hidden beneath the Harlington-Straker film studio, which controls moonbase, a fleet of submarines and land mobiles.

Cast: SHADO Headquarters: Cmdr. Ed Straker (Ed Bishop); Col. Paul Foster (Michael Billington); Col. Virginia Lake (Wanda Ventham); Col. Alec Freeman (George Sewell); Gen. James Henderson (Grant Taylor); Dr. Douglas Jackson (Vladek Sheybal); Lt. Keith Ford (Keith Alexander); SHADO Operative (Ayshea); Miss Ealand (Norma Ronald); Moonbase: Lt. Gay Ellis (Gabrielle Drake); Lt. Nina Barry (Dolores Mantez); Lt. Joan Harrington (Antonia Ellis); Skydiver Submarine Crew: Capt. Peter Carlin (Peter Gordeno); Lt. Lew Waterman (Gary Meyers); Masters (Jon Kelley); Skydiver Navigator (Jeremy Wilkin); Skydiver Operative (Georgina Moon); With Voice of SID (Mel Oxley).

Created by: Gerry and Sylvia Anderson, with Reg Hill; *Producer:* Reg Hill; *Executive Producer:* Gerry Anderson; *Century 21 Fashions by:* Sylvia Anderson; *Special Effects Supervisor:* Derek Meddings; *Music:* Barry Gray; *Director of Photography:* Brendan Stafford; CBS/ITC Entertainment; 60 minutes.

UFO was an action-packed series loaded with spectacular hardware: A moonbase that launched interceptor spaceships; a fleet of submarines that launched missile-carrying aircraft; SID, a satellite with a booming British voice that announced the trajectory of incoming UFOs; and vehicles that included Commander Straker's bubbletop car (actually a modified Zephyr—Zodiac MK 1V).

On the bad guys' side was a seemingly inexhaustible supply of alien flying saucers that zoomed across the galaxy with masochistic determination. Most of the saucers were blown apart by the interceptors before reaching Earth. A few of the hostile marauders did land on Earth to kidnap unwitting humans. The aliens couldn't live in Earth's atmosphere long, however. After a few days, their bodies aged and their spaceships began to deteriorate.

UFO was the first live-action series created by the husband-and-wife team of Gerry and Sylvia Anderson. Previously, the English couple had produced such children's adventure programs as *Thunderbirds* and *Captain Scarlet*. These Super Marionation puppet series enjoyed huge international success.

UFO benefited from a no-nonsense approach to its subject matter. Despite the comic-strip premise, many plots had a remarkably adult subtext. The photography was first-rate, the editing exceptional and the theme music exciting. Conceptually, the show's weakest link was the aliens. They traveled millions of light years across space, clad in red spacesuits and breathing green liquid, to raid human beings of their body organs. It was an unpleasant and impractical premise. For the aliens to get away with a couple of hearts and a lung didn't seem to justify the weekly destruction they faced from Earth's defenses.

In later episodes, the aliens' motives for attacking Earth grew murkier. The concept of Earth as an intergalactic grocery store gave way to a straight "us or them" conflict as the aliens tried to destroy all of mankind.

Portraying a weekly war on a TV budget was a formidable task. Dozens of alien saucers were created exclusively for the series, and dozens were blown up by the special effects men. This became too expensive, and the technicians learned to rely on quick editing to insert shots of exploding magnesium rather than destroy any more saucers.

Before *UFO* began production, ITC Entertainment hoped that the series could be sold to one of the American networks. With this in mind, Ed Bishop was chosen as the lead. Bishop had moved to England from America in the early 1960s and had worked for the Andersons in their 1969 film *Journey to the Far Side of the Sun*. Bishop portrayed Straker with a steely determination.

Producers Gerry and Sylvia Anderson on the set of *UFO*. Copyright 1969 ITC/Century 21.

turmoil to satisfy him. Straker always came to the fore under great pressure."

The female characters on *UFO* were caught between a futuristic vision of equality and and the leering sexism of the 1960s. Women controlled moonbase, and they did their jobs coolly and efficiently. On the other hand, they were dressed in skin-tight leotards and wore purple wigs and abberant eye shadow. The most heroic female character was on Earth, Col. Virginia Lake (Wanda Ventham). She could compete with the men in the most hazardous of missions, but she retained a dignified femininity.

"It was very important to me to have women characters represented as strong and courageous as opposed to being merely decorative," says Sylvia Anderson. "However, as I was a lone voice at the executive level, I was by no means happy with all of the female characters. They were written by an all-male team of writers. For the time, I felt *UFO* made some steps forward."

The first 18 episodes of the series were filmed in early 1969 at MGM studios in England. The remaining eight episodes were shot at Pinewood studios later that year. Prior to filming, an enthusiastic Gerry Anderson interviewed UFO experts and solicited scientists' advice on the liquid-breathing biology of the aliens.

When the series premiered in England, it boasted the largest regular cast in TV history. However, several key actors didn't last the season. Peter Gordeno, who played submarine Captain Peter Carlin, was soon dismissed from SHADO duty. "Peter was considered a nonactor" by executive management, says Sylvia

Beneath the cool exterior, Bishop hinted at a sensitive, tragic man who had been given the job of saving the universe at any cost. His dedication ultimately cost him his marriage and his son's life. When one character suggests Straker go home and get some rest, Straker bitterly replies, "What home?" SHADO became his total existence.

"Straker was one of those guys who had a singleness of purpose," says Bishop. "In his life, there was very little grey. Everything was black and white, right and wrong. He put everything through his own personal sieve and it came out the way he wanted it. With a hard-ass like Straker, you could throw anything at him and he would field it. Nothing fazed him. He was also one of those guys who was constantly in turmoil. If you removed the turmoil, he'd find another source of

Anderson of the singer and dancer. "Therefore, his contract was not renewed. I, personally, thought that was a mistake. His character was interesting [Carlin's sister had been killed by the aliens], and Peter's personality overcame his lack of acting experience."

Straker's right-hand man, Alec Freeman, was characterized with a quiet sensitivity and humor by George Sewell. He was also phased out by the season's end in an effort to sell *UFO* to America for syndication. "The American networks found George Sewell not as attractive as their second leads in America normally were," says Sylvia Anderson. "As a result, I cast Michael Billington [Col. Foster] to replace him."

The third major change was the loss of Lt. Ellis (Gabrielle Drake) from Moonbase. Drake left the series to pursue other acting jobs.

Straker's foil during the series was his superior, the gruff General Henderson. Some of the series' best scenes were provided by the clashes between the two men. The late Grant Taylor played Henderson, and it was to be his last role. "Grant was a terrific guy," recalls Bishop. "He was an Australian actor who came to England during the early 1960s. He had been a boxer, football player and star athlete. He was a magnificent actor, but his career never really took off. He was still a very employable actor, and he was wonderful as General Henderson. Grant was a very uninhibited guy who lived life to its fullest.

"After we shot the 18 episodes at MGM, we had a holdover for four months before filming resumed at Pinewood. When Grant showed up, he had lost half his body weight. He was gaunt, thin and drawn. He had cancer. He was no longer the gregarious guy who was on the set six months earlier. He was now very quiet and rarely spoke to anybody. He did his lines and sat in a chair, reading a book. If you'd go over and try to talk to him, he was very monosyllabic. It was totally unlike him."

Realizing he only had weeks to live, Taylor invited his closest friends to a last dinner party. "He gave a farewell party," says Bishop, "He said to everybody, 'Look, I'm dying. This is the last time you'll see me, so say your goodbyes.' That's the way Grant went out, with a sense of style. He died either just before *UFO* finished filming or immediately after. It was certainly the last job Grant ever did."

Under the action-laden premise of the series were some surprisingly adult dramas dealing with the sacrifices SHADO demanded of peoples' lives.

Unlike many science fiction series, *UFO* improved as it went on, breathing life into its limited format with stories of time warps, mind-altering drugs and undersea alien installations. In the ultimate surreal adventure, "Mindbender," Straker finds himself in a nightmare world where SHADO is merely a TV show. The episode follows Straker's travels from set to set in his effort to find reality. It offered an intriguing look at the *UFO* sets and studio background.

"The strengths of *UFO* were the special effects and the visual presentation," says Bishop. "Sylvia Anderson was largely responsible for how the show looked. The main weakness of the series was our format. It was a very narrow channel. Every week the aliens came, we went on red alert and scrambled to meet them. That was the basic formula. If you compare that to *Star Trek*, where the universe was their oyster, you realize how constricting *UFO* was."

Having seen a few of the episodes recently, Bishop observes, "As an actor, the stories I liked the most were ones about Straker's personal relationships. The breakup of his marriage and the story about his son. Give me the beautiful Suzanne Neve [who played Straker's wife] anytime over a radar screen! Yet, seeing them now, I don't feel those personal elements on *UFO* worked that well."

Bishop's favorite episode was "Sub Smash," where the commander struggles to survive in a capsized sub after a UFO attack. "When I first accepted the role of Straker, I said to myself, 'I'm going to act the part as if I don't know the ending of the script.' Because you can usually see behind a hero's eyes. They know they're going to be back next week, so any danger they face is qualified. I wanted to get away from that.

"In *Sub Smash*, Straker really thinks this is the end, and I tried to convey that." With only minutes of air left, Straker begins to hallucinate. "Straker never mentioned religion, but as he's sitting there, dying, he says a simple line of, 'We wait for the day of resurrection.' It was an interesting facet of Straker to play, but there was great controversy over that. People said, 'No, No! That's pretentious. It's horseshit.' The guy who did the post-production hated it so much he tried to drown it out with music!"

UFO scripter Terence Feely recalls the show as well made and satisfying to work on. "It was certainly ahead of its time. It shared something with TV's *The Prisoner* in that Gerry Anderson found it easy to take on lateral thinking and the

Col. Lake (Wanda Ventham) and Cmdr. Straker (Ed Bishop) find their world frozen in time in "Timelash!" Copyright 1970 ITC/Century 21.

United States markets, five of them owned by CBS. A successful North American run could have revived production of the series.

UFO premiered to good ratings. Most Americans were unaware that the episodes were over three years old, and the series' deft camera-work, sharp editing and futuristic presentation gave the show a contemporary look.

Ironically, as *UFO* made a splash in America, its star, Ed Bishop, was also in the United States, toiling away at odd jobs. "We finished filming *UFO* in 1969," he says, "and frankly, my phone didn't ring. I didn't get any offers of work. It could have been that when the show was over, people in the business presumed that, 'Oh, Ed just did a big TV series. He's not interested in the sort of bread and butter acting jobs we used to give him.' Also, *UFO* was not a successful series in England. I think a lot of people thought I was lousy in it. So for a time, I didn't make any money, and I had a young family to support. My wife was very supportive. She became a schoolteacher, and she helped considerably, but I had to do something."

In 1972, Bishop decided to try his luck in America. With only 200 dollars in his pocket, he boarded a plane for America, his arrival coinciding with *UFO*'s launch.

"I had one important asset," he says. "A very dear friend of mine had a wonderful apartment in Central Park West in New York. I stayed with him while I called up agents, trying to get work."

Between acting roles, Bishop supported himself by doing odd jobs. "I'm quite good at what you call self-help—electricity, plumbing, wallpapering, and construction. I did that between acting appointments."

It led to one of the strangest events in

surreal. Gerry has a mind that understands the powerful logic of the surreal." Feely, who later wrote for Anderson's *Space 1999* series, says, "*UFO* was easier to write for than *Space 1999*. *UFO* gave me an opportunity to write better plots, while *Space 1999* had better characters. That's often the choice in science fiction." The writer didn't resent the special-effects nature of both series. "The effects were a blessing. They can cover a multitude of writing blemishes."

UFO premiered in England in 1970, but its scheduling broadcasts were erratic. Science fiction was generally regarded as children's fare, and TV programmers were baffled by *UFO*'s adult content. Some episodes were broadcast in late evening slots to protect younger viewers from their intense themes.

As *UFO* endured a choppy and ineffective run in its native England, the series' 26 episodes were enjoying a highly successful 1970-71 broadcast in Canada on the CTV network. America held its option on *UFO* until the fall of 1972, when the episodes began a major launch on 91

Lt. Ellis (Gabrielle Drake), Col. Foster (Michael Billington) and Cmdr. Straker (Ed Bishop) on moonbase in "Kill Straker!" Copyright 1969 ITC/Century 21.

Bishop's life. "This story serves as a moral for anybody who is dazzled by the glamour of show-biz," he says. "I got a wallpapering job in the Bronx one Saturday morning. A very nice couple wanted me to wallpaper their kitchen for 75 bucks. So I arrived with my bucket and paste. I began what was a slow, fiddly-like job. I was there all day, and around 6 p.m. the couple and their teenaged daughter went into the living room to watch TV. Meanwhile, I concentrated on getting this wallpapering job done. At 7 p.m., I heard this music from the TV. I stopped working and said, 'My God! That's the UFO theme music!' I got off my step ladder, put down my bucket and peered into the living room. They were watching me on UFO. I didn't know whether to laugh or cry. I probably did both. It was so bizarre! Here I am, the leading guy on this TV show, and I'm wallpapering their kitchen. When I finished at 9 p.m., they paid me my 75 dollars and off I went. To this day, those people don't know who I was! It's just as well," Bishop laughs. "If they had known, it would have been extremely embarrassing!"

When Bishop returned to England in the mid-1970s, work had picked up for the actor. UFO concluded a successful run on American TV in 1973. In March 1973, TV Guide critic Cleveland Amory gave UFO a negative review in his column. Viewers angrily protested his swipes at the series. Amory later admitted that UFO generated a surprising amount of favorable mail.

Gerry and Sylvia Anderson waited to see if the American affiliates were interested in a second season of UFO. Though the series had been filmed four years ago, many of the props had been stored, and some of the cast was available. The late Tony Barwick, UFO's story editor, wrote several scripts in case UFO was revived. However, affiliates were more interested in the creation of the Andersons' Space 1999 series, which began an American run in 1975.

"A second season of UFO was highly anticipated," says Sylvia Anderson. "Had it continued, it would have been set entirely on the moon. This is, of course, what did happen with Space:1999."

UFO vanished from most screens after 1975. Ten years later, the show slowly sizzled back into the consciousness of British and American audiences. Isolated reruns sparked fan clubs, and several successful conventions in England reunited the *UFO* cast. Episodes of *UFO* were also released on video, and the series enjoyed a run on America's Science Fiction cable channel. The series found tremendous success in Japan, where toys based on the series' hardware continue to sell well.

"*UFO* didn't receive the acclaim and popularity it deserved during its first run," acknowledges Sylvia Anderson. "Science fiction wasn't highly regarded in the creative world of British TV. In other words, it was ahead of its time." In Anderson's view, the series holds up well today, but she notes the show's weaknesses included "some substandard scripts and a lack of subtle direction."

Ed Bishop says, "*UFO* had the moonbase, subs and planes to protect England from UFO raids. In many ways, it was like the battle of Britain all over again. But that premise also restricted the show. It was too confining. I would have liked to have seen, in a second year, that storyline expanded somehow."

Bishop has been a guest at several British *UFO* conventions in recent years. He's gratified by the series' sustained popularity. "The spectrum of questions from the fans is amazing," he says. "They ask very astute and perceptive things. It's flattering to meet people who remember your work."

The fan reaction has made Bishop ponder the possibility of a *UFO* film. "I think there's a very good feature film struggling to get out of the ashes," he notes. "I'd be interested in being a part of that. There was still a lot of mileage in ol' Straker."

Bishop doesn't feel a *UFO* revival would require all of the hardware. "It could simply be about some of the characters on *UFO* and what became of them. Did they defeat the aliens? Was SHADO shut down? It would be interesting to find out what became of Straker. Maybe he's an alcoholic living in Sydney, Australia, or Elephant Breath, Wisconsin. He tells everybody about the SHADO days and nobody listens. People are going, 'Oh, here comes that nut case again! Give him a drink!' Someone with a corkscrew imagination could write a good film script. I think there's certainly a creative vein there, waiting to be dug."

CAST NOTES

Ed Bishop (Straker): Born 1936. After graduating from the Boston University Theatre Division in 1960, Bishop moved to England. He provided the voice for Captain Blue in the Gerry Anderson puppet series *Captain Scarlet* in the 1960s. His film credits include *You Only Live Twice* (1967) and *2001: A Space Odyssey* (1968). He's one of England's top voice artists.

Michael Billington (Foster): Born 1948. Billington played Barbara Bach's Russian boyfriend who is killed by James Bond at the beginning of *The Spy Who Loved Me* (1977). He later came to America to co-star in the ill-fated series *The Quest* (1982). He returned to England, where he became a schoolteacher.

Wanda Ventham (Col. Lake): Born 1938. Ventham made news headlines in 1992 during her starring performance in the stage comedy *It Runs in the Family*. A middle-aged audience member leaped up on stage and claimed she was his mother. The actress used good humor to get the man offstage, and the show went on.

Gabrielle Drake (Lt. Ellis): Born 1945. Her first acting role was on stage at the age of six. A businesswoman and stage actress, Drake was one of the stars of the English hit series *The Brothers* in the mid–1970s. She spent three years playing the boss on the soap opera *Crossroads* (1985–88).

George Sewell (Alec): Born 1924. Sewell caught *UFO* producer Gerry Anderson's attention in 1968 when he co-starred in his film *Journey to the Far Side of the Sun*. He also starred in the successful English crime drama series *The Branch*. He continues working as a British character actor.

Peter Gordeno (Capt. Carlin): A former ballet dancer, Gordon continued acting after *UFO* and had a featured role in the 1980s film *Carry On, Columbus*.

Vladek Sheybal (Dr. Jackson): Born 1932 in Poland. Sheybal often played a bad guy, as in the James Bond film *From Russia, with Love* (1964). His later appearances included the mini-series *Shogun* (1980). Sheybal was also a writer and director. He died in 1992.

Episode Guide

Identified
The secret origin of the aliens is partially revealed when a dead alien is found inside a crashed saucer. Wr: Gerry Anderson, Sylvia Anderson, Tony Barwick. Dir: Gerry Anderson.

Minister (Basil Dignam); Dr. Schroeder (Maxwell Shaw); Co-Pilot (Shane Rimmer); Alien (Gito Santana/ Stan Bray); Mark (Harry Baird); Kurt Mahler (Paul Gillard); Ken Matthews (Michael Mundell); Phil Wade (Gary Files); Dr. Harris (Matthew Robertson); Nurse (Annette Kerr).

Flight Path
Alec's close friend, a SHADO operative, is being blackmailed by the aliens to reveal space coordinates for an attack on the moon. Wr: Ian Scott Stewart. Dir: Ken Turner.

Paul Roper (George Cole); Carol Roper (Sonia Fox); Dawson (Keith Grenville); Dr. Schroeder (Maxwell Shaw).

The Computer Affair
While hunting for a downed UFO in northern Canada, Straker investigates an interracial romance that might have caused the death of an astronaut. Wr: Tony Barwick. Dir: David Lane.

Mark Bradley (Harry Baird); Dr. Schroeder (Maxwell Shaw); Ken Matthews (Michael Mundell); Dr. Murray (Peter Burton); Moonbase man (Nigel Lambert); Mobile #3 man (Hugh Armstrong); Shadow crew #1 (Hein Viljoen, Dennis Plenty).

Confetti Check A-OK
Flashbacks recall the building of SHADO in 1970 and the toll it took on Straker's marriage. Wr: Tony Barwick. Dir: David Lane.

Mary Straker (Suzanne Neve); Lt. Grey (Julian Burton); CIA man (Shane Rimmer); Mary's father (Michael Nightingale); Hotel clerk (Geoffrey Hinsliff); Potter (Frank Tregear); Estate agent (Donald Pelmear); Doctor (Tom Oliver); Nurse (Penny Jackson); Officer (Michael Forrest); English delegate (Jack May); U.S. delegate (Alan Tilvern); French delegate (Jeffrey Segal); German delegate (Gordon Sterne); SHADO man (Jeremy Wilkin); Technician (Jon Kelley).

The Responsibility Seat
Straker finds himself seduced by the charms of a beautiful news reporter, who has evidence that may expose SHADO. Meanwhile, Alec tries to stop a runaway Russian vehicle from colliding with moonbase. Wr: Tony Barwick. Dir: Alan Perry.

Jo Fraser (Jane Merrow); Russian commander (Patrick Jordan); Astronaut (Mark Hawkins); Russian astronauts (Janos Kurucz, Paul Tamarin); Operative (Anouska Hempel); Film director (Ralph Ball); Stuntman (Royston Rowe).

A Question of Priorities
Straker must chose between saving his critically injured son or rescuing an alien who could bring an end to the invasion. Wr: Tony Barwick. Dir: David Lane.

Mary Rutland (Suzanne Neve); Rutland (Philip Madoc); Dr. Segal (Peter Halliday); Mrs. O'Connor (Mary Merrall); Dr. Green (Russell Napier); John Rutland (Barnaby Shaw); Alien (Richard Aylen); Operative (Penny Spencer); Nurse (Andrea Allan); Car driver (David Cargill).

Exposed
A pilot witnesses a UFO being destroyed by Sky 1. His relentless efforts to expose SHADO put his life in danger, for SHADO must protect its secrecy at all costs. Wr: Tony Barwick. Dir: David Lane.

Janna Wade (Jean Marsh); Kofax (Robin Bailey); Jim (Matt Zimmerman); Dr. Frazer (Basil Moss); Nurse (Sue Gerrard); Tsi (Paula Li Schiu); Louis Graham (Arthur Cox); Mark (Harry Baird).

Conflict!
Two pilots are killed mysteriously while reentering Earth's atmosphere. Foster disobeys orders to fly the same path and discovers an alien plot to destroy SHADO headquarters. Wr: Ruric Powell. Dir: Ken Turner.

Steve Maddox (Drewe Henley); Crewman (David Courtland); Steiner (Michael Kilgarriff); Pilot (Gerard Norman); Navigator (Alan Tucker).

Kill Straker
Paul returns from a mission a changed man. Consumed with hatred for Straker, he embarks on a campaign of intimidation to remove Straker from SHADO. Wr: Donald James. Dir: Alan Perry.

Craig (David Sumner); Mark Bradley (Harry Baird); Guard (Steve Cory); Nurse (Louise Pajo).

Ordeal
Paul is abducted by aliens, and SHADO personnel are divided over whether to destroy the UFO or try to recover Paul before the saucer leaves Earth's atmosphere. Wr: Tony Barwick. Dir: Ken Turner.

Sylvia Graham (Quinn O'Hara); Joe Franklin (David Healy); Mark (Harry Baird); Dr. Harris (Basil Moss); Perry (Peter Burton); Medic (Joseph Morris); Woman at party (Sylvia Anderson).

The Square Triangle
A woman's plot to murder her husband takes a strange twist when she accidentally kills an alien instead. Wr: Alan Pattillo. Dir: David Lane.

Liz Newton (Adrienne Corri); Cass Fowler (Patrick Mower); Jack Newton (Allan Cuthbertson); Alien (Anthony Chinn); Gamekeeper (Godfrey James); Mobile man (Hugo Panczak).

Close-Up
A space probe is sent to the aliens' home planet. Straker tries to analyze the bizarre photographic evidence that it sends back. Wr: Tony Barwick. Dir: Alan Perry.

Kelly (Neil Hallett); Young (James Beckett); Pilot (Mark Hawkins); Controller (Frank Mann); Operative (Alan Tucker).

ESP

Controlled by the aliens, a man uses ESP to lure Straker into a death trap. Wr: Alan Fennell. Dir: Ken Turner.

John Croxley (John Stratton); Stella Croxley (Deborah Stanford); Dr. Ward (Douglas Wilmer); Dr. Shroeder (Maxwell Shaw); Mark (Harry Baird); Gateman (Donald Tandy); Guard (Stanley McGeogh).

Survival

Paul is stranded on the lunar surface with the alien who killed his astronaut friend. Working together for survival, the two build a fragile friendship. Wr: Tony Barwick. Dir: Alan Perry.

Tina Duval (Suzan Farmer); Alien (Gito Santana); Grant (Robert Swann); Mark (Harry Baird); Pilot (Ray Armstrong); Rescuer (David Weston).

The Dalotek Affair

An alien device on the moon is causing communication blackouts on the moon, resulting in tragic disasters on moonbase. Wr: Ruric Powell. Dir: Alan Perry.

Jane Carson (Tracy Reed); Tanner (Clinton Greyn); Mitchell (David Weston); Blake (Philip Latham); Read (John Breslin); Doctor (Basil Moss); Dr. Frank E. Stranges (Himself); Lunar pilot (Alan Tucker); Captain (John Cobner); Lt. (Richard Poore).

Court Martial

Solid evidence has convicted Paul Foster of espionage. Unless Straker can clear him, Foster will be executed by SHADO. Wr: Tony Barwick. Dir: Ron Appleton.

Diane (Pippa Steel); Carl Mason (Neil McCallum); Webb (Jack Hedley); Agent (Noel Davis); Miss Scott (Louise Pajo); Miss Grant (Georgina Cookson); A.D. (Paul Green Halgh); Singleton (Tutte Lemkow); Guard (Michel Glover).

Sub Smash!

Straker and five SHADO colleagues struggle for survival when their submarine plunges to the sea floor after a UFO attack. Wr: Alan Fennell. Dir: David Lane.

Lt. Lewis (Paul Maxwell); Lt. Chin (Anthony Chinn); Pilot (Burnell Tucker); Mary (flashback) (Suzanne Neve); John (flashback) (Barnaby Shaw); SHADO divers (John Golightly, Alan Haywood).

The Sound of Silence

Marauding aliens from a submerged flying saucer threaten a couple living in the countryside. Wr: David Lane, Bob Bell. Dir: David Lane.

Russ (Michael Jayston); Anne (Susan Jameson); Culley (Nigel Gregory); Alien (Gito Santana); Stone (Richard Vernon); Dr. (Basil Moss); Technicians (Tom Oliver, Malcolm Reynolds); Pilot (Craig Hunter); Co-pilot (Burnell Tucker); Moonbase operative (Andrea Allan).

Destruction

A Navy ship's efforts to dispose of nerve gas at midsea is threatened by attacking UFOs. Wr: Dennis Spooner. Dir: Ken Turner.

Sarah Bosanquet (Stephanie Beacham); Captain (Philip Madoc); Sheringham (Edwin Richfield); Officer #2 (Peter Blythe); Skydiver Capt. (David Warbeck); Engineer (Barry Stokes); Astronaut (Steven Berkoff); Rating (Jimmy Winston); Radar (Michael Ferrand); Radar officer (Robert Lloyd).

The Cat with Ten Lives

An alien Siamese cat controls an astronaut and directs him to destroy moonbase with an interceptor. Wr and Dir: David Tomblin.

Jim Regan (Alexis Kanner); Jean Regan (Geraldine Moffat); Miss Holland (Lois Maxwell); Morgan (Windsor Davies); Muriel (Eleanor Summerfield); Albert (Colin Gordon); Astronauts (Al Mancini, Steven Berkoff); Operative (Anouska Hempel).

The Man Who Came Back

A long-lost astronaut returns, brainwashed by the aliens to kill Straker during a space mission. Wr: Terence Feely. Dir: David Lane.

Craig Collins (Derren Nesbitt); Col. Grey (Gary Raymond); Miss Holland (Lois Maxwell); Sir Esmond (Roland Culver); Chauffeur (Mike Stevens); Operative (Anouska Hempel); Nurse (Rona Newton-John); Moonbase Dr. (Robert Grange); Moonbase operative (Andrea Allan); Housekeeper (Nancy Nevinson); Doctor (David Savile); Porter (Fred Real).

Trivia Alert: Rona Newton-John is the sister of singer Olivia Newton-John.

Psycho Bombs

Three ordinary people are given super-powers by the aliens and turned loose on SHADO's installations. Wr: Tony Barwick. Dir: Jeremy Summers.

Linda Simmons (Deborah Grant); Daniel Clark (David Collings); Mason (Mike Pratt); Lauritzen (Tom Adams); Executive (Alex Davion); Skydiver navigator (Christopher Timothy); Security men (Nigel Gregory, Hans de Vries); Room 22 guard (Aidan Murphy); Detective (Oscar James); Cop (Gavin Campbell); Tracker station officer (Peter Blythe); Tracker guards (Peter Davies, Derek Steen); Skydiver capt. (Robin Hawdon); Skydiver engineers (Mark York, Peter Dolphin).

Reflections in the Water

Weird happenings lead Skydiver to an undersea world where aliens have made an exact duplicate of SHADO. Wr and Dir: David Tomblin.

Lt. Anderson (James Cosmo); Operative (Anouska Hempel); Skipper (Conrad Phillips); Skydiver capt. (David Warbeck); Navigator (Barry Stokes); Producer (Richard Caldicott); Helmsman (Gordon Sterne); Crewman (Fredric Abbott); Cameraman (Mark Griffith); Director (Keith Bell); Insurance man (Gerald Cross); Astronaut (Steven Berkoff).

Timelash!

Straker and Col. Lake hunt a traitorous SHADO crewman who has frozen the entire SHADO base in time and is leaving it open for alien attack. Wr: Terence Feely. Dir: Cyril Frankel.

Turner (Patrick Allen); Casting agent (Ron Pember); Actor (Jean Vladon); Actress (Kirsten Lindholm); Engineer

(Douglas Nottage); Guard (John Lyons); Security man (John J. Carney).

Memory Flash—Terence Feely: "'Timelash' was the episode that worked best for me. My abiding memory of producer Gerry Anderson was the contrast between the softness of his speech and the diabolical speed with which he drove!"

Mindbender
Plunged into a nightmare where SHADO is a weekly TV series, Straker journeys from set to set to find his way back to reality. Wr: Tony Barwick. Dir: Ken Turner.

Howard Byrne (Stuart Damon); Conroy (Al Mancini); James (Charles Tingwell); Dale (Craig Hunter); Operative (Anouska Hempel); Operative #2 (James Marcus); Guards (Stanley McGeagh, John Lyons); Director (Stephen Chase); John (flashback) (Barnaby Shaw); Mary (flashback) (Suzanne Neve); Rutland(flashback) (Philip Madoc); Minister (flashback) (Basil Dignam); Astronaut (Steven Berkoff); Bandits (Larry Taylor, Richard Montez, Bill Morgan); A.D. (Norton Clarke); A.D. #2 (Paul Greaves); Cyclist (Jack Silk).

The Long Sleep
A young woman awakens from a ten-year coma and tries to retrace her steps in order to prevent the destruction of the Earth from a time bomb. Wr: David Tomblin. Dir: Jeremy Summers.

Catherine (Tessa Wyatt); Tim (Christian Roberts); Van driver (John Garrie); Bomb expert (Christopher Robbie); Operative (Anouska Hempel).

V

October 1984–July 1985

Earth is confronted by the Visitors, aliens who offer peace, friendship and protection. While many accept them at face value, the square jaw and Aryan features leave others more cynical about their true intentions. Donovan, a television cameraman, sneaks aboard the alien space vessel and captures a glimpse of the aliens' true form—behind a rubber mask lies a reptilian visage. The Visitors take the world by storm, controlling the human population by means of a tight-fisted fascist police state; it's up to an intrepid band of resistance fighters to stop them.

Cast: As the Resistance: Mike Donovan (Marc Singer); Julie Parrish (Faye Grant); Ham Tyler (Michael Ironside); Kyle Bates (Jeff Yagher); Elizabeth (Jennifer Cooke); Elias (Michael Wright); Robin Maxwell (Blair Tefkin); *As the Visitors:* Diana (Jane Badler); Willie (Robert Englund); Lydia (June Chadwick); Martin/Philip (Frank Ashmore); Lt. James (Judson Scott); *Also Starring:* Nathan Bates (Lane Smith); Mr. Chiang (Aki Aleong); Howard K. Smith (Himself).

V (Mini-series): Created by: Kenneth Johnson; *Executive Producer:* Kenneth Johnson; *Producer:* Chuck Bowman; *Associate Producer:* Patrick Boyriven; *V: The Final Battle: Executive Producers:* Daniel H. Blatt and Robert Singer; *Co-Producer:* Patrick Boyriven; *Produced by:* Dean O'Brien; *V (the series): Executive Producer:* Daniel H. Blatt, Robert Singer; *Producer:* Dean O'Brien, Skip Ward, Donald R. Boyle, Ralph R. Riskin; *Supervising Producer:* Steven de Souza, Garner Simmons; *Associate Producer:* Michael Eliot; NBC/Warner Brothers; 60 minutes.

The brutal events of World War II, the Nazi oppression and the battleground landscape of European underground resistance fighters in France and Denmark served as inspiration of this popular "War of the Worlds"—style science fiction drama.

When he sat down to write a script about vigilantism in the United States several years ago, Kenneth Johnson never realized that his fascination with the novel *It Can't Happen Here* by Sinclair Lewis would lead him to the creation of *V*, a highly acclaimed four hour mini-series. The novel was about the rise of fascism in the United States.

"If you look at the strength of the religious right and the fundamentalists of this country you'll see the reality of the novel," says Johnson.

At the time, Johnson was writing a screenplay "about a vigilante-type organization growing and growing until suddenly we're no longer in the same country. Overnight we would become a police state. We'd become a right-wing, fascist state. Of course, there'd be a group of people determined to fight against them and try to bring the United States back the way it's supposed to be.

"Brandon Tartikoff [then head of NBC Television] saw that script and was nervous about the whole fascist thing. It was a contemporary script, taking place wherever you wanted. Brandon felt that Americans would have a hard time believing it," recalls Johnson. " 'Couldn't the bad guys be Soviets? Or the Chinese?' I said, 'No, I don't think the Soviets or the Chinese could sustain a protracted occupation of the United States.' Jeff Sagansky, who was the second in command at the time, was sitting over in the corner of this meeting, and he said, 'How about if aliens come in?' and we said, 'Oh, god! Jeff! We're sick of that!'"

But that set some tumblers whirling in Johnson's brain. He began thinking about how he could transplant this rise-of-vigilantism fiction into a science fiction arena.

"I thought maybe there was a way to parallel the Nazis' falling in Denmark. They sort of rolled in Denmark and said, 'Hi, we're going to be your friends. We're here to protect you from the imperialistic English, you lucky people.' So I thought about spacecraft being like the Nazi coming into Denmark. And I realized there was a way to do that, that a totalitarian society like the aliens could come in here, showing us one face if you will, but underneath, guess what?

"In the case of *V* the face underneath is, literally, the face underneath! They were not humans at all—they were reptilian. Again, this goes back to my studies in evolution and where we could have gone...."

Fascinated with the parallels he could draw by allegory, Johnson picked a real person as inspiration for the character of Julie Parrish, played by Faye Grant. "Faye's character," he says, "is based on an 18-year-old French woman who ran the underground lines. She lived in France and one day walked into a British outpost in Barbados, Spain, with half a dozen British fighters who had been downed in France. She said, 'Here, I brought them to you.' And they said, 'How did you bring them here?' They asked her to bring out more ... and smuggle them back to England. She became one of the leaders of the French resistance."

Johnson provided Grant the key to her characterization in this woman. "I brought it forth to her, and as a matter of fact, I think Faye even met the woman after the show on a trip to Europe," he says.

"Marc [Singer], his character was one of the major leftovers of my original script. It was from the point of view of a cameraman. I wanted a cameraman because like the camera, he doesn't blink. You know, when anybody else is dazzled by

these people, he's a cynic. He's the one that says, 'I'm not sure!' He's the one that's looking all the time."

Only one scene remained from the "fascist" script version of *V*: the moment when Donovan is coming back from the mothership and "walks in with the videotape, and he's about to go on the air and he's going to blow the lid off of everything [with] the tape of Diana swallowing the guinea pig. The network has been taken over by the aliens at that point, and the Visitors now control all our communication, and you're essentially screwed. That scene was verbatim from my original fascist script before it became lizards and aliens."

For Johnson, *V* was emotionally and creatively satisfying. "I was very excited and proud of it as a piece of work because it really spoke to the heroism in all of us. Really, what *V* was about was *power*. *V* was about people reacting to power. Whether it was sucking to it, like Donovan's mother does out of the desire to increase her own stance and power in the community"—or like another character, whose reaction Johnson describes as, " 'Don't worry, everything's going to be OK. This is better.' Or like David Packer's character (Daniel), who gets seduced into being the new Hitler youth out of a desire to gain power, prestige—particularly if they are a troubled youth. It gives them something to hold on to, and if you put a gun to someone's head, their real personality begins to emerge. Why doesn't someone like Faye, who doesn't think of [herself] as a powerful person, give in? And yet, because it's innate in her nature, she rises to the top to become a heroine of peace."

Johnson believes very strongly that "everybody, one way or another, gives in to the desire of, the seduction of, power—or they fight against what they know [is] wrong even if it puts them into mortal danger. That's what the piece is about, and that's what I intended the series to be. I did not ever want the series to be a comic book piece. I did not ever want it to be the power station of the week we're going to blow up.

"I wanted it to be a really tense, suspenseful psychological drama about the interrelationships of those people. Essentially, the science fiction retelling of the French, Dutch and Danish resistance during World War II."

Ratings for the first mini-series were so strong—as it had been seen by some 65 million people—that Warner Brothers and NBC wanted a second mini-series, this time a six-hour piece

Kenneth Johnson stands by a Los Angeles billboard advertising his blockbuster mini-series *V* on NBC. Photo courtesy of Kenneth Johnson.

budgeted at $14 million and titled *V: The Final Battle*. But Johnson did not do the second mini-series.

"When NBC decided not to do it as a one-hour show, and they knew they had a gold mine and asked me to do a sequel, Warner Brothers did not want to do a sequel because it was so expensive," explains Johnson.

To encourage Johnson and Warner Brothers to film the sequel, NBC promised both parties a 12-hour blind series commitment. "'Blind' means [NBC] was guaranteeing Warner Brothers an entire other series, something yet to be determined, with me producing," explains Johnson. Warner Brothers agreed to the deal. But the wheels just set in motion came to a screeching halt when Warner Brothers went to Johnson and "asked if I could do it quick, cheap and dirty." Johnson threatened to abandon the project. "And then they said, 'OK, you can get started on the blind 12-hour series commitment.' I said, 'No, you don't understand, I'm leaving. I don't want to do this.'"

Now agitated, Warner Brothers was amazed at Johnson's audacity in so easily dropping 12 hours of television production. "And they said, 'You can't take that [NBC] commitment and go somewhere else!' I said, 'I know that. But that's a million dollars out of our pocket!' I said, 'I know that. A lot of people are working here!' I replied, 'I don't like how you screwed me here with the budget on the first show!' And they were pretty amazed. It was pretty foolish of me because they brought in some people who could not have the investment I had on the show"—"who, Johnson says, went about the business of totally revising, trashing the script I had."

Johnson supervised the writing and shared a story credit on the second mini-series with Diane Frolov, Craig (Faustus) Buck and Peggy Goldman. Each had written a teleplay for two hours of the six hours prepared. Colleagues Harry and Renee Longstreet had written additional scripts for the series which were incorporated into the Frolov, Buck and Goldman teleplays.

"For the record, NBC was elated with our six-hour script—and very upset after Daniel Blatt and Robert Singer took on the project when I left and had it 'fixed up' by another writer," says Johnson. "NBC felt their new version was apparently not as good, but were so close to production they had to go with it. I did take my name off, replacing it with my pseudonym, 'Lillian Weezer'—the name of my dog!"

Johnson believes the new team completely

Mike Donovan (Marc Singer) battles an alien assassin (Tom Callaway) while trying to rescue his son in "The Sanction." Copyright 1984 NBC/Warner Bros.

she's doing, and she doesn't like the fact that it makes her think. And because of that she spins around and out of the blue, kills the priest. The way the scene [was] written was amazing because you really saw her character; she had three dimensions, and was a very interesting person."

In Johnson's original treatment, Ham Tyler was in a wheelchair, and in the rewritten aired version, an entire 'scientists are evil' subplot— Johnson's parallel to the Holocaust—was shredded. Also in Johnson's second mini-series script, he introduced the Alliance, the Visitors' enemies in space. But Johnson says that was a red herring to falsely bolster the Resistance's spirit for help. New writers grabbed that and used it as a plot point.

Johnson disowns a subplot regarding the half-lizard, half-human child Elizabeth, who, in the conclusion of *The Final Battle,* grabs the control panel of the mothership just before the self-destruct mechanism can complete its countdown, and she mysteriously glows and saves the ship.

missed the subtlety and psychological depth he intended for the second six hours of *V.* Johnson has never seen the sequel or the television series, but he was informed by friends and colleagues of the end product. By accident, one day while flipping through channels on TV, he ran across a scene of the second mini-series and saw how his original vision had been mangled in the rewriting process for the second.

"We had written one scene where a priest had given Diana [the lead alien] a Bible and gave Diana some real second thoughts," explains Johnson. "The way the scene was originally written was as a very hip, young priest. Somebody cool to play this priest. And Diana begins to wonder about herself and where she's going and what

Johnson had definite plans for resolving the premise. "The way the original six hours ended was the Earth being saved and the spacecraft leaving, but leaving with our people on it. But Marc and Faye decided they couldn't deal with that and they had gone after them. Marc flies a shuttlecraft into the saucer as it was leaving. And that's the way we ended it."

V has become so popular worldwide that, Johnson reports, "in Germany alone, on video, it made a million dollars! It aired in South Africa and … the white government saw this as, 'Wait! This has white people and black people working

Alien commander Diana (Jane Badler), a lizard under the skin, cold-bloodedly plots against humanity with a comrade who has shed his human facade in *V*. Copyright 1984 NBC/Warner Bros.

Brothers really shot themselves in the foot."

Contemplating a revisit to *V*, for Johnson, is just an exercise in futility. "I don't know what I can do now that they haven't already screwed up," he says disgustedly. "It's like trying to go back and ... recreate a painting.

"There's one thing you should understand that's very important. One of the toughest days I've had in this town was when I sat down to watch the first cut of *V*. Usually, when you see the film first cut together you [say], 'Oh my god! That's not what I did! How do I deal with the film?' In the case of *V*, I was sitting and watching this screening, and this is before putting in any of the special effects, laser stuff, spacecraft, any of that. But it sang like a million bucks. The reason why is because of the *characters*. Any science fiction, or any good drama, is all about [good characters]. People are always asking me, 'Why isn't there any good science fiction on television?' Because people get all caught up on the effects. But the real heart and soul is in the *people*. Let the people work. Make them strong and solid."

The editing process provided interesting problems. "After I cut it down, it's four hours and fifteen minutes," says Johnson. "It had to be four hours with commercials. I called Brandon and said, 'I have a problem, I can't cut this down to four.' And he said, 'Oh, come on, this is a director who can't cut his own work?' So I said, 'Take a look at it, see what you think.' He looked at the whole picture, and he came back and said, 'Well, we're going to have fifteen more minutes Sunday

together,'" says Johnson excitedly. "The response was the same as when Europe saw it; the black people started spraying big red *V* all over," as they saw the allegorical comments on a repressive society. "Ain't that great! I loved it!

"We were also huge in Japan. I was on a promotional tour to Japan and you couldn't walk down the street without seeing signs for *V*. Germany closed the schools to make sure everybody watched it."

When it arrived in England, it aired opposite the 1984 Olympics, stomping the games in the ratings. "Truly! It's just been received with astonishment all over the world. As I said, Warner

night!' When *V* aired, the first two hours was two hours and fifteen minutes. There was too much good material, and Brandon agreed with me that it could not be cut."

Johnson remembers that early in the process of making *V*, he made an interesting suggestion to NBC chief Brandon Tartikoff. "I told Brandon, 'Let me have Sunday night every five weeks and I'll give you a continuing saga.' Now, three years later, Brandon came to me and said, 'You know that's what we should have done with *V*.' I said, 'How's that?' 'We should have put it on Sunday nights, like once every five or six weeks.' I replied, 'I'm the one that gave you that idea!'"

When the second mini-series aired with an amazing 50 million viewers glued to their screens, NBC felt they had no choice but to develop a series. Executive producers Robert Singer and Daniel Blatt came in to take the reins that once were held by Johnson. New characters were introduced to further the story.

For Michael Ironside, who played the distrustful ex–CIA agent Ham Tyler in both the second mini-series and the series, *V* was an opportunity to make friends. In the second mini-series, he says, "the very first scene we shot—Mickey Jones and I walk into the rebel headquarters and confront Donovan and say, 'You guys are doomed, they know who you are'—was the actual first day of shooting. When I first met Mickey Jones, who plays Chris Farber, Ham's backup, we became instant friends. He was best man at my wedding. I have a pickup truck I bought off him." Much later, they would appear together in the feature film *Total Recall* (1990).

"Faye Grant, I see fairly regularly, on and off over the years. She's married [to actor Stephen Collins, best known for *Tales of the Gold Monkey*], and has a baby. Jennifer Cooke is a good friend, although I haven't talked to her in a while. She married a guy ... and they live in Boulder, Colorado. I saw Marc Singer recently at an audition. We were actually going up for the same part in a movie. I haven't seen Michael Wright in a long time.

"That's what [the business] is all about. The people you meet."

Thirteen episodes into the series, Ironside, Jones and Blair Tefkin left the show, ostensibly for their characters to fight the aliens in Chicago. The elimination of characters was an attempt at reducing the number of different players and trimming storylines.

"I wanted to leave," says Ironside candidly.

"It's very difficult work, week after week, to feel fresh with that character. When I was given the opportunity to take him to Chicago, I gratefully took it. I was coming up to an opportunity to work on *Jo Jo Dancer* with Richard Pryor and *Top Gun* with Tom Cruise. I'd rather have done those. Also in the contract, if they got the [second] season, I'd be back."

The two mini-series created a tremendous problem for the network and the studio when the decision was made to continue as a weekly television series. In *The Final Battle*, the humans had won their fight against the Visitors by disabling them with the red dust spread across the world. For answers on how to continue the war, the network turned to producer and writer Steven E. de Souza.

"The mini-series was a complete story which ended with the triumph against the aliens," recaps de Souza. "The aliens were utterly defeated at the end of the mini-series. It was sort of saying World War II ended after the Japanese surrendered. When Warner Brothers and NBC said, 'We want to pick this up after we left off,' I said, 'You can't pick it up where you left off. You've created an impossible situation to resurrect it. The only thing you can do is start it up again.' In my opinion the mini-series worked at its best in the earlier episodes when there was sort of a political stalemate. So my intention was to get back to that stalemate situation."

To get it back to the heated status quo of the first mini-series required some creative exercises. In the process, de Souza's mind leapt to *Casablanca*. "*Casablanca*, many people say, is one of the greatest art pictures ever made," says de Souza. "It works well, has great drama, because the cafe that Rick has is a neutral ground where the Nazi and the freedom fighters meet on equal ground. So you have very intense scenes between Victor Lazlo (actor Paul Henreid), leader of the French underground, and the Nazis. They're threatening each other, and yet no one pulls out a gun and shoots the other person! This was the political construction of *Casablanca* at the time, and that gives you drama. So, I set up a nightclub in the series, analogous to that, to create that situation."

Believing this to be a good foundation for dramatic scenes, de Souza embellished the idea by "making Los Angeles in the series a neutral city—an open city. For the series to work, you've got to be able to have the heroes and villains get in the same room to have scenes together. So if you have

A TV cameraman (Marc Singer, kneeling left) and a scientist (Faye Grant, kneeling right) are among the leaders of the Resistance against human-like lizards from outer space. The aliens (standing) include Diana (Jane Badler) and Martin (Frank Ashmore). Copyright 1984 NBC/Warner Bros.

a full-scale war like they had in the last two to three hours of the first mini-series, they never can have scenes with each other! If you ever have Marc Singer get in the same room with Jane Badler in the mini-series, they would shoot each other! Whereas if they were in the same room in the fifth hour of the series, they would have a very tense melodramatic scene. That's good, because you have got to have the characters interact with each other!"

Michael Ironside played Ham Tyler in *V*.

Although he set up the foundations of drama so the saga could continue, de Souza left the show after six episodes because of "creative differences."

"There was a great deal of impatience at the network for the ratings to go up," he sighs. "Again, in short-sighted thinking, they remembered the highest rating was the last two hours of the first mini-series. That's where it was non-stop combat. Of course, I want action every week too, I don't want these people standing around talking. The problem is you have to have the underlying society of your story. Look at *Star Trek*: They didn't have a space battle with Klingons every week. The Klingons were out there. The series was a gunboat diplomacy show, where you had the Klingons and the Romulans who were the bad guys. And they would be mentioned all the time. There were many episodes about a new planet discovered, that we have to defend these people because it's an important outpost that the Romulans might get. It was an analogy to the Cold War. But they did not have a shooting battle with the Klingons every week. They never said, 'This week on *Star Trek*, all-out war breaks out!' The next 13 episodes is, like, war against the Klingons in outer space. The series would have degenerated to a military show every week, where everyone is on a military mission."

De Souza argued for balance, but "[the net-work] came to me and said, 'We want a higher rating. We want you to have complete, total war because these were the highest ratings of the last two hours of the first mini-series.' First of all, action is very expensive. We had action every week, but within the context of resistance fighters who are trying to go out and destroy the enemy in small, guerrilla actions—which we can afford to do. You know, like sabotage, blowing things up, capturing people, making them talk."

De Souza told the network, "If *V* becomes a complete war we can't do it because now the Air Force gets involved. Now, we have to spend all of our money on special effects shots of flying saucers shooting missiles at the city! I wanted the show to take place in a neutral place like Vichy, France [during World War II]. That's exactly what I wanted to do. In Vichy, France, there were no armies coming and going. I wanted a middle ground where small groups of commandos and guerrillas would engage each other. That can be done. I was overruled. I left the show. The minute I was gone, two weeks later, they got rid of a whole bunch of characters. And the wrong ones, by the way! The show ended in stalemate. And immediately, the show failed!

"First of all, the people behind the show had so little understanding of science fiction, and they didn't even pay attention to the show. Towards the end, they had an episode where someone came on the show and said, 'I must leave now and return to our own galaxy.' In the mini-series almost a year and a half ago, they identified a character as coming from a planet around the star Sirius, which is a very close star to us! In our own galaxy! So no one even gave a care to their own ground rules."

Of the many plots and subplots running throughout the saga, de Souza believes that one of the best didn't get the airplay it deserved: the conflict between Donovan and Tyler.

"No one was able to make it work," he says. "It wasn't used enough. I don't know why, but the networks said, 'We don't want the heroes fighting. We want them fighting the villains.' I loved that and I wanted to continue it. The network studio executives say, 'Why are you having these guys bicker? You should have them fight the aliens together.' I had people say to me, 'Steve, you are inconsistent. You are talking about *Star Trek*. That's your dream role model; they never fought [among each other].' I said, 'Watch it again!' There was a great deal of conflict between Captain Kirk, Mr. Spock and Dr. McCoy. It could never get as intense as it could get with Marc and Michael because [the Enterprise officers] were in a military situation and at a certain point you get court martialed!"

Many actors worked hard on the saga, de Souza says. "Everybody wanted to stretch their characters. Everybody wanted to go in new areas. It was my impression that they were very disheartened when the show changed. ... My impression was that morale really went down after they let a lot of the characters go. Everybody had an understanding of their characters when the mini-series was going. [But then] inconsistencies crept in. They were very quick to find it. They'd ask, 'Why am I doing this? This doesn't make any sense to me!'"

The move from mini-series to weekly episodes presented further story problems. For example, at the end of *The Final Battle*, Donovan and Parrish had, with the help of the friendly Visitor Martin, captured a mothership. As soon as *V* went to series status, de Souza realized in alarm that if they were to reestablish the status quo, the Resistance could not be in possession of the aliens' technology.

"One of the first things I said was, 'We have to get rid of the mothership.' The network executive said, 'Why are you doing this storyline about the mothership then [for the second episode, "Dreadnaught"]?' I said, 'Because if the mothership has been captured, and the aliens attack again, we would immediately take the mothership apart, right? You can't just resume the war because any 12-year-old with common sense would say, 'They've captured the mothership. They understand how all the weapons work.'

"So the network executive said, 'Don't even bother with that. Our audience won't even think of that.'"

Disgusted with this attitude, de Souza argued for continuity, as well as respect for the audience.

"They'd say, 'Maybe they put [the mothership] in the Smithsonian Institute and the Smithsonian people will turn it over to the Pentagon.' I said, 'Are you serious?' You've got to say that this is being examined and taken apart. You have to pick it up at that point. That was our plan, and we spent the first hour getting rid of the mothership. It was like a magic ring. You never give your heroes a magic ring or there's no series! It's like giving Angela Lansbury a crystal ball in *Murder She Wrote* and it tells her who the killer

is. There's no show! The fact they think that our audience is too *stupid* to think that through indicates the score that they have of the audience."

Making a move from a mini-series to a weekly series has important implications for story development. For a mini-series, structure demands a beginning, middle and end. But a weekly series automatically becomes melodramatic, and "the ongoing saga" here was not unlike a soap opera, with twists and turns in every chapter, as de Souza remembers.

Because *The Final Battle* ended with Diana taking off from the mothership and Donovan saying, "I'll get her later," de Souza suggested a story for the first episode of the series: "'Let's catch her, and then we have a second hour.' We picked up like the Saturday morning serials, right from where we left off. Donovan shoots her down and captures her. She gets away, and now we just continue the chase. The trial would have been a different situation, so we did a Lee Harvey Oswald. On the way to the trial she was shot. And she's faked her death. They substitute the body. And the people who did this ran the scientific corporation. We invented a new character [Lane Smith as Nathan Bates] and we said, off camera, he was the chemical genius that invented the poison that killed the aliens [the red dust used in the second mini-series]. He was like a Howard Hughes kind of character. We had him kidnap her because he wanted her to help his scientists understand the spaceships so he could make money selling the technology. Finally, she escapes and brings back the aliens.

"Someone at the network said, 'I don't understand why you have this whole complicated thing where he gets her and fakes her death, kills her like Lee Harvey Oswald, and she has her own plans and then she escapes. You go through all that stuff to have her escape. But she can escape in one second. You can save thousands of dollars in filming.'"

The executive suggested that Diana use alien powers to free herself. "I said, 'Well, how does she do that?' He said, 'Because, she's an alien, she has hypnotic power.' But I said, 'We never established anything like that!' And this is a top network executive who just cannot understand that you just can't keep changing the rules every week!"

Some four years after the *V* series ended its run, it seemed as though another page would be added to its history. Intrigued with the idea of reviving *V*, Warner Bros. in late 1989 commissioned screenwriter J. Michael Straczynski, of *Capt. Power*, *Twilight Zone* and *Babylon 5* fame, to write *V: The Next Chapter* to resolve the saga. The four-hour, two-part script, entitled "Rebirth," was an exercise in violent science fiction for television.

Straczynski's vision for the final fate of our band of freedom fighters begins with a complicated prelude: While peace is being declared on Earth, the Visitors violate the truce and massively attack the planet using 15 motherships. Elias (Michael Wright) is killed in battle, Willie (Robert Englund) is executed as a traitor, and Lydia (June Chadwick) disintegrates along with her mothership. Diana (Jane Badler) is reassigned elsewhere, while Julie Parrish (Faye Grant) flees the U.S. for Australia and disappears. Mike Donovan (Marc Singer) ends up as a prisoner of war on the Visitors' home planet. Many cities of the world get crushed into rubble in the process.

"Rebirth" takes place five years after Earth's surrender to the Visitors and deals with members of the Visitors' enemies, the Alliance, meeting with Earth's last rebel forces in a desperate bid to regain the planet. Straczynski takes what was meant as a false message, a red herring, in Johnson's original treatment, as a real event within the story.

After an extensive feasibility study, Warner Bros. rejected Straczynski's script as being too expensive to produce.

Both Ken Johnson and Michael Ironside said that Warner Bros. wanted to bring back *V* as a feature film and NBC wanted it as another four-hour mini-series to complete a syndication package.

"I've known that for years," scoffs Johnson. "They couldn't afford it then, they can't afford it now. Warner Bros. absolutely fumbled the ball."

Ironside echoes Johnson's belief that Warner Bros. and NBC have different ideas for the next incarnation. "We hear about it once a year or so. I think Warner Bros. doesn't want to pay for it. It's like a million and a half a week, and NBC would like the four hours to be done so they can get their syndication into place. Warner Bros. is not interested in footing the bill for that, because they never make enough revenues off of it. They are more interested in the feature film concept. So maybe when they stop bickering over it, someday it'll get done.

"It's getting more and more expensive. You've got people like Robert Englund as Freddy Krueger. Myself, I've gone off and done things, so my salary is higher now."

For now, the Visitors have Earth in their clutches. And if Straczynski's effort is any indication, it will be a long, difficult road before this mega-series comes alive once again and humans regroup their forces to destroy the lizards.

CAST NOTES

Marc Singer (Mike Donovan): Born in 1948 in Vancouver, Canada, he first came to attention in a leading role in *The Taming of the Shrew* for PBS. His features include *Go Tell the Spartans* (1978) and *If You Can See What I Hear* (1982), and he starred in two *Beastmaster* films (1982 and 1992). He also has been busy with films for video like *Silhouette* with Tracy Scoggins and *Watchers II—The Outsiders* (1989), and with television appearances like *Twilight Zone*, *The Hitchhiker*, *Simon and Simon* and *Highlander—The Series*.

Faye Grant (Julie): Born in Detroit, Michigan, Grant started out in *Greatest American Hero* as one of the high school kids. She became very proficient in commercials and guest roles.

Michael Ironside (Ham Tyler): Born 1949. Excels as villains, including the nasty assassin in *Total Recall* (1990) and *Highlander II: The Quickening* (1991). But he also co-produced small films like *Chaindance* (1991).

Jane Badler (Diana): First came to attention on the daytime soaps *One Life to Live* and *The Doctors*. Later appeared on *The Highwayman* (1988) with Sam Jones.

June Chadwick (Lydia): This English-born actress has starred in feature films like *This Is Spinal Tap* (1984) and *Forbidden World* (1982) and co-starred in the TV movie *Sparkling Cyanide* (1983). Later, she had a recurring role in Stephen J. Cannell's *Riptide* (1986).

Lane Smith (Nathan Bates): Born 1935. Smith's features include *Rooster Cogburn* (1969), *Network* (1976), *Prince of the City* (1981) and *Frances* (1982). Television credits include *Something About Amelia* (1984) and *Special Bulletin* (1983). He's also appeared in *Chiefs* (1983) and *Kay*

O'Brien (1986). Most recently, he landed the role of editor Perry White on *Lois and Clark: The Adventures of Superman* (1993).

Robert Englund (Willie): Born 1947. Became famous as Freddy Krueger in *Nightmare on Elm Street* horror feature series. Later the character moved into television under the title *Freddy's Nightmares* (1989–90).

Blair Tefkin (Robin): Has appeared in *Fast Times at Ridgemont High* (1982) and *Johnny Dangerously* (1984) and guest-starred in series such as *Quincy*, *Shirley* and *Marcus Welby, M.D.*

Michael Wright (Elias): Was named best actor at the Venice Film Festival for his performance in *Streamers* (1983). By answering a newspaper ad, he was cast in the feature film *The Wanderers* (1979), which led to his role in *V*.

Jennifer Cooke (Elizabeth): Potrayed the demure young Morgan Nelson on the daytime drama *The Guiding Light* for two years. She's a veteran of more than 200 commercials.

Jeff Yagher (Kyle): Was a first-year graduate student on a scholarship at Yale Drama School where he won the role of Kyle. He starred in the Oscar-winning *The Refuge* (1984). He returned to the science fiction genre in *The Bionic Showdown* (1989), the second reunion tele-film with the six million dollar man and the bionic woman.

EPISODE GUIDE

V (May 1983 mini-series)
(**Part One**) Simultaneously, in 31 cities around the world, the Earth is visited by gigantic UFOs. The supreme commander seeks Earth's help, but cameraman Donovan suspects sinister motives and joins a resistance group. (**Part Two**) Donovan becomes a fugitive when trying to reveal to the world the truth about the aliens. But they've got his son. Donovan boards the mothership but fails in his mission. Donovan is saved by one of the aliens, Martin. He learns that they plan to steal Earth's water and take humans as slaves, soldiers and food. Wr: Kenneth Johnson. Dir: Kenneth Johnson.
  Mike Donovan (Marc Singer); Diana (Jane Badler); Dr. Robert Maxwell (Michael Durrell); Dr. Juliet Parrish (Faye Grant); Brian (Peter Nelson); Daniel Bernstein (David Packer); Eleanor Donovan (Neva Patterson); Josh (Tommy Peterson); Robin Maxwell (Blair Tefkin); Elias Taylor

(Michael Wright); Helena Bernstein (Bonnie Bartlett); Abraham Bernstein (Leonardo Cimino); John (Richard Herd); Tony (Evan Kim); Dr. Ben Taylor (Richard Lawson); Stanley Bernstein (George Morfogen); Steven (Andrew Prine); Arthur Donovan (Hansford Rowe); Christine Walsh (Jenny Sullivan); Catherine Maxwell (Penelope Windust); Hard Hat (Michael Alldredge); Ruby Brown (Camila Ashlend); Martin (Frank Ashmore); Caleb Taylor (Jason Bernard); Cop (Michael Bond); Sancho (Rafael Campos); Harmy (Diane Civita); Willie (Robert Englund); Denny (Ron Hajak); Ruth (Mary-Alan Hokanson); Dr. Metz (David Hooks); Marjorie Donovan (Joanna Kerns); Barbara (Jenny Neumann); Brad (William Russ); Cop (Michael Swan); Asst. director (Stephanie Faulkner); Sen. Burke (Tom Fuccello); Sec. general (Wiley Harker); TV director (Dick Harwood); Quinton (Myron Healey); A woman (Bonnie Johns); Sean Donovan (Eric Johnston); Jankowski (Curt Lowens); Katie Maxwell (Marin May); Visitor soldier (Denny Miller, uncredited); Donovan's trooper (Mike Monahan); Reporter (Jennifer Perito); Reporter (Clete Roberts); Reporter (Nathan Roberts); Howard K. Smith (Himself); El Salvador leader (Robert Vandenberg); Newswoman #3 (Momo Yashima).

V: The Final Battle (May 1984 mini-series)
(**Part One**) Four months have passed since alien invaders have taken over Earth. Visitors have manipulated world opinion via the media, and are determined to eradicate the Resistance. Many humans are now cooperating with the Visitors. When Diana, one of the alien leaders, makes a public appearance, the Resistance finds an opportunity to expose the Visitors to the world. Meanwhile, Robin's pregnant by a Visitor. (**Part Two**) Reunited with his son, Donovan joins international Resistance forces headed by Ham Tyler and Chris Farber. First priority is freeing fellow fighter Julie, who is being held in the mothership. Meanwhile, Robin goes into labor. (**Part Three**) Donovan turns himself over to the aliens to save his son. Meanwhile, Diana hears her colleagues plot against her. She tells her leader only she can succeed because of a spy among the Resistance. Elsewhere, Willie, a friendly alien, submits to tests so Julie can find a biological weapon against the aliens. The stakes go higher when Martin tells Donovan that Diana has a nuclear device to ensure victory. (**Part One**) Wr: Brian Taggert and Peggy Goldman, story by Lillian Weezer (Kenneth Johnson), Peggy Goldman, Craig Faustus Buck, Diane Frolov, and Harry and Renee Longstreet. (**Part Two**) Wr: Brian Taggert and Diane Frolov, story by Lillian Weezer (Kenneth Johnson), Diane Frolov, Peggy Goldman and Craig Faustus Buck. (**Part Three**) Wr: Brian Taggert, Craig Faustus Buck, story by Lillian Weezer (Kenneth Johnson), Diane Frolov, Peggy Goldman. Dir: Richard T. Heffron.
  Mike Donovan (Marc Singer); Diane (Jane Badler); Dr. Robert Maxwell (Michael Durrell); Willie (Robert Englund); Dr. Juliet Parrish (Faye Grant); John (Richard Herd); Father Andrew Doyle (Thomas Hill); Ham Tyler (Michael Ironside); Brian (Peter Nelson); Daniel Bernstein (David Packer); Eleanor Donovan (Neva Patterson); Steven

(Andrew Prine); Mark (Sandy Simpson); Robin Maxwell (Blair Tefkin); Elias Taylor (Michael Wright); Maggie Blodgett (Denise Galik); Caleb Taylor (Jason Bernard); Sancho (Rafael Campos); Pamela (Sarah Douglas); Arthur Donovan (Hansford Rowe); Martin (Frank Ashmore); Elizabeth (age 8) (Jenny Beck); Harmy (Diane Civita); Chris Farber (Mickey Jones); Katie Maxwell (Marin May); Freedom fighter (Jenny O'Hara); Christine Walsh (Jenny Sullivan); Fred (Mark L. Taylor); Ruby Brown (Camila Ashlend); Lorraine (Greta Blackburn); Elizabeth Maxwell (Brandy Gold); Sean Donovan (Eric Johnston); Pascall (Dick Miller); Black alien captain (Stack Pierce); Reporter (Clete Roberts); Dr. Walter Corley (Don Starr).

Season Episodes

Liberation Day

As the world celebrates the end of the war with the Visitors, Diana is on trial, but she's spirited away by industrialist Nathan Bates, who has covert plans for Los Angeles. Wr: Paul Monash. Dir: Paul Krasny.

Young Elizabeth (Jenny Beck); Robert Maxwell (Michael Durell); Martin (Frank Ashmore); Good Old Boy (Ed Call); Dirk Small (Rod Browning); Sergeant (Kirk Scott); Keith Chavez (Val DeVargas); Steve Roller (Burt Marshall); Debby (Debby Davison); Anchorman (Hal Fishman); Woman reporter (Haunani Minn).

Dreadnaught

Diana plots the destruction of Los Angeles with the help of Nathan Bates. Wr: Steven E. de Souza. Dir: Paul Krasny.

Air Force general (Linden Chiles); Visitor technician (Barry Jenner); Visitor officer (Don Maxwell); Young Elizabeth (Jenny Beck); Robert Maxwell (Michael Durell); Steve Roller (Burt Marshall).

Breakout

Locked in an alien workcamp, surrounded by a giant sand monster, Ham and Mike try to organize a breakout. Wr: David Braff. Dir: Ray Austin.

Annie (Pamela Ludwig); Pilot (J.D. Hall); Steve Roller (Burt Marshall); Guard (Fiona Guinness); Foreman (Michael Abelar); Isaac (Xander Berkeley); Col. Hoya (Charles McCaulay); Male driver (Greg Zadikov); Female diner (Mary Baldwin); Billy Henley (Christian Jacobs); Vanik (Herman Poppe); Mother (Patrice Allison).

The Deception

Kyle Bates, Nathan's son, joins the Resistance. When Mike's captured, he's reunited with his son. Meanwhile, Diana has captured Elizabeth, the starchild. Wr: Garner Simmons. Dir: Victor Lobl.

Alien captain (Sandy Lang); Sean Donovan (Nick Katt); Pilot (Randall Brady); Alient sergeant (Anthony Ellis).

The Sanction

To assist in defeating the Resistance, Diana recruits Klaus, a Visitor commando who uses Mike's son, Sean, as a pawn to draw him in. Wr: Brian Taggert. Dir: Bruce Seth Green.

Sean Donovan (Nick Katt); Klaus (Thomas Callaway); Visitor officer (Casey Sander); Guard (James Ingersoll);

Theatre mgr. (David J. Partington); Ticket taker (Rob Stone).

Visitor's Choice

A Visitor food processing machine, the Encapsulator, is brought in to speed up the processing of people. Wr: David Braff. Dir: Gilbert Shilton.

Rodrigo (Martin Azarow); Raymond (Thomas Bellin); Barry Boddicker (Jonathan Caliri); Mary Kruger (Sybil Danning); Gen. Maxwell Larson (Robert Ellenstein); Security guard (Steve Itkin); Dean Boddicker (Chad McQueen); Fisher (Jason Ross); Edmund (Gustav Vintas).

The Overlord

The Resistance is lured into a trap when bikers help the Visitors. Wr: David Abramowitz. Dir: Bruce Seth Green.

Glenna (Sheryl Lee Ralph); Garrison (Michael Champion); Daniel (Robert Thaler); Marcus (C.E. Grimes); Frank (Rion Hunter); Amon (Kay E. Kuter); Dr. Jeffords (Richardson Morse); Kenneth (Craig Zehms); Helmsman (Michael Ashley Adams); Technician (Barry Buchanan); Driver (Anthony Henderson); The guard (Eric Lawrence); Billy Jeffords (Ricky Stout).

The Dissident

The Visitors have a deadly new weapon, a force field. The Resistance kidnaps its inventor. Wr: Paul F. Edwards. Dir: Walter Grauman.

Jacob (John McLiam); Visitor (Richard Manheim); Galen (Anthony De Longis); Technician (Robert MacKenzie); Security officer (Armand Gerami); Brian (Peter Nelson).

Reflections in Terror

The Visitors obtain a sample of Elizabeth's blood and create an evil clone. Meanwhile, the Resistance saves orphan children. Wr: Chris Manheim. Dir: Kevin Hooks.

Chris Farber (Mickey Jones); Elizabeth clone (age 8) (Jenny Beck); Dennis (James Daughton); Laird (Anthony James); Rev. Turney (William Wellman, Jr.); Jennifer (Keri Houlihan); Ferris (Robert Rothwell); Old woman (Connie Sawyer); Policeman in park (Charles Walker); Saleswoman (Debra Armani); Vendor (Jim Boelsen); Manager (Tom Lowell); Newscaster (Tawny Schneider).

The Conversion

Kyle and Ham are captured by Diana. The Resistance captures Lydia, unaware that Ham has been converted to kill Mike. Wr: Brian Taggert Dir: Gilbert Shilton.

Chris Farber (Mickey Jones); Lin (Catherine Nguyen); Charles (Duncan Regehr); Mira (Nicole Rowe); Female technician (Marin Mazzie); Technician (Vince McKewin); 2nd female technician (Syl Farrell); Rebel (Dominic Hoffman); Lizard #1 (John C. Mooney); Lizard #2 (Kurt Smildsin).

The Hero

The Visitors hold hostages and demand the surrender of the Resistance fighters. The aliens' real goal is to plant a spy into the Resistance's ranks. Wr: Carleton Eastlake. Dir: Kevin Hooks.

Lt. James (Judson Scott); John Langley (Bruce Davison);

Chris Farber (Mickey Jones); Charles (Duncan Regehr); Carol Caniff (Judyann Elder); George Caniff (Robert Hooks); Visitor (Jeff Kober); Reggie (Ernest Harden, Jr.); Plainclothes cop (Beau Starr); Glen (cop) (Chris Capen); Dr. Liz Talbot (Nancy Lenehan); Also with Christopher Patterson.

The Betrayal

Willie nearly dies when shot by the Visitors, but a kidnapped Visitor medical student agrees to operate on him. Wr: Mark Rosner. Dir: Gilbert Shilton.

Lt. John Langley (Bruce Davison); Charles (Duncan Regehr); Howie (Richard Minchenberg); Doctor (Robert Dowdell); Officer (Dean Abston); Guard #1 (John Allen); Orderly (Gary Dubin); Mel (Jonah Pearson); Simon (Michael Tulin).

The Rescue

As the Resistance regroups, Julie's old friend Alan needs her help in delivering his wife's baby. Meanwhile, Charles plans to get rid of Diana by marrying her. But Diana has her own plot to murder him. Kyle manages to make peace with his father before the elder Bates is killed. Wr: Garner Simmons. Dir: Kevin Hooks.

Lt. James (Judson Scott); Charles (Duncan Regehr); Alan Davis (Terence Knox); Jo Ann Davis (Darleen Carr); John Davis (Ian Fried); Marta (Gela Jacobson); Lizard priest (Ralph Drischell); Guard #1 (Richard Epcar); Cary (Cynthia Frost); Ensign (Sandy Lang); Female (Mindi Miller); Angelo (Leland Murray); Louis (Christopher Shobe).

The Champion

Mike helps organize a Resistance force in a small town. Philip (Martin's brother) arrives to investigate Charles' death. Wr: Paul F. Edwards. Dir: Cliff Bole.

Lt. James (Judson Scott); Philip (Frank Ashmore); Sheriff Roland (Hugh Gillin); Kathy Courtney (Deborah Wakeham); Jesse Courtney (Sherri Stoner); Messenger (Steven Barr); Chief juror (R.D. Call); Commander (John H. Evans).

The Wildcats

While a medical crisis rages through a community, the Resistance are mistaken for invaders by teenagers in the town. Wr: David Braff. Dir: John Florea.

Lt. James (Judson Scott); Philip (Frank Ashmore); Ellen (Rhonda Aldrich); Tony (Jeffery Jay Cohen); Andy (Adam Silbar); Marta (Gela Jacobson); Cal (Ashton Wise); Bart (Reggie Johnson); Oswald (Peter Elbling); Mary (Nancy Warren); Cindy (Cathy Wellman); Guard and Visitor guard (Fritz Ford); Girl (Paige Matthews).

The Littlest Dragon

Philip, the alien brother of Martin, blames Mike for Martin's death. But Philip forms an alliance with Mike when he learns Diana was the killer. Wr: David Abramowitz. Dir: Cliff Bole.

Robert (Brett Cullen); Glenda (Wendy Fulton); Angela (Leslie Bevis); Ensign (Christopher Shobe).

War of Illusion

Kyle's old friend, a computer wizard, taps into the Visitors' communications network. This incites the aliens to hunt for the boy. Wr: John Simmons. Dir: Earl Bellamy.

Lt. James (Judson Scott); Philip (Frank Ashmore); Oswald (Peter Elbling); Dr. David Atkins (Conrad Janis); Henry Atkins (Josh Richman); Blanche Butler (Louise Fitch); Also with David Abbott, Ted Lehmann, Chip Heller.

The Secret Underground

Sneaking aboard the mothership to retrieve a deadly Resistance list, Julie discovers an old flame, a scientist. He's being held against his will by the aliens to create viruses. Wr: David Braff and Colley Cibber, story by David Abramowitz and Donald R. Boyle. Dir: Cliff Bole.

Lt. James (Judson Scott); Philip (Frank Ashmore); Dr. Steven Maitland (John Calvin); Jonathan (Derek Barton); Judith (Debbie Gates); Oswald (Peter Elbling); Nigel (Lydia's brother) (Ken Olandt).

The Return

To sabotage a truce by her leader, Diana plans to stop the aliens' arrival on Earth with a well-planted bomb. Wr: David Abramowitz and Donald R. Boyle, story by David Braff and Paul Edwards. Dir: John Florea.

Lt. James (Judson Scott); Philip (Frank Ashmore); Thelma (Marilyn Jones); Cal (Ashton Wise); Newscaster (Tawny Schneider).

Voyage to the Bottom of the Sea

September 1964–September 1968

The submarine Seaview *carries out dangerous missions for the United States government, and encounters strange life forms under the sea. Built by Admiral Nelson, the Seaview has a crew of 125 men. Voyage's first year was set in 1973. The second year spanned 1973–78. The last two seasons were set from 1980 to 1982.*

Cast: Admiral Harriman Nelson (Richard Basehart); Captain Lee Crane (David Hedison); Chief Francis Sharkey (years 2–4) (Terry Becker); Lt. Cdr. Chip Morton (Robert Dowdell); Kowalski (Del Monroe);

Patterson (Paul F. Trinka); Stu Riley (year 2) (Allan Hunt); Chief Curley Jones (year 1) (Henry Kulky); Sparks (Arch Whiting); Doctor (Richard Bull); Kelly, the sonarman (year 1) (Nigel McKeand).

Created by: Irwin Allen; *Associate Producers:* Allan Balter, Joe Gantman (year 1); William Welch (year 2); Bruce Fowler (years 3–4); *Executive Producer:* Irwin Allen; *Special Effects:* L.B. Abbott; *Main Director of Photography:* Winton C. Hoch; *Music Composers included:* Leith Stevens, Nelson Riddle, Jerry Goldsmith; ABC/Twentieth Century–Fox; 60 minutes; black and white (year 1); color (years 2–4).

When Shakespearean actor Richard Basehart heard about a new TV series called *Voyage to the Bottom of the Sea,* he asked his agent to set up a meeting with producer Irwin Allen. Having wound up a successful film career, Basehart was intrigued by the idea of doing a submarine series that would take him to exotic ports of call each week. A week later, Basehart sat in Allen's office. The producers excitedly told the actor of an upcoming storyline where the *Seaview* would be grabbed by a prehistoric monster. Basehart broke into laughter. He stopped laughing when he realized they were serious.

"Richard confided to me that he couldn't turn down the pilot because the money was too good," recalls actor Mark Slade, who played crewman Malone during the first season. "He was sure that it wouldn't sell. Well, on the first day of filming, he came up to me and said, 'My God, it sold!'"

The series was based on the 1961 motion picture starring Walter Pidgeon and Joan Fontaine. It was an updated version of Jules Verne's *20,000 Leagues Under the Sea.* The slightly eccentric Admiral Nelson, like Verne's Captain Nemo, had built his own submarine. When producer Irwin Allen pitched a weekly version of *Voyage* to ABC, the network was interested. Allen, who would go on to produce disaster films such as *The Poseidon Adventure* and *The Towering Inferno,* was dubbed the dean of TV science fiction when *Voyage* and his later *Lost in Space* took off in the ratings.

"Allen was one of the most creative people in the science fiction arena," says Thomas Moore, former president of ABC. "He grasped the Jules Verne material with an immediate recognition as to its convertibility to television. He surrounded himself with talented young writers, directors and special effects people."

With Richard Basehart signed up as the admiral, producer Allen had to reel in actor David Hedison for the part of the sub's skipper, Lee Crane. Hedison wanted nothing to do with the series. "I had worked with Irwin Allen before on the *Lost World* film," says Hedison. "As much as I liked him, I vowed never to work with him again or do that kind of a film again. In 1961, Irwin sent me the script for the *Voyage* feature. He wanted me to play Captain Crane. I read six pages and turned him down flat. I lied to Irwin and told him I was doing another movie. I thought that was the end of it."

Robert Sterling was cast as the captain in the feature film, but when the series bobbed to the surface, Allen was determined that Hedison would play Crane. The actor found the character a one-dimensional bore and turned it down again. "Irwin called me in New York," says Hedison. "I thanked him for thinking of me and told him I wasn't interested. I flew to the Cairo Film Festival, and he called me there. I made up more excuses. When I arrived in London a few days later to do a guest shot on *The Saint* with Roger Moore, Irwin was on the phone. It was 7 a.m. I said no! I said no again. I was looking for a different kind of show. I pleaded: 'Irwin, I'm half asleep. I can't think!' Then he said the magic words. No, not money. He said, 'Richard Basehart will be playing the admiral.' That did it. If Richard Basehart can do this shit, so can I.

"Working with Richard was a joy. He wasn't an easy person, but we hit it off from the start. What a gentleman … what an incredible human being … and my God, what an actor! He made bad dialogue breathe. I learned a lot from him."

With his actors cast, Allen began filming the series in 1964. The series' first year, filmed in black and white, emphasized enemy agents and espionage, but there were also nightmarish scenarios where the submarine was pitted against killer robots, giant whales, humanoid amphibians, and monsters that slurped down corridors and ate people.

Despite the first season's preference for adventure over drama, the stories were treated in a suspenseful, serious manner. The series was an immediate hit and dominated its time period for its first few months on the air.

Mark Slade recalls how Richard Basehart narrowly averted tragedy on the series' set during the filming of an early segment, "City Beneath the Sea." "We were ready to shoot a scene where the submarine is hit by a torpedo. We rehearsed the scene on the deck of the plywood sub on the backlot tank, and the explosives were set. For some reason, Richard asked to see the explosives go off before the scene was shot. His request caused some tension because it would delay filming, but Richard held out. The special effects crew set off the explosives, and it blew out a huge chunk of the sub's deck, right where the actors would have been standing. Richard just stood there and began singing, 'There's no business like show business,' and he went to lunch."

Another guest star, Joey Tata, recalls trying to fast-talk Irwin Allen into signing him up as a regular. "Irwin told me, 'Joey, I have enough cast members as it is. Don't worry—you'll work.' He was put to work in an early episode, "The Mist of Silence," as a crewman who is dragged from a South American prison and shot. "That scene was so powerful it was almost cut out," explains Tata. "Director Lenny Horn said to me, 'Joey, I don't know if we'll get away with this, but let's play this really straight.' So when the soldiers grabbed me, I yelled and screamed and struggled

An aquatic beauty (Diane Webber) is recruited by Captain Crane (David Hedison) to save California's coast in "The Mermaid." Copyright 1967 ABC/Twentieth Century–Fox.

like crazy. After the rehearsal, somebody said to Lenny, 'Irwin's not going to like this scene.' Irwin didn't like drama unless it was well lit with explosions. Lenny looked over at me and winked. We shot the scene, and it was left in. After it was over, Del Monroe [Kowalski] said, 'Holy shit, Joey ... I got a terrible feeling watching that.'"

Another first season guest star, John Anderson, had second thoughts about accepting the role of a scientist in "Cradle of the Deep" (an episode David Hedison ranks as his least favorite). "When I read the script, I said, 'God almighty! All this guy does is blab about unlocking the secrets of life.' It was a one-dimensional

character, and I wondered why I had even accepted the part."

As Anderson struggled with the character, he noticed some unsettling behavior on the set. "By noon of the fourth day, I noticed that Richard Basehart, who had suffered through 25 segments by this time, was poking fun at the lines and snickering over inside jokes. I was shocked that Basehart, who was a good friend, was engaging in such destructive and insensitive behavior. After several hours of watching Dick indulge in this kids' shit, I decided to settle it. We went for lunch. I lit up my cigar and he had a drink. I said, 'Dick, I'm going to describe a situation that's been bothering me. You may not like it, but since you're the star of the show…' and he said, 'Yeah, damn it! I know I am.'

"I stopped him and said, 'Don't tell me your troubles, Dick. You're paid a lot of money to do this show, right?' He nodded. I said, 'Don't you have any other reasons for doing this show?' He replied, 'John, it's these damn scripts. They're the same thing every week.' I shook my head and said, 'Dick, I have tremendous respect for you. You're one of the greatest living talents in this business. But do you have any idea how hard it is for me, as a guest star, to make this thinly drawn character work while you're making jokes about the script?' He looked at me very grimly. I wasn't out to hurt him, but I could see that I had really gotten through to him. 'You're right, John,' he said. 'It's easy for me to kid the script, but it's got to stop.' He thanked me profusely and we went back to work. There was no more bullshit."

Anderson's co-star in the episode was a rapidly expanding blob aboard the *Seaview*. "I concentrated on making the story work," he recalls. "I couldn't look at the blob and say, 'Jesus Christ! What a sorry piece of shit that is! It's a pulsating bag with red ink in it. Do we really have to work with this dumb piece of shit?' Instead, I figured, 'Well, by God, it's a low-budget show and damn, that's the best blob they could come up with. So let's do it.'"

Novelist Jerry Sohl (*Costigan's Needle*) recalls that veteran writer Sy Salkowitz took an inventive approach to get out of writing a script. "Sy's agent had set up a meeting with Irwin Allen and Sy wasn't interested. He decided the best way to lose the assignment was to give Irwin the worst story ever. So when the two met, Sy said, 'Irwin, let's do a story where the president and the head of Red China board the submarine for a summit meeting.' Irwin just looked at him and said, 'Uh-huh,' with absolutely no enthusiasm.

"Sy continued, 'The president suffers a stroke and is incapacitated.' Irwin showed a little more interest. 'Fortunately, there's a brain surgeon aboard and they fix him up.' 'Oh, that's interesting,' Irwin deadpanned. Sy continued, 'And the surgeon, who is one of the Red Chinese, is a woman!' Irwin just looked at Sy blankly. And Sy goes, 'And she's got tits that stick way out to here!' Irwin yelled, 'I'll buy it! I'll buy it!'" (And he did—at least the idea, for the episode "Hail to the Chief.")

Voyage had surfaced in the top 30 during its first year, but it lacked the complete audience that

ABC was seeking. To attract teenagers, a hip young sailor named Riley (Allan Hunt) was added during the second season. When Henry Kulky (Chief Jones) died of a heart attack while reading his script during the first year, Terry Becker was brought in as the new CPO, Chief Sharkey. The second season would be in color. The *Seaview* was also given a sleek refurbishment. The addition of a small flying sub allowed the writers to get the characters to different parts of the world.

Although Richard Basehart and David Hedison had campaigned to get a female regular on the show, a half-hearted attempt to make actress Susan Flannery a recurring character wasn't successful. Research showed that viewers wanted more monsters and action, not women. Indeed, female guest stars began to disappear as the second season progressed. It was a cost-cutting measure instigated by Irwin Allen. Under orders from the network to reduce budget expenditures, Allen grew to resent the extra time required to provide women with hairstyles and makeup. He put his money toward building bigger and better monsters.

Terry Becker, now cast as Chief Sharkey, recalls, "My agent at the time didn't think I was right for the role. But the show's casting director, Joe D'Agosta, showed some film to Irwin from a show I had done called *The Men*, and Irwin wanted to meet me.

"So we met and he said, 'Okay, you're going in at minimum salary. If you show me that you can do this role, I'll raise your salary.' So we agreed on a raise. I went through the year and at an appropriate time, I said to Irwin, 'Am I coming back for another year?' He said, 'Yeah.' So I mentioned the raise. He said, 'What raise? Forget it!' So I said, 'Okay, then kill me off.'"

At the conclusion of the episode "The Sky's on Fire," Sharkey was blasted from the series. "Chief Sharkey commits hara-kiri by jumping on a grenade to save the ship," explains Becker, "and that was that. Irwin read every actor in town to replace the chief. I recall Harvey Lembeck was up for the part. However, during the screen tests, Irwin kept turning to director Harry Harris and saying, 'That's not my chief.' Harry replied, 'Look, you want Terry Becker. Call him and make a deal!' So he called me in. He's trying to charm me and I'm trying to charm him and we're both disgusting. I said, 'Look, all I want is my money.' So we came down to a 50 dollar difference. I started to get up to leave, and Irwin said, 'All

The stars of *Voyage* clown around with "The Deadly Dolls." Left to right: Richard Basehart, guest star Vincent Price, David Hedison. Copyright 1967 ABC/Twentieth Century–Fox.

right! All right! I'll give you 49 dollars.' And I stayed."

Sometimes Allen had to get inventive in attracting actors to play the monsters of the week. Actor Vic Lundin, who had played Friday in the 1964 film *Robinson Crusoe on Mars,* admits that his role as the Lobster Man "probably wouldn't have been played by any other actor unless they were really hungry!" Lundin was cast as the crafty crustacean after receiving a call from Allen. "He asked me if I could do an English accent. I said, 'Why, certainly, old man!' So I read for the director, got the part and went for makeup. I got a cup of coffee, sat in the chair, and suddenly everything went dark. They had put an object over my head, and seconds later they cut away slits for my eyes so I could see. Behold, I was Lobster Man! They dressed me up in a wetsuit that weighed 40

pounds, and they marched me over to see Irwin. He was in a conference when I walked in. I could barely talk through this mask. I said, very muffled, 'Irwin, answer me one question. Why the hell do I have to do an English accent for this thing?' He agreed to cut away part of the mask so that my mother could at least recognize me. Aside from the costume, it was a really good part. With the suit on, though, it became a spoof."

Lundin found out that Richard Basehart had an aversion to monsters. "Basehart was adamant about never being filmed with a monster. I was near him one day when a publicity photographer stopped to take a picture of the two of us. Basehart went absolutely ballistic on me and the photographer. I really thought he was going to kill us! He didn't want any photos taken of him with 'a monster.' He was a dedicated actor but very difficult to work with. From then on, I stayed away from him and just did my scenes."

Voyage played out its last three years on Sunday nights, cornering a modest but loyal audience consisting mainly of children and women. One of the series' trademarks became the "*Seaview* stomp." Allan Hunt, who played crewman Riley, explains: "Every week, the submarine would be rammed or blown up and we'd go crashing from side to side. Actually, the sub set stayed level. They just tilted the camera to create the illusion that the sub was rocking. The explosions were just little puffs of smoke. When the sound guys added the big sound effects in the editing room, the result was devastating. It looked and sounded great."

"Everyone who worked on the submarine got burned," claims actor Joey Tata. "When Irwin did explosions, he really did them. And a lot of times you'll see us closing these big, heavy doors on the sub, but they were really made of balsa wood. The sound guys added a heavy clank, but sometimes you can see the doors bounce."

"The propman would sit with a tin can and hammer," recalls director Sutton Roley, "and when he hit the tin can, the actors would fake their falls. It bothered the actors to do it this way. Richard Basehart was particularly embarrassed by the tin can, but it worked."

Roley, whose distinctive style includes extreme close-ups and inventive dolly sweeps with the camera, incorporated his style into the creepy segment "The Phantom." Alfred Ryder guest-starred as the ghost of a World War I U-boat captain who demands Captain Crane's body.

"Irwin had a very cut-and-dry approach," explains Roley. "He was a great believer in storyboarding. He had his artists draw every shot of the script beforehand. I can't work that way. Whenever you surprised Irwin by doing something different, he could be quite a shouter."

Roley decided to shoot a seven-page scene by having the camera dolly back and forth as the crew tries to track the approaching ghost ship in the control room. "The sub's control room was built like a real submarine, totally enclosed. I asked the grip, 'Does this sub come apart?' He said the whole side did. So I said, 'Rip the whole thing off!' and it was unbolted. This way I could shoot over the computers and give the scene some visual leeway.

"We set it up and the cameraman shook his head. 'You're gonna get blurred images,' he said.

I replied, 'Is that right? Well, this is the way we're gonna do it.' So the cameraman called up Irwin, and I was called to the phone. 'What are you doing down there?' Irwin yelled. 'You've got everybody upset.' I said, 'It's gonna work, Irwin. And I think you're gonna like it.'

"As we shot it, I had everybody against me, except for Richard Basehart and David Hedison. After the shot was completed, Basehart said, 'I knew we were okay, Sutton, as soon as I saw half of that Goddamned submarine set taken away. I'm tired of being stuck in here. It gives me claustrophobia.' We wrapped the scene at 2:30 that afternoon, which was unheard of. In the dailies the next day, everyone was watching as my shot came up. When the scene was over Irwin suddenly tapped me on the shoulder. 'It really did work, didn't it?' They loved the episode so much that they made a sequel to it."

Terry Becker recalls a scene in "The Fossil Men." "Richard and I were supposed to be exploring this island, and I said to him, 'You know, Richard, this scene could be kinda funny.' He said, 'Yeah?' I said, 'Yeah. Watch me.' So we're looking around and I see these rocks walking toward us. I say, 'Admiral?' And he goes, 'Yeah?' and I say, 'Sir, the rocks are moving,' and he goes, 'Aw!' He turns and sees them. 'Yeah, the rocks *are* moving,' he says. We got right into it.

"Well, when the episode was run for the ABC executives, they cracked up. They fell on the floor in hysterics. Irwin stormed up to me and Richard and yelled, 'What are you guys doing? You're making a comedy out of this show. It's not a comedy!'"

While Becker and Basehart developed a good working relationship on the show, Becker had to coax his co-star into becoming more sociable on the set. "Basehart would go to his dressing room or read a book because he didn't want to deal with people. I felt that when we had visitors on the set, we had a responsibility to go out and greet them. I'd ask Richard to join me and he'd say, 'Well, I want to read.' I'd say, 'Read outside. Say hello to the people. What are you, a recluse? This is part of your job.' So he did. Eventually, he grew to enjoy it."

By *Voyage*'s third year, TV critics regularly fumed that it was a silly show and lambasted it for its outlandish plots. *Voyage* continued to serve up magic elves, mermaids and lobster men without pretension. The series never winked at its audience, and its relentless storylines of fossil men, clowns and mummies were played straight.

The *Seaview*'s crew prepares for action. Left to right: Richard Basehart, David Hedison, Del Monroe, Robert Dowdell and Terry Becker. Copyright 1967 ABC/Twentieth Century–Fox.

Voyage had metamorphosed into true camp and bore very little resemblance to the semi-realistic stories of the first year.

Another transformation occurred with the crew. During the first year, the *Seaview*'s background sailors often had brief lines of dialogue. By the second year, budget cuts pared the extras to a bare minimum. "The *Seaview* supposedly had a crew of 125 men," recalls writer Robert Vincent Wright. "But you never saw more than a half-dozen or so actors."

The budget also rendered the background crewmen mute. Protocol requires that when a superior officer gives an order to a sailor, the

David Hedison boxes with a visiting *Lost in Space* monster (Robert Maffei) on the studio backlot. Courtesy of costume designer Paul Zastupnevich.

only be attacked by so many denizens of the deep. A writer would come in and say, 'Hey, I've got a great story about a giant frog!' Irwin would say, 'We've had too many giant frogs! Think of something else.' Once, Irwin asked me if I had something new. I said, 'Sure. How about an episode where the *Seaview* is attacked by a giant anchovy? There's a terrible battle, but the *Seaview* kills it.' Irwin asked, 'What happens then?' I said, 'The crew makes the biggest Caesar salad known to man.' Irwin snapped, 'Very funny!'"

By the fourth year, Terry Becker and his fellow cast members all shared the weariness of having to deal with weird creatures every week. "Certainly, as actors, we didn't want to do monsters. Just seeing another guy in a monster suit drove us up the wall.

sailor must verbally acknowledge that order. To save money on dialogue, the crewmen were reduced to acknowledging their orders either by nodding or by having an old voice-track of "Aye, sir!" dubbed over the scene.

Being a *Seaview* crewman was also hazardous. By the time the submarine had finished its travels, a total of 77 crewmen had been blasted or vaporized. Although Captain Kirk on *Star Trek* always did a song and dance over losing a crew member, the redundancy of mourning his losses became a drag for Admiral Nelson. While watching the body of "Simpson" being taken away in "The Mummy," Nelson expresses his regret in such a weary tone that one surmises he couldn't care less.

As the series continued its monster-of-the-week format, the writers became desperate for new ideas. "There got to be a sameness with the series," says Robert Vincent Wright. "You can

"We wanted to do other stories, but it was cheaper to put a guy in a rubber suit than to go out on location. We hardly ever got off that sub. When I joined the show, my hair was just thinning, and Irwin wanted me to wear a toupee. He said the chief might get involved with women. I said, 'Hey, that's an interesting idea. A woman falls in love with a bald guy and he scores!' But all of those ideas got cut out. We ended up making love to giant lizards."

"Richard Basehart was a consummate actor," says Sutton Roley, "and he just stuck his tongue in his cheek and played the thing. I'd catch him on occasion and say, 'Richard, you're doing a little number here.' He'd smile and say, 'Ah, you caught me again.'"

"Richard got himself screwed up with the amount of money he had to pay for his divorce," recalls casting director Larry Stewart. "*Voyage* was a way to make money. One day, network people

Left: Admiral Nelson (Richard Basehart) and Captain Crane (David Hedison) are under the watchful eyes of a sea monster as they chart their next course. *Right:* Crewman Patterson (Paul Trinka) finds himself on hazardous duty. Both photos courtesy of costume designer Paul Zastupnevich.

from Japan visited the set. Through an interpreter, they asked him, 'How do you enjoy the scripts?' Richard replied, 'All I can tell you is that every Friday, someone in Irwin Allen's office flushes the toilet and the script ends up here.' The interpreter tried to explain this to the visitors and they looked totally bewildered."

A year before his death in 1984, Basehart shared his perspective on the series. "I enjoyed doing *Voyage* part of the time," he said, "but a great deal of it was a chore. The trouble with any TV series is that it's going to be the same thing every week."

Allan Hunt recalls that, while Basehart and David Hedison were good friends, there was an amusing cultural gap between them. "Richard read books on Churchill; David sang Beatles' songs. Between scenes, David would sing little melodies. Richard was always very silent, deep in thought. At the time, there was a hit song called "Henry the VIII" by Freddy and the Dreamers. David was singing 'I'm Henry the VIII, I am' to himself and Richard turned to him and said, 'What are you singing?' David said, '"Henry the VIII." Don't you ever listen to KROA?' David launched into this 'I'm Henry the VIII, I am.' Richard just looked at him and said, 'That's terrible.'"

Voyage's success with young viewers inspired

a flood of merchandise, including a comic book series, games, bubblegum cards and *Seaview* models. There was also a spoof on the prestigious *Hollywood Palace* TV show in 1967. David Hedison was invited to take part in the skit. "I played Captain Crane, of course, and Milton Berle played a crazed, desperate crewman," chuckles Hedison. "When the *Seaview* started its rock and roll, the audience was thrilled. The laughter was nonstop. The skit was very successful."

After sailing through some plausible—and many implausible—adventures, the *Seaview* was dry-docked. With 110 episodes completed, there was a consensus that four years of nautical mayhem had exhausted the *Seaview*'s mission roster.

"The overall strengths of *Voyage* were the acting and the photo effects," reflects Hedison. "The weaknesses were too many monsters, and not very creative ones at that. I would have been happy to continue with the series if I had a guarantee that I'd never see another monster. But by year four, I knew it was doomed. The storylines were ludicrous, the writing team of William Woodfield and Allan Balter had left, and we had lots of plant men, fossil men, fish men, you name it. Four years was nice. Four years working with Richard Basehart was particularly nice. I still miss him."

The series found some success in syndication after leaving ABC in 1968, and it has spawned its share of fan interest. "Recently, I did an L.A. talk show," says Joey Tata, "and the hostess said, 'I remember you from *Voyage to the Bottom of the Sea*!' So I got up and I did the *Seaview* stomp … four steps to the left, four steps to the right. The audience was on the floor! It's great to find out that you're part of a cult show."

CAST NOTES

Richard Basehart (Admiral Nelson): Born 1914. His film career included *Titanic* (1953), *La Strada* (1954) and *Moby Dick* (1956). The Emmy award–winning actor was the main title announcer for the series *Knight Rider* (1982–86). Basehart died shortly after providing the closing narration for the 1984 Summer Olympic Games in Los Angeles.

David Hedison (Captain Crane): Born 1929. Hedison is known to fans as *The Fly* (1958). Shortly after *Voyage* wrapped up, he moved to England and got married. He returned to America in the early 1970s and became one of TV's most visible guest stars. He also appeared as Felix Leiter in the James Bond films *Live and Let Die* (1973) and *License to Kill* (1989). Hedison played a recurring villain in the daytime series *Another World* (1990–95).

Terry Becker (Chief Sharkey): Born 1932. A New York stage actor who turned to producing and directing in 1968, Becker recently returned to acting, explaining, "It's a group called Theater West in L.A., and I'm having fun." He finds people still recognize him as Sharkey. "I went to Pittsburgh for a trade show and everyone recognized me as the chief. There's an audience out there that still respects the show."

Robert Dowdell (Chip Morton): Born 1933. Initially, producer Irwin Allen didn't want Dowdell for the Chip Morton role. Recalls Allan Hunt: "Irwin and David Hedison were screening a scene from the TV series *Stoney Burke* (1963). Bob Dowdell was playing a rodeo rider whose back was broken, and he was dying in Jack Lord's arms. When the lights came up, David was very moved by Bob's performance. Irwin just had a blank look on his face and said, 'I don't like him … he doesn't have a sense of humor.'" Neverthe-

less, Dowdell landed the *Voyage* role. A real estate expert, he continues acting in TV guest roles and commercials.

Del Monroe (Kowalski): Born 1931. Monroe was the only *Voyage* cast member who also appeared in the 1961 *Voyage* film (his movie debut). "Del was a rather shy, extremely gentle, hard-working actor," recalls actor Mark Slade. "During *Voyage*'s first season, he was also moonlighting at an aerospace plant to support his family." Monroe continued acting into the 1980s.

Allan Hunt (Riley): Born 1945. As a science fiction buff, Hunt found his role on *Voyage* a dream come true. However, in 1966 he was drafted by the army and had to leave the series. He resumed his acting career in the 1970s. He's also a director.

Paul Trinka (Patterson). Trinka's last TV appearance was on *Rod Serling's Night Gallery* in 1972. He was in his early thirties when he died in 1973.

Henry Kulky (Chief Jones): Born 1911. A former wrestler, Kulky began his acting career in the 1940s, usually as a thug. His TV series included roles on *The Life of Riley* (1953–58) and *Hennesey* (1959–62). Kulky died of a heart attack in 1965, during production of the *Voyage* episode "Cradle of the Deep."

Richard Bull (Doc): Born 1924. Best known as the patient Mr. Oleson on *Little House on the Prairie* (1974–83).

Arch Whiting (Sparks): Whiting left acting in the late 1970s shortly after starring in the Saturday morning series *Run Joe Run* (1974–75). "Arch told me he was going to Paris to become a cinematographer," says actor Joey Tata. "That's the last time I saw him."

Nigel McKeand (Kelly): McKeand is astonished when he learns that his *Voyage* character had a name. "I usually had one line per week, like, 'We're sinking!' or 'There's a monster dead ahead!'

The actor manned the *Seaview*'s sonar controls for the series' first season. He admits the role didn't stretch his acting abilities. "I never left the submarine. I'd just sit there twiddling the dials. I had always considered *Voyage* as basically a kids' show, but the cast was terrific."

McKeand and his wife Carol later produced the 1970s series *Family*.

EPISODE GUIDE

Season 1: 1964-65

Eleven Days to Zero

Seaview's mission to prevent a quake is threatened by a giant octopus and enemy agents. Wr and story: Irwin Allen. Dir: Irwin Allen.

Dr. Fred Wilson (Eddie Albert); Gamma (Theodore Marcuse); Claude Selby (John Zaremba); Malone (Mark Slade); Chairman (Booth Colman); John Phillips (William Hudson); Sonarman (Christopher Connelly); General Chairman (Hal Torey); O'Brien (Gordon Gilbert); Army general (Barney Biro); Junior officer (Derrik Lewis); Enemy technician (Paul Kremin); Helmsman (Jim Goodwin); Narrator (Dick Tufeld); Enemy Voice (Werner Klemperer); Scientist (Walter Reed); Asians (Mike Ferris, Oren Curtis); Driver (Ron Rondell); Crew (Buck Kartalian, Fred Zendar, Bill Kinney, Chuck Courtney).

Memory Flash—Mark Slade: "During the filming of the pilot in November 1963, I was walking outside the soundstage. Someone said President Kennedy had been assassinated. I ran back to the stage and told an older crew member. He got angry and said, 'That's not funny!' A few moments later, everyone knew it was true. The reaction on the set of the *Seaview* was the same as it was around the country."

City Beneath the Sea

Crane and a woman diver find a dangerous undersea world ruled by a scientist. Wr: Richard Landau. Dir: John Brahm.

Melina Galnerez (Linda Cristal); Leopold Zeraff (Hurd Hatfield); Dimitri Gournaris (Al Ruscio); Round Face (John Alderson); Zanthos (Peter Brocco); Nicholas (Peter Mamakos); Crewman (Mark Slade); Atlas (Joey Walsh); Operator (Dennis Cross); Clerk (Athan Karras); Georgio (Paul Kremin).

The Fear Makers

Something made 125 men on the submarine *Polidor* die of sheer terror. Wr: Anthony Wilson. Dir: Leonard Horn.

Arthur Kenner (Edgar Bergen); Martin Davis (Lloyd Bochner); Capt. Anders (William Sargent); Agent (Martin Kosleck); Dan Case (Walter Brooke); Philip James (Ed Prentiss); Murdock (Robert Payne); O'Brien (Derrick Lewis); Pryor (Robert Doyle); Scientist (Paul Kremin); Connors (Chuck Courtney); Crew (George Spicer, Pat Colby, Robert Beech).

The Mist of Silence

Nelson races against time to save Capt. Crane and his men, who are being executed one by one by a South American dictator. Wr: John McGreevey. Dir: Leonard Horn.

Detta Casone (Rita Gam); Ricardo Galdez (Alejandro Rey); Estabon Dalvarez (Mike Kellin); Farrell (Joey Tata); Chairman (Booth Colman); Capt. Serra (Henry Darrow); Alejandro Fuentes (Edward Colmans); Williams (Doug Lambert); Soldier (Armand Alzamora); Oriental (Weaver Levy).

The Price of Doom

The last screams of a young newlywed couple, who were eaten alive by plankton, hold the answer to saving the *Seaview*. Giant plankton specimens are slurping through the corridors, devouring anyone in their way. Wr: Cordwainer Bird (Harlan Ellison). Dir: James Goldstone.

Dr. Julie Lyle (Jill Ireland); Karl Riesner (David Opatoshu); Philip Wesley (John Milford); Robert B. Pennell (Steve Ihnat); Karen Joyce Pennell (Pat Priest); General (Dan Seymour); Commander (Ivan Triesault); Smiling Jack (James Frawley); Helmsman (Jim Goodwin); Fox (Fred Stromsoe); Doc (Garth Benton); Man (Paul Kremin).

Memory Flash—Pat Priest: "I had never been eaten by plankton before," says the actress best known as Marilyn on *The Munsters*. "When they told me what the story was about, I thought, 'Come on! How can I be eaten by plankton? It's practically microscopic. It would take great special effects to pull it off.' But I liked how they did it. The problem was to act fearful when you see a guy crouched under the plankton, supporting it as it comes after you. We had a lot of rehearsals because it had to be timed perfectly. Jim Goldstone was a wonderful director. I had never done science fiction before. *Voyage* was really one of the forerunners of the genre."

The Sky Is Falling

Seaview encounters a submerged flying saucer inhabited by friendly aliens who need to escape from Earth before Navy planes destroy them. Wr: Don Brinkley. Dir: Leonard Horn.

Walter Tobin (Charles McGraw); Chief (Adam Williams); General (Frank Ferguson); Technician (Joe Di Reda); Murdock (Robert Payne); Courtney (Chuck Courtney); Pilot (Don Wilbanks); Crewman (George Spicer).

Turn Back the Clock

Jason Kemp makes a spectacular escape from a giant lizard on a prehistoric world in Antarctica. He goes to elaborate lengths to prevent *Seaview* from exposing his life of infamy on the island. Wr: Sheldon Stark. Dir: Alan Crosland, Jr.

Jason Kemp (Nick Adams); Carol Denning (Yvonne Craig); Dr. Denning (Les Tremayne); Ernst Ziegler (Robert Cornthwaite); Crewman (Mark Slade); Native girl (Vitina Marcus); Navy doctor (Robert Patten); O'Brien (Derrick Lewis); Native (John Lamb); William (Paul Kremin).

Memory Flash—Sheldon Stark: "Nick Adams' performance was quite good, and it was an exciting show. But it was a very simple story. Irwin Allen was jumping up and down over this old earthquake footage he had. He asked me to write a story around it. For a writer to come in cold like that and find fuzzy earthquake footage waiting there was a help."

The Village of Guilt

The deaths of two fishermen eaten alive by a giant squid and the discovery of huge catfish lead the *Seaview* to Norway, where experiments have created an undersea monster. Wr: Berne Giler. Dir: Irwin Allen.

Lars Mattson (Richard Carlson); Sigrid Dalgren-Mattson (Anna Lisa); Oscar Dalgren (Steven Geray); Otto Hassler (Frank Richards); Dr. Anderson (G. Stanley Jones); Gertera (Erik Holland); Bartender (Torben Meyer); Homer (Kort Falkenburg); Crewman (Mark Slade); O'Brien (Gordon Gilbert); Boy (Gregor Vigen); Newscaster (Irwin Allen); Rolvaag (Clyde Cameron); Assassin (Al George); Reporters (Brendan Dillon, Peter Bourne).

Hot Line

A nuclear satellite from Russia crashes near the California coast, forcing the two superpowers to work together to disarm it. However, one scientist aboard *Seaview* is an imposter. Wr: Berne Giler. Dir: John Brahm.

Gregory Malinoff (Michael Ansara); Gronski (Everett Sloane); Chairman (John Banner); Clark (Paul Carr); President (Ford Rainey); Larry Tobin (James Doohan); George (Robert Carson); Official (Arthur Peterson); Man (Al George); Russians (Maurice Manson, Gene Benton).

Submarine Sunk Here

Derelict mine fields send the *Seaview* to the bottom, where the men fight against flooding compartments. Wr: William Tunberg. Dir: Leonard Horn.

Blake (Robert Doyle); Harker (Eddie Ryder); Collins (George Lindsay); Bishop (Paul Comi); Doctor (Wright King); Evans (Carl Reindel); O'Brien (Derrik Lewis); Officer (Wes Liston); O'Mare (Frank Graham); Crew (Hal Needham, Mark Russell, Peter Dixon).

Memory Flash—George Lindsay: "It was one of the best shows they ever did," says the actor best known as Goober from *The Andy Griffith Show*. "I was cold and wet all of the time, but it was a fun show. Richard Basehart was a real pro." The actor still hungers for dramatic shows. "I've been 'Goobered' to death."

The Magnus Beam

Crane joins a group of freedom fighters who are battling a sadistic general; meanwhile, a giant magnet threatens to crush the *Seaview*'s hull. Wr: Alan Caillou. Dir: Leonard Horn.

General Gamal (Malachi Throne); Major Amadi (Mario Alcalde); Luana (Monique LeMaire); Valider (Joseph Ruskin); Abdul Azziz (Jacques Aubuchon); Jerry (Jon Locke); Sulimani (Richard Hale); Arab (Dehl Berti).

No Way Out

Defector Anton Koslow refuses to cooperate with Nelson unless his girlfriend is rescued from a hostile country. Wr: Robert Hamner, story by Robert Hamner, Robert Leslie Bellum. Dir: Felix Feist.

Victor Vail (Jan Merlin); Anna Ravec (Danielle de Metz); Anton Koslow (Than Wyenn); Lascoe Dupoff (Oscar Beregi); Warren Parker (Richard Webb); Gen.

(Tyler McVey); Guard (Patrick Culliton); Wilson (Don Wilbanks); Asian (John Mamo); Man (Will White).

The Blizzard Makers

Freezing storms lead *Seaview* to an island where a weather machine is disrupting the Gulf Stream. Wr: William Welch, story by William Welch, Joe Madison. Dir: Joe Leytes.

Fred Cregar (Werner Klemperer); Charles Melton (Milton Selzer); Mrs. Melton (Sheila Matthews); Pilot (William Boyett); Doctor (Kenneth MacDonald); Lineman (Biff Elliot); Boy (Roger Bacon); Doc (Joey Tata).

The Ghost of Moby Dick

A grief-ridden father uses the *Seaview* to track down the giant whale that crippled him and killed his 12-year-old son. Wr: Robert Hamner. Dir: Sobey Martin.

Dr. Ellen Bryce (June Lockhart); Dr. Walter Bryce (Edward Binns); Jimmy Bryce (Bobby Beekman); Crewman's voice (Irwin Allen).

Trivia Alert: Producer Irwin Allen often supplied his voice as a crewman during the first season. In this episode, the producer's best line is, "If that whale hits us again, we've had it!"

Long Live the King

A young prince, the target of death threats, develops a friendship with Old John, a mysterious man rescued by *Seaview* near Christmas Island. Wr: Raphael Hayes. Dir: Laslo Benedek.

Old John (Carroll O'Connor); Col. Meger (Michael Pate); Countess des Roche (Sara Shane); Prince Ang (Michel Petit); Georges (Jan Arvan); Johnson (Peter Adams); Cookie (Tony Monaco); O'Brien (Derrick Lewis); Junior officer (Robert Payne); King (Sol Gorge).

Memory Flash—Michael Pate: "Laslo was a wonderful, sensitive director. He was terribly patient with the young boy. When Michel Petit began to behave as a nasty little boy on the set, most everyone was lining up to kick him!"

Hail to the Chief

The president must be operated on aboard the *Seaview*, but the chief surgeon has orders to kill him. Wr: Don Brinkley. Dir: Gerd Oswald.

Dr. Laura Rettig (Viveca Lindfors); Monique (Nancy Kovack); Steno girl (Susan Flannery); George Beeker (John Hoyt); Morgan (Edward C. Platt); Clark (Paul Carr); Larry Tobin (James Doohan); Dr. Jameson (Malcolm Atterbury); Chairman (Berry Kroeger); Dr. Kranze (David Lewis); Dr. Taylor (Tom Palmer); Joe Oberhansley (Lorence Kerr); Secretary of state (James Seay); Crewman's voice (Irwin Allen); Secretary (Viola Harris); Man (Paul Sorenson).

The Last Battle

Nelson tries to rally four POWs into revolting against modern-day Nazis, who have lured *Seaview* into submarine nets. Wr: Robert Hamner. Dir: Felix Feist.

Alfried Shroder (John Van Dreelan); Alejandro Tomas Brandy (Rudy Solari); Anton Miklos (Joe de Santis); Ben Brewster (Ben Wright); Gustav Reinhardt (Dayton Lummis);

Deiner (Eric Feldary); Stewardess (Sandra Williams); Lady (Miriam Schiller); Man (Charles Horvath).

Mutiny
Nelson is on the edge of a nervous breakdown after he sees a giant jellyfish eat an American submarine. Wr: William Read Woodfield. Dir: Sobey Martin.

Ad. Jiggs Starke (Harold J. Stone); Jim Jefferson (Jay Lanin); Fowler (Steve Harris); Jackson (Lew Brown).

Doomsday
A young officer on *Seaview* jeopardizes his career by hatching a daring plan to scare the world into nuclear disarmament. Wr: William Read Woodfield. Dir: James Goldstone.

Lt. William Corbett (Don Harron); Casey Clark (Paul Carr); President (Ford Rainey); Gen. Ashton (Paul Genge); Corporal (Sy Prescott); Radarman (Patrick Culliton).

Memory Flash—William Read Woodfield: "It turned out to be a fine show. Richard Basehart and David Hedison both wanted to meet me after they read the script. They said, 'This is the best script we've ever had. Please stay and write more.'"

The Invaders
The crew awakens a strange creature from a glass coffin, where he has been in suspended animation for over 20 million years. Wr: William Read Woodfield. Dir: Sobey Martin.

Zar (Robert Duvall); Foster (Michael McDonald); Sailors (Richard Geary, Bill Kinney).

The Indestructible Man
The crew is pitted against a super-robot. Wr: Richard Landau. Dir: Felix Feist.

Ralph Brand (Michael Constantine); Robot (Scott McFadden, William O'Douglas, Jr.).

The Buccaneer
An army garrison takes over the *Seaview*. Under the leadership of Mr. Logan, they steal the Mona Lisa from a French warship. Wr: William Welch, Al Gail. Dir: Laslo Benedek.

Logan (Barry Atwater); Captain (Emile Genest); Igor (George Keymas); Guard (Gene Dynarski); Guard #2 (Dick Dial); Crewman (Ray Didsbury); Men (Dennis Cross, George Sawaya, John Cliff, Peter Dixon, Paul Kessler).

The Human Computer
Crane is stalked by an enemy agent who has orders to kill him. Wr: Robert Hamner. Dir: James Goldstone.

Ralph Reston (Simon Scott); Agent (Harry Millard); Admiral #2 (Walter Sande); Foreign general (Ted de Corsia); Admiral #1 (Herb Lytton).

The Saboteur
Nelson is unaware that Crane has been brainwashed to kill him. Wr: George Reed (William Read Woodfield). Dir: Felix Feist.

Mason Forrester (Warren Stevens); Ernst Ullman (Bert Freed); Fred Parker (Russell Horton); O'Brien (Derrik Lewis); Spencer (James Brolin); Conditioner (Werner Klemperer); Crewman's voice (Irwin Allen); Lt. (John Ward); Guards (John Durran, Vince Carroll).

Cradle of the Deep
A scientist's experiment in evolution aboard *Seaview* creates a huge blob that keeps growing and growing. Wr: Robert Hamner. Dir: Sobey Martin.

Wesley Janus (John Anderson); Bill Clark (Paul Carr); Andrew Benton (Howard Wendell); Helsman (Robert Payne); O'Brien (Derrick Lewis).

Memory Flash—Robert Hamner: "The episode drove the network crazy. They wouldn't approve it. They said its theme was anti–Christian. I said, 'This is science fact. It's Charles Darwin!' It became a very big problem. I finally wore them down and it went on."

The Amphibians
The *Seaview* is disabled by two scientists who are turning divers into humanoid amphibians. Wr: Rik Vollaerts. Dir: Felix Feist.

Jenkins (Skip Homeier); Winslow (Curt Conway); Angie Maxxon (Zale Parry); Danny (Frank Graham); Divers (Paul Stader, George Robotham).

Memory Flash—George Robotham: "Paul Stader and I were in the water tank at Fox. We were playing *Seaview* divers snared by this net. We got totally entangled in the thing. We sank to the bottom, stuck. Our air was running low, and Paul and I exchanged looks of, 'Well, where do we go from here?' The special effects guy, Glen Galvin, finally hauled us up to the surface. It was a little on the life-threatening side!"

The Exile
Nelson and a dictator find themselves stranded on a life raft. Wr: William Read Woodfield. Dir: James Goldstone.

Aleksei Brynov (Edward Asner); Josip (David Sheiner); Semenev (James Frawley); Konstantine (Harry Davis); Mikhil Brynov (Jason Wingreen); Garrett (Michael Pataki); Survivor (Paul Kremin); Also with Ron Burke, Denver Mattson, Bob May, Bud Garrett.

The Creature
A young engineer watches a monster fish kill his crew. Unless he can convince the authorities the creature exists, he faces a court martial. Wr: Rik Vollaerts. Dir: Sobey Martin.

Wayne Adams (Leslie Nielsen); Radioman (Robert Lipton); Radarman (William Stevens); Helmsman (Patrick Culliton); Cutter (Jim Wetherill).

The Enemies
The loss of an American submarine was caused when two of its officers got into a savage fight. *Seaview* finds an island where hate experiments are being conducted. Wr: William Read Woodfield. Dir: Felix Feist.

General Tau (Henry Silva); Dr. Shinera (Malachi Throne); Jim Williams (Robert Sampson); Frank Richardson (Tom Skerritt); Helmsman (Robert Lipton); Crewman (Patrick Culliton); O'Brien (Derrick Lewis).

Secret of the Loch

A giant serpent kills three top scientists at Scotland's Loch Ness, putting the *Seaview* on the trail of the legendary monster. Wr: Charles Bennett. Dir: Sobey Martin.

Alistair McDougall (Torin Thatcher); Lester (Hedley Mattingly); Andrews (John McLiam); Angus (George Mitchell); Macroft (Joe Higgens); Crofter (Tudor Owen).

The Condemned

A presidential order turns *Seaview* over to a scientist who is trying to break the crush depth, but his experiments are disturbing a giant sea creature. Wr: William Read Woodfield. Dir: Leonard Horn.

Bentley Falk, Jr. (J.D. Cannon); Archer (Arthur Franz); Hoff (Alvy Moore); Tracy (John Goddard).

The Traitor

Crane is devastated when he learns that Nelson is giving away secret missile locations to save his kidnapped sister. Wr: William Welch, Al Gail. Dir: Sobey Martin.

Gen. Fenton (George Sanders); Hamid (Michael Pate); Edith Louise Nelson (Susan Flannery); Waiter (Paul Kremin).

Memory Flash—Australian actor Michael Pate: "George Sanders was a charming, easy man to work with. He was one of the greatest actors of all time. I remember him murmuring through this role. It's a pity that he had to act in such shit as this episode in the twilight of his career."

Season 2: 1965-66

Jonah and the Whale

Crane and his divers crawl into the stomach of a prehistoric whale to recover Nelson and a Russian scientist. Wr: Shimon Wincelberg. Dir: Sobey Martin.

Dr. Katya Markhova (Gia Scala); Winchman (Patrick Culliton); Sonar (Nigel McKeand); Helmsman (Robert Payne); Aleksei's voice (Paul Kremin).

Trivia Alert: This episode introduced two new regulars to *Voyage*: Terry Becker (as Chief Sharkey) and Allan Hunt (as Riley). Actor James Doohan was originally offered the Sharkey role, but he turned it down in favor of playing Scotty on *Star Trek*. Walter Koenig, Chekov on *Star Trek*, was one of the actors tested for the Riley role.

Time Bomb

Nelson's mission to inspect Russian reactors is imperiled when he's unknowingly injected with a chemical that turns him into a time bomb. Wr: William Read Woodfield, Allan Balter. Dir: Sobey Martin.

Litchka (Ina Balin); Katie (Susan Flannery); Ad. William T. Johnson (John Zaremba); Li Tung (Richard Loo); Dr (Dr. Harold Dyrenforth); Dwarf (Frank Delfino); Soldier (Lee Millar); Tal (Richard Gilden); Policeman (Jon Kowal).

And Five of Us Are Left

The prospect of rescue for five men trapped under a volcano for 28 years threatens to open up old wounds from World War II. Wr: Robert Vincent Wright. Dir: Harry Harris.

James Ryan (Phillip E. Pine); Tony Wilson (James Anderson); Esaka Nakamura (Teru Shimada); Frank Werden (Robert Doyle); Burgar Johnson (Kent Taylor); Brenda (Françoise Ruggieri); Hill (Ed McCready); Newsman (Fred Crane).

Memory Flash—Phillip E. Pine: "I liked my character's quiet strength. He also had an acceptance of Teru Shimada's character: a natural, unprejudiced treatment of his prisoner. It was a well-written show." Pine recalls a snafu during production. "In the opening scenes, Teru was having difficulty with pronouncing English words. After two fluffs, producer Irwin Allen came down and berated Teru and Harry Harris. He insulted both men and made everyone very nervous. Irwin screamed to Harris, 'If he messes up one more time, cut him out of the scene!' I had enough. I told him he had hired Teru in the first place. Now he was blaming him for having a Japanese accent! I told him I wouldn't continue working unless he left the set. He left, and Teru and Harris both thanked me. I didn't work for Irwin Allen again."

The Cyborg

Nelson befriends a beautiful android who may be the key to stopping Dr. Ullrich's plan to turn the world over to cyborgs. Wr: William Read Woodfield, Allan Balter. Dir: Leo Penn.

Tabor Ullrich (Victor Buono); Gundi (Brooke Bundy); Patricia Sweetley (Nancy Hsueh); Reporter (Nicholas Colasanto); Cyborg (Fred Crane); Technician (Tom Curtis); Crewman (Stanley Schneider).

Escape from Venice

Crane is pursued by enemy agents and the police in Venice after he's framed for murder. Wr: Charles Bennett. Dir: Alex March.

Bellini (Vincent Gardenia); Count Ferdie Staglione (Renzo Cesana); Julietta (Delphi Lawrence); Lola Hale (Danica D'Hondt); Betty Harmon (Margot Stevenson); Alicia (Rachel Romen); Antonio (Tommy Nello); Croupier (Freddie Roberto); Gondolier (Ken Tilles); Musician (John Paul Gerardi); Newsman (Fred Crane).

The Left Handed Man

Nelson and Tippy Penfield are targeted by an assassin when they try to stop Tippy's father, a beloved politician, from becoming secretary of defense. Wr: William Welch. Dir: Jerry Hopper.

Tippy Penfield (Barbara Bouchet); George W. Penfield (Regis Toomey); Noah Graften (Cyril Delevanti); Angie (Judy Lang); Left handed man (Charles Dierkop); Joe Cabrillo (Michael Barrier); Fred Lasher (Fred Crane); Pilot's voice (Ray Didsbury); Newsman's voice (Arch Whiting); Men (Roy Sickner, Paul Stader).

The Deadliest Game

As Crane and the president struggle to survive in a

flooding undersea base, Nelson tries to stop a general's plan to start World War III. Wr: Rik Vollaerts. Dir: Sobey Martin.

Gen. Mark Hobson (Lloyd Bochner); Lydia Parish (Audrey Dalton); President (Robert F. Simon); Reed Michaels (Robert Cornthwaite); Sailor (Ron Stein).

Leviathan
The death of a diver, who was eaten alive by a giant fish, is the first clue that an undersea fissure has turned sea life and Dr. Anthony Sterling into giants. Wr: William Welch. Dir: Harry Harris.

Cara Sloane (Karen Steele); Anthony Sterling (Liam Sullivan); Diver (Mike Donovon).

Memory Flash—Liam Sullivan: "I played a scientist who grows into a giant and attacks the *Seaview*. The tank was 12 feet deep, and Harry Harris directed from behind a glass window. After the third take, I was supposed to jump up and catch one of the wires stretched over the tank. I missed the wire and fell back into the tank, totally out of breath. Two divers plunged into the tank and pulled me to the surface. It was a close call. I nearly drowned! Three weeks later, Irwin Allen looked at the footage and decided my makeup wasn't scary enough. So we did the whole damn thing over! Yech!"

The Peacemaker
Everett Lang develops a super-bomb and tries to blackmail the world's leaders into nuclear disarmament. Wr: William Read Woodfield, Allan Balter. Dir: Sobey Martin.

Everett Lang (John Cassavetes); Su Yin (Irene Tsu); Bill Conners (Whit Bissell); Policeman (Lloyd Kino); Hansen (Walter Wolff King); Premier (Dale Ishimoto); Scientist (George Zaima); Captain (Lee Kolima); Lang's friend (George Young); Cop (Owen Song).

The Silent Saboteurs
Crane flies to Asia to knock out a weapon that destroyed a manned spaceflight from Venus. Wr: Sidney Marshall, story by Max Ehrlich. Dir: Sobey Martin.

Moana Yutang (Pilar Seurat); Li Cheng (George Takei); Halden (Bert Freed); Lago (Alex D'Arcy); Stevens (Phil Posner); Astronaut (Robert Chadwick); Astronaut #2 (Ted Jordan); Technician (Phil Barry).

The X Factor
Nelson struggles to escape from an enemy scientist who has been sending kidnapped scientists out of the country in a state of suspended animation. Wr: William Welch. Dir: Leonard Horn.

Alexander Corby (John McGiver); Henderson (Jan Merlin); George Shire (William Hudson); Randall Liscomb (George Tyne); Technician (Anthony Brand).

The Machines Strike Back
Nelson discovers his friend, a rogue admiral, is using unmanned submarines to carry out attacks on America. Wr: John and Ward Hawkins. Dir: Nathan Juran.

Adm. Alex Halder (Roger C. Carmel); Capt. Verna Trober (Françoise Ruggieri); Kimberly (Bert Remsen); William T. Johnson (John Gallaudet); Murphy (Al Shelley); Jones' voice (Ray Didsbury).

The Monster from Outer Space
A creature found clinging to a space capsule takes over the minds of the *Seaview*'s crew one by one. Wr: William Read Woodfield, Allan Balter. Dir: James B. Clark.

Commander (Hal Torey); Flight control (Preston Hansen); Technician (Lee R. Delano); Doctor (Wayne Heffley); Sonarman (Ray Didsbury); Divers (Bill Hickman, Jim Van Niekerk).

Memory Flash—cast member Allan Hunt: "The story was about this big walking blob. This was done in the days before satire. We were encouraged to play it as real as possible. If the story was ridiculous—and it was—it was up to us to make it work. To play it absolutely straight was the key."

Terror on Dinosaur Island
A search for Nelson on a prehistoric island is hampered by dinosaurs and a crewman who plans to kill Crane. Wr: William Welch. Dir: Leonard Horn.

Benson (Paul Carr); Crewman (Ron Stein); Grady (Frank Graham).

Killers of the Deep
Crane is held hostage on an enemy sub while Nelson pursues the sub with a crippled Navy destroyer. Wr: William Read Woodfield, Allan Balter. Dir: Harry Harris.

Tomas Royez (Michael Ansara); Lt. Frazer (Patrick Wayne); Manola (James Frawley); Richard Lawrence (John Newton); Enemy sonar (Gus Trikonis); Bosun's mate (Bruce Mars); U.S. sonar (Dallas Mitchell); Crewman (Robert Yuro); Men (Rick Warwick, Paul Stader).

Deadly Creature Below
Two gun-toting convicts take over the *Seaview*, but they accidentally plunge the submarine into the arms of a giant seaweed creature. Wr: William Read Woodfield, Allan Balter. Dir: Sobey Martin.

Francis J. Dobbs (Nehemiah Persoff); Joe Hawkins (Paul Comi); Doctor (Wayne Heffley); Monster (Sig Winguard); Crewman (Hubie Kerns).

Memory Flash—Paul Comi: "Nehemiah Persoff and I spent most of our time laughing at the absurdities of the script and the lines we had to say. Sobey Martin couldn't figure out what we were laughing at. It was very tough to be serious on that show."

The Phantom Strikes
A long-dead World War I U-boat captain is relentless in his efforts to take over Crane's body. Wr: William Welch. Dir: Sutton Roley.

Captain Gerhardt Krueger (Alfred Ryder); Junior Officer (Ron Stein).

Memory Flash—Sutton Roley: "The point was to scare people, and it did. It worked very well. Irwin Allen loved it, and they asked me to do a sequel. It wasn't as good, but it was okay."

The Sky's on Fire

A raging fire in the Van Allen belt threatens to destroy the Earth. Nelson's plans to put out the blaze are threatened by a fanatical U.N. official. Wr: William Welch, story by Irwin Allen, Charles Bennett. Dir: Sobey Martin.

Eric Carleton (Robert H. Harris); August Weber (David J. Stewart); McHenry (Frank Marth); Sparks (Anthony Brand).

Graveyard of Fear

A giant jellyfish sinks a research ship. Dr. Crandall Ames needs to recover immortal serum from the wreck before his girlfriend ages to death. Wr: Robert Vincent Wright. Dir: Justus Addiss.

Crandall Ames (Robert Loggia); Karyll Simmons (Marian Moses); Helmsman's voice (Jim Goodwin).

The Shape of Doom

Seaview pursues a giant whale that has swallowed a nuclear bomb. Wr: William Welch. Dir: Nathan Juran.

Alex Holden (Kevin Hagen); Sonar (Nigel McKeand); Ray (Ron Stein); First mate (Dave Dunlap).

Dead Men's Doubloons

Two divers die mysteriously in an undersea graveyard. This leads *Seaview* to modern-day pirates who are terrorizing the seven seas. Wr: Sidney Marshall. Dir: Sutton Roley.

Alfred Brent (Albert Salmi); Howard (Robert Brubaker); Sebastion (Allen Jaffe); Pirate (Bob Swimmer); Sailor (Stan Kamber); Ray (Ray Didsbury); Henderson (Garrett Myles); Travis (Robert Johnson).

The Death Ship

Nelson, Crane and eight scientists aboard *Seaview* are stalked by a killer who has orders to take over the sub. Wr: George Reed, Michael Lynn (William Read Woodfield, Allan Balter). Dir: Abner Biberman.

Tracy Stewart (Elizabeth Perry); Ava Winters (June Vincent); Arthur Chandler (David Sheiner); Judson Stroller (Lew Gallo); Glenn Carter (Herb Voland); Frank Templeton (Harry Davis); Eric Klaus (Ivan Triesault); Roarke (Ed Connelly); Chairman (Ross Elliot); Assistant (Al Shelly).

The Monster's Web

Mike Gantt claims his submarine was attacked by a giant spider. His claim is substantiated when *Seaview* comes across a giant spider web. Wr: Peter Packer, Al Gail, story by Peter Packer. Dir: Justus Addiss.

Mike Gantt (Peter Mark Richman); Bill Balter (Barry Coe); Sonarman (Sean Morgan); Doctor (Wayne Heffley); Ray (Ron Stein); Crew (Howard Curtis, Vince Deadrick).

Memory Flash—Sean Morgan: "I was cast at 6:30 in the morning. Casting director Joe D'Agosta called me in a panic. They had forgotten to cast the role of the sonarman. Would I do it? They paid me $500. I later told Joe I would have done it for scale, which was $180. When the giant spider grabs the sub, the control panels blew up. Some sparks landed on my ankle and burned a hole through my socks. I said, 'Geez, I'm glad I'm not doing this show every week!'"

The Menfish

A scientist creates an army of lizard-fish monsters. One creature grows into a giant and attacks the *Seaview*. Wr: William Read Woodfield, Allan Balter. Dir: Tom Gries.

Ad. Roy Park (Gary Merrill); Dr. Sten Borgman (John Dehner); Hansjurg (Vic Lundin); Johnson (Roy Jenson); Diver (Lawrence Mann); Doctor (Wayne Heffley); Bailey (George T. Sims); Manfish (Frank Graham); Forrester (Ron Stein); Collins (Ray Didsbury); Crewman (Lou Elias).

Memory Flash—Vic Lundin: "John Dehner's character was an evil scientist who was like the father of my character, Hansjurg. At the end, I strangle him. I wanted to show Hansjurg's emotion at having to kill him. There was a ten-second close-up of me with tears in my eyes. When Irwin Allen saw the rushes, he screamed to Tom Gries, 'What the hell do you think we're doing? Playhouse 90?!' It was too intense for him, and they cut it down to two seconds. Irwin wasn't a director who was sensitive to actors. He went for special effects."

Trivia Alert: Gary Merrill was almost signed to replace Richard Basehart as the admiral for the remainder of the series. Stricken with a bleeding ulcer, Basehart was unable to appear in several second-season segments. He recovered in time for the third season.

The Mechanical Man

An android refuses to stop drilling for a new power source beneath the Earth even though his undersea mining operation is tearing the planet apart. Wr: John and Ward Hawkins. Dir: Sobey Martin.

Peter Omir (James Darren); Paul Ward (Arthur O'Connell); Jenson (Seymour Cassell); Van Drutan (Cecil Linder); Ralph Vendon (Robert Riordon); Repairman (Scott McFadden); Newsman (Bart La Rue).

Return of the Phantom

Nelson teams up with the ghost of a Hawaiian girl to stop the spirit of Capt. Krueger, who has possessed Captain Crane's body. Wr: William Welch. Dir: Sutton Roley.

Gerhardt Krueger (Alfred Ryder); Lani (Vitina Marcus); Ray (Ron Stein).

Memory Flash—Sutton Roley: "The series was a comic strip. I mean that literally. The stories were way out, and reality was flown to the wind. Irwin was mainly enamoured with the submarine and its Christmas lights. He tended to treat the actors like buffoons. I didn't like that attitude."

Season 3: 1966-67

Monster from the Inferno
A glowing blue brain is brought aboard the submarine, where it becomes a terrifying menace. Wr: Rik Vollaerts. Dir: Harry Harris.
> Lindsay (Arthur Hill); Brain's voice (Dick Tufeld); Crewman (Buddy Van Horn).

Werewolf
Efforts to destroy an erupting volcano are threatened by a young scientist: He's been turned into a murderous werewolf by a radioactive virus. Wr: Donn Mullally. Dir: Justus Addiss.
> Dr. Hollis (Charles Aidman); Witt (Douglas Bank); Corpsman (Jim Arnett); Pilot (Ralph Garrett).

Memory Flash—George Robotham: "The guy who doubled for Charles Aidman's wolfman character turned out to be a real looney. He was a half-assed stuntman who wanted to be an actor. This guy really believed he was a wolf. He got caught up in the tragedy of this poor guy trapped with a wolf's head. He was obsessed with establishing the wolfman's motivation.

"I doubled for David Hedison in one scene, and I was up on a ledge with the werewolf guy. There's an earthquake, and we're both supposed to fall off the cliff. This guy was so busy acting like a wolf, he wouldn't fall off the ledge. I pretended to stumble and I shoved him off. Unfortunately, he landed on my landing pads. I had nowhere to fall. Luckily, I missed the rocks and landed safely."

The Day the World Ended
Nelson uses the flying sub to search for human life, which has vanished from the face of the Earth. Wr: William Welch. Dir: Jerry Hopper.
> Sen. William Dennis (Skip Homeier); Sonarman (Ron Stein).

Night of Terror
A tidal wave throws Nelson, Sharkey and a geologist onto a prehistoric island inhabited by a giant lizard. Wr: Robert Bloomfield. Dir: Justus Addiss.
> Dr. Elton Sprague (Henry Jones); Pirate (Jerry Catron).

The Terrible Toys
The crew battles six indestructible toys which are intent on destroying the Seaview. Wr: Robert Vincent Wright. Dir: Justus Addiss.
> Sam Burke (Paul Fix); Old man (Francis X. Bushman); Alien voice (Jim Mills); Ray (Ray Didsbury).

Memory Flash—Robert Vincent Wright: "Francis X. Bushman was a famous silent screen idol in the 1920s. This turned out to be his last role. He died three weeks later. He hadn't worked in years. I was glad that he got even this minor part."

Day of Evil
Nelson makes a Faust-like deal with an alien who agrees to save Crane's life, but secretly plans Earth's destruction. Wr: William Welch. Dir: Jerry Hopper.
> None.

Deadly Waters
Trapped on the sea floor, the Seaview's only chance of rescue is an experimental diving suit, but Kowalski's brother Stan is too scared to use it. Wr: Robert Vincent Wright. Dir: Gerald Mayer.
> Stan Kowalski (Don Gordon); Kruger (Lew Gallo); Commander Finch (Harry Lauter).

The Thing from Inner Space
A TV host accidentally incites a sea monster to attack and kill his camera crew. To cover his guilt, he lays the blame on Patterson's father. Wr: William Welch. Dir: Alex March.
> Bainbridge Wells (Hugh Marlowe); Monster (Dawson Palmer).

The Death Watch
Nelson and Crane are racing around the empty sub trying to kill each other. Wr: William Welch. Dir: Leonard Horn.
> Computer voice (Sue England).

Memory Flash—Writer William Read Woodfield: "William Welch told me he had finally written a *Voyage* episode that had absolutely no content in it whatsoever. It was about *nothing*. He seemed very proud of himself."

Deadly Invasion
Nelson and Sharkey are held captive by alien creatures who are using an undersea base to power their destructive spaceships. Wr: John and Ward Hawkins. Dir: Nathan Juran.
> Sam Garrity (Warren Stevens); Gen. Haines (Michael Fox); Peters (Brent Davis); Kelly (Ashley Gilbert).

The Haunted Submarine
A fun-loving poltergeist turns out to be Nelson's long-dead ancestor, who will destroy Seaview unless Nelson accepts his gift of immortality. Richard Basehart plays Capt. Shaemus O'Hara. Wr: William Welch. Dir: Harry Harris.
> None.

Memory Flash—Robert Vincent Wright: "William Welch was very interested in the occult. He told me that if a high-quality tape recorder is left running in an empty room, it will record spirits of the dead. He seriously believed it. I listened to the tapes, and there were bits and pieces of spoken words on them!"

The Plant Man
Telepathic twins battle each other for control of giant plant creatures on the sea floor. Wr: Donn Mullally. Dir: Harry Harris.
> Ben/John Wilson (William Smithers).

The Lost Bomb
An old friend of Sharkey's is sabotaging Seaview's

underwater laser battle with an enemy submarine. Wr: Oliver Crawford. Dir: Gerald Mayer.

Dr. Bradley (John Lupton); Athos Vadim (Gerald Mohr); Zane (George Keymas); Vulcan crew (Gene Le Bell, Richard Geary, Orwin Harvey, Paul Stader).

Memory Flash—Gerald Mayer: "Richard Basehart was a marvelous actor. He was absolutely wasted in the series. One couldn't feel sorry for him because he was making a barrel of money. He was obviously unhappy with the show because he could deliver the character of the admiral in his sleep."

Brand of the Beast
Looking for a werewolf? Try Nelson—an overdose of radiation has turned him into one! Wr: William Welch. Dir: Justus Addiss.

None.

The Creature
While walking toward California, a giant seaweed monster is taking over the minds of *Seaview*'s crew one by one. Wr: John and Ward Hawkins. Dir: Justus Addiss.

Dr. Horace King (Lyle Bettger).

Death from the Past
Two Nazis, awakened from suspended animation after 40 years, plan to use *Seaview* to carry out their schemes. Wr: Sidney Marshall, Charles Bennett, story by Sidney Marshall. Dir: Justus Addiss.

Gustav Von Neuberg (John Van Dreelan); Erich Froelich (Jan Merlin).

The Heat Monster
An invisible scientist and a living flame from outer space threaten the *Seaview*. Wr: Charles Bennett. Dir: Gerald Mayer.

Olaf Bergstrom (Alfred Ryder); Sven Larsen (Don Knight); Creature's voice (Jim Mills); Anderson (Ray Didsbury).

The Fossil Men
Lumbering rock men invade the *Seaview*. Their plan: turn the crew into living fossil men. Wr: James N. Whiton. Dir: Justus Addiss.

Capt. Jacob Wren (Brendon Dillon); Richards (Jerry Catron); Rock men (Gary Epper, Dave Dunlap).

The Mermaid
Crane enlists the aid of a friendly mermaid to locate a super-bomb hidden off California's coast. Wr: William Welch. Dir: Jerry Hopper.

Mermaid (Diane Webber); Crewman (Roy Jenson); Thompson (Ron Stein); Monster (Frank Graham); Crew (Tom Anthony, Bob O'Neal).

The Mummy
A 3,000-year-old mummy refuses to be shipped to a Middle Eastern nation and prowls the *Seaview*. Wr: William Welch. Dir: Harry Harris.

Mac (Patrick Culliton); Crewman (Ted Jordan); Mummy (Scott McFadden); Simpson (Phil Barry).

The Shadowman
A creepy black shadow from outer space delays a space probe launching by taking over the *Seaview* officers' minds one by one. Wr: Rik Vollaerts. Dir: Justus Addiss.

Gen. Blake (Tyler McVey); Shadowman (Jerry Catron); Shadowman's voice (Jim Mills).

No Escape from Death
Swallowed by a giant jellyfish, Crane and his men must survive in the creature's stomach until help can arrive. Wr: William Welch. Dir: Harry Harris.

Clark (Paul Carr); Crewman (Carl Reindel); Repairman (Ray Didsbury).

Doomsday Island
Seaview's discovery of a six-foot egg leads the crew to an island where amphibians are planning a world takeover. Wr: Peter Germano. Dir: Jerry Hopper.

Lars (Jock Gaynor); Ray (Ray Didsbury); Crewman (Ted Jordan); Creature (Darryl McFadden).

Memory Flash—Jock Gaynor: There was always a monster of the week on *Voyage*. Although they offered me the role of Lars, anybody could have done it. It was a paycheck. The costume I wore was rubber. It was made from scuba gear, and under the hot lights I lost about 12 pounds. The series in general was a children's show. High camp. It was not to be taken seriously."

The Wax Men
A crazed circus clown and his army of living wax dummies take over the *Seaview*. Wr: William Welch. Dir: Harmon Jones.

The clown (Michael Dunn).

The Deadly Cloud
An alien cloud is causing worldwide disasters. An alien version of Crane boards the sub with orders to kill Nelson and destroy the *Seaview*. Wr: Rik Vollaerts. Dir: Jerry Hopper.

Jurgenson (Robert C. Carson); Bill (Bill Baldwin); Cloud invader (Darryl McFadden).

Destroy *Seaview*!
Brainwashed by enemy agents, Nelson seals Crane in an underwater cave and returns to destroy the *Seaview*. Wr: Donn Mullally. Dir: Justus Addiss.

Dr. Land (Arthur Space); Enemy voice (Gregory Morton); Patrol leader (Jerry Catron); Thug (Dave Dunlap).

Season 4: 1967-68

Fires of Death
A 500-year-old immortal and a raging volcano pose problems for the *Seaview*. Wr: Arthur Weiss. Dir: Bruce Fowler.

Albert Turner (Victor Jory); Brent (Joey Tata); Adam (Chuck Couch); Corpsman (Brent Davis).

Memory Flash—Joey Tata: "The volcano set was magnificent. Before filming, Irwin Allen said to me,

'Joey, I know you're very animated, but don't touch the rocks. They're made of foam and they'll bend if you touch them.' When Chuck Couch, who plays the golden man, falls into the lava, you can see his hand hit a rock. The rock sinks in like rubber. Irwin screamed, 'Did you see that! He touched the rock!' I said, 'So? Look at all of the rubber rocks floating in the lava.' Irwin said, 'You're not supposed to see those!'"

The Deadly Dolls
Living puppets take over the *Seaview*. They pilot the submarine to a glowing creature on the sea floor that needs a new shell. Wr: Charles Bennett. Dir: Harry Harris.
   Prof. Multiple (Vincent Price); Puppeteer (Ronald P. Martin); Burns (Ted Jordan).

   Memory Flash—David Hedison: "I was always cutting up and being rather silly on the set between takes. Vincent Price said during one of my particularly manic phases, 'David, when we did *The Fly* together, you were always so terribly earnest. What happened?' I said, 'Dear Vincent, playing an insect was a very earnest experience!'"

Cave of the Dead
Living skeletons and ghostly ships haunt Nelson as he tries to escape from the curse of the Flying Dutchman. Wr: William Welch. Dir: Harry Harris.
   Peter Van Wyck (Warren Stevens); Pirate's voice (Bart La Rue).

Journey with Fear
Stranded on Venus, Crane and Morton encounter aliens who fear man's aggressiveness and want to block the U.S. space program. Wr: Arthur Weiss. Dir: Harry Harris.
   Centaur one (Gene Dynarski); Centaur two (James Gosa); Robert Wilson (Eric Matthews).

Sealed Orders
With his crew disappearing one by one, Nelson encounters horrifying illusions as he tries to disarm a superbomb. Wr: William Welch. Dir: Jerry Hopper.
   Jackson (Jack Anthony Basehart); Monster (Dawson Palmer).

   Trivia Alert: Jack Anthony Basehart is the son of *Voyage* star Richard Basehart.

Man of Many Faces
Seaview races to destroy a huge underwater magnet that is drawing the moon toward the earth. An intruder, capable of changing his appearance, threatens the mission. Wr: William Welch. Dir: Harry Harris.
   Randolph Mason (Jock Gaynor); Reporter (Howard Culver); Page (Bradd Arnold); Driver (Wally Rose).

   Memory Flash—Jock Gaynor: "I turned down the role of Chip Morton and recommended another

longtime friend, Bob Dowdell. Richard Basehart was a wonderful actor. He hated the show. He did it for the money. Producer Irwin Allen had a great imagination. He ate, drank and lived show business. He also screamed a lot."

Fatal Cargo
Nelson agrees to transport a giant white gorilla to Santa Barbara, unaware that a civilian controls the monster. Wr: William Welch. Dir: Jerry Hopper.
   Leo Brock (Woodrow Parfrey); Dr. Pierre Blanchard (Jon Lormer); Gorilla (Janos Prohaska).

Time Lock
Nelson is transported to the far future by a scientist who wants to add him to his collection of historical zombie figures. Wr: William Welch. Dir: Jerry Hopper.
   Alpha (John Crawford); Guard (Patrick Culliton); Androids (Gil Perkins, Roy Sickner); Zombies (Alex Rodine, Charles Horvath).

Rescue
A saboteur on *Seaview* hampers Nelson's efforts to fight off an enemy submarine and rescue Crane from the crippled flying sub. Wr: William Welch. Dir: Justus Addiss.
   Beach (Don Dubbins); Crewman (Marco Lopez).

Terror
Possessed by a pregnant flower, Nelson is turned into a super-human juggernaut. He uses the nuclear reactor to hatch the plant's seedlings. Wr: Sidney Ellis. Dir: Jerry Hopper.
   Thompson (Damian O'Flynn); Dunlap (Patrick Culliton); Storage guard (Jerry Catron); Reactor man #1 (Brent Davis); Reactor man #2 (Thomas Brann); Crewman (Charles Picerni); Brinks (Robert Johnson).

A Time to Die
Seaview is transported to 1 million B.C., where the crew encounter dinosaurs and a time traveler named Mr. Pem. Wr: William Welch. Dir: Robert Sparr.
   Mr. Pem (Henry Jones); Creature (Dawson Palmer).

Blow Up
Crane's loyalty to Nelson is tested when an accident turns the admiral into a tyrannical Captain Bligh. Wr: William Welch. Dir: Justus Addiss.
   None.

The Deadly Amphibians
Amphibians need the *Seaview*'s reactor to rule the seas. Wr: Arthur Weiss. Dir: Jerry Hopper.
   Proto (Don Matheson); Corpsman (Joey Tata); Guard (Patrick Culliton); Amphibian (Scott McFadden).

The Return of Blackbeard
The ghost of Blackbeard takes over *Seaview* and turns the crew into pirates. Wr: Al Gail. Dir: Justus Addiss.
   Edward Blackbeard (Malachi Throne); Guard (Ted Jordan).

The Terrible Leprechaun
Seaview becomes the battleground for two elves in the Irish sea. Wr: Charles Bennett. Dir: Jerry Hopper.

Mickey/Patrick O'Shaughnessy (Walter Burke); Sommers (Ralph Garrett); Crewman (John Bellah); Jenson (Seymour Cassel); Corpsman (Patrick Culliton).

The Lobster Man
A lobster man proclaims peace, but after he hits Patterson, sabotages the reactor room and destroys communications, Nelson suspects the crustacean has malevolent motives. Wr: Al Gail. Dir: Justus Addiss.

Lobster man (Vic Lundin).

Memory Flash—Vic Lundin: "Irwin Allen wanted Lobster Man to speak with an English accent. He thought it would provide him with character. But if you do it too much, it becomes comical. I did just enough to make him happy, and it turned out well. I understand 'Lobster Man' is something of a cult show. People still ask me about it."

Nightmare
Crane is pitted against an alien aboard the empty *Seaview*. If Crane fails to survive the alien's test of human resourcefulness, the Earth will be destroyed. Wr: Sidney Marshall. Dir: Charles Rondeau.

Jim Bentley (Paul Mantee).

The Abominable Snowman
A ferocious snowbeast is loose on the *Seaview*. A manhunt is organized to capture the creature. Wr: Robert Hamner. Dir: Robert Sparr.

Hawkins (Bruce Mars); Rayburn (Dusty Cadis); Corpsman (Frank Babich); Paulson's voice (Bart La Rue); Snowman (Darryl Scott McFadden).

Secret of the Deep
Enemy agents have created an armada of giant sea monsters which will destroy Atlantic shipping unless their demands are met. Wr: William Welch. Dir: Charles Rondeau.

John Hendrix (Peter Mark Richman).

Man Beast
Experiments in the diving bell unlock the primitive man in Crane, turning him into a Neanderthal monster. Wr: William Welch. Dir: Jerry Hopper.

Dr. Kermit Braddock (Lawrence Montaigne).

Memory Flash—David Hedison: "It was one of my favorite episodes. My stuntman and friend, George Robotham, usually did all of the dangerous stunt work. But I wouldn't let him do *anything* on 'Man Beast'! I wanted to do it all. Why? Because I'm an actor and I'm crazy! It was great to play a monster."

Memory Flash #2—Lawrence Montaigne: "My character was confined to a wheelchair and between takes, I would ride the wheelchair around. Then Richard Basehart grabbed it and he rode it around. Then some of the crew got a hold of it. Let's face it, we were like a bunch of kids."

Savage Jungle
An alien and his three toy soldiers turn the interior of *Seaview* into a prehistoric jungle. Wr: Arthur Weiss. Dir: Robert Sparr.

Keeler (Perry Lopez); Toy #1 (Patrick Culliton); Toy #2 (Nick Dimitri); Toy #3 (Scott McFadden).

Flaming Ice
Ice creatures at the North Pole encase *Seaview* in a block of ice. The aliens also cause worldwide floods in their efforts to recharge their flying saucer. Wr: Arthur Browne, Jr. Dir: Robert Sparr.

Gelid (Michael Pate); Frost man (Frank Babich); Frost man #2 (George Robotham).

Memory Flash—Michael Pate: "Gelid was a spectacular character to play. I gave a kind of Grand Guignol/Lon Chaney Sr. bravura performance. The makeup was only 75 percent successful. It could have been better with more production time. It was the standard 'near enough is good enough' for series TV. The sets and special effects were top class. Richard Basehart was one of the greatest actors I have ever met."

Attack!
Crane joins up with a peace-loving alien named Robek who morally opposes his people's plan to attack Earth. Wr: William Welch. Dir: Jerry Hopper.

Robek (Skip Homeier); Kemal (Kevin Hagen); Aliens (Troy Melton, Denver Mattson).

The Edge of Doom
Mistakenly thinking Crane is an imposter, the *Seaview*'s officers stage dangerous pranks to make him crack. Wr: William Welch. Dir: Justus Addiss.

General (Tyler Mcvey); Helmsman (Scott McFadden).

The Death Clock
Crewman Mallory discovers an island in the fourth dimension, and subjects Crane to a series of terrifying adventures. Wr: Sidney Marshall. Dir: Charles Rondeau.

Mallory (Chris Robinson).

No Way Back
Seaview is transported to the eighteenth century where Mr. Pem and Benedict Arnold plan to change the outcome of the Revolutionary War. Wr: William Welch. Dir: Robert Sparr.

Benedict Arnold (Barry Atwater); Mr. Pem (Henry Jones); John Andre (William Beckley).

Voyagers!

October 1982–July 1983

The voyagers are time-travelers who monitor history to make sure that it's on track. Each voyager carries a device called an Omni, and when it flashes red, it means history has been disrupted and must be corrected. It flashes green to tell the voyagers that their mission for that time period has been successful.

Phineas Bogg, an ambitious and impulsive voyager, is traveling to the past when he accidentally lands in New York, 1982. He's befriended by a 12-year-old orphan, Jeffrey. After Jeffrey's dog eats Bogg's guidebook to history, Bogg reluctantly agrees to take Jeffrey with him as his historical expert in order to correct twists in history.

Cast: Phineas Bogg (Jon-Erik Hexum); Jeffrey Jones (Meeno Peluce).

Created by: James D. Parriott; *Producer:* Jill Sherman; NBC/Universal; 60 minutes.

The premise of this show was to take history and toss it up into the air. When it comes back down in a jumble, the Voyagers have to put it back together like a jigsaw puzzle. What if Franklin Roosevelt had become a movie director instead of a politician? What if the Russians had landed on the moon before the Americans? What if the Mona Lisa had gone down with the *Titanic*? The fun of *Voyagers!* was in its speculation about what *could* have happened in history. Every week, the two voyagers fixed history and imparted some historical knowledge to their (mainly) youthful audience.

Voyagers! secured only a small audience, but it did succeed in conveying the romance of going back in time and meeting famous people. Creator James Parriott had wanted to do the show for years. "Jeff Sagansky [at NBC] and I got our heads together, and we came up with *Voyagers!* Jeff called the concept 'Time Cop.' It was always conceived as a 7 p.m. show that would deal with history and appeal to kids. We didn't set out to portray history with absolute accuracy. The idea was to get kids excited about a character or theme. We had a lot of teachers who wanted to know what episodes would be coming up. This way they could base their studies around them. Scholastic put out a Weekly Reader in schools, and *Voyagers!* soon became part of the magazine."

Cast as Bogg was the late Jon-Erik Hexum, an ex-model. "Originally, Bogg was conceived as an older man. Jon-Erik's only acting experience had been in a soap opera. He was a very raw actor. We literally bought him his Screen Actors Guild card. But he was just right. He read for the part, and after he walked out of the room, I turned to the other people there and said, 'That's the guy!' He had a magical, magnetic presence."

Associate producer Dean Zanetos had been much more cynical. "When Jon-Erik walked in, I thought, 'Oh, God. Just another pretty guy off of *GQ* magazine. It was almost embarrassing. The guy was too good-looking. I didn't even want to watch his reading. I thought he would be horrible. But we had already seen a lot of other guys, and they had all been bad. Jon-Erik began his scene, and he brought the character to life. It was astounding. He was an amazing performer. He would have been an incredible actor." (Hexum died accidentally in 1984 during production of his series *Cover Up*.)

"Jon-Erik was absolutely the right choice," says producer Jill Sherman-Donner. "His last series [*Cover Up*] didn't do him justice."

For the part of Jeff, Meeno Peluce was cast. "He was the best kid we read," says Parriott, "although he was a little too old for the part. I wanted someone a year or two younger, but Meeno turned out to be great. He and Jon-Erik were a pleasure to work with."

"Jon-Erik had done some stage in New Jersey, but he was very new to TV," says director Paul Lynch. "He was in his twenties, while Meeno was 12 or 13. One day I walked by them and Meeno was telling Jon how to act in the upcoming scene. Jon was listening very intently. It was a wonderful moment. Meeno was fabulous."

Sherman-Donner recalls that Hexum returned the favor. "My husband, Robert Donner, played Buffalo Bill in one episode. He was privy to a conversation between Jon-Erik and Meeno. Meeno had to film an episode and miss The Who concert. The Who were making their final tour. The comforting that Jon-Erik did was remark-

President Lincoln (John Anderson) visits with the time travelers (Meeno Peluce, center, and Jon-Erik Hexum. Copyright 1982 NBC/Universal.

I worked on *The Incredible Hulk*, and I was very taken with the *Voyagers!* pilot film. It was a wonderful concept."

To plot the voyagers' adventures, Sherman-Donner pondered how she could tweak history. "I looked at certain historical eras. For instance, in 'Cleo and the Babe,' Lucky Luciano and Babe Ruth were alive at the same time. I thought, 'Who would be an attractive woman for Luciano to meet?' He had a reputation as a womanizer, and I thought of Cleopatra. I studied her life and thought, 'What would happen if she had picked another man other than Marc Antony?' There are always ifs in people's bios. Turn a different corner or make another decision than the one you've already made and your life goes off in a totally different direction. Magnify these decisions in the context of history's most important people and it's easy to imagine, 'What if.' 'Cleo and the Babe' turned out to be my favorite episode in a totally comedic way. It was fun to take a fish out of water."

The titles of *Voyagers!* were often charming and whimsical. Sherman-Donner says, "We often used the original titles we came up with while pitching the stories. The more serious the topic, the more difficult it was to come up with a title. You didn't want to crack wise about something serious."

Several of the episodes did deal with history on a relatively serious level. They included topics such as Jack the Ripper, the *Titanic* and the Salem witch hunts. "*Voyagers!* wasn't a kids' show, although it certainly included them," Sherman-Donner notes. "It worked on two levels. Most of

able. So much of the time, Meeno was the adult of that duo because he was so precocious and experienced. In this instance, it was Jon-Erik who was being the 'big brother.' They had a sweet relationship. There was never any temperament."

Parriott admits that the series was not conceived as dead-serious fare. "We were doing a whimsical show. The toughest thing was keeping within our budget. Bogg and Jeffrey went into at least two time zones per show. But we had the whole Universal backlot to work with, and they didn't charge us for it."

Sherman-Donner was invited by Parriott to produce the series. She jumped at the chance. "I was raised on *The Outer Limits*, *Twilight Zone* and *Night Gallery*," she says. "I knew Jim from when

the time we dealt with history in a rather light-hearted manner. We did touch on some intense moments in history. The *Titanic* was pretty heavy. I think we could have touched on the diary of Anne Frank but we would never have gone into Auschwitz, which is the most intense time that I can think of."

Despite occasional visits to violent eras, *Voyagers!* tried to soften the rougher edges of history. For this reason, Dean Zanetos was astonished when the series was hit over the head for its content. "We were in a children's time slot, 7 p.m. Sundays. This made us subject to a lot of pressure from Standards and Practices. There was a group in Chicago that reviewed television's most violent shows. To our surprise, *Voyagers!* was rated as the most violent. It threw us into a complete tailspin. We couldn't understand what they were talking about. We were very careful not to have the kid placed in danger. We later learned the study's criteria for violence was the number of explosions heard on the soundtrack. If Bogg and the kid landed in the middle of a battlefield, every explosion you heard in the distance was counted as an act of violence. At the same time, we were a borderline show in terms of ratings. The violence thing was another notch against us."

It was a different criticism that soured things slightly for producer Sherman-Donner. "We were told by a gentleman at Universal, who shall remain nameless, that the characters of Napoleon, Josephine and Harriet Tubman [all of whom appeared in episodes] didn't have a high enough TVQ rating [a system used to the determine popularity of characters]. That was very disappointing.

Jeff (Meeno Peluce) and Phineas Bogg (Jon-Erik Hexum) leap through time. Copyright 1982 NBC/Universal.

Voyagers! was a show that was supposed to educate. For example, Harriet Tubman was a woman instrumental in the making of the Underground Railroad [for black slaves in the mid–1800s]. Half of the fun of the series was finding out different aspects of famous people and learning about people that the audience may not know. When you're told that your historical characters need to have a high TVQ rating, it gets discouraging. It kind of knocked the steam out of me. If we had gone another year [22 episodes], we would have had to come up with 44 characters that everybody easily recognized. But you can only do Ben Franklin and Cleopatra so many times. It would have been more fun to come up with more little-known characters who contributed to history."

Filmed on a standard budget, the series had to accommodate two, sometimes three, time eras per show. "We had the Universal backlot, which included the old castle for the Robin Hood movies," says Sherman-Donner. "We also had the forests to run through, and a Roman Colosseum. Jim Parriott was able to use the sets for maximum effect. You couldn't do *Voyagers!* today because most of the Universal backlot has been torn down."

"I researched every historical film that had ever been made by Universal," says Dean Zanetos. "I traced the history of the footage to see if it was available for the show. We would construct episodes around the stock footage that was available. This saved us millions of dollars in terms of matte paintings and extras."

While Bogg and Jeff survived history's most dangerous eras, they couldn't survive a mere 60-minute challenge from the other network. "If NBC could get the ratings *Voyagers!* got against *60 Minutes* today, they would pass out," says Sherman-Donner. "*Voyagers!* did so much better in the ratings than it was given credit for. Kids and their parents had fun watching it together. Everyone was surprised when it was canceled."

"We did a good job on *Voyagers!*" says Zanetos. "Brandon Tartikoff [NBC's president at the time] said later that it was his biggest disappointment to cancel the series."

"It was a fun show," says James Parriott, "and a great educational thing as well. It got a 20 share in the ratings. We were replaced by a news show called *Monitor*. It got a nine share. NBC said, 'Oh, that was a mistake.' We did better in that time slot than anything they've had since."

"It was an interesting show," says director Paul Lynch, "but they never had the money to do it correctly. Although the pilot was very impressive, there was pressure after the first two shows to cut back on budget. If we couldn't shoot a show in seven days, they were thinking of canceling the show. The scripts were very good and in general, the show was very good. They just needed more money."

Shortly after cancellation, the series was put into syndication and did very well. In 1984 there was brief talk of reviving the show for syndication.

"*Voyagers!* hit its potential 90 percent of the time," concludes Sherman-Donner, "and that's a really good average. I've noticed on *The Young Indiana Jones Chronicles* that they've included their characters with real-life people in interesting ways. It's nice to see that echo of *Voyagers!*"

The producer remains gratified by the show's continued visibility. "It's even shown up in video stores," she says, "and I still get residuals from the episodes. There's a little cult thing around *Voyagers!* We didn't make many episodes, but it continues to have a life of its own."

CAST NOTES

Jon Erik-Hexum (Bogg): Born 1957. His promising career was cut short in 1984, when he accidentally shot himself with a gun filled with blanks on the set of his TV series *Cover Up*.

Meeno Peluce (Jeff): Born 1970 in Amsterdam. He's the brother of actress Soleil Moon Frye. "Meeno was interested in getting into film production," says producer Jill Sherman-Donner. "Meeno was involved in a rock-and-roll band the last I heard," says producer Dean Zanetos.

EPISODE GUIDE

Voyagers!
Bogg and Jeff travel back to Egypt, 1450 B.C., where they encounter a baby Moses. The travelers later meet the Red Baron during World War I and journey to 1903 Ohio to discover why the Wright brothers didn't get off the ground. Wr and Dir: James D. Parriott.

Mary (Faye Grant); Orville Wright (Donald Petrie); Wilbur Wright (Ed Begley, Jr.); Eddie Rickenbacker (Peter Frechette); Aunt Elizabeth (Jeanie Bradley); Agnes Spence (Sondra Currie); Tom (Terrence O'Hara).

Created Equal
In Rome, 73 B.C., Bogg and Spartacus are sentenced to die in the Arena. In 1847 Hannibal, Missouri, Jeff and Sam Clemens try to free Harriet Tubman from the bonds of slavery. Wr: Nick Thiel. Dir: Virgil W. Vogel.

Harriet Tubman (Fay Hauser); Spartacus (Dan Pastorini); Cicero (Jay Robinson); Octavia (Leigh Hamilton); Sam Clemens (Rossie Harris); Calpurnia (Robin Ignico); Bitiatus (Ian Ambercrombie); Sheriff (Duke Stroud); Sandy (Gary Allen); Cabin boy (Darin Willis); Woman (Dorothy Chace); Junior (Tony Epper); Andrew (Dave Cass); Guards (Chuck Hicks, Gary Epper, Terry J. Leonard, Sal Land); Butch Bastaine (Ed Bakey); Also with Tim Rossovich.

Bully and Billy
The rebels in the Cuban Revolution are jeopardized when Teddy Roosevelt is shot dead by Billy the Kid

in 1889. The voyagers also meet an exasperated Ben Franklin. Wr: B.W. Sandefur. Dir: Virgil W. Vogel.

Teddy Roosevelt (Gregg Henry); Billy the Kid (Frank Koppala); Rita Dela Rose (Gina Gallego); Ben Franklin (Fredd Wayne); Remington (Jon Lindstrom); Davis (Gregory Itzan); Charlie (Alan Stock); Manuel (Wilfredo Hernandez); Sheriff (Sid Conrad); Maggie (Lee Kessler); Bartender (Don Maxwell); Ned Dawson (Michael Sandovel); Soldier (Robert O'Sullivan); Jorge (East Carlo).

Agents of Satan
The voyagers and Ben Franklin's mother are sentenced to hang during the Salem witch hunts. Their only hope is from Houdini, who has given up magic for a pursuit of ghosts. Wr: James D. Parriott. Dir: Alan J. Levi.

Abiah Folger (Jennifer Holmes); Noyes (Guy Stockwell); Houdini (Michael Durrell); Margaret (Marta DuBois); Betty Parris (Shannen Doherty); Rev. Parris (Earl Boen); Judge Sewell (David Hooks); Francis Scott Key (Andy Wood); Abigail Williams (Kim Marie); Suzanne Martin (Katie Budge); Reporter (Robert Nadder); Old man (Zachary Berger); Woman (Gwendolyn Brown); Scientist (James Cook); Old woman (Helene Heigh); Ghost (Douglas Blair).

Worlds Apart
Bogg befriends Lawrence of Arabia, who is fleeing for his life; meanwhile, Jeff meets Thomas Edison and helps him with the light bulb. Wr: James D. Parriott, Jill Sherman. Dir: Ron Satlof.

Lawrence of Arabia (Judson Scott); Thomas Edison (Steven Keats); Mary Edison (Mary Kate McGeehan); Taurus (Lawrence Dobkin); Medina (Shanit Keter); J.P. Morgan (Robert Ackerman); John Kruesi (Arthur Rosenberg); Prisoner (Marius Mazmanian); Upton (Michael Horsley); Boehm (Tony Brafa); Omen (Nicholas Khan); Lowrey (Lynn Seibel).

Memory Flash—Ron Satlof: "It was a happy series. I had a wonderful time on the show. The stories were lovely. It had a perfect, Disney time slot for Sunday night. *Voyagers!* was probably much more closer to [the film] *Time Bandits* than to *Quantum Leap*."

Cleo and the Babe
The travelers propel Cleopatra to the 1920s, where she gets involved with gangster Lucky Luciano. The voyagers try to stop Lucky from blocking Babe Ruth's sixtieth home run. Wr: Jill Sherman. Dir: Bernard McEveety.

Cleopatra (Andrea Marcovicci); Babe Ruth (Bill Lucking); Lucky Luciano (Michael Gregory); Ed Barrow (Ken Swofford); Marc Antony (Norman Snow); Roman senator (George Sawaya); Sir Isaac Newton (Dan Kern); News vendor (Ed McCready); Announcer (Clint Young); Reporter (Charles G. Stevenson); Doorman (Michael London); Reporter #2 (John Achorn); Men (David Blackwood, Don Boughton); Telegrapher (Richard Morof).

The Day the Rebs Took Lincoln
Abe Lincoln is kidnapped by the traitorous Jane Phillips, causing the North to begin losing the war. The voyagers (and Charles Dickens) also pursue Fagin and the Artful Dodger in England when they steal the Omni. Wr: Robert Janes. Dir: Bernard McEveety.

Abe Lincoln (John Anderson); Jane Phillips (Alexa Hamilton); Charles Dickens (Alex Hyde-White); Sykes (Robert Phalen); Fagin (Gerald Hiken); Mrs. Lincoln (Rachel Bard); Bates (Donald Durrell); Guard (Alex Daniels); Officer (Ross Evans); Rebel (Ray Colbert); Artful Dodger (Nicky Katt); Nancy (Melissa Ann Fuller); Steve (Cameron Dye); Lincoln guard (Glenn Morrissey); Ad lib people (Julian Barnes, Suki Goodwin); Gate guard (Ross Evans); Marion (Karen Dotrice).

Old Hickory and the Pirate
The hanging of pirate Jean Lafitte puts New Orleans under British control in 1815. To prevent his death, the voyagers must go back to 1798, where they encounter Lewis and Clark. Wr: Robert Janes. Dir: Peter Crane.

Jean Lafitte (James Carroll Jordan); Anne (Tricia O'Neil); Andrew Jackson (Lance Le Gault); Lizzy (Andra Akers); Black Bill Scraggins (George Innes); Pierre Lafitte (Eric Mason); Jim (Michael Baldwin); William Clark (Michael Bond); Meriwether Lewis (William McLaughlin); Blind man (John Dullaghan); Maria (Ruth Britt); Scar (Robert Feero); York (Mik One); Man (Dominic Barto); Pirate (David Cadiente); Soldier (Stacy MacGregor); Soldier #2 (Roger Rook); Also with William Bryant.

The Travels of Marco Polo and Friends
Isaac Wolfstein is a retired voyager who retires to an island, unaware it's been set for atomic testing. Meanwhile, Jeff is captured by hostile tribesmen while visiting Marco Polo. Wr: James D. Parriott. Dir: Paul Lynch.

Isaac Wolfstein (Michael Fox); Marco Polo (Paul Regina); Kublai Khan (Keye Luke); Nicolo (Paul Comi); Albert Einstein (Nathan Adler); Maffeo (Pat Renella); Oxen (Manu Tupou); Auctioneer (Julius Harris); Jennie (Wendy Hoffman); Clara Barton (Patricia Donahue); Mover (John Brandon); Sung-Tarter (Richard Lee); Karauna guard (Michael Yama); Kharis guard (Jesse Borja); Reporter (Dale Reynolds); Jailkeeper (Mako).

Memory Flash—Paul Comi: "They put me in a wig and costume as Marco Polo's father. I ended up looking like one of the Andrews Sisters!"

An Arrow Pointing East
The travelers help Robin Hood rescue Maid Marian. In 1927, Charles Lindbergh needs assistance during his flight of the *Spirit of St. Louis*. Wr: Jill Sherman, Nick Thiel. Dir: Ernest Pintoff.

Maid Marian (Wendy Fulton); Robin Hood (Dan Hamilton); Charles Lindbergh (Jonathon Frakes); Friar Tuck (Mills Watson); Sheriff of Nottingham (Alex Rebar); Little John (Denny Miller); Lane (Vernon Weddle); Mrs. Lindbergh (Jan Stratton); Harold Bixby (Michael Currie); Blythe (William Wintersole); Doc Kimball (Bryan O'Byrne); Prince Jon (Jon Slade); Reporters (George Caldwell, Howard Schechter, Howard Goodwin); Will (Chuck Howerton).

Merry Christmas, Bogg

Christmas Eve, 1776, finds George Washington on the British side! In Pittsburgh, the pair encounter Jeff's grandfather, who is defending Sam Gompers. Bogg soon feels Jeff would be better off staying with his grandfather. Wr: Bruce Shelley. Dir: Ron Satlof.

Washington (Peter Donat); Amy (Anne Lockhart); Sam Gompers (Joe Dorsey); Stephen Jones (John O'Connell); Mrs. Washington (Kelly Jean Peters); Englishman (Don Knight); Young Washington (Mike Brick); Ben (Terrence Evans); Man with pipe (Jack Kosslyn); Fred (Ken Letner); Schmidt (Cecil Reddick); Mayor David (Jeff Reese); Harker (Roger Hampton); Nathan (Ed Brodow); Sarah (Sarah Lilly); Lt. (Joe Nagengast).

Buffalo Bill and Annie Oakley Play the Palace

When the British princess marries a Russian duke, Britain's involvement with the Russian revolution begins one year earlier. While trying to stop the wedding to keep history on track, the voyagers meet Buffalo Bill and Annie Oakley in 1857. The voyagers also meet Albert Schweitzer and help him bring medical supplies to a dying African chief. Wr: Jill Sherman. Dir: Alan J. Levi.

Buffalo Bill Cody (Robert Donner); Annie Oakley (Diane Civita); Albert Schweitzer (Christopher Cary); Queen Victoria (Lurene Tuttle); Massandi (Raymond St. Jacques); Aide de camp (Tom Troupe); Granddaughter (Robin G. Eisenmann); Grand Duke Michael (Stan Sells); Rapp (Erik Stern); Hagson (John C. McLaughlin); Soldier (Terence Marinan); Joseph (Stuart K. Robinson).

The Trial of Phineas Bogg

Bogg chases a fellow voyager who has framed him for crimes by tampering with the Omni; during the chase, the travelers meet Sam Houston, who is sentenced to die. Wr: Jill Sherman. Dir: Sigmund Neufeld, Jr.

Drake (Stephen Liska); Garth (Harry Townes); Susan (Jenny Neumann); Sam Houston (William McLaughlin); Brindle (Barbara Beckley); Kane (Will Gill, Jr.).

Sneak Attack!

While trying to prevent Gen. MacArthur's death at Pearl Harbor in 1941, the travelers accidentally transport a naval officer back to 1860 Utah, where the trio aids Bill Cody against outlaws. Wr: Nick Thiel. Dir: Paul Stanley.

Jackie Knox (Brianne Leary); Gen. MacArthur (Frank Marth); Jack Knox (Dana Elcar); Buffalo Bill Cody (Ike Eisenmann); Corp. Baker (Robin Haynes); Mike (David Graf); Max (Christopher DeRose); Tina (Robin Hoff); Tom (Mark Rowland); Buck (Nicholas Shaffer); Jones (Tim Haldeman).

Voyagers of the *Titanic*

The voyagers meet another voyager, Olivia, who has orders to get the stolen Mona Lisa off the ship before it sinks. The three travelers also land in Paris, where Jeff is bitten by a rabid dog. Louis Pasteur tries to save him. Wr: James D. Parriott, Jill Sherman. Dir: Winrich Kolbe.

Olivia Dunn (Tracy Brooks Swope); Louis Pasteur

(Will Kuluva); Molly Brown (Fionnuala Flanagan); Dr. Bernard (John McLiam); Ismay (Sam Chew, Jr.); Suzzanne Brandes (Suzanne Barnes); Capt. Smith (Hugh Reilly); Haggerty (Lee de Broux); Murdock (Dennis Robertson); Policeman (Albert Carrier); Crewmen (Don Maxwell, William Lodge); Newsboy (Chris Vore).

Memory Flash—Winrich Kolbe: "I wish *Voyagers!* had gone on. It was a back-breaking show to work on, but it was an interesting show. Jon-Erik Hexum was very open about his lack of acting experience. He knew his limitations and was willing to work on them."

Pursuit

A visit to watch the *Apollo 11* lift-off reveals that rocket genius Werner von Braun was convicted as a traitor by the Russians in 1945. This results in the Russians reaching the moon first. The travelers set on a complicated journey to reverse history. Wr: Harry Longstreet, Renee Schoenfeld Longstreet. Dir: Alan Myerson.

Werner von Braun (David Olivier); Erika (Monique Van De Ven); Otto (Bo Brundin); Klaus (Robert O'Reilly); Willy (Patrick Gorman); Ernst (Gregory Itzin); Gen. Kamnler (Barrie Ingham); Wally (Dan Barrows); Schneiker (Cliff Taylor); Kurt (Vincent Caristi).

Destiny's Choice

1928 movie star Veronica Bliss befriends the heroes after Bogg is accused of sabotaging a movie set. They also discover the film's director is Franklin Roosevelt, who has abandoned his political career. Wr: Jill Sherman. Dir: Paul Stanley.

Veronica Bliss (Bonnie Urseth); FDR (Nicholas Pryor); Eleanor Roosevelt (Ellen Geer); Mama Roosevelt (Angela Clarke); Sam (Oliver Clark); Franz Rubin (Joseph Leader); Child (Roger Duffy); Monroe Jones (Robert Dunlap); Guard (Robert Carnegie); Mailman (Bill McLean); Stagehands (Buddy Farmer, Karl Johnson).

All Fall Down

In 1938, Bogg agrees to box against Joe Louis, who is prepared to give up his fight against Max Schmeling. In 1970, Jeff must land a 747 jet after foiling a skyjacking. Wr: Harry Longstreet, Renee Schoenfeld Longstreet. Dir: Ron Satlof.

Joe Louis (Sam Scarber); Robert Stewart (Robert F. Lyons); Jack Blackburn (John Hancock); Dorfman (Michael Swan); Max (George P. Wilbur); Billy (Steve Buckingham); Archer (Richard Alden); Patty (Leigh Kavanaugh); Dave (Lee Weaver); Broadcaster (Misha Hausserman); Fred (David Cadiente); Phyllis (Momo Yashima); David (David Kotch); Jimmy Carter look-a-like (Walt Hanna); Ground control (Jim B. Smith); Seth (Roger Robinson); Brooks (Jim McKrell); Also with L.Q. Jones.

The Barriers of Sound

The travelers play matchmaker between Alexander Graham Bell and a deaf girl to put the inventor back on track, but Boggs falls in love with the woman instead. The travelers also aid in the birth of Dwight Eisenhower in 1890 Texas. Wr: Nick Thiel. Dir: Bernard McEveety.

Mabel Hubbard (Lou Mulford); Alexander Bell (Kenneth Gilman); Watson (Linwood Boomer); Hubbard (John Randolph); Policeman (Read Morgan); George (Kevin Kovacs); Walter (Dan Frischman); Maid (Paddi Edwards); Thomas (Bill Erwin).

Jack's Back

Drake, the corrupt voyager who tried to frame Bogg earlier, returns, posing as Jack the Ripper in England. An 1889 detective tries to nail Bogg as the killer. The travelers also ensure that Nellie Bly launches her trip around the world, and help Sir Arthur Conan Doyle cure his writer's block. Wr: James D. Parriott, Sarah Parriott. Dir: Dean Zanetos.

Nellie Bly (Julia Duffy); Drake (Stephen Liska); Arthur Doyle (Michael Ensign); Barkeep (Michael Hadlow); Cockney #1 (James Garrett); Bobbie (B.J. Turner); Cockney #2 (Peter Ashton); Cockney #3 (Terence Pushman); Cockney #4 (Wayne Wasserman); Spectator (Joi Staton); Spectator #2 (Dean Dittman); Inspector Lestrade (Gerry Gibson).

War of the Worlds

October 1988–May 1990

Based loosely on H.G. Wells' classic novel of alien invasion from Mars, the series actually takes its premise from the 1953 George Pal feature film of the same name. In the series, 35 years have passed since the 1953 invasion, and the alien menace has returned. Aliens once thought dead and buried are actually lying dormant, waiting to be reawakened. A scientist, a military man, a communications expert and a biologist are teamed to fight a secret war against this new invasion.

Cast: The Heroes: Harrison Blackwood (Jared Martin); Colonel Paul Ironhorse (year 1) (Richard Chaves); Suzanne McCullough (Lynda Mason Green); Debbie McCullough (Rachel Blanchard); Norton Drake (year 1) (Philip Akin); Kincaid (year 2) (Adrian Paul). *The Aliens:* Urich (aka Advocate #2) (year 1) (Ilse Von Glatz); Chambers (aka Advocate #1) (year 1) (Richard Comar); Einhorn (aka Advocate #3) (year 1) (Michael Rudder); Malzor (year 2) (Denis Forest); Mana (year 2) (Catherine Disher); Ardix (year 2) (Julian Richings).

Creator: Greg and Sam Strangis (year 1); *Executive Producer:* Herbert Wright (year 1); Frank Mancuso, Jr. (year 2); *Producer:* Jonathan Hackett (year 1); *Supervising Producer:* Jon Anderson (year 2); Syndicated/Paramount; 60 minutes.

When Orson Welles broadcast his pseudo-documentary based on H.G. Wells' story "War of the Worlds" (Martians landing to plunder Earth), many of the radio listeners of 1938 mistook the drama for the real thing. One man came home to find his wife about to drink poison, preferring to die that way rather than be incinerated by the Martian death rays.

H.G. Wells' 1898 novel also inspired a 1953 motion picture starring Gene Barry and Ann Robinson. And in the 1980s, Martian invasion was still a compelling theme, ready for updating in a TV series.

The *War of the Worlds* series was essentially a continuation of the George Pal film. The premise picks up the story some 35 years later, with the Martian war machines crated up and stored in military warehouses and the aliens buried in steel drums and forgotten. Enter: Dr. Harrison Blackwood, an astrophysicist; Suzanne McCullough, a microbiologist; Norton Drake, a wheelchair-bound radio astronomer; and Colonel Paul Ironhorse, a military man.

Neill Fearnley, a director of four episodes of the first season, admits that the very first science fiction book he had ever read was *War of the Worlds.*

"To be a part of [the story], in any fashion, was a lot of fun!" laughs Fearnley. "In the H.G. Wells story, the aliens all died of a cold virus—a common cold, and then Orson Welles came along and he concocted his premise [updating the location and time of the story to modern-day New Jersey], which was clever, and then the movie came along, and so they decided to fashion [this television series] somewhat after the movie. The stumbling block was that [the aliens] had died in the film."

To do a series based on dead aliens was a difficult chore for the show's creators. Greg Strangis, who assembled *War of the Worlds* for Paramount Television, says that "the George Pal film really was a homage to the novel, and it was a pretty reasonable adaptation of the radio broadcast. ... I thought, 'OK, ... how do we deal with it in the '80s? It's many years later and the aliens are still here.' And that was the jumping-off point. I made every effort to be respectful to the source material and still have the requirements of a continuing series."

To make sure that the reviving aliens who were defeated by Earth's bacteria would not be defeated again by the very same germs, Strangis says, "My reasoning was that radiation protected them from the virus. Radiation killed the virus."

"They were in hibernation, and they would all come back to life, which was very clever," interjects Fearnley. "I think where the show ran into problems, personally, is the idea they would enter a human body and somehow their molecules combine with a human's molecules. And you could have an alien sitting right there. Again, a clever idea, and given today's technology, if you were to promote the series today, you might get away with it because of morphing.

"If we had today's computer morphing effects, the way that *Terminator 2* has been done, we might have been able to do some really extraordinary things. But in those days the idea was that [the alien invaders] would be a hole inside of you and come out of you. That doesn't really work emotionally, but worse, technically. For a show filmed in six days, it's virtually impossible to satisfy the demands for excellence that the audience has, and to have them see that as anything but a rough attempt to approximate the effect."

Fearnley believes that *War of the Worlds* was "a very grand idea for a limited budget," and adds, "A lot of people had difficulty on that show. For me, it was great fun. I enjoyed myself thoroughly. ... I don't remember bad things about it. It *was* very, very difficult, and the hours were very long and it hurt making it. But it was fun. We had a good time. We tried very hard; we were very sincere about what we were doing. But sometimes it doesn't work out, and it didn't for us on that show for whatever reasons."

Among the challenges they faced was dealing with a very abrupt and jarring Writers Guild Strike in Los Angeles, which affected production severely. Strangis says the writers' strike almost brought the show to a screeching halt.

"We started principal photography of the two-hour premiere episode on or about the same time as the writers' strike," he recalls. "There were no scripts being developed. The pilot was completed. The strike was still going. The pilot was delivered. Basically I was out of work until the resolution of the strike. When I came back when the strike was resolved, scripts were apparently being written by strike scabbers. Some of those shows were not in the best of shape, so we put them up on the shelf and scrambled and tried to come up with product in a very short amount of time so we could keep producing."

"It affected things badly," says Fearnley, who was in Toronto where the show as filmed. "In a way, you almost had to write your own scripts. They didn't have access to a broad spectrum of people—[just] the few who were working on the show, and those scripts were done under pseudonyms. Who knows who wrote them? The scripts needed a lot of work."

Fearnley's comments shed light on several suspicious teleplay credits for the show's first season. On "Epiphany," Sylvia Van Buren was credited. Sylvia Van Buren was Ann Robinson's character from the George Pal film (and in fact Robinson guest-starred in early episodes). "That's right. That was the gag," responds Fearnley to this reminder. "Who wrote that show? I don't know. There were a few others [with pseudonymous screenwriters].

"Whoever wrote those shows—and they weren't really written—I had the right to rewrite. I would start rewriting, and I'd give it back to the producers. I wouldn't get credit for it, but you do it all the time. You say, 'Look, this isn't working,' and [the producers] say, 'Oh, why?' 'Well, for these reasons,' and they say, 'You're right!' So the first few scripts were very unwieldy, very difficult, basically not very good."

Strangis says the strike polarized the studios and the writers. "Put yourself in the various different positions in terms of the studios. It's very important for us to have and maintain at least a semblance of a business as usual. The creators are very protective from an editorial perspective ... being a writer, I didn't want to do anything that would breach the Writers Guild." As a result, the station owners were concerned about having product. "Everybody wanted the best of all possible worlds, and it's a matter of compromise. I think the show suffered."

Ilse Von Glatz, who was one of the three semi-regular villains on the show, recalls, "The first thing I thought with the advent of the strike was that my job was on the line! We kept shooting, but everything was thrown into a panic, especially since this happened so close to the

War of the Worlds cast, year one, left to right: Jared Martin, Richard Chaves, Philip Akin and Lynda Mason Green. Copyright 1988 Paramount Television.

beginning. Everybody became somewhat demoralized because we really didn't know what was going on. Were these scripts, during that time, the real thing or some slapdash thing just thrown together? A sense of cohesiveness was certainly lacking."

Of his scripts, Fearnley recalls "Epiphany" as being definitely affected, and possibly "Multitude of Idols," but the last two were in fine shape. "You know," he says, "it improved a lot once the writers [returned]. We tried very hard on a very difficult thing in a short period of time," Fearnley adds. "I think more planning would have delivered a better show. On a show like that, the planning is essential, and I think we rushed into it. And it might be simply that the writers' strike got in our way. You can't do anything without the writers. Who knows? It might have been because of the strike that it came together.

"In the end, it was fun. I think it was one of the first times I had the chance to just *be* creative and *not* be told what to do. The show was wide open. We were making up the universe as we went along."

Coming back from the strike was harder than starting from scratch, says Strangis. "After the strike, by and large, it was a long process because we were really trying to catch up in terms of material. There was never enough time to develop stories. First, a series requires so much time, and there was none of that available to us. But slowly and surely we found out what things were working and what things weren't. The one thing everybody forgets is it takes a long time to develop special effects. After writing down something on a page, it takes awhile to make it work, and then you have to turn it over to other craftsmen. And it was tough trying to deal with schedules. The show as coming along very nicely.

Also lost in the Writers Guild strike was the explanation that as our intrepid team battled the aliens, no one in the world remembered the invasion of 1953—the war that (in the George Pal film) destroyed, among other things, the Eiffel Tower, the Taj Mahal and the Los Angeles city hall. The episode "Eye for an Eye" also explored the first invasion in 1938. Actor Philip Akin says, "It was never explained to anyone's satisfaction, ever. Just one of the blips that we had to keep glossing over and use smoke and mirrors to try and shy away from it..."

Further inconsistencies developed because years one and two had different production personnel, whose interpretations were in contrast to each other.

"They changed the rules again," declares Fearnley. "And that's okay. Where the problem lies is within the season. *If* you break the rules, then you get into trouble."

Asked if he felt the radical retooling of the show for second season was too much, Fearnley responds, "And did that contribute to the downfall of the show? As a viewer, I think so. As somebody working there, I can't say so because I didn't work on the second season. I don't know all of the reasons for the changes. Some executive somewhere wasn't happy. But as a viewer I preferred, in a funny way, the premise of the second season, where the aliens had accomplished a lot of their ends. The Earth was in dire straits. I liked that. That was kind of interesting. I preferred that apocalyptic, 'Max Headroom' kind of approach to the universe."

Of the cast of characters assembled for the series, Fearnley enjoyed the four-person team consisting of a scientist, a military man, a communications expert and a biologist. But, he says, "Richard Chaves and Philip Akin were not as well served as they could have been. Those characters had handicaps placed upon them.

"They put [actor Philip Akin] in a chair in a basement in front of a computer screen, and they didn't give him much of an opportunity. ... I mean, here was a character who's dynamic and filling the screen and yet we only cut to him every two seconds when we go to the TV screen. We had to get him involved in the story! He's tremendous! Very few shows had had people physically handicapped before, so nobody knew what to do, and we said, 'Why not put him in a truck? Give him a facility. Get him outside and make him human. Get him away from the screen and office and into the world.' I think that was a big bonus, but I don't think the character was served as well as it could have been. He's a terrific actor. I don't take credit for [the van idea], but after a lot of discussions, we were able to do that."

Philip Akin maintains, "Neill was responsible for Norton getting out and about. However, subsequent directors and the producers began, I felt, to feel it was too much of a hassle. In retrospect, it was as if they loved the idea of the wheelchair but not the reality [of working with it]."

Fearnley points out that to include a disabled character in the show was a challenging and daring move on the part of the creators. "It's a melting pot," he reflects. "Somebody's saying [in casting the lead characters of this show], 'Well, let's include in our group all of the different social aspects of America that we can think of and put that mix together,' and somebody gets the idea, 'We'll put one guy in a wheelchair...'" That requires a conscious decision. ... And *War of the Worlds* was one of the first shows where somebody at least made the effort to portray somebody functioning in society who had a physical handicap ... and made him one of the best characters of the whole show."

Working with a wheelchair gave Akin opportunities to innovate and incorporate some personal skills into the show. "I am quite a physical person and actor. I train in Aikido, Kung Fu and Tai Chi as well as being an avid bicyclist, so the wheelchair forced me to work in many different ways than what I was used to. I couldn't use the physical stuff that I'm so fond of using. It was a bit of a stretch to try not to use my legs, thus I started to use a strap to tie my legs together so that it would be a constant reminder not to move. It did cause some problems on the set as they kept designing 'Norton things' that were better suited to a leg-user and not a wheelchair user. A case in point was the alarm buzzer in the 'Second Wave' script. They had it set on the floor, and the director could not see the problem or the incongruity of a floor switch for a wheelie. In one other case, I found it impossible to loop any of my lines standing up. It all had to be done seated as that position changed my breath and vocal patterns."

Regarding other characters of the show, Fearnley says that Col. Ironhorse could have done a lot more, too. Yet he believes that the show's focus was more on Blackwood and Ironhorse than on some of the other characters and says there should have been a better balance. "It was all very politically correct, too. We had everything from the very right wing to the very left wing."

Playing one of the three alien advocates like a German terrorist was Ilse Von Glatz's ticket to the show. She confesses *War of the Worlds* "was not a show that I would watch on TV myself. Dormant aliens brought back to life ... to wreak havoc on the world—come on! You must understand, actors are not necessarily concerned with concept. Nobody ever really explained [to me] what the concept really was. You go in there, do the job as best as you can—usually totally uninformed. I had absolutely no idea what was going on at the audition. Some terrorist thing, I was told. 'Look stern. Dress in black.' I was handed a couple of pages of script that made no rhyme or reason. I guess I have the look they wanted, and [the fact] that I could play a German terrorist, with a German accent, got me the job.

"We had pretty good ratings for the first few shows. We were all pretty hyped. The PR machine was working at full tilt. Richard Comar, Michael Rudder and I got our photos in full fright makeup, on the front page of the entertainment section of USA Today. But by the time I was just doing ADR (looping dialogue) in the studio, I was so far removed from the whole thing. I would only find out sporadically how things were going."

At first, says Von Glatz, "we bad guys had the upper hand and were actually visible to the audience. To be quite honest, I don't think they should have ever allowed us—the triumvirate, the Advocates—to become unrecognizable. ... The audience, believe me, love to cheer on the villains too! They're usually more interesting. I knew we were 'disintegrating,' but surely they could have come up with some miracle cure for us."

As resident aliens on the first season, Von Glatz, Rudder and Comar never really interacted with the main cast. As a result, says Von Glatz, "Richard, Michael and I, as we always appeared together, became quite the team. Working so closely, I really got to love those guys. Making jokes, clowning around, trying to make sense of the script, sweating under all that makeup ... the filmmaking experience really boiled down to the camaraderie we shared.

"For the time that I was there, I can only laud the production values. The work, the sets, a location at the Quarry in the first three episodes, were anything but low-budget. The set for the aliens in the studio was unbelievable. I was stunned when I first saw this immense cave that was to become our 'home.' Shooting for TV is always rushed, but I was never aware of any 'low-budgetness' for the time I was actually on the set."

As for her character, "I must say that my role never really developed," laments Von Glatz. "The most work I did was at the beginning as far as character was concerned. That's when I played Urich the terrorist. After that, as aliens, we were directed to be as monotone and unemotional as possible. The challenge was restricted to the limitations imposed by the prosthetics, the costume."

Remembering audience reactions to her character, Ilse laughs: "Ha! I got one fan letter from a visually impaired fellow who thought I 'looked' really hot as a terrorist. He requested a full length photo." She also remembers, "One day Richard and Michael and I headed off in the car during lunch break. No big deal, except that we were in full horror makeup and costume. Caused quite a few traffic jams!"

In summary, says Von Glatz, "I can't say that I really had that much to do. For the most part we were instructed to act half dead and monotone. The real challenge came in the ADR studios. You're handed scripts in which you don't know what's going on and tape dialogue. It really works!"

When it comes to guest-starring in War of the Worlds, John Colicos, a respected actor famous as Baltar in Battlestar Galactica, remembers his appearance on "The Prodigal Son" very fondly. "It was a marvelous part," he says, "and in fact, one of the best science fiction parts ever created! [It was] one of the best science fiction scripts I think I've ever read. Greg Strangis, the producer, thought so highly of it that he put me up for an award, which unfortunately I did not get, as best performer in a guest role for a series."

Colicos describes his character on "Prodigal Son" as a "half-alien, half human sort of character. It was a character who was in constant conflict with himself, whether he would let the human side or the alien side of himself take over."

Did the character regard himself as human or alien? "That's the conflict," replies Colicos. "That's what we were trying to develop." He adds, "You would never know from week to week; was he an enemy or was he a human or was he trying to bridge the gap?"

The character was to continue in the series, but the show went into a different direction. Colicos regards the loss of the character and the show as unfortunate. "Had it gone in the direction that Greg Strangis wanted to, I think it would have filled a marvelous void because there is a great audience out there for good intellectual science fiction. Unfortunately, producers thought otherwise, and they wanted blood and gore and that usual stuff you find on television, so it was canceled."

Philip Akin believes his character on the show "was a strong individual with ideas and a great sense of humor and less of a compu-droid. I feel that within the parameters that I had to work in, I was pleased to go as far with him as I

War of the Worlds cast, year two, left to right: Catherine Disher, Denis Forest, Jared Martin, Lynda Mason Green, Rachel Blanchard, and Adrian Paul. Copyright 1989 Paramount Television.

was able to. However, the full growth of the character was never realized. In that first year, he still remained somewhat stunted. By the end of the season there was progress, but still he was left somewhat stillborn.

"In the last episode [of the first season] there was a great opportunity to have Norton healed. However, the producers backed away from the option that had been provided to them by the writers."

Instead, at the start of the second season, Norton Drake and Col. Ironhorse were killed ("The Second Wave") as part of a radical facelift for the whole series, now under the guidance of a new producer, Frank Mancuso. The aliens were executed in this episode by new aliens, the Morthren, who took over attempting their own invasion of Earth.

Of his departure, Akin says, "I thought the script was inconsistent and pathetic even for the genre. There were better, classier ways for people to leave than what they did. I have no real knowledge of why two of the most popular characters were killed off. I never got any other explanation except that the new producers wanted to go in another direction."

Richard Chaves, who played Col. Ironhorse,

says that like Akin, he was anguished at the decision to kill his character. "I [had] gone through the whole gambit, the whole spectrum of emotions. I was hurt. I couldn't understand and it blew me away. At first I was very upset, and very angry, and I didn't understand. And one of the things that fueled that negative reaction was that everybody kept telling me, 'Richard, you're the greatest.' Everyone kept telling me my fan mail was like five-to-one."

Series star Jared Martin provides an insight to the thought processes leading to the death of Ironhorse. "His character was sort of painted into a corner, and they couldn't deal with a sort of crisp, neatly pressed military person in the world which the show was going into," he remarks. "[That was] very much a *Blade Runner, 1984* world as opposed to a brightly lit, by-the-book, military-operation kind of world. They wanted to introduce a character—more of a roguish, offbeat, Mad Max character—and the Ironhorse character was just not going to work. It was a real tough decision. I know that Frank Mancuso spent many late nights thinking about it. He was killing off, arguably, the most popular cast member, which you don't do lightly."

Filming the scenes was very emotional for Chaves. "My last night of filming was very strange, and the first time I recounted what happened was to Peter Bloch Hanson, the guy who did the *Starlog* interview. And Peter isn't just a professional press person that I have worked with; he's a friend. He asked me what the last night was like, and I started telling him about it. The next thing I knew, I got real emotional and I fell apart. It was very, very difficult. It was a long, long night, and the most poignant moment of the entire time was when I took off my uniform for the last time and said goodbye to a very, very dear friend."

But as time went on, Chaves says, he steered himself to the positives. "I knew something better would come along."

Whatever shortcomings the show had for Philip Akin, being associated with *War of the Worlds* was worthwhile for him overall because of the impact his role made on the people who watched the show.

"I have received lots of fabulous and caring mail from many people. At one conference a lady came up to me and told me of her friend's class of disabled kids who loved the show because Norton was so independent and capable. It was that kind of response that made it all quite special."

One cast member who continued into the second season was Lynda Mason Green, as microbiologist Suzanne McCullough. "When we first started working on *War of the Worlds*, I was very happy with the script," she says. "I liked the writing, the characters, the idea. I saw lots of potential for Suzanne. She was a woman who interested me. I liked her and looked forward to being a part of her evolution and the challenge of playing a successful scientist who was also a single mother.

"For me, the best part of the [two-hour premiere episode] script was its humor. I felt that the tone and the wit that had been established by Greg Strangis in that script was a lot of fun. At times, 'wit' slammed into 'camp' but I, as a viewer, have always appreciated a series that had its tongue firmly implanted in its cheek and resisted taking itself too seriously. I looked forward to a lot of the same in future episodes."

Green was concerned that the updated approach to the Pal adaptation of the Wells novel would not have the strong foundations for a long run. "Audiences these days have very sophisticated tastes, and expectations of SF drama are high. After *Close Encounters* and *Star Trek* and its subsequent generations, it's become hard to sell the 'evil rubber suit Martian' without a healthy dose of humor. Since that seemed to be integral to the show at the beginning, I felt optimistic about our future." She

was troubled, however, when the humor she appreciated became the first casualty of the writers' strike. "It seems in retrospect that we never quite got back on track after that, even after the strike was finally resolved. Writing seems to be a fragile process in need of a lot of TLC. I admit that it was a disappointment for me that we never seemed to get to that wonderful point where everything begins to pulse with the same rhythm."

Further, Green recalls, "I was stunned to hear that we would be losing two important cast members. I had become friends with Phil Akin and was especially disappointed that he would not be back." However, she says, "By the end of the first season, we knew that we would have a new producer if there was to be a second season. Frank Mancuso, Jr., who became the new producer, had some very exciting changes to make. I liked what I heard so much that I could hardly wait to get back to work.

"As the second season progressed, the style and the look that had been designed by Frank was maintained by our wonderful creative staff and their crews. The scripts also took on a more intense, darker, more dangerous tone and texture as well. We were now to become a *Blade Runner*-esque action/drama. The show bore so little resemblance to the first season that it was hard to relate the two. I personally preferred it. Mostly it gave me an opportunity to get out of the lab and to develop the relationship with Debi [played by young actress Rachel Blanchard] much more. Almost everything about the new season was much more interesting for Suzanne and therefore for me as well."

One of the most important improvements for Green was changing the nature of the adversaries. "The aliens became more humanoid. Denis Forest and Catherine Disher were wonderfully arch Nazi-esque aliens. They updated the threat, made the aliens much more intelligent and consequently much more scary. I thought they were great. Julian Riching and Pat Phillips were also strong new members of the alien cast.

"I was also glad to have Adrian Paul come aboard [as Kincaid]. His character was much more of the romantic action-adventure hero, a rogue warrior. We needed him in the second season, especially since we were now out of our element and the environment had completely changed. We were forced onto Kincaid's turf. It was an easy adjustment."

Discussing audience response to the drastic

changes between seasons, Green says, "We were effectively two completely different shows connected by a thread of consistency that was barely more than a rumor. We lost a lot of fans that had been attached to the conservatism of the first season. The second year was much darker, oppressive, anarchic, and the 'good guys' did not always win. Many of the more enthusiastic fans of the first season did not make the transition." On the other hand, "many did like it better, and we apparently gained a lot of new fans as they discovered the show."

Green was unable to offer any concrete reasons for the show's demise. "Cast is rarely privy to such information until someone says, 'The show is over. Your check is in the mail!' I assume we didn't have enough support in the syndication market, that our support at Paramount waned, that audiences were confused by the radical shift between seasons that was never really explained adequately. It's pure speculation on my part. I would have been happy to do one more season, but I think we took it as far as we could under the circumstances, and it was time to move on."

Jared Martin says he's proud of the second season of War of the Worlds, which he called "immeasurably better." In a 1988 interview during the second season, while he was looping dialogue, Martin said that the show was "more consistent, it has a point of view, and we seem to have taken that last ounce of effort that makes something extra good.

"I think the show last year was perceived as an attempt to reach different kinds of audiences. We kind of went hat-in-hand to the audience and went, 'Look at us! Won't you please watch our show and like it?' This year, we're building the show first, and we're making a statement. If we collect an audience, that's fine. Last year, I think we were concerned too much with demographics. This year, because of our executive producer, Frank Mancuso, Jr., our attitude is, 'Let's swing for the fences on this one.' And if we fail, fine. If we get canceled, life goes on, but if we don't and we're going to have a hit that makes us more concerned with the show ... and indeed it's already kind of paid with a good review in Variety."

The radical format change between seasons one and two served to "open it up," Martin said. "Our show is based on the almost-tomorrow; therefore the things that we do are more recognizable and have to be based on reality. The more you base a show on reality, the more it starts swinging to a cops-and-robbers type of action-adventure show. We're trying to leverage out the concept of the show.... We're dealing in more pure science fiction terms. It's not just the good guys versus the bad guys from outer space [any longer]. That would get stale.

"We're more urban-based this season," he continued. "What seems to be happening in the world is happening in the cities. There's Beirut, New York, you name it. We've moved into the city. What's happening in the cities are the real problems of the advancing world, how do we deal with them? We can make a statement and score some points if we stay in an urban environment."

With the Morthren setting up shop on Earth and taking over where the Advocates failed, the second season's "new" aliens provided a deadlier threat to the world. Jared Martin said, "The strings are being pulled by the aliens. It's been personalized and we get to see more of their point of view. Why they're here and what they're about. They are not just stock villains in vacuum cleaner suits like they were last year, so the show is moving to the tune of the alien agenda, and this represents a shift other than us chasing them. [This time around] they are chasing us. We're living underground and are in more desperate circumstances, which makes for a more interesting show.

"How do 250 or so aliens take over the earth? They don't have the weaponry at this point, they are cut off from their planet, [but] they [do have] superior intelligence and technology. How do they do it? They attack several nerve centers of the socioeconomic, political aspects of the earth. Basically, they are here to disrupt, destroy and take over.

"The stewardship of Earth has been marred by all sorts of ecological disasters; nuclear explosions and constant warfare. We just don't get on with each other and we're not really taking care of this planet very well. I mean, there's an underlying ecological message to this series, which has to be well decorated with action-adventure or else people just wouldn't tune in." It's there if you look for it, he said.

Martin also believed that with proper care, the show would be further exposed to audiences via overseas sales, cassettes, and syndication reruns. And in fact, the Sci-Fi Channel promptly picked up War of the Worlds when the station first went on the air in the fall of 1992.

"It's a timeless thing," insisted Martin.

"Most science fiction is. It's not going to fade as quickly as a lot of action-adventure, sit-com or dramatic shows might."

Martin waxed romantic at the notion of the show going for five years. "Well, I'd like to. I like the character. I like the people [I work with], I like the set-up, and in terms of my acting this is my signature series. Right now I'm very involved with it and I'd hate to think that we will close down at the end of this [second] year."

Unfortunately for Martin, the *War of the Worlds* did just that.

CAST NOTES

Jared Martin (Dr. Harrison Blackwood): See *Fantastic Journey*.

Lynda Mason Green (Suzanne McCullough): Before *War of the Worlds*, Green starred in *Night Heat*, with appearances in *Adderly* and the ABC mini-series *Amerika*. Over the last few years Lynda has been writing, directing and producing corporate videos. She continues to pursue an interest in mainstream TV and film as an intern director on Canadian TV series.

Philip Akin (Norton Drake): Has appeared in many film and television roles. They include the features *FX2* (1991), *Millennium* (1989), *Switching Channels* (1988), *The Park Is Mine* (1985), and *Iceman* (1984). TV appearances include *Top Cops*, *E.N.G.*, *Night Heat* and the *Cagney and Lacey* pilot and Akin snagged a regular role in *Highlander*'s second season (1993-94) with fellow warrior Adrian Paul.

Richard Chaves (Col. Ironhorse): Born October 9, 1951, Chaves had extensive stage and television appearances. He was in *Dallas*, *Hill Street Blues*, *St. Elsewhere*, *Eight Is Enough* and the TV movie *Fire on the Mountain* (1981). He also had a small part in Irwin Allen's *The Swarm* (1978) and *Predator* (1987).

Rachel Blanchard (Debi McCullough): For a girl who's never had a formal acting lesson, Blanchard is a veteran of many commercials. Blanchard has also appeared in *The Littlest Hobo*, *Kids of DeGrassi Street*, and the TV movie *Glory Enough for All*. For the latter, she had to do a scene explaining to another girl that they both were going to die of diabetes. "I had to cry," explains Blanchard. "When I finished the scene, I looked up and the cameraman was crying, everyone was crying. It was a moment of achievement for me.

"I'm very athletic. I love to play ice hockey and tennis, and I enjoy swimming, skiing and dancing." A B-plus student, Blanchard's favorite classes are drama and gym.

Adrian Paul (Kincaid): London-born, Paul went from playing a Russian ballet dancer in *The Colbys* to fighting aliens in *War of the Worlds*. Paul's first break was on the London stage as a dancer in a play aptly named *The Break*. After that, he got roles in an NBC TV movie, *Shooter*, and a guest role in *Beauty and the Beast*.

"I like the way the show has been set up. And I like the character of Kincaid," said Paul during the second season. "He's very interesting and very complex. Kincaid is mercurial—he's charming. But he's a loner. He's tough, obstinate and capable of ferocious anger. It's a role that will allow me to grow as an actor."

After *War of the Worlds*, Paul starred in the hit SF syndicated series *Highlander*, filming in Vancouver, British Columbia, and Paris, France.

EPISODE GUIDE

Season 1: 1988-89

The Resurrection (2 hours)
At an army disposal site where toxic and radioactive wastes are kept, terrorists accidentally revive aliens from the invasion of 1953, who take over their bodies. To combat the aliens, General Wilson assembles a specialized team to exterminate the aliens who go after their spaceships. Wr: Greg Strangis. Dir: Colin Chilvers.
 Chambers (Richard Comar); Charlotte (Gwynyth Walsh); Urich (Ilse Von Glatz); Sgt. Gordon Reynolds (Eugene Clark); Einhorn (Michael Rudder); Mrs. Pennyworth (Corinne Conley); Mr. Kensington (Larry Reynolds); General Wilson (John Vernon); Mossoud (Frank Pellegrino); Finney (Martin Neuffeld); Teal (Ric Sarabia); Orel (Desmond Ellis); Doc (Jack Mather); Sheriff Deak (Harry Booker); Dr. Efrem Jacobi (David Hughes); Dr. Jeffrey Gutterman (Donald Tripe); Corporal #1 (Steve Atkinson); Corporal #2 (Kevin Fox); General Arquette (Ted Follows); Pilot #1 (Judah Katz); Pilot #2 (Jeff Knight); Signal corps technician (Daryl Shuttleworth); Hunter #1 (Richard Sali); Hunter #2 (Don Keppy).

The Walls of Jericho
Just when General Wilson is ready to mothball the team, aliens steal blood from steers and have been

appropriating plastic material to make environmental suits. When it comes to Harrison's attention, he believes the two events are related. Wr: Forrest Van Buren. Dir: Colin Chilvers.

Milkman #1 (Mark Humphrey); Advocate #1 (Richard Comar); Advocate #3 (Michael Rudder); Advocate #2 (Ilse Von Glatz); Major Kensington (Larry Reynolds); Mrs. Pennyworth (Corinne Conley); General Wilson (John Vernon); Sheriff (Ted) (Dale Wilson); Rancher (Zeke) (Jim Bearden); Detective #1 (Les Carlson); Young wife (Louise Cranfield); Detective #2 (Kris Ryan); Woman worker (Brenda Adams); Computer technician (Rob Jeffernan); Ralph (Michael Carvana); Farmer (Chris Potter); Foreman (Eric Keenleyside); Milkman #2 (Stephen Makaj); Chin (Detective) (Robert Lee); Chinese woman (Mrs. Lau); Guard (Ted Hanlan); Cop (Paul de la Rosa).

Thy Kingdom Come

Four deer hunters run into body-snatching aliens, who send signals into space. Their mission is defined: Retrieve more fellow aliens from the bottom of a Canadian lake. Meanwhile, Sylvia van Buren is having a bad night and tells Harrison that the aliens are nearby in Montana. Wr: Herbert Wright. Dir: Winrich Kolbe.

Sylvia van Buren (Ann Robinson); Advocate # 1 (Richard Comar); Advocate #2 (Ilse Von Glatz); Advocate #3 (Michael Rudder); Alien hunter (Alar Aedma); Prison Guard (Walker Boone); Beckwith (Michael Fletcher); Mom (Joy Thompson); Daddy (John Blackwood); Granny (Helen Carscallen); Bobby (Stuart Stone); Nurse Hamilton (Diane Douglass); Old man (John Dee); Attendant (Paul Bettis); Sheriff Dumas (Steve Mousseau); Police captain (Len Doncheff); Hunter #1 (Paul MacCallum); Hunter #2 (David Blacker); Hunter #3 (Kenneth W. Roberts); Hockey Player #1 (Michael-Michael Sokovin); Hockey Player #2 (Robbie Rox); Hockey Player #3 (Al Therrieu); Goalie (Gary Robbins); Officer/Guard (Aaron Ross Fraser); Jordan (Colleen Embree); Nun (Dolora Harvey); Nun (Valerie Boyle); Military Guard #1 (Brian Hall); Military guard #2 (Freddy) (Elliot McIver).

Trivia Alert: Ann Robinson starred in the 1953 *War of the Worlds* feature in the same role.

A Multitude of Idols

An investigative reporter hot on a trail of radioactive waste disposal witnesses a body-snatching. Meanwhile, someone steals a list of hazardous waste shipments from the Department of Transportation, alerting General Wilson and the team to alien activity. Wr: Tom Lazarus. Dir: Neill Fearnley.

Elyse Conway (Michele Scarabelli); Reverend (Neil Vipond); FBI Leader (Ray James); Alex (Von Flores); Blanche (Jackie Richardson); Simons (Garfield Andrews); Driver #1 (Roger McKeen); Driver #2 (Tedd Dillon); Judy (Judy Sinclair); Frank (Chick Roberts); FBI #1 (Richard Gira); FBI #2 (Jim Walton); FBI #3 (Joseph Matheson); Voice of advocate #1 (Richard Comar); Voice of advocate #2 (Ilse Von Glatz); Voice of advocate #3 (Michael Rudder).

Eye for an Eye

At Grover's Mill, the fiftieth anniversary of the Orson Welles 'War of the Worlds' radio broadcast is underway. Harrison and the team arrive and interview anyone who remembers the war of 1938. Meanwhile, the aliens uncover a working heat ray device. Wr: Tom Lazarus. Dir: Mark Sobel.

Flannery (Jeff Corey); Harv (John Ireland); Bill (Jack Jessup); Sam (Jack Ammon); Red (Mark Holmes); Miss Daly (Rita Tuckett); Dog (Kevin Rushton); Marla (Mary Beth Rubens); Biker #1 (Sergio Galli); Biker Chick (Linda Singer); Biker #2 (Kenny Maclean); Biker #3 (Sascha Tukatsch); Officer #1 (Richard Fitzpatrick); Officer #2 (Michael Fawkes); Orson Welles#1 (Frank Knight); Orson Welles #2 (Giovanni Paldino); Worker (Alanna Cavanaugh).

The Second Seal

When Norton locates Project Deep Ice (containing massive information about the aliens), the team is soon heading for an army base—and so are the aliens, disguised as a news team. When Norton and his co-workers find a strange pyramid-shaped object, their personalities are strangely altered.Wr: Patrick Barry. Dir: Neill Fearnley.

Lt. Amanda Burke (Lynne Griffin); General Masters (Greg Morris); Lt. Michael Hamill (Michael McKeever); Captain Murphy (James Kidnie); Newswoman (Anne Farquhar); Sgt. Hancock (Kirk Dunn); Ellen (Sgt.) (Miriam Newhouse); Cameraman (Roy Lewis); Alien MP/courier (Paul Eves); Officer at the bar (Wally Bonderenko); Guard (Todd Schroeder).

Goliath Is My Name

When aliens learn some biological warfare has been accidentally released, they head into a university laboratory where the vials are kept. And when Suzanne's upset at the disappearance of a colleague, she brings Harrison and Ironhorse to the same lab to investigate. Wr: Tom Lazarus. Dir: George Bloomfield.

Student (Jeremy Ratchford); Jefferson (Eric Bruskotter); Pete (Jason Blicker); Alien #1 (Hume Baugh); Advocate #2 (Ilse Von Glatz); Debra (Carolyn Dunn); Kim (Kelly Rowan); Robert Parkins (James Kee); Dean Holden (Terry Doyle); Samuel (Alex Karzis); Gabriel (Kevin Frank); Patty (Jill Hennessey); Alien #2 (Darren O. Donnell); Alien #3 (Damon D'Oliveria); Lab technician (T.J. Scott); Officer Helfrich (George Merner).

To Heal the Leper

To ward off chickenpox, the aliens need human brains to distill and administer to the sick alien. Meanwhile, Norton's picking up alien signals just when Harrison is becoming more obsessed than ever with finding the aliens. Wr: David Tynan. Dir: William Fruet.

Sylvia van Buren (Ann Robinson); Scott (Kim Coates); Beth (Guylaine St-Onge); Leo (Paul Boretski); Advocate #1 (Richard Comar); Advocate #2 (Ilse Von Glatz); Detective Harley (Neil Dainard); Nurse Hamilton (Diane Douglass); Old man (John Dee); Fred (Philip Williams); Attending alien (Len Carlson); Officer Roberts (Ross Manson); Desk Honey (Elizabeth Leslie); Teen queen (Krista Bridges); Dean (Claude Rae); Guard (Harold Luft).

The Good Samaritan

Aliens have developed deadly spores administered in food. Using a billionaire industrialist as their pawn, they plan on implanting the spores into an international "feed the world" grain that will soon be distributed. But Suzanne and the team have already been investigating the man and his grain products. Wr: Sylvia Clayton. Dir: Warren Davis.

Terri (Lori Hallier); Franklin (Warren Davis); Marcus Madison Mason (Alex Cord); Advocate #1 (Richard Comar); Advocate #2 (Ilse Von Glatz); Advocate #3 (Michael Rudder); Mrs. Pennyworth (Corinne Conley); Larson (David Gardner); Helen (Sharolyn Sparrow); Joyce Mason (Micki Moore); Hewlit (Barry Flatman); Commander (alien) (Michael Kramer); Cook (Mr. Cook) (James Oregon); Busboy (Mr. Stein) (Mark Krause); Waitress (Miss Marshall) (Mung Ling Tsui); Matron #1 (Billie Mae Richards); Matron #2 (Maxine Miller); Matron #3 (Anne Mirvish); Bodyguard (Michael Woods); Dr. Adams (J.R. Zimmerman); Longshoreman (George Kash); Doctor (John Baylis); Nurse (Djanet Sears); College Boy #1 (Darrin Baker); College Boy #2 (Andrew Gunn); Cheerleader (Laura Cruickshank).

Epiphany

During a US-USSR disarmament conference, aliens determine that humans can exterminate themselves by "petty tribal warfare" and all they need is some help. Towards this end, aliens steal 12 kilos of plutonium to make nuclear bombs. Wr: Sylvia Van Buren. Dir: Neill Fearnley.

Dr. Kayta Rhodan (Deborah Wakeham); Policeman (David Ferry); Major Valery Kerov (Patrick McNee); Advocate #1 (Richard Comar); Advocate #2 (Ilse Von Glatz); Advocate #3 (Michael Rudder); Commander (alien) (Michael Kramer); Mrs. Pennyworth (Corinne Conley); Worker #1 (John Liddle); Worker #2 (Frank Crudell); Female worker (Maggie Huculak); Journalist (Bob Dunn); Nun #1 (Patti Gail); Nun #2 (Brenda Kaminc); Nun #3 (Jackie May); Small boy (Paul Brogren); Pre-teen #1 (Nick Kantos); Pre-teen #2 (Troy Di Berto); Old lady (Stella Sprowell); Young hood (Gary Chessman); Cabby (Marty Galin); Driver (Conrad Coates); Co-worker (Stephen Walsh); Reporter (Paula Barrett); Parking officer (Rita) (Barbara Barnes Howard); Security guard (Paul Martin Charters); Young girl (Sarah Lynn Campbell); Uniformed cop (Andrew Thompson); Tow truck driver (Patrick Patterson).

Among the Philistines

After an attempt to capture some aliens fails, the team approaches Dr. Bouchard, a noted communications expert, who has intercepted alien transmissions. Wr: Patrick Barry. Dir: William Fruet.

Dr. Adrian Bouchard (Cedric Smith); Mrs. Pennyworth (Corinne Conley); Mr. Kensington (Larry Reynolds); Advocate #1 (David Calderisi); Advocate #2 (Ilse Von Glatz); Chubs (Gregory Cross); Alien trucker (Cliff Woolner); Alien driver (Richard Beach); Soldier (Clyde Whitham).

Choirs of Angels

When aliens sabotage a musician's latest recordings, a pre-release copy falls into Harrison's hands via Suzanne's old teacher, who attracts the aliens because he's developing a vaccine that will render them immune to Earth's bacteria. But the alien-doctored music has caused Harrison to snap. Wr: Durnford King. Dir: Herbert Wright.

Alien #1 (John Novak); Alien #2 (Alex Carter); Alien #3 (Heidi von Palleske); Dr. Eric Von Deer (Jan Rubes); Billy Carlos (Billy Thorpe); Advocate #3 (Michael Rudder); Advocate #2 (Ilse Von Glatz); Advocate #1 (David Calderisi); Receptionist (Karen Wood); Policeman (Wally Bolland).

Dust to Dust

When an archeologist sneaks into an Indian territory to steal artifacts, he witnesses an Indian ritual. Ironhorse, who sees a report on TV, believes he stole the items. But the aliens recognize the objects as pieces from their warships. Wr: Richard Krzemien. Dir: George Bloomfield.

Mark Newport (R.D. Reid); Alien BIA agent (Elias Zarou); Joseph Lonetree (Ivan Naranjo); Grace Lonetree (Robin Sewell); Darrow Lonetree (Eric Schweig); Advocate #3 (Michael Rudder); Advocate #2 (Ilse Von Glatz); Connie (Linda Goranson); Pat (Joseph Zeigler); Lawyer (George Bloomfield); Detective Bob (Gairey Richardson); Guard (Tim MacMenamin).

He Feedeth Among the Lilies

Using an appropriated ambulance, aliens now kidnap humans for medical experiments and implant devices in them for "harvesting." Meanwhile, Harrison and the team study victims of strange abductions, and he becomes attached to one particular blonde lady. Wr: Tom Lazarus. Dir: George Bloomfield.

Karen McKinney (Cynthia Belliveau); Estelle Robards (Maria Del Mar); Pat Thistle (Carole Galloway); Arnold Thistle (Graham Batchelor); Malter Hayden (Myron Senkus); Advocate #3 (Michael Rudder); Advocate #2 (Ilse Von Glatz); Advocate #1 (David Calderisi); Alien doc #1 (Mary Pirie); Paramedic #1 (Mark Wilson); Paramedic #2 (Dana Anderson); Alien doc #2 (Faye Cohen); Alien doc #3 (Diana Rowland); Man with hat (Julian Richings); Doctor (Larry Mannell); Nurse (Bonnie Gruen); Aide (Andrea Nevitt); Cop (Chris Trace).

The Prodigal Son

The team are off to New York for a secret briefing session with the U.N. Security Council on alien activity. Meanwhile, Harrison meets with Quinn, an eccentric sculptor who turns out to be an alien from the invasion of '53, and they are pursued by three aliens who locate Quinn's studio. Wr: Herbert Wright, story by Patrick Barry. Dir: George McCowan.

Alien detective (James Purcell); Sgt. Fitzpatrick (Robert Morelli); Quinn (John Colicos); Alien cop (Boris Khaimovich); Cop (Elliott McIver); Advocate #3 (Michael Rudder); Advocate #2 (Ilse Von Glatz); Advocate #1 (David Calderisi); Margo (Randall Carpenter); Hwang (Jim Yip); Sanchez (Dan Delabbio).

The Meek Shall Inherit

In an effort to break down society, the aliens muck

up the phone system, which results in chaos. But when an alien absorbs a street person, a witness is left behind. Wr: D.C. Fontana. Dir: William Fruet.

Molly Stone (Diana Reis); Sylvia van Buren (Ann Robinson); Dayton (Michael Copeman); Sensky (John Gilbert); Pollito (Sam Malkin); Sgt. Coleman (Norah Grant); Crp. Alexander Stavrakos (Vito Rezza); Sgt. Derriman (Steve Pernie); Bull (Gene Mack); Nurse Hamilton (Diane Douglass); Advocate #1 (David Calderisi); Advocate #2 (Michael Kramer); Advocate #3 (Martin Neufeld); Lineman (Steve Makaj); Hooker (Kim Caver); Mom (Mary McCandless); Dad (Will Finlay); Daughter (Susan Lowry); Stan (Jed Dixon).

Memory Flash—D.C. Fontana: "In the final version of my script (and I was not given a chance to do more than the first draft), there were many contradictions and confusions, many things left unclear as to what the aliens were doing and why. Those did not exist in the first draft I turned in. I did like the fact that the character of Sylvia Van Buren had a strong presence in my script and that was left in; also her relationship with the young bag lady Molly Stone was left pretty much intact. The general theme was a comment on the 'invisibility' of street people and the fact that no one really cares if something happens to them. They are considered to be 'disposable.' I don't think that's a healthy attitude, and the story was meant to underline the value of any human life, no matter what financial circumstances the person is in."

Unto Us a Child Is Born
At a shopping mall to test a bacteriological weapon, one of the aliens, in an attempt to escape from a guard, switches to a pregnant woman—who immediately goes into labor. Meanwhile, Norton detects alien signals nearby and the team head to the hospital. Wr: David Braff. Dir: George Bloomfield.

Alien #1 (Brent Carver); Mrs. Nancy Salvo (Amber-Lea Weston); Colin (Geoffrey Bowes); Young (Clark Johnson); Howard Hugo (Peter Boretski); Peggy (Martha Irving); Alien Mutant #1 (Mark Parr); Sgt. Coleman (Norah Grant); Saleslady (Deborah Theaker); Ken (Albert Schultz); Advocate #1 (David Calderisi); Advocate #2 (Michael Kramer); Advocate #3 (Martin Neufeld); Alien mutant #2 (John Ferguson); Lang (Ken Girotti); Guard (Walker) (Daniel Kash); Nurse (Michele Claire); Dr. Melish (Tim Koetting); Nurse (Heather Clifford); Blanche (Jacqueline McLeod); Bernie (James Mainprize); Alien toddler (Jonathan Ursini); Alien toddler (Brandyn Ursini).

The Last Supper
When the team attends a secret meeting of foreign representatives to discuss the global alien problem, the Advocates make a desperate push to find the meeting and kill all the attendants so the resistance movement can be quashed. Wr: Tom Lazarus. Dir: George McCowan.

Dr. Leonid Arghochev (Colm Feore); Gabriel Morales (Efrain Figueroa); Dr. Soo Tak (James Hong); Jerry Raymond (Barry Kennedy); Dr. Sunethra Menathong (Suz-

anne Coy); Dr. Morris Burnobi (Abbott Jones Anderson); Advocate #1 (Ilse Von Glatz); Advocate #2 (Ric Sarabia); Advocate #3 (Michael Copeman); Nurse (Brenda Kamino); Businessman (Ron Payne); Sgt. Coleman (Norah Grant).

Vengeance Is Mine
When an innocent human is killed during an alien theft of optical lenses, Ironhorse feels tremendously guilty. Meanwhile, needing more lenses to build their weapons, the aliens attempt to buy more from dealers. Wr: Arnold Margolin. Dir: George Bloomfield.

Psychiatrist (Bernard Behrens); Martin Cole (Denis Forest); Sarah Cole (Carolyn Dunn); Samantha (Alannah Myles); Alien #1 (Peter Millard); Alien #2 (Paul Jolicoeur); Alien woman (Julie Khaner); Milton (Don Allison); Henchman (Roger Montgomery); Stavrakos (Vito Rezza); Advocate #1 (Ilse Von Glatz); Advocate #2 (Ric Sarabia); Advocate #3 (Michael Copeman); Woman student (Mismu Vellani); Reverend (David Mulholland); Guard (Simon din Toit); Human captive (Nick De Kruyff).

My Soul to Keep
Alien eggs are deteriorating, so the Advocates move storage to an ice plant. Meanwhile, Suzanne's reporter ex-husband, Cash, wants to see Debi and threatens to reveal what he knows about the Blackwood Project. Wr: Jon Kubichan. Dir: William Fruet.

Cash McCullough (Michael Parks); Quinn (John Colicos); Farmer/Alien (Michael Dyson); Guard (Bruce McFee); Advocate #1 (Ilse Von Glatz); Advocate #2 (Ric Sarabia); Advocate #3 (Michael Copeman); Stavrakos (Vito Rezza); Cabbie/Alien (Mohsin Sherazee); Old clerk (Handy Atmadja); Cooper (Robert Bidaman); Camera Crew #1 (Peter Van Wart); Camera Crew #2 (Andre Mayers).

So Shall Ye Reap
Aliens are having a hard time again. Drugs that try to turn humans into homicidal maniacs don't work well; subjects keep dying too fast. To find out what the aliens are up to, Harrison and the team pose as DEA agents working with the local police. Wr: Michael McCormack. Dir: George Bloomfield.

Envoy (Jill Jacobson); Lt. Teri Novak (Dixie Seatle); Det. Jack Sawyer (Jonathan Welsh); Scientist (Angelo Rizacos); Sherry (Isabelle Mejias); Other woman (Carolyn Scott); Director (Peter McNeill); Streetwalker (Shelly-Lynn Owens); Alien driver (Andrew Scorer); Advocate #1 (Ilse Von Glatz); Advocate #2 (Ric Sarabia); Advocate #3 (Frank Pelligrino); Megan (Charlene Richards); Businessman (Charles Gray); Cop #1 (Allen Kosonic); Cop #2 (Phil Jarrett); Sergeant (Reg Dreger); Bartender (Gene Mack); Nasty alien (Vince Guerriero); Man (Myron Senkus); Busboy (Benson Simmonds); Bum (Charles Hayter); Coroner (John Grima).

The Raising of Lazarus
In Wisconsin, a USAF team uncover an alien spacecraft. The Blackwood team members arrive and discover an intact alien aboard, but their efforts to examine the ship are hampered by a colonel. Wr: Durnford King. Dir: Neill Fearnley.

Dr. Frederick Alexander (Nicolas Coster); Lt. Perry (Janet Bailey); Sgt. Tex (Dale Wilson); Ray (Hugh Thompson); Lab Tech #1 (Tim Lee); Lab Tech #2 (James Rankin); Lt. Col. Manning (Thomas Hauff); Worker (John Tench); Man #1 (Hume Baugh).

The Angel of Death

Many aliens are being killed within a short time period and the team realize they have an alien assassin on Earth. The killer is a synthetic being from the planet Qar'To who captures Ironhorse and brainwashes him to believe she is a friend. Wr: Herbert Wright. Dir: Herbert Wright.

Q'Tara (Elaine Giftos); Jake (alien) (John Evans); Housewife #1 (Rachel Stephens); Housewife #2 (Denise Baillarceon); Housewife #3 (Maryanne McIssac); Stavrakos (Vito Rezza); Max (David McKnight); Advocate #1 (Ilse Von Glatz); Advocate #2 (Ric Sarabia); Advocate #3 (Frank Pellegrino); Fireman #1 (Dwight Bacquie); Fireman #2 (Peter James Haworth); Fireman #3 (Alan Fawcett); T.J. (Gerry Mendecino); Fred (Richard Blackburn); Man with glasses (Doug Hughes); Janitor (Art Nefsky); Beggar (Adrian Pellett).

Season 2: 1989-90

The Second Wave

New aliens are on Earth. Malzor and Mana are from a world that has exploded, and they want to make Earth their new home. The Eternal, the Morthren's god, arrives and orders them to get rid of Earth's inhabitants. When Harrison attempts to meet General Wilson, he's attacked by aliens but then is saved by John Kincaid, an ex-member of Ironhorse's team. Hunting for the new aliens, Ironhorse is captured and deposited into a cloning chamber. Wr: Michael Michaelian and Jonathan Glassner, story by Michael Michaelian. Dir: Francis De Lia.

Norton Drake (Philip Akin); Lt. Col. Paul Ironhorse (Richard Chaves); Female Newcomer (Sonya Delwaide); Alien guard (James Kirchner); Plato (Aaron Ross Fraser); Addict 1 (Greg Kramer); Guard (Michael Woods); Young hooker (Marion Bennett); Tough kid (Richard Zeppieri); Marine 1 (Paul Eves).

No Direction Home

In shock over losing the lives of Norton and Ironhorse, the remaining members of the Blackwood team leave the wreckage of their home. They find the new aliens' warehouse location and Harrison picks up a valuable engram that uses mental powers to reveal memories and images. Wr: Nolan Powers, story by Thomas Baum. Dir: Mark Sobel.

Father Tim (Angelo Rizacos); Ralph (Peter Blais); Lady at mission (Denise Fergusson); Ex-biker (Kevin Rushton).

Doomsday

A heatwave is raging and water has become precious because a strange alien membrane is stopping the distribution. The aliens' cloned bodies are also hav-

ing a hard time, so Ardix suggests using the water treatment plant to cool them down. Meanwhile, Ardix studies the Bible for a way to create a "miracle" so humans will look to the Eternal for salvation. Wr: Tony Di Franco. Dir: Timothy Bond.

Reverend Thomas Solter (Kurt Reis); Grace Solter (Diana Reis); Steven Solter (Nathaniel Moreau); Bayda (Patricia Phillips); Gates (Stephen Black); Jones (Donnie Bowes); Barrows (Vince Guerriero); Desperate man (Frank Blanch); Parishioner (Gerry Pearson).

Terminal Rock

The punker group Scorched Earth incites youths to "go out and destroy!" nearly killing Ardix and other aliens. And when Debi plays their music at the shelter, John and Suzanne are fed up. The Morthrens snatch the band's leader and turn the band into obedient slaves. Wr: John Groves. Dir: Gabriel Pelletier.

Rosa (Shannon Lawson); Larry (Jaimz Woolvett); Sol (Dennis Lawson) (Paul Bettis); Mr. Ripper (Lawrence King); Scavenger 1 (Dylan Real).

Breeding Ground

The aliens implant a seed into a young man at a hospital to breed a new species, but Harrison witnesses their failure on a test subject and, with John, he investigates. Wr: Alan Moskowitz. Dir: Armand Mastroianni.

Katie Barrows (Helen Hughes); Dr. Emil Gestaine (Gerard Parkes); Bayda (Patricia Phillips); Eddie (James Knapp); Mailman (John Dee); Nurse (Elizabeth Leslie); Fifth floor nurse (Sandra Caldwell).

Seft of Enum

With their power crystals low, the aliens revive Lady Seft and use her as a pawn to further their goals. When she encounters Harrison, he falls in love with her, but John is the enemy blocking her way. Wr: J.K.E. Rose. Dir: William Fruet.

Seft (Laura Press); Blade (Victoria Snow); Torri (Illya Woloshyn).

Loving the Alien

An underground agent known to Suzanne has discovered what he believes is an alien weapon. To retrieve their weapon, the aliens capture his daughter and torture her. Meanwhile, Debi runs away and falls in love with an alien boy. Wr: Janet Maclean. Dir: Otta Hanus.

Marcus Crane (Eugene Glazer); Ceeto (Keram Malicki-Sanchez); Dix (Elliott Smith); Jo Crane (Mia Kirshner); Cappy (Cal Wilson); Packrat (Louis Tucci); Mercenary (Larry McLean).

Night Moves

A nationwide food shortage forces Suzanne to bring Debi to her parents' farm away from the city. But an alien has taken over her stepfather's body. Wr: Lorne Rossman. Dir: Mark Sobel.

John Owen (Ken Pogue); Rebecca Owen (Sally Chamberlin); Paul Fox (Wayne Best); Shirley (Meg Hogarth); Roy (Dale Wilson); Scoggs (Belinda Metz); Farmer (Leonard Chow); Guard (John Thallon); Morthren Worker (Ted Ludzik).

Synthetic Love

Disguised as the head of a pharmaceutical firm, Malzor uses the legalization of drugs for his nefarious schemes. Meanwhile, John discovers his friend "Mr. Jimmy" strung out and checks him right into the clinic where Malzor is operating. Wr: Nancy Ann Miller. Dir: Francis De Lia.

Laporte (Vlasta Vrana); Mr. Jimmy (James Wilson) (Sam Malkin); Renee Laporte (Kathryn Rose); Aide (Richard Sali); Bayda (Patricia Phillips); Lunatic (Andrew) (Andrew Scorer); Nurse (Ellen Horst); Drug dealer (Dean Richards); Young woman (Gigi DeLeon); Druggist (R. D. Reid); Scientist (Elizabeth Beeler); Man in bar (Real Andrews).

The Defector

Gone awry, an alien experiment with human computers kills John's friend and stuns an alien as well. Kincaid's mystified, and he investigates. Wr: Sandra Berg and Judith Berg. Dir: Armand Mastroianni.

Kemo (Charles McCaughan); Scoggs (Belinda Metz); Ace (Charles Kerr); Lonelyheart (Alan Feiman); Roller (Paul Jolicoecur).

Time to Reap

Ordered to go back in time to prevent Earth's bacteria from destroying the invasion, Malzor prepares for a time jump. Meanwhile the team's in the eye of a hurricane they believe is a result of alien activity or another invasion. Wr: Jim Trombetta. Dir: Joseph L. Scanlan.

Miranda Watson (Paula Barrett); General Mann (George E. Robertson); Sylvia Forrester (Martha Irving); Young Harrison (Amos Crawley); Tommy (Seirge LeBlanc); Aide (Brian Furlong); Reporter #1 (Alan Argue); Reporter #2 (Lorne Pardy); Cab driver (Gerry Quigley).

The Pied Piper

An alien child born on Earth has aged rapidly. The boy comes to the attention of a professor at an experimental school, who contacts Suzanne for her help. But the aliens hope to access the genetic files at the school. Wr: Nancy Ann Miller, story by Alan Moskowitz. Dir: Allan Eastman.

Adam Warner (Joel Carson); Dr. Martin Daniels (Ron Lea); Julie (Lisa Jakub); Miss Gholston (Tanya Jacobs); Bill (Domenic Cuzzocrea); Patrick (Marc Marlt); Man (Michael Copeman); Mrs. Janet Daniels (Nadine MacKinnon).

The Deadliest Disease

When a medical cell vital to the aliens' survival is stolen from a lab, John Kincaid gets recruited to help find it. Wr: Carl Binder, story by Wilson Coneybeare. Dir: William Fruet.

Brock (James Purcell); Bing (Joon B. Kim); Abraham (Elias Zarou); Jerry Brock (Alex Karzis); Tao (Aki Aleong); Colonel West (John Evans); Wiley (Gene Mack); Chin (Deni Artyama); Vendor (Robert Lee); Thief (Matt Birman).

Path of Lies

A reporter accidentally photographs Blackwood and Kincaid destroying an alien. Meanwhile, Ardix and Malzor are pursuing access to a dying millionaire's communications satellite. Wr: Rick Schwartz and Nancy Ann Miller, story by Rick Schwartz. Dir: Allan Eastman.

Marc Traynor (David Ferry); Ed Jennings (Bernard Behrens); Mrs. Bebe Gardner (Barbara Gordon); W.R. Samuels (Maurice Evans); Rob Nunn (Martin Doyle); Maureen (Nadia Capone); Salo (Ken Quinn).

Candle in the Night

While aliens test a new surveillance device against the humans, Suzanne is concerned about Debi's upcoming birthday and her daughter's ensuing depression. Meanwhile, the alien probe malfunctions. Wr: Carl Binder. Dir: Armand Mastroianni.

Nate (Noam Zylberman); Gunther (Sandy Webster); Sam Fisher (Gema Zamprogna); Ralph (Marlow Vella); Lisa (Krista Houston); Joe (Nicolas Van Burek); Sal (Sam Moses); Grace (Jayne Eastwood); Zeel (Rob McInally); Pitcher (Pat Mastroianni); 2nd Baseman (Nigel Tan).

Video Messiah

The aliens have cloned a "video messiah" whose self-help platitudes have made him a millionaire. Using his subliminal messages, the aliens hope to incite humans to violence. But with a new alien watcher, the team discover Van Order's insidious plans. Wr: Norman Snider. Dir: Gabriel Pelletier.

Dr. Van Order (Roy Thinnes); Mindy Cooper (Lori Hallier); Clark (Alex Carter); Hardy Galt (Larry Joshua); Bob (Keith Knight); Jane (Angela Dorffman); Kurt (Michael Caruaa); Sara (Denise McLeod); Staff member (Suzanne Coy); Thief (Randy Butcher).

Totally Real

The aliens have a deadly new game, a battle arena where crowds bet on the outcome. Debi and a friend have stumbled upon the simulator, and Debi's high score targets her as the next contestant. Wr: Jim Trombetta. Dir: William Fruet.

Nikita (Colm Feore); David Nash (Trevor Cameron Smith); Scoggs (Belinda Metz); Sendac (Micheal Woods); Gambler #1 (John Tench); Gambler #2 (Elena Kudaba); Hood (Antony Audian); Stoner (Peter Szkoda).

Max

Flashbacks explore the death of Max Kincaid, John's brother, who was shot by Mana. Presently, Mana has created a cyborg in Max's image—the prototype of an indestructible army to save her people. The cyborg is ordered to find weapons and to target John as his next victim. Wr: Naomi Janzen. Dir: Jorge Montesi.

Max Kincaid (Michael Welden); Col. James Bradley (Chuck Shamata); Scoggs (Belinda Metz); Zak (Z. Gallagher) (Michael Rhodes); Scott (Jill Hennessey); Desk clerk (Marcus Parilo); MP (Barclay Hope); J. Gomez (Jorge Montesi).

The True Believer

When the team ambush aliens to get blood samples, the aliens disguise three warriors as Harrison, Suzanne and Kincaid and promptly rob a bank so that the police will find and put away the real team. Wr: Jim Henshaw. Dir: Armand Mastrioanni.

Thresher (Timothy Webber); N. Nash (Michael Hogan); Hook (Vincent Dale); Guard (Leslie Toth); Newscaster (Sandi Stahlbrand); Dutch (Jon Andersen); Alien Cop #1 (Matt Birman); St. Hunter #1 (D. McLean); St. Hunter #2 (J.J. Nakaro); St. Alien #1 (Marco Bianco); St. Alien #2 (Denis Christensen); St. Alien #3 (Ken Quinn); St. Alien #4 (T.J. Scott); St. Alien #5 (Shane Cardwell); St. Alien #6 (Ted Hanlan).

The Obelisk

With time running out to conquer Earth, Malzor accesses the Obelisk, an all-knowing device, and decides to use the Talasian spores to destroy all life on the planet except the aliens. But a test is witnessed by Ceeto, who warns Debi and the team. Wr: Rick Schwartz and Nancy Ann Miller. Dir: William Fruet.

Lord Tallick (John Gilbert); Ceeto (Keram Malicki-Sanchez); Tila (Cynthia Dale); Bayda (Patricia Phillips).

(The New, Original) Wonder Woman

April 1976–November 1976; December 1976–September 1979

From a hidden Bermuda Triangle island comes a superhuman female, Wonder Woman, who fights world evil during World War II. In her secret identity as Diana Prince, she works for Major Steve Trevor. In the second year, Diana Prince helps Steve Trevor's son battle crime in the 1970s, working for a top-secret government agency.

Cast: Diana Prince/Wonder Woman (Lynda Carter); Maj. Steve Trevor (Lyle Waggoner); Gen. Blankenship (year 1) (Richard Eastham); Etta Candy (year 1) (Beatrice Colen); *At the I.A.D.C.:* Joe Atkinson, IADC's Director (year 2) (Norman Burton); Eve, Steve's Secretary (years 2–3) (Saundra Sharp); Voice of I.R.A.C. (years 2–3) (Tom Kratochzil).

Wonder Woman created by: Charles Moulton; *Developed for television by:* Stanley Ralph Ross; *Executive Producers:* Douglas S. Cramer (years 1–3), Wilfred Baumes (year 2); *Producer:* Wilfred Baumes (year 1), Mark Rodgers (year 2); *Supervising Producer:* Charles B. Fitzsimons (year 2); *Theme Music:* Charles Fox, Norman Gimbel; CBS/Warner Bros.; 60 minutes.

First appearing in comics in 1941, Wonder Woman was the creation of a psychologist, Dr. William Moulton Marston. Using the pen name Charles Moulton, Dr. Marston attempted to create a female superhero character as popular as Superman.

Endowed with superhuman strength, Diana Prince comes from the hidden Paradise Island in the Bermuda Triangle, inhabited completely by powerful women with a remarkable history: Centuries ago, when the war god Ares and the love goddess Aphrodite quarreled about whether strength or love should rule, Ares sent soldiers to enslave women. In reply, Aphrodite created from clay a race of warrior women—the Amazons. Their powers were derived from a magic girdle worn by the queen Hippolyte. But when mighty Hercules stole the girdle, the Amazons were all caught and held prisoners. After Aphrodite rescued them, she gave them a home at Paradise Island, where no man is allowed.

As the *Wonder Woman* legend goes, when Major Steve Trevor, during World War II, crash-landed on Paradise Island, the queen decreed that a champion had to go into the world of men to fight evil. After a long and arduous competition (well documented in the pilot for the series) Diana Prince, the queen's own daughter, won the games and was appointed Wonder Woman. To aid her in the world of men, Diana was given an invisible plane, a magic golden lasso that would compel captives to tell the truth, and the famous bracelets that bounced bullets away from her.

The story of Wonder Woman's graduation to television goes back to the late 1960s when Stanley Ralph Ross, a screenwriter, was working on the *Batman* TV series. Says Ross, "William Dozier, executive producer of *Batman*, came to me and said he had acquired the rights to *Wonder Woman*. I was a comics expert and agreed to give it a try. He said he was going to do it as a half-hour comedy."

A script by *MAD* magazine staffers Stan Hart and Larry Siegel was not working out, so Ross pitched in and gave it a try.

"I made it over the top," he says. "I made it more campy than what the other guys did. We shot a seven- or eight-minute example. It was like

Lynda Carter ready for action as the superhuman *Wonder Woman.* Copyright 1977, CBS/Warner Bros.

turning down the job?' I said, 'Yes.'"

John D.F. Black got the screenwriting job, and in 1974, audiences witnessed the TV movie with Crosby, co-starring Ricardo Montalban as the villain Abner.

This *Wonder Woman* bore very little resemblance to her comics progenitor. The film was a modern-day, straight action-adventure treatment that strictly avoided the campiness of the comics. Cathy Lee Crosby wore, instead of a one-piece star-spangled suit, a polyester track suit intended to update the character's image for the modern world.

"The show got treacherous reviews but pretty good ratings. Which indicated to them that the idea was a good one," recalls Ross. "Then, they came back to me again and said, 'Ok, how would you do it?'"

Sending ABC the meticulous notes he had been keeping for years, Ross finally landed for himself a role in bringing Wonder Woman to life, not from clay, but from celluloid film.

"They liked what they saw, and I wrote it based in the 1940s," says Ross. "I based it partly on the Morton bomb site—a real place, by the way. If you see the pilot, there's a Morton bomb site. So I used a lot of truth in the story. And I really saw it as a comedy. Now, Leonard Horn was signed to direct. Doug Cramer came to me and said, 'Stanley, this is too funny! You have to punch it *down*!'

"The normal expression is 'punch it *up*' when you talk about adding jokes. He wants me to punch it *down* because it's too funny. 'No, I don't think so.' 'Yes it is! If you don't take it down, Stanley, I'll get someone else and you'll wind up with half a credit.'"

a presentation, directed by Leslie Martinson. It was then presented to the guy at Fox, Douglas Cramer."

But Cramer did not like what he saw. Ross describes what followed: "Dissolve. Years go by. Doug Cramer is now on his own. He calls me up and says, 'I'm thinking of doing *Wonder Woman.* I know you were there the first time. I know I didn't want to do it, but what you did was good. How would you like to do this?' I said, 'Tell me what you've got set already.' He said, 'We got Cathy Lee Crosby set,' and I said, 'Cathy Lee Crosby is wrong! Wonder Woman has dark hair!' He said, 'What are you talking about?' I said, 'Cathy is a nice lady. I've played tennis with her. But she's wrong for the part.' Doug answered, 'No, no, no! We're going to do it with Cathy.' 'It's wrong! I'm not going to do it!' He said, 'You're

Mumbling under his breath, "If this turns out to be a series, I don't want to do this," Ross went back to the typewriter, "and made it a lot duller than my original. Leonard Horn, the director, took a copy of the original—which is why he was excited about taking the job—and made copies of it, and he gave it to the actors. He said, 'This is what I'd like to do.' Then he gave them the final script, and said, 'This is what I have to do.'"

According to Ross, he wanted *Wonder Woman* to be funny because "I wanted it to have ample humor. Joy. I was a *Batman* writer. I like to write fun! I don't like to write a dull, serious show. I mean, that's why *Batman* was so successful. And shows like *Columbo with* humor don't work."

Eventually, Lynda Carter won the part of Wonder Woman, but other casting decisions were made at an earlier stage: in the writing. For instance, while walking through the CBS parking lot one day, Ross bumped into Lyle Waggoner. "Lyle is trying to get close to me. 'Stanley, ever since I've done *Carol Burnett*, nothing's happened! Do you know anything I can do?' I said, 'Let me see if I can come up with anything.'"

Back to the typewriter. Taking a sheet of paper, Ross tapped the following passage into the script: "'Steve Trevor, a Lyle Waggoner type—better yet, get Lyle Waggoner.'" No actor could ask for a better recommendation.

"I wrote it for Lyle," reveals Ross. "Specifically, for Lyle. And in the pilot, I wrote the Nazi guy specifically for Kenny Mars. He does Nazis the best. He did it in *The Producers* and in *Young Frankenstein*. And I wrote his assistant for Henry Gibson, a friend of mine. I like him, and I like to write for them. I wrote for people I know."

Asked about Ross's story, Lyle Waggoner says simply, "I've known Stanley for a long time. I don't know this parking lot story, but that may have been the case. Yes, he did write the part for me in mind."

Waggoner agrees that making the show less funny was not a good idea. Indeed, Waggoner professes to enjoying the first season of the show much more than the subsequent two seasons, when it moved over to CBS in a straight action-adventure format that distanced itself from the camp roots installed by Ross. Should producers have kept the approach more cartoon-like? "No question about it," says Waggoner. "Absolutely. That was the way they did *Batman*, and *Batman* was funny and entertaining. Doing a dramatic show out of a cartoon character—that's ridiculous. I much preferred to stay in the 1940s period, during World War II, so we [could] have some fun with it."

Waggoner feels Maj. Steve Trevor had the same relationship with Wonder Woman that Lois Lane had with Superman, albeit with the roles reversed. He says that he didn't really have any problems with the fact that the characters were fairly one-dimensional. *Wonder Woman* was a comic book, and he liked the show best when there were no pretensions to anything serious.

Waggoner says it was "fun going to work on the studio lot, to have a regular job on a national series." He also enjoyed the exposure it gave him to an important segment of the viewing public: children.

"In my experience on *The Carol Burnett Show*, we were playing to an older group. And now, I was being introduced to the kids! They would recognize me for many years to come, and that was fun. But it was even more interesting to be able to entertain kids but at the same time do double entendre so that adults would appreciate the humor."

Waggoner says he found that adults appreciated mostly the first-season segments. "We'd do tongue-in-cheek jokes and the kids wouldn't even get them, you know? [But we lost that] when we went to the modern format."

One of many directors for the first season of the show was actor and director Stuart Margolin.

"I remember directing a segment in particular ["Last of the Two Dollar Bills"]—a counterfeiting plot," he reminisces. "I remember it fondly because I think it turned out very well. We shot a lot of film at the beach and at the backlot of Warner Bros., and I thought some scenes worked very well. It was my first experience working with Lynda. She was pretty new to the business at the time and, oh, she was perfect for the role. I think she was in a rock-and-roll band prior to doing the show. She was very eager to work, obviously stunningly beautiful. I recall walking onto the lot on the street and seeing a woman coming toward me. And I thought, 'This woman is stunning!' and I didn't recognize her because she didn't have her Wonder Woman hairstyle or clothes on. I think probably a part like that, with somebody who is not well trained, is a difficult career move—difficult to move away from that. She was certainly a good Wonder Woman, and I think she probably could have done a lot more things, and maybe she will. But

I don't know, at that point in her career, if she had the 'chops' to tackle other things."

For a second segment, "Bushwackers," Margolin got to work with legendary star and cowboy, Roy Rogers. "Having watched him in my childhood, walking up to Roy Rogers and saying 'Roy, I want you to ride that way' was thrilling.

"If I recall correctly, Roy Rogers made a pass at Wonder Woman, albeit a very nice one. Nothing salacious—just a very charming, kind of flirtatious comment, which I thought, considering his age, was fabulous. I don't blame him at all. I don't think *I* had the courage to make a pass at Lynda Carter."

Stephen Kandel, a screenwriter on *Wonder Woman*, recalls his work on the show as a fun stint. "I've always enjoyed science fiction and fantasy as a genre," says Kandel, who has worked on a number of other science fiction shows, such as *Star Trek*. "One two-parter I wrote ["Mind Stealers from Outer Space"] involved an extraterrestrial court passing a sober judgment on our species, deciding whether humanity deserved to exist. True, the balance was tipped in our favor by *Wonder Woman* herself, but I was able to pose the question quite seriously."

Kandel says that the reason for the format change from a campy, spoof approach to a straighter, action-adventure style, was "to make it more relevant to an audience which didn't remember World War II. It also opened the format up a little, making a wider range of stories possible."

Calvin Clements, Jr., the screenwriter of "The Bermuda Triangle Crisis," remembers that "it was great fun—you can't take it seriously. You take it tongue-in-cheek. My children ... were proud as they could be. They went around telling their friends that their dad had been chosen to do a *Wonder Woman*. And they loved the episode, and so did I."

Like Clements, Margaret Armen, who wrote the first series episode ("Wonder Woman Meets Baroness Von Gunther") enjoyed making her contributions to the show. "I was doing a quick last-minute rewrite [on "Baroness Von Gunther"] and they were casting the episode," she recalls. "The only office they could put me in was the associate producer's, and they were also reading the actors in that office. So, I was at the typewriter, writing, and these actors would be coming in, reading for the role of one of the heavies, one of the Nazi criminals, and they were just going for broke and I'd stop the typewriter when-

ever they started reading. It was all cold readings, and about five came in, and the director [Barry Crane] didn't like any of them. The sixth guy came in and just threw himself into the role, and the director had his back to me, watching. And I was motioning, to the story editor, over the director's head as though I had a hammer and was hammering him on the head because I wanted to finish typing my two scenes. Suddenly, the director turned around and I was stuck with my fist raised in the air. Fortunately, the sixth guy got the role and I could finish my scenes. [Crane] was a perfectionist."

Armen has a varied and productive background as a writer. She served three terms on the board of directors for the Writers Guild; she was a member of the board of governors with the Television Academy; and she has written westerns, TV movies and, of course, science fiction and fantasy shows.

For Armen, *Wonder Woman* "was a cute show. It didn't take long to write the scripts. You mainly tried to come up with as interesting antics for Wonder Woman as you could. For what it was, the show was well done. I never felt that it would be lasting, but it was a refreshing departure from the steady diet of murder and cop shows. The emphasis was on action rather than broad comedy, and certain 'sexy' scenes (played for comedy value) were toned down at the request of the producer. One scene had pursuing heavies frozen with admiration when they glimpsed Wonder Woman minus usual attire and wearing only a satin sheet. No real porno stuff, of course, but she did have a great body.

"I wish we had some more such escape shows on the air now. I'm really tired of 'reality shows' which are doctored up for dramatic purposes."

Summing up the show, Clements says, "It appealed to younger people. Some TV shows take themselves very seriously. *Star Trek: The Next Generation* takes itself very seriously, and the people who watch it are very serious about it. They follow the characters, and care about these people and get all worked up over it. But *Wonder Woman*, nobody gets serious about. They just enjoy it."

CAST NOTES

Lynda Carter (Diana Prince/Wonder Woman): Born 1951. Carter was a Miss World USA Beauty

Pageant winner in 1973. After the series, she went to Las Vegas with a successful musical nightclub act as well as a CBS musical special. She's starred in several TV films and the series *Partners in Crime* (1984) with Loni Anderson.

Lyle Waggoner (Maj. Steve Trevor): Born 1935. Lyle was one of the cast of the variety series *The Carol Burnett Show* (1967–74). Today, Lyle owns and operates Star Waggons, a rental business specializing in motor homes for the film industry.

Richard Eastham (Gen. Blankenship): Born 1918 in Louisiana. Eastham later had a recurring role in *Falcon Crest* (1982–83).

EPISODE GUIDE

The New, Original Wonder Woman (1975. TV movie, 90 minutes)
During World War II, Major Steve Trevor crashlands on the hidden Paradise Island in the Bermuda Triangle. The queen declares a tournament to choose the strongest and nimblest of the Amazons to go into the world of men and fight evil—against the Nazis. The queen's own daughter, Diana, wins the games and becomes Wonder Woman. Wr: Stanley Ralph Ross. Dir: Leonard Horn.
     Blankenship (John Randolph); Norman (Red Buttons); Marcia (Stella Stevens); Kapitan Drangel (Eric Braeden); Bad guy (Severn Darden); Doctor (Fannie Flagg); Nikolas (Henry Gibson); Col. von Blasko (Kenneth Mars); Queen Mother (Cloris Leachman); Nurse (Helen Verbit); Cop #2 (Tom Rosqui); Sales lady (Fritzi Burr); Rena (Inga Neilson); Teutonic woman (Maida Severn); 2nd Amazon (Jean Karlson); Taxi driver (Anne Ramsey).

Season 1: 1976-77

Wonder Woman Meets Baroness Von Gunther
Wonder Woman meets up with the evil female Nazi Baroness Von Gunther, who heads a spy ring endangering the United States. Wr: Margaret Armen. Dir: Barry Crane.
     Baroness Paula Von Gunther (Christine Belford); Warden (Edmund Gilbert); Hanson (Ed Griffith); Tommy (Christian Juttner); Arthur Deal III/Thor (Bradford Dillman); Guard #1 (Jude Farese); Guard #2 (Cletus Young); Woman (Ruth Warshawsky); Police sergeant (John Brandon).

Fausta: The Nazi Wonder Woman
The Nazis recruit their own superwoman, Fausta, an ex–German Olympic champion. Her mission: Go to America and capture Wonder Woman and bring her back to Germany. Wr: Bruce Shelly and David Ketchum. Dir: Barry Crane.

Kesselmann (Bo Brundin); Fausta (Lynda Day George); Rojack (Christopher George); Peasant girl (Mary Rings); Soldier #1 (Gene Biegouloff); Soldier #2 (Kenneth Smedburg); Cabbie (Angelo Gnazzo); M.C. (Larry Ellis); Radio man (Ron Lombard); Also with Colby Chester, Jeff Cooper, Keene Curtis, Bill Fletcher.

Beauty on Parade
German saboteurs use a traveling beauty contest as a cover for their nefarious schemes. Wr: Ron Friedman. Dir: Richard Kinom.
     Lola Flynn (Anne Francis); Jack Wood (Dick Van Patten); Col. Flint (William Lanteau); Monty Burns (Bobby Van); Susan (Jennifer Shaw); Tina (Lindsay Bloom); Rita (Christa Helm); Mitzie (Paulette Breen); Betsy (Linda Carpenter); June (Eddie Benton); Betty Lou (April Tatro); Rosalie (Derna Wylde); Captain (Wayne Grace); Stagehand (Henry Deas); Sentry (Bill Adler); Lieutenant (John David Yarbrough).

The Feminum Mystique, Part 1
A Nazi scientist, Captain Radl, becomes interested in the secret of Wonder Woman's strange metal bracelets, which are impervious to bullets. He decides to capture her and learn their secret but instead mistakenly captures her sister Drusilla (Wonder Girl). Wr: Jimmy Sangster, story by Barbara Avedon and Barbara Corday. Dir: Herb Wallerstein.
     Captain Radl (John Saxon); Queen (Carolyn Jones); Peter Knight (Charles Frank); Wertz (Paul Shenar); Hemmschler (Kurt Kreuger); Drusilla/Wonder Girl (Debra Winger); Gen. Ulrich (Curt Lowens); Dalma (Erica Hagen); Magda (Pamela Susan Shoop); Harris (Kurt Grayson); Tommy (Jay Fenichel); Joey (Brad Rearden).

The Feminum Mystique, Part 2
Once the Nazis have subdued the Amazons on Paradise Island, it takes the combined efforts of Wonder Woman and Wonder Girl to rid the island of them as well as to stop their final attempt to steal the experimental plane, the XPJ-1. Wr: Jimmy Sangster, story by Barbara Avedon and Barbara Corday. Dir: Herb Wallerstein.
     Radl (John Saxon); Queen Mother (Carolyn Jones); Peter Knight (Charles Frank); Wertz (Paul Shenar); Drusilla/Wonder Girl (Debra Winger); Dalma (Erica Hagen); Magda (Pamela Susan Shoop); Lt. Weil (Rayford Barnes); Harris (Kurt Grayson); Tommy (Jay Fenichel); Destroyer commander (Newell Alexander).

Wonder Woman vs. Gargantua
To defeat Wonder Woman, the Nazis unleash a trained and powerful gorilla. Wr: David Ketchum and Tony DiMarco. Dir: Charles R. Rondeau.
     Hans Eichler (Robert Loggia); Erica Belgard (Gretchen Corbett); Conrad Steigler (John Hillerman); Carl Mueller (Tom Reese); Dr. Osmond (Herb Voland); Circus guard (Jerry Fitzpatrick); Sergeant Henderson (Jim Driskill); Corporal Rogers (Curtis Credel); Soldier (John Zenda); Gargantua (Mickey Morton).

The Pluto File
When a scientist's revolutionary paper on the

formation of earthquakes is stolen, the Irish mercenary thief is unaware that he is carrying the bubonic plague. Wr: Herbert Bermann. Dir: Herb Wallerstein.

Sean Fallon (Robert Reed); Prof. Warren (Hayden Roarke); Charles Benson (Albert Stratton); Frank Willis (Michael Twain); Dr. Barnes (Kenneth Tigar); James Porter (Jason Johnson); Dr. Norris (Peter Brandon); Bobby (Sean Kelly); Sergeant Evans (Gary Oakes); Camilla Moret (Mikki Jamison-Olsen); Customs agent (Brigid O'Brien).

Last of the Two Dollar Bills

Nazis threaten the U.S. economy with fake $2 bills. Wr: Paul Dubov and Gwen Bagni. Dir: Stuart Margolin.

Wotan (James Olson); Maggie (Barbara Anderson); Hank (David Cryer); Doctor (John Howard); Frank Wilson (Richard O'Brien); Dan Fletcher (Dean Harens); Jason (Victor Argo); Dentist (Don Eitner); S.S. colonel (Michael Dan Wagner); Customer (Naomi Grumette).

Judgment from Outer Space, Part 1

Andros is sent from the Council of Planets to Earth to pass judgment because earth people are "war-like savages who are beginning to develop atomic power." Andros' mission is to determine if this is true and, if so, to destroy the planet to protect the rest of the galaxy from us. Wr: Stephen Kandel. Dir: Alan Crosland.

Andros (Tim O'Connor); Von Dreiberg (Kurt Kasznar); Sakri (Janet MacLachlan); Paul Bjornsen (Scott Hylands); Gen. Kane (Archie Johnson); Gorel (Vic Perrin); Gormsby (Patrick Skelton); Sergeant (Fil Formicola).

Judgment from Outer Space, Part 2

With Earth hanging in the balance, Wonder Woman has to rescue Andros, who has been kidnapped by the Nazis. Wr: Stephen Kandel. Dir: Alan Crosland.

Andros (Tim O'Connor); Von Dreiberg (Kurt Kasznar); Sakri (Janet MacLachlan); Mallory (Christopher Cary); Paul Bjornsen (Scott Hylands); Gorel (Vic Perrin); Graebner (Hank Brandt); Lisa Engel (Christine Schmidtmer); Gen. Clewes (George Cooper); Nazi Grau (Erik Holland); Berghoff (Ted Roter).

Formula 407

Undercover, Steve Trevor and Diana trail enemy agents to Buenos Aires, where a scientist has perfected a formula for turning rubber into the strength of steel. It's up to them to get to the professor before the Nazis. Wr: Elroy Schwartz. Dir: Herb Wallerstein.

Prof. Moreno (Nehemiah Persoff); Maria (Marisa Pavan); Major Keller (John Devlin); Schmidt (Peter MacLean); McCauley (Charles Macaulay); Lydia Moreno (Maria Grimm); Antonio Cruz (Armando Silvestre); S.S. general (Curt Lowens); Otto Dietrich (Gary Cashdollar).

The Bushwackers

When a man begins selling beef on the black market for huge profits, Steve investigates, and Wonder Woman tags along to make sure he doesn't get into trouble. Wr: Skip Webster. Dir: Stuart Margolin.

Mr. Hadley (Roy Rogers); Walter Lampkin (Henry Darrow); Jeff Hadley (Lance Kerwin); Emmett Dawson (Tony George); Sheriff Bodie (David Clarke); Linc (Christoff St. John); Babette (Christelle Pierrette Gaspart); Freddie (Justin Randi); Charlie (David Yanez); Sen (Carey Wong); Maria (Rita Gomez); The man (Murray Macleod).

Wonder Woman in Hollywood

When war heroes arrive in Hollywood to film movies about their exploits, the Nazis kidnap them. Wr: Jimmy Sangster. Dir: Bruce Bilson.

Mark Bremer (Harris Yulin); Jim Ames (Robert Hays); Gloria Beverly (Christopher Norris); Kurt (Charles Cyphers);. Director (Alan Bergmann); Queen (Carolyn Jones); Drusilla/Wonder Girl (Debra Winger); Lt. Bill Rand (Ross Bickell); Sergeant Harry Willard (David Himes); Freddy (Barry Van Dyke); George (Danil Torpe); Roger (Eric Boles); Destroyer captain (Alex Rodine); Receptionist (June Whitley Taylor); Guard (Carmen Filpi).

Season 2: 1977-78

The Return of Wonder Woman

When Steve Trevor, Jr., crash-lands on Paradise Island 32 years after the events of World War II, the ageless Diana decides to return to the world of men. In the opener, disguised as Trevor's secretary, Diana helps Steve defeat an international terrorist. Wr: Stephen Kandel. Dir: Alan Crosland.

Dr. Solano (Fritz Weaver); Asclepia (Bettye Ackerman); Gloria (Jessica Walter); Queen (Beatrice Straight); Maj. Gaines (David Knapp); Colonel Acevo (Carlos Romero); Evadne (Dorrie Thomson); Manageress (Argentina Brunetti); Pilot (Edward Cross); Dr. Ross (Johana Dewinter); Samuels (George Ives); Logan (Frank Killmond); Kleist (Russ Marin); Kalten (William Tregoe); Dr. Andrea (Raye Sheffield).

Anschluss '77

Nazis in South America clone Adolph Hitler and recreate the Third Reich. Wr: Dallas L. Barnes. Dir: Alan Crosland.

Fritz Gerlich (Mel Ferrer); Von Klemper (Leon Charles); Cloned Hitler (Barry Dennen); Koenig (Kurt Kreuger); Gaitan (Julio Medina); Rogel (Tom Ormeny); Strasser (Peter Nyberg).

The Man Who Could Move the World

A Japanese soldier with telekinetic powers seeks revenge against Wonder Woman for crimes during World War II. Wr: Judy Burns. Dir: Bob Kelljan.

Takeo Ishida (Yuki Shimoda); Dr. Wilson (Lew Ayres); Oshima (James Hong); Security guard (Alan McRae); Taft (J. Kenneth Campbell); Ishida, as a boy (Steven Ken Suehiro); Masaaki, as a boy (Peter Kwong); Masaaki (Arthur Song).

The Bermuda Triangle Crisis

Steve and Diana investigate the disappearance of an intelligence plane in the vicinity of the Bermuda Triangle. Wr: Calvin Clements, Jr. Dir: Seymour Robbie.

Raymond Manta (Charles Cioffi); The queen (Beatrice Straight); Sergeant (Herman Poppe); Radar man (Barry Hamilton); Lt.-Cmdr. Mansfield (Larry Golden); Driver/Guard (George Ranito Jordan); Guard #1 (James Staley); Radio man (Joseph Chapman).

Knockout

When Steve Trevor disappears in Los Angeles, Diana investigates. Wr: Mark Rodgers. Dir: Seymour Robbie.

Carolyn (Jayne Kennedy); Tom Baker (Burr DeBenning); John Kelly (Arch Johnson); Tall man (Frank Marth); Pete (Ted Shackelford); Officer Fernandez (Abraham Alvarez); Angel Valasquez (Alex Colon); Lane Curran (Frank Parker); Ted (K.C. Martel).

The Pied Piper

A rock musician employs alluring music to mesmerize his followers and use them for stealing. His powers may be too strong even for Wonder Woman. Wr: David Ketchum, Tony DiMarco and Brian McKay, story by David Ketchum and Tony DiMarco. Dir: Alan Crosland.

Hamlin Rule (Martin Mull); Carl Schwartz (Denny Miller); Elena Atkinson (Eve Plumb); Gatekeeper (Bob Hastings); Manager Amos Hoffman (George Cooper); Lieutenant McMasters (Melvin F. Allen).

The Queen and the Thief

To catch an international thief, Steve poses as the leader of a foreign country and Diana as a maid. Wr: Bruce Shelly. Dir: Jack Arnold.

Queen Kathryn (Juliet Mills); Evan Robley (David Hedison); Ambassador Orrick (John Colicos).

I Do, I Do

Using an Arizona spa, spies pull secrets from the wives of U.S. government officials. Wr: Richard Carr. Dir: Herb Wallerstein.

Dolly Tucker (Celeste Holm); Sam Tucker (Simon Scott); Christian Harrison (John Getz); David Allen (Henry Darrow); Justice Brown (Kent Smith); Denny Lake (Brian Avery); Smitty (Thomas W. Babson); Johnny (Steve Eastin); Desk clerk (Scott Mulhern).

The Man Who Made Volcanoes

A mad scientist invents a powerful laser that he uses to explode volcanoes and other targets, holding the world hostage. Wonder Woman steps in to defeat his plans. Wr: Brian McKay and Dan Ullman, story by Wilton Denmark. Dir: Alan Crosland.

Jack Corbin (Roger Davis); Mei Ling (Irene Tsu); Lin Wan (Richard Narita); Professor John Chapman (Roddy McDowall); Kalanin (Milt Kogan); Tobirov (Ray Young); Col. Minh (Philip Ahn); Dave Pruett (James R. Parkes); Technician (Grant Owens).

Mind Stealers from Outer Space, Part 1

Diana reteams with the alien Andros to fight against the evil Skrill, who are stealing the minds of the world's most brilliant scientists. Wr: Stephen Kandel. Dir: Michael Caffey.

Andros (Dack Rambo); Debbie (Kristin Larkin); Johnny (Vincent Van Patten); Chaka (Earl Boen); General Miller (Barry Cahill); Dr. George Hess (Del Hinkley); Sell (Barbara O. Jones); Dr. Rand (Allan Migicovsky); Connie (Anne Ramsey); Dr. Ruth Blaine (Linda Ryan); Capt. Parelli (Sol Weiner); Rossman (Gary Bisig); Cleaning lady (Betty Cole); Karen (Lana Marie Hendricks); Kim (Lori Ann Hendricks).

Mind Stealers from Outer Space, Part 2

After Andros' mind is stolen by the Skrill, Wonder Woman must find their location to save him as well as save the Earth from being decontaminated. Wr: Stephen Kandel. Dir: Alan Crosland.

Andros (Dack Rambo); Carla Burgess (Pamela Mason); Johnny (Vincent Van Patten); Chaka (Earl Boen); Sell (Barbara O. Jones); Dr. Rand (Allan Migicovsky); Nordling (Curt Lowens); Prof. Eidleman (Rege Cordic); Karen (Lana Marie Hendricks); Kim (Lori Ann Hendricks); Security guard (Walt Davis); Woman delegate (Phyllis Flax); Senator Wainright (Eric Mason); Zambezia delegate (Dee Dee Young); Debbie (Kristin Larkin).

The Deadly Toys

A villainous toymaker uses androids to steal government secrets. Wr: Anne Collins, story by Carey Wilber. Dir: Dick Moder.

Dr. Orlich Hoffman (Frank Gorshin); Dr. Prescott (James A. Watson Jr.); Maj. John Dexter (John Rubinstein); Dr. Tobias (Donald Bishop); Dr. Lazar (Ross Elliott); Guard #2 (Michael W. Kinney); Intruder (Mike Kulik); Doctor (Randy Phillips); Guard (Harve Selsby).

Light-Fingered Lady

Diana infiltrates a gang of criminal masterminds to catch master thief Anton Caribe in the act of the crime. Wr: Bruce Shelly. Dir: Alan Crosland.

Tony Ryan (Christopher Stone); Leech (Joseph R. Sicari); Paul Rojak (Bubba Smith); Grease (Gary Crosby); Michael Sutton (Titos Vandis); Anton Caribe (Greg Morris); Desk sergeant (Stack Pierce); Adler (Larry Ward); Marge Douglas (Judyann Elder); Ross (Ric DiAngelo); Guard (Thomas Hilliard).

Screaming Javelin

A deranged "dictator" kidnaps world-famous athletes to win the favor of the Olympic Games for his imaginary country. Wr: Brian McKay. Dir: Michael Caffey.

Marion Mariposa (Henry Gibson); Bo Taggart (Robert Sampson); Nadia Samara (Melanie Chartoff); Tom Hamilton (Rick Springfield); Lois Taggart (E.J. Peaker); Eric (Vaughn Armstrong); Bill (Roger Callard); The twins (The Kearney Twins); Runner (Sam Freed); Pole vaulter (Dennis M. Madalone).

Diana's Disappearing Act

Count Cagliostro, an evil alchemist, plans to drive up the international price of oil by selling large amounts of gold that will become lead after three days. Wr: S.S. Schweitzer. Dir: Michael Caffey.

Count Cagliostro (Dick Gautier); Harold Farnum (Ed Begley Jr); Jazreel (J.A. Preston); Dr. Hutchins (Allen Williams); Emir of Quiana (Aharon Ipale); Morgana La Fay (Brenda Benet); Shopkeeper (George Skaff); Ambassador (Maurice Sherbanee); Magician #1 (James Mark Wilson); Magician #2 (Don W. Brockhaus); Mime #1 (Peter DePaula); Mime #2 (Kathlyn).

Death in Disguise

Diana's life is in jeopardy when she serves as a bodyguard to a millionaire. Wr: Tom Sawyer. Dir: Alan Crosland.

Woodward Nightingale (Joel Fabiani); Violet Louise Tree (Jennifer Darling); Marius (Lee Bergere); Starker (Charles Pierce); Carlo Indrezzano (George Chakiris); Krug (Arthur Batanides); Beamer (Christopher Cary); Major Finley (Carol Worthington); Corporal (Katherine Charles); Plotkin (Jack Kissell); Maitre d' (Maurice Marsac).

IRAC Is Missing

A computer genius uses the memories and programs of the world's largest computers in his bid to take over the world. Wr: Anne Collins. Dir: Alex Singer.

Bernard Havitol (Ross Martin); Dirk (Lee Paul); Dick (W.T. Zacha); Cori (Tina Lenert); Guard (Lloyd McLinn); Technician (Mathias Reitz); Sgt. Dobson (Jim Veres); Official (Cletus Young); Director (Colin Hamilton).

Flight to Oblivion

A villain focuses his hypnotic powers in a campaign against the U.S. Air Force. Wr: Patrick Mathews. Dir: Alan Crosland.

Lt. Stonehouse (Michael Shannon); Capt. Ann Colby (Corinne Michaels); Maj. Alan Cornell (Alan Fudge); Mitch (Mitch Vogel); Edmund Dante (John Van Dreelan); Lieutenant (Walt Davis).

Seance of Terror

High-ranking officials are being influenced by a child psychic. Wr: Bruce Shelly. Dir: Dick Moder.

Koslo (Rick Jason); Theodora (Kres Mersky); Matthew (Todd Lookinland); Yamura (John Fujioka); Ms. Kell (Hanna Hertelendy); Bakru (Adam Ageli); Eric (John Birk); Mrs. Bakru (Christine Avila); Dekker (Jean-Ivan Durin); Yamura Sr. (Tad Horino).

The Man Who Wouldn't Tell

A janitor finds himself in danger when he discovers the ingredients of a secret explosive. Wr: Anne Collins. Dir: Alan Crosland.

Meg (Jane Actman); Rudolph Furst (Philip M. Thomas); Ted (Michael Cole); B.W. (Millie Slaven); Alan Akroy (Gary Burghoff); Tom (Tony Brubacker).

The Girl from Ilandia

A young girl from another dimension is kidnapped by criminals. She was given special jewelry that gives her super-strength equal to Wonder Woman's. Wr: Anne Collins. Dir: Dick Moder.

Simon Penrose (Harry Guardino); Tina (Julie Ann Haddock); Bleaker (Allan Arbus); Doctor (Buck Young); Nurse (Pamela Toll); Davis (Fred Lerner); Thompson (Chuck Hicks); First mate (Mike Kopcha); Bully (Todd Hoffman).

The Murderous Missile

Diana is trapped in a ghost town while traveling to a missile test site. Wr: Dick Nelson. Dir: Dick Moder.

George (James Luisi); Luther (Mark Withers); Sheriff Beal (Warren Stevens); Mac (Steve Inwood); Flo (Lucille Benson); Hal Shaver (Hal England); Ernie (Sam Edwards); Lieutenant (Alan McRae); Corporal (Maurice Sneed); William Ryan (Neil Elliot).

Season 3: 1978-79

My Teenage Idol Is Missing

A teenage celebrity is kidnapped and replaced with a look-alike, and it's up to Wonder Woman to save him. Wr: Anne Collins. Dir: Seymour Robbie.

Ashton Ripley (Michael Lerner); Morley (Michael Baseleon); Whitney Springfield (Dawn Lyn); Raleigh Crichton (Albert Paulsen); Lane/Mike (Leif Garrett); Bodyguard (Herman Poppe); Cabbie (Lanny Duncan); Benjamin Springfield (Robert Patten); Sampson (Tony Brubacker); Ludwig (David Ellis); Girl #1 (Abbie Wolfsen); Girl #2 (Suzanne Crough); Girl #3 (Michele Laurita).

Hot Wheels

Diana Prince must track down a Rolls Royce that contains a top-secret microfilm. Wr: Dennis Landa. Dir: Dick Moder.

Tim Bolt (Peter Brown); Otis Fiskle (Lance LeGault); Alfie (John Durren); Dr. Samson (Don Mitchell); Shadow (Fuddle Bagley); Slim (Marc Ross); Foreman (John Lawrence); Van driver (Frank Doubleday).

The Deadly Sting

When Wonder Woman discovers that football players are being subconsciously manipulated to throw important games, she makes sure that the odds are balanced. Wr: Dick Nelson. Dir: Alan Crosland.

Bill Michaels (Ron Ely); Angie Cappucci (Scott Marlowe); Louis the Lithuanian (Danny Dayton); Beamer (Marvin Miller); Prof. Brubaker (Harvey Jason); Football player (Roman Gabriel); Football player (Deacon Jones); Football player (Lawrence McCutcheon); Football player (Eddie Allen Bell); Broadcaster (Gil Stratton); Nick (Bob Minor); Sam (Craig T. Nelson); Bart (Frank Downing); Gilda (Bobbie Bartosh); Phyllis (Luise Heath).

The Fine Art of Crime

Danger awaits Wonder Woman as she attempts to break up a gang of art thieves. Wr: Anne Collins. Dir: Dick Moder.

Harold Farnum (Ed Begley, Jr.); Joe (Joe E. Tata); Moreaux (Michael McGuire); Henry Roberts (Roddy McDowall); Mrs. Ellsworth (Patti MacLeod); Mr. Ellsworth (Gavin MacLeod); Shubert (Joe Maross); Heavy #1 (George Caldwell); Berkeley student (Mitchel Young-Evans).

Disco Devil

Government engineers are lured to a disco where national secrets are snatched from their brains. Wr: Alan Brennert. Dir: Leslie H. Martinson.

Del Franklin (Paul Sand); Angelique (Ellen Weston); Kathy Munro (Kerry Sherman); Lance (Victor Mohica); Norman (Bob Hoy); Nick Moreno (Michael DeLano); Colonel (Russell Johnson); Infra Red (Wolfman Jack); Andrew Borden (Robert Dunlap); Foreman (Frank McRae); Kerwin (Dennis J. Stewart); Female dancer (Linda Fernandez); Receptionist (Betty Bridges).

Formicida

A scientist develops the proportional strength of an ant and, with her newfound powers, leads thousands of ants against the manufacture of deadly pesticides. Wr: Katharyn Michaelian Powers. Dir: Alan Crosland.

Harcourt (Robert Alda); Doug (Robert Shields); Dr. Irene Janus/Formicida (Lorene Yarnell); Cawley (Stan Haze); Chemist (Ben Young); Receptionist (Carol Carrington); Watchman (Jim Nolan); Foreman (Frank Farmer); Male secretary (Neil Elliot).

Time Bomb

A woman from the year 2155 travels to 1978 and uses her historical knowledge to become a millionaire. Wr: David Wise and Kathleen Barnes. Dir: Seymour Robbie.

Cassandra Loren (Joan Van Ark); Dan Reynolds (Allan Miller); Adam Clement (Ted Shackelford); Foreman (Ivan Naranjo); J.J. McConnell (Fredd Wayne); Guide (Gwenn Mitchell); Guard (Rene Levant); Ellis (Ted Hamaguchi); Reyes (Ernie Orsatti).

Skateboard Wiz

Diana's teenage goddaughter is used as a pawn by a gangster. Wr: Alan Brennert. Dir: Leslie H. Martinson.

Evan Donalson (Eric Braeden); Jamie O'Neill (Cynthia Eilbacher); Leslie O'Neill (Grace Gaynor); Duane Morrisey (Ron Masak); Friedman (Art Metrano); John Key (James Ray); Skye Markham (John Reilly); Ketchum (Neil Flanagan); Kevin Wendell (Peter Wise); Lieutenant (Abraham Alvarez); Chuck (David Cadiente).

The Deadly Dolphin

A trained dolphin is rigged with explosives and ordered to sink an oil tanker. Wr: Jackson Gillis. Dir: Sigmund Neufeld, Jr.

Silas Lockhart (Nicholas Coster); Billy (Britt Leach); Gaffer (Albert Popwell); Henry (Michael Stroka); Darrell (Brian Tochi); Dr. Sylvia Stubbs (Penelope Windust); Goodspeed (Macon McCalman); Admiral (Colin Hamilton); Captain (Gregory Chase); CPO (Paul Tuerpe).

Trivia Alert: Much footage here from the 1973 film *The Day of the Dolphin*.

Stolen Faces

Diana is on guard when she discovers a phony Wonder Woman and Steve Trevor. Wr: Richard Carr and Anne Collins. Dir: Leslie H. Martinson.

Edgar Percy (Joseph Maher); John Austin (Kenneth Tigar); Todd Daniels (John O'Connell); Roman (Bob Seagren); Nancy (Diana Lander); Doctor (Murray MacLeod); Sergeant Cline (Al White); Leslie (Catherine Campbell); Nurse (Daryle Ann Lindley); Boy (Harold P. Pruett).

Pot o' Gold

Wonder Woman helps a friendly leprechaun find his pot o' gold. Wr: Michael McGreevy. Dir: Gordon Hessler.

Pat O'Hanlon (Dick O'Neill); Thackery (Brian Davies); Bonelli (Steve-Allie Collura); Maxwell (Arthur Batanides); Lisa (Sherrie Wills); Rancher (Ric DiAngelo); Mrs. Wells (Jeanne Bates); Gino (Jaime Tirelli); Courier (Gary Epper).

Gault's Brain

The disembodied brain of a billionaire is looking for a new host, and it's up to Wonder Woman to make sure someone isn't on the short end of the stick. Wr: Arthur Weingarten, story by John Gaynor. Dir: Gordon Hessler.

Brandon Stryker (Floyd Levine); Tara London (Cathie Shirriff); Turk (Erik Stern); Dr. Crippin (Peter Mark Richman); Gault's voice (John Carradine); Morton Danzing (David Mason Daniels); Berger (Ari Sorko Ram).

Going, Going, Gone

Black market criminals are in the atomic hardware business, and Diana's job is to go undercover and expose them. Wr: Anne Collins and Patrick Mathews, story by Patrick Mathews. Dir: Alan Crosland.

Zukov (Bo Brundin); Mr. Smith (Charlie Brill); Lucas (Kaz Garas); Capt. Louie (Milton Selzer); Mr. Jones (Marc Lawrence); Mr. Brown (Mako); Como (Hari Rhodes); Heavy (Fil Formicola); Pilot (Jean Ivan Dorin); Officer (Jim Stein).

Spaced Out

Three stolen laser crystals wind up hidden at a science fiction convention, much sought by several parties. Wr: Bill Taylor. Dir: Ivan Dixon.

Kimball (Rene Auberjonois); Sylvester (Steven Anderson); Mr. Munn (George Cheung); Janet (Candy Ann Brown); Simon Rohan (Paul Lawrence Smith); Fan (Rex Riley); Brad (Peter Marc); Desk clerk (Lester C. Fletcher); Guard (J.J. Johnston); Black avenger (Ken Wilson); Robby the robot (Bob Short).

The Starships Are Coming

A big hoax is conjured up that Earth is being invaded by hostile alien forces. Wr: Glen Olson, Rod Baker and Anne Collins, story by Glen Olson and Rod Baker. Dir: Alan Crosland.

Col. Robert Elliott (Tim O'Connor); Henry Wilson (Jeffrey Byron); Aide (James Coleman); Newsman (Frank Whiteman); General (David White); Mason Steele (Andrew Duggan); Mary Lou (Lilibet Stern); Bobbie (Sheryl Lee Ralph); Mrs. Wilson (Doris Dowling); Alien (Jack Kissell); General (Ben Chandler); Woman (Marlena Giovi); Guard (Walt Davis); The reporter (Mario Machado).

Amazon Hot Wax

The recording industry has fallen prey to the extortion racket, and it's up to Diana to break it up. Carter sings "Want to Get Beside You" and "Toto," which she co-wrote. Wr: Alan Brennert. Dir: Ray Austin.

Eric Landau (Curtis Credel); Marty (Bob Hoy); Barbie Gordon (Sarah Purcell); Jeff Gordon (Judge Reinhold); Billy Dero (Martin Speer); Anton (Rick Springfield); Jerry (Danil Torppe); Kim (Michael Botts); Adelle Kobler (Kate Woodville); Jim the engineer (Gene Krischer).

The Richest Man in the World

Wonder Woman searches for a reclusive multi-millionaire who is the key to a guidance missile scrambling device. Wr: Jackson Gillis and Anne Collins. Dir: Don MacDougall.

Marshall Henshaw (Jeremy Slate); Lawrence Dunfield (Roger Perry); Thug (Del Monroe); Prime minister

(Carmen Zapata); Barney (Barry Miller); Lucy DeWitt (Marlyn Mason); IADC officer (Joe Warfield); Foreman (Buck Young); Lab man (Joe G. Medalis); Ambulance attendant (Charles Young); Cab driver (Bobby Baum).

A Date with Doomsday

When a vial of a deadly virus is stolen, evidence indicates a computer dating service could be the culprit. Wr: Roland Starke and Dennis Landa. Dir: Curtis Harrington.

Ward Selkirk (Donnelly Rhodes); Dede (Carol Vogel); Val (Taaffe O'Connell); Dr. Roberts (John O'Leary); George (Bob Hastings); Prof. Zander (Arthur Malet); Mrs. Thrip (Hermione Baddeley); John Blake (Michael Hoit); Codger (Patrick Crenshaw); Claudine (Colette Bertrand); Guard (John Garwood).

The Girl with the Gift for Disaster

A girl becomes involved in the theft of a priceless historical document. Wr: Alan Brennert. Dir: Alan Crosland.

Bonnie Murphy (Jane Actman); Elizabeth Koren (Ina Balin); Neil (Dick Butkus); Bob Baker (Charles Haid); William Mayfield (Raymond St. Jacques); Mark Reuben (James Sloyan); Joan (Renee Brown); Receptionist (Dulcie Jordan).

The Boy Who Knew Her Secret, Part 1

Aliens possess human bodies to search for a criminal from their world who can assume any form—including Wonder Woman. Wr: Anne Collins. Dir: Leslie H. Martinson.

Cameron Michaels (Michael Shannon); Mr. Keller (John Milford); Pete Pearson (Tegan West); Melanie Rose (Lenora May); Dr. Eli Jaffe (Bert Remsen); Skip Keller (Clark Brandon); Mrs. Keller (Joyce Greenwood); Sunny (A.J. Blake).

The Boy Who Knew Her Secret, Part 2

After the alien criminal has made Diana forget that she is Wonder Woman, it is up to Skip to make her remember. Wr: Anne Collins. Dir: Leslie H. Martinson.

Same as Part 1

The Man Who Could Not Die

Wonder Woman faces twin threats: a criminal genius and a man who is invulnerable. Wr: Anne Collins. Dir: John Newland.

Dale Hawthorne (John Durran); Dr. Martin Akers (Robert Sampson); Bryce Kandel/Bret Cassidy (Bob Seagren); Dupris (John Aprea); Professor (Hal Frederick); Joseph Reichman (Brian Davies); T. Burton Phipps III (James Bond III); Admissions clerk (Sherry Miles); Mover (Douglas Broyles).

Phantom of the Roller Coaster, Part 1

An amusement park is suspected as the hideout of a spy organization, but the spies and Wonder Woman are confronted by a phantom haunting the park. Wr: Anne Collins. Dir: John Newland.

Leon/David Gurney (Jared Martin); Pierce (Marc Alaimo); Randy (Ike Eisenmann); Kirk (Fred Lerner); Thorpe (Craig Littler); Harrison Fynch (Joseph Sirola); Ms. Patrick (Jocelyn Summers); Secretary (Jessica Rains); Sergeant (Mike Kopcha); Receptionist (Judith Christoper).

Phantom of the Roller Coaster, Part 2

Wonder Woman aids the "phantom" so that the sabotaged Super Loop doesn't kill its passengers. Wr: Anne Collins. Dir: John Newland.

Leon/David Gurney (Jared Martin); Pierce (Marc Alaimo); Randy (Ike Eisenmann); Kirk (Fred Lerner); Harrison Fynch (Joseph Sirola); Ms. Patrick (Jocelyn Summers); Secretary (Jessica Rains); Sergeant (Mike Kopcha).

World of Giants

1959–1960

Mel Hunter, an Intelligence Bureau agent, is spying on an Iron Curtain missile site when a rocket with experimental fuel explodes. Mel is showered with a strange residue that alters his molecular structure.

He's flown back to the United States, where he gradually shrinks to the height of six inches. Pairing up with normal-sized agent Bill Winters, Mel uses his unique size to conduct further secret missions for the Bureau.

Cast: Mel Hunter (Marshall Thompson); Bill Winters (Arthur Franz); Dorothy Brown (starting with episode 5) (Marcia Henderson); Commissioner H.G. Hall (John Gallaudet).

Producers: Otto Lang, William Alland; *Special Effects:* Stan Horsley; *Art Director:* Jack Collis; *Set Designer:* Robert Kinoshita; Syndicated by CBS through United Artists/ZIV Studios; 30 minutes; black and white.

"You are about to see one of the most closely guarded secrets and one of the most fantastic series of events ever recorded in the annals of counterespionage. This is my story. The story of Mel Hunter, who lives in your world—a World of Giants."—Weekly title narration

Six-inch-high Mel Hunter could be called the live-action equivalent of *Saturday Night Live's*

Mel Hunter (Marshall Thompson) struggles to make a phone call. Copyright 1959 ZIV.

Mr. Bill. Continually put upon by the dangers of everyday life, Mel reflects in one episode, "My own life is in jeopardy every day." In the pilot film alone, poor Mel has barely tumbled out of his mini-sized bed when his giant colleague, Bill Winters, absentmindedly knocks a pencil on the floor, nearly crushing Mel. Minutes later, while being briefed by his giant boss, Mel is bowled over by the hurricane-force wind of an office fan. "Turn off the fan!" Mel screams. The sheepish giants comply, and the meeting goes on.

Nevertheless, Mel always got the job done, scurrying under door frames, climbing up rose bushes and lugging the receivers of giant phones off their cradles to make phone calls. The mighty mite also had all of his comforts provided to him by the Bureau. He lived in a luxurious dollhouse, exercised on a tiny gymnastics bar and was carried around in an attache case by Bill Winters.

Although rarely seen today, WOG (its official nickname) was produced with high hopes by the low-budget studio ZIV. The success of the 1957 film The Incredible Shrinking Man encour-

aged CBS to buy the series for the 1959-60 season. However, the network got cold feet and contracted United Artists to run the 13 episodes in syndication.

William Alland was brought in to replace producer Otto Lang several weeks after production. Alland, the producer of such 1950s films as Creature from the Black Lagoon, It Came from Outer Space and Tarantula, recalls, "William Self, a big-wheel executive at CBS, asked me what I could do with the show. I watched a couple of the episodes, and I thought it was a truly ridiculous idea. The way they were making the show required a million-dollar budget. It should never have been attempted for TV."

Alland found that the giant-sized props were costing ZIV a fortune. There have been misconceptions that World of Giants reused props made for Universal's The Incredible Shrinking Man. In truth, the series built all of its giant props from scratch. "It was crazy," notes Alland. "They were building giant telephones and desks to make Marshall Thompson look like this little guy. The

A tarantula is one of the hazards facing Mel Hunter (Marshall Thompson) in a world of giants. Copyright 1959 ZIV.

"The mathematics of the effects were incredible. Stan would stand in the studio and draw lines and diagrams. The effects were superb."

Alland contends the original production techniques of *WOG* were similar to *The Incredible Shrinking Man,* "which also spent a fortune building giant props. Otto Lang used that approach with *WOG.* I'm guessing that he left because the budget went totally out of sight. The weekly budget for *WOG* was pathetic. With Stan's expertise, we did effects that were not only brilliant but cost peanuts. It's just too bad that all of that talent was wasted on such a ridiculous concept."

As a super mini-spy for the Bureau, Mel had the U.S. government drooling over his ability. Bill Winters discreetly let Mel off at destinations in a briefcase, which came complete with seat and seatbelt for the miniature agent. "The giant briefcase was my idea," notes Alland. "Mel exited from a secret little door on the bottom. But I really had little to do with the scripts. My biggest contribution was solving the technical problems."

Occasionally, Alland still required oversized props. "In one episode, Mel had to hide in a slot machine in Las Vegas. We built a huge slot bar and a few giant silver dollars. We made them out of balsa wood so that they wouldn't crush our actor!"

Marshall Thompson, later the star of the *Daktari* series, was well liked by his producers. "He was a nice guy who took his role very seriously," says Alland. Otto Lang agrees. "Marshall was perfectly cast for the part. He was one of the best actors I've ever worked with."

sets looked great, but they were breaking the budget."

Sizing up the dilemma, Alland called up his friend Stan Horsley. "Stan was a genius for using the camera. Because of his expertise, I made the film *This Island Earth* (1955) for under a million dollars. We worked together to solve *WOG*'s budget problems by doing trick photography rather than construct more giant sets. Stan understood the split-screen technique in a way nobody else did." Using this technology, the pair were able to superimpose their six-inch hero on normal-sized sets, reducing much of the need for giant props. "Without Stan, *World of Giants* couldn't have been done," marvels Alland.

Writer Charles Larson wrote one *WOG* script, "Time Bomb," in which Mel tries to save Winters from a concealed explosive. "I had written a fantasy for the *Climax* TV series, so my agent thought that I and *WOG* would mix well. And we did. I watched the pilot film, which I liked, and days later ZIV approved my script. The script went smoothly, perhaps because ZIV couldn't afford to waste time and money. ZIV in TV was analogous to Monogram [a low budget movie studio in the 1940s]. If it's in English, shoot it!

"I thought the miniaturized secret agent business was basically juvenile and a little silly," he says. "But beyond that, I loved the dramatic dangers this tiny agent faced. To have to struggle through the jungle of an unkempt lawn is bad enough, but to hear the clash of a giant lawnmower coming after you, that was beautiful!

"*WOG* was both exciting and limiting. The problem was to take Mel Hunter seriously. It's difficult to believe that the U.S. will collapse unless your hero can escape a playful kitten. The concept is much more comfortable in comedy, à la *Honey, I Shrunk the Kids* [1989]. *WOG* was great fun to watch once or twice, but then it grew tiresome. That's often the case with gimmicks. However, Marshall Thompson and Arthur Franz were giant pluses for the show. Arthur in particular was a polished professional who could do virtually anything. I was grateful to have so skilled an actor reading my sometimes necessary silly *WOG* lines."

Another writer, Paul King, co-wrote the episode "Teeth of the Watchdog," which found Mel fighting a giant Doberman. King remembers the budget crunches of *WOG*'s early days. "It was by far the most expensive TV series of its day," he reflects. "Otto Lang was very solid in production, which was a prerequisite at ZIV. The show was going over budget, and there was a constant war with the production office over cash. It was an almost hopeless problem: ambitious scripts, not enough money."

King classifies his episode as, "okay, but the series in general was much too simplistic and childish. The emphasis was on the shrink factor. There was little character development. Rather than attract the adults, *WOG* made the fatal error of playing only to a kid audience. It ended up losing both."

According to King, it seemed poor Mel was always beset by snarling canines. "The dog of the week was an inside joke amongst writers," he chuckles.

Thirteen episodes of *WOG* were made and sold for exclusive syndication via CBS/United Artists. By the late 1960s, it had vanished from sight. Otto Lang glances back with fondness at the series. "It was well done for what it was and a challenge to produce. But the cost factors were detrimental, and it caused an early cancellation."

William Alland still thinks highly of *WOG*'s special effects but felt the basic concept was a cropper. "It would have been great as a comic strip," he says. "As a live-action TV show, it didn't fly. If somebody had come to me with the idea of a one-inch G.I. Joe for a movie, I'd have told them to get lost. You can't do anything serious with that kind of hero. If Mel had been an alien who had the ability to reduce his size at will, all right. But to ask the audience to accept that J. Edgar Hoover is having a meeting with a one-inch secret agent is silly. But the special effects remain the greatest."

When the series ended, American scientists were still working around the clock to find a cure for Mel. Paul King recalls that Mel really had only one wish. "The best line in the series was written by Shimon Wincelberg. A giant asks Mel, 'What do you want most in life?' Mel replies: 'A five-inch girl!'"

CAST NOTES

Marshall Thompson (Mel Hunter): Born 1925. The affable Thompson began his career as a leading man in the early 1950s. His later roles included science fiction films such as *Fiend Without a Face* (1958) and *IT!* (1958). He was best known as Dr. Marshall Tracy on TV's *Daktari* (1966–69). He died in 1992.

Arthur Franz (Bill Winters): This veteran character actor starred in several science fiction films, including (in the title role) of *Monster on the Campus* (1955), as well as *Invaders from Mars* (1953). He retired from acting in the 1980s.

John Gallaudet (Commissioner Hall): Born 1903. Gallaudete, a character actor, died in 1983.

Marcia Henderson (Dorothy Brown): Born 1930. As a teenager, this Massachusetts-born actress starred as one of the kids on TV's *The Aldrich Family* (1949–53).

Episode Guide

Special Agent

In his first mission, secret agent Mel Hunter teams with Bill Winters to get the goods on a spy ring. When Bill is knocked out, Mel must battle a giant cat and summon help before enemy agents arrive. Wr: Donald Duncan, Jack Laird, story by Donald Duncan. Dir: Otto Lang.

James Seay, Tom McKee, Craig Duncan.

Time Bomb

Mel discovers a time bomb in Bill's apartment. His efforts to get help are threatened by a variety of giant obstacles. Wr: Charles Larson. Dir: Otto Lang.

Tom Brown, Donald C. Harvey, Don Eitner.

Teeth of the Watchdog

An actress may be involved in espionage. When Bill's undercover status is blown, Mel must carry on the mission, despite the presence of a ferocious Doberman. Wr: Joe Stone, Paul King. Dir: Monroe Askins.

Carol Kelly, Charles Maxwell, Richard Emory.

Death Trap

A car crash knocks out Bill and plunges Mel into a swamp. Mel struggles through the jungle and is attacked by a giant gopher. Wr: Donald Duncan. Dir: Byron Haskin.

Tom Brown, Tom McKee, Keith Richards, Clarence Straight, Wade Cagle, Gay Gadbois.

The Gambling Story

Bill and Mel work against time to bring down a casino which is a front for an underground network. Wr: Richard Carr. Dir: Nathan Juran.

Berry Kroeger, Ivan Triesault, Michael Garth, Frank Scannell, Harry Clexx, Tom Wilde.

The Chemical Story

Mel boards a suitcase to stop the theft of radioactive ore by enemy agents. Wr: Meyer Dolinsky, Robert C. Dennis. Dir: Eugene Lourie.

Peggy Castle, John Van Dreelan, Gavin MacLeod, Byron Morrow, Billy Nelson, Leon Alton, Frank Warren.

Feathered Foes

Investigating a murder, the two agents learn that a spy is using trained pigeons as messengers. Wr: Dan Lundberg, Hugh Lacy. Dir: Nathan Juran.

Brett Halsey, Douglas Dick, Nestor Paiva, Gregg Palmer.

The Pool

Mel, Bill and Dorothy break into a heavily guarded estate to reach a submerged safe that contains microfilm evidence of a spy network. Wr: Laurence Mascott. Dir: Nathan Juran.

Allison Hayes, Bill Masters, Barbara Fuller, Robert Tetrick, Marx Hartmann, Dean Severence.

Rainbow of Fire

Traveling to a small Caribbean island, Mel, Bill and Dorothy try to locate a crashed satellite. Wr: A. Sanford Wolf, Irwin Winehouse. Dir: Harry Horner.

Eduardo Noriega, Eugene Martin, Alex Montoya, Salvadore Baguez, Manuel Paris.

The Smugglers

To free the crew of an American aircraft in Red China, Mel and Bill agree to expose a smuggling operation in Hong Kong. Wr: Fred Freiberger. Dir: Nathan Juran.

Ziva Rodann, John Hart, Walter Reed, Harry Landers, Weaver Levy, Roy Gordon, Donald Lawton, Robert Kino, Frank Harding.

Off Beat

Stolen Egyptian artifacts are sought by the trio. Wr: Kay Lenard, Jess Carneol. Dir: Harry Horner.

Narda Onyx, Bill Walker, Arthur Kendall, Frank Krieg, Johnny Silver, Steve Drextel, Robert Swan.

Unexpected Murder

A supposedly reformed counterfeiter is using his drugstore as a front for a new counterfeiting racket. Wr: Meyer Dolinsky. Dir: Jack Arnold.

Mark Roberts, Pamela Duncan, Harry Lauter, Ed Mills.

Panic in 3-B

Dorothy's well-meaning efforts to help a defecting woman scientist endanger Mel: Enemy agents plan to steal Mel and exploit his shrinking condition. Wr: Irwin Winehouse, A. Sanford Wolf. Dir: Jack Arnold.

Maria Palmer, Edgar Barrier.

APPENDIX A:
HONORABLE MENTIONS

Most of the series covered below (with brief rundowns on their formats and histories) were not science fiction shows per se, but are notable for the ways in which they skimmed the surface of the genre. They are arranged chronologically.

The Man and the Challenge. 1959–60. NBC

A research scientist named Glenn Barton (played by George Nader) used science to test the mental and physical endurance of his subjects at the Human Factors Institute. The Ivan Tors series stressed realism, and every script was painstakingly researched. Guest stars included Julie Adams, Robert Conrad, Jack Ging and William Conrad.

One Step Beyond. Jan 1959–61, ABC

Originally titled *Alcoa Presents* during its network run, *One Step Beyond* was a supernatural anthology that dramatized real-life encounters with the bizarre.

The semi-documentary approach added to the show's spine-tingling suspense. John Newland, who directed all 96 segments of this half-hour series, also served as host. Some noteworthy guest stars included Joan Fontaine, Suzanne Pleshette, Warren Beatty, Robert Blake, Christopher Lee, Charles Bronson, Yvette Mimieux and Elizabeth Montgomery.

"There was a great deal of research that went into the series," says Charles Larson, who scripted five segments. "Creators Merwin Gerard and Larry Marcus did 90 percent of the research for you. I especially enjoyed writing 'Tidal Wave,' about a disabled woman unable to leave her home when a tidal wave threatens to sweep in.

"A passing motorist comes to her aid. When she tries to thank him, she finds out that he's profoundly deaf. He couldn't have heard her cries,

and he didn't know why he had stopped. He had simply been compelled to.

"The episode ended with Newland interviewing the disabled woman on camera. The continued popularity of *One Step Beyond* in syndication is largely to Newland. His attitude, half-skeptic, half-believer, perfectly mirrored the viewers' own shivery doubts."

Thriller. 1960–62, NBC

Boris Karloff hosted and occasionally starred in this horror anthology. The series nearly died while trying to find its identity. The early episodes emphasized suspense over horror, and the ratings plummeted. The producers' decision to go for pure horror resulted in many genuinely frightening stories dealing with zombies, vampires and living scarecrows. Guest stars included Mary Tyler Moore, William Shatner, Ursula Andress, George Kennedy, Cloris Leachman, Richard Kiel and Jane Greer.

Way Out. March–July 1961, CBS

British author Roald Dahl was the host of this macabre "twist ending" anthology. Dahl concluded every episode with, "Good night and sleep well." The stories dealt with disembodied brains, melting faces and a child who turned people into frogs. Such unconventional fare was rejected by the conservative audiences of the early 1960s.

In the 1980s one of the executive producers, David Susskind, gave the 14 episodes to the Museum of Broadcasting in New York, where

Dr. Who (Jon Pertwee).

they've found a more appreciative audience. In addition to good writers (including Larry Cohen and Irving Gaynor Neiman), *Way Out*'s roster included guest stars such as Richard Thomas, Alfred Ryder, Tim O'Connor, Barry Newman, Charlotte Rae, Walter Slezak, Barry Morse, Martin Balsam and Kevin McCarthy.

Dr. Who. 1963–89 BBC

Dr. Who featured a Time Lord from another planet who traveled through time and space and encountered a variety of dangers. Dr. Who had the ability to regenerate himself (taking on new appearances), which was a convenient way to recast actors when they grew tired of the role.

William Hartnell, Patrick Troughton, Jon Pertwee, Tom Baker, Peter Davison, Colin Baker and Sylvester McCoy played Dr. Who over the years. The series' cult following began in North America when the series was exported to the U.S. in the early 1970s. Despite the show's modest production values, its charm attracted guests such as Jean Marsh, Honor Blackman, Richard Todd, Michael Gough and John Cleese.

The Man from U.N.C.L.E. 1964–68, NBC

Two secret agents for the United Network Command for Law Enforcement took on the evil agents of T.H.R.U.S.H.

The series began as a semi-serious spoof of the James Bond genre (007 author Ian Fleming was involved in the preliminary planning of the series). As the series progressed, it turned campy. By series' end, the villains and plots bordered on pure fantasy.

When audiences began to drop in 1967, producer Anthony Spinner was brought in to bring back the realism. However, the series had passed its prime and was canceled in January 1968.

Robert Vaughn starred as Napoleon Solo. His co-star, David McCallum, became the surprise sex symbol as Russian-born Illya Kuryakin. Leo G. Carroll monitored the agents from his control panel at U.N.C.L.E. Vaughn and McCallum reprised their roles in the 1983 TV film *Return of the Man from U.N.C.L.E.*

Guest stars included Jack Lord, Julie London, Michael Rennie, Joan Collins, Nancy Sinatra, Sonny and Cher, Jack Palance and Telly Savalas.

"What made *The Man from U.N.C.L.E.* so good, initially, was its wonderful style, which it lost," says writer Sheldon Stark. "It didn't have a solid foundation. Those are the kinds of shows that waver after two or three years."

The Wild, Wild West. 1965–69, CBS

Although they lived in the 1870s, secret service agents James West (Robert Conrad) and Artemus Gordon (Ross Martin) faced robots, time machines, ghosts, man-made sea monsters and invisible men. One recurring adversary was a dwarf scientist, Dr. Miguelito Loveless (excellently played by Michael Dunn). In one episode, Loveless shrinks West to a height of six inches, and the agent battles a giant cat and spider. The Old West certainly wasn't like this!

Ross Martin was nominated for an Emmy Award for his role during the 1968-69 season. Martin's character was an inspiration to a young fan named Dana Carvey, who grew up to be a master of impressions himself on *Saturday Night Live.*

Some of the actors who visited the West included Ida Lupino, Sammy Davis Jr., Robert Duvall, Michael York, Nick Adams, Boris Karloff, Katherine Ross, Jackie DeShannon, Robert Loggia, Richard Pryor, Peter Lawford and Ricardo Montalban.

Well produced, *The Wild, Wild West* was extremely popular, but it took a lot of flak for its violence. The National Association for Better Broadcasts charged, "It contains some of the most frightening and sadistic scenes ever made for television." That was a strong factor in its cancellation in 1969.

Two TV movies, *The Wild, Wild West Revisited* (1979) and *More Wild, Wild West* (1980) updated the adventures of West and Gordon. Both Conrad and Martin reprised their roles.

Batman. January 1966–68, ABC

The fad of the 1960s, *Batman* was a campy take-off of the considerably more gothic *Batman* character in the DC Comics pages.

The majority of comic book lovers hated the series, feeling it demeaned their superhero. However, the series operated on two levels: action for the kids and a sense of sly humor and satire

Robert Vaughn, left, and David McCallum starred in *The Man from U.N.C.L.E.*

for the adults. (Example: When a laser beam is shot at the Caped Crusaders, it misses Batman's crotch by a few inches. Robin exclaims, "Boy we were lucky, Batman! That could have killed us!" Batman grimly intones, "Or worse, Robin!")

Hollywood's top character actors signed up as guest villains: Burgess Meredith (Penguin), Julie Newmar and Eartha Kitt (Catwoman), Cesar Romero (Joker) and Frank Gorshin and John Astin (The Riddler). Adam West was Batman. Burt Ward played Robin.

Post-production coordinator Robert Mintz recalls that ABC was concerned that *Batman* might be a bust. "The pilot tested horribly with our test audience," he says. "ABC and Twentieth Century–Fox were stunned. They figured out the problem: the audience hadn't realized that *Batman* was a spoof. We tested it again and had an M.C. warm the audience up ahead of time. He told them that it was okay to laugh at the episode. Needless to say, the reaction was tremendously positive. We knew we had a hit."

The Avengers. 1966–69, ABC

The Avengers was a British spy spoof that found a loyal American audience. Patrick MacNee was the suave John Steed and Diana Rigg was the strongly independent Emma Peel. These two agents, Britian's finest, encountered an assortment of weird villains. When Rigg left the series, Linda Thorson stepped in as Tara King for the last season.

The Girl from U.N.C.L.E. 1966–67, NBC

For this spin-off from *The Man from U.N.C.L.E.*, Stephanie Powers was recruited to play secret agent April Dancer. Noel Harrison played her British-born partner, Mark Slate. They had the same boss as the men from U.N.C.L.E., Alexander Waverly (Leo G. Carroll).

The Green Hornet. 1966–67, ABC

Unlike *Batman*, this was a serious effort to bring a superhero to the small screen. However, the once-popular radio character didn't catch on as a TV series. Van Williams played newspaper publisher Britt Reid, who secretly roamed the city as Green Hornet. Bruce Lee was his sidekick, Kato. They buzzed through the city streets in a modified Chrysler Imperial called the Black Beauty.

Journey to the Unknown. 1968–69, ABC

Joan Harrison, one of the producers of the *Alfred Hitchcock Presents* series, executive-produced this English-made anthology. American actors top-lined the stories while sturdy English actors provided the support.

Tales included David Hedison as a reporter who sees the same mysterious people at the site of tragedies; Carol Lynley as a mannequin who comes to life; and Brandon de Wilde as a sailor who encounters a strange woman on a desert island. Other guests included Patty Duke, Roddy McDowall, Barbara Bel Geddes, Robert Reed and Vera Miles.

The Sixth Sense. January–December 1972, ABC

The Sixth Sense took a scientific approach to the occult. Dr. Michael Rhodes (Gary Collins) used the resources of a university to experiment with ESP. It took him to some far-out places. In one episode, he tumbled into a giant spider web. In another show he tried to communicate with the ambulatory skeleton of a murder victim. Dr. Rhodes also met witches, ghostly horses, immortals and lots of hostile poltergeists.

Despite a promising start (with a high-powered writing staff that initially included Harlan Ellison and Dorothy C. Fontana) the series faltered early in its second season.

"We sold *Sixth Sense* in December 1971, and it began airing in January," recalls associate producer Robert F. O'Neill. "It was a madhouse getting it prepared and on the air. But the series worked, and it did fairly well in its first year."

"It actually started as an *ABC Movie of the Week* called *Sweet, Sweet Rachel*," says creator Anthony Lawrence. "Alex Dreier, a well-known news commentator, played the lead. He had a marvelous, powerful voice and gave the movie a sense of reality. The TV movie did very well in the ratings, and ABC decided to do it as a series. One of Universal's contract players, Gary Collins, was cast in the leading role because the studio felt he could do all of the love stories and so on. I was very unhappy about that. I thought Alex was much more interesting in the role."

Although he had created the show, Lawrence's control over *The Sixth Sense*'s content was limited. "I was the story supervisor. I wanted to deal more with ESP and telekinesis. The network and studio wanted it to be ghost-of-the-week. Although we did very well in the ratings that first year, the audience began to drop off because it got to be too much of the same thing every week."

Story consultant Harlan Ellison left the series during the first year after several creative clashes with producer Stan Sheptner. On the day he left, Ellison got up on Sheptner's desk and did a tap dance. "Harlan then went out into the hallway at Universal and let out this shrieking, primal scream," recalls writer Nancy Lawrence. "Everyone came running out of their offices!"

The 25 hour-long episodes were later edited to half-hour segments and packaged with *Rod Serling's Night Gallery* in syndication. "The creative side of me says I hate what they did to it," says Anthony Lawrence of the editing job. "The practical side says I'm very happy because at least it's in syndication. I get residual checks! But they cut them so badly you can't understand them. They were pretty hard to understand in the first place!"

The Evil Touch. 1972–73, Syndicated

This very-low-budget horror anthology was filmed in Australia. British actor Anthony Quayle hosted the series. He stood against a black backdrop with rising smoke. He ended each program with the cryptic, "And remember, there's a touch of evil in all of us."

The stories were varied: Darren McGavin was a doctor chased by a zombie who wanted his heart; James Daly played a crafty politician in the twenty-first century; Leslie Nielsen battled a yacht that had a mind of its own; and Ray Walston was cast as an eccentric who grows protective of a huge sea monster that eats unsuspecting swimmers.

Other guests included Robert Lansing, Vic Morrow, Carol Lynley, Julie Harris, Kim Hunter and Susan Strasberg.

Ghost Story/Circle of Fear. 1972–73, NBC

Sebastian Cabot played host Winston Essex, owner of a creepy mansion. Essex introduced the ghostly tales of this anthology, which was executive-produced by fright master William Castle (*Rosemary's Baby, House on Haunted Hill*). The series received good reviews and was usually in the top 40 in its first few months.

To open up the format, Cabot was dropped in mid-season and the series title changed to *Circle of Fear*. An off-camera voice dared viewers to "live dangerously and step into NBC's Circle of Fear."

Episodes featured demonic dogs, visions from the future, a guilt-ridden vampire, and various ghosts and witches. Some of the guests included Angie Dickinson, Hal Linden, Martin Sheen, Eleanor Parker, Susan Dey, Melvyn Douglas, Patricia Neal, Jodie Foster and James Franciscus.

Of her script "Alter-Ego," writer Dorothy C. Fontana recalls, "It particularly thrilled me because it starred the great Helen Hayes. The script turned out well, and it was a real treat to see Miss Hayes in something I had written."

"*Ghost Story* had a good concept," says story editor Seeleg Lester. "But once again, the network and studio wanted horror. The series was aborted because of ratings."

Search. 1972–73, NBC

Three space-age detectives, each with a transmitter implanted in his ear, globe-trotted around the world. They were monitored by a group of technicians, who watched them on a viewscreen at the Probe division of World Securities. High-tech crime solving was the gimmick. The three stars, Hugh O'Brien, Tony Franciosa and Doug McClure, alternated each week as the detectives.

Burgess Meredith played their boss, Cameron. Cheryl Ladd had a semi-regular role as a Probe agent.

The New Avengers. 1976–77, Syndicated

In this updated version of *The Avengers*, Patrick MacNee returned as John Steed, joined by two young agents: Purdey (Joanna Lumley) and Gambit (Gareth Hunt). The 26 episodes were aired in Britain and Canada and picked up by CBS for late-night broadcasts in 1978. The series did lukewarm business in North America but was a smash hit in the international market.

Tales of the Unexpected. February–August 1977, NBC

William Conrad narrated this suspense-fantasy anthology. The series, which was originally going to be called *Nightmare*, was executive-produced by Quinn Martin. Stories featured crazed canines, alien invasions and weird, ironic story twists. Guest stars included Lloyd Bridges, Roy Thinnes, Linda Kelsey, Van Johnson, Rick Nelson and Robert Foxworth.

Blake's Seven. 1978–81, BBC

Terry Nation created this British space adventure show. After a successful run in England, it exploded to cult status when it was imported to America in the mid 1980s. Despite the low-budget special effects, the series found favor with fans because of its offbeat characters.

The series presented Roj Blake and his mixed band of outlaws as they battled, in true Robin Hood style, a futuristic totalitarian Federation.

The cast included Gareth Thomas as Blake, with Paul Darrow, Sally Knyvette, Michael Keating and Jan Chappell.

The Return of Captain Nemo. March 1978, CBS

A three-segment mini-series from producer Irwin Allen, *Captain Nemo* tried to capitalize on *Star Wars* elements (robots and laser battles) to draw in the viewers.

The story had Captain Nemo (Jose Ferrer) jolted from suspended animation by two Navy divers (Tom Hallick, Burr DeBenning) who discovered his sunken submarine, *Nautilus*. Nemo teamed up with the pair to defeat evil Professor Cunningham (Burgess Meredith) and continue his lifelong quest for Atlantis. Lynda Day George and Warren Stevens co-starred.

The Next Step Beyond. 1978–79, Syndicated

An updated version of *One Step Beyond*, with John Newland back as host. The series, still a half-hour but now in color, barely made a ripple in the ratings. Guests included Majel Barrett, Robert Walker and Mark Goddard.

Cast of *The Outlaws*, left to right: Patrick Houser, Charles Napier, Rod Taylor, Richard Roundtree and Bill Lucking. Copyright 1986 CBS.

Supertrain. February–July 1979, NBC

This big-budgeted fiasco sank like the *Titanic*. A futuristic train carried its passengers into tales of drama, comedy and adventure. The lavishly mounted series (requiring expensive miniatures and luxurious full-sized sets) didn't click with viewers. Edward Andrews, Nita Talbot and Robert Alda were among *Supertrain*'s crew.

Time Express. April–May 1979, CBS

On another train aimed at the heart of fantasy, a mysterious couple (Vincent Price and Coral Browne) guided passengers back in time where they could change their domestic and professional mistakes.

A Man Called Sloane. 1979–80, NBC

UNIT agent Thomas Sloane (Robert Conrad) battled the evil international organization KARTEL. An android who spit fire and a satellite that fired laser beams were two examples of KARTEL's handiwork. With Ji-Tu Cumbuka, Dan O'Herlihy and Karen Purcell.

Darkroom. 1981–82, ABC

James Coburn hosted this supernatural fantasy. He started each show by developing photos in the Darkroom. Each picture represented a bizarre story. Guest stars included Ronny Cox, Billy Crystal, June Lockhart, Andrew Prine, Michael Constantine and Steve Allen.

Wizards and Warriors. February–May 1983, CBS

Special effects distinguished this ambitious series set around sixth century England. Jeff Conaway was Prince Greystone, who battled evil Prince Blackpool (Duncan Regehr). Other cast members included Julia Duffy, Walter Olkewicz and Clive Revill. Bill Bixby directed a number of episodes.

Manimal. September–December 1983, NBC

Dr. Jonathan Chase's father (Don Knight) leaves his son a peculiar legacy: the ability to transform into an animal. Jonathon (Simon Mac-Corkindale) uses this magic power to catch crooks in the big city. The series was noted mainly for its special effects in depicting Jonathan's transformations.

The series' eight episodes played in France in the early 1990s, where they met with incredible popularity and sparked talk of reviving the series for the foreign market.

Manimal's supporting cast included Melody Anderson, Michael D. Roberts and Reni Santoni. William Conrad was the narrator.

The Outlaws. 1986–87, CBS

Sheriff Grail (Rod Taylor) and four outlaws face each other in a showdown in 1899 Texas. A lightning bolt suddenly transports the five into the year 1986. Now dubbed the Magnificent Five, they form their own detective agency and take on contemporary crime.

A December 1986 entry, *The Outlaws* took everyone by surprise by becoming (initially) one of the biggest mid-season hits of the year. However, by spring 1987, the ratings had eroded and the series finished at number 61 out of 81 shows.

Richard Roundtree, Charles Napier, Patrick Houser and William Lucking were the outlaws. Christine Belford played their friend Maggie.

Beauty and the Beast. 1987–90, CBS

A young lawyer discovers an underground world. She becomes increasingly attracted to a "beast" named Vincent who helps her heal from an accident in the pilot. Starring Linda Hamilton and Ron Perlman, *Beauty and the Beast* quickly became an audience favorite for three seasons. Linda Hamilton left the show at the end of the second season to raise her real-life child. Her character, Catherine, was killed in a move that angered many viewers. Eventually, Jo Anderson, who had been playing a police officer named Diana in the series, took up the storyline.

The show boasted the talents of science fiction novelist George R.R. Martin as supervising producer. Directors included Thomas J. Wright, Paul Lynch, Gabrielle Beaumont, Peter Medak and Gus Trikonis, all *Twilight Zone* revival veterans.

The Highwayman. 1987–88, NBC

Capitalizing on the popularity of the hard-edged *Road Warrior* films with Mel Gibson, Glen Larson came up with this hour actioner about a law enforcer on the highways, complete with high-tech trailer rigs and a helicopter. It starred Sam Jones, Jane Badler, Tim Russ and Jacko as the heroic team.

Audiences didn't catch on and after a two-hour telefilm and nine episodes, the series was canceled.

Appendix B: Unsold Science Fiction Television Pilots

There have been some interesting TV pilots over the past 30 years. Some were intriguing, while others were run-of-the-mill dramas. The luckier ones reached the TV movie stage before being rejected as series. Others were stillborn at the script stage. Here's a sample of shows that never were:

Hurricane Island (CBS, 1961—outline). The network asked writer Sam Rolfe to develop a series about shipwrecked survivors landing on an island full of prehistoric beasts. Budget was the main reason that the script didn't reach the filming stage.

Century 21 (ABC, 1964—outline). "It predicted life in the U.S. in the year 2000," says creator Seeleg Lester. "While it created some interest at the networks, it was not sold."

The main character was the executive assistant to the secretary of science. Lester had the opportunity to introduce the *Century 21* character (played by Robert Duvall) in the two-part *Outer Limits* episode "The Inheritors."

Had *Century 21* been picked up as a series, Lester maintains, "it would not have been a show about horror or alien visitors intending to decimate the Earth. Stories were concerned with the leading edge of science. What was on the scientific horizon, and how would it affect our society?

"ESP, time travel, an adventure just a fraction less than 22 seconds into the past, jury by computer, extension of life to 200 years, genetic cloning ... the series concept was unique and original. It was decades ahead of its time."

The Thirteenth Gate (NBC, 1965—one-hour pilot). This ambitious pilot created a lot of interest before it was aired. "It was originally titled *S.D.I.* (Scientific Defense Institute)" recalls Karl Held, one of the show's stars. "The Institute investigated extra-terrestrial phenomena."

In the story, Dr. Jason Banner (David Opatoshu) and his two young assistants, rebellious Steve O'Hara (Alex Cord) and David Matthews (Karl Held), discover that a returning astronaut is being controlled by electrical, one-eyed, multi-legged creatures.

The Paramount production was written by Bob Barbash and directed by Abner Biberman.

"NBC came to me looking for a science fiction series," says Barbash. "I said, 'Why not a government agency that deals with scientific phenomena?' They flipped over it. I wrote and produced it, and it did very well with test audiences across the country, but when NBC's Mort Werner saw it, he wanted David Opatoshu written out of the series. He thought David looked too rabbinical, whatever that means. Werner wanted Michael Rennie to replace him."

Barbash reluctantly began a rewrite for Michael Rennie's character. NBC scheduled the show for Thursdays at 7:30 on NBC, but West–East Coast network politics resulted in *The Thirteenth Gate* getting pulled in favor of the *Daniel Boone* series.

The pilot was unceremoniously aired in the summer of 1966.

The Lost World (ABC, 1965—outline). This series was to be based on producer Irwin Allen's successful 1960 film of the same name. The movie, inspired by Sir Arthur Conan Doyle's story, starred Michael Rennie, Jill St. John, Claude Rains and David Hedison as explorers who find prehistoric creatures in the Amazon.

The proposed series was to focus on a group of explorers who are trapped in a remote tropical jungle. Their efforts to return to civilization are hampered by prehistoric creatures and natives. The series would have used frequent dinosaur clips from the feature film.

The Man from the 25th Century (CBS, 1967). This Irwin Allen–produced pilot materialized only as an 18-minute presentation film. The projected series came within a hair of replacing Allen's *Lost in Space* for the 1968-69 season.

The film used some stock footage from *War of the Worlds* (the 1953 film), *Lost in Space* and *The Time Tunnel*. James Darren starred as Tomo.

As an infant, Tomo was snatched from Earth by hostile aliens and taken to the planet Andro. Given special powers and painstakingly trained as a warrior, Tomo is returned to Earth as a young man. His mission: Pave the way for an alien invasion by destroying America's defense network, Project Delphi (housed under Glacier National Park).

Tomo abandons his mission after he gains an appreciation of the human species. He helps the earthlings repel an intergalactic attack.

The supporting cast included John Napier, Ford Rainey and John Crawford. Joey Tata played Project Delphi's radar man. Tata says he got the role while playing tennis with pal James Darren.

"Jimmy said he was going to do a pilot called *Man from the 25th Century*. I said, 'Oh yeah? And Joey Tata's not in it? All the shows I've done for Irwin Allen and I'm not in it?' Jimmy got embarrassed and just looked at me like, 'Gee, I dunno...'

"So, I asked Jimmy, tongue-in-cheek, 'Do me a favor. When you see Irwin today, tell him, 'Irwin, you SOB, how could you not include Joey Tata?'"

Darren went off to film the pilot and relayed Tata's message word-for-word to Allen. Two days later, Tata got a script in the mail. "Allen had written me in!"

CBS didn't buy the series. "It was a fun story, but Irwin's style was slowly departing by 1968," says Tata. "His shows had that formula that some people sort of outgrew."

In 1970, writers Arthur Weiss and Anthony Wilson revamped the concept as an *ABC Movie of the Week*. It didn't get beyond the script stage.

City Beneath the Sea (NBC, 1967, 1970). Originally produced as a presentation film (budgeted at $100,000) from Irwin Allen, the 1967 test film starred Glenn Corbett as the commander of an underwater metropolis, Pacifica, in the year 2068.

Unlike Allen's *Voyage to the Bottom of the Sea* series, this show (according to Allen's plan) would incorporate actual marine research. The acquanauts would use bubble curtains for doors; tag fish with radioactive markers to study fish migration; and silicone membranes to extract oxygen from the water.

James Brolin, Lawrence Montaigne, Francine York and Lloyd Bochner (as the villain) made up the supporting cast.

Montaigne was cast as Dr. Aguila, a humanoid amphibian. "I was supposed to be a take-off on Mr. Spock," he recalls. "I had done several episodes of *Star Trek*, so perhaps I had that science fiction mystique. I did all of my own swimming. Basically, I was playing a talking fish!"

Although Montaigne praises the pilot as "an exciting concept," it failed to excite NBC as a possible weekly series. The idea was temporarily shelved until 1970, when a 90-minute TV-movie version of *City Beneath the Sea* was filmed. The entirely new cast was headed by Stuart Whitman, Rosemary Forsythe, Robert Colbert and guest star Robert Wagner. Written by John Meredyth Lucas, the film won an Emmy for its special effects, but it failed to win a spot on NBC's schedule as a series.

The Stranger (NBC, 1973—TV movie). This excellent space-age fugitive story kept its science fiction premise in focus. The late Glenn Corbett starred as astronaut Neal Stryker, who crash-lands on an Earth-like planet named Terra. Terra's experimental space program is Stryker's only hope of getting home. However, he's hunted by Terra's totalitarian agents, who want him dead before he can introduce the concept of freedom to the populace.

While struggling to stay alive, Stryker also searches for his two fellow astronauts. The strong supporting cast included Sharon Acker, Cameron Mitchell, Lew Ayres and Tim O'Connor. In a nice piece of special effects wizardry, Terra's night skies were depicted with two moons.

"Michael Landon read the script and liked it,"

The cast of *City Beneath the Sea*, left to right: Burr De Benning, Susan Miranda, Stuart Whitman, and Rosemary Forsythe. Copyright 1970 NBC.

says creator Gerald Sanford. "We had a meeting with Larry White at NBC, and Michael said he was interested. Suddenly, he was called away for a phone call. Meanwhile, Larry said to me, "If Michael Landon does *The Stranger*, you're on for a full season right now."

Sanford's hopes were quickly dashed. "Landon never came back to the meeting. He got a deal for another show called *Little House on the Prairie*."

The Stranger earned adequate ratings as a TV movie, and six scripts were written for a proposed series. "NBC liked the film, but they decided they didn't want to risk the money on a series. We had a great cast and we got good reviews. Daily Variety said, 'If anything deserves to become a series, it's this.'"

Genesis II (CBS, 1973—TV movie). This much-anticipated TV movie was the work of *Star Trek*'s creator, Gene Roddenberry. Scientist Dylan Hunt (Alex Cord) is the subject of an experiment in suspended animation in the Carlsbad Caverns when an earthquake strikes.

Hunt reawakens in the year 2133, and finds that his old world was destroyed in a nuclear war. There are only pockets of civilizations left scattered around the globe.

The supporting cast included Mariette Hartley, Percy Rodrigues, Lynne Marta and Ted Cassidy.

According to Roddenberry, *Genesis II* almost made the schedule. However, CBS's interest was muted when they decided to do the *Planet of the Apes* series instead.

Genesis II was reworked for ABC in 1974 as the TV film *Planet Earth*. John Saxon starred as Dylan Hunt. This time Dylan was enslaved by a society of women led by Diana Muldaur. "Roddenberry expressed his anxiety that the network didn't understand the script's humor," says Saxon. "To me, that was the best part! But this was before *Star Wars* proved sci-fi and humor could go together. So ABC decided *Planet Earth* was a mistake."

The Questor Tapes (NBC, 1974—TV movie). The script of this telefilm was written with Leonard Nimoy in mind as Questor, an android on a search for his creator. Robert Foxworth ended up with the role, and Mike Farrell played his human friend, Jerry Robinson.

The Gene Roddenberry–Gene L. Coon script gave Questor the mission of guiding mankind through the nuclear era.

Roddenberry claimed that the network wanted him to streamline the format into a *Fugitive* mode and eliminate the Robinson character. Roddenberry refused to compromise the concept.

Years later, however, Foxworth admitted that he felt that the TV film said it all and that a TV series could have been redundant.

Larry Alexander, story editor for the projected series, says, "We worked up 13 scripts for a possible series." He recalls some NBC executives were confused by Questor's computerized command center. "Questor used the control center to tune into any place in the world by way of a grid system. He could locate any global problem. NBC literally could not understand how this worked. They said, and I quote, 'Does this mean he has a TV camera in every room in the world?' They just hated the whole basic idea of this. Roddenberry kept trying to explain the set-up to them. He would come back from meetings banging his head against the wall!

"Universal eventually went with *The Six Million Dollar Man*. They felt it was more easily accessible to the general audience. Universal was like, 'Well okay, we've got our science fiction show, so goodbye,' and that was it for *Questor*."

Connecticut Yankee in King Arthur's Court (ABC, 1974—script). A car crash propels a young man named Hank Morgan back in time to A.D. 648 England, where he becomes an aide-de-camp to King Arthur in Camelot. The twentieth-century man dazzles the inhabitants of the sixth century with his 15 centuries' worth of scientific knowledge.

The idea, based on the Mark Twain novel, was developed for television by Irwin Allen. The producers promised that despite the fanciful format, "People will deal with real problems, not situation comedy problems.... Hank Morgan will use his intelligence, shrewdness and technical knowledge to overcome his adversaries."

The Time Travelers (ABC, 1976—TV movie). Despite a lot of publicity, this Irwin Allen telefilm (based on a story by Rod Serling) didn't sell.

Sam Groom and Tom Hallick played scientists who use a time machine to travel back to Chicago, 1871. They hope to find a cure for a virus that has been ravaging 1976.

"It was rather a rehash of Allen's successful *Time Tunnel* series," notes Booth Colman, who played Dr. Cummings. "The plot was fairly good. The great Chicago fire was the main story point. I was the scientist guru who sent the two leads back in time." The film included tinted stock footage of the raging fire from the 1938 film *In Old Chicago*.

Had *The Time Travelers* gone to series, Groom and Hallick would have gone on different time missions each week.

The Man with the Power (NBC, 1977—TV movie). Bob Neill played a Milwaukee high school teacher who is the product of an alien father and terrestrial mother. He could move objects through mental concentration, and in this pilot, he helps an endangered heiress. Guest stars in the pilot included Persis Khambatta and Vic Morrow.

Exo-Man (NBC, 1977—TV movie). Nick Conrad (David Ackroyd) is a professor confined to a wheelchair after being paralyzed by the Mob. He develops a suit that regenerates his limbs. As long as he wears the suit, he's a modern-day superhero. He avenges himself on the Mafia hit men and vows to use his suit to combat crime.

A good supporting cast included Anne Schedeen, Kevin McCarthy, Harry Morgan, Donald Moffatt, A. Martinez, Jose Ferrer and Jack Colvin.

The Clone Master (NBC, 1978—TV movie). Art Hindle is Dr. Simon Shane, who creates 13 duplicates of himself. This enables him to go into overtime, battling international crime.

Robyn Douglass and Ralph Bellamy co-starred.

Dr. Strange (CBS, 1978—TV film). Leaping from otherworldly dimensions as depicted in the comics pages, Dr. Stephen Strange, Master of the Mystic Arts, debuted on television in this offbeat film written and directed by Philip DeGuere. Peter Hooten starred in the title role. Sir John Mills and Jessica Walter as the evil sorceress Morgan Le Fay were his co-stars.

One of the reasons this attempt to bring good-vs.-evil sorcery to television failed was that it aired opposite the second night of the megahit mini-series *Roots*.

"What I remember about *Dr. Strange* was the intense creative frustration of the process. I doubt very seriously if there will ever come a time I can watch that show," says DeGuere. "Whenever I watch anything I've done, I immediately plunge right back into whatever the process was at the time : why this decision was made, or why that cut came out the way it did.

"The original idea of *Dr. Strange* was to progressively push out the normal, everyday sensory reality. What I was looking for was almost psychedelic. I wanted a certain kind of magical glow to the way it looked. It didn't really accomplish that. It's easy for me to blame the script or the amount of money we had to make it for. I think the time factor was also a real problem. Someone had to take responsibility, so I took responsibility."

Captain America (CBS, 1979—2 TV movies). Reb Brown starred as the comic book hero. In the first TV movie (January 1979), Marine Steve Rogers, Jr., is critically injured by the bad guys. He's injected with the FLAG serum that turns him into a superman, Captain America. He goes after the villains who are threatening Phoenix, Arizona, with a neutron bomb. Heather Menzies played the captain's friend, Dr. Wendy Day.

In his second TV film (November 1979), he faces a villain (played by Christopher Lee) who exploits a scientist's aging drug. Connie Sellecca played Dr. Wendy Day in this outing.

The Power Within (ABC, 1979—TV movie). A lightning bolt transforms a flyer named Chris Darrow (Art Hindle) into a super-powered dynamo who quashes crime. In this outing, enemy agents try to unlock the secrets of Darrow's power for their own evil purposes. Eric Braeden, Susan Howard and David Hedison co-starred.

The Aliens Are Coming (NBC, 1980—TV movie). TV producer Quinn Martin felt it was a good time to bring back the format of his *The Invaders* in this pilot film.

Formless extra-terrestrials land in Nevada and begin hijacking human bodies. Dr. Scott Dryden (Tom Mason) and his assistant, Gwen O'Brien (Melinda Fee), battle the aliens who have taken over a hydroelectric dam to replenish their energy.

As in *The Invaders*, the aliens vanished in a glow when killed. However, the film lacked the gritty realism of Martin's earlier science fiction series.

The Time Project (ABC, 1980—script). Producer Irwin Allen called it "the godson" of his earlier series *Time Tunnel*. Herman Miller's script dealt with Project Kronos, a time machine that could carry people back and forth through time. The scientists were forced to use the machine before it could be perfected (the previous travelers had returned as 2,000-year-old skeletons).

"I had a deal with ABC to do a script for them and Irwin Allen had a deal with them to do a project, so they put us together," says Herman Miller. "This way they hoped that Irwin, who sometimes did schlock work, would have a better writer and produce a more literate script than usual."

Voyage of the Shark (CBS, 1989—script). The officers and crew of the submarine *Shark* were the main characters of this undersea adventure with a novel twist: The sub is also a spaceship, traveling to ocean planets in space.

The sub also contains women and children, and in addition to exploration, the *Shark* assists space colonies and participates in rescue missions. Herman Miller wrote the teleplay. The creator of the proposed series was actor and producer Terry Becker, who had charted the seven seas as Chief Sharkey in the series *Voyage to the Bottom of the Sea*.

"CBS was interested in doing an update of *Voyage*," says Becker. "I came up with the idea of a ship that could transform itself from spaceship to sub and vice versa." Becker notes that the success of *Star Trek: The Next Generation* inspired interest in the proposal, but, "We never got to do it. It was a terrific concept. There's only so much you can do in our sea, so I opened up that vista by exploring seas in other galaxies."

APPENDIX C:
EMMY AWARD NOMINEES
AND WINNERS IN
SCIENCE FICTION TELEVISION

indicates a winner

1959-60

Writing in Drama
*Rod Serling, *Twilight Zone*, CBS

1960-61

Drama Series
Twilight Zone, CBS

Writing in Drama
*Rod Serling, *Twilight Zone*, CBS

Cinematography
*George Clemens, *Twilight Zone*, CBS

1961-62

Writing in Drama
Rod Serling *Twilight Zone*, CBS

Art Direction and Scenic Design
Twilight Zone, CBS

Cinematography
Twilight Zone, CBS

1962-63

Cinematography
Twilight Zone, CBS

1963-64

Art Direction and Scenic Design
The Outer Limits, ABC

1964-65

Special Photographic Effects
Voyage to the Bottom of the Sea, ABC

1965-66

Art Direction
Voyage to the Bottom of the Sea, ABC

Set Decoration
Voyage to the Bottom of the Sea, ABC

Cinematography
Voyage to the Bottom of the Sea, ABC

Film Editing
Voyage to the Bottom of the Sea, ABC

Sound Editing
Voyage to the Bottom of the Sea, ABC

Special Photographic Special Effects
Voyage to the Bottom of the Sea, ABC
Lost in Space, CBS

Mechanical Effects
Voyage to the Bottom of the Sea, ABC

1966-67

Drama Series
Star Trek. Gene Coon, Eugene Roddenberry,
   producers, NBC

Supporting Actor for a Drama Series
Leonard Nimoy. *Star Trek*, NBC

Film & Sound Editing
*Voyage to the Bottom of the Sea, ABC
Star Trek, NBC

Special Photographic Effects
Voyage to the Bottom of the Sea, ABC
*Time Tunnel, ABC
Star Trek, NBC

Special Mechanical Effects
Star Trek, NBC
Voyage to the Bottom of the Sea, ABC

1967-68

Drama Series
Star Trek. Gene Roddenberry, producer, NBC

Supporting Actor for a Drama Series
Leonard Nimoy. *Star Trek*, NBC

Cinematography
The Time Tunnel, "Raiders from Outer Space,"
   ABC

Film Editing
Star Trek, "The Doomsday Machine," NBC

Make-up
Lost in Space, "Space Destructors," CBS

Special Photographic Effects
Star Trek, "Metamorphosis," NBC

1968-69

Supporting Actor in a Drama Role
Leonard Nimoy. *Star Trek*, NBC

Art and Set Decoration
Star Trek, "All Our Yesterdays," NBC

Cinematography
Land of the Giants, "The Crash," ABC

Film Editing
Star Trek, "Assignment Earth," NBC

Special Effects
Star Trek, "Tholian Web," NBC

1969-70

Cinematography
The Immortal (TV Film), ABC

Film Sound Editing
Land of the Giants, "A Small War," ABC
*The Immortal (TV Film), ABC

1970-71

Outstanding Single Drama
Night Gallery, "They're Tearing Down Tim Riley's
   Bar," NBC

1971-72

Makeup
Night Gallery, "Pickman's Model," NBC

1975-76

Film Sound Editing
The Six Million Dollar Man, "The Secret of Bigfoot
Pass Parts I and II," ABC

Graphic Design and Title Sequence
The New, Original Wonder Woman, ABC

1976-77

Lead Actress in a Drama Series
**Lindsay Wagner, *The Bionic Woman*, ABC

Film Sound Editing
The Six Million Dollar Man, "Return of Bigfoot,
   Part I," ABC
The Fantastic Journey, "Atlantium," NBC

1977-78

Costume Design
Wonder Woman, "Anschluss '77," CBS

1978-79

Lead Actress in a Drama Series
**Mariette Hartley, *The Incredible Hulk*, "Married,"
   CBS

Art Direction
Battlestar Galactica, "Saga of a Star World," ABC

Costume Design
*Jean-Pierre Dorleac, *Battlestar Galactica*, "Furlon," ABC

Technical Crafts—Special Effects
***Battlestar Galactica*, "Saga of a Star World," ABC

1979-80

Art Direction for a Series
Beyond Westworld, "Pilot," CBS
Buck Rogers, "Ardala Returns," NBC

Cinematography for a Series (Single Camera Production)
The Incredible Hulk, "Broken Image," CBS

Costume Design for a Series
Galactica 1980, "Starbuck's Great Journey," ABC
Buck Rogers, "Flight of the War Witch," NBC

Makeup
Beyond Westworld, "Pilot," CBS

1980-81

Cinematography
Buck Rogers, "Hawk," NBC

Costume Design
Buck Rogers, "The Dorian Secret," NBC

Film Editing for a Series
Greatest American Hero, "Pilot," ABC

Music Composition for a Series (Dramatic Underscore)
**Buck Rogers, "The Satyr," NBC

1981-82

Videotape Editing
Greatest American Hero, "Lost Diablo Mine," ABC

Music Composition for a Series (Dramatic Underscore)
The Incredible Hulk, "Triangle," CBS

1982-83

Makeup
V—The Mini Series, NBC

1983-84

Film Sound Editing for a Limited Series or a Special
V—The Final Battle, Part II, NBC

Makeup for a Series
V—The Final Battle, Part II, NBC

1984-85

Makeup for a Series
V, "The Rescue," NBC

1985-86

Guest Performer in a Drama Series
*John Lithgow, *Amazing Stories*, "The Doll," NBC

Directing in a Drama Series
Steven Spielberg, *Amazing Stories*, "The Mission," NBC

Cinematography for a Series
**Amazing Stories, "The Mission," NBC

Costuming for a Series
Amazing Stories, "Gather Ye Acorns," NBC
Amazing Stories, "Ghost Train," NBC

Editing for a Series (Single Camera Production)
Amazing Stories, "Mummy, Daddy," NBC
Amazing Stories, "The Mission," NBC

Sound Editing for a Series
**Amazing Stories, "The Mission" NBC
Misfits of Science, "Pilot," NBC

Makeup for a Series
Amazing Stories, "Gather Ye Acorns," NBC

Hairstyling for a Series
**Amazing Stories, "Gather Ye Acorns," NBC

1986-87

Cinematography for a Series
Amazing Stories, "Go to Head of the Class," NBC

Art Direction for a Series
Max Headroom, "Blipverts," ABC

Sound Editing for a Series
**Max Headroom, "Blipverts," ABC

Sound Mixing for a Series
**Max Headroom, "Blipverts," ABC

Makeup for a Series
Amazing Stories, "Without Diana," NBC
Max Headroom, "Security Systems," ABC

Hairstyling for a Series
Max Headroom, "Body Banks," ABC

1987-88

Cinematography for a Series
Star Trek: The Next Generation, "The Big Goodbye,"
   Syndicated

Costume Design for a Series
*William Ware Theiss, *Star Trek: The Next
   Generation,* "The Big Goodbye," Syndicated

Sound Editing for a Series
**Star Trek: The Next Generation,* "11001001"
   Syndicated

Sound Mixing for a Series
Star Trek: The Next Generation, "Where No One
   Has Gone Before," Syndicated

Makeup for a Series
**Star Trek: The Next Generation,* "Conspiracy,"
   Syndicated
Star Trek: The Next Generation, "Coming of Age,"
   Syndicated

Hairstyling for a Series
Star Trek: The Next Generation, "Haven," Syndicated

1988-89

Art Direction for a Series
Star Trek: The Next Generation, "Elementary Dear
   Data," Syndicated

Cinematography for a Series
**Quantum Leap,* "Genesis, September 13, 1956,"
   NBC

Costume Design for a Series
Star Trek: The Next Generation, "Elementary Dear
   Data," Syndicated

Sound Editing for a Series
**Star Trek: The Next Generation,* "Q Who?"
   Syndicated

Sound Mixing for a Drama Series
**Star Trek: The Next Generation,* "Q Who?"
   Syndicated

Makeup for a Series
Star Trek: The Next Generation "A Matter of Honor,"
   Syndicated

Hairstyling for a Series
**Quantum Leap,* "Double Identity, November 8,
   1965," NBC
Star Trek: The Next Generation "Unnatural
   Selection," Syndicated

Visual Effects for a Series
Star Trek: The Next Generation, "Q Who?"
   Syndicated

1989-90

Drama Series
Quantum Leap, NBC

Lead Actor in a Drama Series
Scott Bakula, *Quantum Leap,* NBC

Supporting Actor in a Drama Series
Dean Stockwell, *Quantum Leap,* NBC

Guest Actor in a Drama Series
Harold Gould, *The Ray Bradbury Theatre,* "Into
   the Chicago Abyss," USA

Art Direction for a Series
**Star Trek: The Next Generation,* "Sins of the Father,"
   Syndicated

Cinematography for a Series
**Quantum Leap,* "Pool Hall Blues, September 4,
   1954," NBC

Costume Design for a Series
Quantum Leap, "Sea Bride, June 3, 1954," NBC

Editing for a Series (Single Camera Production)
Star Trek: The Next Generation "Deja Q,"
   Syndicated

Sound Editing for a Series
Star Trek: The Next Generation, "Yesterday's
   Enterprise," Syndicated

Sound Mixing for a Series
Star Trek: The Next Generation "Yesterday's
   Enterprise," Syndicated

Makeup for a Series (tied with *Tracy Ullman Show*)
**Alien Nation,* "Chains of Love," FOX

**Music Composition for a Series (Dramatic
   Underscore)**
Dennis McCarthy, *Star Trek: The Next Generation,*
   "Yesterday's Enterprise," Syndicated

Visual Effects for a Series
Star Trek: The Next Generation, "Tin Man,"
   Syndicated
Star Trek: The Next Generation, "Deja Q," Syndicated

1990-91

Drama Series
Quantum Leap, NBC

Lead Actor in a Drama Series
Scott Bakula, *Quantum Leap*, NBC

Supporting Actor in a Drama Series
Dean Stockwell, *Quantum Leap*, NBC

Art Direction for a Series
Star Trek: The Next Generation, "The Best of Both Worlds, Part II," Syndicated
Quantum Leap, "The Boogieman, October 31, 1964," NBC

Cinematography for a Series
Star Trek: The Next Generation, "Family," Syndicated
*Quantum Leap, "The Leap Home, Part II, April 7, 1970," NBC

Costume Design for a Series
Star Trek: The Next Generation, "Devil's Due," Syndicated
Quantum Leap, "Glitter Rock, April 12, 1974," NBC

Sound Editing for a Series
*Star Trek: The Next Generation, "The Best of Both Worlds, Part II," Syndicated
Quantum Leap, "Black On White On Fire, August 11, 1965," NBC

Sound Mixing for a Drama Series
*Star Trek: The Next Generation, "The Best of Both Worlds, Part II," Syndicated

Makeup for a Series
Star Trek: The Next Generation, "Identity Crisis," Syndicated
Star Trek: The Next Generation, "Brothers," Syndicated
*Quantum Leap, "The Leap Home Part I, November 25, 1969," NBC

Visual Effects for a Series
Star Trek: The Next Generation, "The Best of Both Worlds, Part II," Syndicated

1991-92

Drama Series
Quantum Leap, NBC

Lead Actor in a Drama Series
Scott Bakula, *Quantum Leap*, NBC
Harrison Page, *Quantum Leap*, "Song for the Soul, April 7, 1963," (Guest) NBC

Supporting Actor in a Drama Series
Dean Stockwell, *Quantum Leap*, NBC
Richard Kiley, *The Ray Bradbury Theatre,* "Utterly Perfect Murder," USA

Art Direction for a Series
Quantum Leap, "Song for the Soul, April 7, 1963," NBC
Star Trek: The Next Generation, "Unification Part II," Syndicated

Cinematography for a Series
Quantum Leap, "Dreams, February 28, 1979," NBC

Costume Design
Quantum Leap, "A Single Drop of Rain, September 7, 1953," NBC
*Star Trek: The Next Generation, "Cost of Living," Syndicated

Sound Editing for a Series
Quantum Leap, "Hurricane, August 17, 1969," NBC
Star Trek: The Next Generation, Syndicated

Sound Mixing for a Drama Series
Star Trek: The Next Generation, Syndicated

Makeup for a Series
*Star Trek: The Next Generation, "Cost of Living," Syndicated

Hairstyling for a Series
Star Trek: The Next Generation "Cost of Living," Syndicated

Music Composition for a Series (Dramatic Underscore) (Tied with *Matlock*)
**Dennis McCarthy, *Star Trek: The Next Generation*, "Unification Part I," Syndication

1992-93

Lead Actor in a Drama Series
Scott Bakula, *Quantum Leap*, NBC

Supporting Actor in a Drama Series
Dean Stockwell, *Quantum Leap*, NBC

Art Direction for a Series
Quantum Leap, "Blood Moon," NBC

Cinematography for a Series
Quantum Leap, "Trilogy, Part I," NBC

Costume Design for a Series
Quantum Leap, "Lee Harvey Oswald," NBC
Star Trek: The Next Generation, "Time's Arrow, Parts I and II," Syndicated

Editing for a Series (Single Camera Production)
Quantum Leap, "Lee Harvey Oswald," NBC

Sound Editing for a Series
Quantum Leap, "Leaping Between the States," NBC
Star Trek: The Next Generation, "Time's Arrow, Part II," Syndicated

Sound Mixing for a Drama Series
Star Trek: The Next Generation, "A Fistful of Datas," Syndicated

Makeup for a Series
Star Trek: The Next Generation, "The Inner Light," Syndicated

Hairstyling for a Series
Star Trek: The Next Generation, "Time's Arrow, Part II" Syndicated

Music Composition for a Series (Dramatic Underscore)
Quantum Leap, "Leaping on a String," NBC

1993-94

Drama Series
Star Trek: The Next Generation, Syndicated

Art Direction for a Series
Star Trek: The Next Generation, "Thine Own Self," Syndicated

Costuming for a Series
Star Trek: The Next Generation, "All Good Things," Syndicated

Single-Camera Production Editing for a Series
Star Trek: The Next Generation, "All Good Things," Syndicated

Hairstyling for a Series
Star Trek: The Next Generation, "Firstborn," Syndicated

Makeup for a Series
Star Trek: The Next Generation, "Genesis," Syndicated

Music Composition for a Dramatic Underscore for a Series
Star Trek: The Next Generation, "All Good Things," Syndicated

Sound Editing for a Series
Star Trek: The Next Generation, "Genesis," Syndicated

Sound Mixing for a Series
Star Trek: The Next Generation, "Genesis," Syndicated

Outstanding Individual Achievement in Special Effects
Star Trek: The Next Generation, "All Good Things," Syndicated

BIBLIOGRAPHY

Books

Brooks, Tim. *The Complete Directory to Prime Time TV Stars 1946–Present*. Ballantine, 1987.
Brooks, Tim, and Earle Marsh. *The Complete Directory to Prime Time Network TV Shows 1946–Present*. Ballantine, 1992.
Dawidziak, Mark. *Night Stalking*. Image, 1991.
Fulton, Roger. *Encyclopedia of TV Science Fiction*. TV Times Boxtree, 1990.
Gerani, Gary. *Fantastic Television*. Harmony, 1977.
Gianakos, Larry James. *TV Drama Series Programming: A Comprehensive Chronicle 1947–1959*. Scarecrow, 1980.
_____. *TV Drama Series Programming: A Comprehensive Chronicle 1959–1975*. Scarecrow, 1978.
_____. *TV Drama Series Programming: A Comprehensive Chronicle 1975–1980*. Scarecrow, 1981.
_____. *TV Drama Series Programming: A Comprehensive Chronicle 1980–1982*. Scarecrow, 1983.
_____. *TV Drama Series Programming: A Comprehensive Chronicle 1982–1984*. Scarecrow, 1987.
Heald, Tim. *The Making of Space 1999*. Ballantine, 1976.
Hora, Max. *The Prisoner of Portmeirion*. The Six of One—The Prisoner Appreciation Society, 1985.
Inman, David. *The TV Encyclopedia*. Perigee, 1991.
The International Television and Video Almanac. Quigley, 1986–1992.
Javna, John. *The Best of Science Fiction TV*. Harmony, 1987.
Maltin, Leonard. *Leonard Maltin's TV Movies and Video Guide*. Signet, 1989.
Marill, Alvin H. *Movies Made for Television*. Baseline, 1987.
Nemeck, Larry. *Star Trek The Next Generation Companion*. Pocket, 1992.
O'Neil, Thomas. *The Emmys*. Penguin, 1992.
Rogers, Dave. *ITV Encyclopedia of Adventure*. TV Times Boxtree, 1988.
Schow, David J., and Jeffrey Frentzen. *The Outer Limits: The Official Companion*. ACE Science Fiction, 1986.
Steinberg, Corbett. *TV Facts*. Facts on File, 1984.
Taylor, Philip M. *Steven Spielberg: The Man, His Movies and Their Meaning*. Continuum, 1992.
Terrace, Vincent. *Television 1970–1980*. A.S. Barnes, 1980.
Trimble, Bjo. *The Star Trek Concordance*. Ballantine, 1985.
Variety's Directory of Major Show Business Awards. Reed, 1987.
White, Matthew. *The Official Prisoner Companion*. Warner, 1988.
Zicree, Marc Scott. *The Twilight Zone Companion*. Bantam, 1982.

Periodicals

Cinefantastique
The Florida Post, October 1983.
The Hollywood Reporter
Loder, Kurt. "Max Mania." *Rolling Stone*, August 28, 1986, pp. 47–48.
Los Angeles Herald–Examiner, February 1967.
McGuigan, Cathleen. "A Talking Head." *Newsweek*, January 13, 1987.
New York Times, March 1967.
Newsweek, January 1964.
Planet of the Apes, Marvel Comics, 1974.

Roush, Matt. "Max Headroom—It Did Not Compute." *USA Today*, October 15, 1987, p. 3D.

Starlog, 1976–1989.

Thinnes, Roy. "Journey to the Far Side of the Sun—Who Were the Real Stars?" *Science Fantasy Film Classics*, October 1978, pp.48–50.

TV Guide, 1959–1992.

Waters, Harry F. "Mad About M-M-Max." *Newsweek*, April 20, 1987, pp. 58–64.

INDEX

*Titles in **bold** refer to the series that are chronicled in this book.*

791.4565 Phillips, Mark, 1959
PHI   July 22-

        Science fiction
          television series.

$75.00

DATE			